W9-BUZ-443

A MEDITERRANEAN FEAST

ALSO BY CLIFFORD A. WRIGHT

On Cooking

✣

Italian Pure & Simple: Robust and Rustic Home Cooking for Every Day

Grill Italian

Lasagne

Cucina Rapida: Quick Italian-Style Home Cooking

Cucina Paradiso: The Heavenly Food of Sicily

On Politics and History

✣

Facts and Fables: The Arab-Israeli Conflict

After the Palestine-Israel War: Limits to U.S. and Israeli Policy
(with Khalil Nakhleh)

✣

A MEDITERRANEAN FEAST

THE STORY OF THE BIRTH OF THE CELEBRATED CUISINES OF THE MEDITERRANEAN, FROM THE MERCHANTS OF VENICE TO THE BARBARY CORSAIRS

With More Than 500 Recipes

CLIFFORD A. WRIGHT

WILLIAM MORROW AND COMPANY, INC.

New York

It is the policy of William Morrow and Company, Inc., and its imprints and affiliates, recognizing the importance of preserving what has been written, to print the books we publish on acid-free paper, and we exert our best efforts to that end.

LIBRARY OF CONGRESS CATALOGING-IN-PUBLICATION DATA
Wright, Clifford A.
A Mediterranean feast : the story of the birth of the celebrated cuisines of the Mediterranean, from the merchants of Venice to the Barbary Corsairs / Clifford A. Wright. —1st ed.
p. cm.
Includes bibliographical references and index.
ISBN 0-688-15305-4
1. Gastronomy—History. 2. Food habits—Mediterranean region—History. 3. Mediterranean region—Social life and customs.
I. Title.
TX641.W75 1999
641'.01'3091822—dc21 98-49155 CIP

2 3 4 5 6 7 8 9 10

BOOK DESIGN BY FRITZ METSCH

www.williammorrow.com
www.cliffordawright.com

FOR

THE PHILOSOPHERS

AND

THE COOKS

without whom would be served forth

half-baked ideas and thoughtless food

ACKNOWLEDGMENTS

A book of this scope can be written only when the author stands on the shoulders of others. As a result I feel more like the conductor who marshaled an imposing group of people to help me in formulating and concocting a dream. Unfortunately I have stood on so many shoulders that I don't know where to begin to thank people.

I suppose I can start with the people who gave me money, who believed in me, who traveled with me; the libraries that were essential for my research; and the friends who gave groceries and their kitchens for recipe tests spanning more than a decade. My extraordinary editor, Pam Hoenig, understood this book from the moment she read the proposal in what now seems the primordial past. She saw straight to the heart of this book, understood it, loved it, and provided me an advance against royalties to bring the book to completion. And then she had the professional wisdom to say "Okay, great first draft, now . . . " when I thought I was done. Thanks to everyone else at William Morrow—Jennifer Herman and Kate Heddings, editorial assistants; Carole Berglie, copyeditor; Jayne Lathrop, proofreader; Ann Cahn, special projects production editor; Karen Lumley, production manager; Fritz Metsch, designer; Leah Carlson-Stanisic, art manager of cookbooks; and Jeff Ward, map maker.

I am deeply grateful for the financial support of the Oldways Preservation and Exchange Trust, and its present and former directors and staff K. Dun Gifford, Greg Drescher, Nancy Harmon Jenkins, Sara Baer-Sinott, Sara Powers, and Robin Insley. Through the support of Oldways I was able to make extensive progress in my research in Spain, Morocco, and Tunisia. Their work in promoting a Mediterranean diet is a great inspiration.

My agent, Doe Coover, believed in this project from the moment it was a glimmer in my eyes and kept me going over all these years with encouragement to pursue this dream, never once saying, as I suspected she might, "Don't you think you've bitten off more than you can chew?" (a typical food writer's expression).

How could I have endured ("endured" will be explained in a future book) the countless trips to the Mediterranean without my friend Boyd Grove, who accompanied me on so many research trips, ate his way through strange food, strange happenings, strange illnesses in strange countries, yet was the perfect "Zen traveler." And to my friend David Forbes, who accompanied me on one research trip to Turkey and who, with his wife, Ginny Sherwood, provided their kitchen for recipe tests and help with buying food. My other friends who stayed back home in Massachusetts awaiting my return with a cache of recipes to test, Pam Haltom and Harry Irwin, Eric Stange and Barbara Costa, Mark Chalek and Jenny Lavigne, Bob and Marsha Sanders, also lent their kitchens, groceries, and, most important, their friendship and love. My friend Deborah Madison is a constant morale booster and an inspiration for things culinary. Once I moved to California I found wonderful new friends in Martha Rose Shulman, who lent her kitchen during my tumultuous times after first moving, where we shared my recipe tests and hers, and Russ and Kathy Parsons, who shared a number of recipe tests at my house and theirs, and Steve Monas and Maggie Megaw for letting me use their kitchen. Thanks also must go to Martha's husband, Bill Grantham, who read drafts of several chapters and helped me formulate their structure. I want to thank my friends Professors Sidney Mintz of Johns Hopkins University, Larry Wolff of Boston College, and Stephan Haggard of UC-San Diego for reading and critiquing portions of drafts written so early on that I suspect they don't remember.

The notion developed in this book of a culinary revolution that parallels an agricultural revolution, that grows out of the historic poverty of the Mediterranean, influenced by the Arab agricultural revolution, the Age of Exploration, and the Renaissance, was inspired by the writings and conversations I have had over nearly a decade with Professor Emeritus Andrew M. Watson of the University of Toronto, who not only has critiqued my attempts but also performed all kinds of little favors that make the life of a researcher easier.

Writers often forget to thank the libraries where so much work gets done. The library research for this book was extensive and time-consuming. Ninety percent of my library research was completed at the Harvard University libraries, especially Widener and Economic Botany, and at the U.S. Library of Congress, where I can confirm that my tax dollars are being well spent. I also used various libraries and archives in the Mediterranean, especially the Biblioteca Nazionale Marciana and the Archivio di Stato in Venice, as well as the University Research Library of UCLA and my little local public library of Arlington, Massachusetts, whose staff was able to find obscure books for me through interlibrary loan. Thanks also to the staffs of the New York Public Library, the New York Academy of Medicine, and the U.S. National Agricultural Library in Beltsville, Maryland. Without these libraries this book simply could not have been written, and I want to thank their staffs for the help I received.

There are so many others.

My former wife, Professor Najwa al-Qattan, acting far beyond what anyone could expect from an ex-wife, was enormously helpful in many ways, always "on-call" for my myriad scholarly, linguistic, and culinary questions while she finished her Ph.D. at Harvard and after. Our children, Ali, Dyala, and Seri, ate all the food in this book, and are as expert on Mediterranean tastes as any cosmopolitan. My father, Harold I. Wright, let me use his little farmhouse in southwestern France for research purposes and my mother, Helen De Yeso Wright, helped in many motherly ways.

I would also like to thank my late cousin Carlo De Ieso and his wife, Cessarina, and our extended family who helped me enormously, lending their house outside Florence as a base while I pursued my research. I must thank my ex-in-laws Abdul-Muhsin and Leila al-Qattan and their children Hani, Omar, and Lina, who provided everything from recipes and translations to a place to call home while I traveled in Europe and the Middle East. I am grateful to Hind al-Qattan who put my family up while staying in Amman, Jordan, and to Khaled and Bahija al-Qattan for many insights into Arab cooking.

I would also like to thank all the others, whom I list alphabetically by last name or association, and each of whom deserves, if space allowed, a paragraph detailing their extraordinary help and enthusiasm. They are: Hamida Abdel-Magid, Medinet Habu, Egypt; Sari Abul-Jubein, Cambridge, Massachusetts; Professor Janet Abu-Lughod, New School for Social Research, New York; Professor Lila Abu-Lughod, New York University, New York; Professor Dionisius Agius, University of Leeds, England; Messaoud Ben Brahim Agouzal, Meknès, Morocco; Massimo Alberini, Milan, Italy; Clara Maria de Amèzua, Madrid, Spain; Professor Lisa Anderson, Columbia University, New York; Colman Andrews, Editor, *Saveur;*

Bob James, Arlington Public Library, Massachusetts; Rob Arndt, Editor, *Aramco World;* Malik Bachouchi, Bouira, Algeria; Ziad and Haniya Baha ad-Din, Cairo, Egypt; Nancy Verde Barr, Providence, Rhode Island; Edward Behr, Vermont; Chef Rafih Benjelloun, The Imperial Fez, Atlanta, Georgia; Marie-José Bergougnoux, Six-Fours les Plages, France; Irene A. Bierman, Director, Gustav E. von Grunebaum Center for Near Eastern Studies, UCLA; Professor Phyllis Pray Bober, Bryn Mawr College, Pennsylvania; Scot J. Cornwall, Boston Public Library; E. Boutrif, Food and Agriculture Organization, Rome; the late Chef Catherine Brandel, Culinary Institute of America, California; Beth Brownlow, Concord, Massachusetts; Vincenzo Buonassisi, Milan, Italy; Jean Cargill, Harvard Economic Botany Library, Harvard University; Allal Chibane, Rabat, Morocco; Julia Child, Cambridge, Massachusetts; Gaetano Cipolla, Brooklyn, New York; Professor Jon S. Cohen, University of Toronto; Eleonora Consoli, *La Sicilia,* Catania, Sicily; Montse Contreras, Bergueda, Catalonia; Professor William Cole, formerly Harvard University; Giuseppe Coria, Vittoria, Sicily; Professor Santi Correnti, University of Catania, Sicily; Pino Correnti, Catania, Sicily; Darrell Corti, Sacramento, California; Countway Medical Library, Harvard University; Laura Ghittino Courir, Lido di Venezia, Italy; José Crestou, St. Germain-du-Bel-Air, France; Andre Daguin, Auch, France; Dr. Tommaso d'Alba, Bagheria, Sicily; Lubaba al-Daker, Damascus, Syria; Naomi Duguid, Toronto, Canada; Janie C. Morris, Special Collections Library, Duke University, Durham, North Carolina; Essam el-din Adly, Alexandria, Egypt; Martha Imber-Goldstein, Editor, *Encyclopedia of the Modern Middle East,* Macmillan publishers, New York; Asim Erdlik, Turkey; Chef Bobby Flay, Mesa Grill, New York; Salvatore and Frances Fantasia, Gaeta, Italy, and Arlington, Massachusetts; Carol Field, San Francisco, California; Dr. Osman Galal, University of Arizona; Gamal Mohamed, Medinet Habu, Egypt; Benfeghoul Ghali, Ministry of Agriculture, Algeria; Ameena Ghattas, Cairo, Egypt; Chef Pasqualino Giudice, Jonico'a Rutta e'Ciauli, Syracuse, Sicily; Mestan Gökçe, Gökçeler Köyü, Turkey; Gail Zweigenthal, formerly Editor, *Gourmet;* Maria Grazia, Biblioteca Nazionale Marciana, Venice; the late Rudolf Grewe, New York; Sheila Griffin, UC-Irvine; Ihsan Gurdal, Cambridge, Massachusetts; Barbara Haber, Schlesinger Library, Radcliffe College, Cambridge, Massachusetts; Ma'mum and Sahar Haj-Ibrahim, Damascus, Syria; Joseph Halabi, Beirut, Lebanon; Shukri, Amal, and Mimi al-Halaby, Jeble, Syria; Mazen al-Halaby, Damascus, Syria; Maen and Muheeba Haj-Ibrahim, Damascus, Syria; Fatéma Hal, Paris, France; Professor Mustafa and Mrs. Jennifer Hamarneh, Amman, Jordan; Soudiah Hammoudi, Amman, Jordan; Chef Hechmi Hammami, Abou Nawas Hotel, Tunis, Tunisia; Chef Abderrazak Haouari, Hotel Ulysse Palace, Djerba, Tunisia; Nicky Hayward, Madrid, Spain; Brenda Huntley, Six-Fours les Plages, France; Giovanni Inghillieri, Venice, Italy; Mumtaz al-Katib, Damascus, Syria; Kristine Kidd, Editor, *Bon Appétit;* Dr. Perri Klass, Cambridge, Massachusetts; Dr. W. L. Klawe, InterAmerican Tropical Tuna Commission, La Jolla, California; Chef Michele Kayser, Restaurant Alexandre, Nîmes-Garon, France; Khaled Abdul-Karim, Marsa Matruh, Egypt; Sylvia Klemm, Somerville, Massachusetts; Diane Kochilas, Athens, Greece; Mohamed Kouki, Tunis, Tunisia; Moutaz and Nadia Koudmani, Damascus, Syria; Aglaia Kremezi, Athens, Greece; Corby Kummer, Boston, Massachusetts; Nancy Lange, Cambridge, Massachusetts; Robert and Odile La Carrière, Frayssinet, France; Gabriel Larrose, Fenouillet, France; Khaled Lattif, Casablanca, Morocco; Alexandra Leaf, New York, New York; Chef M. P. Lenfant, Grand Hotel, Roquefort-sur-Soulzon, France; Professor Bernard Lewis, Princeton University; Joe Puccio and Dennis Hawkes, Library of Congress, Washington, D.C.; Dr. Paolo Lingua, Genoa, Italy; Kanaan Makiya, Cambridge, Massachusetts; Domenico Manzon, Naples,

Italy; Franco Marenghi, Accademia Italiana della Cucina, Milan, Italy; Professor Manuela Márin, Consejo Superior de Investigaciones Cientificas, Madrid, Spain; Jacques Marquis, Tètou restaurant, Golf-Juan, France; Jean and Anna Masson, Rhodes, Greece; Chef Moncef Meddeb, Concord, Massachusetts; Chef Carlo Middione, Vivande Porta Via, San Francisco; Jackie Mintz, Baltimore, Maryland; Moncef M'zid, Sfax, Tunisia; Fiammetta Oliver di Napoli, Mondello, Sicily; David Smith, New York Public Library; Abdou Ouahab, Tlemcen, Algeria; Khmaïs Ouled-Abdessayed, Qairouan, Tunisia; Chef Özcan Ozan, Sultan's Kitchen restaurant, Boston, Massachusetts; Michele Papa, Catania, Sicily; Chef Claude Patry, Restaurant Relais St. Jean, Levroux, France; Charles Perry, *Los Angeles Times;* Chef Felice Piacentino, Trattoria del Porto restaurant, Trapani, Sicily; Francesca Piviotti, Venice, Italy; Toula Polygalaktos, New York, New York; Hawys Pritchard, Madrid, Spain; Francesco Quinci, Mazara del Vallo, Sicily; Elisabeth Riely, Boston, Massachusetts; Professor James A. Reilly, University of Toronto; Claudia Roden, London; Susan Rossi, Harvard Botanical Museum, Harvard University; Nadim and Kate Rouhana, Arlington, Massachusetts; Christos and Georgia Rozanitis, Arlington, Massachusetts, and Sparta, Greece; Dr. Zak Sabry, Oakland, California; Professor Nina Safran, Harvard University; Chef Lotfi Saibi, Boston, Massachusetts, and Qairouan, Tunisia; Randa and Rafiq Salahiya, Damascus, Syria; George and Jan Sallum, Homs, Syria and Cambridge, Massachusetts; Marina Sambo, Biblioteca Nazionale Marciana, Venice; Professor Alberto Saoner, Palma di Mallorca, Spain; Diane Seed, Rome; Giancarlo Sessa, Somerville, Massachusetts, and Benevento, Italy; Maria Jose Sevilla, London; Shahat Shuhitu, Medinet Habu, Egypt; Enzo Siena, Accademia Italiana della Cucina, Syracuse, Sicily; Mary Taylor Simeti, Palermo, Sicily; Samy Slimi, Sfax, Tunisia; Colin Spencer and Claire Clifton, London; Professor Nikos Stavroulakis, Khania, Crete; Suore Margherita, Pio Istituto Educativo San Benedetto, Catania, Sicily; Conte Emile Targhetta d'Audiffret de Greoux, Venice, Italy; Sam and Sarah Thayer, Winchester, Massachusetts; Éliane Thibaut-Comclade, Ateliers de Cuisine Catalane Traditionelle, Illa de Tet, France; Chef Yves Thuriés, Grand Écuyer restaurant, Cordes, France; Dr. Joyce Toomre, Harvard University; Theodore and Constance Tsikis, Nireas restaurant, Rhodes, Greece; Chef Roger Vergé, Moulin de Mougins restaurant, Mougins, France; Professor David Waines, University of Lancaster, England; Professor Immanuel Wallerstein, Fernand Braudel Center, State University of New York–Binghamton, New York; the late Arlene Wanderman, Foodcom, Inc., New York; John Symery, Wellcome Institute for the History of Medicine, London; Elisabeth Wickett, Cairo, Egypt; John Willoughby, Cambridge, Massachusetts; Paula Wolfert, San Francisco, California; Nacim Zeghlache, Cambridge, Massachusetts, and Sétif, Algeria; Professor Sami Zubaida, Birkbeck College, London. My apologies to anyone I forgot to thank.

Grateful acknowledgment is made to the following publishers for the author's previously published material. The following recipes of the author were previously published in several magazines.

From *Food & Wine*
Habas con Jamón (Lima Beans with Cured Ham)
Salsa de Patatas (Potato Sauce)
Mecerada de Naranja con Coco (Oranges with Coconut)

From *Bon Appétit*
Broccoli Affogato ("Drowned" Broccoli)
Spaghetti alla Siracusana (Spaghetti with the Aromatic Sauce of Syracuse)
Mulinciana 'Muttunate ("Blanketed" Eggplants)

Zuppa di Pesce alla Mazarese (Fish Stew in the Style of Mazara del Vallo)
Pesce Spada col Salmoriglio (Swordfish with Salmoriglio Sauce)
Minestra di Verdure (Vegetable Soup)

From *Radcliffe Culinary Times*
Ḥamām bi'l-Farīk (Pigeon with Green Wheat)

The following recipes or portions of the author's recipes were previously published in several of his books.

From *Grill Italian* (Macmillan)
Salsiccia Fresca (Fresh Homemade Sausage)
Porceddu (Sardinian Roast Suckling Pig)
Salsa Mahonesa (Mayonnaise)

From *Lasagne* (Little, Brown)
Ricotta
Sugo di Umido di Maiale (Rich Pork Stew Sauce)
Pesto alla Genovese
Lasagne Cacate di Mòdica (Shitty Lasagne from Mòdica)

From *Cucina Paradiso: The Heavenly Food of Sicily* (Simon & Schuster)
Caponata
Bottarga (Dried Fish Roe)
Polpette di Baccalà (Salt Cod Fritters)

Someone once said that the more you say the more likely are your chances for saying something wrong. I say a lot in this book, and I may forever be haunted by the idea that I've said something wrong. Although the mistakes in the book are mine alone, I want to assure the reader that I have tried my best to follow the canons of objective scholarship in the historical writing and that I have personally tested all the recipes.

CONTENTS

LIST OF ILLUSTRATIONS AND MAPS

Maps

INTRODUCTION

The mere smell of cooking can evoke a whole civilization.

—FERNAND BRAUDEL[1]

THE MAGICAL UNITY

✣

IN the images of gnarled olive trees, colorful fishing boats in turquoise harbors, crosses and crescents, warm breezes, and whitewashed terraced villages, an enchanting magic draws historian and traveler alike to the Mediterranean. This great middle sea pulls us in awe to its architectural glories, to its dolorous yet eternally hopeful people, and to its evocative pantry of foods. A Mediterranean feast is not only the act of eating together with family and friends, it also refers to the experiences that enrich us whenever we touch upon Mediterranean history and life.

So-called Mediterranean foods are served every day in restaurants in America, yet we can give only an inchoate answer to the question: What is Mediterranean cuisine? The Mediterranean is composed of many different cultures, and there seems to be no single image that represents a "magical" unity. Even with the shared trinity of ingredients (olive oil, wheat, and the vine), Italian food is a world apart from Egyptian food, yet both are Mediterranean.

It says volumes that Americans will cook "Mediterranean" food, while a real Mediterranean cook, whether a Sicilian, Syrian, or Greek, would never dream of cooking any food but his or her own. In fact, I've met Syrians who have never heard of bouillabaisse (page 375), French who've never heard of *kafta* (page 337), and Moroccans who have never heard of Tunisian *brīk* (page 110), even though they have their own variety called *brīwat*. We Americans cook these different foods because we do not have a cuisine, or at most we have an embryonic cuisine. As a young postindustrial nation we are creating our culinary culture as we go, and we are capable and willing to give and receive in all manner of foods.

I propose that by understanding the countries of the Mediterranean in context—in terms of their history, environment, and trade—a diverse Mediterranean unity will emerge that can be reflected and demonstrated in the kitchen. This is a book of food, and a book about food, informed by a history of the environment, an ecology of the Mediterranean, the lives of ordinary people, the importance of trade and transit, the development of towns and capitalism, the beginnings of the nation-state, and the familiar story of great men and wars. But it is also a book about food in history, and about history. It attempts to challenge some notions we have about the food we eat, where it comes from, and how it developed.

Mediterranean food as a gastronomic ensemble was first popularized by the renowned English food writer Elizabeth David. While her lovely portrayal of a rich and bountiful Mediterranean captured its magic, it was, from a scholarly point of view, incomplete.[2] Although she is not a scholar, the popular culinary anthropologist and cookbook writer Paula Wolfert set a standard for a more serious understanding of Mediterranean cuisine than that of David with the publication of her seminal *Couscous and Other Good Foods from Morocco* in 1973. Many popular writers speak of the Mediterranean as a supposedly unique combination of voluptuousness and austerity, but there is also a historical Mediterranean beyond the postcards flush with their blossom-filled villas in Capri or Portofino.[3] The Mediterranean of today is entirely different from the Mediterranean of the classical world. In classical times there were no oranges or lemons, or potatoes and tomatoes, which had yet to arrive from the East and the New World. Asiatic rice, called "the blessing brought by the Arabs," was unknown as were peppers from South America, maize from North America, and coffee from East Africa.[4]

The portrait of a historically bountiful Mediterranean is a false one created by romantically minded food and travel writers who believe that what they see today must have always been. The grandeur of the Mediterranean has led to a conception of a culinarily rich Mediterranean that in reality is a late twentieth-century development based on centuries of evolution. Consider that until relatively recently the picture of the Mediterranean was one of poverty and destitution, even in the richest countries. It was as recently as 1943 that the well-traveled American General George S. Patton Jr. called the Sicilians "the most destitute and God-forgotten people I have ever seen."[5]

In order to write this book, I felt I needed not only a map of the geographical Mediterranean but a philosophical map as well. I found that map in the works of the French historian Fernand Braudel, whose conception of the history of the Mediterranean is the inspiration for this book.

The Mediterranean world of farmers, mariners, traders, bankers, soldiers of fortune, prostitutes, and pirates, all playing on a grand stage and affected by climate, geography, diet, and the rhythms of daily life and trade, was first posed by Braudel in his two-volume masterpiece, *The Mediterranean and the Mediterranean World in the Age of Philip II*. Braudel called the kind of historiography he had undertaken a "total history," a history of the Mediterranean not only woven with treaties, wars, and royal marriages but also one where what some would call the minutiae of Mediterranean life becomes part of the cloth. Braudel felt that "the pursuit of political events is something of a wild goose chase . . . events are the ephemera of history; they pass across its stage like fireflies, hardly glimpsed before they settle back into darkness and as often as not into oblivion." Braudel saw "events" as the flares that intermittently illuminated the historical landscape, providing us a bright but not necessarily a deep understanding of history. The Mediterranean I hope to reveal in this book is not the linear narrative and collection of facts, but is the one that traverses time in multifarious ways. It is based on a diachronic rather than synchronic model of food history. It is a Mediterranean of economic systems, states, societies, civilizations, instruments of exchange, and forms of war and, ultimately, the foods that people grow, cook, and eat, and the cuisines that arise for those foods. This book is a history with recipes. The recipes are not historical—that is, recipes from the medieval era—but rather they are contemporary recipes that exist the way they do because of history, a somewhat different history-telling than you learned in school; they may be considered heirloom recipes pregnant with history itself.

A Mediterranean Feast will seek out the interstices and rhythms of Mediterranean food, moving from field to kitchen, ingredient to recipe, in the hopes of forming a total picture of the Mediterranean reaching beyond traditional cookbooks. I hope to connect the various Mediterranean cuisines in a new, historical way and portray Mediterranean food, not by boundaries or by food groups, but by seeing food as part of the chain of history—where food is as integral to the story as is the farmer who grows the wheat or the merchantman who ships it across Mediterranean sea-lanes. I believe that by weaving in the history of the cuisines we can color the Mediterranean foods we prepare and eat, and endow them with a spirit and meaning. I think a recipe has as much historical meaning as the cartulary favored by archival historians.

A Mediterranean Feast will focus on the foods emanating from historically important cities, villages, seaports, and regions of the Mediterranean. By preparing and tasting a bouillabaisse or a *zuppa di pesce* from scratch, the reader will experience the bounty of the Mediterranean from the standpoint of a simple fisherman or a noble aristocrat. By traveling, both physically and gastronomically, through Andalusia, Languedoc, Provence, Liguria, Sicily, Apulia, Greece, Turkey, Egypt, and all the other regions of the Mediterranean, the reader and home cook will experience the glorious and authentic cuisines of the Mediterranean through recipes that reflect upon centuries of culinary evolution. Just as we all have great-great-grandfathers many times removed, so too every dish we can eat today in the Mediterranean has its genesis and lineage. Even such modern inventions as *tiramisù* have ancestors. Although it is very difficult, if not impossible, to construct a culinary family tree showing where and how each recipe came to be, I hope to draw at least the trunk and main branches of Mediterranean cuisine, to provide the "idea."

A Mediterranean Feast will celebrate the tapestry of Mediterranean cuisines as they exist today and as they reflect on a time when the merchants of Venice struck deals with the spice men of Aleppo, and the corsairs of Barbary scoured the sea-lanes for Spanish merchantmen. The loom of the book will be the history and ecology of the Mediterranean while the warp and woof will be the interconnectedness of life and food. The needle that threads the story will be contemporary recipes that one could find in Mediterranean homes today.

We will come to see that Mediterranean food is not Spanish, French, or Italian food. Because of the complexity of its history, cultures, religions, and geography, Mediterranean food has developed not as national cuisines but as a variety of regional cuisines based on an extreme geography. It is proper to speak of Andalusian, Apulian, Venetian, or Cretan food because they all stand uniquely apart though they are intimately related.

The central thesis of the book is that the Mediterranean cuisines we eat today, represented by the contemporary recipes in this book, did not evolve from the classical era nor were they born in France in the mid-seventeenth century; rather they came about as a result of three great revolutions affecting Mediterranean history: the Arab agricultural revolution of the ninth through twelfth centuries, the Age of Exploration in the fifteenth and sixteenth centuries, and the creative impulse of the Renaissance. The past millennium has formed the Mediterranean food of today. The most important facet of this culinary evolution is the constant historic battle of Mediterranean peoples against famine. I believe that the Mediterranean food we eat today is the result of Mediterranean peoples inspired by, if not completely receptive to, the advanced Islamic culture and agronomy of the early part of the millennium, enhanced by the foods brought to the Mediterranean from exploration and refined by the aesthetic ideals of Renaissance humanism. Mediterranean cuisines developed as a reaction against the monotonous foods of centuries of famine and starvation. The recipes in this book reflect the historical progression of Mediterranean culinary culture as a battle of taste over monotony, of life over death.

MY FIRST MEDITERRANEAN

I FIRST saw the Mediterranean Sea in 1956 when I was five years old. In the 1950s my father was stationed in France for four years with the U. S. Air Force, and our holidays were often spent on Mediterranean coasts, especially Juan-les-Pins, then a quaint little village on the Riviera. Since then I have crisscrossed the Mediterranean countless times while conducting research, on vacations, and visiting family, including my father who lives part of the year in southwestern France; the family of my former wife,

Najwa al-Qattan, in the Arab world; and my mother's family, the De Iesos, in Italy. My grandfather was from a small village in southern Italy, and I remember his preparing foods that I later learned his American children—my mother, aunts, and uncle—wouldn't touch when they were young. Najwa's family were from Palestine and she too remembers the foods of her childhood with great fondness.

What first attracted me to the notion of a culinary history with recipes of the Mediterranean, besides the fact that the food tastes so good, was a longstanding interest in what Fernand Braudel called the two truths that go unchallenged: first, that there is a unity and coherence to the Mediterranean; and second the greatness of the Mediterranean. I also felt that Braudel's concern with food was overly agronomic and alimentary, and not cultural and culinary. Although he didn't ignore the culinary, I felt more attention should be paid to it. The Mediterranean is undoubtedly the sum of many individual histories. Food is one of those histories and, for me, along with art, one of the most immediately satisfying, aesthetically and practically, because we can actually engage our skills and talents and cook food and eat it according to recipes.

THE GOAL OF THE BOOK

CAN a cookbook of Mediterranean foods tell us anything about the Mediterranean and, if it can, how is it that while there is no such thing as "Mediterranean food" we can all agree that we understand this description?

First, we must not think of the Mediterranean as a single sea but rather as a complex of seas linked to the land, where the men were sailors in the summer and peasants in the autumn. The heritage of Mediterranean cuisine is rooted not only in the sea of galleys and roundships but in the seas of the vine and the olive as well.

What is the Mediterranean? Many food writers expend altogether too much of their energy collecting facts and recipes, without the concomitant application of those facts to building a bigger picture that can explain something. This is why most so-called food history is no history at all. I hope to give you the sweep of the Mediterranean, the grand movement and not the bits of the mosaic. To be sure, you could extract the facts that lace the book, but that is not what I hope you will do. As you read this book, I hope that you will let it inform your culinary thinking, your sense of history, but I also hope you will cook from it. That is the whole point of the book: to cook the food. If you are a professional chef or an advanced home cook, you will find recipes that are a great challenge and others that you might use to feed your family on a moment's notice. If you are not a cook or are not a confident cook, taste an olive, read a little, and you will soon start to tackle the simpler recipes and perhaps gain what the Arabs call *al-nafas*, the culinary equivalent of the gardener's "green thumb."[6]

In history we can focus on the princes, wars, and rich men or we can look at the slow, inexorable march of history itself. So, too, in the culinary realm we can dally forever with the mystique of the vine and the olive or we can test the multifarious complexity of the cuisines of the Mediterranean, their oddities, complexities, and commonplaces. I hope to do more than a mere geographical cataloguing of the regions' foods or food products.

A cookbook that purports to be a history of food as well as a collection of recipes must begin with history itself. The story told in this book is a complex one because the lives of people are complex. It is not a traditional history that moves chronologically from beginning to end. A collection of remembered dates or royal family trees do not make history. In order to simplify the morass that history seems to be, historians invent convenient terms that help us categorize and clarify history. Terms like "medieval," "Middle Ages," "Baroque," "Renaissance," or "Early Modern" are meant to assist the reader in placing the themes or events talked about in a framework. Sometimes these terms are amplified with a bevy of dates that further help the reader understand where they are on the historical map. The reader should know that professional historians vigorously debate the usefulness and meaning of ascriptions such as "feudalism," and that all of these terms are problematic. But, with that proviso, I will employ them anyway because something is better than nothing.

In this book you will encounter what may seem an overwhelming number of historical eras, movements, empires, kingdoms, kings, soldiers, and events, not to mention the food. At times you may feel rather daunted. If you are familiar with reading history that "begins at the beginning," you may feel unsettled when you read this book. This is not traditional history, but rather a broad sweep where I hope you come away not with a memory of the importance of 1453 as a date, but with the importance of why Tunisians cook couscous the way they do, why the Spanish love salty food, and why Sicilians sprinkle fried bread crumbs on their pasta. (By the way, 1453 is the date Constantinople fell to the Ottoman Turks, effectively ending the Byzantine Empire.)

The following section will help you put all that you will read later into a traditional historical context. If you feel lost later on, you can always flip back here to see exactly where you are on the historical continuum. The history of Mediterranean food in this book is its history from about the fall of the Roman Empire to the beginning of the modern era, about 1700. Let's then begin at the beginning. If you are familiar with the course of the last two thousand years of history, you can skip this section.

A HISTORICAL CONTINUUM

IN the fifth century A.D. (400–500), the Roman Empire suffered the fatal barbarian blows that were to end a millennium of a glorious civilization. In 410, Alaric sacked Rome and a few years later Spain fell to the Visigoths. By mid-century, Attila the Hun entered Gaul, today's France, and invaded Italy. The traditional date given for the end of the Roman Empire is 476, when Romulus Augustulus, the last emperor of the West (the empire had split into East, with its capital in Constantinople, and West, with its capital in Rome, several centuries earlier) was deposed. The eastern empire actually evolved into the Byzantine Empire, until Constantinople fell first to the Crusaders in 1204 and then finally to the Ottoman Turks in 1453. During this century the emergence of the bishops of Rome would eventually establish that city as the center of Catholicism and the seat of the Holy Father, a single pope.

In the sixth (500–600), seventh (600–700), and eighth (700–800) centuries, often called the Dark Ages, the barbarian tribes settled and established hereditary kingdoms. One of the barbarian tribes, the Franks, established a kingdom under Clovis I in what would become France. There were different branches of Frankish tribes and from one of them, the Carolingians, would emerge the greatest king of this era, Charlemagne, in the eighth century; his Frankish empire included western Europe and northern Italy. He was crowned emperor in Rome in 800.

In the seventh century a new force entered the scene. A dynamic new religion was born on the Arabian peninsula uniting bands of Arab tribes into an effective fighting force inspired by the truth of a monotheistic religion. Within two hundred years a civilization was created that stretched from the Atlantic to beyond Persia. The religion was called Islam and the people were Muslims, which means "those who have submitted to the Will of God." Great Islamic dynasties were established in North Africa and Spain, and Charlemagne was checked in his attempt to reconquer Spain. The traditional date for the beginning of the Muslim calender is A.D. 622, when the Prophet Muhammad fled to Medina in Arabia with his followers. After his death the lands under Muslim rule, very small at this time, came under four of Muhammad's most important followers. Their rule, known as the Orthodox caliphate, lasted until 661. The last of these caliphs was ʿAlī, the son-in-law and cousin of Muhammad. His martyrdom led to a split in the Islamic world. Those who revered ʿAlī became the Shias of today, while the majority of Muslims are Sunni. In 660–661 the first of the great Islamic dynasties, the Umayyad dynasty, was founded in Jerusalem and then moved to Damascus. It lasted until 750, when the Abbasid dynasty based in Baghdad became preeminent and the golden age of Islamic civilization flourished.

In the ninth century (800–900) the Carolingian empire began to break up and the Muslim armies ruled North Africa, Spain, and Sicily. The Idrīsids introduced the doctrines of Shi'ism and ruled in Morocco. The Rustamids ruled in western Algeria, and the Aghlabids ruled eastern Algeria, Tunisia, and Sicily. The Holy Roman Empire found its creation in Germany under Otto the Great. In the east, the Abbasid dynasty, supplanting the Umayyads of Damascus, lasted until about 1100, but its greatest moments were in this century, especially under the enlightened rule of Hārūn al-Rashīd (c. 764–809), of *Arabian Nights* fame, and the caliph al-Ma'mūn. This was a glorious epoch in the history of Islam, and the arts and sciences were richly endowed and encouraged. In the court of the Abbasids we find the first true cuisine developing since the time of the Romans.

In the tenth century, the Byzantine Empire reached its apogee and was the lone bulwark against Muslim expansion. The empire extended from Italy to Mesopotamia (Iraq). Constantinople at this time was the economic and artistic center of the Mediterranean world. The Islamic world also expanded, for during this century Spain, Sicily, and all of North Africa were firmly under Muslim rule and they attacked southern Italy. ʿAbd-ar-Raḥmān III, the most gifted and able ruler of the Islamic dynasty of the Umayyads in Spain, pacified Spain and completed the centralization of government. He encouraged agricultural advances and Córdoba became the greatest intellectual center in the Mediterranean.

In the eleventh century, Sicily was under Arab rule, southern Italy was under weak Byzantine control, and the entire Italian peninsula was a patchwork of small city-states and principalities. Onto this stage rode the mounted Norman knights of northern France, on their way to the Holy City of Jerusalem. These soldiers of fortune were soon to conquer southern Italy, Sicily, Tunisia, and much of the northeastern Mediterranean. The threat of the Muslims was ever present to the Christian Mediterranean, but they did lose the great center of Arab science and learning in Toledo to King Alphonso VI of Castile in 1084, which was a significant strategic setback to the Muslim presence in Spain. This Muslim threat, and the defeat of a Byzantine army by the Seljuk Turks, a Muslim Turkic tribe from Anatolia, at Manzikert (Malazgirt) in 1071, set the stage for the Crusades. The Crusades were military adventures over several centuries by western Christendom attempting to recapture the Holy Land from the Muslims, although eastern Christendom looked upon the effort suspiciously. Most of the Crusades were hopeless ventures by masses of poor people or mercenaries. During the First Crusade (1096–1099) Arab-controlled Jerusalem was captured and forty thousand Jews and Muslims murdered and mosques and synagoges burned. The terror and brutality were so great it is remembered to this day by both Middle Eastern Jews and Muslims. In North Africa, the Zīrids controlled Tunisia while the Almoravids ruled most of the rest of North Africa and parts of Spain.

In the twelfth century, the Crusading movement

dominated the Mediterranean scene and in 1204 Constantinople fell to the Crusaders. But by the end of the century the great Muslim general Saladin recaptured Jerusalem in 1187 without sacking it, an act of great humanitarianism considering the general cruelty of this age. The peripatetic Normans established their kingdom in Sicily, and Palermo became the greatest city in the Mediterranean world for a time. During this century a true urban revolution in the Mediterranean was consolidated, especially in Italy. Soon the names of Venice, Florence, Milan, Pisa, Amalfi, and Genoa would be synonymous with Mediterranean power, both political and economic.

In the thirteenth century, Frederick II, from the house of Hohenstaufen in Swabia in Germany, became king of Sicily and was known as *"Stupor Mundi,"* or wonder of the world. Many historians consider him the greatest of the medieval kings. He was one of the most learned men of his day and was responsible for the translation of many Arabic scientific works into Latin. This century also saw the struggle between Venice and Genoa for the Levantine trade. France came into her own as a Mediterranean power under Philip Augustus (1165–1223), who paved the streets of Paris, walled the city, and began building the Louvre. The Christian reconquest of Spain began earnestly in the thirteenth century and Catalonia started to become a Mediterranean commercial and economic power. There were five more Crusades in this century. The Fourth Crusade, which captured Constantinople from the Byzantines in 1204, was called by the great historian of the Crusades, Steven Runciman, the greatest crime against humanity. In the thirteenth century the Hapsburgs began building their dynasty with roots in southern Germany through territorial expansion and dynastic marriages. In several centuries the Hapsburgs ruled in Spain, Germany, Hungary, Austria, and Bohemia.

In the fourteenth century, the great plague known as the Black Death decimated Europe and the Mediterranean, killing almost half the population in some places. On the intellectual front great poets such as Dante and artists such as Giotto were precursors to the Renaissance that would come into full bloom over the next two centuries. In the eastern Mediterranean, this century saw the beginning of the expansion of Ottoman Turkish power.

In the fifteenth century, Spanish rule of the House of Aragon was at its peak; they conquered the kingdoms of Naples and Sicily and reunited those crowns, to make them the center of the Aragonese Mediterranean. The Muslims were finally defeated completely with the conquest of Granada in 1492, and their many-centuries-long rule came to an end. The Italian city-states were very powerful, especially Florence, the center of the Italian Renaissance. Patrician families such as the de'Medici, controlled the commercial, political, and economic life of the city, and were able, through their fabulous wealth, to be patrons for the artistic and architectural Renaissance and all the elements of fine culture—that is, good living, such as cuisine, fashion, and music. The century from 1450 to 1550 marked the apogee of the Renaissance, as well as the supremacy of Italy in all intellectual and artistic fields. The Italian city-states were always at each other's throats and constantly forming and reforming alliances with foreign powers to do the next city in. A variety of wars against the Turks continued, but the tide turned when the Ottoman Turks under Mohammed the Conqueror captured the Byzantine capital of Constantinople in 1453. The remainder of the century saw wars between the Ottoman Turks and Venice. By the end of the century, Christopher Columbus would sail to a new world and the Mediterannean would never be the same.

The sixteenth century was truly the Age of Exploration. Numerous explorers set out for the New World, and colonies were established and the globe circumnavigated by 1522. France was at war with Spain as well as involved in religious wars with neighbors and internal enemies. Religious fanaticism in this century was the usual cause of all sorts of horrific policies. In Spain, Philip II ruled for nearly a half century and he was determined to stamp out the new cult of Protestantism. These policies led to Spain's involvement in general European affairs, both costly and draining. This century saw the Italian city-states, the Spanish, the French, German mercenaries, and even the Papacy fight vicious battles for control of what was believed to be the fulcrum of the Mediterranean, namely the Italian peninsula. Many of these wars ended with the Treaty of Cateau-Cambrésis in 1559, but it also saw most Italian cities, except Venice, fall directly under Spanish influence. Meanwhile, the Ottoman Turks were still a dangerous threat, attacking Venetian-controlled Cyprus in 1570. They had already captured Syria and Egypt in 1516–1517 and were soon to enter their golden age under Süleiman I the Magnificent (1520–1566). Turkish conquests and wars with Venice continued throughout the century.

In the seventeenth century, the Thirty Years' War consumed most of Europe, but so did Venetian-Turkish wars. The decline of the Ottoman Empire also begins in this century, although it would continue to remain a strong power for some time.

THE ORGANIZATION OF THE BOOK

THIS book is divided into three parts. Part I will explore the relationship of man and his environment, and the food he eats. I call it "An Algebra of Mediterranean Gastronomy" because the various unknowns of Mediterranean cuisines can be considered only if we set up our problem and solution as an algebraic equation. The word *algebra* comes from the Arabic word *al-jabr,* which literally means "the reduction"; the sauce I hope to reduce will reveal the essence of Mediterranean gastronomy. Part I is divided into three chapters. Chapter 1, "The Historical Foundation of Mediterranean Gastronomy," sets the stage, introducing the reader to the technological and economic transformations that reshaped European civilization after the demise of the Roman Empire. The importance of the Arab agricultural revolution, and the concept of the Islamic paradise that underlies this Arab sensibility, will be explored, as will the importance of feudalism, the growth of commerce and industry, and cities. We'll see the effect of the Black Death and the rise of capitalism. The stage will be set to talk about the heritage of our celebrated cuisines and especially the influence of Arab culture.

In Chapter 2, "Harvest of Sorrow, Food of Dreams," the "real" historical Mediterranean will emerge. It is a story of scarcity, climate, the food of dreams. In this chapter we'll see the arrival of the potato in the Old World and how it began to alleviate hunger. Chapter 3, "Feast, Anti-Feast," shows that food determined life. We'll see the importance of bread and the political power of the butcher while we travel through Muslim Spain, Tunisia, the Levant, Spain, Provence, and Languedoc, examining what people ate in the Middle Ages and seeing contemporary recipes that show how the conquering of hunger resulted in a culinary richness.

Part II, "An Ecology of Mediterranean Gastronomy," is devoted to the exploration of the relationship between the geography of the Mediterranean and the populations' interactions with their environment that forms the foundation for the evolution of particular cuisines. The geography of the Mediterranean is a complex of peninsulas and seas ringed by mountains. We pay attention to geography because it tells us about the structural realities that affect the lives of humans. It determines agriculture and fishing and wars and daily life. It determines the food we eat. The first chapter of Part II, Chapter 4, " 'They Eat from One Bowl': Lives in the Mountains, Meadows, Plains, and Deserts," will look at the role of the mountains and mountain people. We'll see the importance of cheese, salt, butter, and yogurt, and we'll examine the Greeks and their role, and look at the transhumant and nomadic populations. Chapter 5 is about the cities, their growth and role in Mediterranean history. The title of the chapter, "Le Serenissima, La Superba, and the Sublime Porte," reflects the three greatest cities of a particular period of the Mediterranean—Venice, Genoa, and Istanbul—but we'll also visit Cairo, the mother of the world; Ragusa, modern Dubrovnik; and see how the expulsion of the Jews and Muslims from Spain affected the lives of cities in the East and North Africa. In Chapter 6, "Frutti di Mare," we will encounter the bulk of the seafood recipes, as well as look at the lives of the people who shaped what the Mediterranean Sea was in the Middle Ages—the shipbuilders, the sailors, the fishermen, and the pirates. Chapter 7, "Islands of Paradise and Isolation," will look at the islands of the Mediterranean. The islands often played an important role in the dissemination of food. Sicily is the most important island, whereas Corsica and Sardinia were isolated. We will also explore the islands of the Adriatic and Aegean, which were once so important for Venice, the quasi-islands, the islets, the presidios, and the islands of the deserts, the oases.

Part III, "A Measure of Mediterranean Gastronomy," is an attempt to see the importance of the two items of trade that made Mediterranean cities rich and how certain cuisines developed as a result. In Chapter 8, "The Spice Orgy," I will examine the role of the spice trade and the markets. Chapter 9, "Grain for Princes, Grain for Dogs," will look at the most important grains—wheat, bulgur, rice, barley, millet—and those who traded these grains. Chapter 10, "Hard Wheat and Its Famous Inventions," covers the most important of grains, wheat, and its most significant inventions, in both an economic and a gastronomic sense—macaroni, couscous, and hardtack.

The final section of the book is the Conclusion, where I will use the literal and evocative sense of the Wandering Jew to make some observations about this Mediterranean Feast.

WHAT THIS BOOK HOPES TO DO

WHAT is the Mediterranean? What does it mean? I can do no better than to quote Fernand Braudel himself:

> The life of the sea, the vital force, takes control of the small and least weighty fragments of land, the islands and coastal margins. Growing more powerful and compelling this force would draw into its orbit larger and larger land masses, the peninsulas, elevating the history of the sea to a higher level. And the greatest moments of all would be when it was strong enough to attract towards it the great continental blocks: moments that saw Caesar in Gaul, Germanicus beyond the Elbe, Alexander on the Indus, the Arabs in China or the Moroccans on the Niger. At such moments the Mediterranean seems to be a concept capable of infinite extension. But how far in space are we justified in extending it? This is a difficult and controversial question; but if we are seeking to explain the history of the Mediterranean, it is perhaps the fundamental question we should be asking.[7]

What is the purpose of a history of food? Is it to know the diet of each historical epoch, to find the *associations alimentaires* (to use Braudel's expression)—that is, how each society confronted economically and socially the problem of survival? Or is it to find the "plant of civilization" or for something else?

This book is not an attempt to answer that question, but it is interested in the "something else" that seems to be linked to the problem of survival in the Mediterranean. It is about what happens in the kitchen, truly a world of women, and is expressed, I hope, by what happens to the reader when he or she brings this book into the kitchen. It is about the creation of cuisine above and beyond food as fuel, as so many Americans unfortunately think of it.

Cuisine is the telos of productive agriculture and husbandry beyond sustenance. For the historian to conclude his or her inquiries with the agricultural and not with cuisine seems to me to miss the whole point. For the food writer to start his history with cuisine without understanding the political, economic, cultural, and agricultural history that underlies cooking is one dimensional. Cuisine is the tactile connection we have to breathing history. History and culture offer us a vibrant living society that we taste through cuisine. All cuisine is a reflection of the society from which it emanates. All cuisine is historical, rooted in the agri-cultures of the region in question. And cuisine has always been rooted in two foundations, the poor and the rich.[8] In the end, cuisine is the result of culture. Food is essential to our lives and our happiness, and the cooking of good food satisfies both. In this book I hope to satisfy some questions about food in the Mediterranean, but I also hope that you prepare it, cook it, and eat it, for this book is a cookbook, and good food will make you happy, and happiness, and the works we engage in to be happy, appear to be the only purpose to our short existence at this time.

[PART I]

An ALGEBRA *of* MEDITERRANEAN GASTRONOMY

IN the ninth century, the word *algebra* was used for the first time in the title of the famous work by the Muslim mathematician Muḥammad ibn Mūsā al-Khwārazmī, *Kitāb al-mukhtaṣar fī-ḥisāb al-jabr wa'l-muqābalah,* which can be roughly translated as "The book of summary concerning the process of calculating compulsion and equation," with the word *al-jabr* giving us the word *algebra. Al-jabr* in the title means restoration and amplification or balancing something incomplete. Al-Khwārazmī did not use any symbolic notation in his book, for his argument was rhetorical. His book was first translated into Latin by Robert of Chester in 1145, and al-Khwārazmī himself gave his name to our English word *algorithm*.

Why does a cookbook begin with the etymology of *algebra*? The reason I've chosen this approach is that there really is no such thing as "Mediterranean cuisine." At the same time, we seem to know what we mean when we use the expression. This paradoxical phenomenon needs to be explained and this book is my attempt to explain it: to inquire into the value of an unknown, call it *x*. I'm using *algebra* as a paradigm for determining the value of *x, x* being the contemporary Mediterranean cuisines that developed from the centuries of struggle that we will encounter in the chapters ahead. I suspect "Mediterranean cuisine" is an invention of Anglo-Saxons, for I have never heard, until the past few years, any native of the Mediterranean (who lives in the Mediterranean) refer to such a thing. But after Elizabeth David published her famous *A Book of Mediterranean Food* in 1950, the expression "Mediterranean cuisine" became common, even though we weren't quite certain what was being referred to. The sense in which I use the word *algebra* is a desire for certainty, for a complete picture.

I hope to expose the foundation of Mediterranean gastronomy, which we will see begins with a consideration of the historical situation in which it arose, as well as the climate, the harvest, the search for food. I will show in Part I that understanding contemporary Mediterranean food is rooted in the history of the Mediterranean peoples and their struggle against poverty and famine. The story of today's celebrated Mediterranean cuisines begins with the fall of the Roman Empire and the rise of Islamic civilization. This is somewhat at variance with the traditional approach, which begins with the ancient Egyptians or the classical Greeks. The story I tell unfolds with the emergence of feudalism and the transition to capitalism. It is a story affected by agricultural revolutions, the plague, innovations in technology, and the Age of Exploration. Once the historical context is set, we can explore where our Western cuisine comes from and how it developed. We will consider how harvests were more of sorrow and food more of dreams in a Mediterranean world where the climate was cruel, scarcity the norm, and vagrants, bandits, the religiously pious, and even the rich struggled for their nourishment. The last chapter of Part I, called "Feast, Anti-Feast," will look at how food determined all. We will look at a sampling of Mediterranean cultures in a variety of historical eras to see how the victory over hopelessness transformed Mediterranean foods from subsistence to cuisine.

❖ I ❖

THE HISTORICAL FOUNDATION OF MEDITERRANEAN GASTRONOMY

Rivers of water unstalling, rivers of milk unchanging in flavor, and rivers of wine—a delight to the drinkers, rivers, too of honey purified, and therein for them is every fruit and forgiveness from their Lord.

—THE KORAN[1]

CABBAGE was one of the most common foods on the Mediterranean table for more than a millennium. In the simple cabbage we find a paradigm for the evolution of Mediterranean cuisine. The horticultural progress of the cabbage from a simple leafy vegetable to the compact tight-headed one of today, from cabbage cooked in water to the following contemporary *minestrone di cavolo* recipe from Pisa in Tuscany, is a metaphor for the evolutionary complexity of Mediterranean cuisine today. How do I define the Mediterranean? What is a cuisine? What is Mediterranean cuisine? How did it develop? These are questions that, if not answered, at least will be addressed in the chapters ahead. But first, fortify yourself for the journey with this cabbage minestrone.

❖ *Minestrone di Cavolo* (Tuscany)

CABBAGE SOUP

The most common dish in the medieval Mediterranean was cabbage soup. The cabbage, today hardly considered a popular vegetable, was a metaphor for nearly a thousand years of Mediterranean food. In many ways cabbage soup was the paradigm of the Mediterranean meal, which only today we can call a Mediterranean feast. Take this recipe, which Pisans claim as their own. It is a delicious, rich, and complex minestrone that everyone will find satisfying in an elemental way, yet it began as nothing more than cabbage cooked in water. Make this soup and the lessons of this chapter can be well digested. (See the box on Italian cooking techniques, page 285, on making a battuto.*)*

½ cup extra virgin olive oil
1 medium-size onion, finely chopped
1 carrot, finely chopped
1 celery stalk, finely chopped
2 ounces pancetta, finely chopped
1 ounce prosciutto fat, finely chopped
½ cup finely chopped fresh parsley leaves
3 tablespoons finely chopped fresh basil leaves
1 pound green cabbage, damaged outer leaves removed, cored, and coarsely chopped
½ pound red cabbage, damaged outer leaves removed, cored, and coarsely chopped
1½ quarts water

½ pound dried *cannellini* or other white beans, picked over, soaked in cold water to cover for 2 hours, and drained
1 pound potatoes, peeled and diced large
Salt and freshly ground black pepper to taste
¼ pound *pennine* or other small macaroni
¼ cup freshly grated Parmigiano-Reggiano cheese

1. In a soup or stockpot, heat the olive oil over medium heat, then cook the *battuto* of onion, carrot, celery, pancetta, prosciutto fat, parsley, and basil until the onion is soft and some fat has rendered, about 10 minutes, stirring occasionally.

2. Add the cabbage and toss with the *battuto* until all the leaves are coated. Add the water and beans. Cover, reduce the heat to medium-low, and cook until the beans are slightly soft, about 1 hour, with the soup only gently bubbling. Add the potatoes and cook just until tender, 25 to 30 minutes.

3. Season the soup with salt and pepper and add the pasta. Cook the pasta, uncovered, until it is al dente, 12 to 15 minutes. Serve with the cheese and more olive oil if desired.

Makes 4 servings

✣ ✣ ✣

ONCE a civilization reaches a point where the availability of food is assured, and its consumption is not purely for subsistence, a cuisine may develop. Then again, this isn't a necessary development because a creative impulse on the part of the society, and not just an individual, is also required. A cuisine cannot be created in the kitchen if it is not desired at the table. A cuisine might not develop at all or it might not develop in all segments of the society. A cuisine transcends simply cooking; turning raw food into cooked food is not cuisine.

There are certain preconditions necessary for the development of cuisine. First, cuisine develops when agriculture is economically productive. Second, a surplus of food must find its way into the kitchen, not merely into a pot over a field fire. Third, once the food has entered the kitchen, the creative talents of a cook must be brought to bear upon the food and the food transformed by a manner of cooking into this thing we call cuisine. Fourth, a cuisine becomes orally codified through the transference of knowledge from master to apprentice (mother to daughter) and sometimes in the written language. Fifth, a cuisine exists when people are eating not simply to fuel up or sustain themselves but because they are emotionally and intellectually relating to culinary creations in the same way they might relate to a work of art. Sixth, the cook cooks for someone; the cuisine must be accepted by someone, for cuisine is not a one-way street nor is the kitchen a vacuum. It is at this point that cuisine becomes art and is more than the act of cooking—it is a meaningful part of material culture. Cuisine becomes a reflection of what that culture values, transformed into taste. Once the flavors of our cabbage soup begin pushing beyond the one-dimensional taste of cabbage, once there is a drizzle of olive oil, or a piece of prosciutto fat, or a certain spicing, we enter a realm of cuisine rather than mere cooking. We can begin to differentiate between different cultures' conceptions of cabbage soup.

I believe that the Mediterranean cuisine of today is better understood when we consider the context in which it arose. That means we need to see cuisine as a product of societal changes that occurred over a period of about one thousand years in terms of the economic, political, agricultural, and social history of the Mediterranean.

Enormous changes occurred in the Mediterranean between the fall of the Roman Empire (fifth century A.D.) and the advent of the modern era (about 1700). The salient parts underlying the Mediterranean culinary story are threefold. First is the rise of Islamic civilization and its role in preserving the Hellenistic tradition and transmitting the Persian, Indian, and Chinese scientific and mathematical heritages to Western civilization, and in making its own unique contributions to modern science and agricultural technology. Second is the transition from feudalism to capitalism and the resultant Renaissance. The third is the Age of Exploration.

The agricultural introductions from the Muslim world and the transition from feudalism to capitalism underlie the evolution of cooking in the Mediterranean from subsistence consumption to the new cuisines that arose from the creative impulse of the Renaissance. A new consciousness was created by the economic transformations resulting from capitalism; both the Renaissance and the Age of Exploration were human endeavors resulting from these capitalist transformations. One part of this new consciousness was to materially transform one's physical surroundings, which we see with the rise of "good living," especially in the realms of fashion, music, theater, art, and cuisine. A true culinary revolution took place in France in the mid-seventeenth century that made the final break with medieval cuisine and its dietetically based style of cooking. The new cuisine, one based on the aesthetic thinking of humanism, is said to have its beginning with the publication of La Varenne's *Le cuisinier françois* in 1652, but we will see that the culinary revolution began earlier in Italy and the Arab world and that the culinary revolution in France was simply the end as well as the beginning of a historical process. Humanism was the philosophical movement that originated in Italy in the latter part of the fourteenth century that recognized the dignity of man and made him the measure of all things. Humanism was the philosophical foundation for Renaissance thinkers as they sought to reintegrate man into the world of nature and history. The humanists rejected the medieval heritage and chose to return to an idealized version of the classical world with its recognition of the place of pleasure in the moral life of man. This led them to the defense of the ancient Greek philosopher Epicurus, whose defense of pleasure appealed to the new conception of man in the universe as conceived by the humanists. In the culinary realm, and put into Hegelian terms, medieval Islamic cuisine was the thesis, Renaissance Italian cuisine was the antithesis, and the French culinary revolution was the synthesis that led to the contemporary Mediterranean cuisine as it is represented in the recipes in this book. This is a very loose formulation, and you will encounter provisos to this statement throughout the book.

The role of agriculture was important also, not only because it provided food but also because the emergence of capitalism was rooted in the profits made from trade, and the overwhelming products of trade were those of agriculture, and especially grain, as we will see in Chapter 9. Once wealth was created through the accumulation of capital on the part of an emerging class of entrepreneurs who were trading in food, several things happened. Cities grew, and so did the refinements of life. The food traded became more than a trade item; it allowed various cuisines to emerge. The cuisine that initally emerged was not widespread but found only in the homes of the extremely wealthy and the kitchens of ducal courts and ecclesiastical residences. In terms of our cabbage metaphor, the leafy cabbage not only developed a head, soup was not only made from it, but the cabbage leaf was manipulated—it was rolled and stuffed.

In this chapter, the foundation will be laid for seeing the emergence of our celebrated cuisines as an unfolding from the cultural and economic poverty of the Mediterranean. Once the economic and historical foundations are laid, we can better understand how the contemporary cuisines of the Mediterranean arose.

The influence of events on the periphery of the Mediterranean, and even on distant shores, has long been ignored in the history of Mediterranean cuisines. We will see that developments in the Arab world and northern Europe had far-reaching profound effects on Mediterranean agriculture. It had effects as well on the rise of feudalism, innovations in technology, the importance of commerce and industry in the growth of cities, the opening of the Age of Exploration, and the rise of capitalism. One of the most important outside influences was the agriculture and sciences of Islamic civilization. We will see how an Islamic aesthetic rooted in the descriptions of the Garden of Paradise in the Koran spawned the agricultural revolution of the Arabs in the Mediterranean. We will also see another agricultural revolution taking place in northern Europe that led to the emergence of the mounted knights and how these knights came to affect developments in the Mediterranean. Three other important outside events affected the Mediterranean: the Black Death from Asia, gold from Africa, and precious metals and new foods from the Americas. All these events had a profound influence on the foods that came to be eaten in the Mediterranean and the cuisines that we celebrate today.

THE ROLE OF ISLAMIC CIVILIZATION IN THE FORMATION OF MEDITERRANEAN GASTRONOMY

The Medieval Green Revolution

THE Dark Ages, that gloomy epoch after the fall of the Roman Empire, is not an entirely accurate term. Although it may be partially accurate to describe the European Mediterranean, the Islamic Mediterranean could hardly be called dark, for in the five centuries from 632 to 1100 a young Muslim civilization showed an extraordinary capacity for receiving and absorbing anything new from other cultures and integrating this knowledge to expand the influence of its own civilization. Although every schoolchild knows where our "Arabic numerals" came from, the Arab contribution in other fields of learning is nearly unknown. Mathematics and astronomy are two areas in which Arab learning gave the Western languages a wealth of terms, from *algebra* and *algorithm* to *zenith* and *zero*. Two of the most consequential areas of Arab scientific endeavor were agriculture and hydrology. A virtual agricultural revolution occurred, leading the economic historian Professor Andrew M. Watson to call it the "medieval green revolution." It is of paramount importance in understanding the evolution of modern European cuisine.

The Romans knew that plants received nitrogen from the air and not the soil, and that by burying plants their nitrogen could be returned to the soil. The Romans called this process "green manuring."[2] Green manuring was instrumental in allowing Roman farmers to successfully grow crop plants, such as cabbage, along with a host of other vegetables. They had a love of cabbages because of its supposed medicinal value. Pliny said it would be a long task to make a list of all the praises of the cabbage. It was believed that eating cabbages could ward off a hangover, as well as act as a laxative. The Romans ate it raw dipped in vinegar or boiled and eaten with lots of oil, a little salt, cumin, and fine barley flour, which was thought to be a cure for colic. The Roman writer Cato, who said the medicinal value of cabbage surpassed that of all other vegetables, recommended that a woman wash her private parts in the urine saved from a person who habitually ate cabbage and she would never be diseased.[3]

Arab agronomists learned many techniques from the Romans but were far more sophisticated in their understanding of agriculture. They studied the structure, temperature, and moisture of soils, the result being that an Arab farmer could predict yields and crop the land more often. For example, in Roman as well as Byzantine Sicily, land was cropped once every two years, while the Arabs cropped four times in the same period. They freed more land for cultivation and created a whole new growing season.[4]

Arab technical innovations led not only to a revolution in agriculture but also to an economic revolution because of all the changes in the lives of people. Innovations in hydrology and irrigation meant that the peasant, by controlling water flow, controlled the number and times of harvests. Crippling famines and crushing poverty were checked as the economy became stable, with more food available.[5]

An enormous variety of new crops were discovered or diffused by the Arabs. These new crops played a central role in a more productive agriculture and were closely linked to important changes in the economy at large. The Arabs introduced higher yielding new crops and better varieties of older ones such as cabbage, increasing the productivity of land and labor. The most important of the new food crops diffused in the Mediterranean by the Arabs were sorghum (*Sorghum bicolor* (L.) Moench.), rice (*Oryza sativa* L.), hard wheat (formerly *Triticum durum* Desf.; currently *T. turgidum* var. *durum*), sugarcane (*Saccharum officinarum* L.), various citrus fruits such as the sour orange, lemon, and lime, bananas and plantains, the coconut palm (*Cocus nucifera* L.), watermelon, spinach, artichoke, taro (*Colocasia antiquorum* Schott.), eggplant, and mangoes.[6] Land use became specialized, irrigation technology was invented or improved, crop rotation became more intensive, and techniques of farming became labor-intensive. As a result the productivity of the whole economy improved. There was a growth in trade, an enlargement of the money economy, a rise in population, and increasing urbanization because more food was available to the cities, produced by more efficient agricultural workers with new agricultural technology.

Popular opinion, and some scholarly as well, has long believed that the Arabs conquered by the sword and brought only ruination when their armies swept through the Mediterranean. This notion can be blamed to a great extent on the conflict between Islam and Christianity. Later, nineteenth- and twentieth-century European scholarship assumed that the remains of Mediterranean irrigation works, castles, and villages all date from Roman times or earlier, and that the Arabs made agriculture less intensive since they had "no agricultural traditions" and "knew only about the raising of stock."[7] The French researcher Professor Marcel Solignac has pointed out that French archaeologists and others working in Tunisia had consistently assigned to the Romans many irrigation works that he showed clearly to be Arab. Modern authors have made this mistake, too.[8] There is a vast literature on irrigation history that minimizes or even discredits the contribution of Muslim science to agriculture, particularly in Spain, North Africa, and Palestine. Much of the irrigation is falsely attributed to the Romans. But the scholarly works of Thomas Glick, A. Pippitone Cannone, and Solignac show that the Muslim contribution was significant. It is interesting to note that the vocabulary of irrigation in the Sicilian language of today is largely of Arabic origin.[9]

What is the context in which the Arabs were responsible for an agricultural revolution that changed what Mediterranean peoples grew and ate? What was the impetus for this revolution? The popular conception of Muslims as a nomadic desert people, without agriculture, is an erroneous one. The first Muslims were not desert dwellers, but Arabs from the commercial center of Mecca and the agricultural oasis of Medina.[10] Islam is a religion of traders and merchants, not peasants, and it is traders and merchants who have the financial and political wherewithal to create a vibrant and innovative agriculture.

One of the reasons the Arabs are not usually associated with agriculture is a fundamental lack of understanding of how Islamic systems of land tenure encouraged productive agriculture. The large estates typical of the Roman and Byzantine Mediterranean were highly inefficient. In Sicily the Arabs successfully broke up large Roman and Byzantine estates known as *latifundia* and established more modest yet more productive farms.[11] These large estates were also broken down by Islamic law relating to the partition of property upon inheritance. Another way in which large estates were possibly broken up was frequent confiscation and regranting (perhaps in smaller units) of property belonging to those who had become too rich or powerful as well as the establishment of smaller holdings by *waqf*s, religious trusts controlled by lawyers, that were more productive. Laws giving the ownership of dead or abandoned land to those who reclaimed it may also have favored the creation of smaller estates.

The lands around Mediterranean cities became dominated by small farms, market gardens, and orchards, often irrigated by a noria (an irrigation method of moving buckets of water upward over short distances). In Sicily many of these gardens were around Palermo, especially in the Conca d'Oro and princely palaces, while in Spain Córdoba and the province of Valencia were well known as horticultural sites.

The owner of a small farm was more likely to innovate when he knew that the benefits would go to his family than if he worked on a large estate where the landowner would profit. In the medieval Arab world, even on the remaining large estates, agricultural workers were free of many oppressive features. There was no demesne, manorial land worked with involuntary tenant labor, which we will encounter later in this chapter in the Christian Mediterranean. Taxation was low, in stark contrast to rural taxation under the late Roman and Byzantine empires, and this also encouraged agricultural innovation.

Long after Arab rule ended these gardens were often tended by Arab cultivators called *ortolani.* The famous Arab geographer of the Norman court, al-Idrīsī, wrote in the twelfth century of these gardens, and the vineyards, but only one olive orchard, meaning that the production of olive oil in the Middle Ages in Sicily was not great. But al-Idrīsī neglected to mention the sugar plantations that we know existed. A half century later, Hugo Falcandis, the historian of the Norman kings whom the contemporary historian Evelyn Jamison argued was not a real person, wrote about the gardens of Palermo as well. In his history of the Norman court from 1154 to 1169 and in a second twelfth-century document called the *Epistola ad Petrum,* both of which were written by the Sicilian admiral Eugenius according to Jamison, there are detailed descriptions of Sicilian gardens. The *Epistola ad Petrum* has a vivid description of the exotic fruits of the Conca d'Oro, which stretches for four miles between the city walls and the mountains. The characteristic Palermitan method of irrigating vegetable gardens, vineyards, and orchards of almonds, date palms, figs, and other fruit trees (the most significant being the Arab-introduced bigerades or bitter oranges, *Citrus aurantium*) is set out in detail. The irrigated gardens grew long, squat cucumbers, gourds, spherical watermelons on trellises, and pomegranates with a hard outer rind, as well as citrons, limes, walnuts, and carobs. The Normans built (although they may have been left over from the Arabs) watchtowers to overlook the gardens or royal pleasure-parties reposing in the gardens.[12]

In the thirteenth- and fourteenth-century gardens of Palermo, truly kitchen gardens, the largest quarter of the garden was given over to growing cabbages, leading the contemporary French historian Henri Bresc to call them the "inevitable cabbage."[13] Contracts from taverns and inns in Palermo in these centuries show the *ortolani* grew only cabbage and onions and ate only cabbage minestrone reinforced with fava and chickpeas, and eaten with stale bread.[14] The Arabs did not introduce the cabbage but they certainly seem to have developed a taste for it.

Another reason agriculture progressed in the Mediterranean was the Islamic legal and institutional framework affecting farming. In the early centuries of the Islamic Mediterranean (A.D. 632–1100) slaves were not used (with rare exceptions) nor was the peasantry reduced to serfdom. The peasantry performed no corvée for the landowner—that is, unpaid labor due from the vassal to the lord—though they were perhaps conscripted for labor on irrigation works. Agricultural workers were free and their labor supplied as self-employed or through sharecropping. Apparently the Arab conquests in the Mediterranean did not bring ruination as much as it did the very opposite: the Arab invasions freed the countryside from many arrangements that were economically backward.[15]

The diffusion of Islamic agriculture was rapid, but once it reached the frontiers of the Christian European Mediterranean it slowed. Spinach was one of the earliest of the new crops to be received in Europe. Spinach is first mentioned in Spain by the late eleventh century, and was the subject of a treatise by Ibn Ḥajjāj in 1073.[16] But it did not appear until the thirteenth century in Italy. Sorghum, too, another new crop, is mentioned in Italy by the late twelfth and thirteenth centuries by the Italian agriculturalist Petrus de Crescentiis (1233?–1321), although its first appearance is as *melega* or *suricum* in an Italian document of 910.[17] Sour oranges and lemons appear to have spread slowly through parts of Italy. The great Arab geographer and historian al-Masʿūdī (died about 956) wrote that the citron and orange were introduced to Oman in the Arabian peninsula, then Iraq, and finally Syria and Egypt by 912.[18] The arrival and progress of the lime in Europe is difficult to detect. Petrus de Crescentiis talks about limes, *lumie,* as *aranci agri* used to make *agresto,* a sour sauce.[19] (The Arab agronomic achievement with citrus rests on the fact that many cultivars of citrus trees are apomictic. That means that the seed contains asexual embryos that retain the genetic material of the mother plant. This mode of reproduction is exceptional among citrus plants, and apomixis, therefore, was a major advantage in domesticating citrus fruit by vegetative propagation before the invention of grafting.[20]) Rice and hard wheat also moved slowly. Two other new vegetables, the artichoke and the eggplant, didn't really become popular and established in Europe until the latter part of the fifteenth century.[21]

The agents of agricultural diffusion were the Arab farmers themselves. In Spain they were particularly conscious of re-creating the landscapes they were familiar with in the East, whether it was from the Fertile Crescent or the lush highlands of Yemen. Recreating one's homeland meant planting the same trees, the same plants, and to "place the same food on the table."[22]

Why did these new crops move so slowly into the European Mediterranean? There may be several reasons. First, as the economic historian Andrew Watson points out, the European peasantry may have lacked the skills required to adopt the new plants agriculturally. Second, the feudal agricultural system, which I will talk about in more depth below, may have been unable to integrate the new crops. A third reason may rest on the fact that irrigation in Europe was limited and the population density lower, which meant that a farmer did not have to struggle to get very high returns from the soil, meaning that they were doing fine with what they already had. Some crops may have been rejected at first because they were perceived to be "Muslim crops," such as eggplant and spinach, and there was an ideological resistance to anything Muslim.

The most efficient way for a new crop to be introduced somewhere is for the original farmer, the person who knows best how to grow it, to move there and start growing the plant or show others how to grow it. In the early medieval Mediterranean the introduction of new crops depended heavily on the Arab peasantry that had migrated and knew how to grow these crops. Sicily provides a good example of this phenomenon. After two centuries of Arab rule Sicily had an experienced peasantry growing a wide variety of these new crops. But with the Christian reconquest of the island and the final expulsion of the remaining Arab-Sicilian peasantry in the early thirteenth century to Lucera in Apulia, many of the new crops died out. In fact, henna and indigo had to be reintroduced to Sicily by Jews from the Maghrib, while the Sicilian king Frederick II had to send to

Tyre in the Levant for "two men who knew how to make sugar," even though Arab Sicily had been a major producer of sugar. The skills needed for growing these crops began to disappear in Sicily after the Norman conquest in 1091 and the slow but sure oppression of the Arab population. Many Arab-Sicilians emigrated to Muslim lands or took flight from the land they cultivated into the mountainous interior of the island. As an aside, at least one of many ideas about the birth of the Mafia supposes that these oppressed mountain Arabs of western Sicily originally formed this now infamous society for their self-protection around 1220, during the reign of Holy Roman Emperor and King of Sicily Frederick II.

The Muslim soldiers who constituted the armies that overran the Mediterranean in the early Islamic centuries (632–1100) were encouraged to settle in the conquered lands through a form of military land grant known as the *iqtaʿ*. This land grant proved to be the foundation for the coming agricultural revolution that in turn was the foundation for the subsequent revolution in the kitchen. Although the early Islamic armies were made up largely of nomads, later armies had large components of Yemenis and others with experience in sedentary agriculture, who contributed to the agricultural development of the regions where they settled.[23] After a short time the Islamic world was populated by an astonishing diversity of people. Visitors to tenth-century Palermo found Greeks, Lombards, Jews, Slavs, Berbers, Persians, Tartars, and sub-Saharan Africans.

Although the Romans knew of many plants, they were not always cultivated. Many were imported from the East—for example, India—and usually for pharmacological reasons—for example, rice. Many of the new crops brought by the Arabs, on the other hand, may have had a beginning in the royal gardens of their rulers. Another possibility is that the crops began in botanical or experimental gardens whose patrons were rulers and whose administrators were the leading agronomes of the day. We know that Arab botanists experimented with three different cultivars of cauliflower, itself derived from the cabbage, and we may assume that they also experimented with cabbage. The first European botanical gardens were not founded until centuries later, the one at Salerno in 1310 being the first.[24] The enchantment with greenery and the description of the Garden of Paradise in the Koran led to a penchant among Arab rulers to collect plants for their kitchen gardens. The kitchen garden was a garden supplying not only food but also natural beauty and it gave rise to a genre of Arabic poetry known as the *rawḍiya,* the garden poem, meant to conjure the image of the Garden of Paradise.[25]

THE GARDENS OF PARADISE

WHAT might account for this interest in and love of growing plants among Muslim communities? Can the philosophical beginning of the Arab agricultural initiative be found in the conception of man derived from the holy book of the Muslims, the Koran? The Koran is not a record of the Prophet's activities, like the New Testament's, but is believed to be the actual Word of God. The Koran provides thorough and comprehensive guidelines on everything from diet to commercial law. For our purposes we are most interested in the Islamic conception of architectural space and the role the garden plays in that space. In the Western tradition there is a concentration on the external look of a building while traditional Islamic architecture is primarily concerned with enclosed space defined by its building materials. The Islamic aesthetic sees the quality of the volume, its light, its coolness, and its decoration as more important than the mass. The result is an internal architecture, inseparable from the fabric of the city, that forges a refuge. This architectural concept of the Islamic dwelling and city is meant to mirror the ideal human condition, which should be disinterested in outward symbols and deeply concerned with space for the inner soul to breathe and develop. The garden should create this refuge both literally and figuratively. It is not much of a leap to see the connection between the garden and the kitchen. These philosophical concerns are mirrored in the Islamic culinary aesthetic.

In this garden, meant to capture the feeling of the Garden of Paradise (or the Garden of Delights), we find the roots of what centuries later in Spain and Italy became the kitchen garden and the horticultural foundation for the culinary imperative. In a way the story of how the Arabs influenced European cuisine begins with the celestial Garden of Paradise described in the Koran. Paradise is the reward for the Muslim faithful. The Muslim paradise is a continuation of the basic Judeo-Christian paradise. The pre-Islamic tradition of a royal pleasure garden and the arid ecology of the birthplace of Islam resulted in a concept of paradise filled with water and plants of all kinds. Water and other liquids are an important feature. "Gardens underneath which rivers flow" is an expression that occurs more than thirty times in the Koran.[26] "Rivers of water unstalling, rivers of milk unchanging in flavor, and rivers of wine—a delight to the drinkers, rivers, too of honey purified, and therein for them is every fruit and forgiveness from their Lord."[27] In the promised garden are vineyards and the faithful will be accompanied by the *ḥūrīyāt,* the buxom black-eyed virgins of paradise "with swelling breasts," and lovely boys, the *ghilmān,* will attend every need.[28] In the Islamic conception of paradise we find the origin of the quartered garden, divided by means of four water channels, all contained within a private walled enclosure. Paradise is a purely sensual image of sight, sound, and taste. The fountains of paradise gush, the greenery is lush, the food delicious, and the elixir called *maʿ al-tasnīm,* literally "water of the ascended to heaven," is the beverage of the blessed in Paradise, giving everlasting life. Green leaves remind the faithful of heavenly gardens where angels and *ḥūrīyāt* are dressed in green silk and brocade.[29] There is more than one garden of Eden and each is planted with fruit trees, the palm, and pomegranate.[30] Abundant fruit trees are mentioned, with rich pavilions set among them where one talks with friends.

The descriptions of Koranic gardens may have been based on the actual gardens of Damascus, the Ghūṭa, which the first Muslims, the Meccan merchants, had seen. The early Arab caliphs and emirs designed luxurious and bountiful garden paradises to reflect the ideal Garden of Paradise. In Islamic Sicily and Spain the gardens of paradise were planted with exotic fruits such as oranges and bergamots and flowers such as asphodel and adorned with fountains where one heard the soothing spray or tinkle of running water while lounging on silken cushions arranged in order on richly spread carpets under the cool shade of broad-leaved trees.[31] A peaceful repose in today's Alhambra palace in Granada or the al-Azim palace in Damascus makes this all clear.

There was nothing like these gardens in Europe of the time. A European traveler gazing upon the fabulous palace garden of the Ṭūlūnid ruler of Egypt Khumārawayh (ruled 884–896) would have been astonished. The garden was filled with sweet-smelling flowers planted to form Arabic calligraphy. In its courtyard was the wondrous pool of quicksilver where Khumārawayh could rest upon inflated leather cushions tethered with silk ropes to silver columns and drink his *raṭl*s of wine and eat rare figs and dates from far-off lands.[32] The Islamic garden was quite different from the gardens of Europe that became famous during the Renaissance. The Muslims had different kinds of gardens serving different purposes. The *būstān* was the garden of the inner court of a house, a formal garden with pools and water channels. The *janna* was an orchard with palms, oranges, and vines irrigated by canals. The *rawḍa* referred in particular to the vegetable garden that produced foods for the cooks.[33] Before long the kitchens of the caliphs saw an explosion of what one scholar called a "culinary *nouvelle vague.*"[34] The Muslim chefs in ninth-century Baghdad were as dazzling cooks as the Michelin-starred chefs of France today, and very much influenced by the cuisine of Persia, which the Arabs had recently conquered. They made involved preparations such as *madfūna,* a dish of eggplant stuffed with finely minced meat previously cooked in coriander and cinnamon with chickpeas, and then simmered in a sauce of onions, broth, and saffron sprinkled with rose water. The next recipe is the first stuffed vegetable with which I am familiar, and by the sixteenth century the Muslim chefs of Ottoman Damascus and Istanbul were stuffing cabbage leaves, too.[35]

Maḥshī Malfūf (Arab Levant)

STUFFED CABBAGE

Arab cooks are the masters of the stuffed vegetable; the repertoire of a competent cook is seemingly endless. These labor-intensive preparations are some of the most rewarding and, if you sit around rolling or stuffing with someone else, really quite joyous to make. Of course, it is traditionally women's work, but this is communal labor where patience and good spirit is rewarded with happy eaters and a contented cook. When I asked my former mother-in-law, Leila al-Qattan, what fifteen recipes must be included in any cookbook on Arab cuisine, she included this stuffed cabbage recipe. Cabbage has been part of the Arab culinary lexicon since medieval times.

1 large head green cabbage (about 2¾ pounds)
1 cup raw medium- or short-grain rice, rinsed under cold running water until clear or soaked in water to cover for 30 minutes and drained
¾ pound ground lamb
⅓ cup very finely chopped onion
2 teaspoons *bahārāt* (page 524)
¾ teaspoon freshly ground allspice berries
½ teaspoon ground cinnamon
1½ teaspoons salt
1½ teaspoons freshly ground black pepper
3 tablespoons dried mint
6 tablespoons extra virgin olive oil
8 large garlic cloves, finely chopped
Juice from 5 lemons (about 1 cup)
3½ to 4 cups water

1. Remove and discard any of the outermost leaves of the cabbage that are blemished. Bring a large pot of water to a rolling boil and plunge the whole cabbage in until the leaves can be peeled away without ripping, about 10 minutes. Drain well and, when cool enough to handle, separate the leaves carefully, setting them aside, and chop the central core. Lay the larger cabbage leaves in front of you and cut out the thick central stem ribs of the leaves with a paring knife, dividing each leaf in two. Leave the smallest leaves whole. Arrange the cabbage stem ribs and chopped core over the bottom of a round stove-top casserole or saucepan a little wider in diameter than a dinner plate.

2. In a medium-size bowl, knead together the rice, lamb, onion, *bahārāt,* allspice, cinnamon, salt, and pepper until well blended.

3. Place about 1 tablespoon of the stuffing along the rib side of each leaf and roll up tightly without folding the sides over. The rice will not expand enough to damage the leaves. Once rolled, the cabbage leaves will look like thin cigars. Arrange the rolled cabbage leaves on top of the cabbage stem ribs in the casserole or saucepan seam side down. The rolled cabbages should be placed tightly next to each other. Once you've got a single layer, sprinkle with more salt and pepper, 1½ teaspoons of the mint, 3 tablespoons of the olive oil, half the garlic, and half the lemon juice.

4. Continue stuffing and rolling the leaves and place a layer upon the first layer, making each row and

each layer compact and neat. Sprinkle with more salt and pepper, the remaining 1½ tablespoons mint, the remaining 3 tablespoons of olive oil, the remaining garlic, and the remaining lemon juice.

5. Pour in enough of the water to barely cover the cabbage rolls. Put an inverted heavy dinner plate over the cabbage rolls to hold them down. Bring to a gentle boil over medium heat, about 20 minutes, then reduce the heat to very low, using a heat diffuser if necessary, cover, and simmer until tender, 3 to 3½ hours. Remove a roll-up to test for doneness. Serve or continue cooking until done.

Makes 6 servings

FOR the gardens of paradise to become reality, the relocated Arab farmers and gardeners needed water. Water was essential to life in the Mediterranean, but with the limited numbers of aquifers and the scanty rainfall it required all the ingenuity of the people to provide water for their crops and sweet water to drink. Arguably, of all the Mediterranean peoples, the Arabs may have the greatest appreciation for water, and the legacy of Arab hydrological technology is evident throughout the Mediterranean. There is the physical evidence of gardens, such as the water *chadar* (water channel) of the Ziza palace in Palermo and the Generalife (from the Arabic *jannat al-ʿarīf,* meaning the inspector's paradise) in Granada, a Naṣrid monument of the late thirteenth century whose villa was one of the outer buildings of the Alhambra. There is also horticultural evidence, such as the fact that Arabs were the first to lay out orchards in a grid to foster easier growth and harvesting, as well as other agricultural, technological, and linguistic evidence.[36]

One of the most important hydraulic technologies that is a legacy of Islam is the *qanāt,* an underground watercourse formed by linking up a series of wells to tap groundwater resources at what may be very considerable distances.[37] It seems that the Arabs made it possible to develop what became the city of Madrid by introducing a sort of *qanāt*. One historian argues that the very name of Madrid comes from the Arabic.[38]

Islamic hydrological technology consisted of a profusion of devices for catching, storing, channeling, and lifting water. Among the more important of these, besides the *qanāt,* were new kinds of dams and a variety of wheels, norias, turned by animal or water power and used for lifting water, sometimes to great heights, out of rivers, canals, wells, and storage basins. Several of these magnificent norias still groan away today in Hama, Syria, where the fourteenth-century Four Norias of Bishriyāt, or the al-Muḥammadiyya, supply the water for the Grand Mosque.

The Arabs did not invent new technologies as much as they modernized older technologies and spread them over wider areas. Arab innovations dramatically improved the quality of irrigation, and it is only a slight exaggeration to say that by the eleventh century there was hardly a river, stream, spring, known aquifer, or predictable flood that went unused. Across the Islamic Mediterranean a patchwork of heavily irrigated areas, some large and some small, transformed a hostile environment into one where a new agriculture could move and where both our old cabbage and the new crops were grown with astonishing success.[39]

The two most important European entrepôts for cultural and technological transfer between the Muslim and Christian worlds were in Sicily and Spain, where the Islamic presence was significant for a long period of time.[40] In Sicily the verdant foliage and abundant springs of the royal gardens of the Arab caliphs, especially in Palermo, were fashioned as productive and peaceful refuges. The royal gardens, beginning as purely decorative gardens, were transformed over time into kitchen gardens that provided the Arab chefs with the raw materials for their culinary inventions. These gardens were not the small household vegetable patches attached to a house that were common in Western Europe but were more a cross between an experimental horticultural station and a royal garden. The gardens were lush with vegetable crops, flowering bushes, and fruit trees, and graced with water fountains and pavilions.[41]

The selecting out of particular vegetable cultivars must have happened early on in these gardens—for example, with cabbage. The glucosinolates that all the Brassicas contain are broken down by an enzyme when wild, and the early varieties of cabbage leaves when chopped or crushed gave off a bitter taste and goitrogenic substances. Arab botanists must have learned to select less bitter-tasting cabbages early on in their domestication.

Spanish agriculture diminished during the Visigothic period, after the fall of the Roman Empire. The arrival of the Arabs in the eighth century saw a new agricultural initiative that was making original contributions to agricultural science by the tenth century. By the eleventh and twelfth centuries, the scientists connected with these advances in agriculture were significant enough to later be identified as the Andalusi Agronomic School. This school comprised at first physicians, botanists, and chemists associated with the caliph ʿAbd-ar-Raḥmān III (912–961) and his son al-Ḥakam II (961–976). The climax of the school led to an agricultural revolution in Spain. During the eleventh century, the Caliphate of Córdoba broke up, creating a decentralized situation in southern Spain. In tune with four specific events, a momentum was created that led to agricultural advances. The first was a comprehensive program to translate Greek, Roman, Byzantine, and Mesopotamian agronomic works. Second, at this time Córdoba was the center of advanced work in medical, pharmacological, and botanical studies. The agricultural treatises of the medieval period of Muslim Spain are notable for their concern with sustainable agriculture, ecology, and, especially, the recycling of nutrients, the use of manure, pest and disease management, and phytohormonal treatments to encourage root growth and propagation. This was in contrast to the agricultural lands of the Christian kingdoms of Spain, which were organized to provide a diet based on wheat, wine, and meat—a less varied and drier agriculture. Third, the growing population of Hispanic-Arab cities created a food supply problem that spurred agricultural improvement and research. Fourth, the new Arab settlers in Spain quickly took advantage of the richness of Spanish soil and the preexisting Hispano-Roman agricultural heritage.[42]

In Spain the caliphs developed vast irrigation projects known as *huertas,* what we would today call truck farms. They were not limited to Spain; in the lower Rhône the Anti-Popes of Avignon grew romaine lettuce in their *huertas*.[43] In Roussillon, peasants in medieval times grew mostly cabbage and turnips in their small *huertas,* called *hortas,* grown no doubt for the cabbage soup that one day would transform into a delicious *l'ollada* (page 15).

In Languedoc the vegetable production of the garden was known as the *ortolagia*. Cabbage was the most common vegetable in the garden, and was eaten almost every day in medieval Languedoc. It was known by three names: white cabbage, green cabbage, and *choux cabus* (large-headed cabbage). In Languedoc documents show that the Bishop of Avignon, clearly a privileged person, ate meat, a soup, and a vegetable every day. On November 5, 1315, the bishop ate fish, peas, and rice (at that time an extremely rare and expensive food) and his servants had cabbage. The *Ménagier de Paris,* an *aide-memoire* written in the late fourteenth century, is detailed about cabbages: that the best are those picked before the frost and that they should be cooked in the morning and served with olive oil. Even so, we don't know a lot about the vegetable component of the Mediterranean diet, except that cabbage was predominant and workers ate it often at midday in soup. We know that the gardens also grew leeks, spinach, squash (Old World gourds), onions, lettuce, herbs, berries, pennyroyal, borage, hyssop, groundsel, fennel, cabbage tops, chickpeas, parsley root, elderberry flowers, cornel berry, chard, and beans (Old World), as well as fruit such as apples, pears, chestnuts, raisins, cherries, and melons. All in all, the repertoire of foods at the market was much more limited than today and many were sold as medicinal plants. In Provence a fundamental food of the peasants and artisans was a soup made of dried peas, fava beans, and lots of cabbage.[44]

L'ollada (Roussillon)

THE STEW

This famous stew of Roussillon, called ouillade *in French, derived from the Old French verb* aeuller, *meaning "to replenish the cask or cauldron," reflects that it would be cooked continuously, constantly replenished with water, beans, vegetables, or meat. In Catalan it is called* l'ollada *and both this word and the Old French word are derived from the Latin. It is a kind of* escudella *(page 170), a thick soup ultimately related to the various* ollas *and* cocidas *made throughout Spain and not far removed from* bollito misto, *pot-au-feu,* yakhna, *and other soups and stews of many Mediterranean cuisines, and the* tafina *of the North African Jews. In the land of Catalonia, which includes the modern-day French province of Roussillon, these one-pot meals are sometimes made in two pots and then mixed, the pots forever kept on the fire, always cooking their stews of chickpeas, potatoes, turnips, cabbage, vegetables, or, in the Gerona and Barcelona provinces of Catalonia, meats.*

L'ollada *is a very old dish. The leading authority on the gastronomy of Roussillon, Éliane Thibaut-Comelade, told me that it is one of four Catalan dishes that she knows of that exist in Roussillon but not in the Catalan lands in Spain, along with* boules de picolat *(page 205),* la bullinada *(page 379), and* la llagostada, *a lobster stew.*[45]

Colman Andrews, author of a book on Catalan food, points out that some scholars believe the dish is a direct descendent of the adafina *of medieval Spanish Jewish cooking (pages 543 and 682), and I believe they are right.*

1/4 pound dried small white beans (1/2 cup), picked over and rinsed
6 quarts water
Bouquet garni, tied together in cheesecloth, consisting of 6 sprigs fresh thyme and 1 bay leaf
3/4 pound leeks, white and light green parts only, halved lengthwise, washed well, and sliced
6 ounces salt pork, cut into small dice
Salt and freshly ground black pepper to taste
3/4 pound Savoy cabbage (about 1/2 a small head), damaged outer leaves removed, cored, and sliced
1 pound potatoes, peeled and diced
1 tablespoon rendered goose or duck fat

1. Place the beans in a stockpot, and cover with the water. Bring to a boil over medium-high heat, then add the bouquet garni, raise the heat to high, and boil for 1 hour, stirring occasionally.

2. Add the leeks and salt pork and cook for 30 minutes. Don't wander away because you need to stir occasionally.

3. Check the seasoning, adding salt and pepper as desired. Add the cabbage and potatoes and cook until tender, about 10 minutes, stirring frequently. Add the goose fat and cook for 3 minutes. Serve.

Makes 6 to 8 servings

✣ ✣ ✣

VALENCIA had its *huertas* and today gives forth wonderful produce, such as fresh lima beans that are cooked with cured ham or made into soups such as the *puré hortelano.* Today, spinach and chard are favorite vegetables of the kitchen gardens of Catalonia, Languedoc, Provence, and Italy, where spinach is married with golden raisins and pine nuts, typically Arab in inspiration or the local mussels of the *étangs* (lagoons). The *huertas* provided the raw ingredients for a proto-ratatouille, the recipe on page 19 being a modern rendition.

Puré Hortelano (Andalusia)

VEGETABLE SOUP FROM THE TRUCK FARMS

This soup puree from the farmlands around low-lying Málaga in Andalusia requires vegetables and plants grown in the local huertas, *the vast irrigated vegetable gardens of the area. There is a family of dishes called* hortalizas, *which are made with the vegetables harvested from the* huertas. *This* puré hortelano *both looks and tastes much like the Egyptian* mulūkhiyya, *a soup made from the mucilaginous vegetable of the same name, also called Jew's mallow* (Corchorus olitorius); *this Andalusian soup has the same flavor and appetizing viscous texture.*

The salicornia (Salsola kali) *called for in this recipe is a green twiglike plant that is also known as saltwort, sea grape, sea asparagus, Jamaica samphire, marsh samphire, and poor man's asparagus. It is grown in marshy areas near the sea. In Spain, another variety of this kind of plant is glasswort,* barilla, *which was once used to make glass and was transported by ship to Marseilles. Although you should be able to find* salicornia *in gourmet greengrocers or farmer's markets, you can replace the saltwort with laver* (Porphyra umbilicalis), *a sea vegetable sold mostly as a dried product in whole food stores.*

2 quarts vegetable or chicken broth (page 54)
2 cups chopped *salicornia,* ends trimmed, or 1 ounce dried laver (page 716)
10 ounces spinach, heavy stems removed, washed well, and chopped
1/4 cup chopped fresh chives
1 head romaine lettuce, central ribs removed and leaves chopped
1 leek, white and light green parts only, cut in half lengthwise, washed well, and chopped
4 cups diced Italian or French bread, white part only
Salt and freshly ground black pepper to taste
2 tablespoons bacon fat
4 to 6 slices Italian or French bread with crusts
1 hard-boiled large egg, shelled and finely chopped

1. In a soup pot, place the broth, *salicornia,* spinach, chives, lettuce, leek, and cubed bread and season with salt and pepper. Cover, turn the heat to medium, and cook for 30 minutes. Reduce the heat to low and cook another 30 minutes.

2. Pass the mixture through a food mill or strainer, pressing as much liquid out of the vegetables as possible. Discard the vegetable pieces that do not pass through the food mill or strainer. Return the soup to the pot and cook for 1 hour over low heat, uncovered. Keep the soup warm until needed.

3. When you are ready to serve, melt the bacon fat in a large skillet over medium-high heat and cook the bread slices until golden on both sides. Place a slice of bread in each serving bowl with a tablespoon or so of the chopped egg, ladle the soup over, and serve.

Makes 4 to 6 servings

Habas con Jamón (Andalusia)

LIMA BEANS WITH CURED HAM

The lima bean (Phaseolus lunatus) *is a New World bean that entered* huerta *production only in the post-Columbian era. There is evidence that the lima bean traveled on Spanish galleons across the Pacific to Asia before it crossed the Atlantic. It arrived on African shores with the slave trade from Brazil and eventually found its way to the Mediterranean by way of inland trade routes by the early sixteenth century.*[46]

Fresh lima beans from the huerta *with the delicate taste of* jamón de Trévelez *(page 716), a cured ham of Andalusia, was a dish I ate with pleasure while traveling through southern Spain. Upon returning home I made* habas con jamón *with both fresh lima beans and frozen baby lima beans in a microwaveable pouch turned into a saucepan in which I had sautéed domestic prosciutto in some olive oil. To my delight even the declassé way of preparing Andalusia's delicious and quite common* hortalizas *was excellent.*

1 pound frozen baby lima beans in a microwaveable pouch
1 to 2 tablespoons extra virgin olive oil
One 1/8-inch-thick slice prosciutto (about 2 ounces), diced
Salt to taste

1. Place the pouch of lima beans in a microwave or saucepan and cook according to the directions on the package. If you have fresh baby lima beans, place in a saucepan with a little water and cook gently over medium-low heat until tender. Drain the lima beans and set aside.

2. Meanwhile, in another saucepan, heat the olive oil over medium heat, then add the prosciutto and cook until heated through, about 2 minutes, stirring. Add the cooked lima beans, salt lightly, stir, and heat through, about 2 minutes. Serve immediately.

Makes 2 to 4 servings

Moules aux Épinards (Languedoc)

MUSSELS WITH SPINACH

This rustic housewife's preparation has roots in the Ménagier de Paris, *a French* aide-memoire, *a bourgeois household reminder book written at the end of the fourteenth century, where one finds mussels seasoned with saffron. But the mixture of mussels, saffron, and spinach is familiar in Languedoc, where one home preparation is known as* boui-abasisso d'espinarc, *a spinach bouillabaisse that is finished with grated Gruyère cheese as in this recipe. If you were to make this preparation in Languedoc, you would be told that your mussels should come from Bouzigues in the Étang de Thau.*

6 pounds mussels, debearded and scrubbed well
4 cups dry white wine
4 shallots (about 2 ounces), chopped
2½ pounds spinach, heavy stems removed and washed well
Pinch of saffron threads, crumbled
3 tablespoons tepid water
2 cups fish broth (page 369)
2 tablespoons *beurre manié* (page 50)
2 tablespoons unsalted butter
Salt and freshly ground black pepper to taste
2 ounces Gruyère cheese, grated

1. Soak the mussels in cold water to cover for 2 hours to purge them of any grit. Pour 2 cups of the wine and half the shallots into a large pot and bring to a boil. Add the drained mussels and cook over medium-high

heat until they have just opened, 8 to 10 minutes, using a long-handled wooden spoon to turn them. Remove the shells from the pot and begin removing the mussels from their shells. Set aside. Discard any mussels that remain tightly shut. Strain the mussel broth through a double thickness of cheesecloth to remove any lingering grit and set aside. You will have about 3 cups of mussel broth. If you don't, as may occur with cultivated mussels, add water to the existing broth to reach 3 cups.

2. Place the spinach leaves with only the water adhering to them from their last rinsing in a large pot, cover, and wilt over medium-high heat, about 5 minutes. Drain well by pressing the spinach in a strainer with the back of a wooden spoon. Chop coarsely and set aside. Steep the saffron in the tepid water.

3. Place the remaining 2 shallots with the remaining 2 cups wine in a medium-size saucepan and reduce the wine by two-thirds over high heat. Tilt the pan occasionally to aid in the reduction and scrape down the sides with a wooden spoon. Add 1½ cups of the mussel broth (freeze the rest for another use) and all of the fish broth. Reduce the heat to medium-low and simmer for 25 minutes.

4. Add the saffron and its soaking water and the *beurre manié* to the saucepan. Stir to mix well and continue to simmer over medium-low heat for another 40 minutes. Strain through a fine mesh strainer. You should now have 1 cup of enriched sauce.

5. Preheat the oven to 500°F. In a large skillet, melt the butter over medium-high heat, add the spinach, season with salt and pepper, and cook for 5 minutes, stirring occasionally.

6. Transfer the spinach to the center of a baking pan. Surround the spinach with the mussels. Cover both with the saffron sauce and Gruyère. Place in the oven until the cheese is melted and some black specks appear, about 10 minutes, and serve very hot.

Makes 6 servings

Spinaci alla Romana (Lazio)

ROMAN SPINACH

This recipe from Rome and the following spinach recipe from Catalonia point not only to the medieval culinary connection between Catalonia and Italy that is so well documented in cookbooks of that time but also to an older and pervasive Arab culinary sensibility in the combination of pine nuts and raisins with a leafy green vegetable such as spinach or Swiss chard. This dish is found throughout the Mediterranean. In centuries past it was also known as a Venetian specialty, where today spinach is more commonly found prepared simply with lemon juice, although Venetian Jews made a specialty with this combination called polpettine di spinassi, *spinach* rissoles, *or fried patties.*

In Andalusia espinacas al sacromonte *is also made with Swiss chard instead of spinach and almonds instead of pine nuts, and is spiced with saffron. The spinach, pine nut, and raisin combination also make the stuffing for* calzone antica *(page 565), an Apulian preparation.*

1 pound spinach, heavy stems removed and washed well
2 tablespoons bacon fat or pork lard
1 tablespoon pine nuts
1 tablespoon golden raisins, soaked for 15 minutes in tepid water and drained
Pinch of freshly grated nutmeg
Salt and freshly ground black pepper to taste

1. Place the spinach in a pot with only the water adhering to it from its last rinsing. Cover, turn the heat to medium-high, and cook until it wilts, about 5 minutes, turning a few times. Drain well in a strainer, pushing out excess water with the back of a wooden spoon.

2. In a medium-size skillet, heat the bacon fat or lard over medium heat and cook the spinach, pine nuts, drained raisins, nutmeg, salt, and pepper until hot and fragrant, about 15 minutes, stirring occasionally. Serve immediately.

Makes 4 servings

❖ *Espinacs amb Panses i Pinyons* (Catalonia)

SPINACH WITH RAISINS AND PINE NUTS

This traditional Catalan dish, also popular in the Balearic Islands, is usually made with Swiss chard. The dish reappears identically in Provence, Languedoc, Lazio (as spinaci alla romana*—see preceding recipe), Liguria (as* spinaci alla genovese*), Sicily, and Attica. It is also an old recipe in Venice, and Iberian Jews know it as a favorite, too.*

2½ pounds spinach, heavy stems removed and washed well
¼ cup extra virgin olive oil
1 garlic clove, crushed
⅓ cup pine nuts
⅓ cup golden raisins, soaked for 15 minutes in tepid water and drained
Salt and freshly ground black pepper to taste

1. Place the spinach in a pot with only the water adhering to it from its last rinsing. Cover, turn the heat to medium-high, and cook until it wilts, about 5 minutes, turning a few times. Drain well in a strainer, pushing out excess water with the back of a wooden spoon. Chop the spinach and set aside.

2. In a medium-size skillet, heat the olive oil with the crushed garlic over medium-high heat until the garlic turns light brown, about 1 minute. Remove and discard the garlic. Add the pine nuts and drained raisins and cook for 2 minutes, stirring, then reduce the heat to medium, add the spinach, season with salt and pepper, and cook until hot and fragrant, about 5 minutes. Serve immediately.

Makes 6 servings

❖ RATATOUILLE (Provence)

This famous preparation is world renowned and has equally delicious cousins throughout the Mediterranean. Even though many people claim that ratatouille is the quintessential Provençal dish, it is not even listed among the 1,123 recipes in J. B. Reboul's classic Provençal cookbook from the late nineteenth century, La cuisinière Provençale. *Ratatouille is actually a relatively modern invention, one that could not occur until the tomato came from the New World. Marimar Torres, author of* The Catalan Country Kitchen, *claims that ratatouille has a connection with* samfaina, *a kind of fried vegetable ragout of Catalonia dating back to when Provence was linked politically with Catalonia and Aragon.*[47] *In any case, throughout the Mediterranean, whenever a regional cuisine attempts to describe its local vegetable ragout, it invariably is described as a "ratatouille." In French military slang* rata, *shortened from ratatouille, means a rough stew, the way it should be.*

There are many ways of cooking a ratatouille, attested to by the fact that there seems not to be a cookbook that doesn't proffer ratatouille or an American food magazine that doesn't present a recipe for it once a month. This recipe is one of the easier ways, but an even better result will occur if you have the time to cook the vegetables separately and then mix them at the end.

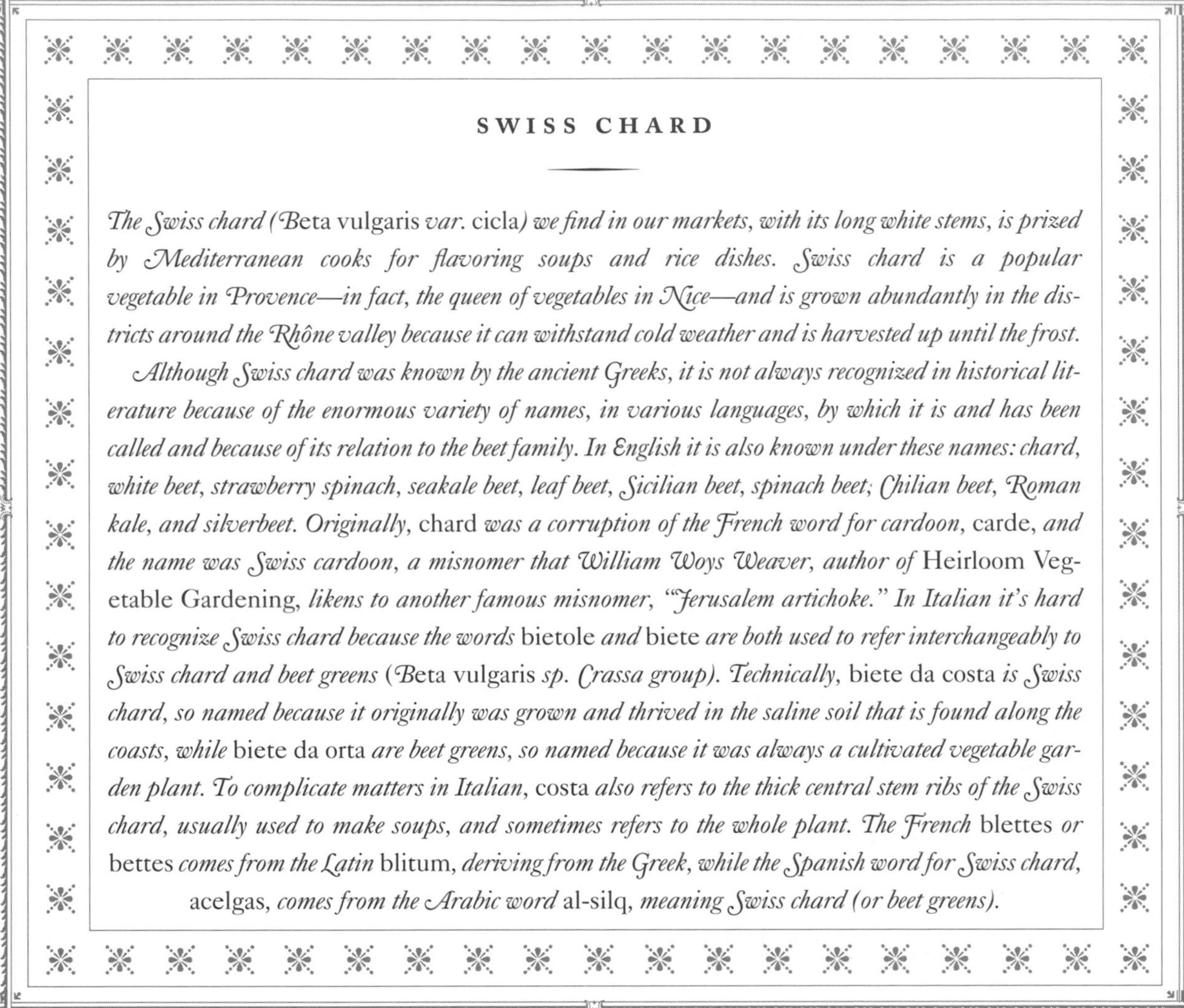

SWISS CHARD

*The Swiss chard (*Beta vulgaris *var.* cicla*) we find in our markets, with its long white stems, is prized by Mediterranean cooks for flavoring soups and rice dishes. Swiss chard is a popular vegetable in Provence—in fact, the queen of vegetables in Nice—and is grown abundantly in the districts around the Rhône valley because it can withstand cold weather and is harvested up until the frost.*

Although Swiss chard was known by the ancient Greeks, it is not always recognized in historical literature because of the enormous variety of names, in various languages, by which it is and has been called and because of its relation to the beet family. In English it is also known under these names: chard, white beet, strawberry spinach, seakale beet, leaf beet, Sicilian beet, spinach beet; Chilian beet, Roman kale, and silverbeet. Originally, chard *was a corruption of the French word for cardoon,* carde, *and the name was Swiss cardoon, a misnomer that William Woys Weaver, author of* Heirloom Vegetable Gardening, *likens to another famous misnomer, "Jerusalem artichoke." In Italian it's hard to recognize Swiss chard because the words* bietole *and* biete *are both used to refer interchangeably to Swiss chard and beet greens (*Beta vulgaris *sp. Crassa group). Technically,* biete da costa *is Swiss chard, so named because it originally was grown and thrived in the saline soil that is found along the coasts, while* biete da orta *are beet greens, so named because it was always a cultivated vegetable garden plant. To complicate matters in Italian,* costa *also refers to the thick central stem ribs of the Swiss chard, usually used to make soups, and sometimes refers to the whole plant. The French* blettes *or* bettes *comes from the Latin* blitum, *deriving from the Greek, while the Spanish word for Swiss chard,* acelgas, *comes from the Arabic word* al-silq, *meaning Swiss chard (or beet greens).*

2 medium-size eggplant (about 2½ pounds), peeled and cubed
Salt
½ cup extra virgin olive oil
2 medium-size onions, chopped or sliced
3 ripe but firm tomatoes (about 1 pound), seeded and quartered
2 medium-size zucchini, peeled and thinly sliced
3 green bell peppers, seeded and cut into thin strips
1 garlic clove, crushed
2 tablespoons dried *herbes de Provence* (page 715), wrapped in cheesecloth
Freshly ground black pepper to taste

1. Lay the eggplant cubes on some paper towels and sprinkle with salt. Leave them to drain of their bitter juices for 30 minutes, then pat dry with paper towels.

2. In a large skillet or casserole, heat the olive oil over medium heat, then cook the onions until translucent, about 6 minutes, stirring occasionally. Add the eggplant, tomatoes, zucchini, peppers, and garlic and shake or stir gently. Add the *herbes de Provence,* season with salt and pepper, and stir to mix. Cover and simmer over medium-low heat until much of the liq-

uid is absorbed and the vegetables tender, 45 minutes to 1 hour, stirring occasionally to prevent sticking. Strain away any remaining liquid and serve at room temperature with bread.

VARIATION

In Step 2, cook each vegetable one after the other, adding more olive oil when necessary, and mix all the vegetables once they are cooked.

Makes 6 servings

WE have seen that the Arab contribution to European agriculture was significant, that the local kitchen gardens and Iberian *huertas* have a lasting debt to Arab initiative and expertise. This is at variance with the traditional explanation attributing much of the agricultural and culinary transfer to the Crusaders.

Food writers, and some scholars as well, have for years popularized the idea that returning Crusaders were responsible for the appearance of this or that food. Writer C. Anne Wilson claimed that the Crusaders had "a considerable impact on the diet of western Europe." Another writer, Reay Tannahill, in her *Food in History,* claimed that the Crusaders imported cooking techniques from the East. There is no evidence to support either of these claims.

The early Crusades were marked by a lack of food, and the constant preoccupation with raiding the surrounding land for grain and vegetables. The Crusaders were religious zealots, mercenaries mostly, off to fight the infidels, without any practical experience in farming or cooking, whose journeys to the Holy Land were military in nature, not alimentary. Their clothes were unsuitable for the climate, their diet was too heavy, they ignored personal hygiene, and they readily succumbed to diseases such as cholera, plague, and leprosy. The Fourth Crusade was a gigantic political folly with no redeeming value to Europeans. The Fifth Crusade, or Children's Crusade, was equally hopeless and pathetic. Later, once Crusader kingdoms were established, we find that their villages tended to raise subsistence, not cash crops, and although they were starting to learn from the local population, their mortality rate was so high that their continued existence was completely dependent on immigration from Europe.[48]

Crusader agriculture barely existed. The lands they occupied were not naturally fertile, except for a few areas such as the coastal strip between the mountains and the sea in Lebanon. Although the Crusader kingdoms could grow their own grain, if harvests were bad they imported grain from Muslim Syria and during the last days of the Crusader kingdoms all grain was imported. In Palestine the Crusaders had orchards and vegetable gardens, and the hills supported sheep, goats, and pigs, and it is possible that they exported olive oil to the West. We also know that rare Palestinian fruits such as the sweet lemon and pomegranates appeared on the tables of the wealthy in Italy. But none of these exports brought any appreciable revenue. The most important of the food products going to the West was sugar that the Crusaders found already under cultivation when they conquered these territories. They learned from the natives and continued its cultivation, with the main center of the industry in Tyre in Lebanon. In fact, nearly all the sugar consumed in Europe during the twelfth and thirteenth centuries came from Outremer (the European name for the Crusader lands in the East). Some spices and herbs were also exported to the West, the most important being balm *(Melissa officinalis),* used in church services. We know that the food the Crusaders ate over time began to resemble the local food but as for Crusader cooking, perhaps a lesson is to be learned in the fact that during the period of the Latin Kingdom of Jerusalem (1174–1277) craftsmen and retailers worked in streets

Pomegranates, a fruit of paradise in the Koran, appeared on the tables of wealthy Italians in the thirteenth century. Giovanna Garzoni (1600–1670). *Still Life with Pomegranate*. Galleria Palatina, Palazzo Pitti, Florence. SCALA/ART RESOURCE.

specializing in their trades and in Jerusalem the Crusader cooks worked in a street named Street of Bad Cooking. As Steven Runciman, the historian of the Crusades put it, apart from castle-building, the West learned nothing from the Crusades. All in all, it is clear that the Crusaders made no impact on Western European cuisine for the cultural contacts were already occurring by virtue of the dominance of Italian merchants in the East.[49]

The "medieval green revolution" was not the result of Crusaders but of Arab agricultural ingenuity whose most important contribution to the eventual rise of Mediterranean cuisines was the opening of a virtually new agricultural season. In Mediterranean lands the traditional growing season had always been winter, the crops being sown around the time of the autumn rains and harvested in the spring; during the long hot summer the land almost always lay fallow, usually even in irrigated areas. Since many of the new crops had their origins in the tropical and subtropical areas of Southeast Asia, India, and the Malay Peninsula, they could be grown only in conditions of great heat. Besides the agricultural achievements of the Arabs, we hardly have to turn to the Crusaders as instruments of culinary transfer because we have, in the East, both Byzantium and the Islamic dynasties that were opulent with grain, wine, olives, and other foods that were exported to Italy from the twelfth century on.

Although the Arabs were responsible for this agricultural revolution in the Mediterranean, it should be understood that Islamic civilization was a perplexing tangle of many other cultures. This, in fact, is the story of the Mediterranean. In the process of expanding, the Muslim community absorbed large bodies of people whose cultural traditions were Hellenistic, and this led in time to a conflict within the Muslim community between Hellenistic traditions and the primitive formulations of Islamic concepts. The Arab contribution to European culture was both an inheritance from the classical Greek and Roman traditions and an original one tempered by the learning of Jews, Persians, Chinese, and Indians. Medieval Islamic civilization was not like the inward-looking, obscurantist, self-doubting, and paranoid Islamic civilization we see today in many postimperialist Muslim countries but, rather, was an outward-looking, dynamic, self-confident, and vibrant civilization both receptive to and giving to other civilizations. In the area of agricultural expertise, there are texts, of course, but much practical knowledge was passed on by ordinary farmers who were generally unlettered and left no records.

The significance of Islamic civilization in the Mediterranean has led several scholars to suggest three important conclusions. First, the advanced civilization of the Arabs contributed to the enrichment of Western Europe mainly in two areas: the improvement of the material basis of society and the refinement of life. Second, Europeans for the most part were backward, ignorant, and illiterate and had little awareness that the science, technology, agronomy, fashion, gastronomy, and other elements of good living they were adopting were Arab and Islamic in character. Third, Arabic literature, with its descriptions of gracious living, may have stimulated the imagination of Europe and sparked the poetic genius of the Romance peoples—the French, Italians, Spanish, and so forth. Whatever one's judgment about these conclusions, it is clear that the rise of feudalism and the transition to capitalism in the European Mediterranean is better understood when we keep in focus the influence of Islamic civilization.

FROM FEUDALISM TO CAPITALISM

Lords, Vassals, and Serfs

WHILE the eastern and southern Mediterranean were in the midst of the golden age of Islam, the European Mediterranean was enveloped in a Dark Age. Although historians have long reminded us that the Dark Ages were not as dark as popularly thought, there still was not a strong centralized power in the Mediterranean during this epoch that could protect people or villages from invasions. The collapse of the Roman system also had adverse effects on the family structure. Families were not as strong and bound together as they once were, so people sought protection wherever they could. The economic system known as feudalism arose as a way that could provide this basic protection.[50] Although *feudalism* is a word used loosely to mean something archaic, inefficient, or oppressive, historians generally use the word more precisely to mean a system of land tenure where the land parcels, called fiefs, were held not for money rent but for services rendered by vassals.[51] These services were usually agricultural labor or military service.

Roman society was a hierarchical society where masters ruled over slaves. Feudal society was an unequal society of chiefs (lords) to whom minions, called vassals and serfs, owed fealty. Although the vassals and serfs were free men, they had a servile relationship to the lord, tending his farms, his livestock, and his manor house or castle. Lords were given land by the king or overlord for services they performed, but a lord's primary responsibility was local: to protect his domain and the people who worked on it. These lands given to the lords were not actually owned by them but "held" in tenure for the king and were mostly devoted to agricultural enterprises.

The magnificent castles that a traveler can visit throughout the Mediterranean reflect the defining basis of medieval feudalism: local chieftains, or lords, formed ad hoc defensive measures in order to protect villages, agriculture, and livestock and the most effective defense was the castle or fortress. Although the castle had a military purpose, it also acted as a commercial and communications center. Around the castle agriculture became the primary economic activity and in the castle the mounted knight found his home.

The lord became part of a growing nobility that exacted a price for the protection they afforded their populations. The vassals provided the lord his cavalry and knights while the serfs were peasant farmers who tilled the soil. As people migrated toward the protection of the lord in northern Europe and parts of the Mediterranean, villages became cooperative agricultural communities centered around the manor, the estate of the lord. The lands of the estate *(seigneurie),* or manor, consisted of several parts. First, there was the demesne (the private reserve land of the lord), and all the products of it were taken directly by the lord. Second, there were the tenements, small or medium-size peasant holdings grouped around the lord's court, his manor, and the buildings associated with his dominion such as an armory, granary, and exchequer's office. The bulwark of the defense of the manor or castle was the knight. The mounted knight and technical innovations in agriculture were the two most important components behind the emergence of feudal society.

The Christian Mediterranean was a patchwork of small, sometimes minuscule, principalities centered around castles and manor houses during the feudal period from about 500 to between 1150 and 1350 and was based on a subsistence economy of peasants. The serfs, who farmed tiny plots of land that gave tiny yields, paid large tithes to the lord that left their families on the margins of subsistence.[52]

This is a classic description of western or Christian feudalism. In the Muslim world, there was a different social organization and historians tend not to use the description "feudalism" when referring to it. The "feudal" Islamic Mediterranean village, in Egypt called *ḍayʿa,* from the root word meaning "life," was similar to the feudal village in the Christian Mediterranean in that the peasants were legally free but tied to the soil they worked and to its owner. But these two villages were entirely different, in that the lord of the feudal European village had complete economic control and broad judicial powers and prerogatives. In the feudal Muslim village, the lord was subservient to the state and merely the beneficiary rather than the master of the village.[53]

There were different forms of feudalism throughout the Mediterranean, although generally, along the coastal Mediterranean, knights, in particular, lived in country mansions (manor houses). But living in a manor house did not necessarily mean the arrangement was feudal. In fact, Sardinia, although manorialized, was not feudalized.[54] But the knight in his country home was no "country gentleman." The knight did not become an agriculturalist. When not at war or burdened by administrative duties, the knight engaged in warlike activities, especially hunting, or breeding greyhounds and hawks for hunting. And, of course, there were the famous martial games called tournaments where jousting could get a knight killed.

On these coastal estates along the shores of the Mediterranean Sea it was the peasant who grew the cabbage that went into the minestrone, not the knight. The original Mediterranean cabbage resembled today's rape or kale; it was a field cabbage found along coasts and did not have the "head" we associate with it today. The original cabbage contained a high degree of mustard oil, which had an unpleasant taste. This wild coastal cabbage evolved through cultivation in the gardens of the manor over centuries until it lost its mustard oil and developed into a plant with tender and copious leaves. The cabbage continued to develop under cultivation by the peasant farmer and was bred for fleshier leaves that started to curl in on themselves to form a head. This may have happened earlier than the twelfth century because we know that the famous conservative theologian St. Hildegard of Bingen (died 1179) was familiar with both white and red head cabbages. The ancients, on the other hand, never knew the head cabbage.[55]

The Mediterranean was for centuries an unchanging world of peasants and lords. In the manor house, food shopping and preparation was the duty of the wife. She shopped every day for food in the local village. The market was an unpleasant place, with freshly butchered meat soaking the unpaved streets with rivers of blood and swarms of flies covering the meat and offal that may have dropped to the ground. She would buy her chicken here and, if she could afford it, expensive sugar, honey, and spice. The most common vegetables, if she didn't have a kitchen garden, were cabbage, onions, and leeks. Peddlers were also a part of this market, hawking their sausages, fish, garlic, eggs, cheeses, tripe, pig's blood, wriggling eels, wine, and milk. When the lady got home, she directed the kitchen staff in the cooking of the food, all of which was prepared over an open fire using utensils made of iron, copper, or earthenware. Nearly all food was boiled in cauldrons or roasted on hooks hung from tripods. A cook of the twelfth century prepared huge cauldrons of stew or soup, which almost always contained cabbage as well as local game, maybe a rabbit or chicken, and certainly a piece of salt pork. Puddings or custards were also cooked in the cauldrons, like blancmange, made of chicken paste blended with almond milk and sugar. The cauldrons were raised and lowered over the fire by means of a ratcheting hook. In some open-hearth fires meats were also spit-roasted. The foods cooked were always local produce—nothing came from afar—and the cooks cooked whatever they could get their hands on. There were no cookbooks. Many foods were salt cured to prevent spoilage, especially meats but vegetables too. Meats were eaten with the fingers, soups were eaten with spoons, and people shared bowls.[56]

The impression many of us have of colossal meals at the medieval table is false, for feasting existed only for the rich aristocracy or the papacy, and even for them these feasts were very rare exceptions. The twelfth-century aristocracy often ate the same food that artisans or townspeople were eating. In the morning they ate a kind of soup; in the evening it was soup again or a porridge of vegetables, perhaps with a little salt meat. Herbs were used for flavoring savories or, more often, eaten as we would eat vegetables today, while spices remained out of the reach of common people. Bread was common but any pastry with lots of fat was usually expensive.

Peasants ate more simply than did the townspeople. Their diet was very poor and their hovels did not usually have kitchens, as their cooking was done outdoors or in public ovens. They reserved their best food to sell at the market; millet was the most common food for them.[57] When bread ran out, famine

Peasants selling small quantities of their produce in the town's market. Detail of Lorenzo Lotto's (1480–1556) *Stories from the Life of Saint Barbara.* ALINARI/ART RESOURCE.

ensued. The Anonimo Romano's *Cronica* tells us that during the famine of 1338, people used to eat cabbages "without bread." Cereals, chestnuts, and cabbage were fundamental to the rural diet and an old medieval dietetic tradition identified this produce, especially herbs and roots of all sorts, garlic, onions, leeks, cabbages, and turnips, as typical "popular" food, as opposed to "luxury" food.[58] In the fifteenth century, cabbage and bread were the main elements of the Italian diet.[59]

The agricultural revolution that had its beginning in the tenth century allowed the sylvan-pastoral economy—namely hunting, fishing, and stock rearing—to give way to Mediterranean cereal growing. This resulted from the economic imperative demanded by the growth of population and its integration into a feudal system. The causes of the growth of population are debated, but we know that to feed greater numbers of people required *reducere terram ad panem* (making new arable land for more bread).[60] More bread meant more food to feed the increase in population and to allow the population to continue to grow. But the feudal system did not create enough rewards for farmers to significantly reinvest their profits in agricultural innovation and therefore productivity did not increase at a fast enough rate. Feudalism, once a rational solution to societal problems, was by A.D.1000 hindering the emergence of the state because the various feudal lords in the Christian Mediterranean lacked any homogeneity and had no common loyalty. The only thing that united them was devotion to Christianity.

The greater number of mouths to feed by the year 1000 meant a population crisis was looming. Peasants found it more difficult to get credit and property was seized by a growing aristocracy. Agricultural production during this period did not increase.[61]

Farmer's Plow, Knight's Stirrup, Death's Scythe

HISTORIANS usually place the emergence of a recognizable feudal system in both northern Europe and the Mediterranean shortly after the reign of Charlemagne (died 814). Central to understanding the feudal system were several technical innovations that occurred just before A.D. 1000. One was the adoption of the three-field crop-rotation system. Previously the two-field crop rotation meant one field was planted while the other lay fallow. The three-field system had two fields planted and one fallow, and was more productive. Agricultural productivity rose and with it the peasant society changed, not only in northern Europe but also in parts of the Mediterranean, especially northern Italy, southern France, and portions of Spain.

The most important innovation was the invention of the heavy moldboard plow in northern Europe, which revolutionized tillage. The soil of northern Europe was infused with more clay, unlike the Mediterranean with its sandy loam soil, and as a result the clods of soil were harder to cut and turn, and drainage was a problem. The heavy moldboard plow was a more powerful instrument allowing the farmer to turn his fields without cross-plowing. Cross-plowing meant fields had to be square in shape; the new form of plowing allowed the shape of fields to change from square to long and narrow, which incidentally helped drainage. But to plow through heavy soil with a heavy plow required enormous energy, up to six—even eight—oxen.[62] In later centuries horses were used. This was very expensive to do and the eleventh-century northern European peasant family could hardly afford to plow a field; resources were pooled from several households so more animal power could be brought to bear on plowing.[63] In addition, in his book *Medieval Technology and Social Change,* published in 1962, historian Lynn White Jr. argued that there was a causal connection between the

Farmers using a horse-drawn heavy moldboard plow are sowing grain while pigs feed in the forest to the left. Simon Bening (1483–1561). Da Costa Hours, Bruges, c. 1515. M.399, f. 10v.

THE PIERPONT MORGAN LIBRARY, NEW YORK/ART RESOURCE.

heavy plow and the manor house because the new long and narrow fields, to make economic sense, had to remain unfenced, leading to the growth of powerful village councils of peasants to administer these lands.[64]

In the Mediterranean, the typical plow was the one the Romans had used. There were three major varieties of this type of plow. The first was the deep-share ard, which may have evolved from a digging stick. This was a plow found in Galicia in Spain, parts of Morocco and Algeria, Sicily, Italy, and Sardinia. The second kind of plow was the crook plow; it did not cut deeply into the soil and was used on drier soils such as those found in parts of Spain and Tunisia and the Rif mountain areas of Morocco. In the French Midi, the pitchfork type of plow was used, as was also common in the Mediterranean where plowing never required the kind of raw animal power needed in northern European agriculture because the soil had less clay and was drier and more easily turned.[65] Medieval Mediterranean farming combined Roman methods with new Arab innovations.

The shape of Europe and the Mediterranean began to change radically after the death of Charlemagne but especially after the mounted knights exploded out of northern France in the eleventh century. In classical times, the Greeks and Romans had only light cavalry that could not be used for frontal attack, only flanking maneuvers, meaning the talent of the commander was important.[66] The medieval mounted knight, however, could crush opponents through devastating frontal attacks. The knight, encased in armor, charging with shield and spar, leaning forward over the horse's neck, feet secured with the newly invented stirrup against the shock of the collision, could slice through any known military opponent. In a short time literally a few hundred Norman knights, following Robert Guiscard, a Norman count, swept through Sicily, southern Italy, Tunisia, and Greece. However, this new form of warfare was expensive. Making armor required talented metalworkers and lots of raw material, not to mention the cost of feeding and caring for the horse and man who rode it.[67]

It was the invention of the stirrup that made the mounted knight possible. The stirrup was probably invented by the Sarmatians, a nomadic tribe of the Eurasian steppes, and brought to northern Europe and the greater Mediterranean in the ninth century.[68] Before the stirrup a horseman clung to his steed with pressure from the knees. The rider did not use his sword very much because if he did, and missed his target, he usually fell off the horse.[69] The stirrup gave lateral support to the front and back support provided by pommel and cantle. The horse and rider now became a single integrated fighting unit capable of "a violence without precedence."[70] Here was the early forerunner of the modern tank and it had revolutionary implications, ultimately, in the context of this book, for society, agriculture, and the food we eat.

The duty of the knight was the key to feudal institutions and the determining principle of land tenure, which engendered a social and agricultural revolution. The feudal economy saw a rise in agricultural productivity that was also linked to export trade. A merchant could get rich buying the small amounts of certain spices that were available cheap in the East and selling them dear at home as he did with saffron and cumin, both providing high profit margins. These high profit margins from agricultural surplus combined with manufactured exports helped the Mediterranean lands pay for grain and dried fish from the Atlantic and, later, for sugar. In exchange there was olive oil, the fruits of the south, and raw silk. Export trade in agricultural products made the cities and towns rich because that's where the money flowed.

The feudal mode of production that existed in Europe and the Mediterranean from about 800 to 1350 provided an assured and safer diet but a monotonous one. Although the feudal system worked for so many centuries, a crisis was looming at the end of the thirteenth century. The immediate causes were technological, especially the lack of fertilizer. Arable land in the greater Mediterranean was overworked and the soil needed to be replenished with nutrients from fertilizer in the form of manure. The best producers of fertilizer are cows, but farmers couldn't expand their number because an era of severe winters limited the availability of winter forage for the cattle.[71] The cow is also not the animal best suited to the Mediterranean ecology.

By 1300, the feudal economy had grown inefficient and unproductive. As money flowed toward the towns, an inequality between town and country grew and the feudal system began to weaken. The towns were rich and the countryside was poor, and millions of people lived on the edge of starvation. A crisis ensued and a new economic system slowly emerged based on the new wealth being created by the towns through their financial control of agriculture and export trade. There was a growing distinction between the labor of the land and the towns. New occupations arose that once belonged to the lord of the manor because of the division of labor. More and more people became landless and migrated to the towns to sell their labor. As towns grew, they depended on the country for food and labor.[72]

Compounding the problem in this era of prolonged famines was the holocaust of the Black Death, which dramatically reduced the population by half in some places and created economic havoc. The bubonic plague of the mid-fourteenth century is known as the Black Death and was unimaginably horrific. It originated in Asia. A Tartar army was besieging the Genoese and Venetian trading post of Caffa (Feodsosiya) on the Crimea when the plague decimated its army. In one of the first recorded instances of biological warfare, the Tartars catapulted infected corpses into the city so that the disease would spread to the defenders. But more effective than dead men for spreading plague were live rats. The Black Death arrived in the Mediterranean with a Venetian galley returning to Sicily from Caffa in the fall of 1347. The plague arrived in Egypt at the same time, also on a galley, meaning it must have come from the same Italian Black Sea outposts.[73] In Cairo, ten thousand people died every day.[74] The plague spread quickly throughout Europe, and in Venice 150 years would pass before the population returned to the level before the Black Death. The scythe of the Black Death reached far. Languedoc, in southwestern France, had a population of 1.5 million in 1328 and 1 million one hundred years later.[75]

Plagues were a constant factor of life in the medieval era and their causes and means of transmission completely baffling to the population. People did know that the increase in the rat population was not a good thing, especially since they could see rats contaminating their grain stores, but they had no idea that the plague was actually transmitted by fleas carried by the rats. Because so little was known about medicine and hygiene, losing a third of the population was not unusual. Plagues were usually the endpoint of a vicious cycle; the infection was caused mostly by diseased rats attracted to the large grain stores kept as a hedge against famine, which usually accompanied the plague brought by the rats.[76] The frequent famines occurred because there weren't enough people alive to work the farms providing food for the towns. But meat consumption rose in the Mediterranean in the period after the Black Death because rats could not contaminate meat as they could grain stores.

From Feudalism to Capitalism

A NEW economy developed from these crises that the historian Immanuel Wallerstein called a "world-economy." He argued that in the fifteenth and sixteenth centuries an economy developed that thrived beyond national borders; he called it a "world" system not because it encompassed the whole world but because it was larger than any juridically defined political unit such as a single empire. This world-economy could thrive without national boundaries because of modern capitalism and modern science.[77] A new world-economy meant the affairs of state became both increasingly complex and intertwined, so bureaucracies were created to manage them and the state grew stronger. As the state grew larger and stronger, the manipulation of money became profitable because its nature began to change with the invention of negotiable paper money. Money started to be a commodity, not merely coins in exchange for goods. In the old feudal economy the produce of the agriculturalist was appropriated by the lord on the basis of tribute or rent. In the new capitalist world-economy, agricultural production was greater and more efficient. Wallerstein argued that this transition from feudalism to capitalism was based on an expansion of the geographical size of the world in question, on the development of different methods of labor control for different products and different zones of the world-economy, and the creation of relatively strong state machineries in what would become the core states of this capitalist world-economy.[78] In addition, the population slowly recouped from the Black Death and by 1500 arable land and agricultural productivity was increasing. The dominant crop was wheat, and huge profits were made from the trade in wheat (see Chapter 9).

A world-economy meant that an extensive trading network could arise and things that previously could not be procured became available. Most important, if crops failed domestically, they could now be imported from elsewhere with greater ease. New food inventions made from a certain kind of wheat known as hard wheat *(Triticum turgidum* var. *durum)* alleviated food storage problems (see Chapter 10). Those things that were imported were sold and budding entrepreneurs in the Levant and Western Europe by the thousands looked for goods to sell at a profit. These entrepreneurs created wealth, capital, by helping local crafts develop in order to supply distant markets.[79]

The very nature of society was changing and the once revolutionary knight was now obsolescent. Slow moving (his horse had to carry not only the man but about 150 pounds of armor also), the knight was at a disadvantage against masses of lightly protected but fast-moving infantry. But fast-moving infantry, moving according to tactical and strategic plans, required training and discipline. Training and discipline are expensive and require state-supported standing armies rather than the loose ad hoc formations of knights.[80] Standing armies also need enormous amounts of food because, as the saying goes, "armies travel on their bellies."

Food production increased to feed not only armies but also a rising population, and in the courts cuisines developed. For a thousand years (in Europe) there were only cooks, and now the *chef de cuisine* began to emerge and the first cookbooks began to appear.

They were written for professional chefs who worked at the court, in the homes of the new bourgeois class, or ecclesiastical residences. The new cookbooks found much of their inspiration in the Arab ones. The fourteenth-century Italian chef was as enamored with the cuisine of the "exotic East" (namely, Arab cuisine) as was the ninth-century Arab chef with Persian cuisine or in the same way that American chefs emulate French cuisine today, even though they did not fully comprehend the source for their inspiration in the kitchen. The cuisines emerging in royal and bourgeois kitchens were part of the general refinement of life that was tied to the growing economic power of the merchants, bankers, financiers, and their allied urban lords in the towns. One of the first of these cookbooks, the *Libro della cocina,* was written by an anonymous Tuscan in the late fourteenth century and included several cabbage recipes. These recipes were written for the lord of the manor and they don't sound all that bad, the cabbage now not sounding so plebeian. In one recipe the cabbage tops are boiled in water or broth, then removed and fried in oil with chopped onions, fennel bulb, and a sliced apple. A little broth is added along with spices sprinkled on top; or the cabbage could be cooked with pork lard, scrambled eggs, and spices. In either case the recipe instructs that the dish be served "to the lord."[81]

Commerce, Industry, Gold, Food, and the Age of Exploration

THE foods that go into our mouths are both the beginning and the end of a long chain of events that may be thought of as the cycle of life. The human need for life-giving nourishment leads us to seek plant and animal foods, then to master growing or raising them, which leads to sustenance through agriculture. Once agriculture becomes productive enough to go beyond sustenance, it creates surpluses that can be traded for things in kind or money, and this is commerce. Commerce creates wealth, a by-product of which is the effort to materially change the conditions of our lives, which engenders the creation of cuisine, the transformation of sustenance into art. The cycle begins with food going into our mouths to keep us alive and ends with food going into our mouths to keep us alive *and* happy.

Commerce is the cabbage and onions the peasant woman brings to market, it is the glass of wine the poor man drinks in the rich man's cellar, as well as the goods in the hold of a Venetian *galere da mercato* (merchant galley). But not all goods were handled commercially in the sixteenth century. Economic life was only partly penetrated by the market economy, for the market was everywhere confronted by barter and autarky.

Through commerce towns developed, and through the towns industry rose—the first stages of a city's growth. From the eleventh to the fourteenth centuries, Mediterranean cities came into their own and controlled world wealth. Venice lived off the Ottoman Empire, not vice versa. Mediterranean life revolved around the great commercial centers and Ragusa, modern Dubrovnik, was one of the most important. One family of Ragusan origin, the Gondolas, had branches in Ancona, Venice, Messina, and even London, and handled the exchange of *uve passa* (raisins) and *curanti* (currants) imported from the Levant, ingredients that even today appear prominently in Sicilian and Turkish cooking, for example.

From the time Magellan passed through the Straits into the Pacific Ocean in 1520 until Michelangelo finished *The Last Judgment* in the Sistine Chapel in 1541, the commercial capitalism of the merchant was succeeded by the industrial capitalism of the entrepreneur. The old guild structure of manufacturing was directly affected by industrial capitalism. Previously artisans worked for guilds, the Italian *arti* or Spanish *gremios,* medieval associations of craftsmen who kept profits for themselves. In the new capitalist system the entrepreneur gave the artisan the material to work with for a salary. The financing of this relatively slow production process came from the merchant, who kept the profits from sales and exports instead of the craftsman. Genoa as well as Florence was affected by this new system and by the arrival of silver and gold from America by the early sixteenth century. The merchant, now a full-fledged entrepreneur, saw the expansion and concentration of his young industry. Inefficient methods succumbed to a more rational division of labor that increased production. Industry was also changing in the Muslim part of the Mediterranean, namely the Ottoman Empire.

The rise of the city with its nascent industries was followed by the evolution of banking. The bankers were important actors on this economic stage. The Florentine firm Giucciardini Corsi, which advanced money to Galileo, also had interests in Sicilian grain and in the cloth and pepper trades. Another important trading and banking family were the Capponi, who transported wine and handled shipping insurance. The most famous, of course, were the de'Medici, half of whose interests lay in banking, but who also owned silk workshops in the fifteenth century. The de'Medici were rich and powerful enough to affect national destinies. When Charles VII of France invaded Italy in 1494, he found himself leading a very expensive national army, the first in Europe. When the de'Medici refused to lend him money, he had to borrow from the Genoese banking firm of Sauli at over 40 percent interest.[82] Because of these family networks, the Mediterranean never saw a need to set up the large joint stock companies typical of northern Europe. This reliance on the family for the development of capitalism is a Mediterranean pattern. Industry was expanding throughout the Mediterranean during the sixteenth century and commerce was making the towns grow larger and richer. But the economic stranglehold that the East had on the trade in spices led Mediterranean cities and the newly forming states to seek a way to cut out the Middle Eastern middleman. An age of exploration opened, with Mediterranean sailors sailing south around Africa and west to discover a New World. What ignited the explosive growth in these Mediterranean cities was gold and silver found in the recently discovered Americas. Precious metals in the hands of Mediterranean merchants meant they could trade with the East for the most precious commodity of all: food. Incredible as it might seem, pepper was the motivation behind the search for precious metals, for without the insatiable desire for glittering gold and silver in the East and the equally insatiable desire for spices in the West, little would be traded.

Before the discovery of the New World, precious metals, especially gold, came from Africa. Gold played an important part in the history of the Mediterranean because Africa's supply of gold gradually became the driving economic force for the entire Mediterranean. Gold mined in the medieval Sudanic region of Africa—the Mali and Niger of today—allowed both North Africa and Muslim Spain to become prosperous.[83] Gold from the Sudanic kingdom may also have provided the economic wherewithal for greater production of olive oil in southern Europe because the labor-intensive care of olive orchards was costly. Olive production began to rise in the Mediterranean during the sixteenth century. It was also traded and a change in Mediterranean cooking resulted. This change resulted from local demand. Cabbage soup, the most common dish found on a sixteenth-century Mediterranean table, which we know the students at the Papal school in Tret in Provence ate 125 days out of the year, could now be laced with a fragrant olive oil.[84] The monotony of fast days, almost 150 days a year, could now be alleviated with olive oil.

Our school books told us that the Age of Exploration began with the search for new routes to the spices in the East and for precious metals; that the extraction of gold from the Nubian mines of Africa was exhausted by the thirteenth century and new sources were needed to trade for the *specie* (spices, jewels, drugs, etc.) of the East. This is not an entirely true picture. Staples drive economies, not luxuries. What the Mediterranean needed in the fifteenth century was food and fuel, not saffron and sapphires.

The Age of Exploration opened up new worlds and the most important products returning to the Mediterranean were seeds and metal. The new world of flora introduced to the Mediterranean over the next hundred years fundamentally changed the diet of the Old World. It took time, but today Mediterranean cuisine is unthinkable without the tomato, potato, maize, common bean, chili pepper, and chocolate. But as the prosperity of Mediterranean towns rose in the sixteenth century, so did prices, whether it was the price of goods, labor, or macaroni and tomatoes.

Spaghetti con Salsa di Pomodoro (Campania)

SPAGHETTI WITH TOMATO SAUCE

It is difficult to determine exactly when and where the tomato arrived in Italy, but it seems likely that it was brought first to Naples by the Spanish some time between 1504 and 1544. In the Mediterranean, tomatoes required extra watering and therefore it also seems likely that the first use of the tomato plant was ornamental, perhaps associated with the Neapolitan villas of the Spanish viceroys. In any case, although the tomato arrived in Italy shortly after the discovery of America, it did not become generally accepted into Italian cuisine until the late nineteenth and early twentieth centuries. At the time of the tomato's arrival in Italy, pasta was still being made in Naples in the centuries' old Arab-influenced style typified by the use of lots of sugar and cinnamon, as late as the publication of Antonio Latini's Lo scalco alla moderna *(The modern carver) in 1692. Latini has the first recipe I am familiar with that uses the tomato (a tomato sauce which he calls* salsa di pomadoro, alla spagnuola*), although Costanzo Felici provides a culinary description of the tomato as early as 1572 in his* Del'insalata e piante che in qualunque modo vengono per cibo dell'homo *(Of salads and plants that are foods for man), describing it as better looking than tasting. Not until a century after Latini, in 1790, with the publication of the Neapolitan chef Francesco Leonardi's* L'Apicio moderno *(The modern Apicius) does the spaghetti and tomato sauce of today begin to emerge.[85] This recipe is the classic recipe of my family the De Ieso's of Pago Veiano near Benevento.*

6 tablespoons extra virgin olive oil
1 large garlic clove, crushed
1 medium-size onion, finely chopped
1 large garlic clove (optional), finely chopped
2 pounds very ripe plum tomatoes, peeled, seeded, and chopped
Salt and freshly ground black pepper to taste
8 large fresh basil leaves
1 pound spaghetti
Freshly grated Parmigiano-Reggiano cheese

1. In a large skillet, heat the olive oil over medium-high heat and cook the crushed garlic until it begins to turn light brown, about 1 minute. Remove and discard the garlic. Add the onion and garlic, if using, and cook until the onion is translucent, about 5 minutes, stirring constantly so the garlic doesn't burn. Add the tomatoes and season with salt and pepper. Cook until much of the liquid from the tomatoes has evaporated, about 15 minutes, stirring occasionally and lowering the heat if it splatters too much. Add the basil leaves, turn off the heat, and leave until needed to let the basil leaves steep.

2. Meanwhile, bring a large pot of water to a rolling boil, salt abundantly, and add the spaghetti. Drain the pasta when al dente and toss with the sauce. Sprinkle with Parmigiano-Reggiano.

Makes 4 servings

Inflation, Money, and Capital

PRICES were rising in the Middle Ages and it was not understood why. Food was expensive and people became poorer, lamenting the "good old days," such as the person who wrote in 1560 that in his father's time "there was meat to eat every day, the meals were copious and the wine flowed like water." Gabriel Alonso de Herrera, the famous Spanish agriculturist, said in 1513, "Today a pound of mutton costs as much as a whole sheep used to, a loaf as much as a *fanega* of wheat."[86] Prices were rising, not because of the influx of Americas gold into the economy, but because of demand for food, not only food for sustenance but also food for comfort and profit, namely spices.[87]

There were riches to be made in the Mediterranean and these riches were mostly in the form of agricultural products such as wheat and spices. In the late sixteenth century, the bankers of Genoa and wealthy merchants at fairs established in northern Italy held the keys to the control of the economic life of the Mediterranean and, in fact, to world wealth. The most important fair was the one established at Piacenza in northern Italy in 1579. The French historian Fernand Braudel called it the event of the century in terms of the history of capitalism. It was not in Genoa but in the discreet quarterly meetings of a few businessmen at Piacenza that the rhythm of the material life of the West was dictated.

At the fairs, wealthy merchants invented and refined forms of credit based on bookkeeping and paper that had no real value. This was the age of negotiable paper money. Something new was happening: money began to have an existence separate from the commodities it bought. The rise of paper money meant there was a growing separation between the banker and the financier. It can't be overemphasized how strange this new profession of financier was at the time. Traditionally people assumed money followed trade in commodities. Exchange meant dealing one thing for another. But now money became a commodity itself; this was revolutionary. Finance was created by a change in the public's perception of the nature of money, that it could be a commodity, traded as one would trade the wheat for pasta. This revolution was at the heart of capitalism.

Capitalism can be successful only when there is a network based on cooperation and mutual confidence: capital needs a market. The markets had great appeal not only for economic reasons but social ones as well. The peasant arrived in the towns looking to sell his cabbage and get the money needed to pay taxes. He could even pick up some prepared food sold in stalls run by other merchants, such as "meatballs, dishes of chick peas, fritters."[88] Al-Maqrīzī (1364–1442) tells us that there were thirty-five different markets inside Cairo.[89] Venetian and Genoese merchants employed *fattori,* resident import-export agents, who operated on the quaysides of ports and urban markets throughout the Levant and as far as the Persian Gulf to keep their eyes out for good business and good food, literally, because so much of what was traded was consumable. The European *fattori* were operating in the Levant early on, and they are more likely than the twelfth-century Crusaders to have introduced new culinary concepts to Europe. In 1215 there were 3,000 European merchants in Egypt. In 1400 there were eighteen Venetians, thirty-eight Genoese, fifteen Anconitans, and fifteen Catalan *fattori* in Alexandria. But these *fattori* were only those who registered with a notary; there were in actuality many more. In Aleppo they would have their eyes sharpened for cotton, silk, and fabrics, but also foods such as rhubarb, which was shipped to Venice.[90]

The success of capitalism also required literacy (see Chapter 8). Credit, methods of payment, and the financing of international trade required reading. In a barter economy, a peasant who brought cabbage to market to trade for eggs never needed to read anything. Because the highest literacy rates of the medieval world were among Jewish and Muslim merchants, they played an important role in the development of methods of payment and of financing international trade.[91]

Money was made from long-distance trade, and for the most part trade meant trade in foodstuffs. What mattered was not the volume of trade but the rate of profit. High rates of profit made capitalism grow and as it grew capital was accumulated. Accumulation of capital was the only thing that mattered, and much of it was made in profits from the grain, spice, and drug trades. Accumulation of capital was the foundation for the refinements of life that began to emerge in the towns. These new and wealthy capitalists were the benefactors of these refinements of life. A style of life arose in the cities among these new capitalist merchants, a bourgeois style, that saw its expression in art, fashion, music, and gastronomy. Was this a new gastronomy or a continuation of the Roman one?

THE GASTRONOMIC INHERITANCE OF THE MEDITERRANEAN

Whence Our Celebrated Cuisines?

WHERE does this Mediterranean cuisine touted in our food magazines, served at fancy new restaurants, and encountered in our travels come from? I've suggested that it arose out of the conditions prevalent in the Mediterranean between the fall of the Roman Empire and the beginning of the modern era. The Arab agricultural revolution, innovations in technology, feudalism, and the transition to a capitalist economy were the antecedents to the Age of Exploration and the Renaissance that helped shape the cuisine of today.

Traditionally, food writers have sought the historical roots of Mediterranean cuisine in classical literature rather than looking at the wider picture. A comprehensive food history would rightly begin, if not in prehistoric times, with the works of the first-century A.D. Greek writer Athenaeus (c. 170–230), who lived in Rome. Athenaeus did not write a cookbook per se, but his voluminous works are about food. In the same century there were several Roman writers with the name of Apicius, one of whom wrote what is called the first cookery book, a work that was finally compiled in the fourth century. These writers are usually taken as the beginning of contemporary European cuisine. They are certainly first temporally, but whether there was a continuous development from the classical era to the cuisine of the modern Mediterranean is less certain.[92] The latest scholarly research suggests that during the fourteenth and fifteenth centuries late medieval European court cuisine was not a direct descendent of the cuisine of the classical era, but partly an elaboration of ideas born originally in the kitchens of the medieval Arab Umayyad and Abbasid courts. Medieval Europe was a backward civilization that looked in awe and fear at the advanced Muslim civilization in the East.

Traces of this medieval cuisine are not easy to find.[93] The vast majority of the contemporary Mediterranean cuisines as represented by the recipes in this book barely intimate what the medieval Mediterranean style of cooking looked like. Determining influence is not so straightforward and answers to questions about whether certain foods existed in the classical period, are oftentimes qualified and sometimes even change as new information becomes available. Take, for example, the question as to whether macaroni existed in the classical era. The debate revolves around whether or not the ancients knew of hard wheat (see Chapter 10). Many researchers using modern scientific methods of molecular archeology still cannot be certain as of this writing whether hard wheat existed.[94]

Culinary influence in the Mediterranean is a two-way street, complicated by transferences that occurred in different historical epochs. For example, it is not the whole story to say that the Spanish influenced the cooking of Naples, that the Turks influenced Arab cooking, or that Greek cooking is indebted to the Turks. One must also keep in mind that in these cases, respectively, Spanish cuisine was mostly Arab-influenced during the 700-year era of Islamic Spain, that the Arab dynasties in Baghdad and Damascus of the early Islamic period influenced Turkish cooking hundreds of years before the Ottoman Turks began conquering the Arab world, and that the nomadic Turks spreading throughout Anatolia found a vibrant Greek Byzantine culture whose cuisine may have influenced the new arrivals.

After the Roman cookery book of Apicius there are no European cookery books until the thirteenth century, excepting a codice on dietary matters written in the sixth century by a Byzantine refugee, Anthimus, for the French Merovingian King Theodric I (511–534), son of Clovis, called *De observatione ciborum*.[95] There are other occasional food-related works, mostly dietetic works, from various sources from the fourth to thirteenth centuries, but for the most part they are not important, had no perceptible influence, and are not cookery books in the classic sense.[96]

The degree to which Apicius was known in the Middle Ages, especially before 1450, is unclear. Some people have argued that the classical Roman culinary tradition of Apicius survived in monasteries and in royal courts through the early medieval period in France and Italy.[97] The inventory of the library of the abbey of Saint-Victor in Provence from April 24, 1374, indicates that there might have been a copy.[98] Copies of Apicius's cookery manuscript were made in the court of Charlemagne, and it is from this time that the earliest manuscripts of Apicius date. But an Apicius manuscript was not brought to Italy until 1457 and the first printing did not occur until 1498.[99] It is hard, therefore, to justify the notion of Apicius's influence on Italian cookery when the first Italian cookery manuscripts were written a century before any appearance of Apicius's manuscript in Italy. Also, when we speak of libraries in the Middle Ages, we should not be thinking of a building like those that house today's libraries. A common word for library was *armarium,* which means "wardrobe." A "library" was often nothing more than a couple of shelves in an armoire. Although there was some Latin learning in the early Middle Ages, there was very little access to the Latin classics until the humanists began their widespread translation of these works in the fifteenth century, along with the invention of the movable-type printing press about the same time.

The record is too sparse for us to attribute a classical Roman influence on medieval European cooking. The knowledge of the Roman culinary art, for all practical purposes, was nil among the masses of illiterate Europeans of the Middle Ages, mainly because cuisine was unknown. There are some exceptions—for example, vestigial preparations such as *garum,* a kind of fermented fish sauce used for cooking that probably tasted much like the *nước mắm* of Vietnamese cooking, or *puls,* a porridge made of emmer (a kind of wheat), panic (foxtail millet), millet, or other corns, and a host of simple gruels and breads. The French naturalist Pierre Belon wrote as late as the 1550s, after his travels to the Levant, of the popularity of *garum* in Constantinople made from the entrails of scad or mackerel.[100] This is one of the last references to *garum* as a food used on a daily basis. Shortly it becomes an extinct food in the Mediterranean as more sophisticated food became available. Even among the upper classes, cooking was primitive and the only true cuisines in the early medieval Mediterranean were Arab, especially in Spain, Sicily, and the Levant, and possibly Byzantium.

Although there are some similarities between the recipes of Apicius and those of the first true French chef, Taillevent, a thousand years later, the dissimilarities are more telling. Anne Willan, a well-known food writer, believes these have more to do with an oral tradition going back to the Roman occupation of France than with written works.[101] This may be true; unfortunately, the evidence for an "oral tradition" isn't strong, although circumstantial evidence does pull for both arguments. It's true that the most likely means of the transmission of knowledge in the early Middle Ages was practical rather than by book learning. For example, farmers of the early Middle Ages do not seem to have been familiar with manuring, which was well known by Roman farmers, and yet there were many agricultural techniques employed that show continuity with antiquity. Be that as it may, the collective European memory of Rome had, for the most part, dissolved into the foggy mist of slow disintegration by the Roman Empire. This began the period known as the Dark Ages.[102]

The beginning of the medieval era may be better understood by recognizing that Europe was faced with a new and dynamic Islamic civilization to the east. Muslim civilization was more technologically and scientifically advanced than that of Europe and was richer in every aspect of material culture. By the year 1000, the Mediterranean Sea was very nearly a Muslim lake. Muslims ruled the Holy Land, Egypt, all of North Africa, Spain, and Sicily; they had settlements in Provence and southern Italy and were making incursions into France, Switzerland, and northern Italy. But contacts between Christian Europe and the Muslims were not all violent, for mercantile exchanges increased, too. These two cultures began to exchange material goods as well as ideas, among them aspects of the good life, literature, art, and cuisine. The classical era may have provided the impetus for Europe's rediscovery of her heritage, but it was the explosive power of Islam, the religion of the Arabs, that transformed medieval Europe, in both a negative and a positive sense. In less than one hun-

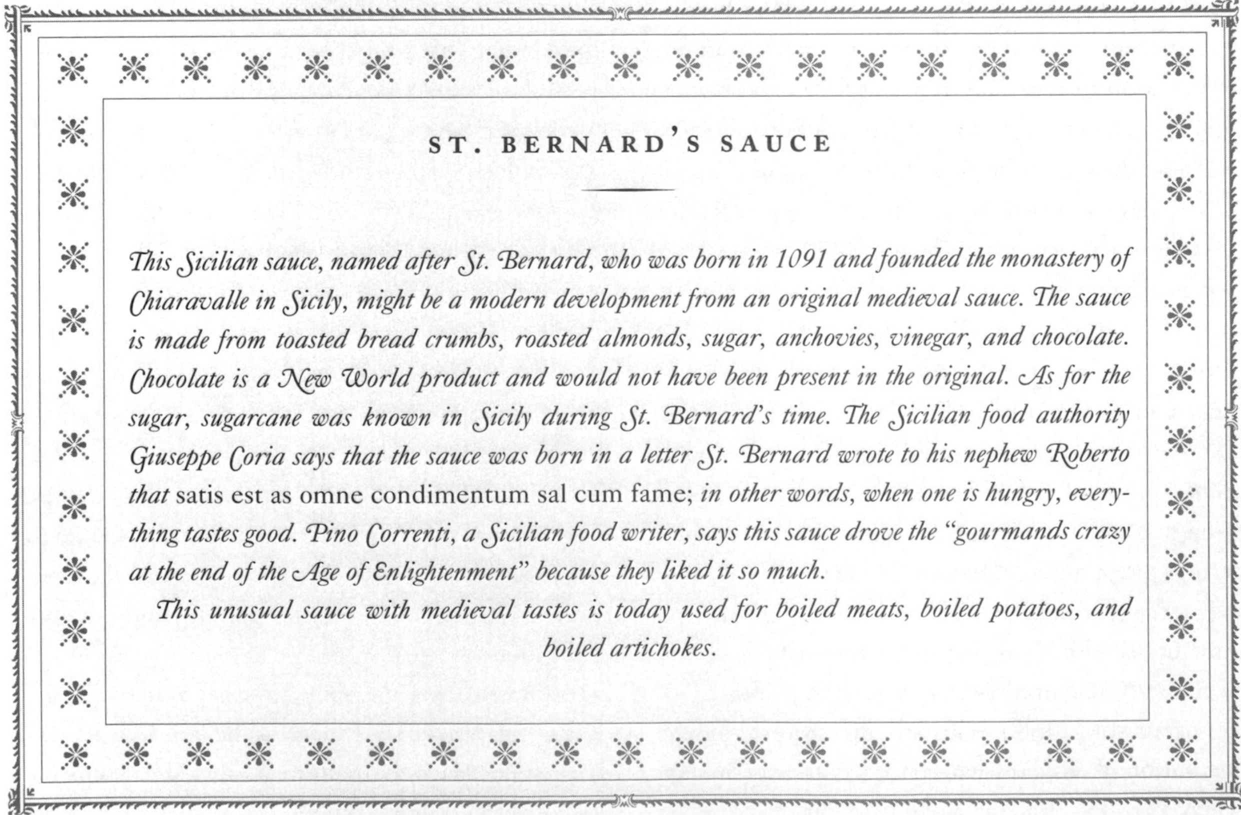

ST. BERNARD'S SAUCE

This Sicilian sauce, named after St. Bernard, who was born in 1091 and founded the monastery of Chiaravalle in Sicily, might be a modern development from an original medieval sauce. The sauce is made from toasted bread crumbs, roasted almonds, sugar, anchovies, vinegar, and chocolate. Chocolate is a New World product and would not have been present in the original. As for the sugar, sugarcane was known in Sicily during St. Bernard's time. The Sicilian food authority Giuseppe Coria says that the sauce was born in a letter St. Bernard wrote to his nephew Roberto that satis est as omne condimentum sal cum fame; *in other words, when one is hungry, everything tastes good. Pino Correnti, a Sicilian food writer, says this sauce drove the "gourmands crazy at the end of the Age of Enlightenment" because they liked it so much.*

This unusual sauce with medieval tastes is today used for boiled meats, boiled potatoes, and boiled artichokes.

dred years, the Arabs created one of the greatest empires ever known to mankind.

In the realm of cuisine, the thirteenth- and fourteenth-century Catalan, French, Spanish, and Italian cookery works reveal more affinity with the medieval Arab cookery manuscripts, than they do with Roman ones (see Chapter 8). In fact, St. Bernard in the twelfth century was already denouncing the culinary exoticism that was growing popular in a medieval Europe fascinated with the sensuousness of Arab culture.[103]

The Arab influence on western European cooking can no more be ignored than can the influence of Arab science on medieval European science.[104] But we must also be careful not to overestimate culinary influence. Eating habits are notable in that they don't change quickly and cultures resist new foods probably as often as they accept them. People are deeply attached to their traditional foods. Occasionally foods appear to be rapidly accepted. An example is the coffee sponge cake called *tiramisù,* meaning literally "pick-me-up," that was invented in the 1960s by the chef at El Toula restaurant in Treviso in the Veneto region of Italy and is now ubiquitous in Italian restaurants in America. The historian of medieval Europe George Duby has even argued that food habits can be so strong that they affect the land use of regions that conquerors enter. His example was the German tribes who overran the western portion of the Roman Empire, carrying with them a preference for a diet of grains and animal products. These food preferences, Duby argued, brought into being the mixed farming methods of the medieval manor.[105] Did a similar situation exist when Christian Europe came into contact with the Muslims? The economic historian Andrew Watson has suggested that maybe Christian Europe was predisposed to reject Muslim culinary concepts that were based on sedentary agriculture, an agriculture that emphasized fruits, vegetables, grains, and legumes and found small need for animal protein. For the common people this seems true.

On the other hand, there is an equal amount of evidence that shows food habits can change very quickly, especially when a new food replaces an old one unavailable through crop failure or is adopted by the upper classes who historically have been adventurous eaters and interested in exotic foods. The new foods slowly entering the largely meat-based diet of Europe of the ninth to twelfth centuries as a result of Arab agricultural technology and horticulture were largely grains, pulses, fruits, and vegetables. The European portion of the Mediterranean rim, countries such as Spain and Sicily that actually had Arab populations for long periods of time, as well as Catalonia, Provence, and especially Italy, all seem to have been more receptive to Arab cookery than northern Europe, probably owing to the fact that they were the first point of contact. Arab farmers were masters of vegetable growing and Arab cooks masters of vegetable cookery. They did wonders with the new vegetables as well as the older ones, such as cabbage.

Salāṭat al-Malfūf (Syria)

CABBAGE SALAD

Arab cooks favored cool salads in the hot and arid climate of Syria. Salads of vegetables and herbs, such as mint, have the hallmarks of preparations that may have come through the ages relatively unchanged. The Arabs knew of the cabbage in medieval times but were not responsible for its diffusion in Europe. In the Middle Ages, cabbage was the most common vegetable and many vegetables were preserved in salt. But, contrary to the way the recipe reads, this salad is not at all salty. This recipe was given to me by George Salloum, who is originally from Homs in Syria.

1 small Savoy cabbage (about 1 pound), damaged outer leaves removed, cored, and shredded
1/4 cup sea salt, or more to taste
6 garlic cloves, very finely chopped
2 tablespoons fresh lemon juice
6 tablespoons extra virgin olive oil
3/4 teaspoon dried mint

1. Toss the shredded cabbage in a large bowl with the salt and let sit for 1 hour.

2. Thoroughly wash the salt from the cabbage by dunking it in water. Taste a piece of the raw cabbage to make sure the salt is washed off. Return to the cleaned bowl. Toss well with the garlic, lemon juice, olive oil, and mint. Check the seasoning, although it should not need any more salt, and serve at room temperature within the hour.

Makes 4 servings

THE elite in Europe began to change their attitudes toward eating, stimulated by the place of food in Muslim theology, as represented in depictions of the Garden of Delights. The sensual pleasures of eating as portrayed in the garden intrigued Europeans, who began to associate luxurious dining with the food of the Arabs. Muslim sensuousness must have appeared attractive as a counterpoint to the ascetic life demanded of Christians.[106] Comparing culinary texts confirms the basic similarity of Arab and European cookery around the fourteenth century, and at least one Arab cookery work was translated in Italy into Latin at this time, the *Liber de ferculis et condimentis* (Book of dishes and seasonings).[107] Already in about 1320, we see an Anglo-Norman cookery manuscript replete with Arab-style recipes such as *blanc desirree, vert desirree,* and *aneserree,* meaning, respectively, "white food of Syria," "green food of Syria," and "yellow food of Syria." The first calls for capon to be boiled with almond milk, then with pomegranates, sugar, ginger, and white wine; the second is about the same but colored with parsley; the third should be the color of saffron. Most of the recipes are heavily spiced with ginger, cinnamon, and sugar, and make use of almond milk; they admonish that the food cooked be yellow, red, or some other color, a type of endoring common to medieval Arab cookery.[108] The tastes of these dishes themselves are purely Arab in inspiration.

The Islamic influence on our Western heritage is often overlooked or discounted.[109] The reasons for this centuries-old distortion of the contributions of Islam can be traced in part to the humanist Petrarch (1304–1374), the Italian poet who led the revival of the spirit of antiquity, and to the Crusading movement of Christian Europe, whose archenemies were the heretical Muslims. Medieval Christians thought that Islam was a false and self-indulgent religion based on the sword. Muhammad, the Muslim prophet, was seen by Christians either as the Antichrist or as the analogy of Christ and therefore a false prophet. Although Muslims were quite insistent that Muhammad was God's messenger, not God's son (in Islamic theology there is only one God and therefore he cannot have a "son"), the distinction fell on deaf Christian ears. Even today it takes only one Muslim psychopath to convince a Westerner that the entire religion is psychopathic.

It was simply impossible for the European mind of the Middle Ages to conceive, let alone admit, that Islam could influence Christian culture. At the same time, in the face of the Islamic cultural threat, Europeans exaggerated the influence of classical Greece and Rome. The valuation of classical knowledge experienced a rebirth during the Renaissance (the meaning of the word, after all) with the discovery of manuscripts and the invention of printing. The humanists of the fourteenth and fifteenth centuries

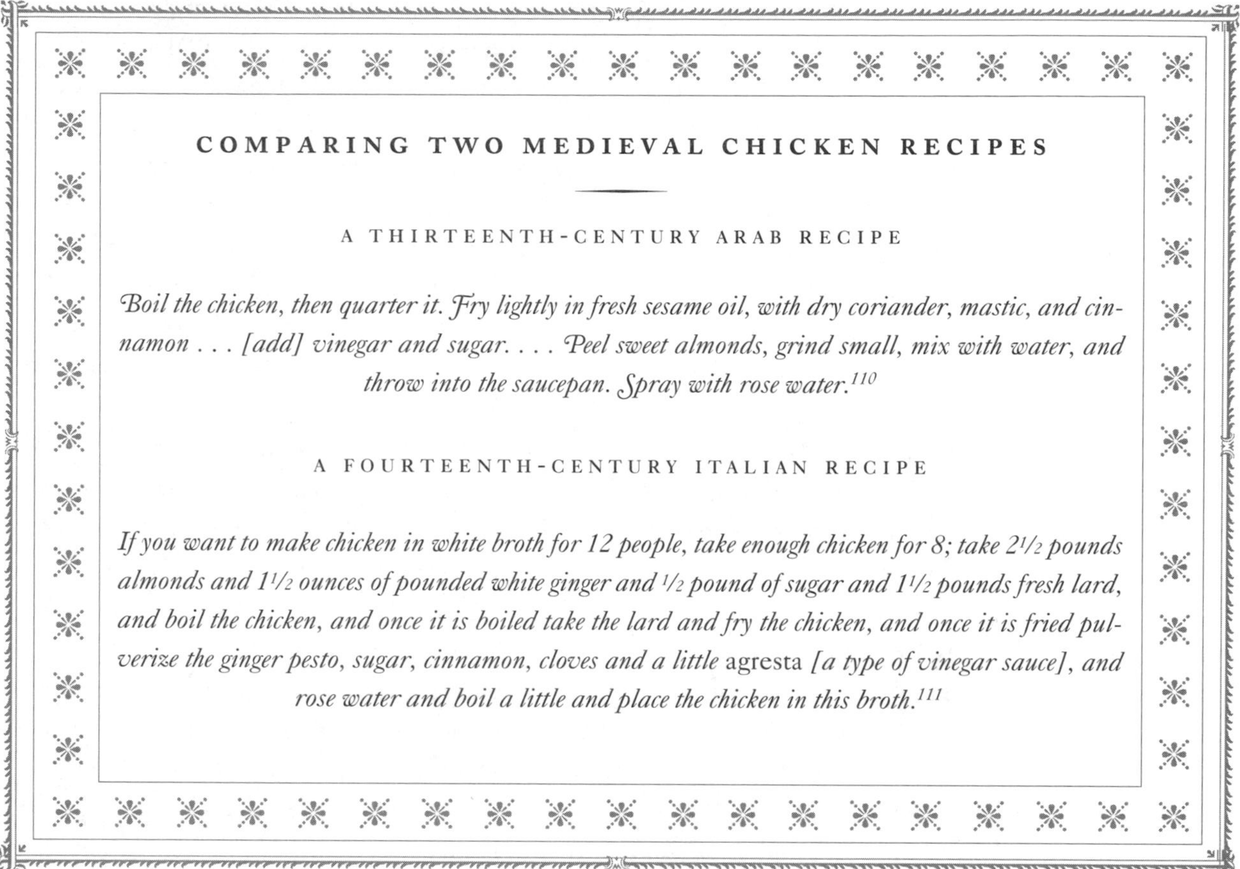

COMPARING TWO MEDIEVAL CHICKEN RECIPES

A THIRTEENTH-CENTURY ARAB RECIPE

Boil the chicken, then quarter it. Fry lightly in fresh sesame oil, with dry coriander, mastic, and cinnamon . . . [add] vinegar and sugar. . . . Peel sweet almonds, grind small, mix with water, and throw into the saucepan. Spray with rose water.[110]

A FOURTEENTH-CENTURY ITALIAN RECIPE

If you want to make chicken in white broth for 12 people, take enough chicken for 8; take 2½ pounds almonds and 1½ ounces of pounded white ginger and ½ pound of sugar and 1½ pounds fresh lard, and boil the chicken, and once it is boiled take the lard and fry the chicken, and once it is fried pulverize the ginger pesto, sugar, cinnamon, cloves and a little agresta *[a type of vinegar sauce], and rose water and boil a little and place the chicken in this broth.*[111]

discovered many ancient texts that had been lost or neglected for centuries.[112] But it was Islam that provided the bridge from the classical era to the Renaissance for Europe.

The Renaissance (c. 1400–1650) was completely different from the Middle Ages (c. 500–1450). The new movement of rediscovery engendered during the Renaissance is known as Neoclassicism. Neoclassicism expressed itself in the validation of the Epicurean idea of pleasure. Eating societies, *convivium,* were a home for humanists, who took on Latin names such the famous Italian poet Francesco Petrarca, who became Petrarch, or the equally famous chef and Vatican librarian, Bartolomeo Sacchi (1421–1481), who became Platina and talked about philosophy. Even food was talked about philosophically. The French essayist Michel Montaigne (1533–1592) noted how the Italian chefs talked philosophically about food, unlike the French of the same period.[113] Early Renaissance people dressed their ideas in the twin cloaks of Greece and Rome without fully realizing that the intellectual inspiration was purely Muslim.

It was during the late medieval period (c. 1100–1400) that Arab influence on European culture affected not only philosophy, science, and technology, which is well documented, but also every aspect of good living.[114] By the thirteenth century, a thriving intellectual movement in western Europe was rapidly assimilating Arab learning in science and philosophy, especially in the royal courts like that of the Holy Roman Emperor Frederick II in Palermo. The court kitchens produced some magnificent foods, all inspired by Arab cookery of the time. Frederick's admiration of Arab culture had its antecedents in the Norman period of rule in Sicily. Roger II, the most illustrious ruler of Norman Sicily, lived in the twelfth century like an Arab caliph with Arab physicians, the most advanced in medical learning in medieval times, and Arab court officials. His attendants included eunuchs and a harem with Muslim women, and his bodyguards were Arabs. The palace kitchen under Roger II was under the supervision of a royal cook who was an Arab and known by the Arabic title *al-nāẓir* (director), who created magnificent dishes served on gold plates by servants dressed in silk costumes. In medieval times, when kings were routinely assassinated by poisoning food, the director of the royal kitchen was an extremely important court post and for the Normans to put an Arab in charge demonstrated the trust the Normans placed in their Arab-Sicilian subjects.[115]

The rising standards for good living in Europe were often due to Arab fashion, as well as some popular customs and beliefs.[116] Hand washing before eating was first introduced through Italy, probably by the Arabs, who had a ritual tradition of washing before praying or eating. The Sicilians, in particular, inherited popular traditions from the Arabs concerning the various magical properties of certain kinds of food. For example, there is a custom in Syria that when a fruit tree doesn't bear fruit the gardener asks a pregnant woman to fasten a stone to one of its branches. This custom is also found in Sicily.[117] The Arabs held that eating birds' hearts made one timorous, sheep's liver strengthened the liver, lamb brains caused stupidity, and sheep's testicles combatted exhaustion. Such Islamic traditions and prohibitions concerning food were significant for Muslim Sicilians. Meat had to be ritually slaughtered and it was unacceptable to get meat from a non-Muslim butcher. Since Jewish food conformed with Muslim rites, it could be eaten. This led to a well-known medieval Muslim proverb giving advice to sleep in Christian beds (which are clean) but to eat Jewish food (which was good).[118] The Jews were highly respected by Muslims for their food, as seen in another proverb, "Of the good things of this world, the Muslims enjoy most sex, the Christians, money, the Persians, status and the Jews, food."[119] There was a prohibition on consuming blood linked to animals that were dead without having been ritually slaughtered and the consumption of carrion was strictly prohibited.[120] Pork was forbidden and considered filthy.

One Arab contribution to European cuisine transmitted through Sicily and Spain was endoring—the coating or coloring of food, for example, with egg yolks or saffron for a yellowing effect, popular because yellow was a symbol of gaiety for medieval Arabs.[121] Red food was attained by using alkanet (from the Arabic *al-ḥinna*), a plant from the borage family whose root gives a red dye. Green was achieved through pistachios, parsley, coriander, and, later, spinach. By the fourteenth century, endoring of food had spread to France.[122]

Along with agriculture and science, culture in general advanced in literature, music, and, of course, gastronomy. A high standard of taste developed for the upper layers of society. In Muslim Spain, a singer named Ziryāb, who lived in Córdoba from 822 to 857 and who had played as a youth before the caliph Hārūn al-Rashīd (c. 764–809) in Baghdad, early on became an arbiter of fashion and taste in general. Ziryāb was an extraordinary individual, and a man of science as well. He is said to have introduced an order in which different dishes were to be served at a banquet; and it seems likely that the order of courses we ourselves follow on the most formal of occasions goes back to Ziryāb.[123]

One part of good living was familiarity with books. The Arabs learned how to make paper from the Chinese, who invented the process. The first paper mill was built by Yaḥyā the Barmakid, the vizier of Hārūn al-Rashīd, in 800 at Baghdad. Paper spread westward, transmitted to Europe through Sicily. The first clear use of paper in Europe is a document of 1090 signed by Roger II, the Norman king of Sicily. As a "people of the book," as were the Jews, Muslims believed all manner of intellectual endeavors could be transmitted among those who were literate and shared the Koran. Scientific texts, agricultural treatises, pharmacological works, health manuals, and cookery books were written and widely read.

Medical practice in Europe was an abomination before the Arabs. Arab doctors scorned European surgical techniques. Although the first hospitals were started around 800 in Baghdad under the caliph Hārūn al-Rashīd, Arab doctors who came to Europe did not find such things as separate wards for infectious diseases or clinical instruction to students in a hospital, then well known in the Arab world. Arab dietetic manuals were the basis for later European ones, and early dietetic manuals and cookery manuscripts were virtually one and the same (see "An Essay on the Sources," page 693).

The scientific literature that became available to Europeans through translation was vast and its influence long lasting.[124] Arab pharmacology, for example, the strongest of the fact-based biological sciences of the Middle Ages, lasted one thousand years, utilized in Europe until the nineteenth century. A center for the translation of Arabic scientific literature existed under the auspices of the royal court of Frederick II in Palermo in the early thirteenth century as well as in Spain, especially in Toledo. For the history of Mediterranean food, the agricultural treatises and pharmacological works are important for understanding the introduction of new plants. The medicinal properties of botanicals known to Arab physicians were essential in their formulation of a theory of dietetics, which in turn was closely connected to cookery. When the Genoese doctor Taddeo Alderott (1223–1303) wrote that chewing fennel seeds or cloves stimulated the appetite and that one should not cook cabbage too much, he was expounding ideas, whether he knew it or not, learned from Arab pharmacology and dietetics. He was also making a culinary recommendation; and the cabbage soup tasted better.[125]

CONCLUSION

In this chapter we saw the simple cabbage as an exemplar of the enormous changes that occurred in the Mediterranean world from the fall of the Roman Empire to the dawn of the modern era. Just as the cabbage was horticulturally transformed from a simple leafy vegetable into the compact head we know today, so too Mediterranean food was transformed from the gruel of subsistence to the pâté of cuisine.

The Mediterranean world was formed by several distinct and interacting phenomena that allowed a cuisine to emerge for the first time since the Romans: the rise of Islamic civilization and its role in modern science and agricultural technology; the agricultural revolutions in the Mediterranean and northern Europe; innovations in technology; the growth of cities and trade; and the transition from feudalism to capitalism, as characterized by the Renaissance and the Age of Exploration. These phenomena underlie the evolution of cooking from the transformation of the raw into the cooked into the new cuisines formed by the creative impulse of the Renaissance.

Capitalism in particular was responsible for a new consciousness on the part of a new class that sought to materially transform their physical surroundings. They sought to live better than they had in the past, and "good living" was as important to their being as was their relationship to their God.

We saw that the Arab agricultural revolution was responsible for the introduction of new and improved agricultural and hydrological technologies that allowed Mediterranean farmers to be more productive. This agricultural revolution was also responsible for the introduction of new plants that materially improved the lot of Mediterranean peoples. One of the most important contributions to the eventual rise of Mediterranean cuisines was the opening up of a virtually new agricultural season.

In addition to the Islamic contribution to Mediterranean agriculture, we saw how feudalism, a system of land tenure that existed from about 500 to 1350, was based on two important components: the mounted knight and technical innovations in agriculture. There was a revolution in tillage, and agricultural productivity increased and the population grew. But several crises occurred in feudal society by about 1350: harsh winters, the lack of fertilizer, and the Black Death ruined the economy and killed off a huge portion of the population. The ensuing crisis saw a diminished rural population heading for the towns to find work. New wealth was being created in the towns and a new economic system arose through the financial control of agriculture and export trade. To manage the increasingly complex affairs of state, bureaucracies were created and the manipulation of money became profitable because its nature began to change with the invention of negotiable paper money. This was a very different system emerging, for in the old feudal economy the produce of the agriculturalist was appropriated by the lord on the basis of tribute or rent. In the emerging capitalist economy, agricultural production was greater and more efficient. Armies began to change and were no longer ad hoc formations but state-supported standing armies requiring expensive training, discipline, and food. Food production increased to feed not only armies but also a rising population, and in the royal courts and homes of rich merchants cuisines developed. Mercantile wealth was made from commerce, and wealth leads people to materially change the conditions of their lives, which engenders the creation of cuisine—the transformation of sustenance into art.

The towns of the Mediterranean grew through commerce. By the sixteenth century, newly discovered gold and silver contributed to this growth in the Mediterranean. But as the prosperity of Mediterranean towns rose in the sixteenth century, so did prices in response to an increased demand for food brought about by a growing and hungry population.

In the age of negotiable paper money, high rates of profit made capitalism grow and capital was accumulated. Accumulation of capital was the foundation for the refinements of life that began to emerge in the towns. Art, fashion, music, and cuisine became important elements in the lives of these new capitalist merchants. The appearance of capitalist modes of production, the rise of finance, the development of cities, and the needs of the growing population for nourishment, and the bourgeoisie for refinement of taste, were answered in many ways by the encounter with spices of the East. From the grain and spice trades riches were made and coincidentally, the monotony of taste overcome, as we will see in more detail in Part III, A Measure of Mediterranean Gastronomy. The rise of capitalist modes of production meant that a new class of people—capitalists, growing rich on trade in food—expropriated for their kitchens new foods and new culinary concepts.

We saw that Neoclassicism was a rebirth inspired by the cultural challenge posed by Islamic civilization and not a continuation of the classical era. The record is too sparse for us to attribute a classical Roman influence on medieval European cooking. Traditionally food writers have seen this rising interest in cuisine only through the lens of Neoclassicism, and they interpret the new gastronomy as a continuation of the Greek and Roman one. I suspect this mistake is a form of the *post hoc ergo propter hoc* fallacy of logical reasoning.

In this journey exploring the byways of Mediterranean food and its origins and transference, we need to reassemble a Mediterranean from the raw material of daily life. To understand the food we eat, we must first explore the milieu in which it arises. Before we move on, we need to complete our algebraic equation by examining, in the next two chapters, the world of the Mediterranean in terms of climate: how it affected the harvest, how agriculture developed, and what the real Mediterranean diet was from the eleventh to seventeenth centuries.

❖ 2 ❖

HARVEST OF SORROW, FOOD OF DREAMS

THE contrast between today's image of the Mediterranean and the actual Mediterranean that existed for centuries could not be drawn more starkly. The world of the Mediterranean past was one in which the climate was cruel and scarcity ruled. In this chapter I will try to give some idea of the daily life of the historic Mediterranean—a world of peddlers, vagrants, bandits, slaves, quacks, herbalists, jesters, deserters, prostitutes, saintly women, and supremely rich people luxuriating in excess while those around them starved. It is a world where *nihil sunt res humanae, nisi umbra et fumus* (human things are naught but shadow and smoke) and the human condition, in the words of one historian, cannot be extricated from the "relentless reproduction of the ineluctable catastrophe of history."[1]

THE CLIMATE, THE HARVEST, AND THE SEASONS

OUR picture of today's Mediterranean, with its ribbons of land filled with vines and olive trees bordering the sea, the rhythm of life set by climate and culture, allows us to forget that the Mediterranean is a poor land without water. The Mediterranean climate is a creation of the Atlantic and the Sahara. The blowing sand and scorching heat of Saharan winds, winds so fierce they have names, affect the weather across the Mediterranean. One might consider these winds one demarcation of the Mediterranean, while another might be the northernmost limit of the olive and vine and the southernmost limit of the palm. This area extends between the thirty-seventh and thirty-eighth parallels, about six hundred miles at its widest. The January isotherm, the line on a map connecting different points having the same temperature at the same time, follows the general shape of the sea, cutting off southern Spain and southern Italy, with southern Mediterranean shores warmer than the northern.

The lands of the Mediterranean, like the islands, were isolated from one another, but people always intermingled by virtue of trade, war, adventure, or immigration. Each region struggled to preserve its own flavor and character in the midst of an extraordinary mixture of races, religions, customs, and civilizations.

On top of it all was the climate; the climate determined the harvest, and the harvest determined life.

The climate speaks volumes about the history of the Mediterranean. Catastrophes are reflected in the growth rings of trees and in the rise and fall of the population. The fourteenth century saw a little ice age that affected cereal growing throughout Europe and the olive groves in Provence. In the Languedoc, a series of frosts killed the olive trees between 1565 and 1624, discouraging planters from attempting its cultivation.[2]

The Mediterranean trinity of wheat, olive, and vine was born of the climate and history. Throughout the Mediterranean one finds an identical agricultural civilization of farmers, peasants, and shepherds. Mediterranean cultures share the same traditional granaries, wine cellars, and oil presses. Daily lives follow the same rhythm. As late as the nineteenth century, fruit vendors in the markets of Palermo and Cairo used the same curious cry to sell their oranges and other fruits so that one never really knew what was being sold. Orange sellers in Cairo yelled "Honey! Oh, oranges! Honey!" while in Palermo they cried out, "Here's the honey," to sell their oranges.[3] There is a shared Mediterranean mentality—languorous, sullen, fatalistic, and dolorous, yet creative, hot-blooded, hospitable, loving, and hopeful. Maybe the inevitability of severe weather causes this mentality or maybe it's the religious passion of Mediterranean peoples. The Word of God, whether through the Talmud, the New Testament, or the Koran, speaks loudly throughout the Mediterranean.

In the sixteenth century, all the coastal regions produced wax, wool, and skins; they all grew mulberry trees and raised silkworms. The entire Mediterranean produced wine and had vineyards, even the Muslim countries, in spite of the Koranic injunction against alcoholic beverages. Muslim poets for centuries extolled the virtues of the vine. In Muslim Sicily of the tenth and eleventh centuries poets such as ʿAlī al-Ballanūbī wrote, "At sunset I drink a sunlit wine reflecting the aurora of its light."[4] In Arabic there is an expression for the two favorite foods, wine and meat, known as *al-'aḥmarān,* "the two red ones."

The Mediterranean climate gives us the impression of sea, sun, and fun—a deceptive image. The climate can be ferocious. Drought is common and irrigation is affected in this region of wadis and *fiumari,* the web of dried riverbeds. The growth of herbaceous vegetation slows with drought. The Mediterranean is a region of shrub culture and fruit-bearing trees, but it is also a bare land lacking an abundance of trees and in constant danger of desertification. The French historian Fernand Braudel noted that the only detail of daily life consistently mentioned in the diplomatic correspondence of the sixteenth century was news of the harvests. King Philip II of Spain (1527–1598) was kept informed by his agents and ambassadors of changes in the weather from seedtime onward. One can see that the price of bread dropped or rose in response to the amount of rainfall.

Climatic change in the Mediterranean is more often associated with scarcity than abundance. If the hot Saharan winds blow, the sirocco or *ghibli* as they are known in Sicily and Libya, before harvest time, the wheat berries will dry up and drop uselessly to the ground. The sirocco is still feared today throughout North Africa and in Sicily. The heat and aridity of North Africa has always been the motivation for cooks of the Maghreb to prepare cool and refreshing foods. Cucumbers, recommended by medieval Arab doctors for their thirst-quenching effect, are popular both as a fruit juice and as a salad, as we see in the following recipe.

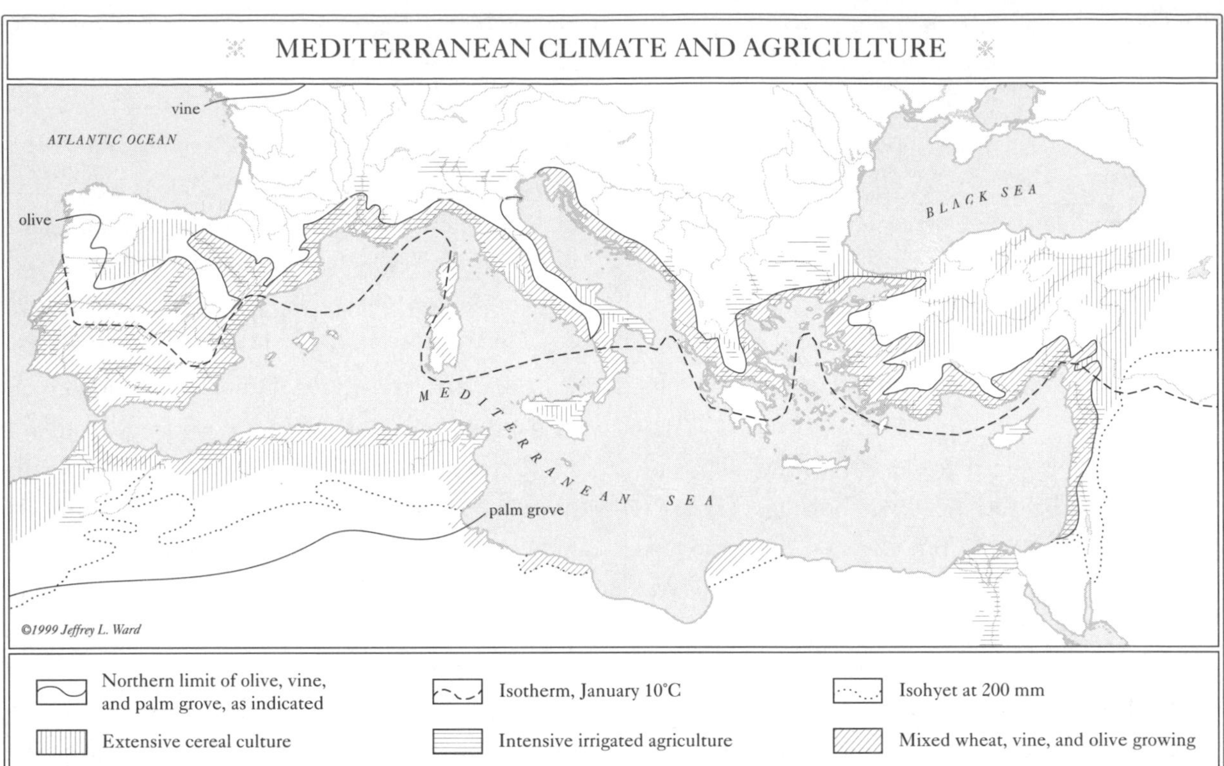

Salāṭat al-Khiyār (Algeria)

ALGERIAN CUCUMBER SALAD

If the great botanist of the nineteenth century Alphonse de Candolle is right, the cucumber has been cultivated in India for more than three thousand years, making it one of the earliest plants to be domesticated. The evidence for the cucumber being indigenous to India is circumstantial because a wild cucumber has never been found but nevertheless compelling because there is a good deal of genetic variety in the cucumbers that do exist in India. Cucumbers spread to the Mediterranean in equally early times since we know the ancient Egyptians grew them.[5]

Although medieval Arab doctors wrote about cucumber seeds and juice in a medical context, they are obviously an important food in dry climates. The cucumber's ability to retain water makes it an attractive vegetable for the cooks of North Africa. This Algerian salad is a natural accompaniment to the fiery hot shakhshūkha al-bisakra *(page 629). Make the salad at the last minute so the water is retained in the cucumber and not the bowl.*

1 large cucumber, peeled, halved lengthwise, seeded, and thinly sliced
1/2 green bell pepper, seeded and cut in half lengthwise
1/3 cup pitted and coarsely chopped imported green olives
4 large fresh mint leaves, finely chopped
2 tablespoons finely chopped fresh coriander (cilantro) leaves
1/2 teaspoon paprika
1/4 cup extra virgin olive oil
3 1/2 teaspoons white wine vinegar
Salt and freshly ground black pepper to taste

1. Toss the cucumber in a salad bowl with the green pepper, olives, and mint.

2. Add the coriander, paprika, olive oil, and vinegar; season with salt and pepper, toss again, and serve.

Makes 2 servings

✣ ✣ ✣

MEDITERRANEAN scarcity also means a lack of pasturage that can support cows in any great number. Cows are rich producers of manure, which is necessary for productive agriculture. The ownership of cattle was associated with prestige, a sentiment inherited from both the Romans and the Germans. The Latin word for money, *pecunia,* is derived from the word for cattle, *pecus,* while the word *fief* is derived from the Old High German word for cattle, *fehu.*[6] But the animal best suited to the Mediterranean climate is not the cow but the sheep. In the sixteenth century, sheep were skinny, reaching about thirty pounds as a maximum weight.[7] These small sheep could not produce as much manure as cows, and therefore Mediterranean agricultural lands were not always productive. Productive land can support people and provide them with the variety of foods that allow cooking to be abundant and interesting. But before the tenth century, Mediterranean peoples do not seem to have applied the knowledge of manuring that we know existed in the Roman Mediterranean.[8]

Winter brought leisure time and festivities. In Christian countries the killing of the pig usually occurred in December and villages broke their monotonous routine with celebrations of fairs and festivities. The generous offer of food was the sign of hospitality and a token of respect. Sixteenth-century university students were expected to lavish a dinner on their professors when they graduated, while a visiting prince or a foreign emissary was always greeted with sumptuous banquets.[9]

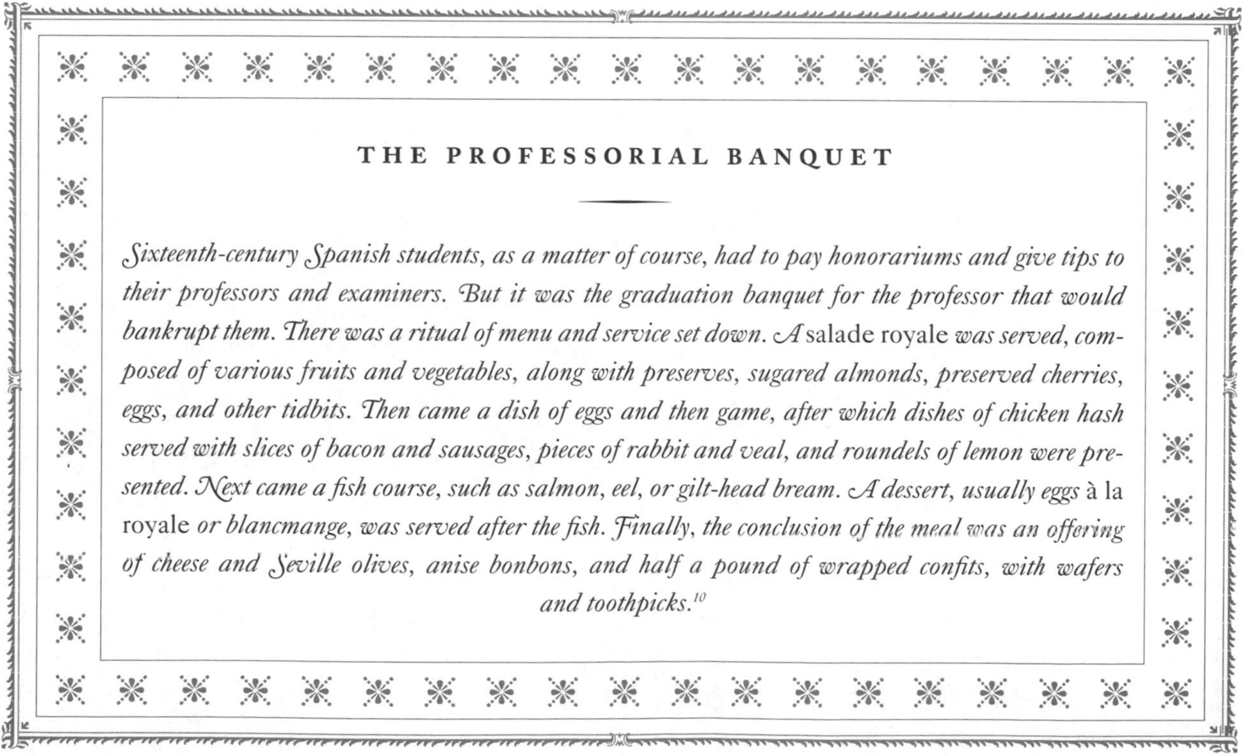

THE PROFESSORIAL BANQUET

Sixteenth-century Spanish students, as a matter of course, had to pay honorariums and give tips to their professors and examiners. But it was the graduation banquet for the professor that would bankrupt them. There was a ritual of menu and service set down. A salade royale *was served, composed of various fruits and vegetables, along with preserves, sugared almonds, preserved cherries, eggs, and other tidbits. Then came a dish of eggs and then game, after which dishes of chicken hash served with slices of bacon and sausages, pieces of rabbit and veal, and roundels of lemon were presented. Next came a fish course, such as salmon, eel, or gilt-head bream. A dessert, usually eggs* à la royale *or blancmange, was served after the fish. Finally, the conclusion of the meal was an offering of cheese and Seville olives, anise bonbons, and half a pound of wrapped confits, with wafers and toothpicks.*[10]

Winter is cold in the Mediterranean and filling the cellars and granaries meant working in haste through a succession of harvests: wheat in June, figs in August, grapes in September, olives in the fall. Shepherds would sell their fleeces in advance to creditors in September for May delivery, allowing them economic survival through the winter. Shipping came to a near halt in the winter because the seas were simply too treacherous.

Summer brought a new enemy—heat—along with the usual scourges of pirate and brigand raids. Shipping became active again in the summer not only because of favorable weather but also because the harvest increased trading. Summer in the Mediterranean was the time for the grape harvest and merrymaking, "a time of madness," as Braudel captured it. Northern boats came to Andalusia for wine as often as they did for olive oil and salt. New wines were an occasion for trading and at Seville *la vendeja* was a kind of wine fair that occurred at the same time each year. Summer was the time for activity on the sea, and it brought the fishermen good catches, especially tuna, which run seasonally. The weather determined entirely how long it took a boat to sail from one port to another. While today the weather is an inconvenience for the most part, in the sixteenth century it was all important. The Messina to Alexandria voyage could take nine days in 1560, while the Leghorn (Livorno) to Alexandria would average thirty-three days.[11]

Summer also brought epidemic diseases. In 1656–1657, forty-five thousand people died of plague in Genoa. Sister Maria Francesca, who was living in Genoa at the time, wrote on June 27, 1657: "It is a miracle that I am still able to write. Everyone has died. The city is ruined and destroyed, the nobility dies without number, all of the Palazzo Ducale is infected, the Archbishopric sick, the senate too, almost all the first, second and third ministers are dead, and if they don't die of the pestilence they die of starvation without any hope of relief."[12] The sick and starving could only dream of food.

FOOD OF DREAMS

MEDITERRANEAN peoples lived in a chronic state of malnourishment under a threatening cloud of starvation. This certainly explains the symbolic value that food acquired in preindustrial Europe. The myth of the land of Cockaigne, that imaginary land of plenty, was an escapist conception that did not disappear until the seventeenth century. The land of Cockaigne, from the Italian *Cocagna,* was the glutton and epicure's home, an imaginary medieval utopia where life was a continual circus of luxurious idleness. The word may have come to the Italian from the Latin *coquere,* "to cook," through a word meaning "cake." So the land of *Cocagna* was literally the land of cakes where the rivers were of wine, the houses built of cake, the streets paved with pastry, and the shops provided goods for nothing. Compare this myth, which finds its first expression in a thirteenth-century French poem, with the vision of paradise in the Koran (see Chapter 1) that was already translated into Latin as *Summa totinus haeresis Saracenorum* in 1150 by Peter the Venerable. It is not hard to see how the Islamic conception of pleasure and paradise may very well have influenced this romantic notion in European literature and how a culinary aesthetic could be absorbed by the literate, and rich, class, eventually trickling down to the masses.

The poor, accounting for about 95 percent of the population of the Mediterranean in the sixteenth century, had no cuisine. In the weeks before the harvest the poor subsisted on the dregs of the last harvest's grains and bran, foods that could become moldy, poisoning them with ergot.[13] When the poor ate unsalted meat, it was often from animals that had died in unknown ways, not those that had been butchered. Even if it were true that the nose knows, starvation will overcome the natural revulsion to putrefying meat.

Our knowledge of the diet of Mediterranean peoples in the sixteenth century comes from all sorts of documents, letters, receipts, official papers, bills of lading, and so forth, but these sources are suspect in the information they can provide about the huge majority who lived on the margins of rich society—the poor, beggars, tramps, and bandits. The menus found in some documents, as well as the recipes of famous Renaissance cookbooks, were for the privileged. The feasts of the Este family, noble Guelphs (who supported the papacy against the Ghibellines, aristocrats who supported the German emperors in medieval Italy), rulers of Ferrara for centuries, were not portraits of the daily cooking of Emilia-Romagna as much as they are today an inspiration for food writers and banqueters. The diet of the poor consisted of not much more than rations of soup, *vaca salada* (salt meat), *bizcocho* (hardtack biscuit), wine, and vinegar. Many of the poor were not even eating in their homes, homes that often lacked cooking facilities, but rather scavenging whatever they could from street vendors or gathering wild herbs or nuts.

As the French historian Fernand Braudel noted, feasts and banquets play a very small role in Mediterranean literature, with the salient exception of the food of dreams—for example, as in Cervantes's *Don Quixote* or Rabelais's *Gargantua and Pantagruel.* In *Don Quixote,* the wedding feast of Camacho is a veritable orgy of excess—a whole steer spitted on a whole elm turning over a burning mountain of wood surrounded by wine jugs each large enough to hold a whole sheep. In the distended belly of the steer were two dozen delicate little suckling pigs, sewn up inside to make them tasty and tender. Scattered about, hanging from the trees, were skinned hares, plucked chickens, and other game, as well as sixty wineskins holding eight gallons of wine each and loaves of white bread and cheeses stacked like bricks making a wall. Two cauldrons of oil were used for frying puddings, which were drained and plunged into another cauldron of honey. There were fifty cooks. The spices seem to have been bought not by the pound but by the baleful and were displayed in a great chest. Sancho's description of this feast is positively exhilarated and the reader is overjoyed at his happiness. He asks one of the cooks if he can dip a piece of bread in the broth and the cook obligingly ladles three hens and two geese.[14] Cervantes wanted to capture the dreams and constant preoccupations of the perpetually hungry peasant.

In Rabelais's *Gargantua and Pantagruel,* the young Gargantua, who is always hungry and thirsty, sees the world as an inexhaustible source of joy and pleasure, a true land of Cockaigne. Later in the book Gargantua's diet changes to a more reasonable one. Although the very rich were eating succulent roast veal and delicate lobsters from the Catalan coasts, the common people would not have these foods for centuries. The two recipes that follow would be considered food for the rich five centuries ago, while today they represent home cooking of the Catalan middle class.

Vedella Lligada (Catalonia)

"TIED-UP" VEAL

Don Quixote said that veal is better than beef or kid, which are both better than goat's meat. Roasted veal with pickle sauce was a dish denied to that famous knight-errant of literature, but today roast veal is a popular Catalan dish. In this recipe the preparation is as straightforward as its name. The veal is tied up to form a regular shape and braised with whole onions, garlic, and spices. The veal is cooled, the sauce defatted, and eaten the next day. This recipe was given to me by Montse Contreras, who is from the Bergueda region of Catalonia, and is, with her husband, William Cole, a professor of Spanish literature, my primary source for understanding Catalan home cooking. Montse told me that vedella lligada *is typical Sunday fare in her mother's kitchen. Some Catalan cooks like to add* llanega, *a kind of mushroom, to the roasting veal.*

¼ cup extra virgin olive oil
One 3-pound veal roast, tied up with kitchen twine
4 cups water
½ cup cognac
2 medium-size onions, peeled
1 head garlic, peeled as much as possible without breaking off individual cloves
1 cinnamon stick
1 whole nutmeg
1 bay leaf
Salt and freshly ground black pepper to taste
1 knob *beurre manié* (see Note)

1. In a large casserole, heat the olive oil over medium-high heat, then brown the veal on all sides, about 5 minutes. Pour in the water and cognac and reduce the heat to low. Add the onions, garlic, cinnamon stick, nutmeg, and bay leaf and season with salt and pepper. Cover and cook until tender, turning several times, 2 to 2½ hours.

2. Remove the veal, let cool 20 minutes, and slice it into 12 to 14 slices, removing and discarding the kitchen twine. Strain the broth into a glass or ceramic bowl and chill it and the sliced veal in the refrigerator overnight.

3. The next day, remove the layer of fat from the broth. Put the broth in a saucepan and reduce over a medium-high heat until you have 1½ to 2 cups. Meanwhile, reheat the veal in a roasting pan in a preheated 200°F oven, covered so it doesn't dry out.

4. Stir the *beurre manié* into the sauce and continue cooking until it is the consistency you like. Transfer the veal slices to a serving platter and spoon the sauce over. Serve immediately.

NOTE: To make a knob of *beurre manié,* mash together 1 tablespoon all-purpose flour with 1 tablespoon room temperature butter until blended.

Makes 6 servings

Llagosta a l'Ampurdán (Catalonia)

LOBSTER FROM THE AMPURDÁN

Although there is no mention of lobster in Don Quixote, *we know that these crustaceans were relatively abundant in the seventeenth century off the Costa Brava, around the island of Minorca, and about the Côte Vermeille of French Roussillon, and found in markets as far north as Montpellier in Languedoc in France. It's possible that they were not expensive. This extraordinary preparation may have some connection to the recipe called* formatgades *in the anonymous Catalan cookery book of* Libre de sent soví *from 1324, where lobster is boiled in a casserole with a mixture of small fish, crushed almonds, and pine nuts, and spiced with saffron and ginger.*[15]

The llagosta *(lobster) used in this Catalan dish from the Ampurdán, the coastal plain south and east of Figueres, is the spiny lobster, which lacks the distinctive claws of the North American lobster. This preparation combines the lobster with snails and is served with a very rich nut sauce. Snails are quite popular in Catalonia and are given to a proverb,* Al juliol ni dona ni cargol *(In July, neither women nor snail), reminding me of a Sicilian proverb (Sicilians also love snails),* Babbaluci a sucari e donni a vasari 'un ponnu mai saziari *(Snails to suck out and women to kiss, that's all one needs to be satisfied). Some people make this dish with chicken instead of snails or shrimp instead of lobster. In any case, these kinds of preparations are called* mar i muntanya *(sea and mountain) or* mar i cel *(sea and heaven), or what we Americans call "surf 'n' turf."*

This recipe was given to me by Éliane Thibaut-Comelade, an authority on Catalan food who lives outside Perpignan in French Catalonia. A Catalonian cookbook from about 1930 describes this dish as being made with chocolate in the nut sauce, a New World addition. Although all the various recipes I consulted seem to indicate that the yield is for two to four people, I found the preparation so rich that six people could be fed or it could be served as a tapas.

The nuts can be ground together. In step 4, removing the meat from the lobsters can take up to 15 minutes, so don't forget to factor in that time when planning the rest of the meal.

3 garlic cloves, peeled
Pinch of freshly powdered saffron (see Note 2)
2 ounces blanched whole almonds, ground very fine in a food processor (about 1/3 cup after grinding)
2 ounces hazelnuts, ground very fine in a food processor (about 1/3 cup after grinding)
8 to 9 slices *crostini di pane per le zuppe di pesce* (page 559)
1 tablespoon finely chopped fresh parsley leaves
Salt and freshly ground black pepper to taste
2/3 cup extra virgin olive oil
2 medium-size onions, finely chopped
One 3 1/4-pound or two 1 1/2-pound live lobsters, cut up (see Note 1 and page 415)
2 cups dry white wine
1 pound ripe tomatoes, peeled, seeded, and chopped
1 teaspoon paprika
1/4 teaspoon ground cinnamon
1/4 teaspoon freshly ground nutmeg
5 dried red chili peppers
Bouquet garni, tied in cheesecloth, consisting of 6 sprigs fresh thyme, 1 bay leaf, and 10 sprigs fresh parsley
20 to 24 canned or fresh snails, drained and washed (if using fresh snails, see Note on page 724)

1. In a mortar, pound the garlic, saffron, ground almonds and hazelnuts, 1 slice of *crostini* with its crust removed, the parsley, salt, and pepper together into a very smooth paste. Do this in batches if your mortar is not large enough. You can also do it in a food processor, but with a less homogenous result. You should have 2 cups. Set aside.

2. In a large, high-sided skillet or enameled cast-iron casserole, heat the olive oil, then cook the onions over medium heat until translucent, about 8 minutes, stirring occasionally.

3. Place the cut-up lobsters in their shells in the skillet with the onions and cook over medium heat until the onions are soft, about another 6 minutes, stirring. Stir in the remaining ingredients, except the snails, and cook, covered, over medium-low heat until the sauce is denser, about 30 minutes. Remove the lobster pieces to a platter. Correct the seasoning if necessary. Add the snails to the sauce, cover, and turn off the heat. When the lobsters are cool enough to handle, remove all the meat, discarding the shells.

4. Carefully stir the nut-and-garlic paste into the sauce over very low heat a little at a time until fully absorbed and cook for 20 minutes. Add the lobster meat and cook another 10 minutes. Remove and discard the chili peppers. Serve immediately with the fried bread.

NOTE 1: This dish must be made with live lobsters because the natural water in the lobster, as well as the coral and tomalley, contribute to the unique taste. The best way to kill a live lobster is to hold the body leg side down with a kitchen towel. Drive a chef's knife into the shell behind the eyes and twist. Chop off the claws with a cleaver and crack them open slightly. Cut up the arms and remove the legs. Break the legs into 2 or 3 pieces. Separate the tail from the body (be careful—strong muscle spasms might make the tail flip back with some force). Remove the meat from the flippers at the end of tail.

NOTE 2: If you have only saffron threads, take a pinch (about 50 threads) and place them on a tray to toast lightly in a toaster oven for a minute. Remove and powder with a pestle in a mortar.

Makes 4 to 6 servings

* * *

THE fanciful world of food that the characters in Cervantes's novel dreamed about was just that—a dream. The real world of food in preindustrial Europe was brilliantly portrayed in a book called *Bread of Dreams* by the contemporary Italian historian Piero Camporesi. Camporesi made the claim that ordinary people lived in an imaginative world of a near permanent state of hallucination owing to their daily intake of toxic plants, rotted food, and bread laced with hallucinogenic herbs, their bodies hosts to scabs and worms. The Mediterranean world was a world of hunger, a Brueghelian hell where everyday folk lived fantastic drug-induced daydreams guided by popular superstitions, herbalists, exorcists, and magicians.[16]

By a seemingly Sisyphean effort did Mediterranean peoples feed themselves and overcome their abject misery. They were confronted by great tracts of land that remained uncultivated or lacking in productivity. Although we hear so much about wheat in the Mediterranean, it was not always abundant nor found everywhere. For example, in the Maghrib poor people may have dreamed of eating *māsh* (or *mʿāsh*), a coarse couscous made from a leguminous plant, or a hard wheat couscous, but they rarely did.[17] Too often it was rather the rough cake of coarsely ground grain, the primitive *kissira,* made with barley and very rarely with wheat.[18]

The Mediterranean world defined by hunger and poverty was noticed by the Flemish traveler Ogier Ghiselin de Busbecq, a linguist, diplomat, antiquarian, zoologist, and botanist, who wrote in 1555:

> The Turks are so frugal and think so little of the pleasures of eating that if they have bread, salt and some garlic or an onion and a kind of sour milk which they call "yoghoort," they ask nothing more. They dilute this milk with very cold water and crumble bread into it and take it when they are hot and thirsty. . . . It is not only palatable and digestible, but it also possesses an extraordinary power of quenching the thirst. . . . At the caravanserais [inns] it is sold along with other relishes. When the Turks are traveling they do not require hot food or meat. Their relishes are sour milk, cheese, prunes, pears, peaches, quinces, figs, raisins, and cornel-cherries all of which are boiled in clean water and set out on large earthenware trays. They eat the fruit relish with bread.[19]

What is so wrong with this diet? It is a subsistence diet, including only a small amount of protein and complex carbohydrates. It is not balanced and the total intake is minimal. Were you to eat nothing but a slice of bread and a pear and drink a glass of buttermilk for weeks on end, the effect would be unpleasant.

Frugality also played a role on the battlefield. The Turkish soldier was a sober soldier content with a little rice, powdered sun-dried meat, and coarse bread cooked in the ashes of the campfire. Busbecq described how Turkish soldiers brought with them a leather sack of the finest flour, a small jar of butter, spices, and salt. This was their nourishment. They would place a few spoonfuls of flour in some water to make a batter and flavor it with salt and spices. The batter was placed in a vessel that was set over an open fire. As the batter boiled, it swelled up and was spooned into a large bowl. They ate this batter two times a day without bread for a month or longer. When a horse died, they would eat it.[20]

The frugality of the Turkish soldier and, in fact, all Mediterranean soldiers, such as the Spaniards, Greeks, and Italians, can be contrasted with the northern soldiers like the Germans or Swiss mercenaries, who demanded better food, otherwise they wouldn't fight. In the latter part of the sixteenth century, the Grand Duke of Tuscany supplied food to the Spanish and German soldiers of Philip II's Spanish army as they crossed from Italy to Spain. He kept an inadequate supply of salt meat for the Germans while the Spaniards were happy with a little rice and biscuit. The bread issued to the Spanish soldiers sometimes would contain "offal, broken biscuits and lumps of plaster."[21] Greeks and Italians could be fed the same. The Mediterranean soldiers might be fed plain watery soups.

Zuppa Pavese (Lombardy)

EGG-DROP SOUP FROM PAVIA

The lessons of an army too well fed can be recounted in this recipe from Pavia in Lombardy. Legend has it that when King Francis I of France (1494–1547) was defeated by Charles V of Spain (1500–1558) at the battle of Pavia in 1525, he took refuge in a nearby farmhouse. The embarrassed, yet deeply honored, housewife was preparing some soup. She had to turn her humble soup into a soup fit for a king, so she fried some stale bread, put it into the soup, and cracked in two newly laid eggs and ladled some broth over the eggs. The whites curdled gently and the yolks remained soft. She served it with grana padano *cheese and the king approved, asking the recipe be given to one of his servants.*

A nice story but typical of what I call the culinary apocrypha. In fact, the badly wounded Francis I was captured immediately by Spanish arquebusiers after his horse was killed under him and he was taken to Madrid as a prisoner. In any case, the Italian food writer Ada Boni, writing in the 1960s, suggested that the cottage where the soup was first prepared for him still stood in a rice paddy just off the main rail link from Milan to Pavia a few minutes before passing the Certosa, the charterhouse of Pavia. I don't know if she believed this story or was repeating the legend.

Fernand Braudel suggested that the Battle of Pavia, besides being a triumph of the arquebusiers, was also the triumph of empty stomachs because Francis's army was too well fed, while the Spanish and Lombards he fought could make do with a simple broth like this zuppa.[22]

The crucial element to this soup is the broth. It should be clear and flavorful. I like to use the broth derived from making cima *(page 354).*

2 tablespoons unsalted butter
4 slices French or Italian bread with crust
1/4 cup freshly grated Parmigiano-Reggiano cheese
1 1/2 quarts veal broth (see variation of next recipe)
4 small eggs
1 tablespoon finely chopped fresh parsley leaves
Freshly ground white pepper to taste

1. Preheat the oven to 200°F. Warm four oven-proof soup bowls.

2. In a large skillet, melt the butter over medium heat, then cook the bread on both sides until golden, making sure you do not blacken the edges.

3. Place a slice of bread in each bowl. Sprinkle 1 tablespoon of the Parmigiano-Reggiano on each slice of bread.

4. Bring the broth to a rolling boil. Without breaking the yolk, crack 1 egg onto each slice of bread and carefully ladle or pour the boiling broth over the egg until the bowl is filled. Sprinkle with parsley and a pinch of white pepper and serve immediately. Add more cheese at the table if desired.

NOTE: The broth must be boiling furiously before you pour it into the bowls, so the eggs, which are small not large, can coddle.

Makes 4 servings

* * *

NORMALLY, a soup with eggs would be a fancy soup, and not eaten by the common folk. The various broths we use today as the basis for more complex sauces were often all that was available in the sixteenth century. Where you see abundant meat flavoring these broths today there would have been only some meatless bones.

Brodo di Carne (Italy)

BEEF BROTH

In times of famine Mediterranean peoples would eat their "water soup," simmered over an open fire with a few stones to give it "flavor." In better times vegetables would go in the pot of water to make a broth, flavored with some meatless bones. Eventually, a good broth evolved as the basis for soups and sauces. This Italian version is a broth that can be frozen for future use. For veal broth, replace the beef with veal; for lamb broth, replace with lamb; and for vegetable broth, omit the meat and add a bunch of spinach and one cut-up leek. For the French method, see the variation.

4 pounds cracked beef marrow, shin, and/or shank bones, with meat on them
1 large onion, cut into eighths
4 ripe plum tomatoes, cut in half (optional)
1 carrot, cut up
2 celery stalks, cut up
10 black peppercorns
Bouquet garni, tied together in cheesecloth, consisting of 3 sprigs fresh parsley, 1 sprig fresh thyme, 2 fresh sage leaves, and 1 bay leaf
4 quarts water
Salt and freshly ground black pepper to taste

1. Put all the ingredients, except the salt and pepper, in a stockpot, bring to a boil, then reduce to a simmer. Skim the surface of foam until no more appears. Partially cover and simmer on a very low heat for no less than 6 hours.

2. Pour the broth through a cone-shaped strainer and discard all the bones, meat, vegetables, and bouquet garni. Now pour the broth through the strainer lined with cheesecloth. Season with salt and pepper.

3. To defat the broth, let it rest in a refrigerator until the fat congeals on the top and can be lifted off. The broth can be frozen for up to 6 months.

Makes 2 to 3 quarts

VARIATION

To turn this broth into a *fond brun de veau*, replace the beef with veal and start by browning the meat in hot clarified butter (page 189) in a large skillet until golden brown, turning with tongs. Remove to the stockpot. Add the onion and 2 peeled carrots cut into rounds to the skillet; when the onion has yellowed, remove all to the stockpot and continue with the recipe. Alternatively, place the meat bones in a roasting pan and roast at 425°F until well browned before using.

Brodo di Pollo (Italy)

CHICKEN BROTH

The most common of nonvegetable broths in the Middle Ages was chicken broth. This is a flavorful Italian-style broth and a good base for other sauces.

8 pounds chicken bones, with meat
2 carrots, sliced
3 celery stalks, with leaves, sliced
1 large onion, halved and separated into layers
10 black peppercorns
Bouquet garni, tied in cheesecloth, consisting of 6 sprigs fresh parsley, 6 sprigs fresh thyme, 6 sprigs fresh marjoram, 2 sprigs fresh sage, and 1 bay leaf
2 cups dry white wine
5 quarts cold water
Salt and freshly ground black pepper to taste

1. Put all the ingredients, except the salt and pepper, in a stockpot, and bring to a boil. Reduce the heat to a simmer and skim off the foam until no more appears. Partially cover the pot and simmer on very low heat for at least 6 hours.

2. Pour the broth through a cone-shaped strainer and discard all the bones, vegetables, and bouquet garni. Now pour the broth through a cheesecloth-lined strainer. Season with salt and pepper. Place the broth in the refrigerator until the fat congeals and remove. The broth can be frozen for up to 6 months.

NOTE: To make rabbit broth, replace the chicken with 4 pounds rabbit bones and reduce the remaining ingredients by half.

Makes 3 to 4 quarts

Fond de Canard (Languedoc)

DUCK BROTH

In southwestern France, duck is ubiquitous and cooked in a variety of ways. One favorite way is as a broth and this duck broth will find many uses.

4 to 5 duck carcasses and necks
1 large onion, quartered
2 carrots, cut up
1 leek with white and green parts only, split lengthwise, washed well, and cut up
1 cup full-bodied red wine
10 black peppercorns
4 garlic cloves, crushed
Bouquet garni, tied in cheesecloth, consisting of 10 sprigs fresh parsley, 6 sprigs fresh thyme, and 1 bay leaf
2 to 3 quarts cold water
Salt and freshly ground black pepper to taste

1. Preheat the oven to 425°F. Arrange the duck pieces in a roasting pan and roast in the oven until browned. Remove the duck pieces to a stockpot, add the remaining ingredients, except the salt and pepper, and bring to a boil. Reduce the heat to very low and skim the surface of foam until no more appears. Simmer for not less than 6 hours.

2. Pour the broth through a cone-shaped strainer and discard the carcasses. Now pour the broth through a cheesecloth-lined strainer, season with salt and pepper, and leave in a refrigerator until the fat congeals on the surface. Remove and discard the fat. Store in the freezer for up to 6 months.

Makes 4 cups

THE Turkish soldier was not the only one who could make do with little. In Istanbul the strong oarsmen, the *caidjis,* working aboard caïques, a kind of light skiff, eating almost nothing but raw cucumbers or dishes of leeks, were as austere in their needs as the servant girls in the Murcia province of Spain who ate only salad, fruit, melons, and, especially, red bell peppers for daily nourishment. These Mediterranean peoples—the soldier, Turkish oarsman, and the Murcian servant girl—may have eaten a fresh vegetable now and then, but they were lacking in the consistent consumption of energy-producing foods needed for their hard labor—that is, protein, fat, and complex carbohydrates.

Austerity was the name of the food game, and that austerity is revealed in recipes such as these, which have their roots in much simpler preparations.

Zeytinyağlı Ekşili Pırasa (Turkey)

TART LEEKS IN OLIVE OIL

The Turkish oarsmen plying the waters of the Bosporus in the seventeenth century could well have eaten a preparation like this. The fresh lemon juice transforms these spring leeks into a tart-tasting dish. In the springtime it is a favorite preparation, along with other vegetable and olive oil dishes. The tomato juice could be squeezed out of a large ripe tomato. My recipe is concocted by adapting the ones found in Nevin Halıcı's and Berrin Ardakoç's cookbooks.

1 pound leeks, white and light green parts only, quartered lengthwise and washed well
1/4 cup extra virgin olive oil
1 small onion, thinly sliced
1/2 cup canned or fresh tomato juice
2 tablespoons finely chopped fresh parsley leaves
4 garlic cloves, finely chopped
1 teaspoon sugar
Salt to taste
1 cup vegetable broth (page 54) or water
2 tablespoons fresh lemon juice

1. Place the leeks in a medium-size skillet with the water clinging to them from their last rinsing. Turn the heat to medium-high and once the water begins to sizzle, leave for 3 minutes, shaking the pan occasionally. Remove and arrange the leeks in a medium-size baking casserole.

2. Preheat the oven to 350°F. In the same skillet you used to cook the leeks, heat the olive oil over medium-high heat, then cook the onion until translucent, about 5 minutes, stirring frequently. Add the tomato juice and stir. Stir in the parsley, garlic, sugar, and salt. Remove from the heat and spread the mixture over the leeks in the casserole. Pour the broth and lemon juice over the leeks, cover, and bake until the broth is bubbling, about 45 minutes.

3. Increase the oven temperature to broil or preheat the broiler. Remove the cover from the casserole and broil the leeks until speckled black, about 10 minutes. Remove the casserole from the oven and let the leeks cool in the casserole and then serve at room temperature.

Makes 4 servings

Zeytinyağlı Pırasa (Turkey)

LEEKS, CARROTS, AND RICE WITH OLIVE OIL

Zeytinyağlılar *are a category of Turkish foods made with olive oil or foods with olive oil poured over them. They are generally eaten at room temperature before the main meal with lots of bread to soak up the flavorful oil. The Turks love mopping up their plates with fresh bread, a gesture not considered rude but a sign of how much they enjoy the cook's preparation. I tend to leave the olive oil behind rather than mop it up.*

1/2 cup extra virgin olive oil
1 pound leeks, white and light green parts only, halved lengthwise, washed well, and cut into 3/4-inch-thick slices
1/4 pound carrots, very thinly sliced
2 tablespoons raw short- or medium-grain rice, rinsed well under cold running water or soaked in water to cover for 30 minutes and drained
1 cup water
1/2 teaspoon salt
2 to 3 tablespoons fresh lemon juice, to your taste

1. In a medium-size skillet, heat the olive oil over medium-high heat and cook the leeks and carrots

until softened, about 10 minutes, stirring occasionally. Add the rice, water, and salt, reduce the heat to very low, cover, and simmer until the rice is soft and plump, 20 to 30 minutes. Set aside to cool.

2. Drizzle on the lemon juice and mix well. Serve at room temperature.

Makes 4 servings

Ensalada Murciana (Murcia)

MURCIAN-STYLE RED BELL PEPPER SALAD

As one travels south along the Costa del Azahar, leaving Valencia and entering Murcia, rice paddies are replaced by orange orchards and huertas, *irrigated vegetable fields. This salad could come into existence only after the introduction of tomatoes and bell peppers from the New World. Today, bell peppers are extremely popular in the Murcia region. In the post-Columbian era of the Middle Ages, Murcians ate these simple vegetables along with several kinds of breads. They ate* bizcocho, *hardtack, which was cooked twice and could be preserved for a long time. They also ate barley or wheat bread, perhaps a mixture of both with rye. They also ate a lot of meat, both wild and domestic. Mutton was the most frequently eaten meat, though it was the most expensive, and the most taxed.*[23]

For this salad you need first to roast the peppers in a baking pan with a little water in an oven preheated to 425° to 450°F until the skins blister black and are easy to peel off, 30 to 40 minutes.

3 tablespoons extra virgin olive oil
2 garlic cloves, finely chopped
1½ pounds ripe tomatoes, peeled, seeded, and diced
1½ pounds red bell peppers, roasted, peeled, seeded, and quartered
Salt and freshly ground black pepper to taste
½ teaspoon freshly ground cumin seeds

1. In a large skillet, heat the olive oil over medium heat, then cook the garlic for 30 seconds, stirring constantly so it doesn't burn. Add the tomatoes and cook until their juices evaporate, about 15 minutes.

2. Reduce the heat to low, add the red bell peppers, and simmer over low heat until soft, about 30 minutes, stirring occasionally. Season with salt and pepper and sprinkle on the cumin. Serve at room temperature.

Makes 4 servings

* * *

THE rich master employing the Murcian servant girl ate more food than she did, and was, in fact, encouraged to do so. Medical science of the day promoted the idea that the poor had digestive systems different from those of the rich. Giacomo Albini, the physician of the House of Savoy, suggested that the rich not eat pottage (a thick soup made, usually, of rotting vegetables common among the poor), which could affect their delicate stomachs, while the poor should not have refined foods because their coarse stomachs would find them hard to digest.[24] The sixteenth-century author Giulio Cesare Croce told a story of a poor man named Bertoldo, who was suffering from stomachaches and eventually died, but before he did, and true to his concerns about his "coarse" stomach, begged his physicians to "bring him a pot of beans with onion in and turnips baked under the ashes."[25] In the sixteenth century the Bolognese doctor Baldassare Pisanelli proposed a nutritive and dietetic regimen based on social differences (*sub species coquinaria,* by culinary types, or, in culinary disguise). The rich were to eat differently from the poor and if either transgressed they would get sick. He said that leeks were the worst and most detestable food and suitable only for country people.[26] (Some people are unable to digest leeks and he may have been one of them.) In Venice, a town rich in food, the novelist Matteo Bandello (1485–1561), a country boy, was dazzled by the markets and the *abbondanza grandissima d'ogni sorte di cose da mangiare* (the great abundance of all kinds of things to eat). Bandello considered a good meal a few vegetables, a little Bologna sausage, some tripe, and a cup of wine.

The Mediterranean solstice or equinox brought bread or famine, a common occurrence until recently. Great, ravishing famines occurred in 1525 in Andalusia, 1528 in Tuscany, 1529 in Perugia, 1540 in Florence, 1575 in Romania, and throughout Italy in 1583, and this is just a sampling. Even the ports dealing in wheat, such as Messina and Genoa, suffered during these famines. When they struck, people would be reduced to eating grass, which is indigestible by humans. The misery of the people was reflected in the diseases they suffered. There was scurvy and ergot as well as pellagra in the seventeenth century, a disease resulting from an exclusive diet of maize. The normal diet for the majority of the population consisted of endless meals of gruel or sops (a piece of food soaked in liquid) or bread made with inferior flours, so hard and moldy it was cut with an axe. In bad times, "the bark of trees and even dirt was utilized in the desperate hope of prolonging the misery of human existence by a few days or hours, the carcasses of animals killed by the plague, even if in a state of advanced decomposition, were roasted to supply miserable hallucinating meals."[27]

THE ARRIVAL OF THE POTATO

THE discovery of the New World and its cornucopia of new foods held some hope for the starving masses of the Mediterranean. The agricultural introduction of these new plants in some cases, however, took centuries.

The Spaniards, who had no interest in the civilization of native Americans, were very much interested in their pharmacopeia and agriculture. In 1570, King Philip II appointed Francisco Hernandes (1517–1578) to collect information on the drugs and medicines of the natives. He eventually produced his monumental classic *Treasures of Medical Matters of New Spain*. New drugs were introduced by virtue of South American Indian pharmacological knowledge—drugs such as cinchona, curare, and ipecac. The Maya also used capsicum, chenopodium, guaiacium, and vanilla for pharmacological purposes.[28] Among the most famous of the New World plants that were of interest to the Spanish was the potato *(Solanum tuberosum)*.

The record of the potato's exact place of origin and how it came to the Mediterranean is scanty. The potatoes originally introduced to Europe were quite knobby and unlike the smooth ovals we see today, a result of cultivators working toward that end. It was also at least one hundred years after its discovery that the potato came to be accepted in any way as a food in the Mediterranean. The common story of the discovery of the potato by Europeans tells of its being found in 1538 by a Spanish soldier, Pedro de Cieza de León, in the Cauca Valley of Colombia, and first introduced as a curiosity to Europe by 1573.[29] Although the latest evidence points to the Chiloé region of Chile as the place of origin, it seems that the first potato to reach Europe must have come from Peru and transshipped through Cartagena in Colombia. The great French botanist Carolus Clusius went to Spain in 1564 with the express purpose of describing rare plants to be found there.

He published his results in 1576 and never mentioned the potato. It seems that so attentive and careful a scholar as Clusius, the greatest botanist of his day, would not have overlooked the potato had it been growing in Spain, although it may have been growing in very localized areas. But since we have definite proof of the potato being eaten at the Sangre hospital in Seville in 1573, it must have reached Spain from the New World in 1569–1570. The story of the sweet potato *(Ipomoea batatis)* is quite different. It was discovered by Columbus in 1492 and brought to Spain from Haiti a year later. The sweet potato was being grown in Spain within a few years. When one encounters references to the "common potato" in early seventeenth-century writers, it is the sweet potato to which they refer. Three tubers—the potato, the sweet potato, and the sunchoke *(Helianthus tuberosus)*—all entered Europe from the New World about the same time, but the potato was the food that became popular. It did so probably because it was easier to digest and its taste was bland enough to allow for greater uses in a household economy. Most important it was the starch in potatoes, its caloric value, that made it so attractive as a food. The potato was grown only in small gardens in Spain in the last part of the sixteenth century, but by the seventeenth century we see the potato more and more in the cuisines of Spain and Naples, then ruled by the Spanish Bourbons.[30] The introduction of both the potato and maize helped reduce the famine problem in Europe, and today the potato is loved in all Mediterranean cuisines.

Salsa de Patatas (Andalusia)

POTATO SAUCE

This sauce from the mountainous region of Andalusia called the Sierra Morena is made with three New World vegetables. In the pre-Columbian era it may originally have been a sauce made with rice or migas *(bread crumbs) and used to embellish chicken. It is not an overpowering sauce, goes very well with fish, and freezes very well.*

¼ cup extra virgin olive oil
¼ pound potatoes (a small potato of any variety), peeled and chopped
2 large red bell peppers, seeded and finely chopped
¾ pound ripe tomatoes, peeled, seeded, and chopped
2¼ teaspoons salt
¾ teaspoon cumin seeds
1 bay leaf
Freshly ground black pepper to taste
1 cup water

1. In a medium-size skillet, heat the olive oil over medium heat, then cook the potatoes until moisture is released, about 6 minutes, stirring occasionally. Add the bell peppers and tomatoes and continue cooking until the flavors are well blended, about 10 minutes, stirring. Add the salt, cumin seeds, bay leaf, black pepper, and water, stir, and cook until denser, about 10 minutes.

2. Pass the sauce through a food mill or potato ricer, then return to the skillet and cook over medium heat until hot, stirring, about 8 minutes. Serve the sauce ladled over fish such as hake or halibut or freeze for later use. If you don't have a food mill it is better to mash by hand with a potato masher rather than an electric mixer or food processor, which will make the potatoes gummy. The sauce can be frozen for 4 months.

Makes 2 cups

Puré de Patatas amb Cansalada (Catalonia)

MASHED POTATOES WITH PORK FATBACK

In the Middle Ages spices were never used for preserving. They were too expensive for that purpose and, besides, there already existed a perfectly fine way to preserve meats, namely salting. One often encounters salted meat in medieval documents as carnsalada *or* vaca salada. *Documents in the municipal archives of Perpignan in French Catalonia describe the use and sale of* carnsalada *(literally, salted meat) in 1276.*[31] *Today, it's called* cansalada *in Catalonia and it refers to this very old form of salted pork fatback used abundantly in Catalan home cooking, especially in preparations where bland food is flavored.*

This recipe is adapted from Montse Contreras who, when describing to me how to make it, warned me several times that this potato dish is very, very good (because of the fat), and I would have a hard time not eating it all. She's right.

½ pound pork fatback, rind removed and saved for flavoring a stew, fat sliced into strips
2½ pounds potatoes, peeled and cut into 2-inch pieces
5 tablespoons unsalted butter
¾ cup hot milk

1. Place the pork fatback strips in a large nonstick skillet and cook over a medium heat until they are crispy brown, 20 to 25 minutes. Remove the rendered pork strips with a slotted spoon, leaving the fat in the pan. Finely chop the pork strips and set aside.

2. Place the potatoes in a large saucepan and cover by 1 inch with cold water. Turn the heat to medium. Once the water begins to boil gently, about 20 minutes, cook until the potatoes are easily pierced by a skewer, about another 20 minutes. Drain the potatoes immediately and pass through a food mill, potato ricer, or strainer back into the saucepan they were cooked in. If you don't have a food mill or ricer it is better to mash by hand with a potato masher rather than an electric mixer or food processor, which will make the potatoes gummy. Beat in the butter and milk a little at a time with a wooden spoon until you have the consistency you like. Stir the chopped crispy fatback into the mashed potatoes.

3. Turn the heat to medium under the fat left in the nonstick skillet. When it is hot, flatten the mashed potatoes into the skillet carefully so you don't splash any hot oil on yourself. Cook the potatoes until the bottom is crispy brown, 15 to 20 minutes. Serve crispy side on top.

VARIATION
Chopped cooked spinach or Swiss chard can be stirred into the mashed potatoes before frying them.

Makes 6 servings

Gnocchi de Patate (Liguria)

POTATO GNOCCHI

We don't know when the potato was introduced to Italy. It seems likely to have arrived via Spain sometime between 1569 and 1588, when it is clearly described in a document as fodder for pigs.

Gnocchi, before the introduction of the potato, referred to little balls of flour or bread or both that were boiled. The earliest of these recipes that I am aware of is the nochi *of the anonymous early fifteenth-century cookbook by the writer known as Anonimo Meridianale. But even by 1692, when Antonio Latini published his* Lo scalco alla moderna, *gnocchi were still made of flour and considered a kind of macaroni. In Genoa gnocchi are today called* tròfie, *but were originally a form of* pasta secca *in the Middle Ages, made from hard wheat flour and not potatoes.*[32]

Eventually the potato was used for making gnocchi and the result was heavenly. Gnocchi are often made heavy, pasty, and unappetizing. The secret to making little puffs of clouds, gnocchi so light they melt in your mouth, will be explained here. The type of potato you use should have a relatively low moisture content. But since you're unlikely to know whether this is the case, simply follow my instructions. Do not use eggs to bind the dough; this will create heavy dumplings. Be very careful with the flour; try not to use any more than I have called for. There should be enough moisture left in the potatoes to help the binding process but not enough to make a heavy gnoccho *(singular). Do not handle the dough very much; use a fork to mix at first and then briefly and quickly knead the dough with your hands. Poach the gnocchi very gently (the water surface should only be shimmering) and remove with a slotted ladle or spoon about 1 minute after they return to the surface.*

3 pounds baking potatoes
¾ cup unbleached all-purpose flour
1½ teaspoons salt
4 quarts water

1. Puncture the potatoes in three or four places with the tip of a paring knife or skewer. Microwave the potatoes in their peel until a skewer glides easily to the center of the potatoes. Alternatively, bake them in their skins at 350°F until a skewer glides easily to the center of the potato.

2. Peel the potatoes while they are still hot and pass through a strainer, potato ricer, or food mill into a large mixing bowl. Add the flour and salt and knead together quickly with a fork. Try not to handle the dough with your hands. Once the potatoes and flour are homogenous, roll out into long ropes about ¾ to 1 inch in diameter. Cut into ¾- to 1-inch segments.

3. Place each piece on a fork and roll it across the tines of the fork, or the largest cheese grating opening on a grater, pressing down gently, and let the *gnoccho* drop to the counter surface. Each *gnoccho* will have indentations on it, perfect for texture and holding the sauce.

4. Bring the water to a gentle boil in a large pot and add some salt. Reduce the heat so the water is shaking a bit, not bubbling. Drop the gnocchi into the water one at a time, slowly, and once they have risen and are floating on top of the water, remove them one at a time after about 60 seconds. If you cook them too long, they will become waterlogged and heavy. Drain and serve with the sauce of your choice.

VARIATIONS

- To make *gnocchi alla bava*, a Piedmontese dish, layer the gnocchi with fontina cheese in a baking dish and bake for 5 minutes at 375°F.
- Serve with *pesto alla genovese* (page 351).
- Serve with *quattro formaggi*, four cheeses, a modern invention from northern Italy. Melt gorgonzola, taleggio, fontina Val d'Aosta, and grated Parmigiano-Reggiano or mascarpone together and toss with the gnocchi with a grinding of black pepper.

Makes 4 servings

Pommes Frites (Provence)

FRENCH FRIES

The most famous potato preparation is the fried potato, the French fry. The commonly accepted story of the origin of the French fry suggests it was first cooked by peasants of the Maas valley in Holland in the seventeenth century. Today, connoisseurs are agreed that Belgium produces the finest French fry. Earlier, in Spain, a kind of potato fritter was made using chũno, *dried potatoes. The French first thought that the best use for potatoes was as fodder.*

French fries are found everywhere in the Mediterranean, sometimes in surprising places. I was having lunch on a rooftop cafe with a Syrian friend in Aleppo once and saw on the menu baṭāṭis bi'l-krīma. *It was some beautiful golden French fries with a spoonful of a creamy yogurt-and-garlic sauce. My fondest memories of the perfect French fry are those I bought many years ago from street vendors in Brussels, wrapped in a brown paper cone with a dollop of mayonnaise, or the light, crisp, golden fries served at a small inn in Switzerland. In fact, the best French fries I ever had was at a little neighborhood restaurant in Allschwil, a suburb of Basel, Switzerland, in the early 1970s when I attended the University of Basel. They were crunchy, light, and golden and served on an oval silver platter.*

As simple as you think making French fries ought to be, they're not, so stick closely to this recipe. The two important "secrets" are washing and drying the potatoes and frying them twice in oil heated to an exact temperature. Keep the cut potatoes in cold water until you need them to avoid their discoloring, but they must be thoroughly dried before cooking by blotting them with paper or kitchen towels.

4 russet potatoes (about 12 ounces each), peeled and cut into 3-inch lengths not more than 3/8 inch thick
2½ quarts peanut or canola oil for deep-frying
Salt to taste

1. Dry the potatoes very well with a towel or multiple sheets of paper toweling. *It is very important that the potatoes be dry.* Preheat the frying oil in a deep-fryer or an 8-inch saucepan fitted with a basket insert to 360° to 365°F. The oil should be at least 2 inches deep and no cooking should happen before that temperature is reached.

2. Cook the potatoes in five batches so the fryer is never too crowded (otherwise the temperature of the oil will drop). Place the potatoes in the fryer basket, lower it into the oil, and deep-fry for exactly 5 minutes. Remove, drain in the basket, and then transfer to a paper towel-lined platter to drain further. Repeat until all the potatoes are cooked. Let the potatoes cool completely, covered with paper towels. Do not salt. You can place them in the refrigerator for 8 hours if you're not to be serving them until later in the day, but do bring them back to room temperature before proceeding.

3. Preheat the frying oil to 370° to 375°F. Cook the fries in five batches again for exactly 4 minutes. Taste one fry and if you like it, fine, otherwise cook for another minute. As you remove the fries to drain on some more paper towels, salt them *immediately*. Transfer the French fries to a platter and serve. Let the frying oil cool completely, strain, and save for a future use. Replace the frying oil completely once its color looks like a light maple syrup.

Makes 4 to 6 servings

Pommes Purées (Provence)

MASHED POTATOES

The first culinary use of the potato in the Mediterranean was in stews. The Spaniard who is credited with discovering the potato, Pedro de Cieza de León in 1538, said that boiled potatoes were as tender as cooked chestnuts. The cooked potatoes were also mashed coarsely and served with oil, vinegar, and pepper. The modern mashed potato, as represented in this recipe, came later and there is a certain mystique to properly cooked mashed potatoes. The knack to it all is adding the ingredients slowly and not overprocessing the potatoes.

1¼ pounds boiling potatoes, peeled and cut into 2-inch cubes
¼ cup (½ stick) unsalted butter
Salt to taste
6 tablespoons warm milk

1. Place the potatoes over the heat in a medium-size casserole or saucepan and cover with cold water by 1 inch or so. Turn the heat to medium and when the potatoes come to a boil, after about 20 minutes, cook another 20 minutes. The potatoes are done when a skewer can glide easily to the center of the potato. Immediately remove the potatoes before they cook any more by pouring the water out and placing the potatoes in a food mill. If you don't have a food mill or potato ricer it is better to mash by hand with a potato masher rather than an electric mixer or food processor, which will make the potatoes gummy.

2. Pass the potatoes through the food mill or ricer back into the casserole or saucepan you used to boil them. Over a very low heat beat in small slices of the butter with a wooden spoon, one at a time, until each is absorbed. Season with salt and slowly beat in the warm milk. Add more milk, depending on the consistency you like. Serve immediately.

Makes 2 to 4 servings

Baṭāṭis Mirḥya (Algeria)

ALGERIAN POTATO PUREE WITH CHEESE

The potato was most likely introduced to North Africa by the Spanish. The acceptance of the potato into local cooking was probably made easier by the similarity between the potato and the native tirfās, *or North African truffle* (Melanogaster variegatus). *In fact, another tuber, the sunchoke, is called* tirfās, *originally a Berber name, in North Africa. This preparation is particularly good with* kalmār ᶜaṣbān *(the stuffed squid recipe on page 454) and is often served with many dishes in Algeria. An Algerian potato puree should not look like our mashed potatoes; it should have a near-fluid cream of wheat consistency. This style of potato puree also appears in Majorca as* puré de patata: *a smooth creamy puree often mixed with grated Mahón cheese, a cheese from Minorca with a sharp Parmesan-like taste. And in the Valencian province of Castellón a thicker potato puree is served with swordfish (page 430).*

2 pounds boiling potatoes
1⅓ cups hot milk
2 tablespoons unsalted butter
¼ cup freshly grated Gruyère cheese
Salt and freshly ground black pepper to taste

1. Wash the potatoes, place in a large saucepan, and cover with 1 inch of cold water. Turn the heat to medium and once it comes to a boil, in about 20 minutes, cook until a skewer glides easily to the center of the potato, about another 20 minutes. Drain the potatoes, peel once cool enough to handle, and pass them through a food mill or ricer back into the saucepan you cooked them in. If you don't have a food mill it is better to mash by hand with a potato masher rather than an electric mixer or food processor, which will make the potatoes gummy.

2. Beat in the hot milk, butter, and cheese a little at a time with a wooden spoon. Season with salt and pepper. Reheat the potato puree over medium heat, stirring with a wooden spoon until it gets hot. Or keep warm and covered until needed.

Makes 4 servings

Matevz (Croatia)

POTATO AND WHITE BEAN PUREE

Croatian cuisine is a finely spiced mix of Austrian, Hungarian, Turkish, and Italian influences. The potato is a very popular vegetable in Croatia, probably second only to cabbage. How the potato came to Croatia is not known. Because Croatia was in the Venetian sphere of influence during the Middle Ages, both political and culinary, a good guess would be that it was an Italian introduction. On the other hand, Croatians provided many captains and sailors to Mediterranean crews, and it could have been one of these merchant-captains who brought the potato back from Spain after its arrival from the New World. This is a recipe from the Croatian hinterland, which we know by the use of smoked pork, typical of inland cooking.

This recipe is concocted from my memory of a dish I had in a restaurant in Zagreb in the early 1970s. It was very late at night and we had driven nonstop from Basel. It was very cold, we were hungry, and this was a quite satisfying dish. I would serve the delicious grilled ground meat fingers called ćevapčići *(**page 346**) with it. This recipe was adapted in part by consulting Vladimir Mirodan's* The Balkan Cookbook.

¾ cup dried haricot beans or small white beans, picked over and rinsed
1 bunch fresh sage (about 8 sprigs), tied together with kitchen string
1 teaspoon salt
2 pounds potatoes
2 tablespoons extra virgin olive oil
1 medium-size onion, chopped
⅓ cup smoked pork fat or lard
2 garlic cloves, finely chopped
Freshly ground black pepper to taste

1. Place the beans in a medium-size saucepan along with the sage and salt, cover with 2 inches of cold water, and bring to a boil. Reduce the heat to a simmer and cook until the beans are tender, 1 to 1½ hours. Drain the beans, saving 2 cups of the cooking water.

2. Meanwhile, place the whole potatoes in a large pot, cover with several inches of cold water, and bring almost to a boil over medium-high heat. Once the water is shimmering, adjust the heat to maintain that and cook the potatoes until a skewer glides easily to the center of the potato, about 20 minutes. Drain and peel the potatoes. Mash the beans and potatoes together in a deep bowl with a fork or in a food processor with three or four short bursts. Be careful using the food processor because it can turn the potatoes gummy.

3. In a deep stove-top casserole, heat the olive oil over medium heat, then cook the onion, pork fat or lard, and garlic, stirring, until the onion is translucent, about 8 minutes. Add the mashed beans and potatoes and reserved bean cooking water a little at a time until it reaches a creamy texture, season with salt and pepper, and, continue to cook over medium heat until it has the consistency of your typical mashed potatoes. Serve immediately.

Makes 6 servings

Musaka od Krumpira (Krompira) (Bosnia, Serbia, Macedonia, Dalmatian Coast)

DALMATIAN-STYLE POTATO AND SHEEP'S CHEESE CASSEROLE

After its arrival in Spain, the potato made its move east, where, along the Dalmatian coast, the culinary influence of the Austro-Hungarian Empire met the influence of the Ottoman Empire in the Balkans and cooking was tempered by a long association with Venice. We can see the meshing of these culinary influences in local preparations such as this potato casserole, which uses smoked bacon, an Austro-Hungarian influence, with sheep's cheese, a Turkic influence, for flavoring the basic potato. This Slavic-style musaka *is influenced by the Greek preparation of the same name; it's a substantial dish and quite appropriate in the winter. This recipe is adapted from Inge Kramarz's* The Balkan Cookbook.

2 pounds potatoes
Salt
¼ pound smoked slab bacon, cut into small dice
6 tablespoons (¾ stick) unsalted butter
¼ cup dried bread crumbs
½ pound fresh sheep's cheese (preferably), crumbled, or kashkaval cheese, grated
1 tablespoons chopped fresh dill
Freshly ground black pepper to taste

1. Place the unpeeled potatoes in a large saucepan, cover with cold water by a few inches, and lightly salt. Bring to a gentle boil over medium heat (this will take about 20 minutes) and cook until the potatoes are easily pierced by a skewer, about another 20 minutes. Drain and, when the potatoes are cool enough to handle, peel them. Cut into ¼-inch-thick slices and set aside.

2. In a small skillet, cook the bacon, stirring, until crispy brown. Remove with a slotted ladle to paper towels to drain and set aside.

3. Butter a medium-size baking pan with 1 to 2 tablespoons of the butter. Sprinkle 2 tablespoons of the bread crumbs over the bottom of the buttered dish, shaking them all around to coat evenly. Arrange the sliced potatoes around the dish. Preheat the oven to 350°F.

4. In a medium-size skillet, melt the remaining butter over low heat and stir together with the sheep's cheese until smooth and bubbling. Stir the crispy bacon, the remaining 2 tablespoons bread crumbs, and the dill into the skillet and season with salt and pepper. Continue to stir until creamy. Pour the contents of the skillet evenly over the potatoes. Bake the potatoes for 20 minutes and serve.

Makes 6 servings

SAUSAGE PEDDLERS, VAGABONDS, AND BANDITS

THE daily consumption of fresh meat began to decline by 1550 as the population was now fully recovered from the Black Death of two centuries before and, as a result, more land was devoted to the more labor-intensive agriculture rather than stock rearing. As fresh meat consumption declined, the salting of meat grew to supply the men of many ships and to form a part of the meager diet of the poor. Salt meat was important for the crews now beginning to reach the Indies through the Indian Ocean and the ships creeping down the coast of West Africa after Henry the Navigator's first foray in the 1440s, not to mention the crews about to explode across the Atlantic to discover another world. Salt meat often took the form of sausages, and the sausage peddler in Italian towns was a familiar character.[33] A document from the Spanish vice-regent in Palermo on January 30, 1415, shows that lamb, pork, or sausages were bought thirteen days out of the month and macaroni only once a month. The sausages were usually purchased from street vendors and eaten for dinner.[34]

Mediterranean sausages of all kinds are justly famous. Farm families would make their own sausage and sell it in town. Muslim countries knew salt meat and sausages as well, made of lamb or beef such as the dried beef of Turkey, *pastırme* (the root of our word *pastrami*), and they were an important part of army rations.

The historic Mediterranean struggle against hunger resulted in a vast repertoire of fresh, dried, and salted sausages and cured meats. Although the origin of sausages is to be found in the classical period, if not earlier, it was during the Middle Ages that sausage making abounded. The list of Mediterranean sausages that follows is not meant to be a definitive accounting but rather a large sampling of contemporary sausages, not all of which can be traced historically. To find any of these products in North America, which is not as impossible as might appear at first glance, you might try the "Mediterranean Food Products Resources," page 727.

Asturiana: A blood sausage from the Asturia region of Spain made with cow's blood, bacon, and onions.

Biroldo: A fresh blood sausage from the Tuscany region of Italy made either sweet with pig's blood, raisins, and pine nuts, or savory with calf's blood, cheese, and pork.

Bisbe: A large blood sausage from Catalonia made with tongue, pork, and pig's offal.

Bondiola or *bondeina:* A kind of *capocollo* (see entry following). A large, round sausage from the Polesine area of the southern Veneto, this is a stuffed ox intestine or pig's bladder made with coarsely ground pork, beef, red wine, salt, and black pepper. Sometimes it is smoked for a month or air-dried for two months.

Bresaola: A salt-cured or air-dried beef product from the Valtellina district of Italy. It is made from very lean beef fillet or loin and sliced extremely thin for antipasto.

Butifarra or *botifarra:* The most common Catalan pork sausage, spiced with cinnamon, fennel seeds, and black pepper. *Botifarra negra* is made with pig's blood.

Camaiot: A *butifarra*-like pork sausage from the Balearic Islands made with less blood that is firmer and coarser, made with diced rather than chopped meat, with a higher fat content.

Capocollo: A two-month-aged boned rolled shoulder of pork, preserved in saltpeter, salt, black pepper, sugar, nutmeg, and wine. Different varieties are made in the Italian regions of Umbria, Apulia, and Calabria.

Cappello da Prete: An expensive Italian sausage (because of its lengthy and complicated production process) made from meat stuffing similiar to that of *zampone* (page 83) but wrapped in a very thin rind from the intestines of the pig. It is served like *zampone*.

Cervellata: A Milanese sausage of pork sirloin with pork and veal fat, Parmigiano-Reggiano cheese, and spices such as saffron and nutmeg. It is also made with pig's brains (hence the name; *cervella* means "brain").

Chorizo: A Spanish sausage that seems to have its origins in the Catalan *xoriço*. There are seventeen officially recognized varieties of chorizo in Catalonia. It is usually made from lean pork, garlic, paprika, red bell peppers, and red pepper flakes.

Ciauscoli: A dry, smoked sausage from the Marches region of Italy made from very finely chopped lean and fatty pancetta mixed with garlic, salt, and black pepper. It is eaten on pieces of lightly toasted bread.

Coppa: An Italian sausage cured for three months, with an earthier taste than prosciutto. It is made from equal parts of lean and fatty boned pig's shoulder rolled with saltpeter, salt, black pepper, and nutmeg.

Coppa Senese: A sausage from Siena made from pork seasoned with garlic, orange and lemon rinds, cinnamon, caraway seeds, and other spices. It must be consumed as soon as it is made.

Coppiette: A Tuscan sausage made from dry- and smoke-cured beef and wild boar seasoned with ginger.

Cotechino: In northern Italy this sausage is made with coarsely chopped pork rind, lean pork, and pork fatback seasoned with salt, black pepper, cloves, and cinnamon, then cured for three weeks.

Culatello: A sausage from Emilia-Romagna made from the top round of a pig's leg stuffed into a pig's bladder and aged for a year. Bonaventura Angeli, in his *Historia della città di Parma,* refers to "culatello" being served in 1322 on the occasion of the wedding of Count Andrea Rossi and Giovanna di San Vitale.[35]

Extremeña: A blood sausage made with chopped meat, potatoes, or pumpkin from the high plains of Spain.

Figatelli: A long, thin, highly flavored smoked pork liver sausage from Corsica, eaten as is or grilled.

Finnochiona: A fennel-flavored Tuscan salami made of pork and garlic and aged about one year.

Grive della Langa: A caul fat *crépinette* from the Piedmont made from beef, pork liver, juniper berries, and nutmeg.

Horiatika: A Greek country pork sausage flavored with orange peel, wine, and oregano.

Insaccato: The general Italian name for all sausages and salami. The word comes from *sacco,* or bag, referring to the casing.

Jabuguito: A small chorizo that is eaten raw or deep-fried.

Jamón de Jabugo: A *jamón serrano* from the western end of the Sierra Morena mountains in Andalusia.

Jamón Serrano: A cured Andalusian ham much used in Spanish regional cooking; similar to prosciutto.

Khlea: See *Qalāya.*

Khlia: See *Qalāya.*

Klaya: See *Qalāya.*

Kokkoretsi: An Easter specialty, this Rumelian (Greek Macedonia) *andouillette* is made of lamb or goat offal and seasoned with lemon juice, oregano, thyme, and garlic. It is usually eaten as part of a *meze* table (page 118). Greek Jews might know it as *gardoumbes*. This Greek sausage lends itself to the Turkish *kokoreç,* a sausage made of sheep's lungs.

Koloface: A fresh Albanian sausage made of lamb's liver and lungs mixed with beef, onion, and rice.

Kranjska Kobasica: A Slovenian sausage made of pork shoulder, slab bacon, garlic, and black pepper.

Llonganissa: See Salchichón.

Longaniza or *llangonissa:* A Spanish pork sausage seasoned with paprika, cinnamon, aniseed, garlic, and vinegar.

Lonzo: A Corsican charcuterie made from rolled fillet of pork cured in brine with herbs and then dried.

Loukanika: A Greek sausage traditionally made in the countryside after the *hirosfagi,* the hog slaughter between mid-November and New Year's Day. Its name derives from the Latin *lucanicus,* said to be the name of a sausage invented by the Lucanians, a people who lived in southern Italy at the time of its Greek settlement and the Roman Republic (but see the comment below for the entry *Luganega*).

Loukanika Nissiotika: Long, thin pork sausage from the Greek islands.

Luganega: A mild Italian sausage with a delicate flavor, also called *salsiccia a metro* because it is sold by the meter. The roots of this sausage can be traced to classical Rome: Varro, Cicero, and Apicius mention it. It is said that the best comes from Monza in Lombardy. Lombardy might also be the birthplace of this sausage, since it also has been argued that the Latin *lucanicus* derives from a Lombard word, not the name of a southern Italian people. In Basilicata it is called *lucanica* or *lucania,* where it is a long, continuously coiled grilled pork sausage flavored with red pepper flakes.

Malagueña: A spicy blood sausage from Andalusia.

Mallegato: A spiced Florentine-style blood sausage with raisins, citron (*Citrus medica* L.), pine nuts, and bread crumbs. It is called *buristo* in Siena.

Maniatika: Half pork and half beef Greek sausage from Máni in the Peloponnesus seasoned with oregano and mint.

Maqāniq: Also spelled *naqaniq;* see page 74.

Maties e saffathes: A Greek sausage made of pork, rice, garlic, cumin, and orange peel usually served before a big Christmas meal. It is first boiled, then fried.

Mazzafegati: A sweet, spit-roasted fresh sausage from Umbria and the Marches made of pig's liver, sugar, pine nuts, golden raisins, and orange peel.

Merguez: See *Mirqāz.*

Mirqāz: A Tunisian sausage, usually transliterated by French and Tunisian writers as *merguez.* See pages 249 and 718.

Mocetta: A specialty of the Val d'Aosta in northern Italy, this is a cured goat-thigh sausage flavored with garlic, herbs, juniper berries, and black pepper. It is salted for twenty days, then hung for four months. It is very hard and needs to be eaten within a year.

Morcilla: A Spanish blood sausage stuffed with rice, paprika, onions, garlic, and spices.

Mortadella: The name is thought to derive from *mortaio* because the mixture was pounded in a mortar. More probably it is derived from the Latin *murtatu,* a sausage seasoned with myrtle.[36] Anna del Conte, author of *The Gastronomy of Italy,* suggests that the first mention of mortadella appears in a document of the official body of meat preservers in Bologna dated 1376, but earlier evidence comes from Boccaccio, who mentions mortadella in the *Decameron,* and it appears earlier still in the statutes of the Cathedral of Nice from 1233.[37] Mortadella is made with a seven-to-three ratio of lean pork meat to fat, flavored with peppercorns, pistachios, wine, sugar, and olives and stuffed into beef bladder casing. The mortadella is steamed an hour for each half-inch of its diameter.

Mortadella di Amatrice: Amatrice is a small town high in the Apennines between Latium (Lazio) and Abruzzi. This lightly smoked mortadella is flavored with cinnamon and cloves and aged for two months.

Morteruelo: A pâté of game from the Cuenca region of Spain.

Mumbar ve Şirdan: Turkish sausage made with the second stomach of ruminants and stuffed with mutton, rice, salt, black pepper, and cinnamon. The fresh sausage is boiled and cooled, then sliced and either fried in butter or dipped in egg and fried. It is probably of Persian origin and also called *bumbar.*

Musetto: From the Veneto and Friuli regions of northern Italy, this is a pork meat and rind sausage seasoned with black pepper, cloves, nutmeg, cinnamon, red pepper flakes, and, sometimes, coriander seeds.

Numbolo: A bacon-flavored sausage from Corfu.

Ortau: A Sardinian *andouillette* made with pork blood, lard, liver, tongue, heart, spleen, and lung, garlic, parsley, salt, and black pepper, usually roasted.

Pancetta: Cured pork belly, the same cut as bacon. There are two types; in one the pancetta is left in its natural state and is used as a flavoring in cooking, while *pancetta arrotolata* is rolled and used at the table as a thinly sliced cold cut for antipasti.

Pastırma (basṭurma): A cured and dried meat originally from Turkey or Armenia, also popular in the Arab world, usually made from beef fillet. Sun-dried slices of meat are coated with a paste made of garlic, fenugreek seeds, paprika, and salt and left to cure. It is usually eaten for breakfast with fried eggs or, in Egypt, with the stewed bean dish known as *fūl* (page 304).

Probusti di Rovereto: A beef-and-pork sausage made with veal kidney fat and garlic from the Trentino-Alto Adige region of Italy.

Prosciutto: The most famous of the cured hams known as *prosciutto crudo* are from San Daniele,

Parma, and Tuscany, although today they are made throughout Italy and North America in local versions.

Qadīd: A preserved meat or jerky from Algeria and Tunisia. There are a number of recipes mixing up either the meats or the spices. Basically, lamb meat is salted and seasoned with garlic and mint. It is remarinated with salt, *harīsa,* and mint and then sun-dried for several days before being cut up and cooked in a mixture of olive oil and sheep's fat. See page 249.

Qalāya (sometimes transliterated as *khlea*): A preserved meat in the Maghrib made from mutton meat, fat, kidneys, heart, and liver and seasoned with garlic, salt, black pepper, red pepper flakes, and other spices. It is cooked in olive oil and kept for two months before being used.

Qawrama: A Levantine Arab preserved meat; see page 126.

Salame: Generic word for salt-cured *insaccati* (see entry)—that is, salami. The word comes from *salare,* "to salt." In Italy there are as many different salamis as there are families that still home-cure them.

Salame da Sugo: A salami specialty of Ferrara made from fat and lean ground pork, minced calf's and pig's livers, and ox or pig's tongue cut into small pieces, all flavored with spices and a full-bodied red wine. The casing is pig's bladder and it is shaped like a small melon. It is dried in a hot room for three to four days and then cured for six to seven months.

Salame di Milano: This salami, along with *salame genovese,* are what most Americans know as "salami." In Italy it is made from pigs fed on cheese by-products. It is flavored with garlic and white wine and cured for four to twelve months.

Salame di Napoli: A pork-and-beef salami, ground coarsely and seasoned with salt, garlic, and red pepper flakes, which distinguishes it from the milder salami of the north. The curing process lasts about four months and sometimes includes smoking.

Salame di Varzi: A salami specialty from the town of Varzi near Pavia. It is made from lean pork shoulder and flavored with red wine, salt, black pepper, and a little garlic.

Salame Toscano: A distinctive salami that is dark and full-bodied in taste, with large "eyes" of fat, flavored with lots of garlic, black peppercorns, and white wine. It is cured for six to twelve months, sometimes in caves, from where its flavor derives.

Salamella: Also called Neapolitan sausage. It contains pork, veal, lard, red pepper flakes, garlic, spices, and wine and is lightly smoked.

Salami di Fabriano: A salami from the Marches region of Italy, flavored with a little garlic and black peppercorns and formed into 1- to 2-pound shapes in natural casings.

Salami Felino: A prized salami that comes from the same area as the prosciutto of Parma. It is made from pigs fed on the by-products of the manufacture of Parmigiano-Reggiano cheese and is flavored with pepper, a little garlic, and white wine.

Salchichón: In Catalonia and the Balearic Islands this sausage is known as *llonganissa;* it is a smoked sausage made from chopped lean pork and pork fat with salt and black pepper.

Salsiccia della Basilicata: A lean pork sausage seasoned with black pepper and red peppers flakes.

Salsicce di Mare: A seafood sausage made from by-products of tuna processing. For a fourteenth-century Italian fish sausage recipe, see page 420.

Salsiccia di Nicosia: A pork-and-rabbit sausage from Sicily.

Sartizzu: A dried Sardinian pork sausage seasoned with black pepper, cinnamon, fennel seeds, and vinegar.

Sheftalia: See page 74.

Sobrasada or *sobrassada:* A Majorcan specialty, a soft, almost pâté-like pork sausage flavored with garlic and paprika. It is not similar to Italian *soppressata,* but rather closer to and less spicy than a Mexican-style chorizo.

Soppressa Veneta: A large, soft pork salami from Valpolicella near Verona made with 35 percent fat.

Soppressata: A salami made in southern Italy, especially Basilicata and Calabria, in a four- or five-to-one ratio of lean pork to a mixture of pork fat and bacon. The meat is coarsely chopped and seasoned with salt and black pepper, with the hotter versions additionally seasoned with red pepper flakes, paprika, and wine. The sausage is lightly smoked and pressed to eliminate air pockets (hence the name; it's "pressed").

Sosizza cu 'u Cimulu: A Sicilian pork sausage with fennel seeds.

Soutzoukaia or *soutzoukakia:* A Greek and Greek Cypriot sausage originally from Smyrna (Izmir) made today with veal or beef instead of the original lamb. Its distinctive flavor is that of cumin, garlic, and wine.

Souzoukaki Politiko: A dried Greek black sausage sometimes made with red pepper flakes.

Speck: An Austrian-type of smoked prosciutto from Alto Adige in northern Italy.

Spetsofai: A *loukanika* (see entry) sausage and black pepper recipe from Mount Pelion. The best known of the Greek sausages.

Strinù: A specialty of Val Camonica in Lombardy, this is a mixture of beef and pork meat, flavored with cinnamon, cloves, black pepper, and nutmeg.

Sujuq (*suguq* in Egypt): Pencil-thin Arab beef sausage flavored with cumin, allspice, cinnamon, garlic, and red pepper flakes popular in Egypt and the Levant; it originated in Turkey.

Thessalias: Greek pork sausage from Thessaly stuffed with leeks.

Voliotika: Small, fat Greek pork-and-beef sausage from Volos seasoned with allspice.

Zampone: Supposedly created in Modena, Italy, in 1511 (see page 83). The pork meat is stuffed into a pig's trotter.

Salsiccia Fresca (Sicily)

FRESH HOMEMADE SAUSAGE

This is the classic Sicilian recipe for sausage, the ur-recipe to what is sold throughout the United States as "Italian sausage." In Italy, families, especially in the south, still make their own sausages frequently.

Because pigs today are grown quite lean, it is necessary to add pork fat in order to make a truly wonderful-tasting sausage. Sausages are made in a three-to-one ratio of meat to fat. If you reduce the fat below this ratio, your sausage will taste dry and crumbly.

Hog casings can be bought from supermarket butchers or any butcher who makes sausages. They are already cleaned and all you need to do is rinse away the preserving salts. Make sure all the ingredients, especially the meat, are very cold, as well as the grinder or food processor blade. Place the blade in the freezer until needed. This prevents the meat and the fat from homogenizing together, looking like a pâté.

The only specialized equipment you will need is a meat grinder/sausage stuffing attachment, which is sold as an accessory to many electric mixers. This recipe is adapted from my Grill Italian *(Macmillan).*

6 pounds boneless pork butt (preferably) or shoulder, with its fat, coarsely chopped or ground
2 pounds pork fatback, rind removed and fat coarsely chopped or ground
6 tablespoons fennel seeds
2 tablespoons salt if using salted pork fatback, 3 to 4 tablespoons if using unsalted fatback
2 tablespoons freshly ground black pepper
1½ cups freshly grated pecorino cheese
1 tablespoon red pepper flakes (optional)
1 cup dry red wine
About 25 feet hog casing

1. In a large bowl, toss together thoroughly the pork, fatback, fennel, salt, black pepper, pecorino,

red pepper flakes, and wine, cover with plastic wrap, and leave refrigerated for 4 hours or overnight for the flavors to blend.

2. Open one end of the hog casing, fit it over the faucet in your kitchen sink, and place the remainder of the casing in a medium-size bowl in the sink. Turn the water on gently to wash out the casings. The casings are sold cleaned; you are merely washing away preserving salts and residue. Now you are ready to start stuffing.

3. Affix one end of the casing over the funnel attached to the sausage stuffing attachment of a stand mixer or meat grinder. Push the entirety of the casing onto the length of the funnel (it will contract and fit fine), leaving about 2 inches dangling from the end. Tie this end in a double knot.

4. Turn the mixer or grinder on and as the sausage stuffing begins to flow into the casing, it will push the casing off the funnel. Have a large bowl or platter ready to catch the sausages. Twist or tie off the sausage with kitchen twine to make links, or leave to make several very long sausages. Do not overstuff the sausage otherwise it will burst, either then and there, or during cooking. Also be careful that the sausage stuffing enters the casing continuously and evenly and that no air bubbles develop. If air bubbles do occur, it is better either to cut the sausage at that point and start a new one, by tying the end off, or to prick the air bubbles with a toothpick.

5. The sausages can be divided into portions of different or the same weights and frozen for later use in freezer bags for 2 to 4 months, or you can cook them immediately. Refrigerate for not more than 2 days. If cooking them, place the sausages in a large pot and cover with water. Bring to a boil and, just as the water begins to bubble, reduce the heat to below a boil and poach the sausages for 10 minutes, if grilling or frying, or 40 minutes if serving them boiled.

NOTE: For grilling sausages, prepare a charcoal fire or preheat a gas grill on low for 20 minutes. Grill the sausages for 45 minutes, turning frequently. (If using a charcoal fire, the sausages should be at least 6 inches away from the coals.)

Makes 8 pounds of sausage

Saucisse de Toulouse (Languedoc)

TOULOUSE SAUSAGE

This recipe for saucisse fraiche du pays *(fresh country sausage), known throughout France, is the* saucisse de Toulouse *that enriches a cassoulet. This recipe is from the sausage maker José Crestou of St. Germain-du-Bel-Air, the next biggest village over from the hamlet where my father owns a farmhouse in southwestern France. It is very simple and when prepared fresh does not need saltpeter or any preservative. Sometimes these sausages are spiced with nutmeg, or sugar is added, but remember that in the sixteenth century nutmeg was affordable only by the rich and these are really nothing but country sausages.*

6 pounds boneless pork butt (preferably) or shoulder, with its fat, cut into small cubes
2 pounds pork fatback, rind removed and fat cut into small cubes
2 tablespoons salt if using salted pork fatback, 3 to 4 tablespoons if using unsalted pork fat
2 tablespoons freshly ground black pepper
About 25 feet hog casing

1. In a large bowl, toss the pork and fatback thoroughly with the salt and pepper. Chill the mixture in the refrigerator for at least 4 hours or overnight for the flavors to blend.

2. Coarsely grind the tossed meat by pushing it through a meat grinder, using the largest-holed blade or process in short pulses in a food processor until the mixture has a consistency somewhere between ground and chopped.

3. Open one end of the hog casing, fit it over the faucet in your kitchen sink, and place the remainder of the casing in a medium-size bowl in the sink. Turn the water on gently to wash out the casings. The casings are sold cleaned; you are merely washing away preserving salts and residue. Now you are ready to start stuffing.

4. Affix one end of the casing over the funnel attached to the sausage stuffing attachment of a stand mixer or meat grinder. Push the entirety of the casing onto the length of the funnel (it will contract and fit fine), leaving about 2 inches dangling from the end. Tie this end in a double knot.

5. Turn the mixer or grinder on and as the sausage stuffing begins to flow into the casing, it will push the casing off the funnel. Have a large bowl or platter ready to catch the sausages. Twist or tie off with kitchen twine to make links, or leave to make several very long sausages. Do not overstuff the sausage, otherwise it will burst, either then and there or during cooking. Also be careful that the sausage stuffing enters the casing continuously and evenly and that no air bubbles develop. If air bubbles do occur, it is better either to cut the sausage at that point and start a new one by tying the end off, or to prick the air bubbles with a toothpick.

6. Refrigerate the sausage for 24 to 48 hours before cooking or freezing. The sausages can be divided into portions of different or the same weights and frozen for later use in freezer bags for 2 to 4 months. To cook, place the sausages in a large pot and cover with water. Bring to a boil and, just as the water begins to bubble, reduce the heat to below a boil and poach the sausages for 10 minutes, if grilling or frying, or 40 minutes, if serving them boiled.

NOTE: For grilling sausages, prepare a charcoal fire or preheat a gas grill on low for 20 minutes. Grill the sausages for 45 minutes, turning frequently. (If using a charcoal fire, the sausages should be at least 6 inches away from the coals.) This sausage can be used in cassoulet (page 195) or for making *saucisse à la languedocienne*. The sausage is rolled up into a spiral and secured with two long skewers or spits. It is cooked in a large covered skillet in pork or goose fat with garlic and herbs and served with a tomato, parsley, and caper sauce.

Makes 8 pounds sausage

ʿAṣbān (Tunisia)

VARIETY MEAT SAUSAGE

In Islam, as in Judaism, the name of God is invoked when an animal is slaughtered. It is a sacramental act and the blood, which is the essence of life given by God, must be returned to the earth. For this reason there are no blood sausages nor very rare steaks in the Muslim world. Lamb was the most common meat in Tunisia centuries ago as well as today, and when the animal was slaughtered, every portion was used except the blood. The innards were often used by the poor, who rarely could afford the better, more tender cuts of meat, to make a variety of sausages and preserved meats such as this sausage called ʿaṣbān *(pronounced us-BAAN and also transliterated as* osban*). It is an offal sausage that the French know as* andouillette, *and it is made from* dawwāra, *the viscera of lamb or kid. The sausages are sometimes stuffed in a small section of reticulum, the second stomach of ruminants, cud-chewing animals.*

ʿAṣbān *always contains some grain, usually barley, couscous, rice, or, rarely, coarse bulgur. My recipe uses hog casing rather than stomach. Although pork prod-*

ucts would never be used by a Muslim sausage maker in a Tunisian recipe, I call for pork caul fat and casing only because it is very difficult to find lamb caul fat or casing, unless you have a kosher/ halal *butcher in your neighborhood. Then again, all the lamb products called for in the recipe are most likely to be found at an ethnic butcher. Sausages freeze very well.*

5 pounds lamb or mutton tripe, rinsed well and very tough portions cut out
10 ounces lamb or pork caul fat, chopped
6 ounces lamb kidney, with any fat that is attached
6 ounces lamb tongue, gristly portion cut off
6 ounces lamb liver, trimmed of arteries
½ pound lamb heart, trimmed of arteries
½ pound *liyya* (mutton or lamb fat; page 717)
Leaves from 1 bunch fresh parsley, chopped
Leaves from ½ pound Swiss chard, chopped
1 large onion, chopped
⅓ cup raw short-grain rice
⅔ cup drained canned chickpeas (about ¼ pound)
3 tablespoons extra virgin olive oil
1 teaspoon *harīsa* (page 523), dissolved in a few tablespoons water
1 tablespoon *tābil* (page 522)
1 tablespoon freshly ground black pepper
1 tablespoon ground red chili pepper, any variety
¼ teaspoon ground cinnamon
½ teaspoon ground dried rose petals (optional; page 727)
½ teaspoon dried mint leaves
3 tablespoons salt
About 20 feet lamb or hog casing

1. Place the cleaned tripe in a large pot with water to cover and bring to a boil. Lower the heat and cook just below a boil until softened but not completely tender, about 3 hours. Drain. Place the tripe in a food processor and process in four or five short pulses, so it looks chopped. Remove to a large bowl and toss with the caul fat. Process the kidney, tongue, liver, heart, and lamb or mutton fat, one at a time, with the same short bursts, transferring each to the same bowl as you finish.

2. In another large bowl, put the parsley, Swiss chard, onion, rice, chickpeas, olive oil, *harīsa, tābil,* black and red peppers, cinnamon, rose petals, mint, and salt and mix well. Add to the processed lamb and toss the mixture with your hands until very well blended. Transfer the sausage mixture to a large colander, place over a bowl, and leave to drain of excess liquid in the refrigerator overnight.

3. Open one end of the casing, fit it over the faucet in your kitchen sink, and place the remainder of the casing in a medium-size bowl in the sink. Turn the water on gently to wash out the casings. The casings are sold cleaned; you are merely washing away preserving salts and residue. Now you are ready to start stuffing.

4. Affix one end of the casing over the funnel attached to the sausage stuffing attachment of a stand mixer or meat grinder. Push the entirety of the casing onto the length of the funnel (it will contract and fit fine), leaving about 2 inches dangling from the end. Tie this end in a double knot.

5. Turn the mixer or grinder on and as the sausage stuffing begins to flow into the casing, it will push the casing off the funnel. Have a large bowl or platter ready to catch the sausages. Twist or tie off with kitchen twine in 3-inch segments to make links. Do not overstuff the sausage, otherwise it will burst, either then and there or during cooking. Also be careful that the sausage stuffing enters the casing continuously and evenly and that no air bubbles develop. If air bubbles do occur, it is better either to cut the sausage at that point and start a new one, by tying the end off, or to prick the air bubbles with a toothpick.

6. If you are going to use these sausages for couscous, then poach for 10 minutes in water to cover that is just shimmering on the surface and then freeze or use for couscous (page 670). If you are going to consume them as is, then boil gently for 40 minutes.

Makes 5 to 6 pounds

❖ *Maqāniq* (Arab Levant)

SPICY LAMB SAUSAGE

Maqāniq *(pronounced mah-AHN-nik) or* naqāniq *is a thin mutton or beef sausage typically served as part of a* mazza *table (page 118) in Lebanon, Syria, Jordan, and Palestine. Lebanese Christians sometimes make this sausage with a mixture of pork and sweet red wine. These sausages are believed by at least one scholar to be derived from the Latin* lucanicae *sausages known by the Romans.*[38] *They are best made with the small intestine, but most hog casing sold is the large intestine, so go ahead and ask the butcher, and then use whatever you find.*

3 pounds coarsely ground mutton or lamb
1½ pounds *liyya* (mutton or lamb fat; page 717), finely chopped
¼ cup white wine vinegar
Juice from 1 lemon
3 tablespoons coriander seeds, crushed
3 tablespoons *bahārāt* (page 524)
Salt and freshly ground black pepper to taste
20 feet hog casing, rinsed

1. In a large bowl, mix all the ingredients (except the casing) well and let marinate in the refrigerator, covered with plastic wrap, for 12 hours.

2. Open one end of the casing, fit it over the faucet in your kitchen sink, and place the remainder of the casing in a medium-size bowl in the sink. Turn the water on gently to wash out the casings. The casings are sold cleaned; you are merely washing away preserving salts and residue. Now you are ready to start stuffing.

3. Affix one end of the casing over the funnel attached to the sausage stuffing attachment of a stand mixer or meat grinder. Push the entirety of the casing onto the length of the funnel (it will contract and fit fine), leaving about 2 inches dangling from the end. Tie this end in a double knot.

4. Turn the mixer or grinder on and as the sausage stuffing begins to flow into the casing, it will push the casing off the funnel. Have a large bowl or platter ready to catch the sausages. Twist or tie off with kitchen twine in 4-inch segments to make links. Do not overstuff the sausage otherwise it will burst, either then and there or during cooking. Also be careful that the sausage stuffing enters the casing continuously and evenly and that no air bubbles develop. If air bubbles do occur, it is better either to cut the sausage at that point and start a new one by tying the end off, or to prick the air bubbles with a toothpick.

5. You can freeze the uncooked sausages for up to 4 months or cook by poaching in water to cover for 10 minutes and then frying with a little olive oil over medium-low heat until cooked through, about 45 minutes.

Makes 4 to 5 pounds

❖ *Sheftalia* (Cyprus)

GRILLED CYPRIOT SAUSAGE

This Greek Cypriot crépinette, *a sausage without skin, uses caul fat, or omentum, the membrane that surrounds the stomach, to wrap the ingredients rather than sausage casing. Caul fat is transparent, fragile, and naturally fatty, so you will not need to baste when grilling. Ask the butcher in your supermarket for it.*

1 pound ground pork shoulder
1 pound ground lamb shoulder or leg
¼ pound pork fatback, rind removed and fat finely chopped

1 large onion, finely chopped
½ cup finely chopped fresh parsley leaves
2 teaspoons salt
Freshly ground black pepper to taste
½ pound pork caul fat

1. In a large bowl, knead together the pork shoulder, lamb, fatback, onion, parsley, salt, and pepper thoroughly and form into small egg-size shapes, slightly flattened.

2. Carefully unravel the caul fat and stretch it out over your work surface. Cut into as many 4- to 5-inch squares as you can. Place a small flattened piece of the sausage mixture on each square and wrap it into a neat little package, shaping it with the palms of your hands. Let the *sheftalia* rest in the refrigerator for 4 hours.

3. The *sheftalia* can be frozen for up to 4 months at this point or you can grill them. Prepare a hot charcoal fire or preheat a gas grill for 20 minutes on high. Grill the *sheftalia* until golden brown, 20 to 30 minutes, moving them around the grill to avoid flare-ups.

Makes 30 sheftalia

✣ ✣ ✣

SAUSAGE peddlers were a common sight, but more so were the vagrants who filled sixteenth-century Mediterranean cities. In Spain the ranks of the *picardia* (rogue's den) included vagrants, adventurers, beggars, pickpockets, even students. They congregated in towns like Sanlúcar de Barrameda. The thieves and tramps came from the dregs of Spanish society and, when not robbing, looked for work and were naturally drawn to the ships heading for the West Indies.

As Spain entered its Golden Age in the late sixteenth century, brigandage was on the rise. In Catalonia, Cervantes described the road from Barcelona to Saragossa as particularly dangerous, filled with as many *bandoleros* as there were *bandouliers* in Languedoc. These bandits were like modern guerilla bands, with the peasants on their side. Cities had to be careful when expelling these dregs of society because they ended up in the countryside robbing travelers. Seville rounded up all its vagabonds in October 1581 and shipped them to the Americas, but they never made it: the four ships sank in the South Atlantic and a thousand vagabonds drowned.[39]

The odd assortment of rogues in Spanish society during this period often became characters in literature. The picaresque novel, derived from the word for "rogue's den," saw the poor rascals become antiheros. They were known as the *sopistas,* the soup eaters living off the handouts of *sopa boba* at monastery doors.[40] Two of the earliest picaresque novels were the anonymous *Lazarillo de Tormes* published in 1554 and Francisco de Quevedo's *La Vida del Buscón* written in 1608. These novels describe down-and-out rascally youths who are preoccupied with how to get food. In *Lazarillo de Tormes,* poor Lazarillo works for an evil priest who gives him one onion every four days. Lazarillo finds a tinkerer to make a copy of the key to the priest's bread box. But he can eat only mere crumbs, like a mouse, so he will not be found out.[41]

The huge number of vagabonds, and lack of strong central authority in Italy, made it a bandit's paradise, especially in Calabria, Sicily, Sardinia, and Corsica. Behind all banditry was the specter of hunger. In Sicily the exploits of the bandits were sung by the *urvi*, blind wandering minstrels who played small violins. There were bandits in North Africa, too, where the noble and ancient *ghazwa,* the razzia or military raid, became nothing more than highway robbery. Turkey, too, eventually became infested with robbers.

Calabria, in southern Italy, was the most infamous for its bands of cutthroats and bandits who committed the most horrifying crimes. They were viciously repressed only to retaliate with ever greater audacity and ferocity. They killed people in churches, raided castles, and entered the towns in daylight. Bandits were often supported by their relatives living in the villages, who stored their food supply and provided shelter. Banditry continued in part because one country delighted in the troubles of another and covertly supported the bandits there. Whether Calabria's rustic cuisine is attributable to its rough historical precedents is an interesting question, but, of course, culinary development doesn't necessarily work that way. Contemporary rustic cuisine is often an outgrowth of historic poverty.

COOKING IN CALABRIA

Historically, and up until the twentieth century, a Calabrian field-worker might eat a milk-soaked bread (sop) with fruit for breakfast or bread with onions or pork innards cooked with lots of pepper. When he returned for the family lunch he might have a typical Calabrian minestra *called* licurdia, *which is prepared with onions fried in lard, bread, and lots of sweet red peppers. The family would also eat zucchini, sweet peppers (*pipi 'ncatenati*), chickpeas, potatoes, and beans (*posa*). His wife might prepare* melanzane alla finitese *(page 77). During the summer they would prepare* melanzane a scapece, *sliced eggplant boiled in water and vinegar and conserved in olive oil in earthenware jars with red peppers, garlic, mint, and salt. During the fall slaughter, they would make* soppressate *and* capicolli *sausages (pages 70 and 66) and* frittule, *pork fried with zucchini flowers, while along the coast it is made with grilled swordfish.*

Mushrooms are very common in Calabrian cooking because they grow everywhere and cost nothing. They are cooked with garlic and a silver coin. If the coin turns black, it is said, the mushrooms are poisonous. Also popular are various bulbs of the onion family because they are readily available, such as cipiduzzi *or* cipuddrizze *or* cipollacci col fiocco, *cooked hyacinth bulbs. The Calabrian peasant is portrayed as a gourmand in many culinary proverbs:* Casu tuostu, pani muollu *(hard cheese, fresh bread);* U pisci feti de capu *(the fresher the fish, the firmer the head);* Si vu mangiari a carni cu gustu prima la vulli e pua l'arrusti *(If you wish to eat good-tasting meat, first boil, then roast).*

Eating in Calabria, as is so often the case in the rural Mediterranean, has ritual significance. The peasant will remove his cap when sitting down to eat, make the sign of the cross, kiss the table, and thank the Lord for the food that is the fruit of his hard work. The soup bowls are filled and no one begins to eat until the father starts. If wine spills on the table during the meal, it is considered a sign of good wishes. But, for good luck, some oil is sprinkled on the spot, three signs of the cross are made, and then a sprinkle of salt is thrown.[42]

"Ferrazzuoli" alla Ricca (Calabria)

MACARONI MADE WITH A *FERRETI* IN A RICH SAUCE

A medieval instrument for forming macaroni is still used today in Calabria. Ferrassoli *or* ferrazzuoli *is a kind of pasta made with a device called a* ferreti, *a thin iron rod. A ball of dough is rolled as thick as a pencil and cut into 2½-inch lengths. One kind of* ferreti *is an iron rod that is greased and placed lengthwise on the rolls of pasta dough and rolled back and forth, wrapping the dough around the* ferreti *until one has 6-inch lengths. The dough slides off the* ferreti *and one ends up with, depending on the diameter of the* ferreti, *a kind of spaghetti with a large hole in the middle—what is called* perciatelli *or* bucatini *today in most parts of Italy, or ziti, rigatoni, or macaroni. Other instruments traditionally used to make this pasta in southern Italy and Sicily have been knitting needles and billiard cues.*

3 tablespoons extra virgin olive oil
½ pound veal shoulder, fat removed and cubed
½ pound turkey breast, skin removed and cubed
1 medium-size onion, chopped
1 cup dry white wine
Salt and freshly ground black pepper to taste
2 pounds ripe tomatoes, peeled, seeded, and chopped
1½ pounds *perciatelli* or *ziti lunghe (mezzani)*
Freshly grated Parmigiano-Reggiano cheese

1. In a large casserole, heat the olive oil over medium heat, then brown the veal and turkey with the onion about 10 minutes. Add the wine and cook, stirring a few times, until it evaporates, about 10 minutes. Add salt and pepper, then the tomatoes. Reduce the heat to low and simmer until denser, about 45 minutes.

2. Meanwhile, bring a large pot of abundantly salted water to a boil and cook the macaroni. Drain when al dente. Add the pasta to the sauce in the casserole, toss, and serve with abundant Parmigiano-Reggiano cheese.

Makes 6 servings

Melanzane alla Finitese (Calabria)

EGGPLANT, THE PERFECT WAY

Arab agriculturists brought the eggplant to the Mediterranean from Persia, or perhaps even from the Arabian peninsula, in the ninth or tenth century. The eggplant was treated with suspicion at first, but soon became a favorite vegetable. In my mind, the Mediterranean crescent of the eggplant kingdom begins in Lebanon and arcs its way through Turkey, Greece, southern Italy, and ends in Sicily. These are the lands of perfect eggplant preparations. Calabrians have seemingly hundreds of different preparations for eggplant and many might agree that this is *the perfect way. The late American food writer Waverly Root claimed that this dish is so called because it is a specialty of San Martino di Finita.*[43]

8 baby eggplant (about 1½ pounds)
Salt to taste
⅔ cup freshly grated pecorino cheese
¼ cup finely chopped fresh basil leaves
Freshly ground black pepper
½ cup extra virgin olive oil

1. Slit each eggplant open in the middle, slicing it lengthwise and making sure you do not cut all the way through. Hollow out a small amount of pulp with a small spoon such as a demitasse or baby spoon. Save the pulp for making the recipe on page 531. Open the

eggplant with your fingers and salt the inside. Leave them on a plate to drain of their bitter juices for 30 minutes, then pat dry the insides with paper towels.

2. In a small bowl, mix the pecorino, basil, and pepper. Using your fingers, stuff each eggplant with the cheese mixture. Close each eggplant with a toothpick if necessary so very little stuffing escapes.

3. In a medium-size skillet, heat the olive oil over medium heat and cook the eggplant until soft, about 25 minutes. Transfer to a serving platter, drizzle with a little olive oil, and let sit for 10 minutes before serving.

Makes 4 servings

Involtini al Grasso con Spaghetti al Ragù (Calabria)

STUFFED PORK ROLL-UP WITH SPAGHETTI IN *RAGÙ*

The invention of the meat roll-up, called in southern Italy a braciola, involtini, *or, in Calabrian dialect,* vrasciola, *is the means employed by the housewife to stretch a meager amount of poor quality meat by stuffing it with bread. Rich and fatty foods were rare for the poor, and highly desired. Even then,* involtini *were not everyday fare, but saved for special occasions. Today, the Calabrians are not so crushingly poor and their* involtini, *as represented by this recipe, are rich in aromatic flavors, such as the pancetta and pecorino, and exotic spicing, such as the cinnamon, a vestige of cooking from the Middle Ages. We can see how prized dishes like this were for the poor, who lacked sufficient calories in their meals, by the fact that the recipe name refers to the fat* (grasso) *so sought after in the Middle Ages. Normally, we would cut the fat off before cooking, but if you want to remain true to the name of the recipe, leave it on. Traditionally, one eats the spaghetti sauced with the* ragù *as a first course to be followed by the roll-ups.*[44]

2 garlic cloves, 2 peeled and left whole, 1 sliced
2 tablespoons pork lard
1 tablespoon finely chopped fresh parsley leaves
6 black peppercorns
2 pounds pork loin, in one piece with its fat, butterflied into a square
3 slices pancetta
½ cup diced pecorino cheese plus 3 tablespoons freshly grated pecorino cheese
Pinch of ground cinnamon
1 ½ cups dry full-bodied red wine
2 pounds ripe plum tomatoes, peeled, seeded, and crushed or chopped
Salt and freshly ground black pepper to taste
½ cup tepid water
1 pound spaghetti

1. In a mortar, pound the 2 whole garlic cloves, 1 tablespoon of the lard, the parsley, and peppercorns together until you have a paste. With a knife, spread the paste over one surface of the butterflied pork. Cover the paste with the pancetta and sprinkle on the diced and grated cheese and cinnamon. Roll up the pork and tie with butcher's twine in four places.

2. In a large casserole, melt the remaining tablespoon lard and cook the sliced garlic over medium heat for 1 minute, stirring constantly so it doesn't burn. Add the pork roll and brown for 10 minutes on all sides. Add the wine and tomatoes, season with salt and pepper, and dilute with the water. Leave the roll-up to cook over medium-low heat until tight and firm to the touch, about 45 minutes, turning occasionally.

3. Meanwhile, bring a large pot of water to a rolling boil, salt abundantly, and add the pasta. Drain when al dente and toss with the sauce the pork is braising in. Serve the spaghetti as a first course and the pork as a second course.

Makes 4 servings

✣ ✣ ✣

THE final group of this sorry lot were the slaves of every race, religion, and origin. Slavery was integral to the life of the Mediterranean; it was not only a New World phenomenon nor solely African in its raw material. In Spain, the tables of the great houses of Valladolid in 1555 were waited upon by Turkish and Slavic as well as African slaves. In fifteenth-century Genoa, all the patrician class had Arab slaves, the women performing the domestic duties of cooking, cleaning, fetching, and satisfying the sexual appetite of the master of the house.

Slave traders dealt in blond slaves (Slavs), yellow slaves (Tartars), brown slaves (Arabs), and, later, black slaves (Africans). Before the fifteenth century, slavery was synonymous with the Slavs, a subjugated people who give their name to the English word *slave*. Both Christian and Muslim corsairs considered each other potential slaves, no matter their race. It was not until the sixteenth century that slavery increasingly became associated with blackness. The first association of blacks and slavery in Venetian documents found by the historian Frederick Lane was in 1490.[45] Slaves could eat well, as they did in some Spanish households, or they could die of starvation; it all depended on the master.

IMMACULATE LAMB, LACTATING BREASTS

✣

THE medieval Mediterranean was a place where religious passion was the source of extraordinary pious acts, as well as the most incredible brutality. Not surprisingly, religious convictions were tied to the struggle for food. Besides the innumerable fast days, the act of eating was intimately connected with religious meaning, whether it was the saying of grace at the table or the food-related religious practices of priests and nuns. The Holy Communion is the Christian sacrament in which bread and wine are taken to represent the flesh and blood of Christ.

Food was an important motive in medieval piety. The historian Caroline Walker Bynum explored the implications of food-related religious practices and food images in the piety of medieval women in particular, to whom it meant more than the men. In the medieval Mediterranean, food was of fundamental economic and religious concern. Food was God-given nourishment and eating was a way of being close to God. At the same time, the desires of the flesh had to be controlled, so fasting was a way of renouncing the sin of gluttony. At a time when hunger and starvation were common, gluttony was only possible among the rich. If a privileged person was pious, he would give food away, fast, or gorge and vomit. The passionate religious belief that led the ascetic Christian to the denial of the self or the world often manifested itself through self-starvation. The Christian resistance to the desires of the flesh was steeped in a powerful mystical element during the medieval period. Eating could give a foretaste of the joy one would encounter in paradise, but, in medieval Europe, eating was not simply about food and eating. The act of eating was also an occasion to be close with fellow man and God. It was God who was given thanks for the food, not the farmer. The Eucharist is, after all, the prototypical meal, where the bread and wine consumed is not just representational but also the actual flesh and blood of Christ. To eat was to become God.[46]

Bynum shows that fasting became an obsession with women in late medieval Europe. Fasting was a spiritual phenomenon where women, by not eating, would deny themselves pleasure so that they could receive Eucharistic visions in their adoration of Christ in the bread and wine at the altar. The bizarre and mystical behavior that transcended the daily hunger of the times, most often exhibited by women, grew as

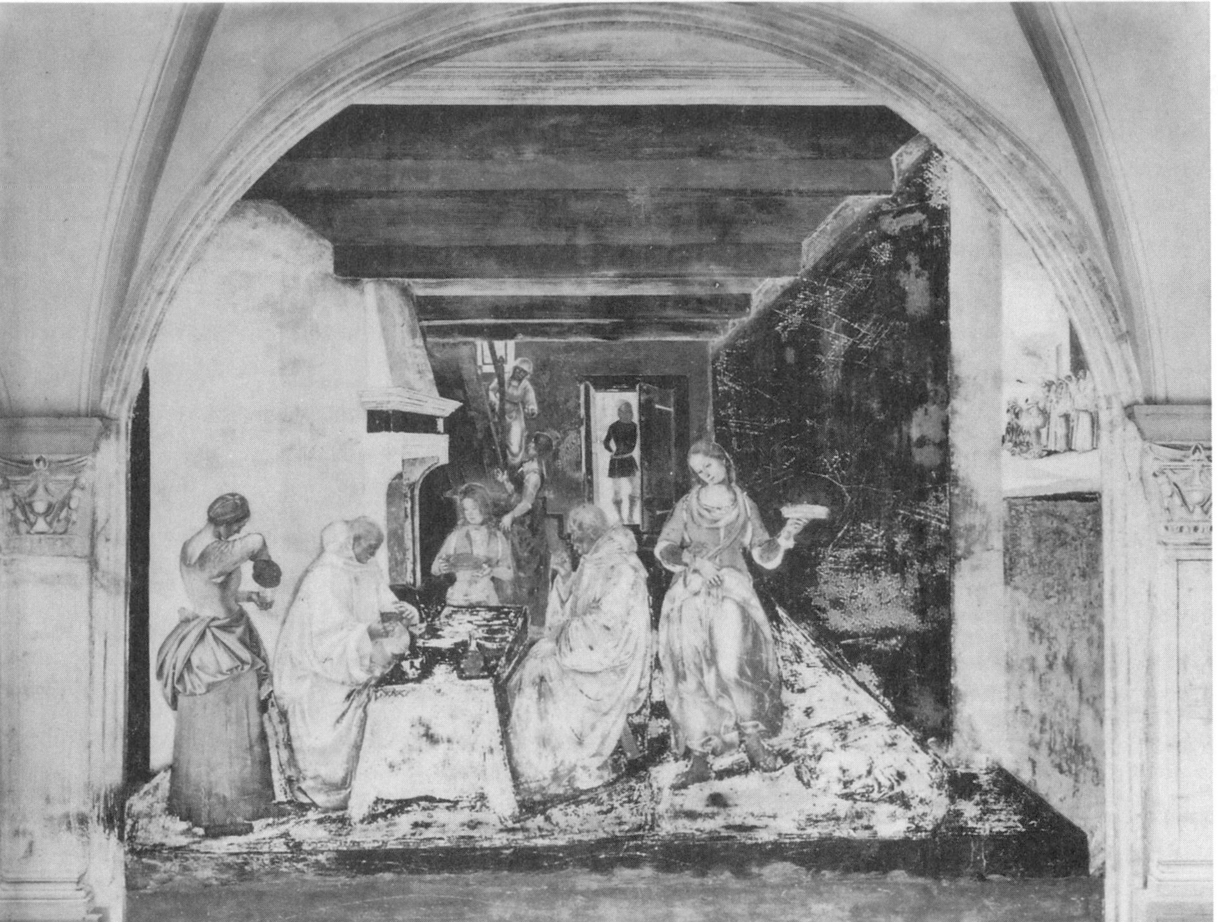

When hunger held sway, as it so often did in the fifteenth century, food was a great temptation for those held to pious standards, such as these two Tuscan monks violating the fast. They are eating well and being served well. Luca Signorelli (1441–1523). Abbey, Monteoliveto Maggiore, Italy. ALINARI/ART RESOURCE.

a result of a new eucharistic piety that appears to have arisen with the growth of medieval towns and cities. In a mirroring of modern life, where bulimia and anorexia occur among young women of means, so too young medieval women of the rising bourgeois class, cut off from the rhythm of village life as the necessity for food diminished and its objectification as a commodity prevailed, engaged in self-destructive actions cloaked in the robe of piety and devotion.[47]

One of the most important foods on the Christian table was lamb. When John saw Jesus coming toward him, he said, "Behold, the Lamb of God." From then on, *agnus dei,* the lamb of God, was used as a symbol of Christ. The immaculate lamb was Christ and we who eat at the table become like the food. To eat lamb (Christ) is to become Christ. As a result of this symbolism, the significance of the eating of lamb cannot be underestimated in the Christian Mediterranean.

Agnello alla Pecora (Calabria)

LAMB SHEPHERD STYLE

Lamb, besides being a popular meat, was associated with Easter in medieval Italy as it is today. One of the greatest of women writers in medieval Italy, Catherine of Siena, wrote that the immaculate lamb (Christ) was food. When the shepherd eats at the table, he becomes like the food (Christ), acting for the honor of God and the salvation of neighbor.[48]

½ cup extra virgin olive oil
3 pounds boneless leg of lamb, trimmed of fat and cubed
2 tablespoons dried oregano
4 garlic cloves, finely chopped
Salt and freshly ground black pepper to taste
2½ cups tomato puree
1 cup water

1. In a large casserole, heat the olive oil over medium-high heat, then brown the lamb on all sides, 6 to 7 minutes. Sprinkle the meat with the oregano and garlic, season with salt and pepper, and toss to mix.

2. Add the tomato puree, reduce the heat to low, and cook until heated through, about 10 minutes. Pour in the water to barely cover the meat. Bring to a boil, reduce to low, and simmer until the meat is tender, about 1½ hours. Serve with roast potatoes or greens.

Makes 6 servings

FOOD is an obsessive feature in the lives and writings of religious women between the twelfth and fifteenth centuries; two of the greatest women writers of medieval Italy were Catherine of Siena (died 1380) and Catherine of Genoa (died 1510). Stories relate how women, and not men, lived for years on the Eucharist alone. They tell of women who drank pus or filth from the sick they cared for, while abstaining from ordinary food, often in defiance of husband or family, and whose bodies excreted healing liquids after death.[49] Women achieved an erotic union through the body of Christ by means of self-flagellation or self-starvation.[50]

Another role played by medieval women had less to do with obsessive religious behavior and more with their role as producers of milk. For the child, of course, women's bodies *were* food. The wet nurse was an important part of the Mediterranean economy. In fact, in Languedoc, the only records of women's wages that are complete for the sixteenth century are those for wet nurses. But the wet nurse provided food for more than babies. Men and women both could feed from the wet nurse, and this was recognized by municipal authorities. Her milk was a source of food in dire times and one abbot's description of the ideal wet nurse dwells at length, and with a coy lasciviousness, on her complexion, the size of her breasts, and her figure.[51]

LUXURY AND ETIQUETTE

THE transformation from the High Renaissance to the Counter-Reformation (1500–1560) did not see the calming of religious passion, but it did see the consolidation of a new class of bourgeoisie. We saw in Chapter 1 the economic importance of this new class, and a new mentality arose as well, finding its expression in the refinements of life, one element of which was a system of rules of etiquette. A number of books on etiquette were published such as the *Galateo,* a famous book by Giovanni della Casa (1503–1556), who was born in Mugello, a region near Florence. He lived through the devastation wreaked upon Italy after the sack of Rome by Spanish and German Imperial troops in 1527 and witnessed the fading power and glory of princes, kings, and popes. If great republics could be destroyed, what could provide the structure for society and the individual? His answer was that order was to be found in a system of rules and manners.[52] One of the most important

THE HISTORY OF THE FORK

The history of the fork has never been written, and when it is, it will be a study of the rules of etiquette in society. Although there is a description of a kind of hook used to pull meats out of cooking pots in the Bible and a five-pronged forklike utensil used for turning roasting meats in Homer's Odyssey, *the first documented use in Europe of a fork with tines at the table while eating is from the eleventh century.*[53] *In the first piece of evidence, the Greek-born Dogissa Maria Argyra in Venice was known to have used a fork to eat.*[54] *St. Peter Damian, the source for this story, was clearly not pleased with its use, having this to say about the diabolical luxury in his condemnation of Maria Argyra: "Such was the luxury of her habits . . . [that] she deigned [not] to touch her food with her fingers, but would command her eunuchs to cut it up into small pieces, which she would impale on a certain golden instrument with two prongs and thus carry to her mouth."*[55] *The second piece of evidence comes from an eleventh-century illustrated manuscript from Monte Cassino of two men using a two-pronged fork.*[56] *We don't hear much of the fork for the next few centuries, except occasionally here and there, until Eustachio Celebrino of Udine writes about the* scalco *(head steward) in 1526, in a work published in Venice called* Opera nova che insegna apparechiar una mensa a uno convito *(New book that teaches the use of banquet table implements).*[57] *Celebrino had table settings of plates with a piece of bread, a cracker* (biscottello), *and a cake* (pignochato) *upon them. The settings were flanked with a knife and fork, which is a very early mention of the dinner fork* (pirone). *In 1599, Jacopo Bassano painted one of the first forks to figure in a Last Supper.*[58] *Charles V of Spain had a dozen forks among his possessions, but the courtiers of Henry III of France (1551–1589) were still laughed at for the amount of food they lost on the way to their mouths.*[59] *He had brought forks back from Venice with him, where they had been known but not really used in the Italian court since 1071.*[60]

Why was the fork invented? The fork has no practical purpose outside of etiquette; the fingers, knife, and spoon are adequate. The fork was invented because of a new consciousness of good taste among a class of people who were urban dwellers, the original meaning of bourgeois. *The genesis of the fork might be found in eighth- or ninth-century Persia, where the Dihqans, members of a family of lesser Iranian nobility, were known as having good table manners. Normally meat was eaten at the Persian table by stripping the meat off the bones with one's fingers and sucking the marrow out, but the Dhiqans were the first to eat meat with a* barjyn *and knife. The term* barjyn *is obscure, but it appears to be cutlery similar to a fork. The word may derive from the Persian word for "glove," so that earlier still they may have eaten with a kind of glove, in contrast to their co-religionists, the Arabs, who ate with their fingers. But we don't know the extent of this custom.*[61] *Whatever the origins of the fork, it was not immediately accepted and did not take root either in Europe or the Middle East, where the fork was still unknown as late as the seventeenth century.*[62]

places where manners began to take hold was at the table. People were beginning to use the knife at the table, but forks were still unknown.

People ate with their fingers, just as they used their fingers to blow their noses. The height of good manners in the Middle Ages was to use only the left hand to blow one's nose at the table. But by the sixteenth century, the middle class had begun to use the sleeve, rather than the fingers.[63] During the Renaissance, the concept of manners grew as the graces of the court grew. One of the most influential works on manners was Baldassare Castiglione's book *Cortigiano (The courtier).* The historian Johan Huizinga said that "It does not overstate the case to claim that every means of beautifying and ennobling the forms of life contain a liturgical element that raises the observance of these forms almost to a religious realm. Only this can explain the extraordinary importance people give to all questions of precedence and etiquette, and not only during late medieval times."[64] In the Renaissance, with the growth of a wealthy urban class, there was, in addition to the pursuit of glory and the protection of honor common in medieval times, a concern too for the life of the mind, the works of man, and an interest in good living, fashion, trade, and food. We call it luxury.

The original Latin was *luxus,* which referred to extravagant eating and drinking. In Venice, a whole world of luxury and etiquette revolved around the table, so much so that the Venetian Senate complained about the expensive feast parties thrown by young noblemen. Marino Sanuto's *Diarii* has preserved some of the menus and prices from these extravagant dinners in the 1520s, with their partridges, pheasants, peacocks, and so on. Luxury meant eating delicacies such as oysters. The popularity of oysters is evidenced in the frequency with which they appeared in the still lifes painted during this time. It was said that when Emperor Charles V of Spain lived in retirement from 1556 to 1558 at the San Jerónimo de Yuste monastery in western Spain, he insisted on fresh oysters, which were brought by horse relay carriers.[65]

Ortensio Lando, in his *Commentario delle piu notabili e mostruose cose d'Italia (Commentary on the most notable and great things in Italy),* attempted to list foods available to charm gourmet palates in the towns of Italy. There was a bewildering range to choose from: sausages and *saveloys* (a dried pig's brain salami) from Bologna, round pies from Ferrara, *cotognata* (quince jam) from Reggio, cheese and gnocchi with garlic from Piacenza, marzipan from Siena, *caci marzolini* (March cheeses) from Florence, *luganica sottile* (thin sausage) and *tomarelle* (mince) from Monza, *fagiani* (pheasant) and chestnuts from Chiavenna, fish and oysters from Venice, even *eccellentissimo* bread (a luxury in itself) from Padua, along with wine and *zampone* (see below) from Modena.[66]

Zampone con Lenticchie (Emilia-Romagna)

STUFFED PIG'S TROTTER WITH LENTILS

Zampone *is stuffed pig's trotter. The foot and shin are boned and stuffed with ground pork snout and other ingredients.* Zampone *is traditionally eaten in Modena on New Year's Eve. Carol Field tells us, in her book* Celebrating Italy, *that the lentils represent money and the sausage stuffing the container that will hold it. Pork is one of the pillars of Emilian cuisine and all kinds of pork products are made there. In Zibello,* culatello, *a cured pork rump, is made, while Bologna offers its famous* mortadella, *and Langhirano makes a cured ham. The other pillars of the cuisine are pasta, especially tortellini, and rich bodied, full-flavored sauces.*

The origin of zampone *is often told as in the follow-*

ing apocrypha: During Pope Julius II's siege of Miràndola in the winter of 1511, the town's people were on the point of starvation and began to use every last piece of a slaughtered pig and invented zampone. *Others are not so sure and suggest its invention in the eighteenth century, or nineteenth century, by a charcutier from Modena.*[67]

Luckily, zampone *is made around Christmas in this country and sold in Italian markets. They freeze very well and can be used later.*

Green lentils can be found in Indian markets. Brown lentils will do fine. Commercially packaged lentils today rarely need soaking; less than an hour of cooking should do it. Some Emilians make a salsa verde, *with walnuts, garlic, and lots of parsley, to accompany* zampone.

One 3½-pound *zampone*
2 cups dried green or brown lentils, picked over and rinsed
2 quarts water
2 medium-size onions, peeled, 1 left whole and 1 finely chopped
3 celery stalks, 2 cut in half and 1 finely chopped
Salt to taste
3 tablespoons extra virgin olive oil
2 ounces prosciutto fat, chopped

1. Prick the *zampone* all over with a couple of corncob holders or toothpicks, and wrap tightly in a double thickness of cheesecloth. Tie off with kitchen twine. Place the *zampone* in a large pot or casserole on its side and cover by 4 inches of cold water. Bring the water to a boil slowly, 45 minutes to 1 hour, then simmer another 4 hours (or about 1 hour per pound of *zampone,* which run anywhere from 2 to 4 pounds). Add boiling water as needed to keep the *zampone* covered.

2. Meanwhile, place the lentils in a casserole with the 2 quarts water, the whole onion, celery stalk halves, and salt. Turn the heat to medium-high and when it begins to bubble, cook for 15 minutes to 1 hour, depending on the age of the lentils. Taste occasionally, and turn the heat off and drain the lentils when they are between al dente and tender, and set aside. Discard the onion and celery.

3. In a medium-size saucepan, heat the olive oil with the prosciutto fat over medium heat and cook 3 to 4 minutes, stirring. Add the chopped onion and chopped celery, and cook until golden, about 8 minutes, stirring.

4. Add the lentils to the sautéed onion and prosciutto fat along with 1½ cups water from the cooking *zampone*. Simmer the lentils until the water is absorbed. If you have accidently overcooked the lentils so they are already soft, do not pour in the water; simply stir the lentils until well combined.

5. Arrange the lentils on a platter. Remove, drain, and untie the *zampone*. Cut it into slices as thick as a finger and arrange on top of the lentils, slightly overlapping them.

Makes 6 to 8 servings

CONCLUSION

IN this chapter, four important phenomena of Mediterranean life were examined. First, we saw that daily life in the Mediterranean of centuries ago was dependent on the weather. The climate determined the harvest, and the harvest determined life. The climate was often the reason for scarcity. Scarcity meant there wasn't enough food for people, nor winter forage for cattle, which are such rich producers of the manure that provides the essential nutrients to the soil necessary to make agriculture productive, and hence food abundant. Second, we saw in this world of starvation and hunger that there was a new class of people getting rich on trade. Third, the staple food, during normal times when people were hungry but not starving, was bread. Supplementing the bread were some vegetables and salt meat, but this did not solve the problem of hunger. Fourth, the precariousness of existence seems behind the growth of religious passion in the Mediterranean. We saw how important food was in the religious piety of the Middle Ages. This piety is contrasted in Mediterranean societies with the consciousness among a class of rich people for the refinements of life, one manifestation being the concern with etiquette and the pursuit of luxury.

In the next chapter I will examine in greater detail what people ate and why. We will see that food determines everything, and with this purpose in mind we'll look at several specific locales in the Mediterranean of the Middle Ages: rural and urban Italy, Muslim Spain and Tunisia, the Arab Levant, and the southern French provinces of Languedoc and Provence.

❋ 3 ❋

FEAST, ANTI-FEAST

RENAISSANCE fairs and medieval feasts are today a popular and festive form of party giving. These fairs or parties have as a component an attempt to re-create a dinner of that era. The recipes for these feasts come from extant cookery manuscripts, written originally for the chefs of the nobility or rich, and they have truly little to do with the life lived by the vast majority of medieval peoples. The "feast," as a recreation of a past era, is not new. During the fifteenth century, the humanist circle of Lorenzo de'Medici held feasts to celebrate Plato and to re-create classical banquets—for example, copying the feast of Agathon's in Plato's *Symposium*.

In this chapter, I'd like to contrast the feasts, those meals we can glean from extant cookbooks written for the well-to-do, with what I call the "anti-feast," the story of the real Mediterranean world, a poor and famine-stricken Mediterranean populated with perpetually hungry people. I have randomly chosen five regions to consider, each to provide a perspective on the whole question of what people ate. This is not meant to be a comprehensive examination. Through a series of alimentary vignettes I want to show that not only was the situation very complex but the crushing monotony of what little the majority of people ate would eventually lead to a reaction against the "millet gruel" that was one of the basic foods of the Mediterranean and result in the wide, and exciting, range of cuisines that one can experience today, as represented by the gustatory delights that are the recipes in this chapter.

I've chosen to look at Italy, Tunisia (and Muslim Spain), the Arab Levant, Spain, and Provence and Languedoc. I said I chose these areas randomly, but perhaps I chose them because the sources are relatively good for these countries, whereas one can find little about the food of medieval Greece. We will see in this chapter the importance of bread in Italy, as well as the human hopelessness and the role of medieval dietetics; the gruel and porridge so typical in Muslim Spain and Tunisia, as well as the food of the rich; the importance of "take-out" food and green vegetables in the Levant, as well as the political importance of the butcher; the rich and poor in Spain, and how bifurcated their world was; and finally, the role of bread and pasta in Provence, and the fact that wine was food.

FOOD DETERMINES EVERYTHING

INFORMATION about the foods people ate in the Mediterranean between the fourteenth and seventeenth centuries has been gleaned from a wealth of documents, many of which give an impression of good living and plenty. But, as that most erudite of historians of the Middle Ages, Johan Huizinga, has warned, "Modern man has, as a rule, no idea of the unrestrained extravagance and inflammability of the medieval heart. A picture based only on documents would lack an important element: the crass colors of the tremendous passions that inspired people as well as the princes."[1] Many food writers have accepted this picture of good living, not questioning the lack of evidence regarding the living standards of the poor.

Luxury is always a more attractive setting for popular food history than poverty, especially when it comes to Mediterranean cuisines. Poverty and famine are depressing. The simple fact is, however, that there was no sophisticated cuisine among the general population in Christian Europe before the thirteenth century.[2] If a peasant had chickens and eggs, calves, lamb, kids, or wheat, they were sold at the market while he and his family ate millet and cabbage every day, and some salt pork once a week.

So many people died during the Black Death in the mid-fourteenth century that there was no one left to care for farms. The farms were abandoned and the land reverted to meadow or forest. The number of husbanded animals, as well as game, increased and therefore more meat was eaten. From the mid-fourteenth to the mid-fifteenth centuries, the European diet consisted mostly of meat. Then, from the late fifteenth to the early eighteenth centuries, the diet shifted to one predominantly of vegetables because the population recovered and was able to bring more land under cultivation and to tend to it. When it comes to caloric sustenance, even today agriculture takes precedence over stock raising.

Food determined everything. In the sixteenth century, yields were small and everything was affected by this, not only in terms of food supply but also politics. Without a good barley crop military strategists could assume that the Turks would not go to war that year because they could not feed their army and navy. On the other hand, one knew that robbery and brigandage on land and piracy on the seas would increase because bandits and corsairs had to feed themselves, and what they had was meager. Pirates in the southeast Peloponnesus may have had a little wheat bread, but typically it was a black cake made of lupine beans *(Lupinus albus)*. Generally beans and barley were luxuries in fourteenth-century Greece and skinny little quail and cactus fruits were part of a regular diet.[3]

Even the diet in trade-bustling Venice was modest. There were summer wheat *(Triticum aestivum* var. *aestivum)* and einkorn *(T. monococcum* var. *monococcum)* and modest amounts of other cereals like rye, millet, and sorghum, beans, and lots of fresh vegetables and condiments, such as salt and rape seed oil *(Brassica napus)*. This constituted the dietetic base of the poorest.[4]

The environment and the climate contribute to local gastronomies in the Mediterranean. But there is more involved because the fact that foods are abundant in one region does not mean people will want to eat them. For example, goats were very popular in Languedoc, but moderately so elsewhere, even though goats were found everywhere. And the Languedociennes also did not like veal, although it was considered the best meat elsewhere.[5] Another example is the porpoise, abundant in the Mediterranean, but not eaten regularly by any Mediterranean peoples. Butter was available in Languedoc, but cooks still cooked their eggs in olive oil.[6]

Omelette aux Pignons (Languedoc)

PINE NUT OMELETTE

The pine trees from which the nuts for this dish come (Pinus pinea *L.) are quite numerous in the Languedoc and this omelette is quite common. On the opposite end of the Mediterranean, the Lebanese also make this omelette, calling it* ʿujja bi'l-ṣanawbar *(eggs with pine nuts), sometimes cooking it with parsley and onions.*

6 large eggs
Salt and freshly ground black pepper to taste
2 to 5 tablespoons extra virgin olive oil or unsalted butter, to your taste
2 to 4 tablespoons pine nuts, to your taste

1. Beat the eggs in a medium-size bowl with some salt and pepper.

2. In a large nonstick omelette pan, heat the olive oil or melt the butter over medium heat. Add the pine nuts and cook until golden, 2 to 3 minutes, stirring. Pour in the eggs and, as the bottom sets, flip up one edge onto the uncooked part, continue rolling it in this manner until it is a cylindrical omelette. Serve immediately.

Makes 2 servings

✣ ✣ ✣

In prosperous sixteenth-century Istanbul, mutton was consumed in prodigious quantities only in the Seraglio (the palace of the sultan); the average resident made do with a third of a sheep per person per year.[7] Egypt, in the same century, was already in decline and even the rich were regularly partaking of meals that consisted of moldy bread, garlic, onion, and sour cheese. A feast meal only meant the appearance of a little boiled mutton. Birds like hazel grouse and ortolans were rare treats. The ortolan, a bird of the vineyard, abounded in Cyprus (from where it was exported to Venice preserved in vinegar in the sixteenth century).[8]

HUNGER, HOPELESSNESS, AND FORTUNE IN ITALY

Dying of hunger, literally dying in the street, was a defining occurrence of the historic Mediterranean. In the countryside grass was found in the mouths of the starved dead or they were found with their teeth sunk into the earth.[9] The great Italian diarist Marino Sanuto describes a heartbreaking scene in Venice during the winter of 1527 of children crying at the Rialto, "Bread, bread, I am dying of hunger and cold." In the morning the children had perished under the portals of the Palazzo Ducale.[10] In 1591, in Palermo "*si trovanno le persone morte nelle strade per la fame*" (you find people dead in the street from hunger) because of bad harvests and unreasonable taxation.[11]

In the chronicles of human hopelessness, the horrible Sicilian account from the anonymous tenth-century Arabic chronicle *Tārīkh jazīrat Ṣiqillīya (History of Sicily)* of parents eating their children in starving desperation stands out as one of the saddest. As horrible still is the common practice of autophagy in times of famine, not to mention the coprophagous habits of starving and diseased Mediterranean peoples stumbling about with open wounds, drifting in a hallucinatory state.[12] This is not a world of Mediterranean food, but rather the paucity of it, hardly the typical topic of cookbooks. But these images are essential for understanding the

Mediterranean food we eat today. The contemporary Mediterranean lusciousness of taste is, I believe, for the most part, a reaction against historic famine, starvation, poverty, and monotony of taste. When you travel in the Mediterranean and, as an honored guest, are served copious amounts of meat, as is customary in all Mediterranean culinary cultures, remember that starvation and poverty stand behind each meal. There is no greater insult in the world of Mediterranean gastronomy than, as a guest, to be served a meal without meat, excepting perhaps to refuse meat offered in all its generosity.

How and what people ate in Italy during the Middle Ages is not as straightforward as simply cataloguing the recipes in the cookbook of a Renaissance chef. The fourteenth-century Italian chronicler Galvano Flamma, referring to an earlier time, tells us that life in Lombardy was hard, that people ate cooked turnips and small amounts of meat three times a week, and they were so poor that husbands and wives ate off the same plate because there weren't enough in the house; nor was there any fireplace in the house to cook in.[13] Eating meat three times a week was taken as a sign of poverty by city dwellers of northern Italy in the late thirteenth and early fourteenth centuries, and chroniclers such as Riccobaldo da Ferrara, canon of the Cathedral of Ravenna, agreeing with Flamma, spoke of a time fifty years before when "the habits of the Italians were unrefined . . . food was scarce and the common people ate fresh meat only three times a week. At midday they ate greens cooked with meat, and in the evening that same meat served cold."[14]

The charitable works of the Misericordia gave food to the hungry and drink to the thirsty. Domenico Ghirlandaio (1448–1494). S. Martino dei Buonomini, Florence. SCALA/ART RESOURCE.

ITALY ABOUT 1494
SWITZERLAND
RAETIAN ALPS
CARNIC ALPS
KINGDOM OF HUNGARY
Rhone R.
Drave R.
Danube R.
DUCHY OF SAVOY
DUCHY OF MILAN
Bergamo
Milan
Pavia
Piacenza
Turin
ASTI
M. OF MONFERRAT
M. OF SALUZZO
M. OF MANTUA
Treviso
Vincenza
Verona
Venice
Padua
Piave R.
Adige R.
Polesina
Po R.
Udine
Triest
Carniola
Zagreb
SLAVONIA
Fiume
Save R.
Istria
Rovigno
Pola
Croatia
VENETIAN REPUBLIC
D. OF FERRARA
REP. OF GENOA
Genoa
D. OF MODENA
Emilia Romagna
Ravenna
Rimini
Pesaro
OTTOMAN EMPIRE
Nice
LUCCA
Pisa
Arno R.
Leghorn
REPUBLIC OF FLORENCE
Florence
DALMATIA (Venice)
Bosnia
LIGURIAN SEA
Spalato (Split)
Mostar
Herzegovina
The Marches
Siena
REPUBLIC OF SIENA
ELBA
Umbria
ADRIATIC SEA
Pescara
Ragusa (Dubrovnik)
Cattaro (Venice)
CORSICA (Genoa)
Tiber R.
Abruzzi
Patrimony of St. Peter
Rome
Molise
Capitanata
Manfredonia
Barletta
Trani
Giovinazzo
Bisceglie
Bari
Benevento
Gaeta
Naples
Campania
Apulia
SARDINIA (Aragon)
KINGDOM OF THE TWO SICILIES
Amalfi
Taranto
Lecce
Otranto
Basilicata
TYRRHENIAN SEA
Cosenza
Aeolian Is.
Messina
Calabria
IONIAN SEA
Trapani
Palermo
Cefalù
Taormina
Marsala
Mazara
Sicily
Caltanissetta
Catania
N
Agrigento
Syracuse
Ragusa
MEDITERRANEAN SEA
Tunis
0 Miles 100
0 Kilometers 100
TUNISIA (Hafṣids)
Note: D.= Duchy; M.=Marquisate
MALTA
©1999 Jeffrey L. Ward

But the friar Bonvesin della Riva, a reliable author who wrote in Latin and the local Milanese dialect, tells us in 1288 that Milan was "fertile, fortunate, fruitful, all kinds of cereals are produced: wheat, rye, millet, panic [a kind of millet] from which bread is made, and all kinds of vegetables which can be cooked and are excellent to eat—beans, chick peas, navy beans, small chick peas, lentils—in such an amazing quantity that after being distributed in different places . . . [they are] distributed to feed peoples beyond the Alps." He goes on to talk about the abundant fruits and nuts that are ground with eggs, pepper, and cheese and used to stuff meats in the winter.[15] In these two different accounts we have two different stories about the availability and quality of food. Can that much have changed in fifty years or is there that much difference between locales in such a small area as Lombardy?

That life was improving slowly in Italy by the end of the fourteenth century was not in doubt. We have the account of the chronicler Giovanni de Mussis who wrote in the second half of the fourteenth century in Piacenza that people lived in a clean and luxurious way, and the crockery was far superior to that of seventy years before (that is, in 1320), and that better wine was drunk.[16] The first indoor fireplace to appear in Piacenza was in 1320, while they were rare in Rome fifty years later. Perhaps this now allowed cooks in Piacenza to bake their *torta de riso bianco* rather than pan-fry it, leading eventually to their famous *bomba,* demonstrated in the following recipe.[17] Today the cooking of Milan is truly sumptuous, as we can see by the *bomba* recipe and the one following, *ossobuco,* traditionally accompanied by a saffron risotto (page 596).

Bomba di Riso alla Piacentina (Emilia-Romagna)

RICE MOLD OF PIGEONS FROM PIACENZA

The cuisine of Piacenza is famous today for its anolini, *a round or half-mooned shaped ravioli stuffed with* straccato, *a beef and vegetable stew cooked for several hours in water and wine, with nutmeg, bread crumbs, and a cured sausage called* coppa. *Another celebrated dish of Piacenza is this* bomba di riso *created for the Festa della Madonna on August 15, while a similar dish is made in Parma with the addition of its famous prosciutto.*

The Emilian cook traditionally makes this flavorful rice mold with plump pigeons. Some cooks enrich the preparation by adding tomato extract to the pigeons, or they add chicken livers and porcini mushrooms. Guinea or Cornish hens can replace the pigeons.

½ cup (1 stick) unsalted butter, at room temperature
2 onions, 1 large and 1 small, chopped separately
2½ pounds pigeons or Guinea or Cornish hens, with hearts, livers, and gizzards sliced
2 tablespoons tomato paste
1 cup dry white wine
Salt and freshly ground black pepper to taste
3 cups chicken broth (page 54)
1½ cups raw Arborio rice
2 cups water
½ cup boiling water if needed
1 cup freshly grated Parmigiano-Reggiano cheese
½ cup cooked fresh or frozen peas
½ pound veal sweetbreads, cleaned of membranes, poached 20 minutes, cooled, and sliced
Dried bread crumbs for coating the mold

1. In a large casserole, melt 2 tablespoons of the butter over medium heat and cook the large onion

until translucent, 5 to 7 minutes, stirring occasionally. Add the whole pigeons or hens along with the hearts, livers, and gizzards and brown the birds on all sides, about 10 minutes.

2. Add 1 tablespoon of the tomato paste to the casserole and cook until the onion and birds are well coated, 2 to 3 minutes, stirring. Pour in the wine and stir again. Reduce the heat to low, season the birds with salt and pepper, and add ½ cup of the broth at a time (using up to 2½ cups) while you simmer the birds until they are tender and cooked through, about 1½ hours, making sure the broth only shimmers on top and does not come to a boil. Remove and bone the birds.

3. Meanwhile, in a heavy saucepan with a heavy lid, melt 2 tablespoons of the butter and cook the small onion over medium heat until it is translucent, about 6 minutes, stirring occasionally. Add the rice, stirring so the grains are coated with the butter. Cook gently for 2 to 3 minutes, then add the water, bring to a boil, and add 1¼ teaspoons salt. Reduce the heat to very low, cover, and cook until the water is absorbed and the rice al dente, about 12 minutes. If the rice is too hard, add the boiling water and continue cooking for another 5 minutes. Once the rice is done, transfer to a large mixing bowl and gently stir in 1 cup of sauce from the birds, the giblets, Parmigiano-Reggiano, 2 tablespoons of the butter, the cooked peas, and sweetbreads. Don't stir too much; fold everything in instead.

4. Preheat the oven to 325°F. In a large round mold, lightly butter the bottom of the pan with 1 tablespoon of the butter and shake in some fine bread crumbs to coat the bottom entirely. Layer some rice on the bottom, then the boned meat of the birds, the remaining tablespoon butter, thinly sliced, and the remaining tablespoon tomato paste mixed with the remaining ½ cup chicken broth. Cover the meat of the birds with the remaining rice, sprinkle some bread crumbs on top, and bake until golden brown on top, about 1½ hours. Remove from the oven and place a round baking tray over the top of the mold. Carefully invert the mold and then slowly and carefully remove the mold from the *bomba*. Serve hot or warm.

Makes 6 servings

Ossobuco alla Milanese (Lombardy)

MILANESE-STYLE VEAL SHANK

Ossobuco, *cut from the shank of veal, is a classic of Milanese cuisine. This famous dish probably had its origins in a farmhouse during the nineteenth century and almost certainly did not originally include tomatoes, a New World discovery which I believe was added by restaurant chefs. It came into its own in the many* osterie *of Milan.*

Ossobuco *is one of the first dishes I ever learned to make. The taste of the veal as it melts away from the bone, the richness of the marrow, and the flavors of the* gremolada*—a seasoning made of lemon zest, garlic, parsley, and anchovies—is truly memorable. A special little spoon is used by the Milanese gourmet for digging out the succulent marrow from the bone; you can use a demitasse or baby spoon.* Ossobuco *is traditionally served on a large platter surrounded by* risotto alla milanese *(page 596) but goes well with mashed potatoes (page 62), too.*

2½ pounds veal shank *(ossobuco)*, cut into 6 pieces 4 inches in diameter, no more than 2 inches thick
All-purpose flour, for dredging
6 tablespoons (¾ stick) unsalted butter
½ cup dry white wine
1 pound ripe tomatoes, peeled, seeded, and chopped
Salt and freshly ground black pepper to taste

FOR THE *GREMOLADA*

1 garlic clove, finely chopped
Grated zest of 1/2 lemon
1/4 cup finely chopped fresh parsley leaves
2 salted anchovy fillets, rinsed

1. Dredge the veal in the flour, patting off any excess. In a large skillet, melt the butter over medium-high heat. Once the butter has stopped sizzling but before it turns color, brown the veal shanks, about 5 minutes per side. Pour in the wine and continue cooking until the wine is nearly evaporated, 5 to 10 minutes. Add the tomatoes, season with salt and pepper, and turn the veal a few times to mix. Cover, reduce the heat to low, and cook until the meat is nearly falling off the bone, about 2 1/2 hours.

2. Meanwhile, prepare the *gremolada*. Mix the garlic, lemon zest, parsley, and anchovies. A few minutes before the veal is to be served, sprinkle this mixture over them and turn several times to distribute the flavors.

Makes 4 servings

Formaggio alla Griglia (Lombardy)

GRIDDLED CHEESE

The cheese production of Lombardy increased in the Middle Ages once there was enough winter forage to justify larger herds. The most famous cheeses were hard salted cheeses, which were expensive, or fresh cheeses such as ricotta. This preparation is very simple; the only difficulty is in finding the right kind of cheese. In Lombardy the cook would use an individual-size wheel of soft ripened cheese like Alpino. If you are unable to find a small individual wheel of cheese, use a larger wheel of cheese such as Brie, which will be runnier than the smaller wheels.

Extra virgin olive oil
One 4- to 8-ounce wheel soft, ripened Alpino or Brie cheese
1 large slice Italian country bread, lightly toasted

1. Lightly oil a griddle with a film of olive oil and place the cheese in it over medium heat. Once it browns, after about 5 minutes flip to other side for another 5 minutes.

2. Remove to a slice of toasted bread and divide into four to six wedges and serve.

Makes 4 to 8 antipasto servings

THE popular diet in rural Italy consisted of more vegetables and greens grown in the kitchen garden than popularly thought. They were eaten raw, in salads, boiled in water, fried in lard or olive oil, or mixed with small amounts of meat. Still-extant "menus" of fifteenth-century taverns confirm the variety of uses for greens, served with bread and a glass of wine for daily meals. The thirteenth-century poet Matazone da Calignano said that the typical peasant's food was "mixed cereals bread, with raw onions, beans, garlic, boiled broad beans, panic pottage [a minestrone made of foxtail millet] and raw turnip greens." *Minestrone,* meaning "big soup," was the most evident culinary vehicle for much of the food available in northern Italy. The origins of minestrone lie in the simple *minestra* of the Middle Ages. Today they can rightly be called big soups, as we see in the minestrone recipe from Genoa.

Minestrone alla Genovese (Liguria)

GENOESE-STYLE MINESTRONE

The Genoese-style minestrone is a very dense and satisfying meal. It utilizes both seasonal vegetables and the famous pesto alla genovese, *made of garlic, basil, pine nuts, and Parmigiano-Reggiano cheese. But, as the Italian gastronome Massimo Alberini has said, as good as minestrone is, it is not a gastronomic specialty but rather an elemental dish composed of seasonal beans and vegetables and bound together by rice or macaroni. It is the quintessential meal of* cucina povera.

In the winter the cook will use dried beans, dried split peas, celery, cabbage, leeks, mushrooms, eggplant, winter squash, Swiss chard stalks, potatoes, and onions. In the summer the beans are fresh, as are the tomatoes, and borage is added for a distinctive flavor. Genoese cooks have perfected the minestrone by using only vegetables, the crust of a piece of Parmigiano-Reggiano cheese for delicate flavoring, and slow cooking, with the addition of the pesto at the very end. The ratio is about three to one, vegetables to water, by volume. In Liguria, for pasta, the cook might use maccheroncini rigati, penne piccole, pennette, tagliatelle fresca, capellini, pastine, bricchetti *(a little pot-shaped pasta), or* scucusu *(a couscous-like pasta), but I call for the easily found* tubetti. *This minestrone needs to be stirred as it cooks to avoid sticking or burning.*

1 cup dried fava beans, picked over, soaked in cold water to cover overnight, and drained
1 small eggplant (about ¾ pound), peeled and diced
Salt
1 cup dried *cannellini, borlotti,* white navy, haricot, Roman, or kidney beans (about ½ pound), picked over, soaked in cold water to cover overnight, and drained
1 medium-size onion, coarsely chopped
2 celery stalks, chopped
2 carrots, cut into small dice
¼ cup finely chopped fresh parsley leaves
½ cup extra virgin olive oil, plus more for drizzling
2 quarts water
6 ounces Parmigiano-Reggiano cheese crusts
1 pound zucchini (about 2), peeled and diced
1¼ pounds potatoes (about 2), peeled and diced
½ pound ripe tomatoes, peeled, seeded, and chopped
2 leeks, white and light green parts only, halved lengthwise, washed well, and chopped
½ pound portobello mushrooms, stems and caps diced
¾ pound orange-colored squash flesh, such as buttercup or pumpkin, diced
½ pound Savoy cabbage, damaged outer leaves removed, cored, and chopped
1 pound borage, collard greens, Swiss chard, escarole, or spinach (stems too only if desired), washed well and finely chopped
½ pound *tubetti* or any short macaroni
6 heaping tablespoons *pesto alla genovese* (page 351)
½ cup freshly grated pecorino Sardo cheese (or any pecorino cheese)

1. Bring a small saucepan of water to a boil and blanch the fava beans for 10 minutes. Drain and peel. Set aside.

2. Lay the eggplant pieces on some paper towels and sprinkle with salt. Leave them to drain of their bitter juices for 30 minutes, then pat dry with paper towels.

3. Put the fava beans, other beans, onion, celery, carrots, parsley, and ¼ cup of the olive oil in a large stockpot, cover with the water, stir, and bring to a boil. Salt to taste, cover, reduce the heat to low, and simmer until the beans are half-cooked, 20 minutes to 1 hour, depending on how old the beans are, stirring occasionally, and tasting for the doneness of the beans.

4. Add the Parmigiano-Reggiano crusts, zucchini, potatoes, tomatoes, leeks, mushrooms, squash, cab-

bage, borage, and eggplant. Pour in the remaining 1/4 cup olive oil. Stir well, cover, and cook over low heat until the minestrone is thick enough for a spoon to stand straight up in it, another 2 to 3 hours.

5. Add the pasta and turn the heat off when it is al dente, about 30 minutes because nothing is being boiled. Stir the pesto into a ladle full of the broth and stir it back into the minestrone. Serve each serving with a drizzle of olive oil and pecorino Sardo cheese.

Makes 8 servings

✣ ✣ ✣

MEDITERRANEAN towns attracted the rich and the poor, artists, merchants, and lords. But the towns also attracted overcrowding and disease, which more affluent urbanites sought to escape. At first, the exodus of rich city dwellers from Rome, Avignon, Milan, Seville, and elsewhere to the country was an escape from epidemics, but it soon became a general movement to country homes set amid fields, orchards, and vineyards. The country manor was a popular bourgeois form of luxury and became fashionable in Venice, Ragusa, Florence, and Seville during the sixteenth century.

In the country, the rich urbanites often had much to be thankful for. The novelist Matteo Bandello (1485–1561) describes how sweet it is in the heat of summer to be in a garden in Milan, to eat mellow fruits, and drink *un generoso e preziosissimo vino bianco* (a fine and full-bodied white wine). The novellas of the sixteenth and seventeenth centuries make frequent mention of the villas outside the cities and their splendid feasts—feasts that perhaps gave birth to dishes such as *ragù d'anitra con luganega e castagne* (see following recipe).

Ragù d'Anitra con Luganega e Castagne (Lombardy)

DUCK, SAUSAGE, AND CHESTNUT STEW

The great twentieth-century Italian chef Luigi Carnacina is thought of by many as the Escoffier of Italy. This gratifying wintertime stew is an adaptation of his recipe, but the original inspiration for this preparation may very well have been from the kitchen of a country manor where the wealthy hunters would return to their lodges with freshly killed duck from the local lakes. Preparing this dish is more or less an all-day affair. Don't let that put you off. Gather around the hearth and keep the kitchen warm on a blustery winter Sunday. Save as much duck fat as possible, as well as the wings, neck, liver, and gizzards, for making confit de canard *(page 200), duck broth (page 55),* alicuit *(page 201), or* salade tiéde de foie et gésiers de canard *(page 194).*

1/2 cup diced salt pork, parboiled for 15 minutes
1/4 cup chopped duck fat, removed from the duck
One 5-pound duck, as much fat removed as possible, cut into 10 serving pieces with a cleaver
1 medium-size onion, coarsely chopped
1 large carrot, sliced
2 garlic cloves, crushed
1 cup dry red wine
2 cups chicken broth (page 54)
1 cup tomato sauce (page 32)
Bouquet garni, tied in cheesecloth, consisting of 5 sprigs fresh parsley, 3 sprigs fresh thyme, and 1 bay leaf
3 tablespoons *burro maneggiato* (*beurre manié;* page 50)
1 pound homemade *salsiccia fresca* (page 70) or commercial mild Italian sausage, parboiled for 10 minutes, cooled, and sliced
15 baby carrots, trimmed, parboiled for 7 minutes, and drained

20 chestnuts, freshly shelled (Step 2, page 479), parboiled in red wine for 15 minutes, and drained
Salt and freshly ground black pepper to taste

1. In a large casserole, brown the salt pork and duck fat together over medium-high heat, about 5 minutes, stirring occasionally. Remove the salt pork with a slotted ladle and reserve.

2. In the fat remaining in the casserole, brown the duck pieces on all sides, about 10 minutes. Remove them with a slotted ladle, and in the remaining duck fat cook the onion, carrot, and garlic cloves, stirring frequently until the onion is soft, about 5 minutes. Remove the vegetables from the casserole with a slotted ladle and set aside. Pour off the duck fat and discard.

3. Return the vegetables and duck to the casserole and heat over medium-high heat, stirring occasionally. Pour in the wine and boil until it is almost evaporated, 12 to 15 minutes. Add the chicken broth, tomato sauce, and bouquet garni, and bring to a boil. Reduce the heat to low and simmer, partially covered, for 1½ hours.

4. Remove the duck pieces from the casserole with a slotted ladle. Pass the broth through a strainer or food mill, discarding the vegetables and bouquet garni. Transfer the broth to a ceramic bowl and place in the refrigerator. Let cool until the fat forms a layer on top, about 6 hours, then remove and discard it.

5. Return the defatted broth to the casserole and heat over medium heat. Stir in the *burro maneggiato* and, once it has melted, stir in the reserved salt pork, duck pieces, sausage, baby carrots, and chestnuts. Reduce the heat to low, cover, and simmer for 1 hour. Taste for seasoning and serve.

Makes 4 to 6 servings

Fagioli al Tonno (Tuscany)

BEANS WITH TUNA

In Boccaccio's Decameron, *a group of men sit down for a breakfast of* fagioli al tonno *and a* fritto misto *of fish.*[18] *The "beans and tuna" those thirteenth-century Tuscan companions ate that morning were probably prepared in a manner similar to this recipe. But the beans they ate were chickpeas, fava beans, lupine beans* (Lupinus albus), *or hyacinth beans* (Dolichos lablab, *syn.* Lablab purpurus [L. niger] *L.*); *the* cannellini *bean and the tomato had not yet arrived from the New World.*

This recipe uses the plump little cannellini *beans. They can be replaced with chickpeas or fava, as well as white haricot, great northern, navy, or white kidney beans. This dish is usually served very hot as a first course, but I also like to serve it at room temperature with a glass of wine and some bread.*

1½ cups dried white *cannellini* beans, picked over and rinsed
1 cup loosely packed fresh sage leaves
½ cup extra virgin olive oil
Salt to taste
2 garlic cloves, crushed
2½ pounds ripe tomatoes, peeled, seeded, and chopped
¼ cup loosely packed finely chopped fresh basil leaves
Freshly ground black pepper to taste
Two 6-ounce cans tuna packed in olive oil

1. Place the beans in a large pot, cover by 3 inches with cold water, and add the sage and 1 tablespoon of the olive oil, and some salt. Bring to a gentle boil, then cook gently over medium-low heat until tender, 1 to 1½ hours, uncovered. Drain.

2. In a large nonreactive skillet, heat the remaining 7 tablespoons olive oil over medium-high heat and

cook the garlic cloves, stirring, until they begin to turn light brown, about 1 minute. Remove the garlic from the pan and discard. Add the tomatoes and season with salt. Raise the heat to high and cook until slightly thicker, about 8 minutes, stirring frequently to prevent sticking, and lowering the heat if it splatters too much.

3. Reduce the heat to low, add the drained beans and basil, season with pepper, and simmer, covered, until the beans are hot, about 10 minutes, stirring occasionally. Turn the heat off, add the tuna and its oil, and stir. Let the skillet rest for 15 minutes. Serve hot or at room temperature.

Makes 8 servings

Fagioli con Cotenne (Tuscany)

BEANS WITH PORK SKIN

In the Middle Ages and until today virtually every part of the pig was used after the slaughter. The skin was prized as a flavoring agent and gave hungry people the illusion of eating meat. Even though these bean recipes from the Tuscan countryside are simple, their flavors are not. In this recipe the pork skin enhances the aromatic influence of the garlic and sage. The pork skin can come off a fresh ham or you can use the skin from a piece of fatback.

1 pound dried small white beans or chickpeas (about 2 cups), picked over and rinsed
4 cups water
1 pound pork skin, cut into 8 pieces
1 cup extra virgin olive oil
6 garlic cloves, finely chopped
6 sprigs fresh sage, tied into a bouquet
2 tablespoons tomato paste
Freshly ground black pepper to taste
Salt to taste

1. Place the beans and the remaining ingredients except the salt in a large nonreactive pot and mix well. Turn the heat to medium and cook for 30 minutes. Reduce the heat to low and cook until the beans are tender, about another 1½ hours.

2. Drain with a slotted ladle, transferring the beans to a serving dish. Check for saltiness, and add some if you like.

Makes 6 servings

THE cooking of everyday people in the countryside was simple, and still is, as these next two contemporary family-style recipes demonstrate, the first from Liguria and the second from Basilicata. The farmyard provided chickens for the cook, although in the Middle Ages the chickens were more than likely anemic-looking things compared to the robust chickens of today.

Ceci a Zimino (Liguria)

CHICKPEAS IN *ZIMINO* SAUCE

In Liguria today, zimino *is the "sauce" left over from cooking beet greens, spinach, or Swiss chard in a little water and olive oil. But it is an old word that Giordano di Pisa used in 1304 in his* Libro della cura delle malattie (Book for the care of illnesses) *to mean a kind of seasoned cooked dish. Modern linguists have made a case that the word derives from the Arabic word* samīn, *meaning fat or something buttery.*[19] *This is a vegetable version of cuttlefish* in zimino *(page 452). In this recipe I've changed the traditional preparation by using the beet roots instead of the greens. Technically, it is a different dish but equally good tasting. Its color is amazingly beautiful and it can be served with nearly everything.*

1 cup dried chickpeas (about ½ pound), picked over and soaked in water to cover overnight
¾ pound beets, rinsed
¼ cup extra virgin olive oil
1 medium-size onion, finely chopped
1 celery stalk, finely chopped
1 tablespoon tomato paste
½ pound ripe tomatoes, peeled, seeded, and chopped, with the juices included
Salt to taste

1. Drain the chickpeas from their soaking water and place in a medium-size saucepan with several inches of water to cover. Bring to a boil and cook over medium-high heat until soft but not breaking apart, about 3 hours, uncovered or partially covered. Drain, reserving ½ cup of the chickpea cooking water. Set the chickpeas aside after rubbing off as much of their thin white skins as possible.

2. Place the whole, unpeeled beets, with 1 inch of their stems, in a medium-size pot of water to cover and bring to a boil. Let boil until easily pierced with a skewer, about 45 minutes. Drain, trim off the stem, peel, and dice. Set aside.

3. In a large nonreactive skillet, heat the olive oil over medium-high heat, then cook the onion and celery until softened, about 4 minutes, stirring frequently. Reduce the heat to medium-low, add the tomato paste and tomatoes with their juices, and cook until some of the water has evaporated, about 10 minutes, stirring a few times. Add the chickpeas and their reserved liquid and cook another 10 minutes. Add the beets and cook until heated through, an additional 10 minutes, seasoning with salt. Gently turn several times to mix the ingredients and serve.

Makes 4 to 6 servings

Pollo con Peperoni (Basilicata)

CHICKEN WITH PEPPERS

Basilicata is the most isolated of Italy's regions and most of its people live in hilltop villages. As a result of its isolation, the cuisine, such as it is, is more rustic and less influenced by outside forces than other areas. Even though Basilicata was ruled from Naples when that city was under the Spanish Bourbons, it was effectively outside any administrative control. Nevertheless, it was the Spanish who introduced the sweet and hot peppers (Capsicum annuum) *to Italy. The New World peppers were, in fact, the most important spice encountered by Columbus at a time when the Mediterranean was very much interested in them. Early Spanish chroniclers of the New World devote a good deal of space to this plant.*[20]

In the dialect of Basilicata in southern Italy, this dish is called adduce cu paparuli, *chicken with peppers. This farmhouse recipe, rich with different colored bell peppers, is best made with a* pollo ruspante, *a free-range chicken, which can be found at natural food stores and specialty butchers.*

2 garlic cloves, finely chopped
3 tablespoons finely chopped fresh parsley leaves
Juice from 1 lemon
1 teaspoon salt
Freshly ground black pepper to taste
One 4- to 5-pound free-range chicken
3 tablespoons extra virgin olive oil
1 garlic clove, crushed
2 red bell peppers, seeded and cut into strips
1 green bell pepper, seeded and cut into strips
1 yellow bell pepper, seeded and cut into strips

1. In a small bowl, toss the chopped garlic, parsley, lemon juice, salt, and pepper together. Coat the chicken inside and out with this mixture and set aside for 1 hour in the refrigerator.

2. Preheat the oven to 350°F. Roast the chicken until golden brown and the leg joints are pliable, about 2 hours. (You need not truss it.) Transfer to a serving platter.

3. Meanwhile, in a large skillet, heat the olive oil over medium-high heat with the crushed garlic until the garlic begins to turn light brown, about 1 minute. Remove and discard the garlic. Reduce the heat to medium, add all the peppers, and cook until they are soft, 25 to 30 minutes, stirring occasionally. Cover the chicken with the peppers and serve.

Makes 4 to 5 servings

* * *

THE rich had not only their country houses but their own doctors as well. In an era when medicine was primitive and hygiene and dietetics not well understood, the few doctors there were provided services only to the high nobility and the very rich. Doctors lived and worked in the cities and towns as university professors or at the courts. The illiterate masses of poor people were still completely guided by popular superstitions when it came to their health and diet. And in rural areas there was no medical care. There was a theory prevalent during the Middle Ages, dating back to Hippocrates and expanded upon by the Greek physician Galen (c. 130–c. 200), attributing to different foods different properties that required different "digestions." These properties produced different "superfluities," which accounts for the great role medieval dietetics had on cooking, for a proper and selective diet was viewed as the road to good health.[21] We can see this attitude surface in a novella by Sabadino degli Arienti (who flourished in the fourteenth century), when the character Zuco Padella, a peasant from the Bolognese countryside, goes into his master's garden every night in order to steal peaches. He is caught one evening and admonished with the following words: *Un'altra volta lassa stare le fructe de li miei pari e mangia de le tue, che son le rape, gli agli, porri, cepolle, e le scalogne col pan de sorgo* (Next time leave my peer's fruit and eat your own, which is turnip greens, garlic, leeks, onions, and scallions with sorghum bread).[22] Doctors in the fourteenth and fifteenth centuries recommended to their rich and noble patients that they avoid fresh fruit because it caused a humoral imbalance, according to the Galenic theory of medicine.[23] Fresh fruit was not eaten in great amounts. More common were dried fruits, eaten because of the influence of Arab medical texts (that had incorporated much of Galen's theorizing) on European dietetics. Dried fruit was inexpensive, storable, and seen as an energetic.[24]

GRUEL, PORRIDGE, AND THE "FIRST FOODS" OF MUSLIM SPAIN AND TUNISIA

THE sixteenth-century Mediterranean diet was still a monotonous one, a lifetime of eating bread, more bread, and gruel. Of course, there were vegetables and meat, but the overwhelming percentage of calories in the diet derived from grain products. In Muslim Spain, the gruel might be made of wheat flour—*sakhīna* or *ʿaṣīda*—cooked in a soup of seasonal herbs, spinach, lettuce, or sorrel, and served in a common bowl for family meals. Or it might be a soup with a few fava beans and chickpeas.[25]

Many of the dishes eaten in Muslim Spain and Tunisia had been traditional for centuries. As early as the tenth century, al-Muqaddasī wrote that he had "eaten '*harīsa*' with the Sufis and '*tharīda*' with the monks and *ʿaṣīda*' with seamen."[26] All these dishes were famous medieval Arab preparations that have their descendents today.

The *harīsa* mentioned by al-Muqaddasī has nothing to do with the spicy hot chili paste with the same name (page 523), other than that both are made by pounding and that the Arabic verb *harasa,* to pound or to crush, gives them their names. From the seventh century until today, *harīsa* was a kind of porridge made from pounded wheat, butter, meat, and spices. *Harīsa* was as famous and as international a dish as pizza is today. During the reign of the Umayyad caliph Muʿāwiya (A.D. 661–680) a delegation of Arabian Jews visited him in Damascus, and the first question he asked them was whether they knew how to prepare the delightful *harīsa,* which he himself had had on a visit to Arabia. The Arabian Jews did in fact know how to make *harīsa,* and it is a dish that has been preserved to this day by Yemeni Jews.[27] This famous dish also traveled to England, where the name was translated into the English of the fourteenth century as frumenty, derived from the Middle French word for "grain." It became in England a kind of wheat stew boiled with milk, cinnamon, and sugar. In the nineteenth century, the famous lexicographer Reinhart Dozy noted that *harīsa* was eaten by Moroccan Jews on Sunday.[28]

Tharīda was basically a bread soup, consisting of bread crumbled with the fingers, then moistened with broth. The name of the dish very likely derives from *tharāda,* meaning, literally, and appropriately, to crumble bread into broth. According to the French scholar Maxime Rodinson, *tharīda* and *ʿaṣīda* were typical foods among the Bedouin of pre-Islamic and, probably, later times. They could also be the food of the wealthy when prepared luxuriously with such extras as eggs and bone marrow.[29]

ʿAṣīda, the name of a variety of similar dishes, but basically a kind of semolina porridge, is rooted in the culinary traditions of Muslim Andalusia. It was as ubiquitous in the medieval Maghrib and Islamic Spain as French fries are today. One of the earliest written recipes for it can be found in an anonymous thirteenth-century Hispano-Muslim cookbook. In the thirteenth century, *ʿaṣīda* was also a porridge—a thick broth stirred into wheat flour, perhaps with butter and honey—usually made for religious holidays, such as Mawlid al-Nabī, the birthday festival of the Prophet Muhammad, or ceremonies such as the *ʿaqiqa,* the traditional hair cutting of the newborn seven days after birth. It was also fed to women in labor.[30] *ʿAṣīda* was known in the Rif, the mountainous region along the Mediterranean coast of Morocco, during the thirteenth and fourteenth centuries, where flour made from lightly grilled barley was used. The famous Arab explorer Ḥasan al-Wazan, who was known as Leo Africanus (c. 1465–1550) in the West, and who journeyed into Africa, gives a recipe: Boil water in a large pot, add the barley flour, stirring with a stick. Pour the gruel into a plate and in the center make a small shallow where one puts the argan seed oil.[31] The argan seed oil he mentions is extracted from the argan tree (*Argania sideroxylon* Roem. et Schult.), a kind of evergreen, the word coming from the Arabic *arjān,* where an oil is extracted from the seed, and is still used today in Moroccan cooking.

Rafis is yet another dish similarly made of wheat flour, dates, honey, and butter and other ingredients that a sheik of Qairouan in the fourteenth century shared once a year in a celebration with the students of his *zāwiyya,* a hospice and theological school. A recipe preserved from the fifteenth century tells us how to make *rafis:* "Take pieces of bread smaller than an olive and mix with dates and honey until it looks like it will break apart. Work the mixture for a long time with the hands not over a fire until you get a *rafis.*"[32]

The reasons these foods were so important around holidays of religious significance were several, including a belief in the medicinal properties of honey. When a bowl of *ʿaṣīda* is eaten in celebration of the Prophet's birthday, Mawlid al-Nabī, it reminds the believer that the holy Koran was recited to Muhammad by the angel Gabriel near Mecca in A.D. 610.

❈ *ᶜAṣīda* (Tunisia, Algeria, Morocco, and Berbers)

SEMOLINA PORRIDGE WITH WARM ORANGE BLOSSOM HONEY

ᶜAṣīda, *best described as a kind of North African polenta, is made in a tin-lined copper pot called a* nuḥāsa. *When would you eat this? For breakfast isn't a bad idea, and in Morocco the family gathers around and eats just that way.*[33]

4 cups hot water
2 teaspoons salt, or to your taste
1⅓ cups fine semolina
1 tablespoon unsalted butter, melted
¼ cup orange blossom honey, heated

1. Bring 2 cups of the water to a rolling boil in a medium-size saucepan and add the salt. In a slow, continuous stream, pour in the semolina, stirring constantly in one direction with a wooden spoon. Reduce the heat to medium. As the water evaporates, the semolina will become harder to stir. At this point, slowly pour in the remaining 2 cups hot water. Continue stirring until you have a smooth porridge, just like Cream of Wheat cereal, 3 to 4 minutes.

2. Pour the porridge onto a platter. Drizzle the butter and honey over the semolina and serve.

VARIATION
In place of honey and butter, use confectioners' sugar, or drizzle with extra virgin olive oil.

Makes 2 servings

WHEN we talk about the food of the Mediterranean, we must talk about the food of the rich. The story of hunger and poverty does not allow one to say much about food because there was so little of it and what there was was so monotonous. But with the food of the rich, we can whet our appetites. After all, the recipes in this book, whether their roots are with the poor or the rich, are contemporary recipes that reflect the contemporary wealth of the Mediterranean (in relative terms, of course). The rich in Tunisia could eat as well as the rich in Italy. The famous Arab geographer al-Bakrī (died 1094) provides interesting accounts of eleventh-century Tunis. He describes Tunis as the most illustrious city of Ifriqiya (the Arabic name of medieval Tunisia) and the richest in excellent fruit, especially an almond called *farīk,* meaning "crumbly," because the shell is so thin it can be rubbed off. The pomegranates are sweet and the citrons delicious. Sweet black figs called *al-khārmī* are big with a thin skin. The quince are huge and sweet. The jujubes are the size of walnuts. Onions are called Calabrian onions *(al-kallawrī)* and are as big as oranges, with a perfect taste. Fish is abundant.[34] He tells us that the soil was improved with human waste.[35] There must have been wine, regardless of the Muslim restrictions, because al-Bakrī reports abundant grape vineyards and sugarcane fields. We also know that Tunis and Bougie (Bejaïa) had famous wine bars because in January 1229, Marseilles regulated the sale of wine to them. Between 1228 and 1236, the Ḥafṣid caliph of Tunisia, Abū Zakariya', made trade agreements with Venice, Pisa, and Genoa and maintained excellent relations with the Sicilian king Frederick II, the greatest king of the medieval world, trading a great deal of food with them all.[36]

The tenth-century Arab writer Abū Bakr al-Mālikī, a pious man from Qairouan in Tunisia during the Fāṭimid dynasty, wrote *Riyāḍ al-nufūs,* one of the richest sources for medieval North African food, and mentions that barley, wheat, fava beans, and chickpeas were grilled before being eaten. In other works there is mention of toasted flour *(duqāq maqlūw)* and three kinds of bread in twelfth-century Tunisia—flour *(duqāq)*, semolina *(samīḍ)*, and coarse flour *(ḥuskār)*—in contrast to Egypt and Syria, where there was only one kind, made from the grinding of wheat, the bran *(al-nukhāla al-kabīra)*.[37] Al-Mālikī mentions that white wheat flour is called *ḥuwwārā*, while the coarser semolina is known as *sawīq*.[38]

Bread was used in a kind of ragout called a *tharīd* (or *thurda*) (page 560). There is mention of a bowl of *tharīd* with wheat bread and fatty lamb, a *thurda* of beet root, and a *tharīda* of lamb with pieces of Swiss chard and chickpeas.[39] *Baysār* was fava beans cooked with butter and milk, cooled, and solidified. Many foods mentioned in the *Riyāḍ al-nufūs* are cooked with *silq,* which today means Swiss chard, but in the twelfth century it may have meant beet leaves. The *Riyāḍ* mentions *samāṣākhiyya,* a synonym for *ḥarīra* (page 668)—al-Mālikī ate this in Sicily when he visited in about 936; *kawākibiyya,* Swiss chard (or beet leaves) and chickpeas; *nīsābūriyya,* which means "heaven is serene," a cut of meat and a dish that is Swiss chard and carrots that derives its name from the famous city of Nīshāpūr in Persia; *fuṣtuqiyya,* Swiss chard and fava (perhaps containing pistachios, too, given the Arabic name; *fuṣtuq* means "pistachio"); *ifrīqiyya,* chicken and olive oil.[40] Medieval Tunisian farmers had learned that plants such as spinach and beets react favorably to the presence of salt in the soil, as was the case along the littoral of Tunisia. These vegetables became popular in Tunisian cooking and still are.

Tunisia saw an active thirteenth-century trade with Genoa, Pisa, Venice, and Sicily while under the dynasty of the Ḥafṣids (1228–1574), named for their eponymous founder Abū Ḥafṣ ʿUmar. By the beginning of the fourteenth century, there was also active trade with Marseilles.[41] Pisans exported Tuscan oil to Barbary and chestnuts came through Marseilles from the Cevennes region of Languedoc, which was scouted by purveyors from Nîmes, who called the area the Châtaigneraie, or chestnut zone. In exchange, figs, walnuts, and almonds were shipped north across the Mediterranean. The Tunisians imported spices and other products in 1500 from the Levant with the same fervor as the northern Mediterranean, including black pepper, cloves, cinnamon, ginger, nutmeg, cassia, manna, aloe, rhubarb, saffron, tartar, mastic, borax, storax, camphor, and scammony.[42] The Tunisians were also well known for their almonds, which were exported mostly to Catalonia, France, and Italy. Even today Tunisian almonds are favored by Europeans. There are four different kinds of Tunisian almonds: *ashagh* (which are the biggest ones), *balsin, zahaf,* and *burat.* The Berbers of the Sahel considered the thinnest almonds (the *burat*) the choicest and they were a good product to trade.

The daily food of Tunisia during the Ḥafṣid period consisted of only a few essentials such as wheat or barley, olives, olive oil, milk, butter, dates, figs, and salt. Milk was used for drinking and making butter. Cheese was made from sheep's or goat's milk. Sugar and honey were popular, as were eggs and chicken. People loved meat, but its consumption was rare, eaten only during festivities.[43]

Events in Spain caused many Andalusian Muslims, beginning in 1462, to settle in Tunis, bringing new culinary preparations such as *mujabbana* (page 103), a cheese cake. Barley played a big role in the kitchen and, to a lesser extent, sorghum and millet. Olives were important and grown on the littoral between Tunis and Tripoli. Figs were important, but not as much as dates, and pistachios were grown in the thirteenth century around Gafsa. Date syrup was made and the dates jarred for consumption.[44] Carobs were grown in Monastir and Djebel Ousselat, while jujubes were cultivated on the plain of Bone (Annaba), called for that reason the "city of *jujubiers.*"[45]

Each region developed fame for a particular product. Bigerades (bitter orange) and citrons were grown in

Tunis and Carthage, while peaches, apricots, prunes, cherries, azaroles, apples, and medlars were grown in Monastir, Djerba, and Zanzur. The pears of Bechari were famous. Quince and almonds also came from Bechari, and Tagiura and Zanzur. Pomegranates were abundant in Tunis, Monastir, Sorman, and Zanzur.[46] Tunisia grew a variety of berries, and cucumbers, parsnips, and melons. Other cultivated vegetables included zucchini, eggplant, turnip, cabbage, cauliflower, Swiss chard, purslane, lettuce, chicory, asparagus, onion, carrots, garlic, and Jew's mallow *(Corchorus olitorius)*. Around Gabes during Ḥafṣid times, chufa *(ḥabb al-ᶜazīz)*, a root, was cultivated and dipped in sugar and sucked.[47] The orchards of Gabes were famed in medieval times for their olives, bananas, apples, dates, and mulberries, much of which was exported to Qairouan, once the capital of Tunisia.[48]

The most common Tunisian herbs and spices, as today, were cumin, caraway, and aniseed, grown around Carthage, Taqyus, Gafsa, Sbibs, and Kerkenna. Henna and madder were cultivated and saffron crocus were grown on the coast of Ebba and later in Djebel Gharian. In the fourteenth century, the commentator Ibn Faḍlallah mentions oregano, myrtle, roses, jasmine, cloves, marjoram, violets, lilies, saffron, basil, thyme, narcissus, and yellow pond lilies, not all of which—obviously—could be eaten, as narcissus bulbs are poisonous.[49]

In Tunisia very little meat was eaten, as is still the case today, although beef was enjoyed by country gentlemen and lots of chicken and mutton were consumed at special times, such as religious feasts. In the country, wheat or barley was the most common grain. Fish was popular along the coast and small birds were sold in the markets. In the south, in Tozeur, Nefta, and Gafsa, dog meat could be bought in the meat stalls of the market. Consumption of dog meat was frowned upon, though, and some Tunisians suspected their neighbors of using it in their *harīsa* soup. Dog is man's best friend only in the West; in North Africa and the rest of the Arab world, dogs are not admired. Ibn Rushd, the famous Muslim philosopher and medical encyclopaedist born in Córdoba and known as Averroës (1126–1198) in the West, said that the worst thing about people of the Maghrib was that they used dog meat.[50]

Valuable descriptions of foods and food customs in fifteenth-century Tunisia also come from Europeans such as the traveler Anselme Adorne, who was born in Bruges, Belgium, in 1424.[51] He describes the perfumes sold before the Grand Mosque of Tunis and the covered stalls of the souk *(sūq)*, the market. He mentions the sanitation workers who washed down the streets to keep them fresh and clean. Water carriers circulated through the souk providing free sweet water to any who wanted it, gladly accepting baksheesh (tips). Adorne tells us that the Tunisians ate magnificently, drinking only milk or water. The rich, though, occasionally drank raisin wine. A favorite drink was sugar water flavored with things such as almond syrup. Fava beans and chickpeas were favorites, as they are today. In Tunis, Adorne ate a lunch of *maqrūḍ* (page 498) prepared with raisins and a *bazīn* (page 248) made with meatballs and boiled in chicken broth, along with chicken, almonds, dates, apples, and, finally, poppy seeds to sleep well during the siesta. In the evening at the same house he ate a meat couscous with cabbage.[52] This was a hard wheat couscous, the same as today, considered a delicate food and popular in the country. Adorne saw it made several times and leaves us a description: The grains are sprinkled with milk or sugar water a little at a time. They are then rolled into little lumps. After the couscous is cooked, it is served with pieces of meat or chicken wrapped in cabbage. The couscous is eaten with five fingers, forming it into a small ball that is placed in the mouth.[53]

Another traveler to Tunisia of the Middle Ages was ᶜAbdalbasiṭ ibn Ḥalīl, an Egyptian, whose two manuscripts detailing his journeys from 1460 to 1470 in Tunisia are in the Vatican library.[54] In Tunis he ate a Spanish cheese cake called *mujabbana* and gives a recipe:

Knead the fresh cheese with your hands as you would dough. Carefully knead in the semolina. Once it has the consistency of a dough of our *zalābiyya* [like New England fried dough or the Italian *zeppole*; recipe on page 113], or a rather thick consistency, then take a piece and spread it out delicately in the palm of your hand. Place a piece of cheese in the center and close it up to make a bonbon. Flatten it a little bit and deep-fry in oil. Remove and sprinkle on powdered sugar and a little powdered cumin.[55]

Mujabbana was known until recently in Tunis as *kayshalīsh,* derived from the Spanish word for cheese, *queso*.[56]

Tunisian home cooking of the Middle Ages was usually not done in the home but in public ovens. During this period Tunisia and Muslim Spain shared many elements of their culture, including culinary culture. In Muslim Spain, too, the bazaar was the public arena for much public cooking, in scenes that must have looked like an evening in the Jammaʿa al-Fināʿ of Marrakech in Morocco today. Customers could have chickens, either *shawwa,* spit-roasters, or *kalla,* fryers, or buy sheep's heads, meatballs, liver, lamb's hearts, and lamb fat *(asfida)* roasted in a brick oven *(tannūr)*. Fried beignets called *isfanj,* moistened with warm honey, were sold, as well as the cheese cakes mentioned above, butter crêpes *(musammanat),* jumbles (ring-shaped cakes also known in Albi in Languedoc), or cracknels (a hard ring biscuit) called *kaʿk,* not to mention nougat, a confection made of almonds and sugar paste.[57]

The kitchen of a prosperous Hispano-Muslim home most likely had a cooking hearth, using charcoal or dung as a fuel, and a *raḍaf,* a warming pan filled with hot coals and probably similar to a modern

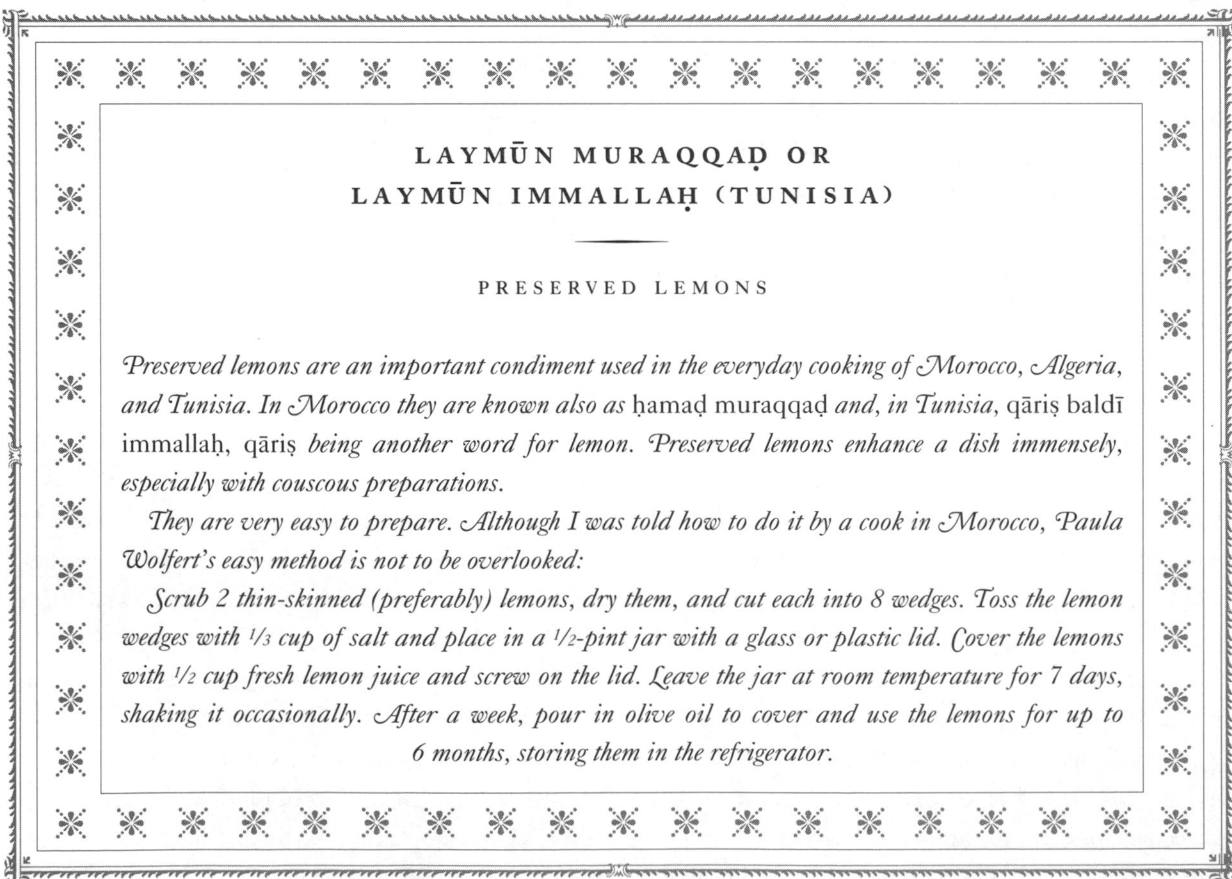

LAYMŪN MURAQQAḌ OR LAYMŪN IMMALLAḤ (TUNISIA)

PRESERVED LEMONS

Preserved lemons are an important condiment used in the everyday cooking of Morocco, Algeria, and Tunisia. In Morocco they are known also as ḥamaḍ muraqqaḍ *and, in Tunisia,* qāriṣ baldī immallaḥ, qāriṣ *being another word for lemon. Preserved lemons enhance a dish immensely, especially with couscous preparations.*

They are very easy to prepare. Although I was told how to do it by a cook in Morocco, Paula Wolfert's easy method is not to be overlooked:

Scrub 2 thin-skinned (preferably) lemons, dry them, and cut each into 8 wedges. Toss the lemon wedges with 1/3 cup of salt and place in a 1/2-pint jar with a glass or plastic lid. Cover the lemons with 1/2 cup fresh lemon juice and screw on the lid. Leave the jar at room temperature for 7 days, shaking it occasionally. After a week, pour in olive oil to cover and use the lemons for up to 6 months, storing them in the refrigerator.

Spanish *brasero,* that was used to set eggs and egg-based sauces, as well as to keep cooked food warm. A variety of leavened and unleavened breads, including puff pastry, was enjoyed, and wheat was a common grain. The origin of *pâte feuilletée* (puff pastry) may very well be rooted in medieval Muslim Spain, according to Charles Perry, a researcher of medieval Muslim foods.[58]

The most common meats were lamb and mutton, and they were cooked on a spit or roasted in an oven. Meat was also pounded in a mortar in a method similar to the contemporary kibbe (page 579). Typical seasonings were coriander, both fresh leaves and seeds, and mint, thyme, fennel, cumin, caraway, and citron leaves. The most popular spices were saffron, black pepper, and cinnamon. A mixture of spikenard (*Nardostachys jatamansi* de Candolle, a rare spice), cinnamon, and sugar was sometimes sprinkled on a dish as a finish and ginger, cloves, nutmeg, and galingale appear occasionally. Prosperous Hispano-Muslims enjoyed a cuisine that employed thickening agents for sauces, such as one with eggs called *khamara,* and one that used a starch like bread crumbs or pounded almonds, called *khaththara*.[59]

Al-Kūsha bi'l-ʿAlūsh (Tunisia)

THE BEST LAMB AND POTATO STEW

This preparation is an old one. The Arabic word kūsha *is used in North Africa to mean "bread oven," thought by some scholars to be a transformation from the Latin* coquere panem, *"to cook bread."*[60] *In the Middle Ages, and until quite recently in certain parts of the Mediterranean, the population of towns like Bizerte on the northern coast of Tunisia would use public ovens to bake bread and foods. Throughout the Mediterranean families left their meals with the baker, leaving their instructions on how they wanted them cooked. He would bake them and the family would pick the meals up later to bring home.*

These simple family-style preparations prove the most surprising. Take this lamb, potato, and long green pepper (peperoncino) *stew that is oven baked in a very flavorful, thin broth of olive oil and lamb juice, with lots of parsley, red pepper, and preserved lemon. I shared this experience with my friend Deborah Madison, a chef and cookbook author, at the Restaurant da Cuisine Tunisienne at the corner of Rue d'Algiers and Rue 20 Mars in Bizerte, after hours of strolling through this former Barbary corsair base with its beige-washed square dwellings.*

This was a workingman's lunch place and completely unassuming. We took our first bite, looked at each other, and in response to my quizzical look, Deborah calmly exclaimed that this was the most delicious potato she had ever had, period. I agreed.

2 pounds lamb shoulder, on the bone, cut into 6 pieces and trimmed of fat
1 small onion, finely chopped
Salt and freshly ground black pepper to taste
1 tablespoon tomato paste
2 quarts water
1/3 teaspoon cayenne pepper
1/4 cup extra virgin olive oil
2 pounds new Russian Banana (fingerling) or Yukon Gold potatoes, peeled and halved or quartered lengthwise
2 long green peppers *(peperoncino),* seeded and quartered lengthwise
Leaves from 1 bunch fresh parsley, finely chopped
1 preserved lemon (page 104), sliced into thinner wedges

1. Preheat the oven to 350°F. Toss the lamb and onion together with salt and pepper and arrange in a baking pan. Mix the tomato paste with 2 cups of the water, the cayenne, and olive oil, pour over the meat, and bake, covered, for 1 hour, spooning the pan juices

over the meat occasionally as it bakes. Add another 3 cups of the water and bake another 1½ hours. Moisten with the remaining 3 cups water as needed to keep the stew from drying out.

2. Arrange the potatocs and green peppers in the baking pan with the meat. Spoon the pan juices over everything. Bake until a skewer glides easily into the potatoes without their falling apart, another 20 to 30 minutes. Check the seasoning.

3. Sprinkle the parsley over the meat and vegetables. Toss well and transfer to a deep serving platter or individual servings with the meat in the center surrounded by the vegetables and preserved lemon slices. Spoon pan juices over everything and serve.

Makes 4 servings

Sidir (Tunisia)

SPICY HOT SEMOLINA BALL SOUP

Sidir *is the name of a soup made with a kind of large couscous also called* sidir. *Actually, this couscous can be called a large pasta ball, also known as* muḥammaṣ *in Tunisia and* burkūkis *in Algeria. It is somewhat unclear what the meaning of* sidir *is. The word generally refers to the jujube* (Zizyphus jujube), *but it can refer also to a variety of Christ's-thorn* (Zizyphus spina Christi), *and in the works of al-Tijānī there is mention of a* sidir misr, *or Egyptian* sidir, *a kind of tree that has fruit bigger than the ones of Tunis.*[61] *Perhaps the fruits in question are small cherries or jujubes. On the other hand, we know that Egyptian peasants until the beginning of the twentieth century used the fruits of Christ's-thorn to make what was called zizyphus bread, and this might be our* sidir misr.[62] *In any case, the couscous (or pasta) form known as* sidir *is supposed to be large, but not as large as a cherry.*

The sidir *soup I had in Tunis was magnificent, and this recipe is adapted from the one given me by a great Tunisian food enthusiast, Hechmi Hammami, the executive chef of the Abou Nawas Hotel in Tunis, who uses* qadīd *for his flavoring (pages 69 and 249). The pasta balls for this recipe can be found sold in Middle Eastern markets under the name* maghribiyya *or* moghrabiyya *(the Arabic name for them in the Levant). Otherwise you can make your own fresh by following the recipe for homemade pasta on page 628 and forming the dough with your fingers into a ball the size of a caper and letting it dry for 48 hours.*

½ teaspoon caraway seeds
5 garlic cloves, peeled
1 teaspoon salt
¼ cup extra virgin olive oil
2 tablespoons tomato paste
7 cups water
1 tablespoon *harīsa* (page 523)
½ teaspoon freshly ground black pepper
¼ pound dried pasta balls (about ½ cup; page 718)
1 tablespoon capers, rinsed
1 preserved lemon (page 104), cut into small dice without the peel
1 tablespoon finely chopped fresh mint leaves (optional)

1. Grind the caraway seeds in a mortar, then pound in the garlic and salt until the mixture is a paste.

2. In a large nonreactive casserole or saucepan, heat the olive oil over high heat and add the tomato paste diluted in 1 cup of the water, the *harīsa,* black pepper, and garlic-caraway paste. It will sizzle violently for a second so remember to keep your face away. Reduce the heat to medium, stir well to mix, cover, and cook for 5 minutes, stirring a few times.

3. Add the remaining 6 cups water, the pasta balls, capers, and preserved lemon and simmer, uncovered, until the pasta balls are soft but not mushy, about 20 minutes. Sprinkle on the mint, if using, correct the salt and serve.

Makes 4 servings

❈ *Ḥarqma* (Tunisia)

SPICY LAMB TROTTERS SOUP

Ḥarqma *is a well-known name in the Maghrib, apparently an introduction from Arab-Andalusian times of the Middle Ages, and a beloved dish during Ramadan.* Ḥarqma *was a word used by Pedro de Alcala in his vocabulary of 1505 to mean "ripe" or "intestines."*[63] *The word was also used to refer to cow's hooves, or to a kind of ratatouille, or to butcher's scraps made into a soup. In Morocco* ḥarqma *is a* ṭājin *of sheep's trotters cooked with wheat and chickpeas, and said to be a breakfast favorite of King Hassan II.*[64] Ḥarqma *also exists farther east in Tunisia, where it is more of a soup, such as in this recipe, but can also refer to a ragout of tripe, feet, and heart. This recipe uses lamb shank. The preparation is so well loved in the Maghrib that North African friends of mine insisted it must be included in this book.*

¼ cup extra virgin olive oil
2 pounds lamb's feet (page 713)
2 pounds lamb shanks
Salt and freshly ground black pepper to taste
2 tablespoons *harīsa* (page 523)
2 quarts water
2 large eggs
2 tablespoons fresh lemon juice

1. In a large stew pot or casserole, heat the olive oil over medium-high heat. Season the lamb's feet and shanks with salt and pepper. Brown the feet and shanks on all sides, 4 to 5 minutes. Stir the *harīsa* into the casserole; once it has melted and blended with the oil, pour in the water. Bring to a boil, reduce the heat to low, cover, and cook until tender, about 2½ hours.

2. Strain the soup. Discard the feet and bones, removing and chopping any meat from the shank. Return the soup and chopped meat to the casserole.

3. Break the eggs into a bowl and whisk in the lemon juice. Whisk a ladle of hot soup into the egg mixture. Once it is blended, whisk in another ladle of soup. Now whisk the entire egg mixture back into the soup. Strain again and discard all bits of gristly meat and fat. Return the soup to the casserole and serve.

Makes 6 servings

❈ *Maraqat al-Safarjal* (Tunisia)

SWEET RAGOUT OF QUINCE AND LAMB

This recipe will help me explain some confusion in Mediterranean culinary terms. In North Africa there are two very different words that mean "stew." In Morocco, a stew is called a ṭājin *(or* ṭājīn*), but in Tunisia a stew is called* maraqa. *In Tunisia, a* ṭājin *is not a stew but the word for a kind of omelette. The Italians have the same kind of omelette, which they call a* frittata. *The Spanish have this, too, but they call their omelette a* tortilla *(it never means a flatbread in Spain), a word the Mexicans use not for an omelette but for a* *kind of flatbread. Now, to complicate matters further, my Arabic-English dictionary (Wehr) translates* maraqa *as a kind of broth or sauce, but, more accurately, it really is what the French call an* etuvé, *a slow-cooked covered stew containing very little fat or liquid, although I call it a ragout since that's the word I believe readers are most familiar with. The* ṭājin *of Morocco is also nearly identical to this French* etuvé. *The word* ṭājin, *although referring to either the stew or the omelette, actually is the name of the shallow earthenware pan that both the stew and the omelette are cooked in, and that word derives from the Greek* teganon, *meaning "frying pan." (By the way,* safarjal *means "quince.")*

The maraqa-*style of cookery had a wide enough influence that one finds it in Provence, probably brought back by the Pied-Noirs, the returned French settlers from North Africa, as evidenced by J.-B. Reboul's recipe for* la marga *in his nineteenth-century cookbook* La cuisinière provençal. *There Reboul has completely changed the concept, but the ingredients are purely North African with the combination of lamb and chicken cooked with fava beans, chickpeas, cardoons, zucchini, artichokes, and onions seasoned with cayenne pepper, cumin, and other spices.*[65]

This sweet recipe can be made with prunes or dried apricots instead of the quince. Dried rose petals are traditionally used as a flavoring. This particular combination of lamb and fruit appears to derive its provenance from Persian cuisine via the Ottoman Turks. Although the Greeks know a similar dish called arni me kithounia *or* kidonia *that they make with veal or pork as well as the cinnamon, it too is probably derived from the Persians through the Turks.*[66]

1¼ pounds boneless leg of lamb, trimmed of all fat and cubed
½ teaspoon ground cinnamon
1 teaspoon dried and ground rose petals (page 727) or ¼ teaspoon rose water
Salt to taste
½ cup extra virgin olive oil
1½ pounds quince (see Note), peeled, cut into eighths, and cored
3 to 4 cups water
1⅓ cups sugar

1. In a medium-size bowl, toss the lamb together with the cinnamon, rose petals or rose water, and salt.

2. In a medium-size casserole, heat the olive oil over medium-high heat and brown the lamb, about 2 minutes, stirring. Add the quince, cover with the water, and bring to a boil. Reduce the heat to medium-low and cook for 1 hour, uncovered. Add the sugar and stir. Cover and cook until the lamb is very tender and the quince soft, about another hour. Remove to a serving platter with a slotted spoon and serve.

NOTE: Quince are like very hard apples. Although there is a sweet variety in North Africa, the quince available in American markets are inedible in the raw state. Use a sharp knife and don't cut them up until you need them because they discolor.

Makes 4 servings

Maraqat al-Khuḍra (Tunisia)

RAGOUT OF GREEN VEGETABLES WITH MUTTON

This vegetable (khuḍra) *ragout* (maraqa) *is typical of home cooking in Tunis. Some cooks might add other leafy vegetables such as spinach, root vegetables such as turnips, legumes such as haricot beans, and even thistles such as artichokes, cardoons, or* *golden thistle (*Scolymus hispanicus *L.). There are as many different* maraqas *as there are families, what* spezzatini *are to Italian families (page 237). In any case, this* maraqa *is cooked midday and often reheated for dinner.*

½ cup extra virgin olive oil
1 pound boneless lamb or mutton shoulder, trimmed of all fat and cut into 1-inch cubes
1½ teaspoons *tābil* (page 522)
Salt and freshly ground black pepper to taste
2 medium-large onions (about 1 pound), chopped
1 pound Swiss chard, washed well, trimmed of the heavier part of their stalks, and chopped
Leaves from 1 bunch fresh parsley, chopped
⅔ cup cooked chickpeas, drained
2 tablespoons tomato paste
1½ teaspoons *harīsa* (page 523)
½ cup water
Juice from 1 lemon
1½ teaspoons freshly ground black pepper
1½ teaspoons ground red pepper, such as Aleppo or cayenne

1. In a medium-size nonreactive casserole, heat the olive oil over high heat. Toss the lamb or mutton with the *tābil,* salt, and pepper. Brown the meat and onions in the hot oil, about 5 minutes, stirring frequently.

2. Reduce the heat to low and add the Swiss chard and parsley with the water clinging to them from their last rinsing. Cook until this liquid is mostly evaporated, about 10 minutes.

3. Add the chickpeas, tomato paste, and *harīsa* diluted in the water, the lemon juice, and black and red peppers. Mix well, cover, and simmer over a very low heat until the meat is very tender, about 2 hours, moistening the ragout with small amounts of water if it is drying out. Serve.

Makes 4 servings

Maraqa bi'l-ʿAdas (Tunisia)

LENTIL RAGOUT

In this maraqa, *the lamb is used as a flavoring condiment for the lentils. The taste is soothing and lusty, although my recipe actually has about twice as much lamb as a typical Tunisian family would use, so reduce the amount by half if you are a stickler for authenticity.*

⅔ cup extra virgin olive oil
1½ pounds lamb neck and shoulder, trimmed of all fat and cut into pieces
Salt and freshly ground black pepper to taste
1 medium-size onion, chopped
2 tablespoons tomato paste
2 cups water
1¼ cups dried brown or green lentils, picked over and rinsed
1 teaspoon freshly ground black pepper
1 teaspoon cayenne pepper
1 teaspoon garlic powder

1. In a medium-size nonreactive casserole, heat the olive oil over medium heat. Season the lamb with salt and pepper. Brown the lamb and onion together until the onion is soft and golden, 8 to 10 minutes, stirring occasionally.

2. Mix the tomato paste with the water. Add the tomato mixture, lentils, black pepper, cayenne, and garlic powder to the lamb. Stir, cover, reduce the heat to very low, and simmer until the lamb is very tender, about 2 hours. Stir occasionally. Serve.

Makes 4 servings

Brīk bi'l-Aḍam (Tunisia)

EGG-STUFFED FRIED PASTRY

In colloquial Tunisian Arabic, a brīk *(pronounced BREEK) is a deep-fried savory pastry popular as a kind of street food. In Algeria they are called* būrak *and in Morocco* brīwat, *all these words coming from the Ottoman Turkish* börek.[67] *The Turkish cookbook writer Professor Ayla Esen Algar mentions one account that attributes the invention of the* börek *to Bugra Khan (died 994), a ruler of eastern Turkistan, from where it gradually spread westward to Khorasan and finally to the Mediterranean. She says that the* börek *appeared in Turkey before the Turks.*[68] *The Turkish* börek *was readily accepted in Tunisian cuisine, although not all Turkish foods were; for example, there is very little pilaf cookery in Tunisia.*

The authentic brīk *dough, called* malsūqa *in Tunisia, is a very thin phyllo pastry-like sheet made from very fine semolina flour. In Algeria this thin dough is called* diyūl, *and* warqa *in Morocco, meaning "leaf," where it is made with sifted white flour.*

Paula Wolfert discovered long ago that Chinese wonton and egg roll wrappers work perfectly for making brīk. *You can also use commercial sheets of phyllo pastry, but the egg roll wrappers work impressively well. There are several ways to fold the dough if it is circular. Fold two sides in, slightly overlapping so you have a rectangle with convex edges. Fold the convex edges over, slightly overlapping to make a square. Place the stuffing in the middle and fold one edge over to make a triangle. Or you can roll the* brīk *up like a cigar. They are then fried in pure olive or vegetable oil until golden.*

Typically a Tunisian brīk *will be crispy brown on the outside with the egg yolk and white being runny. The Tunisians love it this way, but if you are not wild about the idea of runny eggs, use only the yolk from a small egg or use a soft-boiled egg.*

All brīk *are stuffed with an egg, but this* brīk, *called egg* brīk, *is one of the simpler preparations. In the old Barbary corsair hangout of La Goletta on the Gulf of Tunis,* brīk ḥalq al-wād *is the same except for the addition of a couple of finely chopped garlic cloves.*

Tunisians are particular about how they eat a brīk. *A real expert will start right in the middle where the runny egg is, the secret being not to allow any of the egg to fall. Others like to work from the outside in, leaving the egg until last. In any case,* brīk *are meant to be eaten with the fingers.*

6 cups pure or virgin olive, olive pomace, or vegetable oil for deep-frying
1 small onion, grated
1/4 cup finely chopped fresh parsley leaves
Salt and freshly ground black pepper to taste
8 Chinese egg roll wrappers (6 to 8 inches square)
8 small eggs (see Note)

1. Preheat the frying oil in a deep-fryer or an 8-inch saucepan fitted with a basket insert to 375°F.

2. Mix the onion and parsley in a fine-mesh strainer and plunge into boiling salted water for 2 minutes. Drain well, and season with salt and pepper.

3. Place an egg roll wrapper on a plate. Spoon a heaping tablespoon of the onion mixture in the center. Form a small well and break an egg into the center. Sprinkle some salt and pepper over the yolk and fold one corner over to the other, forming a triangle. Seal the edges by rubbing with egg white or water. (Make them one at a time.) Pick the *brīk* up with two hands by the corners, place in the hot oil, and cook until golden brown, 30 seconds to 1 minute. Don't worry if the edges aren't completely sealed, or if some of the egg white has run off, because the hot oil will quickly puff them together and all will be fine.

4. Remove from the oil with a strainer or the fitted basket insert and drain on paper towels for a minute, then serve without utensils, mopping up the egg with the fried piece of egg roll wrapper. Continue making and cooking the remaining *brīk*. Let the frying oil cool completely, strain, and save for a future use.

NOTE: Notice that you use small eggs for this recipe.

Makes 4 servings

Brīk bi'l-Tūnn (Tunisia)

EGG- AND TUNA-STUFFED FRIED PASTRY

Another very popular brīk *is made with tuna and is found throughout Tunisia. Tunisian brands of canned tuna are truly extraordinary, but I do not believe they are imported to this country. The use of Swiss Gruyère cheese in this recipe is not contrived—modern Tunisians are fond of imported cheeses such as Swiss cheese and Parmesan. See the headnote on page 110 before making the* brīk.

6 cups pure or virgin olive, olive pomace, or vegetable oil for deep-frying
1 tablespoon freshly grated Gruyère cheese
1 small onion, very finely chopped
2 tablespoons very finely chopped fresh parsley leaves
One 3½-ounce can imported tuna packed in oil, drained (you may want to save this oil for *farfalle al tonno,* page 635)
1 tablespoon capers, rinsed and chopped if large
1 teaspoon freshly ground black pepper
1 tablespoon *samna* (clarified butter; page 189) or unsalted butter, softened
8 Chinese egg roll wrappers (6 to 8 inches square)
8 small eggs (see Note)
Salt to taste

1. Preheat the frying oil in a deep-fryer or an 8-inch saucepan fitted with a basket insert to 375°F. In a small bowl, mix the cheese, onion, parsley, tuna, capers, pepper, and *samna* (or butter).

2. Place an egg roll wrapper on a plate. Spoon a heaping tablespoon of the tuna mixture in the center. Form a small well and break an egg into the center. Sprinkle some salt over the yolk and fold one corner over to the other, forming a triangle. Seal the edges by rubbing with egg white or water. (Make them one at a time.) Pick the *brīk* up with two hands by the corners, place in the hot oil, and cook until golden brown, 30 seconds to 1 minute. Don't worry if the edges aren't completely sealed, or if some of the egg white has run off, because the hot oil will quickly puff them together and all will be fine.

3. Remove from the oil with a strainer or the fitted basket insert, drain on paper towels for a minute, and serve without utensils, mopping up the egg with the fried piece of egg roll wrapper. Continue making and cooking the remaining *brīk*. Let the frying oil cool completely, strain, and save for a future use.

NOTE: Notice that you use small eggs for this recipe.

Makes 4 servings

Brīk bi'l-Mukh (Tunisia)

EGG- AND BRAIN-STUFFED FRIED PASTRY

Brain is a creamy meat with a mild taste, and in this brīk *a much milder one than that of the tuna* brīk. *Innards, or variety meats and offal, as they are some-*

times called, are popular poor people's food in the Mediterranean, but they also have unique and rich tastes, especially brain. Once when I presented a variety of brīk *to a large group of people during a series of recipe tests, this brain* brīk *was the hands-down favorite, actually surprising all of us. The Parmigiano-Reggiano cheese used in this recipe has an old heritage from the time when Tunisians imported northern Italian and Sicilian cheeses in the Middle Ages.*

1 lamb or veal brain, soaked in cold water to cover for 1 hour, changing the water 3 times, and membrane removed
Salt
2 tablespoons white wine vinegar or fresh lemon juice
6 cups pure or virgin olive, olive pomace, or vegetable oil for deep-frying
1 tablespoon freshly grated Parmigiano-Reggiano cheese
1 small onion, very finely chopped
2 tablespoons very finely chopped fresh parsley leaves
Freshly ground black pepper to taste
1 tablespoon *samna* (clarified butter; page 189) or unsalted butter, softened
8 Chinese egg roll wrappers (6 to 8 inches square)
8 small eggs (see Note)

1. Drain the brains, place in a large nonreactive saucepan, and cover with lightly salted water acidulated with the vinegar or lemon juice. Bring to a gentle boil for 20 minutes. Drain and chop into small pieces.

2. Preheat the frying oil in a deep-fryer or an 8-inch saucepan fitted with a basket insert to 375°F.

3. In a medium-size bowl, mix the chopped brain, Parmigiano-Reggiano, onion, parsley, salt and pepper, and *samna* with a fork until well blended.

4. Place an egg roll wrapper on a plate. Spoon a heaping tablespoon of the brain mixture in the center. Form a small well and break an egg into the center. Sprinkle some salt over the yolk and fold one corner over to the other, forming a triangle. Seal the edges by rubbing with egg white or water. (Make them one at a time.) Pick the *brīk* up with two hands by the corners, place in the hot oil, and cook until golden brown, 30 seconds to 1 minute. Don't worry if the edges aren't completely sealed, or if some of the egg white has run off, because the hot oil will quickly puff them together and all will be fine.

5. Remove from the oil with a strainer or the fitted basket insert, drain on paper towels for a minute, and serve without utensils, mopping up the egg with the fried piece of egg roll wrapper. Continue making and cooking the remaining *brīk*. Let the frying oil cool completely, strain, and save for a future use.

NOTE: Notice that you use small eggs for this recipe.

Makes 4 servings

✣ ✣ ✣

THIS simple Tunisian food was augmented by a more sophisticated cuisine at the upper echelons of society and during special occasions that saw preparations of couscous—today called the national dish of the Maghrib—that I will discuss in greater detail along with the recipes in Chapter 10. On special occasions families would make a variety of pastries, such as *kaʿk* and different kinds of fritters: *sifanj* (or *isfanj,* a kind of deep-fried yeasted beignet served with honey that is probably the origin of the Italian *zeppole*), *faṭīra* (page 307), *jardaq* (a wheat pastry fried in apricot oil), and *zalābiyya* (a kind of deep-fried beignet or puff pastry cake with honey and almonds). They also made *maqrūḍ,* a deep-fried semolina cake stuffed with date paste and served with honey and spices (page 498).[69]

Sifanj (Tunisia)

TUNISIAN FRITTERS

The medieval Arab zalābiyya, *a kind of deep-fried doughnut sprinkled with sugar, exists today, both with that name and many others, including* sifanj. Sifanj, *coming from the Arabic word for "sponge," is a kind of very soft yeasted doughnut made in North Africa that is allowed to rise more than usual to make it airy, and is served with honey or sugar. This* sifanj *exists in Sicily, too, where it is called* sfinci *(or* sfincia*) the word also derived from the Arabic. The thirteenth-century notary Adamo de Citella of Palermo tells us they were sold by a* sfingiarius. *This medieval doughnut was also described in the fourteenth-century Sicilian vocabulary of Angelo Senisio, who tells us that* sfingia *is a fried bread that the common people also call* crispella.[70] *In Algeria they may also be called* khafaf, *in Tunisia,* yūyū.

In Morocco they prefer to make this fritter with white flour, while in Algeria and Tunisia (and Sicily, too) they use fine semolina or white flour. The method of stirring the flour into hot liquid is Sicilian. In Tunisia, sugar and eggs are typically incorporated into the dough. They make these in Libya, too, where you are likely to find them incorporating some milk into the dough. Usually, in both the Tunisian and Sicilian versions, the dough is yeasted, but I prefer using baking powder, as in this recipe.

2 cups unbleached all-purpose flour
2 teaspoons baking powder
1 teaspoon salt
2 tablespoons granulated sugar
2 tablespoons vegetable shortening or lard
4 teaspoons grated orange zest
2 teaspoons orange flower water
Scant ⅔ cup warm water
6 cups vegetable and olive pomace oil mixed for deep-frying
Warm orange blossom honey (optional)
Confectioners' sugar (optional)
Ground roasted almond powder (optional)
Orange flower water-flavored sugar syrup (Step 3, page 498, replacing the rose water with orange flower water; optional)

1. In a medium-size bowl, mix the flour, baking powder, salt, and sugar. Stir in the vegetable shortening or lard, orange zest, orange flower water, and warm water and form into a soft dough. Knead the ball of dough until smooth, about 2 minutes, then cover with a clean dish towel and let rest for 15 minutes.

2. Preheat the frying oil in a deep-fryer or an 8-inch saucepan fitted with a basket insert to 375°F. Take an egg-size piece of dough and roll it out until ¼ inch thick. Cut a small hole in the middle, then cook until golden brown, about 90 seconds per side. Remove with a skimmer or the basket insert and drain on paper towels. Continue making fritters with remaining dough. Let the frying oil cool, strain, and save for a future use. Serve with warm honey, confectioners' sugar, ground almond powder, and orange flower water-flavored sugar syrup, perhaps flavored with vanilla, or let the cooked fritters soak in the sugar syrup until saturated.

VARIATION

Add a handful of raisins, soaked in warm water for 15 minutes then drained, to the dough before it rests. Or add 3 tablespoons of orange juice to the dough in place of 3 tablespoons of water.

Makes 10 to 12 fritters

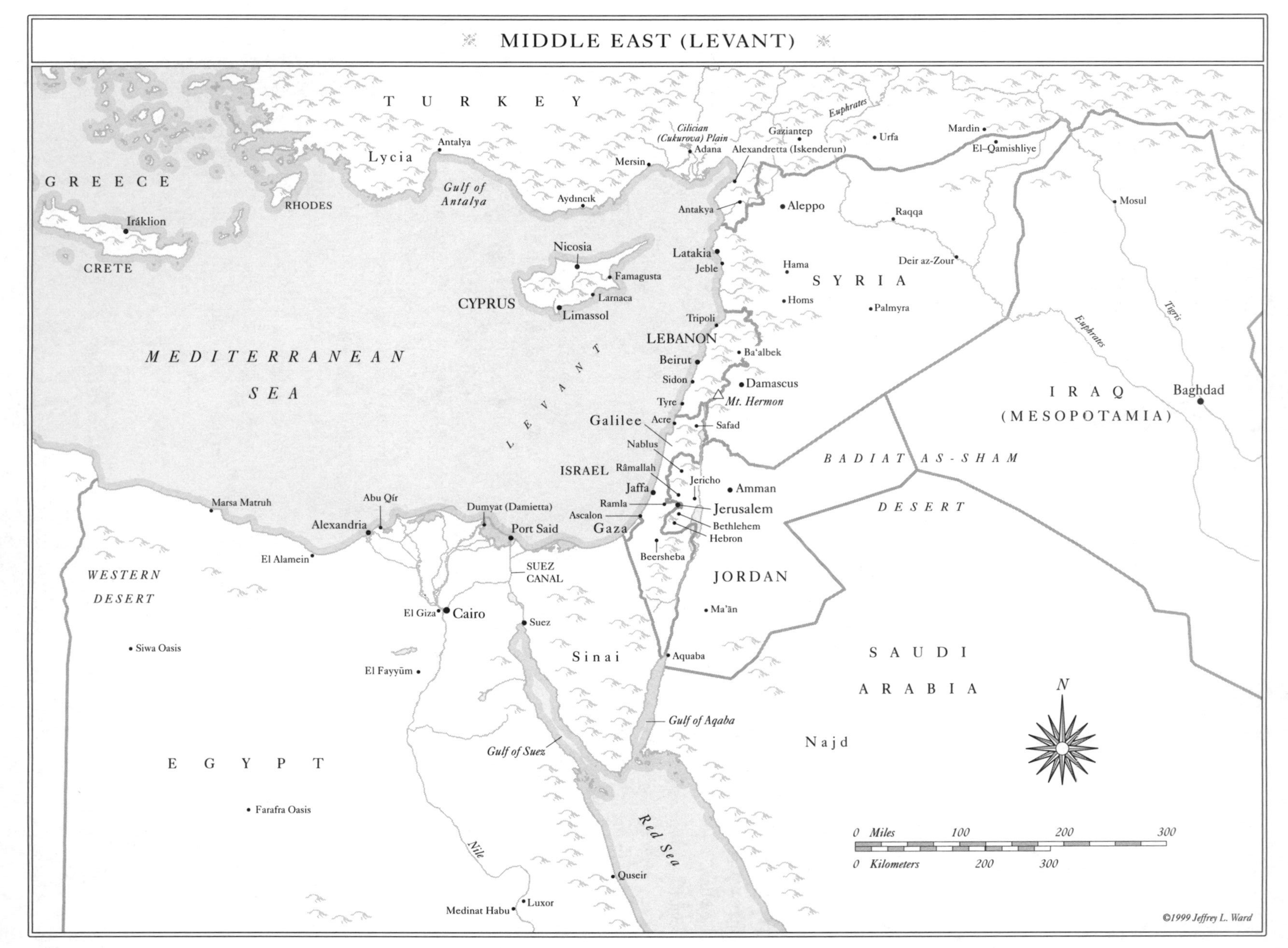
MIDDLE EAST (LEVANT)
TURKEY
GREECE
Iráklion
CRETE
RHODES
Lycia
Antalya
Gulf of Antalya
Aydıncık
Mersin
Cilician (Cukurova) Plain
Adana
Alexandretta (Iskenderun)
Gaziantep
Euphrates
Urfa
Mardin
El-Qamishliye
Mosul
Antakya
Aleppo
Raqqa
Deir az-Zour
Latakia
Jeble
Hama
SYRIA
Homs
Palmyra
Tigris
Euphrates
Nicosia
Famagusta
Larnaca
CYPRUS
Limassol
Tripoli
LEBANON
Ba'albek
MEDITERRANEAN SEA
Beirut
Sidon
Damascus
Mt. Hermon
Tyre
Acre
Safad
Galilee
LEVANT
Nablus
ISRAEL
Râmallah
Jericho
Amman
Jaffa
Ramla
Jerusalem
Ascalon
Bethlehem
Gaza
Hebron
Beersheba
IRAQ (MESOPOTAMIA)
Baghdad
BADIAT AS-SHAM DESERT
JORDAN
Ma'ān
Aquaba
Marsa Matruh
Abu Qîr
Alexandria
Dumyat (Damietta)
Port Said
El Alamein
SUEZ CANAL
WESTERN DESERT
El Giza
Cairo
Suez
Siwa Oasis
Sinai
El Fayyūm
SAUDI ARABIA
Gulf of Aqaba
N
Najd
Gulf of Suez
EGYPT
Farafra Oasis
Red Sea
Nile
Quseir
Luxor
Medinat Habu
0 Miles 100 200 300
0 Kilometers 200 300
©1999 Jeffrey L. Ward

TAKE-OUT FOOD, GREEN VEGETABLES, AND THE BUTCHER IN THE ARAB LEVANT

THE explosion of the Arabs out of the Arabian Peninsula in the seventh century saw their armies at the gates of Damascus and Jerusalem within a decade. The soldiers of these early Arab armies often settled down in the lands they conquered, bringing with them the plants and foods they loved. Although the first soldiers in the earliest armies were nomadic Bedouin, later armies comprised soldiers with experience in sedentary agriculture. It was during the early Islamic centuries that the two most famous of Arab foods, rice and sugar, saw their widespread dispersal. As much as foods were exported, there was also a healthy trade in imported foods from elsewhere that were of particular importance in the Levant, such as dried and salted fish, honey, and hazelnuts from Spain, Italy, or Russia; saffron from Tuscany; cheese from Sicily; and spices from China, India, or East Africa. The hot and arid climate of the Levant encouraged the preserving of foods, and the most important of these preserving methods was with salt and vinegar, which gave its name to a whole range of foods, called *mukhallalāt* (pickled foods).

Eating "take-out" was popular in the Levantine Middle Ages. European travelers to Cairo in the Middle Ages spoke of ten thousand cooks in the streets who sold a wide range of foods, such as the *naqāniqiyyūn,* who sold grilled sausages (see page 74); the *sharāʿiḥiyyūn,* who sold slices of meat; the *ḥalwāniyyūn,* who sold sweets; and the *bawāridiyyūn,* who made and sold cooked green vegetables preserved in vinegar. These cold dishes formed a category of foods called *bawārid* that could also include meat, fowl, and fish.[71]

Some of the more popular street-vending cooks, known as *ṭabbākhūn,* "keepers of the cook-shops," were the *harāʿisiyyūn,* who sold *harīsa,* a porridge of wheat and ground meat cooked in fat.[72] Chicken was also sold from street stalls by itinerant cooks, but it was expensive in fourteenth-century Cairo.[73] People still take out food in the Middle East, and one of the most popular street foods that can be found throughout the Levant today, with different names, is what the Arabs call *shāwurma* or *shāwirma,* a log of spiced meat that grills by turning slowly on a vertical rotisserie and is eaten wrapped in bread.

Shāwurma, Döner Kebabı, Gyro (Arab Levant, Turkey, Greece)

GYRO

The Arabs, Turks, and Greeks all make a variation on the same theme of vertical rotissing seasoned meat. The Turks call it döner kebabı, *the Greeks* gyro *(pronounced YEE-ro), and the Arabs* shāwurma. *It is said that the* döner kebabı *was born in the Anatolian town of Bursa.*

The first time I had döner kebabı *was in Istanbul in 1971, and I remember eating them every chance I had. A few weeks later I found myself in Athens, where I had the Greek version, imported to Greece in the 1920s during the Greek and Turkish frenzy of ethnic "cleansing" that saw Greek and Cretan Muslims transferred in a population exchange with Turkey's Greek population. In Greece, a* gyro *is made with slices of meat rather than ground patties. Several years later I had the Arab* shāwurma *in Amman, Jordan, made with slices of ground meat, but it was quite different from both the Greek and Turkish ones. Far to the east, the Armenians make theirs, called* karski shashlik, *found in the Armenian city of Kars in northeastern Turkey. It is marinated in lemon juice, onions, parsley, and dill.*

In Turkey, döner kebabı *are served either plain or stuffed with onions into* ekmek, *Turkish-style French bread. In Istanbul, the* döner kebabı *is a highly special-*

ized kind of street food with purists declaring certain strict rules about its preparation. Although it's quite common to see electric rotisseries, many feel the hardwood charcoal rotisseries with their vertical shelves for charcoal are the best way to cook the meat. The meat itself is varied with a combination of the best cuts—for instance, a mixture of top sirloin, loin, and shoulder. These cuts are not necessarily ground but rather pounded very thin, layered, seasoned, and skewered. Then they're pressed very tightly together from both sides. This is called yaprak döner *or leaf* döner *because the slices of meat are as thin as a leaf, and it is always served over a bed of plain rice pilaf. There are special cooks who make* yaprak döner *and can be hired for parties.*

Under the name shāwurma, *the* döner kebabı *is found in Lebanon, Syria, Jordan, and Palestine served rolled up in a thin half loaf of Arabic flatbread with onions, tomatoes, and perhaps a tahini-based sauce or, in Syria, with pickled turnip slices and* liyya, *melted lamb fat.*

Contrary to the fact that I'm providing a recipe, this preparation is never made at home in the Middle East, mostly because it is considered street food and requires special equipment. I improvised with the horizontal rotisserie attachment for my grill, which is nearly as good. This particular recipe using ground lamb is closer to the Greek-American gyro. *I also provide a Greek* tzatziki *salad for an accompaniment.*

2¾ pounds ground lamb
3 slices Italian bread with crust, toasted and crumbled
2 teaspoons freshly ground coriander seeds
1¼ teaspoons freshly ground allspice berries
2 garlic cloves, finely chopped
1 medium-size onion, finely chopped
1¼ teaspoons dried summer savory
Salt and freshly ground black pepper to taste
12 thin 2-inch squares lamb fat (best off the leg)
Extra virgin olive oil, for brushing
10 *pide* breads (page 721)
1 recipe *tzatziki* (see Note)
Sliced ripe tomatoes, for garnish

1. In a large bowl, knead together the lamb, bread, coriander, allspice, garlic, onion, savory, salt, and pepper with your hands. The mixture should be sticky and thick and very well blended.

2. Keeping your hands wet so the meat doesn't stick, make twelve balls of equal size from the meat mixture, then flatten each into a hamburger patty. Put one on top of the other, each separated by a thin square of lamb fat. When you are finished, the patty tower should be about 10 inches high. Press down. Holding the top, tip the pile onto its side. Roll gently so that the meat is a smooth cylinder. Cover with plastic wrap and refrigerate overnight.

3. Prepare a low charcoal fire or preheat a gas grill on low for 20 minutes. Push the spit through the center of the meat. Affix the spit-roasting attachment to your grill and set the spit over a drip pan to catch the fat. As the rotisserie turns, the outside will become crusty, about 30 minutes. With a slicing knife or serrated bread knife, slice off sections of crusty meat onto a platter. Let the remaining meat continue to cook, turning continuously with the electric rotisserie or very often if turning by hand.

4. Brush one side of the *pide* breads very lightly with some olive oil and warm them on or near the grill until they are soft. Lay some sliced meat in the center of the oiled sides of *pide* bread; spread 2 to 3 tablespoons of *tzatziki* and a few tomatoes on top. Roll up and serve. Continue in this manner with the remaining gyro.

NOTE: To make *tzatziki,* blend together 2 cups high-quality full-fat plain yogurt with ¼ to ½ cup extra virgin olive oil (use the lesser amount of oil if the yogurt is not thick), 1 small peeled, seeded, and grated cucumber with its water squeezed out, 3 to 5 garlic cloves mashed with ½ teaspoon salt, and 2 tablespoons finely chopped fresh dill.

Makes 6 to 8 servings

✣ ✣ ✣

SOME regions in the Levant used more olive oil than others. The Syrians in particular used lots of it.

Al-Muqqadasī (wrote c. 985–990) relates how fava beans were fried in olive oil and sold mixed with olives. The Christians of Syria prepared foods for their children with great quantities of olive oil, thought to be healthful, and called them "olive oil foods." Iraq and Egypt didn't have local access to great amounts of olive oil, so in Iraq they used sesame seed oil and in Egypt they extracted the oil from the seeds of rape, radish, and lettuce.[74]

In the eastern Mediterranean, vegetables had long been popular in Arab lands. Vegetables were always associated with sweetness in the minds of Arab cooks. We see this mentality manifest in the Arabic expression *'ard ḥulwa,* sweet earth, used to describe land suitable for the production of beautiful vegetables. Arab farmers were usually responsible for the westward diffusion of new vegetables. For example, spinach, which is thought to be native to Nepal and northwest India, slowly made its way from Persia to the Mediterranean by virtue of Arab agriculturalists.[75] The Bedouin of the Levantine deserts, however, never liked fresh green vegetables, perhaps because of their unfamiliarity with them. But among villagers and townspeople vegetables have had an uninterrupted popularity in the Arab world, as is evidenced by the simplicity of the following *ṭayyibāt,* gustatory delights. These are preparations that could very well appear on a *mazza* table today.

Salāṭat al-Khuḍra (Syria)

VEGETABLE SALAD

In the sūq al-khuḍra, *the vegetable market, even in the Middle Ages a cook could find a wide variety of fresh vegetables in cities like Aleppo, Homs, Damascus, and Jerusalem. Historically, the vegetable market was never as economically important as the spice market in Middle Eastern cities because vegetables were raised almost entirely for local consumption.*

In the Syrian town of Homs they like to make simple seasonal salads with very fresh vegetables. The ingredients do not necessarily have to be the ones I use here, although these cucumbers, tomatoes, green peppers, and white onions make for my favorite combination. Once the salad is dressed, the Homsi leave it in a bowl until it becomes soupy from all the vegetable liquids, and that's how they serve it—as a soupy salad.

2 garlic cloves, peeled
½ teaspoon salt
3 tablespoons extra virgin olive oil
2 tablespoons fresh lemon juice
1 tablespoon dried mint
2 tablespoons finely chopped fresh parsley leaves
1 green bell pepper, seeded and cut into small pieces
2 ripe tomatoes, seeded and cut into small pieces
3 small white onions, cut into small pieces
1 cucumber, peeled, seeded, and cut into small pieces

1. In a mortar, pound the garlic with the salt until pastelike. Stir the garlic into the olive oil and lemon juice. Beat in the mint and parsley.

2. Toss the bell pepper, tomatoes, onions, and cucumber together in a large bowl. Pour the dressing over the vegetables and toss again. Check the seasoning. Leave for 2 hours at room temperature before serving. Do not refrigerate.

Makes 4 servings

THE MAZZA TABLE

Nearly every Middle Eastern or Mediterranean cookbook I've ever looked at understandably describes the Middle Eastern and North African mazza *(also transliterated as* meze *or* mezze *following the Greek and Turkish; or called* qimiyya *in Algeria and* ādū *in Tunisia) as "appetizers."* Mazzāt *(plural) are little tidbits served on little plates, and they certainly bear a resemblance to appetizers or tapas. In fact, there is nothing wrong in serving them as appetizers. But, for the record, it is incorrect to speak of the Middle Eastern* mazza *table as appetizers. To think of these small dishes as appetizers is to misunderstand the Arab culinary sensibility. For the Arab, the notion of a food needed to "open the appetite" is completely foreign. The Arab simply starts eating; one is hungry and the stomach enzymes are ready to go to work. An appetizer just slows the process down, so says the Muslim, and the Prophet Muhammad is said to have been in accord with this idea. A* mazza *table can be the entire dinner, thus it is more appropriate to compare* mazza *to the Scandinavian* smörgåsbord, *to which it is more philosophically related.*

The origin of mazza *is unknown, but one food writer offered the explanation that the word comes from the Italian* mezzano, *meaning an intermediary course of foods, introduced by Genoese merchant traders in the fourteenth-century Middle East to refer to certain foods.*[76] *I have never come across this explanation in any of my readings and unfortunately the classical lexica are not much help, but there is a certain plausibility to this explanation. On the other hand, the word* mazza *derives from the root word "to suck," which also gives the word for "acidulous." An Arab writer claims that* mazza *is a colloquial expression meaning "what" in the exclamation* mazza haza *(what is this?). Other Arabs have told me that that explanation is nonsense. And might the word have any connection with the Hebrew word for unleavened foods,* maẓẓot? *I must leave this for a linguist.*

Bābā Ghannūj (Lebanon)

EGGPLANT AND TAHINI PUREE

The Arabs seem to have discovered the eggplant, called bādhinjān *in Arabic, already growing in Persia shortly after their conquest of that country in* A.D. *642, although several ancient Arabic names for the eggplant seem to come directly from Indian subcontinent names, indicating that the plant may have arrived in the Arabian peninsula in pre-Islamic times.*[77] *The Arabs have long been fond of the eggplant and medieval Arabic cookery manuscripts always have lots of recipes.*

Bābā ghannūj *and hummus (page 310) are probably the two most famous* mazzāt. Bābā ghannūj, *although untranslatable, probably refers to the noble position of the eggplant in the Arabic vegetable hierarchy, namely "father"* (bābā) *eggplant.* Ghannūj *is a word that means "cute, easy, soft, coquettish."* Bābā ghannūj *is a Lebanese dish. In Palestine the same dish, using a bit less tahini, is called* mutabbal.

As popular as bābā ghannūj *is in this country, a wonderful example of culinary borrowing, it still seems no one knows how to make it properly. The key in making* bābā ghannūj *is the right proportion of tahini to lemon juice and of the tahini-lemon juice mix to eggplant; you don't want to overpower the eggplant, as sometimes happens.*

4 medium-size eggplant (about 4 pounds)
9 tablespoons fresh lemon juice
½ cup tahini (sesame seed paste)
4 large garlic cloves, peeled
1¾ teaspoons salt

FOR THE GARNISH
Extra virgin olive oil for garnish
2 tablespoons finely chopped fresh parsley leaves
Imported black olives
Pomegranate seeds (optional)

1. Puncture the eggplant all over with a fork. Preheat a gas grill on high for 20 minutes or prepare a hot charcoal fire. Grill the eggplant whole until the skins are black and blistered, about 40 minutes, or preheat the oven to 425°F and roast for 35 to 45 minutes. (Some Arab cooks blister the eggplants over an open burner flame, but I have always found that way messy.) Carefully remove the skins and spoon out the soft pulp just as soon as you can handle the eggplant. Puree the pulp in a food processor, then squeeze or drain out some of the bitter liquid from the eggplant by letting it sit in a strainer over a bowl or the sink for an hour.

2. In a small bowl, slowly mix the lemon juice and tahini together. Pound the garlic and salt together in a mortar until it is a paste, then stir into the tahini mixture. Stir this into the eggplant puree. Taste and add water to thin; *never* thin with more lemon juice.

3. Pour the mixture into a serving platter and garnish with a drizzle of olive oil, the parsley, some black olives, and pomegranate seeds if you desire.

Makes 6 to 8 servings

Baṭarsh (Syria)

BĀBĀ GHANNŪJ IN THE STYLE OF HOMS

This type of bābā ghannūj *is made with yogurt and garlic instead of tahini paste, a style popular in Homs, Syria. Although I call for grilling the eggplant, you can also place them in an oven on a baking pan, turn the heat to 425°F, and bake until blackened, 35 to 45 minutes. Serve with Arab bread for dipping.*

3 large eggplant (about 6 pounds)
4 garlic cloves, peeled
2 teaspoons salt
2 cups high-quality full-fat plain yogurt
4 to 6 tablespoons *labna* (optional; page 186), as needed
Fresh mint leaves for garnish
Pomegranate seeds for garnish

1. Preheat a gas grill on high for 20 minutes or prepare a hot charcoal fire. Place the eggplant on the grill until blackened and the inside pulp is very soft, about 45 minutes, turning to blacken evenly. Remove the eggplant from the grill; when they are cool enough to handle, cut in half. Scrape out all the pulp and transfer to a strainer to drain the bitter juices from the pulp.

2. Transfer the eggplant to a large bowl and beat vigorously with a fork. In a mortar, pound the garlic with 1 teaspoon of the salt until pastelike. Stir the yogurt, garlic, and the remaining salt into the eggplant.

Continue beating with a fork for 1 minute. (If you use a food processor in this step, make sure you use only short bursts so the eggplant doesn't turn into a puree.) Check the seasoning and add a little *labna* if the yogurt is too thin. Transfer to a serving platter. Garnish with fresh mint leaves and pomegranate seeds.

Makes 8 servings

Sabānikh bi'l-Laḥm (Syria)

SPINACH WITH LAMB

Spinach was introduced to the Mediterranean by Arab or Persian farmers, probably in the tenth century, although the routes it took westward are not well known. We do know that the first references to spinach are in the tenth-century works of the famous doctor al-Rāzī, known as Rhazes in the West, and the agricultural treatise by the alchemist Ibn Waḥshīya. The great agronomist from Muslim Spain, Ibn al-ʿAwwām, who wrote in the twelfth century, called spinach the "prince of vegetables."[78]

In much Levantine Arab cooking a vegetable dish is not a vegetarian dish, but a dish where the vegetable is showcased and meat is used as a kind of condiment along with herbs and spices in olive oil or samna *(clarified butter). In this preparation the predominant herb is coriander. In Damascus they like to use lots of fresh coriander pounded in a mortar with garlic, while in the rest of Syria dried coriander is more typical with this spinach preparation. This recipe was given to me by Muheeba Halaby during my sojourn in Damascus.*

2 pounds fresh spinach, heavy stems removed and washed well
Leaves from 1 bunch fresh coriander (cilantro), washed well
4 garlic cloves, peeled
1 teaspoon salt
1 tablespoon *samna* (clarified butter; page 189) or unsalted butter
½ pound boneless leg of lamb or lamb shoulder, trimmed of fat and cut into ½-inch cubes
½ teaspoon *bahārāt* (page 524)
¼ teaspoon freshly ground allspice berries
Salt and freshly ground black pepper to taste

1. Place the spinach in a large saucepan with only the water adhering to it from its last rinsing. Turn the heat to high, cover, and cook until the spinach wilts, 3 to 4 minutes, turning a few times. Drain well in a strainer, squeezing excess water out with the back of a wooden spoon, until almost dry. Chop the spinach.

2. In a mortar, pound the coriander, garlic, and salt together until you have a mushy pesto. In a medium-size casserole or skillet, melt the *samna* over medium-high heat, then brown the lamb on all sides, 7 to 8 minutes, stirring.

3. Reduce the heat to very low, giving the casserole a few minutes to reach the lower temperature. Add the coriander pesto and stir constantly and vigorously for 30 seconds. Add the spinach, *bahārāt,* and allspice and season with salt and pepper. Stir gently to mix, cover, and cook until the lamb is tender, about 30 minutes.

Makes 4 servings

Sabānikh bi'l-Zayt (Arab Levant)

SPINACH WITH OLIVE OIL

Spinach is an annual plant that loves cool weather, so it was quite a feat for Arab agriculturalists of the medieval era to successfully introduce spinach to the warm Mediterranean and have it thrive. Spinach is a popular vegetable in the Arab world, and this recipe an example of the most widespread way of cooking it in Lebanon and Syria. "Italian spinach" is a smooth, or flat-leaved, variety with reddish roots, and is ideal in this preparation, although any spinach is acceptable.

20 ounces fresh Italian spinach, heavy stems removed and washed well
1 medium-size onion, peeled
Salt
½ cup extra virgin olive oil
2 garlic cloves, sliced
½ cup crushed walnuts
Lemon wedges for garnish

1. Place the spinach in a large saucepan with only the water adhering to it from its last rinsing. Turn the heat to high, cover, and cook only until the spinach wilts, 3 to 4 minutes, turning a few times. Drain well by squeezing out excess water in a strainer with the back of a wooden spoon until almost dry. Set aside.

2. Slice the onion horizontally into very thin slices, less than 1/16 inch. Arrange the onion slices on some paper towels, sprinkle with salt, and leave for 30 minutes, covered, with paper towels to absorb moisture.

3. In a large skillet, heat 6 tablespoons of the olive oil over medium-high heat. Add the onion slices and coat them with the oil. Continue turning the onion as the slices turn from white to yellow to brown, spreading them around so they overlap as little as possible. Once they are brown, 8 to 9 minutes, continue to cook until some turn dark brown, another 2 minutes. Remove the skillet from the burner and quickly transfer the onion to a paper towel-lined platter or tray to cool and drain. Once the slices are cool, they will have become crispy.

4. Let the olive oil remaining in the skillet cool a bit and add 1 tablespoon of the remaining olive oil. Turn the heat to medium-high, add the garlic, and let the cloves blacken, 2 to 3 minutes. The cloves will become bitter, but don't worry, this all works. Add the spinach and toss for 2 minutes. Transfer the spinach to a serving platter. Drizzle the remaining tablespoon olive oil over the spinach. Sprinkle the walnuts on top or the side and garnish with lemon wedges.

Makes 4 servings

Ardī Shawkī bi'l-Zayt (Arab Levant)

ARTICHOKES WITH OLIVE OIL

Contrary to the claims of many food writers, the Greco-Roman world did not know the artichoke. There is no reference in classical literature to a plant of this family with edible flesh on the bracts. The Greeks and Romans only knew the cardoon and several other members of the thistle family. The artichoke does not grow wild; it is a cultivated vegetable that apparently was developed from the cardoon by Muslim agronomists. All European languages derive their word for artichoke from the medieval Arabic word kharsūf. *Scholars don't know where the first artichoke appeared; North Africa is a good guess, but so is Syria, where there is a ninth-century reference.*[79]

This Syrian recipe was given to me by Muheeba Halaby of Damascus. When artichokes are in season the Halaby family will eat this and countless other artichoke recipes. The hearts could also be pickled, as is common with a whole range of Arab mukhallalāt *(pickled vegetables). This dish is perfect after the artichokes are cooked and still retain a hint of their warmth.*

8 medium-size to large artichokes (4 to 6 ounces each)
½ lemon and 3 tablespoons fresh lemon juice
¼ cup extra virgin olive oil
½ cup chopped onion
2 garlic cloves, sliced
2 cups water
Salt to taste

1. Trim the artichokes, removing the outer bracts, inner chokes, and fuzzy center of the heart. Rub the hearts with the cut half of a lemon to keep it from discoloring. Slice the hearts and place in a bowl of water acidulated with 1 tablespoon of the lemon juice so they don't discolor.

2. In a nonreactive skillet large enough to hold all the sliced artichoke hearts flat, heat the olive oil, then cook the onion and garlic over medium-high heat until the onion is softened, stirring frequently so the garlic doesn't burn, 3 to 4 minutes.

GETTING TO THE ARTICHOKE HEART

Mediterranean peoples are quite fond of this noble vegetable first introduced as a horticultural development of the cardoon. The artichoke appears to have entered Italy via the Norman kitchen gardens of twelfth-century Sicily, although the first reference is not until the early fourteenth century. The flesh at the bottom of the inside of the bracts (they are not properly called leaves) is edible, as is the foundation or heart of the artichoke. When you pare an artichoke, the hairy choke is removed to reach the heart.

Select artichokes that feel heavy and whose bracts are closed and just beginning to separate. If the bracts have begun spreading wider apart, the artichoke is still usable and fine. Look at the stem for small holes that might indicate worm damage and pass those by. Brown splotches are only frost damage that do not harm the artichoke. The type of artichoke you are most likely to find in the market is the globe artichoke, an Italian cultivar, in various sizes. A specialty greengrocer might carry the Tuscany violet artichokes that taper at top to beautiful purple tips. Store artichokes dry in the refrigerator in a plastic bag no longer than five days.

Preparing a raw artichoke heart is labor intensive, but, as with lobster, one is justly rewarded. It is much easier to do this if the artichoke is boiled first. If you boil the artichoke first, both the flesh at the base of the bracts and the heart are usable; unfortunately not all recipes are suited to previously cooked artichokes. Wash the artichoke and cut off the top half of the bracts with a large chef's knife. Remove the little bracts at the stem. Cut the stem off at the point near the bottom so the artichoke can stand up. Many people throw away the stem, but the flesh inside is edible, so slice off the skin and reserve the stem flesh (much easier to do if the artichoke has been boiled whole first). As you peel, slice or break off the little pale green bracts near the choke, discard them, and, with a paring knife, cut off the woody parts surrounding the bottom, slicing in a circular motion as you hold the artichoke with one hand. Now, from the top, and in a circular motion, cut out the hairy choke. Once the raw artichoke is cut, it will blacken, so you must always keep a cut half of a lemon nearby to immediately rub the artichoke heart when you reach it. As you finish each artichoke, put the heart in a bowl of water acidulated with lemon juice or vinegar to keep it from blackening and continue.

3. Add the drained artichokes, the remaining 2 tablespoons lemon juice, the water, and salt. Reduce the heat to low and simmer, uncovered, until the artichokes are tender and the water evaporated, about 1¼ hours. Serve warm or at room temperature.

Makes 4 servings

Lūbya bi'l-Zayt (Arab Levant)

GREEN BEANS WITH OLIVE OIL

The popularity of vegetables cooked soft and served at room temperature in the Middle East probably has much to do with the general heat and aridity of this area. A typical method in the Middle Ages in Arab countries was to stew the vegetables and then stir in seasoned oil, heating it lightly in a pan, and finishing it by folding in a beaten egg.[80] *This particular preparation, though, could not have been made before the introduction of the green bean from the New World. In this recipe the green beans should be cooked until there is no crunch left but not so much that they discolor and become insipid, a situation that can be avoided by blanching them first. In Turkey a similar dish is prepared and also served at room temperature.*

¾ cup extra virgin olive oil, plus more for drizzling, if you like
2 large onions, chopped
3 garlic cloves, finely chopped
2 pounds fresh green beans, ends trimmed and cut into 2-inch lengths
3 medium-size ripe tomatoes (about 1¼ pounds), peeled, seeded, and chopped
½ cup water
2½ teaspoons salt
¾ teaspoon freshly ground black pepper

1. In a large skillet or casserole, heat the olive oil over medium-high heat, then cook the onions until they are light brown, about 15 minutes, stirring often. Add the garlic and cook 1 minute longer, stirring.

2. Reduce the heat to medium. Add the green beans, tomatoes, water, salt, and pepper, cover, and cook until the green beans are soft, about 1 hour, but keep checking since young green beans will take less time and some older beans can take longer. Add more water if it is evaporating and salt and pepper if that is your taste. When the beans are done there should be very little water left.

3. Remove from the heat and transfer to a serving platter, allowing the beans to come to room temperature. Drizzle with more olive oil if you wish.

Makes 6 servings

ʿAdas bi'l-Ḥāmiḍ (Syria)

LENTILS WITH LEMON

The appearance of pomegranate molasses in the cooked vegetable dishes of Syria usually indicates that the dish is influenced by an Aleppine cook. Syria has long been famous for its pomegranates and Aleppo for its cuisine. The great Umayyad dynasty in Syria in the eighth century was noted for its agricultural achievements as much as its military ones. A branch of the Umayyad dynasty was found in Spain, too. The Spanish Umayyad caliph ʿAbd-ar-Raḥmān I (756–788), perhaps the greatest Arab general who ever lived, defeating in turn his Abbasid enemies in Iraq as well as Charlemagne, sent one of his agents to Syria to bring back an exquisite new pomegranate called the safarī, *which he planted in the garden park surrounding his palace of al-Ruṣāfa outside of Córdoba.*[81]

The combination of pomegranate, garlic, and fresh coriander is a Syrian favorite in this recipe given to me by Nadia Koudmani, a Palestinian living in Damascus. It is one of my favorite lentil recipes, yet no one in Syria could tell me why it is called "with lemon" rather than "with chard," with "garlic and coriander," or "with pomegranate," the other important flavors in the dish.

The garlic should be mashed in a mortar with a pestle—the food processor will not work. Some people find this to be a very garlicky recipe, but it is an authentic recipe and I happen to like it this way, though you can feel free to cut the garlic in half if you must.

1½ cups dried green or brown lentils, picked over and rinsed
¼ cup extra virgin olive oil, plus extra for drizzling
5 large Swiss chard leaves, washed well, stems removed, and sliced into thin strips crosswise
2 tablespoons mashed garlic (about 8 large garlic cloves)
¾ cup finely chopped fresh coriander (cilantro; leaves from 1 to 2 bunches)
1 cup water
1 tablespoon fresh lemon juice
2 tablespoons pomegranate molasses (page 722)

1. Bring a pot of lightly salted water to a boil and cook the lentils until tender, 20 to 45 minutes; check often because the cooking time varies depending on the age of the lentils. Drain and set aside.

2. In a medium-size nonreactive skillet, heat 1 tablespoon of the olive oil over medium-high heat, then cook the Swiss chard until it wilts, 1 to 2 minutes. Remove and drain off any liquid. Set aside.

3. In the same skillet, heat the remaining 3 tablespoons olive oil over medium-high heat. Add the garlic and coriander and cook until sizzling, 1 to 2 minutes, stirring constantly. Reduce the heat to medium, add the Swiss chard, drained lentils, and water, and cook for 10 minutes, stirring frequently. Add the lemon juice and pomegranate molasses and continue cooking until the lentils look mushy, about another 10 minutes. Transfer to a serving bowl and drizzle a small amount of olive oil over it before serving.

Makes 6 servings

Faṣūliya (Arab Levant)
WHITE BEANS IN TOMATOES

Faṣūliya, *the common white bean* (Phaseolus vulgaris *L.) that originated in the New World, is now found throughout the Mediterranean. In this recipe the beans are cooked with tomato juice, the whole preparation being flavored with onion and fresh coriander, morsels of lamb, salt, pepper, and mixed spices. This preparation is ideal served at room temperature or lukewarm. If you use ripe tomatoes instead of the canned ones, they must be very ripe and juicy, enough so you can extract one cup of liquid from them.*

1 cup dried white beans (such as Great Northern), picked over and rinsed
2 tablespoons extra virgin olive oil
¼ pound boneless leg of lamb or lamb shoulder, trimmed of fat and diced
1 medium-size onion, finely chopped
3 tablespoons finely chopped fresh coriander (cilantro) leaves
2 garlic cloves, finely chopped
2 canned plum tomatoes, chopped
1 cup tomato liquid from the tomato can
1 cup water
¾ teaspoon *bahārāt* (page 524)
Salt and freshly ground black pepper to taste

1. Place the beans in a large saucepan, cover with 3 inches of cold water, bring to a boil, and cook until

A plate of white beans by Giovanna Garzoni (1600–1670). Galleria Palatina, Palazzo Pitti, Florence. SCALA/ART RESOURCE.

nearly tender, 45 minutes to 1 hour. Drain and set aside.

2. In a medium-size nonreactive skillet, heat the olive oil over medium-high heat, then brown the lamb, 2 to 3 minutes, stirring. Add the onion, scraping the bottom of the skillet to get up any browned bits. Stir for 2 minutes. Add the coriander and garlic and continue stirring for 30 seconds. Add the beans, tomatoes, tomato juice, water, *bahārāt* and season with salt and pepper. Bring to a boil, then reduce the heat to very low, cover, and simmer until the lamb is very tender, about 1½ hours. Serve warm.

Makes 4 servings

THE contacts between the Arab Levant and the Christian Mediterranean increased not only because of the Crusades but also because of mercantile interests. The Arabs introduced culinary concepts based on lots of vegetables and legumes, but in both the Arab Levant and the West, cereal crops began to recede by the mid-fourteenth century, mostly owing to the effects of the Black Death. The massive scale of death in both the Muslim and Christian Mediterranean led to the expansion of a sylvan-pastoral economy because of the reversion of farmland to pasture.

This phenomenon manifested itself in two ways: the appearance of more meat on the peasant's table and the rising political importance of the butcher. The meat may have been dry-salted for preservation, but it was still meat. This was particularly true in the hills, mountains, and upper plains, where the diet had consisted almost entirely of vegetables because of the lack of area devoted to stock rearing and hunting.[82]

The importance of meat is reflected in the relative political importance of the butcher. In Jerusalem of the sixteenth century, members of the butcher's guild filled the *ḥisba* office, one of the oldest institutions of the Islamic state, responsible for promoting good and forbidding evil as prescribed in the Koran.[83] The *muḥtasib,* the head of the *ḥisba* office, inspected market activities and collected taxes, such as the "butcher's seal tax" guaranteeing the quality of meat. Jerusalem at this time was under Ottoman rule, and the supply of meat to the towns was an important facet of economic activity. Since butchers knew their meat, they often filled these positions as witnessed by their frequent mention in *sijill* records (Ottoman court documents).[84] The butcher was also an important and highly politicized profession in fourteenth-century Provence. The covered markets of Provence were filled with small butcher stalls where they plied their trade over the counters of their *taula,* an Old Provençal word for "table."[85]

QAWRAMA

Qawrama *is the name of a preserved lamb fat—*duhniyāt*—a kind of fat or grease used for cooking in Lebanese and Syrian dishes, and the name of a dish of mutton or beef cut into small pieces and braised with lots of onions and tomatoes. The preserved lamb is made by cooking fatty mutton or lamb's tail (usually), but also shoulder meat, with abundant salt and then pouring the browned meat and its fat into preserving jars. The sheep favored by Arab cooks are the fat-tailed species (*Ovis aries L. platura*), with tails that are very wide and up to two feet long, mostly all fat, that were introduced to the Levant by the Turks.*[86] *Another domesticated species from Arabia (*Ovis aries L. dolichura*) was described by Herodotus as having their long, fat, heavy tails carried by little carts.*[87] *After the preparation is made, a layer of fat solidifies on top. The cook scoops out spoonfuls of it to use in various dishes, including vegetable cookery. None of the Arab recipes in this book uses* qawrama, *but should you feel like giving it a try, grind together equal amounts of lamb fat and lamb shoulder and neck meat. Place this in a stew pot or saucepan and simmer over medium-low heat, adding abundant salt (1½ teaspoons per pound of meat mixture) and a mixture of black pepper and* bahārāt *(page 524), about 1 tablespoon spice mix per pound of mixed meat. Simmer for six hours, and then pour off the fat into a container with some of the meat. Freeze for up to six months and use for the cooking fat in meat recipes.*

❖ *Yakhnat al-Lūbya* (Arab Levant)

GREEN BEAN AND LAMB STEW

In 1560, a great meat market existed in Jerusalem. The highest quality sheep—mutton and lamb being the two most popular meats—were called turkumānī, *referring to the Turcoman tribes who drove their sheep from northeastern Syria and Anatolia to the Palestinian markets. The other kind of sheep available was* balqāwī, *referring to the area east of the Jordan River where Bedouin drove their sheep to the Jerusalem market. The most popular cuts of meat were the* majrūm *(fillet) and the* liyya, *the fat, taillike lower part of the sheep's back which has no bones and is the fat equivalent to fillet.*[88]

In Arab stew cookery, meat is often used as a condiment, a flavoring agent, and is not necessarily the centerpiece of a stew. Take, for example, this long-simmering stew whose Arabic name is simply "green bean stew." It is flavored with a small amount of lamb and spices and can be accompanied by rice (page 602) or made with fava beans for a dish called yakhna bi'l-fūl.

2 pounds fresh green beans, ends trimmed and cut into 2-inch lengths
½ cup *samna* (clarified butter; page 189) or unsalted butter
¾ pound boneless leg of lamb or lamb shoulder, trimmed of fat and cut into ½-inch cubes
2 medium-size onions, chopped
3 ripe plum tomatoes, peeled, seeded, and chopped, with their juices
1 cup water
½ teaspoon ground cinnamon
½ teaspoon *bahārāt* (page 524)
½ teaspoon freshly ground allspice berries
¼ teaspoon freshly grated nutmeg
Salt and freshly ground black pepper to taste
3 garlic cloves, peeled
1 teaspoon salt

1. Bring a large pot of water to a furious boil and blanch the green beans for 3 to 4 minutes. Drain and place the green beans in ice cold water to stop their cooking. Drain from the ice water and set aside.

2. In a large nonreactive casserole or skillet, melt the *samna* over medium-high heat. Brown the lamb on all sides, about 8 minutes, stirring. Add the onions and cook until they turn yellow, about 6 minutes, stirring a few times.

3. Add the green beans and cook for 2 minutes, then add the tomatoes with their juices, the water, cinnamon, *bahārāt,* allspice, and nutmeg. Season with salt and pepper and bring to a boil while stirring. Reduce the heat to low, cover, and simmer until the lamb and green beans are tender, about 2 to 3 hours. Check occasionally for doneness.

4. In a mortar, mash the garlic together with the salt. When ready to serve, stir in the garlic and serve.

Makes 6 servings

❖ *Yakhnat al-Bāmiya* (Lebanon)

OKRA STEW

This is a Lebanese dish, but also popular in Egypt. Okra (Abelmoschus esculentus *[L.] Moench, syn.* Hibiscus esculentus) *is a mucilaginous vegetable in the Malvaceae family, as is cotton. Both Ethiopia and West Africa have been proposed as its place of origin and its date of arrival in the Mediterranean is not known. The cytotaxonomy of okra is so confused that it is possible the plant has an Asian origin.*[89]

Lebanese and Palestinian cooks favor the baby okra, small and tender, about the size of the last joint on your little finger. Unfortunately, the okra sold in American markets is mature, therefore you should cook it 10 minutes more than called for in this recipe. The meatless version of this stew, called bāmiya, *is made with okra, tomatoes, onions, lots of garlic, and lemon juice. In Damascus they would also add lots of fresh coriander, while in Homs and Aleppo the okra would be cooked with copious quantities of garlic, pomegranate molasses, and tomato juice. Serve with rice pilaf and* khubz ᶜarabī *(Arab flatbread or pita bread).*

1 pound fresh young okra
½ cup *samna* (clarified butter; page 189), vegetable shortening, extra virgin olive oil, or corn oil
4 garlic cloves, peeled
1 teaspoon salt
1 teaspoon freshly ground coriander seeds
1 pound boneless lamb shoulder, trimmed of fat and cut into 1- to 2-inch pieces
1 medium-size onion, halved
½ teaspoon freshly ground black pepper
2 tablespoons tomato paste
1 cup water
1 cup tomato liquid (squeezed from ripe tomatoes, not canned tomato juice)
¼ cup fresh lemon juice

1 Trim the stems from the okra, rinse with water, and pat dry with paper towels. In a large nonreactive casserole, heat the *samna* or oil over medium heat until very hot and slightly smoking. Cook the okra until light brown all around, about 6 minutes. Remove with a slotted spoon, drain well, and set aside. In a mortar, crush the garlic with the salt and coriander and pound until it is a paste.

2. In the casserole, brown the lamb on all sides over medium heat, about 5 minutes, turning often. Add the onion halves, garlic mixture, pepper, and more salt if necessary. Cook, stirring, for 2 minutes. Blend the tomato paste with the water and pour over the meat with the tomato liquid. Stir, cover, reduce the heat to low, and simmer for 1 hour.

3. Add the okra and lemon juice, stir once, taste to see if you would like more lemon juice, then cover, and cook until the lamb is tender and the okra heated through, about 10 more minutes, and serve.

Makes 4 servings

Shaqriyya (Syria)

LAMB STEW

This lamb stew from Syria is colored yellow by the use of saffron, and the name of the dish, shaqriyya, *means "the blond [dish]." In the medieval Muslim Mediterranean, as in the Christian Mediterranean, foods were imbued with magical properties. The influence of the alchemists was also felt in the gastronomic world. Alchemy was a quasi-scientific spiritual endeavor and the most important color in this search was the color of gold, namely yellow. Colors had symbolic connections, and yellow was thought to be beneficial or the source of gaiety. Endoring—the coloring of foods, especially the color yellow—was an important part of food preparation, and for that reason saffron, safflower, and turmeric were important spices. Saffron was the rarest, as rare as gold, and the most powerful in its coloring potential.*

The yogurt needs to be stabilized in this preparation, otherwise it will separate while cooking. Serve with rice and Arab bread.

½ teaspoon saffron threads, lightly toasted and gently pounded in a mortar with ½ teaspoon salt
1 quart stabilized yogurt (page 186)

3 tablespoons *samna* (clarified butter; page 189) or unsalted butter
1¼ pounds onions, coarsely chopped
1¼ pounds boneless leg of lamb, trimmed of fat and cut into 1-inch cubes
1½ tablespoons *bahārāt* (page 524)
1 teaspoon dried mint
Salt to taste
3 cups water

1. Stir the saffron and salt into the stabilized yogurt until blended. Leave to steep while you continue the preparation, stirring every once in a while. The more finely you have ground the saffron, the yellower the yogurt will become.

2. In a large casserole, heat the *samna* over medium-high heat, then cook the onions until softened, about 5 minutes, stirring frequently. Add the lamb and cook until it's no longer raw looking, 1 to 2 minutes. Add the *bahārāt* and mint, season with salt, and cook for 1 minute, stirring. Cover the meat with the water, bring to a boil, reduce the heat to medium-low, and cook until the water is evaporated and the meat thick with sauce, about 1¼ hours, stirring occasionally.

3. Pour the yogurt over the meat, stir, reduce the heat to low, cover and simmer until the meat is tender, about 1 hour.

Makes 4 servings

Laban Ummu (Arab Levant)

LAMB IN YOGURT

"His mother's yogurt" is the name of this dish, presumably implying that the meat of the young lamb is cooked in its mother's milk.[90] *This is an old, and popular, preparation among Palestinian Muslims, whereas it was forbidden to Palestinian Jews (Exodus 23:19). There is no religious significance to the fact that Muslims cook lamb or kid in this way; rather, some believe it is rooted in a long-forgotten Canaanite sacrificial custom.*

The cut to be used in this preparation is called mawzāt *in Syria, not to be confused with the similiarly named veal knuckle stew of Egypt. The* mawzāt *is a special cut of lamb, derived from the Arabic word for "banana": it is the banana-shaped meat that runs the length of the shin and is very succulent and tender when stewed for a long time.*

In the sixteenth century butchers played an important role in the economy of Jerusalem (see page 126), but were looked down upon by the populace because they were usually covered with blood and other unpleasant things. The good cook, on the other hand, was quietly exalted, especially when she made a dish as delicious as laban ummu.[91]

1 pound boneless lamb shank, cut lengthwise following the bone or into large chunks
1 quart water
2 teaspoons salt
½ pound small white or white or red pearl onions (page 720), halved
1 quart stabilized yogurt (page 186)
2 tablespoons *samna* (clarified butter; page 189) or unsalted butter
2 garlic cloves, finely chopped
2 teaspoons dried mint

1. Place the lamb in a medium-size pot or casserole and cover with the water. Sprinkle with 1 teaspoon of the salt and add 2 of the white onions, quartered or half a handful of the pearl onions. Bring to a boil, reduce the heat to low, and cook until the lamb is very tender, about 3 hours.

2. Place the stabilized yogurt in a casserole or stew pot large enough to hold the lamb and onions.

3. Boil the remaining onions separately in a large saucepan with water to cover until soft, about 20 minutes. Remove and drain, then stir into the yogurt.

4. Remove the lamb from the pot with a slotted ladle and transfer to the yogurt. Place over medium heat and keep warm, just below a boil, stirring a few times.

5. In a small skillet, melt the *samna*, add the garlic, mint, and remaining teaspoon salt, and cook for 30 seconds to 1 minute over medium heat. Add to the yogurt and cook until heated through, about 20 minutes, stirring occasionally.

Makes 4 servings

Nukhaʿat Maqliyya (Lebanon)

BATTER-FRIED VEAL OR LAMB BRAINS

In Lebanon this preparation for brains is very popular and usually served as part of a mazza *table (page 118). In the Middle Ages, though, especially in northwestern Arabia, eating sheep's brains was not advised because it was thought that it caused loss of memory and would make you stupid, since sheep are stupid animals. Today, connoisseurs know that the mild taste of veal brains and their soft texture make a truly heavenly morsel when batter-dipped and fried to an attractive golden color.*

1 pound veal or lamb brains, any membrane removed
1 tablespoon white wine vinegar
Salt to taste
6 cups pure or virgin olive, olive pomace, or vegetable oil for deep-frying
1 large egg
¾ cup milk
¾ cup all-purpose flour
Lettuce leaves for garnish (optional)
Lemon wedges

1. Soak the brains in cold water for 1 hour, changing the water three times. Bring a medium-size pot of water acidulated with the vinegar to just below a boil. Poach the brains until firm, 15 to 20 minutes. Drain, cut into bite-size pieces, and season with salt.

2. Preheat the frying oil in a deep-fryer or an 8-inch saucepan fitted with a basket insert to 375°F. Make the batter by beating the egg in a medium-size bowl with the milk and flour.

3. Dip the brains into the batter, letting excess batter drip off, and deep-fry in the hot oil until golden, about 3½ minutes. Remove from the oil with a slotted spoon, drain for a moment, and serve immediately on a bed of lettuce leaves, if desired, with lemon wedges. Let the frying oil cool completely, strain, and save for a future use.

Makes 2 to 4 mazza *servings*

Kafta bi'l-Ṣīniyya (Arab Levant)

BAKED MEATLOAF IN A PAN

Kafta *is more than an Arab meatball or meatloaf. It is meat traditionally pounded into a paste in a large marble mortar and mixed with spices before being cooked in a variety of ways. In this preparation the pounded meat is spread in a baking tray, although in the past it would have been cooked in a* ṣīniyya, *a round copper or brass tray set on a stool and used as a table. I became familiar with this recipe by way of my former wife's family who are from Palestine and also call it* kafta. *In Damascus they might call this dish* kiyyfta.

The meat should be ground until smooth and pasty, and a food processor takes care of this task well. Some Arab cooks use mashed potatoes or fried potatoes in place of the sliced baked potatoes in this recipe. Or they will replace the sliced tomatoes with tomato puree or juice. The version with mashed potatoes is quite nice, and if you wish to make it that way, see page 62 for the mashed potatoes.

1 pound ground lamb
3 tablespoons finely chopped onion
1½ tablespoons dried bread crumbs
2 tablespoons finely chopped fresh parsley leaves
¼ teaspoon freshly ground cumin seeds
¼ teaspoon freshly ground allspice berries
Salt to taste
2 tablespoons unsalted butter, thinly sliced
1 small potato, peeled, sliced ⅓ inch thick, and parboiled for 12 minutes, or 1 to 2 cups mashed potatoes
½ cup cooked peas
1 large ripe tomato, sliced, or 1 cup tomato puree or juice
2 tablespoons fresh lemon juice

1. Mix the lamb, onion, bread crumbs, parsley, cumin, allspice, and salt, kneading well with wet hands to avoid sticking. Put the meat mixture in a food processor and process, in batches if necessary, until the meat is creamy smooth, very well blended, and pasty.

2. Preheat the oven to 350°F. Grease a round 9-inch baking pan and press the meat in to cover the bottom. Dot the top with the butter slices and bake for 15 minutes.

3. Lay the potatoes and peas over the meat, and the tomato over everything (or pour over the puree or juice). Drizzle over the lemon juice and return to the oven until the meat feels firm to the touch and its juices run clear, about another hour. Cut into squares or pie slices and serve. If you like, you can spoon some of the accumulated juice and fat over each piece, otherwise discard the excess fat.

Makes 4 servings

RICH AND POOR AND EGGS AND CRUMBS IN SPAIN

THE extreme divide between the rich and poor was captured in *Don Quixote* when Sancho Panza's grandmother said that there were two families in the world, the haves and the have-nots *(el tener y el no tener)*.[92] What distinguished the poor and the rich was not social position but the food they ate: *Al rico llamen honrado porque tiene que comer* (The rich ate gargantuan meals and the rest starved). When the poor *hidalgo* did find food, he sneaked it into his pockets at the court, or when the *pícaro* snatched fruit from a market stall, it was, as reported in *Don Quixote*, a time when "hunger holds no sway."[93] But those days were very rare indeed.

The obsession with food in the sixteenth-century Spain of Philip II was all encompassing. The Spanish picaresque novel, which had its origin about this time when Cervantes wrote, is actually, in the words of one scholar, "an endless preoccupation with food."[94] For weeks people subsisted only on crumbs, barely surviving, always on the edge of starvation. Everyone schemed to get a square meal. Sometimes an orgy of eating would occur, maybe because of a hijacked food convoy for the Imperial troops, all to be quickly forgotten when the pangs of hunger returned. "Hunger's the best sauce in the world, and as the poor have no lack of it, they enjoy their food," Sancho Panza's mother, Teresa, told him.[95] Only by service in the church, the court, army, or shipboard was any kind of regular eating possible. Needless to say, there was a rapid growth in religious orders, as food proved a greater god for the starving.[96]

Painters of Spain's golden age captured the poverty of the table with their stark leitmotifs of hunger. Juan Sánchez Cotán's *Still Life with Quince, Cabbage, Melon and Cucumber*, painted about 1600, is a spare minimalist still life that could pass as a contemporary

An old woman cooks eggs in a *cazuela* set over a brazier. Diego Rodríguez de Silva y Velázquez (1599–1660), painted in 1618.
NATIONAL GALLERY OF SCOTLAND, EDINBURGH/BRIDGEMAN ART LIBRARY, LONDON/NEW YORK.

painting. A quince and cabbage are suspended in midair with strings while a cut melon and cucumber lay on a window ledge. This is all there is to the painting: food as objects to be desired, not actually eaten. Velázquez's melancholy *Old Woman Cooking Eggs*, painted in 1618, is just what it says, a painting of eggs, food that the poor could hope for.

Eggs were a popular food, not only because they were cheap if you owned the hen but also because the supply was dependent on a sure source. As long as the hen was fed, one had eggs.

Caldo del Cielo (Valencia)

HEAVEN'S BROTH

The quantity of eggs (huevos) *used in traditional regional Iberian cooking is truly notable. The* huevera, *or egg dealer, was a common sight in the markets of Valencia in the Middle Ages. The name of this preparation gives some indication of the popularity of eggs.*

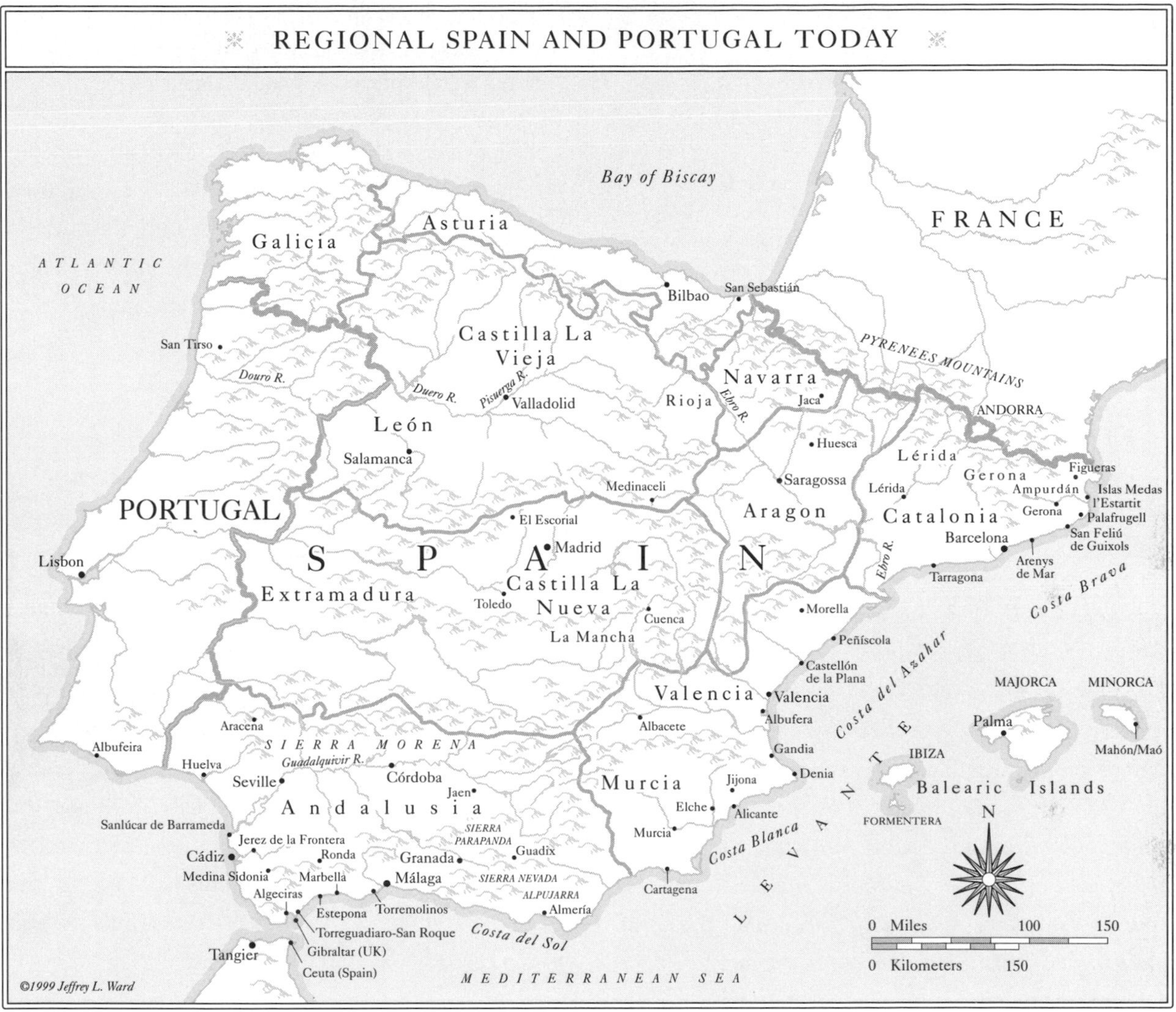

3 tablespoons extra virgin olive oil
1 medium-size onion, cut into eighths and layers separated or very coarsely chopped
2 cups water
¾ pound potatoes (about 1 potato), peeled and diced
¼ pound salt cod, soaked (page 436) and drained
2 sun-dried tomatoes, chopped
1 dried red bell pepper *(ñora)*, chopped
Salt and freshly ground black pepper to taste
1 tablespoon paprika
4 large eggs

1. In an earthenware (preferably) or enameled cast-iron casserole, heat the olive oil over medium heat. Add the onion and 1 cup of the water and cook until soft, about 15 minutes.

2. Add the potatoes, salt cod, dried tomatoes and dried bell pepper, and the remaining cup water. Season with salt and pepper and add the paprika. Stir well and cook until the potatoes can be pierced relatively easy with a skewer, about 30 minutes.

3. Crack the eggs into the casserole and shake the pan so they settle a bit. Cook for 10 minutes, shaking

the pan once in a while so the eggs continue to settle and the whites set. Serve from the casserole as soon as the whites are set.

Makes 4 to 6 servings

Huevos Escalfados (Valencia)

POACHED EGGS VALENCIA STYLE

Egg cookery in Valencia, and for that matter all of Spain, is highly advanced and is considered a measure of culinary skill. A derogatory remark is to say that someone "doesn't even know how to fry an egg." In Alicia Rios and Lourdes March's book The Heritage of Spanish Cooking, *they tell us that eggs can be fried with or without* puntilla *(crispy edges) or* abuñuelados *(encased in puffed-out skin).*[97]

This rich-tasting preparation consists of poached eggs surrounded by poached fish that is covered with a luscious tomato sauce made with fish broth. You must poach a lot of eggs all at once, so make sure you have the eggs lined up ready to go in the method that I use below. Cultivated mussels, often the only mussels available these days, don't really need to be purged, but I continue to do so out of habit.

12 mussels, soaked in water for 1 hour with 1 teaspoon of baking soda, debearded, and washed well
1 tablespoon extra virgin olive oil
10 tablespoon water
½ pound hake or cod fillet
1 small onion, finely chopped
1 garlic clove, finely chopped
Salt and freshly ground black pepper to taste
½ cup (1 stick) unsalted butter
2 tablespoons all-purpose flour
2 tablespoons tomato puree
1 large egg yolk, at room temperature
8 large eggs, at room temperature
1 red bell pepper, seeded and chopped

1. Put the mussels in a small saucepan with the olive oil and 2 tablespoons of the water. Cover, turn the heat to medium-high, and steam until the mussels open, about 5 minutes. Remove the mussels from their shells and set aside. Discard any mussels that remain tightly shut.

2. Put the hake, mussels, onion, garlic, and remaining ½ cup water in a medium-size saucepan and season with salt and pepper. Turn the heat to medium-high and once tiny bubbles start appearing, cook for 4 minutes. Remove the fish and onion with a slotted spoon and reserve the fish broth.

3. Meanwhile, melt 2 tablespoons of the butter in a small saucepan and stir in the flour to make a very light brown roux over medium to medium-high heat. Reduce the heat to low, season with salt and pepper, and slowly whisk in the reserved fish broth and the tomato puree. Cook for 10 minutes, stirring frequently. Over the next 6 minutes, whisk in the remaining butter 1 tablespoon at a time. Finally whisk in the egg yolk. Keep the sauce warm.

4. Have all the eggs lined up and ready to be poached. Fill a large saucepan with water and bring to a gentle boil. Stir the water with a wooden spoon in one direction to start a fast whirlpool. Carefully break the eggs into the swirling water one at a time, in rapid succession, sliding them into the swirling water rather than letting them plop. Keep the water swirling gently. Poach the eggs for about 3 minutes and remove with a skimmer or slotted spoon. Drain the eggs for several seconds or drain in a lightly greased flat colander. Transfer to a lightly greased and warm serving platter. Surround the eggs with the fish, cover with the sauce, and garnish with the chopped bell pepper. Serve immediately.

Makes 4 to 8 servings

Revuelto de Espárragos con Gambas (Valencia)

SCRAMBLED EGGS WITH ASPARAGUS AND SHRIMP

I first ate this dish at the Voramar restaurant in Peñíscola in the Castellón province of Valencia. This peninsula (hence the name of the town) is marked with a castle built by the Templars in the fourteenth century that was the last refuge of the early fifteenth-century antipope Benedict XIII. Benedict was a learned man and remained here until 1422 without ever resolving the schism created with Rome.

This dish is best made with previously cooked asparagus and shrimp. The asparagus should be as soft as those that are canned, which you could certainly use although fresh will taste better.

1 quart chicken broth (page 54)
½ pound thin asparagus, bottoms trimmed
½ pound large shrimp, shelled and deveined if necessary
¼ cup (½ stick) unsalted butter
8 large eggs, beaten

1. Bring the chicken broth to a gentle boil in a medium-size nonreactive saucepan and poach the asparagus until very soft. Drain and cut into 1-inch lengths.

2. Bring a pot of salted water to a furious boil, cook the shrimp for 2 minutes, then drain. Cut each shrimp in half.

3. Melt the butter in a large skillet over medium heat. Add the shrimp and asparagus and cook only until heated through, 1 to 2 minutes. Pour in the eggs and scramble them until they are set but still loose. Serve.

Makes 4 servings

Tortilla al Estile de Granada (Andalusia)

FRITTATA GRANADA STYLE

I know of only three Mediterranean cuisines that serve omelettes as a kind of tidbit: in Spain as a tapa, in Italy as an antipasto, and in Tunisia as an ādū *(another word for* mazza*). This family of Mediterranean omelette dishes served as a kind of* smörgåsbord *is represented by a great number of recipes. The* tortilla *of Spain, the frittata of Italy, and the* maʿqūda *of Tunisia are all served in a similar manner. This* tortilla *from Granada is often served at room temperature as a tapa. If you are not terribly fond of peas, reduce the amount called for by half. For a completely Americanized garnish one can give each square of* tortilla *a drop of Tabasco sauce. The* tortilla *should be consumed the day it is made; I don't care for the consistency if they have been defrosted.*

One ¾-pound boneless veal roast, rolled and tied
¼ cup pork lard or fat
½ cup cooked or frozen peas
3 green bell peppers, seeded and very finely chopped
1 teaspoon salt
6 large eggs
2 tablespoons extra virgin olive oil

1. Preheat the oven to 350°F. Coat the veal with 2 tablespoons of the pork fat or lard, place in a roasting pan, and roast until done, about 1¼ hours, adding a few tablespoons of water to the pan now and then. Let the roast rest for 20 minutes before chopping it. Mix with the peas and bell peppers along with 2 tablespoons of the juice from the roasting pan.

2. In a large skillet or omelette pan, melt the remaining 2 tablespoons pork fat or lard and lightly cook the chopped veal, peas, and peppers with the

salt over medium-low heat until the peppers are soft, about 30 minutes, stirring occasionally.

3. Beat the eggs together with the olive oil and pour into the pan. Cook until the mixture sets, about 3 minutes. Flip and continue cooking for another 3 minutes, or place under a broiler until the top sets. Transfer to a serving platter. Cool and then cut into squares and serve.

Makes 6 tapas servings

Tortilla Murciana (Murcia)

MURCIAN-STYLE FRITTATA

This tortilla *displays the rich vegetable bounty of the* huertas*—vegetable farms—of Murcia. In Spain,* tortilla*, a kind of omelette, is usually served cut into wedges as a tapa.*

1/4 pound eggplant, peeled and diced
Salt
6 tablespoons extra virgin olive oil
1 small onion, finely chopped
1 green bell pepper, seeded and finely chopped
1 small zucchini, peeled, seeded, and diced
1 large ripe tomato, peeled, seeded, and chopped
1/4 pound cooked ham, diced
Freshly ground black pepper to taste
8 large eggs, lightly beaten

1. Spread the diced eggplant over some paper towels and sprinkle with salt. Leave it to drain of its bitter juices for 30 minutes or longer, then pat dry with paper towels.

2. In a large nonreactive skillet or omelette pan, heat the olive oil over high heat, then cook the onion and green pepper until they turn color, about 3 minutes, stirring. Add the eggplant and zucchini and cook until they soften and turn color, about another 5 minutes, stirring a few times. Reduce the heat to medium, add the tomato and ham, season with salt and pepper, and cook until the sauce is denser, about 4 minutes, stirring a few times.

3. Lightly salt and pepper the eggs and pour over the vegetables, shaking the pan to distribute them. Cook until they set and brown ever so slightly, about 4 minutes per side and carefully flip using a wide spatula and tilting the pan as you do, cook for a minute and then transfer to a round platter. Serve at room temperature or warm.

NOTE: You can also cook one side over the burner and the top under a broiler if you feel you are not adept at flipping omelettes.

Makes 4 to 6 servings

SCHOLARS of the Iberian Peninsula have gleaned an idea of what the common people ate by examining the account books of hospitals and monasteries. The account books of the monastery of San Pedro in Toledo for 1455–1458 and 1485–1498, for example, are a rich source of information on the diets of the poor and of the brothers. The brothers ate much better. When and if the poor ate meat at the monastery, it was always boiled tough meat, while the friars enjoyed veal and partridges and chickens stuffed with eggs, saffron, cinnamon, and sugar. The brothers at the San Pedro monastery ate a wide variety of fruit although it was absent from the rations of the poor.[98]

Food historians looking at the Mediterranean diet of the mid-sixteenth century have no shortage of documents to study. But these documents, often with list-

TAPAS

Tapas are tiny plates of food served in bars all over Spain to accompany drinks. The word tapa *means "lid." It was thought that the plate acted like a lid on top of the mug or glass (to keep out dirt, dust, and insects) in bars that originally offered food, probably to attract customers. Anna MacMiadhacháin, in her* Spanish Regional Cookery, *speculates that they are a legacy of the Arab presence in Spain, when, she says, the serving of alcohol was forbidden except with food.*[99] *Although tapas might have roots in the Arab era, they are today not philosophically related to the similar seeming* mazza *or* meze *(page 118) of the eastern Mediterranean. Tapas, unlike* mazza *or* meze, *are not meant to replace dinner.*

Eating tapas is part of the tapeo, *the tradition of stimulating the appetite with friends while trysting and drinking an aperitif. The art of the* tapeo, *Alicia Rio, a Spanish food writer, tells us, "is like a baroque, sybaritic game, as it pleases the five senses by means of multifarious smells, friendly pats on the back, the sight and beauty of the streets. It induces states of inspiration and delight, it gives rise to witty banter on trivial topics and the interchange of snippets of juicy gossip."*[100]

Tapas can be grouped into three main categories, according to how easy they are to eat: cosas de picar, pinchos, *and* cazuelas. Cosas de picar *(meaning "things to nibble") basically refers to finger food, the most famous being the olive—the quintessential Spanish and, in fact, Mediterranean finger food. If a utensil (like* banderillas, *decorated toothpicks that get their name because they look like the darts used in a bullfight) is required to eat the food, the tapa is called* pinchos. Cazuelas *(little dishes) are tapas that usually come in sauce—for example,* albóndigas *(meatballs),* *page 141**, or shrimp fried in garlic.*[101]

ings of menus, are suspect when it comes to the general population, as they pertain most often to the lives of the privileged. As Braudel said, they are particularly suspect because they are "always and without exception *officially* good." The authorities to whom official documents were sent seemed to require the description of abundant food no matter the actual situation.

A man with a regular ration of soup, *vaca salada* (salted meat), *bizcocho* (hardtack), wine, and vinegar was a man doing well, but this was not usually the case, as reflected in the stories told by travelers. One person in sixteenth-century Spain suggested that travelers bring their own food as there were no inns offering room and board, as there were in France and Italy. He recommended bringing bread, eggs, and oil, although sometimes one might meet hunters who would sell freshly killed partridges and rabbits at a reasonable price. The few inns, called *ventas* in Andalusia, that did exist were pitiful and filthy. An Italian traveling in Spain around 1600 described knights-errant (mercenary adventurers) eating bread

Monks eating in the refectory. Il Sodoma (Giovanni Antonio Bazzi, 1477–1549). *Story of Saint Benedict*, detail. Abbey, Monteoliveto Maggiore, Italy.

ALINARI/ART RESOURCE.

baked in the earth with onions and roots.[102] Those of modest means had a slice of kid or lamb, while the rich had two kinds of meat, and the poor ate vegetables, mostly artichokes, beans, and onions, but also some cheese and olives. In Catalonia, vegetables meant a plate of cauliflower. Today, as the next recipe demonstrates, cauliflower is simply prepared, but possesses an elemental feeling of home cooking.

Col-i-flor (Catalonia)

CATALAN-STYLE CAULIFLOWER

Catalan farmers of the Middle Ages, as elsewhere in the Mediterranean, were fond of all the Cruciferae, vegetables from the mustard family. A single species, Brassica oleracea, *has yielded all the cole crops, which include cauliflower, broccoli, cabbage, kale, Brussels sprouts, and kohlrabi. The genetic variability of* Brassica *allowed the farmer, over time, to cluster the flower off the stem of a cabbage, condensing it tightly enough to give him cauliflower, hence the meaning of the word ("stem flower"). Cultivators tie the outer leaves of the plant around the developing head to keep it white instead of letting it develop its natural but unattractive brownish splotches. Many Catalan cooks might agree with Mark Twain, who said, "cauliflower is nothing but cabbage with a college education."*

This recipe came by way of Montse Contreras, a Catalan cook, who tells me that most Catalan home cooking is bland, with very little black pepper used. This is usually served as a first course, followed by meat such as vedella lligada *(page 49). The recipe can be made with the addition of other vegetables, too. For some reason the taste is perfect even though everything is so simple. It must remind a Catalan of his or her mother's cooking as much as mashed potatoes remind us of ours.*

1 pound boiling potatoes, peeled
10 ounces cauliflower florets (from about 1 small head)
Salt to taste
3 tablespoons extra virgin olive oil
2 teaspoons white wine vinegar

1. Cut the potatoes into the same small size as the cauliflower florets. Place both in a large saucepan and cover with 2 inches of lightly salted cold water. Bring to a boil and cook until both are easily pierced with a skewer, about 20 minutes. Drain and transfer to a serving platter.

2. Mix the olive oil, vinegar, and salt to taste, pour over the cauliflower and potatoes, and mix, breaking them up a bit as you do. Serve immediately.

Makes 4 servings

In seventeenth-century Spain, especially in Andalusia, the Muslim influence was still felt. Culinary specialties were unmistakable in their Arab inspiration, and dining customs remained Muslim in many ways—for example, men ate on chairs and women and children squatted at their sides. After the Reconquest, royal Spanish prohibitions forbade women to wear the veil or even to be semi-veiled, but women continued to wear them and they also continued in the odd, and thoroughly unexplained, custom of eating glazed pottery.[103] But the food supply was unrelentingly precarious, no matter whether the rulers were Christians or Muslims, and the famous Spanish meatball, the *albóndigas*, was an old solution to a perennial problem, stretching meat when so little was available.

THE FOOD OF ANDALUSIA

Andalusian food, as with Spanish food in general, is salty. Perhaps the Spaniards have taken too seriously the epigram of their seventh-century encyclopaedist Isidore of Seville (c. 560–636): Nihil enim utilius sale et sole *(Nothing is more useful than salt and sun).*[104]

A great deal of what we know about the historical roots of Andalusian cuisine is found in the works of the historian Professor É. Levi-Provençal, who used Arabic ḥisba *literature to study the early Hispano-Muslim cuisine of the ninth to twelfth centuries.*[105] *Arabic poetry of the time also gives us some information. In the* Kitāb faḍālat al-khiwān fī ṭayyibāt al-ṭᶜam wa'l-alwān, *a late eleventh-century cookery work by Ibn Razīn al-Tujībī, there are recipes for oven-baked bread,* migas de cabeza de ternero *(pieces of calf's head),* sopas de leveadura *(yeast soup),* rosquillas rellenas de miel *(honey-stuffed sweet fritters),* bocaditos del cadi *(the qadi's [magistrate] tidbits),*[106] alcorzas rellas *(stuffed sugar icing),* mantecadas *(a kind of cake),* almojabanas *(cake made of cheese and flour, a kind of cruller),* alcuzcuz *(couscous),* fideos *(a pasta),* guiso de carne de animales salvajes *(a dish of wild game),* gallina asada *(roast chicken),* tortillas de berenjenas *(eggplant omelette), and* guiso de lentejas *(dish of lentils).*

Another commentator on Spanish gastronomy, Professor Solé Sabarís has divided Andalusia into four culinary zones. The zone of meat and game is the Sierra Morena, the tip of the Iberica chain. The zone of wine and olives is in the Subbéticas chain. The zone of cereals, sugar, and oranges is in the Bética depression of the Guadalquivir valley. The zone of fish is between the third and fourth depressions of the Guadalquivir valley.

Although Andalusia is an arid land, the people are gay, enjoying life with a devil-may-care attitude, whereas the northerners are sedate and businesslike. Andalusian cuisine is not a cerebral and complex food, as it often is in the Basque country or in Catalonia; rather, food is prepared in Andalusia with the same abandon and simplicity with which people live their lives.

The three most important native ingredients in Andalusia are olive oil, garlic, and wine. The most widely used herbs are thyme, rosemary, fennel, oregano, bay leaf, plenty of parsley, and, in areas where there was a significant Muslim presence, mint. Politically, Andalusia comprises eight administrative provinces, each with its own distinctive character, fitting into the four culinary zones. The culinary identity of each is dictated by geography, of course, but mostly by the degree to which Muslim cooks were in charge of the historic kitchen. Folklorists say that many Andalusian dishes traveled north to France when Eugenie married Napoleon III in the nineteenth century.

The Andalusian kitchen owes a lot not only to the Arabs and geography but also to the weather and the lack of firewood. Homes did not have indoor ovens because it was too hot and most cook-

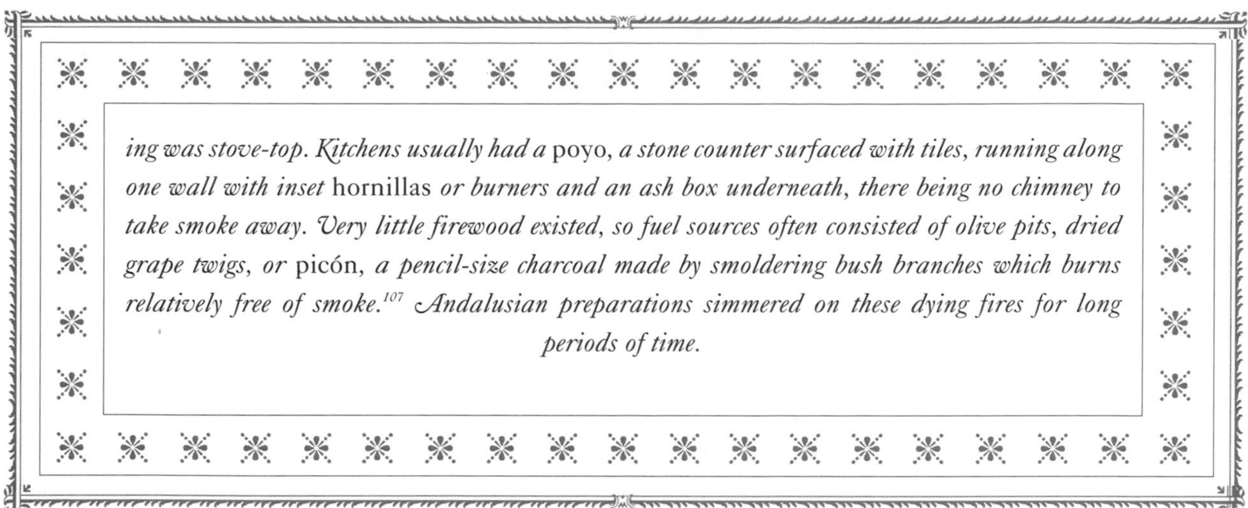

ing was stove-top. Kitchens usually had a poyo, *a stone counter surfaced with tiles, running along one wall with inset* hornillas *or burners and an ash box underneath, there being no chimney to take smoke away. Very little firewood existed, so fuel sources often consisted of olive pits, dried grape twigs, or* picón, *a pencil-size charcoal made by smoldering bush branches which burns relatively free of smoke.*[107] *Andalusian preparations simmered on these dying fires for long periods of time.*

Albóndigas a la Andaluza (Andalusia)

ANDALUSIAN-STYLE CHICKEN, BEEF, AND HAM MEATBALLS

Albóndigas, *the Spanish word for "meatball," derives from the Arabic* al-bunduq, *"hazelnut," meant to evoke their form and size.*[108] *The making of* albóndigas *dates at least back to Islamic Spain, for there are several recipes in the anonymous thirteenth-century Hispano-Muslim cookery book* Kitāb al-ṭabīkh fī Maghrib wa'l-Āndalus.[109] *In fact, the method of frying and then poaching in this recipe, or poaching and then roasting, as found in other recipes in this book, I believe is an Arab culinary influence because we find it employed not only in medieval Arabic texts but also in today's kitchen.*

The delicious combination of ground beef, chicken, and ham, with its uncanny resemblance to veal, is a recipe from the Sierra Parapanda region in Granada. It is spiced with saffron and pimiento and covered with a rich broth, and goes very well with French fries (page 61).

1¼ to 1½ pounds bone-in chicken breasts
One ¾-pound cooked ham slice, with center bone in
2 cups water
2 tablespoons extra virgin olive oil
½ pound ground beef
1 cup fresh or dried bread crumbs
2 garlic cloves, very finely chopped
2 tablespoons finely chopped fresh parsley leaves
¼ cup finely chopped roasted red bell pepper (pimiento)
Pinch of saffron threads, crumbled
2 large eggs, lightly beaten
¾ teaspoon salt
Juice from ½ lemon
6 cups pure or virgin olive, olive pomace, or vegetable oil for deep-frying
All-purpose flour for dredging
1 large egg yolk

1. Bone the chicken breasts and set the bones aside. Discard any fat or skin. In a food processor, chop the chicken breasts with several short pulses. Remove to a medium-size bowl. There should be about ½ pound of breast meat.

2. Cut the ham slice in half. One half should have most of the fat and the other half should have the bone. Grind the half without the bone in a food

These chimneys in Venice about 1500 are evidence of indoor kitchens able to exhaust smoke and odors. Vittore Carpaccio. *Miracle of the Relic of the Holy Cross*, detail. Accademia, Venice. ALINARI/ART RESOURCE.

processor. Remove to the bowl with the chicken. There should be about ½ pound of ham.

3. Place the chicken bones and ham bone in a medium-size casserole or saucepan with the water and olive oil. Reduce the heat to low and simmer for 45 minutes to extract the flavor.

4. Combine the ground beef, bread crumbs, garlic, parsley, roasted pepper, saffron, beaten eggs, salt, and lemon juice with the chicken and ham. Knead the mixture well and form into meatballs with your hands, kept wet with cold water so the mixture doesn't stick. Make 18 meatballs, or, if you have the patience, as many hazelnut-size ones as you can.

5. Preheat the frying oil in a deep-fryer or an 8-inch saucepan fitted with a basket insert to 375°F. Dredge the meatballs in the flour, patting off any excess, and deep-fry in the hot oil until golden, about 2½ minutes (much less if hazelnut-size). Remove from the oil with a slotted spoon, drain on paper towels, and keep warm.

6. Remove and discard the chicken and ham bones from the broth, strain, and return the broth to the casserole or saucepan. Place the meatballs in the broth and poach over low heat until cooked through, about 45 minutes.

7. Remove the meatballs from the casserole and transfer to a serving platter. Whisk the egg yolk into the broth and heat for 1 to 2 minutes, then pour over the meatballs and serve. Let the frying oil cool completely, strain, and save for a future use.

Makes 4 servings

Cabrito en Ajo Caballín (Andalusia)

KID WITH RED BELL PEPPER AND GARLIC SAUCE

The ridiculous Don Quixote, who ate trout with his helmet's visor down, which, of course, is an impossible way to eat, said that the trout was better than beef, and that kid was better than goat's meat. And kid is today still a popular meat from the Sierra Nevada in Granada to Murcia.

A beautiful accompaniment that will balance the richness of this dish is calabacines rellenos al estilo de Andalucía *(page 292). If goat is not available, use lamb, but not before trying Caribbean or Latin American markets in neighborhoods where one is likely to find goat.*

1 cup extra virgin olive oil
1 cup very finely chopped kid or lamb's liver
4½ pounds kid or lamb on the bone, cut into walnut-size pieces from the shoulder or leg
2 tablespoons paprika
½ teaspoon cayenne pepper
1 to 2 roasted red bell peppers (pimientos)
½ teaspoon dried oregano
3 garlic cloves, peeled
¼ pound French or Italian bread, crusts removed and soaked in 3 tablespoons white wine vinegar
½ cup water

1. In a small skillet, heat 1 tablespoon of the olive oil over medium-high heat, then cook the chopped kid liver until it loses its raw color and is cooked through, about 4 minutes, stirring. Set aside.

2. In a large skillet, heat ½ cup of the olive oil over medium heat. Reduce the heat to medium-low and cook the kid pieces until well browned on all sides, stirring occasionally, about 45 minutes.

3. Meanwhile, prepare a paste by pounding the paprika, cayenne, roasted peppers, oregano, garlic, the bread soaked in the vinegar, and the kid liver together in a large mortar. Pound well and then moisten with the water. If you use a food processor, pulse in short bursts.

4. Blend the remaining 7 tablespoons olive oil well with the red pepper paste. Stir into the skillet with the kid, cover, and continue cooking over medium-low heat until the meat is tender, about 30 minutes. Just before serving bring to a boil and then serve.

Makes 6 servings

Cebollas en Cazuela (Andalusia)

CARAMELIZED ONION CASSEROLE

This slow-cooked caramelized onion dish from Jaen is known as a hortalizas *dish, a dish whose vegetables come from the* huertas, *the large irrigated gardens of southern Spain established by the Arabs during the Muslim era. The existence of the* huertas *has not been continuous from that era, though. The Christian Reconquest saw the* huertas *become either pasturage for sheep or devoted to grains and pulses and not the crops introduced by the Arabs. One would like to believe that this delightful and simple recipe does have a continuous history—but it probably doesn't, although the presence of cinnamon certainly is a vestige of the medieval Hispano-Muslim love of that spice.*

4 medium-size onions
3 tablespoons extra virgin olive oil
3 teaspoons sugar
Salt and freshly ground black pepper to taste
¼ teaspoon ground cinnamon

1. Cut off both ends of the onions, peel, and place in a small covered casserole or enameled cast-iron saucepan. Pour the olive oil over the onions and coat them on all sides. Sprinkle the onions evenly with the sugar, salt, pepper, and cinnamon.

2. Turn the heat to low and cook, covered, until the onions are easily pierced to their center with a skewer, 1½ to 2 hours (keep checking and turn them once in a while). Serve.

Makes 4 servings

Callos con Garbanzos, Jamón y Chorizo (Andalusia)

CHICKPEAS AND TRIPE STEW

This long-cooking, hearty tripe stew from Granada is typical farmhouse fare. Tripe is usually sold cleaned, but it still needs to be soaked and boiled for a long time to make it tender. For a modern American family, I would suggest making this recipe on a cold winter weekend, soaking the tripe Saturday night, cooking it Sunday, and serving the stew Sunday night. It's incredibly satisfying.

2½ pounds veal or lamb tripe
Salt to taste
½ cup extra virgin olive oil
2 large onions, finely chopped
2 garlic cloves, finely chopped
¼ pound cooked ham, chopped
5 ripe tomatoes (about 1¾ pounds), peeled, seeded, and chopped
¼ pound Spanish chorizo sausage (see Notes on pages 66 and 712) or Polish kielbasa, thinly sliced
1 cup chicken broth (see page 54)
½ cup dry white wine
2 cups cooked chickpeas, drained
Freshly ground black pepper to taste

1. Soak the tripe in cold water to cover overnight in the refrigerator.

2. Drain and rinse the tripe under cold running water. Cut the tripe into pieces. Place the tripe in a large pot covered by several inches of water with some salt and bring to a boil. Reduce the heat to medium-high and boil until tender but a little chewy, 3 to 7 hours, replenishing the water and salt when necessary. After 3 hours, cut off and taste a small corner to see if it is cooked to the texture you like. Drain or continue cooking.

3. In a large nonreactive casserole, heat ¼ cup of the olive oil over medium-high heat, then cook the tripe until fragrant, 3 to 4 minutes, stirring. Remove the tripe with a slotted spoon and set aside. Add the remaining ¼ cup olive oil to the casserole along with the onions, garlic, and ham and cook until the onions are brown and soft, about 8 minutes, stirring occasionally. Add the tomatoes and cook until the mixture is denser, 6 to 8 minutes.

4. Add the chorizo or kielbasa sausage and stir, then add the tripe and stir to mix. Cook for 1 minute, then stir in the chicken broth and wine. Reduce the heat to low, stir in the chickpeas, season with salt and pepper, cover, and simmer until the sausages are tender and cooked through, about 30 minutes. Serve from the casserole.

Makes 4 to 6 servings

❖ *Garbanzos con Chorizo* (Andalusia)

CHICKPEAS WITH CHORIZO SAUSAGE

The chickpea has been cultivated in the Mediterranean since the third and fourth millennia B.C. *and in Spain since very early times. It is an Old World plant introduced to the New World by Spanish explorers. In this one-pot peasant meal, a satisfying dish nicely spiced for a midwinter dinner and typical Andalusian comfort food, the chorizo sausage is used almost as a condiment. The origin of chorizo is not known, but it is traced to the thirteenth century.*

The Mexican chorizo sausages common in this country are too highly spiced and hot for this dish. If you have a Portuguese community nearby, you may be able to find Portuguese chouriço, *which is closer to the Spanish sausage. Other possibilities are a cooked Italian sweet sausage, chicken sausage, or Polish kielbasa or you can try the recipe on page 71, adding 2 tablespoons paprika to that mixture.*

2 cups dried chickpeas (about 1 pound), picked over, soaked in cold water to cover overnight, and drained, or 4 cups cooked chickpeas, drained
Salt to taste
½ cup extra virgin olive oil
1 medium-size onion, chopped
2 green bell peppers, seeded and cut into strips
2 ripe tomatoes (about 1 pound), peeled, seeded, and chopped
Pinch of saffron threads, crumbled
1 tablespoon paprika
10 ounces cooked Spanish chorizo or Polish kielbasa sausage, sliced
1 cup chicken broth (page 54)

1. Drain the chickpeas, place them with some salt in a pot, and cover with water by 5 inches. Boil until the chickpeas are tender, about 3 hours, adding boiling water when necessary to keep them covered all of the time. Drain. This step is not necessary if you are using cooked chickpeas.

2. In a large nonreactive casserole, heat the olive oil over medium heat, then cook the onion until translucent, 8 to 10 minutes. Add the bell peppers and tomatoes and cook for another 20 minutes, stirring often. Stir in the saffron and paprika and cook, stirring, for 2 minutes. Stir in the chorizo and cook until they are heated, about 5 minutes, then add the chickpeas. Stir in the chicken broth and cook until the sausage is tender, about 15 minutes. Serve from the casserole.

Makes 4 servings

❖ *Garbanzos a la Andaluza* (Andalusia)

ANDALUSIAN-STYLE CHICKPEAS

Garbanzos, *the Spanish word for chickpeas, is a popular legume in Andalusia. The chickpea is native to the eastern Mediterranean, but it had long ago arrived in Spain. In the sixteenth century, chickpeas were the staple diet for the adventurers and soldiers manning the Spanish presidios along the Barbary Coast.*

This recipe is not as old as those soldiers, but I imagine that outside of the green bell pepper they may have eaten something like this. In the province of Granada in Andalusia cooks make this dish in a variety of ways, sometimes adding sweet potatoes or perhaps rice.

1½ quarts water
2 cups dried chickpeas (about 1 pound), picked over, soaked in cold water to cover overnight, and drained
1 medium-size onion, quartered and layers separated
½ pound Canadian or Irish bacon, cut into large dice
1 cup dry white wine
1 bay leaf
Salt to taste
1 tablespoon extra virgin olive oil
1 green bell pepper, seeded and sliced

1. Bring the water to a boil in a large saucepan, add the drained chickpeas, reduce the heat to low, cover partially, and cook for 1 hour. The water should always just cover the chickpeas.

2. Add the onion, bacon, wine, and bay leaf and season with salt. Cover partially and simmer until the chickpeas are soft, another 2 to 3 hours, replenishing with boiling water so the chickpeas are always covered. If they are old you will need to cook them longer.

3. In a medium-size skillet, heat the olive oil over medium-high heat, then cook the sliced rounds of green pepper until soft, stirring frequently, about 20 minutes. When the chickpeas are done, transfer to individual serving bowls or a serving platter, cover with the sautéed green pepper, and serve hot.

Makes 6 servings

Conejo Almogavar (Andalusia)
COMMANDO-STYLE BRAISED RABBIT WITH TOMATO AND CHOCOLATE SAUCE

The almogavar *were commandos trained to carry out raids into enemy territory on the Iberian Peninsula. These soldiers were an important part of armies in the Middle Ages.[110] Whether or not this recipe actually derives from one devised by a mess cook of the Middle Ages is not clear. Probably not, because, first of all, chocolate and tomatoes were discovered with the New World and, second, even in later centuries, both are unlikely to have been available to a field cook. In any case, this seemingly unusual recipe is quite good.*

1 rabbit (about 4 pounds), cut into 4 pieces
Salt and freshly ground black pepper to taste
3 garlic cloves, peeled
6 blanched whole almonds, toasted (page 709)
¼ cup finely chopped fresh parsley leaves
½ teaspoon freshly ground white pepper
1 ounce semisweet chocolate
1 small hard roll (preferably a dried hard wheat biscuit)
1 cup dry white wine
½ cup rabbit or chicken broth (page 54)
2 tablespoons pork lard
1 medium-size onion, chopped
1 cup crushed canned or fresh tomatoes

1. Remove and save the rabbit liver. Season the rabbit with salt and pepper.

2. Put the garlic, almonds, parsley, white pepper, chocolate, hard roll, and rabbit liver in a food processor. Run it in short bursts for about 1 minute and then run continuously while you slowly pour in the wine and chicken broth.

3. In a large nonreactive casserole, melt the lard over medium-high heat, then brown the rabbit pieces on all sides with the onion until the rabbit is golden, about 10 minutes. Reduce the heat to medium-low, add the tomatoes, and cook until the tomato sauce is thick, about 45 minutes, covered.

4. Pour the contents of the food processor over the rabbit and continue cooking until the rabbit is fork-tender, about another 2 hours. Check the rab-

bit to see if it is cooked and add up to 1 cup water if the sauce is drying out. Check the seasoning and serve.

Makes 4 servings

Conejo en Pobre (Andalusia)

"POOR FOLK'S" PEPPERED RABBIT STEW

In the Mediterranean, a rabbit on the table means a hunted wild rabbit. The name of this dish must be purposely ironic because any "poor folk's" stew from the Mediterranean would hardly be flavored with expensive cinnamon, black pepper, and olive oil. There are many such culinary jokes in the cocina córdobesa. *The name refers to the simplicity of the ingredients, not their relative cost.*

The popularity of this rabbit dish is also evidenced in Provence, where lapin à la pebrado, *peppered rabbit, is known to be served with* la sausso au paure ome, *"poor man's sauce." In Andalusia, "*pebre,*" the sauce, is made of garlic, black pepper, parsley, and vinegar and used with various meats.*

1 rabbit (about 4 pounds), cut into serving pieces
$\frac{1}{4}$ cup extra virgin olive oil
2 tablespoons finely chopped fresh parsley leaves
3 garlic cloves, finely chopped
1 to 3 teaspoons freshly crushed black peppercorns, to your taste
2 cups boiling water
$\frac{1}{2}$ teaspoon ground cinnamon
Salt to taste
1 lemon, thinly sliced

1. Brush a cast-iron griddle or skillet and the rabbit pieces with 1 tablespoon of the olive oil. You must have the griddle very hot, so turn the heat to medium-high and once the film of oil is smoking and the griddle or skillet is hot, after about 20 minutes of pre-heating, griddle the rabbit until golden on both sides, 6 to 7 minutes.

2. Transfer the rabbit to a large nonreactive casserole. Sprinkle with the remaining 3 tablespoons olive oil, the parsley, garlic, and black pepper. Toss well, turn the heat to low, and simmer until flavorful, about 30 minutes. Pour in the boiling water, sprinkle with the cinnamon and salt, and cover with the lemon slices. Bring to a boil, reduce the heat to medium-low, and cook until the rabbit is tender and most of the liquid has evaporated, $1\frac{1}{4}$ to $1\frac{3}{4}$ hours.

Makes 4 servings

* * *

ALL of Spain was poor, even after enormous amounts of precious metals began arriving in Seville from the New World in the early sixteenth century. This wealth didn't enter the Spanish economy because it was mortgaged to Genoese bankers, who held the purse strings of Spain during the reigns of Philip II and Philip III. The most precious commodity the Spanish were buying was food, especially grain. The *huertas* were not producing the quantity of vegetables they once had because, being originally Muslim creations, the frenzy of the Reconquest expunged everything Muslim, including many foods perceived as Muslim. The poor ate their chickpeas and turnips, and their cabbage soup, but the rich always had access to more, and the banquets of court life could be memorable.

The banquets of the rich in Spain were as elegant as those in Venice. Francisco Martínez Mo<n>tiño, master chef to King Philip III (1578–1621), in the early seventeenth century served a magnificent Christmas banquet that included a first course of ham, *olla podrida* (page 541), roast turkey from the New World with its gravy, little veal puff pastry pies, roast pigeons and bacon, bird tartlettes over whipped cream soup, roast partridges with lemon sauce, *capirotada* (a batter of herbs and eggs) with pork loin, sausages and partridges, roast suckling pig with cheese, sugar and cinnamon soup, leavened puff pastry with pork lard, and roast chickens. The second course consisted of roast capons, thin, hard-baked cake with quince sauce, chicken with stuffed escarole, roast veal with arugula sauce, seedcake of veal sweetbread and livers of small animals, roast thrush over *sopa dorada* (a highly colored soup), quince pastries, eggs beaten with sugar, hare empanadas, fried trout with bacon fat, and puff pastry tart. For a third course, banqueters were served chicken stuffed with bacon-fried bread, roast veal udder, minced bird meat with lard, roast stuffed goat, green citron tarts, turkey empanadas, sea bream stew, rabbit with capers, pig's feet empanadas, ring dove with black sauce, *manjar blanco* (a dish made of chicken mixed with sugar and milk), rice fritters, and "smothered" or "drowned" *(ahogados)* pigeons.[111]

This last-mentioned cooking technique of foods *ahogados* points to the cross-cultural culinary influences of Spain and Italy probably going as far back as Islamic Spain, perhaps earlier. The vestige of this culinary technique is evident today, as demonstrated in the next three recipes, the first from the Veneto, the second from Sicily, which spent centuries under the rule of the Spanish Bourbons, and the third from Valencia.

Verze Sofegae (Veneto)

"SUFFOCATED" CABBAGE

Sofegao *is Venetian for* soffocato, *the Italian word for "suffocate," the method of cooking food very slowly in a covered pan with very little water so the vegetables "sweat." This method of cooking also appears in Majorca, as evidenced in a document written in the eighteenth century by an Augustine monk, Jaume Martí i Oliver, where a dish is* aufegat, *"drowned," or cooked in very little liquid. But a contrary view is offered by the Italian culinary authority Massimo Alberini, who claims that the method here is of Austrian heritage.*[112] *I don't find his reasoning compelling and suspect we must look south for the origins of this culinary concept—namely to the evidence of the Venetian Jews who also make this dish, but with goose fat and olive oil and effect a sweet-and-sour taste with sugar and vinegar, or to Sicily and Sardinia.*[113] *In a sense the principle behind the method is identical to a Moroccan vegetable* ṭājin *(page 533) or the French* etouffée, *also meaning "smothered," both of which rely on the sweating of vegetables.*

1/4 pound pork lard
1 sprig fresh rosemary
1 garlic clove, finely chopped
1 head Savoy cabbage (about 1 1/4 pounds), outer leaves removed, cored, and sliced into thin strips
Salt to taste
1 cup dry white wine

1. In a large nonreactive casserole, melt the lard over medium heat, then add the rosemary and garlic and cook for 30 seconds, stirring. Add the cabbage and salt, reduce the heat to very low, and cook, covered, until wilted and a little crunchy, about 1 hour, stirring occasionally.

2. Pour in the wine, cover, and cook until the cabbage is soft, about another hour. Remove to a serving bowl with a slotted spoon and serve.

Makes 4 servings

❈ *Broccoli Affogato* (Sicily)

"DROWNED" BROCCOLI

The concept of "drowning" food—the meaning of the word affogato*—is usually thought to be a Sicilian method, but variations of this dish are found throughout Italy. The original method may have been imported from Spain. The difference between "drowning" and "suffocating" is slight, but in the former more liquid is used. Pino Correnti, a leading Sicilian culinary authority from Catania, suggests that it be made with the inflorescence of the broccoli, the unfolding flower buds. In Sardinia they make it with tomato sauce and it's called* sufugadu*, meaning "suffocated." The color and presentation of the dish will be improved if you blanch the broccoli first, although it is not necessary for taste.*

½ cup extra virgin olive oil
2 medium-size white onions, thinly sliced
6 tablespoons finely chopped fresh parsley leaves
2 pounds broccoli (about 5 stalks), trimmed, stems thinly sliced lengthwise, broken into small florets, preferably blanched for 4 minutes, and plunged into ice water
10 salted anchovy fillets, rinsed and chopped
4 ounces *caciocavallo, pecorino pepato,* or imported provolone cheese, cut into tiny dice
2 ounces imported black olives (12 to 16 olives), pitted and chopped
Salt and freshly ground black pepper to taste
½ cup dry red wine

1. In a large nonreactive skillet or casserole, heat the olive oil over medium-high heat, then cook the onions, parsley, and broccoli until the onions are soft and translucent, 13 to 15 minutes, stirring frequently.

2. Stir in the anchovies, *caciocavallo*, and olives, season with salt and pepper (but not very much), and cook for 1 minute, stirring. Pour in the wine, stir, cover, and reduce the heat to low. This is the "drowning" of the broccoli. When the wine has almost evaporated, it's done, 20 to 35 minutes; keep checking. Serve with a slotted ladle to leave behind the remaining liquid.

Makes 4 to 6 servings

❈ *Fritanga Alicantina* (Valencia)

FRIED RED PEPPER, ZUCCHINI, AND TUNA PLATTER FROM ALICANTE

Red bell peppers are a favorite vegetable in Murcia and Alicante. In this vegetable preparation they are smothered in copious amounts of olive oil with onion, zucchini, and fresh tuna. They are then transferred to a casserole and simmered for an hour to sweat the vegetables and let the aromatic flavors blend with the paprika.

1 cup extra virgin olive oil
4 red bell peppers, seeded and finely chopped
1 medium-size onion, finely chopped
Salt and freshly ground black pepper to taste
2 zucchini (about ¾ pound), halved lengthwise, then quartered crosswise
¾ pound fresh tuna, cut into bite-size pieces
1 pound ripe tomatoes, peeled, seeded, and chopped
2 garlic cloves, finely chopped
1 tablespoon paprika
1 teaspoon sugar
½ cup vegetable broth (page 54)

1. In a medium-size nonreactive casserole, heat the olive oil over medium heat, then cook the red peppers and onion until soft, about 8 minutes, stirring occasionally. Season with salt and pepper. Remove from the casserole with a slotted spoon and set aside.

2. In the olive oil remaining in the casserole, cook the zucchini over medium heat until soft, about 8 minutes, stirring gently. Add the tuna and cook until it turns color on all sides, about 1 minute.

3. Pour off the olive oil and juice from the casserole and return the red peppers and onion to the zucchini and tuna. Add the tomatoes, garlic, paprika, sugar, and broth. Check the seasoning. Cover and simmer on a very low heat, using a heat diffuser if necessary, until the mixture is fragrant and soft, about 1 hour. Serve immediately.

Makes 4 to 6 servings

BREAD, WINE, AND PASTA IN PROVENCE AND LANGUEDOC

PROVENCE today is a mecca for food lovers, but in the Middle Ages it was as poor as the rest of the Mediterranean. The traditional food of Provence is a bit difficult to pin down. René Jouveau, the author of an important book on Provençal food, captured this feeling when he wrote that "There is a Provençal cuisine and popular traditions that do not coincide exactly with the cookbooks in the sense that the cookbooks do not give an idea of the manner in which the Provençal actually eat."[114] Those who have traveled or lived in Provence have detected this, especially if we are also familiar with the gastronomic history of Provence, particularly the important period beginning in the fifteenth century. Scholars have noted that between 1350 and 1480, there was the appearance for the first time of kneading troughs and in-house ovens in the homes of a variety of classes in Provence. Both the troughs and the ovens were principally used for bread making, and bread was the basis of the Provençal diet. There were three quite distinct professions involved in the business of bread making. First were the *fourniers*, the bread bakers, usually people of a lower class and modest means. Second were the *pistres*—that is, a *boulanger*, a seller of bread with a shop—and third were the *pâtissiers*, the people who kneaded and made the dough. The *boulanger* had the more remunerative profession.[115]

But the Provençal did not live entirely on bread. A good deal of beef was eaten and the butcher, in both the Christian and Jewish communities in Provence, had as much political influence as the butcher in Palestine mentioned earlier. Among the well-to-do in fifteenth-century Provence there was some good eating to be done, including spit-roasted meats with onions and garlic, *pibrada* (beef covered with a black pepper sauce), and tripe cooked with a sauce of saffron and cheese. Provençal sauces were usually made with eggs, almonds, and garlic. Fava beans and eggs were also fried, always in olive oil, though in Avignon there is a mention of eggs cooked in lard and in Sisteron eggs were prepared with rose water. Incidentally, rose water was so prevalent in medieval Arab cookery that ninety-four of the one hundred and fifty-five recipes in the early thirteenth-century Baghdad cookery book, the *Kitāb waṣf al-aṭʿima al-muʿtāda*, use rose water.[116] A sauce made of almonds and garlic or the use of rose water points to Arab culinary influence. How and when this influence was transmitted to Provence we can't quite be sure, but that it came via Italy or Catalonia is the most likely explanation.

Jean-Jacques Bouchard, a traveler from northern France, mentioned in 1630 that food in Provence was usually prepared *à l'italienne,* meaning with lots of spices and highly seasoned sauces. The cooking of Provence at this time was more closely connected with the Italian city-states than it was with any so-called French cooking. *À l'italienne* meant the use of Levantine-style spicing, typical of Arab-influenced cookery that had taken root in Italy and was associated with Italian cooking between the fourteenth and seventeenth centuries. Bouchard learned how to make a dish that he called excellent, and provided the recipe:

> Take lamb that has been cooked and allowed to cool, cut it into pieces, add as much cheese as there is meat, and boil with bouillon; when it is done, add egg yolks and the juice of bitter oranges and pour this over the meat just before taking it from the fire, because if the orange juice boils it will lose all of its flavor. Then . . . add a little nutmeg.[117]

This recipe might be called *à l'italienne*, but it is more Arab than Italian, being not far removed from the recipe called *nāranjiyya* in the thirteenth-century Baghdad cookbook, with its use of bitter oranges and nutmeg.[118]

Italian cuisine was influencing France as early as the thirteenth century; the statutes of the Cathedral of Nice in 1233 report ravioli, *crosete siue rafiole* (ravioli pie), and mortadella being served for varied meals or holidays. The influence of Italian cuisine was felt in England a century later, where we find another recipe for ravioli called *raffyolys* in a cookery book.[119]

❉ *Crosete siue Rafiole*

A COOK'S CONCEPTION OF A FOURTEENTH-CENTURY RAVIOLI PIE

Although there are a good number of late medieval ravioli recipes, we can't be absolutely sure what they tasted like or how they were cooked. I devised this recipe based upon my reading of several recipes—in particular the two recipes called de rauiolis *in the anonymous* Liber de coquina *of the fourteenth-century Angevin court in Naples, the* rafioli commun de herbe vantazati *in the anonymous fourteenth-century Venetian* Libro per cuoco, *the* ravioli *recipe in the anonymous fifteenth-century* Libro B *of the Anonimo Meridionale, and the* ravioli in tempo di carne *in Maestro Martini's fifteenth-century* Libro de arte coquinaria.[120]

1 recipe *pasta frolla* (short dough; page 550)
1 cup béchamel sauce (Step 2, page 283)
¼ teaspoon freshly grated nutmeg
Salt and freshly ground black pepper to taste
4 cups chicken broth (page 54)
9 ounces homemade or store-bought fresh cheese ravioli
1 tablespoon unsalted butter
1 teaspoon finely chopped fresh basil leaves
¼ cup freshly grated Parmigiano-Reggiano cheese

1. Make the *pasta frolla* and refrigerate for 1 hour.

2. Make the béchamel sauce, seasoning it with the nutmeg and salt and pepper.

3. Preheat the oven to 400°F.

4. Bring the chicken broth to a boil in a large saucepan, add the ravioli, and cook until done, about 8 minutes. Drain and return the ravioli to the saucepan with the butter, béchamel, basil, and 2 tablespoons of the Parmigiano-Reggiano. Set aside and keep warm.

5. Cut the short dough in half and roll out two disks, one larger than the other. Cover the bottom and sides of a lightly greased 9-inch straight-sided cake pan with the larger piece of short dough. Prick the dough all over with a toothpick or fork. Fill the pie with the ravioli and sprinkle the top with the remaining 2 tablespoons Parmigiano-Reggiano. Cover with the remaining piece of dough, crimping the edges sealed with the overlapping bottom piece with the tines of a fork. Score the pie in several places.

6. Bake until the top is golden brown, 35 to 40 minutes. Remove and let set 10 minutes before plac-

ing a large round platter over the pie. Invert the pie onto the platter, holding firmly. Cut into wedges and serve.

Makes 6 servings

✣ ✣ ✣

SOME of the most magnificent eating at the Provençal table in the fifteenth century and earlier was at the pope's table. The eloquent Pope Clement VI, who did much to stem the anti-Jewish wave that accompanied the Black Death, kept an elegant court in Avignon.[121] Avignon in the Middle Ages was an important trading city situated on the routes of great commerce. It was the capital of Latin Christianity and a fortified city of forty thousand.[122] Pope Clement VI's coronation was one of legend. The quantity of food—118 cows, 1,023 lambs, 101 calves, 914 goats, about 10,000 chickens—required fourteen butchers simply to cut up the meat. There were fifteen barrels of salt, thirteen barrels of mustard, and thirteen barrels of garlic, along with 38,000 eggs and 36,000 apples to make 50,000 dessert tarts.[123] There was meat and fish, the rare rice, and expensive spices. Pâtés were much appreciated, and the pope in Avignon ate one every day, made from all sorts of meats and birds.

Cooking foods *au gratin*, the quick browning of the top of a prepared dish with high heat, may have had an early start in Provence, as indicated by the word *gratoneya*, which appears in certain Provençal archival documents related to cooking foods.[124] Many accounts of the delights of the rich Provençal pantry come from travelers, such as Bouchard, who journeyed there from northern France in 1630 and marveled at gardens producing foods he had seen only in markets, like oranges, lemons, citrons, quinces, and pomegranates. In Toulon he ate little meat pies made of chopped tripe and cheese, and near Aubagne he had chicken fricassee in oil "that was not as unpleasant as one might imagine."[125] Butter was more commonly used in northern France, and the unpleasantness Bouchard referred to might be the taste, unfamiliar to him, of the olive oil.

A ravioli pie *(crosete siue rafiole),* reported in the statutes of the Cathedral of Nice in 1233, was a dish for the well-to-do in Provence, who had other favorite preparations such as a soup made of salted meat and its fat. A lot of fish was eaten, too, in fifteenth-century Provence because there were 151 fast days in this almost entirely Catholic country. Fish was always lightly floured, fried in a *poêle* (pan) with oil, and seasoned with lemon juice. Most of the fish eaten on Avignon tables came from the fishermen of the Martigue, who could barely make a living.[126] The poor didn't have fresh fish but rather ate salted anchovies they bought from barrels.

Official documents don't talk about the very poor because officialdom did not provide for them. The vast majority of people in Provence were wretchedly poor and their world remains hidden except for an occasional glimpse, such as an incident at Aix-en-Provence on May 27, 1597, when a church was giving out bread to the twelve hundred poor gathered, many of whom died in the mad crush for food. Food typical of the poor in Provence was chestnuts. The region of the Cevennes, the mountainous area to the west of the Rhône, in the sixteenth century was known as the zone of chestnuts. Workers were paid in pounds of fatback and white chestnuts, the everyday food of the people of this region. The chestnut was a basic food of the Cevenols, who roasted it, dried it, or pounded it into flour for black bread.[127]

One study of the cooking of Aix-en-Provence in the last quarter of the fourteenth century shows that only 42 percent of the fifty-three Aixoise homes inventoried had kitchens, called *focanea, saleta sive focanea*, and, less common, *coquina*. Although these homes didn't have kitchens, they still had a room where food could be prepared, even if not a kitchen

PERCENTAGE OF FOOD BUDGET, THREE PROVENÇAL INSTITUTIONS 1364–1430			
ITEM	STUDIUM PAPAL	SAINT-ESPRIT	ARCHBISHOPRIC
Bread	32.0	30.0	24.5
Meat	15.5	33.1	23.0
Fish, eggs	5.3	12.6	13.5
Fruit, vegetables	3.0	3.6	2.5
Spices, cooking fat, cheese	3.1	4.5	5.5
Wine	41.0	15.3	31.0

Source: Stouff 1970: 226.

proper. These homes had tripods, spits, warmers, and even frying pans, mortars, graters, sieves, and basins for washing, yet they had no hearth, indicating that, as in Sicily (see page 464), there was no cuisine. Most interesting, one fourteenth-century *auberge* in Provence had in its inventory a kind of pot, narrow at the bottom, bulging in the middle, and narrow again at the top, called an *ydres*, that appears to be identical to a cooking vessel used in Egypt during the same period of time, an *idra*, used in Cairo to cook *fūl* (page 304).[128]

The French historian Louis Stouff asks, in his book *Ravitaillement et alimentation en Provence aux XIVe et XVe siècles (Provisioning and food in Provence in the 14th and 15th centuries)*, published in 1970, whether there was an original Provençal cuisine of the fourteenth and fifteenth centuries. He does not think so, even though there is evidence of a certain taste for olive oil, garlic, aromatic herbs, and a preponderance of mutton meat. But this is an equally apt description of other Mediterranean cuisines. Stouff thought that there was the "cuisine of the rich," which was a cosmopolitan cuisine independent of "poor people's cuisine." But there may have been a regional cuisine among small landowners, middle-ranking ecclesiastics, and the various lesser bourgeoisie.[129] Stouff looked at the food budgets of three institutions—the Studium Papal of Tret in the year 1364–1365, the Saint-Esprit Hospital of Marseilles in 1409, and the Archbishopric of Arles in 1429–1430. The figures seem consistent (see table above).

What do these figures tell us? Without question they tell us that, in Provence, wine is food and the vaunted "Mediterranean vegetables" barely existed. Most notable is the extraordinary bread and wine consumption—nearly 800 liters of wine per person yearly in Arles in 1442. This was much more than Florence and Genoa in the same period, where people drank 286 liters of wine and ate 250 kilos of bread, perhaps because the Italian cities had more refined cuisines.[130] Another question not answered by this study is whether grain was exclusively eaten in the form of bread. There must have been porridges made from grain. A small amount of *pasta secca* (macaroni) was probably made in fifteenth-century Provence from wheat, although most was likely imported from Genoa, Naples, and Sicily. We don't usually associate pasta with Provence, but the rich were eating it in the fifteenth century and it is still eaten today, more frequently than we realize.

Taiarin à la Veniciano (Provence)

TAGLIARINI IN THE STYLE OF VENICE

Pasta (that is, macaroni) was a favorite Provençal food in the sixteenth century. The earliest references to pasta secca *in Provence appear at about the same time as they do in Italy, and by the fifteenth century Marseilles was the third largest producer of macaroni after Naples and Genoa.*[131] *The anonymous* Thresor de santé *(Treasury of health), published in 1607, is rich in descriptions of some of the pasta specialties of Provence. There were* macarons *(macaroni),* vermisseaux *(vermicelli), and* fidaux *(spaghetti, from the Spanish word* fideos, *which in turn derives from the Arabic* al-fidawsh, *meaning "spaghetti"). These sixteenth-century Provençal pasta dishes were made with cinnamon, nutmeg, and sometimes rose water, or with almond milk, grated cheese, or goat's milk.*[132] *Not only can all these combinations be found in the early Italian cookery books, but they are all purely Arab in inspiration.*

Taiarin *is the Provençal word for* tagliarini, *a pasta thinner than tagliatelle and wider than fettuccine. This recipe is adapted from the cookbook of Jacques Medecin, an author and former mayor of Nice.*

Salt to taste
1 pound *tagliarini* or fettuccine
6 tablespoons (3/4 stick) unsalted butter, 2 tablespoons of it melted and reserved
3 tablespoons all-purpose flour
2 cups milk
1/4 pound sliced boiled ham or Canadian bacon, julienned
1/4 pound mushrooms, stems removed and caps cut into julienne
1/4 pound boneless, skinless chicken breast, cut into julienne
2 cups freshly grated France-Comté or Parmigiano-Reggiano cheese

1. Bring a large pot of water to a rolling boil, salt abundantly, and add the pasta. Drain when al dente.

2. Meanwhile, in a large saucepan, melt 3 tablespoons of the butter over medium heat. Add the flour and stir to make a roux, stirring for 2 minutes. Remove the saucepan from the heat and slowly whisk in the milk. Season with salt and let set for 2 minutes. Add the ham or bacon, mushrooms, and chicken breast to the white sauce. Place over low heat and simmer for 10 minutes.

3. Preheat the oven to 400°F. Toss the pasta with 1 cup of the cheese and toss again with the sauce. Grease a baking pan with 1 tablespoon of the butter and pour the pasta into it. Sprinkle with the remaining cup of cheese and pour the reserved 2 tablespoons of melted butter over the pasta. Bake until speckled golden brown on top, about 15 minutes, and serve.

VARIATION

Reduce 2 quarts of *fond brun de veau* (see Variation on page 54) to 2 cups over medium heat. Transfer to a small saucepan and reduce again over low heat to 1/2 cup. This thick syrup is called *glace de viande* and can be spread over the top of the baked spaghetti before serving.

Makes 4 to 6 servings

Lu Spaghetti où Pistou (Provence)

SPAGHETTI WITH NIÇOISE-STYLE PESTO

*Pasta appears more often than one would think in the home cooking of the Niçoise because, until recently, Nice was always more closely associated with Italian dynasties such as the House of Savoy than with France. The city's proximity to Genoa also meant that a culinary culture could be shared. In this famous preparation, the key is the pesto—*pistou *in Provençal, meaning pounded—an addition also stirred into soup, just as is done farther east in Genoa. Some Provençal home cooks sprinkle grated Gruyère on top of the finished dish.*

3 garlic cloves, peeled
½ teaspoon salt
Pinch of freshly ground black pepper
60 large fresh basil leaves, washed well and thoroughly dried
2 tablespoons pine nuts
¼ cup extra virgin olive oil
3 tablespoons freshly grated Parmigiano-Reggiano cheese
1 pound spaghetti
1 cup freshly grated Gruyère cheese

1. Pound the garlic, salt, pepper, basil, and pine nuts together in a mortar until completely mushy. Slowly pour in the olive oil as you continue pounding gently. Stir in 2 tablespoons of the Parmigiano-Reggiano. This can also be done in a food processor, although I generally don't care for the result.

2. Bring a large pot of water to a rolling boil, salt abundantly, and add the pasta. Drain when al dente and divide into individual serving portions. Sprinkle the remaining tablespoon of cheese on top of each portion, then divide the pesto into dollops of equal portions. Serve with the Gruyère on the side at the table.

Makes 4 servings

* * *

BREAD and wine were the foods of Provence centuries ago. Although the very few cookbooks that existed did have recipes called "Provençal dishes," there really is no way to tell if there was actually a regional Provençal cuisine. Today, of course, there is such a cuisine, and it is defined by olive oil and aromatic herbs; products from the New World such as tomatoes, bell peppers, and haricot beans; and foods originally from the Arabs, via Italy—namely, artichokes, spinach, and sugar, as well as native produce often grown in the coastal manor houses, such as garlic, Swiss chard, beets, and, of course, the ubiquitous cabbage.

Languedoc, the region to the west of Provence, shared many alimentary parallels with Provence, especially the prevalence of bread and wine in the diet. In his study of the peasants of Languedoc during the last third of the fifteenth century, the French historian Emmanuel Le Roy Ladurie compared the diet of the farmworkers of Narbonne to the bourgeoisie of Béziers, using household accounts.[133] The bourgeois family of Béziers, the Rocolles, consisted of a widow, her two daughters, and a female servant. The four of them consumed about two thousand liters of wine a year. Again, as in Provence, we see that wine was food. The Narbonne farmworkers drank even more—about 650 liters of red wine a year per person. The farmworkers were not demanding, insisting only on money in the pocket, white bread on the table, and a glass of good wine. Although rations did not decline between 1480 and 1580, the quality did because employers skimped on it. As Ladurie said, "The workers ate white bread under Louis XI and black bread under Henry III." In 1480, the farmworkers and the Rocolles's could eat bread made from fine wheat and drink hearty red wine, while one hundred years later it was a ration of black bread and *piquette*.[134] In later centuries the gastronomy improved again and the farmyard produced many chickens, ducks, and geese, which are evident in the local cooking today. This next recipe is a classic example of the bourgeois cooking of Toulouse, although it apparently may have had an earlier start to the south in Spain.

Poularde à la Toulouse (Languedoc)

CHICKEN IN THE STYLE OF TOULOUSE

This rich dish that exemplifies the bourgeois cooking of the late nineteenth century is fortified with a substantial amount of butter and bacon. Coastal traders of the sixteenth century would have bought butter in Villefrance and vinegar and bacon in Toulon. The recipe may have had its genesis in the brouet *of chicken found in the early French cookery book* Le ménagier de Paris, *where the elements of the dish are cooked separately and then joined together at the end of the process. A very similar recipe, also familiar in the Languedoc, is called* poularde à la d'Albufera, *a reference to the large lagoon south of Valencia that feeds the* huertas, *or "truck farm" vegetable gardens. The* sauce d'Albufera *is similar to this sauce here except for the addition of pimiento butter. It is unclear how the name of Albufera was transferred north, but perhaps at some point the New World bell peppers* (Capsicum annuum *var.* annuum) *were grown in the* huertas *of Valencia by mid-sixteenth century and were familiar to the great number of French in Valencia (there were more of them there than in Catalonia), who were there to make money.*[135] *This preparation, adapted from J.-B. Reboul's classic* La cuisinière provençale, *can be served as a rustic peasant dish or you can fuss a bit, with decoration and what not, and serve it for a bourgeois dinner, as I've done in this recipe.*

6 thick strips bacon (about 1/4 pound)
1 large onion, sliced
1 carrot, sliced
1 bay leaf
1 sprig fresh thyme
1 chicken (about 5 pounds), trussed, giblets saved
Salt and freshly ground black pepper to taste
1 cup dry white wine
1 1/2 cups chicken broth (page 54)
1/2 cup water
1 prepared recipe *quenelles ordinaires* (optional; page 574)
4 to 6 slices *foie gras de canard* (optional; see Note)
1/4 cup (1/2 stick) unsalted butter
2 large egg yolks
1 tablespoon heavy cream
Juice from 1 lemon
1 tablespoon all-purpose flour
1/2 pound small mushrooms, stems removed

1. In a large, heavy casserole, layer the bacon, onion, carrot, bay leaf, and thyme. Place the chicken on top, scatter the giblets around the sides, and season with salt and pepper. Cover and cook the chicken over low heat until the onion and bacon begin to stick a bit to the bottom of the casserole, about 30 minutes. Turn the chicken and simmer in its juices and fat for

another 15 minutes. Pour in the wine and let it reduce while the casserole remains covered for another 20 minutes. Add 1 cup of the chicken broth and the water and let the chicken cook, covered, for 1 hour over low heat. It is not necessary to turn the chicken, but you can if you like.

2. Meanwhile, prepare the quenelles and slice the foie gras, if using. In a small skillet, heat 1 tablespoon of the butter over very low heat; once it has melted, cook the foie gras slices until heated through. Alternatively, put them in the microwave with an extremely thin slice of butter on top of each slice for 15 seconds on low or medium power. Keep warm on the side.

3. In a small bowl, beat together the egg yolks, heavy cream, and lemon juice and set aside. If the chicken is done, with the joints very pliable and the meat almost falling off the bones, remove to a platter and keep warm until needed. Slice the chicken giblets. Strain the sauce in the casserole through a fine-mesh strainer and set aside in a saucepan or the casserole you cooked it in.

4. In a medium-size saucepan, melt the remaining 3 tablespoons butter and stir in the flour over

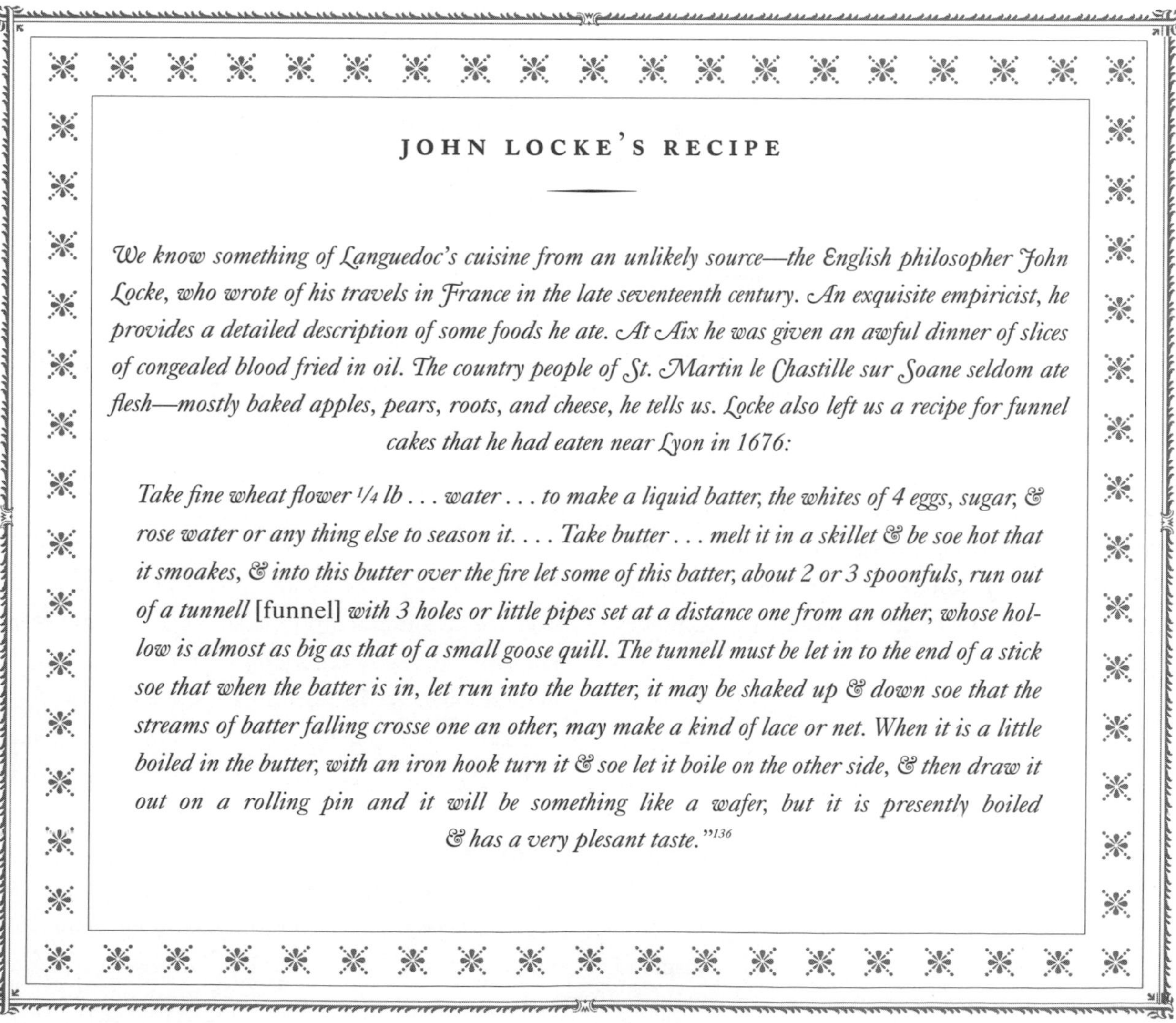

JOHN LOCKE'S RECIPE

We know something of Languedoc's cuisine from an unlikely source—the English philosopher John Locke, who wrote of his travels in France in the late seventeenth century. An exquisite empiricist, he provides a detailed description of some foods he ate. At Aix he was given an awful dinner of slices of congealed blood fried in oil. The country people of St. Martin le Chastille sur Soane seldom ate flesh—mostly baked apples, pears, roots, and cheese, he tells us. Locke also left us a recipe for funnel cakes that he had eaten near Lyon in 1676:

> *Take fine wheat flower 1/4 lb . . . water . . . to make a liquid batter, the whites of 4 eggs, sugar, & rose water or any thing else to season it. . . . Take butter . . . melt it in a skillet & be soe hot that it smoakes, & into this butter over the fire let some of this batter, about 2 or 3 spoonfuls, run out of a tunnell* [funnel] *with 3 holes or little pipes set at a distance one from an other, whose hollow is almost as big as that of a small goose quill. The tunnell must be let in to the end of a stick soe that when the batter is in, let run into the batter, it may be shaked up & down soe that the streams of batter falling crosse one an other, may make a kind of lace or net. When it is a little boiled in the butter, with an iron hook turn it & soe let it boile on the other side, & then draw it out on a rolling pin and it will be something like a wafer, but it is presently boiled & has a very plesant taste."*[136]

medium-low heat. Moisten this roux with the remaining ½ cup chicken broth and 1¼ cups of the reserved sauce from the casseroled chicken (save any remaining sauce for another use). Bring the sauce to a boil over high heat. Reduce the heat to very low and simmer. Spoon a few tablespoons of the sauce into the egg yolk mixture while whisking constantly, then bind the sauce with the egg yolk mixture, pouring it in slowly and whisking constantly as you do.

5. Add the mushrooms to the sauce and carefully slide in the quenelles, if using. Sprinkle the pieces of chicken giblets into the sauce and let simmer until the quenelles are poached through and springy to the touch, about 20 minutes.

6. Place the chicken in the middle of a large serving platter. Arrange the mushrooms and quenelles around the edges. Drape a sheet of aluminum foil over the chicken to keep it warm or place in a warm oven as you continue the preparation. Slip the foie gras into the sauce for 1 minute and remove to the platter. Pass the sauce through a fine-mesh strainer and return to the casserole, reducing it to a glaze over medium-high heat. Pour the glaze over the chicken and serve.

NOTE: *Foie gras de canard* is sold in cans, the better quality ones being satisfactory for this preparation. Some gourmet markets make their own that are very good, and there are mail-order possibilities (page 727).

Makes 4 servings

* * *

THE prodigious amount of wine being consumed by people in the French Mediterranean—nearly two liters a day per person—would lead one to believe they were always drunk. The accounts and chronicles, however, are revealing about the level of public drunkenness. As the German-speaking merchant of Montpellier Fèlix Platter noted in 1556, all the drunks were German. Platter was embarrassed by his compatriots, red as lobsters, pouring wine over each others' heads, pissing in their pants, and lying in the streets dead drunk.[137] Even today throughout the Mediterranean, with its vast wine consumption, the public nuisances are often northern Europeans. This was true for Catalonia as well: in Barcelona of 1595, one could find hundreds of prostitutes in the dives of the port quarter but apparently, no drunks.

The recipes that follow are contemporary recipes, but each one has an intimate connection to the historical foods of Provence and Languedoc.

Aperó-Chic Super (Languedoc)

OLIVE, BEAN, AND NUT MIX

Les Halles de Nîmes is the central food market in Nîmes. In Les Halles one can find rocambole, *or sand leek* (Allium scorodoprasum *L.*), *a mild type of red garlic grown in the south of France, also known as* ail d'Espagne, *Spanish garlic. Among many other delicacies was this delightful mix of olives, nuts, and beans that my friend Boyd Grove and I bought with some other food and brought over to the nearby Jardin de Fontaine to eat.* Aperó *is a colloquial word meaning "aperitif." Cooked lupine beans are sold in every supermarket, usually in jars; they should be drained, and if large the hard skin peeled off before using.*

3 cups imported green olives with a mild, unflavored brine
1 cup cooked lupine beans, drained and peeled
1 cup blanched whole almonds
1 cup hazelnuts, blanched if desired
½ cup roasted red bell peppers (pimientos), chopped
½ cup extra virgin olive oil
1 garlic clove, finely chopped
1 *rocambole*, chopped (optional)
1 tablespoon very finely chopped fresh basil leaves
1 teaspoon very finely chopped fresh thyme leaves
Salt and freshly ground black pepper to taste

Mix all the ingredients, cover, and leave for 24 hours at room temperature, then refrigerate. It is best after 1 week.

Makes about 2 quarts

Fougasse (Languedoc)

PUFF PASTRY WITH OLIVES AND ANCHOVY

This fougasse *is a flat puff pastry stuffed with anchovies and olives or walnuts. But the shapes, and even the dough, can vary according to the mood and artistic talent of the baker. It can be like lacework, in the shape of an* N, *or as a flower petal.*

A fougasse *can be made with frozen store-bought* pâte feuilletée *(puff pastry) and baked until light and fluffy in any shape you wish. In Aigues-Mortes, one can find* fougasse noël, *a large flat rectangle of dough, yellow from a glaze of yolks, spongy, light, and frosted with sugar. In Bouzigues, one can find the* fougasse *(or sometimes* faugasse *or* fougassette) *stuffed with ground walnuts. This recipe uses chopped imported black olives and salted anchovies, and is my favorite.*

1 package (1 pound 1¼ ounces) frozen commercial *pâte feuilletée* (puff pastry), defrosted according to package instructions
⅔ cup chopped imported black olives
12 salted anchovy fillets, rinsed
1 large egg, beaten

1. Roll out each sheet of puff pastry to an 11 × 14-inch rectangle on a floured work surface, following the directions on the package for handling. Cut each in half widthwise. Fold each of the four pieces in half and cut out two triangles on top and bottom to form an N.

2. Mix the olives and anchovies, spread this stuffing on one side of each sheet of pastry, and fold the other side over, crimping the edges with the tines of a fork. Place on a baking sheet and brush with some beaten egg. (It is not necessary to grease the baking sheet as the pastry has plenty of butter worked into it).

3. Preheat the oven to 350°F. Bake until golden brown, about 20 minutes. Cool slightly on a wire rack and serve.

Makes 4 to 6 servings

Feuilletée aux Anchois (Languedoc)

ANCHOVY IN PUFF PASTRY

It's hard to imagine that these crunchy, fluffy pastry pies, so popular with anchovy lovers, were once the food of the poor (in vastly altered form). In the Middle Ages, the typical fish eaten by the common people were salted anchovies or sardines sold from barrels. They could be

FOUGASSE

Fougasse *is a flatbread, sometimes stuffed, with a long history. In Languedoc and Provence, its roots go back to the twelfth century and maybe earlier, deriving from the Italian words* fugata, fugaza, *or* foga*—that is, a focaccia.* Focaccia *is rooted to the late Latin word* focacia, *which appeared in the dictionary of the seventh-century lexicographer Isidore of Seville as meaning "to cook with a* focolàre,*" a kind of cooking stone.*[138]

During the Middle Ages, fogassia, *along with* menudeta *and* placentula, *was a kind of bread known as* pain fantasie *(made usually for special festivals), including various kinds of cakes or rolls.*[139] *The earliest documented reference to* fougasse *is in a charter from Toulouse in 1173, distinguishing between leavened bread,* panis levatus, *and* fogasse. *Most unleavened bread was made with the highest quality flour in monasteries to be distributed at the benediction ceremony. Besides being baked in an oven,* fougasse *was also cooked under the ashes,* subcinericius.[140] Fougasse *is omnipresent in the south of France and has been known in Italy since the eleventh century.*

In Roussillon, the French part of Catalonia, now the southernmost portion of coastal Languedoc, the aristocracy ate wheat bread while common people ate fogaces, *described as a kind of cake.*[141] *Spanish texts also mention* fougasse *less frequently, known today as* hogaza, *a festive bread not made very much.*

In the anonymous fourteenth-century Venetian cookbook Libro per cuoco, *the recipe* pan de noxe maravigliosso e bone *(a marvelous and good nut bread) makes a reference that sheds light on the popularity of* fougasse. *The recipe calls for pounding together nuts, herbs, grated onion, sweet and strong spices, and sugar. A dough is made with fine flour and rolled out like a* lasagne grande. *The nut mixture is laid in between the layers and the whole is baked "in the way a* fugaza *is," which must mean that it was well known.*

On Corfu, peasants still make a fogatsa, *a sweet bread baked at Easter time. They flavor the bread with* mahlepi, *the powdered pits of the St. Lucie's cherry, and orange zest, and they decorate it with slivered almonds.*

eaten with some poor quality bread, the better quality bread made from fine wheat flour being reserved for the wealthy. For real excellence you need to find the salted anchovies; this recipe will not be as delicious if one uses the oil-cured anchovy fillets in the little cans.

10 ounces salted anchovy fillets (about 40 fillets), rinsed
2 tablespoons unsalted butter, softened
Pinch of cayenne pepper
1 package (1 pound 1¼ ounces) frozen commercial *pâte feuilletée* (puff pastry), defrosted according to package instructions

1 small egg, beaten
1 tablespoon finely chopped fresh parsley leaves (optional)

1. Preheat the oven to 450°F.

2. Reserve eight of the anchovy fillets and mash the rest together with the butter and cayenne. Roll the puff pastry out until it is about ⅓ inch thick or less. Cut as many 2 × 3½-inch rectangles as you are able.

3. Place half the rectangles on a baking sheet and brush with the beaten egg. Bake until light golden, 7 to 8 minutes.

4. Spread the anchovy butter on the remaining rectangles and top with a small piece of anchovy. Place in the oven and bake until golden. Remove from the oven and let cool on a wire rack. Reduce the oven heat to 350°F (or you can reserve the baked rectangles at this point and refrigerate for later use if desired).

5. Cover each anchovy-slathered rectangle with a plain rectangle and place in the oven until deep golden, about 10 minutes. Sprinkle with parsley if desired before serving.

Makes 8 generous hors d'oeuvre servings

Feuilletée aux Escargots à la Languedocienne (Languedoc)

LANGUEDOCIAN-STYLE SNAILS IN PUFF PASTRY

Snail hunting is a popular pastime in the large vine-growing areas of Languedoc and Provence. Snail hunting today is a regulated season, and the gathering becomes rather frenzied in the narrow window of time allowed. But in the Middle Ages snails were collected whenever and wherever, and the gathered snails fed on aromatic herbs that grow in the garrigue, *or moors, of Languedoc.*

This recipe is adapted from the one given to me by Chef Patrick Lenfant of the Grand Hotel in Roquefort-sur-Soulzon and the one consulted in Anne Willan's French Regional Cooking.

36 large fresh or canned snails
6 salted anchovy fillets, rinsed
½ cup milk
¾ cup crushed walnuts
1 garlic clove, finely chopped
2 tablespoons finely chopped fresh parsley leaves
3 tablespoons extra virgin olive oil
1 tablespoon tomato paste
1 cup chicken broth (page 54)
2 tablespoons cognac
2 ounces cooked ham, chopped
2 ounces bacon, chopped
Freshly ground black pepper to taste
2 tablespoons fresh bread crumbs
1 package (1 pound 1¼ ounces) frozen commercial *pâte feuilletée* (puff pastry) for *vol-au-vent* hors d'oeuvres, defrosted according to package directions (see Note if *vol-au-vent* puff pastry is unavailable)

1. Rinse the snails if canned or purge if fresh, according to the instructions on page 724, and then precook. Soak the anchovies in the milk for 30 minutes.

2. Drain the anchovies and chop with the walnuts, garlic, and parsley. Transfer to a small bowl and stir in 1 tablespoon of the olive oil. In another small bowl, mix the tomato paste with the chicken broth and stir in the cognac.

3. In a medium-size heavy skillet, heat the remaining 2 tablespoons olive oil over medium-high, then brown the ham and bacon, about 5 minutes, stirring. Reduce the heat to medium-low, add the walnut mixture, and simmer for 1 to 2 minutes, stirring. Stir in the tomato paste mixture, bring to a boil for 3 to 4

minutes, and add the snails. Reduce the heat to low and simmer for 10 minutes. Sprinkle with pepper and stir in the bread crumbs. Set this stuffing aside until needed.

4. Bake the *vol-au-vent* pastries according to the package instructions. Arrange attractively on a serving platter, stuff each one with a snail and its sauce, and serve.

NOTE: If *vol-au-vent* puff pastry for hors d'oeuvres is not available, roll sheets of commercial *pâte feuilletée* out thin and cut out 72 circles each 1½-inches in diameter. Cut out a ¾-inch hole in half of the pastry disks. Lay the doughnut-shaped disks on top of the whole ones. Arrange on an ungreased baking sheet and bake according to the instructions on the package. Remove from the oven and cool. Fill each disk with a snail and sauce and reheat to serve.

Makes 36 hors d'oeuvres

Escargots à la Sommièroise (Languedoc)

SNAILS IN THE STYLE OF SOMMIÈRIES

Recipes for snails abound in the Languedoc. Traditionally the snails were gathered by the local people in the wild moors of Languedoc known as the garrigue, *where spiky holm oak, prickly broom, thistly scrub, wild mints, thyme, rosemary, and wild lavenders form a dense ground cover.*

The popularity of snails is evidenced in the number of recipes one encounters: there are the escargots à la Lodevoise, *made with sautéed onions, ham, spinach, Swiss chard, parsley, chervil, and mint; and* à la Narbonnaise, *made without spinach but with egg yolks and almonds. Snails* à la Nîmoise *means the snails are boiled with onions, spices, thyme, bay leaf, and fennel seeds and then cooked with shallots, onions, ham, anchovies, spinach, parsley, and chervil.*

Older versions of this preparation from Sommièries, a small town on the Vidourle River, west of Nîmes, call for blettes *(or* blèa *in patois), a French word that can refer to white Swiss chard, white beet leaves, or strawberry spinach* (Blitums capitatum *or* B. virgatum). *Some Sommièroise soak the live snails in vinegar first and then add some orange peel to the sauté mixture.*

Although ideally made with fresh snails, which must be purged and cooked in a court-bouillon, this recipe is for canned snails. The French use an escargotière, *a little plate with six indentations for the shells, and a small long-pronged curved snail fork and spring-loaded snail holder when eating snails. You do not need to make a special purchase of this equipment, as handy as it is, but keep your eyes open for used forks and holders at garage sales and flea markets, or when traveling in France—they make great gifts and souvenirs. Lacking such instruments, serve the snails in a wide, shallow bowl, such as a pasta bowl. This will be a little messier because you will need to hold the shells steady with your fingers as you pick out the snails.*

10 ounces fresh spinach, heavy stems removed and washed well
¾ pound Swiss chard, leaves removed from stems and washed well
½ cup extra virgin olive oil
Salt to taste
2 ounces pork fatback, blanched in boiling water for 2 to 5 minutes, drained, and cut into tiny bits
1 tablespoon pork lard
4 salted anchovy fillets, rinsed and mashed
1 garlic clove, finely chopped
24 canned snails and shells (see Note)
Extra virgin olive oil for drizzling
⅓ cup coarsely chopped walnuts
½ cup dry white wine
1 tablespoon finely chopped fresh parsley leaves

1. Put the spinach and Swiss chard leaves in a large pot with only the water adhering to them from their last rinsing with the olive oil, and wilt over medium heat, about 8 minutes, covered, tossing occasionally. Drain well in a colander, pressing on the leaves with a spoon until almost dry, salt, and chop.

2. In a medium-size casserole, cook the blanched pork fatback in the lard over medium heat until rendered a bit, about 5 minutes, stirring. Add the anchovies, garlic, spinach, and Swiss chard and cook until the anchovies have melted, about 10 minutes, stirring occasionally. Add the snails and turn off the heat and let sit for 10 minutes.

3. Put the snails into the shells and arrange the stuffed shells in a single layer in a large skillet. Drizzle with olive oil and cover with the spinach mixture. Cover and simmer over medium heat until fragrant, about 20 minutes, shaking the skillet every once in a while. Add the walnuts and cook another 5 minutes. Pour in the wine and continue cooking until the mixture is soft and aromatic, about another 5 minutes.

4. Place the snail shells on individual *escargotières* with some of the sauce. Sprinkle with the parsley and serve with a snail fork and shell holder and a small spoon for the sauce.

NOTE: Canned snails are sometimes sold with 12 shells included. Save the shells for reusing. I have cleaned them in the top rack of a dishwasher without ill effects.

Makes 4 servings

Petits Pâtés de Pézenas (Languedoc)

LAMB SWEETMEAT

These little pastries stuffed with a sweet mincemeat made of mutton are still made today in the town of Pézenas, probably little changed from the time of Rabelais. Mutton was popular in Languedoc in the Middle Ages since we know that agricultural workers in the fifteenth century could afford to buy 108 grams (about ¼ pound) of mutton a day, while in Venice, by comparison, they could afford only 52 grams of salted pork a day.[142] *This recipe can also be made with puff pastry if desired.*

3 cups unbleached all-purpose flour, sifted
3 large egg yolks
1½ teaspoons salt
¾ cup (1½ sticks) unsalted butter
½ cup boiling water
10 ounces boneless leg of mutton or lamb, trimmed of fat
Salt and freshly ground black pepper to taste
2 ounces lamb or mutton kidney fat
Very finely chopped or grated zest of 1 lemon
1 cup firmly packed dark brown sugar
½ cup raisins
1 large egg, beaten

1. In a large bowl, knead together the flour, egg yolks, and salt. Melt the butter in the boiling water, then knead the melted mixture into the flour. Form into a ball and leave in the refrigerator for 1 hour wrapped in waxed paper.

2. Season the lamb or mutton with salt and pepper and grind it with the lamb or mutton kidney fat through the fine blade of a meat grinder or with short bursts in a food processor. Remove to a medium-size bowl and mix in the lemon zest,

brown sugar, and raisins. Check the taste of the seasoning.

3. Preheat the oven to 400°F. Roll out the dough on a floured work surface until it is ¼ inch thick. Cut out fourteen 4-inch rounds and fourteen 2-inch rounds (you may need to reform and roll out the dough twice or thrice). Place some of the lamb mixture in the middle of the large rounds and lift up the sides to form walls in a teardrop shape. Pinch the four corners closed with the tines of a fork. Place a 2-inch round on top and lightly press down. Continue with the rest of the rounds and filling placing them on a baking sheet. Refrigerate for 15 minutes.

4. Poke holes with a toothpick through the 2-inch disks that lay on top of the pies. Brush each pie with some beaten egg and bake for 30 minutes. Cool on a wire rack and serve at room temperature.

Makes 14 pies

Les Oreillettes Montpellieraines (Languedoc)

MONTPELLIER EARS

In the area of Montpellier, a number of sweets are traditionally made during carnival period, beginning around January 6 and lasting until Mardi Gras. This recipe is one of them. Their history is old and they are very likely inherited from a class of Arab sweets in North Africa and Syria known as qaraṣ, *a word referring to a disk- or lozenge-like dough, or* galette. Les oreillettes *are identical, in fact, to the Algerian* qaraṣ *(or* qiriyyūsh), *typically made in the city of Tlemcen.*

Another sweet in this category is a kind of galette *called* langues-de-chat, *"cat tongues," for which Dijon is famous.* Langues-de-chat, *named for its shape, is today a crisp, dry biscuit made with sugar, cream, and egg whites that keeps for a long time. Their history can be traced to Syria. Syrians ate many different pastries, such as those from Baalbek, made with lots of sugar, cornstarch, and orange flower water, as well as* khubz al-abāzīr, *spice bread, that may have passed into Europe by way of the Crusaders or, more probably, merchants. This so-called spice bread was, in fact, the sugar-covered galette called* langues-de-chat.[143]

3 cups unbleached all-purpose flour
3 large eggs, beaten
½ cup granulated sugar
6 tablespoons (¾ stick) unsalted butter, cut into bits
Grated zest from 2 lemons
2 tablespoons milk
2 tablespoons light rum
1 teaspoon orange flower water
6 cups pure or virgin olive, olive pomace, or vegetable oil for deep-frying
Confectioners' sugar (optional)

1. Pour the flour onto a work surface and make a well in the center of it. In the well put the eggs, granulated sugar, butter, lemon zest, milk, rum, and orange flower water. Work the dough well with your fingers to incorporate all the ingredients and knead until an elastic ball is formed. Cover with plastic wrap and leave to rest at room temperature for 2 hours.

2. Flour the work surface. Cut off a handful of dough. Roll the dough out very thin, then cut into any shape you want, about 6 inches in diameter.

3. Preheat the frying oil in a deep-fryer or an 8-inch saucepan fitted with a basket insert to 375°F. Fry the dough shapes in batches until golden, about 2 minutes, turning once. Dust with confectioners' sugar if desired. Drain on paper towels and serve once cool. Let the frying oil cool completely, strain, and save for a future use.

Makes 12 "ears"

CONCLUSION

IN this chapter I have tried to question the impression of the Middle Ages as a time when people "feasted." We have seen that the overwhelming majority of the Mediterranean population was living in abject poverty and we know little about their daily diet. The poor peasant ate millet and some cabbage, not much more. The rich, on the other hand, for whom we have menus and various accounts, provide a more sumptuous story.

This chapter surveyed a little of what we know about food in some selected areas of the Mediterranean. I hoped to give a broad idea of what people ate in this region. Clearly, bread was prevalent in the diet, wine was food, and barley was eaten by the poor. The period after the Black Death saw a rise in meat availability, though.

This chapter concludes the "Algebra of Mediterranean Gastronomy." The equation was set up by seeing the importance of the political, economic, and agricultural history of the Mediterranean in forming a gastronomy. By looking at how the climate affected harvests, and how harvests determined what people really ate, we can now move on to see how the geography and ecology of the Mediterranean must be added to this equation to round out the picture of Mediterranean gastronomy. In the next part of the book we will travel to the mountains, meadows, plains, and deserts, then to the cities, and finally to the sea and its islands.

[PART II]

An ECOLOGY *of* MEDITERRANEAN GASTRONOMY

AN ecology of Mediterranean gastronomy is not complete if it is only a catalog of geographical formations and their populations. Geography plays a role in the ecology of a place by determining where agriculture can thrive, and what kinds of foods are grown or raised and how much food can be produced. The amount of food produced by agriculture will determine how often women get pregnant, and how many children they can raise and feed, which determines the level of population in a geographical area.[1] Whether the area is an island, mountain, or city, the amount of food produced there will lead to population changes. As enough food is produced to feed nonfood producers such as bureaucrats, merchants, and soldiers, the taste of food becomes ever more important and a cuisine can develop.

Food and geography is a complex story of mountains, meadows, hills, deserts, cities, seas, and islands. An ecology of Mediterranean gastronomy is the story of the interaction of geography and the movements of people. These movements are so often about food; in this part of the book we will encounter contemporary recipes that reflect the historic struggle of Mediterranean peoples against their environment. It is a wide-ranging story that will touch upon medieval Sicilian cooking, Spanish military presidios on the North African coast, rats that contaminate grain stores, mountain superstitions, land reclamation, the expulsion of people from one place and their acceptance in another, nomadism, the riches of Venice, the addiction to sugar, the urban monster of Istanbul, the financial power of Genoa, fishermen and cutthroats on the high seas, and how dead reckoning changed the lives of corsairs and galley cooks alike. An ecology of the Mediterranean will lead us to the measure of Mediterranean gastronomy, the topic of Part III.

4

"THEY EAT FROM ONE BOWL": LIVES IN THE MOUNTAINS, MEADOWS, PLAINS, AND DESERTS

The peninsulas of the Mediterranean are the key actors.

—FERNAND BRAUDEL

BEHIND those beautiful Mediterranean sea coasts stand mountains, hills, and deserts. Food writers have traditionally focused on the sea and coasts of the Mediterranean, but a proper culinary understanding of the Mediterranean must encompass its complete geography. The mountains had resources, such as snow and wheat, and of course people. Because the mountains were isolated from the main flow of culture, life was crude and the people superstitious. The mountains were also home to bandits.

Mountain culture and hill towns were responsible for the most overlooked of food staples in the Mediterranean: cheese, salt, butter, and yogurt. Meadows grew in importance because, with the decrease in population following the Black Death, stock rearing increased. So often the story of the "real" Mediterranean is a tale of the movements of people. People moved down from the mountains to the plains to seek a better life. Other people, known as transhumants, moved their sheep into mountain pastures and back again like an endless tide. But the most "movable" of peoples in the Mediterranean were those quintessential nomads, the Bedouins, who found their homes in the vast reaches of the empty desert and the Jews, the inadvertant nomads, who we will encounter in greater depth in the conclusion of the book.

SNOW AND STRANGE CLOTHES

THE Mediterranean is tied together with a variety of geographical, historical, commercial, and culinary strings. The Mediterranean is coastal Mediterranean, but is also mountain villages and highlands, snowy and isolated, far from where orange trees blossom. In Montenegro, the snows can last until midsummer. After I drove through the rugged and raw Taygetus Mountains in Greece I descended into the semitropical plains of Sparta, today filled as far as the eye can see with the silver-green leaves of endless olive trees and the darker green dots of clustered orange groves. The same trip was made in 1553 by a Flemish traveler, Peter Coeck of Alost, who mentioned rain and snow and hail while crossing the mountains, to be greeted in the lowland plains of Greece by "women who bring provisions such as . . .

barley, oats, wine, bread or round loaves baked in hot embers."[1]

The snows of Mt. Hermon in Lebanon provided the offering made by Saladin, the great Muslim general and nemesis of the Crusaders, to Richard the Lion-Hearted (1157–1199). Mountain snow was a commodity of some value in the Mediterranean. Travelers in Syria noted merchants selling snow water for a few coins in Tripoli on the Lebanese coast. Istanbul received boatloads of snow, and the pashas exploited ice mines in Anatolia. The Egyptians saw snow arrive from Syria via a kind of pony express. The rugged men of the Spanish presidios of the Barbary Coast, such as the outpost at Oran, received snow from the brigantines of the Intendance, the administrative office of the Spanish monarchy. The Knights Hospitalers, the military religious order that grew out of an eleventh-century hospital for pilgrims in Jerusalem, after settling in Malta, were delighted with the luxury of receiving snow from Naples. The snow would be tightly packed in large "bales," wrapped in straw to keep it from melting. Sicilian folklore proposes that it was in the tenth century that Arab-Sicilians began culinary experiments with the snows of Mt. Etna, resulting in the first sherbets.[2] The wide use of snow in the Appenine Napoletano and Sicily explains the early development of sherbet, *granita*, and ice cream in southern Italy. Petrus Casola reports, in his *Viaggio a Gerusalemme*, that pilgrims traveling in Syria in July 1494 were astonished to see a merchant-captain selling sacks of snow from his boat. The Venetian traveler Gradenigo reported in 1553 that the Arabs would sprinkle snow on their food as the Venetians would sugar or we would salt.[3]

A first glimpse of the Mediterranean is often by way of descent from the mountains. But the traveler, as well as the historian, overlooks the mountains because he is drawn to the sea. The sea leads one to think that this is where the story or unity of the Mediterranean lies. The key, though, is the mountainous peninsulas. That is where wheat, vines, and olives were grown, as we can see today in the Anti-Atlas Mountains of Morocco. For daily life, the importance of the mountains played another role: they were a refuge from the incessant trepass of soldiers and pirates. Ultimately, the populations of the mountains were insignificant, as civilizations are the result of lowlands and urbanity, and the mountains remained primitive. Mountain people understood this and, to escape the oppressive poverty, would head toward the attraction of good wages in the towns of the plains. A Catalan proverb captures this sentiment: *Baixar sempre, mountar no*, Down always, up never. Undoubtedly, once the Catalan shepherd reached the plains, heartbreaks would await him, but perhaps, if he were lucky, a good *escudella* would remind him of home.

Escudella (Catalonia)

CATALONIAN STEW

Escudella *means "bowl," and in Catalonia it is the name of a big stew-soup,* escudella i carn d'olla*, usually made for Christmas. The rustic taste of this stew is evident in the bones and feet, whose gelatin give such an unctuousness to the dish, and in the rough vegetables such as cabbage and turnips that were so common in the mountains and hills. Every family might make it a little different, perhaps using pasta, as well as cabbage, white beans, chickpeas, or various winter vegetables such as turnips. In the Middle Ages, the family* escudella *was not nearly as delicious sounding as this recipe and was likely to have been eaten from one bowl, as they were too poor to have individual bowls. Like the* cocido *(page 541) of Andalusia or the* ouillade *(page 15) in Roussillon in the French part of Catalonia,* escudella *is meant to be a hearty one-pot meal. Its preparation in Catalonia is notable enough for Colman Andrews, a thoughtful student of Catalan cuisine, to* *have called it the ur-Catalan specialty. Joseph Pla, the great Catalan gastronome, said that a good* escudella, *the way it once was made, is today worth a fortune.*[4]

This recipe is "the way it once was made," adapted from one described to me by Montse Contreras as made by her mother, who uses rodanxa *(a slice of lamb ankle) for flavoring the soup and white* butifarra *sausage for the meatball. Commercially made chicken sausage is close in taste to* butifarra *sausage, which is made with veal. I also use the shank, which is farther up the leg than the ankle and has more meat on it. Taste a small bit of your prosciutto to make sure it is not too salty. If it is, remember this when you salt later.*

Once you eat this escudella, *you will see why it is a favorite cold-weather dish: it has wonderful, memorable flavors that are warming for soul and stomach. By the way, all those feet and bones in the stew are essential for the real and full taste, and although supermarkets are increasingly aware of the needs of authentic cooks and may have them, you probably will need to make a special trip to a butcher.*

2 chicken feet, skinned, or 1 chicken neck
1 chicken gizzard
1 lamb foot and ankle
1⅓ pounds lamb shank
1 prosciutto bone (about 2 pounds) or ¼-pound piece prosciutto with its fat
2 pounds beef or pork marrow (soup) bones
5 quarts water
1 slice stale French bread, crust removed
1 large egg, beaten
½ pound ground pork
½ pound *butifarra* (page 711) or chicken sausage, casings removed and meat crumbled
2 garlic cloves, finely chopped
¼ cup finely chopped fresh parsley leaves
Salt and freshly ground black pepper to taste
¼ cup fresh bread crumbs, if needed
1 potato (about ½ pound), peeled and cut into chunks
1 carrot, cut up
1 pound Swiss chard, stems removed and leaves chopped
All-purpose flour for dredging

1. Place the chicken feet or neck, chicken gizzard, lamb foot and ankle, lamb shank, prosciutto bone or piece of prosciutto, and beef or pork marrow (soup) bones in a large stew pot. Cover with the water and bring to a boil. Boil for 2 hours, turning the meat occasionally. Replenish the water if necessary.

2. Meanwhile, make the large meatball. Soak the slice of bread in water. Squeeze the water out and place in a medium-size bowl with the beaten egg. Add the ground pork, *butifarra* or chicken sausage, garlic, and parsley and season with salt and pepper. If the meatball doesn't hold together well, add some of the bread crumbs. Form the meat into a single large ball and set aside in the refrigerator.

3. After the meat bones have been boiling for 2 hours, turn the heat off and remove the bones. Remove the marrow from the soup bones and the meat from the lamb shank, cut it up, and discard all the bones. Transfer the marrow and meat to a stew pot or large casserole. Strain the broth and add it to the stew pot. Bring to a boil and add the potato, carrot, and Swiss chard. Season to taste with salt and boil for 10 minutes. Dredge the meatball evenly in flour, tapping off any excess, add it to the broth and boil until firm, 20 to 25 minutes, replenishing the water if necessary. Serve immediately. The meatball can be divided by each diner.

Makes 6 servings

Escalivada (Catalonia)

A CATALAN VEGETABLE MEDLEY

Escalivar *means "to cook in hot ashes." Typically the vegetables in an* escalivada *are grilled, and the dish is served with grilled meats. Mountain shepherds were adept at packing their rucksacks with some cheese and wine, perhaps, and building a hardwood fire near a revetment of their sheep's pasture, where they could grill a medley of vegetables. Some writers call this a Catalan-style ratatouille, but* escalivada *more closely resembles the Tunisian* salāṭa mishwiyya *(page 503), to which it may be historically related. The excellence of this dish comes from absolutely fresh vegetables. Since not everyone has a grill, I provide this alternative to grilling; otherwise, pull out the grill and follow the variation.*

1 eggplant (about 1½ pounds), peeled and sliced
Salt
6 cups pure or virgin olive or olive pomace oil for deep-frying
5 tablespoons extra virgin olive oil
1 large onion, chopped
1 green bell pepper, peeled, seeded, and quartered
8 ripe but firm plum tomatoes, peeled and seeded if desired and cut in half
Freshly ground black pepper to taste

FOR THE VINAIGRETTE SAUCE (WHISKED TOGETHER)
¼ cup extra virgin olive oil
2 tablespoons red wine vinegar
1 garlic clove, finely chopped
1 tablespoon finely chopped fresh parsley leaves
Salt and freshly ground black pepper to taste

1. Lay the eggplant slices on some paper towels and sprinkle with salt. Leave them to drain of their bitter juices for 30 minutes, then pat dry with more paper towels.

2. Preheat the frying oil in a deep-fryer or an 8-inch saucepan with a basket insert to 375°F. Fry the eggplant slices in batches until golden brown, 7 to 8 minutes. Drain on paper towels and let cool. Let the frying oil cool completely, strain, and save for a future use.

3. In a large stove-top and ovenproof casserole, heat 1 tablespoon of the extra virgin olive oil over medium heat, then cook the onion until translucent, 6 to 7 minutes, stirring occasionally. Add the eggplant slices, bell pepper, tomatoes, and a sprinkling of salt and pepper. Mix gently. Pour the remaining ¼ cup extra virgin olive oil over the vegetables and bake, uncovered, for 1 hour. Let cool, then serve with the vinaigrette poured over.

VARIATION

Prepare a hot charcoal fire or preheat a gas grill for 15 minutes on high. Grill the whole unpeeled and unseeded green pepper until its skin blisters black, about 45 minutes. Slip off the skin, remove the core and seeds, and cut into quarters. Pat dry the eggplant after leaching its bitter juices, brush with olive oil, and grill until the pieces have attractive grid marks, about 10 minutes on each side. Boil the whole onion in water to cover for 10 minutes. Peel, split in half, brush with oil, and grill for 30 minutes over a low or dying fire until it is browned and easily pierced with a fork. Mix the grilled pepper, eggplant, and onion and serve with the vinaigrette.

Makes 4 servings

✣ ✣ ✣

MOUNTAIN dwellers went down to the plains at harvest time because there was no work in the mountains; their lives were hard. The typical Mediterranean mountain man was a peddler who specialized in reselling, someone without too many scruples, selling bean meal as a remedy for mange and traveling all over Italy with baskets slung over his neck, like a precursor of the American snake-oil salesman. Displaced mountain people became vagabonds, camp followers, and often soldiers, like the Albanians, who appeared in Cyprus, Sicily, Venice, Mantua, Rome, and Naples, always spoiling for a fight, as did the Corsicans. The Corsicans left their mountainous island for everywhere in the Mediterranean. Hasan Corso, a Corsican converted to Islam, was even the king of Algiers from 1518 to 1556.

Mountain people were physically isolated, as in the Nurra region in Sardinia. This meant they were isolated from the political, social, and economic systems of feudalism, and led an existence that was unstable, primitive, backward, and exceedingly poor. Life was crude in the mountains of the sixteenth century and the food was considered coarse by outsiders. A typical mountain house was a shepherd's hovel built for animals rather than humans—filthy, with a stench so awful that most travelers preferred to sleep outside. There were no roads in or into the mountains. Most mountain people shepherded for a living or were woodcutters, and they had to contend with the massive snows of winter, a lack of food, and precarious shelter. Foraging for fuel, food, and their animals was a constant preoccupation. The mountain family was often confronted by the incursion of pirates or bandits.

Magic and superstition guided mountain people, who also harbored crude concepts of right and wrong, as the medieval concepts of justice never penetrated into the mountains. For this reason one finds the vendetta, the blood feud, in mountainous regions such as the Sicilian Madonie, Corsica, Sardinia, Calabria, Albania, and the Berber lands.[5] There was no

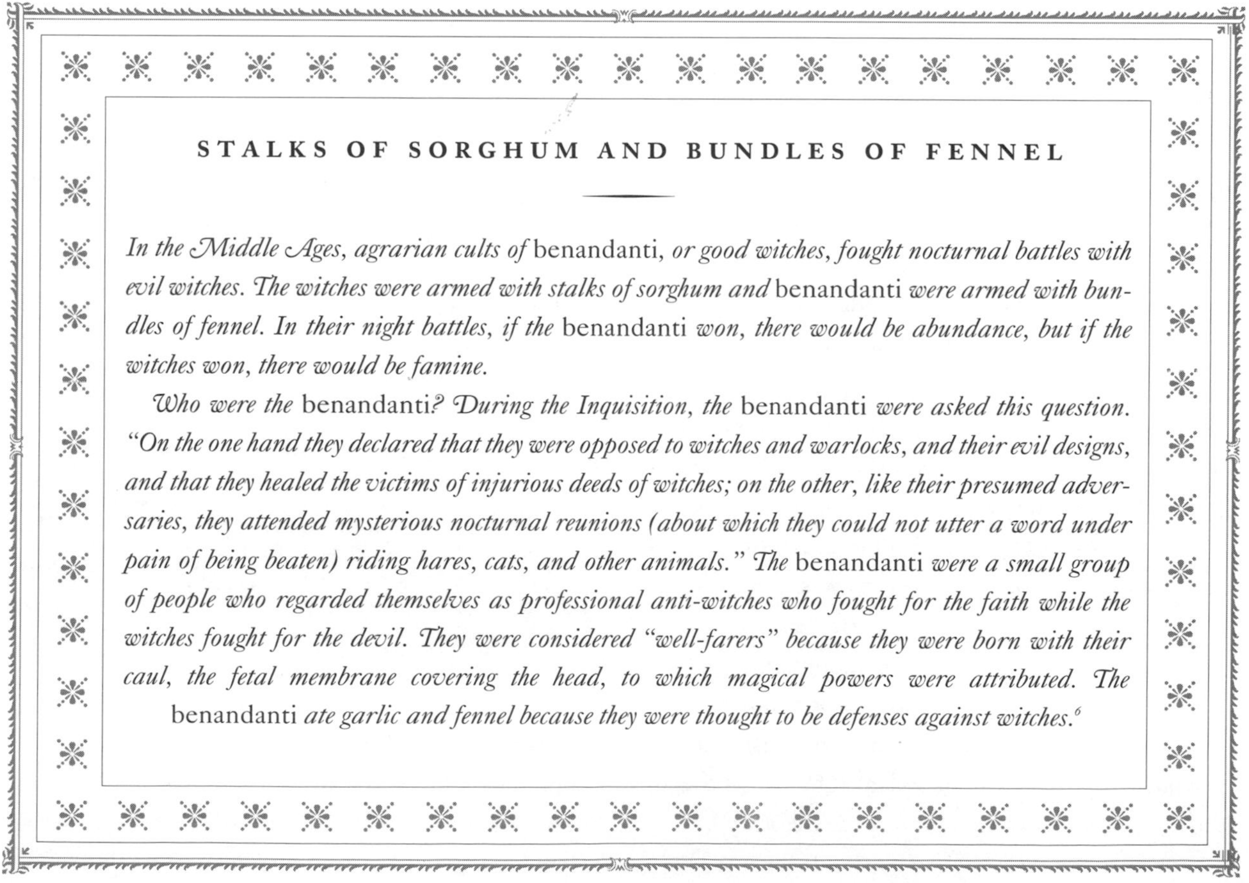

STALKS OF SORGHUM AND BUNDLES OF FENNEL

In the Middle Ages, agrarian cults of benandanti, *or good witches, fought nocturnal battles with evil witches. The witches were armed with stalks of sorghum and* benandanti *were armed with bundles of fennel. In their night battles, if the* benandanti *won, there would be abundance, but if the witches won, there would be famine.*

Who were the benandanti*? During the Inquisition, the* benandanti *were asked this question. "On the one hand they declared that they were opposed to witches and warlocks, and their evil designs, and that they healed the victims of injurious deeds of witches; on the other, like their presumed adversaries, they attended mysterious nocturnal reunions (about which they could not utter a word under pain of being beaten) riding hares, cats, and other animals." The* benandanti *were a small group of people who regarded themselves as professional anti-witches who fought for the faith while the witches fought for the devil. They were considered "well-farers" because they were born with their caul, the fetal membrane covering the head, to which magical powers were attributed. The* benandanti *ate garlic and fennel because they were thought to be defenses against witches.*[6]

landed aristocracy in the mountains and therefore no rich, well-fed clergy to provide guidance and inspiration. The mountain priest was as destitute as the people he served. There was no cuisine in the mountains, merely sustenance.

Documents show that the mountain priests of Corsica were ignorant of Christian practices such as the Lord's Prayer or how to make the sign of the cross. Corsica was idolatrous and barbaric; magic and superstition were integral to everyday life. Murder was rampant, and priests were known to kill in their own churches. Primitive magic and the black masses flourished in the mountains, where aberrant cults found a secure refuge among ignorant people who looked to sorcery and witchcraft to solve their daily problems. At the end of the week, mountain people would have their black sabbath, since Christianity was almost nonexistent at the higher elevations.

The resources of the hills and mountains were important to the entire Mediterranean. On Mediterranean hillsides, a fragile economy of terraced crops such as was to be found in Languedoc, Provence, Sicily, Tuscany, or the Sahel of Algiers, where vines mingle with the trees, oats with vetch for the mules, and wheat with vegetables such as asparagus, was important both locally and for trading with the towns. In Andalusia they even have a name for the asparagus that grows with the wheat, *espárragos trigueros.* In the Abruzzi was Aquila, famous for its saffron, while wheat and barley were important exports of Apulia. From Mt. Etna came vines for wine and grapes, as well as chestnuts, not to mention mineral resources. Animal resources in the mountains were sheep or goats, and for this reason one finds today excellent lamb preparations coming from the mountains. Greece, which is nearly entirely mountainous, offers some intriguing dishes, such as *arni exohiko,* a rustic-tasting preparation made from baby lamb that was brought down from the mountain pastures in the spring.

Revoltijo de Espárragos (Andalusia)

ASPARAGUS MEDLEY

Although both cumin and saffron were known by Hispano-Romans, the presence of these spices here is a possible indication of medieval Arab influence, maybe even introduced by Ziryāb, the ninth-century Arab arbiter of taste, who is known to have popularized the then unpopular asparagus.[7] *Asparagus, native to Europe and eastern Asia, was also cultivated by the ancient Greeks. This dish is made with* espárragos trigueros, *the perennial asparagus that grows in the wheat fields of Andalusia. The asparagus and the sauce should both be very hot when served.*

1 pound thin asparagus, bottoms trimmed
6 tablespoons extra virgin olive oil
2 garlic cloves, peeled
1 slice Italian or French round country bread, crust removed and cut into cubes
Pinch of saffron threads, crumbled
1 teaspoon cumin seeds
2 tablespoons all-purpose flour
6 tablespoons water
3/4 cup dry white wine
Salt and freshly ground white pepper to taste

1. In a large nonreactive saucepan, place the asparagus in lightly salted water brought to a gentle boil and cook until tender, about 12 minutes. Drain well and keep warm.

2. Meanwhile, in a medium-size skillet, heat 3 tablespoons of the olive oil over medium heat, then cook the garlic cloves and bread cubes until golden, about 8 minutes, tossing frequently to keep the garlic from burning and to coat the bread with oil. Remove the garlic and bread to a mortar and pound together

with the saffron, cumin, and another tablespoon of the olive oil until it is completely mixed and mashed.

3. In a medium-size skillet, heat the remaining 2 tablespoons olive oil over medium heat and stir in the flour. Cook, while stirring until the roux is blended and turning ever so slightly light brown, then remove the skillet from the heat and slowly whisk in the water and wine. Stir well to blend and season with salt and pepper. Return to the heat, stir in the bread mixture, and cook for 1 minute. The sauce should have the consistency of a thick mayonnaise; thin with water if necessary.

4. Reheat the asparagus if necessary so it is very hot. Arrange the asparagus on a serving platter, cover with the hot sauce, and serve immediately.

Makes 4 servings

Arni Exohiko (Greece)

COUNTRY-STYLE LAMB

Exohiko *means "countryside" in Greek. Diane Kochilas, the author of* The Food and Wine of Greece, *tells us that this style of food is called* klephtica, *or "of thieves," in reference to the Klephts—early nineteenth-century mountain fighters against the Ottomans—who cooked their foods in buried ovens so they wouldn't give away their positions. Whether this preparation actually derives from the Klephts and, if it did, whether they also used phyllo pastry, seems unlikely to me.*

However, I believe this method of "buried" cooking predates the Greek War of Independence in 1820–1821 because there are similar dishes elsewhere in the Mediterranean, some made in hermetically sealed earthenware jugs dating back to the Arab era of Sicily and even earlier, as well as buried foods in Corsica, Sardinia, and Tunisia. Baking foods underground was more likely a convenient and inexpensive alternative to building an expensive above-ground oven. This recipe is based on my first taste of this country-style lamb in a small taverna in Larisa many years ago.

6 boneless lamb loin chops (about 1¾ pounds), trimmed of some fat
Salt and freshly ground black pepper to taste
10 tablespoons (1¼ sticks) unsalted butter
1 potato, peeled and cut into 12 slices
6 small ripe plum tomatoes, peeled, seeded, and chopped
1 cup fresh or frozen peas
½ pound commercial phyllo pastry (usually 14 × 18-inch sheets; see page 224 on its handling)
½ pound *kasseri* cheese (page 716), cut into 12 slices
2 tablespoons chopped fresh parsley leaves

1. Season the lamb with salt and pepper. In a large skillet, melt 2 tablespoons of the butter over high heat; once it stops sizzling, brown the chops on both sides, about 10 minutes. Remove the lamb with a slotted ladle, scraping the bottom of the skillet, and set aside.

2. In another large skillet, melt 2 tablespoons of the butter over medium-high heat, then cook the potato slices with salt and pepper until golden brown, about 5 minutes per side. Add the tomatoes and cook until soft, about another 5 minutes, then set aside. In a small saucepan, boil the peas in water to cover for 5 minutes and set aside.

3. Preheat oven to 375°F. Melt the remaining 6 tablespoons (¾ stick) butter in a small saucepan and set aside. Brush a sheet of the phyllo pastry with some of the melted butter, using a 2-inch-wide brush. Fold the sheet in half and brush with butter again. Put a lamb chop on the phyllo sheet, along with 2 tablespoons of the peas, two potato slices, a little of the tomato sauce, and two slices of the cheese. Sprinkle with salt, pepper, and a little of the parsley and wrap

into a small square or cylindrical package. Continue in this manner with the rest of the lamb, buttering each sheet of phyllo.

4. Butter a large baking pan and arrange the lamb pies in it. Bake until golden brown, about 40 minutes. If the tops of the phyllo squares begin to burn, cover with a piece of waxed paper oiled on both sides.

Makes 4 to 6 servings

CHEESE, SALT, BUTTER, AND YOGURT

MILK products, such as cheese, butter, and yogurt, and salt are the two great foods of the Middle Ages that are often overlooked by food history writers. Butter and yogurt were staples and were products of the mountains, as was salt. But the salt mines of antiquity found new competition in the salt pans of the Mediterranean Sea, which proved to be economically important. Peccais (Languedoc), Venice, and Trapani (Sicily) all exported salt to the Swiss cantons, whose people needed it for making cheese and salting meat and fish. Salt was used for making *bottarga* in Provence, Sardinia, and Sicily and for the home preserving of asparagus, fresh peas, mushrooms, morels, artichoke hearts, and sardines in the Veneto.[8] A decree of Venice on February 21, 1439, made the salt trade a state monopoly and salted products such as sardines became, and still are, justly famous (see page 434).[9]

Spaghetti alla Bottarga (Sardinia)

SPAGHETTI WITH *BOTTARGA*

The salting of fish roe, called bottarga *in Sardinia and Sicily, derives from the Arabic* baṭarikh, *which in turn derives from the Coptic* pitaoichon *or the Greek* tarichoe, *meaning salted fish or meat.*[10] *It is an old art, and in Sardinia one of the favorite ways of using* bottarga *is with spaghetti. In this dish* bottarga *is grated onto and tossed with spaghetti, and it almost looks like curry—it's golden and glistens from the olive oil.* Bottarga *in Sardinia is either* di tonno *(tuna) or* di muggine *(gray mullet) and restaurant menus often specify which. Fluff the spaghetti a few times and taste the extraordinary. When I first tasted* spaghetti alla bottarga *in the Trattoria Gennargentu in Cágliari, I also noticed that other people were eating very thinly sliced or grated* bottarga *with raw crunchy celery, a popular Sardinian antipasto.*

1 pound spaghetti
Salt
½ cup extra virgin olive oil
1 large garlic clove, crushed
2 to 3 ounces *bottarga* (page 435), finely grated
3 tablespoons very finely chopped fresh parsley leaves (optional)

1. Bring a large pot of water to a rolling boil, salt lightly (not abundantly as instructed elsewhere because the *bottarga* is salty), and add the pasta. Drain when al dente.

2. Meanwhile, in a large skillet or casserole, gently heat the olive oil over low heat with the crushed garlic and all but 2 tablespoons of the grated *bottarga* until the *bottarga* begins to sizzle. Turn the heat off and wait until the spaghetti is ready. Remove and discard the garlic cloves. Add the spaghetti to the casserole and toss well with two forks or tongs until

completely coated with *bottarga*. Serve with a sprinkle of the remaining *bottarga* and the parsley, if using.

Makes 4 to 6 servings

CHEESE was important in the Middle Ages because it was, along with clarified butter (see the *samna* recipe on page 189), the only dairy product that kept for a long time. Sardinian cheeses, such as *caciocavallo* and *salso*, were exported to Naples, Rome, Leghorn, Marseilles, and Barcelona. Cheeses from Candia (Iráklion) on Crete were sold in Venice. Petrus Casola leaves us a vivid description in his diary *Viaggio a Gerusalemme* of the marketing of feta cheese in Candia, expressing surprise when he sees how much of it was loaded onto his own galley because he thought feta was too salty for Italian tastes.[11] In Marseilles they ate the cheeses of the Auvergne in 1543, but a large portion of Marseilles's imported cheese came from Sicily; imports of *fromages de Palerme* were second only to its imports of Sicilian sugar.[12] A combination of these two important products is excellently represented in the Sicilian dessert cannoli.

Cannoli (Sicily)

The convents of Sicily are the great repositories of Arab-influenced desserts, the so-called dolci di badia, *or abbey sweets. Other examples are* muccunetti, *an almond dough stuffed with fruit conserve from Mazara del Vallo and sweets from the Convento di Santa Caterina on Piazza Bellini in Palermo, where they make cannoli as well as* pasticcini farciti con conserva di arance e bergamotto *(pastries stuffed with orange and bergamot preserves) and* marzapane di mandole e pistacchio *(marzipan of almond and pistachio). The great Sicilian gastronome, medical doctor, and Arabist Alberto Denti di Pirajno proposed a theory as to how the convents became home for so many Arab-influenced sweets. During Arab rule in Sicily (827–1091), the inland town of Caltanissetta was called* Qalʿat al-nissa, *the castle of women, because of the fame of the harem of the emir of that city. In the hours when they awaited their masters, the women prepared sweets and cakes. After the Normans conquered Caltanissetta, the harems disappeared but the Muslims did not. They were driven into the mountains, and some converted—perhaps the women found refuge as crypto-Muslim nuns in the convents, bringing their secret recipes along with their secret religion to be handed down through the confines of the convents.*[13]

It was just a matter of time before someone would think to combine sugar and ricotta. Homemade cannoli taste like nothing you've had before. A freshly made cannoli is an extraordinary taste of celestial paradise, a perfect conclusion to a feast. I recommend purchasing some specialized equipment that will make your task significantly easier. First, you need cannoli forms to wrap the pastry around. These tubular metal forms are usually sold in baking supply stores and Italian markets. A pasta-rolling machine is very convenient for rolling the dough into thin sheets. A deep-fryer for home use has regulated temperature controls and will allow you to fry the cannoli pastry to a perfect golden color. You will also need a pastry bag and nozzle for piping the stuffing into the pastry forms and pliers to hold the hot metal forms when they come out of the oil.

Traditionally, cannoli have bits of candied citrus peel and chocolate mixed into the ricotta.

2 cups unbleached all-purpose flour, sifted
1 tablespoon pork lard or unsalted butter
1 tablespoon granulated sugar
½ teaspoon salt

½ cup sweet Marsala wine
6 cups pure or virgin olive oil or olive pomace oil for deep-frying
1 large egg
2 pounds fresh ricotta cheese, preferably homemade (page 467)
¾ cup confectioners' sugar
2 teaspoons orange flower water
7 teaspoons Cointreau or other orange liqueur
½ cup chopped candied citron, orange, or lemon (optional)
6 tablespoons pistachios, crushed
½ cup Maraschino cherries, quartered
Confectioners' sugar for sprinkling

1. On a countertop surface or in a medium-size bowl, combine the flour, lard, granulated sugar, and salt. Make a well and add the Marsala a little at a time until you can form the dough into a ball, picking up any loose pieces. Now begin to knead the dough into a smooth, pliable ball, pressing down with your palms and kneading for 7 to 8 minutes. Form the dough into a ball and let rest at room temperature with the bowl inverted over it. The dough can be refrigerated for later use at this point, although you must let the dough return to room temperature before you can work it.

2. Cut the ball of dough in two and roll out one section in a pasta-rolling machine until it is as thin as a sheet of no-boil lasagne, about 1 millimeter thick. Cut out 4-inch circles with a cookie cutter and continue gathering and rolling and cutting the remaining dough until you have 24 circles.

3. Preheat the frying oil in a deep-fryer or an 8-inch saucepan fitted with a basket insert to 375°F. If you don't have a fryer basket, have a slotted spoon available. Beat the egg in a small bowl. Line a platter with paper towels and set it next to the fryer. Have a pair of pliers handy to grab the hot metal forms when they come out of the oil. Arrange the dough circles and cannoli forms near you. As you will likely have only four to eight cannoli forms, you will need to keep using them until all 24 circles are cooked. The forms do not need to be greased. Take the bottom portion of dough and fold it over on top of the form. Dab your finger in the beaten egg and smear it on top of a small portion of the dough where the top portion will affix itself, making sure you don't get any egg on the metal form. Fold the top portion of the circle over the edge of the bottom portion on the form. Gently roll the form with the dough surrounding it between the palms of your hands to seal the two edges. If you don't do this, the seal will be broken when it fries and the pastry will slip off and puff up.

4. Place the metal form with the pastry in the fryer basket, no more than three at a time, and fry in the hot oil until golden brown, less than 1 minute. Raise the basket or remove the forms with a slotted spoon to the platter using the pliers to pick up the very hot metal forms. When the pastry is cool enough to handle, the metal won't be, so hold the metal form with the pliers and pull the pastry off with your hand, making sure you don't touch the metal. It will either slide off easily or you will have to grasp the pastry and twist firmly but gently. Set the cannoli pastries aside while you finish frying the remainder of the circles. (The cannoli pastry shells can be frozen at this point if desired.) Let the frying oil cool, strain, and save for a future use.

5. In a large bowl, stir together the ricotta, confectioners' sugar, orange flower water, Cointreau, and candied peel, if using, until well blended. Fill the pastry bag with this mixture and then pipe it into the pastry forms when you are within 3 hours of wanting to serve the cannoli. The ricotta should just be poking out of the ends of the pastries. Dip each end of the cannoli into a dish filled with the crushed pistachios and place a quartered piece of cherry into one or both ends of the cannoli. Refrigerate until just before serving. Dust with confectioners' sugar and serve.

Makes 24 cannoli

* * *

SICILIAN cheese was well known in the Middle Ages. Sicilian Jews were involved with the export of cheese to the Jewish community in Alexandria in the thirteenth century, even though there were perfectly fine Egyptian cheeses, such as *ḥalūm* (or *ḥallūm*), a semisoft brined cheese. Egyptians thought that European cheeses were more durable, and there might also have been a snobbish reason for the popularity of Sicilian cheese among the Egyptian upper classes because it was foreign. Salted cheeses tended to be expensive because of the more time-consuming curing process and the cost of salt.[14] When meat was not available, cheese was a replacement. The combination of cheese and pasta in Sicily is as popular today as it was centuries ago. The difference is that cheese and pasta were both expensive in the thirteenth and fourteenth centuries, and eaten only by the better-off people of the cities, and then only about once a month. Today many Sicilian pasta and cheese recipes are involved preparations stemming from the later Baroque era (see page 472), as we see demonstrated in *pasta 'ncaciata*.

The *ḥalūm* cheese mentioned above still exists today, and it is popular for breakfast in Lebanon and Syria, as we see in the recipe following the next one.

Pasta 'Ncaciata (Sicily)

CHEESED PASTA IN A MOLD

There are two famous versions of this classic baked pasta dish from Sicily, sometimes confused by food writers. The first is a molded dish lined with eggplant and stuffed with macaroni, veal, peas, chicken livers, and tomato sauce from Ragusa and called pasta 'ncasciata, *meaning "encased pasta." The second is this recipe from Messina, also molded but with a golden cheese crust of pecorino, called* pasta 'ncaciata, *or "cheesed pasta." There are variations on these two themes, and in place of the eggplant one could also find broccoli, fennel sausage, red wine, pine nuts, and red pepper flakes in other cooks' versions.*

½ cup plus 2 tablespoons extra virgin olive oil
2 garlic cloves, crushed
3 pounds ripe tomatoes, peeled and chopped
½ cup finely chopped fresh basil leaves
2 to 4 eggplant (about 3 pounds), sliced ⅜ inch thick
Salt
6 cups pure or virgin olive oil or olive pomace oil for deep-frying
½ pound ground beef
½ cup dry white wine
1¼ pounds macaroni
½ cup dried bread crumbs
1 cup very finely diced pecorino or *caciocavallo* cheese
Freshly ground black pepper to taste
2 hard-boiled large eggs, shelled and sliced
½ pound fresh mozzarella cheese, sliced
1 ounce *sopressatta* or any other salami, chopped
1 ounce mortadella, chopped
Freshly grated pecorino cheese to taste

1. In a large nonreactive casserole or skillet, heat ¼ cup of the olive oil over medium heat, then cook the garlic cloves, tomatoes, and 2 tablespoons of the basil together until the mixture is somewhat denser, about 20 minutes. Remove and discard the garlic. Remove and reserve ½ cup of tomato sauce for step 6.

2. Lay the eggplant slices on some paper towels and sprinkle with salt. Leave them to drain of their bitter juices for 30 minutes, then pat dry with paper towels.

3. Preheat the frying oil in a deep-fryer or an 8-inch saucepan fitted with a basket insert to 375°F. Fry the eggplant slices in batches until brown, 3 to 4 minutes per side. Remove and drain on paper towels. Let the frying oil cool completely, strain, and save for a future use.

4. In a medium-size skillet, heat another 1/4 cup of the olive oil over medium-high heat, then cook the ground beef until browned, 4 to 5 minutes, breaking it up with a wooden spoon or fork. Pour in the wine and cook until it evaporates. Stir in 1/4 cup of the tomato sauce from the casserole.

5. Meanwhile, bring a large pot of water to a rolling boil, salt abundantly, and add the macaroni. Drain when very al dente and toss with the tomato sauce in the casserole. Preheat the oven to 400°F.

6. Coat a deep baking pan or casserole with the remaining 2 tablespoons olive oil and sprinkle with the bread crumbs, shaking them around the pan so it is evenly covered. Pour in a layer of half the sauced macaroni, then a third of the diced pecorino, then all of the cooked beef, pepper to taste, half the fried eggplant, another third of the pecorino, the remaining 6 tablespoons basil, the sliced eggs, mozzarella, salami, and mortadella, the last third of pecorino, and make a last layer of the remaining macaroni, and the eggplant. Spread the top with the 1/2 cup reserved tomato sauce and sprinkle grated pecorino on top. Bake until the cheese on top is golden brown, 30 to 40 minutes. Let it rest for 10 minutes and then unmold and serve.

Makes 6 to 8 servings

Jubna Ḥallūm Maqliyya (Arab Levant)

FRIED *HALLOUMI* CHEESE

One of the first mentions of ḥallūm *cheese is in an account by the tenth-century Arab writer al-Muqqadasī, who said that this salted cheese was being used in Egyptian cuisine.*[15]

Ḥallūm *or* halloumi *cheese is very popular in Syria and Lebanon, although most of today's production is in Cyprus.* Halloumi *is a semisoft cheese made from raw sheep's milk sometimes mixed with goat's milk. The cheese is formed into blocks 6 × 4 × 1 inch. These blocks are then cooked in the hot whey, after which they are salted, folded over on themselves, and submerged in brine.*

Halloumi, *once in the home, is soaked in several changes of fresh cold water for 24 hours, then sliced lengthwise and fried in clarified butter. I usually eat* jubna maqliyya *in the Arab style, as a breakfast dish with some Arab bread, olives,* zaʿtar *(page 524), and* labna *(page 186). This recipe can also be made with* jubna bayḍā', *Syrian white cheese, both readily available in Middle Eastern markets and increasingly in well-stocked supermarkets.*

2 tablespoons *samna* (clarified butter; page 189), unsalted butter, or extra virgin olive oil
1/4 pound *halloumi* cheese or Syrian white cheese (*jubna bayḍā'*; page 716), soaked in water to cover for 24 hours, drained, and sliced into 2-inch squares about 1/2 inch thick

1. In a large skillet, heat the *samna* over medium-high heat; when it begins to bubble, add the cheese slices. Cook until their bottoms are golden brown, 2 to 3 minutes, then turn with a spatula, making sure to scrape up the burnt crust.

2. Cook for another 2 to 3 minutes and serve.

Makes 2 servings

Saganaki (Greece)

FRIED CHEESE

Athenaeus (c. 170–c. 230), the Greek food writer, relates that Pherecrates, author of The Slave-Teacher, *waxed poetic about "melted cheese sizzling."*[16] *The Greeks still love melted cheese and they use a* saganaki, *a small two-handled pan, to make this preparation of the same name. Many Greeks will admit that* saganaki *is secretly their favorite* meze, *which is a little tidbit to be had with a glass of ouzo. They say "secretly" because as gourmets they shouldn't be admitting to loving a dish so simple. In Nea Mystra we had some beautiful* mezedes *(plural) of Kalamata olives and* saganaki *with lemon wedges and ouzo. Do not salt since the cheese is salty enough.*

½ pound *kefalotyri* cheese (page 716), cut into wedges 3 × 2 × ¼ inch
All-purpose flour for dredging
½ cup pure or virgin olive oil
Freshly ground black pepper to taste
Lemon wedges for garnish

1. Soak the cheese in water for 30 minutes. Pat dry with paper towels and dredge in flour, tapping off any excess.

2. In a small cast-iron skillet, heat the olive oil over medium heat until it begins to smoke. Add the pieces of cheese and cook until golden brown, about 2½ minutes in all, turning only once. Sprinkle with pepper and serve with lemon wedges.

VARIATION

Place under the broiler until bubbling.

Makes 3 to 4 servings

ALTHOUGH the cookery books of the time do not give much notice of cheese, it was the protein par excellence for sixteenth-century Mediterranean peoples. The first authoritative Italian work on dairy products, the *Summa lacticiniorum* by Pantaleone da Confienza, written in the latter part of the fifteenth century, describes some of the best cheeses, mentioning the cheeses of the Val d'Aosta as being very tasty—perhaps a description of fontina.[17] The best

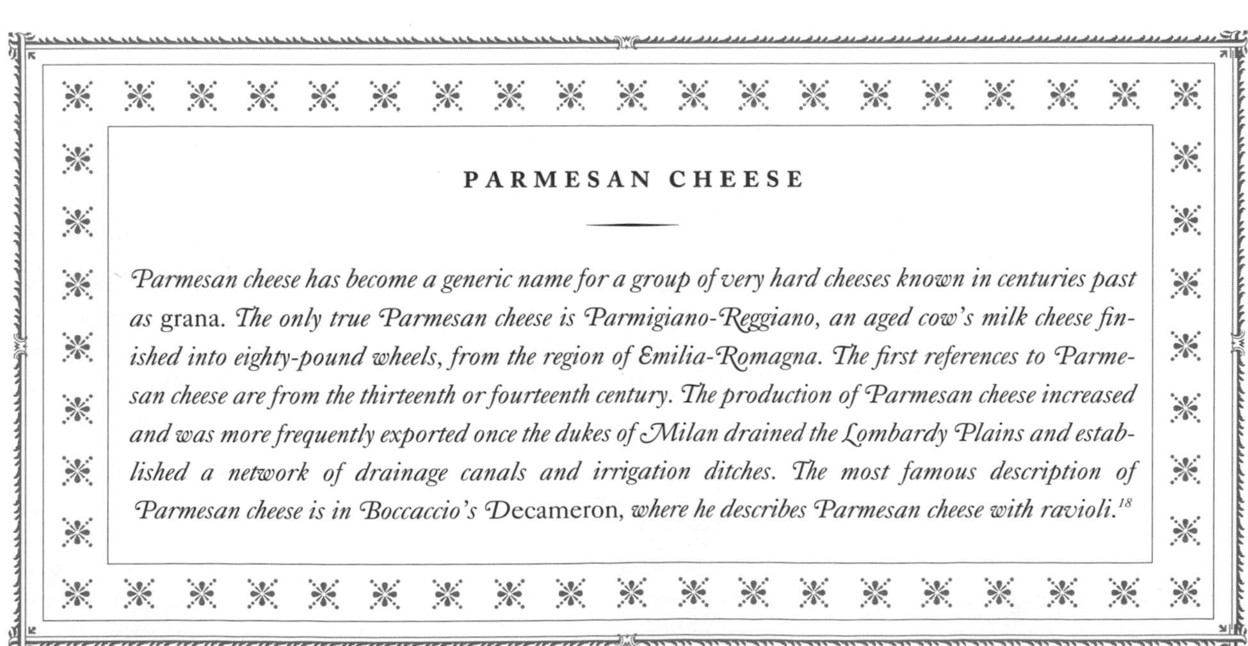

PARMESAN CHEESE

Parmesan cheese has become a generic name for a group of very hard cheeses known in centuries past as grana. *The only true Parmesan cheese is Parmigiano-Reggiano, an aged cow's milk cheese finished into eighty-pound wheels, from the region of Emilia-Romagna. The first references to Parmesan cheese are from the thirteenth or fourteenth century. The production of Parmesan cheese increased and was more frequently exported once the dukes of Milan drained the Lombardy Plains and established a network of drainage canals and irrigation ditches. The most famous description of Parmesan cheese is in Boccaccio's* Decameron, *where he describes Parmesan cheese with ravioli.*[18]

cheeses were considered to be those made from cow's or ewe's milk, while goat cheese was considered inferior for some reason. The cheeses of Sardinia and Corsica were famous in the Middle Ages. Sardinian cheese was exported all over the Mediterranean of Philip II's day (the second half of the sixteenth century), while the hilly and mountainous regions of Languedoc became important sources for cheeses such as the famous one from Roquefort-sur-Soulzon. In fact, in 1702 a noted medical writer, without explaining why, listed only three great cheeses: Roquefort, Parmigiano-Reggiano, and those from Sassenage in Dauphiné, the province of which Grenoble is the capital.[19] Cheeses were kept in leather pouches called *tulum* or made in wheels or balls, like the famous mountain cheese of Wallachia, the region of the lower Danubian plain of Romania, *cascaval.* The latter was exported to Istanbul and Italy, where it became known as *caciocavallo. Cascaval* is a ewe's milk cheese repeatedly boiled, as is *caciocavallo* in Sardinia and Italy.[20]

Today, cheese is the star of two contemporary Roquefort preparations from Languedoc.

Tarte au Roquefort (Languedoc)

ROQUEFORT TART

In the mountainous Rouergue is the small village of Roquefort-sur-Soulzon, where they make the famous ewe's milk cheese with its distinctive blue veins of Penicillium roqueforti. *Roquefort is probably France's oldest cheese, although perhaps not as old as some people claim—since it is mentioned in Pliny's* Natural History.[21] *Called the doyen of French cheeses, Roquefort is made by mixing the curds with ground dried bread crumbs that have developed a green mold.*

The geology of these limestone plateaux called causses *is highly permeable, so water seeps into the ground to carve caves and grottos. Here in one of these systems of underground caves and tunnels the cheese of Roquefort is allowed to ripen for up to a year. The caves provide an environment suited to the growth of the green mold, which turns ordinary white ewe's cheese into blue cheese. Only the blue-veined sheep cheeses that are made in these caves of Roquefort are allowed by law to be called Roquefort. In the Aude and Ariège, the same caves also supported communities of prehistoric peoples, who left their artwork on the cave walls.*

If you are using a square or rectangular piece of pâte feuilletée, *you can either cut and crimp the excess dough or simply flip it over into the pan over the filling.*

8 to 10 ounces commercial *pâte feuilletée* (puff pastry)
2 large eggs
1 cup crème fraîche (page 712)
Freshly ground black pepper to taste
¼ pound imported Roquefort cheese, crumbled

1. Preheat the oven to 425°F. Roll the puff pastry out slightly on a floured work surface so that it can cover the bottom of an 8- to 9-inch tart or shallow pie pan. Fit the puff pastry into the pan and prick the bottom carefully with a toothpick. Trim the edges if desired.

2. In a medium-size bowl, beat together the eggs, crème fraîche, pepper, and Roquefort. Pour the mixture into the pan and, if you have not trimmed the pastry, flip the edges over on top of the filling. Bake until the top is speckled brown, about 25 minutes.

Makes 6 servings

Pavé Croustillant de Saumon au Roquefort Effeuillé d'Épinards (Languedoc)

SALMON IN PUFF PASTRY WITH SPINACH AND ROQUEFORT

Although Roquefort was made in the mountains, mountain people rarely ate much of it in times past, exporting most of it to elsewhere in France, and later abroad. In 1411, Charles VI granted the people of Roquefort-sur-Soulzon the monopoly of ripening the cheese in their caves as they had been doing for several hundred years. This elegant preparation—what appears to be an unusual combination of fish with a cheese sauce results in a fresh, light taste—is purely a restaurant specialty and not part of home cooking. But I chose this recipe, a modern creation given to me by Chef Patrick Lenfant of the Michelin one-star Grand Hotel in Roquefort-sur-Soulzon, because it accepts rather than rejects some of the historical elements of the local food, such as the spinach, the Roquefort, and the pâte feuilletée.

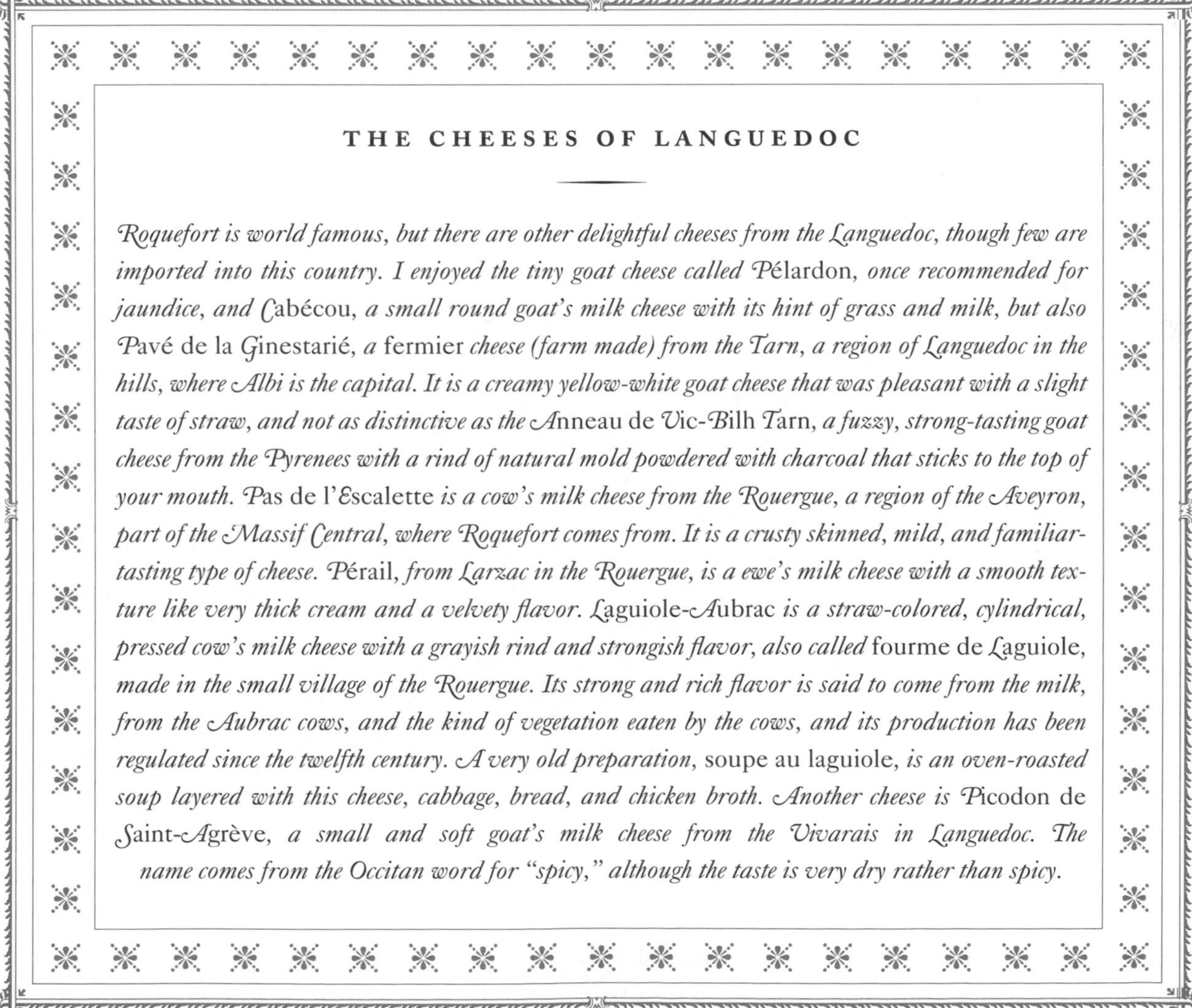

THE CHEESES OF LANGUEDOC

Roquefort is world famous, but there are other delightful cheeses from the Languedoc, though few are imported into this country. I enjoyed the tiny goat cheese called Pélardon, *once recommended for jaundice, and* Cabécou, *a small round goat's milk cheese with its hint of grass and milk, but also* Pavé de la Ginestarié, *a* fermier *cheese (farm made) from the Tarn, a region of Languedoc in the hills, where Albi is the capital. It is a creamy yellow-white goat cheese that was pleasant with a slight taste of straw, and not as distinctive as the* Anneau de Vic-Bilh Tarn, *a fuzzy, strong-tasting goat cheese from the Pyrenees with a rind of natural mold powdered with charcoal that sticks to the top of your mouth.* Pas de l'Escalette *is a cow's milk cheese from the Rouergue, a region of the Aveyron, part of the Massif Central, where Roquefort comes from. It is a crusty skinned, mild, and familiar-tasting type of cheese.* Pérail, *from Larzac in the Rouergue, is a ewe's milk cheese with a smooth texture like very thick cream and a velvety flavor.* Laguiole-Aubrac *is a straw-colored, cylindrical, pressed cow's milk cheese with a grayish rind and strongish flavor, also called* fourme de Laguiole, *made in the small village of the Rouergue. Its strong and rich flavor is said to come from the milk, from the Aubrac cows, and the kind of vegetation eaten by the cows, and its production has been regulated since the twelfth century. A very old preparation,* soupe au laguiole, *is an oven-roasted soup layered with this cheese, cabbage, bread, and chicken broth. Another cheese is* Picodon de Saint-Agrève, *a small and soft goat's milk cheese from the Vivarais in Languedoc. The name comes from the Occitan word for "spicy," although the taste is very dry rather than spicy.*

8 to 10 ounces commercial *pâte feuilletée* (puff pastry)
1 cup crème fraîche (page 712)
7 ounces imported Roquefort cheese
1 tablespoon cognac
Salt and freshly ground black pepper to taste
1 pound fresh spinach, heavy stems removed and washed well
3 tablespoons extra virgin olive oil
1 garlic clove, finely chopped
One 1¾-pound skinless salmon fillet, cut into 6 equal-size pieces

1. Preheat the oven to 350°F.

2. Roll the sheet of pastry out a bit, following the instructions on the package, and cut the pastry sheet into 12 equal triangles. Place on an ungreased baking sheet and bake until golden brown, about 20 minutes. Remove to a wire rack to cool and set aside.

3. In a medium-size heavy saucepan, warm the crème fraîche, then crumble the Roquefort into it with the cognac. Lightly salt and pepper the sauce. Keep warm, not letting it get too hot, and never to a boil.

4. Meanwhile, bring a large saucepan of lightly salted water to a boil and cook the spinach for 1 to 2 minutes. Drain the spinach and plunge into ice water to stop the cooking. Drain very well, pressing out as much liquid as you can with the back of a wooden spoon, and then blot with paper towels.

5. In a small, heavy saucepan, heat the spinach over medium-low heat with 1 tablespoon of the olive oil, the garlic, and 2 tablespoons of the Roquefort sauce. Keep warm.

6. In a large skillet, heat the remaining 2 tablespoons olive oil over medium heat, then cook the salmon, seasoned lightly with salt and pepper, until the fish can be flaked, about 10 minutes. Turn only once, lifting with a spatula occasionally to avoid sticking. Remove from the skillet and keep warm covered with a sheet of aluminum foil.

7. Rewarm the pastry triangles in the oven for a few minutes. On six individual plates or one serving platter, arrange six triangles of baked pastry. Layer them with the spinach and place a salmon piece on top. Place the six remaining pastry triangles on top of each piece of salmon and pour the Roquefort over. Serve immediately.

Makes 6 servings

IN Turkey, and other Muslim lands, milk, butter, and cheese played a great role in providing nutritionally rich food. Yogurt was an important food for the poor. Depending on the season, it was eaten with cucumbers or melons, onions or leeks, or stewed dried fruit. The Bedouin could transport their dried yogurt, *jamīd*, from place to place without spoilage (see page 244). Another Turkish staple was a milk product called *kaymak*, a slightly salted boiled cream (see page 185).

Yoğurt (Turkey)

HOMEMADE YOGURT

Yogurt, *a Turkish word, is a semisolid cultured or fermented milk containing the bacteria* Bacillus bulgaricus *and* Streptococcus thermophilus.[22] *These organisms present in the "starter," given warmth, will ferment whole or skimmed fresh milk overnight.*

Yogurt may have been known by the ancient Greeks as pyriate. *Andrew Dalby, who wrote an important study on classical Greek gastronomy, argues that the Greek physician Galen (c. 130–c. 200) was correct to identify this older term,* pyriate, *with the* oxygala *familiar in his own day, which was a form of yogurt and was eaten on its own or with honey.*[23] *The first unequivocal description of yogurt is found in a dictionary called* Divanu luga-i turk, *compiled by Kaşgarli Mahmut in 1072–1073 during the Seljuk era in the Middle East (1038–1194).*[24] *Yogurt spread rapidly throughout the Levant, but it hardly penetrated the western and northern Mediterranean. The use of yogurt was first recorded in France in the sixteenth century, when it was said to have cured the ailing King Francis I. The yogurt was administered daily by a Jewish doctor who had traveled on foot from Constantinople accompanied by a flock of sheep, and that was the last France saw of yogurt until the nineteenth century.*[25]

The Turks are far more picky about yogurt than Americans, and as a result one finds very high-quality yogurt in Turkey. Most yogurt is made from cow's milk, with some made from sheep's milk, while goat's milk yogurt is rare in Turkey. Yogurt is a staple food in the Middle East and is now ubiquitous in the United States, where very high-quality yogurt can occasionally be found.

1 quart whole cow's milk, preferably fresh and unhomogenized
3 tablespoons high-quality full-fat plain yogurt

1. In a medium-size heavy saucepan, bring the milk to a gentle boil over medium heat, making sure you do not scald the bottom of the pot. Once the milk is shimmering on the surface, simmer for 2 minutes. Pour the milk into a large bowl and let cool until you can keep your little finger submerged in it to a count of 10.

2. Stir a few tablespoons of the hot milk into the yogurt and then quickly stir this back into the hot milk. Cover the bowl and leave overnight, wrapped in

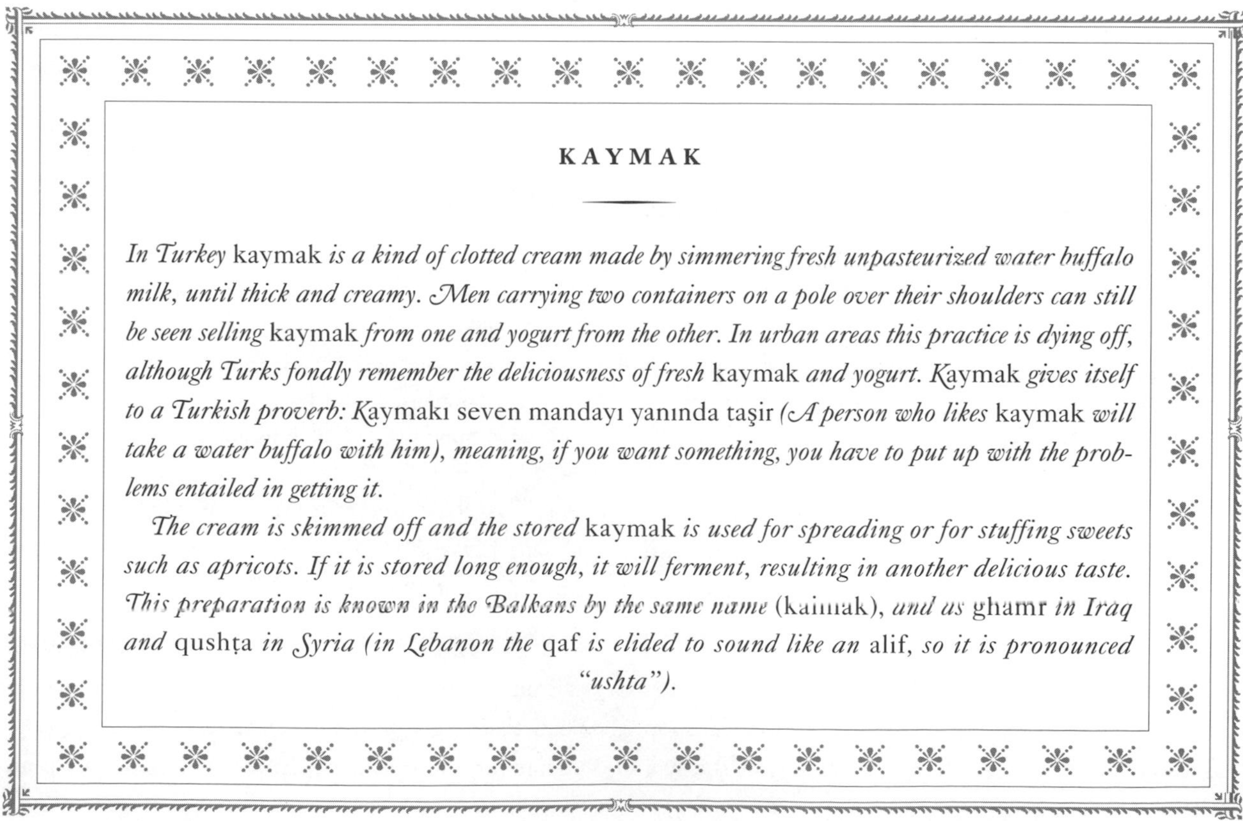

KAYMAK

In Turkey kaymak *is a kind of clotted cream made by simmering fresh unpasteurized water buffalo milk, until thick and creamy. Men carrying two containers on a pole over their shoulders can still be seen selling* kaymak *from one and yogurt from the other. In urban areas this practice is dying off, although Turks fondly remember the deliciousness of fresh* kaymak *and yogurt.* Kaymak *gives itself to a Turkish proverb:* Kaymakı seven mandayı yanında taşir *(A person who likes* kaymak *will take a water buffalo with him), meaning, if you want something, you have to put up with the problems entailed in getting it.*

The cream is skimmed off and the stored kaymak *is used for spreading or for stuffing sweets such as apricots. If it is stored long enough, it will ferment, resulting in another delicious taste. This preparation is known in the Balkans by the same name* (kaimak), *and as* ghamr *in Iraq and* qushṭa *in Syria (in Lebanon the* qaf *is elided to sound like an* alif, *so it is pronounced "ushta").*

a wool blanket or inside a turned-off oven. The next morning you will have homemade yogurt that will keep for a week. You can save some of this homemade yogurt as your starter for the next batch.

NOTE: To make strained yogurt (*labna* in Arabic; *süzme yoğurt* in Turkish), pour the yogurt into a linen towel or several layers of cheesecloth, tie off, and hang from a kitchen sink faucet to drain overnight. In the Middle East, strained yogurt is used as a breakfast spread for Arabic bread, served as a dip for hot foods, or is eaten plain with some olive oil or honey.

Makes 1 quart

Stabilized Yogurt

Cow's milk yogurt will separate when heated beyond a certain point, so for cooking purposes it must be stabilized before heating. This process is necessary in all dishes requiring cooked yogurt.

1 quart high-quality full-fat plain cow's milk yogurt
1 large egg white, beaten
1 tablespoon cornstarch
1 teaspoon salt

1. Beat the yogurt in a large, heavy saucepan with a fork until smooth. Beat in the egg white, cornstarch, and salt.

2. Put the saucepan over high heat and start stirring in one direction with a wooden spoon. As soon as it starts to bubble, about 6 minutes, reduce the heat to medium and boil gently until it is thick, about 5 minutes. Now the yogurt is ready to use in other dishes. It will keep for a week in the refrigerator.

Makes 1 quart

Cacık (Turkey)

YOGURT AND CUCUMBER SAUCE

Cacık *(pronounced JA-juk) is so common throughout Turkey that it becomes a comforting sight, a relish for virtually any prepared food, especially good with kebabs and* köfte *(grilled meatballs), although many Turks actually eat it alone as a* meze*. In the Anatolian town of Bursa, men like to blow bubbles into the* cacık *with a straw to make it frothy, in identical fashion to what American parents admonish their children not to do with their milk.*

1 large cucumber, peeled, seeded, and grated
Salt to taste
3 garlic cloves, mashed
2 cups thick, high-quality full-fat plain yogurt (see Note)
1 tablespoon chopped fresh dill
¾ teaspoon dried mint
1 tablespoon extra virgin olive oil

1. Toss the grated cucumber with a light sprinkling of salt. Leave for 30 minutes. Drain the cucumber, squeezing out all the liquid.

2. Pound the garlic in a mortar with 1 teaspoon salt until completely mashed. Stir the garlic into the yogurt and beat with a fork until smooth. Stir in the cucumber, the dill, mint, and olive oil and stir until

the consistency of a thick soup. Refrigerate for 1 hour and serve cold.

NOTE: If the yogurt you usually buy is not thick, stir some *labna* into it (strained yogurt; page 186).

Makes 3 cups

Açili Esme (Turkey)

SPICY TURKISH-STYLE YOGURT DIP

Ogier Ghiselin de Busbecq was a multifaceted Belgian and imperial ambassador to the Ottoman Empire in 1554. He wrote many letters describing his stay, and the foods he encountered. One food that he found fascinating was yogurt, which the Turks, he told us, diluted with very cold water and crumbled bread into it and took it when they were very hot and thirsty.[26] *This preparation is a simple blend made with yogurt and garlic, a spiced-up* cacık. *You eat it with pieces of bread and scallions, but I also loved to dip* köfte *(page 336) into it.*

1 teaspoon salt
4 garlic cloves, peeled
3/4 cup high-quality full-fat plain yogurt
6 tablespoons *labna* (strained yogurt; page 186)
1/2 teaspoon cayenne pepper
1 teaspoon chopped fresh dill
Extra virgin olive oil for drizzling
Whole scallions for garnish
French bread

1. In a mortar, pound the salt and garlic together until mushy.

2. In a small bowl, blend the garlic with the yogurt, *labna*, cayenne, and dill. Drizzle with a small amount of olive oil and serve with scallions and good French bread.

Makes 4 servings

Yoğurtlu Patlıcan Biber Kızartması (Turkey)

FRIED EGGPLANT AND PEPPERS WITH YOGURT AND GARLIC SAUCE

Since before the days of Süleiman I the Magnificent (1494–1566), yogurt has been a staple food in Turkey, and a class of dishes prepared with yogurt are known as yoğurtlu, *which means "dishes prepared with yogurt." This simple one with fried eggplant and peppers is one of my favorites. As the name indicates* (kızartması *means "to roast"), one can also roast rather than fry the eggplant and peppers.*

2 eggplant (about 3 pounds), peeled and sliced into 3/8-inch-thick rounds
Salt
3 large garlic cloves, peeled
6 cups pure or virgin olive oil or olive pomace oil for deep-frying
6 poblano chili peppers (about 3/4 pound)
2 cups high-quality full-fat plain yogurt

1. Lay the eggplant slices on some paper towels and sprinkle with salt. Leave them to drain of their bitter juices for 30 minutes, then pat dry with paper towels. Mash the garlic with 1 teaspoon salt in a mortar until completely mushy.

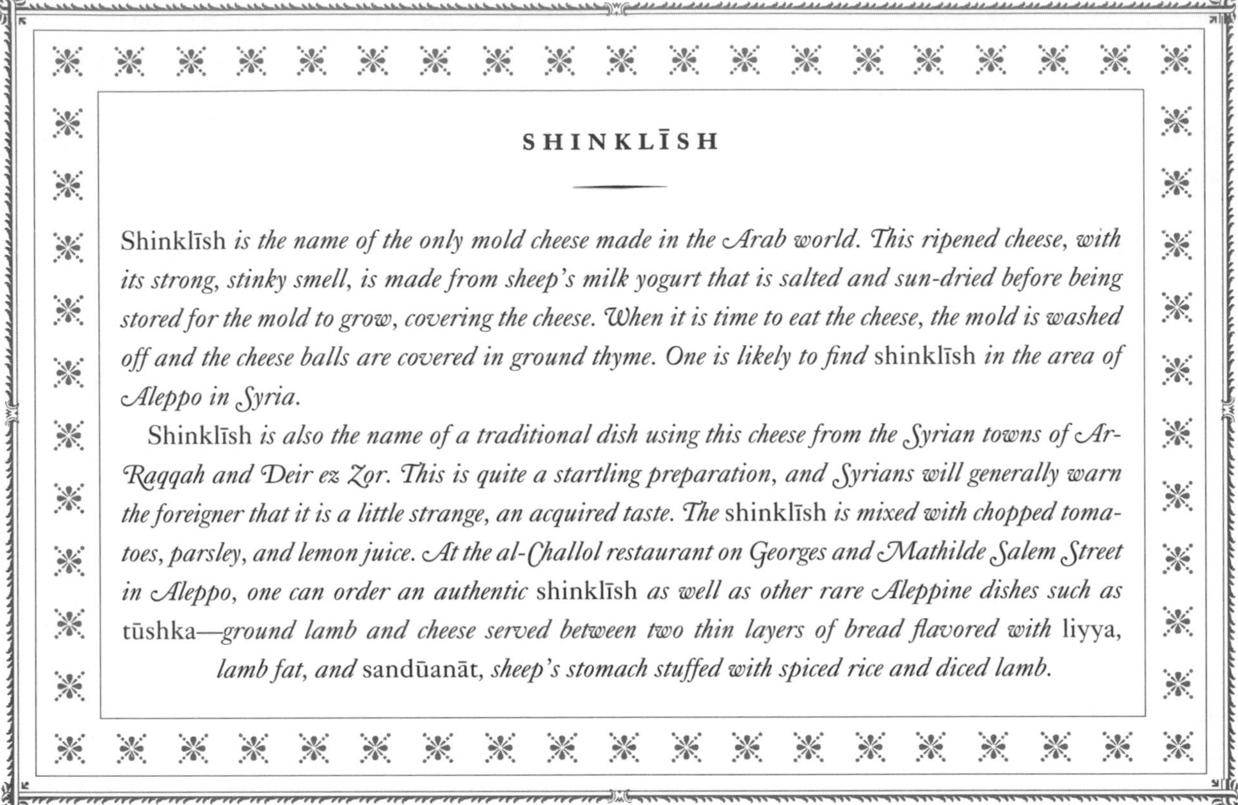

SHINKLĪSH

Shinklīsh *is the name of the only mold cheese made in the Arab world. This ripened cheese, with its strong, stinky smell, is made from sheep's milk yogurt that is salted and sun-dried before being stored for the mold to grow, covering the cheese. When it is time to eat the cheese, the mold is washed off and the cheese balls are covered in ground thyme. One is likely to find* shinklīsh *in the area of Aleppo in Syria.*

Shinklīsh *is also the name of a traditional dish using this cheese from the Syrian towns of Ar-Raqqah and Deir ez Zor. This is quite a startling preparation, and Syrians will generally warn the foreigner that it is a little strange, an acquired taste. The* shinklīsh *is mixed with chopped tomatoes, parsley, and lemon juice. At the al-Challol restaurant on Georges and Mathilde Salem Street in Aleppo, one can order an authentic* shinklīsh *as well as other rare Aleppine dishes such as* tūshka—*ground lamb and cheese served between two thin layers of bread flavored with* liyya, *lamb fat, and* sandūanāt, *sheep's stomach stuffed with spiced rice and diced lamb.*

2. Preheat the frying oil in a deep-fryer or an 8-inch saucepan with a basket insert to 375°F. Deep-fry the eggplant slices in batches until golden brown, 7 to 8 minutes, turning once. Drain and transfer to a platter covered with paper towels to drain further. Arrange on a serving platter.

3. Deep-fry the peppers in the hot oil until the skins are crispy and peeling, about 3½ minutes, turning once. Arrange over the eggplant slices. Mix the yogurt and mashed garlic, stirring well, spoon over the eggplant and peppers, and serve. Let the frying oil cool completely, strain, and save for a future use.

Makes 4 to 6 servings

Yoğurtlu Şalgam (Turkey)

FRIED TURNIPS WITH YOGURT

In the mountainous Anatolia of the thirteenth century, turnips were a common food, along with vegetables like leeks, celeriac, onions, garlic, cucumbers, black-eyed peas, lentils, chickpeas, and fava beans. The literary works of the Persian mystic Jalal al-Din Muhammad Din al-Rumi, who lived in the thirteenth century and whose followers founded the Whirling Dervishes, contain many references to food, which he categorized—for example, meats stewed with vegetables or foods with yogurt.

This recipe of turnips and yogurt is adapted from a much later date, from Turabi Effendi, the author of one of the first Turkish cookery books translated into Eng-

lish in the mid-nineteenth century. I never would have thought of turnips and yogurt together, but after tasting this I think you will agree they are naturals.

1 pound small turnips
All-purpose flour for dredging
1/4 cup (1/2 stick) unsalted butter
Salt
2/3 cup beef broth (page 54)
1 to 2 cups high-quality full-fat plain yogurt, to your taste
Freshly ground black pepper to taste

1. In a large saucepan, boil the turnips whole in water to cover until they can be pierced with a skewer, about 25 minutes. Drain, peel, and cut into 1/4-inch-thick slices.

2. Preheat the oven to 350°F. Dredge the turnip slices in the flour, tapping off any excess. In a large skillet, melt 3 tablespoons of the butter over medium-high heat, then cook the turnips, salting to taste, until golden on both sides, 8 to 10 minutes. Remove to a baking pan.

Harvesting turnips in October in fourteenth-century Italy. Officium Beatae Virginis. Italian codex. Biblioteca Civica, Forli, Italy.
SCALA/ART RESOURCE.

3. Pour the beef broth over the turnips and bake until tender, about 15 minutes. Remove from the oven and coat with the remaining tablespoon butter. Cover with the yogurt and a grinding of pepper and serve.

Makes 4 servings

Samna (Middle East and North Africa)

CLARIFIED BUTTER

Samna *is butter that is clarified, a process that removes the milk solids to render the butter more suitable for cooking purposes, as milk solids burn, and to increase its shelf life. It is also known as* sman *(sometimes transliterated as* smen*) and by the Hindi word* ghee. *Shepherds would make their own clarified butter, to use some themselves and sell the surplus at the market. Arab gourmets insist that* samna *is ideally made from water buffalo butter, although today in the Arab world butter is mostly made from cow's milk. In the Middle East and North Africa, the clarified butter is strained through salt into an earthenware container for storage, then aged, acquiring a unique taste. The Bedouin of the Sinai and Negev flavor their* samna *with the leaves of* nafal (Trigonella arabica), *a kind of clover.*

I cannot recommend buying canned, commercially made ghee. *It is made from vegetables and has, as far as I'm concerned, a ghastly rancid taste. Given the number of recipes in this book cooked in* samna, *I think it worth your while to make this amount fresh.* Samna *will keep for six months in the refrigerator.*

2 pounds (8 sticks) unsalted butter, quartered

1. In a large, heavy saucepan, melt the butter over low heat until completely melted or until you detect the first sign of bubbling, in which case turn the heat even lower or use a heat diffuser. Turn the heat off and let the butter cool but not solidify.

2. Tilt the saucepan, then carefully gather all the foam to one side, spoon it off, and discard. Carefully pour or spoon the liquid butter into the container you are using to store it, being careful not to let any of the milk solids on the bottom of the pan pour in. Alternatively, pour the butter through a damp cheesecloth-lined strainer into the container.

VARIATION

I've made *samna* in a microwave, and it was the easiest method of all. Place the butter in a microwavable container and run at medium power until the butter is melted. Carefully pour the clarified butter into your container, making sure no milk solids fall in.

Makes 1½ pounds (3 cups) samna

RECLAIMING THE LAND

WHILE the mountains were locked in their archaic ways in the sixteenth century, it was on the once stagnant plains of the Mediterranean that a vibrant new agronomy was forming on reclaimed land. Big trading cities such as Venice, Florence, and Milan, whose long-term trade provided contacts with the rest of the world and high profit margins, were able to utilize accumulated capital to turn their hinterlands, usually plains, into productive agricultural areas. The French historian of the Mediterranean Fernand Braudel suggests that perhaps the reason Italy did not play a great role during the Age of Exploration was its preoccupation with reclaiming land. Francesco Guicciardini (1483–1540), in his *History of Italy*, notes that "Italy is cultivated right up to the mountain tops."[27]

Venice began major dike improvements around 1574 by establishing a system of *ritratti*—networks of dikes, canals, and trenches—to drain marshes and irrigate. Agriculture in the Roman *campagna* flourished in the fifteenth century, and great estates were built with huge farms that rotated their crops, wheat being the chief produce; large-scale stock farming found its labor coming from the mountainous Abruzzi region.

The populated plains of Apulia we see today are the result of centuries of toil involving land reclamation. The mountain villages became indispensable to the life of the towns and plains. Many people came from the mountains, such as the Lombards—mountain dwellers who left their homes for the south. Researchers have found numerous Lombard surnames appearing in documents from thirteenth-century Sicily and sixteenth-century Naples.[28] But reclamation was a slow process. The plains were not completely drained even by the sixteenth century, for the population was still rebuilding itself one hundred and fifty years after the Black Death.

Land reclamation proceeded in Turkey as well, where marshes were turned into productive lands through the efforts of rich noblemen, who created new villages of *ciftliks*—serfs who worked the land.

As early as the twelfth century, Languedoc drained its marshes, the abbeys and monasteries often leading the way, employing vast amounts of capital and labor. The brackish waters between Nîmes, the Rhône, and the sea were turned into virgin soil and the marshland into plowland. Land was reclaimed not only along the coasts but also up toward the mountains. Towns began to spring up as the population increased, which in turn stimulated the rise of irrigated market gardening on the alluvial plains—around Béziers, for example. Saffron was grown and exported from Albi, and cabbage was a popular vegetable in these market gardens; but Languedoc was also sprouting Catharism, a heresy soon to be crushed by the Pope in the Albigensian crusade. Languedoc was experiencing a booming spice trade as well as Catharist turmoil, and the lords of Béziers were "collectors of cabbage tithes before they became pillars of heresy."[29]

Gras-Double Safrané à l'Albigeoise (Languedoc)

ALBI-STYLE TRIPE STEW WITH SAFFRON

Albi, capital of the Tarn region in the Haut-Languedoc, from the tenth to fourteenth centuries was the center of a widespread sect of heretical Christians known as the Cathars. They were dualists who believed in a good God and a bad God, and that all people were ultimately saved. One Catharist declared that if he could "get hold of the false and perfidious God of the Catholics who created a thousand men in order to save a single one and damn all the rest, he would break him to pieces and tear him asunder with his nails and spit in his face."[30]

The Cathars, especially the holy men, lived by extremely hard rules, abstaining from all flesh except fish. They could not eat cheese, eggs, or milk because they were per viam generationis seu coitus, *produced through coitus. The Catholic church rejected Catharist philosophy, and Papal armies under northern leadership viciously wiped out the Cathar heresy during the Albigensian crusade of the early thirteenth century. There is no evidence of the Cathars today, or their beliefs, although the massive red fortresslike cathedral of Albi was certainly built to intimidate and awe any who did not follow the Church of St. Peter.*

I first ate this magnificent dish in the shadow of the church, a preparation that would tempt any Catharist monk. L'Auberge Saint-Loup is run by the obstreperous gastronome M. Bernard Valette, who serves les spécialitiés albigeoises. *His restaurant was recommended to me by one of the most famous chefs of southwestern France, who told me that the house specialty was* gras-double safrané à l'albigeoise, *a very satisfying and hearty winter tripe stew with ham, veal shank, carrot rounds, and parsley in a brown ragout flavored with saffron. He told me* sotto voce *that he couldn't serve this peasant dish in his Michelin-starred restaurant, but here in M. Valette's cozy cellar restaurant delights of the local home cooking could be sampled, and it was the best in the region. Albi was one of very few areas in the Mediterranean where saffron was grown, and one finds it used in the local cooking.*

This is very rich, rib-sticking peasant food, and quite good. It is cooked all day, and its aroma on a cold winter day will drive you mad with desire. The tripe doesn't quite melt in your mouth, but has a soft bite to it. The dish is traditionally accompanied with boiled potatoes covered with capers. The night that we ate this, we started with a salade composé *of lettuce, diced potatoes and tomatoes, rice, onions, and black and green olives covered with a vinaigrette.*

If desired, refrigerate overnight, then remove the fat and reheat the stew before serving.

2 pounds beef or lamb tripe
2½ pounds veal or pig's feet and lamb's feet (the veal or pig's feet split, the lamb's feet whole)
3 tablespoons pork lard
½ pound fresh ham
1 pound veal shank
Bouquet garni, tied in cheesecloth, consisting of 10 sprigs fresh parsley, 6 sprigs fresh thyme, and 1 bay leaf
1 leek, white and light green parts only, halved lengthwise, washed well, and chopped
3 carrots, sliced
1 large onion, halved
1 head garlic, outer peel removed and left whole
¼ cup extra virgin olive oil
Salt and freshly ground black pepper to taste
2 cups dry white wine
2 quarts beef or veal broth (page 54)
2 pinches of saffron threads, crumbled
3 tablespoons tepid water

1. Bring a large pot of water to a boil and blanch the tripe and feet for 5 minutes to remove any particles or scum. Drain and set aside.

2. Rub the bottom of a large stew pot or casserole with the lard. Arrange the veal or pig's feet on the bottom. Place the tripe in one piece on top. Next, layer the ham, veal shank, lamb's feet, bouquet garni, leek, carrots, onion, and head of garlic, drizzle over the olive oil, and sprinkle on some salt and pepper. Pour in the wine and broth. Cover and cook over very low heat, using a heat diffuser if necessary, until the meat is tender but still attached to the bone, about 6 hours.

3. Remove the ham from the pot and cut into pieces. Set aside. Continue cooking the other meats until the tripe is soft, with a little bite to it, and the other meats are falling off the bone, another 2 to 4 hours. You can test for doneness during this period of time by cutting off a tiny piece of the tripe and tasting to see if it has a soft bite; if it is chewy, continue cooking. Remove the veal shank and tripe and cut both into pieces. Discard all the bones, the bouquet garni, and onion. Return all the meats to the pot to reheat.

4. Meanwhile, steep the saffron in the tepid water for 30 minutes. Stir the saffron into the casserole. Remove all the meats with a slotted ladle to serving bowls and serve with boiled potatoes, capers, and cornichon (gherkins).

Makes 6 servings

LANGUEDOC'S fortunes were soon to take a further terrible turn. The population had grown through the thirteenth century. Then from 1302 until 1348, the region was rendered desolate by famine, amounting to twenty of the forty-six years in this period. Harvest failures were frequent. In 1310, torrential rains drowned the harvest and started a cycle of crop failures that lasted until 1313. There were crop failures in 1322 and 1329 as well, and the populace usually vented its desperation on the Jews, lepers, and "sorcerers." By 1332, most people were living on a diet of nothing but herbs throughout the winter. Bad harvests continued until 1347, when it finally seemed over. Then came the Black Death in 1348.[31]

The Black Death resulted in a contraction of agriculture and viticulture in Languedoc that lasted until 1500. Much of the frontier conquered through reclamation in the eleventh and twelfth centuries reverted to swamp, woods, and wastelands.[32] This may account, in part, for the rise in duck farming. The most famous duck of Languedoc today is the *canard mulard*, a cross between the Barbary duck and the Rouen duck, and is prized for making foie gras and *confit de canard.*

Not until the seventeenth century was maize, a New World introduction, called *mil gros*, widely grown in the Haut-Languedoc, where it significantly alleviated the problems of sustenance in the mountains and plains. The flour milled from it was called *milhas*, an Old French word, as well as a Portuguese word from where it may derive, once referring to either millet or sorghum, and from it were made two famous preparations. In one, the *milhas* is boiled quickly in water until it reaches the consistency of an oatmeal and is eaten with bread. It can accompany sauced meat or be served just with an egg, sardine, and milk. *Milhas remué* is cooked a little longer and is more refined. It can be eaten for dessert with honey or jam or be pan-fried and sugared or salted.[33] The cooking of the Haut-Languedoc is earthy and usually very satisfying, especially if one likes duck, lamb, oxtail, sausages, and beans.

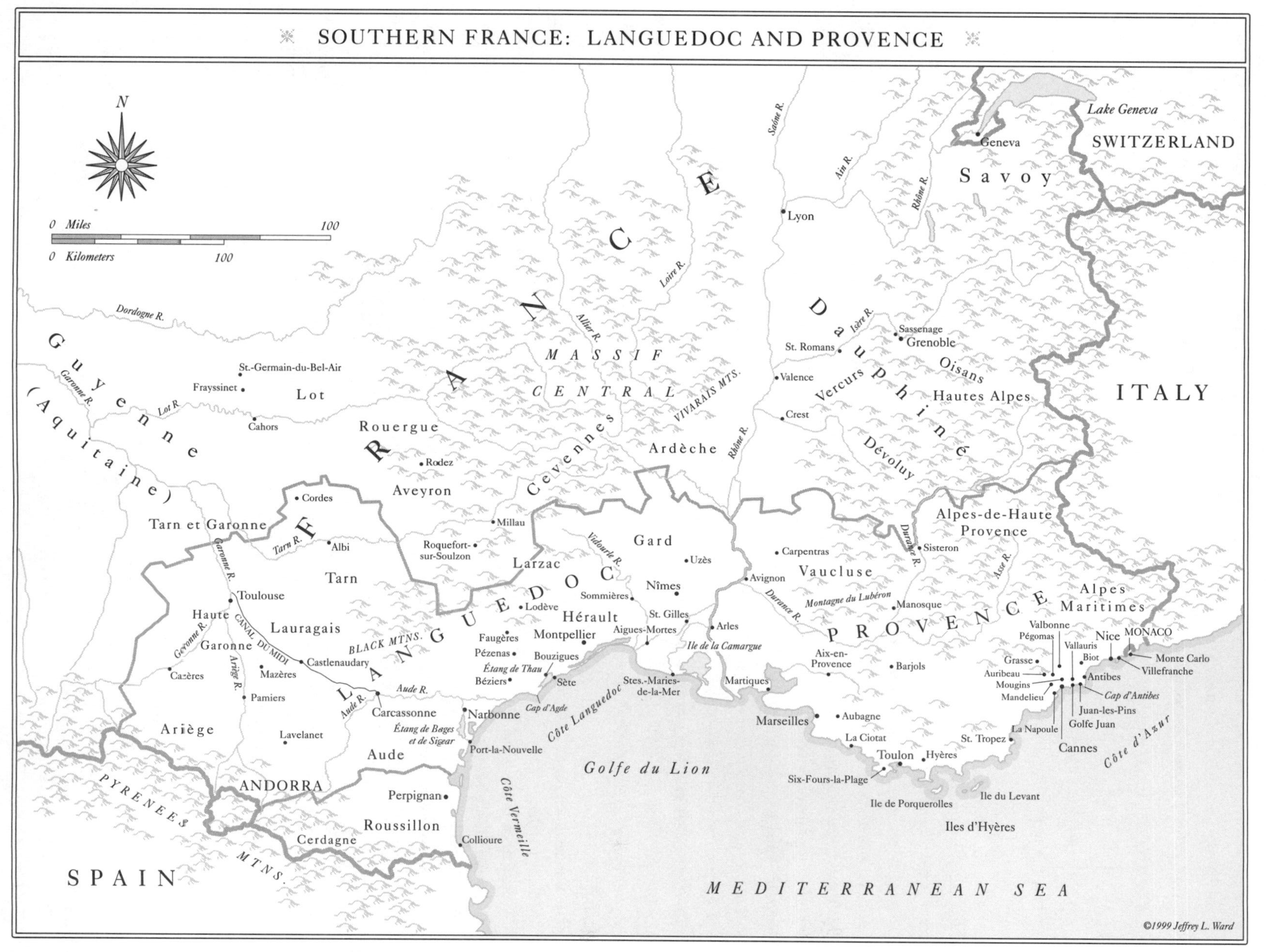
SOUTHERN FRANCE: LANGUEDOC AND PROVENCE
N
0 Miles 100
0 Kilometers 100
FRANCE
LANGUEDOC
PROVENCE
Dauphiné
Savoy
Guyenne (Aquitaine)
SWITZERLAND
ITALY
SPAIN
ANDORRA
MONACO
Lake Geneva
Geneva
Lyon
Saône R.
Ain R.
Rhône R.
Loire R.
Allier R.
Dordogne R.
Garonne R.
Lot R.
Tarn R.
Isère R.
Durance R.
Asse R.
Vidourle R.
Aude R.
Ariège R.
Gevonne R.
MASSIF CENTRAL
VIVARAIS MTS.
Cevennes
BLACK MTNS.
CANAL DU MIDI
PYRENEES MTNS.
St.-Germain-du-Bel-Air
Frayssinet
Lot
Cahors
Rouergue
Rodez
Aveyron
Cordes
Tarn et Garonne
Albi
Tarn
Millau
Roquefort-sur-Soulzon
Larzac
Toulouse
Haute Garonne
Lauragais
Castlenaudary
Cazères
Mazères
Pamiers
Ariège
Lavelanet
Carcassonne
Aude
Étang de Bages et de Sigear
Narbonne
Port-la-Nouvelle
Perpignan
Roussillon
Cerdagne
Collioure
Côte Vermeille
Golfe du Lion
Côte Languedoc
Cap d'Agde
Béziers
Pézenas
Faugères
Étang de Thau
Bouzigues
Sète
Lodève
Montpellier
Hérault
Sommières
Aigues-Mortes
Gard
Nîmes
Uzès
St. Gilles
Stes.-Maries-de-la-Mer
Ile de la Camargue
Arles
Ardèche
Avignon
Carpentras
Vaucluse
Montagne du Lubéron
Manosque
Martiques
Marseilles
Aix-en-Provence
Aubagne
La Ciotat
Toulon
Six-Fours-la-Plage
Hyères
Ile de Porquerolles
Ile du Levant
Iles d'Hyères
Barjols
St. Tropez
La Napoule
Cannes
Golfe Juan
Juan-les-Pins
Cap d'Antibes
Antibes
Mandelieu
Mougins
Auribeau
Grasse
Pégomas
Valbonne
Vallauris
Biot
Nice
Villefranche
Monte Carlo
Côte d'Azur
Alpes Maritimes
Alpes-de-Haute Provence
Sisteron
Dévoluy
Hautes Alpes
Oisans
Vercurs
Crest
Valence
St. Romans
Sassenage
Grenoble
MEDITERRANEAN SEA
©1999 Jeffrey L. Ward

Salade Tiéde de Foie et Gésiers de Canard (Languedoc)

WARM SALAD OF DUCK LIVER AND SLICED GIZZARD AND GREENS

This salad is typically served at the mechoui, *the festive communal dinners that little villages in the Haut-Languedoc or Lot hold several times a year for national holidays or harvest celebrations. Evidence that the Arab influence remained in the Languedoc is the fact that the word* mechoui *comes from the Arabic word for "grilled,"* mishwī, *a word that in Morocco today refers to a whole spit-roasted lamb or goat.*

I keep a little zippered-top plastic freezer bag filled with duck livers and gizzards from other preparations, and when I have enough I make this salad. Make sure all your greens are completely dry after washing them.

10 ounces duck livers
Milk as needed
4 cups duck broth (page 55)
1 pound duck gizzards
3 tablespoons Armagnac or brandy
Salt and freshly ground black pepper to taste
2 tablespoons unsalted butter

FOR THE VINAIGRETTE

2 tablespoons white wine vinegar
½ teaspoon salt
¼ teaspoon freshly ground black pepper
1 teaspoon Dijon mustard
⅓ cup heavy cream
1 shallot, finely chopped
6 tablespoons extra virgin olive oil
1 teaspoon finely chopped fresh parsley leaves

TO FINISH THE SALAD

½ pound mixed salad greens (mesclun, arugula, lamb's lettuce, frisée, etc.)
1 head romaine lettuce, leaves stripped from the stems and torn
1 head Boston head lettuce, torn into small pieces

1. Soak the duck livers in milk to cover for 3 hours in the refrigerator.

2. Meanwhile, bring the duck broth to a gentle boil in a large saucepan and add the duck gizzards. Reduce the heat to medium-low and cook until tender but a little chewy, about 1½ hours. Remove the gizzards with a slotted spoon and slice thin. Set aside in a bowl.

3. Drain the livers and pat dry with paper towels. Discard the milk. Place in a bowl and marinate in the Armagnac for 2 hours with salt and pepper. Drain and pat dry the duck livers.

4. In a small skillet, melt 1 tablespoon of the butter, then cook the livers gently over medium heat until firm but not overcooked, 6 to 7 minutes. Remove with a slotted spoon and slice. Mix the duck livers and gizzards in a bowl and set aside.

5. Prepare the vinaigrette. In a medium-size bowl, whisk together the vinegar, salt, pepper, mustard, cream, and shallot. Slowly whisk in the olive oil, in a slow stream, so it emulsifies. When you are ready to serve, heat the vinaigrette very gently over very low heat in the top of a double boiler over simmering water and whisk in the parsley.

6. Arrange the greens in a large bowl or platter, tossing well. In a medium-size saucepan, melt the remaining tablespoon butter, then heat the duck livers and gizzards until warm. Sprinkle the warm duck livers and gizzards over the salad and toss gently. Pour the warm vinaigrette over the salad, toss, and serve. Save the duck broth for a future use.

Makes 8 servings

❈ Cassoulet (Languedoc)

Cassoulet is a bean stew cooked in an earthenware casserole, hence the name. It is one of the classic dishes of the Languedoc, and of France. This famous bean stew—and "bean stew" hardly conveys the complexity of its flavors—is subject to much debate about what constitutes a "true" cassoulet. Cassoulet is a paradigm for a culinary understanding of the Languedoc, for there is a different recipe in every kitchen.

The history of cassoulet is a history of Languedoc. One legend places the birth of cassoulet during the siege of Castelnaudary by the Black Prince, Edward the Prince of Wales, in 1355. The besieged townspeople gathered their remaining food to create a big stew cooked in a cauldron. Apocrypha aside, a more appropriate historical question can be asked: Is the prototype of cassoulet the fava and mutton stews of the Arabs, as suggested by Julia Child and Paula Wolfert (but denied by Waverly Root)? Was the Languedoc the northern limit of the cooks, if not the commandos, of ʿAbd-ar-Raḥmān I and the yakhna bi'l-fūl *(fava bean stew, page 127)? Etymology alone provides some circumstantial evidence pointing to the celebrated cuisine of the Arabs as the provenance of cassoulet, already having made its mark on the bean stews to the south in Muslim Spain.*

The word cassoulet *derives from the earthenware pot it is cooked in, the* cassolle *or* cassolo, *a special vessel made by the local potteries from the* terre d'Issel, *Issel being a village in the vicinity of Castelnaudary. The word* cassolo *comes directly from the Spanish. But where does the Spanish word* cassa, *meaning "a receptacle for carrying liquid," from which it derives come from? Possibly it is the Mozarab word* cacherulo, *derived from the Arabic* qaṣʿa, *a large shallow bowl or pan, or it may be derived from a proto-Hispanic word.*[34]

We also cannot forget the proximity of Catalonia and the close historical association of Languedoc with the Aragonese-Catalan empire. Cassoulet has much in common with the bean and sausage dishes of Catalonia's northernmost province, Roussillon, with its l'ollada *(page 15, although I have left out the sausage in that recipe), that in turn is related to the* escudella *of Catalonia (page 170). This, of course, leads us to the* olla *of Castile and Cervantes (page 541). The bean in all these early bean stews must be the fava bean or hyacinth bean, because* Phaseolus vulgaris*—the white bean so closely associated today with cassoulet—did not appear in Europe until after Columbus's second voyage in 1493, and one of the first references in Languedoc to this bean is in Clermont-sur-Lauquet in 1565, by the name* monges.[35]

The life of this famous bean stew begins in Castelnaudary. The cassoulet of Castelnaudary, a pleasant village in the Aude along the Canal du Midi, is certainly the oldest of the three cassoulets, the other two being from Carcassonne and Toulouse. Some authors speak of a fourth and fifth cassoulet, but in reality you can speak of three or a thousand. The Castelnaudary version is the most rustic, using only water from Castelnaudary and the produce of the Lauragais. In older times the cassoulet was simmered in a cauldron over an open hearth fire of gorse wood collected in the Black Mountains of the region. During hunting season the Carcassonnais will throw several red partridges and some lamb shoulder or leg into their cassoulet. In Toulouse it is enriched with confit of goose, pork skin, and saucisse de Toulouse, *a simple pork sausage with a distinctive flavor (page 71).*

A proper understanding of the importance of cassoulet to local cuisine can be captured by a famous saying: Le Cassoulet est le dieu de la cuisine occitane. Un Dieu en trois personnes: Dieu le père est celui de Castelnaudary, Dieu le fils est celui de Carcassonne et le Saint-Esprit qui est celui de Toulouse. *(Cassoulet is the god of Occitan cuisine. A god in three persons: God the father is that of Castelnaudry. God the son is that of*

THE WORLD OF LEGUMES

The members of the botanical family known as Leguminosae were among the first cultivated plants in the Mediterranean. Legumes or beans (strictly, beans are a genus in the family Leguminosae) were also one of the first domesticated plants in the New World, appearing before 6000 B.C. Beans have among the highest protein content of all plant foods and are, for that reason, known as poor people's food, and are nutritionally important for people who cannot or choose not to eat meat. The amino acids found in beans are perfectly complemented by those in cereals, and these two foods are the first ones found preserved in archeological sites. When we see Mediterranean dishes with wheat and beans, or rice and lentils, or maize and peas, they are dishes that come very close to fulfilling our protein needs. But, in the words of the botanist Charles B. Heiser Jr., this was a "happy accident," because primitive people knew nothing about amino acids or proteins.

Legume plants are also important for another reason. No other cultivated food plant has the ability that most legumes do of being able to obtain nitrogen from the atmosphere through the action of special bacteria that live in nodules on their roots. This nitrogen goes into the production of protein that makes itself available to humans when we eat the seeds. When the legume plant dies, the nitrogen is returned to the soil, helping other plants grow and building up soil fertility. Historically, this "green manuring" was important for the nutrient-poor Mediterranean soil. The Book of Daniel (1:12) gives a sense of the importance of beans: "And let them give us pulse to eat, and water to drink."

The Mediterranean legumes are of great variety, such as carob or St. John's bread (Ceratonia siliqua). *The pods of carobs, native to Syria, are eaten by some people in the Mediterranean because of their high sugar content, although they are used mostly for livestock feed. The grasspea or India pea* (Lathyrus sativus) *is a legume eaten in the Mediterranean as well as Asia, and when eaten in quantity without other foods can cause a disease known as lathyrism, which leads to a paralysis of the lower limbs that can be permanent. In the seventeenth-century Moroccan medical compendium* Tuḥfat al-aḥbāb, *this legume is described as an aphrodisiac.*[36] *The chickpea* (Cicer arietinum) *is native to the Near Eastern Mediterranean, as are lentils* (Lens esculenta) *and the fava bean* (Vicia faba), *also known as the broad bean, Windsor bean, horse bean, Scotch bean, and English bean. A wild form of this plant is no longer known. The lupine bean* (Lupinus albus) *is native to the Near Eastern Mediterranean and so is bittervetch* (Vicia ervilia) *and the cultivated pea* (Pisum sativum), *of which there are of two kinds—the field pea, used mostly for dried peas and forage, and the garden pea with its high sugar content. Several Mediterranean legumes originated in Africa, such as the hyacinth bean* (Lablab niger), *native to the East African savanna or India, and the cowpea* (Vigna unguiculata *[L.] Walp. subsp.* unguiculata), *also known as the black-eyed pea; native to East or West Africa, according to the latest thinking.*

Today, the Mediterranean's most famous beans, after the fava bean, lentil, and chickpea, are the New World beans. Phaseolus *is the genus that has provided the most edible species of beans. This genus was unknown in the Mediterranean before the return of Columbus from his second voyage to the New World in 1493. Old World beans that were once classified as* Phaseolus *are now assigned to the genus* Vigna. *Four different species were domesticated in the Americas. Two of them, the scarlet runner bean (*Phaseolus coccineus*), originally from Mexico, and the tepary bean (*P. acutifolius*), are either grown for ornamental reasons or are now making a small comeback in some American culinary circles. Of the other two, the lima bean (*P. lunatus, *also called butter or sieva bean) is cultivated extensively and is originally from Peru. Lima beans' distinctive taste comes from cyanogenetic glucoside, a cyanide-containing compound that appears in very small amounts in the beans grown in the United States.*

*The common bean (*Phaseolus vulgaris*), or kidney bean, snap bean, French bean,* haricot verts, *flageolet, garden bean, filet bean, green bean, and string bean, is the most widespread bean. The common green bean is a variety of this species whose pod is eaten at an immature stage. Horticultural or shell beans are* P. vulgaris *that have been picked when the pods have swelled but before the beans inside have dried. All the famous named beans you may have heard of—Kentucky Wonder, Blue Lake,* cannellini, *Jacob's Cattle, and so on—are cultivars of* P. vulgaris, *of which there are now more than five hundred varieties.*

Two other New World legumes have not made the jump to the Mediterranean kitchen: pacae *beans (*Inga feuillei*), whose pods are nearly a yard long with seeds covered with a sweet white pulp that is sucked off; and jícama, a legume with an edible root.*

Carcassonne, and the Holy Spirit is that of Toulouse).[37] *Anatole France, writing in the late nineteenth century, described cassoulet as having a "taste, which one finds in the paintings of old Venetian masters, in the amber flesh tints of their women." He claimed in his* Histoire comique *that the cassoulet he used to eat at Chez Clemence on the Rue Vavin, a favorite establishment in Paris, had been cooking for twenty years, the water, beans, and meats replenished daily.*[38]

Where does one find the best cassoulet? Undoubtedly, in the kitchen of a farmer's wife. One French authority declared that a good cassoulet could not be a restaurant dish under any circumstances. Opinions of cooks and chefs are strong on the composition of a cassoulet. Some chefs say that mutton and confit can't go together. Other cooks look down on the bread crumb crust, saying that it is a restaurant invention done to make it look better.

No matter which cassoulet you make, it is important to follow several important rules. Use the very best ingredients. If you are traveling in Languedoc you couldn't bring back a better souvenir than the best medium-size haricot beans you can find, such as the lingot de Lavelanet *or the haricot beans of Mazères, Pamiers, or Cazères.*[39]

The water for a good cassoulet is quite important. It

In the *Bean-Eater,* painted by Annibale Carracci c. 1585, the man is eating a bowl of black-eyed peas (*Vigna unguiculata* [L.] Walp. subsp. *unguiculata*), an Old World bean native to Africa. The New World beans had not yet been integrated into Mediterranean cuisine. Galleria Colonna, Rome.

ALINARI/ART RESOURCE.

should be hard and calcareous, which allows the beans to maintain their shape better. Also, patience is required. There is much preparation, and the cooking is long, with the fire being adjusted if necessary.

Last, you should know about the so-called secret of the seven skins: a film develops over the cassoulet while it cooks. This skin or film must be broken seven times to make a perfect cassoulet, culinary folklore instructs.

I have eaten many cassoulets and I'm not sure of my favorite, but I remember well the experience of a great cassoulet. *My cassoulet de Castelnaudary came in a large earthenware casserole with an inviting golden crust of bread crumbs. I plunged my spoon into the crust and noticed the white haricot beans, soft and separate. The tomato sauce was not heavy or in great evidence, but its influence was clearly there. The meat, confit of duck, pork, and Toulouse sausage, was well cooked, nearly falling to pieces when touched with my fork. The cassoulet was spicier than I expected and the broth was not a sauce, but almost soupy and very rich. The flavors are incredible, strong, luscious, and fatty.*

My recipe devolves from years of patient experimenting. For the most part I began with an idea given to me by Odile La Carrière, my father's neighbor in

*Frayssinet, the little farming hamlet where he lives in southwest France. Odile's husband, Robert, is a sheep farmer and, as with all farm wives, she has strong opinions about food. I have amended her basic suggestions to fit my fantasy of the perfect cassoulet, based on that cassoulet I had at the Hotel Restaurant du Centre et du Lauragais in Castelnaudary. Odile's cassoulet is quite straightforward. She makes a rough-and-ready everyday type of dish with a pound of dried white beans—not too small, she says—*collet de mouton *(mutton neck),* poitrine fumé *(smoked pork breast),* echine de porc *(pork back),* saucisse de Toulouse *(pork sausages from Toulouse), and* confit de canard *(fat-preserved duck). She simmers the meats in water on the stove top until done, flavored with garlic, tomatoes, onions, and carrots. How easy it all seems when I'm in France where the* saucisse de Toulouse, *duck confit, pig's knuckles, and salted pork breast can be found at the local* boucherie. *For those of us trying to capture authentic tastes here at home, we must go through some rigmarole, and I apologize for that, but this recipe will be worth it—you will eat very happily and your guests will think you are a genius. It would be best to think about preparing an authentic cassoulet at least several months in advance so you can prepare the* saucisse de Toulouse *and duck confit. If this is simply too much work for you, then replace the Toulouse sausage with mild Italian sausage and get the confit through mail-order (see "Mediterranean Food Products Resources").*

My recipe is a rich, authentic, full-bodied feast best served around two in the afternoon on a very cold winter day to your friends. Cassoulet is heavy. It is said that you can reduce the amount of flatulence often associated with eating beans by following the instructions that I provide, although frankly I'm not convinced it accomplishes anything. If you wish to make a full production of a fête languedocienne, *serve* tielle de poulpe sètoise *as a starter (page 441) and follow the cassoulet with a* salade tiéde de foie et gésiers de canard *(page 194) and* les oreillettes montpellieraines *(page 164) for a sweet. Cassoulet is a forgiving preparation and even if you mess up, you'll be rewarded.*

2 pounds ham hocks, semi-salted with 1 cup coarse salt (see Note 1 on page 200)
2 pounds medium-size dried white haricot or Great Northern white beans (about 4 cups), picked over, soaked in water to cover overnight, and drained
2 pounds *confit de canard* (page 200)
½ pound salt pork (brisket cut)
¼ pound pancetta (not an authentic ingredient, but meant to replace the traditional *petit salé,* a lean salt pork)
1 pound fresh pork skin (see Note 2 on page 200)
½ cup duck fat from the confit
1½ pounds *saucisse de Toulouse* (page 71)
1¾ pounds pork shoulder, trimmed of fat and cut into smaller pieces (ask the butcher to do this)
1½ pounds mutton or lamb shoulder, trimmed of fat and cut into smaller pieces (ask the butcher to do this)
2 medium-size onions, peeled, and each studded with 2 cloves
1 large carrot, sliced
1 pound ripe tomatoes, peeled, seeded, and finely chopped
3 tablespoons tomato paste
10 garlic cloves, crushed
Bouquet garni, tied in cheesecloth, consisting of 10 sprigs fresh parsley, 10 sprigs fresh thyme, and 2 bay leaves
2 quarts bottled imported Evian or other bottled spring water
Salt and freshly ground black pepper to taste
2 cups fresh bread crumbs made from a French baguette in a food processor with the crust

1. Prepare the semi-salted ham hocks with the salt.

2. Bring a large pot of water to a boil and blanch the drained beans for 5 minutes. Drain and let them soak in cold water to cover for 1 hour. Set the terrine or casserole that contains the duck confit in a pan of hot water so the duck fat softens.

3. Bring a large saucepan of water to a gentle boil and blanch the salt pork and pancetta for 10 minutes.

Drain and slice the skin off the salt pork. Slice the salt pork and dice the pancetta. Set aside. Reserve the salt pork skin with the fresh pork skin.

4. In a 6- to 8-quart casserole or stockpot, melt 5 tablespoons of the duck fat from the confit terrine over medium heat. Puncture the *saucisse de Toulouse* with corn cob holders or toothpicks so it doesn't burst while cooking. Brown the sausage, about 10 minutes, turning occasionally. Remove the sausage and set aside. Brown the pork shoulder cubes in the same casserole, 8 to 10 minutes. Remove and set aside. Brown the ham hocks in the casserole, about 5 minutes. Remove and set aside. Brown the mutton shoulder, 8 to 10 minutes. Remove and set aside. Brown the salt pork and pancetta, about 4 minutes. Remove and set aside. Brown the duck confit, about 4 minutes. Remove the duck and set aside with the other meats.

5. Add the clove-studded onions and sliced carrot to the casserole and cook until the onions turn color, 4 to 5 minutes, stirring occasionally. Add the tomatoes, tomato paste, garlic, bouquet garni, bottled water, and some salt and pepper. Return all the meats, including the duck to the pan, along with the fresh and salt pork skins. Bring to a boil, then reduce the heat to medium-low, cover, and simmer until the meats are tender, about 2 hours.

6. Remove the ham hock, salt pork, Toulouse sausage, pork shoulder, lamb shoulder, and duck. Cut the meat off all the bones. Chop the salt pork. Slice the sausage into thick rounds. Remove the bones from the duck. Discard the bones and remove any fat from the meat, reserving the fat from the ham hocks. Strain the broth through a colander or conical strainer, discarding the vegetables and saving the broth.

7. Preheat the oven to 275°F. Line the bottom of a heavy 6- to 8-quart casserole (it can be the same one you just used, thoroughly washed and dried) with the pork skins, fat side down, and the fat from the ham hocks. Pour in half the beans, then layer the meat from the pork shoulder, ham hock, lamb shoulder, duck confit, salt pork, pancetta, and the sausages on top. Cover with the remaining beans. Pour enough of the reserved broth into the casserole until it just reaches the top of the beans. Sprinkle the top with the bread crumbs and dot or drizzle the remaining 3 tablespoons of the duck fat. Bake, uncovered, until the crust is golden brown, breaking the crust seven times by pushing down slightly with the back of a ladle, about 4 hours. Serve immediately after the seventh time.

NOTE 1: Roll the ham hocks in the coarse salt and arrange in a glass or ceramic bowl or tray. Leave in the refrigerator for 2 days. Wash the salt off before using in step 4.

NOTE 2: The fresh pork skin is an essential flavoring for cassoulet. If you are unable to get it from your butcher, use the rind from a piece of fatback. Blanch for 5 minutes in boiling water to soften it and remove the salt.

Makes 12 servings

Confit de Canard (Languedoc)

FAT-PRESERVED DUCK

Preserving duck is an old method in Languedoc from a time before refrigeration. Perhaps the best way to begin making confit de canard *is to read Paula Wolfert's monumentally thorough method in* The Cooking of South-West France. *She has done a great service for anyone wishing to capture the true taste of southwest France. That being said, my recipe is different from hers. My method is the one described to me by Odile La Carrière, my father's neighbor in the southwest of France where he lives part of the year. Mde. La Carrière, who makes her own confit as easily as we would shape a hamburger patty and also uses her twenty ducks to produce foie gras, described the making of confit in such a matter-of-fact way that I will never hesitate doing it myself. The only real difficulty in making* confit de canard *is getting ahold of all the duck fat you need for it. One way is to save the fat every time you make a duck recipe. Another is to buy the fat through mail order (see "Mediterranean Food Products Resources"). In any case, this recipe is specifically for use in cassoulet (page 195).*

1 duck (about 5 pounds)
½ cup salt
½ teaspoon freshly ground black pepper
1 teaspoon dried thyme
1 bay leaf, crumbled
4 to 5 cups rendered duck fat (see Note)
1 cup melted pork lard

1. Separate the duck with a heavy cleaver or poultry shears into two thighs, two wings, two legs, and two breasts. Divide each of the breasts in two. Rip away and pull off all the fat and skin. Chop the fat into small pieces and set aside. Remove the wing tips and save for making *alicuit* (page 201). Save the neck for *fond de canard* (page 55), and save the liver and gizzards for *salade tiéde de foie et gésiers de canard* (page 194).

2. Mix the salt, pepper, thyme, and bay leaf and toss with the duck pieces in a large bowl. Arrange the duck pieces in a ceramic or glass baking dish and let marinate for 24 hours, covered, in the refrigerator.

3. Preheat the oven to 300°F. Put all the cut-up duck fat and skin in a medium-size casserole and place in the oven for 1½ hours. Pour off the liquid fat and let cool. Add to the other rendered duck fat. Cover and set aside. Discard the duck chitterlings (the crispy bits), unless you want to eat them, in which case chop them up and toss with some spaghetti, parsley, and black pepper.

4. In a medium-size heavy casserole or saucepan, place all of the rendered duck fat and melt over very low heat, about 25 minutes. Rinse the duck pieces and dry with paper towels. Add the duck thighs to the completely melted duck or goose fat so they are covered. If you do not have enough fat, cook in batches. Cook the duck thighs for 30 minutes, then add the remaining duck pieces and cook for 1 hour, making sure all the pieces are covered with fat. Turn the heat off and let everything cool and solidify.

5. Sprinkle salt on the bottom of a ceramic or glass casserole or terrine. Skim off the top layer of duck fat and cover the bottom of the bowl or terrine with it. Place the pieces of duck over the fat. Melt the remaining fat again and pour it over the duck to cover, making sure you do not include any meat juices, and let it cool until solid. Melt the pork lard again and cover the duck fat layer with a ¼-inch layer of lard. Cover with plastic wrap and leave in the refrigerator for 4 to 6 weeks before using in cassoulet.

NOTE: Rendered duck fat is merely the fat collected in the baking pan after roasting a duck. Pour off the fat, making sure you don't collect any of the meat juices, cool, then refrigerate until needed. It will keep indefinitely.

Makes 1 confit *of duck*

Alicuit (Languedoc)

DUCK WING STEW

Alicuit *is traditionally eaten in the Languedoc countryside after the duck slaughter. The name of the dish comes from the word for "wing,"* aile, *and the word for "neck,"* cou. Alicuit *is a very flavorful and home-style*

THE CUISINE OF LANGUEDOC

Languedoc was a dominion of the Counts of Toulouse—independent principalities in southwestern France—until the thirteenth century, when it became a possession of the French Crown. There were two medieval French dialects spoken, oc, *spoken in the south, and* oïl, *spoken in the north, derived from their respective words for "yes." The language of the south, Occitan, known as* langue d'oc *(language of "yes"), was a Romance language that flowered from the eleventh to thirteenth centuries, when troubadours composed lyric courtly love poems called* canso *and traveled to the seigneurial courts reciting their works.*

The land of Oc circles from Roussillon, near the Spanish border, to the Rhône River. In the past many French people considered the Languedoc a desert of French gastronomy. But the rich tradition of cooking in Languedoc was evident long ago if we consider the dramatist Jean Racine's comment, who first remarked, while staying in Uzès in 1661, that twenty caterers could make a living there but a bookseller would starve to death, and that Languedoc had the best olive in the world. Many people think of Languedoc as mountainous, while others see it as a poor man's Côte d'Azur. A culinary confusion has arisen as well. Is the food ducks and beans or is it fish stews and salt cod? The geography of Languedoc is responsible for some of this confusion. The cuisine of Languedoc is divided into three areas and each feels a culinary influence from its neighboring region. The hills and mountains of Haut-Languedoc are home to cities such as Toulouse, Carcassonne, Albi, and Cordes and feel its greatest influence from three sources, the Quercy, the Auvergne, and coastal Languedoc. The cuisine of the Haut-Languedoc is characterized by the use of pork and bird fat, especially duck, and by local products. Besides cassoulet (page 195) and poularde à la Toulouse *(page 156),* daube languedocienne *is famous, as is* pâté de fois gras *made with truffles, a specialty of Toulouse, Cazères, and Albi.*

The second area is the Bas-Languedoc, the plains and sloping hills that run to the coast. The Bas-Languedoc, like neighboring Provence, is characterized by a more interesting cuisine and elaborate fish preparations that are found all along the coast. From the Bas-Languedoc come preparations such as la brandade de Nîmes *(page 438).*

The third area is the Côte Languedoc, almost a part of Provence on one end and Catalonia on the other. Here one finds les petits pâtés de Pézenas, *pastry of lamb sweetmeat (page 163), and the* bourride de Sète, *a fish stew made with saffron and a vegetable-enchanced garlic mayonnaise. Along the* côte, *bordering Spain, is Roussillon or French Catalonia, mostly influenced by Catalan cooking. This Catalonian influence goes all the way to the mouth of the Rhône, and one sees this today in the appearance of paella (admittedly not very good) as far east as Nîmes.*

The dishes of the Roussillon and Languedoc range from the Catalan snail, pork sausage, and lamb chop grilled repast known as cargolade *to the Camarguais* gardiane, *a bull, red wine, and black olive stew (page 206). Other dishes are smoked tuna; fricassee of wild* girolles *(a species of chanterelle mushroom) with garlic and herbs;* crème catalane, *a lemon, vanilla, and fennel seed custard;* moules de Bouzigues, *the cultivated mussels of the lagoon;* boules de picolat, *seasoned meatballs with white beans (page 205);* salade catalane *or* Collioure, *greens with anchovies, peppers, and tomatoes (page 209);* cigalle de mer, *sea cricket, a tiny crayfish-like creature, served grilled; and* l'ollada *(page 15).*[40]

The gastronomy of Languedoc grew as a result of the influence of Spain. A Spanish tide flowed over the Pyrenees to towns like Toulouse, Béziers, Narbonne, and Montpellier. The wave it rode upon was the great body of Arabic learning that emanated out of the intellectual center of Toledo. By the fourteenth century, we find traces of the new Arab astronomy, astrology, philosophy, medicine, and dietetics in the Languedoc, with the University of Montpellier playing an important role in their dissemination. The Jews played a great role, too, in this intellectual movement, for the largest share of translators were Jewish, often translating Arabic works from the Hebrew or the original Arabic.

In the kitchen, bean stews became more popular and a certain Arab flavoring using spices such as saffron and cinnamon became obvious, not to mention the great body of sweet confections.

dish in this region of duck farmers. Outside of Languedoc this preparation can become expensive, especially if you don't have lots of ducks or geese around, so I suggest other bird wings in the recipe besides duck. Wings are not always sold separately in supermarkets, so you might need to collect them over a period of time and keep them frozen until needed. In any case, at least 50 percent of the wings should be duck or goose because that's where the special flavor comes from.

1 tablespoon goose or duck fat
4 pounds duck, chicken, turkey, or goose wings and necks (or any combination of these, with the majority being duck and goose)
6 thick carrots, sliced
2 large onions, sliced
2 cups dry white wine
2 cups chicken broth (page 54)
Bouquet garni, tied in cheesecloth, consisting of 2 sprigs fresh thyme, 1 celery stalk, 1 bay leaf, 4 sprigs fresh oregano, and 1 sprig fresh sage
3 garlic cloves, crushed
Salt and freshly ground black pepper to taste

1. In a large casserole, heat the goose fat over medium heat, then brown the wings until golden on both sides and there is juice in the casserole, about 20 minutes. Remove the wings and set aside. Add the carrots and onions and continue cooking until the onions are yellow, about 20 minutes, stirring occasionally. Deglaze the casserole with the wine and chicken broth, scraping the bottom and sides of the casserole to get up any brown bits.

2. Bring the wine and broth to a boil and return the wings to the casserole. Reduce the heat to low, add the bouquet garni and garlic, season with salt and pepper, and simmer until the wings are falling apart and easily pierced by a fork, about 2 hours.

Makes 4 servings

Pistache de Mouton ou d'Agneau (Languedoc)

DRUNKEN MUTTON OR LAMB

In the Aude, a region of Languedoc, during the Middle Ages, laborers, whose heavy work required a lot of energy, would eat lamb stew, an omelette, or mutton tripe for breakfast. At ten o'clock, the men would take a break and eat bread ends and levar l'ega, *drink a cup of water. At midday, they ate soup, cabbage, or other vegetables with a piece of meat. At three was another* l'ega, *or water break. At six they ate cassoulet or* pistache. *At nine, they would have some* aiga bolhida *(a soup) and a salad.*[41]

The pistache *does not refer to pistachios, which do not appear in this recipe, but to the expression* avoir sa pistache, *"to be drunk," from all the wine and garlic the meat is cooked in. This dish is also known as a preparation* à la Catalane. *If you were living in Languedoc, you would insist on using* pré-salé, *the sheep raised in salt marsh meadows near the sea, which have a distinctive taste. Serving this dish with* moules aux épinards *(page 17) provides a delightful balance.*

3 pounds boneless lamb or mutton shoulder, trimmed of fat, rolled, and tied
Salt and freshly ground black pepper to taste
2 tablespoons rendered goose or duck fat
1 carrot, sliced
1 large onion, sliced
½ pound fresh ham, diced
2 cups dry red wine
3 cups chicken broth (page 54)
Bouquet garni, tied in cheesecloth, consisting of 6 sprigs fresh parsley, 1 bay leaf, 4 sprigs fresh marjoram, and 6 sprigs fresh thyme
1 long strip orange rind, without the white pith
50 garlic cloves, peeled
2 tablespoons *beurre manié* (page 50)
Imported black and green olives for garnish (optional)

1. Preheat the oven to 350°F. Rub the lamb or mutton with salt and pepper. In a large ovenproof stove-top casserole, melt the goose or duck fat over medium heat, then brown the lamb on all sides with the carrot, onion, and ham, about 20 minutes, turning frequently.

2. Pour in the wine and chicken broth and add the bouquet garni. Cover and place in the oven for 45 minutes. Add the garlic cloves and bake until the meat is tender, another 20 to 25 minutes.

3. Remove the roast from the casserole and set aside to a deep serving platter, keeping it warm. Remove 2 cups of the sauce from the baking casserole and transfer to a saucepan with the *beurre manié*. Reduce the sauce for 5 minutes over high heat, stirring constantly. Remove the twine from the roast and cover with the sauce. Garnish with the olives and serve immediately.

NOTE: Rather than buy a whole shoulder roast, tie boneless lamb or mutton shoulder slices together with butcher's twine into the shape of a whole roast. When the roast is done, the meat will have gently fused together. Simply cut off the twine and pull the slices apart.

Makes 4 to 6 servings

Boules de Picolat (Roussillon)

ROUSSILLON-STYLE MEATBALLS

Meatballs, pâtés, sausages, and cured hams are all popular in the Roussillon and made by specially trained people. The butifareres *are women of "portly and funereal aspect" who hire themselves out to make sausages, blood puddings, and pâtés. In the Vallée de Carol, they make a pâté of izard. This tradition is quite old, as the hams of the Cerdagne were mentioned by Strabo in the first century* B.C. *and praised by Martial.*[42]

I learned this Roussillon recipe from Chef Claude Patry, formerly chef de cuisine *of Le Chapon Fin-Park Hotel in Perpignan. It goes very nicely with white haricot beans or fried potatoes (pages 96 or 61) or preceded by* tarte au Roquefort *(page 182), a dish of the Rouergue region of the Haut-Languedoc.* Boules *is French, from the Catalan word for "meatball,"* boles.

For convenience, try asking the butcher to grind the beef and sausage meat together, although he might not want to mix meats in his machine. Keep your hands wet with cold water when forming the meatballs so they do not stick.

1 pound ground beef
1 pound sausage meat (see Note)
4 garlic cloves, very finely chopped
2½ tablespoons very finely chopped fresh parsley leaves
1 tablespoon very finely chopped fresh tarragon or basil leaves
Ground cinnamon to taste
1 large egg, beaten
Salt and freshly ground black pepper to taste
All-purpose flour for dredging
½ cup extra virgin olive oil
1 pound fresh or canned tomatoes, peeled, seeded, and finely chopped
1 large shallot, finely chopped
Pinch of cayenne pepper
1 cup chopped pimiento-stuffed green Spanish olives (optional)
¼ cup chopped fresh ham (optional)
1 cup veal or chicken broth (page 54)

1. In a large bowl, knead together the beef, sausage meat, garlic, parsley, tarragon or basil, cinnamon, egg, salt, and pepper. Form the mixture into meatballs the size of a small egg, wetting your hands so they don't stick, and set aside.

2. Dredge the meatballs evenly in the flour, tapping off any excess. In a large nonreactive skillet, heat the olive oil over medium-high heat until the oil is almost smoking, then brown the meatballs until golden, about 5 minutes, turning frequently. Remove the meatballs from the oil with tongs and set aside. Discard all but 3 to 4 tablespoons of the oil and rendered fat.

3. Reduce the heat to medium, add the tomatoes, shallot, and cayenne, and cook until the tomatoes have reduced to a sauce, about 15 minutes. Return the meatballs to the skillet with the olives and ham, if using, then pour in the broth and cook until the meatballs are cooked through, about 20 minutes. Remove the meatballs and set aside, keeping them warm. Reduce the sauce by half over medium heat, then cover the meatballs with the sauce and serve.

NOTE: You can't go too wrong with the kind of sausage you use here, so try homemade *salsiccia fresca* (page 70) or store-bought mild Italian sausage, fresh Spanish or Portuguese-style chorizo, fresh Polish kielbasa, or chicken or turkey sausage. They all work.

Makes 6 servings

Taureau Sauvage à la Gardiane (Provence)

BULL STEW IN THE STYLE OF THE CAMARGUE

This rich dish from the Camargue of Provence is known as gardiane de taureau, boeuf à la gardiane, *or simply* la gardiane. *Some people also make* gardiane *with lamb. In Córdoba in Andalusia, there is another braised bull dish called* rabo de toro, *with equally luscious flavors (page 207).*

The bulls of the Camargue are a twentieth-century introduction, for in the sixteenth century large-scale summer transhumance controlling the sheep flocks of the Camargue defined this area, then infested with mosquitoes and afflicted with a high rate of unemployment (see page 442). A remarkable effort of rural land development transformed the region at that time into a productive sheep-rearing land. But today the bulls are the predominant presence in the Camargue and gardiane, *or bull stew, is a famous local specialty. I remember an excellent* gardiane *at the seaside restaurant of À la Brise de Mer in the small coastal town of Les Saintes Maries-de-la-Mer in the Camargue. One arrives at Stes. Maries by following a solitary road from Arles through the Camargue, a marshy land of alluvial deposit, past grazing lands and horse farms. Legend has it that this was where St. Marie-Jacobé, St. Marie-Salomé, and their servant St. Sarah landed after being set adrift off the coast of Palestine by the Jews of Judea in the first century A.D. The Romany, or Gypsies of the Camargue, consider St. Sarah their patron saint, and in May and September there are processions of* gardianes, *or Camargue cowboys, who drive the bulls through the streets to the bullring for nonlethal bullfighting or to a pool for a strange sport called* taureau piscine, *where amateur bullfighters dodge the bulls in the water-filled pools.*

The stew is excellent with French fries (page 61).

1/4 cup extra virgin olive oil
4 pounds oxtail (weighed with bone) or 3 pounds beef shank, well trimmed of fat and cut into 2-inch pieces (ask the butcher to do this for you)
1 tablespoon pork lard
2 medium-size onions, finely chopped
1 pound potatoes, peeled and diced
2 cups beef broth (page 54)
1 cup dry red wine
Bouquet garni, tied in cheesecloth, consisting of 5 sprigs fresh parsley, 15 sprigs fresh thyme, and 5 sprigs fresh savory or tarragon
Peel from 1 orange, without the white pith, in 1 long spiral
1 medium-size onion, peeled and studded with 1 clove
1 bay leaf
1 garlic clove, crushed
1 tablespoon tomato paste
1/4 cup chopped imported pitted green olives
1/4 cup chopped pitted black Niçoise olives
Salt and freshly ground black pepper to taste

1. In a large, heavy casserole, heat the olive oil over medium-high heat, then brown the oxtail or shank pieces on all sides, about 5 minutes. Remove the oxtail from the casserole and set aside, keeping it warm.

2. In the same casserole, melt the lard over medium-high heat, then cook the chopped onions and potatoes until the onions are golden, about 8 minutes, stirring frequently and adding small amounts of water to scrape the browned bits off the bottom of the casserole if necessary.

3. Return the meat to the casserole. Pour in the beef broth and wine along with the bouquet garni, orange peel, clove-studded whole onion, bay leaf, garlic, tomato paste, and chopped olives. Season with salt and pepper.

4. Reduce the heat to low and simmer, uncovered, until the sauce is thick and the meat tender and falling off the bone, about 4 hours. Remove and discard the

orange peel, bouquet garni, whole onion, and bay leaf. Serve immediately.

Makes 4 to 6 servings

✣ ✣ ✣

THE bullfighting of the Camargue is not nearly as famous as the home of bullfighting, Andalusia, and especially Ronda and Seville. The origins of bullfighting are obscure. Some people think it may have derived from Roman games, while others attribute it to the Arabs, and some have claimed that medieval mounted knights faced the bulls with their lances. What is known is that the first rules laid down for modern bullfighting appeared in Ronda, located in the mountains of the Málaga district of Andalusia, in the late eighteenth century. After the bull was killed it was butchered and the meat fed the town.

Bullfighting is not a sport in Spain, but rather is considered one of the arts. Bullfighting is an important element of Spanish culture that expresses the drama of Spanish fatalism, the universal struggle of life and death, with a finale worthy of a Greek tragedy. Bullfighting cannot be judged in terms of animal cruelty, any more than the wearing of the veil in Muslim countries can be judged in terms of women's rights, for both are expressions of the soul of a culture and can only be understood, or criticized, within the context of that culture.

❈ *Rabo de Toro* (Andalusia)

BULL STEW

This famous dish of cocina córdobésa*—the cooking of the city of Córdoba in the heart of Andalusia—is* rabo de toro*, bulltail stew. Córdoba was the greatest city in the world when Islamic Spain was a cultural center of the Mediterranean.*

Córdoba is in the heart of bullfight country. After the fight, the bulls are butchered and the tails go into this highly flavored stew. A quite similar dish is found in the Camargue of Provence, where bulls are also raised for Provençal-style bullfighting in which the bull isn't killed (see page 206).

Rabo de toro *is found on the menu of many Córdoban restaurants. I had it first in the famous El Caballo Rojo restaurant, opposite the Mezquita, the extraordinary eighth-century mosque built during the reign of ʿAbd-ar-Raḥmān I, the founder of the Spanish Umayyad dynasty.*

½ cup extra virgin olive oil
2 pounds onions, finely chopped
4 pounds oxtail, well trimmed of fat and cut into 2-inch pieces (ask the butcher to do this for you)
1 cup water
2 cups dry white wine
1½ pounds carrots, sliced
1 pound mushrooms, sliced
1½ pounds ripe tomatoes, peeled, seeded, and chopped
6 garlic cloves, chopped
1 tablespoon paprika
Pinch of saffron threads, crumbled
1 bay leaf
1 tablespoon finely chopped fresh parsley leaves
Salt and freshly ground black pepper to taste
10 ounces fresh or frozen peas
1 recipe French-fried potatoes (page 61)

1. In a large nonreactive casserole, heat the olive oil over medium-high heat, then cook the onions until translucent, about 8 minutes, stirring frequently. Remove the onions from the casserole and set aside.

2. Place the oxtail pieces in the casserole and brown on all sides over medium-high heat, about 5 minutes, turning frequently. Add the water and scrape the bottom of the casserole to pick up any

browned pieces of meat. Add the reserved fried onions, the wine, carrots, mushrooms, tomatoes, garlic, paprika, saffron, bay leaf, and parsley and season with salt and pepper. Bring to a boil, reduce the heat to medium, and cook for 10 minutes, uncovered, skimming the foam off the top as it appears. Reduce the heat to low, cover, and cook for 1 hour, then uncover and continue cooking until the oxtail pieces are very tender and falling off the bone, about 3 hours. Add the peas 30 minutes before serving.

3. Meanwhile, prepare the French fries. Serve the oxtail with a helping of French fries on top.

Makes 4 to 6 servings

Tendrons de Veau à la Gardiane (Provence)

BRAISED VEAL IN THE STYLE OF THE CAMARGUE

The powers to be in sixteenth-century Arles launched a serious effort of reclamation that turned the malaria-infested Camargue into a land that could support modest stock rearing on its alluvial lands. Young calves were not in great abundance—they were little and skinny—but by the nineteenth century there were greater numbers of cattle and they found their way into braised dishes, a popular means of cooking because the pot could be left unattended.

This recipe is adapted from Jean-Noël Escudier's Provençal cookbook. It is excellent served with spaghetti moistened with the remaining sauce or with risotto alla milanese *(page 596).*

10 ounces pearl onions (about 3 cups)
3 tablespoons extra virgin olive oil
One 3½-pound veal breast with bone in or veal rib roast, trimmed of fat
Salt and freshly ground black pepper to taste
3 garlic cloves, lightly crushed
¼ pound button mushrooms, thinly sliced
1 cup dry white wine
1 cup finely chopped fresh or canned tomatoes
12 imported green olives, pitted and chopped

1. Bring a large saucepan of water to a boil and blanch the pearl onions for 3 minutes to make it easier to peel them. Drain and slice off the root ends with a sharp paring knife. Peel by squeezing to pop off the skins.

2. In a small skillet, heat 1 tablespoon of the olive oil over medium-high heat, then cook the onions until softened, 3 to 4 minutes, stirring. Remove and set aside.

3. In a large casserole, heat the remaining 2 tablespoons olive oil over medium-high heat, then brown the breast or rib roast on both sides, 4 to 5 minutes. Season with salt and pepper. Add the garlic, mushrooms, and the onions. Stir to distribute around the casserole and pour in the wine and tomatoes. Reduce the heat to low and cook for 2 hours, stirring the sauce occasionally. Add the olives and cook another 15 minutes.

4. Transfer the veal breast to a serving platter. Surround the breast with the remaining vegetables in the casserole using a slotted ladle. Spoon some sauce over the veal breast and serve.

Makes 4 servings

Salade Collioure (Roussillon)

MIXED SALAD FROM ROUSSILLON

Collioure is a small Catalan fishing village on the Côte Vermeille, the coastal Mediterranean of the French province of Roussillon, which is considered a part of Languedoc. Today, this little gem of a harbor is populated with tourists, but in the twelfth century the large castle overlooking the town was built by the Majorcan kings and it provided protection for this tiny but strategic port. Little beaches are sprinkled around the coast and outdoor cafes always offer this colorful salad, also called salade catalane. *It is a pleasant and light salad identical to the Tunisian* salāṭat tūnisiyya bi'l-tifāḥ.

FOR THE SALAD

1 head Boston lettuce, torn into pieces
½ head radicchio, torn into pieces
One 6-ounce can imported tuna in olive oil
2 ripe plum tomatoes, quartered
2 hard-boiled eggs, shelled and quartered
6 salted anchovy fillets, rinsed and cut in half
1 small red potato, boiled until tender, drained, and cut into eighths
20 imported black olives

FOR THE VINAIGRETTE

⅓ cup extra virgin olive oil
2 tablespoons red wine vinegar
½ teaspoon *herbes de Provence* (page 715)
1 small garlic clove, finely chopped

1. Arrange the lettuce and radicchio attractively on a large serving platter. Scatter the remaining salad ingredients decoratively around and on top of the lettuce.

2. Whisk together the vinaigrette ingredients, pour over the salad, and serve.

Makes 4 servings

THE *COLTURA MISTA:* WHERE MOUNTAIN AND PLAIN MEET

We come down from the mountains to the plateaux, foothills, and hills. This narrow region where mountain and plain meet is distinguished by its beauty and richness, where waters from higher elevations provide irrigation for the cultivation of gardens. Vines, wheat, and olives are grown in this region. Some people see this narrow strip as the "real" Mediterranean, where the *coltura mista*, mixed cultivation—orchards, market gardens, and sown fields—grow in the foothills. A stellar example of this geography is in Apulia. One coastal string of towns, Barletta to Bari to Lecce, runs parallel to an inland route of Andria to Bitonto to Putignano. This accessibility for commerce was the result of centuries of human works. By the sixteenth century, Apulia was wealthy as a grain store and olive oil reservoir for the whole of Italy.

This narrow strip is repeated throughout the Mediterranean—for instance, on the other side of the Adriatic in the Dinaric Alps from Istria to Ragusa. In the sixteenth century, this was a wild area, a frontier zone facing the Turks populated by the Zagorci, the legendary *uskoks*, natural-born soldiers and bandits who ranged the mountains of Albania and Montenegro, and who were in a sense tamed by the coastal civilization of orchards, vineyards, terraced gardens, and thriving towns with their narrow streets and closely packed houses. This Dalmatian strip, we will see, was intimately linked by the Adriatic with Italy, and the food was heavily influenced by the Italians.

Zagrebaćke Glive s Makaronem (Croatia)

ZAGREB-STYLE BAKED MUSHROOMS AND MACARONI

The Italian culinary influence, mixed with other legacies, survives in Croatia partly because of the proximity of Venice over the centuries, but also because Croatian sailors, especially ships' captains, regularly traveled to the Italian peninsula. Unlike most of the former Yugoslavia, Zagreb escaped Turkish domination in the sixteenth and seventeenth centuries and therefore the culinary influences are mostly Italian and Austro-Hungarian. In this baked macaroni dish, with a gorgeous orange golden crust and rich with the flavor of field mushrooms, we see the pasta coming from the Italians, while the use of cream is an Austrian tendency. Mushrooms were found by local foragers usually in the forest, not in the fields. In this recipe, adapted from Inge Kramarz's The Balkan Cookbook, *I use the common domestic white (button or field) mushrooms that you can find in your supermarket.*

2 tablespoons extra virgin olive oil
½ pound button mushrooms, chopped
1 medium-size onion, chopped
2 tablespoons finely chopped fresh parsley leaves
1 tablespoon all-purpose flour
1½ cups heavy cream
½ pound *pappardelle* or other wide pasta
1 large egg, beaten
2 tablespoons unsalted butter
Freshly ground black pepper to taste
2 tablespoons dried bread crumbs
2 large eggs
½ cup freshly grated Parmigiano-Reggiano cheese

1. In a large stove-top and ovenproof (preferably) earthenware casserole, heat the olive oil over medium-high heat, then cook the mushrooms until browned and soft, but not until they have shrunk, about 8 minutes, stirring frequently. Add the onion and cook another 5 minutes more, stirring. Sprinkle with the parsley and flour. Pour in 1 cup of the heavy cream.

2. Preheat the oven to 400°F. Meanwhile, bring a large pot of water to a rolling boil, salt abundantly, add the pasta, and drain when half cooked. Add the pasta to the mushroom casserole along with the beaten egg and butter and season with salt and pepper. Toss well. Sprinkle the bread crumbs over the pasta. Beat the remaining 2 eggs with the remaining ½ cup cream and pour over the casserole. Sprinkle with the cheese and bake until golden, about 30 minutes.

Makes 4 servings

✦ ✦ ✦

It was the nascent class of wealthy capitalists that profoundly changed the land of the Mediterranean during the fifteenth and sixteenth centuries. Canals were built originally to improve trade and help the dukes of Milan build a regional state, but soon they led to irrigation improvements. The network of drainage and irrigation canals throughout the Lombardy plain made it possible to run dairy farms, which in turn led to the development of an industry producing Parmesan cheese, which would find markets far from home.[43]

The central markets of the towns were fed by surrounding vegetable gardens and wheat fields. Spain saw the same kind of development. A Venetian ambassador passing through Castile in the sixteenth century wrote of the wide *paramos* (barren wilderness) where sheep grazed and the *secanos* (unirrigated land) reserved for wheat, all of which appeared to him as barren countryside. But he also saw the green patches of irrigated land around the towns, the orchards at Valladolid, and the gardens bordering the banks of the Pisuerga River.

Land reclamation and irrigation eventually enriched the towns, such as Valladolid in northwestern Spain. Valladolid was the financial capital of Spain in the sixteenth century, and merchant families such as the Ruiz got rich on the wheat trade. The city was crowded with milk-laden donkeys brought from the countryside to the cheese, butter, and cream making centers in town. This was a luxury in Spain. The riches made by budding capitalists who reclaimed surrounding land and made it productive are evident, too, when we look at what was eaten. The Valladolid poultry market saw seven thousand birds sold daily, the mutton was considered the best in the world, and the people were consuming twenty-six kilos of meat per person a year.[44]

The same link between the towns and agriculture appeared in sixteenth-century Provence, with new land being brought under cultivation in Mandelieu, Biot, Auribeau, Vallauris, Pégomas, Valbonne, Grasse, Barjols, Saint-Paul-de Fogossières, and Manosque. Market gardens were developed all along the Durance Valley. Many of them embraced New World discoveries such as sunchokes *(Helianthus tuberosus)*, zucchini, and tomatoes within a century of their introduction, growing them alongside traditional chard and spinach.

❈ *Topinambours en Daube* (Provence)

WINE-STEWED SUNCHOKES

The sunchoke, or Jerusalem artichoke (Helianthus tuberosus), *is a tuber related to the sunflower. It is a New World food that first entered Italy in 1617 and was grown in the Farnese garden in Rome with the name* girasole articiocco *(sunflower artichoke). The English name "Jerusalem" has long been claimed to be a corruption of* girasole, *but the agricultural historian Redcliffe Salaman pointed out that the name Jerusalem was used to refer to Jerusalem artichokes before* girasole *came to be used. He argues that "Jerusalem" is a corruption of Terneuzen, a town in Holland from where the Jerusalem artichoke was first introduced to England.*[45]

The sunchoke was first introduced to France from Canada not before 1607 by the lawyer and historian Marc Lescarbot and the explorer Samuel de Champlain (1567–1635).[46] *It entered Provence about the same time as it did Italy, and recipes are rarely found anywhere else in the Mediterranean but these two locales, although it is known in Algeria and Tunisia as* tirfās, *an Arabic word for a North African truffle, which the sunchoke resembles in appearance, although they also once called it* kamāiya balād al-Āmrīk, *or American truffle.*[47] *The French name,* topinambour, *comes from the name of a Brazilian tribe, and its application to this tuber has nothing to do with the origin of the plant. Sunchokes are native to Canada, look like a knobby potato, and taste similar to an artichoke heart. They go well with meats and goose. Because the tubers can turn black when cooking, do not use an aluminum pan.*

2 tablespoons extra virgin olive oil
1 small onion, finely chopped
1 pound sunchokes, peeled and diced
3 garlic cloves, crushed
Bouquet garni, tied in cheesecloth, consisting of
6 sprigs each fresh parsley, thyme, and oregano
Salt and freshly ground black pepper to taste
1 cup dry white wine
1 cup water

1. In a medium-size nonreactive casserole, such as an enameled cast-iron one, heat the olive oil over medium heat, then cook the onion until yellow, about 8 minutes, stirring frequently.

2. Add the sunchokes, garlic, and bouquet garni and season with salt and pepper. Pour in the wine and water, reduce the heat to low, cover, and simmer until tender, 45 to 50 minutes. Drain with a slotted ladle and serve.

Makes 2 to 4 servings

Tian d'Épinards (Provence)

SPINACH GRATIN

Spinach was introduced to the Mediterranean by the Arabs. It is not known when spinach arrived in France, but we do know that Arnold of Vilanova, who taught at the University of Montpellier in the mid-fourteenth century, said it was a common food in his time.[48] *Spinach was popular cooked in a* tian, *an Old Provençal word for a type of earthenware pan. The root is the Greek* teganon, *which also gives us the Arabic* ṭājin *and the Italian* tegame, *all referring to pans. This* tian *recipe is a popular one in home cooking and very simple, although restaurant chefs are known to fancy it up.*

2 pounds spinach, heavy stems removed
Salt and freshly ground black pepper to taste
Extra virgin olive oil
¼ cup all-purpose flour

1. Preheat the oven to 425°F. Wash the spinach well and spin dry in a salad spinner or damp-dry with paper towels. Transfer the slightly moist spinach to a large bowl and toss with salt and pepper.

2. Lightly oil a baking dish. Arrange the spinach evenly about the dish. Drizzle with a little olive oil. Sprinkle the flour evenly over the spinach, drizzle with a little more olive oil, and salt lightly. Bake until the flour is speckled golden, 15 to 20 minutes.

Makes 4 servings

Tian de Coucourdeto (Provence)

GRATIN OF ZUCCHINI

Zucchini is a species of the genus Cucurbita. *Other members of this genus are squash as diverse as the Halloween pumpkin and crookneck, acorn, spaghetti, and pattypan squashes. Zucchini is a New World vegetable domesticated twice, once in northeastern Mexico and a second time in the midwestern United States. Zucchini was introduced to the Mediterranean in the sixteenth century and joined the Old World* Cucurbita, *the bottle gourd* (Lagenaria siceraria), *muskmelon* (Cucumis melo) *and cucumber* (Cucumis sativas). *This gratin of zucchini is a very nice accompaniment to rabbit or chicken.*

4 salted anchovy fillets, rinsed
3 tablespoons unsalted butter
2 tablespoons extra virgin olive oil
1 small onion, finely chopped
1¼ pounds zucchini, peeled, seeded (if large), and diced
Freshly ground black pepper to taste
3 hard-boiled large eggs, shelled and thinly sliced
4 to 5 tablespoons fresh or dried bread crumbs

1. Place the anchovies in a large saucepan with 2 tablespoons of the butter and the olive oil. Turn the heat to medium-high and, once the anchovies have disintegrated, add the onion and cook until translucent, 5 to 6 minutes, stirring frequently. Add the zucchini and cook over medium heat until soft, about 10 minutes. Season with pepper to taste.

2. Preheat the oven to 450°F. Transfer the zucchini to a large bowl and toss with the sliced eggs. Transfer to a baking dish. Cover evenly with the bread crumbs and remaining tablespoon butter, slivered, and bake until the top is dappled with golden spots, about 10 minutes.

Makes 4 servings

❈ *"Poumo d'Amour" à la Provençal* (Provence)

PROVENCE-STYLE TOMATOES

Once the conquest of Mexico was completed by Hernando Cortés (by 1523) the tomato was brought to Europe. Seville, which dominated the American trade, was probably the first place in Europe where it was grown. Although it is sometimes claimed that the tomato originated in Peru—and its wild ancestor did—it was in Mexico that the tomato was first domesticated. Spanish herbals published in the mid-sixteenth century do not mention the tomato. The first description of the tomato in the Mediterranean was in 1544, by the Italian botanist Pierandrea Mattioli. He was describing a yellow-fruited variety, and it has been suggested that the Italian word for tomato, pomodoro *(apple of gold), derived from this variety. How this word was transformed into the apple of love* (poumo d'amour), *as it was known in Provence, is not clear, although it may have taken on aphrodisiacal properties in the minds of people. Another theory of the origin of* pomme d'amour *is that it is a corruption of* pomme des mours, *"apple of the Moors," in recognition that two important members of the Solanaceae family, the eggplant and the tomato, were favorite Arab vegetables.*[49] *At first the tomato was used only as an ornamental plant in Mediterranean gardens because growers recognized it as a member of the nightshade family, then known as comprising only poisonous plants such as mandrake.*

The quality and ripeness of the tomatoes in this traditional Provençal-style tomato recipe are paramount, therefore this is strictly a summer dish. If the tomatoes come from your garden, all the better. The tomatoes are cut in half and arranged in a baking pan or frying pan and cooked in a very different way than you would expect: slowly, with a sprinkling of garlic, parsley, and salt or perhaps garlic, sugar, and another herb. Some people put bread crumbs on top and finish them in the oven. The same recipe can be done with mushrooms. Because ripe tomatoes will differ in their shape, water content, and firmness, it is best to keep a close eye on the tomatoes as they cook, using the times I suggest as a guide.

3 tablespoons extra virgin olive oil, plus extra for drizzling
Salt to taste
4 medium-size ripe but firm tomatoes, cut in half and hollowed out
1 garlic clove, very finely chopped
3 tablespoons finely chopped fresh *herbes de Provence* (page 715) or mixed fresh herbs (parsley, basil, marjoram, oregano, chervil)
Several pinches of sugar
3 tablespoons fresh or dried bread crumbs (optional)

1. In a large nonreactive skillet, heat 2 tablespoons of the olive oil over low heat. Salt the tomatoes, and arrange in the heated skillet cut side down, and cook until softened, about 40 minutes, pushing them around gently so they don't stick.

2. Turn the tomatoes carefully and sprinkle the garlic, fresh herbs, a pinch of sugar, and salt in the hollow of each one. Drizzle the remaining tablespoon olive oil over the tomatoes. Continue cooking until the flavors have melded, about 15 minutes. Serve or go to step 3 if you would like to have a bread crumb topping.

3. Preheat the oven to 450°F. If you desire, sprinkle each tomato half with about 1 teaspoon of the bread crumbs. Transfer the tomatoes to a baking dish, drizzle with a little olive oil, and bake until the bread crumbs are speckled golden, about 5 minutes. Remove the tomatoes, let them cool for 10 minutes, and serve warm.

Makes 6 to 8 servings

"Poumo d'Amour" à l'Antiboise (Provence)

TOMATOES STUFFED IN THE STYLE OF ANTIBES

Along the Côte d'Azur, tiny villages dot the rocky littoral with its craggy promontories and occasional sandy beaches. In the fifteenth century they were fishing villages that rigorously asserted their fishing rights against the next village. The best fishing places were called cales or calancae ad piscandum *(fishing waters), and an arbitrage document of May 16, 1470, settled a dispute by having the fishermen of Cannes and Antibes split the fishing grounds.*

Perhaps it was the new market garden of nearby Grasse in the sixteenth century that provided tomatoes to Antibes, although probably unlikely, for the Scottish novelist Tobias Smollett (1721–1771), who wintered in Nice in 1764, does not mention tomatoes in his review of local vegetables. The Antiboise were probably as late coming to the tomato as were the Neapolitans.

In any case, this recipe from Antibes, a continuation of the idea in the previous recipe, probably is a recent invention. I would serve these tomatoes with a poisson grillé *(page 412) with* pommes frites *(page 61). This preparation should be made only when you have access to firm, vine-ripened tomatoes.*

2 cups (2 to 3 ounces) diced white part of French bread
½ cup milk
6 salted anchovy fillets, rinsed and finely chopped
3½ ounces imported canned tuna in olive oil, finely chopped with its oil
2 garlic cloves, finely chopped
2½ tablespoons *fines herbes* (equal parts finely chopped fresh parsley leaves, tarragon, chervil, and chives)
4 medium-size ripe but firm tomatoes
Salt and freshly ground black pepper to taste
1 teaspoon dried or fresh thyme
8 pinches of fennel seeds
1 tablespoon finely chopped fresh parsley leaves
Extra virgin olive oil for drizzling

1. Soak the bread in the milk for a few minutes, then squeeze the milk out with your hands, as if forming a snowball. Place the bread in a medium-size bowl and blend well with the anchovies, tuna, garlic, and *fines herbes*.

2. Cut the tomatoes in half and scoop out the pulp. Season the hollows with salt and pepper. Stuff the tomatoes with the stuffing mixture and sprinkle each with thyme, a pinch of fennel, parsley, and more salt and pepper.

3. Preheat the oven to 475°F. Arrange the tomatoes in a lightly oiled baking pan, drizzle with olive oil, and bake until some of the herbs on top look like they might be drying out, 15 to 20 minutes. Serve hot.

Makes 6 servings

Sou Fassum (Provence)

STUFFED CABBAGE IN THE STYLE OF NICE

Sou fassum, *the Provençal name, is known in French as* chou farci à la niçoise. *It is a specialty of the region around Grasse. Traditionally, the stuffed cabbage leaves are placed in a net made of thick threads called a* fassumier, *which is then lowered into a good chicken broth to be cooked. Although cabbage was part of the daily diet in the Middle Ages, it is not now as popular a Provençal vegetable, although this preparation is.*[50]

1 head Savoy cabbage (about 2½ pounds), cored
⅔ cup medium-grain rice
1½ pounds homemade *salsiccia fresca* (page 70), *saucisse de Toulouse* (page 71), or commercial mild Italian sausage, casing removed and meat crumbled
2 large garlic cloves, finely chopped
3 tablespoons unsalted butter
1 medium-size onion, finely chopped
6 ounces pork tenderloin, cut into small dice
3 ripe plum tomatoes, peeled, seeded, and chopped
½ cup frozen or fresh peas
Salt and freshly ground black pepper to taste
1 quart beef broth (page 54)
½ pound boneless lamb or mutton neck or shoulder meat, trimmed of fat and cut into small pieces

1. Remove and discard any of the outermost leaves of the cabbage that are blemished. Bring a large pot of water to a rolling boil and plunge the whole cabbage in until the leaves can be unrolled without ripping, about 10 minutes. Drain well and, when cool enough to handle, separate the leaves carefully, setting them aside to be rolled later. Finely chop the innermost section of the cabbage, about ½ pound of cabbage. Set aside.

2. Place the rice in a small strainer and dip the rice-filled strainer into a pot of lightly salted boiling water for 1 minute. Blanching or rinsing the rice removes the starch that would otherwise make it sticky. Remove and set aside. Toss the sausage meat with the garlic.

3. In a large skillet, melt 2 tablespoons of the butter over medium-high heat, then cook the onion until translucent, about 5 minutes, stirring occasionally. Add the remaining tablespoon butter; once it has melted, add the diced pork tenderloin and brown, 3 to 4 minutes, stirring. Set aside.

4. Lay the cabbage leaves in front of you on a work surface and layer the pork and onion, the chopped tomatoes, rice, peas, and sausage meat on one side, in that order, on top of one another. Season with salt and pepper. Roll the cabbage leaves up, tucking in the sides. It will be a package the shape of a ball. Repeat with the remaining leaves and filling. You should have about 12 stuffed cabbage leaves.

5. Arrange the stuffed cabbage in a casserole that will hold all of them tightly in one or two layers. Cover with the beef broth and lamb or mutton neck meat. Cover and bring to a gentle boil over medium-high heat. As soon as the water starts to bubble, reduce the heat to low, and simmer until the rice inside the cabbage is tender, about 3½ hours.

Makes 6 servings

Petits Oiseaux Grillés (Provence)

SPIT-ROASTED SMALL BIRDS WRAPPED IN GRAPE LEAVES

Farmers and vineyard workers in Provence love to grill small birds. Marie-José Bergougnoux, who lived in Six-Plages, a coastal community near Toulon, told me that farmers and vineyard workers in Provence might shoot buckshot at a flock of sparrows, larks, wheatears, culroussets *or figpeckers, then collect them and prepare a recipe such as this one. This recipe uses the more easily found quail. The birds are rolled in an aromatic blend of bread crumbs and fennel seeds, then wrapped in fresh grape leaves before spit-roasting.*

FOUNDATIONS OF PROVENÇAL CUISINE

According to the great writers on Provençal cuisine, there are three foundations to this cookery: olive oil, garlic, and the aromatic herbs, such as herbes de Provence *or aromatic condiments such as* pissalat, *a puree of anchovies blended with olive oil.*[51] *Jean-Noël Escudier, the author of an important book on Provençal food,* La véritable cuisine provençal et niçoise, *said that the king of Provence is the olive tree, the essential element to Provençal cuisine. There is no good cuisine without good oil and there is no Provençal cuisine without garlic.*

C. Chanot-Bullier, the author of a subregional cookbook of Provençal cuisine, Vieii receto du cousino prouvençalo, *divided the cuisine of Provence into four regions. The first she called the region of Marseillaises, Martegalle, and Aixoise (or* Marsiheso, Martegalo, *and* Sestiano *in the Provençal language). This is an area of fish stews and soups, bouillabaisse (page 375) being the most famous. All kinds of shellfish are important, too. The Provençal version of* allioli *(page 513), called* rouille *(page 514), is a famous accompaniment to many fish dishes. The meat of this region is prepared in a variety of ways, with daube being the most popular; the meat is slowly cooked in red wine and stock along with black olives. The nearby hills of Aix provide an abundance of rabbit and small birds (page 215), which are favorites for the cooks. The vegetable dishes are often cooked as* tian *(see page 212). The desserts have a certain Arab feeling to them, such as the baked* maniclo, *made of leavened dough, sugar, and orange flower water, or the* cacho-dènt, *baked fingers of flour and sugar dough made with eggs, ground almond, and orange flower water.*

Chanot-Bullier called the second of Provençal cuisines that of Arlesiennes and Camarguaises-Comtadines (Arlatenco-Camarguenco-Coumtadino). *In this region, vegetables play a role above all. In the Comtat-Venaissin, a typically excellent plate is* le tian, *made in many different ways, although* tian d'épinards *(page 212) is quite famous. (A* tian *is a vegetable dish cooked in an earthenware pan called by the same name.) After spinach and Swiss chard, the most common vegetables are eggplant, cardoon, and zucchini, although artichokes are popular, too.*

The third cuisine is of Toulonnaise and Varoise (Toulounenco-Varesco). *This is the cuisine of the Côte d'Azur, the kingdom of* coquillages, *shellfish, eaten raw or cooked in fancy sauces. She includes* tapenade, *the famous paste of black olives, anchovies, tuna, and capers, as being a part of this cuisine.*

Fourth is the cuisine of Nice (Niçarda), *where it is typical to see the use of pasta. Nice has been part of France only since 1860, and has historically been more closely associated with Italy than with France. For five hundred years, Nice—except for a brief period during the Napoleonic era—belonged to the House of Savoy, whose dominions included Savoy, Sardinia, and the Piedmont. Nice's culinary traditions are closely tied with that of the Italians, especially the Genoese, and for that reason pasta has played a role in the cuisine of Nice since the thirteenth century. Ratatouille is famous here (page 19).*

Provençal cooks are very particular about how a dish is prepared. They are fussy about ingredients, especially the olive, the king of Provençal cuisine, and about methods of cooking that can appear baroque to the outsider. The origin of the culinary baroque, a voluptuous, almost Rubenesque cooking style, seems to be rooted in the age of Louis XIV. The baroque philosophical sensibility of the Provençal cook is captured in a well-known story concerning an imaginary dish called olives Provençal. *A green olive is stuffed into a thrush. The thrush is stuffed into a chicken, which is stuffed into a goat that in turn is stuffed into a pig, which is stuffed into a pony that is stuffed into a cow. The stuffed cow is roasted on a spit for a long time, nearly a day. When it is done, you discard the cow, pony, pig, goat, chicken, and thrush, remove the olive, and eat it. This is not a story about profligacy; it is a story about the proper way to eat an olive.*

Much of the writing about Provençal food is very misleading when it comes to the historic roots of the cuisine. During the Middle Ages, cabbage was virtually the major source of food for the Provençal masses.[52] *But in the contemporary cookbooks cabbage is hardly mentioned, and we read instead about tomatoes, zucchini, and potatoes as if these New World foods have had a long history in Provence. It seems likely they became popular in the cuisine only recently, perhaps around the end of the nineteenth century.*

12 small birds, such as quail
Salt and freshly ground black pepper to taste
3 tablespoons extra virgin olive oil
⅔ cup dried bread crumbs
1 tablespoon freshly ground fennel seeds
24 large fresh grape leaves (see Note if using brined grape leaves)

1. Prepare a medium charcoal fire or preheat a gas grill for 20 minutes on medium.

2. Place the birds in a ceramic or glass dish, season with salt and pepper, and cover with a light film of olive oil. Mix the bread crumbs and fennel seeds, then roll each bird in the bread crumb mixture. Overlap two grape leaves, unless they are quite large, and place a quail on one end. Carefully wrap each bird in the grape leaves. Skewer the quail on the spit, packed tightly, so they don't spin on the skewers while spit-roasting. Affix the spit-roasting attachment.

3. Once the fire or grill is ready, add some grape twigs or shoots, apple wood chips, or hazelnut or other nut shells to the fire and spit-roast the birds until golden brown, 30 to 40 minutes.

NOTE: If using fresh grape leaves, boil them gently in water to cover for 5 minutes before using. Brined grape leaves are sold in jars and work fine; however, if they have been jarred a long time they might disintegrate, so it is best to use them sooner rather than later.

Makes 6 servings

WHITHER AND WHENCE THE GREEKS

AMONG the mountain peoples of the Mediterranean, those of the Greek peninsula and its archipelago are salient. Could Greek cuisine be the font of all contemporary Mediterranean cuisine? We know that some of the earliest written references to cuisine in the Mediterranean are Greek. But some scholars point out that the Greeks of today have not an ounce of classical Greek blood and are in fact a mixture of Albanians, Slavs, and Turks. This is certainly overstating the case, but there is an element of truth. Even so, the story is more complicated than Greek food writers have admitted. A look at the contemporary food of Greece is enlightening. At first glance it appears indebted entirely to Turkish food; and, in fact, many of the names of Greek dishes attest to this. But we should remember that culinary influence flows two ways. This two-way flow is complicated by the fact that when Turkish tribes expanded their control over Anatolia in the twelfth and thirteenth centuries, leading to the establishment of the Seljuk and, later, the Ottoman empires, the population was hugely Greek. Before the arrival of these Turkic tribes from Central Asia, Anatolia was part of the Greek Byzantine Empire. Many of these Greeks converted to Islam. Today scholars are not sure the extent to which a Byzantine Greek cultural substratum influenced the nomadic Turks moving into Anatolia. There are other influences on Greek cuisine, too, such as Italian. When we think of the contemporary tension between Greece and Turkey, we sometimes forget that the Greeks once hated the Venetians far more than they did the Turks. The Italian influence shows up clearly in many dishes from Ionian islands, and the Turkish influence is felt in the Dodocanese archipelago in the form of pilaf and in the use of spices and seeds such as cumin and sesame seeds. I've been told of other culinary traces, such as spit-roasting on Crete, a method that is said not to have existed before its introduction by Albanians.[53]

As any of the latest naval standoffs between Turks and Greeks in the Aegean shows, the Greeks are not much amenable to the idea that their food might be indebted to Turkish cooking. It is commonplace for Greek food writers to introduce Greek cuisine as one "shaped through over three thousand years of history."[54] The sumptuous feasts described by Homer or Plato and menus from Athenaeus—all this will be described as part of the Greek culinary heritage. Sometimes it can get rather silly, such as the comment of one writer that "When you start your day with rolls and coffee, you are following an ancient Greek custom."[55] One Greek writer went so far as to state that Greek cuisine is twenty-five centuries old and is the ur-cuisine that the Turks, Italians, and other Europeans borrowed from, not the other way around.[56] Nicolas Tselementes was a noted Greek food authority who claimed the Greeks influenced western European foods via Rome; he traced the ancestry of such dishes as *keftedes*, dolmades, moussaka, and *yuvarelakia* to ancient Greek preparations that subsequently became masked behind Turkish and European names. He also said that bouillabaisse was an offspring of the Greek *kakavia*.[57]

The Greek food writers are right about one thing: Greece is the source of an original European cuisine, just as it is the source of Western philosophy. The Hellenist influence on the Mediterranean is no doubt a powerful and important one and should not be underestimated. But whether it is the only font of Mediterranean cuisine is another matter. Greek culinary nationalism has hindered any reasoned debate and research on this question of the degree to which the Greek people preserved and maintained the classical heritage through twenty-five hundred years, including Roman occupation, barbarian invasions, and five hundred years of occupation by the Turks, not to mention interference and occupation by Venetians, Genoese, and Catalans. They ignore the fact that the majority population of peninsular Greece in the Middle Ages was Slav.[58] They also underemphasize the importance of the Byzantine Empire, the Greek successor state to the Roman Empire in the East.

The Byzantine Empire saw its most glorious period in the sixth century. A new period of splendor also occurred in the ninth and tenth centuries, but after the Turkish victory at Manzikert in 1071 the fortunes of Byzantium declined. The empire broke up when the Crusaders captured Constantinople in 1204 during the Fourth Crusade, and continued as a truncated state, ever-shrinking in the face of the Ottoman Turks and vainly begging for aid from the West. Finally, Constantinople fell to Mohammed II in 1453, and the Byzantine Empire was extinguished forever. But this Greek civilization certainly left important culinary artifacts, and these culinary influences from Byzantium are a more likely Greek contribution than that from classical Greece, as claimed by so many writers. We know that there were Byzantine mechanical devices such as one for preparing dough using animal power, apparently invented at the end of the tenth century. We can surmise that there were other important culinary transfers as well. Unfortunately, there are no comparative historical studies of Greek and Turkish food by disinterested third-party scholars, although at least one Greek scholar believes his countrymen claim too much ownership.[59] In any case, all claims regarding the heritage of Greek food must be taken with a grain of salt, for Greek culinary history still awaits its Maxime Rodinson, the French historian who treated culinary history with objective scholarship. As the scholar of medieval Hellenism, Speros Vryonis Jr. warned: "In matters of cuisine the conquerors undoubtedly absorbed some items from the conquered, but the problem is again obscured by a similarity in Byzantine and Islamic cuisine which probably existed before the appearance of the Turks."[60] For my part, I am convinced of the possibility that contemporary Greek food, when it is not directly taken from the Turks or Italians, has its roots more properly in Greek Byzantium than it does in the classical era.

The history of Greek food is as complicated as Greek history. Listening today, one would think that the boundary between Greek and Turkish is true and clear—but it isn't, for although Greece was part of the Ottoman Empire for a long time, the Greeks themselves sometimes benefited from a pax turcica. In the Middle Ages, the Greek peasants of Anatolia rose up against the towns where their Greek landlords lived, converted to Islam, and welcomed the Turkish nomads arriving from the East. Remember, too, that the Greeks helped the Turkish expedition against Crete in the seventeenth century because they hated the Venetians. Before the Turks, Greece was under the scourge of the Catalans, who took Athens in 1311 and set up their own dynasty, not to mention the Florentines in the late fourteenth and early fifteenth centuries. By the mid-fourteenth century, parts of Greece were falling to the Turks and the great Greek capital of Constantinople fell in 1453, a momentous event. Some of the most famous admirals in the Turkish service were Greeks, such as the corsair Khayr al-Din (Barbarossa) and possibly Kemal Re'is, whose fleet defeated the Venetians off Modon in 1500. When the Turks overran Greece, they populated the fertile plains of Thessaly and western Macedonia, but were never really able to conquer the mountains. These mountain Greeks, the famous Klephts, often raided the plains, attacking both Greeks and Turks. The Turks sometimes used the institution of the Greek *armatoloi* (men at arms) to track down the Klephts. There were also Greek tribal communities left completely untouched by the Ottoman forces, such as the Suli of Epirus, the Máni in the Peloponnesus, and the Sphakia on Crete. These tribes were semi-autonomous communities left unmolested by

GREECE, TURKEY, AND THE BALKANS
BOSNIA–HERZEGOVINA
CROATIA
Split (Spalato) (Venetian)
Makarska
BRAČ
PELJEŠAC
HVAR
KORČULA
LASTOVO
MLJET
Dubrovnik (Ragusa)
SERBIA
Niš
Pirot
(FORMER YUGOSLAVIA)
MONTENEGRO
KOSOVO
Wallachia
BULGARIA
Sofia
Plovdiv (Philippopolis)
BLACK SEA
Bosphorus
Edirne (Andrianople)
Istanbul (Constantinople)
Scutari (Ushküdar) (Shkodër)
İzmit (Kocaeli) (Nicomedia)
Tekirdag (Rodosto)
Sea of Marmara
Gallipoli (Gelibolu)
Erdek
Bursa
Ankara
Shkoder (Scutari)
Uskub (Skopje)
MACEDONIA
ADRIATIC SEA
Thrace
Kavalla
Tirana
Strouga
Durrës (Durazzo) (Venetian)
Bari
Salonika (Thessaloniki) (Venetian)
ALBANIA
Macedonia (Rumelia)
ITALY
Brindisi
Vlorë (Valona)
SAMOTHRÁKI
LEMNOS
Çanakkale
Troy
Balikesir
TURKEY
ANATOLIA
Lecce
Strait of Otranto
BOZCAADA (VENETIAN)
Edremit
Ayvalik
Pergamon (Bergama)
Gulf of Taranto
Kerkira
CORFU (KERKIRA) (VENETIAN)
Piros
Ioannina
Thessaly
Mt. Pelion
Vólos
GREECE
NORTHERN SPORADES
LESBOS
Çandarlı
Aegean Sea
Konya
Dhomokós
Lamia
Menemen
İzmir (Smyrna)
AKDAĞ MTNS.
IONIAN SEA
IONIAN ISLANDS
Préveza
Sterea
NEGROPONTE (EUBOEA) (VENETIAN)
CHIOS
Ortaklar
Aydn
Gökçeler Koyu
Denizli
S. MAURA (LEVKÁS) (VENETIAN)
Lepanto (Návpaktos) (Venetian)
(ATTICA)
Boetia
Athens
Gulf of Corinth
ANDROS (VENETIAN)
SÁMOS
Geyre
Tavas
CEPHALONIA (KEFALLINÍA) (VENETIAN)
Patras (Pátrai) (Venetian)
TÍNOS (VENETIAN)
Milâs
Muğla
Antalya
Piraeus
PÁTMOS
MÍKONOS
Bodrum
ZANTE (ZÁKINTHOS) (VENETIAN)
Argos (Venetian)
Napoli di Romania (Návplion) (Nauplia) (Venetian)
HYDRA
CYCLADES
NÁXOS (VENETIAN)
KOS
Lycia
Gulf of Antalya
N
Taygetos Mtns.
Peloponnesus (Morea)
Kalamata
Nea Mystra
Sparta
Mirtoan Sea
DODECANESE
SÍMI
Marmaris
Rhodes
Kaş
Zonchio (Pílos) (Venetian)
MÍLOS
ÍOS (VENETIAN)
Monemvasia (Venetian)
STAMPALIA (ASTIPÁLALA) (VENETIAN)
Líndos
Modon (Methóni) (Venetian)
Koron (Koróni) (Venetian)
RHODES
Máni
Sea of Crete
MEDITERRANEAN SEA
0 Miles 100 200
CERIGO (KÍTHERA) (VENETIAN)
Canea (Khaniá) (Venetian)
0 Kilometers 100 200
Kalithea
Candia (Iráklion)
SCARPANTO (KÁRPATHOS) (VENETIAN)
CERIGOTTO (ANDIKÍTHERA) (VENETIAN)
CRETE (VENETIAN)
Note: Several Venetian possessions during the Middle Ages shown in parentheses.
Retimo (Réthimnon) (Venetian)
©1999 Jeffrey L. Ward

the Ottomans in their impregnable mountain confederations. They rarely interacted with the Turks, except occasionally when the Ottomans compelled them to pay tribute if they had sufficient troops in a local area to do so.[61]

The rivalry between the Houses of Anjou and Aragon over the island of Sicily affected Greek history of the late thirteenth century more than any other cause. Once peace came to Sicily, the Catalan auxiliaries of Aragon sought their mercenary adventure in Greece, wreaking havoc on the Greeks and the Frankish rulers of the Levant. The Catalans ruled Attica and Boetia for seventy-five years, until Athens was taken by Nerio Acciaiuoli, a member of a famous Florentine banking and arms manufacturing family in 1388 and the Greeks subjugated. The position of the Greeks during this time is reflected in Catalan, Sicilian, and Florentine documents where, when concerned with Greece, the Greeks remain nameless.[62] For a hundred years Greece was dominated by this conflict, only to fall to the Ottoman Turks in short order.[63] By the late fourteenth and early fifteenth centuries, there was an upsurge in Greek ethnic awareness that sustained the Greeks as a people through four centuries of Turkish rule. This spirit was fostered and guided by the Greek Orthodox Church. Whatever exists in the way of a unique Greek cuisine more than likely derives from the efforts of the orthodox church in sustaining Greek Byzantine culture, rather than from the classical period, and was influenced by mountain Greeks who were not so easily subjugated by occupying powers.

Unfortunately, we don't have any information about what culinary traditions or recipes may have been preserved in Greek Orthodox monasteries outside of folkloric apocrypha. The number of fasting days in the Greek Orthodox calendar are numerous, and the Greeks are a devout people, so many preparations were created for special religious occasions or for the particular needs of fasting. The most important holiday for the Greeks is Easter, celebrated by Christians as the anniversary of the resurrection of Jesus Christ.

The following recipes are some examples of foods that might find their way onto a menu for a variety of religious holidays.

Kotoletes Arniou Souvlas (Greece)

SPIT-ROASTED LAMB LOIN

The Greek name for this literally means "chops of lamb on the spit-grill," a souvla *being a spit. Professor Nikos Stavroulakis, an authority on Greek and Cretan food, tells me that spit-roasting on Crete is an Albanian introduction. This preparation is seasoned with a* ladolemono *sauce, a dressing made of two parts olive oil to one part lemon juice, seasoned with a little oregano. The meat is marinated eight hours until it is tender. Some cooks also add dried mint and thyme to the marinade. Serve with French fries (page 61), any Greek salad, and lemon wedges.*

½ cup extra virgin olive oil
Juice from 2 lemons
2 teaspoons dried oregano or thyme
Salt and freshly ground black pepper to taste
One 3½-pound lamb loin roast (7 to 8 ribs)

1. Whisk together the marinade of olive oil, lemon juice, and oregano seasoned with salt and pepper. Place the lamb roast in a large glass baking dish, pour the marinade over it, making sure to coat the whole thing, and let marinate in the refrigerator for 8 hours, turning every hour.

2. Prepare a hot charcoal grill or preheat a gas grill on high for 20 minutes. If spit-roasting, secure the whole lamb loin tightly to the spit and rotate

about 10 inches from the heat for 1¼ to 1½ hours. If grilling, cut the lamb into chops before marinating and then grill for 20 minutes per side. Serve immediately.

Makes 4 servings

Keftedakia Marinata (Greece)
MARINATED MEATBALLS

The pre-Lenten carnival season in Greece is a period of feasting and drinking. The carnival of Apokreos occurs during the week preceding Lent. The event begins on Sunday, and on this day and during the week meat is consumed and the foods are called kreatinis, *referring to meats. This recipe is typical of the foods eaten at this time.*

Travelers who are unable to eat in a Greek home—where the best Greek food is—might run across very good preparations of keftedakia, *moussaka, or* pastitsio *at roadside tavernas. This recipe is in fact based on one I had at a truck-stop taverna outside Ioannina, after consulting the recipe in Vilma Chantiles's* The Food of Greece.

2 cups cubed Italian or French bread, white part only
¾ cup water
1¼ pounds lean ground lamb
½ cup finely chopped fresh parsley leaves
2 tablespoons finely chopped fresh mint leaves
1 teaspoon ground coriander seeds
1 small onion, grated
2 large garlic cloves, mashed
Salt and freshly ground black pepper to taste
6 cups pure or virgin olive oil, olive pomace oil, or vegetable oil for deep-frying
All-purpose flour for dredging
2 tablespoons extra virgin olive oil
1 small onion, chopped
2 large garlic cloves, finely chopped
2 pounds ripe plum tomatoes, peeled, seeded, and chopped
1 cup dry red wine
1 cinnamon stick
2 tablespoons fresh savory leaves or 1 teaspoon dried savory

1. In a large bowl, soak the bread cubes in the water until sodden. Squeeze the water out between your palms as if you were making a snowball. In a large bowl, knead together the bread, lamb, 6 tablespoons of the parsley, the mint, coriander, grated onion, and mashed garlic and season with salt and pepper. Cover and refrigerate overnight.

2. Preheat the frying oil in a deep-fryer or an 8-inch saucepan fitted with a basket insert to 375°F. Remove the meat mixture from the refrigerator and form meatballs the size of a walnut, keeping your hands wet with cold water so the meat doesn't stick to them. Dredge the meatballs in the flour, tapping off any excess. Deep-fry the meatballs in batches in the hot oil until light brown, 3 to 4 minutes. Drain on paper towels and set aside. Let the frying oil cool completely, strain, and save for a future use.

3. In a large earthenware casserole or enameled cast-iron casserole, heat the extra virgin olive oil over medium heat, then cook the chopped onion until translucent, about 8 minutes, stirring occasionally. Add the chopped garlic, tomatoes, wine, cinnamon stick, remaining 2 tablespoons parsley, and the savory and season with salt and pepper. Stir well to blend and simmer for 45 minutes. Remove the cinnamon stick and discard. Add the meatballs to the sauce, stir, reduce the heat to low, and cook until thickened a bit, another 15 to 30 minutes. Serve warm, not hot.

Makes 4 to 6 servings

❈ *Spanakopitta* (Greece)

SPINACH PIE

Apokreos is the week preceding Lent, and tradition calls for eating meat, while during the next week of Lent eggs, butter, and milk products are eaten. This recipe, and the two following, are typically prepared during this period.

Although spanakopitta *is found in nearly every Greek-American fast-food joint, in varying degrees of quality, I still love this spinach pie and provide this recipe so you can make it at home. Diane Kochilas, author of* The Food and Wine of Greece, *tells us that the capital of* spanakopitta *making is in Epirus in northwestern Greece. Her recipe is more complicated than mine, but very good and rewarding. In Turkey an identical pie is made called* ıspanaki peynirli tepsi böreği *which means "spinach-cheese small tray-pie." It might be made with feta cheese and flavored with scallions and dill.*

3 pounds spinach, heavy stems removed and washed well
13 tablespoons unsalted butter
3 large eggs, beaten
1 cup freshly grated *kefalotyri* cheese (page 716)
1 tablespoon finely chopped fresh parsley leaves
¾ cup béchamel sauce (see Step 2, page 283)
1 teaspoon salt
Freshly ground black pepper to taste
¼ cup extra virgin olive oil
¾ pound (about 12 sheets) commercial phyllo pastry (usually 14 × 18-inch sheets; see page 224 on handling it)

1. Put the spinach in a large pot with only the water clinging to it from the last washing, cover, and cook over medium heat, turning occasionally with a long wooden spoon or a fork, until the spinach has wilted, 15 to 20 minutes. Drain very well, pressing the water out with the back of a wooden spoon, and chop.

2. In the pot you cooked the spinach, melt 6 tablespoons (¾ stick) of the butter, then cook the spinach over medium heat for 10 minutes, stirring. Remove from the heat and turn into a large bowl. Add the beaten eggs, *kefalotyri* cheese, parsley, béchamel, salt, and pepper.

3. Preheat the oven to 350°F. Melt the remaining 7 tablespoons butter with the olive oil in a small saucepan. Grease a 9 × 12-inch baking pan with this mixture using a brush. Unravel the phyllo pastry following the directions on page 224. Lay in six of the phyllo pasty sheets, brushing each with the melted butter and oil. Brush the first layer liberally. Keep the phyllo pastry sheets humidified with a wet kitchen towel draped over them as you work so they don't dry out. The pastry should go up the sides of the pan. Spread the spinach evenly over the top of the pastry sheets. Cover the spinach with six more sheets of pastry, brushing each with butter. Fold the edges of any phyllo pastry sheets over and liberally brush the top with the remaining olive oil and butter.

4. Bake until the top is golden, about 40 minutes. Cool for 20 minutes, cut into squares, and serve at room temperature.

NOTE: You may add a little chopped scallion or dill to the spinach.

Makes 8 servings

❈ *Tyropitakia* (Greece)

CHEESE PASTRIES

Tyri *means "cheese" in Greek, and this cheese pie is typical of a wide range of dishes that cover cheese with pas-*

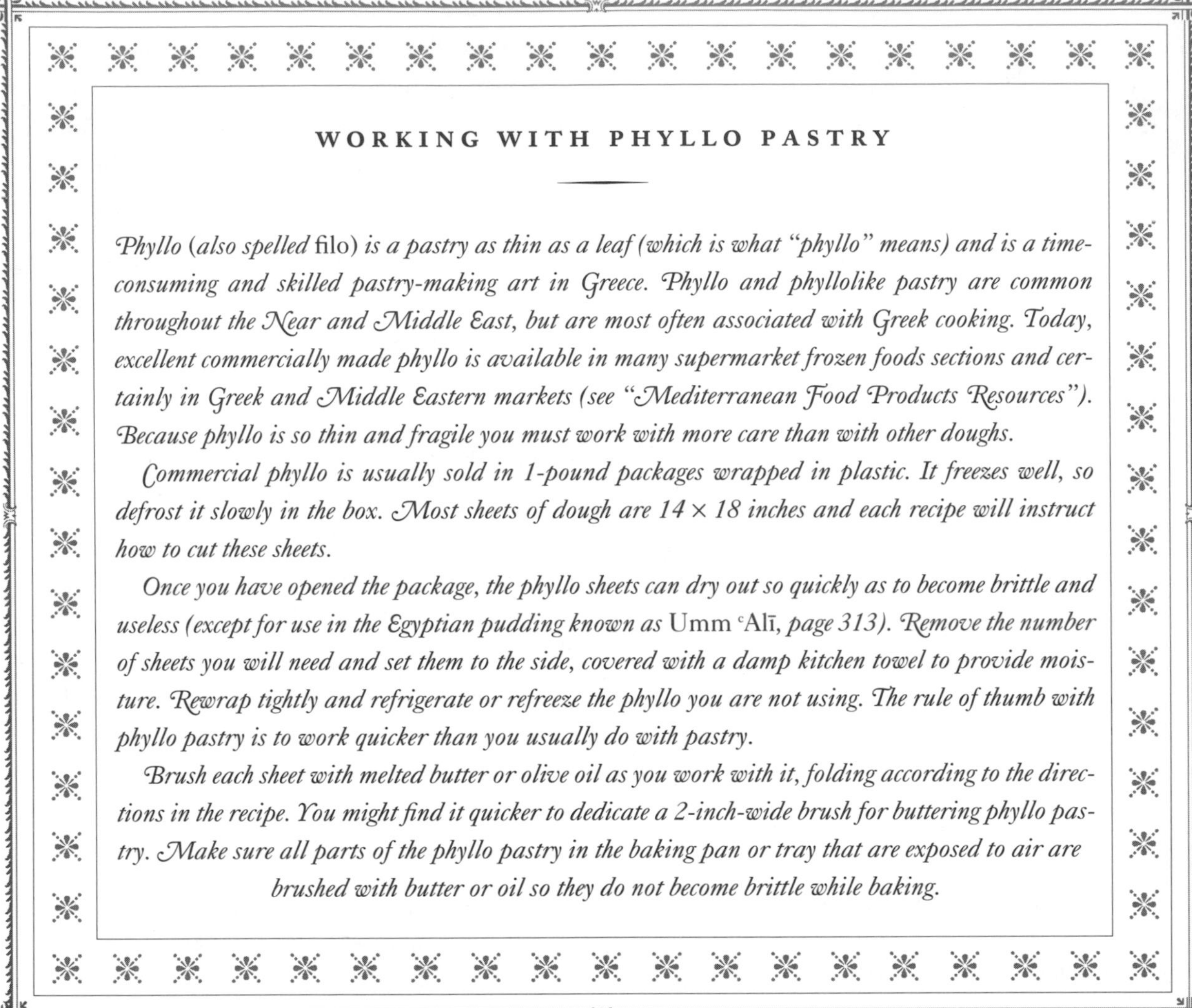

WORKING WITH PHYLLO PASTRY

Phyllo (also spelled filo) is a pastry as thin as a leaf (which is what "phyllo" means) and is a time-consuming and skilled pastry-making art in Greece. Phyllo and phyllolike pastry are common throughout the Near and Middle East, but are most often associated with Greek cooking. Today, excellent commercially made phyllo is available in many supermarket frozen foods sections and certainly in Greek and Middle Eastern markets (see "Mediterranean Food Products Resources"). Because phyllo is so thin and fragile you must work with more care than with other doughs.

Commercial phyllo is usually sold in 1-pound packages wrapped in plastic. It freezes well, so defrost it slowly in the box. Most sheets of dough are 14 × 18 inches and each recipe will instruct how to cut these sheets.

Once you have opened the package, the phyllo sheets can dry out so quickly as to become brittle and useless (except for use in the Egyptian pudding known as Umm ʿAlī, page 313). Remove the number of sheets you will need and set them to the side, covered with a damp kitchen towel to provide moisture. Rewrap tightly and refrigerate or refreeze the phyllo you are not using. The rule of thumb with phyllo pastry is to work quicker than you usually do with pastry.

Brush each sheet with melted butter or olive oil as you work with it, folding according to the directions in the recipe. You might find it quicker to dedicate a 2-inch-wide brush for buttering phyllo pastry. Make sure all parts of the phyllo pastry in the baking pan or tray that are exposed to air are brushed with butter or oil so they do not become brittle while baking.

try. It is a preparation made during Apokreos, the period before Lent when dairy products are eaten. This recipe mixes feta, a sheep and goat's milk curd cheese that is salted and stored in brine, and mezithra *(also transliterated* mizithra *and* myzithra*), a kind of Greek ricotta salata, or* kefalotyri*, a hard grating cheese usually made of sheep's milk, though sometimes goat's milk. Another traditional cheese mixture would use* manouri*, a soft, unsalted white cream cheese made of the whey of sheep and goat's milk (see page 717) and grated* kefalotyri*. It is made as one large baked pie, although pastry triangles are typical, too.*

Many Greek-Americans replace the Greek cheeses with an Italian pecorino Romano, and with cream cheese, cottage cheese, or muenster cheese. Because I have never had difficulty finding Greek cheeses in this country, I prefer the traditional way of making tyropitakia *(also spelled* tyropittes*) and provide this recipe from Nafpliou (Návplion or Nauplia), a town once occupied by the Venetians and known as Napoli di Romania. There are many recipes for this dish, the ingredients depending on the region or even island. For instance, in Thessaly, a short dough of flour, water, and vinegar is used. Sometimes a puff pastry is used or shortbread in a pie called* kouroumbougatses*. In Rumelia, a* tyropitakia *is made with nearly a dozen* *eggs.*[64] *Another name for this is* kalitsounia, *as it is known on Crete. In Greece they are all generally called* pittes *or pies.*

6 tablespoons (3/4 stick) unsalted butter
3 large eggs
6 ounces *mezithra*, crumbled, or *kefalotyri* cheese, grated
14 ounces feta cheese, crumbled
1 tablespoon very finely chopped parsley leaves
Pinch of freshly grated nutmeg
3/4 pound (about 12 sheets) commercial phyllo pastry (usually 14 × 18-inch sheets; see page 224 on handling it)

1. Melt the butter in a small saucepan and keep warm. In a large bowl, beat the eggs and toss together with the *mezithra* or *kefalotyri* cheese, feta, parsley, and nutmeg.

2. Unravel the phyllo pastry following the directions on page 224. Keep the phyllo sheets humidified with a wet kitchen towel draped over them as you work. With a pastry brush, butter the bottom of a 9 × 12-inch baking pan and layer in seven or eight sheets of phyllo, brushing butter on each layer. Let the phyllo edges droop over the sides of the pan. Pour in the cheese mixture, making sure it is spread evenly over the pastry. Fold the edges of the phyllo over into the pan, and butter them, too.

3. Preheat the oven to 350°F. With the remaining five to six phyllo sheets, cover the pan, buttering each sheet and tucking the edges over and into the pan. Bake until the top is golden brown, about 40 minutes. Remove, let it rest for 15 minutes, and then cut into squares. Serve warm.

VARIATION
You can make about fifty individual cheese pies by cutting the phyllo into 3 × 14-inch strips. Place a heaping teaspoon of the cheese mixture at one end and fold one corner over to the opposite edge of the phyllo to form a triangle. Continue in this way up the strip until you end up with a triangular pie. Continue the preparation. These individual cheese triangles freeze well and make very appetizing *mezedes* for surprise guests.

Makes 8 servings

Bourekakia apo Tyri (Greece)

CHEESE ROLLS

Bourekakia *comes from the Turkish word* börek, *also meaning a pastry. This phyllo pastry roll can be filled with any combination of crab, shrimp, chicken, chicken liver, ground lamb, spinach and cheese, mushrooms, and artichokes, or be made as a sweet. One Greek-American food writer claims that thirteenth-century Crusaders wrote home about this dish after having tasted it in Constantinople.*[65] Graviera *is a Greek version of Gruyère cheese.*

1/2 pound feta cheese
1/2 pound *graviera* or Gruyère cheese, grated
10 tablespoons (1 1/4 sticks) unsalted butter
1/4 cup all-purpose flour
1 cup milk
2 large eggs, beaten
1 tablespoon finely chopped fresh parsley leaves
Pinch of freshly grated nutmeg
3/4 pound (about 12 sheets) commercial phyllo pastry (usually 14 × 18-inch sheets; see page 224 on handling it)

1. Crumble the feta and mix with the *graviera* or Gruyère. In a medium-size saucepan, melt 1/4 cup (1/2 stick) of the butter over medium heat, then blend in the flour to make a roux and cook for 1 minute. Remove the saucepan from the burner and whisk in the milk a little at a time. Return to the burner and

cook over medium heat until it is a thick white sauce, 3 to 4 minutes, stirring constantly. Remove the white sauce from the heat and let cool slightly. Add the cheeses, eggs, parsley, and nutmeg and stir well to combine. In a small saucepan, melt the remaining 6 tablespoons (3/4 stick) butter.

2. Preheat the oven to 350°F. Cut the phyllo sheets in half lengthwise. Keep the phyllo sheets humidified with a wet kitchen towel draped over them as you work. Lay one sheet down and brush with the melted butter using a 2-inch brush. Lay another sheet on top and brush with butter. Spoon 2 tablespoons of the cheese stuffing on one end of the sheet and fold the top over lengthwise. Fold 1 inch of each side over, brush with butter and roll up. Arrange the pastry cylinders in a buttered baking dish, seam-side down. Bake until golden, about 30 minutes. Remove, cool, and serve warm or freeze for later use.

Makes 18 to 20 rolls

Angourodomatosalata me Feta (Greece)

TOMATO AND CUCUMBER SALAD WITH FETA CHEESE

At the end of the workday, men gather in tavernas to drink ouzo, wine, or beer and eat a variety of mezedes, *small dishes of specially prepared foods to be eaten with drinks. Although this preparation is often served as a straightforward salad in Greece, it is popular too as a* meze. *The tomato was not adopted wholeheartedly in Greece until the nineteenth century. Feta cheese, the quintessential Greek cheese, may originally have been Italian. The word does not exist in classical Greek; it is a New Greek word, originally* tyripheta, *or "cheese slice," the word* feta *coming from the Italian* fette, *meaning a slice of food. Although cheeses are mentioned frequently in the writings of the ancient Greeks, it is never clear what kind of cheese they are talking about. The description of cheesemaking in Homer's* Odyssey *(Book 9: 278–79) sounds more like the Sicilian cheeses known as* tuma *or* canestrato *than it does a brined cheese like feta. In the anonymous fourteenth-century Venetian cookbook, the* Libro per cuoco, *there are two recipes that call for* formazo di Candia, *a cheese made on the then Venetian island of Crete, that may be the first feta cheese. One recipe specifically calls for the cheese to be washed, as you would feta. Greek feta cheese is a soft, white cheese made by mountain shepherds from goat or ewe's milk whose curd, once solidified from rennet, is placed in wooden barrels or boxes to drain and is then rubbed with salt and sold in a salted brine. In the United States, feta cheese is made from cow's milk. Be sure that this dish is served at room temperature.*

8 ripe but firm plum tomatoes (about 1 1/4 pounds), sliced
2 cucumbers, peeled, cut in half lengthwise, seeded, and sliced
1 green bell pepper, seeded and sliced
1/2 pound feta cheese, crumbled into large chunks
12 imported black Kalamata olives
1/4 cup extra virgin olive oil
Juice from 1/2 lemon
2 tablespoons red or white wine vinegar
1 garlic clove, chopped
3 tablespoons finely chopped fresh mint leaves
Salt and freshly ground black pepper to taste

1. In a large mixing or salad bowl, toss the tomatoes, cucumbers, green pepper, feta, and olives together.

2. In a small bowl, whisk the olive oil, lemon juice, vinegar, garlic, and mint together and pour over the salad. Toss to coat evenly and season with salt and pepper. Toss again and serve at room temperature.

Makes 6 servings

Patzaria Salata (Greece)

BEET SALAD

This salad might be made during one of the fasting periods when abstinence from meat and poultry is observed, such as on Palm Sunday or when preparing for Holy Communion. Greek cooks like to gather beets that are young and small, and they use the beet leaves for a horta *preparation (page 492). An attractive way to make this is to combine orange beets with the regular beets.*

8 small beets (about 2 pounds)
3 tablespoons extra virgin olive oil
2 teaspoons white wine vinegar
Skordalia sauce (page 515)

1. Slice off the green leaves without puncturing the beets and set them aside. Place the beets in a medium-size pot and cover with water. Boil until tender, when easily pierced by a skewer, about 45 minutes. After the roots have been boiling for 30 minutes, add the beet greens. Drain. Set the beet greens aside if using in the *horta* recipe, otherwise use them in step 2.

2. Peel, then slice the beets thin. Lightly oil the bottom of a serving platter and arrange the beet greens on top. Now arrange the beet slices on top of the greens. Whisk the oil and vinegar together, drizzle over the beets and beet greens, and serve at room temperature with *skordalia* sauce on the side.

Makes 4 servings

Pastitsio (Greece)

BAKED MACARONI

The traditional method of baking in Greece was to use a beehive-shaped oven, called an avli, *built on the side of a house. Those who couldn't afford an oven would send their food to the local baker's* fourno *(oven) for cooking.* Pastitsio, *baked macaroni with meat sauce and white sauce, with its Italian-derived name but Muslim-derived baking technique of mixing meat and pasta, is a favorite dish for the Sunday of Apokreos, the week before Lent, when meat is typically eaten.* Pastitsio *is also frequently found in tavernas, and a recipe appears in every Greek cookbook. This recipe is a combination of an old recipe from a Greek cookbook of the 1950s modified by the* pastitsios *I have had in Greece and loved so much. A certain kind of pasta is used for this preparation and the Greeks call it "macaroni for* pastitsio," *which is what the Italians call* ziti lunghe *or* mezzani.

¾ cup (1½ sticks) unsalted butter
¾ cup all-purpose flour
Salt and freshly ground black pepper to taste
4 cups hot milk
4 large egg yolks
2 large egg whites, whipped to form firm peaks, but not dry ones
Pinch plus 1 teaspoon freshly grated nutmeg
1½ cups freshly grated *kefalotyri* cheese (page 716)
2 tablespoons extra virgin olive oil
1 large onion, finely chopped
1½ pounds ground beef
1 large garlic clove, finely chopped
3 cups crushed or chopped fresh ripe or canned tomatoes
1 tablespoon tomato paste
1½ teaspoons ground cinnamon
6 whole cloves, ground
1½ teaspoons freshly ground allspice berries
1 pound *ziti lunghe* or *mezzani*

1. In a large saucepan, melt 1/4 cup (1/2 stick) of the butter over medium-high heat. Stir in 1/4 cup of the flour and cook this roux until it begins to turn very light brown or golden, 6 to 7 minutes, stirring frequently. Lightly season with salt and pepper. Whisk 2 tablespoons of the hot milk into the egg yolks. Remove the saucepan from the heat and whisk 2 cups of the hot milk into the roux. Return the saucepan to medium-low heat and cook a few minutes, stirring. Remove from the burner again and stir in half of the beaten egg yolks and milk. Set aside.

2. Make a thicker béchamel by following the instructions in step 1 using another 1/4 cup (1/2 stick) of the remaining butter, the 1/2 cup remaining flour, the remaining hot milk, and the remaining beaten egg yolks. Once the sauce is made, stir in the whipped egg whites, a pinch of the nutmeg, and 1/2 cup of the *kefalotyri* cheese.

3. In a large skillet, heat the olive oil over medium-high heat, then cook the onion until translucent, 5 to 6 minutes, stirring. Add the beef and brown with the garlic, 3 to 4 minutes. Add the tomatoes, tomato paste, cinnamon, the remaining teaspoon nutmeg, the cloves, and allspice and season with salt and pepper. Mix well, reduce the heat to low, cover, and simmer until well blended and fragrant, about 30 minutes, stirring occasionally.

4. Meanwhile, bring a large pot of water to a rolling boil, salt abundantly, and add the pasta. Cook until very al dente. Drain.

5. In a small skillet, melt the remaining 1/4 cup butter; once it turns brown, pour over the pasta. Toss the pasta with the thin béchamel from Step 1; you want the pasta just coated, not soggy, with béchamel, so you might not need to use it all.

6. Preheat the oven to 350°F. Butter a 9 × 11 × 2-inch baking or lasagne pan. Cover the bottom of it with half the pasta. Sprinkle with 1/4 cup of the *kefalotyri* cheese. Pour the meat sauce over the pasta, spreading it evenly. Sprinkle with another 1/4 cup of the *kefalotyri*. Cover with the remaining pasta, and sprinkle with another 1/4 cup of the cheese. Cover the pasta with the thick béchamel from step 2. Sprinkle the remaining 1/4 cup *kefalotyri* evenly on top. Bake until golden brown, 50 minutes to 1 hour. Let rest 10 minutes before serving.

Makes 8 servings

Arni Yahni (Greece)

LAMB STEW

The Easter lamb is famous in Greece, and although spit-roasted lamb would be typical for Easter dinner, this lamb stew is served throughout the year when not observing a fast requiring abstinence from meat. Sometimes lamb shoulder is used for braising instead of leg, known by its Italian name spala.

There are as many variations and recipes for this as there are families in Greece. This recipe is based on the one I had after I was released from several days in a Greek army hospital in Lamia, recuperating from a car accident in the mountains near Dhomokós. Arni yahni *was very welcome after hospital food. Serve with pilaf (page 602) or* manestra *(the Greek word for orzo-type pasta) browned in butter.*

2 tablespoons extra virgin olive oil
1/4 cup (1/2 stick) unsalted butter
2 pounds boneless lamb cut from the leg, trimmed of fat and cut into 1/2-inch cubes
1 large onion, chopped
1 cup canned or freshly made tomato puree
2 garlic cloves, crushed
1/2 cup water
1/2 cup dry white wine

1 bay leaf
Juice from ½ lemon
Salt and freshly ground black pepper to taste

1. In a large casserole, heat the olive oil with the butter over medium heat; once the butter has melted and stopped sizzling, lightly brown the lamb in it on all sides, about 10 minutes. Remove the meat with a slotted ladle and set aside. Cook the onion in the casserole until lightly browned, 12 to 15 minutes, stirring occasionally.

2. Return the lamb to the casserole and add the tomato puree, garlic, water, wine, bay leaf, and lemon juice and season with salt and pepper. Reduce the heat to low, cover, and braise until the lamb is tender, about 2 hours.

VARIATION
Arni yahni is usually served with a vegetable addition to the stew. Chickpeas, winter squash, celery, okra, cauliflower, carrots, and cabbage might be added at the same time as the lamb, or vegetables such as zucchini, spinach, or peas might be added when there is only 45 minutes left to cooking the lamb.

Makes 4 to 6 servings

Melitzanes Mousakas (Greece)
EGGPLANT MOUSSAKA

Mou-sak-KA is a baked lamb and eggplant casserole covered with a thick layer of béchamel sauce that becomes golden and crusty. It can be made with other ingredients besides eggplant, such as beef or zucchini, potatoes, or artichokes. Moussaka is the best known of all Greek foods. Greeks believe that moussaka was introduced when the Arabs brought the eggplant, although Arabs, especially in Lebanon, think of it as a Greek dish. Moussaka is also found in Turkey.

No one knows what the origin of moussaka is, but the following recipe from the thirteenth-century Arabic cookbook known as the Baghdad cookery book was proposed by the writer Reay Tannahill as the ancestor of moussaka.[66]

Maghmūma or Muqaṭṭaʿa

Cut fat meat small. Slice the tail thin and chop up small. Take onions and eggplant, peel, half-boil, and also cut up small: these may, however, be peeled and cut up into the meat-pot, and not be boiled separately. Make a layer of the tail at the bottom of the pan, then put on top of it a layer of meat: drop in fine-ground seasonings, dry coriander, cumin, caraway, pepper, cinnamon, ginger, and salt. On top of the meat put a layer of eggplant and onion: repeat, until only about four or five fingers' space remain in the pot. Sprinkle over each layer the ground seasonings as required. Mix best vinegar with a little water and a trifle of saffron, and add to the pan so as to lie to a depth of two or three fingers on top of the meat and other ingredients. Leave to settle over the fire: then remove.

It seems likely that the Greek moussaka has Arab origins and may be related to the Palestinian musakhkhan *(page 555), with the word* moussaka *perhaps derived from this Arab word.*

One potential problem with making a traditional moussaka is the amount of fat that might remain after baking. To avoid this I've developed this recipe, which removes a lot of fat but also retains the authentic flavor.

FOR THE EGGPLANT
3 pounds eggplant, sliced ⅓ inch thick
½ to ¾ cup extra virgin olive oil

FOR THE MEAT

1½ pounds ground lamb
2 tablespoons extra virgin olive oil
1 medium onion, chopped
2 garlic cloves, finely chopped
½ cup dry white wine
1 large tomato (about ½ pound), peeled, seeded, and chopped
¼ cup finely chopped fresh parsley leaves
¼ teaspoon dried oregano
1 bay leaf
3 whole cloves
1 teaspoon sugar
1 small cinnamon stick
¼ teaspoon freshly ground allspice berries
1 teaspoon salt
½ teaspoon freshly ground black pepper
2 large egg whites (save the yolks for the white sauce), beaten to form stiff peaks
2 tablespoons dried bread crumbs

FOR THE WHITE SAUCE

9 tablespoons unsalted butter
9 tablespoons unbleached all-purpose flour
3 cups milk
1 teaspoon salt
½ cup freshly grated *kefalotyri* or *kashkaval* cheese
Pinch of freshly grated nutmeg
2 large egg yolks

TO FINISH THE MOUSSAKA

1 teaspoon unsalted butter
2 tablespoons dried bread crumbs

1. Lay the eggplant slices on some paper towels and sprinkle with salt. Leave them to release their bitter juices for 30 minutes, then pat dry with paper towels.

2. Heat a lightly oiled cast-iron griddle over medium-high heat for 10 minutes. Brush each slice of eggplant on both sides and cook until golden brown, about 4 minutes a side. Brush and cook the remaining slices. Remove and set aside on a paper towel–lined platter to absorb more of the oil.

3. In a medium-size skillet, brown the lamb over medium heat until it loses most of its fat, about 10 minutes. Remove with a slotted ladle, pressing down each scoop with the back of a wooden spoon to squeeze out more fat. Clean the skillet, then heat the olive oil over medium-high heat and cook the onion and garlic until translucent, 5 to 6 minutes, stirring frequently so the garlic doesn't burn. Add the meat and crumble it further with a wooden spoon. Add the wine, tomato, parsley, oregano, bay leaf, cloves, sugar, cinnamon stick, allspice, and salt and pepper, reduce the heat to medium-low, cover, then cook until the meat is soft and flavorful, about 30 minutes. Remove and discard the bay leaf and cinnamon stick. Cool, then fold in the beaten egg whites and 2 tablespoons bread crumbs and blend well.

4. Make a thick white sauce by melting the butter in a saucepan over medium-high heat. Form a roux by stirring in the flour and cook until very light golden, about 3 minutes. Take the saucepan off the heat and slowly whisk in the milk. Return to a medium heat and cook until thick, 10 to 15 minutes, stirring occasionally and adding the grated cheese at some point. Reduce the heat if it is bubbling. Stir in some grated nutmeg and the egg yolks. Turn the heat off.

5. Preheat the oven to 400°F. Lightly butter the bottom and sides of a 9 × 12 × 2-inch baking dish and sprinkle 1 tablespoon of the bread crumbs over the bottom, shaking and tilting the dish so all sides are lightly coated with bread crumbs. Line the bottom of the baking dish with two layers of eggplant slices, cover with the meat sauce, and layer the remaining eggplant slices on top. Cover with the white sauce and then sprinkle the remaining 1 tablespoon bread crumbs on top. Bake until the top is golden, about 30 minutes. Remove from the oven. As there still may be a good deal of fat remaining, cut out a 2-inch section from the moussaka in one of the corners, then rest the baking dish tilted so that liquid runs to that corner. After several minutes spoon away any accumu-

lated fat and continue to let the fat run into the corner for another 30 minutes. Place the moussaka in a warm oven until ready to serve.

Makes 6 servings

Hirino me Selino Avgolemono (Greece)

PORK AND CELERY WITH AVGOLEMONO SAUCE

Pork is a traditional meat during the pre-Lenten carnival in Greece. In Monemvasia, a medieval village clinging to the mountain walls of a promontory jutting into the Mirtoan Sea in the southeastern part of the Peloponnesus, the Matoyla restaurant serves some traditional foods on a terrace, under market umbrellas and the natural shade of pomegranate and fig trees. Monemvasia's strategic importance to Venice during the Middle Ages is not in doubt, for even today you can see how defensible its position is.

The chef prepared a delicious braised pork and spinach dish, made with the classic avgolemono, an egg (avgo) *and lemon* (lemono) *sauce whipped together with pan juices. In this recipe I have replaced the spinach with the equally authentic celery.*

1 bunch celery (about 2 pounds), coarsely chopped, including leaves
Salt
½ cup plus 1 tablespoon extra virgin olive oil
2 pounds boneless pork shoulder, trimmed of fat and cut into pieces
½ cup grated onion
Freshly ground black pepper to taste
2 large eggs
½ cup fresh lemon juice
Crumbled imported feta cheese for garnish

1. Blanch the celery in lightly salted boiling water for 8 minutes. Drain, saving 2 cups of the blanching water and set aside.

2. In a large casserole, heat ½ cup of the olive oil over high heat and cook the pork until deep golden brown on all sides, about 10 minutes. Remove the meat from the casserole with a slotted ladle and set aside. Pour off and discard all the fat.

3. Heat the remaining tablespoon olive oil in the same casserole over medium heat and cook the onions until deep golden, stirring constantly. Return the pork to the casserole. Pour in the reserved 2 cups celery water, season with salt and pepper, stir well, cover, reduce the heat to low, and simmer for 1½ hours, shaking the pan occasionally. The meat should be tender and the water nearly evaporated. If there is still a good amount of pan juices left, remove the meat again and reduce the liquid over high heat until it is more syrupy, 3 or 4 minutes, and then return the meat to the casserole. Add the celery to the casserole, mix well, and cook until it has lost its crunch but is still firm, with a bite, about 30 minutes. Taste the celery as it cooks so you don't overcook it.

4. Meanwhile, make the lemon-and-egg sauce. Beat the eggs together in a medium-size bowl, then beat in the lemon juice a little at a time. Add a few tablespoons of the pan juices, beating all the time. Pour the sauce over the pork, shaking the casserole to distribute it. Sprinkle on some pepper. Take off the heat and let it sit 5 minutes. Serve with feta cheese.

Makes 4 servings

Arni me Anginares ke Spanaki Avgolemono (Greece)

LAMB WITH ARTICHOKES AND SPINACH IN AVGOLEMONO SAUCE

Greece's long connection with the Venetian Republic accounts for some of the culinary influences that appear Italian. But it does seem that the Venetians learned a thing or two from Greece. For example, the Venetian manzo alla greca *derives from the Greek original as seen in (besides the name) the basic avgolemono, or lemon and egg yolk sauce.*[67] *This sauce was popular in Venice and was also used in another preparation known as* bollito alla cortigiana, *courtesan's boiled beef (page 257). However, at least one scholar believes the influence on both the Greek and Venetian dishes may come much later, from French cuisine, because of the use of eggs in the sauce, derived from French-style compound sauces.*[68]

This delicious preparation is served at the highly recommended Costayannis restaurant in Athens, from where this recipe is adapted. Serve with rice pilaf (page 602).

1/4 cup (1/2 stick) unsalted butter
1 tablespoon extra virgin olive oil
2 pounds lamb shoulder on the bone, then boned, trimmed of fat, and cut into large pieces
1 medium-size onion, chopped
1/2 cup dry white wine
1 1/2 cups water
10 baby carrots
Salt and freshly ground black pepper to taste
8 medium-size fresh artichoke hearts (about 3 pounds whole artichokes; see page 122 for handling), quartered
Juice from 1 1/2 lemons
10 ounces spinach, heavy stems removed, washed well, and chopped
2 tablespoons chopped fresh dill
2 large eggs

1. In a large casserole, melt the butter in the olive oil over medium-high heat, then brown the meat, about 8 minutes, turning occasionally. Add the onion and cook until soft, stirring with the meat, about 6 minutes. Add the wine and cook until evaporated, about 5 minutes. Reduce the heat to medium-low, add the water and carrots, season with salt and pepper, and cook until the carrots are tender, about 45 minutes.

2. Add the artichoke hearts and one-third of the lemon juice to the casserole. Reduce the heat to low and simmer for 20 minutes. Add the spinach and dill, stir, and cook until the artichokes are tender, about another 20 minutes.

3. Meanwhile, beat the eggs together in a bowl until frothy. Pour in the remaining lemon juice, beating well as you pour. Slowly beat in about 1/2 cup of the broth from the casserole into the egg mixture. Pour the lemon sauce over the meat in the casserole and shake the pot until the sauce has thickened, about 12 minutes. Serve hot.

Makes 4 servings

Youvetsi (Greece)

LAMB WITH ORZO

This dish is traditionally made in an earthenware pan called a youvetsi *(or* giouvetsi, *from the Turkish word* güveç, *meaning the same).*[69] *A typical Greek pasta is orzo, an Italian word that means "barley," referring to the shape of the pasta. The Greeks call this type of pasta* manestra *(cantaloupe seeds) or* kritharaki *("barley"), which is what they look like. You can replace the lamb with veal knuckle, shank, or shoulder. In Greece the preferred veal is called* mosxhari, *a yearling steer rather than the younger calf.*

½ cup extra virgin olive oil
4 pounds lamb or veal shoulder on the bone, trimmed of fat and cut up
1 medium-size onion, chopped
3 cups fresh or canned crushed tomatoes or tomato puree
2 garlic cloves, finely chopped
1 teaspoon dried savory
3 cups hot water
Salt and freshly ground black pepper to taste
1 pound orzo (*manestra*)
1 cup freshly grated *kefalotyri* cheese (page 716)

1. Preheat the oven to 350°F.

2. In a large earthenware (preferably) stove-top and ovenproof casserole, heat the olive oil over medium heat, then brown the lamb on all sides, about 12 minutes. Add the onion, tomatoes, garlic, savory, and water and season with salt and pepper. Mix well, cover, and bake until the lamb is tender, about 1¼ hours.

3. Remove 2 cups of liquid from the casserole and set aside. Add the orzo to the casserole, stir, and return to the oven to bake for 15 minutes, uncovered. If the liquid in the casserole has dried out and the orzo is not yet cooked, add some of the reserved liquid. Sprinkle the casserole with the cheese and continue baking, uncovered, until brown specks form on top, about 15 minutes, then serve.

Makes 6 servings

Pihti (Greece)

ASPIC OF PIG'S FEET

Greek food writers tell us that this preparation has a history reaching back to the ancient Greeks. It's true that Athenaeus mentions in several places the boiling of pig's feet, but there is nothing resembling a recipe in his writings.[70] *The use of cloves probably is old, too, for even though the center of their origin and the locale from which they were imported is the five volcanic islands of the northern Moluccas in today's Indonesia, they were known in the then mostly Greek city of Alexandria in Egypt in the second century A.D.*

Today one often finds pig's feet on the Christmas table, though some cooks make this dish with pig's head. Although the taste is slightly sweet, this preparation isn't for everyone.

2 pig's feet (about 2½ pounds), cleaned and split
5 cups water
2 medium-size onions, peeled and each studded with 10 cloves
¾ cup plus 1 tablespoon white wine vinegar
10 black peppercorns
1 bay leaf
1 garlic clove, crushed
Salt and freshly ground black pepper to taste
¼ cup all-purpose flour
¼ cup fresh lemon juice
3 garlic cloves, peeled

1. Place the pig's feet in a large casserole and cover with the water. Add the clove-studded onions, ¾ cup of the vinegar, the peppercorns, bay leaf, and crushed garlic clove, season with salt and pepper, and cook over medium heat for 5 hours. Remove to a deep platter or serving dish, placing the split pig's feet next to each other. Pour 4 or 5 ladlefuls of broth over the feet and set aside to cool.

2. In a small bowl, dissolve the flour in the lemon juice, season with salt and pepper, and pour in several tablespoons of hot broth from the pig's feet. Crush the garlic cloves in a mortar to a paste and moisten with the remaining tablespoon vinegar and a few tablespoons of the broth. Check the seasoning and stir until well blended. Pour this mixture over the pig's feet. Set aside until completely cool and then refrigerate for 3 hours. Serve at room temperature.

Keep refrigerated for up to a week. Serve at room temperature as a *meze.*

Makes 4 to 6 servings

Bamies Laderes (Greece)

STEWED OKRA

This is a preparation typically made for a Greek Lenten menu. Ladera *means "oily," and is a general description of a Greek method of cooking a variety of vegetables, reminiscent of the Turkish* zeytinyağlı sebze yemekleri *(olive oil vegetable foods). An exact amount of olive oil is poured into a pan and the vegetables are cooked swimming in oil and some water. The pot remains covered while the vegetables cook, and they are salted at the end. The vegetables are often cooked with a tomato sauce and some herb. Okra was domesticated in either Ethiopia or West Africa but it is not known when it arrived in the Mediterranean. But because the cytotaxonomy of the plant is so confused it's possible that it may originate in Asia.*

In this recipe I use okra, seasoned with other vegetables, but some other popular combinations suggested in Vilma Liacouras Chantiles's excellent The Food of Greece *are cabbage with dill and bay leaf; eggplant with garlic, oregano, and allspice; green beans with mint and nutmeg; peas with dill and onions; lettuce with onion or leek; onions or leeks with wine or vinegar, cloves, cinnamon, bay leaf, and sugar; potatoes with rosemary, oregano, dill, or mint; spinach with mint and nutmeg; tomatoes with cinnamon and basil, mint, or marjoram; and zucchini with onions, green pepper, and oregano or thyme. If you try any of these combinations (for which I don't provide recipes), keep in mind that they require about 1 cup of olive oil for each 1 to 2 pounds of vegetable, 3 cups tomato sauce, 3 tablespoons of the herb, and 1/4 teaspoon of the spice if you are using it. Remember that you* cook *in this amount of oil, you don't eat all this oil (although both Greeks and Turks will sop up everything with bread).*

I first had this delicious vegetable dish in Sparta. The okra was stewed with onions and tomatoes, but also had the addition of peperoncini *peppers, celery, and a tiny amount of eggplant.*

1 pound small okra, ends trimmed
1/4 cup red wine vinegar
Salt to taste
1 cup extra virgin olive oil
1 medium-size onion, chopped
1/4 cup finely chopped celery
1 long green pepper (*peperoncini*), seeded and finely chopped
1/2 cup peeled and finely chopped eggplant
4 garlic cloves, finely chopped
3 cups fresh or canned crushed tomatoes with their liquid
1 tablespoon tomato paste
1 teaspoon sugar
Freshly ground black pepper to taste

1. Soak the okra in the vinegar with a sprinkling of salt for 1 hour.

2. In a large casserole, heat the olive oil over medium heat, then cook the onion, celery, green pepper, eggplant, and garlic until soft, 6 to 8 minutes, stirring occasionally. Add the tomatoes, tomato paste, and sugar. Stir well and cook for 10 minutes. Add the drained okra, season with salt and pepper, and add more water if necessary to keep the okra moist instead of oily. Cover, reduce the heat to low, and simmer until the water is evaporated, about 4 hours. Serve warm using a slotted ladle.

Makes 4 to 6 servings

Briami (Greece)

BAKED MIXED VEGETABLES

Briami, briam, *or* tourlou, *considered Greece's contribution to the genus of Mediterranean vegetable dishes that melds flavors together through long baking or stewing, is a preparation one might find on a Lenten menu. There are many similar dishes around the Mediterranean, such as in Provence where one finds ratatouille, in Catalonia where there is* escalivada, *and, in Turkey,* türlü. Briami *is best served lukewarm, perhaps with* skordostoumbi *(page 491).* Briami *is also excellent as a leftover, served either at room temperature or rebaked.*

1 pound eggplant, peeled and sliced into ½-inch-thick rounds
Salt to taste
2¼ pounds ripe tomatoes, peeled, seeded, and chopped
1 pound potatoes, peeled and sliced into ¼-inch-thick rounds
1 pound zucchini, peeled and sliced into ½-inch-thick rounds
1 pound small okra, ends trimmed
Freshly ground black pepper to taste
2 tablespoons white wine vinegar
1 small onion, finely chopped
3 large garlic cloves, finely chopped
½ green bell pepper, seeded and finely chopped
2 tablespoons finely chopped fresh parsley leaves
1½ cups extra virgin olive oil

1. Lay the eggplant slices on some paper towels and sprinkle with salt. Leave them to drain of their bitter juices for 30 minutes, then pat dry with paper towels.

2. Arrange half the tomatoes in a large nonreactive baking pan. Season with salt. Cover with the potatoes, zucchini, eggplant, and okra in that order, lightly seasoning each layer with salt and pepper. Sprinkle with vinegar. Lightly season again with salt and pepper.

3. Mix the onion, garlic, green pepper, and parsley and spoon evenly over the vegetables. Cover with the remaining tomatoes.

4. Preheat the oven to 350°F. Pour the olive oil over the vegetables, cover the baking pan with aluminum foil or a lid, and bake until the potatoes are completely tender when pierced with a skewer, about 2 hours. Remove from the oven and let the temperature of the *briami* cool to a little warmer than room temperature. Serve.

Makes 6 to 8 servings

Arakes me Anginares (Greece)

PEAS WITH ARTICHOKES

The ancient Greeks did not know the artichoke, which was developed from the cardoon by Arab agronomists in the early Middle Ages. The Greek philosopher Theophrastos (c. 372–287 B.C.) tells us that the stem of the kaktos *is eaten, a description of the cardoon. He mentions another thistle, the* pternix, *whose receptacle but not bracts are edible. None of the thistlelike plants described by the first-century doctor Dioscorides appears to be the artichoke.*[71]

Today, Greeks are very particular about fresh seasonal vegetables. During the Lenten season this very pretty dish, bright green and excellent in the spring with newly arrived artichokes and peas, is a favorite. It is a preparation one is likely to encounter throughout the Levant. Leave the artichokes in cold water acidulated with lemon juice while you prepare them to prevent discoloration.

4 large fresh artichoke hearts (about 2 pounds whole artichokes; see page 122 for handling), cut in half
1 lemon, cut in half
½ cup extra virgin olive oil
6 scallions, white and light green parts only, sliced
1 cup fresh or canned tomato puree
¼ cup water
2 tablespoons finely chopped fresh parsley leaves
1 tablespoon chopped fresh dill
1 teaspoon sugar
Salt and freshly ground black pepper to taste
2 cups fresh or frozen peas

1. Once you've trimmed and cleaned the artichoke hearts, rub them with the cut lemon and squeeze the rest of the lemon juice into a bowl of water where you will leave the hearts while you continue the preparation.

2. In a large skillet, heat the olive oil over medium-high heat, then cook the scallions until translucent, about 5 minutes, stirring frequently. Add the tomato puree, water, parsley, dill, and sugar, season with salt and pepper, and stir. Add the peas (if using fresh; add frozen peas later) and artichokes and stir to blend. Cover, reduce the heat to medium-low, and simmer until the artichokes are tender, about 40 minutes. If the pan looks dry, add a few tablespoons of water. If using frozen peas, add them after the artichokes have been cooking for 30 minutes.

Makes 6 servings

Anginares a la Polita (Greece)
CONSTANTINOPLE-STYLE ARTICHOKES

"Artichokes in the style of the City" is the name of this perfect spring vegetable dish, usually served on the Greek Easter table. The city referred to in the name of this preparation is not Athens but the great Greek Byzantine city of Constantinople, today's Istanbul. Constantinople was a cosmopolitan center of the Mediterranean, and the roots of many contemporary Greek dishes might properly be traced to Byzantium rather than classical Greece, when not to the Ottoman Turks.[72]

The potatoes, which were likely added to the preparation at a later date, should be very small, the size of marbles. Leave the skin on. In Corfu they make nearly the same preparation with an avgolemono sauce. I cook the vegetables a bit less than would be typical in Greece.

10 medium-size fresh artichokes hearts (from whole artichoke weighing about 6 ounces each)
2 lemons
¾ cup extra virgin olive oil
6 scallions, white and light green parts, chopped
12 small white onions, 1 inch in diameter (about ½ pound), peeled
½ pound baby carrots
¾ pound small new potatoes (about the size of a big marble; quarter them if larger)
2 tablespoons all-purpose flour
1 cup water
Salt and freshly ground black pepper to taste
2 tablespoons chopped fresh dill

1. Prepare the artichokes according to the instructions on page 122, rubbing the hearts with the cut half of one of the lemons and placing in a bowl of cold water. Squeeze the juice from this lemon into the bowl of water while you continue preparing the remaining artichokes.

2. Line a lightly oiled wide saucepan with the scallions. Arrange the onions, carrots, potatoes, and artichoke hearts over the scallions. Dissolve the flour in the water and the juice of the remaining lemon. Pour the water and olive oil over the vegetables so they are barely covered. Season with salt and pepper and sprinkle 1 tablespoon of the dill around.

3. Bring to a boil, reduce the heat to medium-low, cover, and simmer until the vegetables are tender, about 1½ hours. There should be little liquid left. Remove with a slotted ladle to a serving platter and serve at room temperature. Garnish with the remaining tablespoon dill.

Makes 4 to 6 servings

SHEPHERDING, TRANSHUMANCE, AND NOMADISM

THE wandering life of the sailor is sometimes described as a nomadic existence, but it is more akin to that form of Mediterranean pastoral life hardly seen these days, transhumance: the movement of shepherds and their herds from winter grazing plains to summer pastures in the hills and back again.

Mediterranean transhumance traditionally involved only the shepherds, not the women and children, who seasonally shifted their lives between lower-level grazing lands and mountainous pastures. In the sixteenth century, Mediterranean transhumance was limited to the Iberian and Italian peninsulas and the south of France. In Anatolia, North Africa, and the Middle East, transhumance merged with nomadism.

The transhumant routes, about twelve yards wide, bore different names, called *canadas* in Castile, *camis ramaders* in the eastern Pyrenees, *drayes* in Languedoc, *carraires* in Provence, and *trazzere* in Sicily. In Apulia, then part of the Spanish dominions, King Alfonso V of Aragon, "the Magnanimous," organized these transhumant sheep routes (there called *tratturi*), the connecting tracks (called *tratturelli*), and the resting pastures (called *riposi*) in 1442, making them privileged and compulsory for the shepherds, toll roads, in essence. Peasants, vines, olives, and especially wheat could not encroach on these routes. By 1548 the royal grazing lands in the Apulia represented about half of the 870,000 acres. The flocks moved through land rented to and tended by the peasants for six-year periods.[73] The flocks naturally fertilized these fields and accordingly wheat yields reached record levels in Apulia. As a result of high wheat yields, macaroni production increased as well (see Chapter 9).

Summertime saw the animals moving into the mountains to graze. This transhumance usually came into conflict with the mountain people, who resented the movements of people and flocks through their lands, interfering with their lives. There rarely was armed conflict though, because these sheepwalks, sometimes up to 320 feet wide, were *regalia del Principe*, royal lands, and severe penalties could result from any interference including the death penalty after 1575.[74] The shepherds and their families, not surprisingly, ate lots of lamb and there are a great variety of lamb stews on the Italian peninsula that can sometimes be called *spezzatini*, which simply refers to the stew.

Spezzatino d'Agnello (Campania)

CAMPANIAN-STYLE LAMB STEW

Spezzatini *are rustic country-style stews of meat, usually lamb, cut into smaller pieces and cooked slowly on a stove or in an oven. There are many such dishes throughout Italy. In the Piedmont, a* spezzatino *is called a* rustida. *In the Middle Ages, vegetables were put into* spezzatini *and seasoned* cum almuris idest salmuria et oleo etc *(with* almorí, *pork fat or meat, and oil, etc.).*[75] Almuris *(or almoreí) was a popular condiment, probably inherited from the Romans or perhaps originally introduced by the Arabs via Andalusia (see page 530), made of fermented barley or wheat with spices and honey that gave it an ever so slightly sweet taste.*

Meat was cooked in a variety of ways during the Middle Ages, but spit-roasting and boiling were the most common. Another popular preparation was in piccatiglio. *The finest cut of meat was chopped finely with cheese, spices, and aromatic herbs and used in timbales,* pasticci *and, especially, in oven-baked stuffed tortes. Both the rich and poor ate this* in piccatiglio, *the rich more often, and accompanied it with a vinegar sauce, a sweet-and-sour sauce, or a hot sauce. The poor, when they ate meat, usually ate boiled meat with* pulmentum, *a kind of polenta made from millet or barley, and vegetables.*[76]

3 tablespoons extra virgin olive oil
2 garlic cloves, crushed
2 pounds boneless leg of lamb, trimmed of fat and cubed
Salt and freshly ground black pepper to taste
1 small bay leaf
2 tablespoons finely chopped fresh marjoram leaves
2 tablespoons finely chopped fresh basil leaves
½ cup dry white wine
1 pound ripe tomatoes, peeled, seeded, and chopped
1 cup water

1. In a large earthenware or enameled cast-iron casserole, heat the olive oil with the garlic cloves over medium-high heat and continue to cook the cloves until they begin to turn light brown. Remove and discard the garlic.

2. Damp-dry the lamb with paper towels. Salt and pepper the lamb, then brown it in the hot oil on all sides over medium-high heat, about 6 minutes. Add the bay leaf, marjoram, and basil, stir, and cook for 2 minutes. Pour in the wine and reduce until it is nearly evaporated, about 10 minutes. Reduce the heat to low and add the tomatoes and water, just enough to almost cover the lamb. Check the seasonings and cook, partially covered, until the lamb is tender and the sauce thick, about 1½ hours. Serve.

Makes 4 servings

La Pigneti (Basilicata)

LAMB STEW

The pigneti *is an earthenware* marmite *or jug used for cooking. The word comes from a Latin word* pinguia, *meaning "a jug used to store fat." In Basilicata, families hermetically seal the earthenware jug with clay and then place the* pigneti *in the embers of a fire to cook. This method locks in all the flavors.*

3 pounds boneless leg of mutton or lamb, trimmed of fat and cut into 2-inch cubes
2 pound potatoes, peeled, halved, and sliced
1 large onion, cut into eighths and layers separated
6 large ripe tomatoes (about 3 pounds), peeled, seeded, and chopped
⅓ pound pecorino cheese, diced
1 dried red chili pepper, crumbled
¼ pound *soppressata della Basilicata* or any hot spicy salami or pepperoni, cut into small pieces
1½ cups water
Salt to taste
All-purpose flour for making a rope

1. Put all of the ingredients, except the flour, in a large enameled cast-iron or earthenware casserole, a *marmite,* or the bottom portion of a *couscousière.* Toss well and cover. Make a paste from flour and water and form it into a rope. Seal the pot and lid together with this rope.

2. Turn the heat to medium-low and cook for 1½ hours, shaking occasionally. Remove the flour-and-water rope and check to see if the lamb is tender and

the potatoes cooked. If they aren't, reform a rope of flour, reseal the pot and lid, and continue cooking until tender, up to 30 minutes more. Serve immediately.

Makes 6 servings

Agnello con Funghi (Basilicata)

LAMB WITH MUSHROOMS

Mushrooms are the food par excellence in sylvan-pastoral cuisine, and in Basilicata a cook would use cardoncelli (Lactarius deliciosus), *mushrooms that are unavailable to us. In their place a mixture of portobello, oyster, and chanterelle mushrooms would provide an equally lusty taste. If you are unable to find these exotic mushrooms, use the common mushroom (button or field) mixed with dried porcini mushrooms that have been previously soaked and drained. Do not wash the mushrooms—brush or wipe them clean. This recipe from Matera is perfect for cold weather.*

2 pounds boneless leg of lamb, cubed (with a little fat left on)
1½ pounds mushrooms (see above)
2 garlic cloves, chopped
1 dried red chili pepper, crumbled
¼ cup extra virgin olive oil
Salt to taste

1. Preheat the oven to 325°F. Put all the ingredients in a large enameled cast-iron or earthenware casserole, a *marmite,* or bottom portion of a *couscousière.*

2. Toss well, cover, and place in the oven, and bake until tender, about 1½ hours, stirring every 10 minutes. Serve.

Makes 6 servings

Castrato alla Brace (Apulia)

GRILLED WETHER CHOPS

The simplicity of this preparation points to the kinds of foods that shepherd families still eat. The cooking fire is made from forage woods, herb twigs, and even nut shells. Once the fat begins to drip, the aromas have what Apulians call il sapore omerico, *a Homeric taste. Grilled lamb chops are popular throughout the south, and one does not always have to use the expensive rib chops, as you can see by this recipe.* Castrato *is the Italian word for "wether," a castrated sheep, which one finds regularly in the cooking of southern Italy.*

20 dried thyme twigs
1 cup hazelnut shells
1 cup almond shells
6 mutton or lamb shoulder chops (about 2½ pounds)
Salt to taste

1. Prepare a low charcoal fire using a lot of charcoal briquets or wood if making a hardwood fire because it must burn for an hour, or preheat your gas grill on low for 20 minutes. Soak the thyme and nut shells in some water and then throw them onto the fire or place them in a wood-burning receptacle if your gas grill has one.

2. Place the chops on the grill with a sprinkle of salt, and put the hood partially down if the grill has one, and grill slowly, turning once in a while, for at least 1 hour.

NOTE: Grilling with the hood completely down on modern charcoal grills will often produced metallic, poor-tasting food. The small holes on the top of the hood are too small to let escape the enormous amount of smoke being generated. Ideally you'd like some smoke, so, if you can jury-rig your grill, have it partially covered, always so the better part of the smoke can escape.

Makes 4 to 6 servings

Agnello con Lasagnette all' Abruzzese (Abruzzi)

LAMB WITH ABRUZZI-STYLE *LASAGNETTE*

Although sheep rearing is not as important today in the Abruzzi as it was in the Middle Ages, the legacy of lamb cookery is embedded in the culinary culture. Under the Aragons the shepherds of the Abruzzi would drive their sheep in the winter to Tavoliere di Puglia along prescribed tracks with customs—a toll road, in essence.

In this deeply flavorful and hot preparation, the lamb can be eaten with the lasagnette *as part of an Abruzzese* panarda, *a gigantic feast.*[77] *The use of red chili peppers, called* diavolino *(little devils), in such abundance in the Abruzzi, has never been adequately explained. It certainly doesn't exist in the surrounding culinary areas. Is this a matter of taste or endoring—the coloring of food—especially after the decline of the saffron-growing economy in Aquila in later centuries?*[78] Lasagnette *is a pasta narrower than lasagne and wider than* pappardelle, *either of which can be used in the preparation. Another traditional Abruzzi-style pasta that might be used is* cazzarelli, *fresh homemade durum wheat-and-water pasta in the shape of a sliced squid ring, with which, incidently, it goes very well.*

2½ pounds leg of lamb, trimmed of some fat
1 garlic clove, slivered
Leaves from 1 sprig fresh rosemary
¼ pound pancetta, cut into 6 slices
¼ cup extra virgin olive oil
Salt and freshly ground black pepper to taste
1½ teaspoons cayenne pepper
1½ cups dry red wine (preferably Montepulciano d'Abruzzi)
4 garlic cloves, crushed
2½ cups fresh or canned tomato puree
2 tablespoons finely chopped fresh parsley leaves
2 tablespoons finely chopped fresh oregano leaves or 1 teaspoon dried oregano or thyme
1 pound *lasagnette*
¼ cup (½ stick) unsalted butter, cut into pieces
6 tablespoons freshly grated Parmigiano-Reggiano cheese

1. Make several incisions in the lamb with a sharp knife point and stuff them with the slivers of garlic and some rosemary. If the lamb is boneless, tie it up with kitchen twine so that its shape is uniform if it isn't already. Boil the pancetta in water to cover for 5 minutes. Drain and set aside.

2. In a large casserole, heat the olive oil over medium-high heat. Season the lamb with salt, black pepper, and cayenne. Brown the lamb on all sides, about 3 minutes. Add the pancetta and pour in the wine. Reduce the wine for 10 minutes, then add the crushed garlic. When the wine is almost evaporated, after about 4 more minutes, add the tomato puree, parsley, oregano, and more salt if desired. Reduce the heat to low and cook until the lamb is tender, about 1 hour and 20 minutes, covered. Remove the lamb and let it rest for 10 minutes.

3. Meanwhile, bring a large pot of water to a rolling boil, salt abundantly, and add the pasta. Drain when al dente. Place the lamb in the center of a platter if you are not going to serve it as a second course. Place the slices of pancetta on top and moisten with several tablespoons of the sauce. Toss the *lasagnette* with the butter, cheese, and remaining sauce and serve immediately with more Parmigiano-Reggiano on the side.

Makes 4 servings

❈ *Funghi Mista in Umido* (Calabria)

A STEW OF EXOTIC MUSHROOMS

A mushroom stew is the quintessential sylvan-pastoral meal in Calabria and Sardinia. Elsewhere in northern Italy the forager-cook might use wild herbs such as catnip, collected on the same mushroom foraging trip. I once made this stew with a pound each of portobello and button mushrooms and an assortment of lobster, trumpet, black trumpet, shiitake, oyster, crimini, and enoki mushrooms. If you use the greater amount of olive oil called for in the ingredients list, the final dish will be richer and, of course, fattier. Serve with crostini di pane per le zuppe di pesce *(page 559) or spaghetti.*

4 pounds mixed mushrooms (at least 5 different types)
3/4 to 1 1/2 cups extra virgin olive oil, to your taste
4 large garlic cloves, finely chopped
4 teaspoons dried oregano
Salt and freshly ground black pepper to taste
2 pounds ripe tomatoes, peeled, seeded, chopped, and drained
2 dried red chili peppers
6 tablespoons finely chopped fresh mint leaves

1. Clean the mushrooms, when necessary, by brushing and trimming them with a small knife, not by washing. Slice into large pieces, including the stems. Leave the smaller mushrooms whole.

2. In a large casserole, heat the olive oil with the garlic and oregano over medium-high heat for 2 minutes, stirring so the garlic doesn't burn. Reduce the heat to medium-low, add the mushrooms, and season with salt and pepper. Toss the mushrooms well so they are coated with olive oil. Slowly cook the mushrooms for 15 minutes, tossing and stirring occasionally.

3. Add the tomatoes, chili peppers, and mint. Cook until the stew is unctuous, about 30 minutes. Check the seasonings and serve.

Makes 6 servings

❈ *Maccheroni alla Pastora* (Calabria)

MACARONI SHEPHERD STYLE

In medieval Calabria, the shepherds engaged in an inverse transhumance. They came down from the mountains to find the markets for sheep and milk in the lowlands.[79] *This macaroni dish is called a shepherd's dish because it is simple and made with ewe's milk pecorino and ricotta. It was a fortifying meal, and the amount of butter and lard called for in the recipe is meant to give you an idea of traditional and authentic tastes, but feel free to reduce the amount by half.*

Salt
1 pound homemade (preferably) macaroni (page 628), cut into 5-inch lengths
1/2 pound homemade ricotta cheese (page 467)
6 tablespoons (3/4 stick) unsalted butter, melted
1 tablespoon melted pork lard
1/2 cup freshly grated pecorino cheese
Freshly ground black pepper to taste
1/8 teaspoon cayenne pepper

1. Bring a large pot of water to a rolling boil, salt abundantly, and add the pasta. Drain the pasta when al dente, reserving 1/4 cup of the cooking water.

2. Stir the reserved cooking water into the ricotta, blending until it looks creamy. Toss the macaroni with the melted butter and lard. Toss again with the ricotta

and pecorino cheeses, sprinkle with black pepper and cayenne, and serve.

Makes 4 to 6 servings

* * *

TRANSHUMANCE existed in Spain, where in the north the *rabadanes*, professional Castilian shepherds, moved their sheep using slings and long crooks, packing only their mules and cooking pots. Shepherds roamed with their flocks through the summer pastures of the vast empty plains of Extramadura, La Mancha, and Andalusia. Spanish sheep were cross-bred with sheep imported from North Africa, and these sheep were more important to the Spanish economy than olives, grapes, copper, or even the treasures of Peru, the economic historian Roberto Lopez has argued.[80] Castilian wool was inexpensive and, with the drop in exports of English wool, the thriving Italian textile industry looked to Spain to fulfill its needs for raw material.

In the hill country of Castellón in Valencia, goatherds would boil their stew in a copper pot over an open fire.

Tombet de les Useres (Valencia)

GOAT STEW FROM THE HILLS

This is a typical dish of the hill country of Castellón in Valencia. It is traditionally cooked in a copper kettle called a perol *or* peroles. *These kinds of goat stews were celebrated by Cervantes (1547–1616), as we know from the episode when Don Quixote was welcomed by some goatherds boiling goat's meat in a pot over a fire. They spread the cooked goat's meat on a sheepskin in large chunks and ate. Afterward they spread some acorns to eat with a very hard cheese, drinking wine.*[81]

Many dishes in southern Spain, with their use of saffron, point to a Muslim heritage. Although culinary historians generally recognize the influence that both Muslim Spain and later Aragon had on Sicily, there was evidently Sicilian, possibly Muslim Sicilian, culinary influence on Muslim Spain, as seen in the thirteenth-century recipe called the "Sicilian dish" in the anonymous Hispano-Muslim cookbook the Kitāb al-ṭabīkh*: a lamb stew made with a huge amount of onions and seasoned with olive oil, black pepper, cinnamon, "Chinese cinnamom" (possibly cassia,* Cinnamomum cassia, *the ground dried bark of a tree in the laurel family), lavender, and meatballs. After the stew was cooked, saffron dissolved in beaten eggs was whipped in and allowed to set.*[82]

½ cup extra virgin olive oil
2 pounds goat leg or shoulder meat on the bone, trimmed of fat and cut into small pieces
Salt to taste
2 cups water
Pinch of saffron threads, crumbled
1 bay leaf
15 black peppercorns
10 garlic cloves, finely chopped, or 40 garlic cloves, peeled

1. In a large casserole, heat the olive oil over medium-high heat, then brown the goat meat, seasoned with some salt, on all sides, about 10 minutes. Cover with the water and add the saffron, bay leaf, and peppercorns. Bring to a boil, then reduce the heat to low, cover, and simmer until the meat is quite tender, about 2½ hours, shaking the casserole occasionally.

2. Add the garlic to the casserole, reduce the heat to very low (or use a heat diffuser), and simmer for another hour. Serve by draining the meat with a slotted ladle and transferring to a serving platter.

Makes 4 servings

✣ ✣ ✣

TRANSHUMANCE was also a major factor in the economy of sixteenth-century Provence. In Arles, the flocks of the Camargue, and especially of the Crau, moved along the Durance Valley into the high pastures of the Oisans, the Dévoluy, and the Vercurs.

Transhumance doesn't much exist today, many people having settled into a semi-sedentary life, such as the former transhumants of the little villages of the Akdağ Mountains west of Denizli in western Turkey. One tribe, the Gökçeler Köyu, still tends its sheep, following old shepherding routes high in the mountains and makes a living from exquisite kilim weavings. The food of the Gökçeler Köyu is simple but earthy, such as the grilled *ayabalık*, trout from cold mountain streams, or spinach and rice, as in the next recipe, simply called "spinach."

Ispanak (Turkey)

SPINACH

On one of my research trips to Turkey, I spent some time in the Akdağ Mountains west of Denizli. It was mid-March, and I was told that nearly three feet of snow had just melted. It was still bitterly cold when I stayed in the three-room inn run by Mestan Gökçe in the hamlet of Geyre. Just one little communal room of the inn was open, because it was the only room that had a wood-fired stove. My friend David Forbes and I ate well here, but one favorite dish was this recipe given to me by Mestan, who says it is how they make spinach in his village, Gökçeler Köyu, even farther up in the mountains. He simply called it "spinach," even when I pressed him for its name. It is very good, and should look gooey when done.

The Turks save the roots and stems of the spinach to make into a soup. Their flavor is different, more bitter, and therefore eaten with yogurt. Many Turkish dishes excel in twofold contrasts, between bitter and sweet and hot and cold. The hot spinach would get a dollop of cool yogurt for a delightful taste and texture. And everything would get cleaned up with fresh bread.

10 ounces spinach, heavy stems removed and washed well
1/4 cup extra virgin olive oil
1 medium-size onion, finely chopped
1 celery stalk, finely chopped
1/2 teaspoon freshly ground coriander seeds
Salt and freshly ground black pepper to taste
3 tablespoons cooked long-grain rice (page 602)

1. Bring a pot of lightly salted water to a boil and plunge the spinach in for 3 to 4 minutes. Drain, saving 1 cup of the spinach water. Coarsely chop the spinach and set aside.

2. In a medium-size saucepan, heat the olive oil over medium heat, then cook the onion and celery, stirring, until soft and translucent, 10 to 12 minutes. Add the spinach, 1/2 cup of the spinach water, and the coriander, season with salt and pepper, reduce the heat to low, and cook until the spinach is gooey looking, 15 to 20 minutes, adding more spinach water if necessary to keep it saucy. Stir in the rice and continue cooking for 3 to 4 minutes. Serve.

Makes 4 servings

✣ ✣ ✣

NOMADISM is different from transhumance in that it has historically involved whole communities, not just shepherds. Nomadism is a means of human adaptation to the harsh environment of the desert, and when the nomad finds verdant land, he uses it for pasture and growing plants. The desert made the nomads who they were because of its harsh environment—the livelihood of the clan or tribe depended on moving to where resources could be found. Nomads could also be agriculturalists, planting olive, date, or almond trees, although they might consider this activity beneath their dignity because they are foremost herders who see little pride in the sedentary life.

Nomadism doesn't really exist today in the Mediterranean, except perhaps for small groups of people in southern Algeria, Libya, eastern Jordan and Syria, and the Western Desert of Egypt. The quintessential Mediterranean nomad is the Arab Bedouin, the word "bedouin" coming from the Arabic word for "desert dweller." Bedouin cooking was so often mere subsistence cooking, but there are Bedouin culinary contributions to our celebrated Mediterranean cuisines, most particularly the unusual dairy by-product of strained, defatted, and dried yogurt known as *jamīd* and the feast meal called *mansaf*.

Mansaf (Palestinian and Jordanian Bedouin)

A BEDOUIN LAMB AND RICE FEAST DISH

A magnificent repast, and a sign of great generosity, prepared by the Bedouin of Jordan and Palestine is called mansaf. *It is prepared for joyous occasions such as big festivals or family reunions. In Palestinian households it is traditionally made when there is an abundance of lamb.*

Mansaf *is perhaps taken even more seriously in Jordan. Palestinians make up a large portion of the population of Jordan today, but native Jordanians are, for the most part, of Bedouin descent. Among Jordanians, great debates can ensue about the preparation of* mansaf. *One Iraqi woman told me that her relationship with a Jordanian man broke up because she admitted to not caring for* mansaf.

My former brother-in-law, Omar al-Qattan, a Palestinian connoisseur of a great feast, told me that one of the root meanings of the word mansaf *is "explosion," and it is truly that: the tastes and aromas are an explosion of flavors. The flavors come not so much from spices but from a curious little dried yogurt product called* jamīd. Jamīd *is defatted and dehydrated yogurt made from sheep or goat's milk and sold in rock hard nuggets prepared in the spring and summer. It may have been originally a nomadic Turkish invention. The butterfat of the yogurt is separated by churning, accomplished by shaking the yogurt in a goat skin bag called a* shakwa. *The separated butterfat is then used to make* samna, *clarified butter (page 189). The defatted yogurt, called* makhīd *at this point, is strained under high pressure through a cloth, concentrating it into* jamīd. *The* jamīd *is salted and formed by hand into small balls to be placed in the sun and dried until hard. To reconstitute the* jamīd, *which is now 50 percent protein, it is soaked in water and then melted, giving its distinctive earthy flavor to the* mansaf.

Jamīd *is made in the home for the most part, although one can find it in stores in Amman. It would be a perfect culinary souvenir to bring back from a trip to the Middle East. Though it probably is impossible to find here, you might seek out a Middle Eastern market in this country, especially one run by Palestinians or Jordanians. If you are unable to find any, you must settle for my suggested, and not entirely satisfactory, substitute given in the Note.*

How one eats mansaf *is as important as how it tastes. Several overlapping sheets of a thin fine wheat flour flatbread, the size of a small pizza, called* marqūq, *are laid directly on the table or a large communal platter and are covered with the meat and rice. Another bread can be used, called* shrak, *a whole wheat flatbread baked on a domed griddle over an open fire. It is very thin, as is* marqūq *bread. Everyone eats with his hands in a ritualized manner with a high degree of eti-*

quette. Hands are first washed and the right sleeve rolled up. Guests sit or stand around the table sideways, with their right side tilted slightly toward the food and eat only with the first three fingers and thumb of the right hand. Each person stakes out a small area of the mansaf *that is in front of him and moistens it with the bowl of* jamīd *that is passed around. Grace is given,* al-ḥamdu lillāh *(Thanks be to God), and the eating begins.*

One eats in one of two ways. Small amounts of rice and meat are picked up, compacted slightly, and brought up to the mouth. No food should fall from the hand or the mouth as you eat, nor should your fingers touch your mouth; the food is flipped into the mouth from about an inch away. In another method, diners form a ball of rice in the palms of their hands, constantly flipping the ball in the air because it is quite hot. Then, for those who are dexterous and talented, the rice ball is flipped, sometimes from a foot away, into the mouth. In some situations the host will form the rice ball in his own hand for the guest of honor.

There are several essential ingredients in making mansaf, *besides the* jamīd. *One is the spice mixture known as* bahārāt. *It is easily found in Middle Eastern markets but can be made at home. Another is the cooking fat called* samna, *clarified butter.* Marqūq *bread is sold in the Middle Eastern and Greek markets and, in increasing numbers, supermarkets in the United States under a variety of names (see page 717), but most often by the Armenian name* lavash. *Once you've experienced this* mansaf *feast, remember to praise God for his generosity, whether you're a believer or not,* al-ḥamdu lillāh. *This recipe is derived from the first time I had a* mansaf, *prepared by Mustafa Hamarneh, a Bedouin friend who lives in Amman.*

6 pieces *jamīd* (about 1/2 pound) or see Note on page 246
3 quarts plus 2 cups water
10 tablespoons *samna* (clarified butter, page 189)
4 1/2 pounds lamb shoulder on the bone, cut into about 3/4-pound pieces and trimmed of excess fat
2 tablespoons *bahārāt* (page 524)
3 cups raw long-grain rice, soaked in water to cover for 30 minutes and drained or rinsed well under running water until the water runs clear
3 to 4 cups boiling water
1 tablespoon salt
1/2 cup blanched whole almonds
1/2 cup pine nuts
2 pieces *marqūq, shrak,* or *lavash* (Armenian flatbread), left whole, or 4 large *khubz ʿarabī* (Arab flatbread or pita bread), split open to make 8 pieces

1. Soak the *jamīd* in cold water to cover for 24 to 48 hours. Drain and melt the *jamīd* in a pot with 1 quart of the water over medium heat. Add the remaining 2 quarts water as it evaporates until the mixture has the consistency of yogurt. This could take up to 2 hours and you should ultimately have about 2 quarts liquid *jamīd*. Strain the *jamīd* through a sieve and set it aside. Save three-quarters of the *jamīd* for the meat and the rest for the rice, which you will cook separately.

2. In a large, preferably earthenware casserole, heat 5 tablespoons of the *samna* over medium heat, then cook the lamb until browned on all sides, about 20 minutes. Remove the meat from the casserole with a slotted ladle and set aside. Pour off all the excess fat and liquid. Return the meat to the casserole with the reserved three-quarters of *jamīd*, reduce the heat to low, add the remaining 2 cups of water, sprinkle on the *bahārāt*, and cook, uncovered until the meat is falling off the bone, 2 or more hours. Do not use any salt because the *jamīd* is salty, but if you are using the stabilized yogurt (see Note), you need to salt the meat to taste. Stir the meat so it is mixed well with the spices and yogurt.

3. Meanwhile, prepare the rice. In a heavy casserole or saucepan with a heavy lid, melt 3 tablespoons of the *samna* over medium-high heat, then cook the rice for 2 minutes, stirring. Pour in 3 cups of the boiling water and the salt, bring to a boil, reduce the heat to low, cover, and cook until the rice is tender and all the liquid is absorbed, about 20 minutes. Do not lift

the lid to look at the rice and do not stir the rice as it cooks. After 20 minutes, if the rice is not done, keep adding boiling water until the rice has absorbed the additional water and is tender. When the rice is done, stir in the remaining quarter of the *jamīd*, to make the rice a little watery.

4. Meanwhile, melt 1 tablespoon of the *samna* in a small skillet and cook until golden, 2 to 3 minutes, shaking the skillet. Remove and set aside. Melt the remaining tablespoon *samna* in the small skillet and cook the almonds until light golden, about 5 minutes, tossing the nuts. Add the pine nuts and cook until they are golden, about another 3 minutes. Set aside.

5. Clean off a serving, dining, or kitchen table with soap and water and then rinse well and dry, unless you are using a very large tray or serving platter. Arrange the *marqūq* or other bread directly on the table or tray, overlapping them some, and spread some *jamīd* from the cooked lamb on it so it becomes soft. Strain the meat and place it over the bread, now soft and broken. Spoon the rice over next and put the remaining *jamīd* sauce from the lamb in a separate bowl with a serving spoon. Sprinkle the pine nuts and almonds over the rice. Pour the reserved 1 tablespoon melted *samna* over everything. Gather your guests around the table, hands properly washed, with their right hands closest to the food. Begin eating.

NOTE: In place of *jamīd*, stir 3 tablespoons tahini (see page 725) into 2 quarts stabilized yogurt (page 186).

Makes 6 to 8 servings

* * *

As a modern Iraqi scholar of the Arab world said, "Anyone who has tasted the food of the Bedouins will never escape from its spell."[83] Because Bedouin food was subsistence food, I suspect he meant that the meager food was as soul-satisfying as the possibility of Bedouin desert life was astonishing. Before the advent of "black gold," the desert dweller lived in an extraordinary world of famine cooking. The Tuareg, a nomadic Muslim Berber tribe of the Aïr, a region in the Sahara in northwestern Niger and southeastern Algeria, use over twenty plants for food, notably the seeds of the *drīn* (the fruit of a kind of nard, *Aristida pungens*, and with *Calligonum comosum*, it also formed the principal food of their camels), wild *fonio* or *founi* (*Digitaria exilis* Stapf.), *tawit* (the white mulberry, *Morus alba*), *mrokba* (panic, *Panicum turgidum*), grains of *cram-cram* (sandbur, *Cenchrus biflorus* or *Pennisetum distichum*), and the rhizomes and young shoots of the *berdi*. The Tibu, another nomadic tribe of the Sahara and neighbors of the Tuareg, get their bread from the fruit of the *dum* (dwarf palm).[84] The Bedouin hunted for food: wild sheep, donkey, oxen, camel, gazelle, and antelope. Rat was a favored game, a delicacy in the Badiet esh-Shām, the heart of the Syrian Desert.

A proper study of Bedouin culinary culture has never been undertaken, but we can glean elements of this culture from anthropologists working in other areas, such as Lila Abu-Lughod's valuable *Veiled Sentiments: Honor and Poetry in a Bedouin Society*.[85] The heart of understanding the desert life of the nomad is the camel and dromedary. The Koran assures the Bedouin that the camel is a gift of God, although these "desert Arabs" are not the most sincere of believers.[86] The camel driver almost never eats their flesh and barely makes a living from their milk, butter, and cheese. In fact, Abu-Lughod's study of the Awlad ʿAlī tribe of Bedouin in the Western Desert of Egypt, who are descendants of the banū-Sulaym and banū-Hilāl, Arab invaders of the Najd who swept through North Africa in the eleventh century—tells us that Bedouin families kept large sheep herds and camels for prestige, not for sustenance.

Bedouin families planted olive and almond trees and regularly pressed olive oil for their own consumption. Today they own agricultural land, sowing barley from which they hope to make a profit.[87] The Awlad ʿAlī conduct most of their trading in the coastal town of Marsa Matruh, a dusty, small settlement one hundred and seventy-five miles west of Alexandria. Their sheep are sold here and various supplies can be bought.

Muḥammar (Egypt)

FRIED LIVER

The long drive to the west from Alexandria takes one through the desert and the famous World War II battleground of El Alamein, where in October 1942 British General Bernard Montgomery finally defeated German General Erwin Rommel to end the Nazi threat to the Middle East. Finally one reaches Marsa Matruh, the site of the ancient Ptolemaic city of Paraetonium. The town not only is a trading terminus for the local Bedouin tribes but also is graced with beautiful beaches where cows help themselves to a little sunbathing.

This recipe was given to me by Khaled Abdul-Karim, the lamb butcher of Marsa Matruh. Other meats are sold by other butchers, but lamb is sold by Khaled. The lamb liver is fried in olive oil over very high heat very quickly, with garlic, salt, cumin, and red chili pepper. The taste is extraordinary.

3 tablespoons extra virgin olive or vegetable oil
1 pound lamb liver, trimmed of arteries
2 garlic cloves, finely chopped
¾ teaspoon freshly ground cumin seeds
½ teaspoon ground red chili pepper
Salt to taste
1 to 2 tablespoons water, as needed

In a large skillet, heat the oil over medium-high heat until very hot and smoking, then cook the liver, sprinkled with the garlic, cumin, ground chili pepper, and salt until springy to the touch, about 6 but not more than 7 minutes, turning frequently to mix the spices. Add the water if the garlic is burning. Serve immediately.

NOTE: Although it might appear strange to an Egyptian, I have made this dish with turkey livers and it was excellent.

Makes 2 to 4 servings

* * *

THE Bedouin family is tight-knit, so much so that they would describe a household as one where "they eat from one bowl."[88] Food images and proverbs also extend to other areas of Bedouin life, such as the feeling of nostalgia, which is strong among them. Nostalgia is expressed as "the gazelle or the umbellifer [carrot family] that whets the appetite, or the tea that cures."[89]

It is said that the dream of every Bedouin is to possess *al-aswadān*, "the two black ones," water and dates. The Awlad ʿAlī have wonderful date dishes such as *mafrūka*, a kind of sweet snack made with wheat dough stuffed with dates. *Mafrūka* derives from the same word that the hard wheat product called *farīk* does, meaning "rubbed." For other Bedouin tribes, *mafrūka* is a kind of flatbread that is cooked in and covered with the ashes of a fire spread out in the sand. The Awlad ʿAlī eat a lot of rice and lentils and make use of spices such as black pepper, cumin, and coriander. They also make their own couscous from scratch, called *kiskisk*. Their flatbread is good, as is their *malih*, a cheese like Lebanese *labna*. A very rich Bedouin dish is made of rice and boiled lamb cooked with buttermilk and *samna*, usually made from goat's milk curdled overnight and the butter separated in a goatskin bag.[90]

Although the desert runs right to the sea from Sfax in Tunisia to Alexandria in Egypt, except for the Jabal al-Akhdar of Libya, the sea has never played a big part in the lives of the Bedouin; their poetry of natural beauty is reserved for the desert. The Bedouin range across the North African Sahara, and in Libya the entire population is Bedouin and their food equally simple.

Shūrba Libiyya (Libya)

LIBYAN SOUP

Libyans will tell you that their region was always too poor to have developed a cuisine. Like much of the cooking in Egypt, everything appears vaguely familiar, from other regions. The Italian influence is strong, especially in restaurants, and Libyans eat lots of pasta secca. *Whether this was the result of the Italian occupation or an addition to a preexisting substratum of macaroni cookery, as I believe to be the case in neighboring Tunisia (see page 618), is uncertain.*[91]

Contemporary Libya can be divided into the historical regions of Tripolitania to the west and Cyrenaica to the east. The Gulf of Sirte, in the middle, could be considered the "couscous line" of North Africa. That means, to the west of this line couscous is a staple food and the people eat couscous from here all the way to the shores of the Atlantic, while to the east of the line, to the Suez, couscous is occasionally eaten, but is not a staple food. Libyans living to the east of the line eat mostly Egyptian-style food, although their olive oil consumption today is the highest in the world, at seventy grams a day, about twice that of the Italians.[92]

If any dish can be considered a "national" dish, it is either bazīn *or* shūrba Libiyya. Bazīn *is an old preparation, a kind of polenta made with semolina and water and sometimes yeast, found along the southern Tunisian and Libyan littoral. It is related to the simple meal of barley flour, olive oil, and water called* basīssa, *known since medieval times by the people in North Africa. This was a preparation that, in his* Prolegomena, *the fourteenth-century philosopher Ibn Khaldūn called the "first food" of Ifriqiya (Tunisia).*[93] *The dish can also be made with fish.* Bazīn *is often made for the ʿĪd al-kabīr, the holiday feast celebrating the sacrifice of Abraham, in the Sfax and Sousse regions of Tunisia. This recipe was given to me by Professor Lisa Anderson, a scholar of modern Libya at Columbia University, who tells me that it "summarizes Libyan cuisine, such as it is."* Shūrba *means "soup," and this is Libyan-style soup.*

½ cup extra virgin olive oil
1 tablespoon *samna* (clarified butter; page 189)
1 large onion, finely chopped or grated
1 pound boneless beef chuck or lamb shoulder or leg, trimmed of fat and cubed
6 very ripe plum tomatoes (about 1 pound), peeled, seeded, and chopped
2 tablespoons tomato paste
5 cups water
½ cup cooked chickpeas, drained
½ cup finely chopped fresh parsley leaves (from about ½ bunch parsley)
1 teaspoon ground red pepper (cayenne, chili, or Aleppo)
¼ teaspoon ground cinnamon
1 teaspoon *bzar* (see Note on page 250)
1 teaspoon salt
½ cup *pastina* (soup pasta)
1 teaspoon dried mint

1. In a medium-size casserole, heat the olive oil with the *samna* over medium-high heat, then cook the onion until translucent, about 5 minutes. Brown the beef or lamb on all sides, 2 to 4 minutes.

2. Add the tomatoes, the tomato paste dissolved in 1 cup of the water, the chickpeas, parsley, red pepper,

MIRQĀZ AND *QADĪD*, NORTH AFRICAN PRESERVED MEATS

These two preserved meats from North Africa were made by Bedouin as well as the population at large. Mirqāz (*also transliterated as* merguez) *is a fresh or dried lamb sausage, also made with veal, usually formed in thin 4-inch links and used in a variety of Tunisian preparations. Tunisians prefer the dried variety that is stored in olive oil-filled earthenware containers.*

The first written recipe for mirqāz *sausage is in an anonymous thirteenth-century Hispano-Muslim cookery book.*[94] *Today there are several varieties, such as* mirqāz kibda bi'l-liyya, *made in the ratio of two thirds mutton liver to one third fat (liyya) and seasoned with* harīsa *(page 523),* tābil *(page 522), and salt.* Mirqāz ṣayim *is a sun-dried sausage preserved in olive oil after frying and is made with two parts lamb or mutton meat to one part fat and seasoned with* harīsa, *cinnamon, dried rose petals, salt, and black pepper.* Mirqāz baqri *is sun-dried veal sausage seasoned with preserved lemon (page 104), aniseed,* harīsa, tābil, *salt, and black pepper.* Mirqāz dawwāra *is a sun-dried veal offal sausage preserved in olive oil after frying. It is made with coarsely chopped veal kidneys, tripe, heart, lung, and liver and seasoned with preserved lemon,* harīsa, tābil, *aniseed, salt, and black pepper.*

I am not providing a recipe, but if you would like to make your own, you can follow the directions for making fresh sausage on page 70, mixing 2 pounds diced boneless lamb shoulder with 1 pound diced lamb fat and seasoning it with 4 pounded and mashed garlic cloves, salt to taste, 1 teaspoon ground fennel seeds, 1 teaspoon harīsa, *1/2 teaspoon ground red chili pepper, and black pepper to taste. Pass the mixture through the coarse grinder of a sausage stuffer and stuff the sausages, twisting them into 4-inch-long links using hog casing (readily available compared to the hard-to-find but available lamb casing). If you would like to make dried* mirqāz, *leave them in hot, dry, direct sunlight for 48 hours, protected against insects and animals, puncturing the sausage with a skewer so they dry better. Once they are dried, heat some olive oil, turn the heat off, and submerge the dried* mirqāz *in the oil for 20 minutes. Store them in glass or earthenware jars filled with the same olive oil.*

In place of making your own mirqāz, *the D'Artagnan company (see "Mediterranean Food Products Resources") makes an excellent fresh* mirqāz *that they spell* merguez.

Qadīd (*also transliterated* kedide) *is lamb jerky, a cured lamb meat prepared for the ʿĪd al-aḍḥa festival (also called the ʿĪd al-kabīr), the holiday feast in Algeria and Tunisia celebrating the sacrifice of Abraham.* Qadīd *is said to have been introduced to North Africa by the Arabs.*[95] *Lamb meat is rubbed with garlic and lots of salt and left to dry for a day. Then the meat is rubbed with a mix of ground red pepper, ground caraway, ground coriander seeds, and dried mint and then sun-dried for some time. The* qadīd *is submerged in hot olive oil, as the* mirqāz *is, and then stored in glass or earthenware jars with the oil.*

cinnamon, *bzar*, and salt and cook for 10 minutes. Add the remaining 4 cups water and cook, covered, until the meat is tender, 1 to 1¼ hours. Add the pasta and cook, uncovered, until done, about 10 minutes. Just before serving stir in the mint.

NOTE: The Libyan spice mix known as *bzar* is usually made of equal parts of black pepper, cinnamon, cloves, nutmeg, turmeric (or zedoary *[Curcuma zedoaria]* or galingale), ground ginger, and a smaller part cumin.

Makes 4 servings

✣ ✣ ✣

THE Bedouins have a whole food classification system that remains unstudied. They praise the *nawāshif*, the good "dry" food of desert life—the cereals, dates, and milk products. The Bedouin regard fresh vegetable stews as unhealthy because vegetables are not considered "dry" food. Traditionally, it seems that they considered vegetables unhealthy because there weren't any to be found. Today, vegetables are part of their diet, but many older Bedouin still consider them unhealthy because of the pesticides used in their growing. The Bedouins also find pleasure in the milk products of the springtime, such as the milk of ewes who feed on *shīh*, aromatic wormwood. For the Bedouin, spring is not a season but a state of being. They don't say "spring," but rather speak of *rabīᶜ*, which is the "state of pasture when the desert is green from rain."[96] The Bedouin appreciation of food is reflected in the male's conception of feminine beauty. The Awlad ᶜAlī find skinny women disgusting, while a beautiful woman shines with the rosy glow of good health and has a robust figure.

Nomads have fought over grazing lands for their flocks of sheep, goats, or camels. The resources are so meager, the desert so empty, yet the Bedouin love the desert with the same inexplicable intensity that the Inuit love the Arctic. This is why the Bedouin used to raid and attack in Egypt and Syria, where people put up very little resistance.

One problem with talking about the Bedouin as nomads is that there are Bedouin tribes that are seminomadic as well as those in a stage of quasi-urbanity. Nomads can plant fields filled with barley as well as bring sheep to pasture, and, today, be tourist guides at archeological sites. The variety of nomadic life is seen in certain activities that define the Bedouin—sheep or camel raising, hunting, and raiding (the last mentioned no longer occurring in today's world). Agriculture is not a major preoccupation of many Bedouin, but was for the seminomadic. In the spring, the seminomadic tribes would reap the barley, millet, sorghum, or wheat planted the previous autumn. The Awlad ᶜAbdalā tribe of Algeria was witnessed by the sixteenth-century chronicler Diego Suarez as sowing the coastal region. They vigorously protected their crops from neighboring tribes, and they preserved their own meat fried in its fat *(qadīd)* and made dried sausages of *mirqāz*. They harvested their hard wheat and made their own couscous, which they called *alcuzcuzu* (page 660), and drank sour milk called *lubint*.

The eleventh-century Arab traveler al-Bakrī provided a rich description of the foods and lives of the nomads in what is today's Saharan regions of Mauritania, Mali, and northern Niger. The population of Aoudaghast, in northern Niger, was composed of Tunisians. He tells us that "Negresses are employed as very good cooks, who know how to make very appetizing dishes such as '*djouzinkat*' [walnut cake] and '*kataif*' [a kind of crêpe batter]."[97] The town of Tadmekka (probably in today's Agadez region of northern Niger) was described by al-Bakrī as peopled by Muslims and Berbers. They ate meat, milk, and "a grain from a wild plant." (The plant in question is *Pennisetum distichum* Barth.)[98]

Nomadic movements could be large scale, from the steppe to the coast and back to the desert. Indeed, the Shabbiyya tribe of Qairouan, once the capital of Tunisia, would appear and disappear. But these back-and-forth movements of the nomads had nothing to do with the image of a convoy of camels melting away into the orange glow of the shimmering desert sun. Those great caravans crossing the desert were part of merchant activity that was half commercial and half religious. The report of a magnificent caravan that took weeks to form in 1586 outside Cairo, on its way to the holy city of Mecca, was not a nomadic movement but virtually a merchant city on the move. The numbers are mind boggling—forty thousand mules and camels and fifty thousand people. Merchants preceded the caravan, selling their silk, coral, tin, grain, and rice. They traveled between two in the morning and dawn to avoid the heat. Six hundred soldiers with field artillery provided escort. This escort was to protect the caravan against the Bedouin, who would attack at will—the ancient and noble form of raid called the razzia—as essential a part of their traditional culture as the camel was for transportation.

CONCLUSION

MOUNTAIN life in the Middle Ages was primitive and the people were isolated from the political, social, and economic systems of feudalism, leading to a life that was unstable, backward, and exceedingly poor. Life was crude in the mountains of the sixteenth century and so was the food. In the end, the mountains were too poor to support their populations and mountain people escaped their poverty by heading for the towns of the plains.

On the hillsides of the Mediterranean, a fragile economy of terraced crops existed, such as that found in Languedoc, Provence, Sicily, Tuscany, and the Sahel of Algiers, where vines mingle with the trees, oats with vetch for the mules, and wheat with vegetables. The mountains and hills produced milk products such as cheese, butter, and yogurt, along with salt. In Turkey and other Muslim lands, milk, butter, and cheese played a great role in providing nutritionally rich food. Yogurt was also an important food for the poor.

Cities such as Venice, Florence, and Milan utilized their accumulated capital derived from long-distance trade to turn their hinterlands into productive agricultural areas. Canals were built and towns began to spring up as the population increased, which in turn stimulated the rise of irrigated market gardening on the alluvial plains. Orchards, market gardens, and sown fields spread through the foothills and reclaimed plains. The network of drainage and irrigation canals built in different Mediterranean regions made it possible to run dairy farms, which in turn led to the development of an industry producing cheeses, whose products would find markets far from home. In this chapter we saw the role of transhumance—the movement of shepherds and their herds from winter grazing plains to summer pastures in the hills and back again—and nomadism.

The mountains, meadows, plains, and deserts, and the peoples and foods that populated them, were always secondary to the cities, from where wealth emanated. From the great cities of the Mediterranean sprung not only the impetus for new social, political, and economic structures but also the capital that allowed the expansion and revolutions in agriculture that saw their eventual manifestations in the kitchen. Now we move on to the cities, especially the five great Mediterranean cities of the Middle Ages—Venice, Genoa, Istanbul, Cairo, and Ragusa. It is here in the cities that was born the true revolution in Mediterranean cuisine, in the royal court and in the kitchens of the new bourgeoisie.

5

LA SERENISSIMA, LA SUPERBA, AND THE SUBLIME PORTE

The attainment of the superfluous causes greater spiritual excitement than the attainment of necessities. Man is a creature of desire and not a creature of need.

—GASTON BACHELARD

FOOD might be grown in the countryside, but cuisine is an urban phenomenon. In the last chapter, we saw how the role of the mountains, meadows, plains, and deserts pointed to the cities. In this chapter, we turn our focus to towns and cities. During the fourteenth to sixteenth centuries, La Serenissima (Venice), La Superba (Genoa), and the Sublime Porte (Istanbul) were the greatest cities of the Mediterranean. There were other great cites—Seville, Barcelona, Marseilles, Milan, Florence, Palermo, Naples, Ragusa, Algiers, Cairo, Jerusalem, and Damascus, to mention a few. The French historian Lucien Febvre wrote that the Mediterranean was the sum of its routes and often a tale of triumph of one route or port city over another. The importance of the rise of these Mediterranean port cities, and the towns in the hinterland that relied upon them, cannot be underestimated. French historian Fernand Braudel believed that the development of these towns was more important than the historic rise in prices in the early sixteenth century, known today as the price revolution (see "Inflation, Money, and Capital" in Chapter 1), than the Turkish conquests, and the discovery and colonization of America.

Historically, family relations defined economic relations in the Mediterranean. But beginning in the eleventh century, a great number of very effective ad hoc corporations emerged in Italian city-states that transcended family connections. Once people were able to interact with wider groupings beyond blood relatives—for instance, townspeople, speakers of the same language, or believers in the same faith—a new and more powerful set of economic relations could arise. In the Mediterranean, the entrepreneurs of the Italian city-states were unique in this respect compared, for instance, to the Greeks, Jews, and Arabs, who, although they were effective merchants, had not by that time succeeded in transcending blood lines.[1] A self-contained system of budding capitalists operating out of and living in cities emerged. The focal point of this self-contained system in the fifteenth and sixteenth centuries was a narrow strip running from Venice through Milan and Florence to Genoa. The rise of these and other cities and their insatiable demand for food changed the Mediterranean economically, as well as gastronomically.

In this chapter, we will focus on five cities that are representative of the historic Mediterranean as a whole—Venice, Cairo, Constantinople (Istanbul), Ragusa (Dubrovnik), and Genoa—and we will see that the central problem for the cities was food supply.

CIBORUM LAUTICA (MAGNIFICENT FOOD)

VENICE and Genoa were the two great cities of the sixteenth-century Mediterranean, and they were able to exploit the whole world. In the East their rival was Constantinople, the great polis of Byzantium that later became Istanbul, the capital of the Ottoman Empire, where all power flowed from the Sublime Porte—the name that the offices of the Grand Vizier was known by and the symbol of the Ottoman government itself. Venice actively traded with and lived off the Ottoman Empire. Genoa was as rich as Venice and it, too, had a rich appetite that was fed by the productive gardens of its riviera and Corsica, a Genoese dominion. Genoa's empire was based on her trading colonies beyond Constantinople, at the edge of the Byzantine Empire, and in Sicily. These distant colonies made huge profits—for example, Messina, where in 1561 the Genoese made a killing in wheat, silk, and spice. By 1570, Genoa was also the world center for the distribution of American silver.

Venice had traded with Constantinople since early Byzantine times, but its commercial interests increased dramatically on June 18, 1265, when the Byzantine Emperor Michael VIII granted Venice privileges whereby Venetian traders operating in the empire became exempt from taxation. An important commodity of trade for the Venetians in Constantinople was wine. They imported it from their Cretan colony and from territories they did not hold in Greece. They also owned many of the taverns in Constantinople and therefore could sell wine at highly competitive prices.[2] Venice's relations with Byzantium were governed by concessions granted by the emperor called *Chrysobulls*, or Golden Bulls, the first being granted to Venice by Emperors Basil and Constantine in 992. The concessions forbade the detention of a Venetian ship for more than three days without good cause and limited the amount of tariffs levied on Venetian ships sailing to and from Byzantine ports. The Venetians weren't the only outsiders in Constantinople, where their agents *(fattori)* and merchants lived on the southern shore of the Golden Horn in their own community. To the east of them lived the Amalfitans, then the Pisans, and finally a colony of Genoese, who later moved to Galata.[3]

The Peace of Lodi in 1454 marked Venice in its heyday. The fall of Constantinople to the Ottomans the year before galvanized the principals to the peace—Naples, Venice, Milan, Florence, and the Papal States—to set aside their differences in order to confront the Turks. The Ottoman Turks had attempted unsuccessfully to capture Constantinople in 1397, but in 1453 Mohammed the Conqueror tried again and met with victory, thus ending one thousand years of the Eastern Empire (that is, the Eastern Roman Empire and Byzantium).

At this time, Venice was the undisputed center of the Mediterranean world. Venice was a city in love with money, bills of exchange, fabrics, foods, spices, and shipping—la Serenissima was a self-confident city-state, superior and wealthy, although it had lost Salonika (Thessaloniki) in 1430 and the wheat-growing island of Negroponte (Euboea) in 1470 to the Turks. Venice was the leading city-state at the time, and Venetian patricians who chartered state-owned *galere da mercato* (merchant galleys) made enormous profits. Venice's sea link to the Mediterranean was the Adriatic, and for some time the city had controlled many of the ports along the Dalmatian coast, both for trading purposes and security. Venice had eliminated its competition from the east coast of the Adriatic, so the *galere da mercato* putting in at Pola (Pula), a small port on the Istrian coast, could take on crew, oarsmen, and provisions.

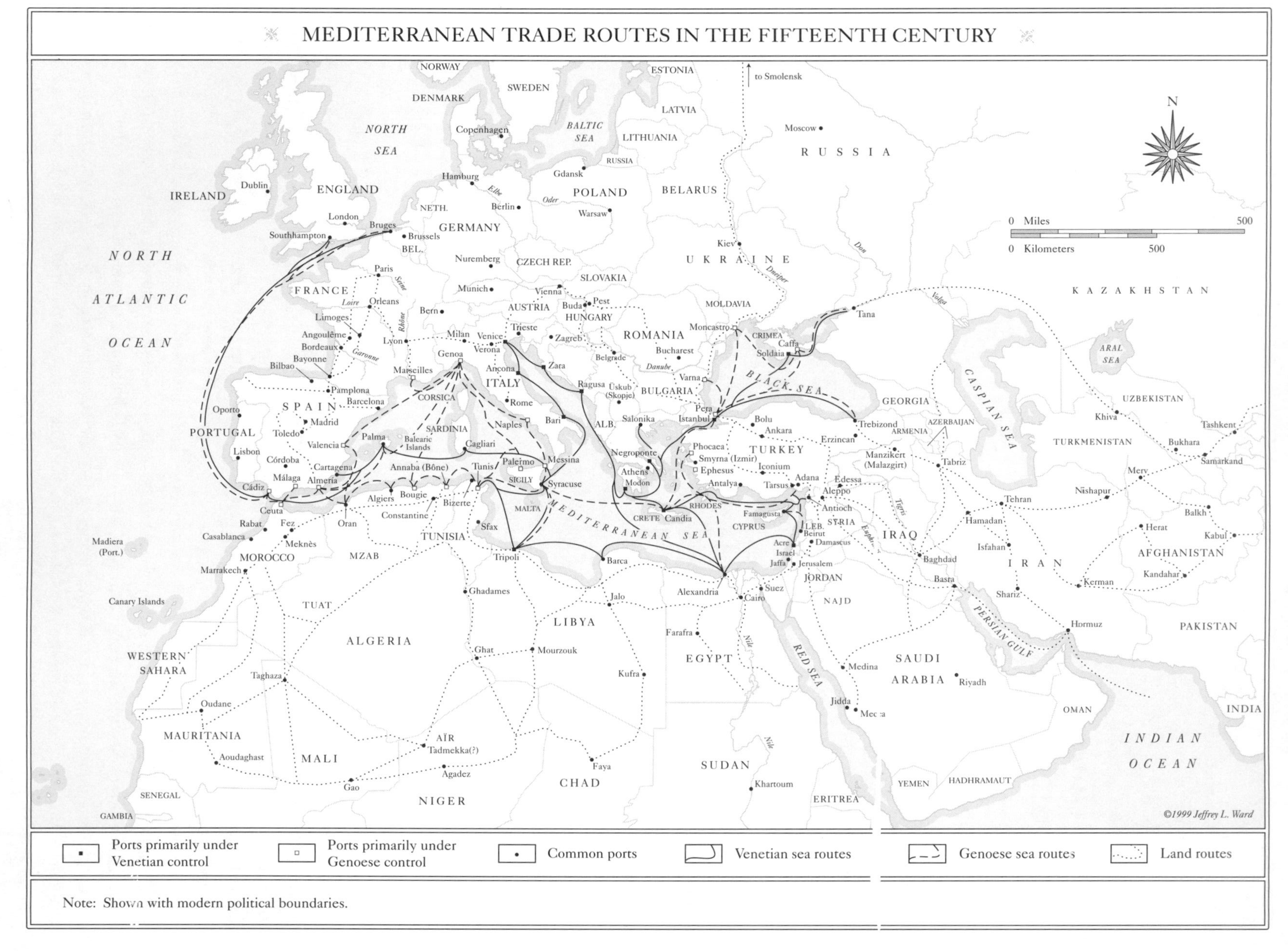
MEDITERRANEAN TRADE ROUTES IN THE FIFTEENTH CENTURY
N
0 Miles 500
0 Kilometers 500
NORTH ATLANTIC OCEAN
NORTH SEA
BALTIC SEA
MEDITERRANEAN SEA
BLACK SEA
CASPIAN SEA
ARAL SEA
RED SEA
PERSIAN GULF
INDIAN OCEAN
IRELAND
ENGLAND
NORWAY
DENMARK
SWEDEN
ESTONIA
LATVIA
LITHUANIA
RUSSIA
POLAND
BELARUS
RUSSIA
UKRAINE
NETH.
BEL.
GERMANY
CZECH REP.
SLOVAKIA
AUSTRIA
HUNGARY
ROMANIA
MOLDAVIA
FRANCE
SPAIN
PORTUGAL
ITALY
CORSICA
SARDINIA
SICILY
MALTA
ALB.
BULGARIA
TURKEY
GEORGIA
ARMENIA
AZERBAIJAN
KAZAKHSTAN
UZBEKISTAN
TURKMENISTAN
AFGHANISTAN
PAKISTAN
INDIA
IRAN
IRAQ
SYRIA
LEB.
Israel
JORDAN
NAJD
SAUDI ARABIA
OMAN
YEMEN
HADHRAMAUT
ERITREA
SUDAN
EGYPT
LIBYA
TUNISIA
ALGERIA
MOROCCO
WESTERN SAHARA
MAURITANIA
MALI
NIGER
CHAD
SENEGAL
GAMBIA
MZAB
TUAT
AÏR
CRETE
RHODES
CYPRUS
CRIMEA
Balearic Islands
Canary Islands
Madiera (Port.)
Dublin
London
Southhampton
Bruges
Brussels
Paris
Orleans
Limoges
Angoulême
Bordeaux
Bayonne
Bilbao
Pamplona
Barcelona
Madrid
Toledo
Valencia
Córdoba
Cartagena
Almeria
Málaga
Cádiz
Lisbon
Oporto
Lyon
Marseilles
Genoa
Milan
Verona
Venice
Trieste
Bern
Munich
Nuremberg
Hamburg
Berlin
Copenhagen
Gdansk
Warsaw
Vienna
Buda
Pest
Zagreb
Belgrade
Bucharest
Zara
Ancona
Rome
Naples
Bari
Ragusa
Üskub (Skopje)
Salonika
Negroponte
Athens
Modon
Candia
Palma
Cagliari
Palermo
Messina
Syracuse
Tunis
Bizerte
Annaba (Bône)
Bougie
Algiers
Constantine
Oran
Ceuta
Fez
Meknès
Rabat
Casablanca
Marrakech
Sfax
Tripoli
Barca
Alexandria
Cairo
Suez
Jalo
Farafra
Kufra
Ghadames
Ghat
Mourzouk
Faya
Khartoum
Taghaza
Oudane
Aoudaghast
Gao
Tadmekka(?)
Agadez
Moncastro
Varna
Pera
Istanbul
Phocaea
Smyrna (Izmir)
Ephesus
Antalya
Iconium
Tarsus
Adana
Famagusta
Bolu
Ankara
Erzincan
Trebizond
Soldaia
Caffa
Tana
Kiev
Moscow
to Smolensk
Manzikert (Malazgirt)
Tabriz
Edessa
Aleppo
Antioch
Beirut
Damascus
Acre
Jaffa
Jerusalem
Baghdad
Basra
Medina
Jidda
Mecca
Riyadh
Hamadan
Tehran
Isfahan
Shariz
Kerman
Hormuz
Nishapur
Merv
Herat
Kandahar
Kabul
Balkh
Khiva
Bukhara
Samarkand
Tashkent
Danube
Dnieper
Don
Volga
Elbe
Oder
Seine
Loire
Rhône
Garonne
Tigris
Euphrates
Nile
©1999 Jeffrey L. Ward
Ports primarily under Venetian control
Ports primarily under Genoese control
Common ports
Venetian sea routes
Genoese sea routes
Land routes
Note: Shown with modern political boundaries.

Venetian seamen flocked to Pola because it was the best-stocked market for cloth made from coarse wool, which came from the Istrian and Dalmatian hinterland. The cost of living in isolated regions on the coast was less than in the major cities. At Fasana (Fažana), a little port near Pola, veal sold for a quarter the price as in a large town such as Venice. A Venetian traveler described Fasana as a place for *buonissimo vivere*, good living, and perhaps he enjoyed a *punjena teleća prsa* (stuffed breast of veal). At that time the food from the Croatian hinterland was rough and simple. Today, Croatian cuisine evidences the culinary influence of both Venice and Venice's nemesis, the Austrian Hapsburgs. Recipes such as the following one became popular among many Croatian families.

Punjena Teleća Prsa (Croatia)

STUFFED BREAST OF VEAL

Since the collapse of the greater Yugoslavian state in the Balkans in the 1990s, many people imagine Croatia as a particularly brutal place. During the Middle Ages there was a similar attitude, the results of the actions of people in Croatia called the Uskoks. The Uskoks were a ghastly, violent, and butcherous people, originally Christian refugees from the eastern side of the Dinaric Alps, who had escaped from the Turks. As the chronicler of Venice, Jan Morris, has written, "They were epic villains." The Venetians were fearful of them and believed the Uskoks were supernaturally guided by wise women who in lived in caves. In 1615, the Austrian Hapsburg archduke lent his protection to the Uskoks, who usually attacked Venetian interests. Combat with these pirates became more savage on both sides. Once Venice celebrated a victory by setting up the heads of slaughtered Uskok pirates around the piazza. In revenge the Uskoks waylaid a Venetian commander and rejoiced by killing him and eating his heart at a banquet.

Much of what survives today in Croatia seems a cultural struggle among Italian, Slavic, and Hapsburg influences. The dominating influence of Italy, especially Venice, was felt during the Middle Ages, and the lingua franca of Croatia and the Dalmatian coast was, in fact, Italian. In recipes we also see the influence of the Italians, as in this stuffed veal preparation. But we see, too, the influence of the Austrian Hapsburgs in the presence of sour cream.

4 pounds boneless veal breast
Salt and freshly ground black pepper to taste
1/4 cup pork lard
1 slice bacon, finely chopped
1 small onion, finely chopped
1/2 cup chicken livers, trimmed of membranes and finely chopped
3 cups small French bread cubes with crust
2 large eggs
1/2 cup sour cream
1 tablespoon finely chopped fresh parsley leaves

1. Cut a pocket into the veal, making sure you don't puncture the sides, and season the veal with salt and pepper inside and out (see Step 2 on page 355).

2. In a medium-size skillet, heat 3 tablespoons of the lard with the bacon over medium-high heat, then cook the bacon until sizzling, about 4 minutes. Add the onion and cook until translucent, about 4 minutes, stirring. Add the chicken livers and brown for 2 minutes, stirring.

3. Preheat the oven to 400°F. Place the bread cubes in a large bowl and pour the fried onion mixture over them. Beat the eggs together and whip in the sour cream, parsley, and salt to taste. Pour over the bread and mix the stuffing well. Stuff the veal (not too tightly) with this mixture and sew up the opening or interlace with a 10-inch-long wooden

skewer. Rub the veal with remaining tablespoon lard.

4. Roast the veal in a lightly oiled roasting pan for 1 hour, uncovered, moistening it with the pan juices and water as needed. Cover and roast until the meat is tender, about another hour. Transfer to a serving platter and let rest for 10 minutes. Slice into serving portions and serve.

Makes 4 to 6 servings

✣ ✣ ✣

BUSINESS was good in the Mediterranean and that meant towns got bigger. Venetian ships were in the thick of it, and their agents were located in both gateways to spices, silk, and other products of the East, Syria and Egypt. The success of the merchants of Venice depended on these gateways, Syria perhaps being the more important of the two, assisting in the growth of the ancient city of Aleppo, the terminus of a number of trade routes. The riches made from this trade with both Syria and Egypt were incredible because the demand was incredible. Venice did have manufactured products to trade, but in reality it sacrificed all its valuable metal currency to meet the powerful demand for black pepper, spices, drugs, cotton, linens, and silk. The trade between Egypt and Venice, usually transhipped through Crete, was intense even in 1350.[4] Crete was an entrepôt for spices from Beirut and Alexandria, too. As Venice grew richer, people flocked to the city and its territories, and had flocked perhaps for some time if we consider the purported origin of the name Venice: from *veni etiam*, come and come again.[5] These were somewhat halcyon days for Venice in terms of trade, for Syria and Egypt were both part of the Mameluke governance, a Muslim Egyptian dynasty, at this time and the historical turning point of the Ottoman victories of 1516–1517 had not yet occurred, "so Venice slept the sleep of the rich," as Braudel put it.[6]

In the fifteenth century, growing towns became rich towns populated by rich people who saw in land ownership their only protection against the long-term effects of inflation. Rich Venetians began building villas on their vast lands in the countryside, such as the famous ones built by Andrea Palladio (1508–1580), while keeping their *palazzi* in the city. They also sought refuge in their country villas from the urban oppressiveness. There was heat in the summer, but they also wished to escape the festering city-born diseases, the surrounding poverty, and famine with its attendant desperate people. The Venetian patricians who owned land "beyond the Brenta," a river in the rich plain of Padua, were by the end of the sixteenth century investing heavily in farming. Advances in new kinds of hydraulic works, canals, and locks to drain wetlands meant reclaimed land (see Chapter 4) that was used for livestock and meat production.[7] Though originally built for elitist reasons, by the sixteenth century many country villas had been turned into profitable agricultural enterprises.[8]

Farm activity outside the walls of fourteenth-century Siena is depicted in Ambrogio Lorenzotti's *Allegory of Good Government: Effects of Good Government on the City and Country*, 1337–1340. Palazzo Publico, Siena. GIRAUDON/ART RESOURCE.

Festivals and banquets would be held in the country villas, their cellars full of grain and wine presses. This was such an important activity that Vincenzo Tanara wrote a book in 1651 that was published in Venice, called *L'economia del cittadino in villa* (The economy of the city dweller in the country). The book is a guide to the rural economy for the rich villa owner. He suggests fish farming as the best way to feed the family and provide the *companatico* (food to accompany bread) for his farmhands.[9]

Venice was fantastically rich, and the merchants of Venice could be found all over the world. In 1512, ships brought sixty thousand tons of wheat to Venice; this was enough to feed three hundred thousand people, more than twice its own population.[10] In 1569, a Neapolitan document gives us the names of five hundred Venetian merchants who bought wine and wheat in Apulia. William Shakespeare's merchant of Venice was a real character, resembling today's businessman rather than today's merchant, whom we think of as a shopkeeper, a retail seller of goods. The Venetian merchant was often the head of a manufacturing enterprise, a moneylender, and a trader all at the same time. He was a wholesaler and retailer, the distinction not really existing in the Middle Ages. He often operated as an international merchant, although there were local ones, too.[11]

Life in Venice was grand for the rich. The great diarist Marino Sanuto describes sumptuous feasts in Venice. Both Venetian and foreigner alike referred to the government of Venice as *La Serenissima*, "the serene republic." The courtesan life was in full bloom in the sixteenth century and the *commedia dell'arte* emerged. Venetian style meant fashionable people who listened to music, engaged in witty conversation, all with the proper doses of the theater, gambling, drinking, and fine dining.

Bollito alla Cortigiana (Veneto)

COURTESAN'S BOILED BEEF

The courtesan life was in full bloom in Venice during the sixteenth and seventeenth centuries. These Venetian prostitutes were legendary in the Mediterranean, and were considered necessary by the authorities to preserve the pleasant life in Venice. They were not like prostitutes as we think of them today and were often quite erudite. The Renaissance humanists felt the need to be with women who understood their philosophizing, or who at least gave the impression they did. Love to the humanists was a form of mental stimulus and the courtesans, with their refinements of speech and taste, suited this attitude. The courtesans were admired and respected. Artists, in fact, had to pay them more to take off their clothes and paint them than to merely take off their clothes. The pimps for the courtesans were known as mangiamarroni, *chestnut eaters.*[12]

If we are to take the name of this dish literally, the courtesans prepared delectables like this recipe for their lovers.

2 pounds boneless stew beef, trimmed of fat and cut into 1-inch cubes
All-purpose flour for dredging
1/4 cup (1/2 stick) unsalted butter
1 large or 4 *cipolline* onions, chopped
1 ounce dried porcini mushrooms, soaked in tepid water to cover for 15 minutes and drained
Salt and freshly ground black pepper to taste
1/4 teaspoon freshly ground nutmeg
3 cups dry white wine
2 cups beef broth (page 54)
1 large egg, beaten
Juice from 1 lemon

Dredge the meat in the flour, tapping off any excess. In a medium-size casserole, melt the butter over medium-high heat and cook the meat, onions, and mushrooms until the meat browns, about 8 minutes, stirring. Season with salt, pepper, and nutmeg and pour in the wine and beef broth. Reduce the heat to low and cook until the meat is tender and the sauce thick, about 3 hours. Add water if the sauce is too thick. Turn the heat off, beat in the egg and lemon juice, and serve.

Makes 4 to 6 servings

Paolo Veronese's (1528–1588) *Marriage at Cana* is more than a story from the gospel. It is a Mediterranean feast, for all those depicted, except Christ, are real people of the time, including Queen Mary of England and the Ottoman emperor Süleiman I the Magnificent. Veronese himself is in the center foreground playing the viola. Louvre, Paris. GIRAUDON/ART RESOURCE.

THE artists Titian (c. 1490–1576) and Albrecht Dürer (1471–1528) portrayed Venetian courtesans and used them as models for both pagan and sacred scenes. The luxury of the Venetian banquet is seen in Paolo Veronese's (1528–1588) *The Marriage at Cana* (1563), now in the Louvre, although it depicts a semireligious setting of a not-too-obvious Christ at a lush table of food. Another example of a bountiful banquet is Sandro Botticelli's (c. 1444–1510) painting of the wedding banquet of Nastagio degli Onesti depicting a scene from Boccaccio's *Decameron.* On the intellectual front, there was the influence of nearby Padua with its university and famous medical school, where anatomists carried on the tradition of Andreas Vesalius (1514–1564) and Gabriello Fallopio (1523–1562), who gave his name to the oviducts he discovered.[13]

The printing industry of Europe was centered in Venice because of the city's commercial connections. Between 1495 and 1497, of the 1,821 publications known to have been issued from all existing printers, 447 were printed at Venice, whereas Paris, next in importance, printed only 181. Some of the first cookbooks were printed in Venice. Although the heart of the Renaissance beat in Florence, the most famous publisher was in Venice, the humanist Aldus Manutius, who invented the type called italic and printed the Greek classics in the 1480s. Bookstores were opened up in Venice, and the famous humanist philosopher Desiderius Erasmus (1466–1536) worked in one owned by Manutius's father-in-law. Erasmus had many complaints, not only about Scholasticism but about Venetian cuisine as well, one being that they liked plenty of meat and had no use for a "morsel of shellfish caught in the sewer."[14] I believe Erasmus was speaking of *canocchie*, and the Venetians certainly have use for it now.

Canocchie (Schile) Agio e Ogio (Veneto)

MANTIS SHRIMP IN GARLIC AND OLIVE OIL

The humanist philosopher Erasmus claimed that the Venetians in the sixteenth century had no use for shellfish. Today shellfish is very popular. This simple preparation from Venice for canocchie (*also* canocie, canoce, *or* schile), *a shellfish that is a kind of cross between a shrimp and a crayfish called* Squilla mantis, *found in the Venetian lagoon, can be made with shrimp or prawns, although both are entirely different animals. Mantis shrimp cannot commercially be found in this country, so this recipe is best saved for that one time during the year when a local shrimper will have fresh crayfish or prawns, the shellfish closest in taste to mantis, usually in March or April.*

Years ago canocchie *could be found abundantly in the canals of Venice, Erasmus's "sewer." Housewives would walk down to the end of their local* calle *to a canal and pick them off the sides of the buildings just under the water line.* Canocchie *were once considered part of* cucina povera, *but today are as expensive as* scampi *(that is, prawns,* Nephrops norvegicus *Linn.) at the Rialto fish market. Surprisingly, I later learned that the North Atlantic relative of mantis shrimp* (Squilla empusa *Say) does live in mud holes below the low-water mark along the eastern U.S. seaboard, but I have never seen them in a market, nor does anyone seem to know anything about them as seafood.*

4 pounds fresh shrimp with their heads (2 pounds without heads) or 5 pounds fresh crayfish in their shells
1 tablespoon sea salt
½ cup extra virgin olive oil
3 garlic cloves, very finely chopped
½ cup finely chopped fresh parsley leaves

1. Rinse the shrimp or crayfish in cold water. Place the shellfish in a large pot with just enough water to cover. Add the salt to the water and set the heat on high. After 10 minutes, before the water has reached a boil and is frothing, drain and rinse the shellfish under cold water.

2. Place the shrimp or crayfish, in their shells and with their heads, in a large skillet or casserole with the olive oil, garlic, and parsley. Set the heat to high and cook, shaking and turning often, until bright red or orange and fragrant, about 7 minutes. Remove to a platter and eat with your hands. Salt if necessary.

VARIATION 1

Remove the shrimp from their shells after boiling for 1 minute and season with heated or unheated olive oil, lemon juice, parsley, salt, and pepper.

VARIATION 2

Skewer the shrimp and grill them until a deep golden, then season with unheated olive oil, parsley, salt, and pepper.

VARIATION 3

Drain the boiled shrimp, pile on a platter, and pour a sauce made from unheated olive oil, lemon juice, white wine vinegar, parsley, salt, and pepper over them.

Makes 4 antipasti *servings*

THE pursuit of good living in Venice led to the passing as early as the fourteenth century of what were known as sumptuary laws, which attempted to limit the more flagrant excesses of extravagance and luxury. Fashions in clothing and food became various and vibrant, and knew no bounds. This abundance of food is called *ciborum lautica*, magnificent food, in the texts, and the sumptuary laws were passed because excessive displays of wealth in a time when the common people were generally destitute was considered a threat to social equilibrium.[15] These sumptuary laws affected every aspect of a patrician's life. At one time or another the laws forbade the yearly, and expensive, changes in women's fashions or the wearing of pearls braided into the hair; pheasants, peacocks, partridges, and doves were banned from banquets in a law passed on January 12, 1472. The serving of more than three kinds of foods at banquets, besides sweets, was forbidden, and this law from 1512 went on to say that the waiters were required to inform the authorities where the banquet was to be held and to lead the authorities on an inspection tour of the banquet hall. If anyone threw "bread or oranges" at the heads of the inspectors, the waiters were required to refuse service to the banquet. Feasts late at night were also forbidden.[16]

The Venetians were considered quite strange by other Europeans. They were entirely city dwellers, with canals piercing their city, who neither sowed nor reaped but bought their food abroad in exchange for services and salt. This was true in Venice's early history as well as centuries later. Venice's waterways enabled it to bring everyday foodstuffs and sheep cheese from as far off as Casalmaggiore in Lombardy and its shipping routes were ideal for the transport of wheat, oil, wine, fish, and meat on the hoof. Venice's ships brought wheat from its normal suppliers in Sicily and Apulia and from Egypt and the Black Sea in times of shortage.

Venice was strange in another way. The city was a republic with a form of government that we today associate with limited democracy in an era of autarky. The doge, the ruler of Venice, was elected by a general assembly of noblemen. Even the doge's palace, the Palazzo Ducale, was unique when compared to other seats of power in Italian cities, where they were built to be large, dark, and foreboding, like the Palazzo Vecchio in Florence, reflecting the terror that governments could routinely bring to bear on their citizens. In Venice, in contrast, one perceives the doge's palace as a white, light, and airy palace open to all and located on the water, feeling no need to create a fortresslike effect.[17] The Sala di Maggior Consiglio in the Palazzo Ducale was the seat of the governing body of the republic. Built in 1340, this hall was large enough to hold all seventeen hundred Venetian patrician members; it was so well constructed that there have never been any repairs.[18] Here are located three great paintings depicting three great events in the history of the republic: the meeting in Venice of Frederick Barbarossa and Pope Alexander in 1177; the Fourth Crusade in 1202 that captured Constantinople; and the triumph of Doge Contarini after his victory over the Genoese in the Battle of Chioggia in 1379. Here, too, is *Paradise* by Tintoretto (c. 1592), the largest oil painting in the world at 21 by 72 feet.

Soon the Venetian "sleep of the rich" would be disturbed, for once Constantinople became Istanbul and the capital of the Ottoman Empire and its population reached seven hundred thousand in the late sixteenth century, sucking up all the wheat within reach to feed this enormous population, Venice had to seek supplies closer to home.[19] Venice was consuming 500,000 *staia* (about 1,150,000 bushels) of wheat around 1600, as well as rice, millet, and rye.[20] The population of the city was about 140,000 with another 50,000 in the adjoining territories. In 1555, each Venetian ate approximately five hundred pounds of food a year.[21] Whether it was the radicchio of Treviso or, later, the *borlotti* beans of Lamon, the Venetian cooks of patrician families did not go without.

Radicchio Rosso di Treviso (Veneto)

RADICCHIO FROM TREVISO

A famous indovinello, *a ditty, about the red radicchio of Treviso gives some indication of its popularity:* Se lo guardo, egli è un sorriso. Se lo mangio, è un paradiso, il radicchio di Treviso *(If you see it, it's so nice. If you eat it, it's paradise, the radicchio of Treviso).*

Radicchio is a kind of chicory first developed in Treviso in the Veneto region of northern Italy. The small, tight red radicchio found in the United States is actually radicchio di Verona, *while the leafier kind is* radicchio di Treviso. *It is common in the old traditional cuisine of Venice to fry it in corn, nut, or grapeseed oil instead of olive oil. Giuseppe Maffioli, a noted authority on the gastronomy of the Veneto, suggests a very small radicchio dipped in batter and deep-fried in olive oil as an alternative to this recipe.*

6 cups sunflower seed, corn, or canola oil for deep-frying
4 red radicchio (about 3/4 pound), washed, patted dry, cut in half, and bruised outer leaves discarded
All-purpose flour for dredging
1 large egg, beaten
Dried bread crumbs for dredging
Salt and freshly ground black pepper to taste

1. Preheat the frying oil in a deep-fryer or an 8-inch saucepan fitted with a basket insert to 360°F.

2. Dredge the radicchio halves in the flour, tapping off any excess. Dip in the egg and then roll in the bread crumbs. Deep-fry until golden in the hot oil, 1 to 2 minutes. Drain on paper towels immediately, season with salt and pepper and serve. Let the frying oil cool completely, strain, and save for future use.

Makes 4 antipasti *servings*

Fondi di Carciofi in Tegame (Veneto)

PAN-FRIED WHOLE ARTICHOKE HEARTS

The latest thinking about the origin of the artichoke is that it was developed from the cardoon by Arab or Berber horticulturalists sometime before the thirteenth century. There are ambiguous references to what might be the artichoke in the twelfth- and thirteenth-century Levant, Spain, and North Africa, and it does seem fairly clear that the ancients did not know the artichoke, only the cardoon. The first clear reference to the artichoke in Italy is in Tuscany about 1466, and the sixteenth-century Italian botanist Pierandrea Mattioli said it was brought to Naples from Sicily, where it seems to have been grown for the first time in Europe.[22]

At the Campo San Margherita in Venice, where there is also a small fish market, one can find fresh artichokes and other vegetables. Vendors sell fresh artichoke hearts, the bracts cut off, ready for cooking. The hearts are kept in containers of acidulated water to keep them from turning color, and they are sold to housewives looking to save themselves some work. This method of preparing the artichokes is described in Giacomo Castelvetro's (1546–1616) book on vegetables, although he also seasons them with bitter orange juice.

16 medium-size artichokes (about 6 pounds), trimmed (page 122)
1 lemon, cut in half
Salt to taste
6 tablespoons extra virgin olive oil
2 garlic cloves, crushed
1/4 cup very finely chopped fresh parsley leaves

1. Rub the artichoke hearts when you remove them with the cut half of the lemon and place the hearts in a bowl of water acidulated with the juice from the lemon halves so they don't turn color.

2. Bring a pot of lightly salted water to a boil and cook the artichoke hearts until a skewer can be pushed in with only a little resistance. Drain, saving 6 tablespoons of the water.

3. In a large saucepan, heat the olive oil over medium heat with the crushed garlic cloves until they begin to turn light brown. Remove and discard the garlic. Reduce the heat to medium-low and add the artichoke hearts, 2 tablespoons of the parsley, salt to taste, and the reserved artichoke water. Cover and cook until the artichokes are soft, about 12 minutes. Sprinkle with the remaining 2 tablespoons parsley and serve.

Makes 4 servings

Pasta e Fasioi (Veneto)

PASTA AND BEANS

Pasta e fasioi *is a peasant bean stew found in many parts of Italy and made in Venice with* borlotti, scozia *(red-speckled beans), or white navy beans, and* pasta sciutta, *dried pasta. This Venetian version reminds me of a soupy Egyptian* fūl mudammas *(page 304).* Pasta i fazoi *is the Dalmatian version of this dish, Croatian cooks making it with smoked meats and bacon. My favorite Venetian* pasta e fasioi *preparation, and the one this recipe is based on, was the one I had at the Ostaria al Milion, a small* ostaria *behind the church of San Giovanni Crisostomo on the Calle Corte de Milion in Venice.*

Pasta e fasioi *is made with about six parts* borlotti *beans to one part pasta*—tagliatelle, *or a Venetian pasta form called* cannolicchietti *being traditional, but I use* tubetti *or* ditalini. *The* tagliatelle *of the Veneto is cut wide and is made with durum wheat and water, not eggs, as is common in Emilia-Romagna to the south. The beans are important; they should not be too old. A Venetian would use Lamon beans, red pinto or kidney beans that come from Lamon, north of Feltre. They are very tender and melt into the stew.*

The prosciutto bone is an essential flavor in this dish, but it may be difficult to get. Often when a prosciutto ham is finished, proprietors in the United States of Italian delicatessens and salumerie *usually keep the bones for themselves, but at larger supermarkets they think of it as garbage (unless they're in the know), so if they sell prosciutto on the bone you can try asking them for the finished bone. As an alternative, buy the end cut, in one piece, of an inexpensive domestic prosciutto, which, unfortunately, is the closest you can get to the real thing (and often too salty). The pork skin required in the ingredient list can be taken from a piece of salt pork or ask the butcher for fresh pork skin, which he will have.*

½ prosciutto bone or ½ pound end-cut of an inexpensive prosciutto, soaked in water to cover overnight to remove salt
½ pound pork skin
2 cups (about 1 pound) dried *borlotti*, pinto, red speckled, or red kidney beans, picked over, soaked in water to cover overnight, and drained
3 quarts cold water
Freshly ground black pepper to taste
2 tablespoons finely chopped pancetta (optional)
1 tablespoon extra virgin olive oil (optional)
¼ cup finely chopped onion
1 garlic clove, finely chopped
1 celery stalk, finely chopped
¼ cup finely chopped fresh parsley leaves
2 cups peeled, seeded, and chopped tomatoes
½ pound *tubetti*

1. If you have a prosciutto bone, boil it with the pork skin for 10 minutes. Drain and scrape the fat off the bone and the skin. Chop the fat from the prosciutto bone (or prosciutto end cut, if using it) and the pork skin very finely. Reserve the fat.

2. Put the beans in a medium-size pot and cover with the cold water. Season with pepper. Add the prosciutto bone or end cut and the skin and bring to a boil, then reduce the heat to medium and cook until the beans are tender, about 2 hours, stirring occasionally.

3. Meanwhile, in a medium-size casserole, cook the chopped prosciutto fat and pork skin fat over medium-high heat until at least a tablespoon of fat has been rendered. If you do not have enough fat scraped off the end cut piece of prosciutto, use the optional pancetta and olive oil to get enough fat to cook the vegetables in. Add the onion, garlic, celery, and parsley and cook until softened, about 6 minutes, stirring. Add the tomatoes, season with pepper, and cook over medium heat for 10 minutes, stirring occasionally.

4. When the beans are cooked, remove the prosciutto bone or chunk and pork skin. Remove the meat from the prosciutto bone and chop fine or chop

1 cup of prosciutto from the chunk. Discard the pork skin. Add this prosciutto meat to the cooked vegetables. Remove half of the cooked beans and push them through a food mill or strainer. Return the bean puree to the pot with the whole beans.

5. Meanwhile, bring a large pot of abundantly salted water to a boil and add the *tubetti* when the water is rolling. Cook until al dente, then drain and add the pasta to the beans. Add the cooked vegetables to the beans. Stir well and simmer for 10 minutes and serve.

Makes 4 to 6 servings

THE grain and flour entering Venice were controlled by a grain office that also controlled sales. Flour could be sold only in two city markets, one near San Marco and the other at the Rivoalto (Rialto). The doge was informed of warehoused supplies, and once they dwindled to a year's supply the Collegio, an arm of government where state business was conducted, was notified.[23] When the food supply of Venice was endangered, no ship carrying wheat was safe in the Adriatic. Venice would capture grain ships along the Apulian coast and unload them at Corfu, Spalato (Split), or back in Venice. Once Venice lost Apulia as a grain and wine cellar, its position became more precarious in times of famine or need. This situation was compounded by the fact that Venice's usual sources of food supply during crisis were Egypt or the Black Sea, whose food was now diverted as tribute to the hungry urban monster of Istanbul.

The Rialto was for centuries the most important market in Venice, once the most important mercantile exchange in the Mediterranean. Merchants, exchange agents, middlemen, notaries, and insurance and maritime agents all converged around the Portego del Bancogire and in the vicinty of the Calle della Sigurtà. Among the most important denizens were the pepper merchants, who fixed daily prices.[24] Speculation in spices was very important for Venetian merchants, as the arrival or loss of a galleon could make or break them. In the Rialto, Venetians could sell the spices and silks of the East to the Lombards and Florentines, with their metalwork or cloth, or to the Germans for whom a joint inn and warehouse *(caravanserai)* had been built next to the bridge, the Fondaco dei Tedeschi, in 1318, that stills stands as the local post office.[25]

Today, tourists in Venice tend to congregate around the Piazza San Marco and the arteries that lead to the Rialto. They miss the fabulous *scuole*, not to mention the chiarascuro of La Serenissima. The *scuole* were lay confraternities, associations of middle-class people who shared a particular craft or national origin and were involved in a charitable service. They built lodges for themselves, usually consisting of a banquet hall on the ground floor and archives, offices, and rented rooms on the second. The *scuole* played an important role in the Venetian Republic.

At the base of Venice's political structure was the Maggior Consiglio, the Great Council, consisting of nearly two thousand members. After the Maggior Consiglio became a closed group of patricians in 1297, one would think that the middle class would have revolted against their being shunted from power. But in five hundred years the Venetians never really revolted. The reason they didn't was that the patrician aristocracy never claimed for itself a natural right of superiority. A sense of justice developed in Venice, and serving the public good in the republic became a guiding principle. Interactions between classes were common and vehicles such as the sumptuary laws limited the power and excess of the aristocracy. The middle classes had their *scuole* whereby they could feel a oneness with the polity. One of the most satisfying *scuola* for today's traveler is the seventeenth-century Scuola Grande dei Carmini, a Carmelite confraternity devoted to the Virgin of Carmelo at one end of the Campo San Margherita, with its stunning ceiling by Giambattista Tiepolo. Another *scuola* you may want to visit is the Scuola Grande di San Rocco, built by the Confraternity of St. Rocco, the saint whose name is invoked against the plague, which contains nearly fifty paintings by Tintoretto. Finally, there is the Scuola di San Giorgio degli Schiavoni, founded in 1451 to protect the Dalmatian community, mainly sailors, in Venice. It is a tiny place with a wonderfully enjoyable series of paintings by Carpaccio detailing the lives of three famous Dalmatian saints, St. Jerome, St. George, and St. Tryphone.

Many visitors miss the *scuole* and often miss the specialties of Venetian cuisine, as they sadly order a most unserene *pizza Margherita*, a prosaic choice in the face of *la cucina venexiana*, such as the extraordinary *seppie nero con polenta*, or sliced cuttlefish in its own sauce of ink and tomatoes with a mound of bright yellow polenta (page 449) or *polenta e osèi* (below). The middle classes had their foods, and many of these preparations may very well have had their genesis in the kitchens of the *scuole* that were used for banquets and daily meals.

Polenta e Osèi (Veneto)

POLENTA AND SMALL BIRDS

This delicacy was once found on the menus of all the ostarie *of Venice and is the subject of a Venetian proverb:* Polenta e osèi, magnàrli con i dèi *(Polenta and small birds, eat them with penitence), meaning, thank the Lord for this delicious dish. The popularity of small birds goes back quite a way in Venice, where one finds the Maggior Consiglio, the parliament of the republic, regulating them in 1275.*[26]

In the Veneto region, especially in Vicenza, cooks once spit-roasted songbirds such as larks, thrushes, warblers, and blackbirds, as well as aquatic birds such as duck, teal, and crane, over a fire of mixed wood. Spit-roasted crane was a delicacy in the Middle Ages, as we know from Boccaccio's story in the Decameron *about the Venetian chef Chichibio. Chichibio was the cook to Currado Gianfigliazzi, who one day brought home a plump crane. As the well-seasoned crane was cooking, Brunetta, a young girl Chichibio fancied, smelled the aromas and asked him for a leg, which he gave her. Later at the dinner table his master noticed that the crane only had one leg. The cook told him that cranes only have one leg. The master flew into a rage at this ludicrous statement, even as the cook insisted that in the morning he would prove it. When morning came the two set out, Chichibio quite worried since he hadn't a clue as to how he would prove that cranes have only one leg. Coming upon a flock of sleeping cranes on one leg, as is their nature, the cook pointed to his evidence. Currado didn't believe this for an instant and yelled "Oho!" whereupon the cranes put down their other legs and flew away. Currado turned to Chichibio and said, "What do you have to say?" And Chichibio replied, "Well, you didn't say 'Oho' last night, and if you had the other leg would have appeared." Currado roared with laughter at this clever answer and was no longer angry.*[27]

Osèi *is the Venetian dialect word for* uccelli, *small wild birds. You can use quail or Cornish hens in the place of small birds.*

8 quail or 4 small Cornish hens
6 ounces pancetta, cut into thick slices
1 bunch fresh sage leaves
Salt
8 slices cooked polenta (page 615)

1. Prepare a charcoal fire or preheat a gas grill for 15 minutes on medium-low heat. Affix the spit-roasting attachment. Truss the birds and secure tightly to the spit interspersed with the pancetta and

sage leaves. Sprinkle with salt. Make sure the bird's weight is evenly distributed so the spit rotates smoothly and that the holding prongs are tight. Tie the birds to the spit with butcher's twine if necessary so they will not slide while the spit turns.

2. Place a pan under the roasting birds to catch the melting fat and grill the polenta dipped in this. The birds are done when they are golden brown and the juices run clear when pricked in the thigh joint with a skewer, about 1¼ hours for the Cornish hens and about 35 minutes for the quail.

Makes 4 servings

THE doges celebrated major holidays with great banquets. The forty days after Easter were known as *la Sensa* in Venetian, and celebrated along with other holidays such as the *Redentore* in July and the *Salute* in November. *La Sensa*, or Ascension Day, was a movable feast that celebrated the campaign of Doge Pietro Orseolo II against the Dalmatians in 1000. The *Redentore* is a day of thanksgiving for the deliverance of Venice from the terrible plague of 1575–1577 that took a quarter of the population, and the *Salute* celebrates the end of the plague of 1631. For *la Sensa*, the *scalco maggiore*, major carver or manager, would pick up the table silver from the Zecca, the silver repository, and organize the banquet. The doge sat at an oval table seating nine or eleven guests. Guests would first wash their hands with perfumed water. Banquets began with eleven *ordover*, a Venetian word for hors d'oeuvre. The first course might include green ginger with small lemons, walnuts, or other candied fruits, plates of fresh fruit, small pastries, salted tongue, and Florence salami. The main courses were usually meat such as veal tripe, stuffed meatloaf, chicken, roast veal, grilled lamb offal, a soup of biscuits with Malvasia wine, fresh artichokes, one bowl for every two persons of fresh cheese perfumed with rose water and sugar, bowls of chicken, trencher boards with pheasant, partridge, a bowl of thinly sliced sweet lemons with sugar and rose water, a different pie—for example, of pears—meat jelly, boiled capon, veal and tongue served with a soup of sage and rice or with blancmange or ravioli, accompanied by bowls of mustard with cinnamon and sweet spices, and hare with bowls of pepper sauce. Vegetables like asparagus, artichokes, and fennel served at room temperature would cleanse the palate. Some time around the end of the fourteenth century, it became fashionable in Italy to have meals begin and end with a sweet confectionary, so a final course was marzipan. The festival of San Vito e Modesto on June 15 required *risotto coi peoci*—that is, with mussels—and for San Marco, *sfogi in saòr*, and on Good Friday, *bigoli in salsa*.[28]

The *ordover* of the Venetian Republic are in evidence today, for the Venetians are fond of delicate *antipasti* such as the *canocchie*, mantis shrimp (*Squilla mantis* L.); or *gamberetti*, small shrimp; *schlie*, small gray shrimp; *moleche*, small crabs; *moscardini*, baby octopus; and *uova di seppie*, cuttlefish eggs, from the lagoon. There is the world-famous antipasto invented by the Venetian restaurateurs Giuseppe and Arrigo Cipriani in the twentieth century—carpaccio, or ultra-thin slices of beef tenderloin with a mayonnaise-based dressing—and an old recipe going back to the time of the doges, *pâté de fegato*, liver pâté. Some famous Venetian recipes follow.

Risotto coi Peoci (Veneto)

MUSSEL RISOTTO

In the days of the Venetian Republic, La Serenissima would spare nothing to properly regale the ambassadors to St. Marks with all the pomp and splendor befitting such a noble position. The state dinner was a notable event, and the master chefs of the doge would prepare an exquisite minestra di riso *that centuries later evolved into the risottos we know today.* Risotto coi pedocchi *or* peoci *(Venetian dialect for mussels) is traditionally served on June 15 for the Feast of San Vito and Modesto and throughout the summer months. This preparation is also called* alla gondoliera, *the way the gondoliers liked it, pulling the clinging mussels off the sides of the buildings.*

Mussels are cultivated along a stretch of coastline that runs parallel to the Lido di Venezia up to the village of Malamocco. In A.D. *1000, a mighty tidal wave destroyed much of the Lido, but the local fishermen rebuilt their lives and their livelihood—the cultivation of mussels.*

The mussels used for this should be large. Clean the mussels under running water and pull off their beards.

4 pounds mussels, debearded and washed well
3 cups fish broth (page 369)
3 tablespoons extra virgin olive oil
5 tablespoons unsalted butter
1 small onion, very finely chopped
2 garlic cloves, very finely chopped
1½ cups Arborio rice
Salt to taste
3 tablespoons finely chopped fresh parsley leaves
Freshly ground black pepper to taste

1. Soak the mussels in cold water to cover for 30 minutes. Place the mussels in a large pot or casserole over high heat and shake until they have opened, 8 and 10 minutes. Remove them from the pot; when they are cool enough to handle, remove the mussels from their shells and set aside. Discard any mussels that remain tightly shut. Strain the mussel juice through a double thickness of cheesecloth and save 1 cup of it, mixing it with the fish broth. Save some shells for decorating the serving platter if desired.

2. In a medium-size casserole, heat the olive oil and 2½ tablespoons of the butter over medium heat. Once the butter has melted, cook the onion and garlic until the onion is translucent and slightly golden, 7 to 8 minutes, stirring frequently so the garlic doesn't burn. Pour in the rice and stir for 2 minutes to coat it. Now pour in 1 cup of the mussel-and-fish broth. Taste the broth and add salt if necessary. Once the liquid evaporates, pour in another ½ cup of the broth. Continue adding the remaining broth in smaller and smaller amounts as it evaporates and is absorbed and cook until the rice is between al dente and tender, stirring almost constantly.

3. When the rice is done, stir in the reserved mussels, the parsley, the remaining 2½ tablespoons butter, and the pepper. Stir until the butter melts, transfer to a serving platter, decorate with the mussel shells, and serve immediately.

Makes 4 servings

Sardine o "Sfogi in Saòr" (Veneto)

MARINATED SARDINES OR SOLE

This dish, traditionally made with baby sole or fresh sardines, is a special preparation for the Festa del Redentore, *on the third Sunday of July when Venetians celebrate the Holy Redeemer with fireworks and food. Private and public gondolas and motor launches and other boats fill the Grand Canal, the Canale della Giudecca, and the quays of the Bacino di San Marco, Giudecca, and the Zattere. The* Redentore *itself is a Franciscan church designed by Palladio and built in 1577–1592 as a thanksgiving for delivering Venice from the horrible plague of 1575–1577, which left a quarter of the population dead.*

Several dishes are traditional for this celebration

besides sfogi in saòr. *Roast duck, beans, and snails* (bovoletti) *with garlic and olive oil are also prepared, usually shipboard.*

This is a perfect dish for a sultry summer day. Any kind of fish could theoretically be used for a pesse in saòr, *marinated fish, but in Venice it is made with* sfogi, *baby sole, and more commonly with sardines. If you are unable to find fresh sardines (canned will not work), look for small sole or flounder, butterfish, porgies, small red snapper, or even smelts.*

Saòr *is a Venetian word that means "flavor," and particularly flavor by way of marination. The marination of fish goes back to the classical Greeks, and very possibly earlier, because of the necessity of preserving food through salting or marination in an acid. In Greece today,* psari savori *or* psari marinata *is a similar marinated fish served at room temperature.*

My own thought is that sfogi in saòr *is related to the* pesci 'ntammaru *of Sicily, an Arab-influenced dish that is identical.*[29] *Although the Romans are known to have preserved fish with hot vinegar, the recipes from the Middle Ages appear Arab influenced because they use methods and spicing different from those of the Romans.*[30] *These recipes find the addition of cinnamon, ground coriander, cloves, pomegranate juice, ginger, and bay leaves to the marinade, an indication of Muslim provenance. In the anonymous fourteenth-century cookery manuscript* Liber de coquina, *from the Angevin court in Naples,* de scapeta piscium *is fish fried in oil with raisins, wine, vinegar, and saffron.*[31] *The fourteenth-century* Libro per cuoco *by an anonymous Venetian also contains an identical recipe called* savore de pesse, *where the fish is fried in oil and covered with vinegar, raisins, and saffron or galingale (a culinary spice made from a root related to ginger).*[32] *Even the southern Italian manuscript known as* Libro B *of the Anonimo Meridionale (Book B of the Anonymous Southerner), from the early fifteenth century, has a recipe that calls for the fried fish to be covered with wine, vinegar, onions, almonds, maraschino cherries, and "dates from Alexandria."*[33] *The relationship between medieval Arabic cookery manuscripts and the early Italian cookery works has been noted by several scholars.*[34]

Sardines are the fish traditionally most used by the poor because they were the best fish suited for salting. Venetians also use other fish, such as papaline *(sprat),* anguele *(sand smelt),* passarini *(flounder),* pesse popolo *(any small fish),* gò *(goby),* murèi de bisata *(moray eel), and* trotelle *(small trout), most of which can be found at the Rialto fish market every morning in today's Venice. In this preparation you can leave the head on or off, and you can remove the backbone after frying if you have difficulty removing it when the fish is fresh and uncooked (see Step 1, pages 388–389, for removing sardine backbones).*

1½ cups extra virgin olive oil
All-purpose flour as needed
2 pounds fresh (or defrosted frozen) sardines, sand dabs, or porgies, cleaned and gutted
Salt to taste
2¼ pounds white onions, very thinly sliced
1¼ cups white wine vinegar
¼ cup golden raisins, soaked in tepid water to cover for 20 minutes and drained
¼ cup pine nuts
Pinch of ground cinnamon

1. In a large skillet, heat the olive oil over medium-high heat until 375°F, until it begins to smoke. Meanwhile, flour the sardines or porgies, tapping off any excess. Fry the sardines without crowding them in the hot oil until golden, about 1½ minutes per side (the sand dabs and porgies will need 1 to 2 minutes a side longer), and drain. Place the fish on paper towels to drain some more and season with salt.

2. Reduce the heat under the skillet to medium. Allow 10 minutes to pass for the temperature of the oil to reduce sufficiently. Once the olive oil has cooled, cook the onions until soft, about 30 minutes, stirring occasionally. The onions should still look white after they are cooked, although some people cook them until golden, or even brown. Pour off or

ladle out ½ to ¾ cup of the frying oil. Increase the heat under the skillet to medium-high and add the vinegar, raisins and pine nuts, to the remaining oil, being careful about splattering oil, and cook for 5 minutes, stirring.

3. Arrange the sardines or porgies in a large ceramic or glass baking dish. Sprinkle over the cinnamon. Cover with the onions and all the liquid from the skillet. Cover with plastic wrap and refrigerate for 2 days. Remove from the refrigerator 2 hours before serving, transfer to a serving platter, and serve at room temperature.

Makes 6 servings

Bigoli in Salsa (Veneto)

WHOLE WHEAT SPAGHETTI WITH SALTED SARDINE SAUCE

Bigoli in salsa *is an old and beloved Venetian preparation made on Good Friday. A Venetian would know that* bigoli in salsa, *which means "spaghetti in sauce" in dialect, is nothing other than this unctuous concoction also called* bigoli con le sardelle. *Today the dish is made with anchovies, although I use the sardines of the older fashion in this recipe, which Venetians would get from Chioggia, in the southern portion of the lagoon, and salt themselves. Other recipes using this pasta might include duck livers sautéed in butter and seasoned with duck broth, onions, and sage.*

Bigoli in salsa *is a typical preparation of the lowlands, where the pasta was once made in the home with a special press called a* bigolaro *or* bigolo.[35] *Today, Venetians rarely make their own* bigoli *(a Venetian dialect word pronounced BEE-go-wee) as it is easily obtainable around the city, made by artisanal pasta makers and sold in gourmet stores.* Bigoli *is the Venetian word for "spaghetti," actually "vermicelli," but refers to any kind of spaghetti. In this preparation a very long, dark whole wheat spaghetti is used and it is kept long while cooking and not broken in two. The origin of the word is unknown, but some scholars believe it comes from the Italian* baco, *worms.*[36]

Bigoli *is also used in a preparation called* all'ajada, *a dialect word indicating how the pasta is cut: it is meant to resemble the swathing with which the Madonna wrapped the infant Jesus. It is traditionally served in the lower Lombardy on Christmas Eve. The domain of this dish extends into France, where in the Haute-Provence it is known as* crouzets *and eaten on Advent Eve.* Crouzets *is a* bigoli *made with a sauce of walnuts, fresh bread crumbs, garlic, and milk.*

You can make bigoli in salsa *very nearly identical to the Venetian one by observing a few rules. Make sure the onions are finely chopped; no piece should be bigger than this "O." You will need the salted sardines described on page 434 or you can mix sardines and anchovies as explained in the Note.*

¼ pound salted sardines
½ cup extra virgin olive oil
1 large onion, very finely chopped
6 tablespoons water
Salt
1 pound whole-wheat spaghetti
Freshly ground black pepper to taste

1. If using the homemade salted sardines, first wash, then peel the fillets off the backbone and chop fine; otherwise, see the Note. In a large casserole, heat the olive oil over high heat, then cook the onion and sardines until they begin to turn color, about 5 minutes, uncovered, stirring occasionally. Add the water, cover tightly, and reduce the heat to low. Cook until the onion is soft and golden, 25 to 30 minutes, stirring occasionally.

2. Meanwhile, bring a large pot of abundantly salted water to a boil and add the pasta when the water is rolling. Cook until al dente, drain, and add to the casserole with the sauce, tossing. Sprinkle with

the pepper and toss again. Serve immediately without cheese, but pass the peppermill around.

NOTE: If you do not have homemade salted sardines, mix 3 ounces sardines canned in olive oil with 6 salted anchovy fillets, previously rinsed, and continue with the preparation.

Makes 4 servings

Risi e Bisi (Veneto)

RICE AND PEAS

Risi e bisi, rizi e bizi, *or* bisi e risi *is today internationally famous, and not just a Venetian dish. In Padua and Verona there are identical recipes except for the addition of pieces of goose confit. Originally* risi e bisi *was served for the grand festivals of the doges, such as the Festival of St. Mark's on April 25. It was a special preparation because peas were only newly popular around 1650, although they had been grown in the Near East since Neolithic times. The fact that rice was expensive and the season for peas short must have contributed to the specialness of the dish.*

You will want fresh "new" sweet peas for this dish and a rich, flavorful chicken and pea pod broth. These new peas are called magnatuto *(meaning "eat it all") in Venetian.*[37] *New peas are ready in the spring, and rows upon rows of staked bean and pea plants can be seen in the fields fronting the lagoon on the islands of Torcello, Burano, and Murano, and along the lagoon side of the Lido as it stretches to Chioggia. Travelers today can see the gardens of local residents growing their peas and other vegetables by taking the no. 12* vaporetto *from Fondamente Nuove to Torcello and back.*

Risi e bisi *is not as dry as a risotto nor is it cooked like a risotto. In fact, it is not a risotto but a kind of* minestra*, cooked like a thick soup as they did in the Middle Ages. The rice should be cooked* all'onda*, wavelike, as they say in Venice, so that if you were to tilt the bowl the rice would slowly run out like molasses. The proportion is one-third uncooked rice to two-thirds new or baby peas.*

1/4 cup (1/2 stick) unsalted butter
2 tablespoons extra virgin olive oil
1 small onion, very finely chopped
Two 1/8-inch-thick slices pancetta, finely chopped
Two 1/8-inch-thick slices boiled ham, finely chopped
3 cups fresh new sweet peas (from 2 1/2 pounds pea pods; save 1/2 pound of the pods for the broth)
2 tablespoons finely chopped fresh parsley leaves
Salt and freshly ground black pepper to taste
5 cups chicken and pea broth (page 270)
1 1/2 cups Arborio or Vialone rice
3 tablespoons freshly grated Parmigiano-Reggiano cheese

1. In a large, heavy casserole or saucepan, heat 2 tablespoons of the butter and all of the olive oil together over medium heat. Once the butter has melted and is sizzling, cook the onion, pancetta, and ham until the onion is translucent, about 5 minutes, stirring a few times. Add the peas and 1 tablespoon of the parsley, season with salt and pepper, and cook for 1 minute, stirring to coat the peas. Add 1 cup of the broth and increase the heat to high. Stir constantly.

2. When the peas are softer, after about 5 minutes, add 2 cups of the remaining broth, then the rice. Stir continuously, but very gently, making sure you don't break the peas. Add more broth every time the previous amount is absorbed until you have just a ladleful left, after 18 to 20 minutes. Remove the casserole from the heat and add the remaining broth, which should make the *risi e bisi* somewhat soupy. Fold in the remaining 2 tablespoons butter and 1 tablespoon parsley and the Parmigiano-Reggiano and serve immediately.

Makes 4 servings

Brodo di Pollo e Piselli per Risi e Bisi (Veneto)

CHICKEN AND PEA BROTH FOR *RISI E BISI*

Because I feel that risi e bisi *is such a special Venetian preparation, I provide this recipe for the broth that will make it so excellent.*

2 to 4 pounds chicken feet, necks, bones, or carcasses
1 carrot, sliced
2 celery stalks, with leaves, sliced
1 medium-size onion, cut in half and layers separated
½ pound pea pods
10 black peppercorns
Bouquet garni, tied in cheesecloth, consisting of
6 sprigs each fresh parsley, thyme, and marjoram
2 sprigs fresh sage, and 1 bay leaf
1 cup dry white wine
3 quarts cold water

1. Put all the ingredients in a stockpot and bring to a boil. Reduce the heat to a simmer and skim off the foam. Partially cover and simmer over very low heat for 6 hours, continuing to skim off any foam.

2. Strain the broth through cheesecloth and place the broth in the refrigerator so the fat can congeal on the top. Skim it off. Pour the defatted broth into containers for freezing. A more convenient method for freezing broth is to pour it into ice cube trays and once the cubes are frozen, empty into large zippered-top plastic freezer bags. The cubes can stay in a freezer for 6 months.

VARIATION

To make a vegetable broth, replace the chicken with 2 pounds Swiss chard and simmer for 3 hours.

Makes 6 to 8 cups

Pâté di Fegato (Veneto)

LIVER PÂTÉ IN THE STYLE OF VENICE

The theory that people of the Middle Ages fancied pâtés made of finely chopped meat presupposes that they did because of their poor teeth. We know, however, that pâtés have had an uninterrupted popularity since Roman times among all kinds of people with both good and bad teeth. In Venice this liver pâté is said to have been popular with Doge Nicolò Tron (d. 1473), the only doge whose head appears on a Venetian coin.[38]

The cooked liver should be cool before processing. If the pâté appears very soft and you are unable to mold it with your hands, that may be because too much liquid was left in the original liver preparation or because the whipped butter began to melt from the heat generated by the food processor. In either case, nothing is lost: Place the liver on a sheet of aluminum foil and twist the ends before placing in the refrigerator. The pâté will take its form once it's cool.

1 recipe *fegato di vitello alla veneziana* (page 273)
¼ pound whipped unsalted butter, at room temperature

1. Place all of the cooked, and cooled, liver in a food processor and run until pastelike. Add the whipped butter and continue to process until it is all blended.

2. Remove, form with your hands into a sausage shape, and place on a sheet of aluminum foil. Roll it up and place in the refrigerator. Serve at room temperature.

Makes 4 servings

THE banquets of the doges and princely courts have received most of the attention of food writers, but a close look at the merriment of bourgeois eating can be had in the Ca'Rezzonico, a museum of sixteenth-century Venice housed in a *palazzo* on the Grand Canal. On the second floor is the Pietro Longhi (1702–1785) room. Longhi was a genre painter of domestic life and here you can see *La venditrice di fritole*, a vendor selling her fried food, *La polenta,* showing a woman dumping a huge mound of polenta onto the table for two men, and *L'allegra coppia*, the merry cup, with a voluptuous woman serving wine to some men. In Gaspare Diziani's the *Festival of Santa Marita*, men are pan-frying food over an open fire while women in a nearby boat eat fish fillets (or are they eggplant slices?) with wine. Many of these sumptuous dishes are impossible to find in today's Venice. But the frying of foods in oil is more ubiquitous in the Mediterranean than the proponents of the "Mediterranean diet" would like to admit. Street vendors in Italian cities sold a variety of "take-out" foods, especially fritters of one kind or another, perhaps similar to the two following contemporary recipes from Emilia-Romagna. And in Venice, a favorite food since at least Roman times, and certainly during the era of the doges of the Venetian Republic, is veal liver, often fried in olive or grapeseed oil. Venetians have delightful ways of preparing it, as in the three recipes following those from Emilia.

The fry vendor selling her street foods in Venice. Pietro Longhi (1702–1785). *The Seller of* Fritole. Ca'Rezzonico Museum, Venice.
ALINARI/ART RESOURCE

Frittelle di Ricotta (Emilia-Romagna)

RICOTTA FRITTERS

Fritelle *or* frictelle *are small fritters, fried foods, of great variety that were very popular in the Middle Ages and often sold from street vendors. The anonymous fourteenth-century Venetian cookery book* Libro per cuoco *has an important-sounding recipe called* fritelle da imperadore magnifici *(the magnificent emperor's fritter) that is quite similar to this contemporary preparation. In the fourteenth century, they made it with fresh cheese, beaten egg whites, flour, and pine nuts and sprinkled it with sugar when finished.*[39] *Today, these simple fritters are considered a* passatempo, *a kind of small cocktail snack had with a drink before any formal dining begins.*

1 cup fresh ricotta cheese (page 467)
¾ cup all-purpose flour
Salt to taste
1 large egg
1 tablespoon Marsala or rum
6 cups pure or virgin olive, olive pomace, or canola oil for deep-frying

1. Blend the ricotta, flour, salt, egg, and Marsala with a fork in a medium-size bowl. Cover with plastic wrap and leave to rest for 30 minutes in the refrigerator.

2. Preheat the frying oil in a deep-fryer or an 8-inch saucepan fitted with a basket insert to 375°F. Deep-fry several soupspoonfuls of the ricotta dough at a time without crowding the fryer until golden, 4 to 5 minutes, turning if necessary. Let drain on paper towels. Let the frying oil cool completely, strain through a porous paper filter and save the oil for a future use.

Makes 4 passatempo *servings*

Mortadella Fritta (Emilia-Romagna)

FRIED MORTADELLA

Mortadella is a quite lean pork sausage with "eyes" of fat, flavored with peppercorns, pistachios, wine, sugar, and olives and stuffed into beef bladder casing, giving the final product a huge shape. The earliest mentions of mortadella that I am aware of demonstrate that it is a very old Mediterranean sausage. Although there is no direct evidence that the Romans made mortadella, the name is thought to derive from the Latin murtatu, *a sausage seasoned with myrtle.* Mortadella *is also mentioned in the statutes of the Cathedral of Nice from 1233 as being made for holidays such as Easter, pentecost, or Christmas. In the fourteenth century, mortadella is mentioned again in the anonymous* Liber de coquina, *apparently written by someone familiar with the Neapolitan court then under the sphere of Charles II of Anjou, and in the* Libro per cuoco *by an anonymous Venetian, where it is made with the addition of pig's liver.*[40] *Today, this preparation is an unusual* passatempo, *delicious, but you must soak the mortadella in milk during the day or overnight before cooking to remove any saltiness.*

½ pound mortadella, in one ¾-inch-thick piece
Milk for soaking
All-purpose flour for dredging
1 large egg, lightly beaten and salted
Dry bread crumbs for dredging
3 tablespoons unsalted butter
3 tablespoons extra virgin olive oil

1. Cut the mortadella into 3-inch squares about the thickness of a finger. Place in a small bowl, cover with milk, and let soak for 6 to 8 hours in the refrigerator. Drain.

2. Dredge the mortadella pieces in flour, shaking off any excess flour. Dip in the beaten egg and then dredge in bread crumbs. Set aside on a plate in the refrigerator for 30 minutes.

3. In a small skillet, melt the butter with the olive oil until very hot, almost smoking, over medium-high heat and cook the breaded mortadella until golden on both sides, 2 to 3 minutes. Drain on paper towels and serve.

Makes 4 servings

Figà coi Fighi (Veneto)

VEAL LIVER AND FIGS

In ancient Rome it was popular to raise geese fed exclusively on a diet of fresh figs. The meat, and especially the liver, came to have a special and refined fla-

vor that was much prized. It was called iecur ficatum, *or liver with figs. When people bought such liver at the market, they asked for* ficatum *(with figs). Over time,* ficatum *became* figà *in Venetian and* fegato *in Italian.*[41]

This dish of veal liver and figs is certainly not found in restaurants and few housewives make it anymore. But it is a rewarding recipe for veal liver, and extraordinary with goose liver. Because it is easy to overcook veal liver, making it unappetizing, you must pay close attention to the cooking.

1 pound fresh figs (about 12)
1 pound veal, goose, or duck liver, arteries removed
1 cup water
3 tablespoons white wine vinegar
¼ cup extra virgin olive oil or grapeseed oil
1 large onion, thinly sliced
Juice and grated zest from 1 lemon
1 teaspoon fennel seeds

1. Split the figs in half, scoop out the flesh with a teaspoon, chop it, and set aside. The skin is edible but you will not use it in this preparation. Cut the liver into thin strips and place in a medium-size bowl containing the mixed water and vinegar and set aside for 1 hour in the refrigerator. Drain the liver and mix with the chopped figs, tossing well.

2. In a large skillet, heat the oil over medium heat, then cook the onion until translucent, 12 to 15 minutes, stirring occasionally. Increase the heat to high and when the onion slices are sizzling, add the liver slices and chopped figs and cook for 1 minute, stirring. Add the lemon juice, lemon zest, and fennel seeds and cook for 1 more minute. Immediately remove from the heat, transfer to a serving platter, and serve.

Makes 4 to 6 servings

Fegato di Vitello alla Veneziana (Veneto)

VEAL LIVER IN THE STYLE OF VENICE

Fegato alla veneziana, *or* figà a la venexiana *in Venetian, is a truly plebeian dish. There is an identical preparation in Catalonia and a similar one in Egypt. It is common to see in Venice today, perhaps at a* rosticceria, *working people at a counter eating* fegato, *always with a steaming square of yellow polenta. I used to order this from the Rosticceria San Bartolomeo on the Calle del Bisse in Cannaregio, near my apartment, for lunch after coming home from school, and ate it standing up at the counter like everyone else.*

It is important that the liver be cooked over very high heat in a very hot pan, tossed almost constantly. Make sure you don't overcook the liver. By doubling the recipe and saving the excess, you can make the famous Venetian specialty, pâté di fegato *(page 270).*

1 pound veal liver, arteries removed
1 cup milk
¼ cup extra virgin olive or grapeseed oil
1 large white onion, thinly sliced
Salt to taste
Juice from 1 lemon
2 tablespoons very finely chopped fresh parsley leaves
Freshly ground black pepper to taste

1. Cut the liver into thin strips, place in a medium-size bowl, marinate for 1 hour in the milk, and drain.

2. In a large skillet, heat the oil over medium heat, then cook the onion until translucent, 12 to 15 minutes, stirring occasionally. Increase the heat to high, add the liver, and cook for 2 minutes, tossing often.

Season with salt and stir in the lemon juice. Remove the skillet from the heat, sprinkle on the parsley and black pepper, and serve with hot polenta (page 615).

Makes 4 servings

✣ ✣ ✣

THE descriptions we have of the Venetian markets of the sixteenth century sound like the markets of the rich. But most Venetians were poor, and offal, particularly tripe, was one of their everyday foods.[42] A very popular bourgeois dish in sixteenth-century Venice was *fongadina* or *coratella di capretto*, goat's pluck stew (heart, liver, lungs, and windpipe). The pluck are boiled, cut into small pieces, and fried in a casserole with a little lard. Some chopped aromatic herbs are put in, along with raisins, pepper, cinnamon, saffron, and some broth.[43] The poor of sixteenth-century Venice could also receive bread tickets from the city authorities for a half pound wheat bread or a ten-ounce millet bread.[44] The perennial problem for Venice, and for every Mediterranean city, was feeding the population.

FEEDING THE CITIES

THE great cities of the western and southern Mediterranean are all near the sea, the great trade route. In the eastern Mediterranean the great cities are inland, their faces pointed toward the important trading roads through the desert. Desert caravans finally reached the sea at Tripoli on the Barbary coast, Tunis, or Algiers. In Syria, Aleppo was located as a way station for the Mediterranean–Persian Gulf route.

The most serious problem for these huge cities—in fact, for all cities—was the food supply. Supplying them with food was a crushing problem throughout the Mediterranean. Although there was a competitive economy in the fourteenth-century Mediterranean, the total volume of exchange was small, prices were low, and the distances goods could be transported were short. The primary commodities were foodstuffs that could be transported without spoilage, such as almonds from Provence, salted tuna or meat, sacks of dried beans from Egypt, and casks of oil and grain, for which there was the greatest demand.

Padua was, and is, a famous university town, but it was also a big agricultural center, taxing competitors from other towns for hens, geese, pigeons, capons, eggs, vegetables, and fruits leaving the city. Florence obtained its olive oil, vegetables, poultry, wine, and game and birds (which peasants sold in bunches at the city gates) from the surrounding *contado* (suburban agricultural land). The control of food supplies was carefully regulated in Florence. The Abbondanza was responsible for the production and supply of cereals, and another governmental body, the Grascia, set up production and exchange controls for all other foodstuffs. When heavy rainfalls in the autumn of 1589 flooded Florentine warehouses and cellars, and made sowing difficult, orders were given, in anticipation of a poor harvest, for rapeseed to be sown on 5 percent of all arable land to provide both oil and a vegetable.

Florence was a rich city that, in 1337, supported one hundred and forty-six bakeries. The bakers needed 2,310 bushels of grain every day to bake their bread. Each year the city consumed 4,000 oxen and calves, 60,000 mutton and sheep, 20,000 goats, and 30,000 pigs. During the month of July, 4,000 loads of melons came through Porta San Friano.[45] Fernand Braudel suggested that fluctuations of the cost of living in sixteenth-century Mediterranean could be identified by scholars simply by examining the cost of eggs in Florence.[46]

The foods eaten in the cities of the European Mediterranean were heavily influenced by the prevailing theory of dietetics, then a wholly Arab science having incorporated Hellenistic learning. The Arab style of cooking influenced the upper classes of Europe at the end of the Middle Ages in part because of these dietetic theories, based on philosophical and scientific works written in Arabic. Even today we can see evidence of how intellectual influence goes hand in hand with aspects of daily life—for example, in the westernization of Asian and African peoples today, which always begins with the upper classes.

The premier school for the study of dietetics and medicine in the Middle Ages was established at Salerno in Italy in the ninth century and was completely under the influence of Arab science. Under the patronage of the Holy Roman Emperor Frederick II, King of Sicily, the University of Salerno, in the early thirteenth century, became the center for the study and translation of Arab medical and dietetic texts. It is not too surprising that Arabic culinary texts were also translated, such as the one for the Angevin court in Naples.[47] The precepts of dietetics developed by the doctors at Salerno came to be known as the Salerno regimen. Medical doctors of the sixteenth century, still following these precepts of the Salerno School, recommended eating eggs, which were popular everywhere, fresh and not overcooked, because they were thought to increase coitus and the yolks were warm and moist, an antidote to cold and dry temperaments.

Mercantile relations could also affect the food that cities ate. Bakers in Florence were forbidden to use flour for any other purpose but bread baking, and Ferdinand I (1503–1564), younger brother of Spanish King Charles V, ordered Florentine merchants to start purchasing their wheat abroad because of low supplies, and for the first time a Hanseatic vessel berthed in Leghorn (Livorno) in December 1590.[48] The Hanseatic League was a mercantile association of German and northern European towns that had formed over the years to protect themselves against piracy and overcome foreign competition and trade restrictions. The arrival of one of their vessels in the Mediterranean meant competition would be fiercer, and the cities able to exploit this trade would grow larger, as did Leghorn, where ships and sailors from many lands could be found and where the cuisine associated with that city was often food from the sea.

Spaghetti coi Granchi (Tuscany)

SPAGHETTI WITH CRAB

Leghorn (Livorno) in the Middle Ages rose from a small village to an important shipping center where, as with Gibraltar, there was a thriving trade in contraband and a base for Christendom's pirates. The Hanseatic merchantman arriving from Hamburg with a cargo of lead, copper, and salt fish was engaged in a three-cornered trade. The merchantman picked up the specie *(spices in the wide sense)—raisins, raw cotton, spices, bales of silk, or even Malmsey wine—which enabled goods to be bought in the Levant, Zante (Zákinthos), Cyprus, or Syria.[49] In the words of Fernand Braudel, as Leghorn grew richer, the city was "one of the most disposed to convert its wealth into luxury."[50] This wealth is reflected in the food of Leghorn, a cuisine that is richer and spicier than that of other Tuscan cities and where seafood is expertly prepared with full-bodied, flavorful sauces.*

1 small onion, very finely chopped
3 garlic cloves, very finely chopped
1 poblano chili pepper, seeded
1 small carrot, very finely chopped
½ cup extra virgin olive oil
1 pound ripe tomatoes, peeled, seeded, and finely chopped
½ cup dry red wine
½ pound crabmeat, picked over for cartilage and shells
1 teaspoon cayenne pepper (optional)
Salt to taste
¾ pound spaghetti
¼ cup finely chopped fresh parsley leaves

1. Make a *battuto* (page 285) with the onion, one of the chopped garlic cloves, the chili pepper, and carrot. In a medium-size casserole, heat the olive oil over medium heat, then cook the *battuto* until soft, 7 to 8 minutes, stirring frequently. Reduce the heat to medium-low, add the tomatoes and 1/4 cup of the wine, stir, cover, and cook for another 10 minutes.

2. Pound the crabmeat in a mortar or pulse it in a food processor a few times until a little mushy. Add the crabmeat, the remaining 1/4 cup wine, and the cayenne if using, to the casserole, stir, cover, and cook until the sauce is thicker and flavorful, about 5 minutes.

3. Meanwhile, bring a large pot of abundantly salted water to a boil and add the pasta when the water is rolling. Drain when al dente. Toss the pasta with the sauce in the casserole and then again with the parsley and remaining chopped garlic and serve.

Makes 4 servings

Fagiolini Fresca alla Pomodoro (Tuscany)

FRESH BEANS WITH TOMATOES

The great cities of northern Italy during the Middle Ages found their trade both far and near, but their essential food supplies had to come from the farms of the contado *(suburban agricultural land) within thirty kilometers of the city. The vegetables, oil, wine, poultry, game, and other birds that were sold by peasants at the city gates of Florence all came from surrounding* contado. *Among the vegetables, the most common beans before the discovery of the Americas were fava beans, but once the American green bean arrived it became popular in local cooking.*

This preparation can be served along with meat, but it is also very nice as an antipasto. In Tuscany cooks will sometimes use the asparagus bean, fagiolo di Sant' Anna (Vigna unguiculata *var.* sesquipedalis), *a slender green bean more than a foot long, and a similar preparation is favored with Arabs* (lūbya bi'l-zayt, *page 123*) *and Turks* (zeytinyağlı taze fasulye, *page 326*).

Salt to taste
1 pound green beans, asparagus beans, or runner beans, ends trimmed
1/3 cup extra virgin olive oil
1 medium-size onion, sliced
2 garlic cloves, crushed
2 ounces pancetta, cut into very thin strips
1 pound ripe tomatoes, peeled, seeded, and coarsely chopped
Freshly ground black pepper to taste

1. Bring a pot of lightly salted water to a boil and blanch the beans for 3 minutes. This will keep the beans bright green. Remove from the heat, drain, and cool immediately in cold water. Return to a boiling pot of water and cook for another 8 minutes. Drain.

2. In a large skillet, heat the olive oil with the onion, garlic, and pancetta over medium heat and cook until the pancetta begins to get crispy, 12 to 14 minutes, stirring occasionally, so the onion doesn't burn. Add the tomatoes and green beans, season with salt and pepper, and cook until the green beans are between al dente and tender, 20 to 30 minutes, depending on the age of the beans, stirring occasionally. Let the beans return to room temperature before serving.

Makes 4 servings

* * *

THE cities, no matter how big or powerful, had to find their essential food supplies within a radius of about twenty miles. This was also true of the smaller towns such as Nîmes and Montpellier, the two biggest towns of Mediterranean Languedoc in 1550, each with a population of about ten thousand people, a quarter of whom were peasants and farm laborers.[51] Montpellier was the industrial center, and the surrounding countryside of Nîmes still produces some fine vegetables and herbs, especially tarragon.

Beurre de Montpellier (Languedoc)

HERB BUTTER FROM MONTPELLIER

As one comes down the Aude River in southern France, the hills are left behind and the road slowly glides into the plains with the Étang de Bages et de Sigear straight ahead. The gently sloping hills are covered with vineyards, and cypress trees punctuate the flat land dotted with small farm outbuildings of beige stucco and adobe-tiled roofs.[52] A spear of straight railroad tracks leads off to Port-la-Nouvelle, wispy flat clouds and gently rolling hills with the Mediterranean just beyond. As one heads north to Béziers or south to Perpignan, one encounters many a grilled fish served with the beurre de Montpellier.

Montpellier was an important trading center in the Middle Ages, and its spice merchants are said to have given the city its name. They were located on a hill back from the coast that was named Mount of the Spice Merchants (from the Latin monspistillarius, *mountain of the mortar pounders). Montpellier was also the industrial center of medieval France, and it attracted large numbers of Arabs and Jews, especially after their expulsion from Spain in 1492. Its medical school was established in A.D. 1000 by Jewish physicians, but it was the celebrated Catalan doctor Arnold of Vilanova (1240–1311) who became an influential professor of medicine at Montpellier and who translated the works of the Arab philosopher and medical encyclopaedist Avicenna, who wrote extensively on dietetics promoting the medicinal virtues of many spices and herbs.*

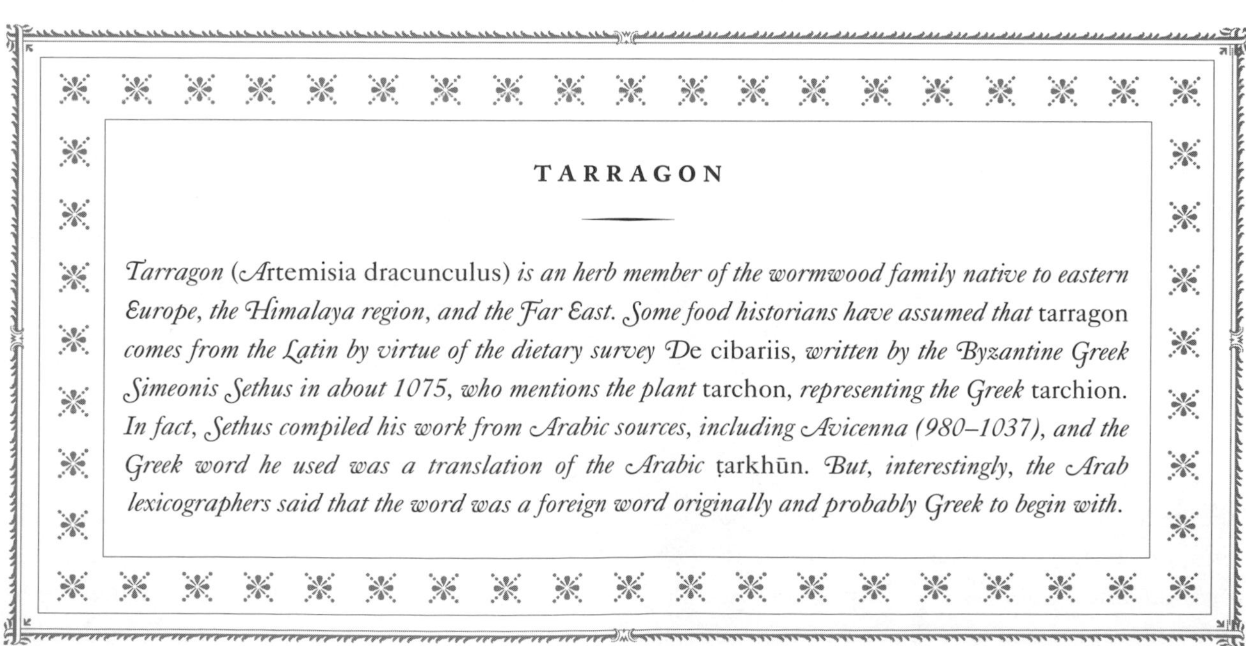

TARRAGON

Tarragon (Artemisia dracunculus) *is an herb member of the wormwood family native to eastern Europe, the Himalaya region, and the Far East. Some food historians have assumed that* tarragon *comes from the Latin by virtue of the dietary survey* De cibariis, *written by the Byzantine Greek Simeonis Sethus in about 1075, who mentions the plant* tarchon, *representing the Greek* tarchion. *In fact, Sethus compiled his work from Arabic sources, including Avicenna (980–1037), and the Greek word he used was a translation of the Arabic* ṭarkhūn. *But, interestingly, the Arab lexicographers said that the word was a foreign word originally and probably Greek to begin with.*

This fragrant herb butter, which an old English edition of Larousse gastronomique *says is edible but only used for decoration, is, in the French edition, usually served over a grilled tuna steak or other firm-fleshed flavorful fish such as bass. I use it over two of my favorite fish for grilling, Spanish mackerel* (Scomberomorus maculatus) *and kingfish* (Menticirrhus saxatilis), *both similar in taste, although in Montpellier tuna would be typical.*

6 leaves spinach, heavy stems removed
Leaves from 1 bunch watercress
5 sprigs fresh chervil
5 sprigs fresh chives
Leaves from 5 sprigs fresh parsley
Leaves from 5 sprigs fresh tarragon, oregano, or summer savory
2 garlic cloves, peeled
5 salted anchovy fillets, rinsed
3/4 cup (1 1/2 sticks) unsalted butter, softened
1 tablespoon extra virgin olive oil
1 tablespoon capers, rinsed and very finely chopped
1 sweet gherkin, very finely chopped
Salt and freshly ground black pepper to taste
2 large egg yolks (optional)

1. Wash the spinach, watercress, and herbs well in cold water, make sure no stems are remaining, and place in a metal strainer that will fit into a pot. Bring the pot of water to a boil and plunge the strainer in for 3 seconds (yes, 3 seconds). Remove and drain, pushing the water out with the back of a wooden spoon. Drain further with paper towels until very little moisture is left. Check for and remove any remaining stems and chop everything together very fine.

2. In a mortar, pound the garlic and anchovies together until a paste forms. Add the herb mixture to the anchovies and garlic and continue pounding until well incorporated. Turn into a larger bowl with the butter and whip together with a fork. Add the olive oil, capers, and gherkin, season with salt and pepper, and whip some more. Add the egg yolks, if using, and whip again. Place the butter on a sheet of aluminum foil and fold to cover. Roll the butter into a cylindrical shape and store in the refrigerator until needed.

NOTE: Keep refrigerated for up to 1 week.

Makes 1 1/2 cups

IN terms of population, the two greatest cities of the sixteenth-century Mediterranean were Naples and Istanbul, although any city over twenty thousand people was considered large. In 1348, Venice and a few other cities topped a hundred thousand people before their populations were cut in half by the Black Death.[53] The population of Naples was 280,000 in 1595, twice that of Venice, three times that of Rome, four times that of Florence, and nine times the population of Marseilles.

Marseilles was the "unchallenged mistress" of the Provençal coast in 1543. It was the entrepôt for spices, black pepper, drugs, wool, and leather from the Barbary Coast, cheeses from Sardinia, barrels of fish, cases of dates, and oranges from the islands of Hyères off the Provençal coast, Turkish carpets, silks, rice from the Levant, steel from Piedmont, alum from Civitavecchia just north of Rome, and Malmsey (Malvasia) wine from Greece. It was in Marseilles that France first experienced coffee in 1646, arriving from either Egypt or Syria.[54]

Marseilles was rich in every way. The food in 1560 was sumptuous by any standard: bread, wine, meat, and fish. The annual ration per person was 605 pounds of bread, 160 quarts of wine, 100 pounds of meat (beef, mutton, pork), but only 22 pounds of fish (salt cod came from Brittany beginning in the six-

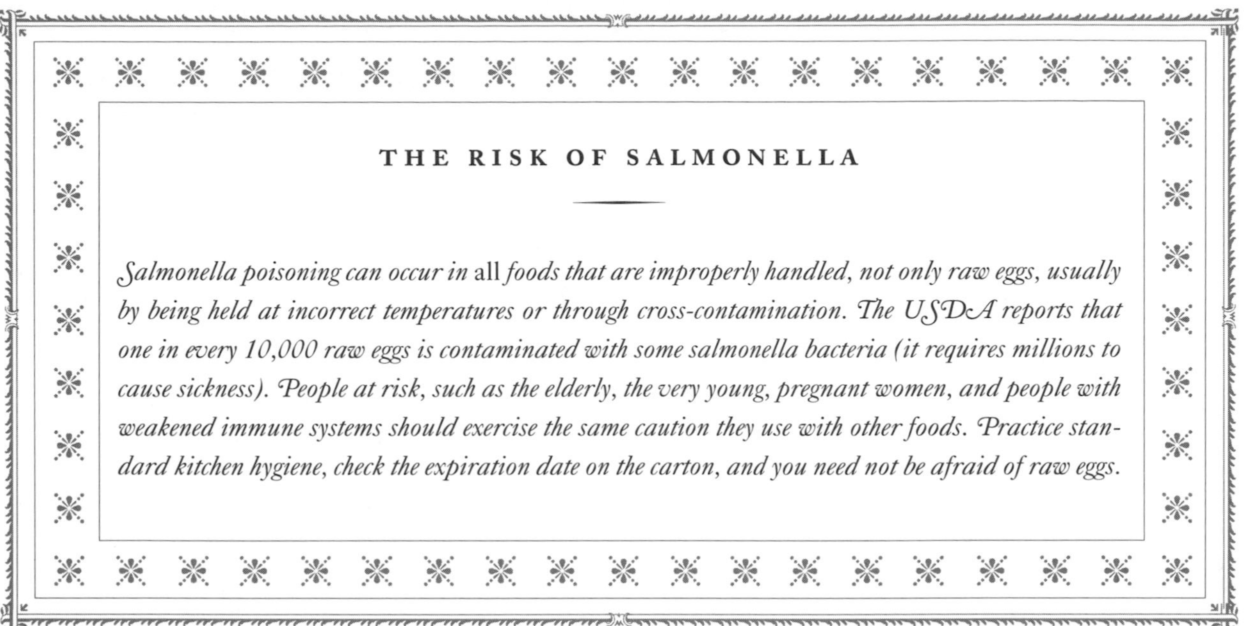

THE RISK OF SALMONELLA

Salmonella poisoning can occur in all *foods that are improperly handled, not only raw eggs, usually by being held at incorrect temperatures or through cross-contamination. The USDA reports that one in every 10,000 raw eggs is contaminated with some salmonella bacteria (it requires millions to cause sickness). People at risk, such as the elderly, the very young, pregnant women, and people with weakened immune systems should exercise the same caution they use with other foods. Practice standard kitchen hygiene, check the expiration date on the carton, and you need not be afraid of raw eggs.*

teenth century). There were some vegetables, honey, and imported oranges.[55] The Jews of Marseilles controlled most of the Levant trade while Christian pirates enjoyed a safe haven in the port of Marseilles. The mysterious plunder of Ibiza in August 1536 was revelatory in what was taken: the raiders carried off several sides of salt pork, a delight for the French pirates but forbidden to Muslim corsairs. The Christian pirates of Malta were considered too far away to have been the culprits.

For all her power, Marseilles was still at the mercy of the food supply. In 1584, Marseilles, with forty-five thousand people, was consuming fifteen hundred tons of meat including fresh beef, pork, charcuterie, veal, lamb, and horses per year.[56] By 1588, she was making appeals to Spain and requests to Oran and Sicily for grain to feed her increasingly hungry population.

When we speak of Sicily or southern Italy in this period, it often means Naples, to which everyone, rich or poor, flocked. Genoese merchants found Naples a good place to do business and gave their name to a famous Neapolitan macaroni dish, *la genovesa*.

La Genovesa (Campania)

BRAISED VEAL SHOULDER IN *RAGÙ* WITH MACARONI

In the fifteenth century, Genoese merchants found Naples a rich place to do business. They have even given their name to a famous Neapolitan macaroni dish called la genovesa. *This dish has nothing to do with Genoa, where the preparation is not known, but is traced to Genoese merchants in the second half of the fifteenth century when the city was under Aragonese rule. It is made with macaroni, beef or veal, prosciutto or pancetta, lots of onions, celery, carrot, marjoram, lard, Parmigiano-Reggiano cheese, and wine.*[57]

One 2-pound veal shoulder roast
2 ounces pancetta, cut into strips
Salt to taste
2 tablespoons pork lard
3/4 cup (1 1/2 sticks) unsalted butter
1/4 cup extra virgin olive oil

1 ripe tomato (about ½ pound), peeled, seeded, and chopped
¾ pound onions, chopped
1 carrot, chopped
1 celery stalk, chopped
1 handful fresh basil leaves, chopped
Freshly ground black pepper to taste
2 cups beef or veal broth (page 54) or water
1 cup dry white wine
1 pound macaroni or *maccharoncelli*
½ cup freshly grated Parmigiano-Reggiano cheese

1. Lard the veal roast with strips of pancetta using a larding needle or making holes with a thick skewer and stuffing them in. Season with salt. Tie the veal roast into a regular shape with some kitchen twine.

2. In a casserole, melt the pork lard, butter, and olive oil over high heat, then brown the veal on all sides, 3 to 4 minutes. Add the tomato, onions, carrot, celery, basil, and season with salt and pepper. Cook until the liquid is reduced some and the onions are soft, about 8 minutes. Pour in the broth and reduce the heat to medium-low, cover, and cook until the veal is firm, about 1 hour. Pour in the wine and cook, covered, until very tender, about another 1½ hours. Remove the veal to a platter, turn the heat to high and reduce the sauce by a quarter, about 15 minutes.

3. Pass the sauce through a food mill and return the veal to the sauce to moisten and heat for 10 minutes. Remove the veal, cut off the twine, and slice into serving portions.

4. Meanwhile, bring a large pot of abundantly salted water to a vigorous boil and add the pasta. Cook until al dente and drain well. Transfer the pasta to the sauce and mix well with the Parmigiano-Reggiano cheese. Serve the pasta as a first course with some of the sauce and the veal as a second course.

Makes 6 servings

TRADITIONALLY, meat did not play a great role in this dish nor in other Neapolitan dishes whose roots are traced to this era. But once meat consumption increased as the population became better off, especially in the twentieth century, these basic recipes began to include copious amounts of meats—for example, the following one.

Sugo di Umido di Maiale (Campania)

RICH PORK STEW SAUCE

This rich sauce is typical of Naples and is used to sauce various lasagne, macaroni dishes, and timpani *(timbales).*[58] *The finished sauce will contain a substantial amount of fat, traditionally a prized source of calories for the poorer population. In this recipe I call for the removal of the fat, which is essential in the flavoring but not in the taste of the final product. Traditionally, the lasagne is eaten as a first course with the pork served as a second course with the remaining sauce.*

1 pound homemade *salsiccia fresca* (page 70) or mild Italian sausage, punctured with a toothpick or corn cob holders in several places
¼ cup *'nzugna* (freshly rendered pork fat; see box, page 281) or pork lard
1 small onion, finely chopped
1 carrot, finely chopped
½ celery stalk, finely chopped
2 garlic cloves, finely chopped
2 tablespoons finely chopped fresh parsley leaves
1 tablespoon unsalted butter
2 ounces mushrooms, cleaned and finely chopped
2 pounds boneless pork shoulder or loin chop, in one piece
¼ pound chicken livers, trimmed membranes and finely chopped

Salt to taste
½ teaspoon red pepper flakes
1 cup dry white wine
3 pounds ripe tomatoes, peeled, seeded, and chopped
1 quart water

1. Prepare the sausage if making homemade. Prepare the *'nzugna.*

2. In a large casserole, melt 1 tablespoon of the *'nzugna* or lard over medium heat, then brown the sausages, about 12 minutes. Remove with a slotted ladle and set aside.

3. In the same casserole, melt the remaining 3 tablespoons *'nzugna* or lard along with the fat from the sausages over medium heat, then cook the onion, carrot, celery, garlic, and parsley until they turn color, about 4 minutes, stirring frequently. Add the butter and mushrooms and cook until the butter melts. Add the pork shoulder or loin chop and chicken livers, mix well, and sprinkle with salt and red pepper flakes. Brown the pork and livers on all sides, about 10 minutes, turning occasionally.

4. Pour in the wine and reduce until evaporated. Add the tomatoes, water, and the reserved sausages, mix well, and bring to a boil. Reduce the heat to low and cook, uncovered, until the mixture is dense, 3 to 4 hours. Add water if the sauce gets too thick and stir occasionally to keep it from sticking.

5. Remove the meat from the casserole, keep warm, and serve as a second course with some of the sauce if desired. Pour the sauce through a strainer.

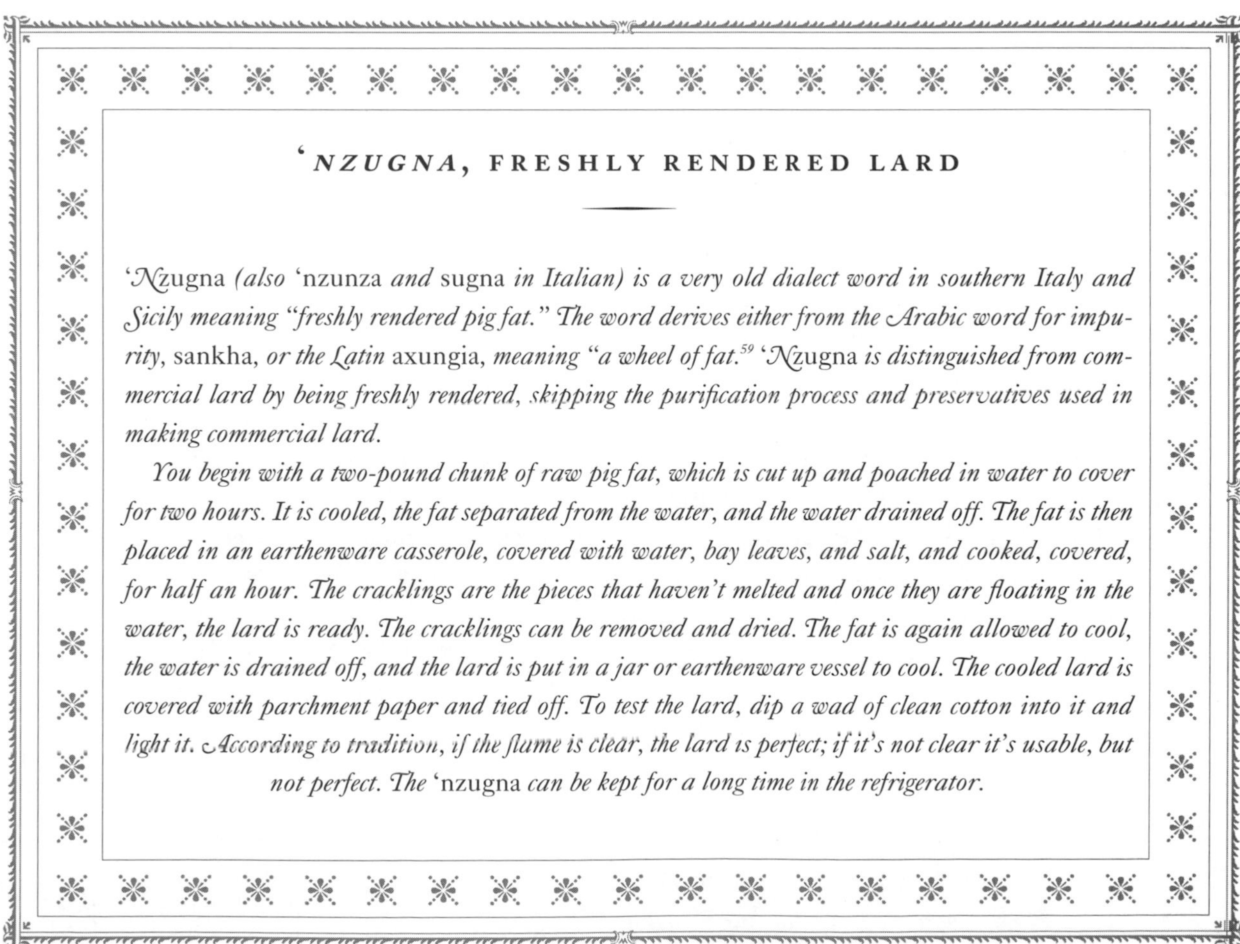

'NZUGNA, FRESHLY RENDERED LARD

'Nzugna *(also* 'nzunza *and* sugna *in Italian) is a very old dialect word in southern Italy and Sicily meaning "freshly rendered pig fat." The word derives either from the Arabic word for impurity,* sankha, *or the Latin* axungia, *meaning "a wheel of fat.*[59] 'Nzugna *is distinguished from commercial lard by being freshly rendered, skipping the purification process and preservatives used in making commercial lard.*

You begin with a two-pound chunk of raw pig fat, which is cut up and poached in water to cover for two hours. It is cooled, the fat separated from the water, and the water drained off. The fat is then placed in an earthenware casserole, covered with water, bay leaves, and salt, and cooked, covered, for half an hour. The cracklings are the pieces that haven't melted and once they are floating in the water, the lard is ready. The cracklings can be removed and dried. The fat is again allowed to cool, the water is drained off, and the lard is put in a jar or earthenware vessel to cool. The cooled lard is covered with parchment paper and tied off. To test the lard, dip a wad of clean cotton into it and light it. According to tradition, if the flame is clear, the lard is perfect; if it's not clear it's usable, but not perfect. The 'nzugna *can be kept for a long time in the refrigerator.*

Whatever won't go through, push through a food mill. Mix all the sauce, reheat, and serve with a first course of spaghetti or sheets of lasagne, or set the sauce aside to cool down. Place in the refrigerator until the fat congeals. Once the layer of fat has formed on top, remove and discard it.

Makes 6 cups; 4 to 6 servings

✦ ✦ ✦

NEAPOLITAN food during the Renaissance consisted mostly of vegetables, and Naples was known as a city of *mangiafoglie* (leaf eaters), eating the leaves of cabbage, Swiss chard, spinach, dandelion, and others. Although this was meant to be a derogatory description, Neapolitans began to appreciate good food in the Middle Ages and, in fact, an anonymous poet of the sixteenth century wrote: *Amci miei, magnammo e po' bevimmo 'n fino ca 'nce sta 'uoglio alla lucerna! Chi sa si all'auto munno 'nce vedimmo! Chi sa si all'auto munno 'nce taverna!* (My friends, we eat and then we drink until we are alive! I wonder whether we will see ourselves in the next world! I wonder whether there is a tavern in the next world!)[60]

In the seventeenth century, bourgeois families in Naples employed professional chefs who created many new dishes, but the peasants and poorer people continued in their traditional ways, which consisted of eating lots of vegetables, such as those represented in the next two Neapolitan (Campanian) recipes.[61]

Fava con le Olive (Campania)
FRESH FAVA BEANS WITH OLIVES

The fava bean (Vicia faba L.) *has enjoyed a high reputation in Italy since the days of Pliny* (A.D. *23–79), who said that, of the legumes,* inter quae maximus honos fabae *(the highest place of honor belongs to the fava bean). The seventh-century lexicographer Isidore of Seville, following Pliny, called fava the first food of man. In the thirteenth century, the Bolognese agronomist Petrus de Crescentiis (1233?–1321) recognized the importance of fava beans and suggested they be planted from November to February.*[62]

Because fava beans were often used as fodder, as in Egypt, it was always considered the food of the poor in Italy. This labor-intensive recipe is best prepared imagining the traditional Campanian massaia, *housewife, sitting around the table with her mother, daughters, daughters-in-law, or neighbors chatting about events of the day while painstakingly peeling the fava. The reward is not only a delicious and very beautiful dish but the spirit of community and family fostered by sharing experiences over food preparation.*

4 pounds fresh fava beans in their pods
20 imported black Gaeta olives
Estate-bottled extra virgin olive oil
Salt and freshly ground black pepper to taste

1. Shell the beans and set aside in a bowl until needed.

2. Bring a pot of lightly salted water to a rolling boil and blanch the fava beans until the peels can be pinched off, about 6 minutes. Drain.

3. There is also a thin, light green peel covering the fava bean that must be removed in this preparation. It

pops right off by pinching and squeezing the cooked fava bean. Place all the peeled fava beans on a platter, sprinkle the olives around, drizzle with olive oil, and sprinkle with salt and pepper. Serve at room temperature.

Makes 4 servings

Finocchio alla Besciamella (Campania)

FENNEL WITH BÉCHAMEL SAUCE

The use of béchamel in Neapolitan cooking is more prominent than one would think, perhaps introduced by the French-influenced chefs of aristocratic and bourgeois families beginning in the seventeenth century. The traditional history of béchamel sauce traces its invention to the steward of Louis XIV's court, a Louis de Béchameil. The often unreliable Waverly Root reports that the town of Cesana in Emilia-Romagna claims the sauce as its own, invented in the fourteenth century. Whatever the true history of the sauce, the first written Italian recipe with this name appears in Francesco Leonardi's L'Apicio moderno *published in 1790, where it seems to be a sauce used in different forms for stuffing purposes. In the end the best claim for the invention of béchamel sauce might lie with the ancient Greeks, for we have the Alexandrian writer of scurrilous verse, Sopater of Paphos (c. 300* B.C.*), describing a "white sauce" that covers a stew of sow's miscarried matrix.*[63] *They ate differently then.*

Salt to taste
2 fennel bulbs (about 2 pounds), hard stem and fronds removed and bulbs quartered
3 tablespoons unsalted butter
3 tablespoons all-purpose flour
1½ cups hot milk
Freshly ground white pepper to taste
Pinch of freshly grated nutmeg
½ cup freshly grated Parmigiano-Reggiano cheese or diced fresh *fior de latte* or mozzarella cheese (optional)

1. Bring a pot of salted water to a boil and cook the fennel bulbs until easily pierced by a skewer, 10 to 12 minutes. Drain well.

2. Make the béchamel sauce. In a medium-size saucepan, melt 2 tablespoons of the butter, then stir in the flour to form a roux, cooking for 1 minute over medium heat. Remove the saucepan from the heat and whisk in the milk a little at a time until it is all blended. Sprinkle with salt and white pepper and the nutmeg. Return to the heat and cook, stirring almost constantly, until thick, 6 to 7 minutes. Remove from the heat and stir in the cheese if using, reserving 3 tablespoons of grated or diced cheese.

3. Preheat the oven to 375°F. Arrange the drained fennel in a baking dish and cover with the béchamel. Sprinkle with the remaining cheese and dot with slivers of the remaining tablespoon butter. Bake until the top of the béchamel is slightly browning, about 45 minutes. Serve immediately.

Makes 4 to 6 servings

Peperoni alla Napoletana (Campania)

NEAPOLITAN-STYLE BAKED PEPPERS

Bell pepper, paprika (a blend of several highly colored, mild red peppers), cayenne pepper, jalapeño, and serrano peppers are all varieties of a single species, Capsicum annuum. *They are a New World vegetable first described by a European, Diego Alvarez Chanca, a physician to the fleet in 1494 after Columbus's second voyage. These first peppers encountered by Europeans must have been hot because their piquancy is noted in the early descriptions. The chronicle of Gonzalo Fernández de Orviedo y Valdés (1478–1537),* Historia general y natural de las Indias *(General and natural history of the Indies), published in 1526, informs us that the pepper was brought to Italy by the Spanish some years before that date, very probably to Naples from where this recipe originates.*[64]

The colorful peppers are grilled first and then tossed with aromatic ingredients before being coated with fresh bread crumbs for a gratinate *finish. This is a splendid preparation for bell peppers and is most enjoyable served at room temperature.*

4 yellow bell peppers
4 red bell peppers
3 tablespoons capers, rinsed and chopped if large
3 tablespoons chopped imported black olives
8 salted anchovy fillets, rinsed and chopped
3 tablespoons pine nuts
Salt to taste
3/4 cup extra virgin olive oil
1 1/2 cups fresh bread crumbs

1. Prepare a charcoal fire or preheat a gas grill on high for 15 minutes. Grill the peppers until their skins blister black on all sides, about 40 minutes. When cool enough to handle, peel, core, seed, rinse, and quarter the peppers. Drain for a few hours or damp-dry with paper towels.

2. In a large bowl, toss the peppers with the capers, olives, anchovies, and pine nuts and season with salt.

3. Preheat the oven to 425°F. Lightly oil an 8- or 9-inch-square baking pan with 1 tablespoon of the olive oil and fill with the pepper mixture, pushing down to make sure it is compact. Sprinkle the bread crumbs over the peppers and lightly drizzle them with the remaining olive oil. Bake until the top is golden, about 35 minutes. Serve warm or at room temperature.

Makes 4 to 6 servings

Frienno e Magnanno (Campania)

GRAND NEAPOLITAN MIXED FRY

Life was always hard in Naples, but it was Spanish rule that created the poverty still evident today. In 1585, large-scale exports of grain from Naples to Spain had caused domestic famine. The Neapolitans were forced to eat bread di castagne e legumi *(made with chestnuts and pulses). One of the merchants hoarding grain, Giovanni Vicenzo Storaci, was challenged by an angry crowd who said they would not eat such bread. He unwisely replied* mangiate pietre *(eat stones); the crowd murdered him and dragged his mutilated body around the city.*[65]

The Neapolitans are passionate about food. The foods might be simple, but are evocative and vibrant, as in this frienno e magnanno, *which means "fry and eat" in Campanian dialect and is typically served for special occasions. The fry usually consists of several different ingredients deep-fried in a combination of olive oil and* 'nzugna *(page 281), unadulterated freshly rendered pork lard. I like a mixed fry to consist of small fish such as smelts, sardines, anchovies, or other small fish, called* cecenielli *in Neapolitan dialect. You can often find these small fish sold seasonally at ethnic fish stores, especially those catering to a Greek, Italian, or international clientele. I have also had luck finding them in the freezer section of my supermarket occasionally, usually imported from Peru.*

But you don't have to fry fish—try mixed offal, such

as veal liver, sweetbreads, and brain, all breaded and fried. You can also try cubed pieces of breaded mozzarella; or make a bread crumb–coated fritter of hard-boiled egg yolks dipped into a very thick béchamel sauce and fried whole; potato-and-ricotta croquettes; rice croquettes; breaded cauliflower florets; artichoke hearts; zucchini or batter-coated zucchini flowers; or fried béchamel croquettes (extremely thick white sauce dropped in hot oil).

In this recipe I use three different foods, but you can easily use more if you have the time, patience, and energy to prepare these suggestions.

ITALIAN COOKING TECHNIQUES

One occasionally hears mention of the following terms in Italian cooking—battuto, soffritto, trito, crudo, *al dente, and* insaporire. *What do they mean?*

Battuto, *which is often used in the same sense as* soffritto, *means "beaten." A* battuto *is usually a very finely chopped mixture of salt pork, pork fat, or pancetta along with garlic and onions. It can also contain celery, carrots, hot or sweet peppers, and other ingredients as long as they are all very finely chopped. The mixture, because it so finely chopped, almost looks like it's beaten together. Once it is sautéed with some olive oil, it becomes a* soffritto.

A soffritto *at its most basic is a sauté of finely chopped onions in olive oil. Although most dictionaries translate* soffritto *as "sauté," it really means to fry very gently, to underfry (*sotto friggere*). A* soffritto *is often the beginning point of a sauce or more involved dish. A more complex* soffritto *would also sauté finely chopped garlic, celery, and herbs, usually parsley, in the olive oil. As the onions begin to turn yellow, tomatoes or whatever else the dish requires, such as meat or vegetables, are added. The* soffritto *concept also exists in Catalan cooking, where* sofregit *means the same thing.*

A trito *is the same as a* battuto *except that it usually doesn't contain pork; it's very finely chopped vegetables, usually including some combination of onions, celery, garlic, carrot, and parsley. The concept also exists in French cooking, where it is called* mirepoix.

Crudo *can refer to a* mirepoix *of vegetables and herbs or other ingredients that are added uncooked to a dish or sauce, and then cooked. It can also be a* mirepoix *of herbs and vegetables, or any combination of these, that is put directly on or mixed with cooked food—for example, tossed with freshly cooked pasta.*

Al dente *is a term used in reference to pasta cooking. It means "to the teeth," saying that the pasta should have a slight bite to it, still offer a bit of resistance, after cooking.*

Insaporire *means "to enhance the flavor." One would do this with an* insaporiti, *a mixture typically consisting of olive oil or butter perhaps flavored with onion, garlic, and parsley added during or after the cooking.*

3 Yukon Gold potatoes
1 cup fresh ricotta cheese, preferably homemade (page 467)
2 large eggs
Salt to taste
All-purpose flour for dredging
Dry bread crumbs for dredging
6 cups pure or virgin olive oil, olive pomace, or vegetable oil for deep-frying
1½ pounds small fish
1½ pounds squid with tentacles, cleaned (page 448) and bodies cut into rings
Lemon wedges for garnish

1. Place the potatoes in a large saucepan covered with cold water. Bring to a gentle boil, 20 to 25 minutes, and cook until the potatoes are easily pierced by the tip of a skewer, about another 20 minutes. Drain, peel, and push through a food mill. Push the ricotta through the mill, too. Stir in 1 beaten egg and season with salt. Form the mixture into walnut-size balls and dredge in the flour, tapping off any excess, then dip into a bowl containing the other beaten egg. Dredge evenly in the bread crumbs and set aside in the refrigerator while you continue working.

2. Preheat the frying oil in a deep-fryer or an 8-inch saucepan fitted with a basket insert to 375°F. Deep-fry the small fish in batches until golden, about 4 minutes. Drain on paper towels, salt, and keep warm in the oven. Deep-fry the squid until golden and crispy, about 4 minutes. Drain, salt, and keep warm in the oven. Deep-fry the potato-ricotta croquettes in batches until golden brown, 3 to 4½ minutes (depending on the size). Drain, salt, and serve with the remaining food and some wedges of lemon. Let the frying oil cool completely, strain, and save for a future use.

Makes 4 servings

VALENCIA, on Spain's Mediterranean coast in the province of the same name, was a great city surrounded by gardens. Certainly this was recognized in the anonymous picaresque story of the stingy priest who gave Lazarillo a key to a cupboard, as if "the key could open the storehouse of all the fruit and vegetables in Valencia," even though the only thing in it is some onions.[66] Valencia produced a significant amount of rice, which accounts for the excellence of rice preparations in the region. It was also an importer of grain from Egypt. Valencia was reclaimed in 1238 during the Christian Reconquest, but its culinary culture was forever branded by Muslim sensibilities and tastes. The expulsion of the Muslims hurt Valencia to a great extent. As the Archbishop of Valencia put it, "Who will make our shoes?" while the lords of the *lugares de moriscos* (Muslim hamlets) thought, "Who will farm our land?"

All i Pebre (Valencia)

GARLIC AND PEPPER

The name hardly conveys the seriousness of this famous specialty of the Albufera lagoon south of Valencia. Nearly every restaurant in the area proclaims its expertise in the preparation of all i pebre. *I first ate* all i pebre *at the Port restaurant in La Palmar, a dead-end town on the lone road that leads through the rice paddies of the Albufera (from the Arabic diminutive of "sea"), the great* huerta *lagoon of Valencia. La Palmar is a town that takes its* all i pebre, *paella, and* arròs a banda *(page 425) seriously. There are countless restaurants specializing in these Valencian preparations and little else.*

All i pebre *is always served some time between eleven in the morning and the early afternoon but*

LA COCINA LEVANTINA

La Cocina levantina, *the cuisine of Valencia, is truly a cuisine of rice, and its most famous preparation is* la paella. *The earliest mention of a dish resembling a paella is a preparation from Somalia cited by the famed fourteenth-century Muslim traveler Ibn Baṭṭūta, called* kūshān, *a dish made with rice, chicken, meat, fish, and vegetables. But the Spanish paella is a rice dish containing various ingredients cooked in a pan called a* paella, *a word derived from the Latin for "pan." Paella is not a seafood or meat preparation but a rice preparation, and an authentic paella, say the purists, does not combine meat with seafood. The ingredients used in a paella are variable, open to discussion and argument. But without argument is the claim that Valencia is the mecca of paella cookery. It is cooked in a flat, low-sided pan with two handles. It is traditionally cooked over an outdoor wood fire or at least a gas-fired grill. It also seems traditional for men to cook paella, not women. Paella pans come in many sizes, depending on the number of people to be served—from eleven inches in diameter for two people to three feet for ten people. Specialty paella pans exist, mostly for restaurant and catering use, that measure up to thirteen feet in diameter.*

The cooking of paella is a source of great debate and pride. My first memory of an authentic paella valenciana *was in a modest workingman's cafeteria in Valencia. There were three 4-foot-diameter paella pans from which a counter man served. A plate arrived piled high with rice, brilliant yellow with saffron, sticky and glutinous looking, with several pieces of well-cooked chicken and pork, green bell peppers, and lupine beans stirred in, and all quite tepid. It was a very flavorful paella made with the local Calasparra rice.*

I also ordered a horchata, *a vaguely almond-tasting beverage in Valencia made from a milk, extracted from a tuber less than ½ inch in diameter, called the chufa or tiger-nut* (Cyperus esculentus); *the chufa is cultivated in only one area of Valencia, though it is also known in the Maghrib.*[67]

before the mid-day meal, which may begin as early as two. I was surprised to see it served at this time of day, but after eating all i pebre *I understood why. It is so rich that to eat it late at night, the usual Spanish dining time, one would not have time to digest before sleeping. The star ingredient of this dish is the common eel that comes directly from the lagoon and its canals. The eel is cut up and served with a sauce enriched by tomatoes and sweet red peppers, heavy with garlic and olive oil. It is a messy dish and best eaten with a fork, a spoon, and lots of bread.* All i pebre *also makes an excellent tapas-size serving.*

If you are not able to find eel, ocean pout (ling) is almost identical in texture and very close in taste. Monkfish will be identical in texture but not in taste, and mackerel fillets or pieces of sand dab, striped bass, mahimahi, kingfish, or Spanish mackerel would also be very fine substitutes.

3/4 cup extra virgin olive oil
4 fresh or dried red chili peppers
4 garlic cloves, finely chopped
2 red bell peppers, seeded and cut into thin strips 1 inch long
1 cup water
1 tablespoon tomato paste
Salt to taste
1 pound common eel, skinned and cut into 1-inch pieces
Freshly ground black pepper to taste

1. In a large skillet or casserole, heat the olive oil over medium heat. Add the chili peppers and garlic and cook for 1 minute, shaking the skillet constantly so the garlic doesn't burn. Add the bell peppers, water, and tomato paste, and season with salt. Cook until a nice sauce forms, 25 to 30 minutes, stirring occasionally.

2. Add the eel or other fish and cook until it can easily be cut with a fork, about 30 minutes, stirring frequently. The red peppers will dissolve and the skillet will look oily. This is the way it should look. Season with black pepper and serve with bread and beer or red wine.

Makes 4 to 6 tapas servings or serves 2 to 4 as a main dish

Arròs i Fesols i Naps (Valencia)

VALENCIAN RICE WITH WHITE BEANS AND TURNIPS

La Palmar is a small town at the end of a long road in the Albufera, the great huerta *lagoon of Valencia. Surrounded by rice paddies, with orange groves in the distance, and bisected by canals, the town seems to be nothing but eating establishments serving* all i pebre, *paella, and* arròs a banda *(page 425). Several restaurants also serve the rustic* arròs i fesols i naps—fesols i naps *(beans and turnips) for short—and proudly announce that fact on their billboards. It is cooked with* judias *or* fesols*—that is, small dried white beans. Sometimes* pebreras torrades, *a dish of roasted green and red peppers covered with sardines fried in olive oil, is served before or after a heavy* fesols i naps.

This dish was the subject of a poem by the Valencian poet Teodoro Llorente, who found it worthy of waxing poetical and you might, too.

1/2 pound dried small white beans (about 1 cup), picked over
3 quarts cold water
One 3/4-pound piece boneless beef chuck
1 pig's foot
2 pig's ears
1/2 pound Canadian or Irish bacon in one piece, diced
3/4 pound veal sausage (see page 71 for homemade sausage, replacing the pork with veal) or store-bought turkey or chicken sausage
6 turnips (about 2 pounds), peeled and cut up
1 1/2 cups raw short- or medium-grain rice
Salt to taste

1. In a large earthenware casserole such as a Spanish *cazuela* (see "Mediterranean Food Products Resources") or stew pot, place the white beans, water, beef, pig's foot and ears, bacon, sausage, and turnips. Bring the water to a boil, reduce the heat to low, cover, and cook until the beans are tender and the meat breaks apart, about 3 hours, occasionally skimming any foam from the surface.

2. Add the rice and some salt and cook until the rice is to your taste, about 20 minutes. Serve in a large platter. Discard the pig's foot and ears, cut all the meat up, and serve on top of the rice and beans.

Makes 8 servings

✣ ✣ ✣

SEVILLE, along with Genoa, Leghorn (Livorno), Venice, Ancona, and Naples, was one of the great commercial centers of the Mediterranean in the sixteenth century. The riches of America flowed to Seville exclusively because it was in direct line of the trade winds and had a legal monopoly on that trade. The soil was productive and olives and vines prospered in lower Andalusia during the sixteenth century. At that time, half the population of Andalusia were still Muslim. As Seville and Andalusia prospered, they looked outward. Venetian ambassadors regularly described Andalusia as a splendid land. Wheat was the leading product of trade in Andalusia; nevertheless, Seville was often short of grain, while neighboring towns Puerto de Santa María, Jerez de la Frontera, and Málaga had abundant food. One solution to the crisis of Seville's food supply was a product from the New World, the potato, although it didn't become fully integrated into Spanish cooking until the mid-seventeenth century, where it is represented in Bartolomé Estéban Murillo's (1617?–1682) painting showing the poor of Seville eating potatoes, the food of the humble, from a cauldron.

The sources for the feeding of Seville, as with all Mediterranean cities, were confined to the territory within carting distance of Seville. Fish came from Cádiz and other nearby villages on the coast. Pork came from Ronda, Aracena, and other towns on the fringes of the Sierra Nevada and Sierra Morena. Rice was from Valenica and raisins came from Almería. Wheat came from local farms, and a little from France and North Africa, and some cheese was later imported from Germany, Flanders, and the Canaries. At the beginning of the seventeenth century, there was a decline in Andalusian agriculture, and provisioning shifted from domestic to imported. By 1617, salt pork came from Ireland and salt beef from Flanders.[68]

By the mid-sixteenth century, the Genoese controlled the American trade and exerted a powerful influence over the economic life of Seville because of their superior understanding of the mechanisms of finance and their access to capital (see page 147). Society in Seville was changing from a medieval one where the nobility defined its virtues in terms of valor, to one where profit making motivated a new class of people looking to acquire luxury items and live well.[69] The population of Seville was ninety thousand in 1594; it was the largest city in Spain. The Guadalquivir River was the mainspring of Seville's economic life, bringing the fabulous riches of the Indies to the city.[70]

EXPULSION

✣

SOON the very nature of Seville and Valencia and all of Spain—town and country—would forever be changed. The Lérida plain was still being worked by *fallāḥīn* in the sixteenth century, as was the Rioja in the Ebro Valley. The *fallāḥīn* were the peasant farmers who were originally Muslim but converted to Christianity. These were the Moriscos, the name given to the descendents of the converted Muslims. The *fallāḥīn*, like the Lombard rice workers, were very poor (see page 587). In the Mediterranean, the rich were very rich and the poor, very poor. You can see this today in Morocco, where the very rich own vast tracts of olive and argan trees.[71]

In the end, even the Moriscos were driven out of Spain in the final great expulsion of 1609–1614. In 1609, the Moriscos accounted for one-third of the total population of Valencia. Although they controlled Valencia's fertile *huertas* (large vegetable gardens), without an aristocracy to lead them there was no organized resistance to their oppression. There were occasional revolts, such as one on Christmas night in Granada in 1568, but the decision to eradicate any Muslim presence in Spain had already been made by Philip II. Muslim costumes were forbidden, speaking Arabic was forbidden, women were forbidden to wear the veil, and all traces of Muslim civilization were banished. By 1614, three hundred thousand Moriscos had been expelled out of an overall population of eight million. They were expelled because they never assimilated and they were hated for it. But hatred could not wipe out the thousands of Arabic words and place names in Spain, the black eyes of the Andalusians, nor the rich, evocative cuisine that conveys the taste of the celestial paradise of the *dar al-Islam* (house of peace), as the next three recipes demonstrate.

Alboronía (Andalusia)

AN ARAB-ANDALUSI VEGETABLE RAGOUT

There are two opposing theories as to the origin of this famous vegetable preparation from Andalusia. Either the Spanish name derives from the Arabic al-būrāniyya, *meaning "the dish of Būrān," the wife of the Abbasid caliph al-Ma'mūn (786–833), son of Hārūn al-Rashīd; or the Arabic name derives from the Spanish name* alboronía, *a dish made of eggplant, gourd, tomatoes, and peppers, or another dish called* beraniya, *made of lamb breast, butter, eggs, cardoons, grated cheese, and lots of spices.*[72] *I believe the first explanation is the more likely one.*

In the anonymous thirteenth-century Hispano-Muslim cookbook of the Almohad dynasty, there is a recipe for a fish and eggplant būrāniyya *made with spices. The attribution to Būrān of various recipes appears in a number of other medieval culinary texts. The late eleventh-century* Kitāb faḍālat al-khiwān fī ṭayyibāt al-ṭᶜam wa'l-alwān *by Ibn Razīn al-Tujībī; the thirteenth-century cookery books, the* Kitāb al-wuṣla ila l-ḥabīb fī waṣfi aṭ-ṭayyibāt wāṭ-ṭīb*; and the Baghdad cookery book* Kitāb waṣf al-atᶜima al-muᶜtāda *(or* Kitāb al-ṭabikh)*; and the sixteenth-century* Kitāb al-ṭibaḥa *all have forms of* būrāniyya.

The būrāniyya *in the Baghdad cookery book is a meat plate seasoned with salt, coriander, cinnamon, onions, cumin, black pepper, and mastic. The meat is formed into balls and cooked with fried eggplant and onions in sesame oil or other fat. On top of the dish is sprinkled* almorí *(a kind of condiment; page 530), saffron, dried coriander leaves, rose water, and cinnamon. Also in the Baghdad cookery book there is a* būrāniyya *of calabash (an Old World squash also called bottle gourd,* Lagenaria siceraria *(Mol.) Standl.), which follows the same preparation. In medieval Damascus,* būrānī *was made with Swiss chard. If there is one common thread in all these dishes and theories, though, it is the eggplant.*[73]

This dish is a hortalizas *(page 16), and similar to what we know today as a ratatouille, but I don't feel that it stands on its own. Accompany it with a salt cod, rabbit, or a chicken recipe, although it may be best with* albóndigas a la Andaluza *(page 141).*

1 large eggplant (about 2 pounds), peeled and cut into small dice
Salt
1/2 cup extra virgin olive oil
1 pound onions, chopped
4 green bell peppers (about 2 pounds), seeded and chopped
2 zucchini (about 1 pound), peeled and cut into small dice
1 1/4 pounds ripe tomatoes, peeled, seeded, and chopped
2 1/2 tablespoons paprika

1. Lay the eggplant pieces on some paper towels and sprinkle with salt. Leave them to drain of their bitter juices for 30 minutes, then pat dry with more paper towels.

2. In a large casserole, heat the olive oil over medium heat, then cook the onions until translucent,

about 12 minutes, stirring occasionally. Add the eggplant, the peppers, and zucchini and continue cooking over medium heat, stirring occasionally, for another 20 minutes. Add the tomatoes, cover, and cook for 30 minutes, stirring every once in a while. Sprinkle in the paprika and 1 tablespoon salt and cook another 15 minutes. Serve a little warmer than room temperature, not hot.

Makes 6 servings

Berenjenas con Queso (Andalusia)

EGGPLANT WITH CHEESE

Berenjenas con queso *is another famous eggplant preparation with roots in the thirteenth century, mentioned in the* Kitāb faḍālat al-khiwān fī ṭayyibāt al-ṭʿam wa'l-alwān *by Ibn Razīn al-Tujībī and the cento dealing with Hispanic-Maghribi cooking of that time. Lourdes March, a Spanish culinary authority, cites later evidence of the popularity of this dish by quoting the writer and sailor Baltasar de Alcázar, who praised the dish in the sixteenth century: "Three things have my heart imprisoned, the beautiful lady Inés, ham, and eggplant with cheese."*[74] *The sixteenth-century chef Ruperto de Nola, in his* Libre del coch, *called the dish "Moorish eggplant" and his original recipe reads:*

> Hull the eggplants and cut into four quarters; cut off the peel and put them on to cook; when they are well cooked, take them off the stove, and then press them between two wooden blocks to get rid of all water, then chop them up with a knife, and put them into a pot and fry them very well with good bacon fat or with oil which is sweet, because the Moors do not eat bacon, and when they are well fried, cook them in a pot with good thick broth; and the meat fat, and finely grated cheese, and ground coriander with everything, and then stir them as if they were squash, and when they are almost cooked, put the yolks of beaten eggs to them, as if they were squash.[75]

The squash mentioned in this translation is undoubtedly the Old World gourd and not a *Cucurbita* squash of the New World.[76]

This recipe is similar to the *polpette di melanzane* of the Sicilians, which appears to be an Aragonese elaboration of an Arab concept.[77] If you are unable to find the Spanish cheese I call for after looking at "Mediterranean Food Products Resources," use a pecorino cheese.

2½ pounds eggplant, peeled and chopped
Salt
1 tablespoon extra virgin olive oil
1 medium-size onion, finely chopped
1 teaspoon dried mint
1 large hard-boiled egg, shelled and chopped
½ cup dried bread crumbs
¼ pound Spanish sheep's milk cheese, such as Manchego or Idiazábal, or Spanish goat cheese such as Ibores, grated
Salt and freshly ground black pepper to taste
⅛ teaspoon ground cloves
⅛ teaspoon ground cinnamon
Pinch of freshly grated nutmeg
1 teaspoon sugar
6 cups pure or virgin olive or olive pomace oil for deep-frying
1 cup all-purpose flour
2 large eggs, beaten
Freshly ground cumin seeds for sprinkling

1. Boil the eggplant in salted water to cover for 10 minutes. Drain very well, pressing out all liquid, otherwise you will be unable to form the eggplant into patties in the next step. Process the eggplant in a food processor until smooth. Transfer to a fine-mesh strainer and leave to drain for another 45 min-

utes or more if it still looks liquidy. Transfer to a large bowl.

2. In a small skillet, heat the oil over medium-high heat, then cook the onion until yellow, 3 to 4 minutes, stirring. Add the onion to the eggplant and mix well. Add the mint, hard-boiled egg, bread crumbs, and cheese and mix again. Season with salt, pepper, cloves, cinnamon, nutmeg, and sugar and mix well. Form the mixture into patties about 2½ inches in diameter.

3. Preheat the frying oil in a deep-fryer or an 8-inch saucepan fitted with a basket insert to 360°F. Dredge the eggplant patties in the flour, tapping off any excess, then dip into the beaten eggs and dredge again in the flour. Deep-fry the eggplant patties in batches until golden, 7 to 8 minutes. Drain of excess oil on paper towels and serve lukewarm with a sprinkle of cumin. Let the frying oil cool completely, strain, and save for a future use.

Makes 6 tapas servings

Calabacines Rellenos al Estilo de Andalucía (Andalusia)

ANDALUSIAN-STYLE STUFFED ZUCCHINI

Muslim civilization has left its traces in Andalusian cities. In Córdoba, the Mezquita, the city's most noteworthy building, is today a cathedral but was originally constructed in the eighth to tenth centuries as Europe's largest and most beautiful mosque. Once Córdoba fell to the Reconquest in 1236, the capital of the Arab dominions moved to Granada, founded in the eighth century by the Arabs. The palace of the caliphs, the Alhambra, remains as the most important vestige of Granada's splendid Muslim era. Seville also has many landmarks from the Muslim era—for example, the Alcazar, a royal palace built by the Arabs in 1181. Traces of early Arab civilization are seen in its small and winding streets as well as squat white houses, courtyards with fountains, and the remains of a wall that once surrounded the city.

In Andalusia, the centuries-long influence of the Arabs is still apparent in the cuisine as much as in the architecture, even in dishes like this stuffed squash that had to await the discovery of the Americas years after Muslim rule. It is worth your while having a corer on hand to hollow out the zucchini without breaking their sides. Middle Eastern markets sell very useful tools for hollowing out vegetables, such as a naqqāra *(in Arabic) used for zucchini. Otherwise, use a long-handled iced tea spoon.*

This stuffed squash dish from Andalusia is a delicious balance for the richness of a dish like cabrito en ajo caballín *(page 143) and is especially popular in Seville.*

4 large eggs
1 cup chicken broth (page 54)
4 medium-size zucchini or yellow summer squash (about 2 pounds)
2 medium-size onions, finely chopped
1 cup extra virgin olive oil
¼ pound boneless pork or veal shoulder or rump, trimmed of fat and chopped
Salt to taste
½ cup chopped imported green olives
½ cup raisins
½ cup all-purpose flour
1 cup dry white wine
2 tablespoons ground roasted almonds (page 709)

1. Hard-boil two of the eggs. Finely chop the hard-boiled eggs. Peel the zucchini and hollow them out with a corer or spoon, being very careful not to break the sides, starting from the blossom end. (Reserve the zucchini pulp to make the variation of *'ujja bi'l-bādhinjān*, page 531). Carve off the stem using a small utility knife, being careful not to break through to the

hollow part. Set ½ cup of the chopped onions to the side.

2. In a large skillet, heat 3 tablespoons of the olive oil over medium-high heat, then cook half the remaining onions until translucent, about 6 minutes, stirring frequently. Add the chopped pork or veal and season with salt. Mix well and cook for 2 minutes, stirring. Remove the skillet from the heat, stir in the olives and the raisins, then stir in the chopped hard-boiled eggs. Stuff the zucchini with this mixture, tamping it down slightly. Cover the zucchini with a tablespoon each of the reserved chopped onions. Set aside while you make the sauce.

3. Return the skillet to the burner and heat another 3 tablespoons of the olive oil over medium-high heat, then cook the remaining onions until translucent, about 6 minutes, stirring frequently. Add 1 tablespoon of the flour and stir it into the onions and oil. After about 1 minute, pour in the wine and let it reduce for 4 to 5 minutes. Pour in the chicken broth and let it reduce for 7 minutes, keeping the heat on medium-high. Remove from the heat, pour the sauce through a fine-mesh strainer or food mill, and set aside while you continue the preparation of the zucchini.

4. Again return the skillet to the burner, pour in the remaining ½ cup plus 2 tablespoons olive oil, and heat over medium heat. Break the remaining 2 eggs into a flat dinner plate and beat lightly. Spread the remaining 7 tablespoons flour on some waxed paper. Roll the zucchini in the flour, tapping off any excess, then dip in the beaten eggs and place in the skillet—it will spurt a little. Cook the zucchini for 15 minutes, turning carefully with two spoons several times so they don't stick. Pour in the reserved sauce, reduce the heat to low, and cook until a skewer glides easily into the zucchini, 15 to 20 minutes.

5. Transfer the zucchini carefully to a serving platter that can hold liquid, being careful not to break them, and cover with the sauce. Sprinkle the ground almonds on top and serve.

Makes 4 to 6 servings

THE great expulsion of Muslims and Jews from Spain saw Jews leaving for France, especially Montpellier, the Netherlands, and Germany, and for Turkey and Greece, particularly the cities of Smyrna (Izmir), Istanbul, and Salonica (Thessaloniki), where they came to be known as Sephardim. The Muslims went to Morocco, Algeria, and Tunisia, and they brought with them a rich culinary heritage that merged with an existing Berber-Arab foundation. Some of the Jews who had converted to Christianity, the Marranos, left for North African cities like Tunis, Algiers, and Fez, where their foodways showed a pronounced Hispanic influence. We don't know too much about medieval Iberian Jewish food because there are no extant Jewish cookbooks from that period. But David Gitlitz and his wife Linda Kay Davidson, both of the University of Rhode Island, in their *A Drizzle of Honey: The Lives and Recipes of Spain's Secret Jews,* have culled about ninety food references from Inquisition trial testimony. These food references, combined with extant Hispano-Muslim cookbooks, give us a better idea of how these communities ate. Although they ate very much the same foods their Christian neighbors ate, there is an emphasis on sugar and oranges, olive oil, and on vegetables. One of these Jewish foodways was a proclivity for vegetables that, in Fez in particular, caused the local Muslim population to shun them.[78] Some of the dishes brought by these people from Spain evolved into preparations found today, such as the famous pigeon pie know as *basṭīla*, the apex of Moroccan cooking.

A CULINARY HISTORY OF MOROCCO'S FAMOUS PIGEON PIE

Basṭīla *is a pigeon pie, a sumptuous, utterly rich, and magnificent preparation made for special occasions in Morocco such as holidays, weddings, or when esteemed guests arrive. The pie is surrounded by a very thin pastry leaf called* warqa *(which means "leaf"), the top of which is sprinkled with powdered sugar and a latticework of ground cinnamon.* Warqa *pastry begins as a spongy dough that is tapped or slapped against a hot convex sheet of pounded metal, a kind of pan called a* ṭubsil *set over a hot charcoal brazier, in a series of overlapping concentric circles to form a large film of pastry. This collection of leaves, now forming a whole thin sheet, is carefully but quickly peeled off the metal and set aside.* Warqa *pastry is a bit thinner than phyllo pastry, although phyllo pastry is what I use in the recipe on page 296. If you wish to make your own* warqa *pastry, excellent instructions with suggestions for alternative equipment are found in Paula Wolfert's* Couscous and Other Good Foods from Morocco *and very helpful photographs are found in Robert Carrier's* A Taste of Morocco.[79]

The name of the pigeon pie, basṭīla *or* basṭal, *comes from the Spanish word for pastry,* pastilla, *after the transformation of the phoneme "p" into "b" that is specific to the Arabic language.*[80] *D. Francisco Javier Simonet's* Glosario de voces ibéricas y latinas usadas entre los mozárabes *(Glossary of Iberian and Latin words used by the Mozarabs) tells us that* bestila [sic] *is the Mozarab* pastel *from the Latin* pastillum, *a diminuitive of* panis, *"bread."*[81] *This Mozarab* bestila *becomes the dialectal Moroccan Arabic* besthila [sic], *also meaning* "pastel."[82] *Rudolf Grewe, a researcher of Hispano-Muslim cuisine, thought that the dish called* jūdhāba *in the anonymous thirteenth-century Hispano-Muslim cookbook, a chicken pie enclosed in many paper-thin sheets of dough, was a clear antecedent of the Moroccan* basṭīla.[83]

Contemporary Moroccan cuisine is essentially an Arab and Hispano-Muslim cuisine set upon the foundation of an older and simpler Berber sustenance diet, with outside influences from sub-Saharan West Africa and colonial-era France. The Arabs arrived in Morocco soon after the death of the Prophet Muhammad and continued on into Spain by the early eighth century. The Arabs and Muslimized Berbers in Spain merged with the existing Hispano-Roman population then ruled by the Visigoths, a German military aristocracy, and they later came to be known by historians as Hispano-Muslims and by popular writers as Moors. Between 1462 and 1615, this population emigrated to Morocco and other areas of North Africa as a result of the Christian Reconquest of Spain and governmental policies that led to the Great Expulsion of 1609–1614.

Paula Wolfert suggested in her cookbook of Moroccan food that b'stila [sic] *was not a Hispano-Muslim-influenced dish because she could find no trace of the dish today in Spain, and it* seemed inconceivable to her that such a great recipe disappeared.[84] She no longer maintains this, but was led to believe it years ago based on her conversations with the leader of one of the Moroccan Berber parties who was a gastronome as well, and from her reading of Emile Laoust, a French scholar of the Berbers who taught in Rabat in the early part of this century, who described bestila [sic] as chicken cooked with saffron, which Wolfert presumed to be a Berber word describing the base stuffing for the basṭīla.[85]

Although the point is now moot, this never seemed likely to me for several reasons. First, the contemporary nonexistence of a similar pastry pie in Spain does not seem compelling. Ninety-five percent, if not more, of the dishes described in the great Italian and Spanish cookery works of the fourteenth through sixteenth centuries no longer exist. These were famous dishes of their day, yet there are no vestiges of them. Ninety percent of the black pepper and spice trade that made Mediterranean cities so fabulously rich went to northern Europe, whose cuisine today is anything but spicy.[86] So what happened? Food tastes change more frequently and rapidly than scholars of nutrition and diet have led us to believe.

On the other hand, a closer look perhaps reveals some evidence of vestigial remains of the basṭīla or pastel around the Mediterranean. Perhaps the original Spanish dish migrated to Turkey with the Jews, as suggested in Claudia Roden's description of the dish called pasteles of the Turkish Jews.[87] Patricia Smouha, the author of a Middle Eastern cookbook, also tells us of an "old Syrian dish" called pastelis [sic], which is a pie stuffed with either fried beef, onions, and pine nuts or brains.[88] In any case, we know that as late as the sixteenth century, Spain's King Philip II was still eating pastel.[89] That pastelis traveled is not in doubt. Besides the evidence of the eastern Mediterranean, pastelis eventually appeared in Puerto Rican cookery stuffed with almonds, raisins, and cornmeal.

There is other evidence of the Andalusian origins of and inspiration behind basṭīla.[90] Andalusia had a rich court life under the Spanish branch of the Umayyad dynasty (756–1031), and the Almohad (1130–1269) and Naṣrid (1230–1492) caliphates and a concomitantly rich cuisine, whereas the Berbers did not. Pre-Islamic Berber cooking in Morocco was subsistance cooking, not cuisine.

The French were making a kind of pie or cake called pastillus, a word that was transformed into gastellus, guastellus, wastellus, and gastiel—all names of different stuffed cakes that appear in texts from 1129 to 1200 in the areas of Champagne, Île-de-France, and Picardie. It was a luxury pastry made with very fine, good-quality flour, and stuffed with meat or fish and spices and fat, corresponding to the Moroccan basṭīla. The term crosses the English Channel, where the Scottish king William the Lion served wastelli dominici to Richard the Lion-Hearted. It also appears in yet a different guise in Sicily as guastedde or vastieddi, a kind of spleen calzone (page 566).[91] It still appears today in Corsica as bastella, a meat-and-vegetable-filled pie pastry.

Basṭīla (Morocco)
A GRAND MOROCCAN PIGEON PIE

Basṭīla is a huge pigeon pie traditional in Fez, and found throughout Morocco.[92] One Moroccan cookbook starts a recipe for basṭīla *by saying that one must have a* dada *come to the house to prepare it. A* dada *is a black professional woman cook from Saharan and sub-Saharan Africa employed in bourgeois and aristocratic households in Morocco to this day.*

My most memorable basṭīla *was at the huge villa of Moulay Messaouad Agouzzal outside Meknès, where our conference party of one hundred sixty people dined on magnificent Moroccan culinary treasures. Moulay Agouzzal is a gracious landowner and olive oil producer who put on an incredible feast with extraordinary modesty and great delight. After I had spent some time in the kitchen quizzing cooks about the food we were to eat, I returned to my table and was fortunate enough to be seated next to Paula Wolfert, the author of many books on Mediterranean cuisines, and who, although I nitpick with her about historical things, knows how to cook and eat* basṭīla. *Guided by her inimitable enthusiasm I learned how to eat* basṭīla *the correct way, with my fingers, and how to pay attention to the sequence of tastes and cacophony of smells.*

This recipe is re-created from my conversations with the cooks. I find the combination of fowl (my idea) to be a very close approximation of those plump and flavorful pigeons one can enjoy in North Africa. Of course, if you can find affordable, good-quality unfrozen plump pigeons (squab) in your market, then by all means use them. Before proceeding, make sure you have a 16-inch-diameter baking pan and that it fits in your oven. If you have never made basṭīla *before, allow plenty of time, read the recipe several times, and work patiently.*

5 pounds pigeons or one 5-pound free-range chicken; alternatively, try 2 Cornish hens (3 pounds total), 1 pheasant (1½ pounds), and ½ pound turkey thigh or breast
6 large garlic cloves, peeled
1 tablespoon salt
1 cup *samna* (clarified butter; page 189), melted
1 pound blanched whole almonds
1 cup confectioners' sugar, plus more for dusting
1 tablespoon plus ¼ teaspoon ground cinnamon, plus more for garnish
2 cups water
1 tablespoon orange flower water (page 720)
1 pound (4 sticks) unsalted butter
1 large onion, chopped
1 teaspoon ground ginger
½ teaspoon Moroccan spice mix (page 522)
¼ teaspoon freshly ground allspice berries
2 good-size pinches of saffron threads, pounded in a mortar with a little salt
¼ cup finely chopped fresh parsley leaves
¼ cup finely chopped fresh coriander (cilantro) leaves
Salt to taste
10 large eggs plus 2 large egg yolks
1 package (1 pound 1¼ ounce) (20 to 24 sheets) commercial phyllo pastry (usually 14 × 18-inch sheets; see page 224 for handling it)

1. If you are using chicken, pull off as much fat as possible. In a mortar, pound the garlic and salt together until mushy and rub the fowl inside and out with this paste. Set the fowl aside for 1 hour in the refrigerator.

2. In a large skillet, melt 1 tablespoon of the *samna* over medium-high heat, then cook the almonds until golden, about 8 minutes, stirring or shaking the skillet almost constantly after the first 4 minutes. Cool completely, then grind in a food processor and mix with the confectioners' sugar and 1 tablespoon of the cinnamon.

3. Put the fowl in a large casserole or stew pot with the water, orange flower water, 1 pound butter, onion, ginger, spice mix, allspice, saffron, the remaining ¼ teaspoon cinnamon, the parsley, and fresh coriander

and season with salt. Bring to a boil, reduce the heat to low, cover, and simmer until the meat is falling off the bones, about 3 hours. Remove the birds and separate the meat from the bones and set aside. Discard the bones.

4. Remove 5½ cups of the poaching liquid from the casserole or stew pot. Beat the eggs and egg yolks into 2 cups of the poaching liquid. Pour the remaining 3½ cups poaching liquid back into the casserole and reduce to a little less than 1 cup over high heat, about 8 minutes. Set aside.

5. Preheat the oven to 425°F. Grease the bottom and sides of a 16-inch round baking pan with some of the remaining *samna*. Cover the bottom of the pan with a layer of six sheets of phyllo dough, overlapping so some sheets drape over the side of the baking pan. Liberally brush the phyllo with melted *samna*. Layer another six sheets of phyllo and brush again liberally with *samna*. Fold the overlapping sheets in and bake until browned, about 5 minutes. Remove from the oven.

6. Sprinkle half the almond-and-sugar mixture over the pastry. Ladle half of the egg-and-broth mixture over the almond-sugar mixture, making sure that none runs over the edges. Arrange the reserved meat from the birds around the entire pie and spread with the glaze made of the reduced broth. Cover with the remaining egg-and-broth mixture, again making sure it does not run over the sides. Cover with the remaining almond-and-sugar mixture and cover with the remaining 12 sheets of phyllo, in two layers, brushing the layers with the remaining *samna*. Tuck the overlapping edges of phyllo into and under the pie, lifting the sides up gently. Brush the top of the pie with *samna*. Also brush the sides of pie well with *samna* where you tucked the phyllo under at the edge of the pan, using up all but 1 to 2 tablespoons of the remaining *samna*.

7. Bake until the top of the pie is golden brown, 15 to 20 minutes. Tilt the pan, spoon out any excess *samna*, and reserve. Loosen the sides of the pie with a spatula. Place a large buttered 18- to 20-inch pizza pan over the top of the baking pan and invert the pie in one quick motion. Given the size of the pie pan, this will seem like madness, but don't be intimidated—hold tight and flip quickly. Practice the movement a couple of times with an empty pie pan filled with some books and *absolutely* do not hesitate when you do it. Return the pie to the pan by sliding it in quickly from the pizza pan, brush the top with the remaining *samna*, and bake until golden brown, another 15 to 20 minutes.

8. Remove the pie to a serving platter, and let rest for 10 minutes. Dust the top with confectioners' sugar and make crisscross lines with ground cinnamon. Serve and, if eating authentically, seat your guests around the *basṭīla* and eat with your fingers.

Makes 12 servings

SUGAR AND EVERYTHING NICE

In the sixteenth century, the use of sugar was sometimes excessive in the pursuit of the good life among the rich. Naples consumed the unbelievable quantity of fifteen hundred tons of sugar every year. Syrups, preserves, and *altre cose di zucaro* (other kinds of sugary things) were major exports from Naples. In medieval Italy, a typical stuffing for ravioli consisted of chopped pork, eggs, cheese, and parsley, served with fried bacon and sprinkled with sugar. Another sweet dish was a pâté of tench (a freshwater fish) and eel mixed with dates, raisins, pine nuts, and spices.[93] Sugar is found vestigially in Italian ravioli to this day, as in the following recipe from the Abruzzi.

Ravioli all'Abruzzese (Abruzzi)

ABRUZZI-STYLE RAVIOLI WITH VEAL *RAGÙ*

The history of ravioli is quite old. Leaving aside for the moment as to whether the Central Asian mantı *can be considered a ravioli (page 330), the earliest evidence we have of ravioli in the Mediterranean is found in the statutes of the Cathedral of Nice in 1233, which report of* crosete siue rafiole, *a ravioli pie (page 151). In the anonymous fourteenth-century cookbook from the Angevin court in Naples known as the* Liber de coquina, *a ravioli recipe is made without pasta dough. It is simply a stuffing of pork belly and liver flavored with aromatic herbs, saffron, and other spices pounded in a mortar with beaten eggs and then wrapped in caul fat and fried in oil. The author instructs the cook, though, that if he likes, he can stuff thin pasta dough with this stuffing, fry it in oil or other fat, and then serve it with a sauce of honey.[94] This recipe from the Abruzzi has vestigial medieval elements, but its taste is not medieval at all; it is unctuous and robust.*

FOR THE SAUCE

1/4 cup (1/2 stick) unsalted butter
1/4 cup extra virgin olive oil
1/2 pound ground veal
1 medium-size onion, chopped
3 garlic cloves, finely chopped
2 whole cloves
Salt and freshly ground black pepper to taste
1/2 cup dry white wine
3 pounds ripe tomatoes, peeled, seeded, and chopped
1/2 teaspoon meat extract mixed with 3 tablespoons water

FOR THE PASTA DOUGH

4 cups unbleached all-purpose white flour
5 large eggs
1 tablespoon extra virgin olive oil
1 teaspoon salt
Pinch of saffron threads, crumbled

FOR THE STUFFING

3 1/2 cups fresh ricotta cheese, preferably homemade (page 467)
2 teaspoons sugar
Pinch of ground cinnamon
1 large egg
1 teaspoon water

FOR THE GARNISH

1 cup freshly grated pecorino cheese

1. In a large casserole, melt the butter with the olive oil over medium-high heat, then brown the veal, onion, garlic, and cloves, about 4 minutes, stirring frequently. Season with salt and pepper, stirring occasionally. Add the wine and let it evaporate, about 8 minutes, stirring frequently. Add the tomatoes and meat extract diluted with water. Cover, reduce the heat to low, and simmer until thick, about 4 hours, using a heat diffuser if the sauce is bubbling too vigorously.

2. Meanwhile, prepare the pasta dough. Pour the flour onto your work surface. Make a well in the middle, piling up the flour around it so that it resembles a volcanic crater. Crack the eggs into the well and sprinkle with olive oil, salt, and saffron. Incorporate the eggs with the flour by breaking the yolks with your fingers a little at a time, drawing more flour from the inside wall of the well. Make sure you don't break through the wall, otherwise the eggs might run. Scrape off any dough on your fingers and knead into the dough.

3. Once the flour and eggs are combined and you can form the dough into a ball, knead for 8 to 10 minutes. Do not add more water or egg. As you press down while kneading, use the ball to pick up any loose clumps of dough. Don't add any liquid until you've kneaded for at least 3 minutes. If the dough is too dry at this point and you must add water to help it bind, do so only by wetting your hands, as many times as you need. If the dough is too wet—meaning if there is any sign of stickiness—dust with flour. Continue kneading, pressing down with the full force of both palms, until

a smooth ball is formed. Wrap the dough in waxed paper or plastic wrap and leave for 1 hour at room temperature.

4. Unwrap the ball of dough and dust with flour. Place on a floured work surface, pressing down with your palms to flatten. With a rolling pin, roll the pasta out until it is about 12 inches in diameter and cut into thirds. Roll each third with the rolling pin until it is thin enough to fit into the widest setting of a pasta machine. Roll once at the widest setting. Close the setting one notch and roll again. Gather the sheet of pasta, fold in thirds, and roll through the roller so you have a nice rectangle.

Continue ratcheting down the setting until the dough reaches the thinnest or next to the thinnest setting. Dust the dough on both sides with flour at the slightest sign of stickiness. If necessary, continue to dust with flour as you roll through narrower and narrower settings; otherwise the dough will become hopelessly stuck together. By this time you will have a very long, thin ribbon of pliable dough that looks and even feels like a velvety chamois cloth. Cut the ribbon of pasta into lengths that will fit over a ravioli mold, if using one, always dusting with flour at any sign of stickiness. Or lay a length of thin pasta dough on the counter with an equal length nearby.

5. In a large bowl, mix the ricotta, sugar, and cinnamon. Arrange a sheet of pasta over the ravioli mold and press down into the wells. Beat the egg and water together and brush each well. Place teaspoonfuls of the stuffing in the wells. Lay a sheet of pasta over the stuffing and, with a rolling pin press down hard to seal the two sheets. Carefully turn the ravioli mold upside down and peel the ravioli out, arranging them on a floured baking tray while you continue the preparation. Dust the ravioli with flour. Dry for a couple of hours on a floured baking tray in the refrigerator.

If you don't have a ravioli press, lay a sheet of pasta down on a surface and place teaspoon-size dollops of stuffing side by side (assuming the sheet of pasta from your machine is at least 4 inches wide) all along its length. Drape the other equal-size sheet of pasta over the bottom sheet and carefully press down so that you can cut through them easily. Use a pastry-cutting wheel to cut the ravioli into individual pieces. Dust with flour and arrange on a baking or jelly roll pan in the refrigerator until needed.

6. Meanwhile, bring a large pot of abundantly salted water to a vigorous boil and add the ravioli. Cook until they have puffed up and are floating on the surface, 8 to 10 minutes. Drain well and serve with the sauce and a sprinkling of pecorino cheese.

Makes about 100 ravioli (about 2 pounds) for 6 to 8 servings

This sugar-master is making syrup from the loaves of sugar resting on the small table. Many sugary things were traded in medieval Italy. *The Making of Syrup, with Sugar Loaves*, from Dioscurides' *Tractatus de Herbis*. MsLat.993, L.9.28, f.142r. Biblioteca Estense, Modena, Italy. GIRAUDON/ART RESOURCE.

Siroppa di Lampone (Campania)

RASPBERRY SYRUP

Perhaps one of these altre cose di zucaro *that was exported from Naples was* siroppo di lampone, *raspberry syrup. We know that one of the biggest importers of Neapolitan sugar products was Tunisia, and it's not farfetched to think that they used raspberry syrup with their* zalābiyya *(page 113).*

I tend to make this recipe during the window of time when raspberries come to market and are relatively inexpensive. It is excellent with crespelle *(crêpes), pancakes, waffles, tarts, poached pears, and plain cakes.*

4 pounds fresh raspberries
9 cups sugar
Juice from 1½ lemons

1. In a large bowl, squeeze the raspberries with your hands until they are completely mashed. Put the mashed raspberries in a ceramic bowl and leave for 3 days, stirring a few times each day. The raspberries will begin to ferment.

2. After 3 days, strain all of the raspberry juice and pulp through a fine-mesh sieve, pushing with the back of a wooden spoon or with a pestle, or pass through a food mill. Add the sugar and mix well. Add the lemon juice and mix again.

3. Transfer the raspberry juice to a large nonreactive saucepan and bring to a boil slowly. Simmer for 35 minutes while stirring. Turn the heat off and skim the foam off the top. Pour into a bowl to cool. Skim some more if necessary. Once it is cool, pour it into a glass container and store in a cool place. Refrigerate once opened. The syrup should be used within one month.

Makes 2 quarts

Mecerada de Naranja con Coco (Andalusia)

ORANGES WITH COCONUT

The origin of the orange, following the work of the foremost botanist on the genus Citrus, *Professor Tyozaburo Tanaka, is an area in southeast China around the provinces of Yunnan and Kwangsi. The date of domestication of the orange is not known, and its taxonomy is quite confused. It is known that the orange arrived in the Mediterranean with the Arabs, and by* A.D. *976 the chamberlain al-Manṣūr planted the Patio de los Naranjos (Courtyard of the Oranges) in Córdoba, this being one of the earliest mentions of the orange in Spain. The only citrus fruit cited in the anonymous agricultural treatise the Córdoban Calendar, written in 961, is the citron, larger than a lemon and used for perfumes, medicines, and liqueurs. By the twelfth century, oranges were being grown in the courtyards of palaces, mosques, and many houses in Spain. This was the sour or bitter orange; the sweet orange came later, although some sour oranges are relatively sweet.*[95]

The coconut that is used in this preparation is probably a modern culinary invention, but the Spanish may have been introduced to the coconut by Portuguese explorers at the end of the fifteenth century. The origin of the coconut has long been in dispute, but because of genetic variability and the number of local names, it is now thought that the place of origin is Southeast Asia, perhaps the Malay Peninsula. In any case, the coconut seems to have been brought to the Mediterranean by Arab sailors familiar with the plant that they found on the islands of the Indian Ocean.[96]

I first had this surprisingly simple dessert after a main course of fritture de pescado *(page 424) in the Meson Andaluz restaurant in Granada, and found it the perfect balance to the fried fish.*

3 Valencia juice oranges, peeled and white pith removed
2 tablespoons sugar
½ cup sweetened coconut flakes
Whipped cream to taste

1. Slice the oranges ⅜ inch thick and arrange on a serving platter in an attractive way.

2. Sprinkle the sugar over each slice. Sprinkle the coconut over each slice, place a dollop of whipped cream on each slice, and serve.

Makes 4 servings

Dilìzia di Pérsichi (Sicily)
PEACH DELIGHTS

The peach was introduced to Europe from Persia, but the evidence for its origin in western China is strong because of the present distribution of wild species and because early Chinese writings describe it before it is mentioned in the West.[97] *In Sicily, one word for peach,* pérsichi, *meaning "Persian," acknowledges this fact. Today, Italy is one of the world's largest producers of peaches, and this recipe from Sicily is a delightful way to prepare them. Sugar was introduced to Sicily by the Arabs, where they established a great industry. Its cultivation had died out by the early thirteenth century, though, because Frederick II had to send representatives to Tyre on the Lebanese coast to find someone who knew how to grow and refine it.*[98]

1 large egg
⅔ cup sugar
½ cup all-purpose flour, plus more for dusting
¼ teaspoon pure vanilla extract
⅛ teaspoon salt
¼ cup milk
1 tablespoon unsalted butter
1½ pounds ripe peaches, peeled, pitted, and sliced

1. Preheat the oven to 350°F.

2. In a medium-size bowl, beat the egg with ⅓ cup of the sugar. Slowly add the ½ cup flour, stirring continously. Once it is blended, stir in the vanilla and salt. Pour in the milk and beat with a fork until it has the consistency of crêpe batter.

3. Butter an 8 × 10-inch baking pan and lightly flour it, tapping out any excess. Layer the peaches in the pan. Cover with the batter. Bake until the top is light golden, about 30 minutes. Sprinkle the top with the remaining ⅓ cup sugar and serve out of the pan.

Makes 4 servings

VALENCIA was another prodigious consumer of sugar. Foreign companies played a large role in the Spanish sugar industry of the fifteenth century, especially Genoese, but also southern German and Swiss firms. Between 1420 and 1430, the Swiss company Diesbach-Watt of Bern Saint Gall and the Grand Company of Ravensburg established factories near Valencia.[99] It was at the beginning of the fifteenth century that sugar began to replace honey in the making of sweets and pastries. Cookbooks of the time, such as the Catalan *Libre de sent soví*, were explicit in their directions to use *molt sucre blanch* (lots of sugar). For the wedding of Princess Anna, daughter of the king of Valencia, to the Count of Medinaceli at Saragossa, the pharmacist Johan Gilabert was employed to exercise his knowledge of confectionary, often the job of medieval pharmacy. He used nine hundred pounds of comfit and confitures to make the confections. The masterpiece of his efforts was fifty marzipan cakes (*marçapans* or *massepains*), a legacy of the Arabs. Even kings concerned themselves with sugar, as we know from King Philip III (1578–1621), the bigoted

Spanish king responsible for the final expulsion of the Moriscos in 1609, who thought that the Viceroy of Valencia should distribute more sweets and *turrón* (similar to an almond nougat) among the poor of the city to celebrate Christmas.[100]

Perhaps the most voracious medieval consumers of sugar were the Arabs, who had many sugar factories throughout the Middle East and Sicily. One can see in Arabic chronicles of the thirteenth and fourteenth centuries the enormous quantities of sugar stored and consumed at the great banquets. In Cairo, the Ayyūbid sultan al-Malik al-ʿĀdil II gave a great banquet in 1239 in honor of his brother, who had been captured and imprisoned by his enemies. He offered his guests sugar loaves weighing in all about 1,215 tons. There are many stories of even more copious amounts being eaten.[101] To this day, Arab sweets are the sweetest in any Mediterranean cuisine.

CASSATA

Cassata *is arguably the most famous and the most extraordinary sweet of Sicily, possibly sharing that title with the* cannoli *(page 177). It may be traced to the Arab era, or to the Arab-influenced kitchens of Norman-Sicilian monasteries, as a very simple concoction of eggs and flour. It is today a richly decorated baroque cake of aristocratic proportions. The foundation of* cassata *is an egg cake—*pan de Spagna*—known by the English misnomer "sponge cake," that is sprinkled with a sweet liqueur such as Maraschino cherry and orange flower water and has a filling made from strained fresh ricotta mixed with sugar, pistachios, cinnamon, candied fruits, and chocolate. Baroque decorations are added using sugar icing and colored candied fruits, apricot preserves, and marzipan delights such as miniature pears, cherries, kumquats, and slices of candied citron twisted into bows or rosettes.*

Cassata *was, from early on, traditionally made as an Easter specialty by the monastery nuns or for Purim by Sicilian Jews.* Cassata *was so delicious and seductive that as late as 1574 the diocese of Mazara del Vallo had to prohibit its making at the monastery during the holy week because the nuns preferred to bake and eat it than pray.[102] That this cake was an important part of the celebrations of two major monotheistic religions and possibly derived from a third, Islam, is a testament to how close these populations were in medieval Sicily, and it illustrates the statement of that great historian of science Charles Haskins, who said that nowhere else (but in Sicily) did these great civilizations "live side by side in peace and toleration."[103] Documents show that large purchases of ricotta were made before the end of Lent. The ancient relationship of* cassata *to the period around Lent is noted, for the Jews, by the explicit reference to* festum Judeorum nuncupatum di li Cassati *(for the Jewish festival it is called* cassati*), which must be Passover, as contrasted to Easter, which the reference* festum Azimorum *in the documents must mean (*Azimorum *means "unleavened").[104]*

Popular Sicilian tradition sometimes places the origin of cassata in the fourteenth century, and food writers such as Giuliano Bugialli incorrectly claim an unequivocal Latin derivation. Although the etymology of cassata is not yet settled, the notion that cassata comes from the Latin caseus, the word for "cheese," because it can be made with cheese, was called "far-fetched" by the famous etymologists da Aleppo and Calvaruso.[105] The Latin derivation is not likely. First, cassata is born of a fascination with sugar, not cheese, and sugar was not cultivated in Sicily during the Roman era. It was only when the Arabs brought sugar to Sicily and an energetic sugar industry took root in the tenth century that sweet inventions using this product appeared. Second, the proposed derivation from the Latin caseus doesn't make sense because the Sicilian word for "cheese," which does derive from the Latin word, is casu, not cassu. The more likely derivation is from the word for the baking tray or earthenware bowl cassata was cooked in, the Arabic qaṣʿa.[106]

The earliest reference to cassata as a specifically Sicilian cake made with ricotta cheese, as it is today, is from a delivery contract of 1409 to a Jew named Sadon Misoc.[107] But the first mention of the possible ancestor of cassata appears in the Paris manuscript of the Riyāḍ al-nufūs, a tenth-century description attributed to a certain Abū Bakr al-Mālikī. He reports that Abū al-Faḍl, an orthodox jurist from the Aghlabid capital in Tunisia, refused to eat a sweet cake called a kaʿk because it was made with sugar from Sicily, then ruled by unorthodox Shias.[108]

Although pan de Spagna is today known as sponge cake, in the Middle Ages it was called bizcocho in Spain, a word that today refers to the egg cake as well as hardtack. In the twelfth-century cookbook of Abū Marwān ibn Zuhr, Kitāb al-aghdhiya (literally meaning, book of diet), a kaʿk is described as a kind of twisted ring of bread or cake fried in oil and finished with pistachios, pine nuts, or almonds, rose water, and honey. It is spoken of in the same breath as bishmaṭ or bizcocho.[109]

Michele Amari, the preeminent historian of the Arabs in Sicily, was the first to note, in his monumental study Storia dei musulmani di sicilia (History of the Muslims in Sicily) that vestigial Arabisms permeated the Sicilian language. Linguistic researchers of this century have compiled thorough registers of Arabisms that appear in Neo-Latin languages. The culinary language of Sicilian is replete with Arabisms, especially concerning sweets, sweet dishes that are fried, and sweets containing raisins, almonds, ricotta, and/or semolina.[110] For example, there are cubbàita, an almond nougat made with honey and sesame, from the Arabic qubbayṭa, a kind of dried confection made with raisin juice and other ingredients, and the famous Sicilian sfinci, a beignet made of ricotta, associated with the festival of St. Joseph, derived from the Arabic isfanj, a yeast dough fritter eaten with honey.[111] Sfinci is mentioned in Palermo in 1330, where it is sold by the sfingiari.[112] It is still made to this day in both Sicily and Tunisia (page 113).

The Turks liked their sugar, too. The traveler Busbecq, whom we met in an earlier chapter, tells us that, in the mid-sixteenth century, the Janissaries—the elite corps of the Ottoman sultans who were recruited from Christian slaves—were better fed than the general population and loved to eat a kind of pudding made from wine and eggs mixed with plenty of sugar and spice.[113]

MOTHER OF THE WORLD

CAIRO is known to Egyptians as mother of the world, and the city has astonished visitors since its founding a millennium ago. In *The Thousand and One Nights*, an adventurer says: "He who has not seen the city of Cairo has not seen the world." The fourteenth-century Arab philosopher Ibn Khaldūn described Cairo as "the metropolis of the universe, the garden of the world, the nest of the human species, the gateway to Islam." Five hundred years later, the German Egyptologist Georg Ebers made an observation that remains true today: "No man left Cairo without profit or without loss." Gustave Flaubert captured much of living in Cairo when he said, "The raucous semitic syllables clatter in the air like the sound of a whiplash."

Today, Cairo is the largest Mediterranean city. The city now teems with fourteen million people, and that overwhelming crush of humanity, coursing through a crumbling city choked with dust and relentless traffic, remains a challenge for even the most intrepid traveler. Cairo is a Third World megalopolis squeezed into medieval clothing, a demanding place that is neither charming nor beautiful, but is instead a magnificent, bewildering chaos that breathes forth secrets of squalor and splendor. Those moments most vivid in visitors' memories often concern not the ancient tombs but the acts of kindness of simple Egyptian people or the tastes of their equally simple food, such as *fūl* that so many Egyptians eat at any time of the day.

Fūl Mudammas (Egypt)

FAVA BEAN MASH

The rich man's breakfast, the shopkeeper's lunch, the poor man's supper. This Arabic saying captures what fūl mudammas *is.* Fūl mudammas, *a mash of fava beans, is considered the Egyptian national dish, and some claim its roots can be traced to Pharaonic Egypt. But that claim is not so obvious. Although quantities of beans have been found in Twelfth Dynasty tombs (1991–1786 B.C.), some writers have suggested that beans were not commonly cultivated in ancient Egypt, and Herodotus, in the fifth century B.C., mentions the fact that the Egyptians "never sow beans, and even if any happen to grow wild, they will not eat them, either raw or boiled."*[114]

Fūl *(pronounced FOOL), which means "fava bean," is often eaten for breakfast. The word* mudammas *was originally Coptic, meaning "buried," and its use here might mean that the beans are buried in the pot.*[115] *Although there are countless ways of embellishing* fūl, *the basic recipe remains the same. Once the* fūl *is cooked, it is salted and eaten plain or accompanied by olive oil, corn oil, butter,* samna *(clarified butter), buffalo milk, béchamel sauce,* basṭurma *(pressed and dried beef fillet seasoned with cumin, garlic, and other spices), fried eggs, tomato sauce, tahini, fresh lime juice, or other ingredients.*

There are different kinds of fava beans and different cooking times, depending on their size, so you must make sure you use the right kind. The only fava bean used for making the prepared dish known as fūl *is the smaller, rounder one called* fūl ḥammām *(bath fava) by the Egyptians. They should be cooked until soft; there should be no "bite" to them. The other kinds of fava bean used by Egyptian cooks are* fūl rūmī, *the large kidney-shaped fava beans you may be more familiar with; and* fūl baladī, *country beans, of middling size.* Fūl nābit (*or* nābid) *are fava beans sprouts,* fūl akhḍar *are fresh fava beans, and* fūl madshūsh *are crushed fava beans.*

There is an interesting story about how fūl ḥammām *came to be known as "bath beans." Professor Janet Abu-Lughod, whose authoritative book on Cairo published by Princeton University Press is now a classic, told me the story of* fūl. *In the Middle Ages, the making of* fūl *was monopolized by the people living around the Princess Baths, a public bath in a tiny compound near today's* sabīl *(public drinking fountain) of Muḥammad ʿAlī Basha, a block north of the two elegant minarets of the Mosque of Sultan Muʿayyad Shaykh above the eleventh-century Bāb Zuwaylah gate. During the day, bath attendants stoked the fires heating the* qidras, *huge pots of bathwater. Wood was scarce, so garbage was used as fuel and eventually a dump grew around the baths. When the baths closed, the red embers of the fires continued to burn. To take advantage of these precious fires, huge* qidras *were filled with fava beans and these cauldrons were kept simmering all night, and eventually all day, too, to provide breakfast for Cairo's population.*[116] *Cookshops throughout Cairo would send their minions to the Princess Baths to buy their wholesale* fūl.

My first taste of Egyptian fūl *in Cairo was quite different from the Lebanese-Palestinian version that I was familiar with from my former wife's family. In the Palestinian version of this dish the final result is not as soupy as the Egyptian one, and although it, too, is popular as a breakfast preparation, it is as likely to be eaten as part of a* mazza. *While in Egypt I tried* fūl bi'l-daqqa, *with a garlic sauce;* fūl huṣniyya, *with hard-boiled eggs and a baked béchamel sauce; and, my favorite, the flavorful* fūl bi'l-basṭurma wa'l-bayḍ, *with* basṭurma *(dried and spiced beef) and fried egg.* Fūl *with a drizzle of water buffalo* samna, *a pinch of salt, flatbread, and scallions on the side was also very good.*

Although we had some delicious fūl *dishes at the Filfila restaurant in Cairo, it took my friends Ziad and Haniya Baha ad-Din to show us a "real"* fūl-*shop, as Ziad called it. We met several weeks later at the venerable Cecil Hotel in Alexandria, famous as British headquarters during World War II, and before that as the scenic background of Lawrence Durrell's* Alexandria Quartet. *Ziad, a connoisseur's connoisseur, guided us to a* fūl-*shop on the Shāri ʿAbdul Fattah al-Hadani. His wife, Haniya, is an anthropologist and a fascinating expositor of Egyptian food. We ordered four different* fūl. *The first was "plain," only with butter, one was with fried eggs, one was with tahini, and the fourth was with tomato sauce. They were all quite good, but surprisingly the plainest one, the one with butter, was the best.*

Haniya told me that there are countless ways of making fūl. *They vary around Egypt depending on what is available, but the basic recipe remains the same. Into a big pot, usually a special pot, a* fūl-*pot* (qidra), *narrow at the base, wide in the middle, and narrow again at the top, you put the dried fava beans to soak in water for eight to twenty-four hours. In your kitchen, an ideal pot would be the bottom portion of a* couscousière, *a* marmite, *or a simple stew pot. Then you add the onion, tomatoes, a bit of salt, and a few tablespoons of red lentils, which helps the color, she said. It is simmered over very low heat all night, covered so the beans don't discolor, and is usually eaten in the morning for breakfast, although Egyptians will eat it any time of the day.*

In every case you must salt it yourself since it is never salted. We ate country-style whole wheat bran flatbread, baladī, *with it.*

3 pounds small dried fava beans (about 6 cups), picked over and soaked in water to cover for 24 hours
1 large onion, chopped
2 large ripe tomatoes, chopped
¾ cup dried red lentils, picked over and rinsed
2½ quarts cold water
Salt to taste

1. Drain the fava beans. Bring a pot of water to a boil, add the fava beans, and boil them until they are soft enough to have their peels removed, 10 to 15 minutes. Drain, then remove the peel by gently squeezing each bean so the skin pops off or use a paring knife.

2. Place the peeled fava beans in a stew pot or the bottom portion of a *couscousière* with the onion, tomatoes, and lentils and cover with the water. Bring to a gentle boil, skim the top of foam, and reduce the heat to very low or place on a heat diffuser. Cover and cook for 12 hours. Don't lift the cover at all during the entire cooking time, otherwise the beans will discolor.

3. The cooked fava beans can be eaten whole, slightly mashed, or completely mashed. Season with salt. Serve with extra virgin olive oil, corn oil, melted butter, *samna* (clarified butter; page 189), tomato sauce (page 312), garlic sauce (page 584), *basṭurma* (page 68), fried eggs, hard-boiled eggs, fresh lime juice, or béchamel sauce (Step 2, page 283).

NOTE: You need not halve this large-yielding recipe because *fūl* keeps well in the refrigerator and is excellent reheated.

Makes 10 servings

* * *

CAIRO was founded quite late, in Middle Eastern terms, but was already an important center under Fāṭimid rule (969–1171), who were unorthodox Shias. The original Fāṭimid city of al-Qāhira (the victorious) was planned by the Arab Sicilian Gawhar al-Ṣiqillī for the Caliph al-Muᶜizz in A.D. 969. The name al-Qāhira was later corrupted by Italian merchants into Cairo, as we know it today, although it remains al-Qāhira in Arabic.[117] By 972, the great mosque and university of al-Azhar were built, sometimes called the first university in the world.[118]

The Fāṭimid Caliph al-ᶜAzīz succeeded his father al-Muᶜizz in 975. His reign was a tolerant and humane one, allowing Christians and Jews to participate in his government. This was a period of great luxury and extravagance, and there was development of a cuisine. Al-ᶜAzīz built buildings, and expended sums of money on jewelry and food. He once had cherries sent to him from Lebanon tied to the feet of carrier pigeons. The Fāṭimid empire at its height stretched from the Atlantic to the Persian Gulf.

Caliph al-ᶜAzīz was succeeded by his eleven-year-old son, al-Ḥākim. Al-Ḥākim was an altogether different story, for he was a psychopath who nearly ruined Egypt. At the age of fifteen, al-Ḥākim had his tutor killed and for the next twenty-five years ruled Egypt as a capricious, murderous, and despotic ruler. Laws he promulgated were eccentric, and there was a general climate of violence and fear. He hated Christians, Jews, Sunni Muslims, women, and dogs. His mother was Christian and he had all her brothers executed. He outlawed wine, singing girls, and musical performances. On two separate occasions he had all the dogs in the city killed because their barking annoyed him. He forbade the eating of *mulūkhiyya* (page 309) and the playing of chess. On one occasion he ordered all the honey in Cairo to be dumped into the Nile. Another time he drowned all his concubines as they bathed. One day while strolling through Cairo with his companions he stopped at a butcher's stall, picked up a cleaver, cleaved one of the butchers in half, and walked away as if nothing happened.

Al-Ḥākim was a dangerous man, yet in his library resided the greatest collection of books ever assembled, a goodly number being works on agriculture, botany, and pharmacology.[119]

After the Fāṭimids, the Ayyūbid sultans, beginning with the famous Saladin, ruled Egypt from 1169 to 1250. The grandeur of the Ayyūbid sultans was captured by the famed Chinese traveler Chau Ju-kua (flourished c. 1225), who wrote that when the sultan appeared in public in Cairo, he rode on horseback led by three hundred horses with their saddles decorated with gold and jewels, guarded by a thousand horsemen and three hundred slaves bearing swords. Fifty men held tight the iron chains that led ten

EGYPTIAN SPECIALTIES

Egyptian food has the same poor reputation today among other Arabs that English food has with us. While one can admit that the cooking of Aleppo and Beirut represent the apogee of Arab cuisine, Egypt—this most populous of Arab countries—has a number of specialties that will delight anyone who relishes simple food.

Biṣāra: *A fava bean mash with the consistency of hummus, heavily flavored with mint, fresh coriander, dill, salt, black pepper, and olive oil.*

Faṭīr: *A pan-cooked pastry, a cross between a puff pastry beignet and a crêpe, sometimes served as a savory as well as a sweet. A delicious savory* faṭīr *is* faṭīr bi'l-sakhīna, *there being two varieties of this dish; in the first the pastry is covered with a sauce made of vegetables cooked in vinegar and garlic and the second is a sauce made with chicken poached with onions and water buffalo* samna. Faṭīr, *derived from the word meaning "to break the fast, to breakfast," is, in fact, often eaten at breakfast.*

Fatta: *A feast food prepared after the ritual slaughtering of the lambs during Ramadan. The lamb is cooked in a vinegar, tomato, and garlic sauce, and in Luxor they make* fattat al-Aqṣur *with* faṭīr *(see above).*

Kufta Daūd basha: *Small meatballs cooked in a rich tomato sauce made with lots of chopped onions, garlic, and black pepper, with very thinly sliced charred bell peppers.*

Kawāriᶜ: *A veal ankle and knee joint stew that is very succulent.*

Khalṭa: *A rice pilaf made with chicken pieces and golden raisins.*

Mukhallīl: *Vegetables, such as eggplant, cooked in a vinegar sauce. The name is derived from the word for pickled vegetables.*

Sujuq (pronounced SU-guk in Egypt): *Grilled beef sausage as thin as a pencil seasoned with spices, garlic, and hot pepper.*

Mulūkhiyya bi'l-ārnab: *A stew of Jew's mallow (see box on page 309) flavored with rabbit.*

Mūsā: *A veal or beef knuckle braised until the meat is falling off the bone, served on top of rice flavored with the cooking juices of the knuckle and some tomato and spices.*

Musaqqaᶜa (pronounced mu-SA'a): *A dish of eggplant and meat, probably developed from the Greek moussaka.*[120]

Ruqāq: *A kind of pie made with Arab bread, butter, and ground lamb.*

Ṭᶜamiyya: *An Egyptian version of falafel, but more delicate, spicier, with lots of fresh coriander, shaped into a lozenge about 1½ inches in diameter and deep-fried.*

tigers. Then came a hundred club bearers and thirty hawk bearers. A hundred kettle drummers followed him on horseback. He also noted that the Egyptians survived on cakes and meat and ate no rice, but grew wheat.[121]

Then came the Mamelukes.[122] Slaves converted to Islam, they came to control high military posts in Egypt and eventually took power and established two ruling dynasties, the Baḥrī (1250–1382), made up of Turks and Mongols, and the Burjī (1382–1517), made up of Circassians, a people of the Caucasus who do not speak an Indo-European language but instead a tongue in the Abkhazo-Adyghein subfamily of the Caucasian languages. From earliest times Egypt had provided food to the Mediterranean, and this was still true under the Mamelukes. The Nile delta is today a very productive land, with potatoes, tomatoes, and lettuces in continual production. Cabbage and taro are seasonal and rice is harvested once a year. In Egypt, pulses such as chickpeas, lentils, and beans were considered bread substitutes, and their most popular form in local cookery was as soups.

Çerkez Tavuğu (Circassian)

CIRCASSIAN CHICKEN

In the thirteenth-century Arabic cookbook Kitāb al-wuṣla ilā al-ḥabīb, *there are three recipes for a dish called* ma'ᶜmūniyya *that has some resemblance to Circassian chicken. This is a dish made by Circassians, a people from northwest Caucasia who have communities in a couple of Russian republics and other communities in Turkey, Jordan, and Syria. They converted wholesale to Islam in the seventeenth century. This dish is also popular with the Armenians and Turks. It is a rich and quite elegant preparation. There is a large Circassian community in Amman, Jordan, where I first ate it..*

The walnuts (Juglans regia) *so prominent in this dish are native to southeastern Europe and China. One finds walnuts used a great deal in Caucasian, Armenian, Kurdish, north Syrian, southeastern Turkish, and Persian cuisine.*

1 chicken (about 4 pounds)

FOR THE BROTH

1 medium-size onion, cut up
1 leek, white and green parts only, washed well and chopped
1 large carrot, sliced
6 whole cloves
6 allspice berries
10 black peppercorns
5 bay leaves
1 teaspoon coriander seeds

FOR THE WALNUT SAUCE

6 ounces walnuts, chopped
6 large garlic cloves, crushed in a mortar
¼ pound white part of French or Italian bread
½ cup milk
Leaves from 1 small bunch fresh coriander (cilantro), finely chopped
1 tablespoon walnut oil
Salt and freshly ground black pepper

FOR THE GARNISH

1 tablespoon walnut oil
2 teaspoons paprika
1 teaspoon cayenne pepper
¼ cup chopped walnuts
About 20 fresh coriander (cilantro) leaves

1. Put the chicken in a large stockpot with the broth ingredients and enough water to almost cover the chicken. Bring the water to a very gentle boil, reduce the heat so the water is only shimmering, cover partially, and poach until the chicken legs and

wings look like they could fall off, about 1 hour. It is important that the broth never come to a hard boil, otherwise the chicken meat will become tough. Remove the chicken from the pot and pull off all the meat from the chicken, discarding all the skin, fat, and bones. Shred the meat into thin strips by pulling it apart with a fork. Meanwhile, increase the heat to high under the broth and reduce for 20 minutes. Check the seasoning of the broth and strain.

2. In a food processor or blender, grind the walnuts and garlic together into a paste. Soak the bread in the milk, then squeeze the liquid out in your hands as if you were making a snowball. Add the bread to the food processor and run until homogenous, scraping down the sides when necessary. Transfer the walnut mixture to a large bowl and dilute it with spoonfuls of broth until it has a mayonnaise consistency, using about 1½ cups of broth in all. Add the chicken, mix well, and bind together with a few more tablespoons of the broth and as many teaspoons of walnut oil as necessary until the entire mixture has a creamy consistency. Season with salt and pepper.

3. For the garnish, combine 1 tablespoon walnut oil with the paprika and cayenne and stir. Transfer the chicken to an oval serving platter and decorate the top with the chopped walnuts and the perimeter of the platter with coriander leaves; drizzle the top with the walnut oil mixture. Serve at room temperature with warm French bread or Arab flatbread.

Makes 6 servings

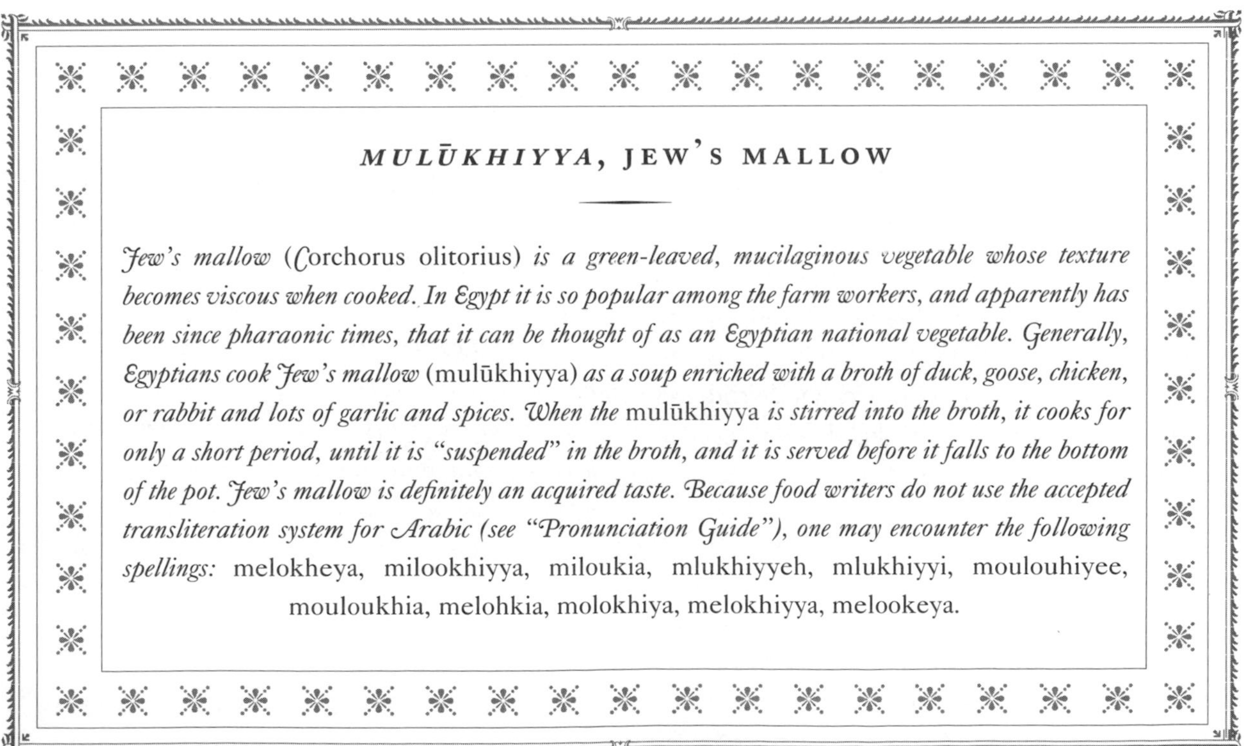

MULŪKHIYYA, JEW'S MALLOW

Jew's mallow (Corchorus olitorius) *is a green-leaved, mucilaginous vegetable whose texture becomes viscous when cooked. In Egypt it is so popular among the farm workers, and apparently has been since pharaonic times, that it can be thought of as an Egyptian national vegetable. Generally, Egyptians cook Jew's mallow* (mulūkhiyya) *as a soup enriched with a broth of duck, goose, chicken, or rabbit and lots of garlic and spices. When the* mulūkhiyya *is stirred into the broth, it cooks for only a short period, until it is "suspended" in the broth, and it is served before it falls to the bottom of the pot. Jew's mallow is definitely an acquired taste. Because food writers do not use the accepted transliteration system for Arabic (see "Pronunciation Guide"), one may encounter the following spellings:* melokheya, milookhiyya, miloukia, mlukhiyyeh, mlukhiyyi, moulouhiyee, mouloukhia, melohkia, molokhiya, melokhiyya, melookeya.

❉ *Shūrbat al-ʿAdas* (Arab Levant)

LENTIL SOUP

This very popular soup in Lebanon, Palestine, and Egypt has a long history, as we know from the story of Esau in the Bible, when he renounced his birthright for a pottage of lentils (Genesis 25:29–34). This recipe is from my former wife, Nawja al-Qattan.

2 cups dried brown lentils
8 cups chicken broth (page 54)
1 large onion, grated
2 teaspoons freshly ground cumin seeds
Salt and freshly ground black pepper to taste
2 tablespoons fresh lemon juice
2 cups pure or virgin olive or olive pomace oil
1 large *khubz ʿarabī* (Arab flatbread or pita bread), cut into ½-inch squares
Extra virgin olive oil for drizzling

1. Wash the lentils under cold running water, picking out any stones. Bring the broth to a boil in a large saucepan and add the lentils and onion. When the broth returns to a boil, reduce the heat to low, cover, and simmer for 1 hour. Do not stir.

2. Pass the lentils and broth through a food mill. Add the cumin and season with salt and pepper. Return the soup to the saucepan and stir. Taste to check the seasoning. Stir in the lemon juice and heat until the soup starts to bubble slightly. Taste again to check the seasoning and add whatever it needs.

3. Meanwhile, heat the olive oil for frying to 375°F in a medium-size saucepan or skillet. Fry the pieces of bread until golden, about 1 minute. Serve the soup with the fried croutons of Arab bread and extra virgin olive oil passed at the table.

Makes 4 to 6 servings

✣ ✣ ✣

In the twelfth century, the poverty and lack of good health of Egyptians was noted by ʿAbd al-Laṭīf al-Baghdādī, a physician from Baghdad, who tells us that children in Egypt were thin, deformed, and stunted and that putrid and phlegmatic diseases affected the population of the Nile. The Florentine Lionardo Frescobaldi made the observation in 1384 that the Egyptians were very feeble (and their bread was very white, meaning it was missing the nutritious bran).[123] Chickpeas were part of the staple Egyptian diet, and the most famous of chickpea preparations from the Levant and Egypt are now firmly ensconced on the American table.

❉ *Ḥummuṣ bi'l-Ṭaḥīna* (Arab Levant)

HUMMUS

This world-famous puree, obligatory on every Arab mazza *table, is loved throughout the Arab world and is now found ubiquitously in the United States. The word* ḥummuṣ *means "chickpea" in Arabic. The tahini is the sesame seed paste that one stirs into the mashed chickpeas. The convenience of prepared hummus is perfect for our harried lifestyles, but unfortunately most prepared hummus is substandard. In the Arab world, every family has its own recipe for hummus, so that the prepared dish does not have such a standardized reputation as it does in this country. For example, in Syria some families make hummus with olive oil, cumin, and allspice instead of tahini and lemon juice. This recipe will give you a more flavorful and personal rendition that I think you will enjoy, but feel free to experiment. For instance, you may want to make a smoother hummus, in which case push the cooked chickpeas through a food mill. No matter how you make hummus, it is important to peel and discard the thin white skins of the chickpeas.*

3 cups dried chickpeas (about 1½ pounds), picked over and soaked overnight in cold water to cover mixed with 1 teaspoon baking soda
¾ cup extra virgin olive oil
Salt
8 garlic cloves, peeled
½ cup tahini (page 725)
½ cup fresh lemon juice
Freshly ground black pepper to taste
¼ cup pine nuts
⅓ cup finely chopped fresh mint leaves and fresh mint leaves for garnish
½ teaspoon sumac (page 724) for garnish

1. Drain the chickpeas and place in a pot of lightly salted water to cover by 2 inches. Bring the water to a boil over high heat until it foams, 5 to 10 minutes. Remove the foam with a skimmer and continue boiling, partially covered, until tender, about 3 hours, so keep checking. Add boiling water to the pot to keep the chickpeas continuously covered. Drain and save 1½ cups of the cooking water. Return the cooked chickpeas to the same pot filled with some cold water so you can rub the skins off the chickpeas with your fingers (many of them will rise to the surface).

2. Process the chickpeas with ½ cup of the olive oil and 1 cup of the reserved chickpea cooking water in a food processor until creamy.

3. In a mortar, pound the garlic with 1 tablespoon salt until it is a creamy mush. In a small bowl, beat the tahini and lemon juice together slowly. If it is too thick, add water—*never* more lemon juice. Stir the tahini-and-lemon juice mixture into the garlic and salt. Stir this mixture into the chickpea puree, adjust the salt, and season with pepper. Check the consistency; if it is too thick, like an oatmeal, then add some of the remaining reserved chickpea cooking water until it is smoother, like a Cream of Wheat. Check the taste and adjust the seasoning if necessary. If you do need to adjust the taste, the process must be repeated—in other words, mash some more garlic with salt or mix a tablespoon of tahini with a tablespoon of lemon juice.

4. In a small skillet, cook the pine nuts in 1 tablespoon of the olive oil over medium heat until light brown, stirring, about 4 minutes. Remove and set aside.

5. Spoon the hummus onto a large round serving platter, not a bowl. Warm the remaining 3 tablespoons extra virgin olive oil. Make spiral or fan-shaped furrows in the hummus and fill with the warm olive oil. Sprinkle the reserved pine nuts around. Garnish the edges with mint leaves and sprinkle the chopped mint on top. Sprinkle the sumac over and serve. Serve with warm *khubz ʿarabī* (Arab flatbread or pita bread).

VARIATION:
Canned cooked chickpeas can be used instead of dried, in which case skip step 1.

NOTE: Other garnishes used are whole cooked chickpeas, black olives, pomegranate seeds, cayenne pepper, red Aleppo pepper, paprika, sumac, or ground cumin.

Makes 6 servings

Ḥamām Mishwī (Egypt)

GRILLED PIGEON (OR DUCK)

Grilled pigeon is a very popular Egyptian dish. Egyptian restaurants tend to specialize in a particular kind of food, and in the cities families will patronize their favorite restaurants. One kind of restaurant is the grill restaurant, where you are likely to encounter this preparation. In rural areas, many homes have their own pigeoncotes where the birds are raised. The pigeon is plucked, singed, washed, and prepared for grilling by being cut in half width-wise and flattened with a mallet. The bird is grilled over a slow wood fire until golden brown, then rolled in chopped parsley. The glistening pigeon is served on a bed of parsley and eaten with one's fingers and pieces of ʿaysh baladī, *a country-style Arab flatbread made with whole wheat bran.*

Guinea hen is close in taste to pigeon, and so is the dark meat of turkey, but for an interesting and still authentic variation, try the duck called for in this recipe. Ask the butcher to prepare the ducks or follow the method in step 1. Save as much duck fat as possible, as well as the duck carcasses, neck, liver, and gizzards for making confit de canard *(page 200),* fond de canard *(page 55), or* salade tiéde de foie et gésiers de canard *(page 194). If you do decide or happen upon pigeons (squab), figure on two per person; for Guinea hens, use four in all; for Cornish hens, use six.*

3 ducks (about 15 pounds in all; see method)
1 head garlic (15 to 20 cloves), separated into cloves and peeled
2 teaspoons salt
½ cup extra virgin olive oil
Freshly ground black pepper to taste
Leaves from 2 bunches fresh parsley, finely chopped
Lemon wedges for garnish
***Khubz ʿarabī* (Arab flatbread or pita bread)**

1. With a heavy cleaver or butcher's knife, cut the ducks in half widthwise. Save the neck, liver, and gizzards for another use. Wash the duck halves and pat dry with paper towels. With the ends of the legs pointing toward you, with a boning or utility knife slice off all the excess fat (much of which is between the legs and carcass) and save. Remove as much fat as you can from the other duck halves (much of which is on the rump), saving it also. Flatten the duck halves with heavy blows from the side of a heavy mallet or cleaver, but not so heavy that you break the bones.

2. Prepare a charcoal fire or preheat a gas grill on low for 20 minutes, allowing for at least one section of the grill to be much cooler than the other by mounding the coals to one side or using only one burner or rack in a gas grill. Place a drip pan under where the ducks are going to be grilled to catch the dripping fat.

3. In a mortar, pound the garlic together with the salt until mushy. Spoon this paste into the olive oil and, using a brush, coat the ducks lightly with it. Season the ducks with pepper. Grill slowly, uncovered, turning often to avoid burning and flare-ups from the remaining fat left on the ducks. If the ducks are flaring up too much, remove them from the fire and slice off any excess fat, and move to a cooler spot on the grill. Baste occasionally with the olive oil-and-garlic mixture. Grill the ducks until golden brown, 50 to 60 minutes.

4. Cover a large platter with the parsley. Place the ducks on top and sprinkle more parsley over them. Serve with lemon wedges and warm pita bread.

Makes 6 servings

Dimʿa Musabīka (Egypt)

EGYPTIAN STEWED TOMATO SAUCE

The Nile delta has been a productive agricultural area feeding Egypt since ancient times. Once the tomato arrived from the New World it became as ubiquitous in Egyptian cooking as it did in all other Mediterranean cooking. So much so, in fact, that among the Bedouins of Egypt's Western Desert, and throughout Egypt in general, vegetables are always cooked biṣalṣa, *with a tomato-based sauce, such as the ubiquitous* dimʿa musabīka *(literally, stewed sauce).*[124] *This sauce is excellent with* kushary *(page 600), on top of spaghetti, or with any vegetable.*

¼ cup extra virgin olive oil
1 medium-size onion, finely chopped
6 garlic cloves, crushed
One 6-ounce can tomato paste
4 cups water
2 teaspoons white wine vinegar
2 teaspoons salt
1 teaspoon freshly ground black pepper
½ teaspoon cayenne pepper

1. In a large skillet, heat the olive oil over medium heat, then cook the onion until translucent, about 8 minutes, stirring. Add the garlic and cook another 2 minutes, stirring constantly so the garlic doesn't burn.

2. Mix the tomato paste and water and add to the onion. Reduce the heat to low while you simmer the tomato sauce for 20 minutes. Stir in the vinegar, salt, black pepper, and cayenne and cook until denser, about another 5 minutes.

Makes 4 cups

Salāṭat al-Girgīr (Egypt)
ARUGULA AND WATERCRESS SALAD

Girgīr (Eruca sylvestris lutea) *is a kind of arugula that tastes slightly of watercress. Arabic-English dictionaries incorrectly describe it as watercress, in fact. It grows wild in Egypt and is served with a variety of dishes but is never cooked. In Alexandria and Marsa Matruh, on Egypt's Mediterranean coast, it is often served with fish. I have concocted this recipe, since it is impossible to get* girgīr *in this country, to taste very close to what I had in Marsa Matruh. It is a variation of the salad served with* samak mishwī, *grilled fish (page 403).*

20 ounces arugula, trimmed, washed, and dried well
Leaves from 1 bunch watercress, washed and dried well
1 small head escarole, washed and dried well
4 ripe plum tomatoes, quartered
1 lemon, sliced very thinly with its peel, about the thickness of a coin
Freshly ground black pepper to taste
Extra virgin olive oil for drizzling
White wine vinegar for drizzling
Salt (optional)

1. Spread the greens over a large platter and scatter the tomatoes around.

2. Cover with the lemon slices, season with pepper, drizzle over oil and vinegar to taste, and add salt if desired.

Makes 4 servings

NOTE: This salad is usually served with grilled or griddled fish *and* Arab bread, not alone.

Umm ʿAlī (Egypt)
ALI'S MOTHER

This famous coconut, milk, and wheat flake pudding is an Egyptian treasure. The apocryphal story of Umm ʿAlī *is that it was invented during the reign of the Ottoman Turks. One day while hunting in the Nile delta, the sultan developed a ravenous appetite and stopped in a small village. The peasants wished to please the sultan, so the best cook of the village, Umm ʿAlī, pulled out a special pan and filled it with the only ingredients she had around: some dried wheat flakes (perhaps stale broken pieces of* gullash, *a phyllolike pastry), sultanas, nuts, and coconut. She covered it with sugar and milk and put it into the village's oven. It was so good that the sultan asked for Umm ʿAlī's dessert the next time he visited. Another story is related by Charles Perry, a food writer for the* Los Angeles Times: *Umm ʿAlī was a pudding learned from an English nurse named O'Malley.*

The coconut came to Egypt by traders, either via Arabs of the southern Arabian peninsula or from East Africa, where it may have been brought by the same Arabs centuries earlier. In any case, although the Arabs were successful in acclimatizing many tropical plants to the Mediterranean, they appear to have been unsuccessful in introducing the coconut to Egypt, according to the fifteenth-century Arab commentator Ibn Iyās.[125]

Take several sheets of phyllo pastry and leave them out until they are completely dry and brittle.

1 tablespoon unsalted butter
¼ pound stale phyllo pastry, crumbled into flakes
3 tablespoons ground blanched hazelnuts
3 tablespoons ground blanched almonds
3 tablespoons sugar
2 tablespoons sweetened coconut flakes
2 tablespoons golden raisins
2 cups light cream

1. Preheat oven to 450°F.

2. Butter a 9 × 12-inch baking pan. Layer the pan with the broken pieces of phyllo. Sprinkle the nuts, sugar, coconut flakes, and raisins over the pastry. Pour the light cream over everything and place in the oven until the cream is bubbling and the top is browning, about 10 minutes. Remove and serve.

Makes 4 to 6 servings

Sharāb al-Laymūn (ʿAsir Laymūn) (Egypt)

LEMONADE

The very first uses for the lemon tree in the Mediterranean were as an ornamental plant in early Islamic gardens. Tracking the progress of the lemon tree from its origin in Assam and northern Burma to China, across Persia and the Arab world to the Mediterranean, is difficult because of the lemon's adaptability to hybridization. This has caused problems for the horticulturist (a variety might not take to a new land), the food historian (unclear references—for example, the "round citron"), and the taxonomist (a proliferation of botanical terms). Although the citron—like a lemon but larger, with a very thick rind and very little pulp or juice—seems to have been known by the ancient Jews before the time of Christ, and perhaps dispersed in the Mediterranean by them, the lemon seems not to have been known in pre-Islamic times. Ilaria Gozzini Giacosa is wrong to claim, in her book A Taste of Ancient Rome, *that the Romans grew the lemon. In fact, the* malum medicum *mentioned by Pliny is the citron.*[126] *Although there are depictions of citrus fruits from Roman mosaics in Carthage and frescoes in Pompeii that bear a striking resemblance to oranges and lemons, this iconographical evidence is not supported by any paleobotanical or literary evidence, suggesting that the artists either imported the fruits or saw them in the East.*[127]

The first clear literary evidence of the lemon tree in any language dates from the early tenth-century Arabic work by Qusṭūs al-Rūmī in his book on farming.[128] *At the end of the twelfth century, Ibn Jamiʿ, the personal physician to the great Muslim leader Saladin, wrote a treatise on the lemon, after which it is mentioned with greater frequency in the Mediterranean.*[129]

Egyptians of the fourteenth century knew of the lemon. Most peasants drank a date-and-honey wine.

Along the Egyptian Mediterranean coast, people drank kashkāb, *a drink made of fermented barley and mint, rue, black pepper, and citron leaf.*[130]

It appears that the all-American summer drink, lemonade, may have had its origin in medieval Egypt. Although the lemon originates farther to the east, and lemonade may very well have been invented in one of the eastern countries, the earliest written evidence of lemonade comes from Egypt. The first reference to the lemon in Egypt is in the chronicles of the Persian poet and traveler Nāṣir-i-Khusraw (1003–1061?), who left a valuable account of life in Egypt under the Fāṭimid caliph al-Mustanṣir (1035–1094). The trade in lemon juice was quite considerable by 1104. We know from documents in the Cairo Geniza—records of the medieval Jewish community in Cairo from the tenth through thirteenth centuries—that bottles of lemon juice, qaṭarmīzāt, *were made with lots of sugar and consumed locally and exported.*[131]

Egyptian lemonade is made with daq *lemons, about the size of a golf ball. These lemons are very juicy and very thin skinned (they don't even have a white pith to speak of, hence the name* daq, *which means "thin"). This method was shown to me by Essam al-Din Adly, at the Baraka restaurant in the Maydān al-Taḥrīr in Alexandria. Throwing the whole lemon into the blender is what makes this lemonade unique, but it can be done only with thin-skinned lemons, not thick-skinned. In this country, the Meyer lemon can be used but not the more common Eureka lemon. A food processor will not work as well as a blender for this preparation. In Egypt, many an intestinally distressed traveler has been magically helped by the elixir of lemon juice or lemonade.*

8 *daq* lemons or 4 Meyer lemons
¾ cup sugar
3 cups cold water

1. Squeeze the juice of 6 *daq* lemons or 3 Meyer lemons and pour it into a blender.

2. Cut up the remaining 2 *daq* or 1 Meyer lemon and put into the blender with the sugar and water and run for 3 minutes. Strain the juice and serve.

VARIATION

Squeeze the juice from 8 Eureka lemons and pour in the blender with the sugar, zest from half a lemon, and water. Blend for 2 minutes, refrigerate, and serve.

Makes 1 quart

BARQŪQ, a Burjī Mameluke, seized the Baḥrī Mameluke sultanate in 1382. His dynasty was supported by the Circassian troops and ruled Egypt for the next one hundred forty years. A great threat to Egypt arose from Persia in the form of Tamerlane, an emir of the Khan, who had marched to the frontier of Syria by 1387. Barqūq was able to hold off Tamerlane for a short time, but under his son Faraj's rule, Tamerlane's march continued and he sacked Damascus in 1400. Although Tamerlane turned east again, Egypt suffered from the enormous expense of defending against his advances. This was followed by a severe famine and plague in 1403.

Egyptian influence in the Mediterranean increased in the early part of the fifteenth century. The eastern Mediterranean was controlled by Egyptian sea power, and trade routes were expanded into the Indian Ocean. Egypt's relations with the Ottomans to the north were friendly under the Mameluke sultan Barsbay. Although the fifteenth century was one of peace in Egypt, the cost of living rose steadily. Crises loomed. The building program of Sultan Qāyt-Bay (1468–1498) placed a great strain on the economy, and the Portuguese found a direct trade route to the Indian Ocean, circumventing Egypt. More dangerous still were the armies of the Ottoman Sultan Selim I (1467–1520). The Ottomans were at war with the Savafids of Persia, and both had eyes on the strategically situated Syria. The Egyptian Mameluke sultan Qānṣūḥ al-Ghawrī was stationed in Syria, observing the outcome of the war. The Ottomans won and then turned toward the Mameluke territories in Syria, forcing Qānṣūḥ al-Ghawrī into battle in August 1516. He died of a stroke on the battlefield and by January 23, 1517, Sultan Selim I was in Cairo, ending centuries of Mameluke rule in Egypt.

This was the second great victory of the Ottoman Turks, after their capture of Constantinople sixty-four years earlier. The West was thrown into crisis, and Egypt declined under the Ottoman administrators. The Egyptians were burdened with taxes and the Ottoman administrators were generally uninterested in Egypt, hoping only to have their tickets punched in furthering their careers before returning to Istanbul. Cairo declined as a cultural center, but not as a religious center. With the decline of Cairo, the rise of all-powerful Istanbul, the center of the Ottoman Empire, tilted the balance of power in the Mediterranean once again.

EGYPTIAN BEVERAGES

The extreme aridity of Egypt means that the most popular drink there is water. Although alcohol is legal in this mostly Muslim country, it is consumed almost wholly by Western tourists. The traveler who spends any length of time in Egypt is advised to counter the heat with soothing drinks of water or fruit juices rather than mind-numbing alcoholic concoctions. Small stands throughout Egypt serve a variety of fruit juices. They are made by throwing the whole fruit in a blender with some ice and sugar water and blending them, a kind of Egyptian smoothie. The most popular fruit juice drinks are farawala *(strawberry),* burtuqāl *(orange juice; called* mangariyya *in the south),* tamar hindī *(tamarind),* granata *or* rummān *(pomegranate),* qaṣab *(sugarcane), and, of course, the very common* ʿasir laymūn *(lemon juice, meaning lemonade).*[132]

Mawz bi'l-laban *is a banana smoothie made with milk and a little sugar.* Karkadiyya *is a unique drink made by soaking dried hibiscus flowers in water for a day and adding sugar. It is found in the north, and the traveler can buy a bag of the dried flowers in the Khan el-Khalili section of Cairo.*

Vegetable juices such as gazar *(carrot),* khiyār *(cucumber), and* qūṭa *(tomato) are also drunk.*

Popular hot drinks, as elsewhere in the Arab world, are tea, especially mint tea, and Turkish coffee, but also "white coffee" (page 329), a drink that can be made by steeping aniseed, caraway seeds, cinnamon, or fenugreek in hot water. In the Sinai, Bedouin tribes make a drink called jaʿdah, *a refreshing thirst-quencher derived from boiling a plant,* Teucrium polium, *with water and sugar.*

PROVISIONING THE URBAN MONSTER

A VAST network of trading routes converged on Mediterranean cities. The pulse of a city was usually located in some central point. In Istanbul, the Great Bazaar was the heart of the city, surrounded by *khans* (warehouses) and courtyards where authorities strictly controlled the food supplies of the city and Seray (the palace of the sultan—that is, Topkapı palace, also called the Seraglio). Istanbul, with seven hundred thousand people, was, in the words of the historian Fernand Braudel, "not a town but an urban monster." Boatmen and ferrymen manned thousands of barks, caïques, *perames, mahonnes*, lighters, and "door ships" for transporting animals from Scutari (Ushküdar) on the Asian side of Istanbul to the European side. The provisioning of a huge city like Istanbul was a great problem for the Sublime Porte (the office of the Grand Vizier and the real seat of power) and *etmek*, bread, enormous amounts of it, was the solution.[133]

In Istanbul, whose population was twice that of Naples, a bill of lading from March 1581 shows that eight ships from Egypt carrying only wheat provided food for just one day. One hundred years later, records showed that Istanbul's inhabitants consumed about five hundred tons of grain a day. In one year, almost two hundred thousand cattle were consumed. Thirty-five thousand of these went into making *pastırma*, a dried meat. Also consumed were four million sheep and three million lambs, as well as many barrels of honey, sugar, and rice, sacks and skins of cheese, caviar, and seven thousand tons of melted butter.[134]

Under the authoritarian planned economy of the Ottoman Empire, drawing riches from all corners, Istanbul could prosper. Prices were fixed, supply zones chosen to suit the methods of transport, and requisitioning was enforced. Istanbul traders were helped by laws that stipulated that merchandise could be unloaded only on the quays of the port of Istanbul. It was at Un Kapani, a few miles up the Golden Horn (an inlet of the Bosporus separating a portion of Istanbul) from the Topkapı palace, that grain from the Black Sea was unloaded. Everything flowed in, including many luxury goods, and very little flowed out, unlike the export centers of Alexandria, Tripoli, and Smyrna (Izmir).

In Anatolia, Antalya and the one-time capital of Bursa also benefited from riches coming from afar. The merchants of Antalya and Bursa were active in the import and export trade with Arab countries, using both land and sea routes.[135] Antalya was ruled by the Seljuk Turks until the Ottoman Turks took over in 1391. The rich merchants of Antalya built much of the charming old quarter known as Kaleiçi, although most of the traditional Turkish wooden buildings still standing are from the eighteenth and nineteenth centuries, delightfully renovated and housing many quaint hotels, inns, and restaurants. Antalya has long been famous for its mussels, as well as its agricultural products such as fresh vegetables and citrus fruits, that go to all corners of Turkey. Mention Antalya today and most Turks will think of the Fluted Minaret that still stands from Seljuk times—and a local *meze* preparation utilizing the mussels that grow on the rocks surrounding the town's harbor and coastline.

Midye Tava (Turkey)

FRIED MUSSELS

The preparation of midye tava *follows certain time-honored rules. The batter that the mussels are dipped in is a beer batter, something I found unusual in Muslim Turkey, although I was assured that that is common. The Antalyan cook will shuck the mussels to order at the last minute and not before. This recipe from the Pink Restaurant on Mermerli Sokak in Antalya was served as a* meze *with* tarator *sauce (see Note) and a cold beer. The restaurant sits on a promontory above the tiny and ancient harbor, and has a magnificent view of the mountains of Lycia in the distance. Those mussels could not have been more perfectly prepared.*

Some of the mussels will clump together as you fry them: don't worry about that, as long as the clumps are not too large.

½ cup all-purpose flour
1 tablespoon tomato juice (from a fresh or canned plum tomato, or tomato paste mixed with water)
2 large eggs, separated
¾ cup beer (lager)
Salt to taste
48 mussels, debearded and washed well
1½ cups pure virgin or extra virgin olive oil

1. In a large bowl, mix the flour, tomato juice, egg yolks, beer, and salt. In a medium-size bowl, beat the egg whites until stiff peaks form, then fold into the batter.

2. Shuck the mussels with a clam knife. Discard the shells and reserve the mussels. Drain the mussels.

3. In a large skillet, heat the olive oil until nearly smoking. Dip the mussels in the batter, let any excess drip off, and fry in batches until golden, 2 to 3 minutes for each, making sure you don't crowd the skillet. Remove with a skimmer or slotted spoon to a paper towel–lined platter to drain. Salt immediately and serve or keep warm until they are all cooked.

NOTE: *Tarator* sauce is made by grinding 1 cup of walnuts to a powder in a food processor, then mixing them with 4 mashed garlic cloves and 2 to 3 cups of diced French bread without the crust, previously soaked in milk and squeezed dry. Beat olive oil and fresh lemon juice into the mixture as one would make mayonnaise, until it reaches the right consistency.

Makes 4 meze *servings*

THE first order of business for the Ottoman government was the provisioning of wheat for the city. The *waqf,* the religious institution, played a major role in provisioning the city, with the *kadı,* a religious magistrate, responsible for the task. The charitably endowed hospices of the city distributed thousands of loaves of bread and meals each day to hundreds of people. The *imaret*s, charitable organizations that fed thousands of people who did not have an independent source of income, had large staffs of cooks and larders. They were the closest thing to today's public soup kitchens and they gave leftover food to widows and children.[136]

According to the seventeenth-century Ottoman scholar Evliya Çelebi's famous study, there were 26,000 cultivated fields in the four districts of the capital and 57,000 farmers. Their production in all likelihood went directly to the imperial palaces of the sultan. Istanbul was a huge entrepôt where the ships of the Black Sea and the Mediterranean, and the caravans of Thrace, the Balkans, and Anatolia came to sell their indispensible products for living. The *kadı* set the base price. The *mübasir* (dock expeditor) or the *yasakçi* (advance man) intervened to speed up the loading of ships and hurry their movements about the capital. Provisioning the capital also meant feeding the imperial troops of the palace and the numerous troops caserned around the city.

The state barley silos at Eminönü received three hundred shiploads a year, over fifty thousand metric tons, assuming a load of one hundred eighty tons per ship. Istanbul's bakers bought their wholesale flour from the state-run flour exchange, the *kapan-i dakik*, located at the entrance to the Golden Horn, which housed four hundred independent shops belonging to flour merchants. The bakers were organized by product, so there were neighborhood bakers and bakers specializing in a product such as hardtack *(peksimid)* for imperial army and navy stores, as well as *ekmek*, a kind of French bread, and *yufka*, a thin wheat flour pastry. Regulations going back to

Mehmed II's reign (1451–1481) required bakers to stock a minimum of one month supply of flour.[137]

There were two types of provisioning going on in Istanbul: one for the population and one for the palace guard and the troops. A document from 1674 gives precise numbers of head of livestock brought to Istanbul for slaughter: 199,900 beef, 3,965,760 mutton, and 2,877,400 lamb. During the same period the palace needed 325,228 mutton and lamb (deducting 96,000 for the Janissaries).[138]

It was prescribed in Islam that one of a ruler's charitable duties was to his people. Because of this responsibility elaborate organizations were set up to fulfill the requirements of feeding people. Large kitchens were built in the palaces and public feasts became important. A public feast was a privilege and a duty of the ruler. In Ottoman society the kitchen had a central importance because it was a social institution. The kitchen, on one hand, was central to the ruling classes who had to feed their huge retinues, numbering thousands of people. On the other hand, the kitchen symbolized the bonds of the people with the ruler. The sultan staffed his kitchens with the most renowned chefs, many of whom came from Bolu on Turkey's Black Sea coast, and many of Turkey's best chefs still do.

Although it was later connected to Islamic theological precepts, the practice of public feast had roots in particularly Turkic customs of Central Asia, as we know from the *Kutadgu bilig (Wisdom of royal glory),* a royal advice book written in Turkish in 1070, that says entertaining people with food and drink are among the chief virtues of a prince.[139] This practice of public feasts (*toy*) was introduced to the Islamic world by the Seljuks, a Muslim Turkish tribe that was the precursor to the Ottoman Turks. The empire they established in Anatolia after the defeat of the Byzantine Emperor at Manzikert in 1071 concerned the Christian West, which saw a new Muslim dynasty in the East as a threat;

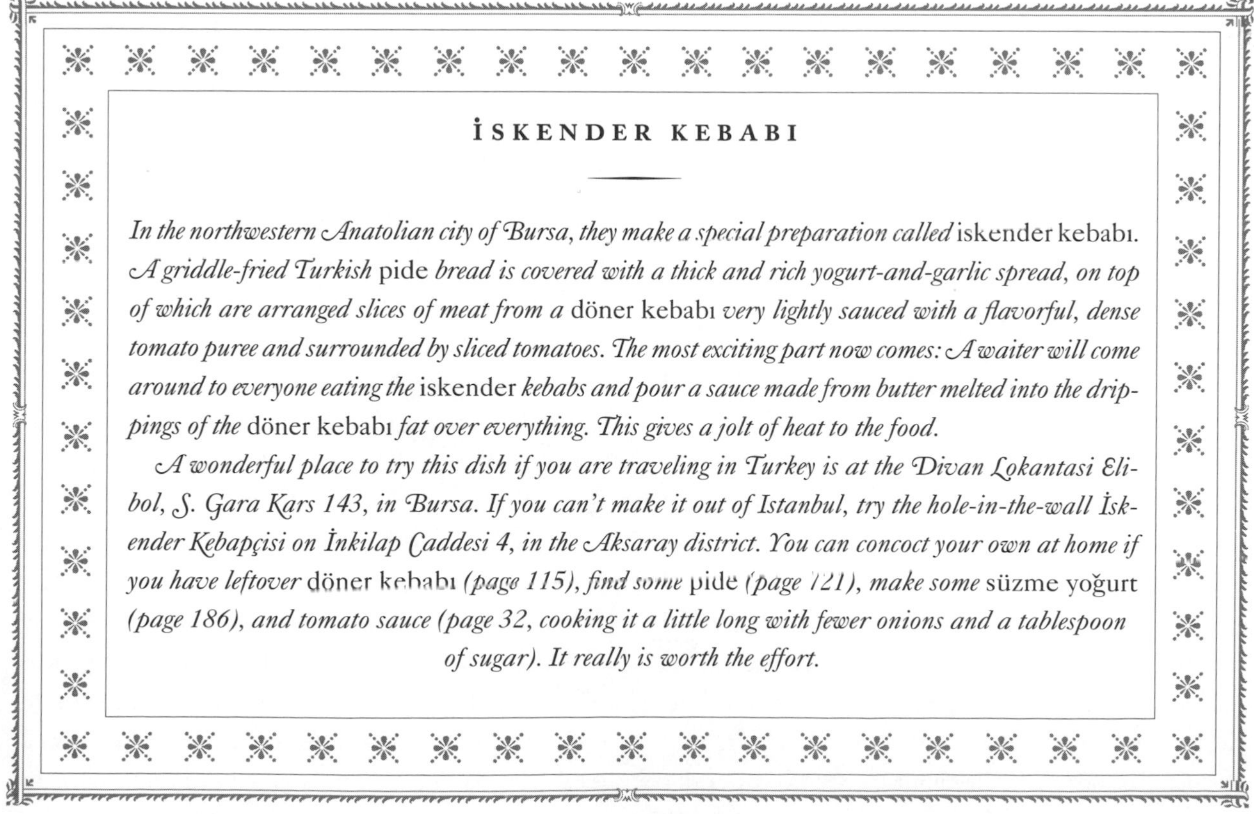

İSKENDER KEBABI

In the northwestern Anatolian city of Bursa, they make a special preparation called iskender kebabı. *A griddle-fried Turkish* pide *bread is covered with a thick and rich yogurt-and-garlic spread, on top of which are arranged slices of meat from a* döner kebabı *very lightly sauced with a flavorful, dense tomato puree and surrounded by sliced tomatoes. The most exciting part now comes: A waiter will come around to everyone eating the* iskender *kebabs and pour a sauce made from butter melted into the drippings of the* döner kebabı *fat over everything. This gives a jolt of heat to the food.*

A wonderful place to try this dish if you are traveling in Turkey is at the Divan Lokantasi Elibol, Ş. Gara Kars 143, in Bursa. If you can't make it out of Istanbul, try the hole-in-the-wall İskender Kebapçisi on İnkilap Caddesi 4, in the Aksaray district. You can concoct your own at home if you have leftover döner kebabı *(page 115), find some* pide *(page 121), make some* süzme yoğurt *(page 186), and tomato sauce (page 32, cooking it a little long with fewer onions and a tablespoon of sugar). It really is worth the effort.*

the establishment of the Seljuk governance was one of the motivating forces of the Crusades.

The sultan became personally interested in the food served because it was considered proof of his concern for society's well-being. Public feasts came to be held on religious holidays, such as the night of the Prophet's birth or the end of Ramadan. Special dishes were created for a variety of holidays, such as the *helva* (sweets) served for the Şeker Baynamı, the feast of the breaking of the Ramadan fast.

The beginnings of a true Turkish cuisine are to be found in the palace kitchens of the sultans. This was a refinement over the army kitchens of the Janissaries (see below), which in turn was a refinement over the food of the original Turkic tribes that moved into Anatolia from Central Asia before the eleventh century, which was mostly boiled and grilled lamb. But even today lamb is the most common meat in Turkish cuisine, where it is used in kebabs such as the *döner kebabı*, thin slices of meat pressed together and spit-roasted, small pieces of meat on a skewer (shish kebab), and meatballs *(köfte)*. Beef is not eaten directly but used to make certain kinds of sausages and, above all, *pastırma*, or dried beef (page 68). In the Middle Ages, there were a hundred *pastırma* shops in Istanbul located mostly in Galata, Top-hane, and Odun Kapisi.[140]

The palace of the sultan was described as a bottomless pit of food because he fed a huge palace population and didn't care about expense. Diners were started off with *meze*, little plates of appetizing food. One report tells us that the sultan's table had salads of "olives, capers, radishes, beets, green garlic, cucumbers, rose flowers and other seasonal things."[141] Vessels called *martaban* were used for carrying meat, such as lamb, spit-roasted chickens cut up into pieces, fricasseed mutton with butter and onions, fried pigeons that were then oven-baked with sugar and rose water, and chickens stuffed with rice and onions and served in a bouillon with eggs and cinnamon. Little meatballs were made with onions and rice and wrapped in borage or hazelnut leaves. Pigeon tortes were served, as was a dish of goose liver chopped with eggs, parsley, almonds, onions, cinnamon, nutmeg, Corinth raisins, and pigeon. The soup might be a puree of green peas with chicken bouillon and fingers of bread fried in butter with egg yolks.[142]

In 1527, there were 5,457 palace servants to feed. The palace kitchen was enormous. The Topkapı palace alone had several kitchens: the imperial kitchen, the confectioner's kitchen, and two bake houses. Within the imperial kitchen was the kitchen for the chief eunuch of the palace (supervising steward) and the kitchen for the palace pages. A special kitchen called the *kuşane* was reserved exclusively for the sultan himself. When Süleiman I the Magnificent rebuilt the palace, it was a grandiose construction with domes and chimneys housing ten kitchens, each serving a special group.[143] By 1679, the head of the imperial larder alone supervised 134 people.

The number of cooks in the imperial kitchens numbered 260 in 1510 and grew to 1,570 by 1570. The cooks were organized into a corps that was then divided into companies, like a military organization. The corps was headed by a chief with the rank of *ağa* (lord or master). He was assisted by a lieutenant and a secretary. As with any profession, there were masters, foremen, and apprentices. Servants in the storerooms formed another corps. Under the head of each corps were bakers, butchers, sweet makers, yogurt makers, vegetable keepers, makers of ring bread (*semit* bread), keepers of ice and snow, keepers of herbs, keepers of poultry, tinners of the copper utensils, makers of candles, water carriers, and wheat pounders. Waiters made up an independent group.[144]

The sultan's cooks competed to please their master by preparing special dishes of their own creation. The sultan showed pleasure by giving rewards. Thus, the Ottoman palace was considered the center of Ottoman Turkish cooking and was where creative chefs were trained and where the imperial Turkish court cuisine evident today developed. For scholars interested in this topic, there are detailed records of the ingredients used in archival kitchen expenditure books.

For the kitchens of the Topkapı palace alone, the annual consumption of lamb was about 1,270 tons. The other three palaces consumed 458 tons annually. Besides cereals, rice formed a good part of the diet of the Turks, especially the well-to-do and the palace. European travelers in Turkey in the Ottoman era always remarked on how the best foods were rice dishes.[145] For centuries rice was at the center of all Turkish cookery. One of the most popular Turkish dishes is pilaf, served with meat or fish. In the sixteenth century, ordinary rice came from Egypt (actually as tribute), the principal supplier of Istanbul, leaving from the port of Damietta. But the highly prized very long-grain or pilaf rice came from Anatolia and Persia, and it was more expensive because of tariffs, and the longer distance in the case of Persian rice. All in all, though, it does not seem that commerce in rice was subject to the severe regulation that wheat and meat were, although there was a corporation of about four hundred rice merchants.[146] After pilaf, one of the most delightful rice preparations was the dolma, or stuffed grape leaf. The dolma is still a very popular preparation in all of the Turkish and Arab Levant.

In the following recipes, we may see a cuisine derived from the Ottoman court. The first recipe uses an unleavened pastry called *yufka* to wrap a fragrant rice pilaf and is clearly a dish created by a chef for the privileged or the sultan.

Yufkalı Pilavı (Turkey)

PILAF IN PASTRY

This preparation has all the hallmarks of the creation of a royal chef in the kitchen of the Topkapı Sarayı, the palace of the sultan in Istanbul during the Ottoman Empire. This rice pilaf is perfumed with finely cut fresh vegetables, herbs, and fragrant spices and wrapped in yufka *pastry, a very thin Turkish pastry nearly as thin as phyllo that, in fact, means "thin." Charles Perry, who has written on the foods of medieval Turkic tribes, has speculated that an ancient Turkish* yufka *pastry described in an eleventh-century dictionary as a thin bread might be the progenitor of the Near Eastern baklava that exists today.*[147] *In this preparation, the* yufka *pastry becomes crunchy and the pilaf inside is like delicious buried treasure. (See page 588 for general instructions on cooking pilafs.)*

10 to 12 tablespoons (1¼ to 1½ sticks) unsalted butter
2 cups long-grain rice, rinsed well or soaked in water to cover for 30 minutes and drained
2 teaspoons salt
4¾ cups water
¼ cup pine nuts
1 small onion, finely chopped
1 cup diced carrots
1 cup fresh or frozen peas
2 tablespoons chopped fresh dill
6 tablespoons dried currants (preferably) or black raisins, soaked in tepid water to cover for 30 minutes and drained
½ teaspoon freshly ground allspice berries
⅛ teaspoon ground cinnamon
½ teaspoon freshly ground cardamom seeds (from about 20 shelled cardamom pods)
1 teaspoon sugar
Salt and freshly ground black pepper to taste
2 sheets *yufka* pastry (about 1 pound) (page 726) or ¾ pound (about 12 sheets) commercial phyllo pastry (usually 14 × 18-inch sheets; see page 224 on handling it)

1. In a large, heavy saucepan or casserole with a tight-fitting lid, melt 3 tablespoons of the butter over medium-high heat, then cook the rice until well coated, 3 minutes, stirring. Add the salt and 4 cups of the water. Bring to a boil, reduce the heat to very low,

cover, and cook until the liquid is absorbed, 12 to 15 minutes, without stirring or looking under the lid. Remove the lid, place a paper towel over the rice, replace the lid. Let stand off the burner for 15 minutes.

2. Meanwhile, melt 1 tablespoon of the butter in a medium-size skillet over medium-high heat, then cook the pine nuts, stirring, until golden, about 3 minutes. Be careful not to burn them. Remove with a slotted ladle and set aside.

3. Melt 2 tablespoons of the butter in the same skillet and cook the onion until translucent, about 4 minutes, stirring a few times. Add the carrots, fresh peas (not the frozen ones), dill, currants or raisins, allspice, cinnamon, cardamom, sugar, and the remaining 3/4 cup water, season with salt and pepper, stir, reduce the heat to medium, and cook for 20 minutes. Add the frozen peas (if using) 4 minutes before the vegetables are done. Stir this vegetable mixture into the rice along with the reserved pine nuts.

4. Preheat the oven to 425°F. Melt the remaining 4 to 6 tablespoons butter. Butter a round 12-inch baking pan and layer a sheet of *yufka* pastry (a round sheet about 16 inches in diameter) on the bottom, letting it hang over the edge. Brush heavily with melted butter. If using phyllo, you will need to overlap up to six sheets, brushing each layer with butter. Cover the pastry sheets with the rice mixture, spreading it evenly around the pan, and cover with another sheet of *yufka* pastry, tucking the sides under and brushing the top with butter. If using phyllo pastry, use six sheets and butter each layer. Bake until the top is light golden brown, 15 to 20 minutes. Invert onto a flat baking sheet. Return to the baking pan and bake the other side until the top is light golden brown, another 15 to 20 minutes. Remove from the baking pan to a round serving platter and serve hot or warm.

Makes 4 to 6 servings

Waraq ʿInab wa Kūsā (Arab Levant)

STUFFED GRAPE LEAVES WITH STUFFED ZUCCHINI

The Arab world was under Ottoman rule for five hundred years, and the Turkish influence is seen in many preparations, such as stuffed grape leaves. But the stuffing of vegetables has its roots in the Arab cookery of the early Islamic empire of the Abbasids in Baghdad, possibly learned from the Persians. Ottoman chefs perfected the stuffing of vegetables, and today nearly everything that can be stuffed is stuffed. The stuffed grape leaf and cabbage leaf are probably the most common and loved of all the stuffed vegetables. Stuffed grape leaves are a popular meze *or* mazza *in Greece, Turkey, and the Arab Levant and are known as* dolmades *in Greece and dolma in Turkey. With Arab cooks, the stuffed grape leaf becomes a little more complex and elaborate. It can be served at room temperature and is called* waraq ʿinab bi'l-zayt *(grape leaves with olive oil) or it can be served hot and is called* waraq ʿinab *(grape leaves).*

This recipe is an even more elaborate Lebanese-Palestinian version of the simple stuffed grape leaf. The recipe is from my former mother-in-law, Leila al-Qattan, and her cook, Ameena Ghattas, and it consists of stuffed grape leaves and stuffed zucchini cooked with mixed spices, lemon juice, fresh mint, and parsley on top of lamb shanks.

3/4 cup extra virgin olive oil
1 1/2 pounds ground lamb
2 tablespoons *bahārāt* (page 524)
2 teaspoons freshly ground allspice berries
1/4 teaspoon ground cinnamon
Salt and freshly ground black pepper to taste
2 cups medium-grain rice, rinsed well or soaked in water to cover for 30 minutes and drained

1¼ cups very finely chopped onions
6 tablespoons very finely chopped fresh parsley leaves
¾ cup very finely chopped fresh mint or coriander (cilantro) leaves
Juice from 1½ lemons
100 to 150 grape leaves (one to two 16-ounce jars, drained), boiled for 5 minutes in water to cover if fresh
3 pounds lamb shanks
10 small zucchini (about 2½ pounds), ends trimmed

1. In a large skillet, heat ¼ cup of the olive oil over medium-high heat, then brown the ground lamb with the *bahārāt*, allspice, cinnamon, salt, and pepper, about 8 minutes, stirring occasionally to break up the meat. Transfer to a large bowl, toss with the drained rice, onions, parsley, 6 tablespoons of the mint or coriander, and 3 tablespoons of the lemon juice, and season with salt.

2. Cover the bottom of a 10-inch stew pot with a drizzle of the remaining olive oil and 6 to 8 large grape leaves and place the lamb shanks on top.

3. Stuff and roll the remaining grape leaves. Set out two dinner plates and one platter. Lay the grape leaves on one dinner plate. On the empty dinner plate, which you will use to do the rolling, lay a grape leaf in front of you with the stem pointing toward you. Place a teaspoonful, or a little more, of stuffing just below the center of the leaf and roll the bottom part over it. Fold the two sides over toward the center and roll up the leaf tightly, but not too tightly. As you finished rolling the leaves, set them on the platter.

4. Hollow out the zucchini using a corer, making sure you do so carefully so as not to puncture the skin. Save the zucchini pulp for making the variation of *ʿujja bi'l-bādhinjān* on page 531. Stuff the zucchini whole with the same stuffing you used to stuff the grape leaves.

5. Pack the stuffed zucchini, then the rolled stuffed grape leaves, tightly and neatly in the stew pot on top of the lamb shanks. Sprinkle each layer with some of the remaining 6 tablespoons mint or coriander and lemon juice, salt, and a light drizzle of olive oil. Finish the top layer with the remaining olive oil, mint, and lemon juice and dash of salt. Invert a heavy plate on top of the grape leaves and zucchini to press them down. Cover and cook over a medium heat for 30 minutes. Reduce the heat to low and cook until the stuffed grape leaves are done, 2 to 3 hours. Test for doneness after 2 hours by tasting one of the grape leaves. If the rice is cooked, it is done, otherwise continue cooking.

Makes 10 servings

Tas Kebabı (Turkey)

LAMB AND SPICE STEW

The first meat of all Turkish cuisine is lamb or mutton. Meat is usually cut up into small pieces and cooked with vegetables for a long time. This method of cooking arose because fuel was scarce and roasting is a profligate way to use up firewood. A second reason this was a popular method of cooking meat was that, although the meat would break down, a wonderful sauce usually resulted from its being cooked with vegetables. A third reason is that long-stewed meat would not be bloody, avoiding the Islamic prohibition against eating blood. Traditionally, tas kebabı, *which means something like "stewed kebabs in a bowl," begins with the cooking of the vegetables in butter, in a method called* yağa vurmak, *"butter-infused," before the meat itself is cooked in the same butter. The stew is stewed in a cooking bowl that is then inverted onto a plate for a dish resembling the upside-down dishes of the Arabs (page 605). I reverse this method of cooking the vegetables first because that is the way I learned it in Turkey.* Tas kebabı *is served surrounded with sultan's delight,* hünkar beğendi *(this page).*

5 tablespoons unsalted butter
2½ pounds boneless lamb stew meat, trimmed of fat and cut into 1-inch cubes
2 medium-size onions, finely chopped
6 tablespoons seeded and finely chopped green bell pepper
¼ cup tomato paste
1½ cups water
½ teaspoon freshly ground allspice berries
¼ teaspoon ground cinnamon
Salt and freshly ground black pepper to taste
¼ cup finely chopped fresh parsley leaves

1. In a large, heavy casserole, melt 2½ tablespoons of the butter over high heat, then brown the lamb in it on all sides, about 5 minutes. Remove the lamb pieces with a slotted spoon and set aside.

2. Reduce the heat to medium. Add the remaining 2½ tablespoons butter to the casserole, melt, and cook the onions and green pepper until the onions are soft, about 8 minutes, stirring. Add the tomato paste dissolved in the water. Stir well, scraping the bottom of the casserole, then add the allspice, cinnamon, salt, pepper, and 2 tablespoons of the parsley.

3. Return the lamb to the casserole, reduce the heat to low, cover, and simmer until the lamb is tender and the sauce thick, about 3 hours. Sprinkle the meat with the remaining 2 tablespoons parsley and serve.

Makes 4 to 6 servings

Hünkar Beğendi (Turkey)

SULTAN'S DELIGHT

The name of this magnificent eggplant recipe, said to have been created for the Sultan Murad IV (1612?–1640), is reason enough to make it. Turkish cookbook author Neşet Eren tells another story of its invention, though. She says that it was so named after being requested by Empress Eugénie, the wife of Napoleon III, when she visited the Topkapı palace in the mid-nineteenth century. Traditionally, hünkar beğendi *is served with* tas kebabı *(page 323).*

2 pounds eggplant
2 tablespoons fresh lemon juice
½ cup (1 stick) unsalted butter
½ cup all-purpose flour
1½ cups hot milk
1 cup grated *kashkaval* or *kasseri* cheese
Salt and freshly ground black pepper to taste

1. Preheat the oven to 425°F. Place the eggplant in a baking pan in the oven until the skins blister black, about 40 minutes. Once they are cool enough to handle, remove the flesh from the charred skins and transfer to a strainer. Leave to drain for 30 minutes to leach them of their bitter juices. Transfer to a food processor with the lemon juice and process until smooth.

2. In a large, heavy casserole, melt the butter over medium-high heat, then stir in the flour to form a roux and cook for 2 to 3 minutes, stirring. Remove the casserole from the heat and whisk in the milk slowly until a thick white sauce without lumps has formed. Return the casserole to the burner.

3. Stir in the pureed eggplant, reduce the heat to low, and simmer for 20 minutes, stirring occasionally. Stir in the cheese and beat well until smooth. Season with salt and pepper and serve.

Makes 4 to 6 servings

İmam Bayıldı (Turkey)

THE IMAM FAINTED

The imam fainted, imam bayıldı, *is the name of one of the most famous of Turkish* zeytinyağlılar *(olive oil foods). It may have medieval roots, if we consider that the* zeytinyağlı *dishes, which are usually eaten cold, fit the prescriptions of the dietetic theory of humors that was the basis for medical theory at that time. It was customary to eat cold and moist foods in the summer during medieval times because that counteracted the hot, dry humor of summer that caused an increase in bile.*[148]

İmam bayıldı *is an eggplant slashed down the middle and stuffed with onions, garlic, and tomatoes and then simmered in olive oil to cover. There are several apocryphal stories about the origins of the dish: the imam (Muslim prayer leader) fainted or swooned when he tasted how good it was; that the imam fainted when he saw how much expensive olive oil was used; that the imam was delighted when a shopkeeper's wife was required to quickly prepare a dish for the imam's unexpected visit. A Turkish proverb casts light on another interpretation:* İmam evinden aş, ölü gözünden yaş çıkmaz *(No food is likely to come out of the imam's house and no tears from a corpse). Perhaps, the meaning is that the stingy imam, when presented with a dish so generous, certainly was delighted, or fainted from delight.*

4 small eggplant (about 1½ pounds)
Salt
10 tablespoons extra virgin olive oil
2 medium-size onions, cut lengthwise and thinly sliced
6 large garlic cloves, chopped
½ pound ripe tomatoes, peeled, seeded, and chopped
¼ cup finely chopped fresh parsley leaves
2 tablespoons chopped fresh dill
1 teaspoon sugar
2 tablespoons fresh lemon juice
¼ cup water

1. Peel off strips of the eggplant skin at 1-inch intervals to make a striped effect. Cut off the stem portion, then cut each eggplant in half lengthwise. Make a deep lengthwise slit along the flesh side of the eggplant, making sure you don't puncture the skin. Cut a very small portion of the skin side of the eggplant to make a flat section so the eggplant can sit correctly in the skillet later. Salt the flesh and set aside, flesh side down, on some paper towels for 30 minutes to leach the eggplant of its bitter juices. Dry with paper towels.

2. In a large skillet, heat ¼ cup of the olive oil over high heat; once it's smoking, fry the eggplant, flesh side down, until golden brown, about 4 minutes. Remove from the skillet to drain on some paper towels.

3. In the same skillet you cooked the eggplant, add the remaining 6 tablespoons oil and heat over medium-high heat, then cook the onions and garlic until soft and yellow, about 5 minutes, stirring frequently so the garlic doesn't burn. Transfer the onions to a medium-size bowl and mix well with the tomatoes, parsley, dill, sugar, salt to taste, and a few tablespoons of the cooking oil.

4. Arrange the eggplant halves in a large skillet or casserole with the slit side up. Gently open the slits so that they can accommodate as much of the stuffing as possible. Season the eggplant with salt, then stuff each one so that the stuffing fills the slits and is spread to cover all the flesh. Sprinkle the lemon juice over the eggplant. Pour any remaining sauce or juices, along with the water, into the skillet, cover, and cook over low heat until the eggplant is soft, about 50 minutes, adding water to the skillet if it is getting too dry. Let the eggplant cool in the skillet and serve whole at room temperature.

Makes 6 servings

❈ *Zeytinyağlı Patlıcan Dolması* (Turkey)

STUFFED EGGPLANT WITH OLIVE OIL

The Ottoman court cuisine began to use olive oil more than had been common. A class of dishes arose called "olive oil foods," zeytinyağlılar. *These were usually vegetables cooked in copious amounts of olive oil and served at room temperature as a* meze. *This eggplant preparation is a favorite and is related to the famous preparation known as* imam bayıldı *(page 325) and eaten at room temperature as a first course.*

8 medium-size eggplant (3½ to 4 pounds)
1 cup extra virgin olive oil
4 medium-size onions, finely chopped
Salt to taste
½ cup short- or medium-grain rice, rinsed well or soaked in tepid water 30 minutes and drained
2 tablespoons pine nuts
1¼ cups water
1 small ripe tomato, peeled, seeded, and finely chopped
2 tablespoons dried currants, soaked in tepid water to cover 30 minutes and drained
1 teaspoon freshly ground allspice berries
Freshly ground black pepper to taste
1 tablespoon finely chopped fresh mint leaves
¼ cup finely chopped fresh dill (about ½ bunch)
1 teaspoon sugar

1. Slice the tops off the eggplant. Hollow out the centers with a corer, being careful not to puncture the skin, and place in salted water for 30 minutes to leach the bitter juices. Rinse the eggplant in plain water, inside and out, and pat dry with paper towels.

2. In a large skillet, heat ½ cup of the olive oil with the onions and salt over medium heat, then cook until the onions are golden, about 40 minutes, stirring occasionally, reducing the heat if it's cooking too fast. Add the drained rice and pine nuts and cook, stirring, for another 2 minutes. Add ¼ cup of the water, the tomato, currants, allspice, pepper, mint, and dill, stir to mix well, cover, and cook for 15 minutes. Remove from the heat, add the sugar, stir, and set aside.

3. Stuff the eggplant loosely with the rice mixture, replace the tops, if desired, and arrange in a large pan or casserole with a cover (you may need to cook the eggplant in two pans). Add the remaining cup water and ½ cup olive oil and season with salt. Cover and cook over medium heat until the rice is cooked and the eggplant is soft to the touch but still firm enough to hold its shape, about 50 minutes. Turn the heat off and leave the eggplant in the pan until cool. Remove the eggplant to a serving platter. Cut into ½-inch-thick slices, slightly overlapping them, and serve at room temperature.

Makes 8 servings

❈ *Zeytinyağlı Taze Fasulye* (Turkey)

GREEN BEANS IN OLIVE OIL

Another popular zeytinyağlı *(olive oil dish) preparation is this dish made with green beans. Turks are very fussy about their green beans. In this preparation the beans should be picked very fresh from the plant about an hour before cooking. In Turkey, so many families have vegetable gardens that preparations such as this one are very popular. A local farmer's market will have the quality of bean necessary for a successful rendition of this recipe if you don't have your own garden.*

Runner beans can also be used in this Turkish preparation served at room temperature. The beans are cooked a long time, until they are completely soft. If your beans are old, you may have to cook them up to 1½ hours, but try to avoid old beans.

1 pound green beans, ends trimmed and halved lengthwise
1 medium-size onion, thinly sliced
2 ripe plum tomatoes, peeled, seeded, and chopped
Salt to taste
⅓ cup extra virgin olive oil
1 cup water
1 tablespoon sugar

1. Put the green beans, onion, and tomatoes in a large skillet and mix well with your hands. Salt and mix again with your hands. Pour the olive oil over the vegetables and cook, covered, over medium heat for 15 minutes. Pour in the water and continue to cook. Sprinkle over the sugar and shake the skillet. Cook until the beans are very tender, soft, 45 minutes to 1½ hours, moistening with more water if necessary. The vegetables should never be swimming in water, only moist.

2. Turn the heat off and uncover the skillet, letting the vegetables cool completely. Serve at room temperature. Drizzle some olive oil over the beans before serving.

Makes 4 servings

✣ ✣ ✣

THE Ottoman rulers had imported slaves—often young Christian boys from lands conquered by the Ottomans—to Istanbul, as well as Egypt, where they were integrated into the military and became the elite guard known as the Janissary Corps. The Janissaries eventually became strong enough to be king makers, and they engaged in numerous revolts against some minister or another and, in several instances, the sultan himself. They were organized on the model of a kitchen. The reason for this may lie in the *futuwwa* (semireligious movement) and Bektashi (an order of dervishes) connections of the corps (and their relationship to the feeding of their members), or in the Turkish custom of *toy*, the institutionalized state feeding of the sultan's subjects. The entire corps was known as the *ocak* (hearth) and was commanded by an *ağa* (master). The *qazan-i şarif*, or sacred cauldron of *şorba* (soup), was the emblem of the whole Janissary corps, and the Janissary headgear was ornamented with a spoon. High-ranking officers were called *şorbadji* ("*soupiers*" or soupmen).[149] Other military ranks were designated by culinary terms—for instance, *aşçıbaşı* (chief cook), the *karakullukçu* (scullion), the *çörekçi* (baker of round bread), and the *gözlemici* (pancake maker).[150] The corps was composed of battalions, *orta*, and each battalion had two or three great *kazans*, cauldrons, to feed the battalion, which could number between one hundred and five hundred troops. Typically the cauldrons were for cooking soup or pilaf. The head cook of each battalion kitchen was the most influential officer in the battalion. Important meetings were held in the kitchen around the cauldron. The Janissaries, who became quite powerful, would "overturn the cauldron" when displeased with the sultan, symbolizing a rejection of the sultan's food, and hence his policies and signaling the beginning of a rebellion. To this day "overturning the cauldron" is an expression in Turkish meaning the same.[151] The Janissaries became so strong, and such a privileged class, that Christian parents soon begged to have their children enrolled.

The common people of Istanbul and Anatolia ate a less elaborate food than the palace people in the Middle Ages. The Istanbulu ate stuffed chickens, or in a ragout, as was popular around Smyrna (Izmir). Other fowl, such as ducks, geese, and pigeons, were reserved for the imperial cuisine. Birds arrived from the provinces at the port of Odun Kapisi, and were delivered to the bird merchants of Stamboul, the *tavukcu taifesi*, which constituted a corporation, and gave its name, *Tavukpazari* (chicken market), to a section of the city. Istanbul had a reputation among Western travelers in the Middle Ages for marvelous fish, the splendor of its fisheries of Stamboul and Galata, and the quality of the species available to buy.[152] A modern traveler can walk down to the Kumkapı Balik Hali to witness the variety of fish or sit down in any of the fish restaurants in the Kumkapı area, or have a fried *uskumru* (mackerel) sandwich prepared by the boatmen near the Galata bridge on the Eminönü side—one of the most memorable foods I ate in Turkey. But we should remember the words of Braudel concerning this sight at Galata: *Mais si le spectacle laisse un souvenir aussi vivace, n'est-ce pas parce qu'il est rarissime?* (But if the spectacle leaves a lively memory, isn't that because it is so rare?)[153]

Many Turkish families in the sixteenth century lived on one ton of rice along with several pots of melted butter and dried fruits for a year. That's a lot of rice, even for a family of four, and therefore there is no mystery why pilaf is so common in Turkey. The midday meal was the most prized and it was often eaten out. An already prepared meal could be bought at the *başhne*, a storehouse for sheep's heads and feet, accompanied with rice or with tripe bought at the *işkembecı*, the tripe merchant, or the *muhallebici*, where you can buy a light dish based on milk, cream, or semolina, with boiled chicken. The evening meal was the meal eaten at home, with the head of the house served by the wife or maid. Food was eaten with fingers, the fork being unknown.[154]

❈ *İşkembe Çorbası* (Turkey)

TRIPE SOUP

In the lifetime of Süleiman I the Magnificent (1494–1566), Istanbulu could buy food for takeout at a variety of shops about the city. Often these meals were bought for the midday meal, and one of the favorite cookshops was the işkembecı, *the tripe merchant's shop, where one could buy a prepared tripe soup that is very popular even today in Istanbul. Today, many Istanbulu will have a* işkembe çorbası, *tripe soup, late at night as they are returning home from a night out on the town. In fact, it is rarely made at home. Folkore has it that it is a comforting antidote for the expected hangover. This recipe is developed from a description by my friend Ihsan Gurdal.*

Tripe has variable cooking times depending on the kind of tripe and the kind of processing it may go through at the butcher, so check after two hours by tasting a small piece. It should be soft and tender but with a little viscous bite to it. Also run your exhaust fan at full blast, and add a few pieces of mastic to the cooking water, if you like, while it cooks to remove any odors, which tend to be strong during the first part of the cooking process.

2½ pounds veal tripe
Several grains of mastic (page 718; optional)
2 medium-size onions, coarsely chopped
3 large garlic cloves, finely chopped
Zest and juice from 1 lemon
1 bay leaf
1 teaspoon dried wild marjoram *(rigani)* or oregano
¼ teaspoon dried thyme
1½ teaspoons salt
3 quarts water
3 garlic cloves
¼ cup (½ stick) unsalted butter
2 tablespoons all-purpose flour
2 large eggs
1 tablespoon paprika

1. Wash the tripe and cut off any fat. Cut the tripe into 6-inch squares. Place it in a stew pot with the mastic grains, onions, chopped garlic, lemon zest, bay leaf, marjoram, thyme, and 1 teaspoon of the salt and cover with the water, adding more if necessary to have the tripe covered by several inches. Bring to a boil, then reduce the heat to a gentle boil, and cook until the tripe is tender, 2 to 7 hours, partially covered,

replenishing the water when necessary to keep the tripe covered and skimming the foam off the surface from time to time. Drain, saving the liquid, by straining through a piece of cheesecloth. Cool the liquid, then slice and chop the tripe into little pieces.

2. Reheat 8 cups of the cooking broth with the pieces of tripe very slowly over medium heat. Crush the garlic cloves with the remaining ½ teaspoon salt and stir into the soup with 1 tablespoon of the lemon juice.

3. In a small saucepan, melt 2 tablespoons of the butter; once it stops sizzling, add the flour and cook for 2 minutes, stirring. Remove the saucepan from the heat and whisk in a few ladlefuls of broth, about 1 cup, to thin the roux. Beat the eggs well and whisk into the roux, also off the heat. Slowly and gradually whisk in the remaining lemon juice.

4. Stir the roux mixture into the broth and bring to a boil. Turn the heat off and let it sit while you prepare the garnish. Melt the remaining 2 tablespoons butter; when it stops sizzling, stir in the paprika.

Serve the soup with a drizzle of the paprika butter.

Makes 4 servings

TRAVELERS noted the frugality of the poor rural population of Anatolia, who were content with raw cucumber and melon. They also mentioned onions and garlic accompanied by bread. The yogurt was excellent, and the Turks were big eaters of vegetables. Garlic came from the region of İzmit (Kocaeli/Nicomedia) and lemons from Chios, Cos, and Mersin (Içel) in Cilicia (Çukurova). Vinegar was a specialty of the region of Brousse. Olive oil and olives were from the region of Erdek, Aydıncık, and Edremit. Spices were transported through Egypt from Arabia and the Indies. Venice played an important role in the importation of spices to the Ottoman Empire and, above all, to Istanbul.[155]

Tommaso Alberti traveled to Istanbul in 1609 and recorded some impressions about the food. The Turks ate lots of bread that was soft and perfect, he wrote. The soup was served with a sauce made of different fruits, including lemon juice and sugar, and was followed by meat. One always eats with the hands, Alberti noted, because the food is "delicately" cooked and perfect. I think he meant that many of the foods were *meze*—that is, finger food. *Antipasti* and pasta were not eaten. After the meat, the Turks finished with several tortes, pies filled with cheese or

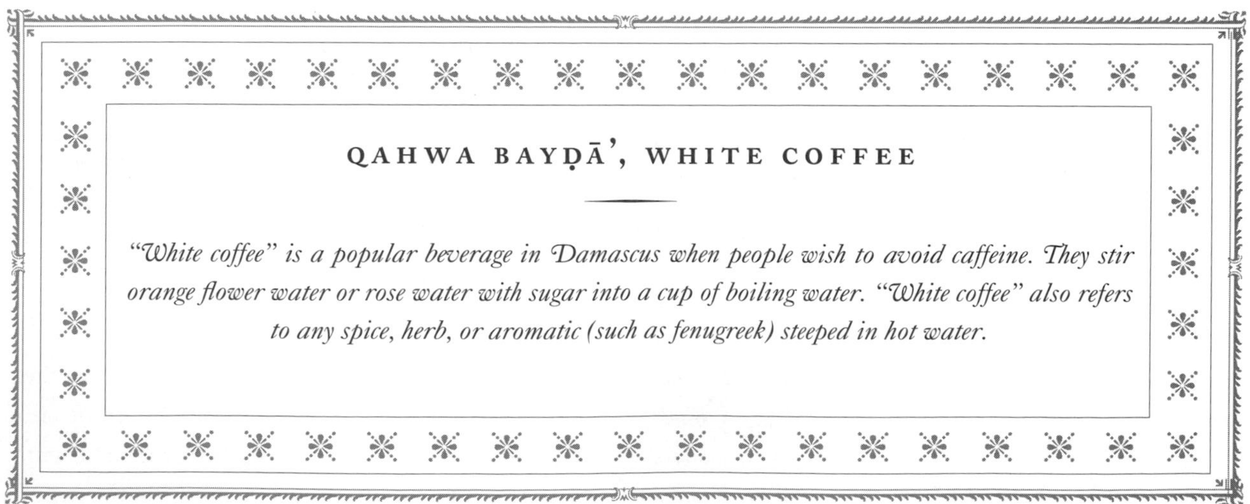

QAHWA BAYḌĀ', WHITE COFFEE

"White coffee" is a popular beverage in Damascus when people wish to avoid caffeine. They stir orange flower water or rose water with sugar into a cup of boiling water. "White coffee" also refers to any spice, herb, or aromatic (such as fenugreek) steeped in hot water.

fruit. Alberti marveled at the kitchen equipment, such as the huge cauldrons and gold serving platters.[156]

A popular drink was flavored with pomegranate syrup. Another was *boza*, a kind of beer made with barley or millet and not very expensive. *Boza* merchants were numerous in Stamboul; there were nearly three hundred shops in 1526.[157] The barley was imported from Anatolia or Thrace and the millet from Tekirdağ (Rodosto). *Müselles* was a kind of *vino cotto*, cooked wine, made from unfermented grape must and sugar and legal to drink as long as one didn't get drunk. *Raki* or *arak*, made from mastic from Chios, was also drunk. Coffee, originating in Abyssinia, appeared in Mecca by 1511, and was introduced to Istanbul by 1517 from the Yemen after the Ottoman conquest of Egypt and the Hijaz. Every year 40,000 *ferde* (5,600 tons) of coffee arrived in Egypt, 50 percent going to Istanbul and the rest to other provinces of the empire. By 1532, coffee appeared in Damascus and in Venice by 1615.[158]

Mantı (Turkey)

TURKISH WONTONS WITH YOGURT-GARLIC SAUCE AND CAYENNE BUTTER

The roots of everyday Turkish cuisine, as opposed to the court cuisine, are found in the Turkic tribes of Central Asia and perhaps the preexisting Greek inhabitants of Anatolia. As the Turkish food authority Nevin Halıcı suggests, a study of the food habits of contemporary Kazan Turks and Tatars might indicate a close relationship between the Turkish foods of today and their historical roots. Mantı *certainly seems a likely candidate.*[159] Mantı *predate the earliest appearance of ravioli in the European Mediterranean, and it is possible that the concept of ravioli derives from this Central Asian precedent.*

The Turkish word mantı *appears to derive from the Chinese via the Uighuric language of a Turkic tribe in eighth-century Sinkiang.* Mantı *is easily translated as "Turkish ravioli," although Turkish wonton might be more appropriate, and even then that description does not capture the painstaking process of making these miniature wontons.*[160] *The dish consists of small wontons of meat served with a yogurt-and-garlic sauce with melted red pepper butter. It is traditionally served at room temperature or warm, not hot.*

Armenians also eat mantı, *and you are likely to find them in the frozen foods section of such a market in the communities where people of Armenian extraction mostly live, in New York, Connecticut, Massachusetts, and California. Alternatively, an excellent substitute is the small meat wontons sold in Chinese groceries, although the smallest Chinese wontons are still about twice as large as the Turkish* mantı. *As a last resort, use small Italian meat ravioli or tortellini.*

1 pound *mantı*, small meat ravioli, or small meat wontons
2 cups chicken or beef broth (page 54)
4 garlic cloves
1 teaspoon salt
1 quart high-quality full-fat plain yogurt, at room temperature
1/4 cup (1/2 stick) unsalted butter
1 teaspoon cayenne pepper
1 teaspoon paprika

1. Preheat the oven to 400°F. Grease a baking pan and arrange the wontons or ravioli over the bottom in a single layer. Bake, uncovered, until golden, about 25 minutes. Pour in the broth and continue cooking for another 15 minutes without turning.

2. In a mortar, pound the garlic and salt together until mushy. Stir into the yogurt and continue stirring until creamy. Melt the butter in a small pan, then stir in the cayenne and paprika. Pour the yogurt

over the wontons, drizzle the melted butter on top, and serve.

Makes 4 servings

Menemen (Turkey)

SCRAMBLED EGGS WITH CHILI PEPPERS AND TOMATOES

Menemen is a small market town off the main highway north of Smyrna (Izmir) that gives its name to this dish of green chili peppers, tomatoes, and scrambled eggs. It's quite possible that this town is the source for the famous shakhshūka *of North Africa, a hash made of eggs, tomatoes, bell peppers, and other vegetables.* Shakhshūka *is not an Arabic word, but in fact derives from the Turkish dish made with peppers, onions, and eggs called* şakşuka, *another name for* menemen.[161]

The population of Turkey until recently was rural. Many Turkish families grew their own vegetables and had small chicken coops where poultry was raised for their eggs. This was a popular preparation for lunch, since eggs are not eaten for breakfast in Turkey. Traditionally, meat is not included in the recipe, although I've had it that way in restaurants in Istanbul. Some cooks use only butter, others only olive oil. Being unable to choose, I've used both. One can also slide a fried egg on top of the finished dish or scramble two eggs in a separate pan and then fold them into the peppers and tomatoes.

1 tablespoon unsalted butter
1 tablespoon extra virgin olive oil
2 long green chili peppers, seeded and chopped
1 long green pepper *(peperoncino)*, seeded and chopped
1½ pounds ripe tomatoes, peeled, seeded, and chopped
5 large eggs
Leaves from ½ bunch fresh parsley, chopped
¼ pound *jubna bayḍā'* (Syrian cheese; page 725) or mozzarella cheese, diced
Salt and freshly ground black pepper to taste

1. In a large skillet, heat the butter and olive oil together over medium-high heat. Once the butter has melted, cook the peppers and tomatoes, covered, until the peppers are tender, about 15 minutes, stirring several times.

2. Beat the eggs together lightly with the parsley. Pour the eggs into the skillet along with the cheese stirred in and season with salt and pepper. Reduce the heat to medium, stir once or twice, and cook until the eggs set, about 6 minutes. Serve immediately.

Makes 3 servings

Türlü (Turkey)

VEGETABLE RATATOUILLE

Türlü *is a preparation from Erzincan in eastern Turkey. It is cold in Erzincan, and this dish is traditionally served as a hearty, piping hot antidote to the cold weather, abundant with corn and root vegetables such as potatoes, turnips, carrots, sunchokes, and celeriac. This recipe is the summer version that you may find replicated throughout the Mediterranean in one way or another.*

Esther Benbassa, in her book Cuisine judeo-espagnole, *describes the Turkish* türlü *as a kind of ratatouille. She tells us the word* türlü *in Turkish means "mixture" or "variety."* Türlü, *also called* güveç yaz *(summer stew) or* güveç kış *(winter stew), is said to be a slang expression for a dish of different foods all artistically combined. Among the Spanish Jews who migrated to Turkey (the Sephardim), the word means "confusion." In Lebanon,* türlü *might be called* yakhnat al-khuḍra *(vegetable stew), while in Egypt it is also known as* tūrlī *and made with small bits of lamb and mint. In Majorcan cuisine, a dish called* tumbet *is very similar to* tūrlü, *with the addition of potatoes. Even in Greece, reflecting its own Turkish domination, the dish known as* briami *(page 235) is also called* tourlou. *From the Yugoslavian part of Macedonia, Bosnia and Herzegovina, Montenegro, and the Dalmatian coast, the same dish appears as* djuveç *(stew) and sometimes contains mutton.*

Türlü *is made in an earthenware* marmite *or a pot called an* oya *among Turkish Jews, probably derived from the Ladino word, the language of the Spanish Jews: in Spain a similar earthenware* marmite *is called an* olla. Türlü *is usually served with grilled meats, as is the Catalan* escalivada *(page 171) and the Majorcan* tumbet.

1 pound eggplant, peeled and cut into cubes
Salt
1 cup extra virgin olive oil
4 medium-size onions, chopped
2 garlic cloves, crushed
½ pound zucchini, peeled and sliced
3 green bell peppers, seeded and quartered
½ pound green beans, ends trimmed and cut in half
½ pound small okra, ends trimmed
5 ripe tomatoes (about 1½ pounds), peeled, seeded, and sliced
Freshly ground black pepper to taste
2 tablespoons finely chopped fresh parsley leaves
Paprika to taste

1. Lay the eggplant cubes on some paper towels and sprinkle with salt. Leave them to drain of their bitter juices for 30 minutes, then pat dry with paper towels.

2. In a large skillet, heat ½ cup of the olive oil over medium-high heat, then cook the eggplant cubes until browned, about 8 minutes, stirring. Remove from the skillet and set aside.

3. Heat another ¼ cup of the olive oil in the skillet and cook the onions and garlic over medium-high heat until the onions are translucent, about 6 minutes, stirring. Set the skillet aside.

4. Preheat the oven to 350°F. In a large casserole, layer the eggplant cubes over the bottom. Cover this layer with the sliced zucchini, half of the peppers, and half of the green beans. Spread some onions over next, then the okra, and then half the tomatoes. Sprinkle on some salt, pepper, half of the parsley, and abundant paprika. Repeat the vegetable layering, finishing with the remaining sliced tomatoes. Sprinkle with more salt, pepper, the remaining parsley, and paprika, pour over the remaining ¼ cup olive oil, cover, and bake until soft, about 1½ hours. Serve lukewarm.

Makes 6 servings

SPIT- and skewer-roasting was popular and still is throughout the Mediterranean, as we see by the following recipes as we travel east to west. Nearly all these preparations are never made in the home but rather are traditionally served in specialty restaurants or are found as street food, that is, city food.

The Turkish penchant for grilling is noted in early works in Turkish from the eleventh century, where men competed against each other in skewering meats.[162] The origin of this interest in grilling is usually tied to the Turkic history of nomadic and seminomadic life, where cooking over open field fires or in open pit ovens was common. But another reason given for grilling's popularity throughout the Mediterranean is simply that Mediterranean life, because of the generally mild climate, is focused on out-of-door activities, historically because of necessity and today because of enjoyment and habit.

Şiş Kebabı (Turkey)

SHISH KEBAB

Who has never heard of shish kebab? In Turkish it literally means "gobbets of meat roasted on a spit or skewers." Probably the most famous preparation for grilled lamb, there seems to be countless recipes. It is said that shish kebab was born over the open-field fires of medieval Turkic soldiers, who used their swords to grill meat. Given the obvious simplicity of spit-roasting meat over a fire, I suspect its genesis is earlier. There is iconographical evidence of Byzantine Greeks cooking shish kebabs.[163] *But surely the descriptions of skewering strips of meat for broiling in Homer's* Odyssey *must count for an early shish kebab.*[164]

In the Arab world, the same preparation is called shīsh kabāb *or* laḥm mishwī *(grilled meat). The true shish kebabs are pieces of marinated lamb affixed to flat or four-sided bladed metal skewers that are grilled over a fire suspended by a skewer holder, without the meat ever touching the grilling grate. The varieties of marinades are wide and could include any combination of olive oil, lemon juice, onion juice, milk, yogurt,* rigani *(wild marjoram), crumbled bay leaves, cinnamon, allspice, and other spices. Using tomatoes, onion wedges, and green bell pepper to separate the meat on the skewers has been suggested by several food writers to be a modern concoction invented by Turkish restaurateurs to make the skewers look more attractive to customers.*

The variety of kebabs is seemingly endless. The word kebab *means "to roast," which is what grilling is, properly speaking.* Orman kebabı *is whole roasted lamb,* çoban kebabı *is a shepherd's-style roast of meat stuck through a stick that is driven into the ground before an open-field fire;* hacci osman kebabı *is a roast on a revolving spit;* süt kebabı *is meat parboiled in milk, then skewered and roasted;* kuşbaşi kebabı *is another skewered and roasted kebab;* koyun kebabı *is a whole lamb roasted in a covered pit;* kabarma kebabı *is a grilled spatchcocked fowl (split open at the belly, kept whole, and flattened with a mallet);* kefenli kebabı *is roast meat wrapped in a "shroud" of bread. Every Turkish cookbook has a chapter called* kebaplar, *where dozens more recipes exist.*

This recipe is based on the countless shish kebabs I have had in Turkey ever since my first visit in 1971 and from Berrin Ardakoç's cookbook, who uses milk to marinate the lamb instead of the yogurt I call for in this recipe. Serve the skewers with pide *bread and* cacık, *if you desire.*

1 cup high-quality full-fat plain yogurt
3 tablespoons extra virgin olive oil
3 tablespoons onion juice (grated from 1 medium-size onion)
Salt and freshly ground black pepper to taste
2 pounds boneless lamb, cut from the leg with its fat into ½-inch cubes
Eight 10-inch metal or wooden skewers
4 *pide* bread (page 721; optional)
1 cup *cacık* (page 186; optional)

1. Stir together the yogurt, olive oil, and onion juice in a glass or ceramic pan or bowl and season with salt and pepper. Add the lamb cubes, coat with the marinade, and refrigerate, covered, for 4 hours.

2. Prepare a charcoal fire and let it die down a bit or preheat a gas grill for 15 minutes on low. Set the skewers in a skewer holder over the fire and grill until golden brown and succulent, turning often, about 20 minutes. Or, lacking a skewer holder, place them on the grill and grill to perfection. Serve with or on a piece of griddle or grill-warmed *pide* bread and the *cacık* on the side.

Makes 4 servings

❈ *Laḥm Mishwī* (Arab Levant)

SHISH KEBAB

In Arabic, the shish kebab is known simply as "grilled meat." Generally, it is not something one prepares at home; it is more likely a dish one would buy at a grill restaurant or from a street corner takeout.

Palestinians and some Syrians have told me that they don't marinate their kebabs, but simply intersperse the lamb meat with lamb fat and a sprinkling of salt and pepper. I don't know how universal this is because this recipe, which uses a marinade, comes from my former wife, Najwa al-Qattan, who is Palestinian. The use of wine in marinades is found among Christian Arabs. Some cooks might add cinnamon, paprika, mint, allspice, or onion juice to their marinade.

The kebabs are served in pita bread (khubz ʿarabī, *Arab bread) or any other flatbread, topped with chopped ripe tomato and raw onion or on a bed of parsley.*

In Cairo, kebab grill shops sell the lamb by weight. A raṭl *of kebab is about a pound. The kebabs are served on a bed of parsley, perhaps sprinkled with cumin.*

1½ pounds boneless lamb, cut from the leg with its fat into ½-inch cubes
3 tablespoons finely chopped onion
¼ cup extra virgin olive oil
1 teaspoon fresh lemon juice
1 teaspoon *bahārāt* (page 524)
Freshly ground black pepper to taste
1 medium-size onion (optional), quartered and layers separated
1 green bell pepper (optional), seeded, cut in half, and each half cut into eighths
8 cherry tomatoes (optional)
Salt to taste
Eight 10-inch-long metal or wooden skewers
***Khubz ʿarabī* (Arab flatbread or pita bread) for garnish**
Finely chopped fresh mint leaves for garnish

1. Place the lamb in a ceramic or glass baking dish to marinate with the chopped onion, olive oil, lemon juice, *bahārāt*, and black pepper for 2 hours in the refrigerator, covered.

2. Prepare a charcoal fire or preheat a gas grill for 20 minutes on medium. Skewer the lamb with the onion and green pepper pieces, if using, ending the skewer with a cherry tomato. Salt the lamb and grill until no longer mushy to the touch, about 20 minutes, turning when necessary. Serve with Arab bread and chopped mint.

Makes 4 servings

❈ *Çöp Şiş* (Turkey)

TINY KEBABS WITH CUMIN

At Ortaklar, basically a truck-stop junction on the highway toward Denizli in the Aydin province of western Anatolia, there are scattered dozens of gaily decorated little kebab stands where you can get çöp şiş, *tiny morsels of lamb grilled over a wood fire and served with tomatoes, peppers, onions, and* pide *bread on the side.*

For these delicious kebabs you need not stop at Ortaklar because when traveling in Turkey I have found that the çöp şiş *are terrific everywhere and I never failed to order some, even when eating other food. The secret to a successful preparation is the little pieces of lamb fat necessary for the tenderizing effect and a pinch of ground cumin sprinkled over the skewers after they're grilled.*

1 pound boneless lamb, cut from the leg with its fat into ⅜-inch cubes
¼ pound lamb fat, cut into ⅜-inch cubes
Salt and freshly ground black pepper to taste
2 tablespoons extra virgin olive oil

Twelve 8-inch-long wooden skewers
1 tablespoon freshly ground cumin seeds
Chopped onions for garnish (optional)
Chopped ripe tomatoes for garnish (optional)
Seeded and chopped green bell peppers for garnish (optional)
Turkish/Greek-style *pide* bread for garnish (page 721; optional)

1. Prepare a medium-hot charcoal fire or preheat a gas grill for 20 minutes on medium. Skewer the lamb and lamb fat, a piece of fat for every four pieces of meat. Season with salt and pepper and drizzle with the olive oil.

2. Set the skewers on a rack over the grilling grate, or directly on the grilling grate, and cook until the lamb is golden brown and the edges of the fat crispy, about 30 minutes, turning occasionally. Remove to a serving platter and sprinkle with the cumin. Serve with chopped onions, tomatoes, green peppers, and *pide* bread, if desired.

Makes 4 servings

Shashlik (Armenia)

GRILLED MARINATED LAMB KEBABS

Shashlik *is a word that refers to a marinated lamb kebab with roots in the Caucasus.* Shasklik, *a version of shish kebab, derives from the* šyšlyk *of the Kazan Tatars, who are from a region centered about four hundred miles west of Moscow on the Volga River. The Armenians of the Caucasus adopted the dish. The Armenians became a Mediterranean people when their migration from the Araxes Valley and Lake Van toward the southwest occurred in the last years of the eleventh century because of Seljuk invasions. The Armenians also make this dish with a variety of marinades, but usually consisting of onions, garlic, bay leaves, olive oil, and paprika. The lamb is skewered and grilled and served with scallions or pomegranate seeds on the side.* Shashlik *can also be made with beef.*

3 pounds boneless lamb, cut from the leg with its fat into 1-inch cubes
2 cups extra virgin olive oil
2 large onions, grated
3 tablespoons paprika
Salt to taste

1. Toss all the ingredients together, except the salt, in a glass or ceramic pan, cover, and marinate the lamb for 12 hours in the refrigerator.

2. Prepare a charcoal fire or preheat a gas grill for 15 minutes on medium. Skewer the pieces of lamb so they don't touch each other. Salt and grill over a medium fire until golden brown, about 45 minutes, turning constantly with tongs.

Makes 6 to 8 servings

Adana Köfte (Turkey)

SPICY GRILLED GROUND VEAL AND LAMB PATTIES FROM ADANA

Adana is a city in southeastern Turkey in the middle of the fertile Cilician (Çukurova) plain. Its history is ancient; this was the area of the Hittite empire (c. 1800 B.C.). The cuisine of Adana has some influence from nearby Syria, but its most famous contribution to Turkish cuisine is the Adana kebab or köfte, *a spicy hot mixture of ground lamb that is grilled. When you come across very spicy Turkish food in western Anatolia, it is a sure sign that it is imported from eastern Anatolia, where they enjoy hotter foods. Adana's interest in spicy foods might have a medieval origin, for in the time of Marco Polo the nearby port of Ayas was an important transhipment place for Asiatic spices and wares; the Venetians, perpetually mesmerized by spices, even had a* bailo *(consul) there.*[165]

¾ pound ground lamb
¾ pound ground veal
2 teaspoons cayenne pepper, or more to taste
2 teaspoons freshly ground coriander seeds
2 teaspoons freshly ground cumin seeds
2 teaspoons freshly ground black pepper
Salt to taste
2 tablespoons unsalted butter, cut into tiny pieces
2 *pide* bread (page 721)
Extra virgin olive oil, melted unsalted butter, or vegetable oil for brushing
2 medium-size onions, sliced
1 tablespoon sumac (page 724)
Finely chopped fresh parsley leaves for garnish

1. In a large bowl, knead the lamb, veal, cayenne, coriander, cumin, pepper, salt, and butter together well, keeping your hands wet so the meat doesn't stick to them. Cover and let the mixture rest in the refrigerator for 1 hour.

2. Prepare a charcoal fire or preheat a gas grill on medium-low for 15 minutes. Form the meat into patties about 6 inches long and 2 inches wide. Grill until the *köfte* are springy to the touch, about 20 minutes, turning often.

3. Meanwhile, brush the *pide* bread with olive oil, melted butter, or vegetable oil and grill or griddle for a few minutes until hot but not brittle.

4. Arrange the *köfte* on a serving platter or individual plates and serve with the *pide* bread, sliced onions, a sprinkle of sumac, and chopped parsley as a garnish.

Makes 4 servings

Bergama Köfte (Turkey)

GRILLED GROUND VEAL AND LAMB FINGERS FROM BERGAMA

The ancient archeological site of Pergamon is just outside the modern town of Bergama in northwestern Anatolia. The town is today an agricultural market surrounded by a well-irrigated plain. Pergamon was at its apogee in the period after the death of Alexander the Great in 323 B.C. *One of the greatest libraries of the ancient world resided here. The medical center of Asclepium, where the most famous doctor of the classical world, Galen, practiced is here at Pergamon. Portions of Galen's medical treatises have survived in Greek and Arabic, and constituted an important part of early medieval dietetics and medicine. In the Middle Ages, Pergamon was captured from the Byzantines in 1212 by the Crusaders.*

Bergama is also known for its köfte *made of ground meat and spices. They are always grilled over a hardwood fire. This recipe is based on the one I had at the Meydan restaurant in the town center.*

½ pound ground veal
½ pound ground lamb
3 tablespoons very finely chopped onion
1 teaspoon freshly ground cumin seeds
1 teaspoon freshly ground coriander seeds
Salt and freshly ground black pepper to taste
Extra virgin olive oil
Lettuce leaves for garish
1 large red onion, sliced
***Pide* bread for garnish (page 721)**

1. In a large bowl, knead together the veal, lamb, onion, cumin, coriander, salt, and pepper very well with wet hands to keep the meat from sticking. Cover and let rest in the refrigerator for 1 hour.

2. Prepare a charcoal fire or preheat a gas grill for 15 minutes. Form the meat into thumb-size pieces.

Brush with olive oil and place on the grill. Grill on medium-low, turning often, until the *köfte* are golden brown and succulent without being mushy to the touch, about 20 minutes. Serve on lettuce leaves with sliced red onions and *pide* bread.

Makes 4 servings

Kafta Mishwiyya (Arab Levant)

GRILLED GROUND LAMB ON SKEWERS

Kafta *is very finely ground spiced lamb meat molded around a skewer that is grilled. Traditionally, it is a typical offering of Lebanese grill restaurants that use flat metal skewers that look like swords. It is also a popular street food from Lebanon to Egypt. In the late Middle Ages, a Damascene housewife from a comfortable background might have refused the hard work of making her own bread and other food at home. If she did not have a household servant, her husband had to provide her with prepared food bought in the market as part of her support.*[166] *Typical among prepared foods were a variety of pickled vegetables, breads, fritters, sweets, and grilled foods such as* kafta.

The meat for the kafta *is well blended and molded by hand around the skewers. The skewers are fitted on a skewer holder, a rectangular metal frame with notches to fit the skewers so that the meat is suspended and never actually touches any part of the grill, then they are grilled over charcoal fires. It always looks very appetizing, smells terrific, and is best eaten in a wrap of thin Arab bread such as* marqūq *(page 717).*

3 pounds ground lamb, cut from the neck or shoulder
3 medium-size to large onions, grated
1 cup very finely chopped fresh parsley leaves
1 tablespoon *bahārāt* (page 524)
2 teaspoons freshly ground allspice berries
1 teaspoon freshly ground cumin seeds
1 teaspoon freshly ground coriander seeds
½ teaspoon ground cinnamon
Salt and freshly ground black pepper to taste
8 flat metal skewers
Extra virgin olive oil for drizzling

FOR THE GARNISH

½ cup coarsely chopped fresh parsley leaves
5 ripe plum tomatoes, chopped
1 large red onion, chopped
¼ teaspoon ground cinnamon
1 tablespoon sumac (page 724)
¼ cup finely chopped fresh mint leaves
6 to 8 large loaves *khubz ʿarabī* (Arab flatbread or pita bread) or *marqūq* bread

1. In a large bowl, knead together the lamb, onions, parsley, *bahārāt*, allspice, cumin, coriander, cinnamon, salt, and pepper until well blended, using wet hands to keep the meat from sticking. Transfer to a food processor in batches and process until the meat is smooth and pasty. Leave the meat to marinate in the refrigerator for 2 to 6 hours.

2. Preheat a gas grill for 20 minutes on low or prepare a charcoal fire and let it die down a bit. Take a handful of meat and press it around a skewer, forming the meat so it surrounds the skewer. Moisten the meat with some olive oil, place the skewers on the skewer holder, and grill until golden brown and springy to the touch, 30 to 40 minutes. Keep the skewers turning, as if on a rotisserie (or use a roto-kebab if you have one).

3. Toss all the garnish ingredients together. Slice an Arabic bread in half and open up the pocket. Remove the meat to the bread pocket and sprinkle on some garnish. Roll up and eat.

Makes 6 to 8 servings

Kafta bi'l-Karaz (Syria)

GRILLED GROUND LAMB AND CHERRIES ON SKEWERS

A famous preparation from Aleppo is called kabāb bi'l-karaz, *kebabs with cherries. A special kind of cherry found around Aleppo is used, the St. Lucie's cherry* (Prunus mahaleb L.), *which is a small, bitter, crimson-colored black cherry. You can use either canned sour cherries or fresh pitted cherries. This recipe is a version in which the lamb meat is ground first as a* kafta.

1 pound ground lamb
2 teaspoons *bahārāt* (page 524)
½ teaspoon freshly ground cumin seeds
½ teaspoon freshly ground coriander seeds
¼ teaspoon ground cinnamon
Salt and freshly ground black pepper to taste
Ten 8- to 10-inch-long wooden skewers
50 pitted fresh black or Bing cherries or canned sour cherries

1. In a medium-size bowl, knead together the lamb, *bahārāt*, cumin, coriander, cinnamon, salt, and pepper, using wet hands to keep the meat from sticking. Transfer to a food processor and process until the meat is smooth and pasty. Form into balls the size of a large olive and skewer them interspersed with cherries, using 5 balls of meat and 4 or 5 cherries per skewer. Refrigerate for 1 hour.

2. Meanwhile, prepare a hot charcoal fire or preheat a gas grill for 15 minutes on high. Place the skewers on the grill and cook, turning occasionally, until the meat is browned and springy to the touch, about 10 minutes.

Makes 4 servings

Shīsh Tawūq (Arab Levant)

GRILLED CHICKEN KEBABS

Shīsh tawūq, *which means "chicken shish kebabs," is probably of Turkish origin, from the Turkish word for chicken,* tavuk. *As with so many grilled foods in the Arab world, this preparation is traditionally served at special grill restaurants in Lebanon. In the halcyon days of pre–civil war Beirut (ante 1976), where my former wife Najwa al-Qattan's family fled after their explusion from Palestine in 1948, the family would occasionally go to her favorite restaurant, the Yaldizlar, a grill restaurant that had a view of the sea.* Shīsh tawūq *was a favorite when she was a child. They grilled it to an orange tinge, and it was brought to the table by waiters in traditional Lebanese costumes. In Damascus, on the other hand,* shīsh tawūq *is white, but still as flavorful. Every cook uses, it seems, a different spice blend, so I give you some options to play with.*

2 pounds skinless, boneless chicken breasts, cut into cubes
½ cup extra virgin olive oil
3 tablespoons fresh lemon juice
1 small onion, grated
½ teaspoon ground cinnamon
½ teaspoon freshly ground cardamom seeds (from about 20 pods)
1 teaspoon dried or fresh thyme leaves
Salt and freshly ground black pepper to taste
1 teaspoon freshly ground cumin seeds (optional)
1 teaspoon ground *bahārāt* (page 524; optional)
½ teaspoon paprika (optional)
Eight 10-inch-long wooden or metal skewers

1. Marinate the chicken cubes in a glass or ceramic bowl or pan with the olive oil, lemon juice, onion, cinnamon, cardamom, thyme, salt, and pepper for 6 hours, covered, in the refrigerator, turning occasion-

ally. Use the optional cumin, *bahārāt*, and paprika, if desired, in your spice mix.

2. Preheat a gas grill for 15 minutes on high or prepare a hot charcoal fire. Skewer the chicken cubes so they touch each other but do not press against each other. If possible, use a skewer rack so the chicken grills without touching the grilling grate. Grill until golden brown, 20 to 30 minutes, turning frequently.

Makes 4 to 6 servings

Kabāb Samak (Egypt)

FISH KEBABS

Modern Egyptian cuisine is much influenced by Greek, Turkish, and Syro-Palestinian cooking. It is generally agreed that kebabs of any kind in Egypt are a Turkish influence. This recipe for fish kebabs, which comes from Egypt's Mediterranean coast, demonstrates its Turkish heritage in the spicing, too, in the use of cumin and bay leaves, which are native to the Mediterranean. As in Lebanon, grilled foods are often restaurant and street foods, and one is likely to find such a preparation in one of the delightful seaside grill restaurants in Alexandria, Abu Qir, Damietta, or Port Said, where the sea bass is typically used.

Juice from ½ lemon
¼ cup extra virgin olive oil
3 medium-size onions, 1 very finely chopped and 2 quartered and layers separated
2 teaspoons freshly ground cumin seeds
Salt and freshly ground black pepper to taste
2 pounds firm-fleshed fish steaks or fillets, such as swordfish, marlin, shark, or sea bass, skin removed and cubed
Eight 10-inch-long wooden skewers
1 green bell pepper, seeded and cut into 20 to 24 square pieces
18 bay leaves, soaked in tepid water to cover for 30 minutes (no need to soak if using fresh)
Lemon wedges for garnish
Chopped fresh parsley leaves for garnish

1. Whisk together the lemon juice, olive oil, 1 chopped onion, cumin, salt, and pepper in a large ceramic or glass baking dish and marinate the fish cubes for 4 to 6 hours, covered, in the refrigerator, turning occasionally.

2. Skewer the fish, putting a piece of quartered onion and a piece of green pepper between the pieces of fish and using 2 to 3 bay leaves per skewer. Continue in this manner until all the ingredients are skewered.

3. Prepare a charcoal fire or preheat a gas grill on high for 20 minutes. Grill the skewered fish for 10 to 12 minutes brushing with the marinade and turning once. Serve garnished with lemon wedges and parsley.

Makes 4 to 6 servings

Xifias Souvlakia (Greece)

SKEWERED SWORDFISH

The Aegean was historically a rich source for a most prized fish, the pelagic Xiphias gladius, *the swordfish. Greek and Turkish seafood cookery is nearly identical when it comes to grilled fish, and I believe that is more evidence of a shared culinary culture than it is of the influence of one culture over another. The Greek Sicilian gastronome Archestratus (flourished 350 B.C.), parts of whose work* Hedypatheia *comes down to us via the writings of Athenaeus (A.D. 170–230), said that when one is in Greece one should get swordfish, where they can be found running in the Bosporus.*[167] *This advice is still relevant today. Serve with rice pilaf (page 602) and a green salad.*

¼ cup extra virgin olive oil
Juice from 1½ lemons
½ cup fresh thyme leaves
2 pounds swordfish steaks, skin removed and cubed
Salt and freshly ground black pepper to taste
10 large bay leaves, broken in half
Eight 10-inch-long wooden skewers
10 cherry tomatoes, halved
1 medium-size onion, quartered and layers separated
2 green bell peppers, seeded and cut into 10 pieces each

1. In a small bowl, whisk together the olive oil, lemon juice, and thyme. Pour the marinade into a glass or ceramic baking dish. Season the swordfish with salt and pepper and toss it in the marinade. Cover and marinate for 2 hours in the refrigerator, turning the cubes a few times. Leave the bay leaves in a bowl of tepid water to soften.

2. Skewer the swordfish, alternating evenly with the tomatoes, onion, green peppers, and drained bay leaves. Try to have three pieces of swordfish per skewer.

3. Preheat a gas grill on high for 20 minutes or prepare a hot charcoal fire. Place the skewers on the grate and grill until blackened on the edges and firm to the pinch, 7 to 8 minutes a side, turning frequently, basting with the marinade.

Makes 4 to 6 servings

Kılıç Şiş (Turkey)

GRILLED MARINATED SWORDFISH

Swordfish, although expensive, is an extremely popular fish in Turkey, and this preparation probably the most famous. The height of the season for swordfish is July, August, and September. Grilling times may change, depending on how far the food is from the fire, so check occasionally for doneness. This recipe was adapted from Tess Mallos's The Complete Middle East Cookbook *and Alan Davidson's* Mediterranean Seafood.

2 tablespoons extra virgin olive oil
¼ cup fresh lemon juice
1 small onion, sliced
1 teaspoon paprika
1 teaspoon salt
Freshly ground black pepper to taste
2 bay leaves, crumbled
2 pounds swordfish steaks, skin removed and cut into 1½-inch cubes
Six to eight 10-inch-long wooden skewers
1 to 2 lemons, sliced and quartered
1 to 2 ripe tomatoes, sliced

1. Prepare the marinade by whisking together the olive oil, lemon juice, onion, paprika, salt, pepper, and bay leaves. Arrange the swordfish in a ceramic or glass baking dish and cover with the marinade. Marinate the swordfish cubes for 3 hours, covered in the refrigerator, turning occasionally.

2. Preheat a gas grill on high for 15 minutes or prepare a hot charcoal fire. Thread the swordfish onto the skewers intermingled with slices of lemon and tomato. Coat the swordfish with some of the marinade and grill until springy to the touch with attractive grid marks, 5 to 6 minutes a side, basting with the marinade. Serve immediately.

Makes 4 to 6 servings

Pinchon Moruno (Andalusia)

MOORISH-STYLE SHISH KEBABS

The spicing, not to mention the name (Moorish skewers), of this Andalusian preparation points to a Muslim heritage. The pork (or lamb, if cooking in the Hispano-Muslim tradition) is cut from the rib, cubed, and marinated in a vaguely "Eastern" style that reminds one of an Indian tandoori, a Turkish çöp şiş *(page 334), or Arab* laḥm mishwī *(page 334), and it is often served as a tapa. After a long marinade and slow grilling, the meat should be succulent and fall apart with each bite. These skewers are typical, too, of that fading memory of the presidios, the Spanish North African enclave of Ceuta, which the Arab geographer al-Bakrī (d. 1094) in the eleventh century described as a town of Berbers and Arabs from the Sidf tribe, originally from the Hadhramaut, a province of Yemen.*[168] *This recipe was the way they did it at the El Cortijo de Don Pedro restaurant in the harbor of Ceuta. Serve with crisp French fries (page 61), tomato slices, and lettuce.*

½ cup extra virgin olive oil
1½ teaspoons freshly ground cumin seeds
2 teaspoons paprika
2 teaspoons salt
Freshly ground black pepper to taste
¼ teaspoon cayenne pepper
2 teaspoons dried thyme
2 bay leaves, finely crumbled
2 pounds boneless pork country ribs, trimmed of fat and cubed
Six 10-inch-long wooden skewers

1. Mix the olive oil, cumin, paprika, salt, black pepper, cayenne, thyme, and bay leaves in a glass or ceramic baking dish. Toss the pork with this mixture and marinate for 24 hours, covered, in the refrigerator, turning the cubes occasionally.

2. Prepare a charcoal fire and let it die down considerably or preheat a gas grill for 15 minutes on very low. Skewer the pork and place on the grill until golden and crispy looking, 50 minutes to 1 hour, turning frequently and making sure the meat is not too close to the fire.

Makes 6 tapas servings

THE ARGOSY RAGUSA

VENICE was the queen of the Mediterranean for several centuries. Venetian power regulated traffic according to what it judged to be its interests, to defend its fiscal system, its markets, its export outlets, its artisans, and its shipping. The Signoria, the inner court of the doge and his advisors, could grant exemptions—for example, permission to load and transport directly through the Adriatic to Ragusa or to Alexandria oils, almonds, walnuts, and chestnuts. In the sixteenth century, the Spanish complained about Venetian hegemony in the Adriatic, but the Venetians responded that the sea was bought not with gold but with their blood "spilt so generously."

Venice was linked to the Ottoman Empire through trade and war. Although Venice feared the Ottomans, competition also came from other quarters, especially the city-state of Ragusa, modern Dubrovnik. Ragusa had its own fleet of merchantmen and competed vigorously with Venice. In fact, shipping was the major industry until the 1950s, when tourism took over. After the fall of Constantinople in 1453 to the Turks, the Ragusans had the foresight to understand that their days were numbered if they didn't establish good relations with the Ottoman Empire, which they promptly did. By 1465, Turkish troops had taken Bosnia and

Herzegovina and were at Ragusa's doorstep.[169] Ragusa played its neutrality brilliantly, as a protégé of the Pope and a vassal to the sultan, in a hostile Mediterranean where its ships could sail unharmed. By the sixteenth century, Ragusan influence on Mediterranean trade was nothing short of amazing, helped by the fact that it had trading colonies throughout the Balkans linked by a network of roads to Sarajevo and Üskub (Skopje), the gateway to the East.

Ragusa was built on extremely poor and barren land that yielded nothing. Food, and especially cereals, had to be imported and so Ragusa maintained good relations with southern Italy, Sicily, and, for that matter, anyone supplying food. Wheat was the primary grain.

The organization of food supply in Ragusa was such that good relations were maintained not only with suppliers but also with the Ottoman Turks, who controlled so many trading routes. Cereal traders and shipowners were strictly controlled by the governing council of the Ragusan Republic and notified a year ahead of time when their turn would come to carry grains to the city.[170]

The purpose of these food regulations is evident when we are told that Ragusa experienced only eight famines in five hundred years, a very un-Mediterranean story. Ragusa had a vast cereal warehousing system. It was supplemented in the beginning of the fifteenth century with the digging of huge pits with a twelve hundred–ton capacity for storing grain. These pits grew in size, and eventually became the enormous edifice called Rupe even today.[171] Rupe means "holes," and above these fifteen holes cut into the rock is a huge three-story building, part of the Municipal Museum.

Through the efforts of the Ragusan government, the city, which had a population of six thousand in the late fifteenth century, always had a sufficient supply of fresh vegetables, especially cabbage and broccoli, which are specialties of the cuisine of Dubrovnik to this day.[172]

Supe od Kupuse (Croatia)
CABBAGE SOUP

The local market in Ragusa was a mecca for Dalmatian farmers who sold their cabbage and broccoli, and where the ubiquitous cabbage soup would be offered by the cooks.[173]

The major influences on Croatian food depend on how far into the hinterland one goes or how far down the Adriatic archipelago one sails. Ragusa (Dubrovnik), being a major seaport, found its culinary influences coming from abroad, especially Italy. But hearty Croatian soups such as this one for the ever popular cabbage show the culinary influence of the Hapsburgs in the use of pork sausages, paprika, and sour cream, while the farther south, and east, you go into Bosnia, the greater the Turkish influence, evidenced by the use of olive oil and yogurt. This delicious soup is best in the late fall.

¼ pound smoked bacon (page 724), cut into small pieces
2 tablespoons pork lard
1 medium-size onion, chopped
1½ pounds Savoy cabbage, damaged outer leaves removed, cored, and chopped
1 tablespoon paprika
Salt and freshly ground black pepper to taste
2 quarts water
2 Polish kielbasa sausages (¾ to 1 pound)
1 tablespoon all-purpose flour
1 large egg yolk
2 tablespoons sour cream
2 tablespoons fresh lemon juice

1. In a large casserole, cook the bacon over medium-high heat until it has been sizzling a bit, about 10 minutes. Reduce the heat to medium and cook until crisp, about another 10 minutes.

2. Add 1 tablespoon of the lard; once it has melted, add the onion. Cook the onion over medium

heat until translucent, about 6 minutes, stirring occasionally. Add the chopped cabbage and sweat for 5 minutes, tossing with the bacon fat until it is well coated. Season with the paprika, salt, and pepper.

3. Pour in the water and boil gently until the cabbage is soft, about 30 minutes. In a saucepan, boil the sausages separately in water to cover for 10 minutes. Drain and slice the sausages.

4. In a small saucepan, melt the remaining tablespoon of lard over medium-high heat and make a roux by stirring in the flour. Cook the roux for 1 minute, then add the sliced sausages. Dilute the roux with 2 ladlefuls of the cabbage broth (about 1 cup), stirring to blend. Pour the roux and sausages into the casserole and stir. Cook for 10 minutes.

5. Beat the egg yolk, sour cream, and lemon juice together in a small bowl. Slowly add several tablespoons of the cabbage broth to the egg mixture and beat it in. Pour the egg mixture into the soup and stir several times before serving.

Makes 4 servings

Prokulica Palačinka (Croatia)

BROCCOLI CRÊPES

Broccoli is a vegetable developed from the cabbage. It spread westward to Italy and Dalmatia, probably in the seventeenth century, from its original home in Crete, Cyprus, or Anatolia. It is unlikely that these early broccoli were the ones with the dense flowering head available in our markets today. They probably were what is today called sprouting broccoli or asparagus broccoli, with edible flower shoots but no head.[174] *Today these broccoli crêpes are favorites of the locals of Dubrovnik, medieval Ragusa, who always have appreciated fine food.*

Salt
½ pound broccoli florets
3 tablespoons all-purpose flour
2 large eggs
¼ cup milk
½ teaspoon salt
¼ teaspoon freshly ground black pepper
1 teaspoon vegetable oil
Sour cream

1. Bring a large pot of well-salted water to a vigorous boil, then cook the broccoli until tender, about 6 minutes. Drain well and puree in a food processor or blender (preferably) for 45 seconds on low speed, scraping down the sides when necessary.

2. In a large bowl, mix the flour and eggs, beating until smooth. Gradually add the milk and then the broccoli. Season with salt and pepper.

3. Lightly oil a medium-size skillet and heat over medium-high until it begins to smoke. Pour a half ladleful of batter into the hot skillet, tilting and twirling the batter so it covers the bottom of the whole skillet. Cook until the bottom is golden, 2 to 3 minutes, then flip with a spatula and cook 2 to 3 minutes more. Transfer to a serving platter and gently smear some sour cream on it and fold in half, if desired. You can keep the crêpes warm in the oven while you continue making the rest. Serve immediately once you finish making all the crêpes.

Makes 4 servings

* * *

THE cuisine of Ragusa was based on olive oil, both locally produced and imported from Apulia. Meat came from the hinterland—small cattle that were consumed fresh, salted, or smoked. An unusual portrait of Ragusa is drawn by the Italian Dominican monk Serafino Razzi, who published his year-by-year account of life in the city in 1595. He tells us that the wine of Ragusa was very good, especially Malvasia; that the weather was perfect, and the markets were filled with fruits such as pears, apples, plums, figs, watermelons, oranges, citrons, and lemons, and lots of fish.[175]

Wine was considered nutritious by the general population and consumed in great quantity. It was imported from Italy as well as the local Ragusan islands of Pelješac and Konvali. Wine from Apulia, with a high alcoholic content, was traded with Dalmatia without going through Venice. A popular wine was the famous Malvasia or Malmsey wine. Malvasia wine is a sweet dark wine with an unusually high alcoholic content made with a special kind of grape that grew, originally, in Cyprus and the Morea. Northern Europeans loved this wine, and in England it came to be known as Malmsey. Malvasia wine was prized and often sent as a gift to Italian cardinals, Venetian doges, or some prince.[176] The development of the wine trade was intimately linked with Malvasia wine and the trade in wool and woolen textiles. Italian merchants brought barrels of Malvasia to England in exchange for the very high-quality English wool. The Italians brought the raw wool to Flanders and Italy, where skilled artisans finished it into fine goods, which were in turn sold all over Europe and the Levant. Once port and Madeira became available in the northern markets beginning in the late fourteenth century, the demand for Malvasia wine began to die out, disappearing entirely by the seventeenth century.[177]

The city of Ragusa was like the rich merchant ships that pulled into port laden with food. In fact, the very word *argosy,* meaning both a large merchantman or a rich supply, comes from "Ragusa." This idyllic-sounding Mediterranean port with its mild climate and sunny days drew all kinds of people to it. There were Croatians, who were seamen, captains, and merchants; Slavs who were couriers; Italians from Venice and Apulia; Tuscans representing the Florentine family firms; Saxon miners; Jewish doctors; and Catalan wool merchants.[178] If famine struck elsewhere, as it often did, the hungry masses would flock to the city, as they did when Ragusa was at war in 1453–1454 with Stephan Vukčić-Kosač, a Herzeg whose camp followers roamed around looking for food, putting great strain on the city, which eventually tried to expel them.[179]

Ragusa was also unique in being one of the first European cities to understand the importance of sanitation in fighting infection and diseases like the plague. The first municipal garbage collection in Europe began in 1415, when the city hired four street sweepers, although the first sanitation official had been appointed as early as 1388.[180] Life was concentrated in the street, squares, and harborfront. Unlike so many cities, Ragusa paved its streets and squares, and installed drainage and sewer systems by the fifteenth century. Garbage, and its awful stink, which is rarely captured or mentioned by writers, was removed regularly. As the city became richer, it also became more aesthetically pleasing, with bigger and more beautiful stone houses, churches, and palaces. Ragusa was a fascinating place to live and a central meeting place of people from all parts of the Mediterranean.[181]

As in Seville, the arrival and departure of ships was always an event of interest to the merchants, captains, and sailors directly involved as well as the population as a whole, whose men were crew members. Foreign ships interested the populace not only because of the goods they carried or took away but also because of the income their crews brought to taverns. All the taverns selling wine in Ragusa were managed by women, reflecting the absence of men, who played a role in the shipping industry.[182]

The abundance of Adriatic trade made the seas dangerous. Ragusa traded with Corfu, Santa Maura (Levkás), and Zante (Zákinthos), from where Greek ships brought fat, lard, ham, salted meat, cheese, oranges, honey, barley, and chickens. There were vast amounts of Apulian and Egyptian wheat, olive oil from Romagna and Apulia, and meat and cheese from Dalmatia going through Ragusa, all of which were enticements to assorted smugglers, local corsairs, and Catalan privateers based in Sicily in the 1400s. The Venetians and Ragusa solved the problem with big armed merchantmen, the argosies.[183]

The normal voyage from Venice or Ragusa to Alexandria, Syria, or Istanbul was not direct. Boats followed the Adriatic coast, stopping in the Peloponnesus, Crete, and Rhodes, not only for rest and commerce but also for safety.[184] Ragusa was ideally located in the Adriatic between Venice and its eastern destinations. Ragusa had the Ottoman Empire to its south and east, Italy to its west, and the Austrian Hapsburg Empire to its north. Ragusa was at the interstices of a number of powerful influences that also affected the history of its cuisine, reflected in contemporary recipes that appear to bridge the meeting of Turks, Italians, and Austro-Hungarians. Only a few miles to the east of Ragusa was Bosnia and Herzegovina, the Dinaric Alps, running north and south, being the natural dividing line. By 1463, the greater part of Bosnia and Herzegovina was under Ottoman rule, many Christian refugees finding their way to Rome, Sicily, Venice, and Ragusa. Although the governor of these territories was usually Turkish, the newly converted aristocracy was Bosnian. Below this feudal nobility and their soldiers the tillers of the soil were Christian serfs, whose sons were frequently pressed into the service of the Janissary Corps (see page 327).

Dolenjska (Bosnia and Herzegovina)

LAMB CROQUETTES IN YOGURT AND PAPRIKA SAUCE

The Ottomans controlled Bosnia and Herzegovina for about four hundred years, and their vestiges are seen in the vernacular architecture and cuisine. Dishes using yogurt and spicing are fairly clearly a result of Turkish influence. Goat, sheep, water buffalo, and cow's milk are sources for the yogurt made in the Balkans. Cow's milk yogurt, from which commercial yogurt is made in this country, will curdle if brought to a boil or heated too long, so the yogurt must be stabilized (page 186) in order to make the sauce for the dolenjska.

1½ pounds ground lamb
Pinch of ground cloves
Pinch of freshly grated nutmeg
¼ cup finely chopped fresh parsley leaves
2 garlic cloves, finely chopped
4 slices stale Italian or French bread without crust
1 cup milk
Juice from 1 lemon
Salt and freshly ground black pepper to taste
6 cups pure or virgin olive or olive pomace oil for deep-frying
1 large egg, beaten
All-purpose flour for dredging
2 cups stabilized yogurt
1 teaspoon paprika

1. In a large bowl, knead the lamb with the cloves, nutmeg, parsley, and garlic, wetting your hands so the meat won't stick to them. Soak the bread in the milk until saturated, then squeeze to drain well and break the bread up, mixing it in with the lamb. Add the lemon juice, salt, and pepper and form the mixture into croquettes about 3 inches long and 1 inch thick.

2. Preheat the frying oil in a deep-fryer or an 8-inch saucepan with a basket insert to 370°F. Dip the croquettes in the beaten egg, then dredge in flour, tapping off any excess flour.

3. Deep-fry a few croquettes at a time until golden brown, 6 to 7 minutes. Drain on some paper towels and place on a serving platter. In a small saucepan, warm the yogurt gently and stir in the paprika. Pour over the croquettes and serve. Let the frying oil cool completely, strain, and save for a future use.

Makes about 12 croquettes

Ražnjići (Bosnia and Serbia)

GRILLED PAPRIKA LAMB KEBABS

Ražnjić *means "skewer" and the lamb, spicing, and use of lemon juice of this recipe shows the Turkish influence in this kind of Bosnian shish kebab (page 333). In Serbia they are likely to make the same dish out of veal or pork.*

2 pounds boneless lamb, cut from the leg with its fat and cubed
2 tablespoons paprika
1 large onion, grated
2 garlic cloves, very finely chopped
Salt and freshly ground black pepper to taste
¼ pound lamb fat or bacon (optional), sliced or diced
Eight 10-inch-long wooden skewers
Juice from 1 lemon
¼ cup extra virgin olive oil
Arab-style flatbread
10 scallions, trimmed

1. Roll the lamb in the paprika, rubbing so all sides of the meat are coated. Toss the lamb cubes with the onion, garlic, salt, and pepper and marinate, covered, for 4 hours in a ceramic or glass bowl or pan in the refrigerator, turning them a few times.

2. Prepare a charcoal fire or preheat a gas grill for 15 minutes on medium.

3. Skewer the lamb and fat, if using, and place on the grill. Whisk the lemon juice and olive oil together and use it to baste the lamb while it cooks, turning occasionally. Grill until brown and tender, about 40 minutes. Serve with flatbread and the scallions.

Makes 6 servings

Ćevapčići (Bosnia, Serbia, Croatia)

SERBIAN *KÖFTE*

The Turkish defeat of Serbia at the Battle of Kosovo in 1389 made the country a tributary state to the Ottoman Empire. But by 1459 the Ottomans annexed Serbia outright, although Belgrade did not fall until 1521. Ottoman rule in Serbia was oppressive, and there were many Serbian revolts, but the last Turkish garrison did not leave Belgrade until 1867. The Turks left vestiges in the culinary realm—for example, these delicious skinless sausages called ćevapčići *(pronounced kev-APP-cheekee or chev-APP-cheechee) in Serbo-Croatian, a language shared by all Yugoslavs but spelled with a cyrillic alphabet by the Serbs. They are small* crêpinettes, *skinless veal-and-lamb sausages, and there are many different ways of making them. Sometimes they're made only with beef or lamb or pork, but the secret to all the recipes is grinding the meat at least three times or processing it to a paste. This recipe is based on my memories of a cold and gray spring day in a long forgotten restaurant in Belgrade.*

4 garlic cloves, peeled
2 teaspoons salt
1 tablespoon water
1¾ pounds slightly fatty veal cut from the shoulder or rump
1¾ pounds slightly fatty lamb cut from the shoulder
1 tablespoon freshly ground cumin seeds
Freshly ground black pepper
1 large onion, grated
Several sprigs of fresh curly parsley for garnish

1. In a mortar, mash the garlic together with the salt until it forms a paste, then add the water and continue pounding until homogenous.

2. In a large bowl, knead together the veal, lamb, cumin, and garlic paste, wetting your hands to keep the meat from sticking to them, then season with pepper. Process the meat mixture in a food processor in batches until it forms a paste, or push through a meat grinder three times. Cover and leave in the refrigerator for 2 hours. With wet hands, form the meat into small sausage-shaped croquettes the size of a large thumb. Set aside on a baking tray, covered, in the refrigerator for another 2 hours.

3. Preheat a gas grill on high for 20 minutes or prepare a hot charcoal fire. Grill the *ćevapčići* until springy to the touch, about 15 minutes, turning with tongs or a spatula, not a fork—make sure you do not prick them. Remove from the grill and arrange on a serving platter surrounded with parsley. Serve with the grated onions on the side.

VARIATION

Here is another recipe that I like very much. I collected it more than twenty-five years ago in Yugoslavia, and I don't remember where or from whom. Follow the method above using these ingredients, processed together in two batches in a food processor: 1¼ pounds ground beef, ¾ pound ground lamb, 1 small peeled and quartered onion, ¼ cup finely chopped fresh parsley leaves, 1 large peeled garlic clove, 2 teaspoons sweet paprika, and salt and pepper to taste.

Makes 6 to 8 servings (variation makes 4 servings)

Dalmatinske Polpete (Dalmatian Coast)

DALMATIAN-STYLE PORK MEATBALLS

The Dinaric Alps present a natural barrier and protection for coastal Dalmatia. A limestone plateau directs water runoff from the mountains into impenetrable canyons, seeping into the ground to emerge at lower elevations. This natural barrier was never penetrated by Ottoman armies. Dalmatia, though, historically had to contend with Venice, which controlled most of the coastal area in the Middle Ages. In the culinary realm the influence is more Italian than Turkish—for example, in this family-style meatball preparation, which is even called by the Italian name polpette *rather than the Turkish* köfte. *Furthermore, it is made with pork rather than the lamb typical of Turkish-influenced cooking. The use of the paprika points to Austro-Hungarian influence, although the Turks use that spice, too. It is delicious accompanied with mashed potatoes and cabbage.*

2 cups fresh bread cubes, white part only
½ cup milk
1 pound ground pork
1 large egg, lightly beaten
1 medium-size onion, finely chopped
2 garlic cloves, finely chopped
1 teaspoon paprika
Salt and freshly ground black pepper to taste

Preheat the oven to 300°F. Soak the bread in the milk and then squeeze dry. Place the bread crumbs in a large bowl with the remaining ingredients and knead until well blended. With wet hands, so the meat doesn't stick to them, form the mixture into balls the size of a walnut. Arrange in a 9 × 12-inch baking pan. Bake until springy to the touch, about 1 hour, and serve.

VARIATION

The meatballs can also be fried in olive oil. In a large skillet, heat ¼ cup olive oil, then cook the meatballs over medium heat until browned and cooked through.

Makes 24 meatballs

GENUENSIS ERGO MERCATOR (GENOESE THEREFORE A TRADER)

GENOA'S position in the Mediterranean is summed up in the medieval proverb *genuensis ergo mercator*, a Genoese therefore a trader. In the eleventh century, the Arabs began losing their position to the Normans in Sicily. The decline of Arab supremacy meant the rise of other powers like Genoa. But by the late fourteenth century, Genoa was in danger of falling to foreign domination and decadence. The enterprising Genoese avoided this fate by exploring new ways to assure a prosperous future.[185]

Commercial interests from northern Europe, with their expertise in building mountain roads, found Genoa suitable for their entry into the profitable shipping trade, and by the fifteenth century Genoa was the leading financial city of the world. Genoa played an early role as an intermediary between Seville and the New World and forged an alliance with Spain in 1528. What allowed Genoa to raise the capital surplus necessary to build the ships that took them across the ocean for trade? Apparently it was agriculture. Land scarcity explains the Genoese motivation to find their food and wealth across the sea, but in the beginning mountain agriculture provided the surplus and mountain trees the timber for the ships. But as we saw in Chapter 4, mountain agriculture depletes very quickly and soon Genoa was in crisis. Genoa's attempt to control the Lombard plain in 1224 was an attempt to assure its food supply, as it could not rely solely on shipments from Provence and Sicily.

The Ariadne's thread throughout Genoese history is the concern for a reliable food supply.[186] In Liguria, chestnut flour had served for centuries as a wheat substitute, but after the Black Death (1348–1350) we hear very little about chestnuts until the sixteenth century, and it seems more wheat is being consumed, indicating a rising standard of living.[187] The Genoese were their own principal customers of food, and the luxuries of the East—which made them rich—were reexported at high profit. Genoa traded with whomever could provide a profit and with whomever could provide food. Therefore, there was always commercial interest in the south, especially Sicily, which provided wheat. In 1191, 18 percent of Genoa's trade was with Sicily, and it rose to 40 percent in 1214, but dropped to 3 percent in 1376 because Genoese traders were taking Sicilian olive oil, cheese, and nuts to Egypt, where they bought Eastern luxuries that they took to Flanders to trade for fine cloth that was sold in Sicily.[188]

This Ligurian city, known as La Superba, the proud, was ahead of its time—a modern city, where the Casa di San Giorgio operated the most sophisticated credit machinery of the Middle Ages. The most innovative form of credit used by Genoese traders was the *commenda*. A ship's captain would receive money from a trader to finance a foreign voyage. Upon the ship's return, the captain would provide the trader with an accounting. If there were profits, three-quarters would go to the trader. The *commenda* was like a loan partnership. But by the fifteenth century, the *commenda* was rare, having been replaced for the most part by the *compagnia*.[189] The *compagnia* was a kind of partnership found between blood relatives. As the *compagnia* developed, it required resources beyond the family, so capital was added to ventures mostly through various forms of participation, including taking deposits. Deposits meant a closer relationship between banking and commercial activities, which was strengthened by the development of the bill of exchange. The bill of exchange was theoretically an instrument for the transfer of money from one area to another. In practice it became the preferred form of credit and speculation.[190] An entire network of exchanges in bills, credit, and correspondence was controlled by a small group of well-informed men who dominated commercial speculation. This was the age of the Italian banker

NORTHERN ITALY AND THE ADRIATIC

and the rise of "finance" (see Chapter 1). Cities such as Ragusa and Seville, which were otherwise commercially prosperous, were *financially* dependent on the Italian cities.

Genoa had big ships because its special trade was in bulky items like the wines of the Levantine islands, such as Malvasia. The Genoese carrack, a huge ship of nearly one thousand tons, was, for a long time, the rational solution to a difficult technical problem.[191]

Genoa's rich appetite, figuratively and literally, was fed by Corsica and the Ligurian coastal rivieras, and by her trading colonies beyond Istanbul, in places like Trebizond, on the northeastern Anatolian Black Sea coast. The Genoese liked to dress, eat, and drink well. Genoese writers provided the city with books on diets and health (see "An Essay on the Sources") and one of her citizens, Christopher Columbus, ventured across the unknown Atlantic to discover a new world. Genoa drained away the natural riches of such diverse places as Tabarka on the Tunisian coast in the form of coral fishing and Messina in Sicily, where the Genoese colony in 1561 made huge profits from trade in wheat, silk, dried fruit, and spices. They ate wild boar and deer from the mountains and drank the Vernaccia wine—a strong white wine similar in a way to sherry—of the Cinque Terre (the coastal area in Liguria between Monterosso and Riomaggiore), which was famous even in the late thirteenth century. Although Genoese recipes are sprinkled throughout the book, here are two that are at the heart of La Superba, and they are superb.

The kitchen of a well-to-do family employing many servants. The old woman with the large marble mortar appears to be making and tasting pesto. Vincenzo Campi (1536–1591). *The Kitchen*. Pinacoteca, Milan. SCALA/ART RESOURCE.

❈ *Pesto alla Genovese* (Liguria)

Genoa is closely associated with its basil and pesto. Pesto is said to be of Persian origin, and although the pounding of coriander and garlic into a pesto is quite old in the Middle East, I believe the origins of Genoese-style pesto may be Roman, as they were known to have made pounded condiments. Although we can't be sure of the first use of pesto, we do know that Genoa was associated with basil, the star ingredient of this pesto, as early as the mid-fifteenth century, from the story of the humanist ambassador and lawyer Francesco Marchese, who won his fame on the basis of a remark he made to the Duke of Milan upon presenting him a tub of basil: if treated well, basil gave off a nice scent; if dealt with harshly, it produced serpents and scorpions. Using a metaphor from the most famous ingredient of Ligurian cuisine was a hint on how Milan should rule Genoa.[192]

The popularity of pesto today is evident in every jar sold in American supermarkets. Pesto is neither time-consuming nor hard to make from scratch, so I recommend you give it a try. Although one can make pesto in a food processor, I don't care to do so because I believe the process is too brutal: the scent of the basil needs to be coaxed from the leaf in a mortar. Furthermore, I take heed of the serpents and scorpions warning. The pesto should be a heavy liquid after you add the olive oil, the highest-quality extra virgin olive oil being essential. This recipe will provide you a liquidy, mildly garlic pesto. To make it stronger, use 3/4 cup olive oil and four garlic cloves, if that is your taste, although in Genoa the garlic in pesto is not the overwhelming flavor that one often finds in the pesto made elsewhere.

Pesto is traditionally stirred into minestrone, but it is also tossed with trenette *(also called* bavette*), which is like fettuccine and* tagliatelle, *and finds its way into lasagne. The type of basil used in Genoa for making pesto is a small-leaved variety sometimes called Genoese basil. I have found this variety in local nurseries and I grow some in a tub, but the recipe calls for the larger-leaved basil you are likely to find in your market.*

1 bunch fresh basil (80 medium-size leaves), washed
2 garlic cloves, peeled
Pinch of salt
2 tablespoons pine nuts, roasted (see almonds, page 709)
3 tablespoons freshly grated Parmigiano-Reggiano cheese
3 tablespoons freshly grated pecorino cheese
1 cup extra virgin olive oil (preferably a Ligurian oil)

1. The basil leaves used for making pesto must be completely dry. Use a salad spinner to remove the water from the washed basil, then damp-dry them with paper towels. Leave the basil leaves spread out on top of paper towels for 1 hour to dry thoroughly. Place the basil, garlic cloves, salt, and pine nuts in a large mortar and begin gently pushing with the pestle. Once the basil begins to mush, pound it more, pressing the leaves clinging to the sides down into the center of the mortar. Pound gently so that you turn the pesto into a paste, not a liquid. Slowly add the cheeses, about a tablespoon at a time every minute, and continue pounding. You will be pounding 9 to 12 minutes.

2. If your mortar is not very large, scrape the pesto once it is a thick paste into a large, deep, and heavy ceramic bowl, and slowly begin pouring in the olive oil, stirring constantly with the back of a wooden spoon, or continuing to use the pestle gently. The pesto can be used now or jarred, topped with olive oil and refrigerated, always retopped with olive oil as you use it. It will keep for six months in the refrigerator as long as you continually replenish the topping of olive oil as you use the pesto.

Makes 1 1/2 cups

Tagliarini con Funghi Porcini alla Ligure (Liguria)

TAGLIARINI WITH PORCINI MUSHROOMS IN THE STYLE OF LIGURIA

The ecology of the mountainous forests surrounding the city of Genoa had a direct effect on the local gastronomy. The most highly prized mushrooms favored by the Genoese gourmet was the porcini mushroom (Boletus edulis). *These mushrooms are common in both coniferous and deciduous forests, where they form a saprophytic relationship with tree roots. The mushrooms cannot be cultivated, contrary to some extravagant claims, and therefore are gathered, making them expensive. Their appearance is also seasonal, with a hot and humid summer increasing their availability.*

Tagliarini *is a pasta in between the size of* capellini *and* spaghettini. *This preparation is one of the best I know for the fresh porcini mushroom. If you cannot find fresh porcini mushrooms, use dried ones soaked in water for 15 minutes.*

2 tablespoons extra virgin olive oil
2½ tablespoons unsalted butter
1 large garlic clove, peeled
1 tablespoon finely chopped fresh parsley leaves
2 teaspoons finely chopped fresh oregano leaves
1 large ripe tomato (about ½ pound), peeled, seeded, and chopped
½ pound porcini mushrooms, brushed clean and sliced
Salt and freshly ground black pepper to taste
3 tablespoons dry white or rosé wine
½ cup freshly grated Parmigiano-Reggiano cheese

1. In a skillet, heat 1 tablespoon of the olive oil over medium heat with the butter and garlic until the butter melts. Add the parsley and oregano and stir. Add the tomato, reduce the heat to medium-low, and simmer until dense, about 30 minutes, adding small amounts of water if necessary so the sauce doesn't become too thick.

2. Meanwhile, in another skillet, heat the remaining 1 tablespoon olive oil over medium heat and cook the porcini, seasoned with salt and pepper, until the greener parts of the porcini look like they are melting, 6 to 8 minutes. Deglaze the skillet by pouring in the wine and scraping the bottom. Transfer the porcini to the first skillet. Correct the seasoning.

3. Meanwhile, bring a large pot of abundantly salted water to a vigorous boil and add the pasta. Cook until al dente and drain well. Mix the pasta with half the Parmigiano-Reggiano and half the sauce. Transfer to a serving platter and pour the remaining sauce over it and sprinkle the remaining cheese on top.

Makes 4 servings

* * *

As Genoa lost its trading colonies in the East to the Turks, its mercantile empire was transformed—by virtue of a financial victory in the West—into a financial empire. Genoa's financial power was unprecedented. The Genoese were pioneers of the new economic structure, but their superiority in the field of finance led them to ignore commerce and the Atlantic trade, which strengthened the position of the merchant capitalists engaged in traditional commerce. With the rise of Dutch capitalism, the financial center of the world slowly shifted away from the Mediterranean to the north over the next hundred years.

The age of the Genoese was the fourteenth to sixteenth centuries, and their financial empire spread over the Western world. Genoese financial control was helped enormously by the establishment in 1579 of the Piacenza fair by the great Italian patrician families. This was more than a trade fair; rather, it became home to the credit machinery of Europe. In fact, the pulse of Mediterranean and Western financial life beat at Piacenza. Genoa's control reached into Spain, where Genoese bankers held the purse strings and controlled the finances of American trade.[193] The Spanish were frustrated and jealous, leading, at one point, the Cortes (the Spanish representative assembly) to react against the foreigners through new regulations. Even in the Spanish picaresque novel *The Swindler*, a character remarks that "We fell in with a Genoese—you know, one of those bankers who've ruined Spain. All he talked about was money; the Genoese are people born with financial acumen. Hardly anyone in business has a conscience, because they've heard it's likely to get in your way, so they leave it behind with their umbilical cords when they're born."[194]

The famous historian Henri Pirenne said that the rise of Genoa as a world power would have been inconceivable without the Muslims: At first, the Muslims were fundamental to the success of Genoa. In the words of Balzac, behind all fortunes lies a crime; in this case, the origins of Genoese greatness was in a capitalism founded on the spoils of piracy, such as the interdiction of Muslim ships and their cargoes, and warfare against the only people in the eleventh- to fourteenth-century Mediterranean who had anything worth stealing: the Muslims, both their property and their persons. In fact, the most common slaves in twelfth- and thirteenth-century Genoa were Arabs; later, there were more Tartar slaves. For example, of the 2,059 slaves in Genoa in 1458, 2,005 were Arab women, and first and foremost they were cooks. They also were responsible for cleaning, carrying water, going to the town ovens to bring and retrieve food, digging latrines, and serving the sexual appetite of their masters. The cheapest slaves were Arab women, and therefore they were popular in the patrician households, the only households that could afford them.[195] Indeed, the role of Arab women cooks in Genoese patrician households in the fourteenth and fifteenth centuries provides an interesting perspective on the development of Genoese cuisine that has been ignored by culinary historians and food writers.[196] Later, the Muslims were important to Genoa as customers; Genoa traded with Muslims in North Africa and in the East. A Spanish Muslim, Abū Abdallah Mūḥammad b. Abī Bakr al-Zuhrī, writing in the twelfth century, recounted a legend that the Genoese were themselves the descendants of apostate Arabs who fled to the west. This story is fanciful, but it highlights the many connections between the Genoese and Muslim history.[197]

Genoa was to remain the fulcrum of international finance for many years. Genoa's wealth and its political reversal in 1528, when the great Genoese admiral Andrea Doria (c. 1468–1560) left the French service to reestablish the republic and ally it with Spain, prepared the way for its age of prosperity, as did its early merchant colonies in Andalusia, such as the one in Seville, where they invested in olive oil. In 1520, the Genoese colony in Seville was the largest foreign entity in Spain. There are a number of reasons the great commercial families of Genoa, such as the Spinola, established branches in Seville.[198] There was civil strife in Liguria and the Eastern colonies were lost to the Turks. Also, the Portuguese had opened the route around Africa and Columbus had discovered America—Seville was the place to be. Actually, the Genoese had had a presence in Seville as early as the twelfth century, and under the Muslim Almohad dynasty garnered large reserves of capital through commerce and money lending.[199] In the Genoese colony in Seville, merchants traded with the New World and capitalists financed the trade of others.[200] They provisioned ships sailing for America, and as early as 1508 Lucas Pinelo sent six casks of vinegar, oil, chickpeas, and calves, among other things, to Hispaniola.[201] By 1580, Genoa was the center for the redistribution of American silver brought back by Spanish ships.

The history of Genoa is not well known. We don't have a clear idea of daily life of either patricians or workers. In part, this is the case because historians have not focused on Genoa. As late as 1996, no one had analyzed the surviving tax records and notarial documents in the Archivio di Stato in Genoa relating to Genoese trade for the period after 1430. There are no portraits extant before one of Admiral Andrea Doria that depict any of the Genoese financiers or doges—men who played an important role in Mediterranean history. The Genoese themselves are a study in contrasts, a fact not allowing any insight into the consciousness of the city. Two of the most famous Genoese, Christopher Columbus and St. Catherine of Genoa, were opposites. St. Catherine, scion of a rich family, never left the city, devoting her life to charity and fasting. Columbus, the son of weavers, left Genoa and never looked back. But he was a Genoese to the core. The old Genoese dream of trading directly with the East, bypassing the Arabs, was, in fact, the motivation for Columbus's expedition to America. Columbus even wrote a letter to the Casa San Giorgio bank in 1502 before his fourth voyage, observing that while his body traveled west, his heart remained in Genoa. He wrote that he wanted Genoa to have a tenth of all his income from the New World in order to reduce the taxes on grain, wine, and other necessities. His artisanal roots are demonstrated in this concern with food and wine of his home city, in contrast to the bourgeois St. Catherine who gave up fruit and ate as little as possible.[202]

The history of Genoese cuisine is also not well studied by scholars, although popular works on Genoese cuisine are numerous.[203] The cuisine of Genoa is also a study in contrasts, as we see in the following recipe for *cima*, an elegant stuffed veal breast that at first glance must be deemed a creation for the financiers. But Ligurian gastronomes assure us that it is not, that the stuffed breast was originally a stuffed paunch (belly) and it was prepared by the common people. The word *cima* means "top" or "summit"—does that mean it is the apex of Genoese cooking or simply that it looks like a mountaintop?

Cima (Liguria)

STUFFED VEAL BREAST IN THE STYLE OF GENOA

The Genoese financiers were powerful and rich men, but the special dishes called finanziera *or* à la financière*, such as* tournedos a la finanziera*, are unlikely to have been contemporaries of the men they were named after. In fact, the word financier referred for a long time to the hated French tax collectors of the late Middle Ages. Dishes that seem to be* à la financière *are not necessarily created for or by financiers. For example, this recipe, as elegant as it is, is said to be an invention of the common folk. The* cima *is a breast of veal stuffed with ground veal, udder, sweetbreads, peas, pistachios, and whole eggs.* Cima *reminds me of two other dishes encountered in my Mediterranean travels, all related, I believe, by culinary exchange and influence: the Sicilian* farsumagru*, a dialect word meaning "falsely lean," and the Lebanese* zunūd al-bint*, "girl's wrists." Both dishes are rolled meats stuffed with whole eggs like the* cima.

Paolo Lingua, in his study of the cuisine of Genoa, calls cima *the queen of Genoese dishes. Once upon a time all the ingredients of a* cima *(pronounced CHEE-ma), a kind of Ligurian galantine called in dialect* çimma pinn-a*, (pronounced SEE-ma), were inexpensive and available. Today, Genoese butcher shops charge as much for what are increasingly considered exotic cuts as do American butchers. In older recipes for* cima *there is a call for butcher's scraps such as* granelli*, testicles, or* mammella*, udder, traditionally* *meats bought by those of lower income, and this points to* çimma*'s role in* cucina povera. Çimma *is considered a family dish, a dish for a merry time, therefore there are hundreds of different recipes ranging from east to west along the Ligurian Riviera and even into Provence, where the* poitrine de veau farcie *described by Reboul in* La cuisinière provençale *is considered by the Italian authority Massimo Alberini a poor hybridization of the true* cima.

Some cooks like to add a chopped carrot for color or artichokes, pine nuts, or dried porcini mushrooms for flavor. The pistachios were originally added to the çimma *stuffing when the dish was made in the wintertime and fresh peas were not available.*[204] *In San Remo,* çimma *is made similarly with the addition of lettuce leaves and panada, a moistened bread mixture (Step 2, page 574). The placing of a weight upon the* çimma *is an old tradition and customarily a steam iron was used. Today you can substitute a cast-iron skillet. Normally, the home cook would not bone the veal breast first. It would be stuffed and poached, or sometimes roasted, on the bone and then the bone would be scraped off after cooking. Leftover* çimma *is sometimes breaded and deep-fried and eaten as a little* passatempo *by connoisseurs. Alberini concluded poetically about the nature of* çimma: Meglio lasciarle la sua fisionomia vera, un po'rustica, ma gentile *(Better to leave its true physiogonomy a bit rustic but nice).*

4 pounds veal breast with bone
½ pound veal brains
1 pound veal sweetbreads
3 tablespoons white wine vinegar or fresh lemon juice
¼ pound pancetta
½ cup veal bone marrow (about 5 ounces), extracted from about 2½ pounds veal bones
2 cups cold water
½ cup (1 stick) unsalted butter
½ pound boneless veal shoulder, trimmed of fat and chopped
1 medium-size onion, finely chopped
4 garlic cloves, finely chopped
¾ cup shelled fresh or frozen peas
2 cooked artichoke hearts (preferably fresh; see page 122 for preparation), finely chopped
2 tablespoons shelled pistachios
4 large eggs, lightly beaten
½ cup freshly grated Parmigiano-Reggiano cheese
2 tablespoons finely chopped fresh marjoram leaves
Pinch of freshly grated nutmeg
Freshly ground black pepper to taste
2 quarts veal or chicken broth (page 54) or quick broth (see Step 6)

1. Soak the brains and sweetbreads separately in cold water acidulated with the lemon juice or vinegar to cover for 2 hours in the refrigerator.

2. Remove the bone from the breast, slicing carefully very close to the bone. Save the bone for veal broth (page 54). You will now have a square piece of boneless veal breast. Carefully begin to form a pocket by making an incision along one side of the breast with a sharp boning knife, enlarging it slowly and carefully, so you don't puncture the pocket. Now enlarge the pocket further by using the boning knife or 6-inch utility knife. Alternatively, ask the butcher to make the pocket for you, if he will, or leave the bone on and form the pocket.

3. Place the brains, sweetbreads, pancetta, and marrow in a large saucepan with the 2 cups water, salt lightly, and bring to just below a boil, so the water is shimmering. Reduce the heat to very low and simmer until the brains and sweetbreads are firm, about 20 minutes. Drain, finely chop all the meat, and set aside.

4. In a large skillet, melt the butter over medium-high heat, then brown the chopped veal, onion, and garlic, stirring often so the garlic doesn't burn, about 6 minutes. Add the brains, sweetbreads, pancetta, and marrow and continue cooking over medium-high heat until the pancetta is rendered a bit and the marrow melted, about 6 minutes. Transfer to a large bowl, add the peas, artichoke hearts, pistachios, eggs, Parmigiano-Reggiano, marjoram, nutmeg, and 1 tablespoon salt, and season with pepper, mixing thoroughly. This stuffing mixture should be relatively smooth.

5. Push the stuffing into the veal breast. It will appear that only half the stuffing will fit, but keep stuffing the pocket until the stuffed veal looks, and feels, like a little pillow. Sew up the opening or skewer it closed with a 10-inch wooden skewer, interlacing it through the meat and cutting off the ends with shears. If, when making the pouch, you cut too close to the surface or you made a little hole, the stuffing may escape. This will be helped out by the fact that you now wrap the *cima* tightly in cheesecloth and tie it up with butcher's twine.

6. Place the veal in a stockpot and cover with the veal or chicken broth. (Or make a quick stock by covering with 2 quarts water, the veal bone, 1 sliced onion, 1 sliced carrot, a few sprigs of fresh marjoram, 10 black peppercorns, and 1 bay leaf). Bring to a gentle boil, reduce the heat a little, and simmer until the *cima* is very firm, about 2 hours at a very gentle boil, uncovered for the first hour and covered for the second.

7. Turn the heat off and let the *cima* cool completely in the broth. Remove from the pot and let it sit for a while. Traditionally an iron weight is placed on top of the *cima*, which helps it assume its traditional rectangular shape. Remove the cheesecloth, string, or skewer from the opening and slice the *cima*. Save the broth for making *zuppa pavese* (page 53).

Makes 8 servings

CONCLUSION

THE political and financial power of cities led to great changes in the fifteenth- and sixteenth-century Mediterranean. The Renaissance was born in the cities enriched by the trade in foodstuffs. The wealthiest of Mediterranean cities was Venice, the undisputed center of the Mediterranean world in 1450, made rich by trading with the East. Venice was in love with money, and its pursuit of good living led to refinements of life, such as good food. Venice became famous for its extravagance and luxury and the abundance of food was called *ciborum lautica*, magnificent food.

Although the Venetian doges, Genoese bankers, and Ottoman sultans celebrated major holidays with great banquets, the perennial problem of the Mediterranean was feeding the cities. Although mercantile relations and dietetic theories could affect the food that people in cities ate, generally, cities, no matter how big or powerful, had to find their essential food supplies within a radius of about twenty miles.

The commerce that made the cities so rich was a trade based on the sea lanes. The story of the sea—the men who sailed the ships, the traders, the ports where they replenished, the pirates who intercepted them, and the fish and fishermen and the food they ate—is told in the next chapter.

6

FRUTTI DI MARE

WHEN God created the Mediterranean, he addressed it, saying: "I have created thee and I shall send thee my servants, those who when they wish to ask some favor from me will say, 'Glory to God' or 'God is very Great,' or 'There is no God but God.' How wilt thou then treat these? "Well, Lord," replied the Mediterranean, "I will drown them." "Away with thee, I curse thee: I will impoverish thy appearance and make thee less fishy!"

THIS story of the creation of the Mediterranean was told by the Arab writer al-Muqaddasī in about A.D. 985, and it means to illustrate the poverty of the sea.[1] The Mediterranean has never been a sea abundant in the *frutti di mare* (fruits of the sea). It is a poor sea where fish and fishermen even today are few. The real *frutti di mare* was the wealth made by trading across the sea. In the Middle Ages, the great wealth of the Mediterranean, its great ports, were all founded on the trade in spices, grain, and other commodities. In this chapter, we will encounter the majority of the seafood recipes in the book, yet these recipes are not those of the fishermen, shipbuilders,

A fishmonger selling what looks like garfish (*Belone belone* L.). Notice the empty counter: fish was never abundant in the Mediterranean. Anonymous, fifteenth century. *The Fish Vendor*. From the sign of Aries. Fresco, Palazzo della Ragione, Padua, Italy.

SCALA/ART RESOURCE.

sailors, or even the pirates. Seafood cookery does not develop on ships and boats, or at the fisherman's quay. It develops through the cooking of landlubbers. Wives and servants find their fish at the market, for the most part, and bring it home to cook. With a few rare exceptions, it is in the kitchens of townswomen that these Mediterranean seafood recipes originate. The fisherman cannot afford to keep the best fish for himself; he must sell it at market. And the ship-builder, sailor, and pirate were looking for treasures greater than fish. In this chapter, we will consider the three activities that defined the Mediterranean Sea: shipbuilding and sailing, fishing, and piracy.

THE PLUNGE

THE slow movement of people to the plains, down from the mountains, took hundreds of years. Eventually many made it to the sea and its ports, large and small, or became seamen themselves. In the Middle Ages, the Mediterranean was an immense sea and conquering one's own fear was the greatest obstacle faced by the sailor. Overcoming the fear of the unknown was known as taking the plunge—*s'engoulfer,* as the French said. The sea had not been conquered (if it can ever be said to be conquered) in 1450, and sailors relied on a few coastal areas and tiny ports for their trade and fishing. Shipping was active only along the coast in a form of sailing called *costeggiare,* coast running. Fishermen stayed close to shore, always in sight of land. Ships, whether merchantmen carrying pilgrims and merchandise or warships prowling for pirates, traveled from one seaport to the next, following the contours of the coastline. One could travel from one seaside inn to another, dining in one and supping in the next. This is how princes and nobles traveled, and it was called "tramping." The princely traveler would buy butter in Villefrance, vinegar and bacon in Toulon, olives in Gaeta, lemons in Salerno, and vermicelli in Trabia. As products were traded along the coast, they left their place of origin and became integrated in the cooking of neighboring regions. The next three recipes are all from small ports along the Tyrrhenian coast of Italy. There's no way of knowing for certain how these developed, although we do know that the seafood was caught locally.

Rombo Fritto (Lazio)

FRIED TURBOT

Rombo (Psetta maxima *L.*)*, or turbot in English, has long been a popular fish in the Tyrrhenian Sea. The recipe called* per friggere il pesce rombo *(fried turbot) in Bartolomeo Scappi's cookbook* Opera, *published in 1570, fries the fish in the manner of this recipe from my former neighbor and fishmonger Salvatore Fantasia, who is originally from Gaeta, north of Naples.*[2] *The sixteenth-century recipe does not call for chili peppers but rather a pomegranate sauce.*

Turbot is a relatively firm-fleshed flatfish that is best replaced with dab if it is not available. A whole six-pound dab will yield about two and a half pounds of fillets. Turbot, as well as dab, is a delicious fish that is best when prepared simply, as in this recipe. If neither of the suggested fish is available, ask for a firm-fleshed sole.

2 cups pure or virgin olive oil
5 dried chili peppers
Salt and freshly ground black pepper to taste
All-purpose flour for dredging
2½ pounds turbot, dab, flounder, sole, or yellowtail fillets, cut into 2-inch squares
Lemon wedges for garnish

1. Preheat the oven to warm (150°F). In an 8-inch saucepan reserved for deep-frying, heat the olive oil

with the chili peppers over medium-high heat until the peppers turn black. Remove and discard the peppers.

2. Salt and pepper the flour in a medium-size bowl and dredge the pieces of fish in it. Transfer the fish pieces to a strainer and shake vigorously to remove any excess flour. Once the oil is hot, nearly smoking, cook three pieces of fish at a time until light golden, 45 seconds to 1 minute per side, turning with long tongs. Remove the fish to drain on paper towels. Keep warm in the oven while you continue to cook the remaining fish. Serve the fish with lemon wedges.

Makes 4 to 6 servings

Spaghetti alla Bucaniera (Lazio)

PIRATE-STYLE SPAGHETTI

The late American food writer Waverly Root stated that preparations such as this one belong to a category of pasta dishes whose names indicate that their spicing is so hot or garlic so strong that only he-men can eat them.[3] *Although we'd like to think that pirates really did eat this food, rest assured that they didn't. Perhaps coast-running Christian pirates of the sixteenth century concocted some* minestre *with pasta aboard their frigates, but this preparation is a creation more probably of a twentieth-century restaurateur in Rome. The Italian culinary authority Vincenzo Buonassisi says that although the name conjures images of faraway seas, it is a preparation typical of* cucina romanesco *(the cuisine of Rome) and that the name is a fanciful one.*[4]

The essential octopus in this preparation prefers rocky coastal areas, and the use of chili pepper is the historic answer to monotonous foods. Most well-known Italian pasta preparations, such as this one, or fettuccine all'Alfredo, have their origins in the twentieth century, or the late nineteenth century at the earliest, usually in a trattoria kitchen. Whatever the recipe's history, the abundant spicy seafood is very appetizing.

½ cup extra virgin olive oil
¾ cup chopped cleaned (page 444) raw octopus
¼ cup water
3 garlic cloves, very finely chopped
½ teaspoon red pepper flakes
1 pound canned or fresh crushed tomatoes
Salt and freshly ground black pepper to taste
½ pound medium-size shrimp, shelled and chopped
1 cup chopped clams
1 pound spaghetti
¼ cup chopped fresh parsley leaves

1. In a small stove-top casserole, heat ¼ cup of the olive oil over medium heat, then add the octopus. Cook for 2 minutes, then add the water and cook for 45 minutes. Any time the juices evaporate, add some more water so that there is always water nearly covering the octopus. Every time you add water, scrape down the sides and bottom of the casserole. Toward the end of the cooking, let the water nearly evaporate.

2. Meanwhile, in a large stove-top casserole, heat the remaining ¼ cup oil over medium heat, then cook the garlic and red pepper flakes for 30 seconds, stirring constantly. Add the tomatoes, season with salt and black pepper, and cook over medium heat for 15 minutes, stirring occasionally.

3. Add the shrimp and clams to the octopus, mixing well, then transfer to the tomato sauce. Increase the heat to high and cook for 3 to 4 minutes, stirring almost constantly.

4. Meanwhile, bring a large pot of abundantly salted water to a boil and add the pasta when the water is rolling. Drain when al dente and place in a serving platter or bowl. Pour the seafood sauce over the spaghetti, sprinkle on the parsley, and toss well. Serve immediately.

Makes 4 servings

Fettuccine col Pesce (Tuscany)

FETTUCCINE WITH FISH

A shipboard meal on a Tuscan galley of the late sixteenth century included daily rations of hardtack, wine, olive oil, and vinegar. There was also salted cheese, salt meat, salt cod, sardines, little tuna (tonnina) or salted tuna, herring, and vermicelli to be used in minestra, *a soupy stew usually containing either pasta or rice. A* minestra *of the time, besides containing pasta, might also have fish or salted meat.*

This contemporary recipe is a reflection of Tuscan cooking that found its inspiration in the sea. To achieve a full flavor, you need at least three different fish, such as monkfish, mahimahi (dolphinfish), and shark or grouper, red snapper, and striped bass.

6 tablespoons extra virgin olive oil
2 medium-size onions, 1 finely chopped and 1 quartered
1½ cups canned or fresh tomato puree
Salt to taste
1 celery stalk
10 sprigs fresh parsley, tied together
1¼ pounds fish fillets (at least 3 of those mentioned above)
¾ pound fettuccine

1. In a large stove-top casserole, heat the olive oil over medium-high heat, then cook the chopped onion until translucent, about 4 minutes, stirring frequently. Add the tomato puree, reduce the heat to medium-low, season with salt, cover, and cook for 20 minutes. Reduce the heat to low and cook until smooth and dense, another 10 minutes.

2. Meanwhile, bring a large pot of water to a rolling boil with the quartered onion, the celery, and parsley bundle. Salt abundantly and put the fish in the boiling water for 2 minutes. Remove the fish with a skimmer and cut into small pieces. Save the water and return to a boil. Discard all the vegetables and add the pasta.

3. Add the fish to the tomato sauce, stir, cover, and simmer over low heat for 15 minutes. Drain the pasta when al dente and add to the casserole. Toss well and serve.

Makes 4 servings

* * *

In the Mediterranean of 1450, "taking the plunge" meant, at its most extreme, going from Rhodes to Alexandria, a voyage of about four days on the open sea, out of sight of land, or from Marseilles to Barcelona. Keep this in mind when we consider the exploits of Columbus, or the Basque fishermen, Irish monks, or Vikings before him, who ventured into what the Arabs called the "Sea of Darkness," the forbidding expanse of the cruel Atlantic. It was truly heroic.

The majority of ships plying the Mediterranean of the fifteenth and sixteenth centuries were not part of blue-water fleets on the high seas but were coast-hugging vessels, like the Genoese *galleass*, a light galley used for short runs to southern Italy and North Africa, that pulled into ports like a traveling bazaar with goods to be exchanged. Small ports were meeting places that provided water, women, and a market, and small villages grew up around these watering stations. They were not the destination-conscious ships of today, with their bills of lading.[5]

Although it flies in the face of popular belief, the Mediterranean is not inhabited by the kind of sailors and fishermen one finds in the northern Atlantic. Mediterranean waters are hardly more productive than the land. The Mediterranean is a deep sea with a limited continental shelf, which is where marine life thrives. Along the coasts are rocky ridges and sandbars leading to sharp drop-offs into the deep.[6] Prevailing currents move newly born fish into the deep where they perish. Mediterranean fisheries provide only a modest yield, except in rare spots such as the lagoons of Comachio in Emilia, the coasts of Tunis and Andalusia, and western Sicily, where there is tuna fishing. The French historian of the Mediterranean Fernand Braudel summed it up: "The scarcity of fish explains the scarcity of fishermen and consequently that of sailors. Between political dreams and reality there always lay this obstacle: the shortage of men capable of building, equipping and handling the fleets."[7] It is also no mystery why the Arabs never had a great navy, although they did have their naval explorers—individuals setting out on their own: They lacked the manpower (not to mention regular access to nearby timber).

Before the great Venetian and Turkish fleets could meet in sea battles, or the corsairs cruise the African coast, the manpower problem had to be solved. The sixteenth century offered its solution through prisoners of war, convicts, and slaves. We know criminals consigned to Spanish galleys were served *mazzamora*, or offal soup, and those on Sicilian vessels may have been given a kind of brined vegetable that their officers may have known as a proto-caponata.[8]

Caponata (Sicily)

The Sicilian antipasto relish known as caponata is said to be of Spanish origin. The Sicilian food authority Pino Correnti believes that the name is derived from the Catalan word caponada, *referring to a similar kind of relish, and says it first appears in a Sicilian etymology of 1709. This Catalan word, which literally means "something tied together like vines," can also refer to an enclosure where animals are fattened for slaughter. But the root word* capón *figures in the expression* capón de galera, *which is a gazpacho or a caponata-like dish usually served on shipboard. In fact, Alberto Denti di Pirajno, the learned Sicilian scholar and doctor, suggested that the dish was born on shipboard as a mariner's breakfast because of the large amount of vinegar used, which would have acted as a preservative. Giuseppe Coria, author of an authoritative tome on Sicilian cooking, offers another suggestion: that the word derives from the Latin word* caupo *(tavern) where* cauponae *was served—that is, tavern food for travelers. Even if this interpretation is correct,* cauponae *certainly wasn't the caponata we know today.*

The earliest recipe I am familiar with of a dish that is a kind of caponata is the cappone di galera alla siciliana *in Francesco Leonardi's* L'Apicio moderno *(The modern Apicius) published in 1790.*

> *Dip a few fresh new beans* [freselle maiorchine, *an esteemed bean from Majorca*] *in Malaga wine, then arrange them on a serving platter, and put over them a garnish of anchovy fillets and thin slices of tuna salami, rinsed of its salt, capers, pieces of citron zest, stoned olives, fried shrimp and squid, oysters poached slightly in their own liquid and several fillets of fried* linguattola [Citharus linguatula, *a kind of flatfish*] *until the platter is well garnished and full. At the moment of serving pour over it a sauce made as follows: in a mortar pound two ounces of peeled green pistachios soaked in olive oil, vinegar, and tarragon or vinegar, salt, and ground pepper.*[9]

Cooking the ingredients separately in the same pan, then mixing them afterward, improves the quality of the dish. Your frying oil should be clean and new. Versions of this famous preparation call for fried pine nuts, almonds, sliced eggs, basil, or ground chocolate. Sicilian restaurants add lobster, shrimp, or bottarga *(dried fish roe, page 435). Other additions found are artichokes, wild asparagus, and baby octopus. The following recipe is the basic one.*

2 medium-size eggplant (about 3 pounds), cut into ¾-inch cubes with their peels
Salt
6 cups pure or virgin olive or olive pomace oil for deep-frying
1 bunch celery, without the leafy tops, cut into 1-inch pieces
½ cup extra virgin olive oil
1 large onion, sliced
One 6-ounce can tomato paste or 3 ripe plum tomatoes, peeled, seeded, and finely chopped
4 teaspoons sugar
1 cup good quality red wine vinegar (not balsamic)
2 tablespoons capers, washed and chopped if very large
½ cup imported green olives, pitted
Freshly ground black pepper to taste
½ teaspoon unsweetened cocoa powder (optional)

1. Lay the eggplant cubes on some paper towels and sprinkle with salt. Leave them to drain of their bitter juices for 30 minutes, then pat dry with more paper towels.

2. Preheat the frying oil in a deep-fryer or an 8-inch saucepan fitted with a basket insert to 375°F. Deep-fry the eggplant cubes in batches without crowding until brown and crispy, 7 to 8 minutes, turning once. Drain on paper towels and set aside.

3. Clean the celery and wipe dry with paper towels. Deep-fry the celery pieces in batches without crowding until the edges are golden, about 2 minutes. Drain on paper towels and set aside. Let the frying oil cool completely, strain, and save for a future use.

4. Take ½ cup of the oil you used to deep-fry the eggplant and celery and mix it with the extra virgin olive oil. In a large casserole, heat this oil mixture over medium-high heat, then cook the onion slices until translucent, about 6 minutes, stirring. Reduce the heat to medium, add the tomato paste mixed with a little water or the tomatoes, stir, and cook for 15 minutes, stirring occasionally. Gently stir in the sugar, vinegar, capers, olives, eggplant cubes, and celery. Sprinkle with salt, if necessary, and pepper and add the cocoa, if using. Cook until the mixture is heated through, about 10 minutes, folding carefully several times instead of stirring. Leave to cool and serve at room temperature.

NOTE: Caponata can be served hot, but does not have a chance to mellow that way, and is preferable at room temperature as an antipasto.

Makes 8 servings

✣ ✣ ✣

WHERE there were seafaring men, a seafood cookery developed—namely along the Dalmatian coast, the Greek islands, the Bosporus, the Syrian coast, the mouth of the Nile, western Sicily, the area around Naples, the coast of Cap Corse, and small coastal regions of Genoa, Provence, Catalonia, and Valencia. However, there are two important points to remember. First, the cookery that developed from the seafood caught was not properly speaking fishermen's food but evolved from the efforts of women. These women were not necessarily the wives of the fishermen but the women of the towns and coastal villages responsible for home cooking who bought their fish at market. And these weren't poor women because fresh fish was too expensive. The poor, when they ate fish, ate salted anchovies, sardines, or herring. Unfortunately for the historian, the women who created this celebrated seafood cookery over the centuries are faceless and nameless. We know almost nothing about their role for they are completely silent in chronicles and documents. Second, fish never played a key role in the Mediterranean diet. But given today's Mediterranean seafood cookery, we will want to understand how it came to be so celebrated.

THE SHIPBUILDERS AND SAILORS

Gondolas and Galleons

THE Mediterranean is not really one sea. There are two great basins, one in the east and one in the west. Each of these seas is cut up again and again by smaller seas that relate to each other through wide or narrow entrances. Throughout these smaller seas are a variety of boats used for a variety of purposes. There are large and small fishing boats, ferryboats for people and animals, barges, flat boats for shellfishing, and a host of others that even today the curious traveler might notice bobbing in picturesque ports. In Collioure, on the coast of the French Roussillon, one can see the *barques catalanes,* strange lateen-rigged fishing boats with their triangular sails that look like an Arab dhow. In Cap d'Agde on the Languedoc coast, the fishermen use a boat called a *tintaine,* with its long prow, to engage in *joute nautiques,* water jousting, using long lances. In the Gulf of Sirte, one sees the *mahunnis* in Sfax in Tunisia with its triangular sails, or the *kamakī* of Djerba, where men fish with a trident; or the multicolored *kaíki* of the Aegean. The most famous of the Mediterranean "little boats" are the Venetian gondolas, with their tall and graceful prows, the origin of which is not known.

On the Arénal (the strand) of Seville, cargo was piled up from the great galleons returning from the West Indies and was moved about by a variety of small boats—that also victualed the ships for their voyages across the Atlantic with dried meat, salt fish, biscuit, oil, and wine, as well as munitions for the cannons of the galleons.[10] They are colorful, these small boats, but by the thirteenth century they were limiting the rise of the great cities, like Genoa and Marseilles. All kinds of boats were coming and going: the graceful xebec, a three-masted sailing ship with long overhanging bow and stern, barques, *galionetti, scafi, leuti*, feluccas, shallops, *saetes*, *navicelloni, caramusali,* tartans, *navi,* and galleons. The last two were the largest and most famous of the great ships of the Mediterranean. The *navi* were huge sailing ships that replaced the galleys because they were more economical. They carried a crew of only sixteen to thirty-two men and were for this reason a pirate's delight because they were easily overcome.[11]

The throngs of little boats in the Mediterranean were a sign of local prosperity, while the big fleets were based in the large ports. Venice had 19,000 tons of shipping in the big class, and 40,000 tons for all classes of ships in 1605. Ragusa, Genoa, Marseilles, Naples, and Sicily had about the same for each of them. The Ottoman Empire had about 80,000 tons and Spain 60,000. The Barbary corsairs had about 10,000 tons. In all the Mediterranean there were about 350,000 tons of shipping, representing about 30,000 men and perhaps over 10,000 ships of all kinds, providing about six million ducats a year in revenue. These figures were extrapolated by French historian Fernand Braudel from the authoritative figures existing for Ragusa. For comparison, and to understand the meaning of 350,000 tons of shipping manned by 30,000 crew, just one modern oil supertanker, with a crew as few as eight, would equal all of the shipping tonnage of all the navies of the sixteenth-century Mediterranean.

Shipbuilding activity traditionally took place in the northern Mediterranean because this is where the forests were. Small coastal villages supplied an inordinate percentage of the sailors and many made names for themselves, such as Salerno and Amalfi, which were active ports in the kingdom of Naples. In the shipyards of Ragusa, the woodcutters and timber merchants were supported by the forests of Mt. Gargano in Apulia, directly across the Adriatic. The Syrian shipbuilding industry was also important until the cedars of Lebanon were exhausted. For the most part, both wood and men were in short supply. Algiers saw its sailors and its oars coming from overseas. Without the large oaks necessary for building hulls, Mediterranean shipbuilding entered a crisis, perhaps explaining why certain maritime technologies and economies developed the way they did.

Shipbuilding in the Mediterranean was an ancient tradition, and the trade saw the creation of a wide range of specialized boats.[12] Navies had sought supremacy on the high seas for centuries, but were foiled by the technical problem of sailing westward exposed to the dangerous mistral, the strong cold winds blowing from the north. Today these technical problems seem so minor—problems such as the kinds of oars available, the shape of hulls, and the tonnage of ships. The solution was found in an entirely different kind of ship, a one-masted, square-rigged, center-rudder ship introduced to the Mediterranean by Basque pirates in 1303.[13] Ships became bigger and now Genoa could send its sailors through the Straits of Gibraltar. By the fifteenth century, huge ships—carracks approaching a thousand tons—were plying the sea.

Nautical Revolutions

A NAUTICAL revolution occurred in the thirteenth century that resulted from technical innovations in shipbuilding, seafaring, and navigation. Two major nautical developments in the Middle Ages came about by contact with ships from outside the Mediterranean. The first was the introduction of the lateen rig. Although the Greco-Romans knew of the lateen rig, it was introduced a second time to the Mediterranean by Arabs who found it being used by Indians sailing in the Sea of Oman. Unlike the square sail, the lateen was a triangular sail fixed fore and aft, which allowed the sailor to beat into the wind with greater ease. The second development came from northern waters when the Mediterranean was introduced to the clinker-built ship, a method of building hulls with overlapping planks, like tiles on a roof, to make for stronger ships, as well as the centerline rudder, an axial rudder operated from inside the ship.[14]

Several major discoveries and inventions also contributed to the nautical revolution. The compass was one invention. Although the origins of the compass are debated, some scholars suggesting a Chinese invention in the twenty-sixth century B.C., it seems likely that the compass was invented independently by the Chinese and either the Italians or the Arabs in the twelfth century. The rudimentary compass consisted of a piece of magnetized stone called a lodestone attached to a stick lying in a bowl of water that would turn in accordance with the magnetic poles of the earth. Later, someone found a way to attach a magnetized needle to a compass card so that it swung freely on a pivot in a box fastened in line with the keel of the ship. This way the captain always knew what course the ship was on. It was far more accurate a system than solely relying on the position of the sun and stars.

Another invention of importance was dead reckoning. As that brilliant historian Frederick Lane wrote in *Venice: A Maritime Republic,* "It was a triumph of mathematical thinking."[15] Mediterranean navigators traditionally used geometry, arithmetic, and experience to determine their direction and the distances traveled. Navigators collected this information over the centuries, and by the mid-thirteenth century, the first book to list the data was produced, called the Port Book. An unknown navigator devised the ingenious conception of dead reckoning by drawing grid lines on navigational maps, allowing the navigator to plot the data on distances and directions listed in the Port Book. Next, this inventor chose a scale appropriate to the map and, using mathematical methods, drew coast lines, locating them according to distances and direction from one landmark to another. What this uncelebrated navigator invented was the first map ever drawn to scale. Because it was derived from the Port Book, it has come to be known as a *portolano* chart, the earliest known one dating from 1270 and called the *carta Pisana.*[16]

The compass, along with traverse tables used by navigators to zigzag along straight lines, beating and tacking to the wind, and the *portolano* or sea chart, allowed dead reckoning to become possible.[17] Dead reckoning with a compass now meant that navigators did not have to rely on clear nights to see the stars; they could travel in cloudy weather. The Mediterranean world became that much smaller, trade increased, and material culture, including foods and culinary ideas, could be exchanged on a greater scale, and faster.

Long Ships and Roundships

SINCE the days of the Phoenicians, the ships of the Mediterranean were of two kinds, long ships and roundships. Long ships were equipped with oars and sometimes sails, and roundships were entirely sailing ships. Long ships were low and narrow and roundships were high and wide.[18] The choice of a ship depended on several conditions, including the kind of commerce engaged in, nautical difficulties encountered, weather, and political conditions.

The most famous of the medieval long ships in the Mediterranean was the galley, with a single flat deck occupied by oarsmen. The roundship might have two or three decks with a forecastle and a stern castle. In the thirteen century, both types of ships were used by the Venetians, including two kinds of roundship, the larger one called a great ship or *buss,* used for precious cargo, and a more defensible ship, and the smaller, called a *tarette,* which carried bulkier items, and was less defensible.[19]

From the first boat ever built at the dawn of Mediterranean history until the seventeenth century, the long ship (the galley or oarship) was the favorite warship because it was sleeker and faster and could accept or decline battle at will. They were fitted for either ramming or boarding, which was important since all medieval naval warfare involved hand-to-hand combat. The long ships were also used to carry passengers and precious merchandise, while the roundships carried the bulkier and cheaper commodities. The medieval oarsmen on Venetian galleys were not slaves chained to benches but were free citizens who would exchange their oars for swords once battle was joined. These were the most able-bodied citizens of Venice who joined at a recruiting station set up in the Piazza San Marco.[20]

The standard Venetian galley between 1290 and 1540 was the trireme, the same design as the Roman galley with its three banks of oars and thirty benches on each side, with three oarsmen to a bench pulling a separate oar.[21] In order to have all the oars parallel so they wouldn't interfere with one another, the benches were slanted obliquely at right angles toward the poop so that their inboard ends were farther aft than their outboard ends. Each oar was about thirty feet long and weighed one hundred and twenty pounds. The other men on board were sailors to tend the rudder and raise and lower the sail on the one-masted lateen-rigged galleys, as well as marines, called bowmen, who were the vessel's shock troops.[22] The arduousness of working a galley meant that the oarsmen and sailors were well fed and their health cared for.

Over time a variety of long ships, mostly smaller light galleys, were built, such as the *fuste, galeotte, bregantini,* and *gregate.*[23] Larger long ships, the great galleys, began to replace light galleys around 1300. The light galley was long and narrow and the great galley wider. A great galley could hold about 250 tons below deck—far more than a light galley—and rode low in the water when fully laden.[24]

We have a description of a great galley from a merchant named Felix Fabri, who wrote in 1483:

> The beak of the prow reaches high up, and from it the belly of the ship begins to swell round against the sea. The stern castle has three stories: the first holds the steersman and compass and he who tells the steersmen how the compass points and the navigators. The middle one is the chamber of the Lord and captain of the ship and his comrades and messmates. The lowest deck is where the noble ladies are housed at night and where the captain's treasure is stored. No light gets in here except through a hatchway in the floor above it. On either side of the poop hang the boats which land people. The poop has its own sail and a flag to show which way the wind is blowing. Two benches beyond the house on the poop, on the right hand side is the kitchen, which is not covered in: beneath the kitchen is the cellar and beside the kitchen is the stable for animals for slaughter, wherein sheep, goats, calves, oxen, cows and pigs stand all together. The whole galley, within and without is covered with the blackest pitch, as are even the ropes, planks, and everything else so that they will not be easily rotted by the water. The ropes for working the sails and anchors take up a large part of the galley, because they are many, and are long, thick, and of manifold kinds. It is a wondrous thing to see the multitude of ropes and their joining and twinings about the vessel. Down below, in the place where pilgrims [Europeans on pilgrimage to the Holy Land] live, is the well for bilge water, just by the middle of the mast, and this well does not contain human filth, but all the water which visibly and invisibly enters the galley filters through and collects in that well and a most loathsome smell arises from it, a worse smell than that from any closet of human odor.[25]

On the deck of the galley, beside the mast, was an open area that acted like a marketplace. The poop was divided into three levels. On the lowest level, called the *pizolo,* distinguished passengers would sleep; it was also reserved for munitions storage and the merchandise belonging to the captain. The poop proper was the middle level, where a table was spread out for meals and where there was a small altar for the captain. At night mattresses were spread out for the pilgrims and passengers. Secured to the ceiling and walls of the middle poop were swords and crossbows for defense. Above the middle poop was the castle, where the captain's quarters were and where a notable person would be bunked if he were on board. Behind the stern castle was an area for managing the rudder that might require the physical labor of several steersmen and the compassman.[26] The very bottom part of the galley was called the sharp hold, and it was filled with sand, for ballast, right up to the deck beams where the pilgrims lay. The pilgrims lifted up the deck to bury in the sand the bottles of wine, their eggs, and other foods that needed to be cool for their voyage.[27]

By 1445, merchant galleys were being built with three masts and were lateen rigged, but also carried other specialized sails depending on the weather. Roundships were still in use because, although it was a matter of time before the oared galleys became obsolete, the galley was practical in the mid-fifteenth century for several reasons. First, they could enter and leave ports quicker and more efficiently than the roundships with only their sails to maneuver. Second, the great galleys were more defensible than the roundships in this era of naval encounters that were essentially land battles transferred to ships. A convoy of four great galleys represented about eight hundred armed men, a formidable military force that could defend itself in all battles with enemies, save the boldest of powerfully armed corsairs. The great galleys were the safest means of transport for two centuries. Although they couldn't hold the tonnage that a round ship could, they were given preference for carrying precious cargo. One fleet of galleys in

1500 left for Alexandria from Venice with three hundred thousand ducats of cash and bales of merchandise and returned in the winter with two and a half million pounds of spices from Alexandria. At every little port they would dock and a miniature fair would be held.[28]

By 1535, the era of the great galleys had come to an end. With their huge complement of men and oars, the galleys were expensive to maintain. They disappeared not only because of improvements made to the roundships but also because of the change in trade routes. In the fifteenth century, rich Mediterranean cities could afford the fleets, but by the sixteenth century they were losing their monopoly on trade with the East because the New World had opened and the English and Dutch were gaining strength. Another factor was the development of naval artillery and the fully rigged ship that deprived the merchant galley of its advantages. An armed roundship could devastate the exposed deck of oarsmen in confrontations.[29] About 1450, the topsail, foresail, and mizzen sail were added to the roundship, making it much more manageable, and in one hundred years it was as safe for long voyages as the merchant galley.

Between 1500 and 1525, roundships replaced galleys as passenger ships for pilgrims. Before then the galleys were preferred by voyagers because they cruised along the coast and put into a port every night; the traveler could always have fresh provisions and see the sights. The roundships did not have fresh food and sailed directly across the sea out of sight of land.[30]

Improvements to Mediterranean shipbuilding occurred once northern ships began entering the Mediterranean after 1300. Basque pirates from Bayonne on the Atlantic were enlightening to Italian mariners in this respect. Their ships were one-masted square-rigged vessels with the rudders attached to the stern posts rather than on the sides, as was traditional in the Mediterranean. Soon Mediterranean shipbuilders began to incorporate these elements into their ships. The castle on the prow and stern was designed into the lines of the ship so that it appeared a more integral part of the hull. The ship that evolved was called a cog, and it was a large merchantman used during most of the fourteenth and fifteenth centuries. The cog was cheaper to build, required fewer men to sail, and was safer to sail than the two-masted lateen-rigged *buss,* which was dangerous to sail with a strong tail wind, although these ships later carried a square sail for just that purpose.[31]

The next nautical revolution in shipbuilding occurred about 1450 with the introduction of the carrack, a ship with a very large and prominent mainmast and a very large square sail. The carrack also had numerous smaller sails added. A small mast on the forecastle was square rigged, which allowed the ship to tack with greater ease, while the mast on the stern was lateen rigged and enabled the carrack to beat to windward. By the end of the sixteenth century, Venetian carracks carried as many as ten sails.[32]

As ships became safer, voyages became more frequent and freight prices dropped. The French historian Fernand Braudel's examination of marine insurance records in the Ragusa (Dubrovnik) archives showed April and May as being the months just before the long voyages.[33] Documents from Leghorn (Livorno) show cargoes of silk and pepper from Alexandria being transported between January and July, and cheeses from Sardinia after October. Ships also became bigger so bulkier items could be carried, such as casks of wine and huge bales of grain. In 1400, the biggest Venetian merchantman was about four hundred tons; by 1450 it was six hundred tons, and roundships built for military purposes were even larger. The famous "ship of the line," the great sailing ship most of us are familiar with from watching swashbuckling movies, was first constructed in the Venetian Arsenal in 1660; it was based on an English model.[34]

Shipbuilding

THE knowledge of shipbuilding was handed down from father to son, and this skill made these craftsmen famous. They needed experience not only in building hulls and masts but also in choosing the proper trees in the forest to build the ships they had in mind. The ship carpenters, the caulkers, and the sawyers formed guilds to regulate professional activity. At first they were formed as *scuole* (see Chapter 5) and later into *arti,* guilds, which existed for worship, economic or professional assistance, banqueting, and settling minor disputes.[35]

The way a ship got built started with the foreman shipwright's going into the nearby forest with his work crew to choose the trees. These trees were brought mostly from the Rhaetian and Carnic Alps to the north to Venice, where the sawyers cut the logs according to the directions of the carpenters, assisted by laborers who would lift the logs onto sawhorses. The next step was to lay the keel. This is when the shipwright, who was usually a celebrated person, would demonstrate his magical and mysterious craft by determining the proportions of the ship and shaping the curves of the ribbed framework as if he were working with clay rather than wood.[36] Then the planking was laid and the cabins and superstructures built. Finally, the seams of the ship's hull were covered in tar and grease, and the galley launched. At this point the deck fixings were fastened, the rigging and mooring set up, and the crew supplied.[37] From the time the tree was cut down until the time the ship was launched could be two years and, with boats having a lifetime of ten years, Venice and other navies worried about having enough ships to feed their cities.[38] These great ships were built in Venice's industrial zone known as the Arsenal.

The feeding of the shipbuilders was the responsibility of the masters, the skilled master craftsmen. Part of their pay was a regular supply of wine. They were allowed to drink wine while they worked, and it would be passed around five or six times a day. The need for a wine steward in the Arsenal grew not only to provide good wine but also to make sure it didn't spoil and to keep the workers from getting too drunk, as sometimes happened. Over time the attraction of free wine drew many workers to the Arsenal and a need developed to keep the wine doors locked and closely watched.[39]

Ports

ALL these ships being built by the Arsenal and by shipyards throughout the Mediterranean meant great ports would thrive. Mediterranean harbors were teeming with people of races and religions of all kinds. Big cosmopolitan ports like Venice, Algiers, Leghorn (Livorno), Marseilles, Salonika, Alexandria, Barcelona, and Istanbul were colorful places of hopelessly tangled cultural threads. Even today it appears to be the same woman grilling corn cobs on the *embarcadero* of Valencia whom we just saw on the Alexandrian *corniche*. The smaller ports, too, had stormy lives and offered great variety. They were the indispensable sources of water for the merchant ships. Besides providing entry to ships carrying spices, the small ports each had their own microcultures, mirrored today in their unique microcuisines. In the Middle Ages, the typical way of cooking fish was frying or grilling. Today one is also likely to find a variety of fish soups, *zuppe di pesce,* a typical way of preparing the locally caught fish. The key to the difference in each community's stew is found in the variety and types of local fish used.

❈ *Fumetto di Pesce* (Veneto)
FISH BROTH

The earliest recipe I am familiar with for a fish broth appears in the anonymous fourteenth-century Tuscan cookery manuscript called Libro della cocina. *There the fish is fried in oil and cooled. Then some onions are fried with almonds, raisins, prunes, and dried elecampane* (Inula helenium *Linn.*)*, a bitter root used in those days as a tonic and stimulant. The broth is finished with wine and vinegar and seasoned with black pepper, saffron, and other spices.*[40]

This recipe is my fish broth for risotto, although it's fine for any other recipe calling for homemade fish broth. Ask your fishmonger for some fish carcasses. He should give them to you for free, although some charge for it. Try to mix the fish, using two or three kinds.

6 pounds mixed fish carcasses, any kind, including at least 1 or 2 fish heads
3 quarts cold water
2 cups dry white wine
2 carrots, cut up
2 celery stalks, sliced
1 onion, quartered
10 black peppercorns
Bouquet garni, tied in cheesecloth, consisting of 10 sprigs each parsley and thyme, 6 sprigs fresh marjoram, and 1 sprig fresh sage

Place all the ingredients in a stockpot. Bring to a boil, then reduce the heat to low and let simmer for 4 hours, skimming the foam that forms on the surface. Strain the broth through a conical strainer. Strain again through a cheesecloth-lined fine-mesh strainer. You can refrigerate up to a week or freeze for up to 6 months.

Makes 2 quarts

❈ *Zuppa di Pesce alla Mazarese* (Sicily)
FISH STEW IN THE STYLE OF MAZARA DEL VALLO

The Sicilian coastal town of Mazara del Vallo is the one of the most important fishing ports in all of Italy. The town has a history that includes incursions by the Phoenicians, Carthaginians, and Romans, but it was during the Arab era (eleventh century) that it became the great terminal for shipment to Egypt. Flax was a major item of trade, as well as cheese and salt.[41] *The most heavily caught fish were sardines and anchovies. Mazara is known for its fish and its fish stew, or* zuppa di pesce. *The white wine is optional, but at least six varieties of fish are needed.*

This particular recipe was given to me by Francesco Quinci, a retired anchovy-packer from Mazara del Vallo, who tells me that it was a favorite of the workers at lunch time when he worked in the business in the 1950s. The anchovies they packed never went into the stew because they were for export. Typically, they would use some of the other fish caught in the nets, which were usually red gurnard, grouper, comber, and sea bream (porgy; scup), as well as some others. I have made it using scorpionfish, yellowtail, croaker (weakfish), dogfish, butterfish, and redfish. Ask your fishmonger for the freshest fish of the day.

½ cup extra virgin olive oil
1 medium-size onion, finely chopped
2 garlic cloves, finely chopped
½ cup very finely chopped fresh parsley leaves
1 large ripe tomato (about 10 ounces), peeled, seeded, and finely chopped
1 quart cold water
1 cup dry white wine (optional)
3 pounds mixed fish fillets (see above)
Salt and freshly ground black pepper to taste
½ recipe *crostini di pane per le zuppe di pesce* (page 559; optional)

In a large, deep casserole or stew pot, heat the olive oil over medium heat, then cook the onion and garlic together until the onion turns translucent, about 5 minutes, stirring constantly so the garlic doesn't burn. Add the parsley and cook for another 3 minutes, stirring. Add the tomato and cook for 2 more minutes. Add the water and wine, if using, and cook for 5 minutes. Add the fish and cook until it is barely able to flake when tugged with a fork, 20 to 25 minutes. Check the fish to make sure it doesn't overcook, which you will notice if it flakes too easily. Season with salt and pepper and serve with the *crostini*, if desired.

Makes 4 to 6 servings

Zuppa di Pesce Siracusana (Sicily)

FISH STEW IN THE STYLE OF SYRACUSE

Syracuse (or Gela) is said to be the home of Archestratus, one of the earliest writers on cuisine whose only known work was a gastronomic poem written about 348 B.C., *called the* Hedypatheia, *which can be translated as the "Life of luxury." During the Greek era Syracuse was known for its elaborate cuisine, and no less than the great philosopher Plato criticized the city's culinary excess.*[42] *As a coastal town on the Ionian Sea, Syracuse has always been noted for its exquisite seafood preparations, and in the twelfth century the famed Arab geographer al-Idrīsī commented on the richness of its port and markets.*

The more fish you use in this recipe, the more delicious and pronounced the taste of the stew. I think four fish at a minimum is right in this Syracusean zuppa di pesce. *Any selection of wolffish (ocean catfish), hake or cod, grouper or red snapper, redfish (ocean perch), monkfish, dogfish, shark, sea bass, halibut, striped bass, mahimahi (dolphinfish), pompano, bluefish, and ocean pout (ling) is fine to use.*

2 pounds mixed fish fillets or steaks (see above), cut into large chunks
1 medium-size onion, thinly sliced
2½ tablespoons finely chopped fresh parsley leaves
3 garlic cloves, crushed
1½ celery stalks, chopped
1 bay leaf
1 large ripe tomato (about 10 ounces), peeled, seeded, and chopped
6 tablespoons extra virgin olive oil
1 cup dry white wine
3 cups water
Salt and freshly ground black pepper to taste
½ recipe *crostini di pane per le zuppe di pesce* (page 559)

1. Preheat the oven to 350°F.

2. Place the fish, onion, parsley, garlic, celery, bay leaf, tomato, olive oil, wine, and water in a large, deep casserole. Season with salt and pepper, and stir well to mix everything. Bake until the fish is about to flake when tugged with a fork, about 45 minutes, and serve with some *crostini* in each serving bowl.

Makes 4 servings

Zuppa di Cozze alla Tarantina (Apulia)

MUSSEL STEW FROM TARANTO

Mussels and oysters have been cultivated in the Gulf of Taranto, the instep of the Italian boot, since ancient times. The beds are located between the Mar Piccolo and the Mar Grande. The Mar Piccolo is a lagoon fed by freshwater and seawater that flows through two channels on either side of the center of the city of Taranto, making it, in effect, an island. The Mar Grande is part of the Gulf of Taranto. The reason the mussels and oysters are so fine in this area is that the tide is significant enough to bring the kind of food the bivalves require, as well as the right amount of salinity in the water to give them their particularly briny taste that is so favored by connoisseurs. This is a simple preparation that allows the mussels all their glory without any masking. The flavors are wonderfully full and appetizing. Most mussels sold today are cultivated mussels and don't need purging. If the mussels are not cultivated, you can purge them of any sand and grit in cold water with one tablespoon of baking soda for one hour, although this is usually not necessary.

2 garlic cloves, peeled, 1 crushed and 1 finely chopped
1 dried chili pepper
¼ cup extra virgin olive oil
¼ cup tomato paste
½ cup water
4 pounds mussels, debearded and washed well
1 cup dry white wine
6 slices *crostini di pane per le zuppe di pesce* (page 559)

1. In a large, preferably earthenware, stove-top casserole, cook the crushed garlic and the chili pepper in the olive oil over medium heat until the garlic begins to turn light brown, about 3 minutes, stirring. Remove and discard the garlic and chili and add the tomato paste diluted in the water. Cook for 10 minutes, stirring occasionally.

2. Add the mussels and cover for 5 minutes, shaking the casserole once in a while until the mussels open. Discard any mussels that remain tightly shut. Increase the heat to high, pour in the wine and the chopped garlic, and cook for 7 to 10 minutes, stirring. Place a piece of *crostini* in each bowl, then, serving the soup from the casserole, pour a ladleful of mussel soup on top. Serve immediately.

Makes 4 servings

❈ *Brodetto de Pesse alla Caorlotta* (Veneto)

FISH STEW IN THE STYLE OF CAORLE

Caorle is an old city in a privileged and secure position on an island located between the Livenza and Lemene rivers between Venice and Trieste. Between sea and land, it has a particular cuisine that relies on the varieties of fish offered by fish merchants. The boats used, called caorline, *were noted as fast boats that could quickly bring fish to market as well as transport fruits and vegetables along inland waterways to Venice. Speed was important to ensure freshness, and even today one can be surprised to find some of the fish one has bought at market wriggling a bit in the shopping bag.*

Chioggia, to the south of Venice, was known for its onions, Venice for its garlic, and Caorle for its bay and parsley. Brodetto de pesse alla caorlotta *(in dialect) was a characteristic dish of the Caorlotti fishermen who make it on their boats using cuttlefish,* cagnoli *(dogfish),* ragni d'alto mar *(a kind of crab),* musi duri *(fish heads),* canocchie *(mantis shrimp), crab, turbot,* lusserne *(tubfish), and the interesting* boche in cao, *star-gazer—literally "mouth-in-the-sky" in Venetian—a fish that has its eyes set upward on the top of its head and is noted for burying itself in the sand (it is called* chiaghia *in Istria). The fish are washed in seawater and quickly cooked in a* soffritto *(page 285) of olive oil and garlic. Traditionally, this fish stew is cooked in a cast-iron pot on board ship in the manner familiar to the fishermen of Murcia (see* caldero murciano *on page*

421). In all there should be two and half pounds of seafood, not including bones or viscera. If available, wash all the seafood in clean seawater.

½ cup extra virgin olive oil
3 large garlic cloves, finely chopped
1½ pounds cuttlefish or squid, cleaned (page 448)
2 tablespoons plus 1 quart water
1 pound dogfish, mako shark, mahimahi (dolphinfish), or kingfish steaks or fillets, cut into large chunks
½ pound firm-fleshed fish (grouper, ocean pout, cod, monkfish, swordfish, etc.) steaks or fillets, cut into large pieces
½ pound other fish (ocean perch [redfish], red snapper, hake, cusk, etc.) fillets, cut into large pieces
¼ pound crabmeat, picked over for cartilage and shells
1 pound fresh medium-size shrimp, heads removed (save for making shrimp broth) or ½ pound headless defrosted shrimp, shelled
Salt and freshly ground black pepper to taste
¼ cup white wine vinegar
1 bay leaf
Bouquet garni, tied with string, consisting of 10 sprigs fresh parsley

1. In a large casserole, heat the olive oil over medium-high heat, then cook the garlic and cuttlefish for 30 seconds, stirring constantly. Reduce the heat to low, add 2 tablespoons of the water, and cook until tender, about 30 minutes, stirring frequently so the garlic doesn't burn.

2. Add all the fish, crab, and shrimp, season with salt and pepper, and cook until firm, about 6 minutes. Cook in batches if necessary. Remove all the fish and shellfish with a slotted spoon and set aside.

3. Increase the heat to medium, pour in the vinegar, the remaining quart water, the bay leaf, and parsley, and reduce the broth for 50 minutes.

4. Return all the fish to the broth, increase the heat to high, and cook until thoroughly reheated, about 6 minutes. Remove and discard the bay leaf and parsley and serve immediately.

Makes 4 servings

Maraqat al-Ḥūt (Tunisia)

FISH STEW IN THE STYLE OF SFAX

In the early twelfth century, al-Idrīsī, the Arab geographer of the Norman court in Palermo during the reign of Roger II, traveled through North Africa and wrote that Sfax was well known for its fish. All during the era of Ḥafṣid Tunisia (1228–1574) fish were a famous product of Sfax.[43]

Sfax today is a bustling Tunisian city where people dress in the latest fashions and the seafood is still justly famous. In Sfax this fish soup is traditional for the ʿĪd al-ṣaghīr *feast, the feast of the breaking of the Ramadan fast, and many Sfaxian cooks make it with raisins. Grouper is usually a part of this stew, but cooks also use scorpionfish, annular bream, hake, and red gurnard. Because of the ease of availability, you will do fine, and capture a Sfaxian taste, by using two of the following fish: grouper, porgy (scup; sea bream), red snapper, redfish (ocean perch), ocean pout (ling), cod, haddock, wolffish (ocean catfish), hake.*

The broth can be eaten as a soup or as a kind of ragout with grilled, toasted, or fried bread or macaroni cooked in the broth. Or each diner can serve himself a piece of fish to be put in the soup bowl.

6 large garlic cloves, peeled
2 teaspoons cumin seeds
½ teaspoon salt
½ cup extra virgin olive oil
1 medium-size onion, chopped
1 tablespoon tomato paste

8½ cups water
½ teaspoon *harīsa* (page 523)
1 tablespoon paprika
1 teaspoon cayenne pepper
½ teaspoon freshly ground black pepper
2 fresh green chili peppers, seeded
2 celery stalks, chopped
3 carrots, sliced
Pinch of saffron threads, crumbled
10 sprigs fresh parsley, tied in cheesecloth
1 bay leaf
Salt to taste
2½ pounds mixed fish (choose 2 of the fish mentioned above, preferably one with its head), scaled, gutted, and cleaned
1 lemon, quartered, or 1 preserved lemon (page 104)

1. In a mortar, pound the garlic, cumin, and salt together until you have a paste. Set aside.

2. In a large, deep stove-top casserole or stew pot, heat the olive oil over high heat, then cook the onion until softened, 1 to 2 minutes, stirring.

3. Meanwhile, dissolve the tomato paste in ½ cup of the water and add to the casserole along with the *harīsa,* paprika, cayenne, black pepper, and garlic paste. Add 4 cups of the water and cook over high heat for 10 minutes.

4. Add the remaining 4 cups water, the whole chili peppers, celery, carrots, saffron, parsley, and bay leaf and season with salt. Reduce the heat to medium-low and simmer for 30 minutes. Strain the broth through a fine-mesh strainer, discarding the vegetables. Return the broth to the casserole or pot.

5. Bring the broth to a furious boil and add the whole fish first, if using any. Cook the whole fish for 5 minutes, then add the remaining fish. Cook for 15 minutes, then remove the fish and bone the whole fish. Serve the broth as a first-course soup and the fish separately as a second course with quartered lemons or preserved lemons, keeping warm in an ovenproof serving platter.

Makes 4 servings

Ṭājin bi'l-Ḥūt (Morocco)

FISH STEW

Traditionally, the ingredients of a ṭājin *are layered in an earthenware casserole with a cone-shaped lid (also called a* ṭājin*) and cooked on top of an earthenware brazier filled with red hot lump hardwood coals for a long time. The reason one cooks in an earthenware* ṭājin *with its conical cover is to achieve that intense, aromatic flavor that results from capturing the steam and juices from all the foods trapped inside. In place of an authentic Moroccan* ṭājin *you can use a Dutch oven or clay oven (be sure to read the directions for use) or enameled cast-iron casserole.*

I learned how to make this fish ṭājin *in Casablanca from Rafih Benjelloun, an effusive Moroccan-American restaurateur from Atlanta whose efficacious approach to Moroccan food was inspiring. The green peppers in my recipe will be ever so slightly crunchy when done. If you prefer them completely soft, cook them first in olive oil until limp before layering them in the* ṭājin.

In place of Mediterranean fish I have found success using swordfish, shark, and sea bass or slightly less firm fish such as grouper or red snapper.

1 recipe *sharmūla* (page 533)
4 firm-fleshed white fish steaks such as swordfish or shark (about 1½ pounds), cut about 1¼ inches thick
1 tablespoon extra virgin olive oil
2 medium-size boiling potatoes (about ½ pound), peeled and sliced ⅛ inch thick
Salt and freshly ground black pepper to taste
2 green bell peppers, seeded and cut into thin strips
2 large ripe tomatoes (about 1 pound), peeled, seeded, and thinly sliced
½ cup tomato puree (preferably fresh)
2 tablespoons finely chopped fresh coriander (cilantro) leaves
2 tablespoons finely chopped fresh parsley leaves

1. Prepare the *sharmūla*. Coat the fish steaks with half of the *sharmūla* and marinate for 2 hours in a ceramic or glass baking pan in the refrigerator.

2. Preheat the oven to 400°F. Lightly oil a *ṭājin*, Dutch oven, earthenware casserole, or enameled cast-iron casserole and arrange the potatoes on the bottom. Lightly salt and pepper the potatoes. Place the fish steaks on top of the potatoes. Cover the fish with the green peppers and then the tomato slices, arranging everything very neatly and decoratively. Lightly salt and pepper again. Spoon half of the remaining *sharmūla* over the tomato slices. Pour the tomato puree over and sprinkle with the coriander, parsley, and more salt and pepper. Spoon the remaining *sharmūla* over everything.

3. Bake the *ṭājin* covered, until the potatoes are tender and the fish cooked, about 1 hour. Do not check until at least 40 minutes have passed. Serve.

Makes 4 servings

Soupe de Poisson (Provence)

FISH SOUP

The peasant reserved his best grain for the market and survived on his inferior grain. So, too, the fourteenth-century fishermen of Marseilles, St. Tropez, and Villefranche were likely to have reserved their most commercially viable fish—the sardines, eels, and anchovies in particular—for the market and reserved the little bony fish, today known as soup fish, for themselves. After the Papacy was moved to Avignon in 1309 by Pope Clement V, many of these commercially viable fish found their way to the opulent papal table.[44]

The soup fish, fish that disappear into a broth and are not actually eaten in any identifiable form, were used exclusively for the fish soups that are today found all along the small ports of Languedoc and Provence. This recipe is typical of Marseilles. In restaurants, soupe de poisson *is ubiquitous on menus, and some chefs use a* chinoise, *a small green orange preserved in brandy, to flavor the fish broth. As with all fish soups and stews, a proper* soupe de poisson *requires a good mix of fish, such as a 1½-pound striped bass, a 1½-pound redfish, a small mackerel, and a few pieces of eel without the skin. In any case, there should be a minimum of four fish, preferably with heads (they provide so much flavor), and at least one of the fish should be an oily fish such as eel, bluefish, sardine, striped bass, kingfish, Spanish mackerel, or mackerel. Ideally, since the fish is used for flavoring the broth and not eaten individually, you can get fish carcasses and heads free by asking the fishmonger for them.*

¼ cup extra virgin olive oil
1 large onion, finely chopped
2 leeks, white part only, halved lengthwise, washed well, and finely chopped
1 small fennel bulb and stalks, finely chopped
2½ quarts cold water
3 to 4 pounds whole fish (choose 4 from those mentioned above), cleaned and each cut into 3 pieces
1 pound ripe tomatoes, peeled, seeded, and finely chopped
1 tablespoon tomato paste
3 garlic cloves, finely chopped
Bouquet garni consisting of 12 sprigs each fresh parsley and thyme and 1 bay leaf, tied in cheesecloth
Pinch of saffron threads, crumbled
½ teaspoon cayenne pepper
Salt and freshly ground black pepper to taste
1 teaspoon grated orange zest or one 10-inch-long strip orange zest
1 teaspoon brandy or cognac
3 ounces vermicelli, broken into 3 pieces
4 heaping tablespoons *sauce rouille* (page 514)
4 to 8 *croûtes* (page 514) or *crostini di pane per le zuppe de pesce* (page 559; optional)
¼ pound Gruyère cheese, freshly grated

1. In a large, deep stove-top casserole or earthenware *marmite,* heat the olive oil over medium-high heat, then cook the onion, leeks, and fennel until wilted, about 6 minutes, stirring occasionally. Add the water, fish, tomatoes, tomato paste, garlic, bouquet garni, saffron, and cayenne, season with salt and black pepper, and stir again. Bring to a boil and let boil for 45 minutes. Add the orange zest and brandy and boil for another 8 minutes. The fish will have disintegrated at this point.

2. Remove from the heat and pass the broth through a food mill, discarding all the vegetables and fish that do not pass through on the first several turns of the food mill.

3. Meanwhile, bring a large pot of water to a rolling boil, salt abundantly, and add the vermicelli. Drain when very al dente.

4. Return the fish soup to the casserole or *marmite*, bring to a gentle boil, add the vermicelli, and cook for 5 minutes. Ladle into individual serving bowls with a heaping tablespoon of *sauce rouille* and 1 or 2 *croûtes* or *crostini,* if desired. Serve with the grated cheese.

NOTE: Normally the cook chooses either the vermicelli or the bread as the garnish, but I like them both.

Makes 4 to 6 servings

Bouillabaisse (Provence)

The most famous fish stew of the Mediterranean is bouillabaisse, and its home is considered to be Marseilles, although it is made in every little port throughout the coastal regions of Provence. The apocryphal story of the origin of bouillabaisse that is popularly told by the Marseillais is that Venus served bouillabaisse to her husband, Vulcan, to lull him to sleep while she consorted with Mars. Greek food writers have laid claim to inventing the precursor of bouillabaisse. They argue that when the Phocaeans, Greeks from Asia Minor, founded Marseilles in about 600 B.C., they brought with them a fish soup known as kakavia *that was the basis of the future bouillabaisse.*[45] *This can be said to be true only in the most general (and meaningless) sense. In fact, we have no idea whether such a soup was "brought" to the western Mediterranean. In the culinary writings of the ancient Greeks, especially as represented by Athenaeus (A.D. 170–230), there are many mentions of boiled fish, cooked in unspecified ways, as well as one fish stew made with grayfish (dogfish), herbs, oil, caraway seeds, and salt.*[46] *The most likely precursor to the Provençal bouillabaisse is an Italian fish stew and, in fact, the closest thing to a bouillabaisse that I have found in a medieval text is the* brodecto de li dicti pisci *that appears in an anonymous fifteenth-century Italian cookery book from southern Italy where sardines and anchovies are boiled in* vino greco *(a strong Neapolitan wine) with black pepper, saffron, and sugar and a little olive oil.*[47]

The most distinguishing characteristic of a bouillabaisse is not the fish, because all fish stews and soups have fish, but the unique flavoring derived from saffron, fennel seeds, and orange zest. A famous Provençal food writer, Jean-Noël Escudier, called bouillabaisse the "magical synthesis." Another famous French epicure, Curnonsky, called it soupe d'or, *soup of gold. The origin of the word* bouillabaisse *has been attributed to the abbess of a Marseilles convent (a pun on* bouille-abbesse, *the abbess' boil?) and, most credibly, to* bouillon abaissé *"to reduce by evaporation."*[48] *One of the earliest uses of the word* bouillabaisse *was in the 1830s, as a term expressing the rapidity of the cooking.*[49] *Stendhal mentioned* bouille-à-baisses, *perhaps referring to a fish stew, in his travels from 1806. But the famous French chef Raymond Oliver, writing in the*

Gastronomy of France, *makes some extraordinary claims about bouillabaisse. He tells us that it is first mentioned in a dictionary from 1785, that its heritage is Phoenician via Greek Sicily, and that the rules for the making of bouillabaisse were laid down in the sixteenth century.*[50] *None of this is supported by any evidence, but in any case, I agree with his estimation that "in 'bouillabaisse' . . . it is essential to retain all the delicacy of the fish and never to debase through too much zeal a symphony of tastes which is so hard to achieve."*[51]

Strong opinions about the proper bouillabaisse are typical from its proponents such as the French writer and gourmet August de Croze, who said it is a culinary heresy to use white wine in a bouillabaisse because wine only changes the nature of the fish. Others, including myself, disagree; it is natural. But I agree with everything else he has to say: live fish in great variety, good olive oil, saffron, and furiously boiling water (the most critical step) are all essential for a successful bouillabaisse. So how did bouillabaisse originate? My guess is that, given all the hallmarks, it was the invention of a nineteenth-century restaurateur of Marseilles. Because of its expense, it most certainly was not an invention of the fishermen.

The memorable tastes of bouillabaisse are rich and heavenly. I have worked my way through countless but always joyful tureens of bouillabaisse. In Golf-Juan, the Tètou restaurant makes a wonderful bouillabaisse, and the proprietor, Jacques Marquis, Monsieur Jacques, may wax poetic about the fragrance of the broth perfumed with leeks, fennel, and saffron and rich with fish like rascasse, *the scorpionfish essential to this famous fish boil of Provence. In Marseilles, an extraordinary bouillabaisse can be found at the Miramar restaurant, while in Cap d'Antibes they say you must not miss the bouillabaisse of the Bacon restaurant.*

Some connoisseurs believe that it is impossible to make an authentic bouillabaisse without fish from the Mediterranean. The famous English food writer Elizabeth David wrote in her French Provincial Cooking *that "It is useless attempting to make a* bouillabaisse *away from the shores of the Mediterranean."*[52] *I have never been attracted to this kind of food snobbery; it isn't true and it limits the culinary imagination. I disagree that one cannot hope to make bouillabaisse outside of the Mediterranean. It can be done, I have done it, and this is the recipe. But, admittedly, you must know your fish, choose carefully, and search for a quality fishmonger—one with a Mediterranean or Asian clientele who demand only the freshest fish, including one-day-old air-freighted fish from the Mediterranean or west coast of Africa. On the other hand, you can make an excellent bouillabaisse without any Mediterranean fish, but this is harder because you must choose fish that bear close resemblance in taste and flavor to Mediterranean fish. I will try to give you the basic information to do this in the recipe.*

First, you must find the rascasse *(scorpionfish) or other member of the* Scorpaenidae *family. Scorpionfish are sometimes sold fresh in ethnic fish stores, but one is likely to find, at times, excellent* rascasse *substitutes in North Atlantic and Pacific* Scorpaenidae *such as bluemouth, redfish (ocean perch), rockfish, and sculpin. Other excellent-tasting fish with similar flesh textures will work well, such as wolffish (ocean catfish), striped bass, sea bass, red snapper, grouper, wreckfish, tautog (blackfish), and tilefish. Without getting into too much detail, one reason the* rascasse *tastes good is its diet among the rocks of the deep waters it inhabits.*[53] *After much experimenting, I believe the taste of scorpionfish can be approximated by using a combination of redfish (ocean perch), the fish closest in taste, or wolffish (ocean catfish), grouper, red snapper, or dogfish (Cape shark) in a one-to-one ratio for the amount of* rascasse *called for.*

There are many recipes for bouillabaisse, including one that features the addition of thinly sliced potatoes, as they make it in Toulon. There are many "keys" or "secrets" to success, and I will tell you mine.

Bouillabaisse should not be made for fewer than eight people. Because a great variety of fish is required, you will need at least that many people to get the bare minimum of fish. You should have both oily and white fish.

Another trick for success is to boil the broth furiously so that the olive oil will emulsify with the broth and not float on top. Once the broth is boiling furiously, you begin to add the fish. This, I believe, is the trickiest part of a good bouillabaisse. If your fish is too cold, it will lower the temperature of the boiling broth too much. The fish should be left at room temperature for twenty minutes before adding it to the broth. Put the fish in one at a time, allowing a few seconds for the broth to adapt to the temperature change.

Making bouillabaisse is expensive and it is work, but I never shy away from preparing it because the flavors are memorable and conversation stopping. You must choose a minimum of four fish from the white-fleshed group and at least two from the oily—the greater the variety, the better. Do not use fragile white-fleshed fish fillets such as flounder or sole because it will fall apart. Ideally you should buy the fish whole and fillet them yourself, saving the head, tail, and carcass for the stock. My recipe calls for about fifteen pounds of whole fish, half of which will be the weight of head, tails, and carcasses.

Traditionally bouillabaisse is eaten as two courses. First, the broth is poured in bowls with some sauce rouille *spread on the* croûtes. *Afterward, the fish platter is served, often with thinly sliced buttered potatoes.*

8 to 10 pounds firm white-fleshed (lean) fish (choose 4 from this group): redfish (ocean perch), red snapper, blue-mouth, rockfish, sea robin (red gurnard), monkfish, cod, porgy (scup; sea bream), grouper, halibut, haddock, dab, turbot, wreckfish, ocean pout (ling), cusk, wolffish (ocean catfish), tautog (blackfish), tilefish, sculpin
4 to 5 pounds oily fish (choose 2 from this group): bluefish, moray eel, conger eel, mackerel, shark, dogfish, striped bass, sea bass, kingfish, Spanish mackerel, mahimahi (dolphinfish)
5 tablespoons unsalted butter
2 medium-size onions, sliced
8 cups cold water
2 bouquet garni, each consisting of 4 sprigs fresh parsley, 6 sprigs fresh thyme, 10 black peppercorns, and 1 bay leaf, tied in cheesecloth
1 cup dry white wine, such as Muscadet, Sancerre, or Cassis (the wine, not the blackberry liqueur)
1½ cups extra virgin olive oil
6 to 8 large garlic cloves, to your taste, finely chopped
Pinch of saffron threads, crumbled and steeped in ¼ cup hot water until needed
2 large onions, finely chopped
3 leeks, white and light green parts only, halved lengthwise, washed well, and thinly sliced
3 celery stalks, finely chopped
2 pounds ripe plum tomatoes, peeled, seeded, and chopped
1 long thin strip orange zest with no pith
1 tablespoon fennel seeds
½ teaspoon saffron threads steeped in ¼ cup tepid dry white wine until needed
Salt and freshly ground black pepper to taste
Boiling water as needed
2 tablespoons tomato paste
2 tablespoons anise liquor such as Pernod or Ouzo
½ cup finely chopped fresh parsley leaves
1 recipe *sauce rouille* (page 514)

1. Gut, scale, and clean the fish. If the fishmonger cleans and fillets your fish, have him save the heads, tails, and carcasses. Cut the fish into 4 × 2½-inch pieces.

2. Prepare the fish broth. Rinse the fish heads, tails, and carcasses in cold water. Break the carcasses into pieces. In a large stockpot, melt the butter over medium heat, then cook the sliced onions until soft but not brown, about 6 minutes, stirring occasionally. Add the fish heads and bones and cover with the cold water. Put in one of the bouquet garni and the wine. Bring to a boil, skimming occasionally, then reduce the heat to low, partially cover, and simmer for 2 hours. Strain the fish broth through a conical strainer and set aside to cool. Discard the solids. You will have 10 cups of fish broth when finished. Clean the stockpot because you will need it for step 4.

3. After you get the fish broth going, marinate the fish in a large ceramic or glass bowl or pan with ¼ cup of the olive oil, half of the chopped garlic, and the saffron steeped in wine for 2 hours in the refrigerator.

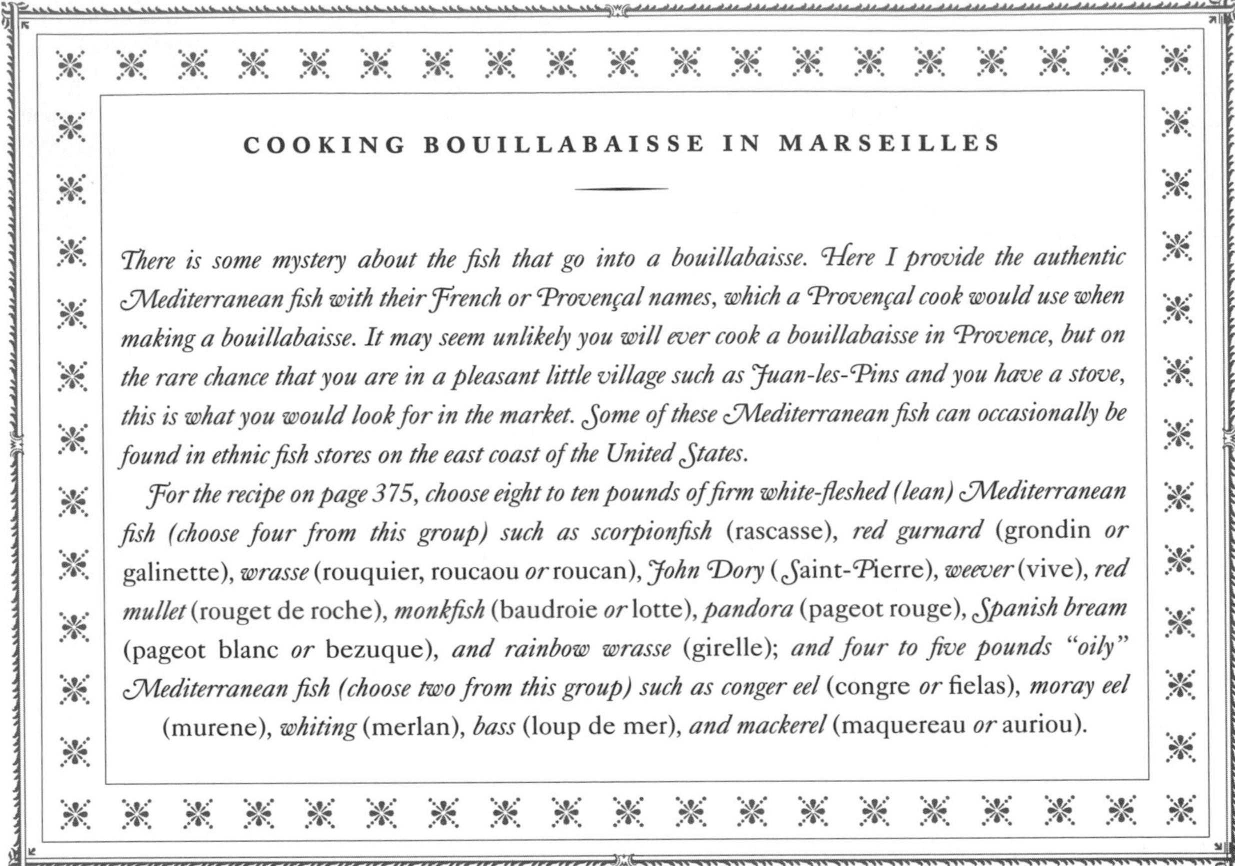

COOKING BOUILLABAISSE IN MARSEILLES

There is some mystery about the fish that go into a bouillabaisse. Here I provide the authentic Mediterranean fish with their French or Provençal names, which a Provençal cook would use when making a bouillabaisse. It may seem unlikely you will ever cook a bouillabaisse in Provence, but on the rare chance that you are in a pleasant little village such as Juan-les-Pins and you have a stove, this is what you would look for in the market. Some of these Mediterranean fish can occasionally be found in ethnic fish stores on the east coast of the United States.

For the recipe on page 375, choose eight to ten pounds of firm white-fleshed (lean) Mediterranean fish (choose four from this group) such as scorpionfish (rascasse), *red gurnard* (grondin *or* galinette), *wrasse* (rouquier, roucaou *or* roucan), *John Dory* (*S*aint-*P*ierre), *weever* (vive), *red mullet* (rouget de roche), *monkfish* (baudroie *or* lotte), *pandora* (pageot rouge), *Spanish bream* (pageot blanc *or* bezuque), *and rainbow wrasse* (girelle); *and four to five pounds "oily" Mediterranean fish (choose two from this group) such as conger eel* (congre *or* fielas), *moray eel* (murene), *whiting* (merlan), *bass* (loup de mer), *and mackerel* (maquereau *or* auriou).

4. In the large stockpot, heat the remaining 1¼ cups olive oil over medium heat, then cook the chopped onions, leeks, and celery for 15 minutes, stirring often. Add the tomatoes, the remaining garlic, the remaining bouquet garni, the orange zest, and fennel seeds. Stir in the reserved fish broth and the saffron steeped in wine and season with salt and pepper. Bring to a boil, then reduce the heat to medium-low and simmer for 40 minutes. The broth can be left like this, covered, for many hours, over very low heat or using a heat diffuser.

5. When you are ready to prepare the final stages of the bouillabaisse, bring the broth back to a furious boil. It should be boiling like mad. Keep the broth boiling furiously so the oil emulsifies. Add the oily fish and boil, uncovered, over very high heat for 8 minutes. Shake the pot to prevent sticking. Now put the firm-fleshed white fish in and boil hard for 6 minutes. Add more boiling water if necessary to cover the fish. Shake the pot occasionally. Meanwhile, mix the tomato paste and anise liqueur.

6. Carefully remove the fish from the broth with a slotted spoon and spatula or skimmer and transfer to a large bowl or deep platter. Arrange the fish on the platter more or less in the order in which you put them into the pot. Keep them warm by covering with a sheet of aluminum foil.

7. Strain the broth through a fine-mesh strainer into a soup tureen or large bowl, discarding what doesn't go through. Whisk in the tomato paste-and-anise mixture. Sprinkle the platter and soup tureen with the parsley and serve with the *croûtes* and *sauce rouille* on separate plates.

VARIATION
Serve the fish with boiled potatoes, thinly sliced and buttered. Some cooks, especially in restaurants, will add a cut-up live lobster at the same time as when the oily fish go in.

Makes 10 to 12 servings

La Bullinada (Roussillon)

FISH STEW

La bullinada (bouillinade *in French) is a typical Catalonian dish from French Roussillon. This is a traditional preparation found in the small coastal villages of the Côte Vermeille. It is made in a glazed earthenware* marmite *with a cover called a* tupí. *Today restaurateurs will make* bullinada *with lobster instead of fish.*

Éliane Thibaut-Comelade, an authority on the cooking of French Catalonia, regrets that this dish is not as famous as bouillabaisse. She recommends placing a small amount of beef or veal marrow, whipped like cream, in the bowl in which you serve the bullinada. Bullinada *can be eaten as two courses. First remove the fish and potatoes to a platter and serve the broth, then the fish.*

3 tablespoons pork lard
1 large onion, chopped
Leaves from 1 bunch fresh parsley (20 to 25 sprigs), chopped
Salt to taste
¼ teaspoon cayenne pepper
Pinch of saffron threads, crumbled
Freshly ground black pepper to taste
1 pound ripe tomatoes (optional), peeled, seeded, and sliced
6 large garlic cloves, finely chopped
2 pounds boiling potatoes, peeled and sliced ⅛ to ¼ inch thick
1 pound red snapper, redfish, or cod fillets, cut into even-size pieces
1 pound monkfish fillets, cut into even-size pieces
1 pound sea bass, striped bass, whiting, or pollack fillets, cut into even-size pieces
1 pound scorpionfish, tilefish, or porgy (scup; sea bream) fillets, cut into even-size pieces
Bouquet garni, consisting of 1 fennel stalk, 6 sprigs fresh thyme, and 1 bay leaf, tied in cheesecloth
About 2 quarts water, salted with 2 to 3 tablespoons sea salt
2 tablespoons extra virgin olive oil
4 to 6 tablespoons veal or beef marrow (optional), to your taste

1. In a large earthenware casserole (preferably) or an enamelled cast-iron casserole, melt the pork lard over medium heat, then cook the onion until golden, about 12 minutes, stirring occasionally. Spread the onion evenly around the bottom of the casserole and sprinkle with parsley, salt, cayenne, saffron, and black pepper.

2. Cover the onion with the tomatoes, if using, the garlic, half the potatoes, and the fish. Cover the fish with the remaining potatoes. Add the bouquet garni and barely cover with the salted water. Cover the casserole and turn the heat to high. Once it starts to boil, in about 14 minutes, add the olive oil and boil furiously until the fish is about to break apart, 10 to 12 minutes.

3. Place a tablespoon of marrow (if using) in each soup bowl, ladle the soup on top, and serve immediately.

Makes 4 to 6 servings

Caldo con Pimientos de Almería (Andalusia)

BELL PEPPER AND FISH SOUP FROM ALMERÍA

One writer described Almería, from where this fish stew originates, as the "most African of Spanish towns."[54] *What he more properly should have said is "the most Arab of towns," for the city's architecture is mostly Muslim inspired. The great Spanish Umayyad ruler 'Abd-ar-Raḥmān III built the mighty fortification, the Alcabaza of Almería, in the tenth century and the city became his most important naval base. When the Spanish Umayyads dissolved as a dynasty in 1031, Muslim Spain politically fragmented. Twenty-three local dynasties arose and the Banū-Ṣumādiḥ ruled in Almería, a time of cultural brilliance, until the coming of the Almoravid conquest of Spain in 1090. The Almoravids were Muslim Berbers from North Africa who were swept up in a wave of religious fervor in the eleventh century. These desert Berbers all wore veils, men and women, and were warriors known as* murābiṭūn *(literally, dwellers of the frontier fortresses), giving us the French word* marabout, *or holy man. They spread a fundamentalist brand of Islam by the faith through the sword. Almería became famous for its sericulture industry, as well as its brassware and glassware. Perhaps, too, although we have no direct evidence, there are culinary vestiges as exemplified by this recipe with its Arab culinary sensibilities.*[55]

This fish stew has at its base salsa de patatas *(page 59), potato sauce.* Mero *(grouper) is very popular in Almería on the coast, as popular as mutton is in the hills. A local proverb goes: Among the meats, mutton, among the fish, grouper.*[56] *If grouper is unavailable, you can use halibut, yellowtail, sea bass, or red snapper in this stew. Traditionally, the fish would be served separately from the broth.*

2 large red bell peppers
5 cups cold water
1 tablespoon salt
1 boiling potato (about ½ pound), peeled and cubed
½ pound grouper, halibut, sea bass, red snapper, or redfish (ocean perch) fillet or steak without bones
1 teaspoon cumin seeds
2 garlic cloves, peeled
Pinch of saffron threads, crumbled
2 teaspoons paprika
1 medium-size ripe tomato, peeled, seeded, and chopped
1 cup beef broth (page 54) or water
6 tablespoons extra virgin olive oil

1. Preheat the oven to 400°F. Place the bell peppers in a baking pan with ½ cup of the water and place the pan in the oven until the peppers blacken on all sides, about 45 minutes. Remove and, once they are cool enough to handle, remove the skins, stems, and seeds. Slice or chop and set aside.

2. Put the remaining 4½ cups water in a pot with the salt and bring to a boil. Add the potato and boil for 12 minutes. Remove the potato with a slotted ladle and set aside. Add the fish and boil for 2 minutes. Remove the fish with a slotted ladle and set aside. Save the broth.

3. In a mortar, pound the cumin seeds with the garlic, saffron, and paprika into a paste. Add the tomato and a few cubes of reserved potato and transfer to a food processor or blender or continue pounding with a pestle until smooth. While the processor or blender is running or you are pounding, add the beef broth or water. The sauce should be homogenous. Whisk in the olive oil in a slow stream, as if you were making mayonnaise (see page 501).

4. Return the remaining potato cubes to the cooking broth and bring to a boil. Add the red bell peppers and cook for 10 minutes over medium-high heat.

Strain the broth through a fine-mesh strainer and pass the vegetables through a food mill back into the broth. Add the reserved fish to the broth and heat gently. Serve.

Makes 4 servings

THE great ports dominated the lives of the little ports, as well as the lives of the pirates who fed off their traffic. Marseilles, Genoa, Ragusa, and Barcelona controlled the sea-lanes near them. The domination of these ports, such as Barcelona, especially after the union of Catalonia and Aragon in 1137, meant the role of the cities in the mercantile life of the Mediterranean was secured. Catalonia developed a thriving sea trade in the eleventh century, brought over by Italian immigrants from Genoa and Pisa. The Catalans traded with North Africa, the Tunisians being big customers, in Valencian olive oil, dried figs in olive oil, and salt from the Balearics, while the Tunisians traded their dates, almonds, hazelnuts, honey, salted tuna, rice, and

wine.[57] By the sixteenth century, Catalonia was in decline, the result of Barcelona's having lost its independence to the Spanish Hapsburgs, then her Jewish community in the inquisition of 1492, and finally her capitalists because of political turmoil, peasant uprisings, and bank failures. The decline of Barcelona meant that corsairs ruled the coasts. The corsairs were either Christian or Muslim. The Christian corsairs of the western Mediterranean were mostly French and Spanish, while the Muslim corsairs were typically Algerians or Tunisians from North Africa, known as the Barbary corsairs. In the eastern Mediterranean, Christian pirates, usually Greeks or Sicilians, were provided with a richer hunting ground than in the western Mediterranean. Here they could play a hiding game in the Aegean while striking at rich prizes, including the lucrative Rhodes-Alexandria route taken by pilgrims and by cargoes of spices, silks, wood, rice, wheat, and sugar.

Food on Ships

IN the western Mediterranean, Seville was the entry point for the American trade. The Casa de la Contratación (House of Trade) was established at Seville on February 14, 1503, to control trade and travel between Spain and the Indies.[58] The ships leaving Seville on their long journeys brought the population out to the riverbanks to see them off. The sails of these magnificent ships would fill slowly and they would drift down the river to the sea, gone for a year or more, or never to be seen again. Merchants as well as sailors' wives were wrought with anxiety because the loss of a ship meant not only the loss of a husband, father, brother, or son but also the loss of entire fortunes. A sinking could bring ruin to the owner of the cargo and his creditors.[59]

The provisioning of these ships was mostly local, but dominated financially by the Genoese.[60] Salt pork came from Ronda, Aracena, and other towns around the Sierra Nevada and Sierra Morena. Cheese, bought in Seville, was usually imported from Germany, Flanders, and the Canary Islands, while the wheat came from France and North Africa. The occasional and small amounts of rice on board came from the fields of Valencia and raisins were bought in Almería. When Andalusian agriculture began to decline in the early seventeenth century, supplies for these ships shifted from local to imported, with salt pork from Flanders and salt beef from Ireland.[61]

Once under way, shipboard life was as rough as one would imagine. Missing mess call meant going without food. However, the diet of sailors and soldiers on board Spanish ships was better than anything on land. In 1560, they could expect a daily ration of one and a half pounds of bread (hardtack), one quart of wine (15 percent alcohol), half a pound of salt beef, cheese, or salt cod depending on the day, about four ounces of beans or chickpeas, and half an ounce of olive oil with some vinegar. Occasionally the ships were provisioned with rice. The daily caloric value was between 3,385 and 3,889.[62] This was simply enormous in the sixteenth-century Mediterranean. Compare it to the diet on a Tuscan galley of the same era, where the daily ration of biscuit was a little less than one and a half pounds along with three-quarters of a quart of wine, less than an ounce of olive oil, and morsels of salted cheese, salt meat, salt cod, sardines, little tuna (*tonnina*) or salted tuna, herring, and vermicelli to be used in *minestra* (soup). The caloric intake ranged from 1,900 on nonmeat days to 2,500 on days with meat.[63]

Galley cooks on a Spanish ship, as one would expect from the Spaniards with their fondness for robust and spicy foods, had a full range of spices to choose from, usually cinnamon, cloves, mustard, parsley, black pepper, and saffron. Surprisingly, there weren't many onions on board and garlic was rationed to last the whole voyage. Along with the copious wine, each man had two quarts of water per day. The men ate their meals on wooden plates. The priests, if there were any on the voyage, ate even better than the seamen, having quince marmalade, olives, hazelnuts, dried figs, and dried plums brought aboard for them.[64] Maybe they ate a *sopa* of almonds and saffron. Because all the cooking on Spanish galleons was done over charcoal or wood, the danger of fire was very great, so during storms the stewards served cheese instead of meat.[65]

Sopa de Almendras (Andalusia)

ALMOND AND SAFFRON SOUP

The roots of sopa de almendras *can be traced to the sixteenth-century cookbook of Ruperto de Nola, chef to King Ferdinand V (1452–1516), Spanish ruler of Naples, who has a similar recipe for almond soup with onions, cinnamon, and sugar.*[66] *The* Libro del arte de cozina *(Book of the art of cooking) by Diego Granado Maldonado, published in 1599, also has a recipe, although it probably was copied from Ruperto de Nola. Earlier still we can see the genesis of these flavors in the sauces used in medieval Arab cookery. Take, for instance, the description of* ibrāhīmiyya *in the medical synopsis of the eleventh-century doctor Ibn Jazla, who tells us it is prepared in the same way as* zīrbāj, *a boiled meat with cinnamon, sesame oil, chickpeas, wine vinegar, sugar water or sugar, sweet almonds, coriander, rue, and saffron.*[67] *In Algeria today, a* maraqat dajāj bi'l-lawz *is a chicken stew with almond and saffron sauce harking back to this medieval combination.*

This thick, creamy green soup typical of Granada is rich and flavorful. The preparation begins with a sofrito *of almonds, garlic, and parsley. Some people like to sprinkle chopped egg or a few drops of very fine vinegar on top before serving.*

½ pound blanched whole almonds
½ cup extra virgin olive oil
2 garlic cloves, peeled
½ cup finely chopped fresh parsley leaves
Pinch of saffron threads, crumbled
5¼ cups water
1 teaspoon freshly ground black pepper
1½ teaspoon freshly ground cumin seeds
Salt to taste
¾ pound Italian or French bread, without crust, soaked in water, squeezed dry, and mashed
1 large hard-boiled egg, shelled and finely chopped
1 cup cubed *crostini di pane per le zuppe di pesce* (page 559; optional)
Slivered blanched almonds (optional)

1. Place the whole almonds, olive oil, garlic, and parsley in a large stove-top casserole or soup pot. Turn the heat to medium and cook until the almonds are a bit browned, about 12 minutes, stirring and shaking the pan occasionally so the garlic doesn't burn. As you do this, steep the saffron in ¼ cup of the tepid water.

2. Remove the *sofrito* of olive oil, almonds, and garlic to a food processor or blender. Add the black pepper, cumin seeds, and steeped saffron and season with salt. Process the mixture until blended and smooth.

3. Return the mixture to the casserole or soup pot and cook for 1 minute over medium heat. Add the bread and continue cooking for 3 to 4 minutes, stirring a few times. Add the remaining 5 cups water, reduce the heat to low, and cook until thick, about 1 hour, covered, stirring occasionally.

4. Pass the soup through a food mill or fine-mesh strainer, return to the casserole or pot, and simmer over very low heat until creamy and smooth, about 45 minutes. Serve hot garnished with the chopped egg, *crostini*, if desired, and slivered almonds, if using.

Makes 4 servings

* * *

WHAT'S missing from this shipboard diet? Clearly the most noticeable deficiency is that of vegetables and fruits. The American historian Earl Hamilton, who studied the inventories of sixteenth-century Spanish ships, found no trace of either.[68] The fertile valley of the Guadalquivir that fed Seville was in full production throughout the year, so the lack of fresh fruits and vegetables on ships must mean that they were not highly prized as food at that time.[69] Fresh fruits and vegetables are perishable, of course, but there isn't even evidence of dried fruits and salted vegetables. Canning was not invented until the eighteenth century, so the absence of fresh vegetables meant that there were none whatsoever on board. The evidence, in fact, points to the complete unpopularity of green vegetables in Spanish cuisine of the sixteenth century. The gout suffered by King Philip II was said to be due to a lack of fruits and vegetables in his diet, he preferring the popular foods of his day—rice and chicken, wine, *pastel* (a savory pie), and empanadas.[70] When the House of Trade bought all the consumables for the Feast of Corpus Christi, a Roman Catholic event commemorating the institution of the Eucharist, which takes place at the height of the vegetable season in May, it did not include any vegetables.[71]

Life on a Venetian galley was as rich as that on a Spanish one, considering the times. In 1310, the daily ration on a Venetian galley included one and a half pounds of *panis biscocti* (hardtack or ship's biscuit), some wine, about two ounces of cheese *(casei)*, two ounces of salt pork (*de porcinis carnibus salitis)*, and three and a half ounces of beans (*fabae*). This amounted to 3,900 total daily calories, 71 percent coming from carbohydrates, 14 percent from fat, and 14 percent from protein. That's a pretty well-fed crew.[72] The Venetian sailor was entitled to carry on board a certain amount of merchandise without paying freight. As with the merchant, he had the right to his own sea chest, his own mattress (a recent Arab introduction), and a personal supply of wood, wine, or water, and flour or biscuits for the voyage.[73]

The galley cooks typically used the salt pork to make a stew with *fabae vel alicuius alterius leguminis* (beans and some other vegetables) that alleviated some of the monotony of the daily meals. The supply officer on each ship, the *scribanus,* furnished the galley cook with three ounces of meat each Sunday for every man on board and half this amount on each of the first four days of the week, Friday and Saturday being fast days.[74]

The distribution of food on board ship was a delicate affair that required serious controls and regulation of the crew to avoid brawls or, worse, mutinies. A legal code that was used widely among ships in the western Mediterranean, regardless of the flag they flew, was the Consolato del Mar, that required crews be fed meat on Sundays, Tuesdays, and Thursdays and *minestra* on other days. But there was no general international law existing stipulating such a requirement, so some sailors fared worse than others. Distributing bread and cheese was not as difficult as the meat and *minestra*. The system employed for food distribution came under the direction of the mate assisted by three crewmen, in rotating appointments, to carry out the task. One crewman was stationed in the poop, one amidship, and one forward to keep control of the situation and nip any developing mayhem in the bud.[75]

Much of what we know about medieval Mediterranean shipboard food comes from Alessandro Magno, a man who kept a diary on his sailing trips to Alexandria on a Venetian merchant ship. He was a noble, entitling him to sit at the first table, the captain's table, along with the mate, the pilot, the purser, the carpenter, the caulker, the gunners, and passengers paying five ducats a month. Dining well depended on the mood of the ship's captain. But the best eating was often found at the second table, with it regular passengers and crew, because this is when the steward and cook ate. The cook reserved the best food for himself. The third mess, with mere deck hands, were better fed than oarsmen on war galleys because they had meat three times a week, with sardines and cheese on the other days, as well as all the *minestra* they wanted.[76]

Minestra di Verdure (Sicily)

VEGETABLE SOUP

Although the American historian Earl Hamilton found no evidence of fresh vegetables on Spanish galleys, fifteenth-century Sicilian documents referring to military rations confirm that fresh vegetables were substituted for meat on Sicilian galleys. When galleys were in port the cooks made minestra di verdure *with fresh vegetables.* Minestra *today refers to soup or to a first course, but in the fifteenth century it was an elemental food, almost like a stew, that could also contain pasta. At sea, rice was reserved for meatless days, and made into* minestra *with fava beans and chickpeas moistened with vinegar and olive oil.*[77]

Although no longer associated with seamen, this soup slowly evolved into recipes such as this one, where a simple list of ingredients elicits an extraordinary taste. Because every cook makes minestra *in a different way, there is no standard recipe.*

3 quarts water
1 cup dried fava beans, picked over
1 cup dried white beans (such as navy, *cannellini*, or great northern), picked over
2 medium-size onions (about 1 pound total), finely chopped
2 carrots, finely chopped
1 celery stalk, finely chopped
1 small Savoy cabbage (about 1 pound), blemished outer leaves removed, cored, and chopped
1 endive, chopped
1 head Boston lettuce, stems trimmed and chopped
Salt and freshly ground black pepper to taste
Freshly grated Parmigiano-Reggiano cheese for sprinkling
Extra virgin olive oil for drizzling

1. Bring the water to a boil in a soup pot. Place the fava beans in a strainer (so you can remove them easily) and boil for 5 minutes. Remove the strainer and, when cool enough to handle, peel the fava beans. Return the fava beans to the boiling water with the white beans, onions, carrots, and celery and cook until the beans are half-cooked, about 30 minutes, partially covered.

2. Add the cabbage, endive, and lettuce, season with salt and pepper, and cook until the beans are fully tender, another 15 to 20 minutes. Transfer to a tureen or individual serving bowls, sprinkle with some cheese, and drizzle with olive oil before serving.

Makes 6 servings

FISHING AND FISHERMEN

Fishing off Sicily

THE most important fishing industry of the medieval Mediterranean was, arguably, in Sicily, and even there fish played a modest albeit constant role in the food of the island. There were two kinds of fish caught in the fifteenth century, the so-called blue fish, mostly sardines and anchovies that had some limited economic importance in Sicily's export trade, and the white fish, such as John Dory, turbot, sea bass, grouper, and comber, which were secondary in economic importance. However, fish had no overall importance in either the diet or the economy of medieval Sicily and the total number of fishermen were few.[78] But the fasting prescriptions of the church assured that fish would always be in demand. In data for the vice-regent from 1415 we see that fresh and dried fish were bought ten days out of the month. On Fridays and Saturdays, fresh fish, eel, salted little tuna, and eggs were eaten instead of meat.[79]

Messina, Cefalù, Termini, Trapani, and Palermo were the five fishing centers of Sicily in the fourteenth and fifteenth centuries, all fishing sardines for the most part. Fish were in seasonal demand and especially during Lent, when church-mandated fasting requirements limited the amount of meat that could be eaten. During the winter, the fishing industry was involved in salting sardines and, especially, *tonnina* (little tuna, *Euthynnus alletteratus*).[80]

The fishermen encircled the shoals of fish with their seine nets and unloaded their catch directly onto the beach. The fish were processed for salting, a small amount perhaps set aside for local cooks of these coastal villages, while the fishermen victualed their boats with bread and wine. Villages of the interior ate freshwater fish from local rivers and streams or eel from the Simeto River near Paternò. In the twelfth century, eel were caught in a complicated device called a *tarusi,* consisting of a series of chambers whereby the eel is unable to turn around and get out.

Palermo was the most important of the five fishing towns in medieval Sicily, and in the fourteenth century the fishermen lived in an area of the city near the sea called the Kalsa. A fisherman's life was a poor and hard one. The Kalsa still exists and even today one finds fishermen, smugglers, and mafiosi (so they say) living there.[81] It was in Palermo where the net makers were and where most of the fishermen could be recruited.

Fishing zones were well demarcated and the fishing of sardines from Termini was the economically most important fishing activity. The zone off Trapani was rich in fish, and we know that agents for the royal kitchen of the Angevin King in Naples, Charles d'Anjou, came here in 1270 to buy *dacteri* (flying fish?) and *cervige* (amberjack?).[82] The zone off Messina was known for its swordfish and still is.

Arriciola alla Brace (Sicily)

GRILLED AMBERJACK

The waters off Trapani and north to the Egadi Islands off the western coast of Sicily are one of the few zones in the Mediterranean where fishing has traditionally been good. Today, as in the fourteenth-century Mediterranean, fish is expensive, usually more so than meat. This tells us volumes about the myth of Mediterranean abundance: there wasn't any. The most expensive Sicilian fish seven centuries ago were the same as today, sarago *and dentex—both a kind of bream—the* sarago *(called two-banded bream,* Diplodus vulgaris) *as well as the dentex* (dentice *in Italian,* Dentex dentex) *being excellent grilling fish, and red mullet and gray mullet.*[83]

This recipe is common to the Egadi Islands, where they use arriciola *(amberjack). The amberjack belongs to the same family as the bluefish, with which it can be replaced in this recipe. You can also substitute pompano, kingfish, halibut, swordfish, Spanish mackerel, scad, jack, or horse mackerel from Atlantic and Pacific waters. Floridians are most likely to have access to amberjack, although I occasionally had some luck with my fishmonger when I lived in New England. If you use whole fish, try red snapper or redfish.*

The sauce poured over the grilled fish is a version of the salmoriglio, *the olive oil, lemon, and oregano sauce used with swordfish (page 390), although this recipe is a little quicker to prepare. Grilling these fish steaks on the beach as the sun sets I suppose is the finest way they*

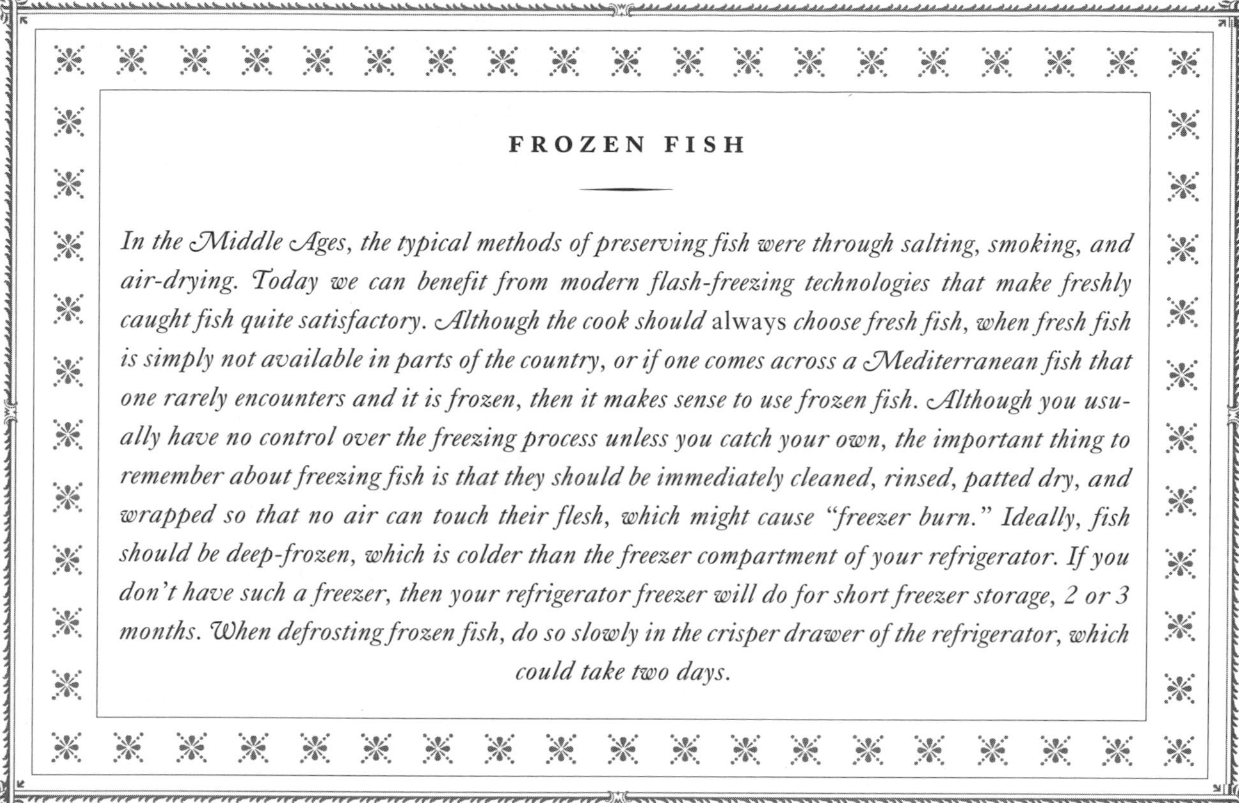

FROZEN FISH

In the Middle Ages, the typical methods of preserving fish were through salting, smoking, and air-drying. Today we can benefit from modern flash-freezing technologies that make freshly caught fish quite satisfactory. Although the cook should always *choose fresh fish, when fresh fish is simply not available in parts of the country, or if one comes across a Mediterranean fish that one rarely encounters and it is frozen, then it makes sense to use frozen fish. Although you usually have no control over the freezing process unless you catch your own, the important thing to remember about freezing fish is that they should be immediately cleaned, rinsed, patted dry, and wrapped so that no air can touch their flesh, which might cause "freezer burn." Ideally, fish should be deep-frozen, which is colder than the freezer compartment of your refrigerator. If you don't have such a freezer, then your refrigerator freezer will do for short freezer storage, 2 or 3 months. When defrosting frozen fish, do so slowly in the crisper drawer of the refrigerator, which could take two days.*

should be had. A whole fish will require a fish grill or a perforated steel sheet (grill topper) to place over the grill in order to lift the fish.

Six 1-inch-thick fish steaks or three 2½-pound whole redfish or red snapper, scaled, gutted, and cleaned, heads and tails left on
Extra virgin olive oil for dipping

FOR THE SAUCE
½ cup extra virgin olive oil
Juice from 1 lemon
2 large garlic cloves, very finely chopped
1 tablespoon very finely chopped fresh parsley leaves
1 tablespoon dried oregano
Salt and freshly ground black pepper to taste

1. Prepare a hot charcoal fire or preheat a gas grill on high for 20 minutes. Dip the fish steaks or whole fish in olive oil and let the excess drip off. Place the fish steaks or whole fish on the grill for 6 to 8 minutes per side, flipping only once. A rule of thumb—and it works—is that a whole fish will take 10 minutes of cooking per inch of fish measured at the thickest part. Whole fish are done when the dorsal fin nearly comes off with a little tug. The fish steaks are done when they are springy to the touch, but not hard.

2. Meanwhile, whisk together the olive oil, lemon juice, garlic, parsley, oregano, salt, and pepper. Remove the fish from the grill and arrange on a serving platter. Pour the olive oil sauce over and serve.

Makes 6 servings

Sardi Fritti (Sicily)

FRIED SARDINES

In the Middle Ages, fishing had little importance in the dietary and economic balance of Sicily. There were not many fishermen, but fish did play a modest role in five fishing centers—Messina, Cefalù, Termini, Palermo, and Trapani. The most often caught and eaten fish were sardines. The bulk of the catch was salted, but the fishermen could always reserve a few for frying, as in this recipe.[84] *This simple preparation is a Sicilian favorite, and if you can get fresh sardines you will see why. If you are using frozen sardines, remember to defrost them in the refrigerater slowly. Canned sardines will not work in this recipe. If fresh sardines are simply out of the question where you live, give any smaller fish, such as a whole red snapper or mackerel, a try.*

2½ pounds fresh sardines, scaled, gutted, and boned, with the head and tail left on
1 cup white wine vinegar
6 cups pure or virgin olive or olive pomace oil for deep-frying
All-purpose flour for dredging
Salt and freshly ground black pepper to taste
Finely chopped fresh parsley leaves for garnish

1. In a large glass or ceramic casserole, marinate the sardines in the vinegar for 1 to 2 hours in the refrigerator, turning them several times.

2. Preheat the frying oil in a deep-fryer or an 8-inch saucepan fitted with a basket insert to 370°F. Preheat the oven to warm (about 150°F). Drain the sardines and roll in a mixture of flour, salt, and pepper in a medium-size bowl until well coated. Transfer to a strainer, vigorously shake off the excess flour, and deep-fry, a batch at a time without crowding, until light golden, about 5 minutes.

3. As the sardines finish cooking, place them on a tray covered with paper towels and keep warm in the oven (but do not cover) while you continue frying. Sprinkle the sardines with parsley and serve immediately. Let the frying oil cool completely, strain, and save for a future use.

Makes 4 to 6 servings

Sarde al Vino Bianco (Sicily)

FRESH SARDINES WITH ANCHOVY BUTTER AND WHITE WINE

Fifteenth-century notary registers from Sicily indicate that the main fishing was for sardines. Sardines are called in the documents "blue fish," as are anchovies, as opposed to the secondary and less commercially viable "white fish" that tended to be locally consumed. The fishing of sardines from Termini with the spiruni *net, a very thin and thinly stitched net, was the economically most important fishing activity. Fishing zones were well demarcated off the coast of Termini and Palermo.*[85]

This recipe is rich and delicious. The remaining broth in the baking pan can be tossed with vermicelli. If you can't find sardines fresh or frozen, you can use whiting or smelts, or small mackerel, red snapper, or redfish.

1¾ to 2 pounds fresh sardines (12 to 18)
10 tablespoons (1¼ sticks) unsalted butter, at room temperature
6 salted anchovy fillets, rinsed
Salt and freshly ground black pepper to taste
1 cup dry white wine

1. Cut off the heads of the sardines and gut them while you separate the fillets down to the backbone

under running water. Open each sardine with your thumbs, laying it flat in your hand or on a countertop, belly side up. Find the end of the backbone nearest the head. Carefully pull it up and toward you, making sure you don't rip the flesh or separate the two fillets. This sounds much more difficult than it is. You should be able to get the hang of it after two or three fish, and once you do, you can whiz right through 2 pounds.

2. Preheat the oven to 350°F. Butter a baking pan with 2 tablespoons of the butter. Mash another 4 tablespoons of the butter together with the anchovies. Rinse the sardines and pat dry each one with paper towels. Lay the sardines open flat with the skin side down in the baking pan and spread a small amount of anchovy butter equally on all the fish. Find a matching-size sardine and lay it on top of the bottom sardine, skin side up. Press down carefully. Sliver the remaining 4 tablespoons butter and sprinkle around on top of the sardines.

3. Sprinkle a little salt and pepper over the fish, pour in the wine, and cover loosely with a sheet of aluminum foil. Bake until all the butter is melted and the pan bubbling, about 20 minutes, and serve.

Makes 4 servings

Ziti con Pesce Spada e Menta (Sicily)

ZITI WITH SWORDFISH AND MINT

The Sicilian fishing industry was a well-organized business as early as the fourteenth century. Fishing grounds and rights were well specified, and the Strait of Messina was the prime hunting grounds for the nomadic swordfish.[86] *The swordfish would spawn in the strait before heading out to the open sea and beyond, past the Strait of Gilbraltar into the North Atlantic. The fishermen of Messina would hunt the swordfish from small boats with a two- or three-man crew using harpoons.*

This preparation from the eastern coast of Sicily is heavily flavored with fresh mint. The unusual combination of fish and cheese is typical in Sicily, Apulia, Calabria, and Campania and one almost never finds it in the north, excepting some old-fashioned home cooking in the Veneto. The pasta I call for here, mezze ziti lunghe, *is a ziti with a hole smaller than ziti but larger than* perciatelli. *Most ziti is already cut, but this kind is left uncut, the same length as a spaghetti strand. It makes for some pretty silly eating, but it's fun and tastes great—this is one time when wearing a bib makes a lot of sense. I always leave the skin on swordfish not only because of its crunchy texture but also because of the delicious thin layer of fat between the skin and meat.*

½ cup extra virgin olive oil
2 large ripe tomatoes, peeled, seeded, and chopped
1 garlic clove, crushed
Leaves from 1 bunch fresh mint (about 15 sprigs), washed and dried
Salt and freshly ground black pepper to taste
One ¾-pound swordfish steak, diced
½ cup water
1 pound *mezze ziti lunghe*
¼ pound fresh mozzarella cheese, cut into tiny dice

1. In a large skillet, heat the olive oil over medium-high heat. Add the tomatoes and garlic, reduce the heat to medium, and cook together until some of the liquid is evaporated, about 12 minutes. Add a quarter of the mint leaves, season with salt and pepper, and stir to mix. Add the swordfish to the skillet. Pour in the water, reduce the heat to low, and cook until the swordfish is a little springy but not completely firm and the sauce slightly reduced, about 20 minutes. Remove the garlic and discard.

2. Meanwhile, bring a large pot of abundantly salted water to a boil and add the pasta when the water is rolling. Drain the pasta when al dente and pour into a serving bowl. Toss with the sauce, mozzarella, and the remaining mint leaves and serve.

Makes 6 servings

Lingue al Pesce Spada (Sicily)

LINGUE WITH SWORDFISH

The only member of the Xiphiidae *family is the swordfish, a nomadic billfish that occasionally ventures into very cold, deep waters and returns to the surface in a stupor after its dive. The swordfish caught in the Strait of Messina have long been famous and figure prominently in* cucina messinese. *The famous Greek Sicilian of Magna Graecia, and the world's first purported cookbook writer, Archestratus, who wrote about 350 B.C., recommended the swordfish from the Strait "hard by the edge of Pelorum's jutting forehand" (that is, Messina).*[87] *This preparation is popular with Sicilian housewives who use a pasta called* lingue *that is wider than linguine and narrower than fettuccine.*

3 tablespoons extra virgin olive oil
3 garlic cloves, crushed
2 pounds ripe tomatoes, peeled, seeded, and chopped
One ½-pound swordfish steak, diced
Salt and freshly ground black pepper to taste
10 large fresh basil leaves
¾ pound *lingue* or linguine

1. In a large skillet, heat the olive oil over medium-high heat, then cook the garlic cloves until they begin to turn light brown. Remove and discard.

2. Add the tomatoes and continue to cook, stirring, until the liquid from them has evaporated, about 6 minutes. Add the swordfish, season with salt and pepper, and reduce the heat to low, stirring for 4 minutes and adding some tablespoons of water if necessary to keep the sauce from becoming too thick. Add the basil leaves, stir, and remove from the heat. Check the seasoning and let the sauce rest for a few minutes.

3. Meanwhile, bring a large pot of water to a rolling boil, salt abundantly, and add the pasta. Drain when al dente and toss with the swordfish sauce. Serve without cheese.

Makes 4 servings

Pesce Spada col Salmoriglio (Sicily)

SWORDFISH WITH *SALMORIGLIO* SAUCE

The finest Sicilian swordfish recipes are usually found in the area of Messina on the northeastern coast. Harpooning was the usual method of catching swordfish in the Mediterranean, and it was always considered a dangerous activity. Pliny (A.D. 23–79), in his Natural History, *describes the danger of trying to spear swordfish and the sinking of harpoon boats pierced by the swordfish.*[88]

Salmoriglio, *or* sammurigghiu *in Sicilian, literally means "brine," but in gastronomic terms it is a sauce whipped with olive oil, lemon juice, garlic, and herbs in a double boiler. In Sicily, where some people associate* salmoriglio *with the* aroma di Sicilia, *it is most commonly used with grilled swordfish. The Greeks use a similar dressing, which they call* ladolemono. *Sicilians do not normally eat swordfish as thick as I call for here, but this is the way I like it.*

½ cup extra virgin olive oil
Juice from 1 lemon
2 tablespoons hot water
Salt and freshly ground black pepper to taste
2 tablespoons very finely chopped fresh oregano leaves or 1 teaspoon dried
6 tablespoons very finely chopped fresh parsley leaves
2 garlic cloves, very finely chopped
1½ pounds swordfish steaks, cut ¾ inch thick

1. Prepare a hot charcoal fire or preheat a gas grill on high for 20 minutes.

2. Bring to a boil an inch or so of water in the bottom of a double boiler. Pour the olive oil into the top of the double boiler and slowly whisk in the lemon juice and hot water. Season with salt and pepper and then add the oregano, parsley, and garlic. Cook for 5 minutes, whisking constantly. The *salmoriglio* will look like a vinaigrette dressing.

3. Grill the swordfish until springy to the touch and streaked with black grid marks, about 5 minutes per side. Turn only once and do not poke or move the fish as it grills. Although I don't find it necessary, you can baste the swordfish with the sauce using a brush made of fresh oregano sprigs. Serve the swordfish, passing the sauce around on the side.

Makes 4 servings

Pesce Spada alla "Stemperata" (Sicily)

SWORDFISH IN SYRACUSEAN SAUCE

Stemperata *is a Syracusean method of cooking that means something like "melting sauce." The idea behind "melting sauce" is to meld a number of aromatic ingredients together by cooking slowly until the sauce or food is infused with flavor. The dish is finished with a sprinkle of vinegar that evaporates, or "melts," into the sauce. Whenever you see a dish described as* stemperata, *you know it is a dish from Syracuse.*

The concept of stemperata *finds its roots in medieval cooking. According to the then prevailing theory of dietetics (see "An Essay on the Sources"), prepared food had properties that would match the temperament of the person eating it. Certain foods were ideal for particular conditions or temperaments. The nature of foods could be changed by tempering the food with additions such as sauces or spicing. In medieval Italian cookbooks one runs across the term* temperare, *which takes on a greater meaning than "to temper." It implies that one corrects the food so it will conform to a dietetic humoral notion. So the Italian* stemperare *has the sense of taking something away, and in this recipe it is the vinegar that "is taken away" through evaporation to moderate the taste of the sauce.*

5 tablespoons extra virgin olive oil
1 medium-size onion, finely chopped
½ celery stalk, finely chopped
1½ tablespoons capers, rinsed and chopped if large
10 large imported green olives, pitted and chopped
1 pound ripe tomatoes, peeled, seeded, and chopped
⅓ cup water
1½ pounds swordfish steaks, cut into ½-inch-thick slices
All-purpose flour for dredging
1 tablespoon white wine vinegar

1. In a large skillet or stove-top earthenware casserole, heat the olive oil over medium-high heat, then cook the onion and celery until softened, 5 to 6 minutes, stirring frequently. Reduce the heat to medium, add the capers, olives, and tomatoes, and stir. Pour in the water, stir again, and cook until denser, about 10 minutes.

2. Dredge the swordfish slices in the flour, tapping off any excess flour. Set aside.

3. Arrange the swordfish slices in the skillet on top of the sauce, spooning some sauce on top of the swordfish. Drizzle the vinegar over the fish, cover, and cook until the vinegar is evaporated, 5 to 6 minutes. Serve.

Makes 4 servings

Pesce Spada "Schibbeci" (Sicily)

SWORDFISH SEVICHE

The boundaries of the Mediterranean are flexible and fluid, depending on what one wants to illustrate. Take, for example, seviche, today a well-known appetizer in America of lime or lemon juice–marinated raw fish. I once read that it was introduced to the United States from Peru by restaurateurs. But seviche is nothing but a Mediterranean method of preserving raw fish. The Latin American Spanish word seviche *comes from the Iberian Spanish* escabeche, *also called* schebbeci *in Sicily, a word that means "marinated fish." The Arabs ruled both Spain and Sicily for centuries, and as a result the word* escabeche *can be traced to the dialectal Arabic word* iskibaj, *which the great lexicographer Joan Corominas describes as deriving from the older* sikbāj, *meaning "a kind of meat with vinegar and other ingredients."*[89] *The autochthonous preparation of Sicily is best represented in this delicious recipe made with swordfish.*

If you are unable to have the swordfish sliced 1/4 inch thick, marinate longer than I call for here.

Juice from 5 lemons
1 large garlic clove, finely chopped
1/4 cup finely chopped fresh oregano leaves
1/4 cup finely chopped fresh parsley leaves
1/4 cup finely chopped fresh mint leaves
1/4 teaspoon red pepper flakes
Salt and freshly ground black pepper to taste
1 1/4 pounds swordfish steaks, sliced 1/4 inch thick
1/4 cup extra virgin olive oil

1. Whisk together the lemon juice, garlic, oregano, parsley, mint, red pepper flakes, salt, and pepper.

2. Arrange the slices of swordfish in a large glass or ceramic baking pan. Cover with the lemon juice and marinate in the refrigerator for 3 hours. The swordfish is ready when a small sliver tastes "cooked" rather than raw.

3. Remove the swordfish slices to a serving platter and cover with the olive oil. Taste a small sliver of marinated swordfish and correct the seasoning if necessary.

Makes 4 servings

* * *

FISH were also caught in more rudimentary ways using traditional techniques that go back to the Arab era and earlier.[90] Usually this meant two men in a boat with a net. The Arab influence on Sicilian fishing and nautical affairs in general is attested to by the Sicilian fishing and nautical vocabulary, which is thoroughly rooted in the Arabic language. Take, for instance, the Sicilian word *xabica,* the big fishing net that is attached to shore and moved seaward in a great sweeping swath by a bark, a small sailing ship. The word derives from the Arabic word *shabaka,* meaning "net." But as some scholars have pointed out, the interplay among Arabo-Berber, Italo-Siculo, Arab, and Turkish cultures was complex enough to find influence a constant two- and even three-way street in the Mediterranean Sea when it comes to nautical matters.[91]

There were fishermen who used another kind of net called a *spiruni,* which was very thin and expensive to purchase. The archdeacon of Cefalù bought three of these nets in 1431. They had eighteen stitchings and cost as much as a ton of fresh fish. Other kinds of nets were the *rizza,* a bit bigger and made of plaited grass cording, used for larger fish. The *nassa* was a complicated device used for catching eels or lobster and those fishermen who used them were called *nassaroli.*[92]

The business of fishing in Sicily was already an ancient profession and well organized by the fifteenth century. But fishing comprised a whole ensemble of activities that went far beyond fishing. There were instrument makers, cordage makers, fishing zone administrators, packers, haulers, net makers, and salters, as well as the fishermen. Curiously, at the end of the fourteenth century and into the fifteenth century, many fishermen came from the tiny island of Lipari off Sicily's north coast.[93]

Pennette con Neonata (Sicily)

PENNETTE WITH SMALL FRIED FISH

In the Middle Ages, church-regulated fast days were quite numerous and a complex relationship arose on the alimentary front between the clergy and the laity. The clergy would demonstrate their austerity by buying only the smallest and least expensive fish at the market.[94] *These were not the choicest fish because the flesh-to-bone ratio was so low, yet these small fish have become very popular throughout the Mediterranean. In Italy and Sicily these little fish are known as* neonata, *literally larval fish, of anchovies or sardines. It is now recognized as a poor idea to use baby fish for culinary purposes because it needlessly depletes the fishing grounds. But they are undeniably popular in the Mediterranean where they appear in many favorite preparations such as this one or the* sartagnano *of Provence, where they are packed into a pancake form and fried in olive oil. This recipe is popular with the fishermen of Trapani in Sicily.*

The difficult part of this recipe is finding the small fish here in North America, but it is an effort that is well rewarded. Small fish species (not baby fish) are occasionally found in Italian, Greek, and Japanese neighborhood fish markets that might sell small fish such as sprat or sand-smelts, or even sand-eel, all often marketed under the name of whitebait. The Italian fishmonger may have sprat, which they call papalina, *while the Greek fishmonger may have sand-smelt, which the Greeks call* atherina *and the Japanese* shirasu. *This preparation is a calcium-rich delight because you are eating all those minuscule fish bones that provide the crunch.*

If you cannot find small fresh fish, a somewhat unusual alternative is to use dried boiled baby anchovies sold in packages at Japanese markets (see "Mediterranean Food Products Resources"). You would first rehydrate them by soaking the fish in water; otherwise, you will have to use cut-up smelts, although much will be lost by way of taste. I occasionally come across frozen anchovies in the supermarket, and they are fine in a pinch, although still twice as large as an ideal fish such as sand-eel. Remember to defrost frozen anchovies (and for that matter all frozen fish) slowly in the refrigerator over a period of several days.

Pennette *are very small quill-shaped pasta, just like* penne *but smaller. They can be found in an Italian market or specialty shop.*

2¼ cups pure or virgin olive oil
2 large eggs
2 pounds whitebait or any fish less than 3 inches long
2 garlic cloves, finely chopped
½ cup finely chopped fresh parsley leaves
Salt and freshly ground black pepper to taste
1 small onion, chopped
1 pound ripe plum tomatoes, peeled, seeded, and chopped
1 pound *pennette* or small macaroni

1. In a large skillet, heat 2 cups of the olive oil over medium-high heat until nearly smoking.

2. Meanwhile, beat the eggs together in a large bowl, then add the fish, garlic, and 6 tablespoons of the parsley, season with salt and pepper, and toss gently so all the ingredients are blended.

3. With a slotted ladle, slide a half ladleful of the fish-and-egg mixture into the hot oil. Do not fry more than four ladlefuls at a time. Cook the patties until golden, about 2 minutes, and turn carefully using a fork and a spatula so you don't splash oil. Cook until a firm golden mass when you remove them, 2 to 3 minutes, more or less. Don't worry too much if they are not completely golden brown. Drain briefly, then transfer to paper towels while you continue to cook all the patties. Never crowd the hot oil with too many patties, otherwise they will turn out greasy.

4. In another large skillet or casserole, heat the remaining 1/4 cup olive oil over medium-high heat, then cook the onion, stirring, until translucent, 5 to 6 minutes. Stir in the remaining 2 tablespoons parsley and the tomatoes and reduce the heat to low. Simmer until the sauce is denser, about 40 minutes, stirring occasionally.

5. Meanwhile, bring a large pot of abundantly salted water to a boil and add the pasta when the water is rolling. Put all the fish patties in the tomato sauce and crush them lightly while they cook for 5 to 10 minutes. Drain the pasta when al dente, mix with the sauce, tossing well, and serve.

Makes 6 to 8 servings

Spaghetti con Sugo "d'Addottu" (Sicily)

SPAGHETTI WITH GROUPER SAUCE

The grouper (Epinephelus guaza L.) *is a large, deep-water fish that prefers rocky bottoms. The grouper is a popular fish in Almería in Valencia and Sfax in Tunisia, but less so in Sicily, where it is, though, a popular prey of Sicilian spearfishermen. There are several varieties of grouper in Sicilian waters, the common one being the "white" grouper, a dark rust brown–colored one called* cirenga *(the appellation "white" referring to the flesh), the deep-water grouper called the* addottu, *and the golden grouper called the* précchia. *The Atlantic grouper is nearly identical in taste and is frequently found in fish markets. The richness and firmness of grouper meat is perfect for a variety of cooking methods, especially as in this* sugo d'addottu *from Sicily. I collected this recipe in Cefalù, on the northern coast of Sicily. If you are using the fish head to flavor the broth, add 1/2 cup water at the same time you add the wine. If you are unable to come across grouper, it can be replaced with striped bass, sea bass, yellowtail, or tilefish.*

1/2 cup extra virgin olive oil
1 medium-size onion, finely chopped
2 pounds canned or fresh crushed or finely chopped tomatoes, with their juice
1 grouper head or other fish head (optional)
1/2 cup water (optional)
3/4 cup dry white wine
4 large garlic cloves, finely chopped
3 tablespoons finely chopped fresh basil leaves
Salt and freshly ground black pepper to taste
1 pound spaghetti
1 one-pound grouper fillet

1. In a large casserole, heat the olive oil over medium-high heat, then cook the onion until translucent, about 5 minutes, stirring frequently. Add the tomatoes, fish head, and water (if using the head), wine, garlic, and basil and season with salt and pepper. Reduce the heat to low, cover, and simmer until denser, about 30 minutes.

2. Meanwhile, bring a large pot of abundantly salted water to a boil and add the pasta when the water is rolling. Drain when al dente.

3. Increase the heat for the broth to high; once it is boiling, add the grouper fillet and cook at a furious boil, shaking, not stirring, the casserole until the fish is cooked firm, about 6 minutes. Transfer the spaghetti to a serving platter or bowl and toss gently with the fish sauce.

Makes 6 servings

THE greatest catch for Sicilian fishermen, and the one they were most famous for, was tuna. The earliest peoples we know of who were fishing tuna off Sicily were the Phoenicians, and it was mentioned by all the great Greek writers. Later, the Byzantines passed legislation concerning tuna fishing off Sicily. But it was the Arabs who are credited with developing important advances in netting and technique. They were already using obstruction nets, nets that blocked passage of fish and headed them off into a desired direction, in the twelfth century, according to the observations of a contemporary, al-Idrīsī.[95] Tuna fishing in Sicily from 1328 to 1390 was a thriving business of the fishermen and *raysi* (captains) of Trapani, Sciacca, and Marsala.

The *raysi,* from the Arabic word for "captain," were the captains of the tuna crews who led the boats out to the *mattanza,* the tuna hunt or killing, where they set out the *madraga,* the tuna nets, to funnel the migrating tuna from larger netted chambers to successively smaller ones, ultimately to reach the *camera della morte,* the death chamber. There the tuna, sometimes weighing up to 750 pounds, would be hooked by their gills, clubbed, and hauled aboard in work that was dangerous and backbreaking. The *raysi,* who came from well-known families that, generation after generation, were engaged in fishing, directed all these activities. These *raysi* families were prestigious families and in documents centuries later the families are still referred to as *raisi.*[96] The tuna crews, the *tonnaroti,* had certain dangers and privileges. There was the danger of capture and enslavement by corsairs, as well as the danger posed by huge fish fighting for their lives. But there was also the allure of good salaries, good food, and legal privileges.

Among the multifarious people living in Palermo and in northwestern Sicily engaged in the tiered structure of the fishing industry were Jews and a number of Tunisians. In fourteenth- and fifteenth-century Calabria and Sicily, the fishing of one variety of tuna, the little tuna, *tonnina,* was an important industry and many of the *tonninarii,* the conservers of little tuna, were specialized artisans and a majority were Jews and Greeks.[97] The Jews in particular were engaged in the salting of tuna roe and the poaching of tuna for preservation. The tuna was cut into steaks or finger-size pieces and were stacked in layers with salt in barrels. The industry was very hierarchical and diversified, and formed a veritable production line. Tuna fishermen would fish at night by torches because the light would attract the tuna.[98] The fish went from the the *tonnaroti* (tuna fishermen) to the *faraticu* (manual tuna laborers on the boats who pulled the huge tuna onto the deck) to the *sparaturi,* the men who hauled the tuna to shore, where they were carried on the backs of the *apindituri* (tuna carriers) to the factory and hung on hooks. There, in the tuna factory, the *taglaturi,* butchers, directed by a *capumastru,* head master, cut the tuna up into choice cuts such as the red meat *(tonnina necta)* or the precious belly-cut, called *surra* or *taglaturi a la bulzunagla.* A hauler carried the meat to a table where the *anictator,* tuna meat washer, cleaned the meat with fresh water before passing it to the *salator,* the tuna salter, who spread the tuna with salt before sending the salted meat on to the *stipator,* the tuna meat packer. From there it went either to the *jarratini,* who weighed and transported the packed barrels of tuna, or to the *salmoriator,* the tuna briners, who used vinegar and oil as a brine, and to the *intimpagnare,* the barrel closers. Finally the barrels went to the bursar for export or dispersement, to the cooks for culinary preparation, or the bread bin for storage. The workers were paid in money and their salaries ranged from 90 *tari* for the season for the head masters to 45 *tari* for the briners to 18 *tari* for the salters.[99] As vibrant as this discussion makes the medieval Sicilian fishing industry seem, the fruits of the Sicilian seas were not reflected in the local cuisine, for nearly all the catch was exported by sea to distant places.[100] This phenomenon makes contemporary Sicilian seafood cookery, as demonstrated in the following recipes, all the more remarkable.

Fusilli con Salsa Rosso di Tonno (Sicily)

FUSILLI WITH RED TUNA SAUCE

Sicilian tuna fishing was a prosperous industry under the ancient Greeks and Phoenicians. But it was the Arabs, arriving in Sicily in the ninth century, who revolutionized tuna fishing through technical innovations, especially in the development of netting.[101] *This delicious preparation is a recipe that I collected in Trapani on the west coast of Sicily many years ago.*

1/4 cup extra virgin olive oil
1/4 cup finely chopped onion
2 garlic cloves, peeled, 1 crushed and 1 finely chopped
3 cups canned crushed tomatoes
Salt and freshly ground black pepper to taste
1 tablespoon pine nuts
1 tablespoon raisins
2 tablespoons finely chopped fresh parsley leaves
One 6 1/2-ounce can imported tuna in olive oil
1 pound *fusilli*

1. In a large skillet, heat the olive oil over medium-high heat, then cook the onion and crushed garlic until the onion is translucent, about 3 minutes, stirring frequently so the garlic doesn't burn. Add the tomatoes and chopped garlic and cook until denser, about 12 minutes, stirring occasionally. Remove from the heat, season with salt and pepper, and add the pine nuts, raisins, and parsley. Once the sauce is cooled, stir in the tuna with its oil.

2. Meanwhile, bring a large pot of water to a rolling boil, salt abundantly, and add the pasta. Drain the pasta when al dente and toss while still very hot with the sauce. Serve without cheese.

Makes 4 to 6 servings

Tunnu 'Nfurnatu (Sicily)

OVEN-BAKED TUNA IN THE STYLE OF FAVIGNANA

Tuna received its name from the Greek word thyein, *darting, because the fish darts through the water in fast, excitable bursts. Tuna fishing in Sicily has been notable since the days of the first Greek settlements.*

Athenaeus (c. A.D. 170 – c. 230) wrote in his Deipnosophistae *that the tuna of Sicily were even better than those found in Greek waters.*[102] *One thousand years later the Arab geographer of the Norman court al-Idrīsī said hyperbolically that the waters around the Egadi Islands were "superabundantly rich in fish" and he described how the tuna nets were stretched in the sea off Bagni Segestani where the tuna were corralled.*[103]

Tunnu 'nfurnatu, *or* tonno infornato *in Italian, is an oven-baked tuna dish that goes by several other names including* tunnu a la matalotta, *which means* a la marinara, *or* alla moda di Favignana, *meaning a preparation from the cooking of the island of Favignana, the main island of the Egadi Islands. One can serve the finished dish with linguine. Some cooks omit the tomatoes and mint while others include potatoes, onions, abundant parsley, and lemon juice.*

6 slices fresh tuna (about 1½ pounds), cut from the belly
½ cup extra virgin olive oil
10 large green imported Sicilian (Paternò) olives, pitted and coarsely chopped (about ⅔ cup)
¼ cup capers, rinsed and chopped if large
1¼ pounds ripe tomatoes, chopped (about 2 cups chopped)
2 tablespoons finely chopped fresh parsley leaves
2 tablespoons finely chopped fresh mint leaves
Salt and freshly ground black pepper to taste
¼ cup dried bread crumbs

1. Preheat the oven to 350°F. Arrange the tuna slices in a lightly oiled baking casserole. Sprinkle the olives on top, then the capers, tomatoes, parsley, and mint and finally season with salt and pepper. Cover this seasoning with a layer of bread crumbs and drizzle the remaining olive oil over.

2. Bake until the tuna is firm, about 20 minutes. Serve immediately with linguine if desired.

Makes 4 servings

Involtini di Tonno (Sicily)

GRILLED TUNA ROLLS

Tuna fishing has been the main activity for the communities ranging from Trapani to San Nicolò l'Arena for centuries. The tunneries of Lanza di Trabia (San Nicolò l'Arena) and of Florio (Arenella and Favignana) were renowned until the 1930s. The mattanza, *or tuna hunt, involves a complicated netting and channeling procedure that funnels the migrating tuna into a series of smaller and smaller chambers that ends in the final chamber, the* camera della morte, *the death chamber, where the tuna are killed in a spectacular frenzy of bloodletting. This is quite an eye-opening, if violent, sight and it has been a tourist show since as early as the eighteenth century. Many famous Sicilian tuna dishes come from this region.*

Tuna is a prize catch off the western coast of Sicily, where they like to grill it as in this preparation. For ease of slicing, let a large chunk of tuna freeze partially, or ask the fishmonger to slice it for you. Instead of grilling, you can cook the roll-ups in the sauce described in the variation below.

Eight ¼-inch-thick slices fresh tuna (about 1½ pounds)
Extra virgin olive oil for drizzling and brushing
1 large hard-boiled egg, shelled and finely chopped
1 tablespoon finely chopped fresh rosemary leaves
¼ cup freshly grated pecorino cheese
2½ tablespoons unsalted butter
Salt and freshly ground black pepper to taste
Eight 8-inch-long wooden skewers

1. Lay each slice of tuna between two sheets of waxed paper and gently pound thin with the side of a cleaver or mallet. Each piece will be about 1/16 inch thick. Be careful you don't break through the flesh.

2. Brush each slice lightly with olive oil. Sprinkle on some egg, rosemary, pecorino, a sliver of butter,

and salt and pepper. Roll each slice up and secure the sides with toothpicks. Continue until all the slices are rolled up.

3. Double-skewer the roll-ups: Hold two skewers parallel to each other about ½ inch apart between your thumb and forefinger. Slide two tuna roll-ups onto each set of skewers.

4. Prepare a hot charcoal fire or preheat a gas grill on high for 20 minutes. Coat the tuna with some more olive oil, salt and pepper lightly, and place on the grill until charred and firm, about 6 minutes per side. Remove the toothpicks and serve on the skewer.

VARIATION

Heat 3 tablespoons olive oil in a casserole with 1 crushed garlic clove until it begins to turn light brown. Remove and discard the garlic. Add 1 small onion, finely chopped, and cook, stirring, until translucent over medium-high heat, about 5 minutes, stirring frequently. Add 1½ pounds ripe tomatoes, peeled, seeded, and chopped, and cook until some liquid has evaporated, about 12 minutes, stirring occasionally and turning down the heat if it sputters too much. Add ¾ cup imported green olives, pitted and finely chopped, and the tuna roll-ups. Reduce the heat to low and cook through, 12 to 15 minutes.

Makes 4 to 6 servings

Bonito "Riganatu" (Sicily)

GRILLED BONITO WITH OREGANO

Although bonito (Sarda sarda *Bloch*) *is found throughout the Mediterranean, it seems to be most popular in Turkey, where only the smaller ones are eaten, and in Spain. In Sicily, bonito, although not as common in the cuisine as swordfish and tuna, is preferably grilled. Typically, a bonito is caught by local or sports fishermen rather than the commercial fleets, and Sicilians especially enjoy such a dish as this grilled over a hardwood fire by the sea as the sun sets.*

2¼ pounds fresh bonito cut into ¾-inch-thick steaks
½ cup extra virgin olive oil
2 large garlic cloves, finely chopped
½ teaspoon salt
½ teaspoon freshly ground black pepper
5 tablespoons dried oregano

1. Place the bonito steaks in a large glass or ceramic pan or bowl and marinate in the olive oil, garlic, salt, pepper, and oregano for 2 hours, skin side up in the refrigerator.

2. Preheat a gas grill on high for 20 minutes or prepare a hot charcoal fire. Place the bonito slices on the grill and cook until streaked with grid marks and springy to the touch, about 6 minutes per side, basting with the marinade. Turn only once and do not poke or move the fish as it grills. Serve with the marinade. Grill longer if the fish is thicker.

Makes 6 servings

Fishing off North Africa and the Near East

THERE weren't many places in the medieval Mediterranean where people could catch fish, feed themselves, and eke out a living on a regular basis. There is also not a good deal of information about the lives of the fishermen in the Middle Ages.

The coasts of Tunisia was one place where there was fishing. The eleventh-century Arab traveler al-

Bakrī describes the fishing off Tunis as being very abundant, with many species, such as *āktūbara* (Octoberfish or salema), a kind of bream, today called *shalba* by Tunisians, which appears only in October, hence its name.[104]

The best fish in Tunisia were from Sfax, still an important port for fishing and famous for its fish since the days of al-Idrīsī's journeys in the twelfth century.[105] The twelfth-century Tunisian markets were selling mullet, bream, bonito, monkfish, ray, saddled bream, meagre, salema, sardine, and other fish hard to identify. In May and June, tuna were caught off the eastern coast of Tunisia. There were also a few people making a living pearl fishing, oystering, and sponging in Sfax.[106] Bizerte was also known for its fish, although its waters were not nearly as prized as those off Sfax.[107] Dried fish, usually sold in jars, was an important commodity both for trade and local cooking since at least Aghlabid times in Tunisia (A.D. 800–909).[108] Tunisian markets still sell a dried fish, called *wazaf* (sometimes transliterated as *ouzaf*), that is an important condiment used in a number of contemporary Tunisian preparations. *Wazaf* are the fry of either a kind of anchovy (*Engraulis meletta* Cuv.) or sardine (*Sardinella aurita* Val.).

The fishing off Algeria was equally small and the most popular fish tended to be the same as in Tunisia. Local fishermen would go out no more than a mile or two from the coast in pairs to catch mostly sardines, squid, and some larger fish, such as bream or grouper.

Sardīn bi'l-Dirsa (Algeria)

SARDINES WITH SPICY HOT MAYONNAISE SAUCE

Dirsa, *a word used in North Africa usually in connection with the crushing of grapes by trampling, is the name of a chili pepper–based hot sauce popular in Algeria with grilled or baked fish, which came about after the introduction of the New World chili pepper. It is made like the Provençal* sauce rouille *(page 514), but without the egg yolks; in fact, it is very much like a traditional* allioli *from Catalonia (page 513). The most popular preparation for* dirsa *is a dish of gutted, headless grilled sardines, but it is also popular with squid and other fish.*

Two 5-inch-long fresh chili peppers, seeded and chopped (about ½ cup)
4 large garlic cloves, peeled
Salt and freshly ground black pepper to taste
5 to 6 tablespoons extra virgin olive oil
1 pound fresh whole sardines (7 to 9), defrosted if frozen, gutted, cleaned, and heads removed
¼ teaspoon freshly ground cumin seeds

1. In a mortar, pound the chili peppers, garlic, salt (at least 1 teaspoon), and pepper together into a paste. Slowly pound in the olive oil. The olive oil can also be incorporated after transferring the garlic and chili pepper mixture to a food processor. Set aside at room temperature.

2. Preheat the oven to 350°F or prepare a hot charcoal fire or preheat a gas grill for 15 minutes on high. Lightly oil a baking pan and bake the sardines until golden, 17 to 18 minutes, or lightly oil the fish and place on a hot grill close to the fire until golden, about 4 minutes per side. Arrange the sardines on a serving platter and coat with the *dirsa* sauce. Sprinkle with the cumin and serve.

VARIATION
Coat the sardines with the *dirsa* sauce before baking.

Makes 4 qimia (mazza) *servings*

✣ ✣ ✣

FOLLOWING the littoral to the east along the North African coast from Tunisia, we do not meet any significant fishing activity until we reach the coast of Egypt. In Marsa Matruh, there are a few fishermen, but in Alexandria and Damietta there are more. The fish of Egypt have been famous since biblical times. In Numbers 11:5, a Jewish crowd, speaking of their exile from Egypt, wept that "we remember the fish we ate in Egypt for nothing." Later the Muslim Egyptians were also infatuated with fish. In medieval times there was such a variety of fish coming from the Nile and deltic Mediterranean that fishmongers were named according to the fish they sold. There were the *tawwān,* sellers of tuna, and the *bunni,* who sold carp pickles (literally, pickled pieces of carp), and the *qardūsi,* who sold sea bass.[109] The Arab doctor from Baghdad, ʿAbd al-Laṭīf (1162–1231), reports that in the Egyptian coastal town of Damietta, they ate a lot of fish cooked in the same way the meat was—that is, with rice and sumac.[110]

The Syrian fishing industry, if it can be called that, was the most meager in the eastern Mediterranean. The catch was small even though 177 of the 324 species of fish in the Levant basin of the Mediterranean are found off the Syro-Palestinian coast. The continental shelf is very narrow, rarely wider than four miles, and cut by submarine canyons that plunge to nearly a mile deep.[111] As a result, there is little for fish to feed on and the local fishing culture is minuscule. The number of port villages, even today, is few and they are only dots along the coast. The catch is consumed locally. However, in the eleventh century, the coast was attractive enough for the *maḥārī,* the catchers of shellfish, based in Alexandria, to make the long journey to catch the little fish such as red mullet that populate the rocky coastline and to dredge for the precious "purple" shellfish—that is, oysters—as they were called.[112] The few fish that are caught along the Syro-Palestinian coast are expertly prepared, and some recipes, such as one for spiced fish (page 407), demonstrate a culinary finesse beyond what we would expect from a food that does not play a major role in the local cooking. Arabs generally eat fish with rice, and fish and rice dishes were first, and particularly, associated with the Khazars, a partly nomadic Turkic people who converted to Judaism in about A.D. 740.[113]

Gambarī Maqlī No. 1 (Alexandria, Egypt)

FRIED SHRIMP

In the sixteenth century, during the months of September and October, favorable winds blew and the sea was open for the merchants trying to reach Alexandria. The fishermen also headed to sea, but as Fernand Braudel said, "If the Mediterranean made the fisherman poor, it made the merchant rich."[114] Although there was a local Alexandrian fishing industry, this was only for local consumption. Shrimp was always a very small part of the catch. It's not even mentioned in the documents, except parenthetically.

There never was a good amount of seafood on Egypt's Mediterranean coast, but the little that there is is expertly prepared, as we see in this preparation for shrimp coated in a cumin-flavored tempura-like batter and deep-fried in vegetable oil.

6 cups sunflower or vegetable oil for deep-frying
1 large egg
½ cup all-purpose flour
½ cup milk
1 tablespoon water
1 teaspoon freshly ground cumin seeds
1 teaspoon salt
Freshly ground black pepper to taste
2 pounds fresh large or jumbo shrimp, heads removed, deveined if veins are large, and shelled (or 1 pound headless defrosted shrimp)

1. Preheat the frying oil in a deep-fryer or an 8-inch saucepan fitted with a basket insert to 370°F. Beat the egg in a medium-size bowl, then stir in the flour, milk, water, cumin, salt, and pepper. It should be a thin batter.

2. Dip the shrimp, a handful at a time, into the batter. Let some of the batter drain off and then deep-fry only two shrimp at first, one until light golden, about 90 seconds, and the other until a bit darker, about 2 minutes. Taste each one, and adjust the cooking time for the remaining shrimp to your liking. Let the frying oil cool completely, strain, and save for a future use.

Makes 4 mazza *servings*

Gambarī Maqlī No. 2 (Marsa Matruh, Egypt)

FRIED SHRIMP

If Alexandrian coasts were parsimonious with seafood, then the coast off Marsa Matruh in the Western Desert of Egypt must be judged as thoroughly insignificant. Yet, there are a handful of fishermen and they prepare some delightful seafood dishes. This catch is so small that although Marsa Matruh is an important market town for local Bedouin tribes, the seafood is not really found any farther inland than the fishermen's boats and the solitary fishmonger directly in the port area. Shrimp can nearly always be bought at the local fishmonger, and this is a favorite preparation. The shrimp are fried in a pan with abundant cumin and salt.

2 pounds fresh large or jumbo shrimp, heads removed, deveined if veins are large, and shelled (or 1 pound headless defrosted shrimp)
2 tablespoons extra virgin olive oil
3 garlic cloves, very finely chopped
Freshly ground cumin seeds to taste
Salt to taste
Cayenne pepper to taste

1. Place all the ingredients in a large skillet and toss. Use your judgment for how much cumin, salt, and cayenne you would like to use. (Try this ratio to start: 1 teaspoon cumin, 1 teaspoon salt, ¼ teaspoon cayenne.)

2. Turn the heat to medium-high and stir or shake the skillet occasionally. Turn the heat off 5 minutes later and serve.

Makes 4 mazza *servings*

Samak Maqlī (Alexandria, Egypt)

ALEXANDRIA-STYLE FRIED FISH

The fish of the Nile, today a deeply polluted river, were apparently abundant and excellent in the medieval era. A twelfth-century Spanish visitor to Cairo reports that fish pickles imported from Alexandria were a common food. There was an Alexandrian shellfishing industry and a Muslim letter writer of the time mentioned that he was horrified to find these Alexandrian shellfishermen drinking beer in Crusaders' taverns in Acre, Palestine.[115]

Today, the poor reputation of Egyptian cuisine has led many people to overlook the highlights of Egyptian seafood cookery, the best of which can be found in Alexandria and along the Mediterranean coast. Fish from the Nile or Red Sea are also eaten, but it is in Alexandria that fish cookery is at its most exalted. Remember that the key to all fish cookery is absolutely fresh fish. Serve with girgīr *salad (page 313).*

EGYPTIAN SEAFOOD COOKERY

Among more cosmopolitan Arabs, "Egyptian cuisine" is something of an oxymoron. Its reputation is somewhat like that of British food. Many Arabs, let alone Westerners, are skeptical, then, when I assure them that there really is an Egyptian seafood cuisine and that it is good. Truly famous Mediterranean fish dishes are found in Alexandria, although great undiscovered fish dishes can be sought in Marsa Matruh, where Cleopatra swam naked for Marc Antony and Rommel made his headquarters, or in the seaside shanty resort of Abu Qir, to the east of Alexandria. The most common and popular Egyptian fish is samak mūsā, *sole, usually fried with a batter. Egyptian culinary folklore traces the sole to Moses. When Moses (Mūsā) parted the sea, a sole—that strange flat fish—got in the way at the moment the sea parted, cleaving the poor sole in half, and that is why the sole is so flat.*

Egyptians prepare fish in four ways. The first is called baladī, *or country style. A whole fresh fish with the scales still on is coated with wheat bran, the same wheat bran used for making the ubiquitous Egyptian country flatbread known as* ʿaysh baladī. *Then the fish is placed on a very hot griddle and cooked, being flipped several times until it is black. It is immediately removed and dipped in a hot water bath seasoned with cumin, hot paprika, salt, lemon, and vinegar. This helps loosen the scales and bran so they can be removed and the fish eaten. This dipping must be done quickly so the scales come off. A second way of cooking the fish is to scale and gut it. The fish is then dipped in olive oil and grilled or griddled and served with lemon and salt. This is very popular in Alexandria and common throughout the Mediterranean. A third way is to bake the fish. The fish is cleaned and scaled, put into a baking pan, and covered with chopped tomatoes, green bell pepper, olive oil, salt, and pepper. Or it is covered with thinly sliced potatoes, tomatoes, onions, and oil and then baked. A fourth way, which is very popular in Alexandria, is to take a cleaned, filleted fish and dip it in a tempura-like batter and deep-fry it.*[116] *Cooks also lightly flour and deep-fry fish in the same manner as elsewhere in the Mediterranean.*

I suppose there is a fifth way if we count fasīkh, *a small salted fermented fish with a very strong odor popular in Egypt, especially around the non-Muslim holiday celebrating the winds that whip up in the spring. The holiday is called* shamm al-nasīm, *literally "to breathe the breeze," and the Muslim authorities don't care to talk much about this pagan holiday.*[117]

The Egyptians also eat freshwater fish from the Nile. Most of these fish are qishr bayāḍī, *a kind of Nile catfish;* bulṭī, *Nile tilapia; and* qarmūṭ, *another kind of catfish. Unfortunately, the Nile is polluted and it is not wise to eat fish that come from the river. Egypt's Red Sea coast also provides fish, although it is an entirely different biosphere than the Mediterranean and the fish are tropical with stunning colors, especially those of the wrasse family.*

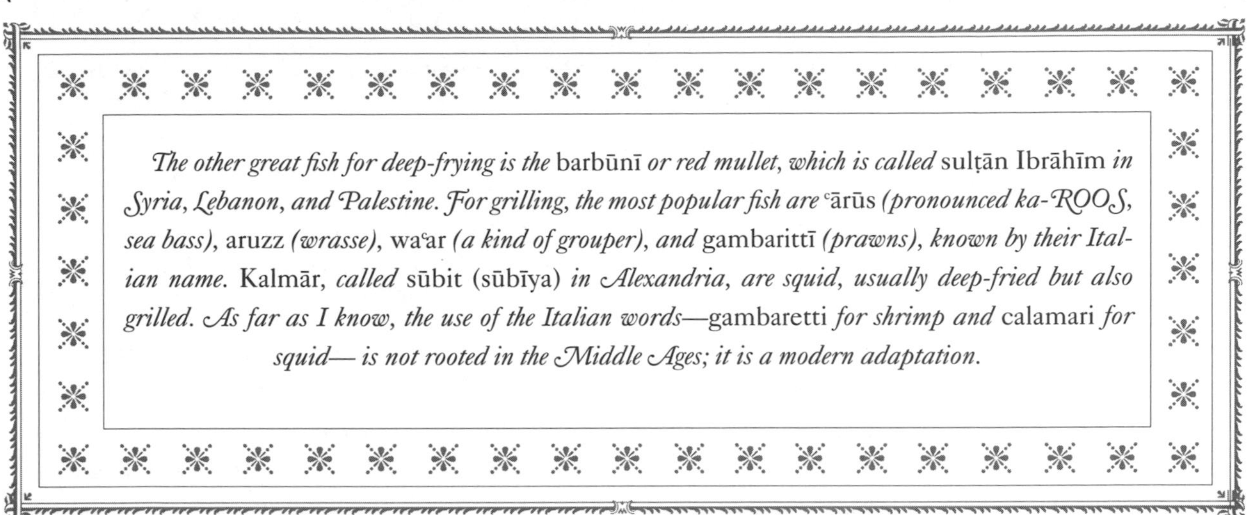

The other great fish for deep-frying is the barbūnī *or red mullet, which is called* sulṭān Ibrāhīm *in Syria, Lebanon, and Palestine. For grilling, the most popular fish are* ʿārūs *(pronounced ka-ROOS, sea bass),* aruzz *(wrasse),* waʿar *(a kind of grouper), and* gambarittī *(prawns), known by their Italian name.* Kalmār, *called* sūbit (sūbīya) *in Alexandria, are squid, usually deep-fried but also grilled. As far as I know, the use of the Italian words—*gambaretti *for shrimp and* calamari *for squid— is not rooted in the Middle Ages; it is a modern adaptation.*

2 garlic cloves, very finely chopped
1 teaspoon freshly ground cumin seeds
1 tablespoon fresh lemon juice
1 tablespoon salt
1 teaspoon freshly ground black pepper
2 cups all-purpose flour
3 pounds large fish steaks (sea bass, striped bass, red snapper, redfish, or halibut)
1 pound whole red mullet (or smelts, sardines, butterfish, whiting, porgies)
½ pound squid, cleaned (page 448), or 1 pound fresh medium-size shrimp with heads or ½ pound medium-size headless defrosted shrimp, shelled
6 cups pure or virgin olive or olive pomace oil mixed with vegetable oil for deep-frying
Leaves from 1 bunch fresh parsley, washed and dried
Lemon wedges for garnish

1. Mix the garlic, cumin, lemon juice, salt, pepper, and flour in a medium-size bowl 2 hours before frying.

2. Wash the fish and cut the large fish steaks into boneless pieces or fillets, although this is not necessary if you are skilled at eating around fish bones. The larger pieces of fish should be the size of a lemon. Keep the smaller fish whole, including their heads, and cut the squid into rings or 1-inch squares.

3. Preheat the frying oil in a deep-fryer or an 8-inch saucepan fitted with a basket insert to 370°F. Dredge the fish in the flour, shaking off any excess quite vigorously in a strainer. Fry the larger pieces of fish first until golden, about 6 minutes. Remove to paper towels and keep warm while you cook the smaller fish until wrinkled, 4 to 5 minutes, and the squid or shrimp until light golden, about 2 minutes. Do not crowd the fryer. Transfer the cooked fish to a serving platter, using the parsley to make a bed for the fish to rest upon. Surround the fish with lemon wedges. Let the frying oil cool completely, strain, and save for a future use.

Makes 4 to 6 servings

Samak Mishwī (Egypt)

GRILLED FISH FROM MARSA MATRUH

I think of "turquoise" as the travel writer's stock phrase to describe very clear water. But here in Marsa Matruh the water really is a startling turquoise. My friend Boyd Grove and I spent the day about five miles west of town skin diving at Cleopatra's Bath, a desolate cove with rock formations a short hike over the dunes where the incestuous Ptolemaic queen allegedly swam naked for Marc Antony. As there were no facilities or transportation, we hitchhiked back to town with some construction workers. We were soon to be mightily surprised in this little town.

Far to the west of Alexandria, near the Libyan border, Marsa Matruh is a dusty coastal town with a military base, a couple of languorous hotels, but, most important, a major trading market for the Bedouin of the Western Desert, like the Awlad ʿAlī tribe.

We arrived in Marsa Matruh by bus, hoping to find a salubrious environment. I had no expectation of discovering any notable food there, our excursion being a last-minute idea to find some R & R from the intensity of Cairo. To our relief, the tourist touts of Cairo and Luxor—the bane of tourists in Egypt—were nowhere to be seen.

We stayed at the only hotel still open in October and, although it was on the beach and very pleasant, it served only poor Western food, which did not please us. So we set out into town with one of the "taxis" of Marsa Matruh, a small donkey-pulled cart driven by young boys. Our sixteen-year-old driver knew a little school-learned English. He couldn't really form a sentence, just as we couldn't really form one in Arabic, but we all knew lots of words in each other's language. Our conversation would consist of the boy's saying a word in Arabic, usually pointing at something that was a noun, and then saying in English "repeat after me." Every time he did this drill with us, we roared with laughter.

We learned from him that there are two seasons in Marsa Matruh, summer, al-ṣayf, *and winter,* al-shitāʾ. *This was the winter season, but the temperature was still 90°F and the water warm. Many things were closed, namely all the restaurants. This was disconcerting since we were starving. He drove us to a fish store, the fishmonger greeting us with a bit of confusion. I asked if we could have some* samak mishwī, *grilled fish. There were no tables, of course—he was a fishmonger, not a fish restaurant. He told me that this wasn't a restaurant, which by now I had realized. He must have taken pity on us and asked if we would like to eat there anyway, and we said yes, indicating to him with looks that we didn't want to put him out. He responded by going off to get some chairs and a table and we began to talk in broken Arabic.*

He brought us over to the cooler, where we chose two būrī, *also called* murgān *(gray mullet), and six* barbūnī *(red mullet), and asked for some bread, for a total of 20 Egyptian pounds, about $6.50. As the fish cooked, we chatted and got to know each other. His name was Khaled Abdel-Karim and he was the butcher—his shop was next door—not the fishmonger. His friend was the fishmonger.*

I asked Khaled about fishing in Marsa Matruh as his friend Zizu pulled up a chair. Zizu was a fisherman and had nothing to say that was encouraging—if you wanted to be a fisherman. Zizu said there were no fish. The only seafood in their cooler besides what we ordered were a couple of waʿar *(a kind of grouper) and a few shrimp.*

As we talked, our fish cooked slowly on the griddle and Zizu went next door to the qaṣab sukkar *shop where the sugarcane man made us some drinks from sugarcane juice. He threaded the six-foot-long ratoons of sugarcane into a huge rolling and pressing machine that squeezed out the frothy and sweet lime-green juice. This was a delicious refreshment—served in beer mugs.*

We sat at the table to eat. The būrī *had been gutted and stuffed with salt, parsley—stems and all—very hot fresh green chili peppers, and chopped tomatoes. The fish were closed up and coated with olive oil and chopped parsley. Both fish were served on a bed of parsley, tomatoes, and lemon halves, in a large round metal bowl with low sides. On the side was a platter of* girgīr (Eruca sylvestris lutea), *a kind of cross between watercress and arugula, very hot fresh green chili peppers, chopped tomatoes, and coarse sea salt. We were given* ʿaysh baladī, *the ubiquitous whole wheat flatbread of*

Egypt, and took pieces of fish off with our fingers and rolled it up in bread.

The fish was some of the freshest I have ever had. It was "griddled" for about thirty minutes, until the skin was blackened and crispy. We peeled off the fish from the bone and with the bread and tomatoes, it was heavenly. Here's the recipe, best grilled in the summertime when you can eat outdoors and wash up with the hose.

4 redfish or red snapper or 8 porgy or gray mullet (about 6 pounds in all), gutted and scaled
Coarse sea salt
3 bunches fresh parsley (leaves only, very finely chopped, from 2 of the bunches)
40 cherry tomatoes, halved
20 fresh green and red chili peppers, seeded and sliced
½ cup extra virgin olive oil
2 lemons, sliced
20 ounces arugula
8 large loaves *khubz ʿarabī* (Arab flatbread or pita bread), warmed

1. Preheat a gas grill on low for 20 minutes or prepare a charcoal fire and let it die down a bit, with a large oiled cast-iron griddle set upon the grilling grate.

2. Season the fish with salt inside and out. Stuff each of the fish with as much of the sprigs of parsley, three-quarters of the cherry tomatoes, and three-quarters of the hot peppers as can fit without overstuffing. Coat the fish with ⅓ cup or more of the olive oil on both sides. Place half of the chopped parsley on a platter and roll the oiled fish in it. Secure the belly opening with toothpicks if necessary. If they don't close well, the fish is overstuffed.

3. Place the fish on the griddle and cook for 30 to 40 minutes, turning several times. The skin of the fish should be black and crispy. Remove from the griddle and lay the fish on a bed of the remaining chopped parsley, 10 of the tomatoes, and all of the lemon slices. While the fish is cooking, prepare the salad of arugula, using the remaining cherry tomatoes and hot peppers.

4. Serve with the salad of arugula, tomatoes, and hot peppers, sprinkling coarse sea salt and the remaining olive oil (or to taste) over the salad. Eat the fish by picking off pieces from the bone, placing it in a piece of Arab flatbread with some parsley, tomatoes, hot peppers, and salad, rolling it up, and eating. You eat with your fingers.

Makes 4 servings

Samak Mishwī min al-Iskandriyya (Alexandria, Egypt)

ALEXANDRIA-STYLE GRIDDLED FISH

The Alexandrian fish market supplied Cairo with pickled fish in the Middle Ages, and salted tuna was exported to the faraway then capital of Tunisia, Qairouan.[118] *Alexander the Great had founded the city, and for millennia the Greek influence has been present. Although we know that the medieval Egyptians delighted in fish cookery, we can only surmise that this was one of the more typical methods by which the fish were cooked. Undoubtedly the Greek community had an influence on seafood cookery, and even today some of the restaurants specializing in seafood that dot the coast from Alexandria east to Abu Qir are Greek owned.*

This recipe instructs you how to grill the fish as it is done at the famous Qaddura restaurant in Alexandria. I hadn't realized it, but most food writers tell us that samak mishwī *is grilled fish when actually, in Egypt, it is "griddled," not grilled. A large cart, whose surface is a steel griddle, is fired by propane gas or wood and the fish is cooked on top.*

If gray or red mullet are not available, use small whole striped bass, red snapper, redfish, or porgy.

2 pounds whole gray mullet or red mullet (about 2 gray and 6 red), scaled, gutted, and cleaned, heads and tails left on, or 1 pound gray or red mullet, scaled, gutted, and cleaned, and 1 pound jumbo shrimp, shelled and deveined if necessary
Juice from 1 lemon
¼ cup extra virgin olive oil
1 medium-size onion, grated
2 teaspoons freshly ground cumin seeds
Salt and freshly ground black pepper to taste
Sprigs of fresh parsley for garnish
Lemon wedges for garnish

1. Marinate the fish, covered, in a ceramic or glass baking pan with the lemon juice, olive oil, onion, cumin, salt, and pepper for 2 hours in the refrigerator, turning several times.

2. Prepare a charcoal fire or preheat a gas grill on low for 20 minutes with a large oiled cast-iron griddle set upon the grilling grate. Score the fish in three places on both sides. Place the fish (and shrimp, if using) on the griddle until the fish is firm and the shrimp completely cooked, turning only once, 16 to 20 minutes for the fish and 8 to 10 minutes for the shrimp. Serve with parsley and lemon wedges.

Makes 4 servings

Samak Baladī (Egypt)

COUNTRY-STYLE FISH

As we have seen throughout this book, the story of Mediterranean food is a story of scarcity, the contemporary richness of its cuisines being, indeed, contemporary. A lesson in all this may be drawn from this recipe. The source of all Mediterranean life, and especially true in Egypt, was bread. In Egypt, bread was called "life," ʿaysh, *in the eleventh century and it still is today. The relatively primitive milling technology in medieval Egypt meant that the finest white bread was often expensive and found in the cities, while the countryside usually had whole wheat bread with large flakes of bran. This recipe demonstrates how some of this bran could be used. It is called country style, which in Egypt means settlements along the Nile or its delta. This interesting way of grilling fish in Egypt is sometimes called* samak al-sun *or* samak bi'l-radda, *fish with bran. It is typical of how country folk grill fish;* baladī *means "country-style."*

Pure or virgin olive oil for the griddle
2 cups wheat bran
4 whole fish (gray mullet, red snapper, grouper, redfish, yellowtail, 1½ to 2 pounds each), scaled (if desired), gutted, and cleaned, with heads and tails left on
¼ cup white wine vinegar
Juice from ½ lemon
3 tablespoons extra virgin olive oil
1 teaspoon freshly ground cumin seeds
½ teaspoon paprika
½ teaspoon cayenne pepper
Salt and freshly ground black pepper to taste
1½ cups hot water

1. Prepare a charcoal fire or preheat a gas grill on low for 20 minutes with a large oiled cast-iron griddle set upon the grilling grate.

2. Pour the wheat bran on a large platter or tray and dredge the whole fish in the bran. Once the griddle is very hot (after 20 minutes of preheating), place the fish on the griddle for 20 minutes total, flipping several times, until the fish are black on both sides and firm everywhere.

3. In a small nonreactive saucepan, stir together the vinegar, lemon juice, olive oil, cumin, paprika, cayenne, salt, and pepper. Add the water and bring to a boil. Transfer this boiling mixture to a hot ceramic or glass baking pan and dip the whole fish quickly into this bath. This helps loosen the scales and bran so it can be eaten. This dipping must be done quickly so the scales come off. Transfer to a serving platter.

Makes 4 servings

Samaka Ḥarra (Syria)

SPICED FISH

The sea at Jeble on the Syrian coast is so unlike the tourist meccas of Spain's Costa del Sol or the French Riviera. It is desolate, quiet, the waves pounding against the sea break, hardly different from how it was in 1550, when a merchantman from Acre might have passed by on his return journey to Venice. Jeble has a tiny port where a handful of fishermen barely make a living. The fishing has never been good in the eastern Mediterranean, and with the lower counts of phosphorus in the water, important for the growth of the plankton that fish live off, it is worse.[119]

Fayez Sayidat, an architect in Jeble, took me on a walking tour of the old town, pointing out the centuries-old ḥammām *(public bath), the Mosque of Sulṭān Ibrāhīm, and the raw coastline without a single tourist facility of any kind as far as the eye could see. I was told that the Arabic name for red mullet,* sulṭān Ibrāhīm, *comes from this sultan, a rich man who gave up everything to devote himself to piety nearly a thousand years ago.*

For lunch we would return to the house of Fayez's mother-in-law, Amal Halaby, so I could follow her in making deep-fried sulṭān Ibrāhīm *and* samaka ḥarra. *There are many different recipes for this spiced fish dish popular along the coast from Latakia in northern Syria to Gaza. Some recipes call for baking the fish whole, such as this one, and others remove the flesh to make a kind of fish hash. This recipe of Amal's, mother of my friend Joseph Halabi, used sea bass and a spiced chili pepper and tomato sauce coating. Amal Halaby lives with her husband, Shukri, a half block from the Mediterranean Sea, and they often have fish because they are virtually at the port. Because the catch is so meager, very fresh fish is consumed in Jeble where they are landed, while Aleppines and Damascenes have only frozen fish available to them. We ate this* samaka ḥarra *right off the bone with warm pieces of* khubz ʿarabī *(Arab flatbread or pita bread).*

6 large garlic cloves, peeled
1½ teaspoons salt
2 fresh red or green long chili peppers, seeded
1 small onion, cut into pieces
1 large ripe tomato (9 to 10 ounces), peeled and seeded
3 tablespoons tomato paste
1 teaspoon freshly ground cumin seeds
1 whole sea bass or red snapper (about 6 pounds), scaled, gutted, and cleaned but left whole with head and tail on
½ cup extra virgin olive oil
Salt and freshly ground black pepper to taste
¼ cup finely chopped fresh coriander (cilantro) leaves

1. In a mortar, pound the garlic and salt together until mushy. Put the chili peppers and onion in a food processor and chop finely. Add the tomato and process in bursts until it is chopped. Remove to a medium-size bowl and stir in the pounded garlic, tomato paste, and cumin.

2. Preheat the oven to 350°F. Rinse the fish and pat dry with paper towels. Score the fish in three places on each side. Lay the fish in a baking pan and coat with the olive oil on both sides. Sprinkle with salt and pepper, then cover with the chili pepper sauce. Bake the fish until the dorsal fin feels as if it will come off with a tug, about 1 hour, basting with the accumulated olive oil in the baking pan. Sprinkle with the coriander and serve.

VARIATION

Preheat a gas grill on low for 20 minutes or prepare a charcoal fire. Place the fish on a rack inside a large aluminum baking pan, for example, the kind you use to roast a whole turkey. Place the aluminum pan on the grilling grate, draw down the hood or cover, and grill until done, 45 minutes to 1 hour, making sure some smoke can escape through vent holes. The fish is done when one of the dorsal fins almost comes off when you pull on it.

Makes 6 servings

In the Pelion region of Greece, fishermen would give up their gardens and hunting and move their families to the streets of the local harbor for the fishing season. In Crete, men routinely joined Turkish ships even a century before Crete fell into Turkish hands. Turkish recruiters would also find Greek sailors in the taverns of Pera on Cyprus. There were many small-time Greek pirates in the islands of the Aegean and along the coasts of the Adriatic, in search of small-time victims and whatever food could be stolen. Although these fishermen-pirates could take from the sea, pirate rations were usually a sack of flour, some biscuits, a skin of oil, honey, a few bunches of garlic and onions, and a little salt. These rations would last a month, or until the next raid or port.

Greek fishermen were truly sailors who found a home all over the Mediterranean. Greek sailors could easily be found manning a Turkish, Spanish, or pirate galley. The infamous brothers, the Barbarossas, were Greek or Turkish sailors from Lesbos who converted to Islam and settled in Djerba, becoming pirates who terrorized the western Mediterranean. By 1518, they ruled Algiers until the last brother's death in 1546.

Psari Fournou me Ambelofia (Greece)

FISH BAKED IN GRAPE LEAVES

The traditional method of baking fish in Greece is called plaki, *where fish such as* sphyrida *(grouper) or* phagri *(Couch's sea bream) are cut up and baked with thinly sliced onions, garlic, tomatoes, herbs, celery, and carrots, perhaps wine, and sometimes cinnamon and even honey.*

The famous turn-of-the-century French chef Auguste Escoffier laid claim to creating a similar preparation. The Greeks, on the other hand, as with the Turks, had long been using grape leaves for all kinds of food wrapping purposes. The secret to this preparation is, quite simply, very fresh fish.

2 whole fish (such as 1½- to 2-pound redfish, red snapper, yellowtail, sea bass, or porgy), scaled, gutted, and cleaned, with heads and tails left on
¼ cup extra virgin olive oil
Juice from 1 lemon
1 tablespoon finely chopped fresh parsley leaves
1 tablespoon finely chopped fresh thyme leaves
1 tablespoon finely chopped fresh dill
Salt and freshly ground black pepper to taste
5 salted anchovy fillets, rinsed and chopped
2 tablespoons unsalted butter, at room temperature
8 to 16 large grape leaves (see Note)
Lemon slices, fennel leaves, or sprigs fresh dill for garnish

1. Score the fish on both sides several times with a very sharp knife. Arrange the fish in a large glass or ceramic pan. In a separate bowl, whisk together the olive oil, lemon juice, parsley, thyme, dill, and salt and pepper. Pour this marinade over the fish, cover with plastic wrap, and leave refrigerated for 2 hours, turning once.

2. In a small bowl or mortar, mash together the anchovies and butter and set aside at room temperature so it will spread easily. Preheat the oven to 350°F.

3. Drain the fish, pat dry with paper towels, and spread the anchovy butter on each side of the fish. Drain the grape leaves and unravel carefully so they don't rip. Wrap the fish in the grape leaves. Lay 4 to 8 large grape leaves on the surface before you with the stem closest to you and the rough side up. Cut off any remaining portion of the stem. Lay a fish over the bottom portion of the grape leaves and roll up carefully. The head and tail should not be covered by the leaf. Arrange the fish in a large oiled baking pan and bake until the eyes of the fish are cloudy and white and the fish is firm, about 35 minutes. Serve garnished with the lemon slices and some chopped fennel or dill sprigs.

NOTE: If using fresh grape leaves, boil them gently for 5 minutes. The jarred grape leaves in brine available in supermarkets do not need any preparation other than draining.

Makes 4 servings

Garides me Feta (Greece)

BAKED SHRIMP WITH FETA CHEESE

Garides me feta, *shrimp with feta, is usually cooked in an earthenware casserole called* youvetsi *(or* giouvetsi*), derived from the Turkish, which is like a Spanish* cazuela. *It is a taverna type of dish popular in the islands. Diane Kochilas, author of* The Food and Wine of Greece, *told me that it is a specialty from Thessaloniki, but it is also well known among the tavernas around Piraeus, the port of Athens. Some people add ouzo or replace the white wine with retsina. This is one of my favorite shrimp dishes and it is easy to prepare at home.*

2 pounds fresh large shrimp, heads removed and shelled and deveined if necessary, or 2 pounds headless defrosted shrimp
2 tablespoons fresh lemon juice
¼ cup extra virgin olive oil
1 medium-size onion or 3 shallots, finely chopped
5 scallions, white and light green parts only, finely chopped
2 pounds ripe tomatoes, peeled, seeded, and chopped
⅓ cup dry white wine
2 large garlic cloves, finely chopped
3 tablespoons finely chopped fresh parsley leaves
Salt and freshly ground black pepper to taste
½ pound Greek or Bulgarian feta cheese, crumbled into large chunks
Fresh parsley leaves for garnish

1. Place the shelled shrimp in a large bowl and pour the lemon juice over. Toss and set aside.

2. In a large skillet or earthenware casserole, heat the olive oil over medium heat, then cook the onion or shallots and scallions until translucent, about 8 minutes, stirring occasionally. Add the tomatoes, wine, garlic, and parsley and season with salt and pepper. Stir well, reduce the heat to low, and simmer until dense, about 30 minutes, stirring occasionally.

3. Preheat the oven to 450°F. Spoon some sauce into a large baking dish. Spread the shrimp around the dish and cover with the remaining sauce. Spread the feta cheese around, pushing the chunks of cheese down into the sauce. Place in the oven and bake until the shrimp are cooked and the cheese melted, about 20 minutes. Remove from the oven and serve garnished with parsley leaves.

Makes 4 to 6 servings

Fishing off Provence

AMONG Christians, the Lenten period is a time of penitential preparation for Easter, beginning on Ash Wednesday, about six weeks before, and is part of a forty-day fast in imitation of Jesus Christ's fasting in the wilderness. In the Middle Ages, fasting regulations were very strict in the Roman Catholic Church and still are in Eastern rite churches.[120] In Provence in the fourteenth century, the number of church-imposed days of fasting without meat, including the period of Lent, reached about 150 days out of every year and important fishing communities sprouted along the coast to fulfill the demand for fish.

Marseilles remained the most important port and the Marseillais were consuming 473 tons of fresh fish in 1556, which sounds like a lot but was still only a quarter of the meat consumption. In one day in 1551 the fishermen of Marseilles landed eight thousand tons (!) of fish, the Provençal writer Quiqueran de Beaujeu tells us.[121] If this figure is correct then most of the catch must have been salted for export because it's at variance with what we know about what was consumed. The type of fish regularly caught were the same as today, but they never were an overly important part of the diet. In 1560, the annual per capita rations of the Marseillais were 275 kilos of bread, 160 liters of wine, 45 kilos of meat (beef, mutton, pork), and only 10 kilos of fish.[122]

In the brackish lagoon water there were eel, carp, pike, tench, gudgeon (a small fish used for bait), and barbel (a freshwater mullet). In the Rhône, the fishermen also found sturgeon; their eggs were not used for fresh caviar as far as we can tell, but rather were salted and dried, according to Quiqueran de Beaujeu. In the saltwater lagoons, the famous *étangs,* they caught gilthead bream *(daurade),* sea bass *(loup),* turbot, gray mullet, shrimp, and tuna. Tuna fishing was not as big an industry as it was in Sicily and Andalusia, but the Provençal liked to grill the steaks, and we know that for Christmas 1515 the master sugarer Berthomeu Blanch prepared a very refined confit of tuna tongue preserved in sugar and stored in earthenware pots.[123] The fish market of Grasse sold twenty-eight kinds of fish including cuttlefish, squid, octopus, and spiny lobster, but the favorites were bream, sea bass, and gray mullet.[124]

How were these fish cooked? The most romantic notion is that the anchovies and sardines were salted and the remaining, less commercially desirable fish were used for fish soups and bouillabaisse. In fact, outside of the highly spiced fish soups in the *Viandier* of Taillevent, there is no mention of fish soups, let alone bouillabaisse, in sixteenth-century Provençal documents and chronicles. The closest thing to a bouillabaisse that I have found in a medieval text is the *brodecto de li dicti pisci* that appears in the anonymous fifteenth-century Italian cookery book known as *Libro A* of the Anonimo Meridionale, where sardines and anchovies are boiled in *vino greco* (a strong Neapolitan wine) with black pepper, saffron, and sugar with a little olive oil. A *brodeto de pessi* (fish broth) was found in the anonymous fourteenth-century Venetian manuscript *Libro per cuoco,* where we find the fish boiled and covered with ground nuts, parsley, bread crumbs, and sweet and strong spices.[125]

The invention of bouillabaisse, in particular, is often attributed to fishermen. I think this is unlikely for two reasons. First, the standard way of cooking fish in sixteenth-century Provence was to fry it in a pan in olive oil. The pan, *poêle* or *sartago,* appeared in 85 percent of Provençal homes, according to one contemporary study, and was used *ad decoquendum pisses* (to cook fish).[126] The other major cooking utensil was the cauldron, and it was used for soups, mostly of meat or vegetables. Second, the famous fish soups, called *soupes de poisson,* as well as the magical bouillabaisse, have all the hallmarks of a nineteenth-century restaurant invention in their sophisticated use of saffron, orange zest, and liqueur.

Scholars have pointed out the difficulty of grasping,

from the extant documents, the nature of the fishing industry in Provence in the fourteenth and fifteenth centuries. They do know that the best fishing places were called *cales* or *calancae ad piscandum* (fishing waters), and rights to fish them were hotly disputed, as we see from an arbitrage document of May 16, 1470, determining that the fishermen of Cannes and Antibes had to split the fishing grounds. Much of their catch was salted, especially anchovy and eel.

The Provençal fishermen used a variety of fishing methods. They had boats linked with nets, often close to shore, where the fish could be pulled onto the beach. There is also a record of nets being used in conjunction with sluice gates to channel fish. A variation of the same method was used in the catching of tuna in Sicily (page 395). In local lagoons, where fish were more easily trapped, canes were stuck into the ground to form netting channels where fish could be more easily beached or boated. These areas were called *bourdigues,* and the most famous were the ones of Martigues.[127] Another method used was called the *palangre,* nets roped together underwater and held stationary by floats and fitted with hooked lines. The biggest of the fish markets was the one at Marseilles, and merchants came from many surrounding towns to buy fish. They came mostly between January and April when the catch was good, and sometimes came from surprisingly distant places up the Rhône, such as Romans, Valence, and Crest.[128]

Filets de Sole Sauce Estragon (Provence)

FILLET OF SOLE WITH TARRAGON SAUCE

The variety of fish available to the Provençal cook of the Middle Ages was great, if the quantity was not. Fish, whether it was fresh, salted, or dried, was an important substitute for meat during fasts imposed by the liturgical calendar. There was bream, shad, carp, trout, salmon, pike, eel, sturgeon, tench, sole, mullet, ray, and many others. Throughout the coastal Mediterranean, from Murcia in Spain to Provence, fish were fried in olive oil in the sixteenth century.[129] *There were two reasons for this. First, in Mediterranean France, the population had been decimated during the Black Death, and the plague was almost an annual occurrence in the Languedoc from 1481 to 1516. But by the sixteenth century, the population's recovery meant demands for more food and employment. As the French historian Emmanuel Le Roy Ladurie showed, the classic Mediterranean response to a rise in population in terms of agriculture when soil nutrients are lacking is irrigation and assarting, the grubbing of forest land to make it arable. Therefore, the sixteenth century saw the growth of arboriculture and viticulture. The population could have reclaimed vacant land or planted trees and vines on old and new assarts. The latter solution occurred in Provence and Languedoc, increasing the returns from agriculture through a more intensive form of land utilization. These were not regular olive orchards but the so-called* camp enholieu *or* camp en olivas*—that is, wheat fields planted with rows of olive trees. Olive oil production increased as a result. Second, the consumer was demanding a certain taste in his food, which was provided by olive oil.*[130] *The frying of fish in olive oil is a method older than the sixteenth century, though, for we know that the Vatican Library and Bibliothèque Nationale manuscripts of the fourteenth-century French cookery work by Taillevent, the* Viandier, *instructs the cook to fry sole in olive oil.*[131]

Tarragon (see page 277), an herb member of the wormwood family, is a popular herb in Provence and is used often with fish, chicken, or eggs. This recipe is adapted from the delightful cookbook of Bernard Loubat and Jeannette Bertrandy, La bonne cuisine Provençale.

FOR THE TARRAGON SAUCE

1 tablespoon unsalted butter
1 tablespoon all-purpose flour
Salt and freshly ground black pepper to taste
1 cup fish broth (page 369)
Bouquet garni, tied in cheesecloth, consisting of 1 bay leaf and 5 sprigs each parsley, tarragon, and marjoram
Pinch of freshly grated nutmeg
2 tablespoons finely chopped fresh tarragon leaves

FOR THE SOLE

8 sole fillets (about 1 pound total)
All-purpose flour for dredging
Salt and freshly ground black pepper to taste
2 tablespoons unsalted butter
1 tablespoon extra virgin olive oil
6 sprigs fresh tarragon for garnish (leaves from 3 pulled off the sprig)

1. Prepare the tarragon sauce. In a small saucepan, melt the butter over medium heat, then stir in the flour to make a roux. Season with salt and pepper and stir for 1 to 2 minutes. Slowly pour in the fish broth, whisking as you do. Add the bouquet garni and nutmeg. Check the seasoning. Cook for 20 to 25 minutes, stirring occasionally. Pass the sauce through a fine-mesh sieve and return to the saucepan. Increase the heat to high, add the tarragon, stir for 1 minute, and remove from the heat. Keep the sauce warm by leaving it on the stove over a turned-off burner.

2. Dredge the sole fillets in the flour, salt, and pepper and shake off any excess flour. In a large skillet, heat the butter and olive oil together over high heat; once the butter has melted and stopped sizzling and is nearly smoking, cook the sole until white and firm, 2 to 3 minutes per side.

3. Ladle some tarragon sauce onto individual plates and lay a sole fillet on top. Garnish with some tarragon leaves and a sprig of tarragon and serve.

Makes 2 to 4 servings

Poisson Grillé (Provence)

GRILLED FISH

In the fourteenth-century French cookery book the Viandier *of Taillevent, some favorite fish for grilling were the freshwater tench* (Tinca tinca), *mackerel, conger eel, salmon, shad, and sole* (Solea solea, *the so-called Dover sole that is firmer than the lemon sole available in the western North Atlantic and more suitable for grilling). Provençal fish were never a staple of the diet, though. In 1560, the annual per capita consumption of fish of the population of Marseilles was only 22 pounds.*[132]

Today, grilled fish is popular along the Côte d'Azur, where small villages, some famous, some not, will sometimes have one or two fishing boats still operating. Although the tourists are the bigger catch for the locals, one can sometimes buy along the quayside a loup de mer *(sea bass) or a* daurade *(gilt-head bream), both excellent fish for grilling. The fish is scored in several places, placed in a hinged fish grill, and grilled over a lump charcoal fire.*

In this recipe, if the grating of your grill is wide enough, the fish and fennel can be laid directly on the oiled grilling grate without using the fish grill. If you don't have a hinged fish grill, but do have a cast-iron griddle, you can lay the griddle on the grilling grate, wait 30 minutes until it is very hot, and griddle the fish for about one hour. The very workable rule of thumb for grilling whole fish (which is called the Canadian method) is to grill about 5 inches from the heat source for 10 minutes per inch of fish measured at its thickest part. Serve with beurre de Montpellier *(page 277).*

One 5-pound whole fish or two 2½-pound whole fish (sea bass, striped bass, red snapper, or redfish), scaled, gutted, and cleaned
1 small bulb Florence fennel, with stalks and leaves, thinly sliced

Salt and freshly ground black pepper to taste
1 tablespoon fresh lemon juice
2 tablespoons extra virgin olive oil

1. Prepare a hot charcoal fire or preheat a gas grill for 15 minutes on high or, alternatively, preheat a gas grill on low for 20 minutes or build a charcoal fire and let it die down a bit.

2. Score the fish diagonally in three places on each side. Carefully stuff each slash with a slice of fennel stalk and leaves. Stuff the cavity with the remaining fennel slices. Season the whole fish with salt and pepper. Pour the lemon juice and olive oil over both sides of the fish, spreading to coat all surfaces with your fingers.

3. Layer a hinged fish grill with fennel stalks, place the fish on top, and then more fennel stalks on top of the fish. Close the hinged fish grill and place on the grill. Cook for 20 minutes over a hot fire, turning once, or 1 hour over a low fire, turning occasionally.

Makes 4 servings

Fricot di Barco (Provence)

BEEF AND ONION RAGOUT OF THE BARK PILOTS OF ARLES

Fricot *is a Provençal word meaning "ragout." The word is a colloquial derivation of* fricassée *in this recipe of the seamen of Arles who piloted the barks—small three-masted sailing ships with their foremast and mainmast square rigged and their mizzenmast fore-and-aft rigged. This dish of stewed beef with abundant onions is traditionally cooked in small earthenware stew pots. The meat and onions are packed tightly and simmered in the manner of a slow-cooked dry stew such as a Moroccan* ṭājin *(page 373). The flavors meld together and the meat falls apart. It is excellent served with boiled parsleyed potatoes, French fries (page 61), or mashed potatoes (page 62).*

¼ cup extra virgin olive oil
2 pounds onions, coarsely chopped
2 pounds beef round, thinly sliced
6 large garlic cloves, finely chopped
10 salted anchovy fillets, rinsed and chopped
Salt and freshly ground black pepper to taste

1. Lightly oil the bottom and sides of a small 2-quart earthenware (preferably) or enameled cast-iron casserole or saucepan with a heavy lid with 2 teaspoons of the olive oil. Layer the bottom with a third of the chopped onions. Lay some beef slices on top of the onions, spread some of the sliced garlic and chopped anchovy on the meat, season with salt and pepper, and cover with more onions. Continue in this order until you have used up all the ingredients, finishing with a layer of onions and salt and pepper.

2. Pour in the remaining 3 tablespoons plus 1 teaspoon oil, cover, and turn the heat to medium for 15 minutes. Reduce the heat to very low and simmer until the meat is very tender and breaks apart with a fork, about 3 hours and 45 minutes without removing the lid. Serve.

Makes 4 to 6 servings

Fishing in the Adriatic

ADRIATIC fishermen employed techniques similar to those used elsewhere. The Ragusan fishermen, whose waters were rocky and a good home for fish, attached one end of their nets to a float and the other to a stone. These seine nets drifted with the currents and were a barrier that intercepted moving shoals, and the fish—mostly mackerel, sardine, and anchovy—became enmeshed. A variety of boats were used for fishing along the Dalmatian coast including the *zoppolo* (*ladva* in Croatian), a large boat hewn out of a single trunk and used by the fishermen of Monfalcone and San Bortolo. The *guzzo* was a small rowing boat used in Quarnero (Kvarner), the strait between the Istrian Peninsula and the island of Cres, for line fishing. These boats were also used off the islands of Quarnero (Kvarner) and in southern Dalmatia, where squid, cuttlefish, conger eel, shark, ray, bass, and gilt-head bream were similarly caught and sun-dried or lightly salted and smoked and stored for the winter. The *batello* was a decked boat of different sizes in use on the west coast of Istria, chiefly at Rovigno (Rovinj), for casting the sardine and anchovy nets. The *sandolo* or *cio* was a small flat boat of about one ton carrying two or three men and used in the lagoons and brackish waters near Grado, west of Trieste, where fishermen could scoop up a lobster for spaghetti or risotto. In Venice, fishermen used similar methods on a flat boat called a *toppo*.[133]

Venetian archers on boats called *toppi* hunting aquatic birds in the lagoon. Vittore Carpaccio (1400–1495). *Hunting on the Lagoon.* J. PAUL GETTY MUSEUM, LOS ANGELES.

❈ *Spaghetti con l'Aragosta* (Friuli-Venezia Giulia)

SPAGHETTI WITH LOBSTER

In the thirteenth century, Trieste's main trade items to Venice were hides and meat.[134] *The Venetians had to worry about Trieste because the city was a great center for selling and reselling, and had the Hapsburgs of Austria as allies.*

The lobster along the Istrian coast was never abundant, so the consumption was always local. Most of the lobster was the clawless spiny lobster (Palinurus vulgaris), *although a very few* astrice (Homarus vulgaris), *the lobster with claws that is similar to the famous ones in Maine* (Homarus americanus), *were caught.*

This recipe is from the Ristorante-Pizzeria "Vulcania" on the waterfront of the harbor in Trieste. The menu is not particularly Istrian, but I asked my waiter to ask the chef if he could prepare something typically Istrian. The waiter wasn't from Istria, so he called his colleague who, without missing a beat, suggested this off-the-menu preparation. The chef prepared this dish and the waiter explained that it is served by housewives as a piatto unico, *an all-in-one meal.*

Traditionally, lobster in Italian cuisine was most often associated with Sardinia, but today it is a popular, if expensive, shellfish found in many regional recipes. It is a superb preparation and I would serve it on a special occasion.

¼ cup (½ stick) unsalted butter
½ cup extra virgin olive oil
1 medium-size onion, finely chopped
2 garlic cloves, finely chopped
1¼ cups dry white wine
¾ cup fish broth (page 369)
2 pounds ripe plum tomatoes, peeled, seeded, and chopped
⅛ to ¼ teaspoon cayenne pepper, to your taste
1 teaspoon dried oregano
10 large fresh basil leaves, 6 left whole, 4 finely chopped
Two 1½-pound live lobsters (Note 1 on page 51)
Salt to taste
1 pound spaghetti

1. In a large stove-top casserole, melt the butter and heat the olive oil together over medium heat, then cook the onion and garlic until translucent, about 7 minutes, stirring frequently so the garlic doesn't burn. Pour in the wine and ½ cup of the fish broth, and add the tomatoes, cayenne, oregano, and whole basil leaves. Reduce the heat to medium-low, cover, and cook until denser, about 35 minutes.

2. Meanwhile, prepare the lobster. The lobster can be split in half lengthwise or chopped into larger pieces. With a heavy cleaver, chop the lobster. If you are squeamish about killing a live lobster this way, you can parboil the lobster first and then chop it up. (I don't like doing it that way because I believe you lose some of the lobster's flavor.) Make sure all of the shells are well cracked and that the meat is easy to get at when served. You will end up eating with your hands anyway. Add the lobster pieces to the sauce, stir, and season with salt. After 10 minutes, add the remaining ¼ cup fish broth. Cover and, if the sauce is bubbling, reduce the heat to low. Cook until the lobster shells are orange-red, the meat firm, white, and cooked, and the sauce dense but not too thick, about 30 minutes. If the sauce is too thick, add a ladleful of hot water.

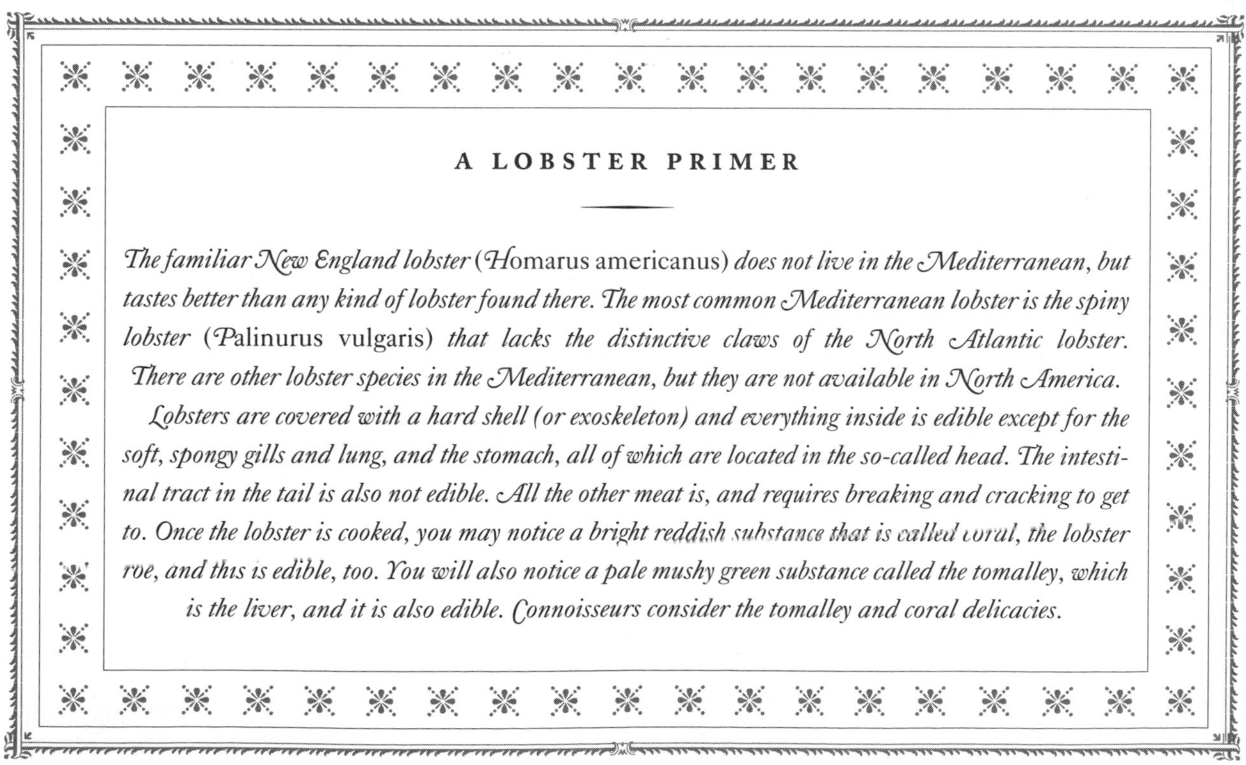

A LOBSTER PRIMER

The familiar New England lobster (Homarus americanus) *does not live in the Mediterranean, but tastes better than any kind of lobster found there. The most common Mediterranean lobster is the spiny lobster* (Palinurus vulgaris) *that lacks the distinctive claws of the North Atlantic lobster. There are other lobster species in the Mediterranean, but they are not available in North America.*

Lobsters are covered with a hard shell (or exoskeleton) and everything inside is edible except for the soft, spongy gills and lung, and the stomach, all of which are located in the so-called head. The intestinal tract in the tail is also not edible. All the other meat is, and requires breaking and cracking to get to. Once the lobster is cooked, you may notice a bright reddish substance that is called coral, the lobster roe, and this is edible, too. You will also notice a pale mushy green substance called the tomalley, which is the liver, and it is also edible. Connoisseurs consider the tomalley and coral delicacies.

3. Meanwhile, bring a large pot of abundantly salted water to a boil and add the pasta when the water is rolling. Drain the pasta when al dente and place in a serving platter. Stir the chopped basil into the sauce, then pour the sauce and lobster pieces over the pasta. Serve immediately.

Makes 4 to 6 servings

Risotto con l'Aragosta (Friuli-Venezia Giulia)

RISOTTO WITH LOBSTER

This preparation is noteworthy for a number of reasons. First, it is a risotto from Trieste, and risottos are not commonly made there, polenta being preferred by the populace. Second, an essential element of the dish is the mash made by pounding the coral, tomalley, and leg meat of the lobster together and thinning it with lobster broth to create a particular sapore, *flavor, that certainly enhances the taste of the risotto.*

2 quarts water
One 2½-pound live lobster
¼ cup (½ stick) unsalted butter
1 small onion, very finely chopped
1 cup Arborio rice
Salt and freshly ground white pepper to taste
1 cup dry white wine
1 tablespoon freshly chopped fresh parsley leaves

1. Place about 2 cups of the water in a big pot and bring to a boil. Add the lobster, cover, and steam until bright red, 25 to 30 minutes. Drain, saving 3 cups of the liquid from the lobster and the water it was steamed with.

2. When the lobster is cool enough to handle, crack the shells and remove all the meat, using a large platter or pan to collect all the juices. (Pour the juices back into the pot, about 1 cup.) Using a spoon, remove the meat from the head (there will be very little) and any coral and tomalley, and transfer to a mortar. Remove the meat from the legs with a lobster pick or toothpick or by breaking and squeezing them. Place it in the mortar and pound with a pestle until it is a mush, then set aside. Chop the remaining lobster meat into small pieces (but not too small) and reserve. Put all the empty shells back into the pot with the water and juices and simmer for 1 hour over low heat. Strain through a fine-mesh strainer and set aside.

3. In a large, heavy saucepan, melt 2 tablespoons of the butter over medium heat, then cook the onion until translucent, about 6 minutes, stirring. Add the rice, season with salt and white pepper, and cook until well coated, about 2 minutes, stirring. Add ½ cup of the wine and cook until it is nearly absorbed. Pour in ½ cup of the reserved lobster broth, then the remaining ½ cup wine. Continue pouring in smaller and smaller amounts of the remaining lobster broth until the rice is creamy and between al dente and tender and all the broth is absorbed, using about 1 quart of lobster broth in all.

4. Add the reserved lobster mash and lobster pieces to the rice and cook for 5 minutes, stirring to mix everything well. Stir in the remaining 2 tablespoons butter, remove from the heat, sprinkle with the parsley, and serve immediately.

Makes 4 servings

✣ ✣ ✣

DALMATIAN fishermen were fond of seafood preparations; they ate sea urchins raw and also ate sea anemones, a kind of polyp whose colorful cluster of tentacles resembles a flower, fried in oil. As in Venice, crabs were a delight boiled with finely chopped garlic and parsley or stewed in vinegar and oil and seasoned with garlic, parsley, and pepper. Mussels were steamed or fried with bread crumbs, parsley, oil, black pepper, and lemon juice. A mussel soup was also made with the addition of rice.[135] The *brodetto* was the favorite way of eating all kinds of fish along the Dalmatian coast. The fish was boiled in seawater and then removed. The broth was seasoned with olive oil, garlic, parsley, and black pepper and served with lots of rice, with the fish served as a second course. Another favorite preparation was *oslić,* a whole hake larded with salted sardines and boiled in cream that seems to show the Hapsburg influence.[136]

Riblja Čorba na Dubrovaćki Naćin (Dalmatian Coast)

DUBROVNIK FISH SOUP

The proximity of the Italian peninsula and the naval dominance of the Venetian Republic during the Middle Ages resulted in a perceptible Italian culinary influence along the Dalmatian coast, where fish soups are called brodet *in Croatian, from the Italian* brodetto. *But this recipe came to me by way of someone calling it a* čorba, *deriving from the Turkish and Arabic words for "soup."*

This simple fish boil from Dubrovnik (Ragusa) will be successful if you have a good mix of fish, at least four kinds, and a whole fish to make the broth from. A good mix would be a whole striped bass, whole porgy (scup), and fillets from bluefish, cod, and salmon.

3½ pounds mixed fish steaks, pieces, heads, carcasses, including whole fish, cut up
12 cups water
Sea salt to taste
1 large ripe tomato (about ½ pound), peeled, seeded, and chopped
¼ cup finely chopped fresh parsley leaves
1 bay leaf
10 black peppercorns
¼ cup extra virgin olive oil
1 cup dry white wine
½ cup medium-grain rice

1. Place the fish heads, tails, and carcasses (1 to 1½ pounds all together) and 1 whole fish in a large pot and cover with 6 cups of the water. Bring to a boil, reduce the heat to medium, and simmer for 1 hour. Strain the fish broth through a cheesecloth-lined strainer and set aside. You should have about 1 quart fish broth.

2. Pour the remaining 6 cups water into a stew pot and season with sea salt. Add the tomato, parsley, bay leaf, peppercorns, olive oil, and wine and bring to a rolling boil. Add the fish pieces to the boiling broth one at a time and boil furiously for 8 to 10 minutes.

3. Meanwhile, bring the reserved fish broth to a boil in a medium-size saucepan and add the rice, cooking it until almost tender (times vary, so keep checking). Turn the heat off.

4. Put 2 to 3 tablespoons of the cooked rice in each individual serving bowl using a slotted ladle. Ladle the fish with broth over the rice and serve.

Makes 4 servings

✣ ✣ ✣

VENICE had a small but robust fishing industry in the twelfth-century Adriatic. The first document listing the major species of fish caught was commissioned by Doge Sebastiano Ziani in 1173. The catalogue of fish reads like a contemporary register of the Rialto fish market: sturgeon, trout, turbot, *variolo* (young sea bass), gilt-head bream, *megla* (?), red mullet, black scorpionfish (*Scorpena porcus),* star-gazer, flounder, sole, large eel, *i lucci cavedagni* (a kind of pike), and tench, a freshwater fish. The variety of fish was so great that clearly the number of recipes in the few extant cookery manuscripts from two centuries later were far fewer than the actual recipes existing.[137] Many of the fish used in Venetian cuisine are locally caught lagoon fish, and one of the most popular of seafoods is cuttlefish. Fishermen from Venice and other lagoon towns such as Chiogga go out in twos and threes using small boats that can navigate the shallow areas of the lagoon to find fish, cuttlefish, and a variety of crustaceans, including mantis shrimp (page 258).

Risotto di Gambaretti (Veneto)

SHRIMP RISOTTO

Shrimp and related shellfish have long been popular in the Venetian lagoon. In a fourteenth-century Venetian cookbook, shrimp is pounded after being boiled and pounded again with herbs, egg yolks, and almonds, and mixed with a kind of vinegar.[138] *The combination of rice and shrimp came much later.*

The secret to this dish is an excellent shrimp broth. For this reason, it would be ideal to use fresh shrimp with their heads still on. The rice should take on a pinkish hue from the shrimp. You can enhance this look by stirring in a tablespoon of tomato sauce. In its true form this dish is made with scampi (Nephrops norvegicus), *which are prawns, a shrimp-size kind of lobster. This dish can also be made with fish such as* branzino *(sea bass) and sole, both very popular in Venice.*

1½ quarts cold water
2 pounds fresh small or medium-size shrimp with their heads (1 pound shrimp without heads)
3 garlic cloves, peeled, 2 crushed and 1 very finely chopped
1 bay leaf
3 tablespoons extra virgin olive oil
¼ cup (½ stick) unsalted butter
1 scallion, finely chopped
2 cups Arborio rice
2 teaspoons salt
¾ cup dry white wine
Freshly ground black pepper to taste

1. Bring the water for the shrimp to a boil in a large saucepan with the 2 crushed garlic cloves and the bay leaf. Put the whole shrimp in their shells into the boiling water and cook for exactly 2 minutes. Remove the shrimp with a slotted ladle or skimmer and remove their shells once they're cool, putting the shells (and heads, if any) back into the water. Chop the shrimp and set aside. Let the broth with the shrimp shells simmer for 1 hour over low heat. Strain the broth through a fine-mesh strainer and set aside.

2. In a large, heavy casserole or saucepan, heat the olive oil and 3 tablespoons of butter together over medium heat until the butter has melted and starts to sizzle. Cook the scallion and chopped garlic for 1 minute, stirring so the garlic doesn't burn.

3. Pour the rice into the casserole or saucepan with the salt, stir, coating all the grains, and cook for 2 minutes. Pour in the wine, stirring constantly. Add the chopped shrimp and 1 cup of the shrimp broth. Once the liquid evaporates, pour in another ½ cup of broth. Continue adding broth in smaller and smaller amounts as it evaporates and is absorbed and cook until the rice is between al dente and tender, stirring almost constantly. You will use about 4 cups of the broth. Once it is cooked, stir in the remaining tablespoon butter and some fresh black pepper and serve.

NOTE: Venetian cooks often stir Parmigiano-Reggiano cheese into the risotto as well, but I don't care for this addition.

Makes 4 to 6 servings

Risotto coi Gò (Veneto)

RISOTTO WITH GOBY

Gò *is the Venetian dialect word for* ghiozzi (Gobius venetorium), *or goby, an ugly little fish common in the lagoon and beloved by Venetian cooks as a soup fish.* Gò *has long been a popular fish in Venice. In 1570, Michele Tramazzini published in Venice the cookbook of Bartolomeo Scappi, known as the Secret Chef to Pope Pius V. Scappi describes how the fishermen of Chioggia and Venice would prepare* gò: *they would fry it in oil and then put it into a stew with Malvasia wine, water, vinegar, and "Venetian spices," with a sauce of pomegranates on top.*[139]

The goby in this recipe can easily be replaced with whiting, butterfish, gray mullet, small Pacific kingfish, or porgy (scup) for a nearly identical taste. This famous preparation of the lagoon is a recipe typical of Chioggia. I learned how to make it from my neighbor in Venice, Leila Bussetta, who learned to make it from her uncle, a fisherman from Chioggia. In fact, it is often called risotto a la Ciosota, *meaning* a la chioggiotta *(in the style of Chioggia).*

Gò *is most often used for broths but also mixed fish frys. A famous preparation for Christmas Eve on the island of Burano in the lagoon is a* risi e fasjoi col brodo de gò, *rice and beans with a broth made of* gò. *Gourmets insist that one never serves cheese with this dish, yet the home cook will toss in the Parmigiano-Reggiano without hesitation at the end of the cooking. I prefer the dish without cheese.*

When I first tested this recipe, I was living in Venice. Since gò *is truly eaten only by the Venetians, the fishmonger was quite surprised and pleased when I, obviously an American, asked for* gò *by name in the Venetian dialect. The recipe is a bit involved but rewarding. Another popular fish in Venetian homes is sea bass,* branzino, *and there is a risotto preparation for that fish, too.*

FOR THE BROTH

1¼ pounds *gò* or substitute (see headnote), cleaned and gutted, with heads left on
¼ cup extra virgin olive oil
1 tablespoon unsalted butter
1 garlic clove, crushed
1½ tablespoons very finely chopped fresh parsley leaves
¾ cup dry white wine
5 cups water
1½ teaspoons salt

FOR THE RICE

¼ cup (½ stick) unsalted butter
1 small onion, very finely chopped
1 garlic clove, finely chopped
2½ cups Arborio rice
¾ cup dry white wine
Freshly ground black pepper to taste

1. Wash the fish and pat dry. In a large casserole with a tight cover, heat the olive oil and butter together over medium heat until the butter melts, then cook the crushed garlic until it begins to turn light brown, about 1 minute. Remove and discard the garlic.

2. Add the fish and parsley and cook for 1 to 2 minutes, pushing the fish around to coat it. Pour in ¾ cup of the wine and cook for 1 minute, then add the water and salt. Increase the heat to medium-high, cover, and cook for 20 minutes. Strain the broth through a fine-mesh strainer, discarding the fish and keeping the broth warm in another saucepan.

3. In another casserole (or wash and reuse the first one), melt 2 tablespoons of the butter over medium heat, then cook the onion and chopped garlic until the onion turns translucent, about 4 minutes, stirring frequently so the garlic doesn't burn. Add the rice and cook for 1 to 2 minutes, stirring constantly.

4. Pour in a ladleful (about 1 cup) of the fish broth and add some salt. Once this amount has been absorbed, add the wine until it too is absorbed. Once

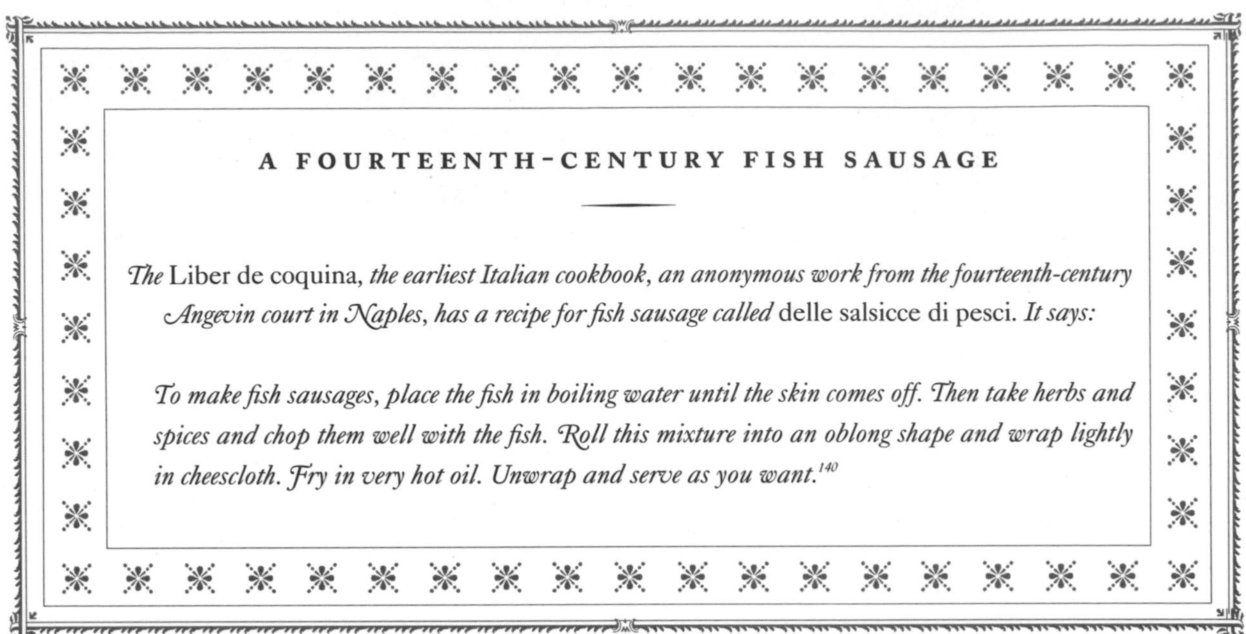

A FOURTEENTH-CENTURY FISH SAUSAGE

The Liber de coquina, *the earliest Italian cookbook, an anonymous work from the fourteenth-century Angevin court in Naples, has a recipe for fish sausage called* delle salsicce di pesci. *It says:*

> *To make fish sausages, place the fish in boiling water until the skin comes off. Then take herbs and spices and chop them well with the fish. Roll this mixture into an oblong shape and wrap lightly in cheescloth. Fry in very hot oil. Unwrap and serve as you want.*[140]

the liquid evaporates, pour in another ½ cup of broth. Continue adding broth in smaller and smaller amounts as it evaporates and is absorbed and cook until the rice is between al dente and tender, stirring almost constantly, about 20 minutes. Stir in the remaining 2 tablespoons butter, sprinkle on the parsley and some pepper, and stir well.

5. Transfer the rice to a serving platter, let it rest for 5 minutes, and serve. The fish, which will have disintegrated in the broth, is not eaten separately. Some Venetians sprinkle a little wine over the rice before serving.

Makes 4 to 6 servings

Fishing off Spain

In the Mediterranean, when one mentions hake one must talk about the Spanish. Although Spain, and Castile in particular, was similar to Sicily in the secondary importance that fish had in the diet and the economy, hake was the most popular of fish.[141] Hake is a gadoid fish (meaning it resembles cod), except it lacks the barbel of the cod and has a long second dorsal and anal fin running from mid-body to the tail fin. Spanish fishermen have caught hake since the fourteenth century, and the Spanish fondness for hake has resulted in a great variety of preparations, as the following recipes demonstrate.

Both the anonymous fourteenth-century Catalan cookbook *Libre de sent soví* and the cookbook of Robert de Nola indicate that some of the typical fish of that time were lamprey, ray, sardine, salmon, eel, moray eel, conger eel, hake, river fish, shad *(sábalo),* sea bass, dentex, gilt-head bream, pandora, red mullet *(salmonete),* meagre *(corvina),* star-gazer *(rata),* bonito, tuna, dried conger eel, salted tuna, langostino, shore crab, cuttlefish, squid, and octopus.[142]

Fishing off Spain was similar to elsewhere in the Mediterranean, with usually two or three men in a small lateen-rigged fishing boat. Generally, they did not cook aboard ship because they were never far from port. But as boats became safer, one does find several dishes that apparently originated on board ship, such as *caldero murciano*.

Caldero Murciano (Murcia)
THE MURCIAN CAULDRON

Caldero murciano, *literally "Murcian cauldron," is an iron cauldron used for cooking on fishing boats. The preparation of* caldero murciano *can be enhanced by looking at the nineteenth-century Spanish painter Joaquín Sorolla's painting* Eating in the Boat *in the Royal Academy of San Fernando in Madrid. Three grizzled fishermen surround a pan under the yawl of their small boat, while three boys (their sons?) eat from the* caldero.[143] *As with many dishes prepared along the coasts of Valencia, Murcia, and Andalusia, the olive oil is first flavored with garlic and* ñoras, *dried red bell peppers. Because of the scarcity of pigs in Murcia in the Middle Ages, most cooking was done with olive oil rather than pork fat.*[144]

Caldero murciana *is eaten in two courses. The fish flavors the broth used to cook the rice. The rice should be a little mushy, like a risotto, and is eaten with a* skordalia *type of mayonnaise sauce (page 501). Then the fish is eaten with its own green garlic sauce. The variety of fish is important for achieving full flavor. I provide a number of possibilities so that you will not be limited by seasonality. My recipe is adapted from Alicia*

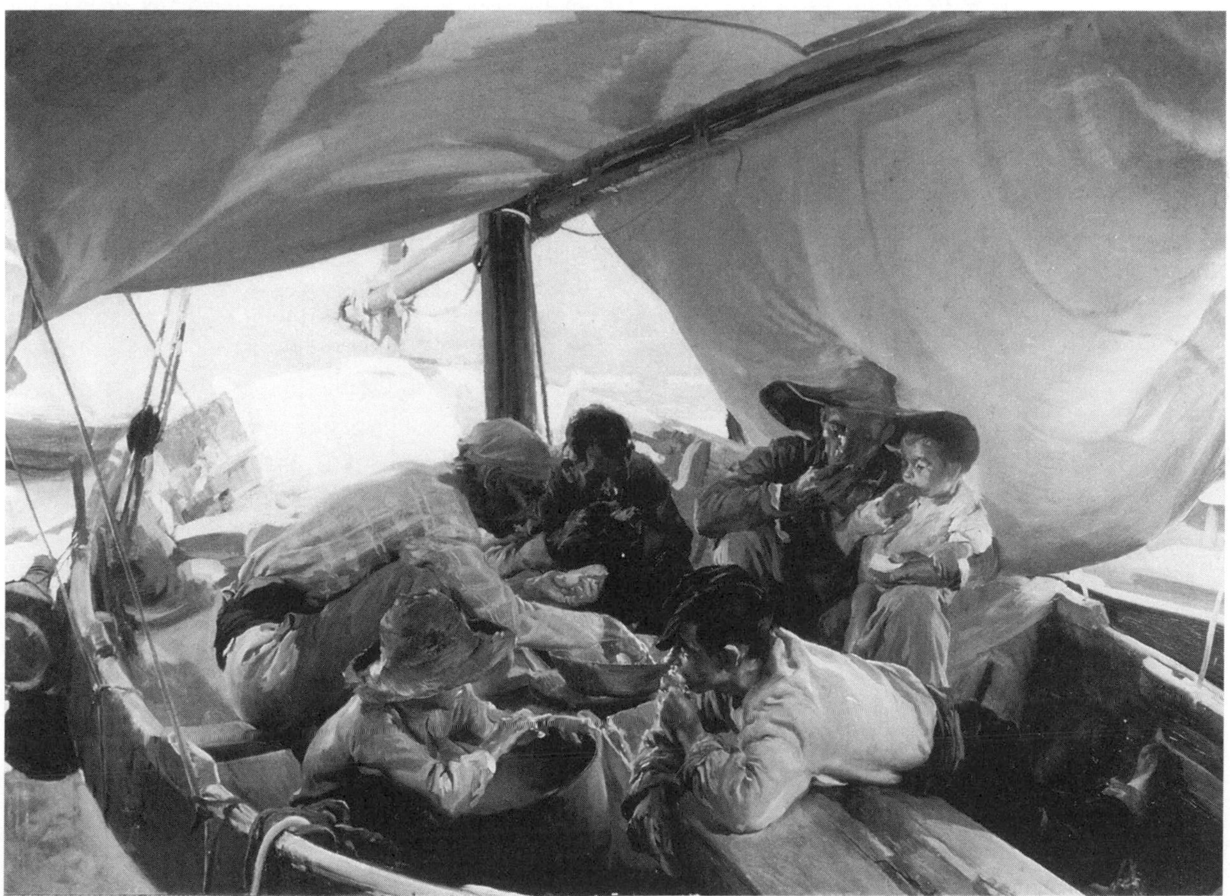

Joaquín Sorolla y Bastida (1863–1923), *Eating in the Boat*. Real Academia de Bellas Artes de San Fernando, Madrid. ALINARI/ART RESOURCE.

Rios and Lourdes March's The Heritage of Spanish Cooking.

1 cup plus 1 tablespoon extra virgin olive oil
3 *ñoras* (page 719)
2 heads garlic
2 ripe tomatoes (about ¾ pound), peeled, seeded, and finely chopped
1 pound gray mullet, porgy (scup), bluefish, or shark fillets
1 pound scorpionfish, red snapper, or redfish (ocean perch) fillets
1 pound sea bass, striped bass, grouper, or monkfish fillets
1½ teaspoons paprika
6 cups boiling water
Salt to taste
1 small boiling potato, peeled and quartered
Pinch of saffron threads, crumbled
2½ cups medium-grain rice
1 large egg yolk
Freshly ground black pepper to taste
3 large garlic cloves, chopped
1 tablespoon finely chopped fresh parsley leaves
Juice from 1 lemon

1. In a large enameled cast-iron casserole or stew pot, heat ¾ cup of the olive oil over medium heat with the *ñoras* and the heads of garlic and cook until the *ñoras* are a little soft, about 12 minutes. Remove one of the *ñoras,* chop, and set aside with 1 head of the garlic.

2. Separate the cloves of the remaining head of fried garlic, peel, put the garlic and the remaining 2 *ñoras* in a food processor, and pulse until the mixture is in tiny particles. Set aside.

3. In a small saucepan, heat 1 tablespoon of the olive oil over medium heat, then cook the tomatoes until soft, about 5 minutes. Remove and set aside.

4. Pat dry the fish with paper towels. Cook the fish in the same oil that the *ñoras* and garlic were cooked in over medium heat for 5 minutes without turning. Pour the processed garlic-and-*ñoras* mixture over the fish. Add the sautéed tomato to the fish. Add 1 teaspoon of the paprika and the boiling water and season with salt. Reduce the heat to medium-low and cook the fish until nearly flaking, about another 10 minutes.

5. Remove the fish with a slotted ladle and reserve, keeping warm. Add the potato quarters to the casserole or pot you cooked the fish in. Cook until soft, about 15 minutes. Remove the potato and set aside.

6. Pass the broth in the casserole through a fine-mesh strainer. Salt if necessary. Remove 1 cup of the broth and set aside, then pour the remaining broth back into the casserole or pot with the saffron. Bring to a boil and add the rice. Reduce the heat to low and cook for 20 minutes, uncovered. The rice should look like a risotto when done (see page 589 on risotto). Keep covered till ready to serve.

7. While the rice cooks, prepare the sauce for the rice. Peel the second reserved head of garlic and crush in a mortar. Add the boiled potato to the mortar and mash well with the garlic. Transfer to a medium-size bowl and slowly pour ½ cup of the reserved fish broth and the egg yolk into the mortar and blend until smooth. While stirring all the time, slowly drizzle in 2 tablespoons of the olive oil until the mixture thickens like mayonnaise. Season with salt and pepper and serve with the rice as a first course.

8. Prepare the fish sauce. In a mortar, pound together the reserved chopped *ñoras,* chopped garlic, and parsley into a paste. Add the remaining ½ cup reserved fish broth, the remaining 2 tablespoons olive oil, the lemon juice, and the remaining ½ teaspoon paprika and season with salt and pepper. Blend thoroughly and serve on the side with the fish as a second course.

Makes 4 to 6 servings

Merluza al Vino (Andalusia)

HAKE WITH WINE

In this preparation from Málaga on the Costa del Sol of Spain, the hake is griddled separately from the sauce. The sauce is made with a panada (a paste of bread and water) sautéed in lard with parsley, garlic, and red pepper, then moistened with white wine. It is excellent with rice. Although hake is probably the most popular Andalusian fish, Professor A. Malpica Cuello of the University of Granada studied and listed the vast variety of fish consumed in the kingdom of Granada at the end of the Middle Ages—there were more than twenty species regularly caught and consumed.[145]

Pure or virgin olive oil for the griddle
2 pounds hake, cut into steaks at the thickest part, each about 1¼ inches thick
3 garlic cloves, peeled
¾ cup loosely packed fresh parsley leaves
3 cups stale ½-inch cubes French bread, white part only, soaked in water and squeezed dry
1 red bell pepper, roasted (page 710), peeled, and seeded
Salt to taste
3 tablespoons pork lard
2 cups dry white wine

1. Preheat a lightly oiled cast-iron griddle over medium-low heat until very hot and the film of oil is smoking a bit, about 20 minutes. Cook the hake until golden, about 10 minutes per side, turning only once. Leave the hake undisturbed as it cooks.

2. Meanwhile, pound the garlic cloves with the parsley, bread, bell pepper, and salt in a large mortar until it is homogenous.

3. In a large skillet, melt the lard over medium heat, then add the panada mixture, pour in the wine, and stir until it dissolves. Check the seasoning. Bring to a boil and continue to boil for 4 minutes. Turn the heat off. Transfer the fish to a serving platter and cover with the creamy sauce.

Makes 4 servings

Merluza en Salsa de Avellanas (Andalusia)

HAKE IN HAZELNUT SAUCE

This recipe from Córdoba seems to show Arab influence with its hazelnuts and delicate flavors, but we can't be sure. The Spanish word for hazelnut, avellanas, *derives from Avellino, the town in the Campania region of Italy that was a major producer and exporter of hazelnuts from the tenth to thirteenth centuries. Medieval gourmets appreciated hazelnuts.*[146] *On board ships, hazelnuts were often reserved for ecclesiastics, who ate better than the crew.*[147] *This recipe is surprisingly quick and easy to prepare.*

6 ounces shelled and peeled hazelnuts (see Note)
1½ cups loosely packed fresh parsley leaves
6 garlic cloves, peeled
About ½ loaf (20 slices) French baguette or Italian bread, toasted
1½ cups dry white wine
½ cup water
2 pounds hake, cut into steaks at the thickest part, each about 1¼ inches thick
Salt to taste

1. In a food processor, grind together the hazelnuts, parsley, garlic, and toasted bread. Transfer to a large bowl.

2. Bring the wine and water to a gentle boil in a large skillet. Reduce the heat to medium-low and

poach the hake until it is firm but not flaking, about 5 minutes. Remove and set aside, keeping warm, and reserve 1½ cups of the broth.

3. Dilute the hazelnut paste with the reserved hake poaching broth, stirring well, and pour it into the skillet with the fish, shaking the skillet to mix. Season with salt and cook until the hake is nearly flaking, another 5 minutes, and serve.

NOTE: If the hazelnuts are not peeled, drop them into boiling water for a few minutes so their peels will come off easily.

Makes 4 servings

Merluza con Almejas (Valencia)

HAKE WITH CLAMS

The twelfth-century Hispano-Muslim tractate on food, the Kitāb al-agdhiya *by Abū Marwān 'Abd al-Malik b. Zuhr, notes that doctors of that era recommended eating fish because, according to the prevailing dietetic theories, fish had a humor that found a natural affinity with man. The most popular Spanish fish, hake, is cooked in a style not far removed from that recommended by 'Abd al-Malik b. Zuhr, who says that the major way to prepare fish is to cook it with some water in an earthenware casserole with olive oil and to finish it with some vinegar and ginger. The cook can add coriander, eggs, and saffron, too, if he or she desires.*[148]

Remember that as flavorful and favorite a fish as it is for the Spanish, hake is also a relatively delicate fish that can fall apart easily, so always handle it carefully when turning or moving. The fried bread is a critical part of this delicious meal.

12 littleneck clams (about 1½ pounds)
1 tablespoon baking soda
3 tablespoons extra virgin olive oil
¼ cup water
1 tablespoon white wine vinegar
1 small onion, finely chopped
Salt to taste
4 hake steaks (about 1¼ pounds)
½ recipe *crostini di pane per le zuppe di pesce* (page 559)

1. Place the clams with the baking soda in a bowl of cold water to cover by several inches and purge for 1 hour. Drain and scrub well with water. Place the clams in a medium-size skillet with 1 tablespoon of the olive oil and the water and turn the heat to high. Cover the skillet and, as soon as the clams open, 10 to 12 minutes, add the vinegar and cook for 1 minute. Remove the clams from their shells. Discard any clams that remain tightly shut. Set the clams and their sauce aside.

2. In large skillet, heat the remaining 2 tablespoons olive oil over medium heat, then cook the onion until translucent, about 5 minutes, stirring occasionally. Lightly salt the hake and cook until it turns color and is imbued with the flavor of onion, about 5 minutes, turning once.

3. Add the clams to the hake, reduce the heat to very low, and cook, uncovered, until the hake flakes, about 30 minutes without turning. Serve with the *crostini.*

Makes 4 servings

Fritture de Pescado (Andalusia)

FRIED FISH PLATTER

Andalusia is known as the land of the fried fish and, for an unknown reason, in documents from the Royal Hos-

pital of Guadix in the late sixteenth century, fritture de pescado *is associated with bandits' food.*[149] *Throughout the region, but especially on the coasts, in cities such as Cádiz or Málaga, one finds the extraordinary Andalusian expertise in frying fish.*

The secret to Andalusian fried fish is threefold. First, the fish must be of the freshest and finest quality. Second, the oil itself should not be too heavy—that is, it should not all be olive oil. Three parts vegetable oil to one part olive oil is ideal. More important is that the oil is clean and hot. Hot means that all the seafood should be cooked at no less than 360°F (you can check the oil with a quick-read candy thermometer if you don't have a regulated home deep-fryer). Remember to let the oil return to 360°F before you cook the next batch of fish. The frying times given here are precise and you really only have a few seconds of leeway, assuming everything is cut the way I describe. This is the way the food fries to a golden orange, cleanly and crisply. Finally, there must be no excess flour on the fish, nor should too many pieces be fried at once.

This recipe is based on the method I observed at the rustic and cozy restaurant Meson Andaluz in Granada. A good combination of seafood to try is swordfish, small shrimp, squid, and fresh sardines (frozen will do; canned will not work). For the amounts of food in this recipe, it may be best to cook in a number of batches. Never should the fryer be crowded, or even remotely crowded, with food. Play it safe and fry as many batches as it takes.

6 cups mixed oil for deep-frying (see above)
Salt to taste
All-purpose flour for dredging
1 pound swordfish, shark, or dogfish steaks, or monkfish fillets, cut into 1-inch cubes
¾ pound medium-size shelled shrimp (about 24)
8 large squid (about 1¼ pounds), cleaned (page 448), bodies cut into ½-inch rings, and tenacles cut off below the eyes and left whole
1 pound fresh sardines, fresh anchovies, or fresh smelt, cleaned and gutted
Lemon wedges for garnish

1. Preheat the frying oil in a deep-fryer or an 8-inch saucepan fitted with a basket insert to 360°F. Preheat the oven to warm (about 150°F). Let all the seafood come to room temperature before frying and season with salt.

2. Pour the flour into a bowl. Toss the swordfish in the flour, dredging well. Transfer the pieces of swordfish to a strainer and vigorously—really vigorously—shake off all excess flour. Carefully place the swordfish pieces in the oil, making sure you are not crowding them, and deep-fry until light golden, about 3 minutes. Remove and keep warm, uncovered, on a paper towel-lined heating tray in the warm oven while you continue frying the other food.

3. Following the method in Step 2, fry the shrimp in batches for 90 seconds, the squid in batches for 2 minutes, and the sardines, two or three at a time, for 3 minutes. Drain well and serve with lemon wedges. Let the frying oil cool completely, strain, and save for a future use.

Makes 4 to 6 servings

Arròs a Banda (Valencia)
SAFFRON RICE AND SEAFOOD

Arròs a banda *is a very old preparation and really quite simple. Traditionally,* arròs a banda *was made on the small* cabotatge, *the coast runners that ran from north to south along the Valencian coast known as the Levante. The boatmen would eat the fish with some hollowed-out pieces of bread. Fishermen also made this dish. As with so many dishes, it begins with a* sofregit, *like the Italian* soffritto, *a mixture of onions, garlic, and other ingredients sautéed in olive oil before the addition of the remaining ingredients; in this case, a rich fish broth is added to be absorbed by the rice.* A banda *means "apart" in Valencian, meaning the rice is served first and apart from the fish, which is served as a second course. It is traditionally served with* allioli, *a pungent garlic mayonnaise (page 513).*

My first taste of arròs a banda *was at the modest seaside Port restaurant on the esplanade of Denia south of Valencia. I later read in Claudia Roden's book* Mediterranean Cookery *that her first taste of this famous Valencian dish was also in Denia at another small restaurant. I read further and discovered that Penelope Casas, author of* The Food and Wines of Spain, *describes her "ultimate" rice dish as being an* arròs a banda, *in Denia, too. I suppose Denia has some extraordinary* arròs a banda.

At a local fish market you would find a variety of shellfish and firm-fleshed fish, so-called soup fish, a category of fish unknown to Americans for the most part. What could be our soup fish is what is considered trash fish by commercial fishermen and retailers and sports fishermen. It is thrown back into the sea as garbage or used for animal feed or bait. For anyone who has seen this form of waste, and who loves fish, it is heartbreaking. In the Denia fish market you might see the rata de mar, *literally sea rat, but with a more appealing and accurate English name of stargazer: the eyes of this fish point directly upward (the Venetians know how to name fish: they call this fish* boche in cao, *mouth-in-the-sky). The* araña *(weever) and* lluerna *(streaked gurnard) are two other small fish found in many Mediterranean fish stews and broths and may be seen along with* gallina *(red gurnard),* salmonetes *(red mullet),* gallo *(fluke), and* rape *(monkfish) that are used in the broth. As for shellfish, clams, crayfish, crab, and shrimp are all popular for flavoring the broth, especially in restaurants. In both this* arròs a banda *recipe and the pasta version,* fideuà al estilo de Gandía *(page 625), the technique called* arrossejat *is used, where either the rice or the pasta is sautéed in olive oil before the addition of any liquid.*

FOR THE CLAM AND FISH BROTHS

12 littleneck clams, scrubbed, purged in cold water to cover with 2 teaspoons baking soda for 1 hour, and drained
¼ cup extra virgin olive oil
1 large onion, chopped
2 large garlic cloves, chopped
3 ripe tomatoes (about 1 pound), peeled, seeded, and finely chopped
5 cups water
1 cup dry white wine
Salt and freshly ground black pepper to taste
Bouquet garni, tied in cheesecloth, consisting of 1 bay leaf, 6 sprigs each fresh thyme and parsley, and 1 teaspoon fennel seeds or 1 fennel stalk with leaves
1½ pounds soup fish—whole fish and fish heads for broth: 2 porgy (scup) or 2 butterfish, and 5 fresh sardines, 1 mackerel, and 1 bluefish or mahimahi head or ½ pound bluefish fillet or mahimahi fillet, cut up
1 pound fresh shrimp, saving the heads and shells (½ pound headless defrosted shrimp)

FOR THE GARLIC MIXTURE

2 garlic cloves, peeled
Pinch of saffron threads, crumbled
1 teaspoon paprika
¼ teaspoon cayenne pepper
½ teaspoon salt

FOR THE FISH

¼ cup extra virgin olive oil
1 small onion, very finely chopped
2 large garlic cloves, chopped
1 ripe tomato, peeled, seeded, and finely chopped
2 tablespoons very finely chopped fresh parsley leaves
2¼ pounds mixed fish steaks or fillets (consisting of ¾ pound monkfish, halibut, hake, cod, scrod, or pollack and ¾ pound striped bass, kingfish, bluefish, Spanish mackerel, dogfish, mahimahi, or shark and ¾ pound red snapper, grouper, redfish, or wolffish)

FOR THE RICE

¼ cup extra virgin olive oil
2 large garlic cloves, lightly crushed

2 dried chili peppers
2 cups medium-grain Spanish rice

1. Put the drained clams in a small pot with 2 tablespoons of the water, cover, and turn the heat to medium-high. Once the clams have all opened, about 6 minutes, remove. Remove the clams from the shells and set aside in the refrigerator. Strain the clam broth through a fine-mesh strainer and set aside. Discard the shells and any clams that remain tightly closed.

2. In a stockpot or large casserole, heat ¼ cup of the olive oil over medium heat, then cook the large onion, garlic, and tomatoes until the mixture looks saucy, 10 to 12 minutes, stirring often so the garlic doesn't burn. Pour in the water, wine, and reserved clam broth and season with salt and pepper. Add the bouquet garni, cut-up whole fish and fish heads, and shrimp heads and shells (keep the shrimp and all other fish refrigerated until 15 minutes before needed). Bring to a boil, reduce the heat to low, and simmer for about 2 hours. Strain the broth through a fine-mesh strainer (you should have about 6 cups).

3. In a mortar, pound together the garlic cloves, the saffron, paprika, cayenne, and salt until completely mashed. Transfer to a 2-cup measuring glass and blend with 1 cup of the fish broth and reserve until step 5.

4. In a large casserole or skillet, heat the ¼ cup olive oil over medium-high heat, then cook the onion, garlic, tomato, and parsley until the onion is soft, about 6 minutes. Add the fish fillets and coat all sides in the mixture, 2 to 3 minutes. Add the reserved fish broth, bring to a boil, and cook for 2 to 3 minutes, shaking the pan occasionally. Add the reserved shrimp and cook for another 2 minutes at a boil, shaking the pan. Remove the fish and shrimp with a slotted ladle, set aside with the reserved clams, and keep warm with a sheet of aluminum foil covering the fish. Strain the fish broth through a fine-mesh strainer, reserving and setting aside 3 cups of it and storing the rest for another use.

5. In a paella pan or large skillet, heat the olive oil over medium heat and cook the crushed garlic and chili peppers until the garlic begins to turn light brown. Remove and discard the garlic and chili peppers. Add the rice and cook, stirring well so the grains are coated with oil, 3 to 4 minutes. Add the reserved fish broth and diluted garlic mixture. Bring to a boil, reduce the heat to low, and cook for 30 minutes, uncovered. There will be an enormous temptation to stir the rice but you must be resolute and absolutely not stir the rice. It must cook undisturbed. Remove from the heat, cover, and let the rice rest until tender, about 15 minutes. Serve the rice first and then the fish, or place the seafood on top of the rice and serve.

Makes 4 to 6 servings

Salmón a la Naranja (Andalusia)

SALMON FILLETS WITH ORANGE SAUCE

In the medieval Hispano-Muslim cookbooks, salmon was called rāʿ, *but it is not a fish mentioned as much as others. The cooking of foods in bitter orange sauce—the juice of the bitter orange the only one known at the time, called the Seville orange today—was a typical Arab method in the Middle Ages. The oranges used in this recipe are the famous Valencia oranges. This dish is a specialty of El Caballo Rojo restaurant in Córdoba. It is a very orange-colored dish because the orange-pink flakes of salmon are enriched by a luscious orange and orange zest sauce that is only slightly sweet. Whether you are making your own fish broth or using bouillon cubes, you can add a salmon head to the broth, if you can get one from the fishmonger; it enriches the broth in a wonderful way. Remember when using bouillon cubes (which I use but am not keen on) that they are quite salty.*

4 Valencia juice oranges
2 medium-size onions, very finely chopped
¼ cup extra virgin olive oil
All-purpose flour for dredging
One 2½-pound salmon fillet, skin removed if desired, cut into 8 strips
2 tablespoons sugar
1 tablespoon white wine vinegar
1 cup fish broth (page 369)
Salt and freshly ground black pepper to taste

1. Remove the peels without the white pith from the oranges and very finely julienne them. Squeeze the juice from the oranges. You should have about 1½ cups. Set both aside.

2. Put the onions and the olive oil in a large nonstick nonreactive skillet and, over medium heat, cook until yellow, about 10 minutes, stirring frequently.

3. Lightly flour the salmon strips, tapping off any excess, and cook them with the onions until they turn color, 4 to 5 minutes, shaking the skillet occasionally.

4. Add the orange juice, sugar, vinegar, and fish broth and cook for 8 minutes over medium heat. Add the very finely julienned orange peel and cook, uncovered, until the sauce is syrupy and the fish tender, about 12 minutes, shaking once in a while. Season with salt and pepper and serve.

Makes 6 servings

Albóndigas de Salmón (Andalusia)

SALMON DUMPLINGS WITH ALMOND AND CAYENNE SAUCE

This recipe has its counterparts in the medieval Hispano-Muslim cookbook known as the Kitāb al-ṭabīkh fī al-Maghrib wa'l-Āndalus *(Cookery book of the Maghrib and Andalusia), such as* al-lūn min al-ḥūt al-kabīr *(dish of big fish), where the flesh is made into balls and cooked with citron juice, garlic, olive oil, vinegar, fennel, cinnamon, dried coriander, cumin, and caraway, among other things.*[150] *Certainly the making of* albóndigas, *meatballs, was known at that time and a typical seasoning was a sauce made of almonds or other nuts. Citrus, especially citron, was used in sauces.*

This recipe is from Córdoba and it can also be made with hake or cod. The dumplings are formed with flour on the hands and will feel soft. They are very light and fluffy tasting before simmering in a smooth almond-flavored tomato sauce.

One 1-pound salmon fillet, skinned
2 large garlic cloves, 1 finely chopped and 1 crushed
½ red bell pepper, roasted (page 710), peeled, and seeded, or from a jar
1 large egg, separated
Salt to taste
All-purpose flour for dredging
6 cups pure or virgin olive or olive pomace oil for deep-frying
2 tablespoons extra virgin olive oil
1 small onion, very finely chopped
24 blanched whole almonds
2 cups tomato puree, preferably fresh
Freshly ground black pepper to taste
⅛ teaspoon cayenne pepper

1. Place the salmon in a food processor with the chopped garlic, bell pepper, and egg yolk and process

until completely blended. Remove to a large bowl and season with salt. Beat the egg white in a small bowl with an electric mixer until it forms stiff peaks, then fold into the salmon mixture. Form the salmon mixture into 8 balls, keeping your hands floured to avoid sticking.

2. Preheat the frying oil to 370°F in a deep-fryer or an 8-inch saucepan fitted with a basket insert. Dredge the salmon balls in the flour. They will feel soft. Tap off any excess flour. Place in the hot oil without crowding and deep-fry until light golden brown, 90 seconds to 2 minutes. Remove to drain on paper towels.

3. In a large skillet, heat the extra virgin olive oil over medium heat, then cook the onion until translucent, whole almonds, and crushed garlic, 6 to 7 minutes, stirring to make sure the garlic doesn't burn. Add the tomato puree, season with salt and black pepper, add the cayenne, and cook until denser, about 10 minutes. Add the fried salmon balls to the sauce and cook for 15 minutes. Serve immediately. Let the frying oil cool; strain and save for a future use.

Makes 2 to 4 servings

El Rape Mozarabe (Andalusia)

A MOZARAB MONKFISH RAGOUT

The first time I tried this dish was at the very popular Córdoban restaurant El Caballo Rojo. They called this dish one of la antigua cocina mozarabe-magribi. *Spanish culinary authority Clara Ma. G. de Amezúa thinks this is all nonsense, claiming that the restaurant never did any research into "old Mozarab-Magribi cuisine" but simply made it all up.*[151] *In any case, this dish, even if invented, is a good example of what any Arab-influenced dish would look and taste like in Andalusia. The fact that this preparation uses cognac does not detract from that statement for two reasons. First, we know that medieval Arabs appreciated good wine and had invented distillation; and second, culinary license must be permitted with inventions. This preparation can also be made with swordfish.*

½ cup extra virgin olive oil
One 2-pound monkfish fillet, cut into 8 pieces
All-purpose flour for dusting
Salt to taste
1 medium-size onion, sliced
1 carrot, sliced
2 tablespoons golden raisins
3 tablespoons cognac
1 cup fish broth (page 369)

1. In a large skillet, heat ¼ cup of the olive oil over medium-high heat. Meanwhile, dust the monkfish with flour and salt, tapping off any excess flour. Cook the fish until lightly golden, about 3 minutes per side, turning only once. Set aside.

2. In a medium-size stove-top casserole, heat the remaining ¼ cup olive oil over medium-high heat, then cook the onion and carrot until softened, about 6 minutes, stirring. Add the monkfish to the casserole along with the raisins and cognac and cover with the fish broth. Reduce the heat to medium and cook until the sauce is thicker, about 15 minutes, adding tablespoons of water if the sauce dries out. Serve immediately.

Makes 6 servings

Anxoves de Cottiliure amb Pebrots Vermells (Roussillon)

ANCHOVIES AND PEPPERS

The anchovies of Collioure, not to mention the bell peppers grown on the terraced hills of the Côte Vermeille in the Roussillon, are as famous today as they were in the Middle Ages, although the peppers were introduced only after the discovery of the New World. I was served this simple preparation at La Café Catalan in Perpignan, and was delighted with the taste as well as the presentation: a simple but very attractively arranged crisscross of anchovy fillets over strips of roasted red bell peppers, sprinkled with parsley and olive oil.

3 large red bell peppers (about 2 pounds)
24 salted anchovy fillets, rinsed
Fresh parsley leaves and finely chopped parsley leaves for garnish
Extra virgin olive oil for drizzling

1. Prepare a hot charcoal fire or preheat a gas grill on high for 15 minutes. Grill the peppers until the skins are charred and blackened, about 40 minutes, or preheat the oven to 425°F and roast until blackened, 40 to 45 minutes. Once the peppers are cool enough to handle, remove the skins, stems, and seeds.

2. Slice the peppers into long, thin strips and arrange them in a crisscross on a serving platter. Arrange the anchovy fillets over the red peppers diagonally. Garnish the edges of the serving platter with parsley leaves and sprinkle the chopped parsley over the peppers. Drizzle some olive oil over the peppers and anchovies and serve.

Makes 4 servings

Pez Espada a la Naranja (Valencia)

SWORDFISH WITH ORANGE SAUCE

This is an instructive recipe both in gastronomic terms and in terms of historical influence. Most food writers assume that many elements of Sicilian food derived from Spanish influence after the expansion of the Aragonese kingdom into Sicily after the defeat of the Angevin in 1282 (see page 495). According to this theory, a Sicilian preparation such as cicirelli all'arancia, *little fish in orange, would be seen as Spanish-influenced. But both Spain and Sicily were under Arab rule during the centuries before the rise of Aragon and at approximately the same time, Arab rule in Sicily ending several hundred years sooner than in Spain. The Islamic civilization of Spain and Sicily had many things in common, including a relatively closely related cuisine. Take, for example, this contemporary recipe from Peñíscola, a small coastal town north of Valencia. It is a very simple recipe that surprises in its good taste. The combination of potatoes and oranges is recognizable in the Valencia region; there is also a salad of potatoes and orange. But the seasoning of food with oranges has as long a heritage in Sicily, as it does in Spain. In the twelfth century, Hugo Falcondis, the historian of the Norman Sicilian kings, wrote of oranges,* arengias, *as flavoring foods. It is known that oranges were regularly sold in the markets of Palermo in 1287, according to documents in the Archivio di Stato di Palermo, one of the first mentions of its appearance in Italy.[152] Cooking fish with orange juice was typical of court cooking in fifteenth-century Italy, and Maestro Martini provides a recipe in his* Libro de arte coquinaria, *probably written in 1450, for sole cooked in orange juice.[153] The original inspiration for using oranges as a food flavoring was Arab, as we see in the* nāranjiyya *of the thirteenth-century Baghdad cookery book.[154]*

The potato puree made for the dish should be quite thick because it will be moistened in the baking by the juices from the swordfish and orange.

3 pounds potatoes
3/4 cup (1 1/2 sticks) unsalted butter, at room temperature
1/2 cup hot milk

Salt and freshly ground black pepper to taste
One 2-pound piece swordfish, cut into 6 slices
2 Valencia oranges, peeled and sliced
Juice from 2 Valencia oranges (about ¾ cup)

1. Place the potatoes in their peels in a large pot and cover by several inches with cold water. Turn the heat to medium and, once the water starts to boil, cook the potatoes until there is no resistance when pierced by a skewer, about 25 minutes. Drain and peel.

2. Push the potatoes through a food mill or strainer into a pot with 8 tablespoons (1 stick) of the butter. With a wooden spoon, beat the potatoes with the butter while slowly adding the hot milk. Season with salt and pepper. The potato puree should be quite thick.

3. Preheat the oven to 350°F. Butter a 9 × 12-inch baking dish and spread the potato puree over the bottom, right up to the sides. Bake for 10 minutes. Remove from the oven.

4. Layer the swordfish slices to cover the potato puree. Salt and pepper the swordfish and place 2 or 3 thin slivers of butter on each slice, using 2 tablespoons of the butter in all. Cover with the orange slices. Cover with a sheet of aluminum foil and place in the oven for 40 minutes.

5. When the baking is nearly completed (when the swordfish feels springy-firm when poked), melt the remaining 2 tablespoons butter in a small nonreactive skillet. Season with salt and pepper, then add the orange juice. Cook over medium heat until it is syrupy, 6 to 8 minutes. Remove the baking pan from the oven, pour the sauce on top, and serve directly from the pan.

Makes 4 to 6 servings

Almejas a la Valenciana (Valencia)

VALENCIA-STYLE CLAMS

The clams favored in Valencian cooking are not actually called clams, but are a variety of bivalves such as cockles (berberechos), *carpet shells* (almejas), *and wedge shells* (coquinas). *This style of cooking clams is popularly served as a tapas in Valencia. Today, the Costa del Sol from Málaga to Marbella is infested with tacky tourist towns. During one of my research trips on the food of coastal Valencia and Andalusia, I decided to base myself in Estepona. It is still hard to find good nontourist food along the coast, but I did make a delightful discovery in the Restaurant Agustino in Torreguadiaro–San Roque on the Cádiz-Málaga road.*

2 pounds littleneck clams
1 tablespoon baking soda
½ cup extra virgin olive oil
2 large ripe tomatoes (about ¾ pound), peeled, seeded, and finely chopped
1 fresh mildly hot green chili pepper, seeded and finely chopped
2 garlic cloves, finely chopped
Salt and freshly ground black pepper to taste
1 tablespoon finely chopped fresh parsley leaves

1. Wash the clams under cold running water, put in a bowl with cold water to cover, sprinkle in the baking soda, and leave for 1 hour. Drain and rinse the clams, discarding any that are open.

2. In a large casserole, heat the olive oil over medium-high heat, then cook the tomatoes and chili pepper until softer, about 4 minutes, stirring often. Add the clams and cook until they all open, about 12 minutes. Discard any clams that remain tightly shut. Once the clams are open, stir in the garlic, salt, pep-

per, and parsley. Serve immediately in bowls with bread to dip in the broth.

Makes 2 servings or 4 as a tapas

✣ ✣ ✣

THE fish caught off Cádiz and nearby fishing villages provisioned the galleons heading for the Indies with salted fish. The Andalusian coasts were known for their bluefin tuna and much of it was salted and exported.[155] The activity of tuna fishing was known as the *almadraba* and has been a part of Andalusian fishing since antiquity. Similar to the Sicilians' development of their tuna fishing industry, the Arabs had contributed to improvements in techniques and netting in Andalusian tuna fishing, the word *almadraba* deriving, in fact, from the Arabic word meaning "the place where the killing (of the tuna) occurs."[156] As in Sicily, every May and June vast shoals of tuna arrived on their spawning run and were driven into nets, clubbed or harpooned, hauled out onto boats, and brought to the processing factories on the coasts where they were cut up, salted, and barreled. The local consumption of fish was as modest as it was in Sicily; and along the Spanish Levante coast fish was prepared in a style favored by fishermen and their boats, cooked *a la marinera* or typically charcoal grilled (griddled).

Merluza de Pincho Fresca a la Plancha (Valencia)

FRESH GRIDDLED HAKE

In Spain, cooking fish on a plancha, *an iron griddle, derives from a time when Valencian cooking was done on wood-burning stoves with a built-in hotplate. This method of griddling fish reminds me a lot of Egyptian fish cookery in Alexandria (see page 402). It requires careful and attentive cooking because of the relative fragility of hake. Any time you see on a Spanish menu that fish is cooked* a la parilla, *it is a grilled fish, while* a la plancha *is griddled fish, as in this recipe. This fresh griddled hake dish, served with a bit of olive oil, lettuce shreds, tomato slices, and fresh peas cooked in a broth with some* jamón serrano, *was perfect at the tidy little Casa Navarro in Valencia.*

Pure or virgin olive oil for the griddle
2 pounds hake, cut into steaks at the thickest part, each about 1¼ inches thick
All-purpose flour for dredging
Salt to taste
4 cups shredded lettuce
2 ripe tomatoes, sliced
4 lemon wedges
Extra virgin olive oil for drizzling

1. Preheat a cast-iron griddle with a light film of oil over medium heat until it is very hot and the film of oil is smoking a bit, about 12 minutes.

2. Meanwhile, dredge the hake in the flour on all sides, tapping off any excess flour, and season with salt. Place on the griddle, reduce the heat to medium-low, and cook without moving or touching until golden brown and blackening slightly, 10 to 12 minutes. Flip carefully with a spatula and cook another 10 to 12 minutes without moving. Check the seasoning and salt the fish a little if desired, and serve on a bed of shredded lettuce and sliced tomatoes, with lemon wedges and a light drizzle of olive oil.

Makes 4 servings

❈ Remolachas con Atún (Andalusia)

BEETS WITH TUNA

The fish most associated with Andalusian cooking is the same as centuries ago—hake, grouper, and tuna. The tuna fishing industry was vibrant but local in the Middle Ages, and most of the catch was preserved in salt or oil. This preparation using tuna in oil is a beautiful maroon color from the beets, and is extraordinarily appetizing. The flavors are enticing and an excellent accompaniment to grilled chicken or fish. Remember that beet juice can stain (the reason it was used as a dye in medieval times), so handle with care around clothing.

10 small beets, trimmed of leaves
One 3½-ounce can imported tuna in olive oil
Salt to taste
¼ cup extra virgin olive oil
2 tablespoons red wine vinegar
2 garlic cloves, finely chopped
1½ tablespoons finely chopped fresh parsley leaves

1. Bring a pot of lightly salted water to a boil and cook the beets whole with a portion of their stems until easily pierced by a skewer, about 20 minutes. Drain and let cool, then peel, trim off the stems and root strands, and dice the beets.

2. Place the beets on a platter and add the tuna with its oil, breaking it apart. Sprinkle some salt, the olive oil, vinegar, garlic, and parsley on top of the beets and tuna. Toss gently, but well, and serve.

Makes 4 servings

Salted Fish

REFRIGERATION and canning had not been invented in the fifteenth and sixteenth centuries, so Mediterranean fishermen had to preserve their catch by salting. Fish was also preserved in brine or in oil, and through smoking and air-drying, but salting was the most common means. The most commonly salted fish were anchovy, eel, sardine, herring, tuna, and tuna eggs in a product called *bottarga* (in Italy) or *poutargue* (in France). Throughout the Mediterranean, a great many products were salted, as we see from the thriving business of salted fish in Languedoc—anchovies and eel—exported from the province of Toulouse, which also exported its prunes and saffron, and imported rice. In Languedoc, anchovies were sold in Narbonne in 1560 and salted eel was transported from Carcassonne to Toulouse, where fifteen hundred salted eel were sold in 1468.[157] All of Toulouse's fish, except for anchovy and eel, came from the Atlantic, the local favorite being *merlus,* hake, just as with the Spanish today. The anchovy and eel were always salted. The commerce in salted fish was profitable because the local packers had access to *le sel narbonnaise,* the salt pans of Narbonne. In January 1424, the buyer for the Archbishopric of Arles went to Ferrières to buy fifty-four salted eel.[158] He could have also bought some locally produced *poutargue,* dried pressed tuna roe.

The salting of fish, mostly sardine and anchovy, was also a major preoccupation along the Croatian coast of the Adriatic. On the west coast of Istria at Isola (Izola), Capo d'Istria (Koper), Pirano (Piran), Rovigno (Rovinj), and on the islands of Lésina (Hvar), Lissa (Vis), and Lagosta (Lastovo), there was an extensive industry of curing of sardine and anchovy, along with, to a lesser degree, mackerel, horse mackerel, and garfish. The fisherman also served as curer and packer. First, he landed the fish and washed them in seawater. Afterward, the fish were packed in small pine boxes, with salt spread between each layer. A weight went on top to press out brine and close up air gaps. This process was repeated until the fish, about fifteen hundred in all, were very compressed.[159]

When a string of bad harvests hit the Mediterranean food supply, coupled with the historically small catch of fish, everyone waited for the arrival of northern grain ships, and increasingly the ships brought salted fish. The discovery of the superabundant Grand Banks off the coast of Newfoundland by fishermen from northern countries, coupled with the poverty of Mediterranean fish stocks, led to a large trade in cod (the most frequently caught fish in the North Atlantic) with the Mediterranean. The large-scale fishing of the Newfoundland banks began as early as the late fifteenth century, although Basque and Irish fishermen were there earlier. In 1598, English ships were docking in Leghorn with 5,613 casks of smoked herring, 268,645 *pesci merluzzi* (cod), and 513 *fardi* (bundles) of *pesci stokfiss* (air-dried cod called stockfish). Salt cod is so well known in Mediterranean countries such as Italy, Greece, Spain, and France that it is hard to remember that virtually all the cod was imported from the North Atlantic.

There are a variety of reasons for this importation. First, of course, is the lack of abundance in the Mediterranean. Although we know that salted fish was exported from Sicily to Palestine in the 1270s, the fish in question was probably herring or tuna and it did not amount to a large trade.[160] Second, the importation of cod increased not only because of Mediterranean demand but also because of favorable trade situations created by the Norwegian famine of 1315–1317. King Haakon of Norway issued an edict on July 30, 1316, permitting the export of stockfish and butter only to those who could import malt, flour, salt, and similar commodities in its place.[161] This northern cod reached Sicily through the port of Trapani. This was necessary because the salt pans of Trapani supplied the northern fishermen with the salt they needed to haul back to the North Atlantic to salt the cod.

Basque, Irish, English, and other northern fishermen had been fishing the waters off Newfoundland from a very early date, but it wasn't until the arrival of countries with the strongest navies that cod fishing became big business. Once the navies of England, Holland, and France entered the fray, the small-time fishermen were pushed out.

The problem faced by open-ocean fishermen of the Middle Ages, after the weather and their fear, was how to preserve the fish in order to get them to market. The solution was immediately to gut the fish on board and pack them in barrels of brine or salt. Alternatively, the fish were dried on land and shipped in that state. The fishing off Newfoundland was especially abundant because of a broad continental shelf and an influx of nutrient-rich water at the sides of the shelf, where spawning takes place.[162] There were light ships, with only twelve fishermen and some more sailors gutting below deck, filling the hold all the way to the bridge with cod. There were also large ships that would salt their cod while still wet, and these were called "green cod." By 1500, thousands of fishermen and seamen were sailing to the Newfoundland banks in a variety of ships and bringing their salt cod either to Brittany, England, Norway, or Holland for shipment or directly to the Mediterranean. Marseilles was a major entrepôt for northern salt cod; it took half of the French catch of dried cod and often reexported it to other parts of the Mediterranean, such as Spain and Greece. Genoa also received a good portion of salt cod.

Sardelle Salate (Veneto)

SALTED SARDINES

Salting fish, especially sardine and anchovy, but also herring and cuttlefish, is an ancient and famed pursuit in Chioggia, at the southern end of the Venetian lagoon. Although it had been wiped out by a tidal wave several centuries before, Chioggia played an important role in the struggle between Genoa and Venice in the late fourteenth century because of its strategic position. The Genoese seized Chioggia and blockaded Venice, a situation entirely unacceptable to the Venetians, who quickly turned the tables and captured the Genoese fleet by 1380. Genoa never again threatened Venetian maritime supremacy. This victory at Chioggia later proved important for Venetian dominance over the rising threat of Ragusa (Dubrovnik) and, later still, the Ottoman Empire.

Salting sardines is not hard, and they can be used in preparations such as bigoli in salsa *(page 268) or* qrīṭfa *(page 653). Finding fresh sardines is more difficult. Before using salted sardines, soak them first in water for at least an hour to eliminate some of the salt. You may even have to soak longer than that if they are hard and stiff from drying. Any recipe calling for salted sardines will work equally fine with salted anchovies, which are readily available in Italian markets. Canned sardines will not work.*

2 pounds fresh sardines
6 to 8 cups sea salt

1. Make an incision along the belly of the sardine from three-quarters down the length of the body to just below the head. Remove the viscera under running water. Wash the sardines well, rubbing off the scales (sardines have very thin, slippery scales that can be rubbed off by hand). Break off the head and save it for making fish broth (page 369).

2. Dry the fish with paper towels and roll them in the sea salt. Place several sheets of paper towels on a wooden board and the sardines on top of the paper towels. Cover with more salt. As the paper towels become wet, change them and add more salt, and continue doing this until the paper towels are completely dry. The best place to leave the sardines as they go through the salting process, a process that should take four to six days, is inside a turned-off oven. When the sardines are completely dry, pack them in coarse salt in an airtight container and store refrigerated.

3. To use, let the sardines soak in water until they are desalted and malleable, anywhere from 1 hour to 2 days. Peel off the fillets and use as the recipe instructs.

Makes less than 2 pounds

Bottarga (Sardinia)

DRIED FISH ROE

Bottarga *is a preparation made of fish eggs in Sardinia and Sicily, but also in Provence and Corsica, as well as Egypt. The method is basically the same: the eggs of either tuna or gray mullet in their ovarian membrane are salted and dried and sometimes pressed into a sausage shape. The final product is dry enough to grate, although crumbly, less dry* bottarga *is fine, too.*

Bottarga *is made commercially and sold in specialty shops in Italy. In Sardinia, home preparation is common and one can find* bottarga *in local* alimentari. *I have seen* bottarga *sold in only a very few select stores in this country and therefore provide this recipe. It is nearly impossible to find tuna roe and, if you do, the cost might be prohibitive (gray mullet is easier to find). Alternatively, ask your fishmonger to save any roe he might find in a large fish such as grouper, dab, halibut, or bonito, and make* bottarga *from this. Examine the roe to make sure the ovarian membrane is not ripped. The bigger the roe, the easier it is to grate once it is dried.*

1 fish roe in its ovarian membrane (1 to 2 pounds), preferably tuna or any other large fish
Extra virgin olive oil
4 cups sea salt

PREPARING SALT COD OR AIR-DRIED COD FOR COOKING

Salt cod products are especially popular in most regions of Italy, France, Spain, and Greece, but curiously nonexistent in the southern Mediterranean, for some reason. The difference between the two cod products, baccalà *and* stoccafisso (*or* stoccofisso), *is that* stoccafisso *is air-dried without salt, as opposed to* baccalà. *From early times, Italy's salt- and air-dried cod has come from northern countries in a trade dating back a millennium. In fact, both Italian words,* baccalà *and* stoccafisso, *probably derive from the Dutch.*[163] *The Italians would trade wine, cloth, and spices, among other things, for salt cod.*

Both cod products are sold with the bone in or out or in chunks. Salt cod is more commonly found in America than stoccafisso *and, being salted, needs soaking in water to remove the salt. Salt cod needs to be soaked in cold water for two to three days, changing the water two or three times a day. Some salt cod products are presoaked and will be so labeled. Any cartilage, bone, or skin can be removed at this point. It is now ready for use in the recipe.*

1. Rinse the roe and pat dry with paper towels. Lightly oil the roe with your fingers and roll in the salt. Arrange the roe on top of several layers of paper towels spread on a wooden board. Place the board with the roe on it inside a turned-off oven. Some people place a heavy weight on top of the roe in order to press it into a rectangular shape.

2. As the paper towels become saturated, roll the roe in more salt on all sides, place them on new paper towels, and return to the wooden board in the oven. Continue until the paper towels remain dry, about 2 days. The roe should be stiff at this time. You can store it refrigerated now or continue drying for another 7 days, using more salt, until the roe is very hard and dry.

3. Wrap the roe, with any remaining salt, in waxed paper and then in a zippered-top plastic freezer bag or plastic wrap. It will keep in the freezer for two years or longer.

Makes about 1 pound

Baccalà alla Livornese (Tuscany)

LEGHORN-STYLE SALT COD

Leghorn (Livorno) was a small village in 1575 when the famous de'Medici family of Florence decided they needed a more reliable port than the one they were using at Pisa. They commissioned an architect to lay out a new city on a grid plan. In gastronomic terms, Leghorn was later renowned for its fish stew, red mul-

let, and salt cod. The cod all came from the North Atlantic and was salted on the fishing ships themselves or on nearby land in Newfoundland, Greenland, or Iceland, while some cod was air-dried in Norway. The trade then shipped the salted cod directly to the Mediterranean or overland through France. In fact, Marseilles absorbed half of the French purchase of dried cod and reexported part of it to Italy.[164] *Salt cod is a popular food along the northern Mediterranean, and after you make this recipe you will see why. All kinds of things can be done with salt cod, ranging from the salt cod with sour cherries recipe of the noted Italian cookbook writer Ada Boni to the batter-fried salt cod with* skordalia *sauce of Greece (page 439).*

If you have any remaining sauce, it can be used with spaghetti or cooked chickpeas. If you desire, and it is quite nice, this dish can be served at room temperature.

1 cup pure or virgin or extra virgin olive oil
1 small onion, thinly sliced
1 large garlic clove, finely chopped
1 large ripe tomato (about ¾ pound), peeled, seeded, and chopped
5 large fresh basil leaves
2 tablespoons finely chopped fresh parsley leaves
Salt and freshly ground black pepper to taste
1 pound salt cod, prepared for cooking (page 436) and cut into 4 × 6-inch pieces
All-purpose flour for dredging

1. In a medium-size casserole, heat ¼ cup of the olive oil over medium-high heat, then cook the onion until translucent, about 4 minutes, stirring a few times. Add half the garlic, the tomato, basil, and 1 tablespoon of the parsley, season with salt (salt lightly because the salt cod might have some remaining saltiness) and pepper, reduce the heat to low, and cook until the sauce is denser, about 20 minutes.

2. Meanwhile, dredge the fish in the flour, patting off any excess. In a large skillet, heat the remaining ¾ cup olive oil over medium heat, then cook the salt cod with the remaining garlic until golden, turning carefully with a fork and spatula, 12 to 15 minutes for thick pieces, 8 to 10 minutes for thinner pieces, and 4 to 6 minutes for very thin pieces. Remove the fish, transfer to the tomato sauce, and cook for 10 minutes. Sprinkle with the remaining tablespoon parsley and serve.

NOTE: Cook the salt cod in batches so you don't crowd the pan. The recipe can easily be doubled.

Makes 2 to 4 servings

Polpette di Baccalà (Sicily)

SALT COD FRITTERS

The first references to baccalà, *salt cod, in Italy date back to the late 1500s, but the idea of frying fish balls* (polpette) *is older. The* Libro de arte coquinaria *of Maestro Martino from about 1450 has several fried fish ball recipes. In one recipe, the unspecified fish is boiled and then pounded with some almond milk, fine flour, sugar, and rose water, formed into whatever shape the cook likes, and is then fried in olive oil.*[165]

These fritters are also found in Languedoc as croquettes de morue, *as well as in Spain.*

1 pound salt cod, prepared for cooking (page 436)
3 large eggs
1 tablespoon golden raisins
½ tablespoon pine nuts
5 tablespoons very finely chopped fresh parsley leaves
1 garlic clove, finely chopped
1 tablespoon very finely chopped onion
Salt and freshly ground black pepper to taste
1½ cups dried bread crumbs
All-purpose flour for dredging
6 cups pure or virgin olive or olive pomace oil for deep-frying
2 cups tomato sauce (page 32; optional)

1. Bring a large pot of water to a boil, add the cod, reduce the heat, and poach at a gentle boil for 15 minutes. Drain well and pat dry, then cut up into chunks.

2. Place the salt cod in a food processor and run until mushy. Beat one egg and add to the fish with a few pulses of the food processor. Transfer the salt cod to a large bowl and mix in the raisins, pine nuts, parsley, garlic, onion, salt, and pepper. Add ½ cup of the bread crumbs, 1 tablespoon at a time, until the mixture has a doughy consistency.

3. Form the fish mixture into croquettes about 3 × 1½ inches, with wet hands so the mixture doesn't stick to them. Beat the remaining 2 eggs together in a shallow bowl. Spread the flour on one piece of waxed paper and the remaining cup bread crumbs on another. Dredge the croquettes in the flour. Dip them in the egg, then roll in the bread crumbs. Let rest in the refrigerator on a plate for 30 minutes.

4. Preheat the frying oil in a deep-fryer or an 8-inch saucepan fitted with a basket insert to 375°F.

5. Deep-fry the croquettes several at a time until golden, 2 to 3 minutes. Drain on paper towels and serve with the tomato sauce, if desired. Let the frying oil cool completely, strain, and save for a future use.

Makes 10 to 12 croquettes

Baccalà Mantecato (Veneto)

"WHIPPED" SALT COD

A curious fact about this preparation is the name. Baccalà *(salt cod) is not used (although it could be), but rather another cod product known as* stoccafisso *(stockfish), air-dried but unsalted cod. This preparation is almost unknown in other parts of Italy. For instance, a fishmonger friend of mine from Gaeta to the south of Rome had never heard of it. But it does appear in Provence, Roussillon, Corsica, and the northern coasts of Spain, as well as in Barcelona, where it is known as* brandada, *and in Languedoc, especially in Nîmes, as* brandade de Nîmes, *the name by which it is most commonly known in the United States. It has been argued that the source for all these varieties of* brandade *is Nîmes, by virtue of the fact that it was an entrepôt for the salt cod arriving from northern countries.*[166]

This Venetian delicacy sounds simple to make but is a bit difficult to get just right. The salt cod or stockfish is reduced to a pulp by whipping and beating, incorporating as much olive oil as one can. Modern methods now beat in milk and even cream.

Mantecato *means "beaten," but one also whisks in the oil. Traditionally, the dried cod was beaten with a stick before it was cooked. You can make this in a food processor, which is most convenient. It is important that the soaked cod be thoroughly drained before beating. Serve the* baccalà mantecato *at room temperature as an antipasto, snack, or party dip. If you serve it as part of a sit-down dinner, it is best accompanied, as with so many other dishes of* cucina venexiana, *with polenta. If you are in Venice you must try the* baccalà mantecato *made by my favorite* salumeria *(delicatessen), Aliani Gastronomia on the Ruga Rialto, 654/655, in San Polo.*

1 pound salt cod *(baccalà)* or air-dried cod *(stoccafisso)*, prepared for cooking (page 436)
About 1 cup extra virgin olive oil or sunflower seed oil
Scant 1 cup milk
1 teaspoon salt
1 garlic clove, peeled
Freshly ground black pepper to taste
1 tablespoon very finely chopped parsley leaves

1. Place the salt cod in a medium-size saucepan and cover with cold water. Bring to a near boil slowly over medium heat, never letting the water come to a boil, then turn off the heat and leave for 20 minutes. Drain very well.

2. Place the salt cod in batches in the food processor, making sure it is dry. Mix the olive oil and milk. Run the food processor and slowly pour in the milk and olive oil. Stop every once in a while and look at the consistency of the salt cod. It should not be stringy; if it is, continue processing. When finished it should look like whipped cream and be a light, fluffy white foam. If there are any solid pieces of salt cod, continue processing.

3. Put the salt and garlic in a mortar and pound together with a pestle until the garlic is completely mashed. Stir the garlic into the salt cod and once the mixture is velvety, season with black pepper and stir in the parsley.

Makes 6 cups

Bakaliaros Tighanitos me Skordalia (Greece)

BATTER-FRIED SALT COD WITH *SKORDALIA*

This preparation is popular everywhere in Greece. A nearly identical preparation of batter-fried salt cod is made in Genoa called baccalà all'aglio, *or* frisciêu *(fritter) in the local Genoese dialect. And the Genoese also have a garlic sauce reminiscent of the Greek* skordalia *derived from the old garlic sauce called* agliata *that has its origins in the* aïoli *of Marseilles (and the* allioli *of Barcelona). In the Greek version of the garlic sauce, the thickening agent is potato while in versions from the western Mediterranean, a panada (a moistened bread mixture) is also not uncommon for thickening the garlic sauce. Although Genoese mercantile companies played a role in medieval Greece, we don't know if the similarity of these culinary preparations is due to that contact or if it is merely serendipitous.*

This recipe comes from the To Meltemi taverna in Methóni, known as Modon in the Middle Ages when it was a major Venetian naval station. It was excellent and quite nice with French fries, too (page 61).

One 1-pound piece salt cod, prepared for cooking (page 436) and cut into 4 pieces
2 cups all-purpose flour
1½ cups water
1 teaspoon baking powder
Salt to taste
2 cups pure or virgin olive or olive pomace oil for frying
1 garlic clove, crushed
A few drops of fresh lemon juice
1 cup *skordalia* (page 515)

1. Place the salt cod in a large skillet filled with water, slowly bring the water to just under a boil, and simmer for about 30 minutes. Remove carefully with a spatula and drain the salt cod well. Let cool.

2. Meanwhile, make a thin batter with the flour, water, baking powder, and salt. In a medium-size skillet, heat the olive oil with the crushed garlic over medium-high heat until the garlic just begins to turn light brown. Remove and discard the garlic. Continue heating the oil until it is about 370°F, using a quick-read thermometer.

3. Dip each salt cod piece in the batter, let the excess drip off, and place in the hot oil, not more than two pieces at a time, until golden, about 2 minutes per side, turning with long tongs so the oil doesn't splash. Remove, squirt a few drops of lemon juice on each, and serve with warm *skordalia*. Let the frying oil cool completely, strain, and save for a future use.

Makes 4 servings

Arròs amb Bacallà i Manxego (Catalonia)

RICE WITH SALT COD AND *MANCHEGO* CHEESE

This recipe from Barcelona is also popular in the Balearic Islands, where we know it has a history from the eighteenth-century cookery book of Jaume Martí i Oliver.[167] *It is ideally prepared in a paella pan, but any large pan will do. The rice is delicately flavored with the spices, seafood, and vegetables; it is not a strong dish. Similar to the Persian love of the crusty bottom layer of rice known as* tah-dig, *Catalonian gourmets prize this crusty rice, which they call* socarrat. *My recipe is adapted from one given to me by Éliane Thibaut-Comelade, who has helped me with my research on Catalan cuisine.*

1⅓ cup plus 2 tablespoons extra virgin olive oil
1 large onion, finely chopped
2 green bell peppers, seeded and cut into small squares
2 pinches of saffron threads, crumbled
2 cups fish broth (page 369)
½ pound salt cod, prepared for cooking (page 436) and cut into 2-inch squares
6 garlic cloves, finely chopped
1 tablespoon finely chopped fresh parsley leaves
1 cup medium-grain Spanish rice
¼ to ½ teaspoon ground cinnamon, to your taste
Salt and freshly ground black pepper to taste
24 mussels, scrubbed, debearded, steamed (page 719), and removed from their shells
½ cup freshly grated *manchego* cheese (substitute pecorino)
1 bay leaf
2 large eggs, beaten
Eight ¼-inch-thick slices French bread, crusts removed

1. In a paella pan or any other large pan, make a *sofregit* (see *soffritto,* page 285) by placing ⅓ cup of the olive oil in the pan with the onion and green peppers, turn the heat to medium, and cook for 30 minutes, stirring occasionally. Meanwhile, steep the saffron in the fish broth.

2. Add the salt cod, garlic, and parsley to the *sofregit* and cook for another 5 minutes, mixing well. Pour in the rice and stir. Cook for 3 minutes, stirring to coat all the grains. Preheat the oven to 375°F.

3. Pour the fish broth into the pan and season with the cinnamon, salt, and pepper. Stir to mix well and add the mussels, 2 tablespoons of the cheese, and the bay leaf. Cook for another 5 minutes. Mix again carefully, increase the heat to high, and cook for 5 minutes.

4. Remove the pan from the burner and cover the rice with the beaten eggs, then a layer of the remaining 6 tablespoons cheese, and finally the slices of bread. Baste the bread slices with the remaining 2 tablespoons olive oil and place in the oven, uncovered, until the top is golden, about 15 minutes. Serve immediately.

Makes 4 servings

Octopus, Squid, and Cuttlefish

SALT cod was an item of trade, imported into the Mediterranean. Octopus, squid, and cuttlefish, on the other hand, were rarely items of trade and were usually consumed locally.

Octopi are eight-armed cephalopods that feed mainly on crabs and lobster, although some are plankton feeders. They live in holes and crevices in rocky areas offshore. The arms of the octopus bear two rows of suckers that have great holding power. At the point where the arms meet, at the center, is a mouth with a pair of sharp beaks that are used for drilling shells and scraping away flesh. The octopus propels itself either by taking water into its mantle and expelling it through a short funnel or by crawling along the sea bottom with its suckers. When it is endangered, the octopus ejects an inky substance that screens its retreat and which, in some species, produces paralysis of the sensory organs of the attacker. The octopus also has highly developed pigment-bearing cells and can change its skin color to an astonishing degree with great rapidity. The octopus is considered the most intelligent of invertebrates.[168] The most typical method of catching octopus was by using a cage contraption that allowed the octopus to enter the chamber, which was baited, but would not let it exit.

Perhaps the popularity of the octopus in Mediterranean cuisines has to do with what it feeds on, or perhaps its intelligence, or simply its taste. In any case, octopus is most popular in Italy, Greece, and Tunisia, and to a lesser degree in Provence and Spain.

In France, octopus is not eaten frequently although it seems to have an old history. In the fish tariff listings of 1182 in the Municipal Archives of Toulouse, there is a mysterious product called *assegia*, which may be octopus.[169] Octopus is still somewhat mysterious in coastal Languedoc and Provence; one almost never comes across it. But in Sète there is a wonderful and rare preparation that I fear is on the edge of extinction. In Aegean waters, abundant squid and octopus have resulted in diverse preparations, and this is true too in the Mezzogiorno and Sicily and across the Sicilian Channel in Tunisia, as the following recipes demonstrate.

Tielle de Poulpe Sètoise (Languedoc)

OCTOPUS PIE FROM SÈTE

The fishing of octopus has always been a secondary activity on the Golfe du Lion, where Sète is a small but important port. We know that octopus was caught on this coast and shipped to Toulouse in the fourteenth century. There are a few extant octopus recipes from the Middle Ages, and one I'm familiar with is an octopus stuffed with mint, parsley, and other herbs found in the anonymous fourteenth-century Catalan cookbook Libre de sent soví.[170]

This recipe from Sète I first tasted in Cap d'Agde, a small, rather pleasant seaside resort in the Hérault department of the Languedoc. Today it is notable as the site of the Quartier Naturisme, a nudist city of about ten thousand people. This delicious tielle, *made in an earthenware pan about five inches in diameter of the same name, is a spicy octopus ragout clothed in a sweet wine-flavored pastry dough. The wine-colored crust glistens golden because of an egg yolk-and-tomato paste glaze. Down the road from Sète, in Bouzigues, a similar preparation is made with mussels and is called* chausson de moule.

FOR THE PASTRY

2 to 2¼ cups unbleached all-purpose flour
3½ ounces pork lard
¼ cup sugar
¼ teaspoon salt
¾ cup sweet red wine

FOR THE STUFFING

1½ pounds octopus, cleaned (page 444)
2 tablespoons red or white wine vinegar
2 tablespoons extra virgin olive oil, plus extra as needed
1 medium-size onion, finely chopped
4 garlic cloves, finely chopped
2 pounds ripe plum tomatoes, peeled, seeded, and crushed
Salt and freshly ground black pepper to taste
¾ teaspoon cayenne pepper
1 teaspoon dried thyme
1 bay leaf
Pork lard or butter for greasing the tart pan

FOR THE GLAZE

1 large egg yolk
1 teaspoon tomato paste

1. In a cold, large metal bowl, work 2 cups of the flour, the lard, sugar, and salt together with your fingers or a pastry cutter until it is pebbly and well blended. Alternatively, pulse in a food processor and then transfer to a cold metal bowl. Add the wine and knead until you have a supple dough, adding more flour if the dough is sticking. Form the dough into a ball, wrap it in waxed paper, and leave in the refrigerator for 2 hours.

2. Put the octopus in a large pot of boiling salted water with the vinegar and boil until tender, about 45 minutes. Drain, rinse with cold water, and peel as much of the skin off the octopus as you can while it is still hot. Chop the octopus into smaller than bite-size pieces.

3. In a large skillet, heat the olive oil over medium heat, then cook the onion, garlic, and octopus until the onion is soft, about 8 minutes, stirring frequently. Add the tomatoes and season the sauce with salt, black pepper, cayenne, thyme, and bay leaf. Reduce the heat to medium-low and let the sauce simmer until the water is evaporated, 1¼ to 1½ hours, stirring occasionally.

4. Preheat the oven to 350°F.

5. Remove the dough from the refrigerator and roll out thin. Cut out sixteen 5-inch disks. Lightly grease eight 4-inch tart pans with lard or butter and cover each with a disk of dough. Prick the dough all over with a toothpick. Spread several tablespoons of the tomato-and-octopus stuffing over it. Cover with the remaining disks and pinch down the edges so they meet the bottom disk. Pinch off any excess dough. Prick the top with a toothpick. Whisk together 2 or 3 drops of olive oil with the egg yolk and tomato paste and brush on the top crust.

6. Bake until a glistening golden, about 30 minutes. Remove the tarts from their pan, arrange on a serving platter, and serve.

Makes 8 servings

Poulpe Rouille (Languedoc)
POTATO AND OCTOPUS SALAD WITH *ROUILLE*

This recipe is from Aigues-Mortes, a medieval walled town in Languedoc, once a port before silt accumulation cut off its access to the sea. The town was founded by Louis IX as an embarkation port for transporting and supplying the Crusades and the merchants who benefited from this trade. By 1270, it was an important port for thriving trade relations with Syria and Palestine. The Aigues-Mortiennes merchants operating in the Levant had a significant enough presence to ask the Muslim authorities for a concession to establish a quarter for themselves in Acre in Palestine as the Venetians had.[171] *Jacques Coeur, Charles VII's (1403–1461) finance minister, was also a merchant who ran a trading link with the Levant from Aigues-Mortes, the aim of which was independence from the Venetian monopoly of trade with the Levant.*[172] *But the town's fortunes changed, and by the sixteenth century Aigues-Mortes had become a little ghost port, buried in the Camargue, infested with mosquitoes and afflicted with a high rate of unemployment. It was also the site of a vigorous scheme of rural land development. Because of its lengthy sunshine, deep soil, and access to water, Aigues-Mortes was an important place for the growing of grain, with its granaries kept nearly bursting, and was a good place to store the spices and bales of cotton that were major items of trade from Egypt and the Levant.*[173]

Maybe this delicious salad was not invented in Aigues-Mortes, but one can find it made expertly there. This octopus and potato salad is mixed with a variation of the rouille *used with bouillabaisse. In the Tarragona province of Catalonia, one finds a* pop estofat amb patates, *a dish that combines octopus and potatoes but without the mayonnaise.*[174] *This recipe yields servings for a big group of people but can easily be cut in half if desired.*

1 recipe *sauce rouille* (page 514)
2½ pounds octopus, cleaned (page 444)
4 pounds new Yukon Gold or red potatoes
1 teaspoon good-quality white wine vinegar
½ teaspoon very fine salt
½ teaspoon very finely ground white pepper
½ teaspoon cayenne pepper

1. Prepare the *sauce rouille.*

2. Put the octopus in a pot and cover by 6 inches of water. Turn the heat to medium-high and boil until tender, 2 to 2½ hours. Drain, rinse with cold water while rubbing off the skin, then slice thin and let cool.

3. Place the potatoes in a large pot and cover with water by 3 inches. Turn the heat to high and boil until the potatoes are slightly resistant to piercing by a skewer, 35 to 40 minutes, then drain, let cool, and quarter with their skin on.

4. Mix 1 cup of *sauce rouille* and the vinegar, salt, white pepper, and cayenne. Toss the mixture with the octopus. Add the potatoes a little at a time and continue to add the remaining *rouille* until it is used up, along with the potatoes, folding in the *rouille* gently so you don't break the potatoes too much. Serve immediately, or refrigerate until ready to serve, but serve at room temperature.

Makes 8 to 10 servings

Polpo in Purgatorio (Abruzzi)
OCTOPUS IN PURGATORY

In the cuisine of the Abruzzi region of Italy, a couple of dishes are known as being cooked in purgatorio. *Generally, these dishes are characterized as food surrounded—in this case octopus, but sunny-side up eggs as well—but not covered by a tomato sauce. These dishes are so called because they are not as hotly spiced as is typical with much of the local cooking. Purgatory, as you may remember, is, in Roman Catholic belief, a state where souls who die with the grace of God go for a time because they have not been cleansed of venial sins. Perhaps we can be guided to an interpretation of this style of cooking by considering the Purgatory of Dante's* The Divine Comedy. *Is a dish* in purgatorio *like a terrace in the climb toward the Earthly Paradise? Or is it a dish that merely piques the appetite as Dante's soul was when* l'anima mia gustava di quel cibo che, saziando di sé, di sé asseta *(My soul tasted that food which, even as it quenches hunger, spurs the appetite)?*[175]

This recipe from the Abruzzi is derived from the one taught to me by the late proprietor of the A. V. Ristorante Italiano in Washington, D.C., Augusto Vasaio, a dedicated culinary traditionalist who prepared "off-the-menu" Abruzzi specialties from his hometown of Pescara for loyal customers. One of my favorite dishes was this octopus stew. The whole octopus swam in a rich, dark broth, and one cut off slices of tentacles and dipped crusty bread into the broth. It was a heavenly dish. This recipe is similar to one made in Vasto, a little farther down the coast, and the Neapolitan specialty called polpo alla Luciana. *Across the Adriatic the Corfiots are also fond of octopus and they make a sumptuous* htapothi yahni, *octopus stew.*

6 tablespoons extra virgin olive oil
3 garlic cloves, finely chopped
¼ cup finely chopped fresh parsley leaves
1 dried chili pepper, crumbled, or ¼ teaspoon red pepper flakes
1¾ pounds octopus, cleaned (page 444)
2 cups fresh or canned tomato puree
Salt to taste
½ recipe *crostini di pane per le zuppe di pesce* (page 559)

Place the olive oil, garlic, parsley, and chili pepper or pepper flakes in an enameled cast-iron casserole with a heavy lid. Turn the heat to medium and, after 4 minutes, stirring occasionally, add the octopus and tomato puree and season with salt. Bring to a gentle boil and immediately reduce the heat to very low. Stir and cover the casserole with a sheet of aluminum foil, pinching the edges down. Cover with the lid. Simmer for 2 hours. Shake every once in a while so the octopus doesn't stick and do not raise the lid until the 2 hours are up, no matter what the temptation. Serve with the *crostini*.

Makes 2 to 4 servings

Polpo alla Luciana (Campania and Apulia)

OCTOPUS STEW

This octopus stew is named after a section of Naples called Santa Lucia, where an old seafood market exists. The area is also noted for its view of Mount Vesuvius and its seafood restaurants lining the quay and a style of old Neapolitan cooking from cucina povera, *the cooking of the poor. In fact, many restaurants describe their cooking as having the* antichi sapori di Napoli, *old flavors of Naples. The nearby Castel dell'Ovo (Castle of the Egg) is of Norman origin, and the octopus caught in the bay would be tenderized by being beaten against the jetty rocks. The stewing of octopus is an old style in central and southern Italy, and there are several early recipes in medieval Italian cookbooks, including one in the early fifteenth-century cookbook known as* Libro A *of the Anonimo Meridionale, called* brodecto di sipie o de polpe.[176]

Among Mediterranean peoples I believe octopus is most favored by the Greeks, but it is also popular in Tunisia, as well as Campania and Apulia. In fact, Carol Field draws our attention to an octopus festival held the last Sunday in July in Mola in Apulia.[177] *The Neapolitans insist on* Octopus vulgaris, *which they call* polpi verace *or "true" octopus, with its two rows of suckers on the tentacles. Nearly all the octopus available to Americans today are these "true" octopus, much of which is imported, already cleaned, from the Philippines and often to be found in the frozen food sections of supermarkets. Canned octopus will not work in this recipe.*

If you have caught your own octopus, it must be cleaned. Turn it upside down and, with a knife, gut it by removing the eyes, head viscera, and small bone (a kind of "beak") in the center. Beat it against a boulder or sidewalk, vigorously and continuously, for 5 minutes to tenderize. In addition, an excellent way to further tenderize octopus is to freeze and unfreeze it once it's been beaten.

Another way to serve this dish is to slice the octopus when it is done, sprinkle the parsley and garlic over it, and return it to the tomato sauce. The bottom portion of a couscousière, *called a* makfūl *in Tunisia, is ideal for making this preparation (see Step 3, page 670).*

2½ pounds octopus, cleaned (see above)
2 tablespoons coarse sea salt
2 cups water
6 garlic cloves, chopped
2 dried chili peppers, crumbled, or ½ teaspoon red pepper flakes
½ cup finely chopped fresh parsley leaves
1 pound ripe plum tomatoes, peeled, seeded, and chopped
Freshly ground black pepper to taste
7 tablespoons extra virgin olive oil
3 tablespoons fresh lemon juice
Salt to taste

1. Clean and tenderize the octopus, if necessary, otherwise put the octopus in an enameled cast-iron casserole or the bottom portion of a *couscousière*. Dissolve the sea salt in the water and cover the octopus

with it. Add half the garlic, the chili peppers or flakes, 2 tablespoons of the parsley, and the tomatoes and season with black pepper. Add more water to cover if necessary.

2. Cover the casserole with a sheet of aluminum foil, pinching down the edges so steam will not escape. Cover with a tight-fitting lid and cook over very low heat for 2 hours. Do not lift the lid. Shake the casserole every once in a while to mingle the flavors and keep the stew from sticking.

3. Meanwhile, prepare the sauce by mixing the olive oil, the remaining garlic, the remaining 6 tablespoons parsley, and the lemon juice and seasoning with salt and pepper. After 2 hours remove the octopus, drain, and slice thinly. Pour the sauce over the octopus and serve.

Makes 4 servings

Polpi sott'Aceto (Apulia)

PRESERVED OCTOPUS

Although not all Mediterranean cultures fancy octopus, the ones that do have a preparation similar to this one, preserved with vinegar and oil. We don't know how old this preparation might be, although Pliny (A.D. 23–79) wrote extensively about the behavior of octopi and there is at least one octopus recipe in the cookbook of Apicius. In the anonymous fourteenth-century cookbook from the Angevin court in Naples, the Liber de coquina, *a recipe for octopus instructs to boil it and then eat it with salt and cumin.*[178]

In Greece, they like their octopus in vinegar, as do Turks along the Mediterranean coast with their ahtapot salatasi, *octopus in olive oil, vinegar, and parsley.*

1 small octopus (about 1 pound), cleaned (page 444)
6 tablespoons white wine vinegar
2 teaspoons finely chopped fresh mint leaves
2 garlic cloves, finely chopped
Salt and freshly ground black pepper to taste
1 cup extra virgin olive oil

1. Wash and clean the octopus if it has not already been done. Put the octopus in a pot and cover with water and add 2 tablespoons of the vinegar. Bring to a boil, reduce the heat to medium-low, and simmer, covered, until tender, about 1½ hours. Drain and wash well in cold water, peeling off the skin if desired.

2. Once the octopus is cool, slice thin and dry by tamping with paper towels. Place in a bowl, toss with the mint, garlic, and the remaining 4 tablespoons vinegar, and season with salt and pepper. Place in a jar and cover with the olive oil. Leave for 48 hours before using. If always covered with olive oil, replenished as you consume the octopus, it will last for several months in the refrigerator. Serve at room temperature as an antipasto.

Makes 2 cups

Yakhna bi'l-Akhṭabūṭ (Tunisia)

DJERBAN-STYLE OCTOPUS STEW

This octopus stew is a specialty of the island of Djerba, where the octopus men catch them using special contraptions made of a series of chambers from which the octopus cannot escape. The traps seem to be a Greek invention because the ancient method of catching octopus in Tunisia during the Roman era, as we know from the octopus mosaic from Dougga in the Bardo Museum in Tunis, was by spearing with a trident. This stew is traditionally cooked in an earth-

enware marmite *that sits atop an earthenware brazier filled with lump hardwood coals. This preparation is octopus as you've never had it: hot, spicy, and luscious.*

1 pound octopus, cleaned (page 444)
6 tablespoons extra virgin olive oil
1 medium-size onion, chopped
3 large garlic cloves, sliced
2 tablespoons tomato paste
7 cups water
1 tablespoon *harīsa* (page 523)
½ teaspoon freshly ground caraway seeds
½ teaspoon cayenne pepper
1 teaspoon freshly ground black pepper
3 cups canned or fresh crushed tomatoes
2 cups peeled, seeded, and diced pumpkin, butternut, turban, or acorn squash (about ½ pound)
Salt to taste
½ cup drained cooked chickpeas

1. Put the octopus in a medium-size pot of water to cover, bring to a gentle boil, and cook for 40 minutes. Drain and, when cool enough to handle, rub off the skin, then cut up into dice-size pieces.

2. In a *marmite* or the bottom portion of a *couscousière* or other deep stew pot, heat the olive oil over medium-high heat, then cook the onion and garlic, stirring frequently so the garlic doesn't burn, until the onion is translucent, about 6 minutes. Add the tomato paste dissolved in 1 cup of the water, the *harīsa,* caraway, cayenne, and black pepper. Stir and cook, covered, for 5 minutes, stirring or shaking the pot occasionally. Add the crushed tomatoes, pumpkin or squash, octopus, and the remaining 6 cups water, season with salt, and boil for 20 minutes. Add the chickpeas and continue cooking until the stew is thick and everything tender, 45 minutes to 1¼ hours. Correct the seasoning and serve.

Makes 4 servings

Oktapodi sta Karvouna (Greece)

GRILLED OCTOPUS

The earliest representation with which I am familiar of what appears to be a Greek octopus trap is from a cup interior attributed to the sixth-century B.C. *Athenian vase painter known as the Ambrosios Painter, held by the Boston Museum of Fine Arts. A naked boy perches on a rock holding a fishing pole in one hand, a creel in the other, and below the water line is an octopus trap luring the nearby octopus.*[179] *In Greece, grilled octopus is typically made during Lent because of the proscription against eating of meat. Properly cooked octopus can be as tender as scampi, and as delicious.*

One 2- to 3-pound octopus, cleaned (page 444)
1 cup white wine vinegar

FOR THE MARINADE
½ cup extra virgin olive oil
1 cup dry white wine
1 teaspoon dried oregano
2 bay leaves
10 black peppercorns
Salt to taste

FOR THE GARNISH
Extra virgin olive oil
Dried oregano
1 lemon, cut into wedges

1. Wash and clean the octopus if this has not already been done. Put the octopus in a medium-size nonreactive pot, cover with water, and add the vinegar. Bring to a boil, reduce the heat to medium-low, and simmer, covered, until tender, about 1½ hours. Drain and wash well in cold water, peeling off the skin.

A naked boy holds a fishing pole in one hand and a creel in the other; below the waterline is an octopus trap luring the nearby octopus. Ambrosios Painter (510–500 B.C.), Greek, Athenian. 01.8024. View: interior.

MUSEUM OF FINE ARTS, BOSTON. HENRY LILLIE PIERCE FUND.

2. Place the whole octopus in a large, deep bowl. Mix the marinade ingredients and pour into the bowl. Place in the refrigerator and marinate, covered, for 24 hours, turning occasionally.

3. Prepare a charcoal fire or preheat a gas grill on medium for 20 minutes. Place the octopus on the hot grill and cook for 8 to 10 minutes per side, basting all the time with the marinade. Remove to a serving platter, drizzle some olive oil over, sprinkle with oregano, and garnish with lemon wedges. Serve immediately or at room temperature.

Makes 4 meze *servings*

SQUID and cuttlefish, along with the octopus, are cephalopods, a class of mollusks (Cephalopoda) with a siphon tube under the head, a group of strong arms around the head with suckers on them, highly developed eyes, and a sack of inky fluid ejected for defense or camouflage. Both squid and cuttlefish make excellent eating, and they have been renowned in the Mediterranean since classical Greek times. The main difference between the two is explained on page 450. Fernand Braudel called dried squid a providential food for the Greek archipelago.[180]

The culinary uses of squid and cuttlefish have a long history in the Mediterranean. Historically, they were never expensive. The price of cuttlefish in the fish market of Venice in 1465 was five *soldi* for a hundred while one turbot cost four *soldi*.[181] They also appear prominently in several fourteenth-century cookbooks, such as the Catalan *Libre de sent soví,* where there is a recipe for *cípies* (cuttlefish) and *calemàs* (squid), and in two Italian books. In the *Liber de coquina,* a cookery book from the Angevin court in Naples, there are several recipes for cuttlefish and squid, including a recipe calling for the cuttlefish to be cooked in the juice of bitter oranges. In the anonymous Tuscan cookery book the *Libro della cocina,* a recipe specifically instructs the cook on using the ink for cooking purposes.[182]

Seppie con Carciofi (Campania)
CUTTLEFISH WITH ARTICHOKES

This seemingly unusual mixture of a cephalopod with the cultivated artichoke actually has a deeper history than is commonly known. The Papacy, which considered Sicilian King Frederick II the Antichrist, found his

CLEANING CUTTLEFISH AND SQUID

Because cuttlefish are messy to work with, make sure your work area is uncluttered, clean, and easy to clean up. Lay the cuttlefish down with the tail pointing toward you. The cuttlefish has an oval-shaped calcified shell that is bone-hard and functions similarly to the plasticlike quill (technically called a chiton) inside a squid. Have this bone side closest to the table, with the "stomach" side facing up toward you. Grasp the body with one hand and, with the other hand, pull out the head, tentacles, and any viscera that attach to it. Cut the tentacles off below the eyes, wash, and set aside.

Slit the belly from top to bottom using a small, sharp paring knife, making sure you don't cut all the way through, which could damage the ink sac. The cuttlefish will be black with ink, but you will not yet have located the sac. Now push the bone through and remove. With your hands, begin to separate the skin from the body and discard all the skin. Rip the body down the middle where you have slit the cuttlefish—carefully, because you don't want to have the ink sac burst on you (although it's not that *fragile).*

The ink sac can be pulled out with your hands. It is a very tiny, narrow white sac with a tube running down. Carefully grab the tube, separating it from the body with your fingers, and pull the sac out, separating it from the surrounding tissue by using your fingers. The ink sac is covered with a white musclelike tissue and will be surrounded on either side by eggs if a female. Don't throw away the white egg sacs; they are a delicacy and can be cooked as directed on page 451.

Remove the mouth, a kind of beak, in the center of the tentacles by popping it out with your fingers. Clean the cuttlefish under cold running water, pulling off all the skin and any other gelatinous-looking tissue. When the cuttlefish is cleaned it will be completely white.

Squid are cleaned in a similar manner, although their skin is easier to pull off but their ink sacs are much harder to work with because they are such small animals.

son Manfred not much more to their liking when Frederick died in 1250. In 1262, Pope Urban IV, in order to undercut the Hohenstaufen claim to the Sicilian crown (the Hohenstaufens were Swabians originally from Germany, who came to rule Sicily in the late twelfth century), offered the crown under papal suzerainty to Charles of Anjou, the brother of French King Louis IX, known in history as St. Louis. Charles invaded southern Italy and defeated Manfred at Benevento in 1266, a day deeply mourned in Sicily. This ended any possibility of a native Italian ruler (Frederick II and Manfred were Italian born) and the hated French took over Naples, Campania, and most of southern Italy. The court of the House of Anjou was in Naples, and the Angevin dynasty lasted until 1435, when the crown, after long diplomatic intrigue and occasional wars, passed to the Aragonese.

It was at the Angevin court in Naples that some of the very first developments in European Mediterranean cuisine arose. At the end of the thirteenth century, an unknown chef wrote for the court the Liber de coquina. *In this manuscript is a recipe called* de sipia *(about cuttlefish) that describes cuttlefish being boiled first, then fried in oil and served with soft vegetables or* salsa verde *(green sauce).*[183] *Here, then, is a modern version that might not be too far removed from the historical* de sipia.

This recipe is a delight whenever artichokes are in season. The flavorings are aromatic and surprisingly complementary in a dish that can also be made with squid. Keep the artichoke hearts in a bowl of cold water acidulated with lemon juice or vinegar while you work to keep them from discoloring.

4 pounds cuttlefish or squid with tentacles, cleaned (page 448) and sliced into rings or strips
2 garlic cloves, finely chopped
2 tablespoons extra virgin olive oil
Salt and freshly ground black pepper to taste
6 salted anchovy fillets, rinsed and mashed into a paste
2 cups dry white wine
6 fresh artichokes hearts, sliced (from about 2½ pounds whole artichokes; see page 122 for preparing them)
1 tablespoon finely chopped fresh parsley leaves

1. Toss the cleaned and sliced cuttlefish or squid with the garlic. In a large skillet or casserole, heat the olive oil over medium-high heat, then cook the cuttlefish or squid, garlic, salt, pepper, and a few tablespoons of water so the garlic doesn't burn until the cuttlefish or squid looks rubbery, 4 to 5 minutes, tossing frequently.

2. Add the anchovies and stir until they have melted. Pour in the wine and reduce to 3 tablespoons, 35 to 40 minutes. Reduce the heat to low and pour in enough water, about 2 cups, to cover the cuttlefish (if using squid, remove with a slotted ladle at this point and reserve until needed). Add the artichoke hearts and cook until the cuttlefish and artichokes are tender, about 1½ hours (after 1¼ hours, add the reserved squid if using). Sprinkle on parsley and then serve immediately.

Makes 4 servings

Seppie Nero alla Veneziana (Veneto)

VENETIAN-STYLE CUTTLEFISH IN BLACK SAUCE

The cooking of cuttlefish in its own ink is a method that goes back at least to the fourteenth century, as we know from an early cookery manuscript where it is cooked with leeks, garlic, and spices to "look like mushroom," which you will recognize when you make this recipe.[184]

The slender squid is a graceful creature when swimming, while the cuttlefish is a stockier-looking cephalopod with thicker meat. Some people have suggested that the timid nature of the cuttlefish accounts for its excellent taste because it is caught relatively motionless and has not had a chance to emit any chemicals associated with fright. However, I am not an ichthyologist so I can't comment on the validity of this theory. Cuttlefish were caught in nets without effort, keeping their ink, and probably it was these fishermen of early Venice who began to use the ink. Choose the smallest cuttlefish available.

The same preparation is made in Chioggia, at the southern end of the Venetian lagoon, without garlic. I must say that cuttlefish appears to be the most popular seafood in Venice; the largest displays at the Rialto fish market are always the cuttlefish. Cuttlefish is usually available around the Christmas season in the United States, especially in ethnic neighborhoods. The recipe can be made with squid, but it just isn't the same, not to mention how difficult it is to get a squid ink sac. Serve with hot polenta (page 615).

4 pounds cuttlefish, cleaned (page 448; save the ink sacs) or squid (see "Mediterranean Food Products Resources" for sources of packaged squid ink)
½ cup extra virgin olive oil or sunflower seed oil
1 medium-size onion, very finely chopped
4 large garlic cloves, very finely chopped
¼ cup very finely chopped fresh parsley leaves
Salt and freshly ground black pepper to taste
2 cups dry white wine
¼ cup tomato sauce (page 32; optional)

1. Prepare the cuttlefish and cut into ½-inch squares.

2. In a large casserole, heat the oil over medium-low heat, then cook the onion and garlic until the onion is translucent, about 10 minutes, stirring frequently so the garlic doesn't burn. Add the cuttlefish and parsley and season with salt and pepper. Continue cooking until the cuttlefish looks rubbery, about 20 minutes, stirring frequently.

3. Squeeze the ink sac into the wine (see page 448 for details about the cuttlefish ink sac) and pour the wine mixture a little at a time into the casserole over the next 10 minutes, adding it whenever the sauce looks like it is drying out. Cook until the cuttlefish is tender, about another 40 minutes, stirring occasionally. Add the tomato sauce if desired and stir. Serve immediately.

Makes 4 servings

Risotto Nero (Veneto)

BLACK RISOTTO WITH CUTTLEFISH

Risotto nero *is a renowned dish of Venetian cuisine where tiny strips of cuttlefish and rice are cooked with a rich fish* fumetto. *The rice is cooked until it is* all'onda, *wavelike, an expression in the culinary language of Venice derived from the proto-risotto preparation of the late Middle Ages, when rice was always cooked as a runny but thick* minestra, *soup, rather than the risotto we know today. Capping this dish the cook squeezes the ink out of the ink sac, stirring it into the rice. I had first tasted a heavenly* risotto nero *at the pleasant Trattoria "da Romana" on the lagoon island of Burano, and knew exactly what kind of taste I wanted to achieve in my own kitchen.*

Early in the morning I left my apartment in Cannareggio, near the Church of San Giovanni Crisostomo in Venice, heading for the Rialto fish market. Normally, I conferred with my friend Francesca Piviotti or our downstairs neighbor Leila Bussetta before leaving to get some ideas about what to buy. One day they were out and I walked to the market on my own. The Rialto fish market is a fish lover's dream, with table after table loaded with all kinds of interesting and fresh fish and crustaceans. Seppie, *cuttlefish, is a Venetian favorite, and many of the tables were covered with these large squidlike cephalopods, dirty looking from their ink. I bought several small cuttlefish, learning later from Leila that I should have bought the big ones—the ones about two pounds each. The smaller cuttlefish are not only more expensive but also harder to use because the ink sac is smaller; they are usually used for grilling. But the taste was the same when I made it again with the larger one.*

This famous dish is difficult to prepare only in that you need to be willing to learn a little about cuttlefish anatomy; locating the ink sac can prove difficult. I think you will be well rewarded for a rare presentation and taste that on the face of it doesn't sound good and looks a bit strange (because the rice will become completely black), but is truly an exquisite taste. Incidentally, squid is not used in this traditional preparation, only cuttlefish. Cuttlefish, which differs from squid by being squatter looking, with thicker meat and a calcified internal shell instead of the squid's chitonous support, is sometimes sold fresh in the U.S. around Christmastime in Italian markets, and more likely in the frozen foods section. If you can't find cuttlefish, then, of course, you can use squid.

The fish broth is quite important; it should be freshly made (page 369). Many Venetians use gò *(page 419) for this broth. Some traditionalists insist that finely chopped beet greens be used instead of parsley. When the rice is finished, it should be served only in a white bowl, making sure you don't blacken the rim. A single leaf of parsley or a single small square of red pepper makes for a beautiful garnish.*

The Catalonians have their own black rice, which they call arròs negre. *Theirs is made with a variety of ingredients, which can range from sweet red peppers to saffron to shrimp to mussels. But in these matters* de gustibus non est disputandum *(taste is not open to dispute), although I follow La Serenissima.*

¼ cup extra virgin olive oil
2 tablespoons unsalted butter
1 small onion, very finely chopped
2 garlic cloves, very finely chopped
2 tablespoons very finely chopped parsley leaves or beet greens
1 to 2 cuttlefish (about 2 pounds in all), cleaned (page 448) and finely chopped (reserve the eggs, if any, and ink sac, page 724 and "Mediterranean Food Products Resources") or 1 pound cleaned squid
½ cup dry white wine
6 to 7 cups fish broth (page 369)
Salt to taste
1 cup Arborio or Vialone rice
1 tablespoon tomato sauce (page 32) or puree
Freshly ground black pepper to taste

1. In a heavy casserole or saucepan, heat the olive oil and butter together over medium heat until the butter has melted and starts to sizzle. Cook the onion, garlic, and 1 tablespoon of the parsley or beet greens until the onion is soft, about 6 minutes, stirring frequently, so the garlic doesn't burn. Add the cuttlefish and cook for 1 minute, then pour in the wine, stirring. Reduce the heat to medium-low and cook the cuttlefish until tender with a little bite to it, 45 to 50 minutes, stirring when needed and adding up to a cup of fish broth if necessary to keep it from drying out. Season with salt.

2. Add the rice when the cuttlefish has just a bit of a bite to it and stir, mixing well, cooking for 1 minute. Add the tomato sauce or puree and another cup of the fish broth. Once the liquid evaporates, pour in another ½ cup of broth. Continue adding broth in smaller and smaller amounts as it evaporates and is absorbed. Cook the rice about 20 minutes before you squeeze the ink out of the reserved ink sacs into the rice and mix well. There will be less than 1 teaspoon of ink from both sacs, but that is more than enough to completely blacken the rice. Continue cooking the rice until it is between al dente and tender, stirring almost constantly. When the rice is done, after about 30 minutes of total cooking time, stir in the remaining tablespoon parsley or beet greens and some black pepper and serve.

Makes 4 servings

Uova di Seppie sott'Olio (Veneto)

CUTTLEFISH EGGS PRESERVED IN OLIVE OIL

Venice has long been in love with the cuttlefish. Uova di mare *are the egg sacs of cuttlefish, harvested in the spring from female cuttlefish. They are shaped like chicken eggs with little golden tails. They are very popular in Venice in May, although never found in restaurants and mostly prepared in homes. Cuttlefish freeze well, as do squid, so save them and then prepare the fol-*

lowing recipe. Save the oil and seasoning when you are done to flavor a plate of steaming pasta.

Uova di seppie *make a very nice* passatempo, *or what the French call an* amuse-gueule *or* amusement, *a small tidbit served before appetizers with drinks. In Venice another popular preparation is* moscardini sott'olio, *baby octopus preserved in sunflower seed oil, but at eighteen dollars a pound in 1992, I didn't try them very much when I lived there.*

Salt to taste
8 cuttlefish eggs, washed in cold water (to prepare cuttlefish, see page 448)
Salt to taste
1/4 cup sunflower oil
2 garlic cloves, very finely chopped
1 tablespoon very finely chopped fresh parsley leaves
Freshly ground black pepper to taste
1 tablespoon fresh lemon juice

1. Bring a pot of salted water to a boil and drop the cuttlefish eggs in. Reduce the heat so the water is rolling gently. Cook for 5 minutes, then drain.

2. When the cuttlefish eggs reach room temperature, salt lightly and cover with the oil, garlic, parsley, pepper, and lemon juice. Serve or place in a jar, top it off with more oil, and refrigerate for up to a couple of months, always replenishing the oil so the eggs stay covered.

Makes 4 to 8 servings

Seppie "aô Zimin" (Liguria)

CUTTLEFISH AND BEET GREENS IN *ZIMINO* SAUCE

Zimino *is a kind of sauce used in Liguria and as far south as coastal Tuscany to cook* seppie *or* totani *(cuttlefish) or calamari (squid). The Ligurian dialect word* zimin *or* zemín *(from which* zimino *derives) can mean any sauce in which foods are cooked or a broth used to cook fatty meats. Strictly speaking,* zimino *once referred to salt cod* (baccalà) *cooked with Swiss chard or beet greens or a fish sauce. The etymology is obscure, but some linguists have made a case that the word derives from the Arabic* samīn, *meaning "fat, or something buttery."*[185]

Some indication of this recipe's possible Roman origins is indicated by the fifteenth-century recipe of Platina, the famous Renaissance chef, whose recipe called de sepia *is reminiscent of Apicius, calling for boiled cuttlefish to be seasoned with asafetida, black pepper, cinnamon, ground coriander seeds, fresh or dried mint, egg yolk, vinegar or verjuice, and olive oil.*[186]

For readers who have encountered the zimínu *found in Sássari, Sardinia, it is not related; it is another kind of preparation composed of donkey offal grilled on an open wood fire.*

1/2 pound beet greens or Swiss chard, leaves only, heavy stems removed
6 tablespoons extra virgin olive oil
1 medium-size onion, finely chopped
2 tablespoons finely chopped celery
2 garlic cloves, finely chopped
2 pounds cuttlefish or squid, cleaned (page 448) and cut into finger-shaped pieces
Salt to taste
1 cup dry white wine
1 tablespoon tomato paste
1/2 cup water
1 dried chili pepper
Freshly ground black pepper to taste

1. Place the beet greens in a large saucepan with just the water clinging to it from its last rinsing. Turn the heat to high, cover, and cook until it wilts, turning a few times, 4 to 5 minutes. Drain in a colander, squeeze the water out with the back of a wooden spoon, and chop. Set aside.

2. In a large casserole, heat the olive oil over medium-high heat, then cook the onion, celery, and

garlic until the onion is translucent, about 4 minutes, stirring so the garlic doesn't burn. Add the cuttlefish or squid, season with salt, and cook for 10 minutes. Pour in the wine, the tomato paste dissolved in the water, and the chili pepper, stir, and cover. Cook until tender, about 45 minutes (30 minutes if using squid), stirring occasionally.

3. Add the beet greens, correct the seasoning with salt and black pepper, stir, cover, and cook for 10 minutes before serving.

Makes 4 servings

Kalamarakia Tiganita or *Marides Tiganita* (Greece)

FRIED SQUID OR FRIED WHITEBAIT

The satisfying small-fry and squid that are so simply cooked in olive oil are a ubiquitous preparation in Greece and most of the coastal Mediterranean. Fry, *meaning "young fish," derives from the Old Norse, while* fry, *"to cook," derives from the Sanskrit through the Greek and Latin. Interestingly, Greek food writers, while claiming all kinds of false provenance for other foods, neglect to mention that* kalamarakia tiganita *and* marides tiganita *do indeed have a classical history. The first mention I am familiar with for fried squid is found in Aristophanes' (455–388 B.C.) play* The Acharnians, *where there is the tortuous image of a dish of sizzling squid being pulled away from the hungry Choregus.*[187] *We also know from Athenaeus that fried squid, although not as common as boiled squid, was eaten.*[188]

The key to frying the tiny whitebait, as well as the squid cut into rings, is to maintain very hot frying oil and to lightly flour the seafood. Coating the fish with bread crumbs, although popular because it's crunchy, diminishes the taste of the seafood by being too heavy.

6 cups pure or virgin olive or olive pomace oil for deep-frying
2 pounds squid, cleaned (page 448), bodies cut into rings, and tentacles cut off below the eyes, or 2 pounds whitebait
All-purpose flour for dredging
Salt to taste
Lemon wedges for garnish

1. Preheat the frying oil in a deep-fryer or an 8-inch saucepan fitted with a basket insert to 375°F.

2. Dust the squid rings and tentacles or whitebait with flour so they are fully coated. Vigorously shake off all excess flour and deep-fry in batches without crowding until golden, about 2 minutes for the squid and 1 to 2 minutes for the whitebait. Test the first batch to see whether you should cook the next batch less or more. Salt as soon as the fish are removed from the oil, drain, and keep warm on paper towels while you cook the rest. Serve with lemon wedges. Let the frying oil cool, strain, and save for a future use.

Makes 4 servings

Kalmār Maḥshī (Tunisia)

STUFFED SQUID FROM DJERBA

In 1560, Djerba grew figs, pears, apples, prunes, apricots, citron, oranges, barley, sorghum, lentils, fava beans, and chickpeas.[189] *The Djerbans had always had a fishing industry, but the fish was for local consumption, and the squid and octopus that inhabited the shores around the island and the continental shelf past Sfax to the north were much appreciated in local cuisine, grilled, fried, or stuffed and braised.*

This delicious prepration from Djerba can be made with cuttlefish (shubay *or* shubya) *or squid* (mantiq *or* kalmār). *When I ate it in Djerba, the cook stuffed the squid with tiny bits of lamb liver, rice, chopped squid, and onions. At the al-Medouia restaurant in the medina of Tunis, I had it again with peas and carrots in a rich tomato sauce. Any leftover stuffing is quite nice mixed with scrambled eggs or in an omelette, a frittata-like preparation that the Tunisians call* maᶜqūda.

½ cup extra virgin olive oil
8 squid (about 2 pounds), cleaned (page 448)
1½ teaspoons unsalted butter
½ cup medium-grain rice, rinsed well or soaked for 30 minutes in water to cover and drained
2½ to 3 cups water
½ teaspoon salt
5 tablespoons finely chopped onion
6 tablespoons finely chopped fresh parsley leaves
4 large hard-boiled eggs, shelled and diced
3 tablespoons freshly grated Parmigiano-Reggiano cheese
Freshly ground black pepper to taste
1 medium-size onion, grated
3 tablespoons tomato paste
2 cups water
4 garlic cloves, finely chopped
1 to 2 teaspoons *harīsa* (page 523), to your taste
½ teaspoon freshly ground cumin seeds

1. In a small skillet, heat 1 tablespoon of the olive oil over medium heat, then cook the tentacles and tail fins of the squid until their liquid has evaporated, 18 to 20 minutes. Chop fine and set aside.

2. In a medium-size heavy saucepan with a heavy lid, melt the butter over medium heat, then cook the rice for 1 to 2 minutes, stirring. Pour in ½ cup of the water and the salt and bring to a boil, then reduce the heat to very low. Cover and cook until the water is absorbed and the rice tender, 15 to 20 minutes. If the rice is still somewhat hard, add ½ cup of boiling water and continue cooking.

3. Transfer the rice to a large bowl and stir in the chopped squid, chopped onion, parsley, hard-boiled eggs, and cheese. Season with salt and pepper and toss to blend. Stuff the mixture into the squid bodies with a small demitasse or baby spoon, making sure you do not stuff too tightly, otherwise the squid might burst when cooking. Close the opening with a toothpick.

4. In the bottom part of a *couscousière* or in a stew pot, heat the remaining 7 tablespoons olive oil over medium heat, then cook the stuffed squid with the grated onion until slightly golden, 6 to 8 minutes, stirring occasionally. Add the tomato paste dissolved in the 2 cups water, the garlic, *harīsa*, and cumin and season with salt. Add water to barely cover the squid if necessary. Bring to a gentle boil, then reduce the heat to very low, cover, and simmer until the squid is cooked and firm, about 40 minutes.

5. Remove the squid from the sauce and keep warm on the side. Increase the heat to high and reduce the sauce until thicker, about 8 minutes. Serve the squid with the sauce on the side or in a bowl with both.

Makes 4 servings

Kalmār Aṣbān (Algeria)

STUFFED SQUID

The Algerian town of Bejaïa, with its modest fishing industry, was a base for Barbary corsairs at the beginning of the sixteenth century, and their activities attracted the Spanish, who attacked the town in 1509. Farther to the west, in the Kabylia, the mountains come right down to the water. There are sheltered bays that once provided refuge for the pirate ships and small fishing villages such as Ziama Mansouria that today have small catches, including squid, which are stuffed. This Algerian version of stuffed squid can be served with baṭāṭis mirḥya, *potato puree (page 63), or boiled rice stirred with butter.*

½ cup medium-grain rice, rinsed well or soaked for 30 minutes in water to cover and drained
2 cups water
¼ teaspoon salt
2½ tablespoons unsalted butter
10 squid (about 1½ pounds), cleaned (page 448)
⅔ cup extra virgin olive oil
1 large onion, very finely chopped
3 large ripe tomatoes (about 1½ pounds), peeled, seeded, and finely chopped
Salt and freshly ground black pepper to taste
6 tablespoons very finely chopped fresh parsley leaves
2 large egg yolks beaten with 2 tablespoons water
1 garlic clove, very finely chopped
½ teaspoon powdered or very finely crumbled bay leaf
¼ teaspoon cayenne pepper

1. Place the rice, water, salt, and ½ tablespoon of the butter in a medium-size saucepan and bring to a boil. Reduce the heat to a simmer, cover, cook exactly 10 minutes, and drain. Set aside.

2. Cut off the tentacles of the squid just below the eyes and chop finely. In a large skillet, heat ⅓ cup of the olive oil over medium-high heat, then cook the tentacles, onion, and one of the tomatoes until some liquid is evaporated, about 10 minutes, stirring frequently. Season with salt and pepper and stir. Add the rice and parsley and stir again, mixing well. Cook for 2 minutes, stirring. Remove the skillet from the heat and transfer the stuffing to a medium-size bowl. Stir in the egg yolks. Let this mixture cool.

3. Stuff the squid three-quarters full with this mixture and secure the opening with a toothpick.

4. In a large stove-top casserole, heat the remaining ⅓ cup olive oil over medium-low heat, then cook the stuffed squid until slightly golden on all sides, about 5 minutes. Season with some salt and pepper, the garlic, powdered bay leaf, and cayenne pepper, add the remaining tomatoes and cook until slightly dense, another 15 minutes.

5. Preheat the oven to 350°F. Place the casserole in the oven with slivers of the remaining 2 tablespoons butter on top of each squid and bake until the butter is melted and the sauce very hot, about 15 minutes. Serve hot.

Makes 4 servings

PIRATES

The Barbary Corsairs

THE great Spanish and Turkish empires were breaking up by the beginning of the seventeenth century, and the Age of the Armada, fleets of a hundred or more heavily armed but cumbersome three-masted galleons, was drawing to a close as faster ships were built. War in the Mediterranean was so expensive that bankruptcy was the usual consequence of victory *or* defeat. The annual upkeep of a galley in 1560 was six thousand ducats, equal to the cost of construction. The great navies couldn't continue forever, and as they retreated from the Mediterranean the vacuum was filled by pirates. Replacing Istanbul, Madrid, and Messina as the capitals of naval warfare were Leghorn (Livorno), Pisa, Algiers, and Malta. Leghorn played an important role as a port for stolen goods that otherwise would have rotted in Barbary ports.

The most celebrated of Mediterranean sailors, if we overlook the famous explorers like Christopher Columbus, were the Muslim pirates, known as the Barbary corsairs. The Barbary corsairs operated off the coast of North Africa (the Barbary Coast) from many different ports and bases, although Algiers was the nominal capital of the Barbary kingdoms. The pirates had wealthy backers who outfitted their vessels and received 10 percent of the prize. Later they were backed by the Ottoman Empire during its struggles with the Christian Mediterranean. The Barbary corsairs used mostly galleys until a Flemish renegade, Simon Danser, taught them to use sailing ships in the seventeenth century.[190] Their favorite ship became the brigantine, a two-masted sailing ship with square rigging on the foremast and lateen rigging on the mainmast.

Piracy had long been a respectable occupation on the North African coast, but it gained in political importance in the sixteenth century when the pirate Barbarossa (Khayr al-Din), a renegade Greek admiral in the service of the Turks, united Algeria and Tunisia as pirate states under the Ottoman sultanate and derived his income from piracy. The favorite hunting grounds of the Barbary corsairs were the waters off Sicily and Naples. Dragut, the most dangerous corsair who lurked in these waters, was a Greek adventurer in the service of Barbarossa and the Turks. He also preyed on Sicilian wheat and captured men for slaves. The Christian Mediterranean made numerous vain attempts to smash the Barbary corsairs, including the expedition of the Holy Roman Emperor Charles V in 1538, which was destroyed by Barbarossa in the Battle of Prevesa off the Albanian coast, securing for the Ottoman navy the control of the eastern Mediterranean. The Christian powers never succeeded in crushing the Barbary corsairs, and as late as the early nineteenth century, a young American navy was tangling with these pirates from the "shores of Tripoli."

Pirates were sea robbers making their daily bread, often literally. If they did not return with food, there was famine. The interdiction of food shipments by Muslim and Christian pirates was considered a respectable activity. Because wheat was a prime target of the pirates, there grew a clandestine land and sea commerce in grain used for bread or *galettes* to avoid this piracy.[191]

Western pirates—that is, Barbary pirates—were based for the most part in Algiers. In the 1560s, pirates were operating off Gaeta and Corsica and were active as far north as the Languedoc, Provence, and Ligurian coasts. The Duke of Savoy was nearly captured by pirates near Villefranche in June 1560. During the same June, stocks of grain and wine in Genoese warehouses ran low because ships from Provence, Corsica, and elsewhere feared putting to sea as long as the pirate threat existed. The pirates plundered everywhere—in Catalonia, Andalusia, and Sardinia. Between 1560 and 1565, the Barbary pirates ruled the western Mediterranean, which saw a near halt to shipping. Finally, there was so little prey that the pirates began heading into the Atlantic as far as Iceland and even Newfoundland.

Algiers' existence depended on the success of the pirates, for there was no other industry there. But make no mistake—this wasn't an anarchic city but rather a disciplined city-state with a judicial system and a caserned army. The port had a lighthouse, solid ramparts, and defense works. In Algiers, ships found the skilled labor, caulkers, gun founders, and carpenters needed to repair and build their vessels. They could find sails and oars (perhaps stolen from other ships) and a market for stolen goods. In the early sixteenth century, the city was a cosmopolitan place of Italians, Berbers, Arabs, Andalusians, renegade Turks, and Greeks. Food and trade circulated in and out of the city. Some of it came from the Sahel with its beautiful gardens while the rest came from caravans and ships, stolen or bartered. Algiers became an important trading port, particularly with the development of the agricultural area in the Mitidja. These plains surrounding the town provided livestock, milk, butter, beans, chickpeas, lentils, melons, cucumbers, poultry, and pigeons. Algiers became rich with perfumes from Spain, woolens from Marseilles, and olive oil and other foods from Djerba, such as figs, pears, apples, prunes, apricots, citron, oranges, barley, sorghum, lentils, fava beans, and chickpeas that were shipped throughout the Mediterranean.[192] We can imagine the harbor of Algiers teeming with pirate and merchant vessels, camels resting in front of the great city gate, the Bab Azoun, and colorfully attired seamen, with their flowing robes in the Ottoman style, enjoying the cooking of food pirated from other ships. Algiers was a luxurious town in the Italian fashion, which in the Middle Ages meant a city of ostentatious good living and, with Leghorn on the Tuscan coast, one of the richest towns of the Mediterranean.

In 1618, Algiers was an extremely wealthy city. The pirate fleet consisted of thirty-five galleys, twenty-five frigates, and a number of brigantines and barks. There were people from everywhere, including twenty thousand captives, and even a few Japanese. There were so many foreigners in Algiers that even a poor Calabrian fisher-boy turned pirate, calling himself ʿUluj ʿAlī, was king of Algiers from 1560 to 1587. Algiers was more Italian than is generally thought, and that fact may have had some influence on the local cooking, although there is no evidence one way or another. The city dominated the entire Mediterranean, its ships plundering as far east as Alexandretta (Iskenderun) in today's Turkey and west past Gibraltar, reaching Iceland in 1627 and England in 1631.

The Christian Pirates

THE Barbary corsairs weren't the only pirates of the Mediterranean. There were Christian pirates operating in the same seas as the Muslims. Christendom's Barbary Coast was in Leghorn and Malta, which had their slave markets and cutthroats. Braudel said it best: "It was not only in Algiers that men hunted each other, threw their enemies into prison, sold or tortured them and became familiar with the miseries, horrors and gleams of sainthood of the 'concentration camp world': it was all over the Mediterranean. Privateering had little to do with either country or faith, it was a way of making a living."[193] The Christian pirates had their own version of Algiers in Malta. Besides piracy, there was a traffic in ransoms that proved profitable. Exchanging prisoners and captured goods led to another kind of commerce that found Tabarka on the northern Tunisian coast, along with Algiers, the active headquarters. These prisoners and escapees would convert back and forth between Islam and Christianity, depending on who captured them. It was a strange world with a colorful group of characters as ransom dealers. There were the Italian renegades who ran the business in Istanbul while Corsican sailors did so in Algiers. French consuls had a monopoly in Tunis, and Jews acted as middlemen everywhere.

Christian pirates also operated along the Dalmatian coast, in the Greek archipelago, and off Valencia and Catalonia in Spain. The pirates along the Dalmatian coast always provided Venice with problems. The Turks entered the Adriatic and seriously increased their activity by establishing bases in the Albanian ports of Stapola, Valona (Vlorë), and Durazzo (Durrës). Farther north on the Istrian Peninsula, Fiume (Rijeka) was a stereotypical hideaway for cutthroats, a base for Uskok pirates, and a rendezvous point for Albanian mercenaries and Slav adventurers. These probably never numbered more than a thousand, but they raided in tiny boats that could access all the channels of the Dalmatian archipelago with deadly efficiency against the Venetian galleys hugging the coast on their way to the Levant. They were nothing but robbers and a devil to pursue, attacking everybody, even their nominal protectors the Turks, and, in fact, were called *diavoli* (devils) by the Venetians. Venice blockaded Fiume, but it did little good because behind Fiume was the great port of Trieste, backed by the formidable power of the Austrian Hapsburgs, who needed it as a center for selling and reselling.

Pirates undercut Venice's market by trading with the itinerant peasant merchant, a familiar figure in the Slav-populated Dalmatian landscape. Although the population was Slavic, the commercial language was Italian. The influence of the Italians penetrated everywhere, including fashion and food, and a pervasive snobbery grew among the higher levels of society, although the influence of Byzantium was still to be felt in the sixteenth century.

The sailors of the Mediterranean came from everywhere, migrating for work. Similar to today, the crews often comprised many nationalities, but especially Greek. There were also small-time pirates cruising the thousands of islands and islets of the Greek archipelago to play cat-and-mouse with victims their own size. These pirates could support themselves for a month on rations of a sack of flour, some biscuit, a skin of oil, honey, a few bunches of garlic and onions, and a little salt. They made a round loaf of bread with their flour. In contrast, mariners in Marseilles had two pounds of bread as daily rations.[194]

Christian pirates also operated out of Catalonia and Valencia, and attacked both Christian and Muslim vessels. In the western Mediterranean, Valencia was a great Christian pirate base.[195] Valencian merchants, who financially backed the pirates, had made their money in the silk trade. Pirate hideouts dotted the coast, and near Pals in Catalonia was the pirate hideout of L'Estartit, where you can see the offshore island of Islas Medes jutting impressively out of the sea, and eat *mar i cel,* sea and heaven, the name of a category of dishes made with ingredients from the land or sky or sea such as a dish made of sausages, rabbit, shrimp, and monkfish or lobster and snails (page 50). Today the town is another beach resort.

The famous Christian military religious orders, the Knights Hospitalers, later known as the Knights of Malta (and also called the Knights of Rhodes or the Knights of St. John), and the Knights of St. Stephen, a Tuscan order founded by Cosimo de'Medici to protect the coast against Muslim pirates, also engaged in piracy. The Knights of Malta were bold Christian corsairs capturing cargoes as far away as the mouth of the Nile. These were rich prizes because they were laden with valuable goods from the markets of Alexandria and were headed for the Levant and Constantinople. In 1564, the Knights of St. Stephen made their first foray into the Levant from their home bases in Tuscany, seizing two rich Turkish vessels. From that time until the end of the century, Christian pirates regularly invaded the Levant in search of booty, usually finding slaves, sacks of rice, spices, dried fish, and carpets.

An orgy of pirating ensued in the last quarter of the sixteenth century, with everyone jumping into the game. The names of these privateers from Sicily who began to launch raids after 1575—Filippo Corona, Giovanni di Orta, Jacopo Calvo, and Giulio Battista Corvaja—became as famous in the Mediterranean as the name Blackbeard would be in the Caribbean. The pirates in their *fregatine* and galliots usually ended up chasing Venetian ships. As Braudel says, "The entire piratical world was eager to settle scores with the Republic of St. Mark," because Venice pursued its interests over all others with a single-minded toughness.[196] Venice protested to Florence and Madrid, both of whom rarely heeded the plea since each was often financing or otherwise supporting the pirates. Finally the Venetians succeeded in getting a ban on piracy from the Spanish King Philip II, which helped stop Spanish-ruled Naples, but Sicily continued in its piratical ways. As with so much in history, insurance rates often tell the story better than any diary—rates went up to 25 percent on the Syria route in 1612.

CONCLUSION

In this chapter we have seen that the Mediterranean does not have rich waters and it cannot be said, as one author states, that the Mediterranean was once much richer in fish than today.[197] When one considers that only the Dalmatian coast, the Greek islands, the Syrian coast, western Sicily, the Naples area, the coast of Cape Corse, the coastal regions of Genoa, Provence, Catalonia, and Valencia truly have seafaring traditions, it is amazing that even if Mediterranean fishing isn't rich, Mediterranean fish cookery is. In the middle of this sea (the meaning of the word, after all) are the islands, big and small. The islands played an important role in the history and the gastronomy of the Mediterranean and they are the subject of the next chapter.

❖ 7 ❖

ISLANDS OF PARADISE AND ISOLATION

Italien ohne Sizilien macht gar kein Bild in der Seele: hier ist der Schlüssel zu allem. (There can be no understanding of Italy without Sicily: Sicily is the key to everything.)

—JOHANN WOLFGANG VON GOETHE[1]

ISLANDS are curiously romantic. The popular image of islands, especially Mediterranean ones, is of spits of land with whitewashed villages on steep inclines and a truly aquamarine sea below—a travel brochure of the Greek islands. In this chapter, we will see why the islands are important and why their popular image has almost nothing to do with their actual history. Sicily is the largest island in the Mediterranean and also the most important from a historical and a gastronomic perspective. Sicily has seemed like a veritable paradise at times to some of her conquerors. On Sicily, we witness the post–Black Death plague phenomenon of greater meat consumption and availability followed in several centuries by the opposite. Other islands, such as Corsica and Sardinia, were outside the main flow of trade and remained isolated. The English word "isolated" derives in fact from the Italian word for island, *isola*. The islands of the Adriatic and Aegean, most of which spent a long time as Venetian possessions, were like pearls on a string for the Venetian overlords. There are also quasi-islands in the Mediterranean, the Spanish presidios, the oases, called islands in the desert, and the little island outcroppings or islets that tell their own stories.

ISLAND CURIOSITIES

ISLANDS are important to the story of Mediterranean food because they often played a crucial role in the dissemination of crops—for example, sugarcane, which passed from Egypt to Cyprus and then to Sicily. The large Mediterranean islands—Sicily, Crete, and Rhodes—are well known, but there are many more smaller islands and their importance is often overlooked. People on the islands lived constantly with the threat of food shortage. Food always came from the sea, either from the meager catch of the fishermen or from trade ships loaded with foodstuffs. Islands generally had monocultures, and they were rarely able to feed themselves. Islands also had culinary curiosities, as on Cyprus, which was known for white apium, a sort of water celery crystallized in sugar, and stuffed pickled buntings, which Cypriots shipped to Venice packed in barrels. On the island of Simi, pie crusts were crimped together with a house key, while a few miles away in Rhodes, the tines of a fork would be used.[2] Unique varieties of leek are native to two other islands, the *Allium melitense* to

Malta and *A. hemisphericum,* typical of the island of Lampedusa off Sicily.

The economic lifelines of the islands were the ships hauling whatever the islands had. The Sicilians traded wheat, cheese, and barrels of tuna fish for the oil of Djerba; the leather, wax, and wool of southern lands; and the gold and slaves of the trans-Saharan trade. The vessels plying the sixteenth-century Mediterranean set sail from the great ports of call such as Leghorn (Livorno), Genoa, and Venice. Often the islands were their destination. A Corsican boat might land at Leghorn with a few casks of salted meat, such as its famous *lonzu,* smoked pork tenderloin, or *ficatellu,* pork sausage, and a few cheeses, perhaps *brocciu sec,* a kind of Corsican ricotta made from the whey, which the captain would sell in the streets of the city, sometimes to the aggravation of local shopkeepers.[3]

Each of the islands had something to offer: Crete and Corfu produced wine, Djerba was famous for its olives, and Sicily its wheat. The islands also "exported" people, especially Corsica, but Sardinia too. When a Corsican, Hasan Corso, became king of Algiers in 1568, it was estimated that six thousand Corsicans were part of the renegade population of the city.

Islands were unique because of their isolation—for example, the Aegean island of Chios.[4] Chios, captured by the Genoese, was run quite differently from feudal governments in other conquests of the western Christians in Greece. The Genoese rule in Chios was the first time in recorded history that the sovereignty of a land was held by a mercantile company of shareholders in a distant country. The Genoese commercial trading company, the Maona of the Justiniani, controlled Chios, though it acknowledged the suzerainty of the Ottoman sultan in nearby Istanbul and paid tribute to the Sublime Porte, the seat of power of the Ottoman vizier. The Genoese ruled the island until 1566, when it was taken by the Ottoman Turks. Chios became an entrepôt for Mediterranean Levant trade with Egypt, and from the thirteenth century on the island imported oranges, apricots, figs, and raisins from the Levant. Chios was the only producer of mastic, a gum that drips from the mastic tree (*Pistacia lentiscus* L.). The Greeks use the gum from a subspecies shrub for chewing.[5] In Egypt, mastic has been used as an odor or taste purgative when boiling foods, even to this day. Chios also produced pitch, derived from the turpentine-producing terebinth tree *(Pistacia terebinthus),* which was exported to Italy and used to waterproof roofs. One of Chios's most unusual items of trade was ginger bread (a real bread, not the cakey cookie we know), exchanged for cloth in 1527.[6]

The histories of the individual Greek islands can be counted as some of the oddest. Take Naxos, which had a Catholic dukedom until 1566, when the Greek inhabitants persuaded Sultan Selim II (c. 1524–1574) to dethrone the duke in the hope of being allowed to farm the island to their benefit. Selim II instead granted the island to a Portuguese Jew, Don Juan Miquez, a wine procurer, who sent a Spanish Catholic, Francis Coronello, to govern the Greeks and collect the taxes. And in the realm of food, there are unexplained oddities, such as dishes from the island of Cerigo (Kythera), which appear no where else in Greece.[7]

Greek island cooking is certainly unique, and although there may be outside culinary influences, these simple preparations are beloved by the islanders with their access to extremely fresh fish or, in the case of the *sfougato* recipe, to fresh eggs, as the following recipes demonstrate.

Psarosoupa (Simi, Dodecanese)

FISH SOUP FROM SIMI

I learned how to make this extraordinary fish soup in the kitchen with Theo Tsatis, who, with his mother, father, and wife, Constance, own the Nireas restaurant located in the walled old town of Rhodes, on the island of the same name. The soup is also called kakavia. *This method of making fish soup is typical on Simi, one of the Dodecanese group of islands north of Rhodes, very near the Turkish coast, from where the Tsatis family migrated some years ago.*

The fish was freshly caught. Three kinds—red gurnard, porgy, and red mullet—were cooked in water with diced potatoes, chopped onions, celery, garlic, salt, and pepper. Once the fish was cooked, it was removed from the broth and set aside. The broth was boiled for several minutes with some rice, then egg whites were beaten with lemon juice and stirred into the soup broth for a few seconds. Normally egg yolks are used, but here it was the whites, which made the whole preparation lighter.

I learned much about the cooking of Simi and Rhodes from Theo and Constance, who are food enthusiasts, preservers of culinary tradition, and owners of one of the very few authentic restaurants in Rhodes in the walled old city (the rest serve Greek tourist food).

1 pound boiling potatoes, peeled and cut up
2 celery stalks, quartered
1 medium-size onion, quartered and layers separated
6 garlic cloves, crushed
½ cup extra virgin olive oil
Salt and freshly ground black pepper to taste
3 quarts cold water
2 porgy (about 2 pounds), also called scup, scaled, gutted, and cleaned
½ pound red mullet, red snapper, or fresh sardines (about 3 red mullet or 4 sardines), scaled, gutted, and cleaned
One ¾-pound haddock, halibut, sea bass, or cod fillet
½ cup raw long-grain rice
3 large egg whites
Juice from 1 lemon

1. Put the potatoes, celery, onion, garlic, olive oil, salt, and pepper in a large pot and cover with the water. Bring to a boil, then reduce the heat so the boil is gentle and cook for 1 hour. Check the seasoning.

2. Bring the soup to a furious boil again and add the porgy. After 2 to 3 minutes, add the remaining fish and cook at a full boil, removing the fish with a spatula before it breaks up, 6 to 8 minutes. Reduce the heat of the soup to a gentle boil. The whole fish can be served as is or you can fillet it by carefully pushing the meat off the bones. Set the fish aside and keep warm.

3. Boil the broth another 2 minutes. Add the rice and cook until soft, 10 to 12 minutes. Beat the egg whites with the lemon juice. Add a little of the broth to the egg white mixture, continue beating, and then add to the broth in the pot and cook for 2 minutes, stirring once or twice.

4. Ladle the broth with some of the rice into each soup bowl, without the potatoes, celery, and onion, and serve the fish separately or let each diner put his or her own mixture of fish into the bowl. Save the remaining broth with its vegetables and process into a puree to use as the base for a creamy soup.

Makes 4 servings

Garides Simio (Simi, Dodecanese)

SMALL SHRIMP FROM SIMI

Off the island of Simi, one of the Dodecanese group of islands north of Rhodes, as well as off Lindos on Rhodes, shrimpers catch very tiny, very red shrimp in October. They are considered a great delicacy and the islanders like to eat them as a meze *(see page 118).*

Sometimes very small fresh shrimp with heads come on the market around the same time from Maine, Georgia, Florida, California, and Louisiana or are imported from Greenland. For this dish they are sautéed very quickly, about 10 seconds, over very high heat in their shells with olive oil, garlic, parsley, oregano, and lemon juice. The result is extraordinary. To do this the shrimp must be no more than half an inch in length including the head. Since the smallest fresh shrimp I have encountered in a North American market are about 1 inch long and often much larger, I developed this recipe.

With the very tiny shrimp, you eat the heads, shells, and all. With larger shrimp, you will have to shell the shrimp, although you can still suck out the delicious juices inside the head. Cook the shrimp in a large skillet or in batches.

2 pounds tiny fresh shrimp with heads on (about 1½ inches in length at the very most, including the head)
3 garlic cloves, very finely chopped
2 tablespoons very finely chopped fresh parsley leaves
1 teaspoon dried oregano
Salt and freshly ground black pepper to taste
2 tablespoons fresh lemon juice
½ cup extra virgin olive oil

1. Rinse the shrimp and damp dry with paper towels. Toss with all the ingredients except the olive oil.

2. In a large skillet, heat the olive oil over high heat. When the oil begins to smoke, add the shrimp and cook until bright red or orange (depends on the variety), about 2 minutes, tossing frequently. Remove from the pan immediately and serve.

Makes 4 servings

Sfougato (Rhodes)

BAKED OMELETTE FROM RHODES

Sfougato, *from the Greek word for sponge,* sfoggos, *is a kind of Rhodes-style omelette. Although it is said to date from the time of the Byzantine Empire (c. 476–1453), I wonder if it might actually be related to the Roman dish known in Latin as* ova spongia, *an omelette recipe that appears in Apicius.*[8] *The Jews of Canea (Khaniá) in Crete make a similarly named dish but with lamb offal. Another delicious omelette is called* froutalia, *from the island of Ándros in the Cyclades, made with potatoes and sausages. This recipe is adapted from Diane Kochilas's* The Food and Wine of Greece.

¼ cup (½ stick) unsalted butter
1 large onion, chopped
1 pound lean ground veal or beef
1 pound zucchini, peeled and cut into small dice
2 tablespoons finely chopped fresh parsley leaves
¼ cup chopped fresh dill
1 cup hot water
Salt and freshly ground black pepper to taste
8 large eggs, beaten
Dried bread crumbs for sprinkling
Feta cheese for garnish

1. In a large skillet or omelette pan, melt the butter over medium heat, then cook the onion until soft and yellow, about 10 minutes, stirring occasionally. Add the veal or beef, breaking it up with a fork and cook until it loses its raw color, about 10 minutes. Add the zucchini, parsley, dill, and hot water and season with salt and pepper. Stir to blend, cover, reduce the heat to low, and simmer until the zucchini is soft and the sauce flavorful, about 30 minutes, stirring occasionally.

2. Transfer the contents of the skillet to a large bowl to cool, using a slotted ladle to drain of excess liquid. Beat the eggs into the bowl. Preheat the oven to 350°F.

3. Sprinkle the bread crumbs lightly on the bottom of a buttered casserole (about 8 × 11 × 2 inches), then pour in the egg-and-meat mixture. Bake until the eggs set, about 25 minutes. Serve warm with feta cheese crumbled on top.

Makes 4 to 6 servings

SICILY

SICILY was unique in many ways, regardless of its fortunes and the forces surrounding it. The island had an important role during the Roman era as a granary providing soft wheat. Later, during the Arab (827–1091) and Norman (1091–1194) eras, Sicily was the bridge at the interstices of geography and history. As the great historian of science Charles Haskins said, "Nowhere else did Latin, Greek and Arabic civilizations live side by side in peace and toleration, and nowhere else was the spirit of the Renaissance more clearly expressed in the policy of the rulers"[9] than in Sicily.

Sicily was certainly held in high regard even at the time. Placido Ragazzoni, a Venetian resident in Messina in 1570, said, "Sicily produces all things necessary for human life, so that she does not need to import anything."[10] But this was a deceptive comment, for Sicily was at that time one of the poorest places in Italy. The reversal in Sicilian fortunes from rich to poor had its origin in the undoing of Arab agricultural successes in twelfth-century Sicily under the rapacious rule of Norman barons allied with the rule of William II. He was known as William the Good by the barons because he allowed them to rape the land. His father, William I, who kept things in check and enjoyed the pleasures of his semi-Muslim court where he could discuss literary and philosophical topics with learned Greeks and Muslims, was called William the Bad by the barons. The Norman barons allowed the ancient Roman and Byzantine *latifunda,* large and inefficient agricultural estates that had been dissolved centuries before during the Arab era, to re-form (see Chapter 1).

The poorest Sicilians were those engaged in agriculture.[11] In the fourteenth century, it is likely that the very poor of Sicily had no cuisine. Medieval Sicilian inventories for the most part mention the *caldaria* (a spit with a tripod), *padella* (a pan), and *sartago* (a fryer), but the rarity of the *foculàri* (slow brazier) and the number of *stricfizarii* (taxes), for instance, on prepared foods (that is, already-cooked foods for take-out) like heads, stomachs, and feet, rather than food for home consumption, suggests the absence or quasi-absence of a cuisine among the poorest.[12] The presence of *foculàri* in the homes of Sicilian peasants would indicate the presence of more sophisticated cooking while the other *batteria da cucina*—spits, fryers, and pans—would indicate the simplest of cooking methods. The fact that there were high taxes on prepared foods sold by vendors indicates that a majority of homes might not have had kitchens and, at the very least, that home cooking was not prevalent.

Sicily was an early entrepôt for vegetables and fruits never before grown in Europe. The Sicilian kitchen garden likely developed during the Kalbite era of Muslim Sicily (947–c. 1040) in the late tenth and early eleventh centuries.[13] The garden had evolved out of the *rawḍa* (see Chapter 1) of the royal gardens of the caliphs, who planted them with decorative vegetation and fruit trees.[14] These gardens did not disappear when the Normans overthrew the Arabs in Sicily. In fact, the Norman overlords, if not the local barons, were thoroughly Arabized, wearing Arab clothing, holding Arab-style courts with harems, and eating Arab food, even if they didn't accept the "Arab" religion. The kitchen gardens were maintained and grew, becoming more sophisticated and hosting a variety of vegetables that were only much later introduced to Italy, as well as old vegetables such as the winged pea (*Tetragonolobus purpureus* Moench.), a food traditionally eaten by the Sicilian poor.[15]

In the fourteenth century and up until the beginning of the eighteenth century, animal fats such as butter, bacon, lard, mutton fat (perhaps a vestige of the Arab presence), and beef suet were used in Sicilian cooking. In fact, the preferred cooking fat in fifteenth-century Sicily was butter. According to the

A sixteenth-century vendor sells an abundance of fruits and vegetables—some recent newcomers to the Old World—such as the winter squash. Vincenzo Campi (1536–1591). *The Fruit Vendor.* Pinacoteca di Brera, Milan. SCALA/ART RESOURCE.

stricfizarii (taxation records), these were the largest purchases. In Corleone, a mountain town of western Sicily, butter was sold in a *quartara,* a kind of narrow-necked earthenware vessel, and was sometimes the only food to accompany the bread available to the agricultural workers who used it frequently in place of cheese.[16]

Although olive oil, the cooking fat most closely associated with Sicilian cooking today, has been produced continually throughout Sicilian history, it was rare and expensive until recently. In the Middle Ages, only the Jews bought olive oil in quantity, as pork fat was forbidden to them (the Muslim Sicilians having suffered their final expulsion in the 1230s). The Jewish cooks' fondness for olive oil is partly behind this, but also most merchants dealing in Sicilian olive oil for export were Jews. Don't let the Sicilian recipes in this book fool you into thinking that olive oil was always abundant in Sicily.[17] When olive oil, with its modest production, was used, it was used on bread or for seasoning dried vegetable soups.[18]

Cheese was of the utmost importance in Sicily, economically and nutritionally. In fact, cheese was the second largest export after grain in fifteenth-century Sicily. The Sicilians greatly appreciated cheese and it was an important part of their diet, especially fresh cheese and ricotta. Cheeses that were made of cow's milk and those that were salted were more expensive because of the expense of salt and the requirements of raising cows. Owing to the effects of the Black Death in Sicily in the fourteenth century, a reduced agricultural population meant a greater number of animals to be corralled or shepherded.

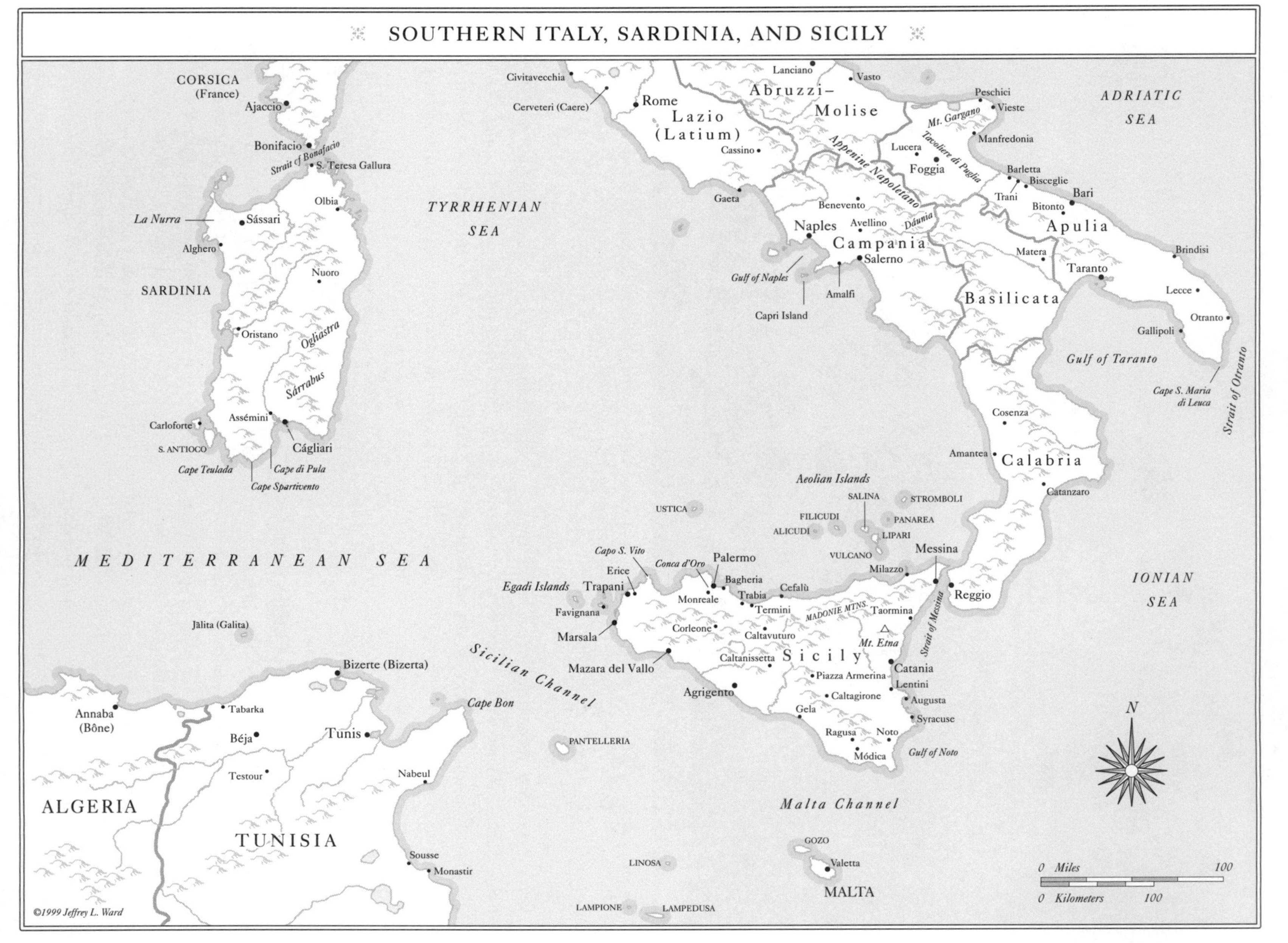
SOUTHERN ITALY, SARDINIA, AND SICILY
CORSICA
(France)
Ajaccio
Bonifacio
Strait of Bonifacio
S. Teresa Gallura
Olbia
La Nurra
Sássari
Alghero
Nuoro
SARDINIA
Oristano
Ogliastra
Sárrabus
Carloforte
Assémini
S. ANTIOCO
Cágliari
Cape Teulada
Cape di Pula
Cape Spartivento
TYRRHENIAN
SEA
MEDITERRANEAN SEA
Civitavecchia
Cerveteri (Caere)
Rome
Lazio
(Latium)
Cassino
Gaeta
Lanciano
Vasto
Abruzzi–
Molise
Peschici
Vieste
Mt. Gargano
Manfredonia
Lucera
Foggia
Tavoliere di Puglia
Appenine Napoletano
Barletta
Bisceglie
Trani
Bari
Bitonto
Apulia
Benevento
Avellino
Dáunia
Naples
Campania
Salerno
Gulf of Naples
Amalfi
Capri Island
Matera
Taranto
Basilicata
Brindisi
Lecce
Otranto
Gallipoli
Gulf of Taranto
Cape S. Maria
di Leuca
Strait of Otranto
ADRIATIC
SEA
Cosenza
Amantea
Calabria
Catanzaro
Aeolian Islands
SALINA
STROMBOLI
USTICA
FILICUDI
ALICUDI
PANAREA
LIPARI
VULCANO
Messina
Milazzo
Reggio
Strait of Messina
IONIAN
SEA
Capo S. Vito
Erice
Conca d'Oro
Palermo
Bagheria
Monreale
Trabia
Cefalù
Egadi Islands
Trapani
Termini
Favignana
MADONIE MTNS.
Taormina
Corleone
Marsala
Caltavuturo
Mt. Etna
Jālita (Galita)
Mazara del Vallo
Caltanissetta
Sicily
Catania
Piazza Armerina
Lentini
Sicilian Channel
Agrigento
Caltagirone
Augusta
Gela
Syracuse
Ragusa
Noto
Módica
Gulf of Noto
N
Bizerte (Bizerta)
Cape Bon
Annaba
(Bône)
Tabarka
Béja
Tunis
PANTELLERIA
Testour
Nabeul
ALGERIA
TUNISIA
Malta Channel
GOZO
Valetta
MALTA
Sousse
Monastir
LINOSA
LAMPIONE
LAMPEDUSA
0 Miles 100
0 Kilometers 100
©1999 Jeffrey L. Ward

Cows were common in Sicily in the late fourteenth and early fifteenth centuries, but by between 1430 and 1460, a cheese made from cow's milk, called *vaccino,* was replaced by a sheep's milk cheese called pecorino or *caciocavallo*. This is indicative of the difficulty of raising cows in a typically arid and vegetatively barren Mediterranean island. More sheep's and goat's milk cheeses were made, and many cheeses were made in the springtime, which also is the time of two important religious holidays, and these cheeses came to be associated with those holidays. *Scaldato,* a cheese like ricotta, was traditional for Easter; it was hardly cooked and cost as much as salted cheese, for some reason. A goat's milk ricotta was used to make a cake called *cassata* (page 302), eaten by Christian and Jewish Sicilians. Sicilian Jews were not only consumers of ricotta and *tuma,* a mozzarella-like cheese, but cheese retailers too, and they usually made it for Passover.[19]

Ricotta (Sicily)

Ricotta is known as an albumin or serum cheese, a cheese made as a by-product of provolone cheese from the recooked whey, hence the name, ricotta, "recooked."

Ricotta cheese, which is generally recognized as having been invented in Sicily, is known in the language of the island by another name: zammatàru, *a word in Sicilian meaning "dairy farmer." This word is derived from the Arabic* zaʿāma, *meaning "cow," leading to the supposition that ricotta might have had its origins in the Arab-Sicilian era.*[20]

The Greek antiquarian who wrote volumes on food, Athenaeus (c. A.D. *170–230), talks about "tender cheese" at a banquet. We don't know if this is ricotta, but he also mentions a cheese from Sicily that was well known.*[21] *Two of the earliest mentions or depictions of ricotta are related to Sicily. Professor Santi Correnti, chairman of the history department of the University of Catania and a preeminent historian of Sicily, told me that during the reign of the Sicilian king Frederick II, in the early thirteenth century, the king and his hunting party came across the hut of a dairy farmer making ricotta and, being ravenous, asked for some. Frederick pulled out his bread loaf, poured the hot ricotta and whey on top, and advised his retinue that* "Cu' non mancia ccu' so' cucchiaru lassa tutto 'o zammatàru" *(Those who don't eat with a spoon will leave all their ricotta behind).*[22] *The first depiction of the making of ricotta is an illustration in the medical treatise known as the* Tacuinum sanitatis *(medieval health handbook), the Latin translation of Ibn Buṭlān's eleventh-century* Taqwīm al-ṣiḥḥa.[23]

The first time you make your own ricotta you will feel an enormous sense of accomplishment and question whether you will ever buy store-made ricotta again. If you are unable to find goat's milk, substitute whole cow's milk, and if you are unable to find non-ultrapasteurized heavy cream, use the regular supermarket cream. Technically this recipe is not real ricotta, which is a by-product of cheese making using rennet, but the taste is identical. To make the Corsican brocciu, *replace the whole cow's milk with whole goat or ewe's milk and replace the 2 cups of goat's milk with goat's or cow's buttermilk.*

4 quarts whole cow's milk
2 cups goat's milk
2 cups heavy cream (preferably not ultrapasteurized)
5 tablespoons fresh lemon juice

1. Pour both milks, the cream, and lemon juice into a large nonreactive saucepan or stew pot. Turn the heat to low and bring to 194°F using a candy/deep-fry thermometer (also called a quick-read thermometer), making sure it does not touch the bottom or sides of the saucepan or pot. This will take about 2 hours.

2. Line a strainer or small colander with cheesecloth. When curds form on the surface of the liquid, remove them with a skimmer or slotted spoon and transfer to the strainer. Increase the heat to medium and after 8 minutes, skim some more, until all the curds are removed and only milky liquid remains.

3. Leave the curds to drain for 1 hour, then transfer them to a container and refrigerate. Fresh homemade ricotta will stay fresh for about 4 days in the refrigerator and may be used in recipes.

Makes 2 pounds

SICILIAN life was primitive, and meat, while widely diffused, was not abundant at the end of the fourteenth century. Typically, Sicilians of the fourteenth century would eat meat for breakfast while dinner consisted of some cheese, cardoons, oranges, bread, and wine. They preferred beef and *castrato* for lunch, pork or sausages for dinner. Fridays and Saturdays, often fast days, people would eat fresh fish such as dogfish *(palombo)* and eel, as well as a salted fish from a member of the tuna family called little tuna *(tonnina),* and eggs.[24] The farmyard must have been nonexistent or very limited because researchers find few references to chickens. This is reflected today in the fact that the smallest chapter, if it exists at all, in Sicilian cookbooks is the one for chicken. We don't know why there were so few chickens in Sicily. Contracts from *locanda,* inns for travelers, and taverns show bread, olives, salted tuna, and cheese available. The *ortolani,* farm workers, grew only cabbage and onions.

But by the early fifteenth century meat consumption had increased as we know from a widow in Palermo who was allotted about two pounds of meat per week and eighty-eight pounds of salt pork a year, while the ration for a vineyard worker was almost four pounds of meat per week. We don't know how many people this had to feed. Bread and wine were daily staples, and vegetables almost so. Every other day, Palermitans might have beef, wether (castrated lamb), which they called *castrato,* or another meat. Fresh fish, dried fish, fruit, and cheese were bought two to three times a week. Macaroni was bought only once a month.[25] Given the amount of beef, veal, and pork being eaten by Sicilians by the end of the fifteenth century, one is not inclined to call it *cucina povera.* But the food was primitive, mostly minestrone based on cabbage reinforced with fava and chickpeas, and eaten with stale bread. In the early sixteenth century a variety of beans, including a small amount of lentils, was grown and mentioned in the records of a garden in Palermo from 1517.[26]

Sicily was always the center of the Mediterranean for those relying on shipping. Today on the western coast of Sicily, in Trapani, stevedores load ships bound for Tunis. On the port side of the cargo vessel, ferries destined for the island of Pantelleria load cars. The sun is low in the sky and the port glistens with the white, blue, and red superstructures of large ships. Five centuries ago, the same scene existed with dark, weatherbeaten men in flowing robes unloading sugar from the cogs, the single-sailed transport ships with their exaggerated prows and poop decks, docked after their two-week journey from Alexandria.

If you were sitting in one of Trapani's quayside trattoria, you might watch this scene while being served a *maccharruni con pesto trapanese,* a pasta dish with vine-ripened tomatoes made into a pesto with almonds, garlic, fresh basil, and olive oil. For a second course, you might choose a *tonno al pomodoro,* a luscious belly-cut of fresh tuna braised with white wine, garlic, onions, tomatoes, basil, and mint.

Maccharruni con Pesto Trapanese (Sicily)

MACARONI WITH PESTO IN THE STYLE OF TRAPANI

New World tomatoes and Old World almonds are key ingredients in this Sicilian pesto, meant to evoke a parallel with the famous pesto alla genovese *(page 351). The twelfth-century historian of the Norman Sicilian kings, Hugo Falcondis, wrote about the abundant vegetable gardens of Palermo and about the cultivation of almonds, which also grew wild there, according to the nineteenth-century botanist Alphonse de Candolle. Shelled almonds were a staple export of Arab Sicily in 1061.*[27] *Tomatoes probably came to Sicily between 1510 and 1540, when Sicily was under Spanish rule.*

Sicilians use this pesto for macaroni. On the island of Lipari, off Sicily's northern coast, they would call it salmoriglio rosso *(page 390), add garlic, parsley, oregano, and vinegar, and serve it with a homemade pasta called* maccheroncello, *a kind of wide spaghetti (wider than* perciatelli) *with a hole up the middle.*

Traditionally, the pesto is made by pounding in a mortar, the preferred method as far as texture goes, but you can use a food processor. Historically, macaroni always meant any variety of pasta secca, *but today macaroni, unless specified, always means a tubular pasta about half an inch in diameter and 1½ to 3 inches in length. Traditionally, cheese is not served with this dish.*

Salt
1 pound macaroni
4 ounces blanched whole almonds
4 garlic cloves, peeled
1 small bunch fresh basil (40 to 50 large leaves), stems discarded
Freshly ground black pepper to taste
½ cup extra virgin olive oil
1 cup fresh tomato puree (not canned), without skins or seeds

1. Bring a large pot of water to a rolling boil, salt abundantly, and add the pasta. Drain the pasta when al dente.

2. Meanwhile, grind the almonds, garlic, basil leaves, salt, and pepper together in a food processor. Slowly add the olive oil in a thin stream through the feed tube while the machine is still running and process until smooth. Transfer to a large bowl and stir in the tomato puree. Toss the macaroni with the sauce and serve.

Makes 4 to 5 servings

Tonno al Pomodoro (Sicily)

TUNA WITH TOMATOES

A great deal of Sicilian tuna comes from the waters off its western coast. In Sicily, fresh tuna is cut into large cubes and slowly cooked in wine and tomatoes, as in this stew. If your fishmonger buys his tuna whole or by the half, ask for a few pieces from the belly, a paler, almost salmon-colored flesh with more fat content, and some cubes from the leaner "shoulder" area (above the pectoral fin). Sicilian culinary folklore always associates mint with Arab-influenced cooking. But this must be a contemporary notion because mint is certainly older than the Arabs, and it is an herb much associated with contemporary Arab cooking rather than medieval Arab cooking.

1½ pounds fresh tuna steaks, cut into 2-inch cubes
½ cup extra virgin olive oil
3 garlic cloves, finely chopped
1 cup loosely packed fresh mint leaves
Salt and freshly ground black pepper to taste
½ cup dry white wine
1½ cups crushed or finely chopped ripe tomatoes
1 small onion, finely chopped
10 large fresh basil leaves
1 recipe *crostini di pane per le zuppe di pesce* (page 559)

1. Toss the tuna pieces in a medium-size bowl with the olive oil and garlic. Finely chop the mint, toss with the tuna, and season with salt and pepper, mixing them in well. Transfer the tuna to a large skillet or casserole and turn the heat to medium-high. Once the tuna has turned color on all sides, 2 to 3 minutes, pour in the wine and evaporate for 4 to 5 minutes.

2. Add the tomatoes, onion, and basil and mix carefully with the tuna, shaking the casserole. Cover, reduce the heat to low, and simmer until the tuna is cooked through and feels firm, 8 to 10 minutes. Add a few tablespoons of water if the sauce is getting too thick. Serve with the *crostini.*

Makes 4 servings

THE rich and evocative cuisine of contemporary Sicily, with its aromatic ingredients and luscious use of olive oil, fresh vegetables, and, of course, seafood, is doubly astonishing once we glimpse the historic poverty of the island. There are two elements constituting the nature of Sicilian cuisine: the culinary mentality that derives from a long history and numerous invaders, and the availability of local food. As Pino Correnti, the noted Sicilian culinary authority, suggested, let's sit at a table spread with the "gastronomical zodiac" of Sicily. The first part of the zodiac is the ancient Greeks, who spawned famous chefs from Syracuse and cultivated the making of wine. The second sector of the zodiac is the Romans, a time when Cicero, Petronius, and Martial celebrated the *siculae dapes* (Sicilian banquets) and Sicily was an enormous granary for Rome. The villas of the rich patricians sported huge kitchens and magnificent dining rooms, as in the Villa Romana del Casale in Piazza Armerina, at its height in the third century. The third part of the zodiac is the Byzantine period, which again introduced Greek influences in hot cheeses and sauces and sweets.

The fourth sector of the zodiac (the "delicious part," as Correnti calls it) is the Arabs, of whom I've already spoken in Chapter 1. The next sector of the zodiac is the Normans and Swabians (originally German). The Normans were responsible for preserving the secrets of Arab-Sicilian gastronomy in their castles and convents. Some people attribute to the Normans the introduction of rotating spits, and the master carvers or seneschals who cut the meat, as well as the smoking of herring and the importation of dried codfish to Sicily. The Swabian king Frederick II, who was born in Italy, was also a famous hunter and gastronome. His richly appointed court, and concerns for earthly paradise instead of eternal life, caused Dante, who had a profound respect for the king, to place him in the sixth circle of hell.[28] The sixth sector of the zodiac is represented by the Angevins and Aragons. The French Angevins, whose hated rule was supplanted by the Spanish Aragons, may have contributed to Sicilian gastronomy in certain methods that today are reflected in various vestigial French words such as *gatto* for *gâteau* (cake) or *rollo* for *roulé* (roll-up). The Spanish viceroys ruled Sicily with an iron hand, forever impoverishing the island but leaving remnants culinary and architectural. During this time New World foods such as tomatoes, potatoes, pumpkins, green beans, and chocolate were introduced to Sicilian cuisine, which now also became more evidently divided between the Baroque cooking of the rich and the simple sustenance of the poor.

After Spanish rule, Sicily disintegrated into the killing fields for a succession of European powers struggling for domination before and after the French Revolution. Even the British left their mark with the introduction of the grapefruit and the beginnings of the fortified wine called Marsala. Sicilian nobles and prelates have, during the last one hundred fifty years, hired professional French-trained cooks, the *monzù* (for *monsieur*) to cook for their big families, and these chefs have developed the secrets of aristocratic cuisine that are characteristically opulent meals. This, then, is the gastronomic zodiac of Sicilian cuisine.[29]

The following recipes seem to defy the historic roots of Sicilian food; they are rich and flavorful, such as the first recipe, a sauce or relish that can be used on pasta or grilled meat, fish, eggplant, or bread. It contains a New World product, the tomato. Next is an example of simple seafood cookery using a kind of shark called the dogfish that is not only popular in Sicily but also sometimes available on the U.S. eastern seaboard and easily replaced by any kind of shark. Then we come to three pasta recipes, the first a rendition from the city of Syracuse that is simply a marvelous example of a later, Baroque style of cuisine of the patrician class. The second is a lustier example of the simple cooking of the plebian class of Syracuse, and perhaps closer to our historic macaroni that was eaten once a month (without the tomatoes, of course). The third is an excellent recipe from the interior city of Módica that uses two of Sicily's famous foods, ricotta and macaroni. It's called a *pasticcio,* or pie, that may reflect the traditional macaroni pies of the Middle Ages (see pages 151 and 623), although this contemporary recipe has no pie crust, but is simply baked like a pie. Finally, we have two eggplant recipes, again modern recipes using the eggplant that first appeared in Sicilian kitchen gardens in the early fourteenth century.

Mataroccu (Sicily)

ALMOND, BASIL, AND TOMATO SAUCE

Mataroccu *is the name of a sauce used in the cooking around Marsala, although it can also mean "silly" and earlier referred to a dish of mashed squash. I don't know how the name came about. The Sicilian food writer Anna Pomar suggests that it may be related to gazpacho.*[30]

Mataroccu *sauce is known by other names and can be made with other ingredients; made with tomatoes, garlic, basil, olive oil, and perhaps a little red pepper, it is called* ammogghiu *(meaning "something wrapped" or "smothered") and used on grilled meat, fish, eggplant, or grilled bread,* bruschette. *But the sauce called* mugghiu—*slang for* sammurugghiu (salmoriglio), *a word which literally means "brine"—is associated with a dipping sauce used for swordfish.* Mataroccu *sometimes includes pine nuts, and parsley or celery leaves, and goes by a variety of other names such as* pesto siciliano, pesto di Favignana, pesto trapanese, pesto marsalese, *or* salsa pantesca a crudo.

12 large garlic cloves, finely chopped
8 large fresh basil leaves, finely chopped
½ cup blanched whole almonds, crushed
2 pounds ripe plum tomatoes, peeled, seeded, and drained well
½ cup extra virgin olive oil

1. Put the garlic, basil, and almonds in a mortar and crush together until mushy with a pestle, or pulse in a food processor. If working in a mortar, transfer the pesto to a deep bowl large enough to hold all the tomatoes.

2. Add the tomatoes to the pesto, first making sure they are thoroughly drained of all their water. Mix and pound the tomatoes into the garlic with the pestle or use the food processor in bursts. This is the *mataroccu*. Toss it with the hot cooked pasta of your choice, or serve it on top of grilled beef or fish.

Makes 4 to 6 servings with 1 pound pasta

Palombo Fritto (Sicily)

FRIED DOGFISH

Dogfish is a kind of small shark called palombo, *popular in Sicily. Its flesh is firm and when fresh is a great favorite on the grill or fried. Dogfish is sometimes marketed on the eastern coast of this country as Cape shark. Dogfish can be replaced with steaks cut from another type of shark, or swordfish, bonito, tuna, bluefish, kingfish, or Spanish mackerel.*

3 pounds dogfish, cut into sixteen ½-inch-thick steaks
1 cup white wine vinegar
Salt and freshly ground black pepper to taste
4½ teaspoons very finely chopped fresh mint leaves
4½ teaspoons very finely chopped fresh oregano leaves
1 cup pure or virgin olive oil
All-purpose flour for dredging
Lemon wedges for garnish (optional)

1. Place the fish in a deep ceramic bowl or pan, cover with the vinegar, season with salt and pepper, and set aside for 30 minutes. Mix the mint and oregano and spread evenly on a wide serving platter for dredging the fish.

2. Pour the olive oil in a 12-inch skillet and heat over medium-high heat until almost smoking. Drain and dredge the fish in the flour, shake off any excess, and then dredge in the herbs. There will not be a lot of herbs. Salt and pepper again, if desired, and cook until light golden in the hot oil, 3 to 4 minutes per side. Cook in batches if necessary so as not to crowd the skillet, and serve immediately with lemon wedges if desired.

Makes 6 to 8 servings

Spaghetti alla Siracusana (Sicily)

SPAGHETTI WITH THE AROMATIC SAUCE OF SYRACUSE

The cooking of Syracuse, the beautiful classical city of Sicily on the Ionian Sea, is marked by highly aromatic foods in combination with fresh vegetables and seafood. This style of cooking is sometimes described as Baroque. The Baroque era in architecture, art, and music was a turning away from the ordered reality of the universe as conceived by the Renaissance to a more fanciful, extravagant, and flamboyant conceptualizing of everyday life. In the realm of gastronomy the Baroque is evidenced in lush flavor melodies, voluptuous tastes, and ingenious combinations of ingredients. This spaghetti recipe showcases the melding of typical Sicilian flavors in a Baroque style of cooking associated with Syracuse.

1 eggplant (about 1¼ pounds), unpeeled and cut into ½-inch cubes
Salt
1 large yellow bell pepper

½ cup extra virgin olive oil
2 garlic cloves, crushed
4 salted anchovy fillets, rinsed and chopped
2 pounds ripe tomatoes, peeled, seeded, and chopped
2 tablespoons capers, rinsed and chopped if large
¼ pound imported black olives, pitted and coarsely chopped
6 large fresh basil leaves, finely chopped
Freshly ground black pepper to taste
1¼ pounds spaghetti
½ cup freshly grated pecorino cheese

1. Lay the eggplant cubes on some paper towels and sprinkle with salt. Leave them to drain of their bitter juices for 30 minutes, then pat dry with paper towels.

2. Preheat the oven to 400°F. Place the bell pepper in a baking dish and roast until the skin blackens, 40 to 45 minutes. Remove and let cool. Peel away the skin, cut open the pepper, and discard the stem and seeds. Slice thin and set aside.

3. In a large skillet, heat the olive oil with the garlic over medium-high heat until the garlic begins to turn light brown. Remove and discard the garlic. Once the oil begins to smoke, add the eggplant, and cook until golden, 7 to 8 minutes, stirring and tossing. Add the anchovies; once they have melted into the sauce, add the tomatoes. Reduce the heat to low and simmer for 10 minutes, stirring occasionally.

4. Add the yellow pepper, capers, olives, and basil. Season with salt and pepper and cook until the sauce is thick, 15 to 20 minutes.

5. Meanwhile, bring a large pot of water to a rolling boil, salt abundantly, and add the pasta. Drain when the pasta is al dente and pour into a serving bowl or platter. Cover with the sauce and pecorino cheese and serve immediately.

Makes 6 servings

Rigatoni con la Salsiccia (Sicily)

RIGATONI WITH SAUSAGE

In Sicily this preparation is a Syracusean family favorite. The ragù *is flavored with pork chops and sausage and then tossed with the macaroni. The best way to eat this dish is in the traditional Sicilian way. First serve the rigatoni with the* ragù, *then eat chops and sausages for the second course. It's a delightful way to linger over some delicious food and enjoy your family and friends.*

½ cup extra virgin olive oil
2 large onions, thinly sliced
6 thin pork chops (about 1¼ pounds)
1½ pounds homemade *salsiccia fresca* (page 70) or mild Italian sausage (1 pound whole links and ½ pound with casings removed and the meat broken up)
2 tablespoons tomato paste
½ cup tepid water
4 cups crushed or chopped fresh or canned tomatoes
Salt and freshly ground black pepper to taste
2 pounds rigatoni
½ pound *ricotta salata* cheese, crumbled or grated

1. In a large skillet or casserole, heat the olive oil over medium-high heat, then cook the onions until translucent, about 8 minutes, stirring occasionally. Add the pork chops and brown, about 2 minutes per side.

2. In a medium-size skillet, brown the crumbled sausage over medium heat until it loses its pink color, about 12 minutes, tossing and breaking the meat up further with a fork or wooden spoon. Remove with a slotted ladle, pressing out any fat with the back of the spoon and set aside.

3. Puncture the casing of the remaining sausages with a skewer or the prongs of a corn cob holder. Fill

a medium-size skillet with water and bring to a gentle boil. Poach the sausages until firm, about 10 minutes. Drain and set aside.

4. Dissolve the tomato paste in the tepid water and stir into the tomatoes. Add the tomatoes to the skillet with the pork chops. Add the parboiled sausages, season with salt and pepper, and add enough water so the pork chops and sausages are covered. Cook over medium heat until the sauce is unctuous, about 30 minutes. Remove the pork chops and keep warm, but leave in the whole sausages. Add the reserved cooked sausage meat to the sauce and cook another 30 minutes.

5. Meanwhile, bring a large stockpot of water to a rolling boil, salt abundantly, and add the pasta. Drain when al dente.

6. Remove the whole sausages from the sauce and keep warm with the pork chops. Toss the macaroni with the sauce and *ricotta salata* and serve as a first course. Serve the pork chops and sausages as a second course or on the side if serving as a *piatto unico,* a one-platter meal.

Makes 8 to 10 servings

Pasticcio di Ricotta (Sicily)

RICOTTA AND MACARONI PIE

Around Módica in Sicily's rugged interior, housewives typically make this baked macaroni preparation for Christmas dinner. In this recipe I call for all the ingredients to be homemade. Normally I don't ask my readers to go through such work, but in this case, because of the simplicity of the dish, the difference between your own preparations and store-bought ingredients is so remarkable that it will seem as if you have two entirely different recipes. This work is not terribly difficult, but you must allow yourself the time to do it. Sicilian homes to this day have resisted processed foods and one will find more homemade foods there than in the rest of Italy. But to make fresh macaroni you will need specialized equipment such as a pasta maker with the correct extrusion dies, so replace it if you must, with commercial dried macaroni or store-bought fresh macaroni.

1 pound fresh homemade macaroni (page 628)
3 tablespoons extra virgin olive oil
1 pound homemade *salsiccia fresca* (page 70), casings removed and meat crumbled
1 pound homemade ricotta cheese (page 467)
Freshly ground black pepper to taste

1. Bring a large pot of water to a rolling boil, salt abundantly, and add the pasta. Cook the macaroni until half cooked. Drain and set aside after tossing with 2 tablespoons of the olive oil.

2. In a medium-size skillet, heat the remaining tablespoon olive oil and brown the sausage over medium-high heat until it loses its pink color, about 7 minutes, breaking the meat up further with a wooden spoon. Remove the sausage with a slotted ladle, squeezing out all fat with the back of the wooden spoon, and toss with the macaroni. Toss again with the ricotta and pepper.

3. Preheat the oven to 350°F. Transfer the macaroni to an earthenware baking dish greased lightly with oil. Bake for 20 minutes and serve.

Makes 6 servings

❖ *Melanzane in Graticola* (Sicily)

GRILLED EGGPLANT

Sicilians and Levantine Arabs seem the most enthusiastic when it comes to devotion to this noble vegetable, which the medieval Arab toxicologist Ibn Waḥshīya (wrote circa 904) said was fatal when eaten raw.[31] *Across Sicily, in every trattoria's* tavola calda, *the large buffet table spread with various prepared dishes displayed in polychromatic serving platters, you will find grilled eggplant, and it is always unforgettable.*

6 small eggplant (about 3 pounds)
Salt
½ cup extra virgin olive oil
2 large garlic cloves, finely chopped
¼ cup finely chopped fresh parsley leaves
Freshly ground black pepper to taste
A brush made from oregano twigs

1. Cut the eggplant into ½-inch-thick slices lengthwise. Lay the slices on some paper towels and sprinkle with salt. Leave them to drain of their bitter juices for 30 minutes, then pat dry with paper towels.

2. Preheat a gas grill on high for 20 minutes or prepare a hot charcoal fire.

3. Stir the olive oil, garlic, parsley, salt, and pepper together. Brush the eggplant slices on both sides with the mixture using the oregano twig brush, then place the slices on the grill. When they begin to brown, about 10 minutes, turn and grill for another 10 minutes, basting if necessary with the marinade. Remove to a platter and pour the remaining marinade over the eggplant, and serve.

NOTE: You can also grill tomatoes, peppers, zucchini, and pumpkin with the same basting mixture.

Makes 4 servings

❖ *Mulinciana 'Muttunate* (Sicily)

"BLANKETED" EGGPLANT

Sicily was one of the first places in Europe where eggplant was grown after being introduced by Arab farmers. It was grown in Spain by the tenth century, although the first clear reference to it in Sicily is from 1309, where it is called melingianas *and is grown in a garden along with cucumber and a kind of gourd (squash).*[32] *Although the eggplant was once called "mad apple"* (mela insana) *because it was thought to produce insanity, this expression is not the etymological root of the Italian and Sicilian words for eggplant,* melanzane *and* mulinciana, *respectively. As Professors Girolamo Caracausi and Giovan Battista Pellegrini have pointed out, the Italian and Sicilian words derive from the Arabic word for the plant,* bādhinjān, *with the influence of* mela *(apple) for the initial m.*[33]

Eggplant is a great favorite in Sicily, where there are very many recipes. This one from Palermo is "blanketed" with a robust and aromatic tomato sauce.

8 baby eggplant (about 1 pound), stems left on, peeled
Salt
6 cups pure or virgin olive or olive pomace oil for deep-frying
1 large garlic clove, cut into 8 slivers
8 large fresh mint leaves
2 cups tomato sauce (page 32)
4½ teaspoons capers, rinsed
3 tablespoons extra virgin olive oil
Freshly ground black pepper to taste

1. Lay the eggplant on some paper towels and sprinkle all over with salt. Leave them to drain of their bitter juices for 30 minutes, then pat dry with paper towels.

2. Preheat the frying oil to 375°F in a deep-fryer or an 8-inch saucepan fitted with a basket insert. Make two small incisions into each eggplant. With the tip of a paring knife, push a garlic sliver into one and a mint leaf into the other. Deep-fry the eggplant until light golden, about 5 minutes. Drain on paper towels. Let the frying oil cool completely, strain, and save for a future use.

3. In a wide saucepan, heat the tomato sauce over medium heat, then add the capers, extra virgin olive oil, and 3 tablespoons of the olive oil in which the eggplant was fried, and season with salt and pepper. Place the eggplant in the sauce and cook for 5 minutes, stirring occasionally, "blanketing" the eggplant with the sauce. Transfer to a serving platter and serve warm or at room temperature.

Makes 4 servings

Eating Meat

BETWEEN 1350 and 1500, the European Mediterranean was eating meat. In Sicily, meat eating was widespread, although not abundant. Eating meat means that, ideally, a stockbreeder needs ample grazing lands that will not interfere or take away from agriculture, although in this era it often did. This was the case in Sicily, and France, too, in the late thirteenth century, where the growth of cities meant more people demanding meat.[34] A century later, cultivated land began to decrease in Languedoc and this increased the consumption of meat, as grazing animals began taking over the previously productive fields.[35] In records kept from 1580 to 1590 from Carpentras in Provence and Valladolid in Spain, the meat consumed yearly was identical: about fifty-seven pounds a head, a good-sized bite of meat a day.[36] In Rome and Jerusalem, it was even higher: sixty-six pounds per person in 1560 for Jerusalem and eighty-four pounds in Rome forty-five years later.[37]

The story of meat in the Mediterranean is directly linked to the holocaust of the Black Death. Nearly half the population of Europe was decimated. Widespread and high levels of mortality meant that there were fewer farm workers, and cultivated lands reverted quickly to meadows and forest when not tended. The handful of people left became shepherds. The result was a rise in meat consumption.[38]

Bistecche ala Siciliana (Sicily)

SICILIAN-STYLE BEEF STEAK

This preparation might have an older history than one would think, given Sicily's poor reputation today for the quality of its meat, which any modern tourist can attest to. Since the seventeenth century, at least, and probably earlier, meat was often unavailable and the population tended to replace it with cheese that was called "fresh" (cascavallo fresco, tuma), *"dry"—that is, salted* (cascavallo duro)*—or "lean," whey-curds (ricotta).*[39] *But earlier still, in the fourteenth century, meat was very common in Sicily for the reasons explained earlier and in Chapter 3. Today, a Palermitan family might consider this recipe a nice dish for* cucina rapida.

3 tablespoons extra virgin olive oil
1 garlic clove, crushed
2 large ripe tomatoes (about 1 pound), peeled and seeded if desired and finely chopped
6 ounces imported black olives, pitted and chopped
½ celery stalk, very finely chopped
1 fresh red or green chili pepper, seeded and finely chopped

2 tablespoons capers, rinsed
Salt and freshly ground black pepper to taste
¼ cup finely chopped fresh oregano leaves
2 pounds beef steak (sirloin, rib eye, or Delmonico), sliced ½ inch thick

1. Prepare a hot charcoal fire or preheat a gas grill on high for 20 minutes.

2. In a large skillet, heat the olive oil over medium-high heat, then cook the garlic, stirring, until it begins to turn light brown. Remove and discard the garlic. Add the tomatoes, olives, celery, chili pepper, and capers and cook until the liquid is almost evaporated, about 8 minutes. Turn the heat off, season with salt and pepper, and stir in the oregano.

3. Grill the steaks to your liking (about 5 minutes a side over a very hot grill will get you a rare steak) and serve with the sauce on top.

Makes 4 servings

Castrato in Graticola di Corleone (Sicily)

GRILLED WETHER OR LAMB IN THE STYLE OF CORLEONE

Castrato *is the Italian word for "wether," castrated young sheep, popular with Sicilians as far back as the fourteenth century. In the Middle Ages, wether was the meat of the Sicilian urban class that couldn't afford veal or beef. As wether is not sold in this country, we can make do with spring lamb.*[40] *This style of grilling is very simple and quite popular in the area around Corleone, a western Sicilian mountain town made famous for Americans by the* Godfather *movies. The lamb chops grill slowly, so move them to a cooler part of the grill if they flare up or blacken too quickly.*

6 spring lamb chops, about ¾ inch thick
½ cup extra virgin olive oil
Juice from 1 lemon
Salt and freshly ground black pepper to taste

1. Place the chops in a glass or ceramic baking dish and cover with the olive oil, lemon juice, and salt and pepper. Marinate for 2 to 4 hours in the refrigerator.

2. Prepare a charcoal fire until the coals are all white with ash and let it die down a bit or preheat a gas grill for 15 minutes on medium-low. Place the chops 8 inches away from the source of the heat and grill for 45 minutes to 1 hour.

Makes 4 to 6 servings

AFTER the end of the fifteenth century, meat became scarce in Sicily as the rural agricultural population recovered from the Black Death and more arable land was worked. It appears that chickens did not replace meat, nor did they play a great role in the farmyard. Documents in the archives of Trapani in 1535–1536 show that a chicken cost thirty-three *grani*, equivalent to 8.1 pounds of pork and 11.4 pounds of veal, while the price of a dozen eggs was twenty-four *grani*.[41] This accounts in part for why there is almost no chicken cookery in Sicily.

Throughout the Mediterranean, when meat availability receded cooks took the precious little meat they had and created ingenious ways to extend it, such as Sicilian recipes for *involtini,* flat pieces of meat that are rolled up with a stuffing of bread usually, or dishes that made use of offal, like this one from Tunisia, a major trading partner of medieval Sicily.

Kammūniyya bi'l-Zuwayd (Tunisia)

SPICY PLUCK RAGOUT

Kammūniyya *derives from the word for "cumin," and this entire ragout takes the name of the cumin. It is a spicy dish utilizing variety meats; in fact,* al-zuwayd *means the animal's pluck (the heart, liver, lungs, and windpipe), although I leave the liver out of this recipe because I feel that it dominates the other delicate meats, and the lungs and windpipe of slaughtered animals are illegal to sell in this country, as far as I know.*

1½ pounds veal sweetbreads, trimmed of membranes
2 tablespoons fresh lemon juice or vinegar
1 pound lamb heart, central ventricle removed
1½ pounds veal kidney, trimmed of arteries
1¾ pounds lamb kidneys, trimmed of arteries
¼ pound lamb fat, cut into small dice
1 tablespoon *tābil* (page 522)
Salt and freshly ground black pepper to taste
½ cup extra virgin olive oil
1 large onion, chopped
1 cup canned or fresh tomato puree
1 tablespoon *harīsa* (page 523)
1 teaspoon cayenne pepper
1 teaspoon freshly ground black pepper
2 cups water
1 teaspoon freshly ground cumin seeds
1 preserved lemon (page 104), diced
1½ cups imported green olives, pitted if desired

1. Place the sweetbreads in a medium-size saucepan with water to cover along with the lemon juice or vinegar. Turn the heat to medium and cook until the sweetbread is firm, about 45 minutes, never letting the water boil. Drain, let cool, cut into bite-size pieces, and transfer to a large bowl.

2. Remove the sinews and veins from the heart. Cut the heart and kidneys into the same-size pieces as the sweetbreads and add to the mixing bowl along with the lamb fat. Mix all the meats with the *tābil,* salt, and pepper.

3. Heat the oil in a large skillet over high heat. Add the onion and meats and cook until the meats turn color, about 8 to 10 minutes, stirring frequently.

4. Add the tomato puree, *harīsa,* cayenne, 1 teaspoon black pepper, and water to cover, about 2 cups. Bring to a boil, then reduce the heat to low, cover, and simmer 1½ hours. Stir in the cumin, preserved lemon, and olives and cook another 5 minutes. Salt, if needed, and serve.

Makes 8 to 10 servings

CORSICA AND SARDINIA

CORSICA and Sardinia were largely isolated, although trade fairs sometimes brought regions into contact with one another. Still, these were closed local economies. On Corsica, the people of Bocognano and Bastelica regarded each other as foreigners. (A few years ago I turned my car back because the mountain road between the two towns was too perilous.) The Corsicans raised their pigs and tended their sheep herds. They grew a limited number of olive trees. Very little was imported or exported. Maybe this isolation is why one finds both lard and olive oil in Corsican cooking, where elsewhere it was one or the other. But Corsica was not totally isolated. Huge boar, stag, and wolf hunts were organized to protect the flocks, and many of these beasts were exported for the menageries of mainland princes.

Corsica was ruled by the Genoese until the French, with Turkish support, wrested the island from them in 1553. The Corsicans hated the Genoese, the nobles because they were forced to submit to them and the people because of the poor harvests that ensued and the fact that the Genoese introduced agricultural methods that disturbed their traditional way of life. The island had few resources and the nearly constant wars didn't help. Mercenaries and soldiers of every kind were based at one time or another on Corsica. There were French, Genoese, Turk, Algerian, German, Italian, and Spanish, and they all looted, spoiled crops, and burned villages. Corsican seacoast towns faced the constant attacks of pirates. Even today a circumnavigation of Corsica demonstrates the scarcity of coastal communities, a result of these piratical depredations. Corsica was a valuable communications center during wartime and an important base for coast watching. Because the Barbary corsairs controlled the passage between southern Sardinia and North Africa, ships sailing from Cartagena, Valencia, Barcelona, Málaga, and Alicante to Genoa, Leghorn, and Naples had to pass within sight of Corsica. Corsica was not often the destination of these ships, and the Corsicans themselves often had to rely on homegrown foods such as chestnuts rather than the fruits of import. In fact, at times, a good portion of what Corsicans ate was based on chestnuts, a habit still to be found in Corsican kitchens.

U Tianu d'Agnellu Incu u Castagne (Corsica)

LAMB AND CHESTNUT STEW

This stew of lamb and chestnuts cooked in an unctuous red wine and tomato sauce is a delicious contemporary concoction of the chef of L'Ondine restaurant in Algajola, on the northern shore of Corsica. The chef uses the ubiquitous chestnut and the concepts of Corsican food from centuries past. It is a perfect example of what a chef with historical sensibilities can do. The chef served it with slices of baby zucchini stuffed with a ragout of ground veal and tomato and a double-layered timbale of red chili and bell pepper custard topped with chestnut custard. Given Corsica's historic isolation, I imagine the tomato was introduced rather late.

One 2¾-pound boneless leg of lamb, sirloin half, tied
24 fresh chestnuts (8 to 10 ounces)
2 tablespoons extra virgin olive oil
1 small onion, very finely chopped
1 garlic clove, very finely chopped
1½ cups dry red wine, preferably Corsican
½ cup canned or fresh tomato puree
1 cup water
Salt and freshly ground black pepper to taste
Finely chopped fresh parsley leaves for garnish

1. Preheat the oven to 425°F. Place the leg of lamb in a roasting pan and roast for 45 minutes. Remove, let cool, trim off the fat, and cut into large cubes. Set aside. Leave the oven on.

2. Meanwhile, lay the chestnuts on their flat sides and carefully make an X on the rounded side with a paring knife, without going too deep. Arrange the chestnuts on a baking sheet and place in the oven for 35 to 40 minutes. Remove and, once the chestnuts are cool enough to handle, peel off and discard the now brittle shell and set the nuts aside.

3. In a large casserole, heat the olive oil over medium-high heat, then cook the onion and garlic together until the onion is yellow, stirring frequently so the garlic doesn't burn, 2 to 3 minutes. Add the lamb cubes and brown for 1 minute.

4. Pour in the wine, increase the heat to high, and reduce the wine by half, about 10 minutes. Reduce the heat to low, stir in the tomato puree and water, season with salt and pepper, and simmer until the lamb is tender, about 1 hour, stirring occasionally.

5. Add the chestnuts and cook until the sauce is a thick ragout, another 20 to 30 minutes. Serve sprinkled with parsley and with a side of rice if desired.

Makes 6 servings

Corsica's isolation has meant that its gastronomy is preserved more than most from medieval days, especially in the area of charcuterie, breads, cheeses, and soups. Most Corsican cheeses, both hard and fresh cheeses, still don't have names and the many varieties are known as either *fromage* (cheese) or *brocciu* (a particular kind of ricotta cheese made from ewe or goat whey). Chestnuts were once the sole source of food during wrenching famines and known as tree bread, but today they find their way into many delicious preparations, such as *suffiantu,* a chestnut and vanilla soufflé, or *maccaredda,* chestnut flour fritters cooked with salt pork.

In the mountains they still eat *misgiscia,* a fillet of goat that is marinated for one or two days in vinegar and then dried with a linen cloth and flavored with rosemary and garlic before being seasoned with salt and pepper and skewered on wood sticks to dry in the sun. It's then cooked in a ragout or over a wood fire. The eating of soup was always filled with meaning, as we see in this Corsican proverb: *O magna a minestra, o salta a finestra* (Eat the soup, or jump out of the window), meaning to pass up food is suicide. Even today Corsican soups such as *soupe paysanne* are thick and dense and often constitute the whole of an evening meal, unlike in the rest of France, where soups are served as a first course and are often quite delicate.

Minestra (Soupe Paysanne) (Corsica)

CORSICAN COUNTRY SOUP

This is the most famous of all the Corsican soups. Shepherds would take some leftovers with them into the mountains to eat cold. Besides the vegetables in the recipe below (the potatoes and tomatoes from the New World) some cooks also use carrots, celery, zucchini, leeks, and dandelion depending on the season.

1/4 pound pork fat, chopped
2 pounds boiling potatoes, peeled and diced
1 small head green cabbage (about 1 1/2 pounds), blemished outer leaves removed, cored, and chopped
3/4 pound Swiss chard leaves (no white part), chopped
1 medium-size onion, chopped
2 large garlic cloves, finely chopped
6 cups water
1/2 pound dried red kidney beans (about 1 cup), picked over
1 ham or smoked bacon chunk with bone (about 1/2 pound)
1 large ripe tomato (about 10 ounces), peeled, seeded, and chopped
6 slices day-old French country bread or 1/4 pound lasagne sheets
1 tablespoon salt
Freshly ground black pepper to taste
Extra virgin olive oil for drizzling

1. In a large casserole or soup pot, cook the pork fat over medium-high heat until there is some fat in the bottom of the pot, about 5 minutes, stirring, then add the potatoes, cabbage, chard, onion, and garlic until the greens are wilted, about 5 minutes. Pour in the water, bring to a boil, then reduce the heat to low, add the beans, ham or smoked bacon, and tomato, and cook until the beans are tender, 2 to 3 hours.

2. Add the slices of bread or lasagne and continue to cook until a spoon can stand straight up in the center of the soup and, if using lasagne, the pasta is tender, about 15 minutes. Season with salt and pepper, drizzle with olive oil, and serve.

Makes 8 servings

Mullade (Corsica)

GOAT CHEESE AND CURDLED MILK CRÊPES

Mullade *are large crêpes made with fresh cheese cooked on a hot stone such as slate, a method known from late antiquity (fifth through seventh centuries* A.D.*) as cooking with a* focolàre. *This was the traditional method of preparation by the shepherds of Corsica. One can approximate this method by using a baking stone over an open hardwood fire, although a cast-iron griddle or skillet will be most practical. It is made with goat or ewe's milk cheese and the more cheese used, the better. Corsican families would keep the batter warm over an all-day wood fire, which shepherd families used for cooking while tending their flocks. These crêpes can be eaten plain for lunch or with various garnishes such as more cheese, or fruit, or with jam.*

2 cups unbleached all-purpose flour
½ cup tepid water
¾ pound homemade goat's milk ricotta (page 467) or soft store-bought goat cheese, crumbled
2 cups curdled milk (see Step 1 of homemade ricotta, page 467)
Salt to taste
Pork lard for greasing the griddle

1. Pour the flour into a large, heavy saucepan and stir in the water and ricotta or crumbled goat cheese. Mix well. Add the curdled milk and salt and mix until you have a batter that is slightly liquid. Add some water if it is too thick; it should be thinner than pancake batter. Heat the batter gently over very low heat or in a preheated 200°F oven.

2. Grease the griddle with lard and heat over medium heat until a droplet of water sizzles rapidly on the griddle. Ladle about ¼ cup of the batter onto the hot griddle, spreading it thin with the bottom of the ladle. When the bottom browns, like a pancake, flip to the other side with a spatula and continue cooking in this manner until they are all cooked.

NOTE: Taste the first crêpe to check the salt. Add some to the batter if necessary. The crêpes can be wrapped in plastic wrap and then frozen in a zippered-style top plastic bag for up to 6 months.

Makes 4 servings

* * *

CORSICA and Sardinia were virtually outside of the main flow of Mediterranean trade. The medieval Sardinian peasant never experimented with new crops, changed his methods, or increased production. He burned the *narboni* (stubble) and did not leave fields fallow. Even today, as one approaches the interior town of Sássari, the burning stubble can be seen polluting the skies for miles.

Sardinia was more pastoral than agricultural in the sixteenth century, and the use of money was largely unknown. The Jesuit fathers in Cágliari accepted gifts in kind: poultry, bread, kids, capons, suckling pigs, good wines, and calves.[42] Sardinian bread was made of hard wheat, perhaps with a little barley. These are the only two cereals mentioned in Sardinian documents. Today there is a variety of traditional breads, some made with white flour, others semolina (hard wheat), breads with bran or sprouts, breads with bread crumbs, or as flat as a sheet of music, called literally *carta di musica,* or *pani carrasau* (dripped bread), a "sheet of music" bread rebaked with olive oil drippings. In Sárrabus, in the south, is a ritual bread made of acorns and clay, which they once ate. In Sardinian cities, public ovens were used to bake traditional dishes such as *panade,* a kind of rustic tort made of bread dough stuffed with small pieces of stewed lamb or eel seasoned with vegetables.[43] Today *panada* is a popular dish in the area around the capital city of Cágliari and in particular in the village of Assémini.

Sardinia was completely backward, yet a major exporter of cheese. Through Cágliari the island was in touch with the rest of the western world, sending its *cavallo* (probably a kind of *caciocavallo*) or *salso* (a salted sheep cheese like pecorino) cheese, going to Leghorn (Livorno), Genoa, Naples, Barcelona, and even Marseilles in spite of the competition of other cheeses from Milan and the Auvergne. Fresh white cheese was made for seasoning soups and minestrone; one such cheese, called *casu e' filixu,* was a fresh cheese layered with fern leaves in the center.[44]

Cheese is still used abundantly in Sardinian cuisine: in soups, in stews, in small ravioli, and in famous desserts such as *sebádas,* semolina, egg, and cheese fritters flavored with sugar, lemon, and honey or the *pardule,* baked buns of semolina stuffed with saffron- and orange-flavored fresh ricotta cheese.

Minestrone di "Viscido" (Sardinia)

SARDINIAN CHEESE SOUP

This minestrone is a mountain farmer's soup. Viscido *is the name in the town of Ogliastra of a kind of sour Sardinian cheese made from goat's milk that is cut into slices and brined. In Nuoro, the cheese is called* merca. *A Greek feta cheese could be substituted or, if you can find it, a dry Sardinian pecorino.* Fregula *is a typical Sardinian durum semolina pasta formed into coarse lumps that resemble couscous. It is possible to find it commercially made now or you can use a small soup pasta such as* pastina *or* acini di pepe, *although the taste and texture will be entirely different.*

2 quarts cold water
1 teaspoon salt
3 potatoes (about 1¾ pounds), peeled and cut into small cubes
⅓ cup dried white navy beans, picked over, soaked in water to cover overnight, and drained
1 small garlic clove, crushed
1 to 2 ounces pork fatback, rind removed and fat cut into ¼-inch-thick × 4-inch-long strips
¼ pound imported Greek feta cheese, cut into 2 slices, or pecorino cheese, grated
¼ cup *fregula*, or any small soup pasta

1. Put the water, salt, potatoes, beans, garlic clove, and pork fat in a large pot and bring to a boil slowly over medium heat. Once it begins to bubble, gently reduce the heat to a simmer and cook until the beans are half done, about 1 hour.

2. Wash the salt off the feta cheese, crumble or cut it into pieces, and add to the soup. Let the soup cook until the cheese melts, about another hour. Add the *fregula* or other pasta until it is cooked, about another 20 minutes. Stir well and often so the pasta doesn't stick, then serve immediately.

Makes 4 servings

✢ ✢ ✢

TYPICAL Sardinian cooking makes use of all kinds of beans: fava beans, white beans, lupine *(Lupinus albus),* chickpeas, and lentils. Parsley, leeks, and especially lots of cabbage were grown and used in soups and minestrone. Onions, chicory, spinach, and beets were also commonplace on the late medieval Sardinian table. The most common fruit was citron.[45] And, of course, there was fish, but only in the few ports. There you might find—and still do today—*cassòla.*

Cassòla (Sardinia)

SARDINIAN FISH CASSEROLE

This zuppa di pesce *has a long history, possibly connected to the Catalan presence in Sardinia, if that is how we interpret the* casola de pex *recipe in the fourteenth-century Catalan cookery book* Libre de sent soví. *The soup is cooked in an earthenware casserole called a* caçols *or* cassòla, *hence the name* cassòla, *a Spanish word for the casserole, derived from the Mozarab word* cacherulo, *itself probably derived from the Arabic* qaṣ'a, *a kind of a earthenware casserole or bowl. On the other hand, the great lexicographer Joan Corominas suggests that this word, also related to cassoulet (page 195), may be a proto-Hispanic word of unknown origin.*[46] *Today* cassòla *is a popular preparation in Cágliari, Pula, and Carloforte along the southwestern coast of Sardinia, where a tourist may very well find it on the menu of a local trattoria.*

Every Mediterranean seafood stew uses different fish, and in this cassòla *the gallery the Sardinian cook chooses from includes dogfish, gray mullet, skate, sea bass, red gurnard (sea robin), scorpionfish, two-banded bream, squid, cuttlefish, octopus, crab, crayfish, common eel, conger eel, small lobster, John Dory, star-gazer,* salici, *weever,* salema, *and striped bream.*[47]

Most cooks of the Mare Ligure (Ligurian Sea) regard the scorpionfish, known as scòrfano *in Italian and* rascasse *in French, as essential to any fish stew. One can try substituting redfish (ocean perch), rockfish, or red snapper. Some other Atlantic and Pacific fish substitutes to look for are yellowtail, croaker (weakfish), butterfish, porgy (scup), pompano, haddock, cod, or bogue (with my favorite scientific name,* Boops boops *L.), a good-tasting stew fish, sometimes found in ethnic fish stores on the eastern coast of the United States.*

You must have at least one cephalopod—squid, cuttlefish, or octopus—and either, but preferably both, lobster and crab, along with at least four different kinds of fish. Some Sardinian cooks replace the fish entirely with chicken gizzards.

4 to 5 pounds mixed fish (see above), cleaned and gutted but heads and tails left on
3½ cups salted water
4 small squid (about ½ pound), cleaned (page 448)
1 small octopus (about 1½ pounds; optional), cleaned (page 444)
1 to 2 cuttlefish (about 1 pound; optional), cleaned (page 448)
1 live lobster (about 1½ pounds) or live crab (about 1 pound) (see Note 1 on page 51 on handling live lobsters)
¾ cup extra virgin olive oil
1 large onion, finely chopped
¼ cup finely chopped fresh parsley leaves
2 garlic cloves, finely chopped
1 dried chili pepper
4 large ripe tomatoes (about 2 pounds), peeled, seeded, and coarsely chopped
½ cup dry white wine
Salt and freshly ground black pepper to taste
6 or more slices *crostini di pane per le zuppe di pesce* (page 559)
Extra virgin olive oil for drizzling

1. Remove the heads and tails from the fish, place in a pot with the salted water, and bring to a boil to make the fish broth. When it reaches a boil, reduce the heat to low, skim the top of foam, and cook for 2 hours. Strain through a fine-mesh strainer and set aside.

2. Cut the larger fish into pieces and leave the smaller fish whole. Rinse the fish off. Slice the squid

into rings and the octopus and cuttlefish, if using, into bite-size pieces. Split the lobster or crab in half lengthwise, including the claws, with a cleaver.

3. In a large casserole, heat the olive oil over a medium heat, then cook the onion, parsley, and chopped garlic together until the onion turns translucent, about 7 minutes, stirring frequently so the garlic doesn't burn. Add the chili pepper and tomatoes and stir. Cook over a medium heat until the tomatoes are denser, about 5 minutes. Pour in the wine and 1 cup of the reserved fish broth. Put the squid, cuttlefish, and octopus in the casserole. Check the seasoning and simmer to let the broth become flavorful, about 15 minutes.

4. Add the firmer-fleshed fish and cook until it turns color, about 5 minutes. Add the lobster and/or crab and cook another 15 minutes. Add the rest of the fish, reduce the heat to low, and simmer until the fish flakes off when pulled with a fork and the lobster is cooked through, about another 15 minutes. Add more fish broth if the *cassòla* is getting too thick; it should be soupy. Place a *crostini* in each individual bowl, ladle the fish and broth over the bread, drizzle with olive oil, and serve.

Makes 6 servings

Fregula con le Arselle (Sardinia)

FREGULA WITH LITTLENECK CLAMS

Fregula *(or* fregola) *are coarse little balls of semolina that look very much like large, rough grains of couscous. In fact, in Malta they call them* kusksu, *but it is definitely not couscous, being closer to what the Tunisians call* muḥammaṣ, *a kind of pasta. But the shape it evokes (of couscous) might be a conscious attempt to emulate an Arab food.* Fregula *is prepared in a variety of ways for* primi piatti *in Sardinia, but this recipe, where it is cooked with tomatoes and baby clams, is my favorite.* Fregula *is one of the harder pastas to find in this country—you can try well-stocked Italian markets or bring some home as a souvenir. I learned how to make this spicy version at the Ristorante Italia in Cágliari.*

24 small littleneck clams (about 2 pounds), scrubbed, soaked in salted water for 1 hour with 1 tablespoon baking soda, and drained
½ cup extra virgin olive oil
2 garlic cloves, crushed
¾ pound ripe tomatoes, peeled, seeded, and finely chopped
2 quarts water
2 teaspoons salt
½ teaspoon cayenne pepper, or more to taste
1½ cups *fregula* (about ¾ pound)
Leaves from ½ bunch fresh parsley, finely chopped

1. Place the drained clams in a large pot or skillet, cover, and turn the heat to high. After 3 minutes, check to see if any clams have opened and begin removing each one that opens, 6 to 7 minutes in all. Discard any clams that remain tightly shut. Separate the shells, discarding the half shell not attached to the clam. Strain the clam broth remaining in the pot through a fine-mesh strainer and set aside.

2. In a medium-size pot or earthenware casserole, heat the olive oil with the garlic over medium-high heat until the garlic begins to turn light golden, stirring so the garlic doesn't burn. Remove and discard the garlic. Add the chopped tomatoes and stir well. Pour in the water, salt, cayenne, and reserved clam juice. Bring to a gentle boil, then add the *fregula*. Cook until al dente, 16 to 18 minutes, then taste and add a little salt if necessary. Stir in the clams and parsley and cook for 2 to 3 minutes, and serve with an extra bowl to collect the empty shells.

Makes 4 servings

❈ *Porceddu* (Sardinia)

ROAST SUCKLING PIG

The slaughter of the pig across the northern Mediterranean is a time of celebration. The whole family and the village partake in the festivities. Although the moment of slaughter is a solemn affair, it immediately turns joyous when Sardinians clean the pig for roasting, as in this porceddu. *If the pig is not to be spit-roasted, it is then butchered, with a use found for every part of the pig. Both the farmer and his wife make lard and* mustela *(pancetta) to season cabbage, wild fennel, or chicory minestrone. The trotter might be stuffed and the head boiled and served as a delicacy. The ham is used to make prosciutto, and the intestines cleaned to make sausages. The blood, carefully collected at the time of slaughter as it drains from the pig, is mixed with pine nuts, raisins, and honey to become a delicious sweet.*[48]

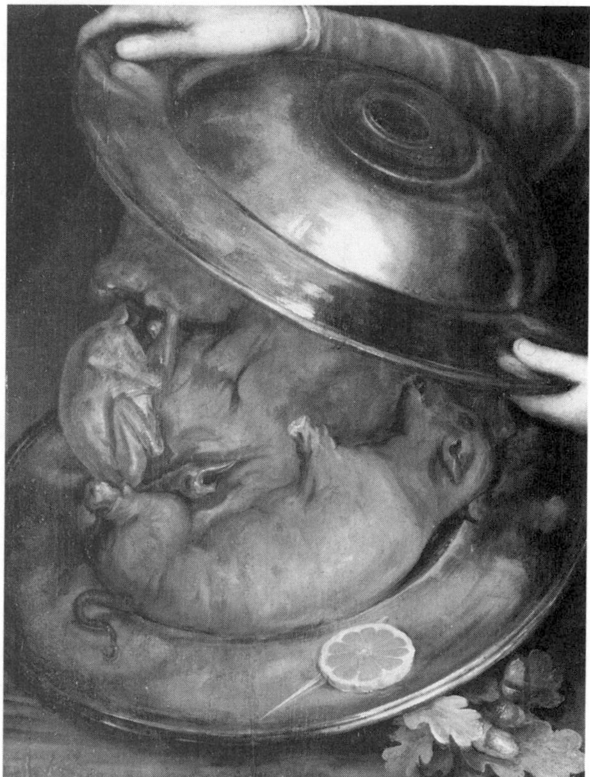

A cook serves suckling pigs. Giuseppe Arcimboldo (1527–1593). *The Cook*. Oil on wood. ERICH LESSING/ART RESOURCE.

There are two ways in which this traditional suckling pig is prepared. For the first method, a large pit is dug in the ground and lined with rocks. A large fire is built upon the rocks, and when it has burned for many hours, the pig is set upon it and covered with hot coals, which are then covered with myrtle branches. The earth is piled on top, leaving no evidence of what is happening under the ground. It is said that this method was typical of the bandits who once populated the desolate reaches of the island's interior.

In the second method, a fire is built with aromatic wood such as juniper, mastic, olive, arbutus, or holm oak. The pig is splayed and affixed to a large strong stick that is pushed into the ground in front of the fire, and basted with a chunk of pork fat. Once the pig is done, it is smothered with myrtle leaves and left for 30 minutes before carving.

In place of the exotic woods, build a fire with whatever wood you have available. Once you begin to roast the pig, throw any combination of leftover nut shells and dried herb twigs such as thyme, marjoram, oregano, mint, or basil, bay leaves, or water-soaked apple wood chips onto the fire to create an aromatic smoke. In this country, myrtle is used only for ornamental plant purposes and it is unlikely you will find pesticide-free myrtle. After experimenting I believe that the closest thing to myrtle is a mixture of bay and sage leaves. If unavailable, use rosemary leaves to smother the finished pig.

This magnificent roast suckling pig requires a grand occasion—perhaps a wedding, holiday, or gathering of great friends. It is well worth the effort. If you lack an outdoor fireplace or do not want to dig a fire pit, you can use your grill by piling all the coals to one side, setting a drip pan in the other side, and jury-rigging the spitted pig over the drip pan, leaning it toward the heat of the coals.

One 15- to 18-pound suckling pig, cleaned
1 pound pork fat or salt pork, in one piece
Myrtle or sage and bay leaves (see page 485)

1. Prepare a hardwood fire in a fire pit or grill and let it burn for 3 hours, replenishing as needed with wood, until you have a good supply of hot coals. Affix the pig to a straight, hard stick that you should be able to find lying around (this might take you 15 minutes) and place 20 inches in front of the fire, chest side toward the fire. (Do not use wood made of composite materials.) The pig should be leaning slightly toward the fire. Make sure there is a drip pan under the pig to catch the melting fat.

2. Roast for 3 hours, basting with the salt pork or pork fat affixed to a meat fork. Turn and continue roasting for another 3 hours. Test for doneness by pulling on one of the ears; it should feel loose. Let the pig sit for 30 minutes on a bed of myrtle or bay leaves before carving.

Makes 12 servings

ISLAND PEARLS

VENICE has its own set of unique islands running down the Adriatic and circling into the Aegean. Look at a map of the Adriatic (page 90) and it is clear why it is a second great sea of the Mediterranean and why Venice once ruled the Adriatic. The Apulian towns of Bari, Brindisi, and Otranto were all occupied by Venice. The gateway to the Adriatic was controlled by Corfu, and that island too was Venetian from 1386 to 1797. Venice was also able to dominate Trieste and Ragusa (Dubrovnik) and in 1602 supported the rebel Ragusan subjects of the island of Lagosta (Lastovo), famous for its seafood.

Venice had long kept vigil against the Turks. Its outposts and coastal watchtowers ran along the shores of Istria, Dalmatia, and Albania, as far as the Ionian Islands and beyond, to Crete and Cyprus. Cyprus was to remain Venetian from 1489 to 1571, but it was always Greek in inspiration and Turkish in its culinary sensibilities, with a predilection for coriander seeds as a spice.

The islands were the secret to Venice's success, islands such as Corfu, Crete, and Cyprus, which, although fertile, could produce only enough grain to last four months, necessitating the export of wine, oil, and flocks of sheep to the mainland.

Hirino Afelia (Cyprus)

BRAISED PORK WITH CORIANDER SEEDS AND RED WINE

Cypriot cooking is a mixture of Greek, Arab, and Turkish cuisines. The Greek Cypriots are very fond of pork, such as the hiromeri, *similar to prosciutto, and* lounza *or* loutza, *a cured pork fillet.*[49]

Afelia *is a Cypriot method of cooking using cracked coriander seeds. The pork is often accompanied with* afelia-*style artichokes, mushrooms, and potatoes, each typically cooked separately. Today corn oil is used more often than olive oil in Cyprus, but I prefer the traditional taste.*

2 pounds boneless pork loin, trimmed of fat and cut into 1-inch cubes
⅔ cup dry red wine
Salt and freshly ground black pepper to taste
2 tablespoons extra virgin olive oil
4 teaspoons freshly and finely ground coriander seeds

1. In a ceramic or glass bowl or dish, marinate the pork in the wine, salt, and pepper for 6 hours in the refrigerator, covered with plastic wrap, turning the pork occasionally. Drain the pork, reserving the marinade. Damp-dry the pork cubes with paper towels. (The pork must be dried, otherwise it will not fry properly.)

2. In a large skillet, heat the olive oil over high heat, then brown the pork cubes on all sides, turning frequently, about 3 minutes. In a small skillet, heat the reserved marinade to a simmer and pour over the pork. Cover, reduce the heat to very low, and braise for 1 hour.

3. Stir in ground coriander and cook until the meat is tender and the wine absorbed, about another 30 minutes. If the wine is not evaporated and the sauce is too thin, remove the meat with a slotted spoon and keep warm. Turn the heat to high and reduce the liquid. Return the meat to the pan and cook until hot again. Serve immediately with rice or a small pasta like orzo.

Makes 4 servings

ITALY in the mid-sixteenth century was dominated by five major city-states: Venice, the strongest; Milan, with the agriculturally productive Po Valley; Florence, the most progressive and the most important in terms of the Renaissance; the Papal States, dominated by highly political popes in Rome; and the kingdom of Naples, a branch of the house of Aragon in Spain. Each of these states constantly tried to destroy the other, often calling in foreigners to help them. As a result, Italy was pockmarked by invasions and interference by outsiders. There were numerous wars and as numerous peace treaties. In 1540, one of these treaties deprived Venice of two precious positions on the Dalmatian coast, Nadino and Laurana (Vrana), and some islands in the Aegean, such as Patmos, Cesina, Ios (the fief of the Pisani family), Stampalia (Astipálaia)—(the fief of the Quirini family), and Páros, belonging to the Venier family. Venice was also forced to give up the important stations of Monemvasia and Napoli di Romania (Navplion, Nauplia) in the Peloponnesus.

Venice also controlled the two Ionian Islands Zante (Zákinthos) and Cephalonia (Kefallinía), and the fortress of Modon (Methóni) in the Peloponnesus. The fact that Venice could hold back the mighty Turkish Empire with a handful of outposts was truly miraculous. Venetian defenses were a triumph of improvisation, of the scrupulous maintenance of the fortresses, of the vigilance of the Arsenale, that mighty industrial compound, of incessant patrols by roundships and galleys, of the loyalty of the frontier population. The entire Venetian empire was nothing but a chain of island bases, pearls on a string, as one chronicler called them, whose populations, except perhaps in Crete, never really amounted to anything. Venice relied as much on bribery and persuasion by its representatives and spies in Istanbul as it did on its roundships and forts.

Modon, modern Methóni, on the southwestern point of the Peloponnesus, was guarded by the most spectacular of Venetian castles, which can be visited today. Modon was like a Venetian Pearl Harbor with its supply warehouses, command posts, repair yard, and rest and recreation centers for Venetian shipping. The Venetians called it the "eye of the Republic." Although it was small, Modon was a vibrant town bustling with the goods of trade, such as spices and silks from Syria and cotton from Cyprus, monkeys for the menageries of the rich, incense from Arabia, and people from everywhere—Mongolian slaves from the Sea of Azov, soldiers, Jewish bankers from Euboea (Negroponte) in Greece, Greek icon-artists, and merchants retiring after a lifetime in Alexandria. Pigs were traded here, supplying all of Venice's bacon.[50]

The foreign intervention that every island experienced, because they often sat smack in the middle of some strategic position, is clear even today. On Cyprus you can see the Venetian and Genoese mansions. On Crete, Canea (Khaniá) sports a huge Venetian *arsenale,* used today for light manufacturing and auto repair, and the old town is filled with Venetian *palazzi.* The Venetian general Giambattista del Monte called the castle at Candia (Iráklion), after it was built in the mid-sixteenth century, *la piu bella fortezza d'Europa,* the most beautiful fortress of Europe. The fortress at Retimo (Réthimnon) was the largest Venetian fort ever built. But in 1538, the pirate Khayr al-Din (Barbarossa) wreaked havoc along the coast of Crete, and Réthimnon, defended by seven thousand men, was sacked and burned.[51]

Soupies me Patatas (Crete)

CUTTLEFISH, POTATO, AND OLIVE STEW

This revealing recipe demonstrates an Arabo-Turkish spicing and the integration of the New World vegetables of potato and tomato. In the covered market of Khaniá in western Crete, there are a couple of workingmen's lunch tavernas that sell very flavorful and filling food. Large serving bains-marie *sit behind a glass counter in the front of the taverna, where the stoves are and the cook works. The Taverna Bonne Petite had some very proud servers and food to be proud of. This stewed cuttlefish was my favorite. At first I couldn't figure out what the delicious yellow wedges were, until after several bites I realized they were the potatoes, having taken on the flavor of the cuttlefish while simmering in a rich tomato and olive oil ragout. If you are unable to find cuttlefish and use squid instead, the amount of time you need to simmer will be reduced, so keep checking by puncturing a piece with a skewer, which should glide somewhat easily into the squid or cuttlefish. For other cuttlefish recipes see pages 447–452.*

1½ cups extra virgin olive oil
1 medium-size onion, finely chopped
2 pounds cuttlefish, cleaned (page 448) and cut into strips
4 large garlic cloves, finely chopped
⅔ cup dry white wine
1½ cups canned or fresh tomato puree
1 cup water
½ cinnamon stick
1 whole clove
½ bay leaf
Salt and freshly ground black pepper to taste
¾ pound Yellow Finn or Russian Banana (fingerling) potatoes, peeled and cut into wedges
1½ cups pitted imported green olives (about 6 ounces)

1. In a medium-size casserole, heat the olive oil over medium heat, then cook the onion until translucent, about 7 minutes, stirring occasionally. Add the cuttlefish and garlic and cook until mixed well, about 2 minutes. Pour in the wine and let it reduce by half, about 8 minutes, stirring a few times. Add the tomato puree, water, cinnamon, clove, and bay leaf, season with salt and pepper, reduce the heat to low, cover, and simmer for 3 hours, stirring once in a while.

2. Add the potatoes and olives and simmer another 1 hour. Serve.

Makes 4 servings

Bourtheto (Corfu)

PEPPERY FISH STEW FROM CORFU

The most illustrious of Corfu's overlords were the Venetians, and we can see their hand in this fish stew flavored with onions, olive oil, tomatoes, paprika, and cayenne. The tomatoes and the two varieties of capsicum, paprika and cayenne, are foods that came from the New World. They are likely to have arrived in Corfu with the Venetians, who controlled the island at the time of Columbus's voyages. One can still find bourtheto *served in the tavernas in Mandouki, the port area behind the New Fortress in town.*

3/4 cup extra virgin olive oil
2 cups water
2 large onions, thinly sliced
2 tablespoons paprika
1 teaspoon cayenne pepper
1 teaspoon salt
Freshly ground black pepper to taste
One 1-pound mackerel or sea bass, gutted, sliced into 1-inch-thick steaks, and head and tail saved
10 ounces redfish (ocean perch), red snapper, or swordfish fillets or steaks, cut into pieces
10 ounces cod, hake, or halibut fillet, cut into pieces
Salt to taste

1. Put the olive oil, water, onions, paprika, cayenne, salt, and black pepper in a 12-inch skillet. Quickly bring to a gentle boil over high heat, about 6 minutes. Immediately reduce the heat to low and simmer until the onions are almost tender, about 25 minutes.

2. Add the fish, placing the mackerel or bass pieces with the head and tail in the center of the pan and the other fish around it. Lightly salt the fish. Partially cover the pan and simmer over medium heat for 20 minutes, shaking the pan occasionally so broth covers the top of the fish. Lift the fish out using a spatula when the whole mackerel's pectoral fin looks like it could come off with a little tug and transfer to a serving bowl or plate. Surround with the onions and pour the remaining sauce over the fish.

Makes 4 servings

Kreatopitta Kefallinitiki (Kefallinía)

MEAT PIE FROM CEPHALONIA

Cephalonia (Kefallinía) is an Ionian island off the western coast of Greece. During the Middle Ages, it first belonged to the Norman kings of Sicily, before becoming a Frankish fief. Italian overlords ruled the island from 1155 to 1478, first under the Orsini family and then the Tocchi family. The Turks captured the island and held it for twenty years until the Ventians supplanted them in 1500, ruling until 1797. As a result, the influence of Italian cookery is still felt in this beautiful pie with a golden phyllo pastry crust and a stuffing that is mild and perfect.

Typically, kreatopitta kefallinitiki *is served on the Feast Day of Analipseos (Ascension Day) and on the day of Apokreas, at the beginning of Lent. This recipe comes from a Greek neighbor in Arlington, Massachusetts, where I once lived.*

1/4 cup extra virgin olive oil
3 tablespoons unsalted butter
1 cup hot water
1 3/4 pounds boneless leg of lamb, trimmed of all fat and cut into bite-size pieces
3 garlic cloves, crushed
1/4 cup finely chopped fresh parsley leaves
Salt and freshly ground black pepper to taste
1/2 cup dry white wine
1/3 cup raw long-grain rice, soaked in cold water to cover for 30 minutes and drained
3/4 pound feta cheese, crumbled
3/4 pound (about 12 sheets) commercial phyllo pastry (usually 14 × 18-inch sheets; see page 224 for handling it)
3 medium-size ripe tomatoes, peeled and sliced
3 hard-boiled large eggs, shelled and sliced
1 tablespoon unsalted butter, melted
2 to 4 tablespoons milk

1. In a large skillet, heat 2 tablespoons of the olive oil with 1 tablespoon of the butter and the hot water over medium heat. Add the lamb, garlic, and parsley and season with salt and pepper. Cover and cook until the lamb is tender, about 1 hour and 15 minutes, adding more water to keep the skillet from drying out completely.

2. Add the wine and cook, uncovered, until reduced somewhat, 12 to 15 minutes. Remove from the heat and toss with the rice and feta cheese. Set aside.

3. Using a tablespoon of butter for each, grease two 9-inch cake pans very well. Divide the phyllo sheets in half. Layer four sheets on the bottom of each pan, brushing each sheet with the remaining 2 tablespoons olive oil. Divide the meat mixture between the two pans and spread over the phyllo sheets. Layer the tomatoes and eggs evenly over the meat in each pan. Cover with the remaining phyllo sheets, brushing each with the olive oil. Brush the top and final layer with the melted butter.

4. Preheat the oven to 350°F. Moisten the edges of the phyllo with water and crimp them together with your fingers. Prick the top of the pie with a fork and make a small hole in the center to vent the steam. Bake until golden brown, about 1 hour, pouring a few tablespoons of milk in the center hole of each while it bakes to keep the stuffing moist.

Makes 8 servings

Tourta (Crete)

MEAT PIE FROM CRETE

The name of this meat pie from Crete derives from the Italian word torta, *a pie or tart. The Cretan version is made in a pie pan called a* tapsi. *Undoubtedly this savory pie has some relationship to the centuries-long rule of the Venetians, but the spicing of cumin and sesame seeds points to the Turks and Arabs. Although it's true that these spices are used more often in the Turkish-influenced Dodecanese group of islands east of Crete, their use here might be modern because it was in the 1920s that a population exchange occurred, transferring Greek Christians from Anatolia to Crete and Cretan Muslims to Anatolia.*

In any case, this recipe for meat pie is typical of Crete and adapted from one I had at the Taverna Despoina Polake in Khaniá. It looks as if there is a lot of meat, but remember that more than a third of the weight is the bone.

3 pounds leg of lamb on the bone, trimmed of all fat
1 cup water
Salt and freshly ground black pepper to taste
4 cups unbleached all-purpose flour, sifted
½ cup (1 stick) unsalted butter, cut into small bits
½ cup milk (optional)
1¼ pounds *mezithra* or *ricotta salata* cheese
½ to 1 teaspoon freshly ground cumin seeds, to your taste
½ cup heavy cream
1 large egg, beaten
1 tablespoon sesame seeds

1. Place the leg of lamb, water, salt, and pepper in a pot or casserole that will fit the leg of lamb snugly. Bring to a gentle boil over medium heat, cover, and simmer until the lamb is partially cooked, about 30 minutes. Remove the lamb from the saucepan and, when cool enough to handle, cut the meat from the bone into bite-size pieces. Remove and discard any remaining gristly pieces of fat. Save ½ cup of the broth if not using the milk.

2. Pour the flour and 2 teaspoons salt into a large bowl and work the butter into it with a fork or your fingers until the mixture resembles coarse meal. Moisten the mixture with the reserved lamb broth or

milk to form a stiff dough and roll into a ball. Knead the dough for 3 minutes, flouring the working surface if necessary to prevent sticking. Divide the dough into two equal pieces. Roll out one piece to a circle about ¼-inch thick and large enough to cover the bottom and side walls of a 9- or 10-inch deep-dish pie pan.

3. Preheat the oven to 350°F. Break up the cheese in a small bowl and, using your fingers, toss with the cubed lamb. Transfer to the pie pan and spread around the bottom, forming a small mound in the center. Sprinkle with the cumin and pour the cream over the filling. Roll the remaining dough out into another circle and cover the pie pan with it. With a sharp knife or scissors trim off the overlapping dough. Crimp the edges closed with the tines of a fork.

4. Brush the top of the pie with the beaten egg and score in several places to vent the steam. Sprinkle the top with sesame seeds and bake until the pie is golden, about 50 minutes. Serve immediately.

Makes 6 servings

Skordostoumbi (Zákinthos)

ZANTE-STYLE GARLIC STEAKS

The Ionian island of Zákinthos (Zante) was ruled by the Venetians from 1485 to 1797. The Venetians loved this island they called Zante, fior di Levante *(Zante, flower of the East), with its mild climate and luxuriant flora. The use of the tomatoes and vinegar in this slow braising of meat flavored with basil and herbs is a typical Italian style of cooking. According to Diane Kochilas, the author of several Greek cookbooks,* skordostoumbi *is the name for the marinade of strong red wine vinegar, lots of garlic, and sometimes walnuts.*

2 pounds veal steak, shoulder, or rib chops, trimmed of fat
Salt and freshly ground black pepper to taste
1 tablespoon red wine vinegar
All-purpose flour for dredging
3 tablespoons extra virgin olive oil
12 garlic cloves, finely chopped
1¾ cups canned or fresh peeled and crushed tomatoes
1 tablespoon sugar
3 tablespoons finely chopped fresh parsley leaves
1 tablespoon finely chopped fresh basil leaves
1 cup dry white wine

1. Bone the veal. Pound the meat between two pieces of waxed paper with a mallet or the side of a cleaver until ¼ inch thick. Salt and pepper the veal and sprinkle the vinegar over it.

2. Dredge the steaks in the flour on both sides, shaking off any excess. Heat the olive oil in a large skillet over medium-high heat and brown the steaks on each side, about 5 minutes per side.

3. Cover the steaks with the garlic and the tomatoes and reduce the heat to low. Season with salt and pepper and sprinkle the sugar, parsley, and basil over the top. Flip the steaks a few times to coat them on both sides with the sauce. Pour the wine over the steaks, shake the pan to mingle the flavors, and cover. Simmer over low heat until the veal is tender, about 1 hour, shaking the pan occasionally.

Makes 4 servings

Pastitsada (Corfu)

CORFU-STYLE PASTA WITH VEAL SAUCE

This popular Corfiot meal is a way to stretch the small amounts of meat available to the housewife. Yearling calf is used and the meat is not like the white milk-fed veal we are familiar with. It's kind of a cross between beef and veal.

In Greece, "macaroni" refers to all dry pasta except spaghetti. In this recipe you use makaronia tirpita *no. 5 (it means "macaroni with a hole in it"), which is the same as Italian* perciatelli (bucatini).

The primary cooking pot of Corfiots is the rihia, *James Chatto and W. L. Martin tell us in their* A Kitchen in Corfu.[52] *This round, flat-bottomed casserole with vertical sides is 4 inches deep, with two small looped handles. It comes in many sizes, similar in purpose to the* olla *or* cazuela *of Andalusia and the* ṭājins *of Morocco.*

Kefalotyri *is a hard, yellow sheep or goat's milk cheese. Most Greek-American cookbooks suggest replacing it with an Italian pecorino or Parmesan cheese, but I feel that provolone is a better choice; in any case I've never had a problem finding it in this country (see "Mediterranean Food Products Resources"). Greeks do not eat pasta al dente as do the Italians; they prefer it cooked well.*

½ cup extra virgin olive oil
2 pounds boneless veal shoulder, trimmed of fat and cut into 1-inch cubes
2 large onions, finely chopped
3 garlic cloves, chopped
Salt and freshly ground black pepper to taste
½ cup dry red or white wine
1 tablespoon white wine vinegar
3 whole cloves
1 cinnamon stick
2 bay leaves
2 pounds ripe tomatoes, peeled, seeded, and finely chopped
1 pound *perciatelli*
¼ cup (½ stick) unsalted butter, melted
1 cup freshly grated *kefalotyri* cheese

1. In a medium-size enameled cast-iron casserole, heat the olive oil over medium-high heat, then brown the veal on all sides, about 6 minutes. Add the onions, stir, reduce the heat to medium-low, cover, and cook until soft, about another 5 minutes. Add the garlic and wine and season with salt and pepper. Stir, then add the vinegar, cloves, cinnamon, and bay leaves. Stir again and add the tomatoes.

2. Cover, reduce the heat to low, and cook until the veal is very tender, about 2½ hours. The sauce should be thick; reduce it if it is not. Remove and discard the bay leaves, cinnamon stick, and cloves (if you can find them).

3. Meanwhile, bring a large pot of water to a rolling boil, salt abundantly, and add the pasta. Drain when soft and pour into a deep serving bowl or platter. Pour the melted butter over the pasta, sprinkle the cheese over, and toss to evenly coat. Ladle the veal sauce over the pasta and serve.

Makes 6 servings

Horta (Crete)

BOILED GREENS WITH OLIVE OIL

In Greece and its islands, horta *is the name of any kind of boiled wild green, derived from the Greek word for "small garden," a word that also gives, through the Latin, the Spanish word for large vegetable garden,* huerta.

In this recipe I use dandelion and sliced zucchini boiled in salted water and drizzled with olive oil and lemon juice. One could also use chicory, arugula, or mizuna, and it is delicious served warm.

10 ounces dandelion leaves, trimmed of tough stems
1 zucchini, cut into ¼-inch-thick slices
Salt to taste
Extra virgin olive oil for drizzling
A few drops of fresh lemon juice

1. Bring a large pot of water to a boil. Drop the dandelion leaves and sliced zucchini in the boiling water and cook until the zucchini slices are tender, about 10 minutes.

2. Drain well, salt, and arrange on a serving platter. Drizzle with olive oil and a few drops of lemon juice. Serve warm.

Makes 2 to 4 servings

Staka (Crete)

HOMEMADE CURD DIP

In Crete, staka *is a rich cream drawn off from water buffalo or sheep's milk when making a ricotta cheese. The milk is boiled and the curds skimmed off. The curds are then mixed with some flour and oil to make a dip. The mountains of Crete have long been a refuge from invaders, such as the Venetians and Turks, and even the Nazis in World War II, and one often finds rustic dishes such as this one there. When I first had* staka, *in the little hamlet of Kalithea in the mountains behind Khaniá, I couldn't stop eating it, even though it is quite heavy. Another preparation of* staka *is a baked delicacy made with eggs, sugar, and lots of sweet butter.*

I base my recipe on goat's milk, which approximates the taste quite closely.

1 quart goat's milk
1 quart unhomogenized (preferably) whole cow's milk
¾ cup heavy cream (preferably not ultrapasteurized)
2 tablespoons fresh lemon juice
1 tablespoon all-purpose flour
Salt to taste
2 tablespoons extra virgin olive oil

1. Pour the goat's milk, cow's milk, cream, and lemon juice into a large nonreactive saucepan. Turn the heat to low and bring the liquid to 194°F using a candy/deep-fry thermometer (also called a quick-read thermometer), making sure it does not touch the bottom or sides of the pot. This will take about 2 hours.

2. Line a strainer or small colander with cheesecloth. When the curds form on the surface of the liquid, remove them with a skimmer or slotted ladle and transfer to the strainer. Raise the heat under the pot to medium and after 8 minutes skim some more, until all the curds are removed and only milky liquid remains.

3. Leave the curds to drain for 1 hour and then beat them together with the flour and salt to taste. Slowly add 1 tablespoon of the olive oil while beating.

4. Preheat the oven to 275°F. Spread in an ovenproof dish and heat until warm in the oven. Drizzle the remaining tablespoon olive oil around the edges and serve warm with warm bread.

Makes 2 to 3 servings

THE PRESIDIOS

At one time the Mediterranean looked like it might become a Muslim lake. Constantinople fell to the Turks in 1453, and its name was changed to Istanbul; by 1522, Egypt, Syria, and Rhodes were under Turkish domination—later, even Vienna was threatened. Muslim supremacy in the southern Mediterranean led to the rise of ports such as Oran, Bougie (Bejaïa), and Algiers. Bône (Annaba) in Algeria, a populous town manufacturing earthenware, consumed a lot of beef and exported wool, butter, and honey.[53] Agricultural produce from the nearby plains flowed into the great market of Algiers and then on to Bougie. Boats from Oued el Harach, off Cape Matifou, transported wool, wheat, and poultry to Marseilles, Valencia, and Barcelona.

Only Melilla and Ceuta, Spanish territories in North Africa and once important presidios, today remind us of the economic and military threats to Spain from this activity in North Africa. To counter the threat from as well as to provide defense against pirates (like ʿUluj ʿAlī, the Bey of Algiers, who drove the Spanish out of Tunis in 1569), the Spanish king Ferdinand V built a line of presidios along the North African coast between 1509 and 1511. To supplement the presidios, the Spanish also built major defense works throughout southern Italy, and by 1567 more than three hundred watchtowers existed throughout the kingdom. The presidios represent a great missed military opportunity for the Spanish because they never moved inland to capture the whole of the Maghrib, the area of western North Africa that includes Morocco, Algeria, Tunisia, and sometimes Libya. The Turkish fleet was stymied and rarely crossed the Naples-Sicily line, where Christian bases at Malta and La Goletta in Tunisia, controlled by the Spanish until 1574, could threaten them. The Spanish also had a base in Messina in Sicily, which held a commanding position in a narrow channel. It had easy access to Sicilian wheat for provisions and was near enough to Naples to receive in short order men, sails, biscuits, hogsheads of wine, vinegar, fine powder, iron cannon balls, oars, and match and rods for arquebuses, the very heavy matchlock guns invented in the fifteenth century.

The presidios grew into little cities, like islands, supported more from the sea than the surrounding lands. Mers-al-Kebir, Ceuta, Melilla, and La Goletta were presidios that had windmills, powder magazines, cisterns, and cavaliers fixed with powerful bronze artillery, the raison d'être of the presidios. The Spanish supply ships plying the sea-lanes of the southern Mediterranean brought the fresh water, fish, and chickpeas needed to feed the presidios. Convoys left the principal port of Málaga to supply the presidios, dodging the corsairs from Algiers or Tetouan who would sometimes capture these ships, reselling their cargo. But at the same time Spanish ships were dodging corsairs, other small boats from Valencia and Andalusia, called *balancelle,* carried rice, perfume, and even contraband to Algiers.

When the corsairs interdicted food shipments to the presidios, famine followed. But when food did arrive at these isolated presidios, dinner was often predictable. The diet of the garrisons along the Barbary Coast in January 1569 consisted of flour, wine, salted meat, lard, chickpeas, tuna, and olive oil.[54] Simple soups and stews were eaten by the adventurers who garrisoned these isolated presidios and the corsairs who attacked them, and they always contained chickpeas. I don't imagine that the corsairs ever had such delicious preparations as the following, but they may have.

Ḥummuṣ bi'l-Kammūn (Algeria)
CHICKPEA SOUP WITH CUMIN

The chickpea was so popular from Egypt to Morocco that Alonso de Pimentel, the commander of La Goletta presidio in Tunisia, wrote in 1570, after receiving large shipments of barley and wheat, "What a misfortune that we have been sent no chickpeas!" This simple soup, a favorite today of Algerian dock workers, is healthy, filling, and has a nice spicy flavor.

3 cups drained canned chickpeas
1 garlic clove, crushed
¼ cup extra virgin olive oil
1 teaspoon freshly ground cumin seeds

1 teaspoon paprika
1 teaspoon *harīsa* (page 523)
1 tablespoon tomato paste
Salt and freshly ground black pepper to taste
1 quart water

1. In a medium-size saucepan, simmer the chickpeas in water to cover for 1 hour over medium-low heat to make them more tender. Drain, remove as much of their white skins as possible, and set aside.

2. Put the garlic, olive oil, cumin, paprika, *harīsa,* tomato paste, salt, and black pepper in a soup pot. Turn the heat to medium, bring to a simmer, and simmer for 5 minutes, stirring occasionally. Pour in the water and bring to a boil. Add the chickpeas and cook for 15 minutes.

3. Using a small strainer, remove the chickpeas and puree them in a food processor or blender. Return the puree to the soup and stir to blend into a smooth veloute. Or you can serve the soup with the whole chickpeas.

Makes 4 servings

CHICKPEAS AND THE SICILIAN VESPERS

Charles of Anjou in 1282 was on the verge of becoming the master of the Mediterranean and ruler of an empire unparalleled since Justinian. His Angevin officials ruled Sicily with an iron hand and his Sicilian subjects detested these Frenchmen. The Sicilians were inflamed by Aragonese agents provocateurs *and enriched by Byzantine agents in the hope they would rise against Charles. The Angevin fleet lay in Messina harbor waiting for the food commandeered from the Sicilian peasants by royal agents to arrive before they set sail to attack Constantinople. In Palermo, at the Church of the Holy Spirit, Easter Monday was being celebrated when a group of drunken French officials joined the festivities. The Sicilians looked on with seething resentment. Soon the younger Sicilian women were being harassed and finally one French sergeant molested a young women, whereupon he was stabbed to death by the husband. The attack unleashed a maelstrom of hate, and within minutes all the French soldiers were dead. At this very moment the church bells rang for vespers, but the Sicilians took the tolling bell as a call to rise up against the oppressor. The streets were filled with angry armed men shouting, "*Moranu li Franchiski*" (Death to the French). The men killed French soldiers on sight and soon French women and children were being murdered. They broke into Dominican and Franciscan convents and dragged out foreign friars who were forced to say the word* ciciri, *Sicilian for "chickpea," a word that the French could not pronounce. Those who couldn't say it were killed. By the next morning, two thousand French men, women, and children were dead and the course of Sicilian history changed once again.*[55]

THIS recipe is misleading, though, in history, not taste. Life in the presidios must have been miserable. The garrison troops were so near the water, yet rations rotted and men died of fever. The hospital in Palermo was crowded with the sick from La Goletta. The soldiers were hungry all year, completely reliant on the supply ships. Later, and only in Oran, did the surrounding countryside provide meat and grain. Even La Goletta, with its excellent location near the inexhaustible supplies of bread, wine, cheese, and chickpeas of Naples and Sicily, suffered as did the rest of the presidios. When Alonso de Pimental took over the garrison at La Goletta in 1569 the troops were living on their reserves of cheese without bread or wine.

Lablābī (Tunisia)

CHICKPEA BREAKFAST STEW

Lablābī *is a popular breakfast stew made with chickpeas, broth, tomatoes, and various toppings such as capers, cumin,* harīsa, *or coddled eggs, eaten in a manner very similar to the way Egyptians eat* fūl *(page 304) or the Syrians* tissaqiyya *(page 554). The word* lablābī *is curious. It is an archaic Arabic word that refers to the hyacinth bean* (Dolichos lablab *L.*), *a bean native to India that is also known as the Egyptian or black bean. The word* lablābī *comes from the Turkish word for roasted chickpea; it is not originally Arabic.* Lablābī *is unknown among the Arabs of the Mashraq, the eastern Arab world. Paula Wolfert suggests it is a food of Tunisian Jews.*[56]

Lablābī *is a favorite winter morning breakfast for stevedores in Tunis. Throughout the city it is a morning offering in the small hole-in-the-wall cook shops that might also sell* brīk *(page 110) and* casse-croûte, *a spicy tuna, tomato, and olive sandwich.*

4 cups drained canned chickpeas
2 tablespoons hot *harīsa* (see variation on page 524)
4 garlic cloves, mashed
1 tablespoon freshly ground cumin seeds
Salt to taste
Juice from 1 lemon
¼ cup extra virgin olive oil

OPTIONAL GARNISHES, TO TASTE

Fresh lemon juice
Coarse sea salt
Coddled eggs
Seeded and finely chopped green bell peppers
Chopped very ripe tomatoes
Dollops of *harīsa*
Capers, rinsed
Pickled turnips
Preserved lemons (see page 104)
Croutons
Finely chopped fresh parsley leaves
Finely chopped fresh coriander (cilantro) leaves
Leftover bread
Extra virgin olive oil

Place the chickpeas in a saucepan and cover with water. Boil until soft, about 30 minutes, then stir in the *harīsa,* garlic, cumin, and salt. Stir well, reduce the heat to medium, and cook for 10 minutes. Stir in the lemon juice and olive oil. Serve with more lemon juice, salt, and ground cumin to taste. Serve with any combination of optional garnishes, including more *harīsa* and olive oil.

Makes 4 servings

WHEN a soldier boarded a ship destined for a presidio, he often would not know his destination and, once there, was not allowed to leave. The famous chronicler Diego Suarez spent twenty-seven years in

Oran in Algeria. The presidios were like prisons and often used as places for deportation, as in the case of Christopher Columbus's grandson, Luis, arrested for trigamy and sent to Oran for a ten-year sentence, where he died.

The presidios resembled little fiefs. Melilla was for many years the province of the Medina Sidonia family, while Oran was the private preserve of the Alcaudete family. The presidios often conducted raids into the surrounding countryside to gather information or food. Sometimes the soldiers would raid out of boredom and as a result were never able to forge a relationship with local populations that could have helped them maintain their presidios. Instead, the Muslims of North Africa became terrified of Spain.

THE OASES AND ISLETS

THERE are also Mediterranean islands not surrounded by water: the oases of the desert. Oases are green, fertile areas in arid regions fed by springs. They are islands of paradise, with date palms *(Phoenix dactylifera)* that provide cool and fragrant refuge from the dry desert. Water determines everything in the oasis. The date orchards are surrounded by mud walls and the palms are fed water through irrigation ditches. Murmuring sounds of water flowing through the gardens and orchards of an oasis are in stark contrast to the silence of the desert. The judicial administration of an oasis is virtually tyrannical, requiring severe discipline of its inhabitants. The oases of Gafsa, north of the huge salt lake called Chott al-Djerid (the Shore of Palms), are today a large town, but during the Ḥafṣid dynasty in the fifteenth century, the caliph al-Muntaṣir built a new kasbah where a variety of desert agricultural produce could be grown, such as apricots, peaches, figs, dates, oranges, pomegranates, and lemons. The delicious *daghlat al-nūr,* dates of light, come from these oases. The date palm is all important, its sap, *lāqmī*, consumed as well as its fruit, sometimes as palm wine, while camels eat the date pits.

Today the *jamʿiyya,* or council of wise men, regulates water usage in an oasis and set rules for irrigation, many of which are a legacy of Arab-Andalusi who migrated there after the Christian reconquest of Spain in the fifteenth century, bringing with them their knowledge of sophisticated irrigation technology. The oases are home to sedentary dwellers who see the desert nomads come and go, their trade carried by the "ship of the desert," the camel. For anyone who has been to an oasis, there is a peaceful timelessness in the umbrellas of date palms piercing the shimmering blue sky, the square houses of local limestone or gypsum supported by beams of palm trunks, the labyrinths of alleyways, corridors, screens, and courtyards that protect private life. I have known people who have been to an oasis without realizing it—it can be huge, like the oasis of Nefta in Tunisia, with its thousand springs.

Farther to the south in the Sahel are the villages of Tataouine and Matmata, where Berbers have forged dwellings in caves and dug cool holes right in the earth, and Cheninni and Guermassa, where *kasrs*, granaries, are filled with esparto grass. Hewn out of the mountainside are mills where blind camels (used so they won't be distracted) turn huge stone wheels to crush olives.[57] Some of these Berber refuges resulted from the ferocious invasions of the banū-Hilāl, Arab invaders from the Najd in the Arabian Peninsula, who swept in from the east in the eleventh century.

Maqrūḍ (Tunisia)

FRIED DATE-STUFFED SEMOLINA CAKES

In Tunisian oases, dates are abundant and popular, especially in making sweets. I'm convinced that this sweet is the original Fig Newton. It is an old preparation, described by the Belgian traveler Anselme Adorne on his visit to Tunis in the fifteenth century, where he ate a maqrūḍ *made with raisins instead of dates. Sweets makers in Tunisia like to use the* āligh *dates, similar to the soft, melt-in-your-mouth medjool dates that grow in the Coachella Valley of California that were originally imported from Morocco in the late nineteenth century. You can also use the* daglat al-nūr *(deglet noor) dates, also grown in California and originally from the stock collected in the nineteenth century at the Algerian oasis of Biskra.*

Date preparations are found everywhere in North Africa and in the Western Desert of Egypt, where the Awlad ʿAlī tribe makes a few wonderful date preparations such as mafrūka, *a kind of sweet snack made with dough stuffed with dates.*

FOR THE SEMOLINA DOUGH

½ teaspoon salt
⅛ teaspoon baking soda
Pinch of saffron threads
2½ cups semolina flour (about 1½ pounds)
6 tablespoons pure or virgin olive oil

FOR THE FILLING

1 pound dates, pitted
¼ cup pure or virgin olive oil
½ teaspoon ground cinnamon
¼ teaspoon ground ginger
2 teaspoons grated orange zest

FOR THE SYRUP

2 cups sugar (about 1¼ pounds)
1¾ cups water
2 tablespoons rose water
½ cup orange blossom honey

2 cups pure or virgin olive oil for frying

1. In a mortar, grind the salt, baking soda, and saffron together. Put this mixture in a large bowl with the semolina and work it into a dough with the olive oil and as much water as needed to form a ball. Add the water by merely wetting your hands. Once a firm, homogenous ball of dough is formed, knead with the palms of your hands for 5 minutes. Roll the ball up in plastic wrap and let rest in the refrigerator for 30 minutes.

2. Meanwhile, mash the dates in a food processor using short bursts until it is a paste. Transfer the mashed dates to a medium-size bowl and incorporate the oil, cinnamon, ginger, and orange zest and mash and squeeze the mixture with your hands until the mixture is pliable and homogenous. Set aside.

3. Place the sugar in a medium-size saucepan with the water and turn the heat to high, stirring until the water and sugar are very syrupy, about 230°F on a candy thermometer, about 25 minutes. Stir in the rose water and turn the heat off. Dissolve the honey in the sugar syrup and set aside, keeping it warm.

4. From the large ball of semolina dough, make three smaller balls, each about the size of an orange. On a sheet of waxed paper, roll the ball of dough out to a cylinder 8 inches long and about ½ inch thick. If the dough is crumbling or breaking apart, squeeze it into shape with your fingers. Take a handful of date paste and roll or shape it into a long, thin cylinder. Flatten the cylinder of dough and place the thin cylinder of date paste in the middle of the semolina dough. Using your hands, lift the sides of the semolina dough and encase the date paste, then roll back and forth until it is the shape of a salami, smoothing out rough parts and cracks. The cracks do not have to be perfectly smooth because it will all hold together anyway when cooked.

Cut into rounds about 3/8 inch thick. Place on an oiled baking sheet while you continue making the rest.

5. In a medium-size skillet, heat the olive oil over medium-high heat until nearly smoking, about 10 minutes. Carefully place the *maqrūḍ* (semolina rounds) in the hot oil a few at a time so the skillet is never crowded, and cook until light golden, about 20 seconds. By the time you have placed the last round in you will have to begin taking the first ones out. Remove from the frying oil with long tongs and place on a paper towel–lined baking tray to drain. Continue cooking the remaining rounds, making sure you don't splash hot oil on yourself and that you don't burn the semolina, because they cook so quickly.

6. Arrange the *maqrūḍ* in layers in whatever container you are going to use as a storage device, such as a cookie tin or a plastic container. Drizzle each layer abundantly with the sugar syrup. Set aside and serve once they are cool. They will keep for 4 months or longer.

Makes 30 or more maqrūḍ

Al-Tamar al-Maḥshī (Tunisia)

STUFFED DATES

In Islam, the Ramadan fast is usually broken with dates and this preparation of stuffed dates is a favorite in Tunisia. In spite of the date's importance as food, the eleventh-century invaders of North Africa, the banū-Hilāl tribe, did not respect date palm production and the trees suffered along with the populace.[58] But by Ḥafṣid times (1228–1574) the date palms had recovered. The daily food of Tunisia during Ḥafṣid times boiled down to a few essential products: wheat or barley, olive oil and olives, milk, butter, dates, figs, and salt. Milk was used for drinking and making butter, but it truly was the date palm, found throughout the Saharan oases, that was of paramount importance to the Bedouin and the Berbers.

FOR THE SYRUP

2 cups granulated sugar (about 1¼ pounds)
1¾ cups water
2 tablespoons rose water

FOR THE FILLING

½ pound blanched whole almonds
1¼ cups confectioners' sugar (about 5 ounces)
2 pounds medjool dates, pitted

TO FINISH

Granulated sugar for dredging

1. Place the granulated sugar in a medium-size saucepan with the water and turn the heat to high, stirring until the water and sugar are very syrupy, about 230°F on a candy thermometer, about 25 minutes. Stir in the rose water and turn the heat off.

2. Place the almonds in a food processor and grind until fine. Transfer the almonds to a medium-size bowl and add the confectioners' sugar and 1 tablespoon water to form a dough with your hands. The dough does not have to be homogenous like a bread dough, just sticky enough so that a thimbleful amount will hold together.

3. Stuff the dates with the filling. Plunge the stuffed dates, holding them with thin tongs or chopsticks, into the sugar syrup, let excess syrup drip off, and then roll the dates in the granulated sugar and set aside on a waxed paper–lined baking sheet or jelly roll pan. Refrigerate, covered, for up to 2 weeks until needed but serve at room temperature.

Makes 6 servings

❈ *ᶜUjja bi'l-Hrūs* (Tunisia)

SPICY EGGS AND SWEET PEPPERS

Hrūs *is the name of a spice mix in Gabes, the coastal oasis town that once was the terminus for the medieval trans-Saharan trade and that had a large Jewish community. The spice mix is made from preserved onions, dried chili peppers, rose petals, and cinnamon. It also appears as a salad of sweet and hot peppers, tuna, olives, capers, garlic, and caraway seeds. But in this recipe,* hrūs*—the puree of hot and sweet peppers—is simmered with eggs in this class of dishes familiar in Tunisia, often served as a lunch dish, called* ᶜujja *(eggs). It is typical in summer. Other important classes of egg dishes in Tunisia are* ṭājin, *a kind of frittata, while* maᶜqūda *is a dish of beaten eggs that set in the oven, derived from the word meaning "to congeal," to set like a pudding. Both these Tunisian egg dishes are identical in purpose and form to the Spanish* tortilla *(page 135), remembering that a Spanish tortilla is a frittata, and not related to the Mexican tortilla, which is a flatbread. The prevalence of New World peppers, both sweet and hot, and the well-developed egg cookery in Tunisia point to strong Spanish influence, the first because those plants were introduced by the Spaniards and the second because of the similiarity of egg preparations and methods of cooking in Spain and Tunisia.*

2 green bell peppers, peeled and seeded
2 fresh green or red chili peppers, peeled and seeded
¼ cup tomato paste
3 cups water
½ cup extra virgin olive oil
1 tablespoon paprika
2 tablespoons hot or mild *harīsa* (page 523)
1 tablespoon caraway seeds
Salt and freshly ground black pepper to taste
8 large eggs

1. Pound all the fresh peppers together in a mortar with a pestle and set aside, or puree in a food processor or blender until green and soupy, about 30 seconds. Dissolve the tomato paste in 1 cup of the water and set aside.

2. In a large skillet, heat the olive oil over high heat, then add the puree of peppers, the tomato water, the paprika, *harīsa,* and caraway seeds and season with salt and pepper. Pour in the remaining 2 cups water and, when it reaches a boil, reduce the heat to medium-low while it cooks and reduces in consistency, about 10 minutes. Then increase the heat to medium for another 10 minutes.

3. Crack the eggs into the pan without breaking the yolks and cook in the sauce over medium heat until they set, about 15 minutes over medium heat. Season with salt and serve.

Makes 4 servings

❈ *ᶜUjja bi'l-Mirqāz* (Tunisia)

SPICY EGGS AND TUNISIAN SAUSAGE

This egg and sausage preparation is a winter specialty of Zarzis, an oasis on the coast south of Djerba, where they typically scramble the eggs. I have also eaten this dish in Djerba, where the eggs can be sunny-side up, a very nice way of preparing it, and the method I use here. In Djerba they served this ᶜujja *with tiny, local black olives and a side plate of mild Berber-style* harīsa *(page 523). Far to the north in Bizerte they also make this popular lunch dish. The* mirqāz *sausages can be found through mail order (see "Mediterranean Food Products Resources") or replaced with a hot Cajun-style andouille sausage or a Mexican chorizo sausage.*

- **6 tablespoons extra virgin olive oil**
- **3 cups canned or fresh crushed or finely chopped tomatoes (about 1 pound)**
- **1 green bell pepper, seeded and thinly sliced**
- **1 tablespoon *harīsa* (page 523)**
- **2 garlic cloves, sliced**
- **½ teaspoon freshly ground caraway seeds**
- **½ teaspoon ground red Aleppo or cayenne pepper**
- **Salt and freshly ground black pepper to taste**
- **1 cup water**
- **¼ pound *mirqāz* sausages (pages 249 and 718)**
- **4 large eggs**

1. Put 4 tablespoons of the olive oil, the tomatoes, bell pepper, *harīsa,* garlic, caraway, red pepper, salt, black pepper, and water in a medium-size saucepan and turn the heat to medium-high. Cook until well blended and fragrant, about 45 minutes, stirring frequently so it doesn't stick, and adding a little water if the juices evaporate too quickly.

2. Add the sausages and continue cooking until they are cooked through, about 30 minutes. Meanwhile, heat the remaining 2 tablespoons olive oil in a nonstick omelette pan and fry the eggs sunny-side up. Transfer the eggs to a round serving platter and surround and cover slightly with the sausage and peppers. Serve immediately.

Makes 2 to 4 servings

THE smaller islands and islets of the Mediterranean are largely ignored because of their smallness. Some of them have histories while others do not. Off Sicily are the Egadi Islands and the Aeolian Islands, where tuna is abundant and so, too, the great white sharks that tourist bureaus prefer to ignore. Farther north are Capri and Elba, and to the south is Malta. Iles d'Hyères sits off the Provençal coast. Finally there are the Balearics, which belong to Spain and had to rely on cereal imports from Sicily to barely support their military and merchant towns. Majorca, Minorca, and Ibiza make up the Balearic Islands. Majorcan cuisine is generally considered to be a subcategory of Catalan cuisine; the peasant cooking derives from many influences, including Arab. The Arabs arrived in 902 and stayed until 1229, when they were driven out by King Jaime of Aragon (1213–1276). The islands stayed independent until 1343, when Pedro IV reunited them to the kingdom of Aragon. The next centuries saw the islands become a base for Christian pirates and suffer the ravages of Muslim buccaneers.

Salsa Mahonesa (Balearic Islands)

MAYONNAISE

It is said that mayonnaise originated in the capital city of Mahón on the island of Minorca, the second largest of the Balearic Islands off Catalonia. One story of its origin holds that Marshal Richelieu, the grandnephew of the infamous eminence grise, *after having expelled the British from Minorca in 1756, was out walking in the countryside and grew hungry. He asked a local peasant women to make something and, realizing that he was important, she improvised a sauce from the few precious eggs she had been hoarding.*

Another story relates that King Carlos III of Spain stopped in Mahón on his way from Barcelona to Naples in 1760 and was fêted by the local governor. The banquet served up lobster, for which Minorca is famous, simply grilled. It didn't look appetizing to the king, so the governor ordered the kitchen to make an instant sauce. As you probably now recognize, these apocryphal stories are found throughout the Mediterranean, all with the same spin (see the recipe for umm ʿAlī, *page 313, and* zuppa pavese, *page 53).*

Seafood is popular in Majorca, and the two most popular fish are cap roig, *scorpionfish, and cleaver wrasse, called* roar (Xyrichthys novacula), *a rare and expensive fish traditionally caught from small family-owned fishing boats known as* llauts. *One of the simplest ways to enjoy some of the local seafood, and especially lobster, is cold with a little dollop of mayonnaise.*

Two famous dishes of the islands are sopes, *a soup made of thin slices of Majorcan country bread,* pan payes, *a round unsalted wheat bread that dates from the Arab era, with vegetables and* tumbet, *a kind of ratatouille dish. Majorcan cuisine has a long written history, as witnessed by the eighteenth-century cookery book of Jaume Martí i Oliver, which contains recipes for* salmoregi, *a kind of marinade or sauce also used in Sicilian cooking (page 390), and* sopa de semola o pastas: fideos, maccarrones, tallarines, *soup of durum wheat or pasta such as* fideos, *macaroni, or* tagliarini.[59]

I include this recipe for mayonnaise because it is, very simply, the most famous and ubiquitous Mediterranean invention, now abused and overused. But everyone should know how to make it: it is part of a culinary education. The traditional method is to painstakingly hand-whisk the oil in drop by drop, but I find the food processor a welcome invention of modernity.

¾ cup light olive oil
¾ cup vegetable oil
1 large egg
1 tablespoon fresh lemon juice or good-quality white wine vinegar
½ teaspoon very fine salt
½ teaspoon very finely ground white pepper

Mix the oils. Put the egg in a food processor and run for 30 seconds. Slowly pour in the oil in a very thin stream with the processor running, 5 to 6 minutes of pouring. Blend in the lemon juice or vinegar for 30 seconds. Add the salt and pepper and continue blending for 30 seconds. Refrigerate for 1 hour before using. Keep refrigerated for up to a week.

Makes 2 cups

THE islet of Jālite (Galite) off the northern Tunisian coast is known for its spiny lobsters, while nearby Malta favors its dolphinfish.

The island of Djerba, off Tunisia's southern coast, today equipped with an international airport flying in hordes of German tourists, was as important as Tunis when Tunisia was ruled by the Fāṭimids (909–1171). During Ḥafṣid times (1228–1574), Djerba was important for its dried raisins, but the common people ate boiled barley for their daily nourishment. For the most part, Djerba experienced enormous and frequent scarcity. Date palms were very important, and a rich source of nutrients, but their production dropped during the banū-Hilāl invasions of the eleventh century. During the famine of 1311, the people of Djerba were reduced to making bread from the sawdust of palm trees.[60] Today the Djerbans have abundant food, and make delightfully cool salads that are pleasant to eat in this region of high temperatures and extreme aridity.

Salāṭat al-Bisbās (Tunisia)
FENNEL SALAD

This fennel salad, a specialty of Djerba, is found in other parts of the country, but I particularly like the mild Berber-style harīsa *that is used in the vinaigrette.*

Fennel was cultivated by the Romans as a garden herb and was described by Pliny as a medicinal plant.

3 tablespoons extra virgin olive oil
2 tablespoons white wine vinegar
1/4 teaspoon Berber-style mild *harīsa* (page 523)
Salt and freshly ground black pepper to taste
3 fennel bulbs, trimmed and thinly sliced lengthwise
2 tablespoons finely chopped fresh parsley leaves
12 imported green olives, pitted or whole
12 imported black olives, pitted or whole
2 hard-boiled eggs, shelled and quartered
4 salted anchovy fillets, rinsed

1. Make the vinaigrette by whisking the olive oil, vinegar, *harīsa,* salt, and pepper together in a small bowl until smooth.

2. Toss the fennel, parsley, and vinaigrette together in a salad bowl. Sprinkle with more olive oil if desired and garnish with the olives, hard-boiled eggs, and anchovies.

Makes 4 servings

Salāṭa Mishwiyya (Tunisia)

GRILLED SALAD

The ingredients of this salad, the New World tomatoes and peppers having been introduced by the Spanish, are grilled, then tossed together. It is a very popular salad throughout the country, and one is likely to encounter it many times in travels to Tunisia. I first ate it in Djerba, where it typically accompanies other grilled food. You can double the recipe easily.

1/2 pound ripe but firm tomatoes
2 green bell peppers (about 3/4 pound)
4 fresh red chili peppers (about 1/2 pound)
1 medium-size onion, quartered
2 garlic cloves, peeled
4 1/2 teaspoons caraway seeds
3/4 teaspoon salt
3 tablespoons extra virgin olive oil
1 tablespoon fresh lemon juice
24 imported black olives, pitted or whole
One 3 1/2-ounce can imported tuna in olive oil, drained and flaked
2 hard-boiled eggs, shelled and quartered

1. Prepare a hot charcoal fire or preheat a gas grill on high for 20 minutes. Grill the tomatoes, peppers, and onion until all have blackened and blistered peels or black grid marks, about 15 minutes for the smaller peppers and tomatoes, and 20 to 25 minutes for the bell peppers and onion.

2. Peel and seed the grilled vegetables, cut them up, and place in a food processor. Process with four or five short pulses and transfer to a medium-size bowl.

3. Pound the garlic, caraway seeds, and salt together in a mortar with a pestle until almost a paste, then stir into the grilled vegetables. Arrange on a platter, drizzle with the olive oil and lemon juice, and garnish with the olives, pieces of tuna, and quartered eggs.

Makes 4 servings

Torta tal-Lampuki (Malta)

MAHIMAHI PIE

Italian and Arab influences are evident on Malta and there are traces of Greek, too. The French occupation (1798–1814) left its mark and so did the English, who ruled 150 years, from 1814 to 1964. Several dishes look like they came directly from Sicily, such as timpana, *which is like a* pasticcio *(a savory pie) of macaroni, and* ross fil-fora, *a baked rice dish with eggs, meat, and saffron that closely resembles the Sicilian* tummàla.

This recipe also has Sicilian overtones. Dolphinfish (mahimahi), so named because its head looks like that of a dolphin, is a member of the family Coryphaenidae. *Caught in the Atlantic and Pacific, this pink-fleshed fish is known in most parts of America by its Hawaiian name, mahimahi. (In the Florida Keys, cooks routinely call this fish dolphin, to the consternation of unknowing mammal lovers.)* Lampuki, *or mahimahi, is to the Maltese what hake is to the Spanish, the sardine to Sicilians, or cod to Bostonians.*

The Maltese are fond of fish, as befits islanders, and are noted for proverbs about the freshness of fish. The Comparative Dictionary of Maltese Proverbs *tells us that "a man who buys fish while it is still in the sea may only get the smell in the end."*[61]

These kinds of fish pies have an ancient ancestry in Malta, but are also popular in the folk cuisine of Sicily, where impanata di Caltanissetta, *made with broccoli, eel, tomatoes, and cheese, is similar to this Maltese preparation.*[62] *Fish pie generally does not keep well, so it is best to consume it on the day it is made.*

FOR THE SHORT PASTRY

3 cups unbleached all-purpose flour (about 1 pound)
½ pound (1 cup) vegetable shortening, cut into little bits
1 teaspoon salt
½ cup cold water

FOR THE PIE FILLING

½ cup plus 2 tablespoons extra virgin olive oil
2 pounds dolphinfish (mahimahi) fillets, cut into big pieces
Salt to taste
All-purpose flour for dredging
1 head cauliflower (about 2 pounds, about 1 pound trimmed)
1 large onion, sliced
3 ripe plum tomatoes, peeled, seeded, and chopped
20 ounces spinach, heavy stems removed and washed well
1 cup water
8 imported green olives, pitted and chopped
¼ cup golden raisins
¼ cup crushed walnuts
2 tablespoons capers, rinsed and chopped

1. Make the short pastry. Keep all the ingredients cold and blend the flour, shortening, salt, and water together with your fingers or a pastry cutter until a dough can be formed, handling the dough as little as possible. Roll into a ball, wrap in plastic wrap, and refrigerate for 1 hour.

2. In a 10-inch skillet, heat ½ cup of the olive oil over medium-high heat until it is almost smoking. Dredge the fish in the salted flour, patting off any excess flour, and cook until golden on both sides, about 5 minutes in all. Remove the fish from the skillet with tongs and set aside to drain on paper towels.

3. Meanwhile, bring a large pot of lightly salted water to a boil and boil the cauliflower whole until it can be pierced in the center with a skewer with just a little resistance, 10 to 12 minutes, but check several times. Drain, let cool, and break the cauliflower into florets.

4. In a large casserole, heat 2 tablespoons of the olive oil over medium-high heat, then cook the onion until softened, about 7 minutes, stirring several times. Add the tomatoes and continue cooking for 4 minutes, stirring. Add the spinach and water and cook until wilted and mixed well, about 12 minutes. Add the cauliflower, olives, raisins, walnuts, and capers, stir to blend, and turn the heat off. Cover and leave for 10 minutes to allow the flavors to mingle.

5. Preheat the oven to 425°F. Cut the dough into two pieces, one a little larger than the other, and roll out on a floured surface to a thickness of 1/16 inch. Line a 9- or 10-inch deep-dish pie pan or a 9 × 12-inch baking dish with the larger of the two halves of the rolled-out dough. Prick the top of this bottom crust with a toothpick. Cover with half of the vegetable mixture. Place the fish on top and cover with the remaining vegetables. Cover with the smaller sheet of dough, pinching the sides closed with the

tines of a fork and cutting any excess dough away with scissors, and score in several places to vent for steam. Bake for 15 minutes, then reduce the oven temperature to 350°F and continue baking until golden brown, about 45 minutes. Remove from the oven and serve.

Makes 6 servings

CONCLUSION

THE islands are important in the history of Mediterranean food because they often played a crucial role in the dissemination of crops. Although the islands had monocultures and were rarely able to feed themselves, they each had something to offer, whether it was Cretan wine, Djerban olives, or Sicilian wheat.

Sicily is the largest island in the Mediterranean and unique in many ways. It lies at the crossroads of Mediterranean geography as well as its cultures. During the Roman era, Sicily provided soft wheat and later was an entrepôt for east-west and north-south trade, including new vegetables and fruits never before grown in Europe. Yet as important as Sicily was, Sicilians themselves were poor.

The two other large Mediterranean islands, Corsica and Sardinia, were isolated and outside the main flow of Mediterranean trade. And Venice had its own set of islands in the Adriatic and the Aegean. These islands, now mostly Croatian or Greek, were the secret of Venice's success islands such as Corfu, Crete, and Cyprus, which, although fertile, could produce only enough grain to last a few months. They exported wine, oil, and flocks of sheep.

Battles over the islands were usually the direct or indirect result of struggles in Italy. Italy in the mid-sixteenth century was dominated by Venice, Milan, Florence, the Papal States, and the kingdom of Naples, a branch of the house of Aragon in Spain. Although each of these states tried to destroy the other, it was the Turkish Empire that posed the greatest threat. Leading the defense of the West was Venice. The southern Mediterranean was also threatened by Muslim supremacy, and the Spanish king Ferdinand V built a line of presidios along the North African coast between 1509 and 1511 to counter this threat. The presidios grew into little cities supported more from the sea than from the surrounding lands. Finally, we saw in this chapter that the islands in the desert, the oases, played a role in the production of food, mostly in the form of dates.

This chapter concludes Part II, "An Ecology of Mediterranean Gastronomy." By examining the history and the recipes of the mountains, plains, hills, deserts, cities, seas, and islands, we have drawn a more complete picture of the Mediterranean. Now we can grapple with the problem of how to gastronomically define or measure the Mediterranean. I propose that the best measure can be gleaned from a look at spices and grain—the two most important items of trade and the topic of the next three chapters of Part III, "A Measure of Mediterranean Gastronomy." The importance of the Mediterranean Sea and its trade routes slowly receded as the Atlantic trade opened up. The wealth made in the spice and grain trades diminished as men sought their fortunes across the Atlantic. From time immemorial the Levant led the West, but after the opening of the Atlantic, the great technological developments emanated from the West and the East had to follow. This was the beginning of the end of the Mediterranean as the center of the civilized Western Hemisphere.

[PART III]

A MEASURE OF MEDITERRANEAN GASTRONOMY

WHAT is a measure of Mediterranean gastronomy? Any historical epoch can be understood, or an attempt can be made to understand it, by seeking the measure of that epoch. Perhaps the great distances that people had to travel in the sixteenth-century Mediterranean is one such measure. The technologies invented to overcome distance and time is another measure. The climate might be a measure, war another. The daily diet of Mediterranean people is a measure. One measure of the Mediterranean diet might be tied to armies: feeding troops on the move was an incredible project, an enormous task even today. It is said that the lead guard of the Spanish troops arriving in the Netherlands in the late sixteenth century saw its rear guard still in Andalusia. All along the way were the wives, valets, and prostitutes that accompanied these armies, and they all had to be fed.

The story of food in the Mediterranean is a story of trade, and without the riches made from the two most important items of trade, spices and grain, there would not have been created the wealth that led to our Mediterranean feasts of today. In this part we will see one measure of the Mediterranean as spice on the one hand and grain on the other. In Chapter 8, we will look at the role spices played in Mediterranean trade and how they came to influence the economy and, by virtue of the economy, the gastronomy. In Chapters 9 and 10, we'll examine the other food item that may have been more important than spices and even more important than the newly found gold and silver treasures of the Americas—grain. In Chapter 9 we see a complex world of different grains and the wheeler-dealers who traded them. In Chapter 10 we look at the most important inventions of the most important grain, hard wheat.

8

THE SPICE ORGY

FRANKINCENSE and myrrh, incense and cinnabar, cinnamon and cassia, and all the spices we associate with long ago times, have traditionally been thought of as arriving in the Mediterranean from the East. The "spices of Araby" found their way to the Mediterranean, the story goes, from the Hadhramaut in the southwestern portion of the Arabian peninsula in a trade controlled by Meccan traders. The spices arrived in Arabia from the Orient or East Africa before continuing their journey north to their terminus in Syria and Egypt, where they were sold to European traders. These Arab traders were said to be in an excellent location and they kept the origin of these spices secret so they could protect their monopoly from their Mediterranean customers. By the seventh century A.D. the trade declined and it was to revive only in the medieval era.[1]

The story of the spices of Araby, told by every food writer, is an exciting story, but is completely untrue. After the publication of the controversial, but compelling, argument made in Patricia Crone's *Meccan Trade and the Rise of Islam*, published in 1987 by Princeton University Press, we must rethink the early history of the spice story. Mecca, which is traditionally described as the center of a far-flung trading empire at the time of the Prophet Muhammad, was not in an "excellent location." Mecca was not at the crossroads of trade, but was off the beaten track. In fact, Crone claims, the Meccans did not trade in incense, spices, and other luxury goods. Their trade was much humbler: clothing and leather, and they could not have founded a commercial empire of international dimensions based on clothing. Arabia is "indelibly associated with the spice trade in the minds of every educated person," and, as the traditional story goes, spices had traded through Arabia for 1,500 to 2,500 years, coming to an end by the time the Arabs conquered the Middle East. Crone says all this is untrue.[2] Some of the famous spices described in antiquity, such as cinnamon and cassia, thought to have come from the East, were not the cinnamon and cassia we know today. It is clear from the classical descriptions of these plants by Theophrastus and Pliny that the plants in question belonged to a genus quite different from that of *Cinnamomum*. They are, in fact, a xerophilous shrub of the kind that proliferates in the thorn woodlands of the regions that border the Red Sea. The cinnamon and cassia known in antiquity were products native to Arabia and East Africa and did not come from the East.[3] This famous "spice route" that went from south Arabia to the Mediterranean was never used for foreign spices but simply for local Arabian aromatics, clothing, and leather.[4] When spices did come from the East, they came from other routes.

The Greco-Roman world imported many Arabian spices in a trade that was quite large. But by the sixth century hardly any spices remained on the market. Six of the most heavily traded spices—frankincense, myrrh, cancamum, tarum, labdanum, and sweet rush—had gone out of fashion, disappeared altogether, or came from within the Greco-Roman world. Two others, aloe and cinnabar, were imported by sea. Cinnamon and cassia, and calamus, were now obtained exclusively from East Africa. One spice, *cardamomum,* has an unsure identity because it clearly is not the cardamom we know today, and two cannot be identified—sweet-smelling bdellium and comacum. Not one of these spices is associated with Meccan trade items.[5] The spice trade dwindled to nothing by the seventh century, and not for another five hundred years would it rise again into a veritable orgy.

There were three reasons for the rise of the medieval Mediterranean spice trade. First, the monotony of a lifetime of consuming bread, more bread, and gruel resulted in a powerful desire, literally, to spice up the food. Even today it is people in the poorest countries of the Third World who are most likely to use spices in their food. Second, there was the need for the emerging new class of bourgeoisie to culturally demonstrate its power and superiority through the purchase of luxury items such as spices, used in food, medicines, and ointments. And third, there was the insatiable desire for gold and silver among the Mediterranean's trading partners in the East, the Chinese and Indians.[6]

MONOTONY OF TASTE

IN the Middle Ages, the term spices was applied to all costly goods (except gems) imported to Europe from the East, and it extended to items no longer commonly called spices, such as dyes, drugs, perfumes, textile fibers, aphrodisiacs, and sugar, as well as what we today call spices, like pepper (meaning peppercorns), cardamom, ginger, turmeric, various herbs, the chili peppers (newly arrived from America), garlic (called the peasant's theriaca by the thirteenth-century doctor Arnold of Vilanova), and saffron, a true luxury.[7]

Food writers have argued two contrary positions about medieval spice use. Some claim that it was a continuation of a Roman tradition, while others claim that spices were actually used sparingly during the Middle Ages. We know that the Romans used spices, but the medieval demand for spices was significantly greater. Medieval cookbooks, no matter what their provenance, fundamentally distinguish themselves from Roman cookery by their enormous use of spices. Take, for instance, the evidence of a recipe for twelve people in the fourteenth-century Italian cookbook the *Libro per cuoco* that calls for a half pound of spice.[8] In fact, saffron, ginger, and pepper stand out in the cookbooks, appearing with the greatest frequency in the recipes.

The love of spices in the West during the Middle Ages was so great that the historian Fernand Braudel called it a "spice orgy." The trade figures alone argue against the notion that spices were used sparingly in medieval European cooking: there were five million pounds of spices going through the spice bazaar of Alexandria alone in 1560.[9] What was this fascination with spices about? Historian Eileen Powers believed that European spice use was due to taste rather than necessity and was a continuation of the practice of the classical world. This is true to an extent, but it doesn't explain the massive increase in the quantity of spices used, as the late Roman world used spices moderately. Although Roman chefs seem to have had a good variety of spices available to them, the spice use in the Roman cookery book of Apicius in no way resembles the use of spices in medieval European cookery manuscripts.[10] In the earliest European cookery books of the fourteenth and fifteenth centuries, spices appear in nearly every recipe.[11] One historian, R. W. Southern, in *The Making of the Middle Ages*, says that we will never know what led to this craving for spices, while another historian, T. Sarah Peterson, believes that the comparative study of late medieval European and Arab recipe manuscripts evidences a spicy style of cooking adopted from the Arabs.[12]

Some food historians have proposed that medieval spice use was huge because of its role in preserving food or masking poor-quality meat. But the argument that spices were used to hide the off flavors of foods (especially meat) or to preserve foods is unfounded. There were far cheaper methods for preserving foods, including salting, sun-drying, air-drying, and smoking. It is well known that the rich—those who could afford spices—ate the freshest meat, meat butchered to order daily, including freshly caught game. As I argued in Chapter 3, because meat was abundant in immediate post–Black Death Europe, about the time that the spice trade was starting its meteroric rise, both the need and the use of preserved meats were low. In any case, the preserving of meats was typically an activity of the poor who couldn't afford spices.[13] The cookery books of the time are explicit in calling for the addition of spices "after" cooking, "at the last moment," says the fourteenth-century *Ménagier de Paris*, meaning that they were used for enhancing flavor, not preserving or masking taste.[14] It seems to me that the medieval Western European love of spices is to be found in changing tastes, not continuing tastes. Europeans, in part awed by the superior culture of the Arabs where spice use was prevalent, delighted in spices because they enhanced the taste of food, not simply made bad food palatable.

Food writers have ignored two other elements in the explanation behind the rise in the use of spices. The Italian historian Massimo Montanari points out that, although it does not explain the spice orgy in Mediterranean gastronomy that began in the thirteenth century, we should not underestimate the role played by spices in the pharmaco-dietetic convictions of the period, as determined by the Galenic theory of humors (see "An Essay on the Sources") that saw the "heat" of spices aiding the digestion.[15] Second, there may have been a snobbish reason on the part of the rising city-born bourgeoise to emulate a foreign culinary culture.

The most important reason for the massive increase in the use of spices is also reflected in another new phenomenon: the appearance of the first cookery books, books written for the newly emerging class of bourgeoise and for the aristocracy. This new bourgeois class of people, the nouveau riche, had the psychosocial need to emphasize their own wealth and importance, and they did so through the purchase of consumables.[16]

Garlic is a spice, yet even though its history in the Mediterranean is very old, the mad desire of Europeans for the exotic spices of the East led them to overlook garlic. Europeans traded gold and silver for the spices of the East, a fact that displeased kings and finance ministers, who thought it a poor trade. Ferdinand of Spain tried to stop the importing of cinnamon and pepper in exchange for silver by saying, "*Buena especia es el ajo*" (Garlic is a perfectly good spice).[17] But popular opinion held that garlic "*sempre è cibo rusticano*" (always is a peasant food), although with the right preparation it could become gentlemen's food. Perhaps garlic is the "plant of civilization." It is the perfect spice, and its appearance in a multitude of Mediterranean recipes, not only in the following one but also throughout the book, testifies to its universality.

Soupe Aïgo Bouïdo à la Ménagère (Provence)

HOUSEWIFE-STYLE GARLIC SOUP

The ordinary housewife in the Middle Ages would hardly have used exotic spices of the East in her soups, but she did have garlic. Garlic and onions were so abundant in the local Provençal horta *(garden) that they were usually the only two products that got transported any distance. The other* ortolagia, *the vegetable products of the garden, were consumed locally.*[18] *Garlic was indispensable for* aïgo bouïdo.

Oil and water or water and bread soups are very old preparations once made by the housewives of Provence. Another simple Provençal "housewife" soup is called aïgo-sau d'iou, *"water and salt," a fish soup made with water and salt, plus a mixture of small white fish, onions, potatoes, tomatoes, garlic, herbs, and olive oil. These soups remind us of how poor the Mediterranean was. They are not limited to Provence, either; on Minorca, the second largest of the Balearic Islands off Catalonia, one still finds the* oliaigua de Pagés *(oil and water soup of Pagés), sometimes with the addition of bread. These poor "family" soups are usually very simple, made with a legume such as lentils or chickpeas or a starch such as rice or potatoes. The aromatic flavoring came from the ubiquitous garlic as well as herbs. In the Gerona region of Catalonia, a family would eat a* sopa de la familia, *family soup, made from potatoes, bread, and garlic.*

Don't expect to find any of these soups on a restaurant menu on your next trip to Provence or Catalonia. They are antique dishes rarely made even in the home now that a pervasive Mediterranean poverty is a thing of the past. But these kinds of soups are notable for being filling, economical, and delicious.

2 quarts water
15 garlic cloves (about 1 head), crushed
Bouquet garni, tied in cheesecloth, consisting of 8 sprigs each fresh parsley, thyme, and marjoram and 1 sprig fresh sage
1 cup extra virgin olive oil
4 teaspoons salt
1/4 teaspoon freshly ground black pepper
6 to 12 slices French bread, toasted golden or not
Finely chopped fresh parsley leaves for garnish

1. Bring the water with the garlic cloves, bouquet garni, olive oil, salt, and black pepper to boil in a 4-quart casserole and boil for 5 minutes. Reduce the heat to low and simmer for 1 hour, uncovered.

2. Place one or two slices of bread in each bowl and ladle the broth over. Sprinkle with parsley and serve.

Makes 6 servings

Soupe à l'Ail (Languedoc)

GARLIC SOUP

In his study of the roots of the cuisine in Provence, the French historian Louis Stouff asks whether there was an original Provençal cuisine. The question is hard to answer because, although one can detect a certain prevalent taste—for example, for olive oil and herbs—we unfortunately cannot deduce much from that because it is equally a description of other Mediterranean cuisines. But in Languedoc and Provence, garlic, although thought of as a vegetable, was used as a spice and appears in everything, such as sauces often made of eggs, garlic, and almonds. Pepper was expensive and when it appeared, it was usually on the table of a noble family or for special occasions, such as this heavily peppered soup that consummates the rite of marriage in traditional ceremonies in Languedoc.[19] *The copious use of both garlic and black pepper in this soup that the wife presents to her new husband on their first day as a couple must be a metaphor for the lives ahead of them and the hope that it will be spiritually, if not materially, rich. This opulent-tasting soup (a result of the eggs) needs hard-toasted bread and lots of pepper, so be liberal.*

2 quarts water
15 garlic cloves (about 1 head), finely chopped
Bouquet garni, tied in cheesecloth, consisting of 8 sprigs each fresh parsley and thyme, and 1 bay leaf
1 cup extra virgin olive oil
Salt to taste
6 large egg yolks
Abundant freshly ground black pepper
8 slices French bread, toasted golden

1. Bring the water with the garlic cloves, bouquet garni, olive oil, and salt to a boil in a 4-quart casserole and boil for 5 minutes. Reduce the heat to low and simmer for 1 hour, uncovered.

2. In a medium-size bowl, beat the egg yolks. Remove the soup from the heat and pour a ladleful of it slowly into the bowl, beating constantly.

3. When the broth has cooled for 5 minutes, pour the egg mixture into the soup, beating all the time. Pepper the soup generously; I leave it up to you the exact amount to use, but it should be heavily peppered. If the soup tastes bland after you've added the pepper, it needs more. Leave to thicken a bit over low heat, making sure the soup does not boil. Divide the bread among individual soup bowls, ladle the soup on top, and serve.

Makes 8 servings

✣ ✣ ✣

SOME of the most famous sauces are rooted in the Mediterranean, often made with spices as wide ranging as garlic or, more recently, the New World cayenne pepper. Emulsions of garlic and olive oil are quite old and found throughout the Mediterranean.

Allioli (Catalonia)

GARLIC MAYONNAISE

A unique use for garlic was as the base for emulsion condiments and sauces made by pounding the garlic and incorporating olive oil. The first apparent mention of anything resembling allioli *is in the writings of Pliny (A.D. 23–79), who was a Roman procurator in Tarragona, on the Catalan coast, for a year and writes that when garlic is "beaten up in oil and vinegar it swells up in foam to a surprising size."*[20] *There is no doubt in my mind that mayonnaise (page 501) was an evolutionary development from* allioli. *Whether all of the emulsions known throughout the Mediterranean are derived from this* ursprung *is less certain. There is a good possibility of serendipitous culinary invention.*

Unlike the aïoli *of Provence and the* aillade *of Languedoc, the true Catalan* allioli (all, *"garlic"*; i, *"and"*; oli, *"oil"*) *is made without eggs, using only garlic, olive oil, and salt. The garlic is placed in a mortar with salt and pounded until completely mashed and smooth. Then olive oil is slowly drizzled in, almost drop by drop, as the continued pounding incorporates the oil into an emulsion with the garlic. This is quite an undertaking, and I wish Colman Andrews had written his classic* Catalan Cuisine *before I slaved away trying to make the authentic* allioli. *He confirms that this is very hard to do and tells us that "the region's most famous chefs openly admit that they can't get the damn thing to work." He also confirms, as I suspected, that* allioli *is regularly made with eggs today, and this is the recipe I give you.*

If you like a heavier, distinctively olive oil taste to your mayonnaise, go ahead and use extra virgin olive oil instead of the so-called light olive oil I call for. Allioli *is traditionally served with rice dishes or fish preparations, although many Catalans use it as a kind of ketchup for anything and everything.*

5 large garlic cloves (about 1½ ounces), peeled
½ teaspoon salt
1 large egg
1 cup light olive oil or ½ cup each pure or virgin olive oil and vegetable oil combined

1. Mash the garlic and salt together in a mortar until it is a paste. In a food processor, process the egg for 30 seconds.

2. Add the garlic paste to the food processor, turn continuously, and slowly drizzle in the oil until absorbed. Cover and refrigerate for 1 hour before using. Keep refrigerated for up to a week.

Makes 1½ cups

Sauce Rouille et Croûtes (Provence)

SAFFRON-GARLIC MAYONNAISE AND FRIED BREAD FOR FISH SOUPS AND STEWS

In the Middle Ages, there was no doubt that saffron was a luxury spice. Saffron was rare and expensive, and grown for export in only three places: Albi in Languedoc, Aquila in Abruzzi, and in Catalonia.[21] A pound of saffron could cost as much as a horse.[22] In Languedoc and Provence, the local saffron may not have been quite that expensive because it did not have to travel very great distances, although it is always expensive to harvest. The saffron was grown in Albi and bought at the Toulouse or Montpellier spice market. The most popular spice mix was black pepper and ginger, with the addition of smaller amounts of other spices such as saffron. When black pepper was in short supply in India, traders would replace it with ersatz pepper such as maniguette (malaguette), *which is known as guinea pepper or grains of paradise* (Aframomum melegueta), *and came from the coast of Guinea from the fifteenth century onward.[23] A recent study showed that black pepper is used in 16 and 19 percent of the recipes, respectively, in the two earliest French cookery works, the* Enseingnemenz qui enseingnent a apareiller toutes manieres de viandes *and* Quomodo praeparanda et condienda omnia cibaria quae comuniter comeduntur, *from the early fourteenth century, and grains of paradise not at all in the first and in 2 percent of the recipes in the second of the manuscripts. But by the time of the famous cookery work, the* Viandier, *by the first notable French chef, Taillevent, later in the fourteenth century, grains of paradise appeared in 14 percent of the recipes, meaning that black pepper was in short supply.[24] Once the New World chili peppers began to arrive in the sixteenth century, they, too, were added to the repertoire of spices used in southern France, their piquancy being noted by early writers.*

Rouille *is the traditional mayonnaise accompaniment to bouillabaisse, containing abundant chili pepper and garlic, a powerful and perilous sauce for many palates. Some cooks add tomato paste for coloring only, but I don't find this necessary because the saffron and cayenne are assertive enough in coloring. In Provençal home cooking, the addition of saffron often allows the cook to call the preparation a "bouillabaisse."[25]*

1½ cups diced French bread, white part only
½ cup fish broth (page 369, or reserve some from the making of bouillabaisse, page 375)

4 to 6 garlic cloves, to your taste, peeled
1 teaspoon salt
½ teaspoon ground red pepper
Pinch of saffron threads, crumbled
1 large egg yolk
Freshly ground black pepper to taste
1¼ cups extra virgin olive oil
5 tablespoons unsalted butter
40 to 50 slices French baguette bread (about 1 loaf)

1. Soak the diced bread in the fish broth. Squeeze the broth out. Mash the garlic cloves in a mortar with the salt until mushy. Place the bread, mashed garlic (saving 1 garlic clove for the *croûtes*), red pepper, saffron, egg yolk, and black pepper in a food processor and blend for 30 seconds, then pour in 1 cup of the olive oil through the feed tube in a slow, thin, steady stream while the machine is running. Refrigerate for 1 hour before serving. Store whatever you don't use in the refrigerator for up to a week.

2. Meanwhile, prepare the *croûtes*. In a large skillet, melt the butter with the remaining ¼ cup olive oil over medium heat with the remaining crushed garlic until it begins to turn light brown. Remove and discard the garlic.

3. Lightly brush both sides of each bread slice with the melted butter and oil and set aside. When all the slices are brushed, place them back in the skillet and cook until they are a very light brown on both sides. Set aside until needed.

VARIATION
Another way to make the *croûtes* is to toast them first and then rub both sides with a cut piece of garlic.

NOTE: If the *rouille* is separating, add 2 to 3 tablespoons of the fish broth and whisk it in until smooth and reemulsified.

Makes 1¼ cups sauce rouille *and 10 servings* croûtes

Skordalia (Greece)

GARLIC SAUCE

Skordalia *is a Greek garlic sauce that appears around the Mediterranean in different guises. In Greece it is used for a variety of foods including being served with beet salad (page 227) and batter-fried salt cod (page 439). The Palestinians and Lebanese use a version with garlic and olive oil, called* thūm bi'l-zayt, *for baked chicken. It is related to the Catalan* allioli *and the* rouille *of Provence. Cooks in Macedonia and Cephalonia (Kefallinía) often add walnuts, and older recipes base the* skordalia *on almonds, leading me to believe that this is the Greek version of the Turkish* tarator *and Arab* ṭaraṭūr *sauces that themselves may owe something to Byzantine food (pages 218 and 318). This particular recipe will yield enough for all the recipes in the book that use* skordalia.

1¾ pounds boiling potatoes
½ cup light cream or more to taste
6 large garlic cloves, peeled
2 cups ½-inch French or Italian bread dice, crust removed
½ cup extra virgin olive oil
3 tablespoons white wine vinegar
Salt to taste

1. In a large pot, place the potatoes in cold water to cover by several inches and turn the heat to medium. Once the water begins to boil, about 20 minutes, continue to boil until a skewer glides easily though the center of each potato, another 25 to 30 minutes. Peel the potatoes once they are cool enough to handle. Pass the potatoes through a food mill or colander and slowly whip in the cream.

2. Pound the garlic in a mortar until mushy. Add the garlic to the potatoes, mixing well. Soak the bread

cubes in a little water until sodden, then squeeze the water out. Pass the bread through the food mill or colander. Blend the bread, potatoes, and garlic together with a fork in a medium-size bowl.

3. Slowly pour the olive oil and vinegar in a steady stream as you continue beating with a fork until the mixture has the consistency of a thick mayonnaise. Do not do this in a food processor because the potatoes will become gummy in their overprocessing. Season with salt and refrigerate until needed.

VARIATION
Add chopped almonds, walnuts, or pine nuts after mashing the garlic.

Makes 3 cups

THE importance of the spice trade, and black pepper in particular, led to spices becoming a status symbol for the rich, who would use copious amounts, for example, in the *peverada* sauce of the Veneto. As soon as their prices fell, spices were not used as much. Trade in new luxuries such as coffee, chocolate, and tobacco rose with the decline of spice use by the eighteenth century.

Peverada Antica (Veneto)

OLD-STYLE PEPPER SAUCE

In patrician households, peverada, *besides being thought of as an aphrodisiac, flavored roasted poultry, boiled meat, game, boar, and dark meat in general. The anonymous fourteenth-century* Libro della cocina *has a recipe for* peverada*:*

> *Take toasted bread, a pinch of saffron, spices and chopped liver and pound in a mortar. Moisten with vinegar or wine and broth, and make it as sweet or sour as you want. Use this peverada with meat, wild game or fish.*[26]

Peverada *sauce was also once flavored with ginger, cinnamon, or pomegranate juice. The panada base of this sauce, made of bread, was diluted with Malmsey (Malvasia) wine, a strong, sweet Madeira-type wine from the Greek town of Monemvasia in the southeast Peloponnesus.* Peverada *was served with roasted chicken with* pién, *a Venetian word meaning* pieno, *"full" (of stuffing). The* pién *consisted of chopped and sauteéd liver and hearts mixed with parsley, lemon rind, sage, rosemary, milk-moistened bread, eggs, nutmeg, black pepper, salted and grated Parmigiano-Reggiano cheese, pine nuts, raisins, crumbled amaretti cookies,* rosolio *or Marsala wine, cinnamon, cloves, sausage, mashed chestnuts, and mushrooms.*[27] *This first recipe is the older one, closer to the tastes of the sixteenth century. The second variation is commonly found today in the more traditional Venetian homes.*

2 cups fresh bread crumbs
½ cup golden raisins, soaked for 15 minutes in tepid water to cover and drained
⅓ cup pine nuts
¼ teaspoon ground cinnamon
Salt to taste
2 teaspoons freshly ground black pepper, or more to taste
½ cup beef broth (page 54), or as needed
½ cup semisweet red Malvasia or sweet Marsala wine, or as needed

1. Place the bread crumbs, raisins, pine nuts, cinnamon, salt, and pepper in a medium-size saucepan.

2. Over low heat, add enough beef broth and wine to make a thick sauce, or of a consistency to your liking, cooking it as long as you think necessary for a taste that you like, stirring occasionally.

Makes enough for 4 servings with roast chicken or boiled meat

Peverada Moderna (Veneto)

NEW-STYLE PEPPER SAUCE

A pleasant way to see Venice is by hopping on one of the vaporetti *that motor their way through the canals. It is sometimes the best way to get a good look at the* palazzi *that line the Grand Canal, as well as other canals. Many of the* palazzi, *such as the Palazzo Barbarigo, can be gazed upon from a bench-lined landing on the opposite side of the canal.*

After you've rested, a spit-roasted chicken with peverada *sauce would be ideal. This is a peppery sauce, so although I leave the final amount to you, 2 teaspoons of freshly ground black pepper would not be considered too much. I like to serve this sauce with roasted split Cornish hens or spit-roasted spatchcocked chicken seasoned lightly with olive oil, salt, and pepper.*

1/4 cup extra virgin olive oil
2 ounces sliced *sopressa Veneta* or Genoa salami, very finely chopped
1/4 pound chicken livers, membranes removed and very finely chopped
1 garlic clove, very finely chopped
2 salted anchovy fillets, rinsed and very finely chopped
1 teaspoon very finely chopped fresh parsley leaves
Zest and juice from 1 lemon (zest, without white pith, very finely chopped)
Salt and freshly ground black pepper to taste
1/2 cup dry white wine

1. In a medium-size saucepan, heat the olive oil over low heat, then add the salami, chicken livers, garlic, anchovies, parsley, and lemon zest. Stir and season with salt and a generous amount of pepper. Simmer for 5 minutes.

2. Pour in the lemon juice and wine. Continue cooking until the sauce is thick and smooth, or a consistency you like, stirring occasionally.

NOTE: The chicken livers can be easily chopped by freezing them slightly first.

Makes enough for 4 servings with roast chicken

Manzo "co' la Pearà" (Veneto)

BEEF WITH PEPPER SAUCE

Pearà *is a Venetian dialect word for* pepe, *pepper.* Manzo "co' la pearà," *with its heavily peppered sauce, is a popular preparation in Verona. It is traditionally cooked in a terra-cotta pot and must derive from the medieval* peverada-*type sauces popular with spit-roasted meats and fowl. Some Veronese cooks use grated horseradish instead of the pepper. Although the sauce can be served as a soup for a first course, it is also used with boiled or braised meats. Marrow can be extracted from inside the bones, sold often as soup bones, using a small spoon or knife.*

2 pounds boneless beef bottom round or any stew meat, in one piece
1 whole clove
1 medium-size onion, peeled
1 celery stalk, sliced
1 leek, white and light green parts only, halved lengthwise, washed well, and sliced
1 carrot, sliced

Salt to taste
¼ cup (½ stick) unsalted butter
½ cup beef or ox marrow (about 5 ounces, from about 2½ pounds of bones)
1¾ cups fresh bread crumbs
2½ to 3 cups chicken, veal, or beef broth (page 54)
¼ cup freshly grated Parmigiano-Reggiano cheese
Freshly ground black pepper to taste

1. In a large casserole, place the piece of stewing meat and cover with water. Stick the clove into the onion and add it, along with the celery, leek, carrot, and some salt, to the casserole. Bring to a boil, reduce the heat to a simmer, cover, and cook until the meat is almost falling apart, about 3 hours.

2. Meanwhile, melt the butter and marrow together in a large skillet, then add the bread crumbs, mixing them in with a wooden spoon. Ladle in the broth ½ cup at a time until you have a smooth sauce. Simmer, uncovered, for 2 hours, stirring once in a while.

3. Once the stew meat is fork-tender, add the Parmigiano-Reggiano, salt, and lots of freshly ground black pepper, at least 1 teaspoon and even more, to the *pearà* sauce. Stir well. Transfer the meat to a serving platter, cover with the sauce, and serve.

Makes 6 servings

THE SPICE BAZAAR

MOST spices came from the East. Black pepper was the most important spice, and its trade was captured by the Mediterranean. Traditionally, the Mediterranean trade used Arab intermediary connections to reserve the superior trade items for itself. The merchants of the East needed the gold coming from Egypt, and later the West, in exchange for the spices. The flourishing Levant trade flowed through the Red Sea, when not coming overland, one route landing at the tiny village of Quseir on Egypt's Red Sea coast and then moving overland to Luxor before flowing down the Nile to Cairo and Alexandria.[28] At the end of these caravan routes were two cities that owed their prosperity to this trade, Aleppo with its port at Tripoli, the terminus of an overland route, and Cairo with its port of Alexandria.

Following the spice routes today means following one's imagination. Near Luxor is the little hamlet of Medinet Habu, where I spent time cooking with a local peasant woman, collecting recipes such as the following and enjoying the use of spices in contemporary Egyptian cookery.

Baṭṭ Muḥammar (Egypt)

FRIED DUCK

*The medieval cardamom (*Elettaria cardamomum *Maton) was one of the spices that arrived in Egypt from India, passing through the Red Sea after a transhipment stop at Jidda in Arabia. This "true" cardamom was not the* cardamomum *of the Greeks and Romans, a plant that grew in Arabia and has not yet been identified.*[29] *Cardamom became closely associated with Egyptian cooking, while the bulk of the trade continued on to northern Europe, where Scandinavian countries became big importers of the spice. Two other spices are also associated with Egyptian cooking, coriander and cumin, both of which grow wild along the banks of the Nile.*

This recipe is from Hamida Abdel-Magid, a peasant women who raises buffalo and tends fields along with single-handedly raising her eight children in Medinet

Habu. Made for me and my friend Boyd Grove, the duck was boiled first before being fried in samna *with a spicing of freshly ground cumin and coriander seeds. We thought it was very, very good. Serve this with* shūrbat al-ᶜadas *(page 310) and* ruzz bi'l-baṭāṭis *(page 598). Mastic grains, the solidified resinous exudate from the mastic tree, is used in Egyptian cooking as a smell purgative. It can be bought at many Middle Eastern markets.*

2 gallons water
1 large onion, peeled
10 mastic grains (page 718)
Seeds from 10 cardamom pods
2 ducks (about 5 pounds each)
½ cup *samna* (clarified butter; page 189)
2 teaspoons freshly ground coriander seeds
2 teaspoons freshly ground cumin seeds
Salt and freshly ground black pepper to taste

1. Bring the water to a boil in a large stockpot. Add the onion, mastic grains, and cardamom seeds. Leave this to boil gently, uncovered, for 15 minutes.

2. Remove the gizzards and necks of the ducks and save for *salade tiéde de foie et gésiers de canard* (page 194). Cut off as much fat as possible from the ducks and save to render for *confit de canard* (page 200). Add the whole ducks to the boiling water and let boil until they turn color and are firm, about 20 minutes.

3. Remove the ducks from the water and leave them to cool. Reserve 1½ cups of the duck cooking broth if you are also going to make *ruzz bi'l-baṭāṭis* (page 598). Let this 1½ cups of broth sit in a refrigerator so the fat solidifies on top. Remove the fat with a spoon and discard or save. Disjoint the duck into breasts, legs, and wings, then bone and cut into pieces. Remove as much fat as possible and save it, if you wish.

4. In a large skillet, melt the *samna* over medium heat, then cook the duck pieces, sprinkled with the coriander, cumin, salt, and pepper, until browned on both sides and tender, about 20 minutes. Remove the duck from the skillet with a slotted spoon, transfer to a serving platter, and serve.

Makes 4 to 5 servings

✣ ✣ ✣

NEARLY all the spices arriving in the Mediterranean followed the famous overland spice route through Central Asia. But once the Mongol states collapsed in the mid-fourteenth century, the trade was thrown into chaos and new routes emerged, finding their terminals in Egypt and Syria. These routes were dominated by Muslim merchants who had the added attraction of being able to combine business with the *hajj*, the Islamic religious obligation of pilgrimage to nearby Mecca. The merchant has an honored place in Islamic society, and the Koran contains a number of theological terms that are borrowed from the commercial usage of the times.[30]

The trade in spices, as with everything else, took time. The distances were great and everything was affected by the weather. The trade in saffron, for instance, depended on a whole series of events to effect its completion. Saffron was packed in linen bags that were grouped in fours and then wrapped in a leather pouch. Payment for the saffron was made in coin. First, the saffron grower hoped for a good harvest, which occurs in October and is labor intensive. Second, the saffron merchant depended on the arrival from Germany of the linen cloth for packing. Third, the bales of leather to make pouches had to come from Hungary, and the copper plate and bars used by the Aquila mint to strike the *cavali* and *cavaluzzi* coins depended on copper from Germany.

This microcosmic story was repeated on a larger scale, as we can see by the Levantine trade in spices, black pepper, drugs, silk, and cotton for silver coins and woolen cloth from the West.

Vermicelli all'Abruzzese (Abruzzi)

VERMICELLI WITH SAFFRON AND ZUCCHINI FLOWERS FROM THE ABRUZZI

In the Abruzzi, the combination of vermicelli and saffron is an old preparation, found as early as the fourteenth century in the anonymous Libro della cucina, *where it is made in the Arab style with almond milk, sugar, and saffron.*[31] *The combination is still popular, as we see in this delicious and colorful dish. Zucchini flowers can be picked the day before you need them and kept in a bowl of ice water or the refrigerator if you do not have enough plants to produce twenty flowers at once. If you can harvest upward of a half pound of zucchini flowers, all the better.*

½ cup extra virgin olive oil
1 medium-size onion, very finely chopped
3 tablespoons finely chopped fresh parsley leaves
2 to 4 ounces zucchini flowers (15 to 20), washed well, dried, and chopped
Pinch of saffron threads
1⅓ cups plus 2 tablespoons beef broth (page 54)
Salt
¾ pound vermicelli
2 large egg yolks
6 tablespoons freshly grated pecorino cheese

1. Pour the olive oil in a medium-size casserole with the onion, parsley, chopped zucchini flowers, and saffron dissolved in 2 tablespoons of the beef broth. Turn the heat to medium and cook until saucy, about 30 minutes, stirring occasionally and gradually adding up to another ¾ cup of the beef broth as it cooks.

2. Pass the mixture through a food mill, return to the casserole with the remaining ½ cup beef broth, and cook over low heat until hot, about 3 minutes.

3. Meanwhile, bring a large pot of water to a rolling boil, salt abundantly, and add the pasta. Drain when al dente.

4. Remove the sauce from the heat and stir in the egg yolks and pecorino. Toss with the vermicelli, transfer to a serving bowl or platter, and serve immediately.

Makes 4 servings

✢ ✢ ✢

THE first mention of spices in Provence was in 1317, where a description in the kitchen accounts of the pontificate of John XXII mentions that a quintal of sugar was bought from François Barral, an Avignon merchant who was the purveyor to the Popes. Gaufridus Isnardi, who was not only the Pope's doctor but also cooked many foods for him, made a *pain d'epices*, a spice bread with rose water and sugared almonds. Isnardi bought large amounts of sugar, cinnamon, ginger, spikenard (a fragrant ointment made from a plant, *Nardostachys jatamansi*, of the valerian family), anise, cloves, saffron, pepper, mastic, nutmeg, and marzipan in the markets of Montpellier.[32] In 1331 it was the Pope's pharmacist, Jaquet Melior, who prepared recipes for the king of France with coriander, rose water, sugared almonds, liquorice, and a mélange of distilled water and oil, mint root, and sugar roux, a kind of paste.

In fifteenth-century Barcelona, a great spice market existed for the trade in the western Mediterranean. Six spices played a significant role in the spice trade, and the two most important were black pepper and ginger. The other four were nutmeg, cloves, cinnamon, and *maniguette (malaguette)*, known as guinea pepper or grains of paradise, a substitute for black pepper (page 514).[33] European spice sellers concocted *les confimens*,

SAFFRON

Saffron (Crocus sativus) *is a perennial herb native to Asia Minor and Persia that was introduced through cultivation throughout the Mediterranean over the past two thousand years. Easy to grow but burdensome to harvest, saffron flowers in October, at which time the stamens and pistils are collected by hand for drying. The yield is quite low: two hundred pounds of flowers give only about three ounces of dried saffron. Saffron is powerful in aroma and coloring: one part saffron can color 100,000 parts of water.*[34] *Besides its medical applications as a sedative in medieval pharmacology, it was used for aromatizing foods and coloring them.*

Although saffron was known in classical times (Pliny wrote about it in detail), its cultivation more or less died out with the passing of Roman administration, and it was the Arabs who were in the main responsible for its reintroduction to the Mediterranean, believing as they did that yellow was a source of gaiety and prizing the yellowing effect of saffron in culinary endoring, the coloring of foods. Is it possible that when the first tomato, which was yellow in color, was introduced to the Mediterranean in the sixteenth century from the New World, one of its first uses might have been ornamental, for endoring, rather than culinary, possibly as an ersatz saffron for coloring foods in place of the expensive true saffron?[35]

Saffron is sold either in thread form or powdered. It is best to buy the deep red-orange-colored threads, which stay fresher longer and are more versatile. In recipes, saffron is called for by the pinch, an inaccurate term that generally means about thirty-five threads or pistils (I actually counted it once). To make the saffron threads more potent, toast them slightly in a pan under a broiler for less than a minute just before using and then pulverize between two sheets of waxed paper or in a mortar with the salt called for in the recipe. Store saffron threads in a zippered-top plastic bag inside a tight-lidded jar in a dark cabinet.

spice mixtures, a phenomenon that one still finds prevalent in North African markets today. The most popular was a mixture of black pepper and ginger called *pebre gingibre*, sold in a powdered form.[36] A statute of 1536 concerning the grocers in the Municipal Archives of Toulouse has preserved three recipes, all with a base of black pepper and ginger. The first recipe calls for a pound of spice *(une livre d'espice)*: eight ounces of ginger, three ounces of black pepper, and one ounce each of cinnamon, cloves, nutmeg, and grains of paradise and a half ounce of saffron. The second recipe is called *espice de lamproye* and is identical to the first except that the proportions of black pepper and ginger are reversed. It was likely used for a kind of eellike sea creature called a lamprey. The richest spice mixture was the third, with six ounces of ginger, three ounces of black pepper, two ounces of cinnamon, one and a half ounces of cloves or to taste, one and a half ounces grains of paradise, one ounce of nutmeg, and one ounce of saffron.[37]

The Toulouse spice market sold the best pepper as *poyvre a la patte de Flandres* (hand pepper of Flanders), while *poyvre marine* (navy pepper) and *poyvre de Calicu* (pepper from Calicut on the Malabar coast of the Indian state of Kerala) were considered medium quality. *Poyvre leger* (light pepper) was sold to foreigners (presumably, non-French). We don't know the exact meaning of the words, but ginger was sold as *mequin* (ginger from near Mecca) or *sorratin* (a ginger from Surat, considered the best). The commerce in the Toulouse market was limited in that very few foodstuffs were traded: olive oil and salt from the Mediterranean and preserved fish from the Atlantic, along with pepper and ginger and other spices, from the Indies.[38] Spices are no longer found in the cooking of Toulouse, with the exception of the occasional pinch of saffron.

For reasons not completely understood, but more than likely related to wealth and poverty, extensive spice use began to recede along the northern Mediterranean while heavy spice use is still prevalent today on the southern and eastern shores, as we can see in the important spice mixes that follow.

Tābil (Tunisia)

TUNISIAN SPICE MIX

Tābil, *which means "seasoning" in Tunisian Arabic, in earlier times was a word used for coriander.*[39] *Paula Wolfert makes the plausible claim that* tābil *is one of the spice mixes brought to Tunisia by Muslim-Andalusi in 1492.*[40] *I agree with her and it does seem possible that* tābil *may have developed in their community of Testour, in the Tunisian plains west of Tunis near Algeria.*[41] *However, although the Muslim kingdom of Granada fell in 1492, the forced conversion of Muslim-Andalusi and other Muslim Spanish did not begin until 1499. Although they departed in small numbers during the intervening years, it was not until 1609 to 1614 that the wholesale expulsion of the Moriscos, Muslim converts to Christianity, occurred, when they left in droves for Morocco, Algeria, and Tunisia, up to half a million of them. Many of these Moriscos then swelled the ranks of the Barbary corsairs.*[42]

Today tābil, *closely associated with the cooking of Tunisia, features coriander seeds and is pounded in a mortar and then dried in the sun and is often used in cooking beef or veal. My recipe uses all dried spices except the garlic, which you should air-dry a bit, otherwise replace it with dried garlic.*

2 large garlic cloves, chopped and dried in the open air for 2 days, or 2 teaspoons garlic powder
1/4 cup coriander seeds
1 tablespoon caraway seeds
2 teaspoons cayenne pepper

In a mortar, pound the garlic with the coriander, caraway, and cayenne until homogenous. Store in the refrigerator or freezer. Keep in the refrigerator if using fresh garlic for up to 2 months or indefinitely if using powdered garlic, although the pungency will decline as time goes by.

Makes about 1/4 cup

Rās al-Ḥanūt (Morocco)

MOROCCAN SPICE MIX

Rās al-ḥanūt, *literally "head of the shop," is a complex spice blend used in Moroccan cooking, but also found in a similiar version in Algeria and a somewhat different one in Tunisia. Spice shops employ experts who concoct the mixture, using up to twenty-seven different spices. But measuring is quite inaccurate because the spices themselves can vary in intensity and flavor depending on how old they are or where they came from. In the Sahel of Tunisia,* rās al-ḥanūt *is usually composed of cinnamon, rose petals, cloves, and black pepper. A detailed description of the Moroccan variety of* rās al-ḥanūt *is found in Paula Wolfert's* Couscous and Other Good Food from Morocco.[43]

2 teaspoons ground cinnamon
1 teaspoon turmeric
½ teaspoon freshly ground black pepper
¼ teaspoon freshly grated nutmeg
¼ teaspoon freshly ground cardamom seeds
¼ teaspoon freshly ground cloves

Mix all the ingredients and store in a spice jar. It will keep indefinitely but lose its pungency over time.

Makes about 4½ teaspoons

Harīsa (Tunisia)

HOT CHILI PASTE

Harīsa *is the most important condiment used in Tunisian cooking, and, in fact, you need to make this recipe and keep it in the refrigerator before attempting any other Tunisian recipe. It's hard to believe that so essential a condiment could evolve only after the introduction of the New World capsicum.* Harīsa *comes from the Arabic word for "to break into pieces," which is done by pounding hot peppers in a mortar, although today a food processor can be used. This famous hot chili paste is also found in the cooking of Algeria, Libya, and even in western Sicily, where* cùscusu *is made. In Tunisia it would be prepared fresh in a spice shop. The simplest recipe is merely a paste of red chili peppers and salt that is covered in olive oil and stored.*

Harīsa *is sold in tubes by both Tunisian and French firms. The Tunisian one is better, but neither can compare to your own freshly made from this recipe.*

I first became intrigued with making harīsa *from a preparation made by Mouldi Hadiji, my Arabic teacher of twenty years ago. I concocted this version, based on a Berber-style one I had in Djerba, from a recipe description given to me by a merchant in the market in Tunis, who unfortunately provided measurements that could last me a century (calling for fifty pounds of chilies). Some cooks also use mint, onions, or olive oil in their* harīsa. *I modified the recipe after much consultation with an illustrious group of opinionated people, including Chef Moncef Meddeb, Mohammed Kouki, the doyen of Tunisian food experts, and cookbook authors Paula Wolfert, Kitty Morse, Nancy Harmon Jenkins, and Deborah Madison.*

Be very careful when handling hot chili peppers, making sure that you do not put your fingers near your eyes, nose, or mouth, or you will live to regret it. Wash your hands well with soap and water after handling chili peppers. After you make your first harīsa, *with all the modern conveniences, I hope you can appreciate what exacting women's work this was, making it in the traditional mortar.*

2 ounces mildly hot dried guajillo chili peppers
2 ounces mild dried Anaheim chili peppers
5 garlic cloves, peeled
2 tablespoons water
2 tablespoons extra virgin olive oil
½ teaspoon freshly ground caraway seeds
¼ teaspoon freshly ground coriander seeds
1½ teaspoons salt
Extra virgin olive oil for topping off

1. Soak the chili peppers in tepid water to cover until softened, 45 minutes to 1 hour. Drain and remove the stems and seeds. Place in a blender or

food processor with the garlic, water, and olive oil and process until smooth, stopping occasionally to scrape down the sides.

2. Transfer the mixture to a small bowl and stir in the caraway, coriander, and salt. Store in a jar and top off, covering the surface of the paste with a layer of olive oil. Whenever the paste is used, you must always top off with olive oil making sure no paste is exposed to air, otherwise it will spoil.

VARIATION
To make a hot *harīsa*, use 4 ounces dried guajillo chili peppers and ½ ounce dried de Arbol peppers.

NOTE: To make *ṣalṣat al-harīsa, harīsa* sauce, used as an accompaniment to grilled meats, stir together 2 teaspoons *harīsa*, 3 tablespoons olive oil, 2 tablespoons water, and 1 tablespoon finely chopped fresh parsley leaves.

Makes 1 cup

Zaʿtar (Arab Levant)
THYME SEASONING MIX

Zaʿtar, *which means "thyme," is a condiment made in Lebanon and elsewhere in the Levant from thyme, sesame seeds, sumac, and salt. Mix several tablespoons of* zaʿtar *with extra virgin olive oil to dip Arabic bread in, as they do for breakfast in Lebanon.* Zaʿtar *can also be bought already prepared in Middle Eastern markets. Sumac is a spice made from the dried red berries of the sumac bush* (Rhus coriaria) *that grows wild throughout the Middle East. It is sold in ground form in Middle Eastern markets and via mail order (see "Mediterranean Food Products Resources").*

2 cups dried thyme
½ cup sesame seeds
2 tablespoons sumac
1 teaspoon salt, or more to taste

Mix all the ingredients. Store in a tight-lidded jar in a dark cabinet. It will lose its pungency over time, but, properly sealed, it can be good for up to a year.

Makes about 2½ cups

Bahārāt (Arab Levant)
SPICE MIX FOR SYRO-PALESTINIAN COOKING

Bahārāt *means "spice" in Arabic, derived from the word* bahār, *which means "pepper," so it is a mixed spice with black pepper. It is an all-purpose spice mix used in Lebanon, Syria, Jordan, and Palestine and found in many prepared savory dishes.*

Bahārāt *can be bought at Middle Eastern groceries and markets, but it is also quite easy to make fresh for yourself and keep stored in a spice jar. There are many different variations, all based on the ingredients of black pepper and allspice. Some mixes might include paprika, coriander seeds, cassia bark, sumac, nutmeg, cumin seeds, or cardamom seeds. This recipe is basic; if you like, you can fiddle with it by adding some of the other spices mentioned.*

¼ cup black peppercorns
¼ cup allspice berries
2 teaspoons ground cinnamon
1 teaspoon freshly grated nutmeg

Grind the peppercorns and allspice together and blend with the cinnamon and nutmeg. Store in a jar in your spice rack, away from sunlight. It will lose pungency as time goes by, but, properly stored, it can be good for many months.

Makes about 1/2 cup

Bahārāt (Tunisia)

TUNISIAN SPICE MIX

Bahārāt *simply means "mixed spices" in Arabic, coming from the root word* bahār, *meaning "pepper."*[44] *This particular spice mix is used in Tunisia, and is quite different from the* bahārāt *spice mix of the Levant* *(page 524).*

- **1 teaspoon ground cinnamon**
- **1 teaspoon dried rose petals (see "Mediterranean Food Products Resources")**
- **1 teaspoon very finely ground black pepper**

Mix the ingredients and store in a small jar.

Makes 1 tablespoon

✣ ✣ ✣

AN obstacle to profits for the Venetian spice merchant was the middleman in the Middle East. Many of the middlemen were Jewish, and Venetian merchants set up colonies in Cairo and Aleppo in order to cut them out. The Venetians, along with merchants from Marseilles and Ragusa, became rich on this trade. The greatest risk to the Venetians involved in the spice trade was the sea voyage to Egypt itself, a venture compensated for by the extremely high rates of return on investment.

Both Syria and Egypt were important to the Venetians, who needed these markets for their manufactured goods and cotton fabrics. In return, they had access to the spice bazaars in Beirut, Tripoli, and Alexandria. In Alexandria, the Venetians had two huge warehouses for their spices, while the Genoese and Catalans had only one, much smaller.[45]

The Venetians were attracted to Egypt not only because of the riches to be made in the spice trade but also because Egypt, since the twelfth century, was a primary source for alum (potassium aluminum sulfate, an important pharmaceutical used as a styptic and emetic), sugar, and wheat and a major market for woods, metals, and slaves. Although Alexandria was an important port, the Venetians found two disadvantages there. First, the Muslim commander of the port ordered ships to turn over their yards and rudders, which left them at his mercy. Second, prevailing winds from the northwest during the summer, which was sailing season, made it difficult, if not impossible, to leave Alexandria.[46]

Acre, on the Palestinian coast, was also favored by Venetian merchants. They lived apart from the native population, with their own church, consulate, warehouse, public oven, bathhouse, slaughterhouse, and perhaps grinding mills. They built huge *palazzi* and other houses for their families and guests who came with the fleets. They also rented these houses to Palestinians and Syrians employed as skilled craftsmen making fancy glass and lace. These *palazzi* and country estates went back to the time of the Crusader's capture of Acre in 1104 with the help of the Venetian doge Domenico Michiel. Here the Venetians came into contact with the famous lemons, oranges, almonds, and figs of Palestine. Syria and Palestine also produced cotton, silks, and sugar to add to the exportable merchandise brought by the caravans from Damascus.[47]

Middle Eastern caravans set out from Syria or Cairo for Mecca, where the routes went east; another route ran from Aleppo to the Tigris. Eventually both routes led to the Indian Ocean. These caravans

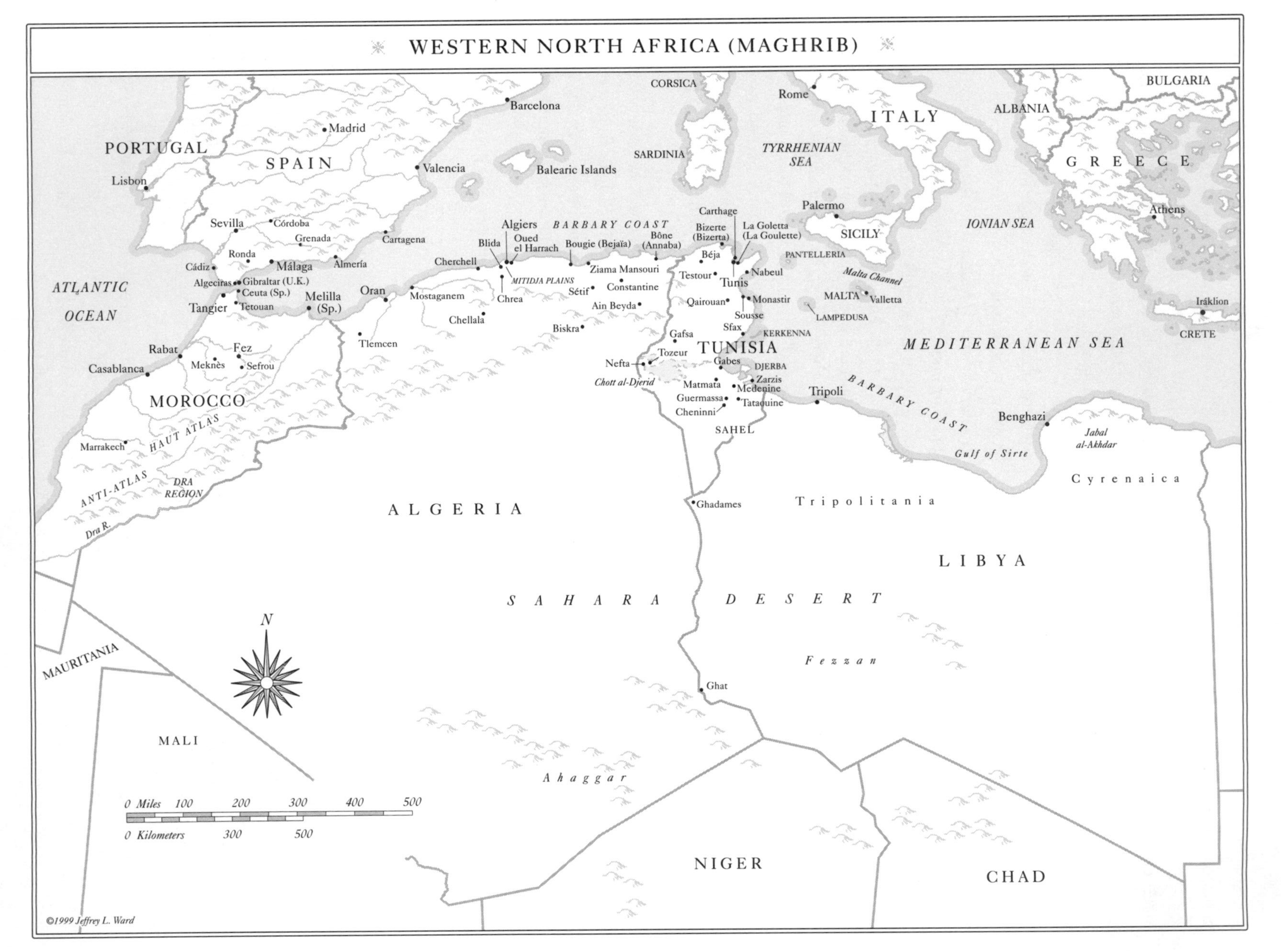
WESTERN NORTH AFRICA (MAGHRIB)
PORTUGAL
Lisbon
SPAIN
Madrid
Barcelona
Valencia
Balearic Islands
Sevilla
Córdoba
Grenada
Ronda
Cádiz
Málaga
Almería
Cartagena
Algeciras
Gibraltar (U.K.)
Ceuta (Sp.)
Tetouan
Tangier
Melilla (Sp.)
ATLANTIC OCEAN
Rabat
Casablanca
Fez
Meknès
Sefrou
MOROCCO
Marrakech
HAUT ATLAS
ANTI-ATLAS
DRA REGION
Dra R.
Oran
Tlemcen
Mostaganem
Chellala
Cherchell
Blida
Algiers
Oued el Harrach
MITIDJA PLAINS
Chrea
BARBARY COAST
Bougie (Bejaïa)
Ziama Mansouri
Bône (Annaba)
Sétif
Constantine
Ain Beyda
Biskra
CORSICA
SARDINIA
Rome
ITALY
TYRRHENIAN SEA
Palermo
SICILY
Carthage
Bizerte (Bizerta)
La Goletta (La Goulette)
Béja
Testour
Tunis
Nabeul
PANTELLERIA
Malta Channel
MALTA
Valletta
LAMPEDUSA
Qairouan
Monastir
Sousse
Sfax
KERKENNA
Gafsa
TUNISIA
Tozeur
Nefta
Chott al-Djerid
Gabes
DJERBA
Zarzis
Matmata
Medenine
Guermassa
Tataouine
Chenini
SAHEL
Tripoli
BARBARY COAST
Gulf of Sirte
Benghazi
Jabal al-Akhdar
Cyrenaica
ALBANIA
BULGARIA
GREECE
Athens
IONIAN SEA
Iráklion
CRETE
MEDITERRANEAN SEA
ALGERIA
Ghadames
Tripolitania
LIBYA
SAHARA DESERT
Fezzan
Ghat
Ahaggar
N
MAURITANIA
MALI
NIGER
CHAD
0 Miles 100 200 300 400 500
0 Kilometers 300 500
©1999 Jeffrey L. Ward

brought the "riches of the Indes" back with them to supply a Mediterranean whose demand for black pepper, spices, and silk was "feverish." This demand certainly existed in the thirteenth century if recipes like *lūn al-miṣra*, found in the anonymous thirteenth-century Hispano-Muslim cookery work, are any evidence. The recipe, which means "Egyptian dish," is a stew of meat with black pepper, ground coriander, saffron, thyme, citron leaves, fennel buds with their flowers, garlic, "lots of olive oil," and soaked *almorí*, a fermented or rotted wheat or barley flour mixed with spices or honey into a paste.[48] So important was this spice trade to the rising city-states of Italy that nearly all of the spices reaching North Africa in the twelfth and thirteenth centuries that came originally from the Muslim lands to the east did so in large part through the entrepôts of Marseilles and Genoa.[49] One can still find the abundant use of spicing in the culinary preparations of Algeria, Morocco, and Tunisia in particular, such as in the following dish for spicy pigeon from the western Algerian town of Tlemcen.

Ḥamām Muḥammar (Algeria)

TLEMCEN-STYLE PIGEON WITH FRESH CORIANDER

In Muslim countries of the Mediterranean—for example, in the mountains of Kabylia in Algeria—the winter solstice brought the feast marking the separation of the sun's cycles, and copious meals of couscous or maybe ḥamām muḥammar *were enjoyed because of the significance they held in symbolizing abundance.*

In the western Algerian town of Tlemcen, a city that grew wealthy in the thirteenth century from the trans-Saharan trade, they like to marinate pigeon, or chicken, in a mixture of abundant fresh coriander leaves seasoned with black pepper, cinnamon, and saffron. This recipe was given to me by Abdou Ouhab, an Algerian from Tlemcen, although I adapted it by consulting Youcef Ferhi's Grandes recettes de la cuisine algerienne.

Mediterranean pigeons are plump, flavorful birds—very popular in all of North Africa and raised for the kitchen. As in Egypt, many homes in Algeria will have their own pigeoncotes. In this recipe I use guinea hen, a delicious bird close in taste to the traditional pigeon used in the Algerian version. Cornish hens, pheasant, or quail can also be used. I have not tried it, but I imagine baby turkey, if there is such a thing on the market, might work well, too. Incidentally, if you find yourself traveling in an Arab country and ask for pigeon, ḥamām, *in a restaurant, be careful you don't stretch the middle "m," otherwise you will be asking for the bathroom,* ḥammām.

2½ pounds pigeons (halved), guinea hen (quartered), or Cornish hens (quartered)
1 cup extra virgin olive oil
½ teaspoon saffron threads, crumbled
1 teaspoon aniseed
Salt and freshly ground black pepper to taste
½ cup finely chopped fresh coriander (cilantro) leaves
1 large sweet (mild) onion, such as Red Florence, Bermuda, Vidalia, Maui, or Walla Walla, very finely chopped
Juice from 1 lemon

1. Put the birds in a large stove-top casserole with the olive oil, saffron, aniseeds, salt, and pepper, turn the heat to medium-high, and brown on all sides, about 10 minutes.

2. Pour in enough water to cover the birds, reduce the heat to medium, cover the casserole, and simmer until the birds are very tender, about 1¼ hours.

3. Transfer the birds to a serving platter, sprinkle with the fresh coriander, onion, and lemon juice, and serve.

Makes 2 to 4 servings

THE INTRICACIES OF ALGERIAN CUISINE

Algerian food is characterized by the interplay of European and Arab influences. The shakhshūkha, barrāniyya, *couscous, and skewered foods are inherited from the Arabs, Berbers, and Turks, whereas the soups, mixed salads, and some desserts are European influenced. The group of dishes known as* shakhshūkha *are vegetables cooked with lots of eggs stirred into them. They derive from a Turkish dish made with bell peppers, onions, and eggs, called* şakşuka.[50] *The category of dishes known as* barrāniyya *are breaded or floured vegetables or meat that are fried with oil and cooked in a sauce. The word* barrāniyya *comes from the Arabic root word meaning "to surround." Another group of dishes are cooked* à la "shaṭīṭha," *a word that means "that which dances," implying that the sauce is so piquant it makes the food jump in your mouth or that it jumps in the skillet, since it is cooked like a fricassee.*

The two main cooking methods in Algerian cuisine are simmering and braising, although the others, such as boiling and grilling are, of course, used also. Two kinds of sauces are used, maraqa ḥamra, *red sauce, and* maraqa bayḍā', *white sauce. Sauces are not usually made separate from the meal, as they are in French cuisine. Some sauces use* aghda, *an emulsifier or binding agent made from finely chopped egg whites and other ingredients. The Algerian white sauces are not the same as classic French sauces for they do not contain milk. They can be differentiated into three kinds. First, the white sauce that is called "white sauce,"* maraqa bayḍā', *and made with a base of butter or oil and seasoned with onion, black pepper, cinnamon, ginger, saffron, or turmeric, is used with couscous or meat cooked with vegetables. The* maraqa ḥulwa, *or sweet sauce, is also made from butter and seasoned with cinnamon, saffron, and honey or sugar and is used for sweet dishes. The third white sauce,* muḥammar, *or roasting sauce (although it's derived from the Arabic word for red), is a butter- or* samna-*based sauce seasoned with onion, cinnamon sticks, and saffron and is used for roasting or spit-roasting meats. Among the red sauces is* maraqa ḥamra, *red sauce, with a base of red bell peppers seasoned with black pepper, salt, and cinnamon, which is used for meat, offal, couscous, and vegetables.* Maraqa bi'l-tūmāṭīsh *is Algerian-style tomato sauce with a base of tomatoes, onions, and garlic seasoned with black pepper and cumin. It is typically used with fish, meat, and on pasta, rice, fried fish, and French fried potatoes.* Shaṭīṭha *(that which dances) is also a word that means red pepper; it is a hot chili sauce seasoned with garlic, caraway, and cumin, and is used for fish and meat. The fourth of the red sauces is the* musharmala, *which is also a highly seasoned sauce for fish or meat, but more so, and contains vinegar or lemon juice. In each of these sauces the cook seasons in accordance with his or her own taste using a variety of other herbs or spices.*

In eastern Algeria, one finds hot red pepper sauces and sweets made with honey or dates. In the central part of Algeria, white sauces and breaded or floured fried meats are found along with desserts made with almonds, such as maqrūḍ, *lozenge-shaped pieces of semolina and almonds. In the west, velouté sauces that are slightly sweet predominate. The two great culinary centers of Algeria are Constantine and Tlemcen, influenced by Muslim-Andalusi. Other major culinary centers are Algiers, Bejaïa, Sétif, and Oran. A favorite Algerian spice is cayenne pepper, a New World spice, while other common spices in Algerian cuisine are black pepper, cumin, ginger, fennel, caraway, aniseed, wild parsley, mint, cinnamon, and cloves. Many dishes involve long simmering.*

The culinary complexity of Algeria is like that of Italy, but because of its remoteness for many Westerners, not to mention the terroristic civil war that erupted in the early 1990s and targeted foreigners, very little is known about Algerian cuisine. There are fascinating preparations that I have only heard about—for example, the Algerian dish of cumin-and-saffron-rubbed whole lamb shoulder wrapped in cheesecloth and placed in the upper portion of a couscousière, *where it is steamed for a day. My friend Nacim Zeghlache described a dish from Sétif of semolina balls stuffed with minced onions and cooked in a sauce of onions and tomatoes, but a man who lived in a village thirteen miles away had never seen or heard of it and asked if the semolina balls grew on trees. Also near Sétif, in the high plains where wheat is grown, farmers store their hard wheat in silos. After a while the wheat adhering to the walls begins to ferment and the farmers' wives scrape it off and cook it.*[51] *They call this silo-scraped fermented wheat* mashruwwbāt, *the plural of the word for alcoholic refreshment, and its odor is curiously similar to that of Gruyère cheese, which may be not too far-fetched an explanation for the popularity of that Swiss cheese in Algiers.*[52] *As far as cheeses go, the people of the Maghrib do not have a large repertoire of cheeses, although they do have high-quality white cheeses such as a soft Algerian cheese with an artichoke heart in the middle.*

Couscous is a staple food. Maṣfūf *is an Algerian-style couscous steamed over broth. Little bits of carrots and peas are sautéed separately in butter and turn into the steamed couscous. Algerians are also fond of couscous with curdled milk. A larger couscous grain is known as* burkūkis, *what the Tunisians call* muḥammaṣ, *basically a pasta ball, but made either in the traditional couscous way, or as an alimentary paste.*

Algerian seafood cookery is found along the coast. The catch is small, but the little that is caught is excellently prepared, the most common fish being the gilt-head bream. Sardines and grouper are also popular.

Tortilla de Berenjenas (Andalusia)

EGGPLANT FRITTATA

Many medieval recipes are unattractive to modern palates because they taste too sweet or are too abundantly spiced. In the thirteenth century, those who could afford sugar used it the way we would use salt, and then some. Honey was a popular sweetener from classical Roman times and one finds it used in many recipes.

There are numerous recipes for eggplant from thirteenth-century Spain. This is notable because eggplant was a relatively new vegetable to Europe, having come from Persia, and this is an early date for its being common. This eggplant-puree tortilla *from Seville is a recipe from the thirteenth-century Arab-Andalusi cookbook of Ibn Razīn al-Tujībī, the* Kitāb faḍālat al-khiwān fī ṭayyibāt al-ṭᶜam wa'l-alwān. *Its relation to the* maᶜqūda *of Tunisia is evident (see page 500).*

The preparation requires a thickening and flavoring paste called almorí, *a concoction from medieval Hispano-Muslim cuisine. The word comes from the Arabic* al-murri, *which is derived from the Latin word (perhaps from the Greek) for brine.* Al-murri *was used as a condiment in the Middle East, too, where it appears in two early Arabic cookery manuscripts.*[53] *Ibn Razīn has several different recipes for* al-murri. *The base recipe for it is barley flour kneaded into balls called* jamajim *that are wrapped in fig leaves and left to dry and rot in the sun for twenty days. Another is made with wheat and barley flour mixed with coriander, nigella, and fennel. In this recipe, identical to the thirteenth-century one, except for a fermented* almorí, *the* almorí *is made with honey, flour, and salt. The spice mixture was popular in the Middle Ages and it also appears in the Piedmont (see page 237).*

This tortilla *is best cut into wedges, drizzled with the sauce, and eaten relatively soon after it has reached room temperature. Serve as a tapas.*

2 pounds eggplant, peeled and sliced
Salt
2 cups fresh bread crumbs
4 large eggs
1 teaspoon freshly ground coriander seeds
1/8 teaspoon ground cinnamon
1/2 cup extra virgin olive oil
Freshly ground black pepper to taste
1 garlic clove, mashed
1 recipe *almorí* (see Note)
1 tablespoon white wine vinegar

1. Lay the eggplant slices on some paper towels and sprinkle with salt. Leave them to drain of their bitter juices for 30 minutes, then pat dry with paper towels.

2. Place the eggplant in a large pot of salted water, bring to a boil, and boil for 30 minutes. Drain well and puree in a food processor. Remove the eggplant to a strainer and let drain some more, pressing out the water. It's important that not too much water remains in the eggplant puree.

3. Combine the eggplant puree in a large bowl with the bread crumbs, eggs, coriander, cinnamon, and 1 tablespoon of the olive oil, season with salt and pepper, and mix well.

4. Prepare the sauce by pounding the garlic in a mortar. Incorporate the *almorí* paste and continue pounding. Slowly pour in 1 tablespoon of the olive oil and continue pounding. Transfer to a medium-size bowl and slowly whisk in 5 tablespoons of the olive oil into the sauce, as you would for making a mayonnaise. Whisk in the vinegar.

5. In a nonstick omelette pan, heat the remaining tablespoon olive oil and pour in the egg-and-eggplant puree. Cook until the bottom sets, then flip it over or place under a broiler for a few minutes to set the eggs. Remove and slide onto a round serving platter. When

the *tortilla* has reached room temperature or is slightly warm, cut into wedges, spoon some sauce over, and serve.

NOTE: A nonfermented mock *almorí* can be made by blending together 1 tablespoon all-purpose flour, 2 teaspoons honey, ½ teaspoon white wine vinegar, and salt to taste in a small bowl until it is a homogenous, sticky paste.

Makes 4 to 6 tapas servings

ᶜUjja bi'l-Bādhinjān (Arab Levant)

EGGPLANT OMELETTE FRITTERS

Arabs of the Levant call allspice, also known as Jamaica pepper, by the word bahār, *which refers to mixed spices in general and to a particular spice mix (page 524) as well. Allspice is not a mixture of different spices, but rather is the dried berry of a Caribbean tree of the myrtle family* (Pimenta dioica). *Allspice was introduced to the Mediterranean after Columbus's voyages to the Americas. It was called allspice because its flavor supposedly combined those of cinnamon, cloves, and nutmeg. Allspice quickly became popular in the Middle East for its aromatic similarity to these spices, and contemporary Levantine cooking is almost unimaginable without it.*

These little fritters can be served as part of a mazza *or on their own. In any case, it is an excellent way of using up the leftover eggplant pulp from any of the stuffed eggplant recipes.*

1½ pounds eggplant, peeled and sliced
Salt
4 large eggs
¼ cup all-purpose flour
¼ cup finely chopped fresh parsley leaves
¼ teaspoon freshly ground allspice berries
Salt and freshly ground black pepper to taste
¼ cup extra virgin olive oil

1. Lay the eggplant pulp on some paper towels and sprinkle with salt. Leave them to drain of their bitter juices for 30 minutes, then pat dry with paper towels. Chop the eggplant.

2. Beat the eggs together in a large bowl and stir in the eggplant, flour, parsley, and allspice and season with salt and pepper.

3. In a large skillet, heat the olive oil over medium-high heat. Put a good-size dollop of egg mixture in the pan and push down so it forms a 4-inch pancake. Cook until it turns golden brown on the bottom, about 2 minutes, and carefully turn to the other side with a spatula and fork, so the oil doesn't splash, and cook until golden brown. Remove to a serving platter and serve hot or at room temperature. Repeat with the remaining egg mixture.

VARIATION
Use zucchini pulp instead of eggplant.

Makes 12 fritters

✣ ✣ ✣

THE profits of the pepper trade were enormous, and there were several attempts to corner the market. The Portuguese were at the forefront of these efforts.[54] After the Portuguese navigator Vasco da Gama rounded the Cape of Good Hope, opening up a new route to the Indies in 1497–1499, several things resulted. First, Venice, at its height in the fourteenth century, found that by 1504 there was no spice trade in Alexandria or Beirut, the trade having been partially diverted by the Portuguese in the Indian Ocean and transshipped to Lisbon. Second, the use of spices increased in the sixteenth century, especially in northern countries where they were used with greater excess than in the Mediterranean. Eventually the famous spice market of Venice and its Fondaco dei Tedeschi moved to Antwerp and then Amsterdam.[55] In order to increase imports of pepper and spices from the Levant, Venice granted permission in 1514 for spices to be transported by any vessel, instead of only the *galere da mercato* (merchant galleys), as they had exclusively been in the past.

The Portuguese efforts in capturing the spice trade were finally not successful, and the Levantine spice trade survived. The major markets in the Levant were in Syria, especially Aleppo and Tripoli. There are documents referring to the purchase of nutmeg in Syria in the summer of 1578, and a year later a list of goods captured by the San Stefano galleys of Tuscany include 936 pounds of sugar, 1,185 pounds of frankincense, 150 pounds of ginger, 1,114 pounds of cloves, 236 pounds of nutmeg, and 7,706 pounds of pepper.

This Levant trade had many stages to it and the whole trading system was actually quite precarious. Imagine the adventures of a sack of peppercorns or cloves. Its final destination may have been a shop in Nuremburg, but it first had to cross the Alps, being transshipped through Venice, and through Aleppo, not to mention all the stops on the caravan route from the distant and exotic Moluccas, where they were harvested.

Arselle alla Pisana (Tuscany)

PISAN-STYLE MUSSELS

The San Stefano galleys of Tuscany unloading spices for Pisa from as far away as the Moluccas carried black pepper, cloves, and ginger. The complete absence of ginger in contemporary Italian cooking doesn't mean that it's not part of Italian tastes, but rather that Italians have lost their taste for it. Spices played a major role in Italian cooking before the sixteenth century, including ginger. But pepper and ginger took first place in the Italian spice trade out of late medieval Egypt, even though ginger was heavily taxed leaving Egypt. Venetian ships were bringing back three kinds of ginger, beledi, micchino, *and* colombino.[56]

This recipe from Pisa is a rare vestige of earlier times, yet it includes the tomato, which was not eaten in Italy on a regular basis until the nineteenth century. How can this dish be explained? Pisa, an important trading city, is perhaps more likely to have retained longer than other Italian cities imported "Eastern" tastes. Unfortunately, I have never seen a recipe for this dish, only a register of its ingredients in an Italian travel book from the 1950s. I developed this recipe with modern tastes and historical intimation in mind.

½ cup extra virgin olive oil
5 pounds mussels (about 60), debearded and washed well
2 garlic cloves, finely chopped
1 teaspoon peeled and finely chopped fresh ginger or ¼ teaspoon ground ginger
¼ cup finely chopped fresh parsley leaves
2 cups peeled, seeded, and chopped fresh or canned tomatoes, with their juice
Freshly ground black pepper to taste

1. Pour the olive oil in a wide casserole or skillet that can hold all or most of the mussels in one layer. Add the garlic, fresh ginger (if using ground ginger, add it in Step 2), and parsley and turn the heat to medium-high. Cook, stirring almost constantly, for about 2 minutes.

2. Add the tomatoes and cook until bubbling, about 8 minutes, stirring frequently. Add the mussels (and ground ginger, if using), and pepper, cover, and cook until they all open, 5 to 6 minutes. Discard any

mussels that remain tightly shut. Serve immediately with crusty Italian bread.

Makes 4 to 6 antipasti *servings*

✣ ✣ ✣

TODAY, one can still smell the allspice, cardamom, cloves, and various *bahārāt* mixtures in their burlap bags and satchels while strolling through the Sūq al-Baḥramiyya and Sūq al-Sakatiyya in Aleppo. In Alexandria, another important Levantine spice market, one could buy all kinds of spices, and in Morocco the cuisine is an ode to spices even today.

Sharmūla (Morocco)

MOROCCAN FISH MARINADE

Moroccan cooks, to cook thicker cuts of fish, use a kind of relish-marinade of herbs and spices called chermoulla, tchermila, chermoula, *or* charmoula, *which are various transliterations for* sharmūla, *derived from the word meaning "to tear lightly." Some cooks gently heat the* sharmūla *in a pan or liquefy everything in a blender. The marinade can also be used with chicken. The suggested amounts in parentheses are in case you decide to put everything in a food processor.*

½ cup very finely chopped fresh coriander (cilantro) leaves (1½ cups lightly packed whole leaves)
½ cup very finely chopped fresh parsley leaves (1½ cups lightly packed whole leaves)
6 garlic cloves, very finely chopped
1 small onion, very finely chopped
Juice from ½ lemon
6 to 8 tablespoons extra virgin olive oil, as needed
1 teaspoon freshly ground black pepper
1 teaspoon paprika
¼ teaspoon cayenne pepper
½ teaspoon freshly ground cumin seeds
¼ teaspoon ground cinnamon
¼ teaspoon powdered saffron or a pinch of saffron threads, lightly toasted in an oven and ground in a mortar
1¼ teaspoons salt

Mix all the ingredients and refrigerate for 1 hour before using.

Makes about 1 cup

Ṭājin Qamama (Morocco)

LAMB STEW

Ṭawājin, *the plural of* ṭājin *(pronounced TAJ-n in Arabic, although ta-JEEN is commonly heard among English speakers), are a category of Moroccan-style dry stews similar to what the French call* etouffé *(which actually means "smothered") or* etuvé, *a slow braise with very little liquid. A* ṭājin *is also the name of the shallow handleless earthenware cooking vessel with its cone-shaped earthenware cover in which the eponymous preparation is made. The Arabic word* ṭājin *derives from the Greek* teganon, *meaning a frying pan. Among the* ṭājins *are several variations:* qidras *are* ṭājins *made with* samna *(clarified butter) or fresh butter cooked in an earthenware* marmite *with lots of chopped onions until they are a puree. The seasoning might include black pepper and saffron. Dishes cooked in olive oil can be known as* muqawllī.[57]

A ṭājin *can be made with a variety of ingredients. The Berbers make* ṭājins *also, such as* tqellia, *made with tripe;* lmorozia, *made with meat and eaten with honey;* nnhorfez, *made with turnips cooked in oil;* bestila, *chicken cooked with saffron; and* gobber dahro, *made with carrots cooked in water and prepared with flour.*[58]

Rafih Benjelloun, a Moroccan chef living in Atlanta, tells me that ṭājins *are special preparations shared with neighbors in Morocco, a tradition that still persists. Khaled Lattif, who is from Casablanca, told me that a* ṭājin *is best when covered and cooked over very low heat for many hours without the cook ever peeking under the cover.*

The ṭājins *called* qamama *are said to be those made with lamb and onions.*[59] Qamama *is an old Arabic word used in the* Thousand and One Nights, *to mean a particular kind of lamb preparation. A man brought a lamb to be butchered and had given it to a* naqib *(an honorific title). He cooked it by making* qamama, *which seems to be a process of wrapping the lamb, or perhaps it meant to smother the lamb. In any case, the method was also known in medieval Arab Andalusia because the historian al-Maqqarī describes this lamb dish in Córdoba.*[60]

This recipe is typical of the rich ṭājins *that would be served as part of a banquet and, as in all of the Arab world, would traditionally be eaten with morsels of bread to convey the food to the mouth. The enormous amount of sugar in the recipe harks back to a medieval time when sugar was thought of as a spice.*

3 pounds lamb shoulder on the bone, trimmed of excess fat
¼ cup extra virgin olive oil
2 large onions (about 2 pounds), grated or finely chopped
3 large garlic cloves, finely chopped
1 teaspoon ground ginger
½ teaspoon ground cinnamon
½ cup sugar
2 pinches of saffron threads, lightly toasted and finely crumbled or powdered in a mortar with a little salt
Salt and freshly ground black pepper to taste
1 cup water
1 cup golden raisins

1. Place the lamb in a *ṭājin*, enameled cast-iron casserole, Dutch oven, or earthenware casserole with a cover along with the olive oil, onions, garlic, ginger, ¼ teaspoon of the cinnamon, 2 tablespoons of the sugar, the saffron, salt, pepper, and water. Toss so all the pieces of meat are coated, then bring to a boil on a burner over medium-high heat, using a heat diffuser if using an earthenware casserole or *ṭājin*. Reduce the heat to low, partially cover, and simmer until the meat is tender, about 2 hours. Remove the meat from the sauce and set aside.

2. Increase the heat to medium-low, add the raisins to the casserole, and continue cooking until the sauce is thick and unctuous, about 45 minutes. Tilt the casserole and spoon out any fat that has collected. Remove the sauce from the casserole to a measuring cup or small bowl.

3. Preheat the oven to 325°F. Return the meat to the casserole and arrange on the bottom. Cover with the sauce and sprinkle with the remaining 6 tablespoons sugar and ¼ teaspoon cinnamon. Place in the oven until the lamb is falling off the bone and very tender, about 1 hour. Serve hot.

Makes 4 to 6 servings

SHIPS laden with spices left every year from Sumatra for Arabia and the Persian Gulf, and ports like Hormuz were open cities with every kind of smuggling and wheeling and dealing going on. The trade route to and from Aleppo was favored somewhat because it was a shorter overland route that avoided the piracy in the Indian Ocean, but mainly because this is where the silk was going through. Silk is mentioned constantly in documents and had an increasingly important position in the European economy. By 1596, Venice had two million ducats in export trade with Syria. The Venetians dropped off their cloth, silk manufactures, trinkets, and glass and packed their ships with raw silk and spices. As the ships returned to Venice, the price of the goods in their hold "increased miraculously," as one chronicler put it. After 1593, the Levant traffic no longer left from Tripoli but from Alexandretta (Iskenderun), which the Venetians made their shipping headquarters because it was nearer to Aleppo.

The Venetian presence in the markets of Cairo and Aleppo meant that they could bring the pepper and spices to their customers quicker than the Portuguese, who had to go around the Cape of Good Hope in southern Africa. Although Portuguese Jews had had a monopoly in Cairo, competition from Venetian merchants and others pushed them out of the Levant and the Portuguese found their solution by going directly to the source. Since nine out of ten customers for pepper and other spices were northerners and not Mediterranean peoples, the supply route through Italy and over the Alps was the most important.[61]

The spice trade brought wealth to Venice, where bags of spices called *sacchetti veneti* were sold in shops called *speciarii, apothecarii*, or *aromatarii*. The bags were used as a means of exchange as well as the *conzàr* (seasoning) for flavoring *luganeghe* (a kind of sausage), other sausages, sauces, and pickling marinades.[62] The merchants of Marseilles and Ragusa (Dubrovnik) also grew rich on spices. In the Piedmont during the fifteenth century, as an example, the most heavily used spices were anise, cinnamon (used especially with meat and game *in umido*, stewed, but also in the making of *vinus claretus*, a red wine, and it had an even larger role as a pharmaceutical), *citual* (a kind of ginger), coriander (popular in *agrodolci* sauces), cubeba (*Piper cubeba*, a kind of pepper), cumin (used in savory tortes and sauces), galingale (imported from Damascus and used in sweet tortes and pharmaceuticals), cardamom (also imported from the Damascus spice market and used in particular as a pharmaceutical), cloves (considered a "refined spice"), grains of paradise (used for therapeutic reasons and as a substitute for black pepper), mace (the fibrous covering of nutmeg used as an aromatic spice for meat and game and also used in medicine), nutmeg (a medieval favorite), pepper (the most famous and widespread of the spices in Middle Ages), mustard (used for sauces for boiled meats), ginger (the best came from Damascus), and sugar (used in the kitchen as a sweetener, where it replaced honey, and as a medicine).[63]

Pepper prices fluctuated with supply and demand. In December 1347, the price of pepper for Venetian merchants in Palestine or Damascus was 112 dinars for one *sporta* (about 450 pounds) while it dropped to 88 dinars in April 1392 and returned to 100 dinars in February 1422. In 1554, the Venetians took 335 tons of pepper from Alexandria. (To understand the proportion, remember that up to 2,250 tons of pepper were flowing annually).[64] The Venetian consul in Cairo reported that 20,000 quintals of pepper (2.4 million pounds) were unloaded at Jidda in Arabia in May 1565. Ginger prices held second place among spices. In 1560, wrote Lourenço Pires de Távora, the Portuguese ambassador to the Papal court, 40,000 quintals (4.8 million pounds) of spices came through Alexandria each year, most of it being pepper.[65] Only when the Dutch became masters of the sea did the Levant trade decline.

The holds of the ships said it all. The *Crose*, a huge Venetian ship (540 tons), sailed for the Levant in 1561 with copper bars, manufactured copper, woolen cloth, silk cloth, kerseys (a coarse ribbed woolen cloth), caps, coral, amber, various trinkets, paper, and coin. On the return journey, she brought back pepper, ginger, cinnamon, nutmeg, cloves, frankincense, gum arabic, sugar, sandalwood, and a host of other exotic goods.[66] And she made a killing on resale. City-states such as Venice grew fantastically rich on this trade, a trade that saw European merchants as bedazzled by Cairo life as by the wealth of the spices they found there.

RAISON D'ÉTAT

As powerful as Cairo, Istanbul, and Venice were, and as rich as they were, the city-state was losing ground. Spices brought them their riches, but confronting these city-states were political and financial challenges they simply could not overcome. The territorial state, rich in land and manpower, was its rival and, in the future, would be able to maintain paid armies, afford costly artillery, and engage in full-scale naval warfare. These great states, Aragon under John II (1397–1479), France under Louis XI (1423–1483), and Turkey under Muhammad II (1429–1481), had their beginnings inland and far from the Mediterranean city-states.

By reasons of state, governments acted; *ragione di stato* or *raison d'état* was an Italian invention. Niccoló Machiavelli's (1469–1527) *The Prince* taught the art of political survival. New governmental structures were appearing, especially in Italy, but in the East, the Ottoman Empire would also act "by reason of state." The Ottoman Empire had its beginning in the northwestern part of Turkey bordering the Sea of Marmara, when a local tribal leader named Osman, from whom the empire received its name, became master of groups of raiders in the thirteenth century. By the mid-fifteenth century the so-called Ottomans were strong enough to challenge western Christendom.

The fall of Constantinople in 1453 sent Latin Christendom into crisis. The Balkans fell to the Turkish conquest and Albanian landlords took refuge in Venetian presidios; Durazzo (Durrës) in Albania remained in Venetian hands until 1501; afterward these Albanians fled to Italy and Sicily and to this day there are several Albanian dishes identified as part of Sicilian gastronomy. Athens was occupied by the Ottoman Turks in 1456. The Ottomans attacked the Mamelukes of Syria and Egypt in 1516. Selim I's army used artillery against the Mameluke army outside Aleppo, and resistance was futile. The capture of Egypt by 1517 meant that the Ottoman Turks could benefit from African gold, and they blocked the Christian West's access to the Indian Ocean. The huge metropolis of Istanbul now had access to extensive wheat-, beans-, and rice-growing regions. Selim I was elevated to Commander of the Faithful, and the Ottomans were recognized as a world power, as they would remain in the Eastern Mediterranean for several hundred years.

By 1550, Turkey was also blessed with a boom in grain, bringing a previously backward country whose social structures were based on life tenure of property into the orbit of a powerful monetary economy already sufficiently strong to disrupt old patterns but not strong enough to create new and truly modern structures. A French traveler in 1528 reported the roads to be safe from robbers in Turkish territories. This certainly couldn't have been said about the brigand-infested lands of Catalonia and Calabria. Throughout the new Ottoman dominions, in the Balkans, Greece, Anatolia, and the Levant, the Ottoman Turks were wise rulers and, for a time, brought a generally well-received *pax turcica*.

In the West, the marriage of Ferdinand V and Isabella I in 1469 joined Castile and Aragon. In short order the reconquest of Granada presented the Spanish kings with a rich agricultural area, a region of productive farming land, and industrious and populous towns. Aragon's Mediterranean possessions—the Balearics, Sardinia, and Sicily—expanded Spanish power. Gonzalvo de Córdoba captured Naples in 1503; his victory marked a triumph for the Aragonese fleet and the creation of the Spanish *tercio* (a combat formation), an event that can rank in military history on a level with the creation of the Macedonian phalanx and the Roman legion.[67] The Turkish threat from the East drew Spain's attention away from the New World to the threatened citadel of Italy, the center of the world as far as a late fifteenth- and early sixteenth-century Mediterranean was concerned. Two great territorial states, rich in manpower, confronted one another.

The sixteenth century was the golden age of these two great states, Spain and Ottoman Turkey. They both lived lavishly. When Süleiman I the Magnificent died in 1566, forbidden things became popular, such as silk clothes woven with gold and silver (he had worn cotton). The luxury of the Seray became unbelievable as sumptuous feasts were regular affairs in Istanbul. Later, the magnificent feasts of Sultan Murad IV (1612?–1640) were prepared at the same time that Turkey was imperiled by war and famine. The golden age in Spain saw an extraordinary flowering of art, luxury, and *fiestas* in a new and rapidly growing city, Madrid, where artists such as Velázquez (1599–1660) and writers such as Lope de Vega (1562–1635) flourished. In both Spain and Turkey, societies were divided: the rich were extravagantly rich and the poor were miserably poor. These great states could not truly afford their "golden age" in this era when governmental bodies were lacking national budgets and a sense of good management. Except for a few Italian examples, states in the late sixteenth-century Mediterranean did not have treasuries or central state banks.

Toward the end of the sixteenth century, it appeared that the "golden age" had depleted the strength of these two empires. Spanish attention was being pulled toward the Atlantic and New World and Spain's struggle was with the Dutch and English; it turned its back on the Mediterranean. The Ottoman Empire also turned its back on the Mediterranean as it pursued policies directed toward Asia. Although the Ottoman court was luxurious in the late sixteenth century, the idea of the Ottoman Empire as the "sick man of Europe" had its beginning at this time. It was also the beginning of the end of the massive spice trade. Tastes began to change in the European Mediterranean with the arrival of other luxury items—coffee from Africa and Arabia, tea from the East, and tobacco and chocolate from the New World. In the kitchen, spices began to recede. It was the beginning of the decline of the Mediterranean. It was a political and economic decline, not culinary.

CULTURAL TRANSFERS

THE variety of people and civilizations is what makes the Mediterranean so vibrant. The mark of a living civilization is that it is capable of exporting itself and absorbing parts of other cultures—it must be able to give and receive. In the Mediterranean, three great civilizations are the Latin, Greek, and Arab. And within these three civilizations are groupings of subcultures constantly sharing with one another, the most important of whom were the Jews, found among all three civilizations.

Cultures could be shared, not forced one upon the other. Islam and Christendom in the Mediterranean, after the Crusades, were not as antagonistic as popular histories have led us to believe. Often there was cooperation, demonstrated in the anecdote about an Algerian ship that raided Gibraltar unsuccessfully in 1540. Once the fighting was all over, the corsairs went with their Christian prisoners into the port and everyone ate and drank happily in the *bodegones*.

Cultures transferred because people transferred. As men and women traveled, their material cultural traveled with them. The Jews who settled in Istanbul and Salonika opened markets. They introduced the first printing presses with Latin, Greek, and Hebrew characters. The Jews are said to have built the first wheeled gun carriages, without which Süleiman I the Magnificent could not have had the artillery that was the secret to his army's success.

How long did it take for cultural transfers to happen? How long for Arabic numerals to replace Roman numerals? How long for sugar to replace honey? Or maize to replace millet or tomatoes to be accepted? Maize, from the New World, changed Italian agriculture and spread rapidly during the early sixteenth century into central Italy, and in some provinces of southern Italy, in the form of polenta, becoming a fundamental food. The tomato, on the other hand, introduced about the same time as maize, was almost completely unknown to Italian farmers as late as the end of the seventeenth century.[68] We know that Arabic numerals came to Antwerp only in the late sixteenth century. How long did it take paper to reach the West? Paper was invented in China out of vegetable matter in A.D. 105. By 751, Chinese prisoners of war revealed its manufacture in Samarkand. Forty-three years later in Baghdad, the Arabs replaced the vegetable matter with rags and began using cloth paper. Not until 1350 did paper replace parchment in the West. Once the transfers happened, the West capitalized and surpassed the East. The paper and textile industry is an example. European success was in its mechanization of the production process and the adoption of the water mill. The Arabs failed to accomplish this productive development.[69] But the great Muslim contribution to medieval economic life was the development of commercial methods based on writing and recording. Not only is the Arab development of paper part of this phenomenon but so too is the high literacy rates of the medieval Muslim world. Literacy meant that the merchant did not always need to be on the move but could now develop large-scale commercial ventures that relied on counting houses.

Literacy was a problem for the development of international trade because not many merchants knew Latin, the language of all European commercial instruments up through the twelfth century. Italian was not yet a full-fledged language and still had to replace French, another language merchants did not know. Literacy was tied to the price of paper. Paper making started at the end of the thirteenth century at the earliest. The oldest extant business documents written in Italian consist of two parchment leaves from the account book of a Florentine banker for the year 1211. These are, in fact, the oldest existing documents in the Florentine dialect, and possibly even in the Italian language.[70] Higher literacy rates means faster cultural transfers, which in turn means culinary transfers.

Cultural transfer takes time, and so does culinary transfer. Did the thirteenth-century recipe for *fuṣtaqiyya*, a chicken stewed with pistachios and sugar found in the *Kitāb al-ṭabīkh*, become the *mirause catellonicum* of the Renaissance chefs Maestro Martino and Platina, a capon spit-roasted, then boiled with almonds, vinegar-and-juice-soaked bread crumbs, cinnamon, ginger, and sugar? We know at least that the entrepôt was Catalonia. How long did it take for *romanía*, a dish of chicken with pomegranates found in the fourteenth-century Italian cookbook edited by Francesco Zambrini, to come to the West?[71] The French scholar of the Arab world Maxime Rodinson pointed out in several written works that certain recipes of early Italian cookery manuscripts adopted Arabic names, and in some cases were identical to the Arab recipe, such as *romanía* (from the Arabic *rummāniyya*, pomegranates); *lomonía*, a dish of meat with lemon juice (from the Arabic *laymūniyya*, lemon); *sommachía*, a dish of chicken, sumac, and almonds (from the Arabic *summāqiyya*, sumac); and *gratonia* (a sugar-flavored sheep's milk and hard egg-white soup); *zeunia* (freshly killed chicken, dove, or other small birds fried in onions, lard, oregano, and wine, with their blood and livers with bread crumbs); and *camollia* (a sauce made from almonds, raisins, cinnamon, cloves, and bread crumbs).[72] Another dish, *mamonia* (*ma'mūniyya*, from the name of the Abbasid caliph al- Ma'mūn), appearing only in the anonymous fourteenth-century Italian cookery manuscript the *Liber de coquina* and not widespread in the West, shows up in English cookery books of the fifteenth century as *momene, maumenye, mawmany, mammenye, malmenye, mammony*, etc.[73] The Italian *mamonia* was a boiled and pounded capon cooked in almond milk with spices, rice, and honey.[74] The English *mammenye* was a concoction made of honey, raisins, sandalwood, cinnamon, wine, pepper, almonds, ginger, salt, saffron, and vinegar.[75] *Mahmūniyya* (or *ma'mūniyya*) appears in the eleventh-century work by Muḥammad ibn Aḥmad al-Muṭahhar al-Azdī called the *Ḥikāyat abī al-qāsim al-baghdādī* as one of the fine feast dishes consumed by gourmets in Baghdad.[76] In the fifteenth century, Ḥalīl al-Ẓāhirī (d. 1468) mentions *ma'mūniyya* as among the dishes prepared for the Mameluke sultans. In the various copies of the thirteenth-century Baghdad cookery book the *Kitāb al-wuṣla ila l-ḥabīb fī wasfi al-ṭayyibāt wāṭ-ṭīb*, *ma'mūniyya* is made in several ways, including as a chicken cooked in sesame oil, thinly shredded and pounded with cooked rice, sugar, and milk. It was served as a kind of paste or thick puree with pistachio nuts.[77]

One cultural transfer seen today is in the legacy of contemporary Spanish cooking. Both the Arabs and the Jews heavily influenced Spanish cooking, the Arabs with their introduction of agricultural products such as saffron and eggplant and the Jews with their use of oil instead of bacon fat.

Berenjenas a la Crema (Valencia)

CREAMED EGGPLANT

One of the earliest written recipes from Valencia may also be the earliest eggplant recipe in the Christian Mediterranean. In a fourteenth-century Valencian cookbook there is a recipe for eggplant cooked with onions, cheese, and spices.[78] This modern recipe is from El Granaino Restaurant in Elche. It is a rich preparation that reflects not only the sumptuousness of the courts of the caliphs but the influence of the Baroque as well. Unfortunately, creamed eggplant doesn't freeze well, so it should be consumed at one sitting.

4 eggplant (about 2 pounds total), split in half lengthwise
Salt
7 tablespoons extra virgin olive oil
Freshly ground black pepper to taste
1 large onion, finely chopped
1 bay leaf
¼ pound mushrooms, finely chopped
1 pound fresh shrimp, heads removed, shelled, and deveined if necessary (½ pound headless shrimp)
3 tablespoons brandy
1 tablespoon all-purpose flour
5 tablespoons heavy cream
Pinch of freshly grated nutmeg
1 cup freshly grated *manchego* cheese (page 717)

1. Preheat the oven to 375°F. Hollow out the eggplant, making sure you do not cut through the skins. Sprinkle the eggplant pulp and hollowed-out halves with salt and lay on some paper towels. Leave them to drain of their bitter juices for 30 minutes or longer, then pat dry with paper towels.

2. Put the eggplant pulp in a baking pan, sprinkle with 3 tablespoons of the olive oil, and season with salt and pepper. Bake for 25 minutes, stirring occasionally. Remove and chop the eggplant pulp.

3. In a large skillet, heat the remaining 4 tablespoons oil over medium heat, then cook the onion and bay leaf until the onion is yellow, about 12 minutes, stirring occasionally. Add the mushrooms and continue cooking until the mushrooms are soft and dark, about 8 minutes, stirring. Add the shrimp and chopped eggplant and cook for 2 minutes. (Save the heads and shells for making stock.) Pour in the brandy and flambé (see Note) until the flame extinguishes itself. Add the flour and stir to mix. Stir in the heavy cream and nutmeg, season again with salt and pepper, and cook for 1 minute.

4. Reduce the oven temperature to 350°F. Stuff the eggplant with the stuffing mixture. Cover the tops evenly with the cheese and bake until dappled with brown specks, about 40 minutes.

NOTE: Flambéing is neither as hard nor as necessary as we are often led to believe. Successful flambéing means letting the alcohol become warm enough to ignite and using your common sense around an open flame in a pan. If the alcohol does not ignite, don't worry, it will eventually evaporate anyway. When working with an open flame in this manner, remember to keep long hair pulled back and sleeves rolled up. Make sure nothing combustible is in the vicinity of the flame. After pouring the brandy into the skillet, give it a few moments to heat up, then light it with a long wooden match. This recipe calls for 3 tablespoons of brandy, and that is sufficient. Do not use too much more than that, otherwise the flame will be too big and last too long. If all this is too intimidating, don't bother.

Makes 4 to 6 servings

Filete Estofar con Cebollas (Spanish Jewish)

SKIRT STEAK WITH ONIONS

Andrès Bernaldez, the chaplain of the Grand Inquisitor and historiographer of the Catholic kings, said, concerning the Marranos, Jews who converted to Christianity:

> *The Jews have never lost their way of eating. They prepare their meat with onions and garlic and fry them in oil which they use in place of lard, because they do not eat lard. And oil with meat is something which gives a very bad odor by their breath and thus their houses smell bad. And this odor is called the Jewish smell.*[79]

I wonder if this Jewish style of preparing beef with onions moved east with the Sephardim in the sixteenth century and then west again to eventually cross the Atlantic and settle on Long Island, New York. I lived on Long Island in the 1960s, and many diners, Jewish-owned, always offered an entree called Romanian steak, my favorite dish. It was beef skirt steak smothered with browned onions fried in olive oil, a delicious dish. This recipe will give you a chance to try it, although skirt steak (cut from the diaphragm), for some reason, is increasingly hard to find. After enjoying this preparation you will see that Bernaldez was as wrong as the Inquisition.

3 tablespoons extra virgin olive oil
1 large onion (about 1 pound), thinly sliced
1 large garlic clove, chopped
One ¾-pound skirt steak
Salt and freshly ground black pepper to taste

1. In a large skillet, heat the olive oil over medium-high heat, then cook the onions and garlic together until the onions begin to brown, about 15 minutes, stirring frequently so the garlic doesn't burn.

2. Add the skirt steak, season with salt and pepper, and continue cooking until rare or medium rare, about 8 minutes, turning occasionally. Serve the meat covered with the onions.

NOTE: The recipe is easily doubled.

Makes 2 servings

SPICES IN ANDALUSIAN CUISINE

THE winding roads of the Mediterranean foothills lead down to the plains, lands that the food essayist Elizabeth David described as filled with plenty and good living. But in the sixteenth century these same plains were swamp infested, their stagnant waters home to malaria. The thickly populated plains of today with their "good living" were the "culmination of centuries of painful collective effort."[80]

In lower Andalusia, dazzling agricultural success in the plains led to the export of olive oil, grapes, wine, and cloth to North Africa, and the import of wheat and spices in turn. Andalusia, the jewel in the crown of whoever conquered Spain, looked outward by virtue of its economic and agricultural wealth, and its culinary wealth gave us *cocida andaluz*. Andalusian cuisine is rich in ingredients like almonds, fava beans, and olives from the land, and porgy, sardine, and shrimp from the sea. Andalusia is the land of gazpacho and olive oil; expertly fried fish is a specialty of the region. And of all the cuisines in the Christian Mediterranean, it is in Andalusia where spices are still used the most.

Ternera con Guisantes (Andalusia)

VEAL ROAST WITH SWEET GREEN PEAS

The Spanish love of saffron has its roots in the Muslim era, although it was known in Roman times, too. As early as the tenth century, the Arab geographer Aḥmad ibn Muḥammad al-Rāzī (888?–955?) advised that the best saffron in color and aroma came from Toldeo.[81]

3 tablespoons extra virgin olive oil
2 large ripe tomatoes, peeled, seeded, and finely chopped
3 garlic cloves, finely chopped
1 bay leaf
½ teaspoon dried thyme
Pinch of saffron threads, crumbled
Pinch of ground cinnamon
Salt and freshly ground black pepper to taste
One 3-pound boneless veal roast, tied to make a regular shape
1 cup beef broth (page 54)
1 cup dry white wine
3 tablespoons cognac
2 tablespoons unsalted butter
2 tablespoons all-purpose flour
2 cups cooked fresh or frozen peas
¼ cup finely chopped fresh parsley leaves

1. Preheat the oven to 350°F. In a large ovenproof casserole, heat the olive oil over medium-high heat, then cook the tomatoes, garlic, bay leaf, thyme, saffron, cinnamon, salt, and pepper together until thoroughly mixed, about 3 minutes, stirring.

2. Add the veal and brown on all sides, about 10 minutes. Pour in the beef broth, wine, and cognac, cover, and bake for 1½ hours. Remove the veal and set aside, covered, to keep it warm.

3. Strain the sauce through a fine-mesh sieve and set aside. In a 2-quart saucepan, melt the butter over medium heat, then add the flour to make a roux, stirring constantly for 2 to 3 minutes. Slowly pour in the reserved sauce, whisking continuously until it becomes a smooth, velvety sauce, about 15 minutes. Add the peas and parsley and stir.

4. Slice the veal and arrange on a serving platter. Spoon the sauce over the veal and serve immediately.

Makes 6 servings

Cocido Andaluz (Andalusia)

ANDALUSIAN STEW

Spiced sausage, cumin, saffron, black pepper, and garlic flavor this stew that some call the national dish of Spain. Some of these spices had their culinary roots in Islamic Spain, but the trade in spices itself was coming through Lisbon to the great spice markets of Seville and Barcelona. This chickpea stew is found throughout Spain in hundreds of versions, also by the name olla podrida, *a name made famous in Cervantes's* Don Quixote, *all made with chickpeas as the base and flavored with a ham bone and other ingredients depending on region, such as* morcilla *(a blood sausage),* oreja

GAZPACHO

There are two Andalusias, the countryside and the seacoast—and represented by gazpacho from the country and pescados fritos *(fried fish) from the sea. Gazpacho is a cold soup-salad made of fresh cucumbers, tomatoes, sweet peppers, and bread moistened with water that is blended with cumin, olive oil, vinegar, and ice and served cold. It is probably Andalusia's best known dish and originated as an Arab soup, an* ajo blanco, *which contained garlic, almonds, bread, olive oil, vinegar, and salt.* Ajo blanco *is today associated with Málaga and made with fresh grapes. Gazpacho comes in a variety of intraregional versions, some of which contain almonds, and no tomatoes and peppers (tomatoes and peppers came to gazpacho after Columbus).*

The Marquesa de Parabere claims, in Historia de la gastronomia, *that garlic soup,* sopa de ajo, *constitutes one of Spain's two contributions to soup making, the other being* cocida *or* olla, *which migrated to France as* pot-au-feu. *The most familiar versions are those from Seville and Córdoba, and the oldest version is probably from Córdoba and was made of bread, garlic, oil, and water. There is also* gazpacho de antequera, *made with homemade mayonnaise made of lemon juice and egg whites and pounded garlic and almonds;* gazpacho de Granada *is made with pounded garlic, cumin, salt, bell peppers, and tomatoes, with olive oil added until creamy, then water and bread on top.* Gazpacho de la serrania de Huelva, *from the mountainous country around Huelva, is a puree of garlic, paprika, onions, tomatoes, and bell peppers with sherry vinegar and olive oil stirred in until creamy and served with cucumber and croutons.* Salmorejo córdobés *(also translated as rabbit sauce) is made with garlic, bell peppers, tomatoes, and moistened bread pounded into a paste, with olive oil stirred in until it has the consistency of a puree. It is served with eggs, oranges, and toasted bread.* Sopa de almendras *is an almond soup;* gazpacho caliente *uses hot peppers. There are also gazpachos with green beans or pine nuts.*

The origin of the word gazpacho *is uncertain, but etymologists believe it might be derived from the Mozarab word* caspa, *meaning "residue" or "fragments," an allusion to the small pieces of bread and vegetables in a gazpacho soup. On the other hand, it may be a pre-Roman Iberian word modified by the Arabic. One will hear a lot about Mozarab when speaking of historic Andalusia. "Mozarab" is a corruption of the Arabic* mustᶜarib, *"would-be Arab," those Hispano-Romans who were allowed to practice their religion on condition of owing their allegiance to the Arab caliph, as opposed to the* muwalladūn, *Hispano-Romans who converted to Islam.*

(pig's ear), rostral *(a part of the spinal cord), and lard, beef knuckle, pumpkin, and cabbage.*

Traditionally, cocido *is served as two, and even three, courses as the important midday meal, not as the evening repast. The poor typically would not have found meat in their* cocido, *excepting perhaps a ham bone for flavor, nor would they have eaten in two courses. Bourgeois households, on the other hand, would strain the broth and eat the first course with rice or* fideos, *a typically Spanish pasta form, a vermicelli broken into 1-inch lengths. The second course consisted of the meat and vegetables, or the vegetables would be saved for yet a third course, served with whatever sausages are in the* olla, *or pot. Beef shoulder would be used by those who could afford it, while goat or lamb would be used by poorer people. As for the pig, every part is used, in making sausages, salted, or thrown into a* cocido. *The chorizo sausage is made with pork, garlic, and pimiento. The vegetables used depend on the local seasonal produce.*

The Spanish culinary authority Luis A. de Vega proposed that cocido *was invented in the late fifteenth century when the Marranos, converted Jews, in order to convince their Christian neighbors of the sincerity of their conversions, began substituting pork for cooked eggs in a traditional Jewish dish known in Spain as* adafina. *The* adafina/cocido *preparation was typical for the night before the Jewish Sabbath, as the pot could remain over a low flame without an attendant, thus avoiding the violation of religious law. The Jews could still have their* adafina, *but the pork would show that they were good converts. Nevertheless, Jewish motives were always suspect and Christian authorities wanted to see not only pork in the stew but also kitchen work on Saturdays. (For a Tunisian Jewish version of* cocido, *see the recipe for* tafīna, *page 682.) I also agree with Rudolf Grewe, a researcher of Hispano-Muslim cuisine, in seeing the earlier roots of* cocido—*that is,* olla podrida—*perhaps in the dish called* ṣinhājī *in the anonymous thirteenth-century Hispano-Muslim cookbook the* Kitāb al-ṭabīkh fī al-Maghrib wa'l-Āndalus, *a preparation cooked slowly in a large pot containing various meats, including meatballs and sausages, root and other vegetables, chickpeas, and spices.*[82] *Some* cocidos *use meatballs called* pilotas *that resemble the hard-boiled eggs of the Jewish* adafina. *They are made with chicken livers, ground meat, bread crumbs, egg, garlic, parsley, lemon peel, cinnamon, and pine nuts.*

The traditional cocido *pot is an earthenware vessel, glazed on the inside and with a tight-fitting lid. In Andalusia today, the pressure cooker is often used in place of the traditional method, in which case you would cook the* cocido *for 45 minutes instead of 4 hours. I am not a fan of the pressure cooker, though. Today* cocido *is something of a preparation for special occasions, a sign of modern times, as traditionally it was nothing more than daily nourishment.*[83]

This recipe from Andalusia is typical of the cocido *found around Granada. Other Andalusian* cocido *recipes would be found in Jaen or Córdoba, such as the next recipe. A robust red wine is ideal with this preparation, and the palate could be cleared with a* salad collioure *(page 209).*

3 cups dried chickpeas (about 1½ pounds), picked over, soaked in cold water overnight, and drained
1½ pounds oxtail
½ pound *jamón serrano*, inexpensive domestic prosciutto, or slab Canadian or Irish bacon, cubed
1 ham bone or one ¾-pound beef shank bone
5 cups water
1 garlic clove, peeled
4 black peppercorns
Pinch of saffron threads, crumbled
½ teaspoon cumin seeds
2 ripe plum tomatoes, peeled and seeded, 1 whole and 1 finely chopped
½ pound green beans, ends trimmed and chopped
4 chicken legs (about 1 pound)
1 Spanish chorizo sausage (about 1 pound) (see Note on page 544 and page 712), sliced
1 potato (about ½ pound), peeled and diced
Salt to taste

1. Put the chickpeas, oxtail, *jamón serrano* (or bacon or prosciutto), and ham bone or beef shank in a large stew pot with 4 cups of the cold water. Bring to a simmer slowly, about 30 minutes, then cook for 1 hour, skimming the foam off the surface occasionally.

2. Meanwhile, in a mortar, pound the garlic, peppercorns, saffron, and cumin together until mushy. Add the whole tomato and continue pounding until

the mixture is homogenous. This step can also be done in a blender or food processor.

3. Add the green beans, chicken legs, chorizo, potato, and the chopped tomato to the stew pot along with the remaining cup cold water. Carefully stir the stew and salt lightly. Add the spice mixture to the pot and stir carefully to blend well.

4. Cook over very low heat for 2 to 4 hours, checking doneness occasionally after 2 hours. The *cocido* is done when the meat is falling off the chicken legs and the potato has lost its crunch, but before it begins to fall apart. Taste and correct the seasoning.

NOTE: A Spanish chorizo sausage is not as hot as the Mexican sausage of the same name. It is best to substitute it with a Portuguese *chouriço* sausage, a Polish kielbasa, or a mild Italian sausage.

Makes 6 servings

Olla Cortijera de Córdoba (Andalusia)

STEW AS THE WIFE OF THE CÓRDOBAN FARMER WOULD MAKE IT

Andalusians are quite fond of cumin as a spice. The plant was brought to Spain from North Africa and entered the cuisine. The famous Spanish Arab agronomist Ibn al-ʿAwwām, who flourished in the twelfth century, wrote extensively about growing cumin.[84]

This one-pot farm meal with the distinctive smell and taste of cumin, an olla *from the hilly farmlands around Córdoba, is an example of the simplest of preparations from* cocina pobre, *the cuisine of the poor, although even wealthy peasants probably ate the same, or at least fed it to their farmhands. This stew cooks for 4 hours but can be frozen and is excellent later in the week.*

5 quarts cold water
2 cups dried chickpeas (about 1 pound), picked over, soaked in cold water to cover overnight, and drained
1 large onion, chopped
3 large garlic cloves, peeled
3 tablespoons extra virgin olive oil
Salt to taste
1 teaspoon freshly ground cumin seeds
½ pound Irish or Canadian bacon, diced
1 small head green cabbage (about 1¾ pounds), outer leaves removed, cored, and chopped

1. Bring the water to a boil in a stew pot. Add the drained chickpeas, onion, garlic, olive oil, salt, and cumin. Reduce the heat to medium and add the bacon after 2 hours. Cook until the chickpeas are soft, about another hour.

2. Add the cabbage to the pot and cook for 1 hour. Taste and correct the seasoning and serve.

Makes 8 servings

Huevos al Plato a la Flamenca (Andalusia)

BAKED EGGS, SAUSAGE, HAM, PEPPERS, ASPARAGUS, AND PEAS

In Andalusian dialect, flamenco *refers to the colorful cuisine of Andalusia. The word also refers to a dance, to the Gypsies of Andalusia, and to buxom women. The colorful* huevos al plato a la flamenca *are served throughout Spain and embody the riches of Andalu-*

sia. There are many variations on this Andalusian preparation, sometimes thought of abroad as a national dish of Spain. Traditionally, this dish is made in individual ramekins, but here I use one dish. See the Note on page 544 for substitutes for chorizo sausage.

½ cup fresh or frozen peas
10 asparagus tips, chopped
10 green beans, ends trimmed and chopped
¼ cup extra virgin olive oil
1 medium-size onion, finely chopped
1 potato (about ½ pound), peeled and diced
¼ pound cured ham (*jamón serrano* or prosciutto), diced
1 large ripe tomato, peeled, seeded, and chopped
¾ red bell pepper, seeded and diced
½ pound commercially cured hard Spanish chorizo sausage or pepperoni, sliced
¼ cup dry sherry
1 tablespoon tomato paste mixed with ¼ cup water
Salt and freshly ground black pepper to taste
8 large eggs
3 tablespoons finely chopped fresh parsley leaves
¼ teaspoon paprika
2 tablespoons unsalted butter, slivered

To serve
4 very thin slices cured ham (*jamón serrano* or prosciutto)
4 very thin slices hard Spanish chorizo
¼ red bell pepper, seeded and cut into 4 pieces

1. Bring a medium-size saucepan of salted water to a boil and blanch the peas, asparagus, and green beans for 4 minutes. (If using frozen peas, add them after the other vegetables have been boiling for 3 minutes.) Remove and plunge into ice water to stop their cooking. Drain and set aside.

2. In a large stove-top ovenproof pan, heat the olive oil over low heat, then cook the onion, potato, and diced cured ham together until the potato is almost soft, about 25 minutes, stirring a few times. Add the tomato and stir together for 4 minutes. Add the bell pepper, beans, peas, asparagus, chorizo, sherry, and diluted tomato paste and season with salt and pepper. Increase the heat to medium and cook for 15 minutes. Remove the pan from the heat.

3. Preheat the oven to 375°F. Break the eggs carefully into the pan over the vegetables. Sprinkle with salt, pepper, parsley, paprika, and the slivered butter. Bake until the whites set, about 15 minutes.

4. Roll up the cured ham slices. Garnish each quarter of the pan with a roll-up of ham, a slice of chorizo, and a piece of bell pepper. Serve immediately from the pan.

Makes 4 to 6 servings

❈ Sangria (Andalusia)

The word sangria *does not appear before the eighteenth century, and the lexicographer Joan Corominas believes the word derives from the Sanskrit through the Urdu* sakkarī, *meaning a sugared wine.*[85] *This beverage of wine, sugar, and fruits probably had its origins in the Spanish American colonies but today is a very popular drink in Spain.*

1 quart red Spanish wine or a hearty burgundy
2 tablespoons fresh orange juice
2 tablespoons apricot or peach liqueur
1 tablespoon sugar
1 orange, sliced
1 lemon, sliced
1 lime, sliced
1 apple or peach, peeled (if desired), cored or pitted, and sliced
1 cup club soda (soda water)
Ice

1. Stir all the ingredients together, except the club soda and ice, and leave in the refrigerator for 4 hours.

2. Add the club soda and ice, stir, and serve.

Makes 2 to 4 servings

DIPLOMATIC correspondence of the Venetian ambassadors in Andalusia constantly praises "a splendid land." By 1503, the riches of the newly discovered Americas added to the splendor. The entry point for these riches was exclusively Seville. Seville, the largest city in Andalusia, held a monopoly on trade because it was in the direct line of the trade winds. Seville, with its surrounding agricultural lands, also produced wine and olive oil, as did Córdoba.

Arroz Córdobés (Andalusia)

CÓRDOBAN-STYLE RICE WITH CHICKEN, VEAL, RABBIT, AND PORK

The active spice trade in Seville assured a cuisine at the upper levels of society that was richly flavored. Once the new plants from the Americas began to arrive, they were incorporated into the cuisine, many of them utilized in a similar manner as older spices. Ground chili and bell peppers in the form of paprika became popular. This contemporary rice preparation from the mountainous region around Córdoba is traditionally made in a large copper kettle called a peroles. *The variety of meat, shellfish, and spices make it a very exciting and satisfying dish for the family table.*

1 cup plus 2 tablespoons extra virgin olive oil
1 large onion, chopped
4 garlic cloves, chopped
3/4 pound boneless veal shoulder, trimmed of fat and cut into small pieces
3/4 pound boneless chicken thigh, skinned and cut into small pieces
3/4 pound boneless rabbit (preferably), homemade hot *salsiccia fresca* (page 70), or commercial hot Italian sausage, cut into small pieces
3/4 pound pork butt or shoulder, cut into small pieces
1 large green bell pepper, seeded and chopped
2 pounds ripe tomatoes, peeled, seeded, and chopped
1/2 pound mushrooms, quartered
1 cup water
Juice from 1 lemon
Pinch of saffron threads, crumbled
1 tablespoon paprika
2 teaspoons salt
Freshly ground black pepper to taste
1 cup dry white wine
12 littleneck clams, soaked in cold water with 1 teaspoon of baking soda for 1 hour, rinsed, and scrubbed well
4 cups medium-grain Spanish rice
10 ounces fresh or frozen peas

1. In a large casserole, heat 1 cup of the olive oil over medium heat, then cook the onion and garlic together until golden, about 10 minutes, stirring frequently so the garlic doesn't burn. Add the pieces of veal, chicken, rabbit or sausage, and pork and brown on all sides, about 12 minutes, tossing or stirring.

2. Meanwhile, in a medium-size skillet, heat the remaining 2 tablespoons olive oil over medium heat, then cook the green pepper and tomatoes together until the pepper is limp, about 15 minutes, stirring occasionally. Add the pepper and tomatoes to the meat. Add the mushrooms to the meat. Pour in the water and increase the heat to high. Season with the lemon juice, saffron, paprika, salt, and pepper. Cook for 15 minutes over high heat, then reduce the heat to medium and cook until the meat is tender, about 45 minutes, stirring occasionally.

3. Once the meat is cooked and soft, add the wine and clams and cook for 10 minutes over high heat. Add the rice, distribute it around the casserole, and cook for 5 minutes. Reduce the heat to low, add the peas, cover, and cook until the water is absorbed and the rice cooked, 45 to 50 minutes. Serve.

Makes 8 servings

CONCLUSION

IT was the monotony of taste that led Mediterranean peoples to seek the spices of the East, which would soon make them rich. We saw that the Mediterranean "spice orgy" was a result of changing tastes, both cultural and culinary. The expensive spices became a status symbol for the rich.

The trade in spices brought people together. There were so many Mediterranean cultures, so many points of contact, exchange, intermingling, that material culture became a kaleidoscope of possibility, a rendezvous for people, religions, fashions, food, and manners. In some sense, one can still feel and see this multifarious Mediterranean world today in ports like Barcelona, Marseilles, Naples, and Alexandria, with the added oddness of a Russian belly dancer in Aleppo, an American tourist in Palermo, and Japanese naval personnel on shore leave jogging on the *corniche* in Alexandria. Untangling the threads of this complex cultural Mediterranean is an impossibility.

The Levantine spice trade remained active until the beginning of the seventeenth century, but with the capture of the Indian Ocean by the Dutch in 1625, it had completely declined. As important as spices were for trade, luxuries were not the basis for the bursts of economic activity in the Middle Ages. In the long run, people need staples—that is, food—no matter how rich one gets from trading in luxuries.[86] The Mediterranean staple par excellence is that golden grain for princes called wheat, the subject of the next two chapters.

9

GRAIN FOR PRINCES, GRAIN FOR DOGS

THE title of this chapter is a play on the dicotomy between the "bread of princes" and the "bread of dogs" described by the sixteenth-century medical doctor at the University of Padua, Giovanni Michele Savonarola. It reflects how two different cultural systems found their focal points in bread. The bread of princes was wheat bread, while the bread of dogs (read: the poor) was millet, barley, or poppyseed bread—breads made from inferior grains. Grain is the basis of all bread, and bread is both the real manifestation and figurative symbol of Mediterranean culture. This chapter is not about bread per se; it is figuratively about bread, about the grains that made bread, that made men rich, salved the hunger of others, and created a vast array of food products and preparations based on grains such as wheat, rice, and maize. Most important, this chapter will follow the trade in grains, the wheeler-dealers who made a killing, those who starved for lack of grain, and some contemporary recipes that make our appreciation of grains so powerful.

WHEAT

THE amber waves of grain that we associate with our American plains could be justly applied to the historic Mediterranean, for it was grain that made possible the defeat of famine and poverty.

There was something magical about grain. That the earth brought forth food was a source of mystery and wonder in the Middle Ages. The image of Mother Earth was not figurative; people thought of a reclining mother when they saw the swelling of two hills close to each other.[1] Mystical agrarian customs were common among the peasants who believed in the vegetable protectress or grain goddess—ideas that were fought by the literate and Latin clerical culture. Grain was the foundation of the most basic food—bread—and bread was the staple food of the Mediterranean.

The tenth- to twelfth-century revolution in agriculture described in Chapter 1 was mirrored by a revolution in diet. Meat consumption began to decline in the mid-sixteenth century as the population recovered from the trauma of the Black Death, from agricultural land reclamation, and from the lack of importation of meat on the hoof from eastern lands after the Ottoman invasion of Hungary. The population became even more dependent on bread for its daily sustenance. From fourteenth-century documents, historians are able to calculate the daily bread consumption in the cities of central and northern Italy as 1¼ to 1¾ pounds per capita. Sicilian bread consumption in the fifteenth century was even higher, over 2¼ pounds per person per day.[2]

In Sicily and Italy, bread became the basis for the diet and was so important and ubiquitous that in the vernacular language people called everything *companaticum*, accompaniments of bread, although fresh fruit played an important role in Sicily as did fish to a lesser extent, if not elsewhere in Italy. Whenever bread was talked about, it was almost always with an obsessive fervor. In medieval agricultural contracts, farm lands were called bread lands *(terre da pane)*, while the produce of the land was the bread harvest *(recoltu panis)*. When tithes or rents were collected, they corresponded to a share of bread *(de pane)*.[3] Even today a decent fellow, or mensch, in Italian is someone who is *buono come il pane*, as good as bread. "Give us this day our daily bread," *panis quotifianus*, was a common expression. In Spanish documents, *los panes* (breads) does not mean merely bread but also a variety of foodstuffs.

What kind of bread was being made? The *constitutiones* of the Abbey of Benevivere in Castile differentiated between the bread called *candidus*, made with wheat without the bran, and the bread called *grossus*, made from other cereals. A *fuero* (statute law) from San Tirso and Castrillino said that the peasants had to receive bread made with 50 percent wheat. More explicit was the *fuero* from Quintanilla del Paramo, which said that bread must be made with wheat and rye, while another town stipulated it be made with wheat and barley.[4]

One's class was evident from the bread one ate. Bread was a status symbol, and its various shades, from black to white, indicated one's social condition. Until the introduction of maize in the sixteenth century, bread was as emblematic of the Mediterranean as was the potato for the Irish in later centuries. Bread was made in a variety of shapes and for different occasions, reflecting the importance it had not only in the daily diet but also in the daily meaning of people's lives. There were round breads, long breads, flatbreads, pizzas, stuffed breads, *galettes*, breads baked under the ashes, and bread made from everything imaginable. The most common bread in Languedoc and Provence was *rotundus*, round bread, but there were also rolls, or *miche*. *Panis lunatus* was made in the form of a crescent. Breads were also made in the form of crowns as offerings, *ex voto*. In Milan, there was *panes coronati* for the festival of Saint Ambrose.[5]

Pasta di Pane e Pizza Casareccio (Sicily)

HOMEMADE BREAD AND PIZZA DOUGH

Antonio Uccello, in his book Pani e dolci di sicilia *(Breads and Sweets of Sicily), tells us of the versatility as well as the sacredness of bread and the role it played in ritual family life in Sicily. The joy and preciousness of children were reflected in the breads made for children. Many breads commemorate certain holidays and take on unusual and highly expressive shapes, such as sleeping lambs for Easter. The family was also seen as sacred and a ritual bread made in the form of a sculpture of the family was called* sacra famiglia. *Breads were also made to memorialize the dead.*[6] *Light-hearted breads were made, such as the randy flatbread known as* sciarbuzzia *that was in the shape of a female pudendum.*[7]

This basic bread and pizza dough can be used for all the empanada and calzone recipes in the book. For recipes calling for bread dough, just leave out the olive oil.

1⅓ cups warm water (not tepid, not hot)
1 tablespoon active dry yeast
1½ teaspoons salt
4 cups bread flour or unbleached all-purpose flour, sifted
¼ cup extra virgin olive oil (only if making pizza)

1. In a large metal bowl previously warmed under hot running water, pour in the warm water. Stir the yeast into the water with a fork. Let it rest for 5 minutes, then add the salt and shake gently.

2. Add the flour (and olive oil only if you are making pizza) and mix until you can knead it with your hands. The dough should stick a little bit for the first few minutes but will then form itself with more kneading and folding into a ball. Once it is formed into a ball, dump it onto a lightly floured wooden surface and knead for exactly 12 minutes. If making bread, do not add flour or water, if needed, until at least the eighth minute of kneading.

3. Once the ball of dough is smooth, place it in a lightly floured bowl, cover with a kitchen towel, and let rise in a warm (80°F) place for 2 hours. For more flavor, let the rising process go on longer: cover the dough with plastic wrap and place in the refrigerator overnight (this is called a cold rise), but let the dough return to room temperature before working it again. Now it is ready for making into a pizza (see Note). If you are making bread, go on to steps 4 and 5 and preheat the oven to 475°F.

4. Punch down the dough. Reform into a round ball, cover with a kitchen towel, and let the dough rise for 1 hour. This slow, second rise is necessary for good-tasting bread. The round shape is the shape you will bake the bread.

5. Score the bread with a razor blade or very sharp knife. Place a pan of water in the oven and then the loaf on a baking stone. Reduce the heat to 425°F and bake until golden brown on top, about 40 minutes, spraying it with water at first. Cool on a rack before slicing.

NOTE: Divide the dough into 4 pieces and roll each out until 9 inches in diameter.

Makes four 9-inch pizzas or one round loaf

Pasta Frolla or *Pâte Brisée* (Italy and France)

SHORT DOUGH

Short dough is the name for the pastry used for savory pies. This recipe is the one that I use for Italian and French recipes, although it is a pan-Mediterranean dough.

1¼ cups unbleached all-purpose flour, sifted
6 tablespoons (¾ stick) cold unsalted butter, cut into bits
2 tablespoons cold vegetable shortening or lard
¼ teaspoon salt
2 tablespoons ice water, or more as needed

1. Blend the flour, butter, shortening, and salt together in a large, cold bowl. Add the ice water. Mix again until the water is absorbed. Add more ice water if necessary to form the dough.

2. Shape the dough into a ball, dust it with flour, and wrap in waxed paper. Refrigerate for at least 1 hour before using, then let rest at room temperature for a few minutes before rolling out according to the recipe.

Makes enough for one double-crusted 10-inch pie

* * *

ALTHOUGH there were a variety of breads made at different times for different occasions, life in the Middle Ages was nevertheless precarious and the struggle to get bread was as notable as the bread gotten. So many people lived on the edge of subsistence that landowners were advised to check their laborers who might be stealing grain, wine, or oil.[8] If there was no bread, there was famine. The desperate cry of the starving, "Bread, bread," could be heard in the streets and many a woman *iettaro loro onore per avere dello pane* (yielded her own honor to have bread). People pathetically tried to prepare turnips *in semmiante de pane* (with the look of bread). During the terrible Emilian famine of 1477, peasants made a bread of dried crushed hornbeam and hawthorn berries mixed with a few grains of wheat. In the Piedmont, starving desperation drove people to make bread by grinding and kneading "straw nodes, fig roots, the rinds of nuts and almonds and even vermillion stones."[9]

The distinctions among kinds of bread were essentially those between the city and the country. The socially inferior country people ate black bread or millet bread, or were bean bread eaters—the bread of dogs—while the city folk ate wheat bread, the bread of princes. Wheat bread was a nutritive bread while the bread eaten by the poor could contain impure ingredients. When the bread contained darnel *(Lolium temulentum),* a deleterious weedy grass, as it often did in times of famine, it became intoxicating. Diets were already precarious and inadequate during the Middle Ages, and people were highly susceptible to infectious diseases. People also suffered from persistent fevers, scrofula, cholera, dropsy, and gangrene, sometimes the result of ingesting breads made from impure flours.

Although wheat appears to be rare in terms of what the overall population ate, it became the most important food product of the Mediterranean in the Middle Ages. Wheat required lots of room to grow. The yields on grains were not very high because the same land could not be sown every year (farmers failed to replenish the land with nutrients through fertilizer). The annual consumption of wheat per person in the sixteenth century was about 220 pounds. Because grain was always scarce in the Mediterranean, people searched for home-grown cereals and ingenious substitutes such as chestnut flour for more common grains such as wheat and barley.

The urban diet consisted mostly of wheat.[10] The urban landowners of farms insisted on wheat growing, and city folk were the ones who bought that wheat. In the fourteenth and fifteenth centuries, wheat in the form of a relatively new product, *pasta secca*—that is, what we today call macaroni, pasta, or noodles, making its first appearance perhaps as early as the eleventh century in Italy, if not earlier in North Africa—was not the food of the poor peasants but of the rich Italian urban dwellers. Even after the appearance of macaroni, bread remained the staple food in the Mediterranean. The peasants preferred crops with higher and safer yields than wheat—grains such as rye (popular in Italy's alpine regions), spelt (eaten in the plains of Lombardy and Emilia), millet, panic, and sorghum throughout Lombardy and the Venetian plains as well as certain places in central Italy, barley in central and southern Italy, and, by the fifteenth century, a new cereal, buckwheat.[11]

In the towns, grain typically was purchased locally and within a small radius encompassing the granaries of the surrounding countryside (what is known as the *contado* of the Italian landscape). The grain traffic was in high-quality wheat known as *grani forti* in Sicily and *grani di Rocella* or *cima delle cime* in Florence, and in a variety of poorer quality grains.

Wheat was as important and as desired in the Middle East as it was in medieval Italy. The best bread, the most desired bread throughout the Mediterranean, was "white bread"—fine wheat flour bread. In the tenth century, the village of Ramla in Palestine was well known for an excellent white bread called *ḥuwwārī*. In the thirteenth century, Burcardus de Monte Sion, a Christian traveler, said he never ate bread as good as the bread in Jerusalem.[12] One such popular

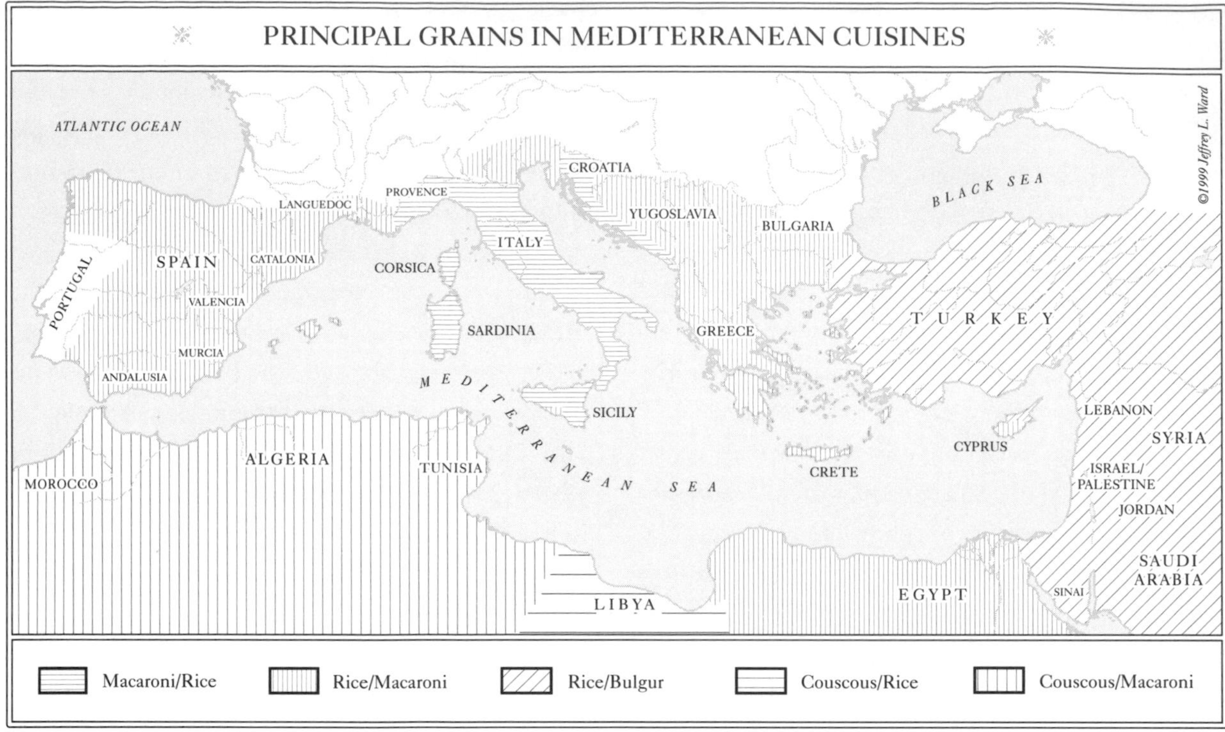

bread in Jerusalem was *kimāj*, a thin bread made without yeast that dried out in a few hours and became tasteless.[13] The Irish monk Symon Semeonis wrote in the 1430s of the bread of Alexandria, and Arab doctors recommended white bread—bread made with the finest flour—for patients.[14] In the Arab world as everywhere in the Mediterranean, bread formed the basis of the meal. But Arab cooks developed some unique and delightful preparations based on bread—dishes known as *fattāt*, crumbled-bread dishes.

Fattat al-Bādhinjān (Arab Levant)

EGGPLANT AND BREAD CASSEROLE

The concept of crumbled bread as a foundation for a culinary preparation is an old one in the Arab world. The thirteenth-century cookbook Kitāb al-wuṣla ila l-ḥabīb fī waṣfī al-ṭayyibāti wāṭ-ṭīb *sometimes attributed to Ibn al-ʿAdīm, a historian from Aleppo and said by some to be the nephew of the great leader Saladin, offers the recipe known as* tharīda raṭba*, a dish made with large pieces of bread crumbled with pomegranate syrup and lamb fat and cooked with chickpeas and meat.*[15]

This eggplant-and-bread fatta *is a simple preparation of Syro-Palestinian cuisine, the cooking of Lebanon, Jordan, Syria, and among Palestinians.*

2 pounds eggplant, cut into 1/4-inch-thick rounds
Salt
1 large *khubz ʿarabī* (Arab flatbread or pita bread)
2 tablespoons *samna* (clarified butter; page 189)
1/4 cup pine nuts
6 cups pure or virgin olive, olive pomace, or vegetable oil for deep-frying
4 large garlic cloves, peeled
1 teaspoon salt
1 quart high-quality full-fat plain yogurt, at room temperature
2 tablespoons finely chopped fresh mint leaves

1. Lay the eggplant slices on some paper towels and sprinkle with salt. Leave them to drain of their bitter juices for 30 minutes, then pat dry with paper towels.

2. Split open the flatbread and toast until hard and golden brown. Lay the bread on the bottom of a baking pan or deep platter. Melt the *samna* in a small pan, then cook the pine nuts over medium heat until light brown, 4 to 5 minutes, stirring or shaking the pan occasionally. Remove the nuts with a slotted spoon and set aside.

3. Preheat the frying oil in a deep-fryer or an 8-inch saucepan fitted with a basket insert to 375°F. Fry the eggplant slices in batches until golden brown, 3 to 3½ minutes per side. Remove and drain on paper towels. While the eggplant slices are still quite warm, arrange them over the bread. Let the frying oil cool completely, strain, and save for a future use.

4. Mash the garlic with the salt in a mortar until completely mushy. Transfer to a medium-size bowl and stir in the yogurt. Stir in half of the mint. Pour the yogurt mixture over the eggplant, covering all the slices. Sprinkle the pine nuts over that and then the remaining mint. Serve at room temperature.

Makes 4 to 6 servings

❖ *Fattat al-Ḥummuṣ* (Arab Levant)

CHICKPEA AND BREAD CASSEROLE

This is known as the poor man's fatta, *while that made with eggplant is the rich man's. Eggplant was not as plentiful as chickpeas and was, after its acceptance as a new vegetable, considered noble because of its taste, shape, and skin color. The* fatta *are the pieces of Arab flatbread that are ripped up to form the bottom layer. In Syria and Lebanon, Arab flatbread is usually used, although some cooks use the local version of French bread. The Homsi (people from Homs, Syria) love to put mint into everything, as in this preparation, while Lebanese and Palestinian cooks prefer frying the bread in oil rather than toasting it.*

1 recipe hummus (page 310)
2 cups dried chickpeas (about 1 pound), picked over, soaked in cold water to cover overnight, and drained
4 to 6 garlic cloves, to your taste, peeled
1 teaspoon salt
2 cups high-quality full-fat plain yogurt
1 to 2 teaspoons dried mint, to your taste
1 large *khubz ʿarabī* (Arab flatbread or pita bread)

1 Prepare the hummus.

2. Place the drained chickpeas in a pot of lightly salted water to cover by several inches. Bring the water to a boil over high heat until it foams, 5 to 10 minutes. Remove the foam with a ladle and continue boiling until tender, about 3 hours; keep checking. Add hot water to the pot to keep the chickpeas continually covered. Drain, place the chickpeas in a pot of cold water, and rub off the thin white skins. Drain again and set aside.

3. In a mortar, pound the garlic and salt together until a creamy mush. Stir the garlic into the yogurt with the mint and beat with a fork until smooth.

4. Split open the flatbread and toast until hard and golden brown. Lay the bread on the bottom of a baking pan or deep platter. Spread the whole chickpeas over the toasted bread. Cover with 1 to 1½ cups hummus (reserve the remaining hummus for another purpose). Pour the yogurt on top of the hummus and serve.

Makes 4 servings

FATTĀT, THE SYRO-PALESTINIAN CRUMBLED-BREAD DISHES

In the Mediterranean, bread was never wasted. During the Middle Ages, bread was almost always eaten stale, sometimes rock hard, but today when bread becomes stale, cooks in Italy make bread crumbs while French cooks prepare a panada (bread and liquid mixture) for quenelles, Spanish cooks use it as migas *(bread crumbs) for soups, and Arab cooks make* fattāt *(plural) or* fatta *(singular).* Fatta *refers to a family of Arab culinary preparations in the Levant in which pieces of stale, toasted, or fresh flatbread are crumbled and used as the foundation of a prepared dish. These preparations developed quite naturally in the Arab world because much of the bread that is consumed there is flatbread, a bread that dries out quickly.*

Two of the most popular fatta *preparations are* fattat al-bādhinjān *and* fattat al-ḥummuṣ *(page 553). Another delicious* fatta *dish is* fattat al-maqādim al-ghanam, *made with lamb shanks, chickpeas, and spices with yogurt spread over the bread. The Bedouins make* fattīta, *a kind of sausage made with bread, sour milk, and lots of butter, and* taftīt, *a food made of crumbled bread and milk. The famous bread salad called* fattūsh, *made with pieces of toasted* khubz ʿarabī *(Arab flatbread or pita bread), cucumbers, tomatoes, scallions, parsley,* baqla *(any wild green, for example, chickweed), and lettuce, is also a member of this class of dishes, as is the equally beloved* musakhkhan *(page 555). So is* fatta, *an Egyptian feast meal, and* fattāt, *a kind of bread soup popular among workers for breakfast in Damascus. I remember fondly the Maṭʿam Jamūriyya on al-Jabri Street next to the overpass in downtown Damascus. I ordered my* fattāt, *which they call* tissaqiyya *(pronounced tessa'EE-ya). A nice bowl of warm chickpeas in hot yogurt mixed with fried Arab bread, a little* bahārāt, *and sunflower seed oil kept me quite happy all morning. It came with a side dish of* ṭurshī, *pickled turnips.*

Fattat al-Dajāj (Arab Levant)

CHICKEN AND BREAD CASSEROLE

The thirteenth-century Arabic cookbook Kitāb al-wuṣla ila l-ḥabīb fī waṣfī al-ṭayyibāt wāṭ-ṭīb *has a recipe for a dish made with crumbled bread, called* ṣifa dīnāriyya, *where the pieces of bread were probably yellowed with saffron and formed to look like gold coins, dinars, as the Arabic name* (dīnāriyya) *implies.*[16] *This contemporary recipe is not meant to impress in the same manner, but is quite delicious.*

My recipe is adapted from two different fatta *dishes, and here chicken and spinach are cooked together and covered with yogurt. Walnuts are sprinkled on top in this version from Damascus, although pine nuts are acceptable, too. Some Damascenes also sprinkle feta cheese, although very little feta is used in Syria. More typical would be tiny cubes of* jubna bayḍā', *white cheese, sold in the United States as Syrian cheese (see "Mediterranean Food Products Resources"). Remember that using olive oil for deep-frying will make the dish delicious, but heavier.*

1 large *khubz ʿarabī* (Arab flatbread or pita bread)
6 cups sunflower seed, corn, or pure or virgin olive oil for deep-frying
10 ounces spinach, stems removed and washed well
¼ cup extra virgin olive oil
1 medium-size onion, chopped
3 garlic cloves, finely chopped
¾ pound boneless chicken breast, trimmed of fat and cut into ½-inch cubes
2 teaspoons *bahārāt* (page 524)
½ teaspoon ground cinnamon
Salt and freshly ground black pepper to taste
1 recipe *ruzz mufalfal* (page 602)
2 cups high-quality full-fat plain yogurt, beaten with a fork
¼ to ½ cup crushed walnuts, to your taste

1. Split the flatbread into its two leaves and cut each into quarters. Preheat the frying oil in a deep-fryer or an 8-inch saucepan fitted with a basket insert to 375°F. Deep-fry the bread until golden, about 1 minute. Set aside to drain on paper towels. Let the frying oil cool completely, strain, and save for a future use.

2. Place the spinach in a pot with only the water adhering to it from its last rinsing. Turn the heat to high and, once the spinach has wilted, 2 to 3 minutes, remove from the heat and drain well, pressing excess liquid out with the back of a wooden spoon. Chop the spinach coarsely.

3. In a small skillet, heat the olive oil over medium-high heat, then cook the onion and garlic until the onion is translucent, about 5 minutes, stirring constantly so the garlic doesn't burn. Add the chicken, spinach, *bahārāt*, and cinnamon, season with salt and pepper, and cook until the chicken is white and tender, about 7 minutes, stirring occasionally. Set aside.

4. Prepare the rice.

5. Preheat the oven to 350°F. Arrange the fried bread on the bottom of a 9 × 12-inch baking pan. Cover with the rice, then spoon the chicken-and-spinach mixture over it. Spread the yogurt over that and sprinkle the walnuts on top. Bake until the yogurt is warm, just a few minutes. Serve.

Makes 4 to 6 servings

Musakhkhan (Palestine)

BREAD-WRAPPED BAKED CHICKEN AND ONIONS WITH SUMAC

In Palestine, a favorite dish made by the peasants is musakhkhan, *a dish that one typically eats with one's hands and that literally means "something that is heated." I have speculated elsewhere that the Greek moussaka may be derived from this Arabic word* musakhkhan. *In any case, the dish is seasoned with sumac, a spice made from the ground dried berries of a bush that grows wild throughout the Middle East and is sold in Middle Eastern markets in this country. Sumac has a sour and vaguely lemony taste.* Musakhkhan *is made by cooking chicken until tender and succulent with an abundant amount of onions. Some Palestinian cooks use more spices, such as allspice or saffron, and garnish the top with fried pine nuts. Once the chicken is cooked, it is wrapped in thin leaves of* shrak *or* marqūq *bread, sold in many American markets today by its Armenian name,* lavash *bread.* Shrak *bread is a thin whole-wheat bread baked on a domed griddle over an open fire, while* marqūq *is a very thin yeasted flat bread. This bread can also be called* sāj, *a bread cooked on a convex metal plate called a* sūrj *or* sāj, *hence the name. All of these breads are stretched until very thin before being cooked.*

This simple preparation is one of my favorites, and the recipe comes from my former mother-in-law, Leila al-Qattan. Her husband, Abdul-Muhsin al-Qattan, usually a penetrating conversationalist, loved musakhkhan *so much that he never talked at the dinner table until he was finished.*

1 free-range chicken (about 3½ pounds)
Salt and freshly ground black pepper to taste
½ cup extra virgin olive oil
4 large onions (about 3½ pounds), thinly sliced
¼ cup sumac
4 sheets *marqūq* bread (see "Mediterranean Food Products Resources," and the Note) or 2 large *khubz ʿarabī* (Arab flatbread or pita bread), split open and separated

1. Cut up the chicken into two breasts, two thighs, two legs, and two wings. Salt and pepper the chicken.

2. In a large, deep casserole, heat ¼ cup of the olive oil, then lightly brown the chicken on all sides over medium heat, about 20 minutes. Remove and set aside. Add the remaining ¼ cup olive oil to the casserole and cook the onions until translucent, about 35 minutes, stirring occasionally. Add the sumac and cook for 2 minutes to mix.

3. Preheat the oven to 350°F. Cover a 9 × 12-inch baking dish with two overlapping halves of the Arab bread or two sheets of *marqūq* bread. Spoon half the onions over each, then arrange the chicken on top of the onions and cover with the remaining onions and the juices from the casserole. Cover with the two remaining half leaves of bread or sheets of *marqūq* bread, crusty side up, tucking in the sides, and spray with water. Bake until the chicken is very tender and almost falling off the bone, about 1½ hours. Before the top cover of bread begins to burn, spray with water again or cover with aluminum foil.

NOTE: The size of *marqūq* bread made and sold in the United States and Canada varies, so use common sense.

Makes 6 servings

✣ ✣ ✣

THE greatest factor in the fluctuation of grain prices was the distance between the fields where the grain was grown and the ports from which it was shipped. In Italy, the grain trade was hindered by poor roads between Apulia and Naples. Yet grain was shipped everywhere, and both merchants and middlemen and entrepreneurs made money. It was cheaper and easier to send grain by sea than by land. Little ports in the proximity of grain-growing areas acted as chief markets. An example of a little port grown wealthy was Lentini in Sicily, which took advantage of the fact that grain-laden ships from Italy preferred crossing to Spain from Sicily rather than from Tuscany owing to the shorter distance, thus encouraging cities with direct sea links to grow.

The main concern of the Spanish viceroys of Sicily was the grain trade. Sicily, with its huge supplies, was a grain supplier since antiquity almost without interruption. In the Middle Ages, Sicilian grain was stored in enormous *caricatori*, warehouses, near the ports. Throughout the sixteenth century, Sicily was exporting at the level of 150,000 to 200,000 *salme* (33,000 to 44,000 tons) a year, with Genoa taking a huge proportion of that amount. But the latter part of the sixteenth century saw a dramatic drop from 144,000 *salme* in 1572 to 41,000 in 1603, marking the rise of Sicilian pauperism, still evident today.

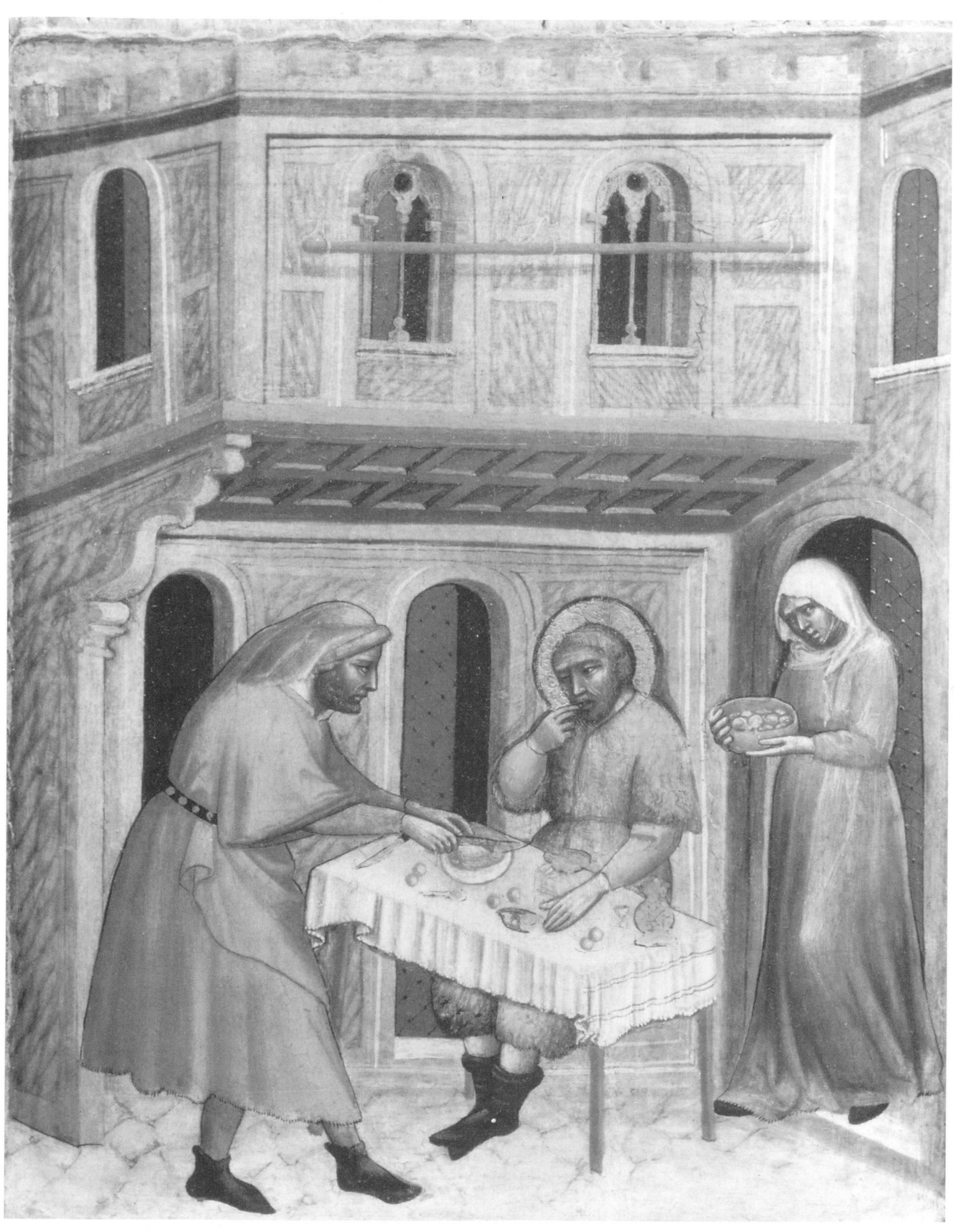

Anonymous, fifteenth century. Florentine: Tending the Hungry. From a series of the *Works of Mercy*. Pinacoteca, Vatican Museums, Vatican State.

SCALA/ART RESOURCE.

The causes for this decrease in production were plagues, government regulation, taxes, and the climate.[17]

The West and the Barbary coast needed Sicilian grain. They found it in the longstanding commercial center of Palermo, which didn't handle transport or loading but rather the *negozio frumentario* (the wheat deal). The landowners lived in Palermo and so did the agents for the wealthy Genoese and Florentine merchants. If you were hungry, you were at their mercy. The famous chronicler Leo Africanus (Ḥasan al-Wazan, c. 1465–1550) relates that the Arabs handed over their children as pledges to obtain Sicilian wheat during times of famine.

Grain merchants took huge risks, and the whole enterprise was speculative. Rains could affect the harvest, gales at sea could sink a ship, and there was always the risk of pirates, not to mention a world of rapacious middlemen. A grain merchant usually had multiple occupations. For example, the Florentine merchants Jacopo and Bardo Corsi were not only lending money to Galileo and selling silk and pepper on credit but also handling massive wheat purchases at Palermo on behalf of the grand duke of Tuscany. The Mediterranean grain trade was so important that the nineteenth-century Italian historian Lodovico Bianchini claimed that grain was responsible for more espionage than the Inquisition.

The grain trade had been important as far back as the classical era. Egypt had been a granary to Rome and its merchants still supplied the Hijaz in Arabia a thousand years later. In Egypt, the Nile carried huge quantities of wheat, rice, beans, and chickpeas. Egyptian grain showed up as far away as Valencia. Indeed, wheeling and dealing in grain was a pan-Mediterranean activity. The marauding light Greek vessels called *caramusalis* brought black market grain from the mainland to Venetian islands like Crete and Corfu. Besides the inherent risks of marauding, there were the Turkish galleys patrolling the sea.

The lessons of the grain trade were simple for merchants and illustrate the political economy of the Mediterranean: grain was cheap in the East and expensive in the West. When scarcity appeared in one place, the price of grain rose. Merchants rushed to this area with their cargoes of grain, and the influx brought prices down again. And so it went.

But merchants could not always meet the needs of the population, as Italy's terrible famine in 1554 showed. Toward the end of the sixteenth century, the food scarcity grew steadily more alarming as wars, plagues, and political machinations interfered with daily life. This, of course, affected the agricultural workers, namely the peasants, who abandoned their farms and flocked to the cities, creating conditions ripe for future plagues and famine. But famines had always been a part of the Mediterranean landscape.

The economic historian Carlo Cipolla expressed the dilemma for the poor in the maxim, "The lower the disposable income is, the higher the proportion spent on food." He argued that people cannot cut down on their food consumption when their income drops, nor can they increase their eating beyond a certain point when their income grows. The poorer the country, the greater the proportionate expenditure on food. A similar argument can be made for the expenditure on bread as a proportion of total expenditure for food. That is, the lower one's income, the more bread and other starchy foods are bought. No doubt we can agree with Fernand Braudel's assessment that bread was the "least expensive foodstuff in relation to its caloric content."[18] Grain in the form of bread was the staff of Mediterranean life. The following bread-related recipes are a sampling from Mediterranean cuisines, for the story of bread in the Mediterranean would require a book larger than this one.

Crostini col "Merollo" (Lazio)

BONE MARROW *CROSTINI*

The marrow inside animal bones has been recognized as a tasty and nutritious food since the dawn of humankind. In the Mediterranean, marrow bones are often used for flavoring soups and stews, as they lend a rich, mellow taste to the pot. Also, bone marrow spread on bread is a Roman snack that went out of style years ago. This recipe is adapted from Ada Boni's book on regional Italian cooking. Once the bone marrow is at room temperature you should be able to spread it with a knife onto the bread.

8 slices Italian bread or French baguette
2 to 3 tablespoons veal or beef bone marrow (from about 3/4 pound bones), at room temperature

1. Preheat the oven to 450°F.

2. Spread some marrow on each bread slice, arrange on a baking sheet, and place in the oven until the marrow has melted.

Makes 4 servings

Tostada de Pan con Aceite y Ajo (Andalusia)

GRILLED BREAD WITH OLIVE OIL AND GARLIC

Tostada de pan *is emblematic of simple bread preparations found all over the Mediterranean. This is the kind of nourishment fieldworkers would make for themselves during the day in the arable lands surrounding Córdoba. Since you're unlikely to fire up a grill simply to cook bread, I suggest you also try* pinchon moruno, *Moorish-style shish kebabs (page 341), as an accompaniment.*

1 round loaf country-style Italian, French, or Spanish bread, sliced
Extra virgin olive oil to taste
Salt to taste
2 large garlic cloves, crushed and cut in half

1. Prepare a hot charcoal fire or preheat a gas grill for 15 minutes on high.

2. Put the slices of bread on a grill or griddle and with a brush dab each slice with some olive oil, then sprinkle with salt. Grill until golden or to your taste. Gently rub each slice of bread on both sides using the four garlic halves.

Makes 8 servings

Crostini di Pane per le Zuppe di Pesce (Italy)

FRIED, TOASTED, OR GRILLED BREAD FOR *ZUPPE DI PESCE*

This is a basic preparation called for in many recipes in this book. Variation 2 below is how I make it when pressed for time.

3 garlic cloves, crushed
1 cup extra virgin olive oil
1 round loaf Tuscan or Italian country bread (about 12 inches in diameter), quartered and sliced, or 1 loaf French baguette, sliced

1. Leave the garlic cloves in the olive oil for 1 hour. Preheat a gas grill for 20 minutes on high or prepare a hot charcoal fire.

2. Brush each piece of bread with the garlic-oil mixture and place on the grill, oiled side down. Brush the top with more oil and grill until the bread is lightly brown, has developed sear marks, or its edges begin to burn. Remove the bread.

VARIATION 1
Brush the bread slices with the olive oil and fry on a griddle over medium heat until golden brown, then rub with a cut half of garlic.

VARIATION 2
Toast each slice until golden, then rub both sides with the cut half of a garlic clove.

Makes 20 or more slices; 8 to 10 servings

Le Mourtaïrol (Languedoc)

OVEN-BAKED SAFFRON CHICKEN BROTH AND BREAD SOUP

Le mourtaïrol *is one of the oldest dishes in European cuisine. The name indicates how the dish was originally prepared: in a mortar, with each ingredient pounded to the desired consistency. There are recipes for this preparation in two anonymous fourteenth-century cookery manuscripts, the* Liber de coquina *from Italy and the Catalan* Libre de sent soví.[19] *There is an old recipe that appears in the late fourteenth-century French cookery work* Le ménagier de Paris *and even in English, in the* Forme of Cury *as "mortrews of Fyssh," and in Chaucer's* Canterbury Tales *as "mortreux."*[20] *Perhaps this broth is originally related to the medieval Arab* lubābiyya, *a preparation made with unleavened bread crumbs, saffron, pistachios, and rose water.*[21] *This peasant soup is a perfect use of leftovers.*

1 pound loaf stale country bread (for example, *pain de campagne* or Tuscan bread)
Pinch of saffron threads, crumbled
2 quarts chicken broth (page 54)

1. Preheat the oven to 325°F.

2. Break up the stale bread in an ovenproof terrine or casserole. Put the saffron in the chicken broth and stir. Pour half the saffron chicken broth over the bread. Keep the terrine in the oven until it is as hot as you like your soup, about 30 minutes, moistening with chicken broth every once in a while.

Makes 4 servings

Tharīd (Tunisia)

BREAD SOUP

Culinary historian and cook alike will find this soup one of the most intriguing. The references in all the classical lexica describe tharīd(a) *as a kind of bread soup or a large earthenware bowl. It has been described as one of the Prophet Muhammad's favorite dishes, in reference to his saying that his wife ʿAisha held a place among women that* tharīd *held among food.*[22] Tharīd *was a food of the Quraysh tribe of the Arabian Peninsula in early Islamic times and, in what may be an apocryphal story, Hāshim, Muhammad's great-grandfather, had cooked this dish, then unknown to non-Arabs, on a visit to Syria for the Byzantine emperor, who liked it so much that he was persuaded to grant the Quraysh mercantile privileges.*[23] *Al-Muqaddasī, the famed Arab*

PA AMB OLI I PA AMB TOMÀQUET (CATALONIA)
BREAD WITH OIL AND BREAD WITH TOMATO

In every Catalan household children love pa amb oli, *bread with oil. A slice of bakery-fresh bread is toasted on the end of a long fork over a fire. Then the bread is coated with olive oil and a sprinkle of sugar or oil and rubbed garlic. Montse Contreras, a Catalan woman who helped me with my research on Catalan home cooking, remembers a children's rhyme from her childhood that goes:*

Volem pa amb oli	We want bread with oil
pa amb oli volem	bread with oil we want
Volem pa amb oli	We want bread with oil
pa amb oli volem	bread with oil we want
Si no ens el donen	And if they don't give it to us
si no ens el donen	And if they don't give it to us
ens el pendrem	We are going to take it

Pa amb tomàquet *is what the adults will eat. Any traveler to Barcelona will notice people in a variety of establishments eating slices of earthy-looking bread coated with something pink. The something pink is a rub of tomato. The whole idea is so typically Catalan, and I have not found a similar treatment anywhere in the Mediterranean, although some* bruschette *from southern Italy are close and that might simply be the influence of the Aragons in earlier times. The simplicity is startling. A very ripe tomato is cut in half, the seeds and excess liquid squeezed out, and then the slice of bread is rubbed with the tomato, leaving a pinkish stain. Olive oil is drizzled on with a sprinkling of salt—and there you have it. You could, of course, begin to add things to accompany the bread, such as anchovies, cured ham, or* butifarra *sausage (page 66), but now you get further from the concept. The secret, if it can be called that, is using high-quality bread, extra virgin olive oil, and a vine-ripened tomato. If the only tomatoes available to you are tasteless out-of-season ones, it is better to use a canned tomato.*

For pa amb oli, *slice the bread 1/2 inch thick and pour on some extra virgin olive oil, spreading it with a knife over the entire slice on both sides. Sprinkle with sugar. For* pa amb tomàquet, *slice the bread (some people toast or grill it lightly first), rub both sides with the cut tomato half, drizzle a little olive oil on both sides, salt to taste, and serve. I usually make one or both for a snack, for my kids, or as tapas.*

traveler who was born in Jerusalem in A.D. *947, says that he ate* tharīda *with the monks, probably meaning the Chaldean monks of Iraq, so the word may be originally Aramaic, Syriac, or Chaldean.*[24] *The* trīd *mentioned by cookbook writers Paula Wolfert and Zette Guinaudeau-Franc as the* basṭīla *(page 294) of the poor in Fez appears to be derived from the word* tharīda.[25] *The role of bread (or* crêpes *as Guinaudeau-Franc not inaccurately calls* trīd*) is prominent and supports Wolfert's claim that the Palestinian* musakhkhan *(page 555) is related because of the use of the very thin crêpe-like flatbread. The role of wheat in general in* tharīd *has led the linguist Professor Dionisius Agius to wonder if there may be a relationship between* tharīd *and the early Arab form of macaroni known as* iṭrīya. *Perhaps the original* tharīd *was really a soup of* pasta secca *and not bread soup.*[26] *In any case, today it is made of bread in Tunis and is a satisfying meal.*

¼ cup drained cooked chickpeas
Bouquet garni, tied with kitchen string, consisting of 1 celery stalk and 5 sprigs fresh parsley
1 young chicken, quartered, or 2 Cornish hens (about 3½ pounds total)
Salt and freshly ground black pepper to taste
2 tablespoons *samna* (clarified butter; page 189)
2½ quarts water
1½ teaspoons *bahārāt* (page 525)
2 large eggs
Juice from 1 lemon
½ cup extra virgin olive oil
About ½ loaf day-old French baguette, cut into croutons

1. Put the chickpeas, bouquet garni, chicken or Cornish hens, salt and pepper, *samna*, and water in a large pot and bring to a gentle boil. Reduce the heat to medium-low, cover, and simmer (just so the water is shimmering) for 1 hour.

2. Remove and discard the bouquet garni. Remove the chicken from the pot. When it is cool enough to handle, separate the meat from the bones. Lightly sprinkle the chicken meat with the *bahārāt* and salt to taste and set aside.

3. Beat the eggs in a bowl with a quarter of the lemon juice. Whisk a few tablespoons of hot soup into the beaten eggs. Transfer the beaten eggs back to the soup, whisking quickly so they don't curdle. Keep the soup warm over very low heat.

4. In a large skillet or casserole, heat ¼ cup of the olive oil and cook the chicken pieces or hens with the remaining lemon juice over high heat for 1 to 2 minutes, turning to brown all sides. Transfer to a serving platter as the pieces finish cooking. Add the remaining ¼ cup olive oil to the pan, reduce the heat to medium, and cook the bread croutons in the olive oil and leftover juices until lightly golden on all sides, 3 or 4 minutes.

5. Place the croutons at the bottom of serving bowls and ladle the soup on top. Serve the chicken on the side or with the soup.

Makes 8 servings

Buke Mevaj me Kripe (Albania)

BREAD SOUP

The towns attracted people, and by the sixteenth century, a full-fledged population revolution was underway. A town developed at Strouga on the Drin River in Albania. A wooden bridge spanned the river and shops began to open where merchants sold sacks of wriggling eels and freshly caught trout, and people ate their bread soup.[27]

Bread forms the basis of this hearty soup that Albanian peasants might make on a winter's night. Some cooks might use yogurt instead of sour cream, but in either case it is a rib-sticking meal. This recipe is adapted from Inge Kramarz's The Balkan Cookbook.

¼ cup extra virgin olive oil
1 medium-size onion, finely chopped
½ teaspoon paprika
1 potato (about ½ pound), peeled and grated
1 quart beef broth (page 54)
4 to 6 ounces French or Italian bread, cut into croutons
½ cup sour cream or high-quality full-fat plain yogurt

1. In a large saucepan, heat 2 tablespoons of the olive oil over medium-high heat, then cook the onion until soft, about 4 minutes, stirring occasionally. Add the paprika and stir, then add the grated potato and broth. Reduce the heat to medium and cook until the potato is tender, 20 to 25 minutes.

2. Meanwhile, heat the remaining 2 tablespoons olive oil in a medium-size skillet over medium-high heat, then fry the bread on all sides until crunchy and golden, about 8 minutes, turning frequently. Add to the soup and bring to a boil. Turn the heat off, whisk in the sour cream or yogurt, and serve.

Makes 4 servings

Calzone Pugliese (Apulia)

APULIAN-SYLE CALZONE

Calzone means "pant leg" in Italian. Calzone are usually associated with Naples, where they can also be made with sausage and mozzarella cheese, but are found, famously, throughout southern Italy, sometimes deep-fried. Every town has its own variation, sometimes with tomatoes, olives, anchovies, sliced onions, and capers, or with abundant fried onions (often sweet red onions), anchovies, capers, and olives and perhaps golden raisins. Other ingredients may include Parmigiano-Reggiano, caciocavallo, *or pecorino cheese or fresh basil and a hard-boiled egg. In the Abruzzi, one finds calzone stuffed with ricotta and mortadella. They also can be found under the names* panzerotti, calzengiedde, *or* caviciuncelli *in Foggia in Apulia.*

Carol Field, author of several books on Italian food, suggests that calzone *may have existed in medieval Latin as early as 1170, according to a reference in Padua, although the historian Luigi Sada, also the author of several Apulian cookbooks, suggests a statute from Bisceglie around 1400 as being the first appearance of the word. Chef Carlo Middione, the author of* The Food of Southern Italy, *makes the plausible suggestion of a Muslim introduction in medieval Arab times. If this is true, then the calzone, not to mention the empanada, is related to the old fried pastry of the medieval Arab world,* sanbūsak *(page 573).*[28]

This is the version often made on the first day of Lent. The rustic flavors of fresh sautéed vegetables seasoned with capers and anchovies make it very popular. Traditional calzone from Apulia are often made with semolina, but you can certainly make this with the pizza dough recipe on page 549. Some versions add tiny diced caciocavallo, *salami, and hard-boiled eggs.*

1 recipe pizza dough
¼ cup extra virgin olive oil
2 large white onions (about 1 pound), sliced
2 cups peeled, seeded, and chopped ripe tomatoes
⅔ cup chopped and pitted imported black olives
1 tablespoon capers, drained and rinsed
6 salted anchovy fillets, rinsed and chopped
2 tablespoons finely chopped fresh parsley leaves
Salt to taste
4 ounces pecorino cheese, cut into ⅛-inch dice (about 1 cup)
1 medium-size egg beaten lightly with 1 tablespoon water
Semolina (durum wheat flour) for sprinkling

1. Prepare the pizza dough and divide into eight balls to rise.

2. In a large casserole, preferably earthenware (which enhances the flavor), heat the olive oil over medium heat, then cook the onions until they are soft and turning color, 12 to 15 minutes, stirring occasionally. Add the tomatoes, olives, capers, anchovies, and parsley, mix well, and season with salt. Cook until thicker, about 10 minutes. Increase the heat to high, add the pecorino, and cook for 2 to 3 minutes, stirring and mixing. Remove from the heat and transfer to a medium-size bowl.

3. Preheat the oven to 400°F. Push the balls of dough down with the palm of your hand and roll or stretch them into eight disks with the thickness of a pizza, about 1/8 inch thick and 8 to 10 inches in diameter. Divide the tomato-and-onion stuffing among them, flip over one half of the dough to form a half-moon, and pinch the edges together with a fork to seal them.

4. Brush the calzone with the egg-and-water glaze mixture. Place on an oiled or semolina-strewn baking sheet or stone and bake until the tops are golden brown, 15 to 20 minutes. Remove and cool on a rack before serving warm.

Makes 8 calzone

Calzone Barese (Apulia)

BARI-STYLE CALZONE

The connection between the Near East and Bari, on the heel of the Italian boot, is an old one, at times reflected in the local cooking, such as this recipe. The population of the region spoke mostly Greek when Bari became an Arab emirate in A.D. 847. By 975, Bari was the capital of the Byzantine province of Lombardy. In the eleventh century, Bari was one of the most important ports in the Adriatic and a rival of Venice. Finally, Bari came under Norman rule, then Swabian rule under Frederick II, both bringing from Sicily their Arab-influenced styles of court living.

This calzone is filled with tomato sauce and fried mackerel, and it reminds me of the same intense flavors of the fried mackerel sandwiches prepared by the boatmen in Istanbul, near the Galata bridge.

1 recipe pizza dough (page 549)
1/4 cup extra virgin olive oil
2 large white onions (about 1 pound), sliced
2 cups peeled, seeded, and chopped ripe tomatoes
Salt and freshly ground black pepper to taste
6 cups pure or virgin olive or olive pomace oil for deep-frying
1 pound mackerel fillets (save the heads, tails, and carcass for the *fumetto di pesce,* page 369)
All-purpose flour for dredging
1/4 cup melted pork lard
1 medium-size egg beaten lightly with 1 tablespoon water
Semolina (durum wheat flour) for sprinkling

1. Prepare the pizza dough and divide the dough into eight balls to rise.

2. In a large casserole, preferably earthenware (which enhances the flavor), heat the olive oil over medium heat, then cook the onions until soft and turning color, 12 to 15 minutes. Add the tomatoes and cook until thicker, about 10 minutes. Season with salt and pepper.

3. Preheat the frying oil to 375°F in a deep-fryer or an 8-inch saucepan fitted with a basket insert. Dust the mackerel pieces with flour, tapping off any excess, and deep-fry without crowding them until golden, about 2½ minutes. Drain on paper towels and set aside. Let the frying oil cool completely, strain, and save for a future use.

4. Preheat the oven to 400°F. Push the balls of dough down with the palm of your hand and roll or

stretch them into eight disks with the thickness of a pizza, about ⅛ inch thick and 8 to 10 inches in diameter. Brush the dough with the melted lard. Divide the tomato sauce among them, spreading it on top somewhat thick, then place several pieces of fish on top. Fold the dough over to form half-moons and pinch together with the tines of a fork. Brush each calzone with the remaining melted lard mixed in with the egg and water.

5. Place the calzone on an oiled or semolina-strewn baking sheet or stone and bake until the tops are golden brown, 15 to 20 minutes. Remove and cool on a rack before serving warm.

Makes 8 calzone

Calzone Antica (Apulia)

OLD-STYLE CALZONE

In Italian cooking, a recipe described as antica, *antique or old, does not necessarily mean it has an ancient history but simply that it is the traditional way of cooking it. One of the first written recipes for calzone appears in the fifteenth-century cookbook of Maestro Martino called* Libro de arte coquinaria. *There it is called a* caliscioni *and the dough is made with sugar and rose water. The traditional calzone is found in rural Apulia, where the cook is as likely to use Swiss chard, beet greens, spinach, or the particularly delightful escarole.*

1 recipe pizza dough (page 549)
⅓ cup raisins
1 cup tepid water
10 ounces spinach, heavy stems removed and washed well
3 tablespoons extra virgin olive oil
1 garlic clove, crushed
⅓ cup pine nuts
1 pound homemade ricotta cheese (page 467)
Semolina (durum wheat flour) for sprinkling

1. Prepare the pizza dough and divide the dough into eight balls to rise.

2. Preheat the oven to 400°F. Put the raisins in the water to soak until you need them.

3. Place the spinach with only the water adhering to its leaves from the last rinsing in a large saucepan and steam over medium-high heat until it wilts, 4 to 5 minutes. Drain well in a colander, pressing the excess liquid out with the back of a wooden spoon, and chop coarsely.

4. In a large casserole, preferably earthenware (which enhances the flavor), heat the olive oil over medium heat, then cook the garlic clove until it just begins to turn light brown. Remove and discard the garlic. Add the pine nuts and cook until they are almost golden, about 2 minutes. Be careful not to burn them. Add the spinach, stir, and cook for 3 minutes. Drain the raisins, add them to the casserole, and cook for another 2 minutes. Remove from the heat and set aside.

5. Push the balls of dough down with the palm of your hand and roll or stretch them into eight disks with the thickness of a pizza, about ⅛ inch thick and 8 to 10 inches in diameter. Stuff each disk with some spinach mixture and a heaping tablespoonful of ricotta cheese. Fold half of the dough over to form a half moon and pinch closed with the tines of a fork.

6. Place the calzone on an oiled or semolina-strewn baking sheet or stone and bake until golden on top, 15 to 20 minutes. Remove and cool on a wire rack.

VARIATION

Steam a head of escarole until wilted and the core or heart is softer. Drain well and chop together with several anchovy fillets and some imported and pitted black olives. Stuff the calzone with this mixture.

Makes 8 calzone

❖ *Calzone Lucana* (Basilicata)

BASILICATA-STYLE CALZONE

This spicy hot calzone is typical home fare from Basilicata. In Matera, these calzone, distinguished by being made with beets, are very popular. Sometimes the beets are replaced with spinach or Swiss chard. Although untraditional with spicy food, adding several tablespoons of ricotta is a very nice touch.

1 recipe pizza dough (page 549)
6 tablespoons extra virgin olive oil
4 medium-size beets (about 1 pound), peeled and very thinly sliced
2 dried chili peppers, crumbled
Salt to taste
¾ pound imported black olives (about 40 olives), pitted and chopped
4 salted anchovy fillets, rinsed and chopped
Semolina (durum wheat flour) for sprinkling

1. Prepare the pizza dough and divide the dough into eight balls to rise.

2. In a large skillet, heat the olive oil with the beets over medium-high heat, then cook until slightly soft, about 20 minutes, stirring frequently. Add the chili peppers, season with salt, and cook for 1 minute, then toss in the olives and anchovies and cook another 2 minutes. Set aside.

3. Preheat the oven to 400°F. Push the balls of dough down with the palm of your hand and roll or stretch them into disks with the thickness of a pizza, about ⅛ inch thick and 8 to 10 inches in diameter. Divide the stuffing mixture among the disks. Fold the other half of the dough over to form half-moons and pinch closed with the tines of a fork.

4. Place the calzone on an oiled or semolina-strewn baking sheet or stone and bake until the tops are golden, 15 to 20 minutes. Remove to a wire rack, cool slightly, and serve.

Makes 8 calzone

❖ *Guastedde* (Sicily)

SICILIAN SPLEEN SANDWICHES ON SESAME SEED ROLLS

In Sicily, guastedde*, also called* vastieddi*, are sesame seed rolls filled with veal spleen, heart, or lung. They can be made* schiette *(unmarried) if only filled with spleen or* maritate *(married) if filled also with fresh ricotta or grated* caciocavallo *cheese. They are sold exclusively from fry-stands called* friggitorie*.* Guastedde *may sound a bit bizarre, but spleen is rather mild in flavor, high in protein, cheap, and has a taste similar to that of very mild veal liver, but you will have to order it from a specialty or local ethnic butcher since supermarkets don't carry it. Spleen does not need any special preparation beyond what is called for in this recipe.*

Very similar to this Sicilian preparation is the crostini de milza *found in Venice made with spleen, pancetta, capers, anchovy, garlic, and parsley. The spleen is poached first in water with carrot, celery, sage, and onion.*[29]

2 quarts water
Salt to taste
Juice and zest from 1 lemon
6 veal or lamb spleens (about 2 pounds)

2 tablespoons extra virgin olive oil or melted pork lard
4 to 6 soft sesame seed rolls
½ pound homemade ricotta cheese (page 467)
¼ pound *caciocavallo* or pecorino cheese, coarsely grated
Lemon wedges for garnish
Freshly ground black pepper to taste

1. Bring the water to a boil in a large pot and lightly salt it. Pour the lemon juice and zest into the water. Reduce the heat until the water is shimmering and poach the spleen in it gently for 1 hour. Drain and cool. Slice off any excess skin and cut the spleen into ⅛-inch-thick slices.

2. In a large skillet, heat the oil or lard over low heat, then cook the spleen slices carefully on both sides until firmer, about 5 minutes. Slice open the sesame rolls and coat the bottom halves with the ricotta cheese about ¼ inch thick. Cover the ricotta

ETYMOLOGY AND COOKING

Culinary history is not yet a serious topic of study in the academic world. Most so-called culinary historians are food writers, such as myself, who are merely consumers of scholarship. Academic historians, when they are concerned about food, are interested more in the economic history of agriculture than in cuisine. This situation is perhaps changing, led by a small number of Italian and French historians influenced by the Annales school of historiography, such as Piero Camporesi, Massimo Montanari, Maurice Aymard, Maxime Rodinson, and Henri Bresc, whose focus is the role of cuisine. Perhaps one of the limiting factors in serious culinary history is that the historian must be conversant with, if not expert in, a variety of practical and academic disciplines beyond cooking and history, such as the knowledge of various languages. Two other of the most important fields of study that a culinary historian will want to be familiar with are etymology and paleoethnobotany. As an example of the etymological approach in culinary history, we can pursue an interesting, some would say convoluted, etymology behind the Sicilian word guastedde *(page 566) to get some sense of how this approach might be fruitful. An eighteenth-century* Vocabulario siciliano-italiano *in the Bibliotheca Comunale di Palermo has an entry for the word* maxhabisu, *a type of focaccia described as the Arabic word for a kind of* guastedde a balata, *a red brick–colored nutritious food cooked in an earthenware bread pan. The word* maxhabisu *comes from the Arabic word* makhābiz, *the plural of* makhbaza, *"bread bakery." The root word for* makhbaza *is* kharbūsha, *an old Syrian Arabic word for a kind of elongated sweet bread stuffed with almonds and hazelnuts that itself comes from the Arabic root word* khubz, *meaning "bread."*[30] Kharbūsha *also gives us* carbuciu, *a Sicilian focaccia that might have its roots in the* khubz al-malla *in Tunisia, a bread baked under ashes.*[31] *The same word is also described by the folklorist Giuseppe Vidossi as a small ball of dough in the form of a female pudendum.*[32] *In the end it's all bread and very delicious.*

with the slices of spleen, then sprinkle with some grated cheese, a squirt from a lemon wedge, and several grindings of black pepper. Put the top of the roll on and serve immediately.

Makes 6 servings

Empanadillas Valencianas (Valencia)

VALENCIA-STYLE SMALL EMPANADAS

Little stuffed breaded things, empanadilla *in Spanish, are very common throughout the Mediterranean. They are simply stuffed bread dough that is fried or baked and eaten as a tapa or sandwich in Spain. In Italy they are to be found in the form of calzone (see the recipes above), and in the Arab world they might be* shūshbarak *(page 571). These are popular foods because they are easy to eat and easy to transport.*

There are a variety of empanada-like preparations even within Spain. In Valencia they are small pies, as reflected in the diminutive name of this recipe. In Galicia and Asturia, to the north, they are made much larger, while in Catalonia they are called coques, *a kind of pizza. The Catalan* coca *(singular of* coques*), Colman Andrews, the author of a book on Catalan food, tells us, is different from a pizza in that it is oval and rarely contains cheese and herbs (see page 570). The same dough appears in a sweet pie of Languedoc called* coque aux fruits. *It is also known in Valencia and Majorca under various names such as* coca fassida, coca fritanga, *and* coco pisto. *In Algeria, a recipe from Bab el-Oued is identical to this last one from Majorca—with a tomato, green pepper, hard-boiled egg, garlic, and anchovy stuffing—which explains why the former French settlers of Algeria known as the* pied-noirs *during the imperial era have their own* coca *similar to the Algerian one.*

The stuffing of dough with previously cooked meats, fish, or vegetables was known early on by the Arabs—for example, in Arab Sicily (827–1091), where a food called sfinci *was presumably stuffed and deep-fried. A kind of stuffed focaccia known as* scacciate *in Sicily is also very old. In fact, in the fourteenth-century Sicilian vocabulary of the lingua franca, the* Declarus *of Senisio, from 1348, one finds a kind of* empanadilla *by the name* pasteda, *which may ultimately be related to the Moroccan* basṭīla, *or vice versa (see page 294). In this same vein, we find in the* Vocabolario latino-siciliano-spanolo *of L. C. Scobar from 1519–1520 a food called* pasticza, *which seems to be a Spanish food. Finally, in Michele Pasqualino's Sicilian dictionary of 1785, we have the entry for* 'mpanata, *which clearly indicates that by the sixteenth century the word had entered the Sicilian language. Various corruptions occurred in Sicily, such as* 'mpanatigghie, 'nfigghiulate, fuazza *(an early form of* focacce, *derived from the Latin, see page 160, but possibly with an Arabic connection),* pastizzu, ravazzata, scacciata, *and* sfinciuni, *the last two being words derived from the Arabic.*[33]

I am providing two different recipes for the empanadilla *dough. The first is a more rustic dough typical of these small pies of Valencia and sometimes used for the larger pies of Galicia and Asturia. The second dough recipe is more appropriate for the* coca *(page 570), but can be used here too.*

For dough 1

6 tablespoons extra virgin olive oil
½ cup water
½ teaspoon salt
3 cups unbleached all-purpose flour
½ teaspoon aniseeds

For dough 2

1 cup tepid water
1 tablespoon active dry yeast

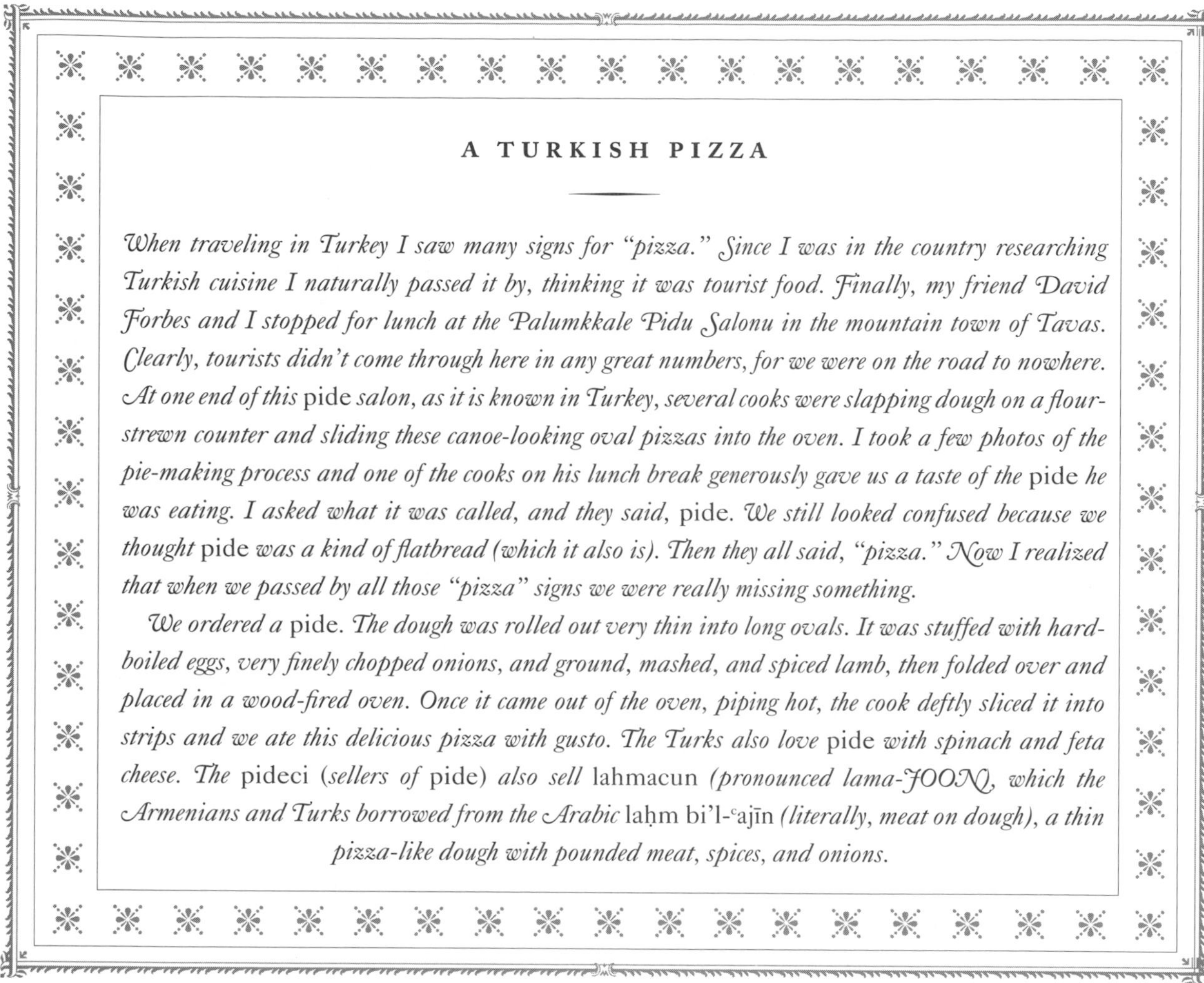

A TURKISH PIZZA

When traveling in Turkey I saw many signs for "pizza." Since I was in the country researching Turkish cuisine I naturally passed it by, thinking it was tourist food. Finally, my friend David Forbes and I stopped for lunch at the Palumkkale Pidu Salonu in the mountain town of Tavas. Clearly, tourists didn't come through here in any great numbers, for we were on the road to nowhere. At one end of this pide *salon, as it is known in Turkey, several cooks were slapping dough on a flour-strewn counter and sliding these canoe-looking oval pizzas into the oven. I took a few photos of the pie-making process and one of the cooks on his lunch break generously gave us a taste of the* pide *he was eating. I asked what it was called, and they said,* pide. *We still looked confused because we thought* pide *was a kind of flatbread (which it also is). Then they all said, "pizza." Now I realized that when we passed by all those "pizza" signs we were really missing something.*

We ordered a pide. *The dough was rolled out very thin into long ovals. It was stuffed with hard-boiled eggs, very finely chopped onions, and ground, mashed, and spiced lamb, then folded over and placed in a wood-fired oven. Once it came out of the oven, piping hot, the cook deftly sliced it into strips and we ate this delicious pizza with gusto. The Turks also love* pide *with spinach and feta cheese. The* pideci (*sellers of* pide) *also sell* lahmacun *(pronounced lama-JOON), which the Armenians and Turks borrowed from the Arabic* laḥm bi'l-ʿajīn *(literally, meat on dough), a thin pizza-like dough with pounded meat, spices, and onions.*

1 tablespoon extra virgin olive oil
1 ounce (2 tablespoons) pork lard, cut into small pieces
1 teaspoon salt
3½ cups unbleached all-purpose flour

For the stuffing
3 tablespoons extra virgin olive oil
1 small onion, finely chopped
1½ cups canned or fresh peeled, seeded, and ground or crushed tomatoes
One 3½-ounce can imported tuna in olive oil
Salt to taste

To deep-fry the *empanadillas*
6 cups pure or virgin olive or olive pomace oil

1. For dough 1: Pour the olive oil, water, and salt in a medium-size bowl, then add the flour and aniseeds. Mix well, then knead until you have a smooth, pliable ball of dough. Wrap in plastic wrap and leave for 30 minutes at room temperature.

For dough 2: Pour the tepid water in a small bowl and stir in the yeast until dissolved. Stir in the olive oil and lard. Let rest for 10 minutes. Sift the salt and flour together into a large bowl. Make a well in the flour and pour in the yeast water. Mix until a ball can be formed, then knead for 12 minutes. Cover with a kitchen towel and leave the dough to rise for 6 hours in a warm place, punching it down twice.

2. Make the stuffing: In a small skillet, heat the olive oil over medium heat, then cook the onion until translucent, about 8 minutes, stirring. Add the tomatoes and cook until thickened, about 20 minutes. Take the skillet off the heat and stir in the tuna and salt, mixing well. Set aside.

3. When it is time to make the *empanadillas*, roll a portion of the dough out very thin and cut out 4- to 5-inch circles. Place a heaping teaspoon of stuffing in the center of each circle of dough and fold over to form a semicircle. Pinch down the edges with the tines of a fork, flip to other side, and pinch the edges down. Set aside until ready to bake or fry.

4. Preheat the frying oil to 360°F in a deep-fryer or an 8-inch saucepan fitted with a basket insert or preheat the oven to 350°F. Deep-fry several *empanadillas* at a time for 1 minute, turning once, or bake on a lightly greased baking tray for 25 minutes. Let the frying oil cool, strain, and save for a future use.

VARIATION

The *empanadillas* can be stuffed with a mixture of chopped tomato, cooked and flaked hake, seeded and chopped green bell peppers, chopped wilted spinach, and toasted pine nuts.

Makes 6 servings

Coca d'Ànec i Olives (Catalonia)

CATALAN-STYLE CALZONE WITH DUCK AND OLIVES

A coca *is a kind of Catalan calzone. The word* coca *comes from the Latin word "to cook" and is used in the Occitan and Catalan languages. This* coca *is popular in the Roussillon, and is adapted from Colman Andrews's* Catalan Cuisine.

Double recipe pizza dough (page 549)
1 duck (about 4 pounds)
2 small onions, chopped
½ celery stalk
1 small carrot, chopped
Bouquet garni, tied with kitchen string in cheesecloth, consisting of 5 sprigs each fresh thyme and parsley, 1 sprig fresh sage, and 1 bay leaf
5 black peppercorns
6 cups water
2 tablespoons extra virgin olive oil
2 ripe tomatoes, peeled, seeded, and chopped
¼ pound prosciutto, chopped
1 cup pitted and coarsely chopped imported green olives
⅓ cup anisette liqueur, like Pernod
Salt and freshly ground black pepper to taste
3 large eggs

1. Prepare the basic pizza dough.

2. Cut off as much meat as you can from the duck. Remove the wings and save for making *alicuit* (page 201). Save all the fat and skin of the duck to render later if making *confit de canard* (page 200). Chop the duck meat, without any fat. You should have about 1½ cups chopped duck meat.

3. Place all the duck bones in a stockpot with one of the chopped onions, the celery, carrot, bouquet garni, and peppercorns. Cover with the water and bring to a boil. Skim the surface of foam, reduce the heat to low, and simmer for 6 hours. If there is less than 2 cups of liquid at any point, add a little water to keep the amount of liquid at about 2 cups by the time it is done. Strain the duck stock through a fine-mesh strainer, discarding all the bones and vegetables. Pour the stock into a glass or ceramic bowl and place in the refrigerator overnight.

4. Remove the layer of fat from the duck stock. In a large skillet or enameled cast-iron casserole, heat the

olive oil over medium-high heat, then cook the remaining chopped onion and the tomatoes for 8 minutes, stirring almost constantly during the last 2 minutes. Add the duck meat and prosciutto and cook until lightly browned, about 4 minutes. Add the olives and stir well for 1 minute. Pour the anisette into the skillet and cook for 1 minute. Add 1 cup of the reserved duck stock, reduce the heat to low, and simmer, uncovered, until the duck is tender, about 1 hour. If the sauce is liquid, remove the meat and olives with a slotted ladle or skimmer and reduce the remaining liquid over high heat until very thick. Return the meat to the skillet, turn the heat off, season with salt and pepper, and leave until completely cool.

5. Beat two of the eggs together, stir into the duck sauce, and mix well. Preheat the oven to 350°F. Roll the two balls of pizza dough into large disks about ½ inch thick. Spoon half of the duck filling onto one half of each pizza disk. Fold the other half over to form a half-moon and crimp the edges with the tines of a fork. Beat the remaining egg, brush the top of each *coca* with it, and place on a baking sheet or stone. Bake until the tops are golden, 50 to 55 minutes. Serve at room temperature.

Makes 2 coques, *6 servings*

Shūshbarak (Arab Levant)

MEAT PASTRIES IN YOGURT, GARLIC, AND CORIANDER SAUCE

Shūshbarak *(or* shīsh barak*) are tiny half-moon pastries stuffed with ground lamb, onions, and pine nuts that are then fried in a skillet until golden and placed in a kind of yogurt soup flavored with garlic and coriander for a final poaching. This is a typical preparation in Lebanon and Syria, although the original dish might be Turkish or Armenian. The pastries are quite time-consuming to make because of their tiny size. But once all is done, the tastes are marvelous and worth the effort. The use of vegetable shortening is quite authentic in contemporary Arab cooking, but for a more intense taste you might want to try using* samna *(clarified butter, page 189) with a little olive oil.*

1 teaspoon extra virgin olive oil
3 tablespoons pine nuts
½ cup plus 1 teaspoon vegetable shortening, or 5 tablespoons plus 1 teaspoon *samna* and 3 tablespoons olive oil
½ pound twice-ground lamb
1 medium-size onion, finely chopped
Salt and freshly ground black pepper to taste
2 quarts high-quality full-fat stabilized plain yogurt (page 186)
6 large garlic cloves, peeled
¼ cup finely chopped fresh coriander (cilantro) leaves
2½ cups unbleached all-purpose flour
½ cup water, or more as necessary

1. In a small skillet, heat the olive oil over medium-high heat, then cook the pine nuts until light brown, 2 to 3 minutes, tossing constantly. Be careful not to burn them. Remove and set aside.

2. In a medium-size skillet, heat 2 tablespoons of the vegetable shortening or 1 tablespoon of the *samna* and 1 tablespoon of the olive oil over medium heat, then brown the lamb with the onion, pine nuts, salt, and pepper, about 12 minutes, stirring and breaking up the meat occasionally. Drain using a slotted spoon and set aside.

3. Meanwhile, pour the yogurt into a large, heavy saucepan and warm over medium-low heat. In a mortar, pound the garlic together with 1 teaspoon salt until mushy. In the skillet used to brown the pine nuts, melt 1 teaspoon of the vegetable shortening or *samna* over medium heat, then cook the garlic and

THE POEM OF *SANBŪSAK*

The great Arab geographer, traveler, and historian al-Masʿūdī (d. 956?) wrote in his Meadows of Gold *of a banquet of culinary poetry sponsored by the caliph al-Mustakfī (944–946). One of the banqueters recited the following poem in praise of the spicy pastries known as* sanbūsaj (sanbūsak) *as originally told a century earlier by Isḥāq ibn Ibrāhīm.*

If thou wouldst know what food gives most delight,
Best let me tell, for none hath subtler sight.
Take first the finest meat, red, soft to touch,
And mince it with the fat, not overmuch;
Then add an onion, cut in circles clean,
A cabbage, very fresh, exceeding green,
And season well with cinnamon and rue;
Of coriander add a handful, too,
And after that of cloves the very least,
Of finest ginger, and of pepper best,
A hand of cumin, murri just to taste,
Two handfuls of Palmyra salt; but haste,
Good master, haste to grind them small and strong.
Then lay and light a blazing fire along;
Put all into the pot, and water pour
Upon it from above, and cover o'er.
But, when the water vanished is from sight
And when the burning flames have dried it quite,
Then, as thou wilt, in pastry wrap it round,
And fasten well the edges, firm and sound;
Or, if it please thee better, take some dough,
Conveniently soft, and rubbed just so,
Then with the rolling-pin let it be spread
And with the nails its edges docketed.
Pour in the frying-pan the choicest oil
And in that liquor let it finely broil.
Last, ladle out into a thin tureen
Where appetizing mustard smeared hath been,
And eat with pleasure, mustarded about,
This tastiest food for hurried diner-out.[34]

coriander together until sizzling, 1 to 2 minutes, stirring frequently. Stir the garlic mixture into the yogurt. Keep the yogurt sauce warm while you continue the preparation.

4. In a medium-size bowl, mix the flour, water, and ½ to 1 teaspoon salt, adding more water if necessary to form a smooth, pliable ball of dough. Knead briefly and then roll out very thin, less than 1⁄16 inch thick. Cut out 125 circles 1½ inches in diameter with a cookie cutter or the rim of a shot glass and place a small amount of the meat mixture on each one. Fold the dough in half and pinch closed, making sure there are no openings, otherwise they will open when cooking. Set aside as you finish forming them.

5. In a large skillet, melt the remaining 6 tablespoons vegetable shortening or 4 tablespoons *samna* and 2 tablespoons olive oil over medium-high heat. Cook the pastries in two batches until golden brown on both sides, 6 to 7 minutes. The pastries are very little so you should be able to do this in two, and certainly three, batches in your largest skillet. Remove from the skillet with a slotted ladle and add to the yogurt sauce. Cook the *shūshbarak* and yogurt over low heat, never letting it boil, until the yogurt and pastries are hot, about 30 minutes. Serve.

Makes 4 to 6 servings

Sanbūsak (Arab Levant)

SPICY LAMB PASTRIES

There is reason to believe that this preparation is the progenitor of the empanada and calzone. Sanbūsak, *an Arabic word that comes from the Persian* sanbūsa, *meaning anything triangular, was first described as a stuffed pastry in the early ninth century by Isḥāq ibn Ibrāhīm (d. 851), a well-known author from Iraq.*[35] *In al-Masᶜūdī's (died c. 956)* Meadows of Gold, *there are foods described that sound like early* sanbūsak. *The twelfth-century dietetic manual, the* Liber de ferculis et condimentis, *which was translated from the Arabic (see "An Essay on the Sources") has a recipe for* sanbasuc, *although there its meaning is closer to a croquette.*[36] *In the thirteenth-century Arabic cookery book of al-Baghdādī,* sanbūsaj *is described as a stuffed triangular pastry fried in sesame oil. Another early written recipe for* sanbūsaq *appears in the thirteenth-century cookbook attributed to Ibn al-ᶜAdīm (d. 1262), the* Kitāb al-wuṣla ila l-ḥabīb fī waṣfī al-ṭayyibāt wāṭ-ṭīb, *where it is described as a small half-moon of puff pastry stuffed with cheese, chopped meat, or* qaymaq *(see the Turkish* kaymak, *page 185). By the thirteenth century,* sanbūsak *appears in Spain, almost as the same recipe, a triangular fried pastry.*[37]

Sanbūsak *are possibly, although not as likely, the origin of the Turkish* börek *and therefore the origin, too, of the savory pastries, the Tunisian* brīk, *Algerian* būrak, *Moroccan* brīwat, *and the Armenian* beoreg, *as well as Spanish, Greek, Italian, and Sicilian versions.*[38]

For the pastry

2½ cups unbleached all-purpose flour, sifted
1 teaspoon salt
½ cup (1 stick) unsalted butter, cut into bits
½ cup cold water

For the filling

2 tablespoons *samna* (clarified butter; page 189)
½ cup finely chopped onion
¾ pound lean ground lamb
¼ cup pine nuts
¼ teaspoon ground cinnamon
1 teaspoon freshly ground allspice berries
Salt and freshly ground black pepper to taste

To deep-fry the pastries

6 cups pure or virgin olive, olive pomace, or vegetable oil

1. Pour the flour and salt into a medium-size bowl. Work the butter into the flour with your fingertips. Add the water slowly to make a soft, pliable dough. Form into a ball, then roll out to ⅛ inch thick and cut into 3-inch disks with a cookie cutter.

2. In a medium-size skillet, melt the *samna* over a medium heat, then cook the onion until translucent, 6 to 7 minutes. Add the lamb, pine nuts, cinnamon, and allspice, season with salt and pepper, and cook until the meat loses all its pinkness, breaking up lumps with a fork or wooden spoon and stirring occasionally to mix the ingredients well. Pour off the excess fat, squeezing the fat out of the meat by placing it in a slotted spoon and pressing with the back of a wooden spoon. Check the seasoning.

3. Put about 1 teaspoon of stuffing on each disk. Fold over and pinch the edges shut with the tines of a fork, forming a half-moon.

4. Preheat the frying oil to 375°F in a deep-fryer or an 8-inch saucepan fitted with a basket insert. Deep-fry the pastries in batches without crowding the fryer until golden, about 4 minutes. Serve hot or at room temperature. Freeze any remaining stuffing for several months. Let the frying oil cool completely, strain, and save for a future use.

Makes 40 to 45 pastries

Quenelles Ordinaires (Provence)
EVERYDAY QUENELLES

One of the simplest uses of bread is in dumplings. In Provençal, quenelo de vedeu *are everyday quenelles, a very light form of dumpling used, for instance, in* poularde à la Toulouse *(page 156), a sumptuous chicken braised with onions, bacon, and wine and covered with a rich egg-based cream sauce. These quenelles are made from a panada, a pasty mixture of bread and other ingredients used to bind stuffings. The English word* panada *comes from a sixteenth-century Spanish word derived from the Latin meaning a "dish boiling bread in water." Panada is a famous preparation in Catalonia, but heavier than these light quenelles.*

½ pound ground veal
3 ounces white bread (French or Italian bread, no crust)
¼ cup (½ stick) unsalted butter, at room temperature
3 large egg yolks
Salt and freshly ground black pepper to taste
Pinch of freshly grated nutmeg
1 quart poaching liquid, either water or homemade broth

1. Put the ground veal in a food processor and process until it is nearly a paste.

2. Soak the bread in some water and then squeeze the water out. Place the bread in a small skillet with 3 tablespoons of the butter and, over low heat, stir with a wooden spoon for 5 minutes, breaking it up. Remove the bread and let it cool completely.

3. Mix the bread, called the panada, with the veal, kneading it together thoroughly, or return it to the food processor and run until it is mixed well. Remove to a heavy, deep bowl. Add the remaining tablespoon butter, the egg yolks, salt, pepper, and nutmeg, and pound the mixture until all the ingredients are homogenous. Don't use the food processor for this last pounding because you might overprocess it.

4. Bring the poaching liquid to a very gentle boil. Form the quenelles by shaping them between two soup spoons; you should not handle them as they are too delicate and will break up or stick to your hands. As you shape the quenelles, drop them into the poaching liquid and poach until firm and cooked

through, about 10 minutes. Remove with a skimmer or slotted spoon, draining the liquid, and serve.

Makes about 12

MEDITERRANEAN archives are rich in detail about grain growing and exporting. The Adriatic, Gulf of Taranto, Abruzzi, Bari, Capitanata, and Basilicata were the grain-producing regions of the kingdom of Naples in 1580. Detailed documents tell us that the 700,000 people living there had access to a wheat harvest of 100,000 *carra* (132,000 tons), of which 8,500 *carra* were exported. An official document from this period says that the yearly per capita consumption was 484 pounds of grain.[39]

The Mediterranean peoples were able to live off their agricultural produce. Only during times of emergency did wheat arrive from abroad. As Ruggiero Romano showed in his important study *Commerce et prix di blé à Marseille au XVIIIe siècle*, published in 1956, the wheat used by Marseilles came from the Provençal plains. The local grain was considered the good grain; in Venice they called it *nostrale*, "our grain."[40] A document in the Museo Correr in Venice quotes Venetian bakers of 1601 as complaining that they "are now being given grain from outside that does not produce such good results as ours."[41] They meant the grain from Padua, Treviso, Polesina, and Fruili.

In Languedoc, several kinds of wheat were distinguished. *Blé blodut*, or *bladette*, was the best, known for its gluten content and prized for flour in bread making. *Blé rousset* was a red wheat appreciated for its seeds. *L'aufegue* or *sarsette* had more coloration than *rousset*, while *blé blanc* or *brun* was rich in starch and desired for baked goods.[42] These distinctions appear after the fifteenth century. Before then the peasants ate barley bread, which gave way to the eating of *méteil*, a mixture of wheat and rye. For most of the late Middle Ages, the staple bread grains of the Languedoc were barley and hard wheat.[43] Bread, along with meat and fish, was taxed, as we know from the *ponderator* of Toulon, the store or produce inspector who set the tax. In Avignon it was the *magister victualium* who had this responsibility.[44]

Agriculture was the leading industry of the Mediterranean in the sixteenth century. Kings and farmers were deeply concerned about grain and about the weather, the yields, and the harvest. For the princes, the success of the harvest determined whether they went to war; for the peasants, whether they lived or died. Wheat yields were good in some places and bad in others. On Cyprus, the yield was six to one on seed sown, while in Apulia, on lands previously used for sheep farming, grain could give exceptional yields of twenty to one, probably the result of manure-rich arable land.

Agriculture did suffer setbacks, for reasons that are unclear. In Spain, in particular, there was the struggle against barren, stony land, the problem of migrant flocks, the regular cultivation of irrigated gardens with their orange, mulberry, and other fruit trees known as the *regadios*, and the dry lands known as *secanos* where vines and olive trees grew, the sown fields with crops of half wheat and half barley every other year, and, last, the fallow lands, the *barbechos*, where beans were often grown. Although the wealth of the New World began to be felt in Seville by mid-sixteenth century, encouraging the expensive and labor-intensive planting of grape vines and olive trees, the olive advanced slowly because the region was already rich in wheat, although not everywhere. Seville lacked wheat while Málaga was rich in wheat. For some unknown reason, the Spanish economy worsened between 1580 and 1590.

In Italy, agricultural production faced a crisis, too, a result of overpopulation, poor weather, a decline in agricultural investment, and foreign wars. Unlike

Spain, Italy found its solution through payments in silver for imported agricultural products. Buying cheap in the Levant and selling at three times the price in Italy meant the merchant could not lose. Venice's food supply had always relied on both home-grown grain and grain arriving by sea. The Venetian government had been exercising a monopoly on the grain trade since the fourteenth century. In fact, the first legislation on cereals was in November 1173.[45]

By 1588, the sea was no longer the chief source of supply to Venice, not only because local cereal production increased, but also because less wheat was being imported from the East. Turkey was entering an age of scarcity and Italy had to look elsewhere for its bread. Istanbul suffered poverty, high prices, spectacular famines, and finally plague. Between 1561 and 1598, according to the dispatches of the Venetian *bailo* (consul), there were eight full years of plague.

Throughout late sixteenth-century Italy, the sylvan-pastoral economy receded as agricultural production increased; hillsides were being cultivated, mountain slopes conquered, the plains reclaimed, and land logically divided between crops and pasturage. In Venice there was large-scale investment in reclaiming low-lying and marshy lands. Travelers such as Montaigne in 1580 were astonished to see, in his words, "mountains all well cultivated and green to their summits, planted with chestnut and olive trees and elsewhere with vines, which they grow all around the mountains, encircling them with rings and terraces. On the outer edge of the terrace raised up a little are the vines; on the inner depression grows wheat."[46]

The constant need to accommodate a growing population displaced grazing lands, reduced the flocks, destroyed trees, and transformed the rural landscape. The lands of feudal and Renaissance Italy were arranged in logical patterns, not hapazardly. For example, in Tuscany these lands were specified as *campi a pìgola*, irregularly shaped fields, or as *alberata*, land in mixed cultivation planted with trees festooned with dense vines, while in the Po Valley a more open, less dense planting was called the *piantata*.[47] This logical arrangement of productive land had an effect on the kitchen: less meat was cooked (animal husbandry was declining, a result of less pasturage) and more vegetables, legumes, and grains eaten. This is the beginning of the so-called Mediterranean diet with its emphasis on grains and vegetables. Cookbooks began to give more precise directions for cooking and became less the *aide-mémoire* of the early books.

BULGUR AND *FARĪK*

THE grain requirements of that "urban monster," Istanbul, were phenomenal. In March 1581, eight ships from Egypt laden with wheat provided food for only a single day. Records from 1660 and 1672 show that Istanbul's inhabitants daily consumed 300 to 500 tons of grain, which provided work for its 133 bakers. In one year Istanbul consumed almost 200,000 cattle, of which 35,000 went to make salt or smoked meat, *pastırma*. Almost four million sheep and three million lambs, plus barrels of honey, sugar, and rice, sacks and skins of cheese, caviar, and 12,904 *cantars* of melted butter (7,000 tons) were also consumed. French historian Fernand Braudel, who examined the archival documents, felt compelled to express his astonishment about Istanbul's consumption by making an aside that "one has to read the figures two or three times before one can believe them."[48]

One solution to Istanbul's huge food needs was bread; another was the easily stored hard wheat product called bulgur, a parched cracked wheat. To make bulgur, in Turkey and the Levant the raw hard wheat was cleaned and sun-dried, traditionally, in the towns on the flat terrace roofs of homes. The wheat berries were separated from the chaff and boiled in water for two hours until they were about to crack open. This process dissolved some of the vitamins and minerals in the outer bran layer of the wheat seeds. As the water soaked into the endosperm, it carried the soluble nutrients to the inside of the grain. The hot water also caused gelatinization of the starch granules and killed germs and insect eggs that might be present. The drained wheat seeds were then dried and occasionally sprinkled with water, which was absorbed by the outer bran layers, making them easily removed by rubbing. The peeled grains were spread to dry again in the sun and then ground into coarse particles. At this point the very coarse grains were ground for the market into coarse, medium, and fine grains of what is called bulgur. Bulgur is cooked in the form of pilafs and is used as the bulk or starchy matter for many Levantine preparations, such as tabbouleh (page 578), kibbe (page 579), and *kishk. Kishk* is a preparation made of yogurt or naturally fermented milk mixed with bulgur or wheat flour. The fermented milk and bulgur are mixed and left in a warm place to ferment for a day. The result is a pasty dough that is formed into balls and left to dry in the sun for a week. Then it is finely ground, packaged, and sold in retail stores.

Bulgur is made from hard wheat grains, but in Arab cookery, semolina of hard wheat is also used in soups, stuffings, gruels, puddings, and sweet pastries. A hard wheat flour is also the basis of many flatbreads in the Levant and North Africa, such as the griddle-fried bread *tabbūna* of Tunisia and the *tabūn* of Syria and Jordan that is cooked on hot gravel, as well as *galettes*, tortes, and some pizzas in Sicily.

❖ *Etli Bulgar Pilavı* (Turkey)

BULGUR PILAF WITH LAMB

This traditional bulgur pilaf from Turkey is flavored with huge amounts of butter. Nutritionally rich foodstuffs such as milk, yogurt, butter, and cheese played a great role in Islam. In Turkey, milk products were almost the sole food of the poor in the Middle Ages, and butter used in large amounts was not uncommon. The butter used was not necessarily fresh creamery butter but often rancid butter.

A bulgur pilaf with lamb is very much a family meal in Turkey, and yours will find it as rewarding and filling. The bulgur, which should have fluffy and separate grains after cooking, can usually be found in Middle Eastern markets and whole food stores. Halloumi *cheese is often sold in Middle Eastern, Greek, and Armenian markets.*

½ pound (2 sticks) unsalted butter
2 large onions, chopped
1½ pounds mutton or lamb stew meat, trimmed of excess fat and cut into bite-size cubes
Salt and freshly ground black pepper to taste
3 large ripe tomatoes, peeled, seeded, and diced
½ cup hot water
2¾ cups raw coarse bulgur
2 cups beef broth (page 54)
¼ pound presoaked *halloumi* cheese (see Note on page 578 and page 715), drained, rinsed, and diced

1. In a large, heavy casserole with a heavy lid, melt ¼ pound (1 stick) of the butter over medium heat, then cook the onions until translucent, about 10 minutes, stirring frequently. Add the lamb cubes, toss with the onions, cover, and cook until they completely turn color, 10 to 15 minutes. Season with salt and pepper, stir in the tomatoes and hot water, cover again, and simmer until the lamb is very tender, 2 to 3 hours. Stir the meat occasionally and add small amounts of additional hot water if it begins to dry out.

2. Meanwhile, melt the remaining ¼ pound (1 stick) butter in another casserole with a heavy tight-fitting lid over medium heat, then cook the bulgur until it looks shiny and has a nutty aroma, about 5 minutes, stirring often. Remove the lamb and onions from their broth with a slotted ladle and save 1 cup of

the lamb stewing liquid, discarding or saving the rest for making a soup later. Add the lamb stewing liquid, beef broth, diced cheese, lamb, and onions to the bulgur and stir.

3. Cover the casserole with several sheets of paper towels, setting the lid on top so that moisture can be absorbed. Reduce the heat to very low, or use a heat diffuser, and cook until the liquid is absorbed, about 35 minutes. If the bulgur is not yet cooked, add a small amount of hot broth and continue cooking until it is (it should have only a slightly chewier texture to it than cooked rice does, although the taste, of course, is entirely different). Remove the paper towels, stir the bulgur, transfer to a serving platter, and serve.

NOTE: *Halloumi* cheese is a heavily salted cheese that needs to be soaked overnight in water to cover before using.

Makes 8 servings

Tabbūla (Arab Levant)

TABBOULEH

Bread wheat (Triticum aestivum) *was not as versatile as hard wheat. One theory deduces that hard wheat developed as a mutation from emmer wheat* (T. dicoccum) *somewhat recently, probably after the period of the Sumerian civilization (5000 to c. 2100* B.C.*, see page 620). Not only can hard wheat be made into macaroni but it also is the basis of bulgur. Tabbouleh, an herb salad dotted with swollen grains of bulgur, vies with hummus (page 310) and pita bread as the most famous Arab foods to have migrated to the United States. In the Arab world, and especially in its home of Syria, Lebanon, and Palestine, tabbouleh is a salad usually made as part of a* mazza *table (page 118). The word* tabbouleh (tabbūla) *derives from the root Arabic word "to season" or "to spice." This root also gives the name to the Tunisian spice mix known as* tābil *(page 522), the Palestinian* mutabbal *(page 119), and the stuffed eggplant dish called* bādhinjān mutabbal.[49] *The seasoning referred to is coriander* (tawābil), *although tabbouleh is usually made with parsley and mint.*

The masters of the tabbouleh are the Lebanese and Palestinians, who prefer, as I do, a tabbouleh where the majority of the salad is composed of the green herbs, not overwhelmed by the bulgur. The taste of a true tabbouleh should not be of wheat but of herbs. The longer the bulgur sits and absorbs the olive oil, lemon juice, tomato, and onion juices, the more it will swell and dominate the salad, so keep that in mind. Many cooks make tabbouleh with a food processor by pulsing in short bursts, although I still prefer the texture of the labor-intensive method of hand-chopping all the ingredients with a large chef's knife. Tabbouleh is properly eaten by scooping up small amounts with pieces of romaine lettuce, not with a fork and knife or pita bread.

½ cup raw medium or coarse bulgur
Juice from 4 lemons
6 cups finely chopped fresh parsley leaves (about 6 bunches)
1 cup finely chopped fresh mint leaves
1 pound ripe tomatoes, very finely chopped
2 large onions, very finely chopped
Salt and freshly ground black pepper to taste
1¼ to 1¾ cups extra virgin olive oil, as needed
1 bunch romaine lettuce, leaves separated, washed, and dried
1 bunch scallions, trimmed

1. Cover a strainer with cheesecloth and place the bulgur on top. Place the strainer in a pot filled with cold water and soak the bulgur for 10 minutes. Pull up the sides of the cheesecloth, encasing the bulgur, and squeeze out all the water. Transfer to a large bowl.

2. Toss the bulgur with the lemon juice. Toss again with the parsley, mint, tomatoes, and onions and season with salt and pepper. Stir in the olive oil and leave to rest at room temperature until the bulgur has absorbed enough liquid to be tender, 4 to 6 hours. Correct the seasoning and olive oil, enough to look shiny and moist but not gooey and oily. Serve garnished with romaine lettuce leaves and scallions.

Makes 6 servings

Kubba Maqliyya (Maḥshiyya) (Arab Levant)

FRIED KIBBE

Kibbe (kubba *among Palestinians and* kibba *among Syrians), a lamb-and-bulgur mixture ground to a paste and formed into a hollow ball for stuffing, is often considered to be the national dish of Lebanon and Syria. The word* kibbe *comes from the verb "to form into a ball." Meat and bulgur are pounded in a very large mortar called a* jūrn *with a pestle called a* madaqqa. *The pounding would go on for quite some time, up to an hour, so a food processor works well here. People who grew up in Lebanon will tell you the fondness with which they remember the slow and rhythmic sounds of kibbe being pounded in their neighborhoods.*

The successful making of kibbe is the zenith of culinary art in Syro-Palestinian cuisine. The key is forming the ball of kibbe into a long, hollow, smooth-skinned oval shell. Women with long, graceful fingers are admired by both sexes because it is rightly assumed that they have the ability to make perfect kibbe with their slender fingers; a man's fingers are too thick.

This recipe I learned from my former wife, Najwa al-Qattan. Najwa learned it from her grandmother Asma, who in turn got the recipe from her sister, who "was an even better kibbe maker than she," says Najwa. Asma would make a heavenly stuffing of ground lamb, chopped parsley and coriander, onions, pine nuts, and bahārāt. *But Asma's sister would make the shell only from bulgur without any meat. As a result the shell was very crunchy.*

There are many ways of preparing the basic kibbe mixture. It can be formed into hollow shells, stuffed, and fried, as in this recipe. When kibbe are charcoal grilled, they are called manqal. Kubba nayya *is raw, the steak tartare version.* Kubba bi'l-ṣīniyya, *or pan kibbe, are kibbe formed in a baking tray or pan, covered with the meat stuffing and then another layer of kibbe. The kibbe are then cut into diagonals in the form of trapezoids or diamonds (see Note).*

All the ingredients should be cold while you work. Since forming the kibbe shell is the most important part of preparing kubba maqliyya, *you will need to pay special attention. Take a ball of kibbe, one about the size of a small egg. Roll it in the palms of your hands until it is smooth. Dip your hands occasionally in a pan of cold water so the meat doesn't stick to your hands; the wetness also helps in smoothing out cracks in the kibbe. Put your forefinger in the center of the ball and begin to make a hole. Use the hand with which you are holding the ball to turn the ball and use your finger as a stationary device that makes the hole, much as if your finger were the spindle on a potter's wheel. The walls of the kibbe shell must be very, very thin. Because the bulgur will expand as it cooks, what you think are thin walls will become thick, so continue flipping the kibbe shell in your palm, pressing your finger against the wall until it is about 1/8 inch thick. This is quite difficult to achieve, so you may want to practice with a ball of kibbe before actually stuffing it.*

If you decide to serve kibbe as part of a large Arab-style dinner table, make the kibbe as described in the recipe. If you are making the kibbe as a mazza *(see page 118), make them a little smaller.*

For the kibbe

2 cups raw fine bulgur
2 teaspoons black peppercorns
2 teaspoons salt
2 pounds ground lamb, cut from the leg or shoulder
1 medium-size onion, grated
1 teaspoon *bahārāt* (page 524)

For the stuffing

½ teaspoon black peppercorns
1 teaspoon salt
6 tablespoons *samna* (clarified butter; page 189)
1 medium-size onion, finely chopped
¼ cup pine nuts
1 pound ground lamb, cut from the leg or shoulder
1 teaspoon *bahārāt* (page 524)

6 cups pure or virgin olive, olive pomace, or vegetable oil for deep-frying

To serve

Fresh parsley leaves for garnish
Plain yogurt (optional)
Scallions (optional)
Pita bread (optional)

1. Cover a strainer with cheesecloth and place the bulgur on top. Place the strainer in a pot filled with lightly salted cold water and soak the bulgur for 10 minutes in the refrigerator. Pull up the sides of the cheesecloth, encasing the bulgur, and squeeze out all the water. Transfer to a large bowl.

2. Grind the peppercorns with the salt in a mortar. Mix the ground lamb, salt, pepper, grated onion, and *bahārāt* in a large bowl. Add the bulgur to the meat mixture. Place the meat mixture in a food processor in batches and process until it is a paste. Remove to a large metal bowl and refrigerate for 1 hour.

3. Meanwhile, make the stuffing. Crush the peppercorns with the salt in a mortar. Heat the *samna* in a medium-size skillet, then cook the onion over medium heat until yellow, about 5 minutes, stirring occasionally. Add the pine nuts and cook for 2 minutes. Add the ground lamb, season with salt, pepper, and the *bahārāt*, and brown the meat until it loses its pink color, 8 to 10 minutes, breaking the meat up further and mixing the ingredients as you cook.

4. Form the ball of kibbe as described above and hollow it out so the wall is ⅛ inch thick. Stuff it with a heaping tablespoon of the lamb stuffing and close the opening with your fingers. Keep your hands wet and gently roll the kibbe in your palms to perfect the teardrop shape, fixing cracks and making the surface very smooth.

5. Preheat the frying oil in a deep-fryer or an 8-inch saucepan fitted with a basket insert to 360°F. Deep-fry the kibbe, not crowding them, until brown, 4 to 5 minutes. Remove the first one, cut it open, and check to see if the timing is correct for doneness. Repeat for the remaining kibbe. Serve the kibbe on a bed of parsley leaves. (Let the frying oil cool completely, strain, and save for a future use.) The kibbe are eaten with one's fingers, plain, or served with yogurt and scallions wrapped in soft and warm Arab bread.

NOTE: To make *kubba bi'l-ṣīniyya*, butter a 14-inch round baking pan and preheat the oven to 360°F. Press half the kibbe mixture to cover the bottom of the pan. Cover with the kibbe stuffing. Cover the stuffing with the remaining kibbe mixture, pressing down carefully so that you do not compact the stuffing. Smooth the top with a spatula. Using a sharp knife, score the kibbe into diamond or trapezoid shapes. Pour up to ¾ cup melted *samna* or olive oil mixed with a little water over the pan. Bake until deep brown, about 30 minutes. Finish cutting the score marks all the way through for serving. Serve with a slotted ladle to leave the fat behind in the pan.

Makes 24 kibbe or one 14-inch kibbe

❈ *Kubba bi'l-Laban* (Arab Levant)

KIBBE WITH YOGURT

An ancestor of the kibbe might be found in medieval Arabic cookery manuscripts, where preparations called mudaqqaqa *or* kubāb *are dishes of ground meat cooked in a variety of ways.*[50] *It is likely that the stuffing of these early meatballs may have resulted from the influence, much later, after the seventeenth century, of Ottoman Turkish cuisine.*

This recipe begins with the kubba maqliyya *on page 579, although it is a good recipe for leftover kibbe, too. Here the kibbe are stirred into yogurt for a very satisfying dish served with rice (page 602); some cooks stir the rice into the yogurt.*

½ recipe uncooked *kubba maqliyya* (12 kibbe), page 579)
1 recipe stabilized yogurt (page 186)
3 garlic cloves, peeled
1½ teaspoons salt
2 teaspoons dried mint
¼ cup *samna* (clarified butter; page 189)
Salt to taste

1. Make the kibbe.

2. Bring the yogurt to a boil in a large, heavy saucepan. Reduce the heat to low and simmer for 5 minutes. Add the kibbe and continue simmering, uncovered.

3. In a mortar, pound the garlic, salt, and mint together until well mashed. In a small skillet, heat the *samna* over medium-high heat, then cook the garlic mixture for 30 seconds to 1 minute, stirring. Stir into the yogurt and taste; salt as necessary. Simmer for 15 minutes without stirring; the yogurt should be thick. If not, simmer 5 more minutes and serve.

Makes 4 servings

❈ *Kibba Mishwiyya* (Syria)

GRILLED KIBBE

The variety of kibbe preparations is enormous.[51] *In this recipe from the Syrian city of Homs, the kibbe are formed by layering two little pancakes of kibbe about 3 inches in diameter together with a stuffing of ground lamb cooked with* shaᶜmī, *a flavorful lamb fat, and seasoned with* bahārāt *and pomegranate molasses. The kibbe are brushed with olive oil, grilled, and eaten hot with* khubz ᶜarabī *(Arab flatbread or pita bread). In El-Qamishliye in northeastern Syria, and in Mardin across the border in Turkey, they are steamed instead of grilled and called* kubbaybī, *little kibbe.*[52] *Serve with the Turkish yogurt-and-garlic dip known as* cacık *(page 186), Arab bread, or* pide *bread (see "Mediterranean Food Products Resources").*

For the kibbe

1 cup raw fine bulgur
1½ pounds ground lamb, cut from the leg or shoulder
Salt and freshly ground black pepper to taste
1 medium-size onion, grated
1 teaspoon *bahārāt* (page 524)

For the stuffing

½ pound ground lamb, cut from the leg or shoulder
2 ounces lamb fat, finely chopped
½ teaspoon *bahārāt* (page 524)
Salt and freshly ground black pepper to taste
1 tablespoon pomegranate molasses (page 722)
Extra virgin olive oil

1. Cover a strainer with cheesecloth and place the bulgur on top. Place the strainer in a pot filled with lightly salted cold water and soak the bulgur for 10 minutes. Pull up the sides of the cheesecloth, encas-

ing the bulgur, and squeeze out all the water. Transfer to a large bowl.

2. Add the ground lamb to the bowl and knead with the bulgur, salt, pepper, grated onion, and *bahārāt* until homogenous. Transfer in batches to a food processor and process to a paste. Remove to a large metal bowl and refrigerate for 1 hour.

3. Meanwhile, prepare the stuffing. Place the ground lamb and lamb fat in a small skillet and turn the heat to medium-high. Add the *bahārāt*, season with salt and pepper, and cook, stirring frequently, until the lamb is browned and the lamb fat pretty much rendered, about 10 minutes. Add the pomegranate molasses and continue cooking another minute, stirring.

4. Remove the meat mixture from the refrigerator and form 28 patties about 3 inches in diameter. Place a heaping teaspoon or more of the stuffing on one patty and cover with another, sealing the edges, until you have 14 hamburger-like patties.

5. Prepare a hot charcoal fire or preheat a gas grill for 15 minutes on high. Brush the kibbe with olive oil and grill until golden brown with black grid marks, about 20 minutes, turning once.

Makes 6 servings

✢ ✢ ✢

FARĪK is another hard wheat product known in the Middle East, but is especially popular in Egypt (in North Africa the word also refers to immature barley grains). *Farīk* has a unique taste that comes from a harvesting process that occurs during a very narrow window of time. Immature hard wheat *(Triticum turgidum* var. *durum)*, sometimes called green wheat, is harvested as the leaves start to turn yellow, when the grains are soft and milky. After drying in the sun, the farmer sets the wheat on fire, carefully controlling the blaze so that only the straw and chaff burn and not the creamy seeds, their high moisture content protecting them.[53] The roasted wheat is then spread out to dry in the sun again. Finally, it is thrashed, a process that rubs off the hull of the seed. It is this thrashing or rubbing process of the grains that gives this food its name, *farīk*, or "rubbed."

Ḥamām bi'l-Farīk (Egypt)

PIGEON WITH GREEN WHEAT

The making of farīk*-based preparations in the Middle East is quite old. We know that in the early thirteenth-century, a dish called* farīkiyya *was described in the Baghdad cookery book. In that recipe meat is fried in oil and braised with water, salt, and cinnamon bark. Then dried coriander is stirred in with young wheat and it is cooked until done and served with cumin, cinnamon, and fresh lamb tail fat.*[54]

This recipe is from Egypt. Fat, plump pigeons are stuffed with the earthy and lusty taste of the farīk*, then they are poached and finally fried in water buffalo* samna *until golden brown. I learned this method during the time I spent in Medinat Habu in Upper Egypt, researching local food with a peasant woman named Hamida Abdel-Magid. I was able to find* farīk *in local Middle Eastern markets in this country and I replaced the pigeons, which are expensive and difficult to locate here, with guinea hens or Cornish hens, both of which worked magnificently in this recipe.* Farīk *is sometimes pronounced fir-EEKY by non-Egyptians. This recipe has enough* farīk *to stuff 6 Cornish hens.*

3 cups *farīk*
1 teaspoon freshly ground coriander seeds

1 teaspoon freshly ground cumin seeds
2 teaspoons plus 2 tablespoons salt
Freshly ground black pepper to taste
½ cup *samna* (clarified butter; page 189)
1½ teaspoons Hamida's *bahārāt* (see Note on page 584)
6 pigeons or large squab, 4 Cornish game hens, or 3 guinea hens (5 to 6 pounds in all)
2 large shallots, halved

1. Pour the *farīk* onto a baking sheet and shake it to see if any small pebbles or chaff remain, picking them out with your fingers. Wash the *farīk* under cold water or soak for 30 minutes, scooping it up with a strainer and discarding anything that floats to the top.

2. Bring a large pot of water to a boil. Season the water with the coriander, cumin, 2 teaspoons salt, and pepper. Add the *farīk* and boil for 12 minutes, uncovered, stirring once in a while. Drain the *farīk*.

3. In a large skillet, heat ¼ cup of the *samna* over medium-high heat. Add the drained and partially cooked *farīk* along with the *bāhārāt*. Stir constantly for 5 minutes. Taste the *farīk* and correct the spices if necessary. The *farīk* should be al dente with the grains more or less separate. It will look like short-grain brown rice, but smell nutty.

4. Bring a large pot of water to a gentle boil. Stuff the *farīk* tightly into the pigeons. You can stuff them tightly because the *farīk* has already expanded through the previous cooking and will not expand anymore. Truss closed using the sharp wing tips to skewer the cavity opening together, or if the sharp wing tips are cut off, in the normal fashion with kitchen twine. The birds will be somewhat misshapen through all this handling, so shape them back to their birdlike look with your hands. Put the remaining 2 tablespoons salt and the shallots in the gently boiling water and slide the birds in. Poach the birds until they are firm, about 35 minutes, keeping the pot half-covered and the water just shimmering, never allowing it to come to a boil, which will toughen the birds. Drain the birds, saving the water (to be used to make *sabānikh bi'l-ḥamām*, page 584). Lightly salt the birds and set aside.

5. In a large skillet, melt the remaining ¼ cup *samna* over medium heat and salt. Pan-fry the stuffed birds until golden brown on all sides, with a sprinkling of salt, about 5 minutes per side. (The *samna* in the pan with the birds will have "blackened"; save 3 tablespoons of this blackened *samna* for the *sabānikh bi'l-ḥamām*). The birds are done now and can be kept

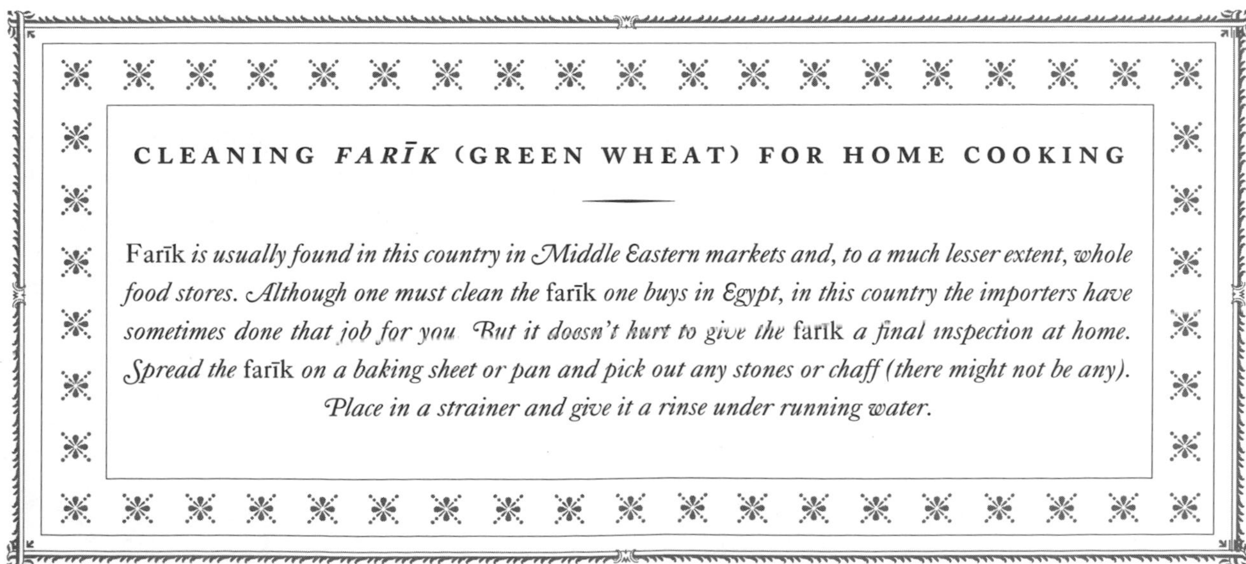

CLEANING *FARĪK* (GREEN WHEAT) FOR HOME COOKING

Farīk *is usually found in this country in Middle Eastern markets and, to a much lesser extent, whole food stores. Although one must clean the* farīk *one buys in Egypt, in this country the importers have sometimes done that job for you. But it doesn't hurt to give the* farīk *a final inspection at home. Spread the* farīk *on a baking sheet or pan and pick out any stones or chaff (there might not be any). Place in a strainer and give it a rinse under running water.*

warm or reheated to eat with the *sabānikh bi'l-ḥamām*.

NOTE: The spice mix *(bahārāt)* is made with equal amounts of cumin seeds, coriander seeds, black peppercorns, and ground red chili pepper.

VARIATION

If there are any gizzards with the fowl you use, poach them for 10 minutes in water just under a boil, drain, and chop finely with ½ small onion. In step 3, cook them until the onion is soft, about 2 minutes over medium-high heat, before adding the wheat.

Makes 6 servings

Sabānikh bi'l-Ḥamām (Egypt)

SPINACH WITH PIGEON BROTH

Although Egyptian cuisine does not have the reputation of the cooking of other Arab countries, there is something magical about being and eating in Egypt. The relation of the fallaḥīn *(peasant farmer) to his food was expressed by Gustave Flaubert in 1850, when he wrote in a letter to a family friend that, "You tear up the meat with your fingers, you dip your bread in the sauce, you drink your water from bowls, the vermin runs up the wall and everyone in the room belches* 'fortissimo'*: it is delightful."*

It is delightful—and this dish is best made at the same time as ḥamām bi'l-farīk *(page 582).*

20 ounces spinach, heavy stems removed and washed well
10 ounces fresh coriander (cilantro) leaves (about 2 bunches), washed
¼ pound fresh dill (about 1 bunch), leaves only
2 quarts pigeon water (see Step 4, page 583)
4 ripe tomatoes (about 1½ pounds), quartered
10 garlic cloves, peeled
1½ teaspoons salt
3 tablespoons blackened *samna* (clarified butter; see Step 5, page 583)
2 tablespoons uncooked *farīk* (page 582), picked over for stones and chaff, soaked in water 30 minutes, and drained
1 teaspoon aniseed
1 teaspoon fennel seeds

1. Chop the spinach, coriander, and dill together. Bring the pigeon water to a boil in a large saucepan or stockpot. Put these greens in the boiling water with the tomatoes, cover, and cook over medium heat for 45 minutes.

2. Pound the garlic in a mortar with the salt until completely mashed. In a small skillet, reheat the blackened *samna*, then cook the mashed garlic over high heat until it just begins to turn light brown, about 1 minute, stirring or shaking constantly. Quickly turn this mixture into the spinach mixture.

3. Stir the uncooked *farīk* into the greens and bring back to a boil. Stir in the aniseed and fennel seeds. Cook, covered, until it is gooey looking, about another 20 minutes. Taste for seasoning and correct. Remove from the heat and twist and beat with a long-handled fork or pronged spaghetti scoop for 2 minutes before serving.

NOTE: The mixture made by pounding garlic and salt together and turning it into the cooked dish is called *taqliyya* (pronounced ta-LIYYA) in Egyptian cookery. Sometimes the cook will add ground coriander to this mixture.

Makes 4 to 6 servings

Firik Pilavı (Turkey)

GREEN WHEAT PILAF

The long-grain rice used for pilaf is highly prized throughout the Middle East, but because it often had to be imported, locally grown hard wheat was, and is, a traditional substitute. Among the common folk, bulgur and green wheat are used in the same manner as rice for making pilafs. This specialty from Gaziantep in Turkey is also a familiar dish in Upper Egypt and across the border in Aleppo, where I had it.

¼ cup (½ stick) unsalted butter
1 small onion, finely chopped
1¾ cups vegetable, lamb, or veal broth (page 54)
1 cup *firik* (page 582), picked over for stones and chaff and rinsed
½ teaspoon salt
Freshly ground black pepper to taste

1. In a medium-size, heavy saucepan, melt 2 tablespoons of the butter over medium-high heat, then cook the onion until yellow, about 4 minutes, stirring constantly. In small saucepan, bring the broth to a boil, then pour it into the saucepan with the onion and return to a boil. Add the *firik* and salt, cover, and cook for 5 minutes over medium-high heat. Reduce the heat to low and cook for 15 minutes, covered. Reduce the heat to very low and cook until the liquid is almost absorbed, about 15 minutes.

2. In a small skillet, heat the remaining 2 tablespoons butter over medium-high heat, then season with pepper and pour over the pilaf. Check the seasoning. Cover the pot with several sheets of paper towels, replace the lid, and leave over very, very low heat for 30 minutes, using a heat diffuser if necessary. Turn the heat off and leave until any liquid is absorbed and the wheat is tender, about 15 minutes.

Makes 4 servings

Shūrbat al-Farīk bi'l-Mukh (Tunisia)

GREEN WHEAT AND BONE MARROW SOUP

Farīk *(pronounced Fir-EEK or FREEK) is an immature hard wheat that goes through a roasting process in its production. In Tunisia,* farīk *also refers to young barley grains and is the name of a kind of almond that will split into two with only the slightest rubbing pressure.* Farīk, *in fact, derives from the Arabic verb for "to rub." Another dish called* farīkiyya *is a kind of* harīsa *(the porridge, not the spicy condiment) made with green wheat instead of the regular hard wheat. This recipe is a* shūrba *(soup) made with* farīk. *If desired, you can let the soup cool completely overnight, remove the layer of fat that congeals on top, and reheat the soup for a nearly fatless version.*

1 cup dried chickpeas (about ½ pound), picked over, soaked in water to cover overnight, and drained
¼ cup finely chopped fresh parsley leaves
1 celery stalk, finely chopped
¼ cup extra virgin olive oil
1 tablespoon tomato paste
7 cups water
1 teaspoon hot or mild *harīsa* (page 523)
½ teaspoon cayenne pepper
½ teaspoon freshly ground black pepper
Salt to taste
2 pounds lamb or beef marrow bones
1 lamb's foot (optional)
1 cup *farīk* (page 582), picked over for stones and chaff and rinsed
2 tablespoons *samna* (clarified butter; page 189)
1 lemon, quartered
***Harīsa* for garnish (page 523)**

1. Put the drained chickpeas, parsley, celery, olive oil, the tomato paste dissolved in 1 cup of the water, *harīsa*, cayenne, black pepper, and salt in a pot and stir to blend. Add the marrow bones and lamb's foot, if using.

2. Turn the heat to high and cook for 10 minutes, stirring or shaking occasionally. Add the remaining 6 cups water and bring to a boil. Add the *farīk*, stir, and reduce the heat to low. Cover and simmer for 2 hours. Add water if desired or necessary while the *farīk* cooks. When the chickpeas are soft and the *farīk* cooked, add the *samna* and check the salt. Serve with lemon wedges and *harīsa*.

Makes 4 servings

Frīkat Laḥma (Syria)

LAMB WITH GREEN WHEAT

"Frīka Laḥma" is a colloquial Damascene expression for farīk bi'l-laḥm *or lamb with green wheat. The preparation of* farīk *is still done "by hand" by the farmers themselves. There was an attempt recently to mechanize the process by Jordanian farmers, without much success. The wheat is harvested while still young and set afire to lend a smoky flavor to the grains. This harvesting and processing method gives the finished wheat a delectable nutty taste and a green aura. In Damascus, they like to prepare the* farīk*—"freeka," as they call it—as you would rice pilaf, but in this recipe it is made with roast lamb, fresh spring peas, and pine nuts.* Farīk *is one of the earthiest grains you can taste and complements lamb perfectly.*

2 pounds leg of lamb on the bone, trimmed of fat
Salt and freshly ground black pepper to taste
½ teaspoon freshly ground allspice berries
Extra virgin olive oil for drizzling
5 tablespoons *samna* (clarified butter; page 189)
1 small onion, very finely chopped
3½ cups boiling beef broth (page 54) or boiling water
2 cups *farīk* (page 582), picked over for stones and chaff and rinsed
1 teaspoon salt
½ teaspoon freshly ground coriander seeds
½ teaspoon *bahārāt* (page 524)
3 tablespoons pine nuts
1 cup fresh or frozen peas
1 green tomato, sliced (optional)

1. Preheat the oven to 325°F. Rub the lamb all over with salt, pepper, and the ground allspice. Coat with a film of olive oil and place in a roasting pan. Roast the lamb until very tender and falling off the bone, about 4 hours.

2. About 1¼ hours before the lamb is done, melt 4 tablespoons of the *samna* in a heavy saucepan over medium-high heat, then cook the onion until golden, about 4 minutes, stirring constantly. Pour in the boiling broth or water and return to a boil. Add the *farīk*, salt, coriander, and *bahārāt*, cover, and cook for 5 minutes over medium-high heat. Reduce the heat to low and cook for 15 minutes, covered. Reduce the heat to very low and cook until the liquid is almost absorbed, about another 15 minutes. Place a heat diffuser under the pot, or turn the heat to very, very low, and leave the *farīk* for 30 minutes. Turn the heat off, cover the top with a paper towel, replace the lid, and leave until the lamb has finished roasting, about another 15 minutes.

3. Meanwhile, melt the remaining tablespoon *samna* in a small pan over medium-high heat and cook the pine nuts until golden, about 3 minutes, shaking the pan almost constantly. Set aside.

4. Bring a small pot of lightly salted water to a boil and cook the peas until tender. Set aside and keep warm, or undercook the peas and leave in the pot

until the *farīk* and lamb are done. Sprinkle black pepper on the *farīk* and toss.

5. Remove the lamb from the oven. Pull the meat off the bone and apart with a fork into serving sizes. Mound the *farīk* attractively on a serving platter. Using a slotted ladle, arrange the peas on top of the *farīk*. Place the meat on top and sprinkle the pine nuts over. Serve with green tomato slices as a garnish if desired.

Makes 4 servings

RICE, BARLEY, MAIZE, AND MILLET

ONE of the unintentional end products of the clearing of the Lombardy plains for the establishment of rice fields in the fifteenth century was risotto.[55] The motivation for the clearing and reclaiming of the plains was simply the demand of the growing towns for food. That demand was met not by rice growers but by budding capitalists who had the financial wherewithal to back the farmers in establishing these rice fields in the Po Valley. One of the earliest references I know of concerning rice in northern Italy is a letter of September 27, 1475, from Galeazzo Maria Sforza to the Duke of Ferrara concerning twelve sacks of rice. I suspect, however, that it was grown even earlier.[56] In both the Po Valley and Valencia in Spain, rice occasionally replaced bread as a staple. It is a typical part of the story that profit margins were kept high as riziculture in Lombardy meant the near enslavement of workers who were not organized, including children exposed to barbarous cruelties, according to a Lombard ordinance of 1590 seeking to stop this practice.[57]

Rice was not new to the Mediterranean. It was known in Roman times, but only medicinally, and was not grown in a regular or widespread way in the Mediterranean until the rise of Islam. Riziculture had its origins in India, Assam, Burma, Thailand, or China, and the plant slowly made its way west, both agriculturally and culinarily. Once there was enough water for irrigation, rice was grown with more frequency in the Islamic world, although its importance never reached that of wheat. In some areas, though, such as desert oases, swamps, and river valleys that flooded, rice became a staple food.[58] By the last half of the tenth century, rice was grown near Baisan in Palestine, in the Fayyūm of Egypt, and in lower Mesopotamia, where it was the most popular food.[59] The writer Ibn Qutaiba (828–889) cites the famous philologist al-Asmaʿī, who said, "White rice with melted butter and white sugar is not of this world," meaning that it is so delicious, it is eaten in paradise. Medieval Arabic cookbooks have many rice recipes, and the great twelfth-century Muslim agronomist Ibn al-ʿAwwām says the best way to eat rice is with butter, oil, fat, and sweet and rich milk, such as ewe's milk.[60] In medieval Aleppo, rice was cooked in fig juice.[61] Even though there are many recipes for rice in the medieval Arab world, rice was still an exotic and expensive food.[62]

The Arabs had established riziculture very early on in Spain and were exporting it from Sicily by the tenth century.[63] Traders could find rice in Levantine ports and in the fourteenth century Majorcan rice was sold at fairs in Champagne. In Venice, a deliberation of the Council of Ten in July 7, 1533, exempts rice from an excise tax because it takes the place of vegetables.[64] The Provençal writer Quiqueran de Beaujeu wrote in 1551 of riziculture in Provence.[65] One can't help but notice that rice was being eaten in Europe before the development of riziculture on the Lombardy plains. The fourteenth-century cookery manuscript by an anonymous Venetian known as

COOKING RICE

There seems to be a great mystery behind rice cookery, probably because there are different ways to cook different rices of different ages. In the Mediterranean, there are three basic ways of cooking rice, methods that are not interchangeable among culinary cultures. An Arab or Turk would consider an Italian risotto an abomination.

Always use raw rice when making rice, never a processed product such as converted rice. I have given the following names to the three main Mediterranean styles of cooking rice: pilaf, arroz, *and risotto, using, respectively, long-grain, medium-grain, and short-grain rice. There is also some steaming of rice for couscous in the Maghrib, but it is not a widespread practice. And rice use does not always fit into these three categories because it is also used for stuffing vegetables, in soups, for desserts, and with stews.*

COOKING RICE PILAF

The most important thing to know about pilaf cookery is the absorptive capacity of the rice you are using, something you can learn only through trial and error. It is best to make pilaf with a rice you have already cooked with. The absorptive capacity of the rice is based mostly on its age; a rice older than six months is best, although it is very difficult for you to know its age. Pilaf *is originally a Persian word, and it seems very likely that the Arabs and Turks learned how to cook rice from them. The best rices for pilaf are the long-grain Basmati or Patna rice, named for places in India. A long-grain American rice is also fine, but not converted rice.*

Pilaf cookery refers to the method of making rice in the cuisines of the Middle East, Greece, and parts of the Balkans. A modified pilaf cookery is also found in Sicily, southern Italy, Provence, and Haut-Languedoc. Once cooked, the rice is tender and each grain is separate and fluffy, not sticky.

First, soak the rice in water for 30 minutes to an hour. Some cooks use hot water, others cold, and some add salt. Alternatively, if you are time-pressed, pour the rice into a fine-mesh strainer and leave it under running water, rubbing with your fingers for a minute. This rinsing or soaking process removes the starch so that the grains will remain separate after cooking. The rinsed and drained rice is often sautéed briefly at this point in cooking fat before the introduction of liquid. Whether you add liquid to rice or rice to liquid, the liquid should be boiling or at least hot, although generally no great harm will be done if you use cold water. The ratio of liquid to rice can be anywhere from two to one (most common) to one to one. Once the rice is in the pot, you must never stir or tamper with it. The rice is always covered when cooking.

According to the Turkish food authority Nevin Halıcı, Turkish families use a number of methods to cook rice. In the salma, *or free-flowing, method, rice is poured in a slow stream into boiling liquid until the liquid is absorbed and then heated fat is poured over. In the* süzme, *or strained, method, rice is boiled in salted water, strained, and then fat is poured over. Last, they might use the* kavurna, *or fried, method: the rice is first fried in fat and then cooked until the liquid is absorbed. I prefer this last method.*

The rice should be cooked in a heavy saucepan that has a tight-fitting lid. I believe a 2- to 4-quart enameled cast-iron saucepan is perfect for rice because it has a very heavy lid that captures the steam. Use either of the two methods below:

- *Bring the broth or water to a boil with the butter or olive oil and salt. Drain the soaked rice and place it in the saucepan. Pour in the boiling broth or water in a steady stream. Return to a boil, then reduce the heat to low, cover, and cook until the liquid is absorbed, about 12 minutes, although times will vary. Remove the lid, cover with paper towels to absorb steam, and replace the lid. Remove the pot from the heat and let it rest off the heat for 15 minutes.*
- *Melt the butter or heat the olive oil. Drain the rice and cook for 1 to 2 minutes over medium-high heat, stirring constantly. Add the salt and hot or boiling broth or water, return to a boil, reduce the heat to very low, cover, and cook until the rice has absorbed the water, about 12 minutes, although times will vary. Sometimes, if I feel I might not be able to pay attention to the rice, I will turn the heat off once it reaches a boil, cover the top with paper towels and then the lid, and leave it undisturbed until all the liquid is absorbed, about 45 minutes.*

COOKING RISOTTO

Risotto is a method of rice cookery in northern Italy. In other parts of Italy where rice is also eaten, the prepared dish is called riso, *and it is not cooked by this special method. The most common rice in Italy is the many varieties of the short-grain rice* Oryza sativa japonica.

My risotto recipes call for one variety of short-grain rice called Arborio rice, a rice that can be found relatively easily in many supermarkets now and certainly in an Italian market. There are four basic varieties of rice used in Italian cooking: riso fino, *a round medium-grain rice that includes a subcategory called* vialone nano, *a rice favored by Venetian cooks in making* minestra *and risotto;* riso semifino, *a longer grain rice used in minestrone;* riso superfino, *which includes the familiar Arborio rice; and* riso comune, *a glutinous short-grain rice, which includes* balilla *rice, used for desserts. In northern Italy one is likely to find a hybrid rice called* carnaroli *or* maratelli, *a rice older than six months, used for risottos. If you are unable to find these rices, use a short-grain Japanese or medium-grain Spanish rice.*

The secret to a perfect risotto is a combination of two elements: a flavorful broth and the broth added to the rice correctly. The goal in risotto is to have a sticky, creamy rice derived from the starch in the rice, not from the addition of cream. Unlike a pilaf, where one rinses the starch from the rice and never touches the rice while it is cooking, in a risotto one leaves the starch and is almost constantly stirring the rice. A risotto is the opposite of a pilaf.

Melt the butter or heat olive oil in a 2- to 4-quart enameled cast-iron saucepan or any heavy saucepan. Sauté the soffrito *(page 285) called for in the recipe, if any. Add the rice, which never gets rinsed because you want to use the starch of the rice to help create the creamy effect. Sauté the rice for a couple of minutes, then add half of the broth called for in a recipe. Stir as you add the broth and continue stirring frequently as it is absorbed by the rice. Continue adding half of the remaining broth, stirring as you do, until the rice is creamy and tender. Zeno's paradox is avoided by making the last addition of broth the last remaining 1/4 cup. This is the single most important feature of a risotto: the broth is never added all at once. (On the other hand, I understand that some Italian cooks add the broth all at once.) The time it takes to cook a risotto depends on the age of the rice, so anywhere between 20 minutes and 1 1/4 hours is possible.*

COOKING *ARROZ* (SPANISH-STYLE RICE)

Spanish-style rice cookery is different from both pilaf and risotto cookery. The best rice to use is a short- or medium-grain rice called Calasparra or Blue Rose (see "Mediterranean Food Products Resources"), or any so-called Spanish rice. The Spanish most often cook their rice in either a wide paella pan or an earthenware casserole called an olla *or* cazuela, *either stove-top or in an oven. The rice is not rinsed and it is sautéed before the addition of broth or water, which is added all at once. The rice cooks uncovered and is never stirred. In the final product the rice is tender, the grains separate yet sticky, but not creamy as in a risotto.*

the *Libro per cuoco* gives a recipe, *rixo in bona manera*—that is, a kind of porridge of rice cooked in almond milk with sugar. In Italy, a person who laughed easily was said to have eaten rice soup, a play on words: *che aveva mangiato la minestra di riso* (he had eaten laughter/rice soup).[66]

In the East, the growing of grain was directly affected by Ottoman land administration, characterized by direct state control of the peasant and the soil. This system had originally been implemented to meet the military and financial needs of an absolutist administration, the main concern of which was to ensure the revenues of the *timar* lands.[67] The *timar* was a military fief, a grant of land to the *sipahi*, cavalrymen, who rendered military service. The *timar* and the feudal Ottoman land system began to break up at the end of the sixteenth century. The regular army grew in importance over the cavalry and the *timar* lands were converted to crown lands leased out to tax farmers without military obligations, in a system called *iltizam*. But heavy taxes caused the peasantry to abandon the soil in droves. The decline of the *sipahi* as a class is pointed to as one of the major reasons for Ottoman decline.[68]

Rice, though, always remained an item of trade and is closely associated with the cuisines of the Venetians, Lombards, Egyptians, Levantine Arabs, Turks, Greeks, and Spaniards, as we see by the representative contemporary recipes following. Rice cookery existed elsewhere as well, in places not usually associated with rice, such as Apulia in southern Italy where *tiella alla pugliese* is a delightful and famous Apulian rice preparation using the local mussels of the Gulf of Taranto.

Tiella alla Pugliese (Apulia)

APULIAN-STYLE CASSEROLE OF MUSSELS, POTATOES, AND RICE

This peasant dish is well known in the south of Italy and is usually served as a minestra, *or first-course soup. In dialect it is called* la tiedda, *which simply means the pie or baking pan in which it it is traditionally made. In Languedoc a similiar pan is used, called a* tielle, *for some preparations (see page 441).*

2 dozen mussels, scrubbed, debearded, and washed well
1/4 cup extra virgin olive oil
1 small onion, finely chopped
1 garlic clove, finely chopped
6 to 8 cups boiling water
1 pound potatoes, peeled and sliced 1/4 inch thick
2 teaspoons salt
Freshly ground black pepper to taste
1 1/2 cups short- or medium-grain rice
4 ripe plum tomatoes, peeled, seeded, and sliced
1 tablespoon finely chopped fresh parsley leaves

1. Place the cleaned mussels in a large pot with 2 tablespoons of the olive oil, cover, and turn the heat to medium-high. Once the mussels have opened, 6 to 7 minutes, remove the mussels from their shells and set aside. Discard the shells and any mussels that remain tightly shut. Strain the juice through a cheesecloth-lined strainer and set aside.

2. In a large casserole, heat the remaining 2 tablespoons olive oil with the onion and garlic over medium-high heat and cook until translucent, about 3 minutes, stirring constantly so the garlic doesn't burn. Add 6 cups of the boiling water, the potatoes, salt, and pepper. Bring to a boil and, after 10 minutes, add the rice and tomatoes. Cover, reduce the heat to very low, and cook for 15 minutes. Stir in the mussel juice and cook until the rice has absorbed the liquid, about 40 minutes, while adding the remaining boiling water 1/2 cup at a time, if necessary, while stirring. Add the mussels and parsley, stir, cook for 2 minutes, covered, and serve.

Makes 4 to 6 servings

Risotto de la "Visilia" (Veneto)

CHRISTMAS EVE RISOTTO

This is a typical Christmas Eve dinner preparation and is unusual for two reasons: it is not cooked according to the risotto method even though it's called a risotto, and it combines cheese with fish. The dish probably evolved from a simple fish pilaf, one using, perhaps, gò *(see page 419), then the eel was added and finally the beans. If you are unable to find eel, striped bass, mahimahi, bluefish, or mackerel might do to provide the rich taste associated with this dish.*

Eel is a traditional food for Christmas Eve in Venice. Grilled eel is popular and it is said that the doge Andrea Gritti died at the age of eighty-four on December 28, 1538, after eating too many grilled eels on Christmas Eve.[69] *The glass workers of Murano created a famous dish with eels,* bisato scotà, *a dish that can't be replicated because it is prepared by the glass workers, who dip the eel into molten glass until it is cooked, then break the glass to eat it.*[70]

The borlotto *bean used in this recipe is a kind of kidney bean in the genus* Phaseolus *with bright stripes of red or pink. Botanists now know that the bean is a New World migrant. The* Phaseolus *mentioned by the classical Latin authors Virgil and Columella probably was another leguminous plant of the genus* Dolichos, *or hyacinth bean. The New World bean appeared in Europe in the sixteenth century, being first illustrated and described by the artist Hieronymous Tragus and the botanist Leonhard Fuchs (1501–1566) in 1542.*

If borlotti *are unavailable, use pinto, Roman, cranberry (red speckled), or red kidney beans, with pinto being a first choice. Common eel is usually sold around Christmastime in some U.S. supermarkets and fish stores.*

2/3 cup (about 6 ounces) dried *borlotto*, pinto, or Roman beans, picked over, soaked in water to cover for several hours, and drained
6 tablespoons (3/4 stick) unsalted butter
1 medium-size onion, very finely chopped
1 celery stalk, very finely chopped
1 carrot, very finely chopped
2 garlic cloves, crushed
1 pound common eel *(Anguilla anguilla)*, skinned and cut into 1-inch pieces (see above for substitutes)
3/4 pound firm fish fillets (such as redfish, wolffish, red snapper, goby, whiting, perch, or porgy)
6 cups water
Salt to taste
1 1/2 cups Arborio rice
1/4 cup freshly grated Parmigiano-Reggiano cheese

1. Put the drained beans in a medium-size saucepan and cover by several inches with lightly salted cold water. Cook the beans over medium heat until soft but not breaking apart, about 1 1/2 hours, but check before that time. Pass half the beans through a food mill or pulse in short bursts in a food processor and reserve. Set aside the remaining beans.

2. In a large casserole or heavy saucepan, melt half the butter, then cook the onion, celery, and carrot over medium heat for 6 minutes, stirring occasionally. Add the garlic, eel, fish, water, and salt and bring to a boil. Reduce the heat to medium and cook until the fish can flake easily, about 30 minutes (but don't flake the fish; keep them whole).

3. Strain the broth through a fine-mesh strainer and return 1 quart of it to the casserole or saucepan. Stir in the pureed beans and mix well. Remove the fish and eel from the strainer and reserve, keeping warm, to serve as a second course.

4. Bring the broth to a boil over medium-high heat and add the rice. Cook, uncovered, until the rice is soft, about 20 minutes. Stir in the remaining butter, remaining beans, and the cheese and serve.

Makes 6 servings

Risotto alla Sbirraglia (Veneto)

THE COP'S RICE

Sbirraglia *is a derogatory word for a policeman. Massimo Alberini, a renowned authority on Italian gas-*

tronomy, says that the sbirri*, in this case military police of foreign occupying powers during the nineteenth century or maybe earlier, would take over a farm and often kill several chickens to cook up with rice, hence the name of the dish. Another version of the story is related by Count Ranieri da Mosto, author of a book on Venetian cuisine, who tells us that the* sbirri *were the police of the Republic and they would make this dish for those long nights on watch in the countryside. Giuseppe Boerio, in his* Dizionario del dialetto veneziano*, attributes the roots of the word to the Arabic* birron *(sic), meaning "justice."*[71] *In other parts of Italy the dish might be called* alla cacciatora *and is more a* piatto unico*, one-pot meal, than a* primo piatto*, first course. In Brescia, an identical preparation is called* risotto alla pitocca*, the beggar's rice, but the chicken is not boned.*

Remove as much fat from the chicken as possible before proceeding.

1 chicken (2½ to 3 pounds)
½ pound beef shank
1 medium-size onion, quartered and separated into layers
2 carrots, 1 sliced and 1 very finely chopped
1 celery stalk, sliced
Salt to taste
1 tablespoon extra virgin olive oil
7 tablespoons unsalted butter
3 ounces pancetta, very finely chopped
1 small onion, very finely chopped
1 celery heart, very finely chopped
Freshly ground black pepper to taste
1 cup dry white wine
¾ pound ripe tomatoes, peeled, seeded, and chopped
2 cups Arborio rice
1½ cups freshly grated Parmigiano-Reggiano cheese

1. Cut all the meat from the chicken. Cut the chicken meat into small pieces. Set the chicken meat, covered, in the refrigerator until needed. Place the chicken bones and gizzards, beef shank, quartered onion, sliced carrot, sliced celery, salt, and water to cover in a stockpot. Bring to a boil, skim the top of foam, and reduce the heat to very low, using a heat diffuser if necessary. Simmer until the water is reduced to 5 cups, about 6 hours. Strain and reserve the broth.

2. In a large casserole, heat the olive oil and melt half the butter over medium heat, then cook the *soffritto* of pancetta, chopped onion, remaining chopped carrot, and celery heart until the onion is translucent, 10 to 12 minutes, stirring occasionally. Add the chicken meat, season with salt and pepper, cover, and cook until well coated with the *soffritto*, about 4 minutes, stirring occasionally.

3. Once the chicken is white, in a few more minutes, pour in the wine and continue cooking until it is half evaporated, about 10 minutes. Add the tomatoes and cook for 1 minute. Pour in the rice and 1 cup of the reserved broth. Once the liquid evaporates, pour in another ½ cup of broth. Continue adding broth in smaller and smaller amounts as it evaporates and is absorbed and cook until the rice is between al dente and tender, stirring almost constantly.

4. Stir the remaining butter and half the Parmigiano-Reggiano into the rice 5 minutes before it is done. Arrange the risotto on a serving platter and sprinkle with the remaining cheese.

Makes 6 to 8 servings

Riso a la Pilota (Veneto)

RICE HUSKER'S RICE

This is a very old rice preparation said to be native to Lombardy, Mantua, or the Veneto. Riso a la pilota *is not cooked like a risotto; rather, it is cooked in a very slow manner, covered, reminiscent of Turkish-style rice pilaf cookery using what the Turks call the* salma *or free-flow-*

ing method (page 589). The difficulty of a dish like this, as with any true pilaf, is that one must know the exact amount of water the particular rice being used can absorb. The most common rice used in the preparation of riso a la pilota *is a short-grain Vialone or Arborio rice that is not washed, meaning its starch content will be higher.*

It is said the name of this rice preparation comes from the process used to winnow the rice, called pilatura. *The rice workers use a* pila di riso, *a wooden tool for husking the rice grains. Another possibility is that* pilota *is a corruption of the Turkish word* pilav, *itself derived from the Persian, which entered the Italian language as* pilao. *This suggestion also seems to be the one that the famous playwright Carlo Goldoni believed when he called a* pilot *a "pilaf." It seems very likely to me that Muslim rice cookery influenced early Italian rice cookery in some way. In Vincenzo Cervio's cookbook* Il Trinciante, *published in Venice in 1581, he specifically calls for rice to be cooked in the Arab pilaf manner:* riso sottestato alla damaschina *(rice cooked under a cover in the style of Damascus).*[72]

Carol Field, the author of numerous works on Italian food, tells us that the pilotati, *the rice huskers, invented this way of preparing the rice. The* risaie *or rice paddies surrounded the great farm houses and workers would prepare these rich dishes. Count Ranieri da Mosto, the author of a book of Venetian cuisine, suggests covering the rice with* pasta matta, *a flour-and-water dough, while it cooks for 1 hour and 45 minutes. Originally the rice was made in a copper kettle called a* paiolo di rame, *the same that is used for polenta.*

Scant 3 cups water
2 teaspoons salt
2 cups Arborio rice
6 tablespoons (3/4 stick) unsalted butter
1 pound freshly ground or chopped boneless pork chops or pork tenderloin
1 ounce pancetta, very finely chopped
2 garlic cloves, crushed
Salt and freshly ground black pepper to taste
1 cup freshly grated Parmigiano-Reggiano cheese

1. Bring the water to a furious boil in a large saucepan and add the salt. Make a cone out of some waxed paper, fill it with the rice, and let the rice slowly run out the other end into the center of the pot of boiling water. When the water returns to a boil, shake the pot or stir with a fork. Reduce the heat to very low and cook until the water is absorbed and the rice just tender, a hair beyond al dente, about 45 minutes. Remove from the heat, cover the pot with a kitchen or paper towels, and leave for 15 minutes.

2. In a medium-size skillet, melt the butter over medium heat, then add the pork, pancetta, and garlic, season with salt and pepper, and cook until the pork is no longer pink, about 10 minutes. Turn the rice into a large bowl and stir in the cooked pork so that it is mixed well. Stir in half the Parmigiano-Reggiano. Pour the rice onto a serving platter. Sprinkle the remaining cheese on top and serve.

Makes 6 servings

Risi in Cavroman (Veneto)

RICE WITH LAMB STEW

This rice preparation may have resulted from Venice's historical contacts with Albania, the Dalmatian coast, or perhaps Palestine during the Middle Ages. The Venetian doges and patrician class, who both loved and could afford the exotic spices of the Levant and Turkey, mixed them with their own home-grown vegetables, creating dishes like this—not so much imported from the East but transformed into a Venetian dish. This is true, too, of the Spanish influence on Venetian cooking. At least two risotto preparations in Venetian cuisine demonstrate this influence from West and East, and East to West and they are similar. Risotto alla spagnola *is made with chicken sautéed with onion, then cooked with tomato paste, saffron, rice, and fresh peas and garnished with a roasted red bell pepper.* Risotto alla turca *is made with onion cooked in lots of butter with the rice. Saffron, chicken livers, prosciutto, and tomato slices are added and it, too, is garnished with a roasted red bell pepper.*

These two dishes, as well as this cavroman *recipe, are very rare preparations, never found in restaurants and seldom if ever in the home today. Recipes go out of style, even when they are good, and this dish fell victim to changing times. It's very flavorful but a bit heavy; you wouldn't want to serve anything but this dish, I think. In developing my recipe I am indebted to my friend Laura Courir, head of the Venetian delegation of the Accademia Italiana della Cucina, whose knowledge of Venetian culinary lore was critical in rescuing this dish from a sure extinction.*

Cavroman *is a Venetian culinary dialect word for* stufato di castrato, *a wether stew (a castrated lamb or calf), a cut used mostly for sauces and* ragù. *The Italian culinary historian Giuseppe Maffioli says that in Venice* castradina *specifically means the castrated lambs of Dalmatia and Albania that are salted and smoked, after which they are soaked and then used in the stew. In place of* castrato *you can use lamb or mutton cut from the neck.*

1/4 cup (1/2 stick) unsalted butter
1 small onion, finely chopped
1 1/4 pounds lamb neck with bone, cut into large pieces and trimmed of fat
1 pound ripe plum tomatoes, peeled and seeded, squeezing out and saving 1/2 cup tomato water
1 cinnamon stick
Salt and freshly ground black pepper to taste
1 3/4 cups Arborio rice
6 cups beef broth (page 54)
1/2 cup freshly grated Parmigiano-Reggiano cheese

1. In a large enameled cast-iron casserole or saucepan, melt the butter, then cook the onion over medium heat until translucent and golden, about 6 minutes, stirring. Add the lamb and brown, turning often so all sides are brown, about 8 minutes. Add the tomatoes, tomato water, and cinnamon stick and season with salt and pepper. Cover and cook over medium heat until tender, 45 to 50 minutes, stirring occasionally with a wooden spoon and scraping the bottom of the pan.

2. Remove the lamb neck pieces from the casserole, cut off all the meat, and scoop out any marrow. Return the lamb pieces and marrow to the now thick tomato sauce, which will look like tomato paste. Add the rice and cook for 2 minutes, stirring often so all the grains are coated.

3. Pour in 1 cup of the beef broth and stir. Once the liquid evaporates, pour in another 1/2 cup of the broth. Continue adding broth in smaller and smaller amounts as it evaporates and is absorbed and cook until the rice is between al dente and tender, stirring almost constantly, about 1 hour. Remove and discard the cinnamon stick. Stir in the Parmigiano-Reggiano and serve.

Makes 8 primi piatti *(first course) servings or 4* piatti unici *(one-pot meal) servings*

Risotto co le Sècole (Veneto)

RISOTTO WITH BACKBONE MEAT

Venice is divided into six sestieri *or "sixths," sections of the city. The* sestieri *are Cannaregio, San Marco, Castello, Dorsoduro, San Polo, and Santa Croce. The two major meat markets in Venice are indicated by streets and plazas called* beccarie. *One is in San Polo near the fish market and the other was historically located in the far west end of Cannaregio, near today's train station. The butchers would sell to those who couldn't afford the better cuts of meat the* sècole, *the gelatinous marrow found between the bones of the vertebrae of beef or veal, although some cooks mean it to refer to the meat left on the joints of the vertebrae after the cow or calf has been butchered.*

The cooking of each of the sestieri *is said by Italian culinary authority Giuseppe Maffioli to be unique enough to be distinguishable by an expert. I developed this old recipe, which might be identifiable by an expert as native to the* sestiero *of Cannaregio, with the assistance of a Venetian cook, Laura Courir, who is head of Venice's delegation to the Accademia Italiana della Cucina. This is another rich, hearty, and flavorful recipe from Venice that one never finds in a restaurant and rarely now even in the home, as it has gone out of style.*

6 ounces veal sweetbreads, trimmed of membranes
2 tablespoons white wine vinegar
¼ cup (½ stick) unsalted butter, plus more to finish the dish, if desired
1 small onion, very finely chopped
1 stalk celery, very finely chopped
1 carrot, very finely chopped
5 ounces beef or veal shank, trimmed of fat and thinly sliced
4 ounces beef or veal marrow (from about 2½ pounds bones), very finely chopped (about ¾ cup)
5 ounces chicken livers, trimmed of fat and membranes and very finely chopped
Salt and freshly ground black pepper to taste
Pinch of freshly grated nutmeg
Pinch of ground cinnamon
¼ cup tomato sauce (page 32)
1 cup dry white wine
2 cups Arborio rice
2 teaspoons salt
6 cups beef broth (page 54)
½ cup freshly grated Parmigiano-Reggiano cheese

1. Put the sweetbreads in a large saucepan of cold water acidulated with the vinegar. Set the heat on high and bring the water to just below a boil. Immediately reduce the heat to low and poach until the sweetbreads are white, about 20 minutes. Drain the sweetbreads and chop. Set aside.

2. In a large casserole, melt 2 tablespoons of the butter over medium heat, then cook the onion, celery, and carrot until soft, about 8 minutes, stirring. Add the sliced beef or veal and brown for 2 minutes. Add the marrow, chicken livers, and sweetbreads, stir, and season with salt, pepper, nutmeg, and cinnamon.

3. Stir the tomato sauce and wine together and pour into the casserole. Stir, cover, reduce the heat to low and simmer until the meat is tender, about 1¼ hours.

4. Meanwhile, prepare the rice. In a large, heavy saucepan, melt the remaining 2 tablespoons butter. Add the rice and 2 teaspoons salt and cook over medium heat for 2 minutes, stirring. Pour in 1 cup of the beef broth and stir. Once the liquid evaporates pour in another ½ cup of the broth. Continue adding broth in smaller and smaller amounts as it evaporates and is absorbed and cook until the rice is between al dente and tender, about 1 hour, stirring almost constantly.

5. When the rice is cooked, transfer it to the casserole with the meat. Fold the rice and meat sauce together and cook for 2 minutes, then transfer to a serving platter or bowl and stir in the Parmigiano-Reggiano and more butter if desired.

Makes 6 servings

Risotto alla Milanese (Lombardy)

SAFFRON RISOTTO

Risotto alla milanese *is a saffron risotto and the traditional accompaniment to* ossobuco *(page 92). The*

Venetian Jews once made an identical preparation simply called riso col zafran. *I believe that the dish was once a kind of saffron pilaf known among the Jews and Arabs of medieval Sicily who traveled north. As early as the sixteenth century, the Renaissance chef Cristoforo da Messisburgo had claimed that he thought* risotto con lo zaffrano *was born in Sicily.*[73]

- **½ cup (1 stick) unsalted butter**
- **1 small onion, very finely chopped**
- **1 ounce veal bone marrow (from about ¾ pound bones), chopped (page 718)**
- **½ cup dry white wine**
- **3 cups Arborio rice**
- **6 to 7 cups boiling veal or beef broth (page 54)**
- **Salt to taste**
- **Good-size pinch of saffron threads, powdered in a mortar and steeped in 3 tablespoons warm water**
- **1 cup freshly grated Parmigiano-Reggiano cheese**

1. In a large, heavy saucepan or casserole, melt ¼ cup (½ stick) of the butter and cook the onion and bone marrow together over medium heat until the onion is translucent, 7 to 8 minutes, stirring frequently. Pour in the wine and continue cooking until the wine is nearly evaporated. Add the rice and cook for 2 minutes, stirring to evenly coat the grains.

2. Add 1 cup of the boiling broth, season with salt, and stir. Once the liquid evaporates, pour in another ½ cup of the broth. Continue adding broth in smaller and smaller amounts as it evaporates and is absorbed and cook until the rice is between al dente and tender, about one hour, stirring almost constantly.

3. A few minutes before the rice is done, add the steeping saffron and stir. Add the remaining ¼ cup (½ stick) butter and the cheese and stir. Cover and leave the risotto for 5 minutes before serving. Serve with more Parmigiano-Reggiano.

Makes 6 servings

Riso e Zucca (Lombardy)

RICE AND WINTER SQUASH

Although Italian cooks in the Middle Ages cooked zucche, *today meaning winter squash or pumpkin, that word then referred to a kind of gourd or melon. The New World winter squash and all its varieties did not enter the Mediterranean until the sixteenth century. In northern Italy, one of the most popular of the* Cucurbita *is the* Cucurbita maxima, *known as Chiogga or sea squash. The flesh of the Chiogga squash is particularly favored in the making of risotto and minestrone.*

This creamy rice and winter squash dish from Lombardy has no cream and is not called a risotto because the method of cooking is different. The end result is a satisfying preparation for a first course in the late fall.

- **6 tablespoons (¾ stick) unsalted butter**
- **1 tablespoon pork lard**
- **2 tablespoons extra virgin olive oil**
- **1 medium-size onion, finely chopped**
- **2 pounds winter squash flesh (pumpkin, hubbard or turban squash), seeded and diced**
- **1 cup dry white wine**
- **4 cups chicken broth (page 54)**
- **2¼ teaspoons salt**
- **2 cups Arborio rice**
- **¾ cup freshly grated Parmigiano-Reggiano cheese**

1. In a large, heavy ovenproof and stove-top casserole, melt 3 tablespoons of the butter with the lard and olive oil over medium-high heat, then cook the onion until translucent, about 5 minutes, stirring frequently.

2. Add the diced squash and wine and cook until the squash is crisp-tender, about 30 minutes, stirring and adding broth if it looks like it is drying out. Add the remaining broth and the salt and bring to a boil. Add the rice, reduce the heat to medium-low, and

cook until between al dente and tender, about 30 minutes, stirring occasionally. Stir in the Parmigiano-Reggiano and remaining 3 tablespoons butter.

3. Preheat the oven to 350°F. Bake the rice until crusty on top, about 10 minutes, and serve immediately.

Makes 6 to 8 servings

Ruzz bi'l-Baṭāṭis (Egypt)

RICE PILAF WITH POTATOES

The knowledge of rice spread into the Mediterranean after Alexander the Great's expedition to the East in the fourth century B.C., *but it was not grown in any widespread way until the rise of Islam in the seventh century* A.D. *The earliest references to rice cultivation in Egypt are from the ninth century. Although rice was grown in limited amounts earlier in Palestine and the Jordan Valley, it does not appear in Egypt until it was grown in the Fayyūm and along the valley of the upper Nile, according to Ibn Ḥawqal, who wrote about* A.D. *988.*[74] *Shortly, Egypt was a major producer of rice, and by the mid-eleventh century exports were going to Sicily on a regular basis, although Egypt would import rice, too, in times of scarcity. In 1120, Cairo had its House of Rice, both a warehouse and market for rice purchases.*[75]

This recipe for rice and potatoes is a simple preparation that I made for the first time with my Egyptian cooking mentor, Hamida Abdul-Magid, along with fried duck (page 518), with which it went very well and was good and spicy.

2 tablespoons *samna* (clarified butter; page 189)
1 boiling potato (about ½ pound), peeled and diced small
1½ cups long-grain rice, rinsed well or soaked in water to cover for 30 minutes and drained
1½ cups duck broth, chicken broth (page 54), or water
1½ teaspoons salt
½ cup boiling water, if needed
2 cups hot Egyptian stewed tomato sauce (*dimʿa musabīka;* page 312)

1. In a heavy saucepan or casserole with a tight-fitting lid, heat the *samna* over medium heat, then cook the potato until yellow, about 5 minutes, stirring often so it doesn't stick. Add the rice and cook for another 2 minutes, stirring.

2. Pour in the broth or water and salt and bring to a boil. Immediately reduce the heat to very low, cover, and cook until all the water is absorbed and the rice tender, 10 to 12 minutes. Do not stir or lift the lid. Check the rice after 10 minutes by pushing a fork to the bottom of the pan. If there is no liquid left and the grains of rice are separate and between al dente and tender, turn the heat off. If the rice is still hard, add the water and let cook a few minutes longer.

3. Transfer the rice to a serving bowl and stir in the heated tomato sauce. Let the rice sit for a few minutes, then serve.

Makes 4 servings

Shalawlaw (Egypt)

RICE PILAF WITH GARLIC, LEMON, AND CORIANDER PESTO

The rice cookery of Egypt is not fancy as some complicated pilafs can be, but rather geared toward daily staples. A beloved rice dish among the fallāḥīn *(peasants) in*

Egypt is shalawlaw, *a Coptic word for a rice dish made with lots of garlic crushed into lemon juice and stirred together with a pungent black pepper and coriander pesto. Another fabulous dish of the peasants is* ruzz bi'l-laban, *boiled rice stirred with buffalo milk that is cooked until soft and eaten with a spoon.*[76] *A very inexact form of this recipe (I'm not even sure it's spelled correctly) was orally described to me by Elisabeth Wickett, an anthropologist then working among Egyptian peasant women in Upper Egypt, so I have never tasted the real thing. I hope my recipe resembles the traditional dish.*

Leaves from 1 bunch fresh coriander (cilantro)
2 teaspoons salt
1 teaspoon black peppercorns
5 large garlic cloves, peeled
Juice from 1 lemon
2 tablespoons extra virgin olive oil
2 cups long-grain rice, rinsed well or soaked in tepid water to cover for 30 minutes and drained
4 cups water

1. In a mortar, pound the coriander, salt, peppercorns, and garlic together until they form a pesto. Slowly stir in the lemon juice. Set aside.

2. In a large, heavy enameled cast-iron casserole, heat the olive oil over medium-high heat, then add the drained rice and cook for 1 minute, stirring. Add the coriander pesto and cook for another minute, stirring. Pour in the water, bring to a boil, reduce the heat to low, and cover the top with two layers of paper towels to absorb water and keep it from falling back into the casserole, and then the lid. Cook until the water is absorbed, without stirring or looking under the lid, about 25 minutes. Transfer the rice to a serving platter and fluff with a fork.

Makes 6 servings

Kushary (Egypt)

EGYPTIAN LENTILS, RICE, AND MACARONI CASSEROLE

Remember that kushary *is a very simple working-class meal; there is nothing elegant to it, and you may wish to make and eat it for the same reason an Egyptian would—it's satisfying, filling, and healthy.*

You will be able to do steps 1, 2, and 3 at the same time if you are well organized. An easy way to serve kushary *to a group of people is to leave the pasta in its colander after draining and rest it over a simmering pot of water. Place the mixing bowl of rice and lentils over another simmering pot of water to keep warm. Leave the tomato sauce in the saucepan you cooked it in and leave the onions in the skillet. Serve by spooning the cooked macaroni in a bowl and then spoon the rice and lentils on top. Spoon a quarter of the tomato sauce on top of the rice and then some onions. Serve the remaining sauce on the side. Eat with a spoon.*

4 large onions, peeled
Salt
½ cup dried brown lentils (should yield 1 cup cooked lentils), picked over
3 cups water
7 tablespoons *samna* (clarified butter; page 189) or 2 tablespoons *samna* and 5 tablespoons extra virgin olive oil
2 cups long-grain rice, rinsed well or soaked in water to cover for 30 minutes and drained
2 cups mixed dry pasta (see Note)
Freshly ground black pepper to taste
2 cups hot Egyptian stewed tomato sauce (*dimʿa musabīka*; page 312)

1. Slice the onions from the stem end into very thin slices, less than 1/16 inch. Arrange the onion slices on some paper towels, sprinkle generously with salt, and

KUSHARY

Among the inexplicable amalgam of sights, smells, and sounds that are modern Cairo is the extraordinarily simple taste of a workingman's lunch called kushary (*also* kusharī, kishiry *and* kashiry). Kushary *is sold in countless hole-in-the-wall cook shops scattered throughout the medieval warrens crowded with Cairo's fourteen million people. Itinerant* kushary *cooks also sell this rice, lentil, and macaroni dish from colorful hand-painted donkey-pulled carts throughout the working-class neighborhoods of the city.*

The food writer John Thorne has argued that kushary *is a recent introduction from India, attributing its arrival in Cairo to the British imperial presence, possibly during World War II. Claudia Roden, a renowned food writer, is an Egyptian Jew who reports that she does not remember* kushary *before she left Cairo in 1952.*[77] *That* kushary *is originally an Indian dish seems sure enough, but its introduction to Egypt appears much earlier than World War II. The first written mention of* kushary *is found in the diaries of the famed Muslim traveler of the fourteenth century, Ibn Baṭṭūṭa.*[78] *In the mid-nineteenth century, the famous British traveler and translator of* Thousand and One Nights, *Richard Burton, identifies* kushary *in the Suez.*[79] *Given* kushary*'s relationship to* mujaddara *(page 602), a dish with roots in the tenth century, its history may be older and more Arab than admitted.*

My own history with kushary *was a bit convoluted. I was determined to have some* kushary *in Cairo, but was often warned away from street food by those in the know, and not unwisely. Still, I had a strong craving for a bowl of this hearty-looking dish that I saw Cairenes eating with such gusto and which was described by the distinguished professor of botany Charles B. Heiser, Jr., as a nearly perfect food for protein enrichment.*[80] *Finally throwing caution to the wind, a friend and I sauntered into a cookshop that would not have met Western hygienic standards, but seemed clean enough to us relative to the countless other filthy places in Cairo. In any case, the food preparation area was clean.*

The cook and his helper, standing behind a counter, were quite delighted to see us, Westerners, walking into their shop on the Sūq al-Turfriyya halfway down from the Shāriʿ Ramses, near the national telecommunications building, far off the beaten tourist path. The name of their place was in Arabic, Kushary Majdiya and Sons.

Kushary *is assembled by spooning into a bowl broken pieces of cooked spaghetti and* tubetti *that are kept warm in a large pan, a cross between a wok and a tub. In another large pan a mixture of cooked rice and lentils is warmed separately and then tossed on top of the pasta, about three parts rice to one part lentils, flavored by being sautéed first in* samna *(clarified butter). In a third, smaller bowl are very brown, slightly crispy, and thinly sliced onions, also cooked in* samna.

We ordered a bowl (which comes in two sizes) for fifty piasters, about fifteen U.S. cents. First the

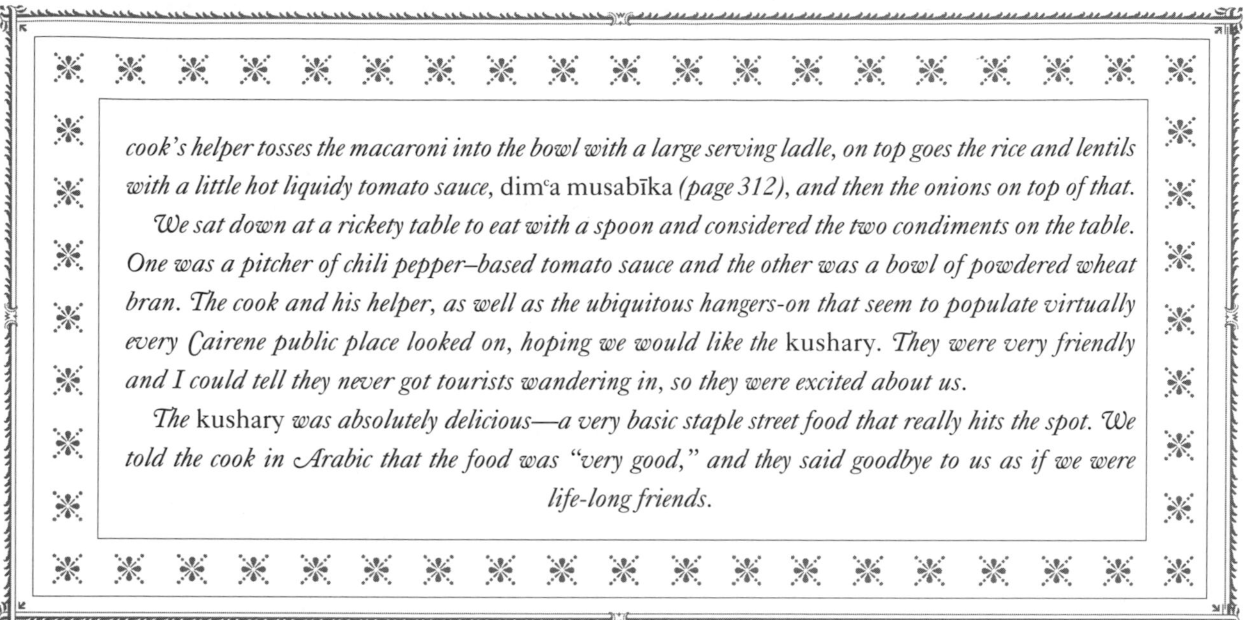

cook's helper tosses the macaroni into the bowl with a large serving ladle, on top goes the rice and lentils with a little hot liquidy tomato sauce, dimʿa musabīka *(page 312), and then the onions on top of that.*

We sat down at a rickety table to eat with a spoon and considered the two condiments on the table. One was a pitcher of chili pepper–based tomato sauce and the other was a bowl of powdered wheat bran. The cook and his helper, as well as the ubiquitous hangers-on that seem to populate virtually every Cairene public place looked on, hoping we would like the kushary. *They were very friendly and I could tell they never got tourists wandering in, so they were excited about us.*

The kushary *was absolutely delicious—a very basic staple street food that really hits the spot. We told the cook in Arabic that the food was "very good," and they said goodbye to us as if we were life-long friends.*

leave for 30 minutes covered with paper towels to absorb moisture.

2. Wash the lentils under running water. Put them in a medium-size heavy saucepan, add 1 cup of the water and 1 teaspoon of the salt, and bring to a boil. Reduce the heat to low and simmer, partially covered, until the lentils are al dente, anywhere from 20 minutes to 1 hour. Check the lentils occasionally so they are not overcooked, since lentil cooking times differ; they should be ever so slightly hard, not completely soft. Add some water to the pot if it is drying out and the lentils are not yet cooked. Drain and reserve the lentils.

3. In another large, heavy saucepan with a tight-fitting lid, heat 2 tablespoons of the *samna* over medium-high heat, then cook the rice for 2 minutes, stirring continuously to coat all the grains, then add the remaining 2 cups water and 2 teaspoons salt. Stir and bring to a boil, then reduce the heat to a simmer and cover while the rice cooks until the water is absorbed, 12 to 15 minutes. Do not lift the lid or stir while the rice cooks.

4. While the lentils and rice are cooking, prepare the onions. In a large skillet, melt the remaining 5 tablespoons *samna* or heat the olive oil over medium-high heat. Add the onion slices and coat with the *samna* or oil. Continue turning the onions as they turn from white to yellow to brown. Once they turn brown, 10 to 20 minutes, continue to cook until some turn dark brown, another 2 minutes. Remove the skillet from the burner, quickly transfer the onions to a paper towel–lined platter to cool, and drain. Once they are cool, they will have become crispy.

5. Meanwhile, bring a large pot of abundantly salted water to a vigorous boil and add the pasta. Cook until soft (not al dente) and drain well. Mix the rice and lentils in a large metal (preferably) bowl with a pinch of black pepper, tossing gently with a fork. Serve according to the instructions above.

NOTE: Half the dry pasta should be short macaroni such as *ditalini*, *tubetti*, or small elbow and the other half should be spaghetti broken into 2-inch lengths. The 2 cups dry pasta should yield 4 cups cooked pasta.

Makes 6 servings

❖ *Mujaddara* (Arab Levant)

RICE AND LENTIL PILAF

Mujaddara *is a classic dish of the family table of Lebanon, Syria, and Palestine, related to* kushary *(page 599).* Mujaddara *literally means "having smallpox." It is unknown if this ascription is meant to be a culinary joke, but it is true that the lentils mixed with the whiteness of the rice gives the impression of a pockmarked visage. In Lombardy there is a rice preparation called* ris in cagnon *that means "maggot rice," so the phenomenon of the edible and inedible in gastronomic terms seems to be a pan-Mediterranean phenomenon. This is an old preparation with roots in medieval Arab cuisine where it once was a rich dish including meat, kebabs, vermicelli, and chickpeas.*[81] *Because I learned to make this preparation from Palestinian cooks, I like to keep the proportion of rice to lentils more or less one to one, whereas elsewhere the proportion of rice would be higher. Serve with* khubz ʿarabī *(Arab flatbread or pita bread).*

1 medium-size onion, peeled
Salt
¼ cup extra virgin olive oil
1 cup dried brown lentils, picked over and rinsed well
1 tablespoon *samna* (clarified butter; page 189)
1 small onion, finely chopped
2 cups boiling water
1 cup long-grain rice, rinsed well or soaked in water to cover for 30 minutes and drained

1. Slice the onion from the stem end into very thin slices, less than 1/16 inch. Arrange the onion slices on some paper towels, sprinkle generously with salt, and leave for 30 minutes covered with paper towels to absorb moisture.

2. In a medium-size skillet, heat the olive oil over medium-high heat and toss the onion slices until coated with oil. Continue turning the onion as the slices turn from white to yellow to brown. Once they turn brown, about 8 to 9 minutes, continue to cook until some turn dark brown, another 2 minutes. Remove the skillet from the burner and quickly transfer the onions to a paper towel–lined platter to cool and drain. Once they are cool, they will have become crispy.

3. Bring a pot of lightly salted water to a boil and cook the lentils until al dente, 20 minutes to 1 hour. Check the lentils occasionally so they are not overcooked, since lentil cooking times differ; they should be ever so slightly hard, not completely soft. Drain and set aside.

4. In a large, heavy casserole or saucepan with a tight-fitting lid, melt the *samna* over medium-high heat, then cook the chopped onion until golden, 7 to 8 minutes, stirring occasionally. Pour in the boiling water, 1 teaspoon salt, and reserved lentils, bring to a boil, and add the drained rice. Return to a boil, reduce the heat to very low, cover, and cook until the water is absorbed and the rice is tender, about 30 minutes. Transfer to a serving platter and garnish with the crispy onions on top.

Makes 6 servings

❖ *Ruzz Mufalfal* (Arab Levant)

PLAIN RICE PILAF

This is the basic rice pilaf recipe used throughout the Middle East. In Arabic, ruzz mufalfal *means "peppered rice" which is essentially rice pilaf. The word* mufalfal *here means "to cook rice" even though the word derives from the word for "pepper"* (filfil)*; it is unclear what the relationship is. The Palestinians and Lebanese use the word* filfil *to mean "spice," too. To make any rice dish successfully, you must know your rice (see page 588* *before making this recipe). Cooking times will vary. The long-grain rice that I buy in bulk is Basmati rice, but even different long-grain rice will have different cooking times. As in all pilaf cookery, the rice must be sautéed first in butter or oil and then is never stirred while the rice cooks; leave it untouched and do not remove the lid to look until 12 minutes have passed.*

2 tablespoons *samna* (clarified butter; page 189)
2 cups long-grain rice, rinsed well or soaked in water to cover for 30 minutes and drained
4 cups water
2 teaspoons salt
½ cup boiling water, if needed
Freshly ground black pepper to taste (optional)

1. In a large, heavy casserole or saucepan with a tight-fitting lid, melt the *samna* over medium-high heat, then cook the rice for 2 to 3 minutes, stirring frequently. Add the water and salt, increase the heat to high, and, once it begins to boil slightly, reduce the heat to very low and cover. Check the rice after 12 minutes by pushing a fork to the bottom of the pot in the middle to see if all moisture has been absorbed. If not, cook for another 3 minutes and check again.

2. If the water is absorbed, turn the heat off and remove the lid. If the water is absorbed but the rice is still hard, add the boiling water and continue cooking until done. Cover the pot with a paper towel, replace the lid, and let sit for 10 to 20 minutes. Transfer to a serving platter, season with black pepper, and serve.

NOTE 1: Many Lebanese cooks break vermicelli into 1-inch lengths, brown them in some *samna*, and add them with the rice to cook until both are tender. This way it is called *ruzz bi'l-shᶜiriyya*, rice with vermicelli.

NOTE 2: The rice can be replaced with the pasta called orzo.

Makes 4 servings

Ruzz bi'l-Fūl (Arab Levant)

RICE PILAF WITH FAVA BEANS

The earliest evidence of the cultivation of fava beans in the Mediterranean comes from a pre-pottery Neolithic B level (a strata at the archeological site) at Jericho in Palestine. They have also been found in Egypt from 1800 B.C. and the Greeks and Romans wrote about the fava bean. So we know that the fava bean is one of the oldest foods in the Middle East. In Syria, the fava bean is a popular legume and often eaten with olive oil. Al-Muqqadasī, who wrote in the late tenth century, tells us that olive oil was a very important element of the food of Syrians, and he relates how fava beans were fried in olive oil and sold mixed with olives in the local markets.[82]

This recipe is from Nadia Koudmani, who lives in Damascus and is the sister of my friend Sari Abul-Jubein. It is a beautiful dish to make with fresh baby fava beans, so young that the beans do not need to be peeled.

2 pounds fresh fava beans in the pods
3 tablespoons *samna* (clarified butter; page 189)
½ pound ground lamb
2 teaspoons *bahārāt* (page 524)
½ teaspoon ground cinnamon
½ teaspoon freshly grated nutmeg
Freshly ground black pepper to taste
1 teaspoon sugar
Salt to taste
1 cup blanched whole almonds
⅓ cup pine nuts
1 recipe *ruzz mufalfal* (page 602)

1. Shell the fava beans. Boil the shelled fava beans for 4 minutes in a large pot of water to loosen the skins (not necessary if they are very young fava beans). Drain, pop the fava beans out of their skins, and set aside. You should have about 1½ cups of beans.

2. In a large skillet, melt 1 tablespoon of the *samna* over medium-high heat, then brown the lamb with the *bahārāt*, cinnamon, nutmeg, and pepper until all the pinkness is gone, about 4 minutes. Remove the lamb from the skillet and set aside in a large bowl.

3. In the same skillet, over low heat, melt another tablespoon of the *samna*, then cook the fava beans with the sugar and salt until tender, about 10 minutes, stirring occasionally. Remove and toss with the meat, keeping them warm.

4. In the same skillet, increase the heat to medium-high, melt 1½ teaspoons of the *samna*, and cook the almonds until golden, about 5 minutes, stirring; be careful not to burn them. Remove and toss with the meat and beans. Add the remaining 1½ teaspoons *samna* to the skillet and cook the pine nuts until golden, about 1 minute, stirring. Remove and toss with the meat mixture.

5. Prepare the rice. Toss all the cooked ingredients together, mold attractively on an oval platter, and serve.

Makes 4 to 6 servings

Ruzz bi'l-Dajāj (Arab Levant)

RICE PILAF WITH CHICKEN

We know that in fourteenth-century Cairo a good quality chicken was very expensive; nevertheless, stewed chickens were sold by itinerant cooks from street stalls.[83] *In the medieval Arab world, there existed a dish called* ma'mūniyya, *which was a famous sweetmeat named after the ninth-century Abbasid caliph in Baghdad al-Ma'mūn. There are three recipes for this dish in the thirteenth-century Arabic cookbook* Kitāb al-wuṣla ilā al-ḥabīb. *In the most refined of the three recipes a chicken is cooked first, presumably by poaching, and then is fried in sesame oil and the meat shredded as finely as hair. Some rice is pounded fine and mixed with sugar-sweetened boiled milk and the chicken. It is cooked until it is as thick as a porridge, then served with pistachios. There is today no evidence of this dish in the Arab world unless we considered Circassian chicken (page 308) to be derivative.*[84] *But rice with chicken, as in this recipe, although it bears no resemblance to the medieval sweetmeat, is testimony to the enduring delight the cook takes in preparing rice and chicken.*

Ruzz bi'l-dajāj *is a family-style chicken pilaf that my former wife, Najwa al-Qattan, remembers fondly from her childhood. The large chunks of poached chicken from the flavorful broth mixed with nuts, lamb, and rice make for a very satisfying dish. It is quite common in contemporary middle-class Arab homes to see vegetable shortening, such as Crisco, replacing the traditional* samna *as the cooking fat.*

1 stewing chicken (about 4 pounds)
Salt and freshly ground black pepper to taste
1 medium-size onion, peeled
1 whole clove
1 cinnamon stick
2 tablespoons extra virgin olive oil
½ cup blanched whole almonds
½ cup pine nuts
3 tablespoons *samna* (clarified butter; page 189), unsalted butter, or vegetable shortening
¼ pound ground lamb
½ teaspoon ground cinnamon
¼ teaspoon freshly ground allspice berries
2 cups long-grain rice, rinsed well or soaked in water to cover for 30 minutes and drained
High-quality full-fat plain yogurt for garnish
***Khubz ʿarabī* (Arab flatbread or pita bread)**

1. Wash the chicken, pat dry, and season with salt and pepper inside and out. Place the untrussed chicken in a large pot in water to cover with the onion

studded with the clove, and the cinnamon stick, and season with salt and pepper. Bring to just under a boil over medium heat. Reduce the heat if necessary so it never comes to a boil and simmer until the meat is almost falling off the bone, 2½ to 3 hours. Do not let the water come to a vigorous boil, or even a gentle boil, otherwise the chicken will toughen; you are just poaching the whole chicken.

2. Drain the chicken, saving the broth, at least 3 cups for this recipe and the remaining to be stored as chicken broth for other recipes. If desired, you can reduce the amount of fat by refrigerating the broth until the fat congeals on top and then remove it. Remove the meat from the bones in large pieces. Set aside and keep warm.

3. In a small skillet, heat the olive oil over medium heat, then cook the almonds until golden, stirring, about 10 minutes. Be careful not to let them burn. Add the pine nuts and cook until they are golden, another 1 to 2 minutes. Set the nuts aside.

4. In a large, heavy saucepan or casserole with a tight-fitting lid, melt 2 tablespoons of the *samna* over medium-high heat and cook the ground lamb seasoned with the ground cinnamon, allspice, salt, and pepper until all the pinkness is gone, about 4 minutes, breaking it up with a fork. Add the rice and continue cooking for 2 minutes, stirring. Add 2¼ cups of the chicken broth, bring to a boil, reduce the heat to very low, cover, and cook until the grains are tender, fluffy, and separate, 15 to 20 minutes, but check if you don't know how your rice responds. If the rice is still al dente, add some boiling chicken broth and continue cooking. Do not stir the rice and do not uncover except to check once.

5. Arrange the rice on a platter, cover with the nuts, and lay the chicken pieces on top or the sides. Serve with yogurt and Arab flatbread.

Makes 4 to 6 servings

Maqlūba (Arab Levant)

UPSIDE-DOWN RICE AND EGGPLANT CASSEROLE

Upside-down dishes have a long history. In the thirteenth-century Arabic cookbook known as the Baghdad cookery book, a chapter is devoted to "fried, marinated, and turned" dishes. Two of the recipes are called maqlūba, *which means "upside down." Although they don't bear any resemblance to this famous preparation of the same name popularly made in Syria, Palestine, and Lebanon, being made mostly with meat, eggs, and spices, the method of inverting the cooked dish is the same.*

This Palestinian recipe for maqlūba *is a rice-and-eggplant casserole made with richly succulent braised lamb and tomatoes. When the casserole is inverted, the top is bright red from the tomatoes that cover golden eggplant. This recipe is from my former mother-in-law, Leila al-Qattan.*

2 medium-size eggplant (about 2½ pounds), peeled and sliced ½ inch thick
Salt
5 tablespoons plus 1 teaspoon extra virgin olive oil
1 large onion, chopped
1½ to 2 pounds boneless lamb shoulder, trimmed of as much fat as possible and cut into pieces
1 tablespoon *bahārāt* (page 524)
1 teaspoon freshly ground black pepper
1 teaspoon freshly ground allspice berries
Pinch of ground cinnamon
Pinch of freshly grated nutmeg
3 cups water
6 cups pure or virgin olive or olive pomace oil for deep-frying
3 large ripe but firm tomatoes (about 1¾ pounds), sliced
1½ cups long-grain rice, rinsed well or soaked in water to cover for 30 minutes and drained
1 cup boiling water

1. Lay the eggplant slices on some paper towels and sprinkle generously with salt. Leave them to drain of their bitter juices for 30 minutes, then pat dry with paper towels.

2. In a large skillet, heat 5 tablespoons of the olive oil over medium-high heat, then cook the onion until yellow, about 10 minutes, stirring occasionally. Reduce the heat to medium-low, add the lamb, *bahārāt*, 1 teaspoon salt, ½ teaspoon of the pepper, the allspice, cinnamon, and nutmeg, and brown for 10 minutes, turning the lamb. Add the water to barely cover the lamb and cook, partially covered, until the lamb is very tender, 2½ to 3 hours, adding a little water to keep the skillet from drying out. Remove the lamb from the skillet with a slotted ladle or skimmer, getting as much of the onion as you can and leaving behind the fat.

3. Meanwhile, preheat the frying oil to 375°F in a deep-fryer or an 8-inch saucepan fitted with a basket insert. Deep-fry the eggplant slices in batches until golden brown, 7 to 8 minutes, turning once. Drain and reserve on paper towels. Let the frying oil cool completely, strain, and save for a future use.

4. Lightly oil the bottom of a round, heavy-bottomed 4- to 6-quart casserole 10 inches in diameter, with a tight-fitting lid, with the remaining teaspoon extra virgin olive oil and arrange the tomato slices on the bottom, overlapping or double layering if necessary. Sprinkle a handful of the rice on top of the tomatoes. Layer the lamb on top, then layer the sliced eggplants on top of the meat. Press down with a spatula or the back of your hand. Pour the rice on top and spread it evenly, pressing down again with a spatula or the back of your hand, and add 1 teaspoon salt, the remaining ½ teaspoon pepper, and the boiling water. Cover tightly and cook over low heat until the rice is tender and the liquid absorbed, about 1 hour. Don't check too often—maybe twice during the whole cooking time. The liquid in the casserole should not be boiling vigorously, so reduce the heat to very low, or use a heat diffuser, if you find that necessary.

5. When the rice is done, take off the lid, place a large round serving platter over the top of the casserole, and carefully invert in one very quick motion, holding both sides very tightly. Slowly and carefully lift the casserole. Serve.

Makes 6 servings

Maqlūbat Qarnabīṭ (Syria)
UPSIDE-DOWN CAULIFLOWER CASSEROLE

This Syrian preparation for maqlūba *is a much lighter version than the previous recipe. It uses cauliflower instead of eggplant. The recipe comes from George Salloum, who, as a young man, learned how to make it while working on a construction crew building a penitentiary in a desolate region of northeastern Syria. The crew's cook was an old Muslim woman from Homs, north of Damascus, named Umm ʿAishi, who took a liking to the young Christian man who was also from Homs. She taught him how to make it and George taught me.*

In Lebanon, cauliflower is called zahra, *which means "flower," to evoke the whiteness of the vegetable, which in this preparation melds with the equally white rice.*

Pressure cooking is quite popular in the Arab world today so if you are using a pressure cooker, do not boil the cauliflower and pressure-cook the dish for 15 minutes. The rice used in Syria is not always long-grain Basmati rice. Sometimes Syrians prefer any long-grain white rice that sticks together a bit after being fried in a little samna.

2 tablespoons *samna* (clarified butter; page 189)
1 cup long-grain rice, rinsed well or soaked in water to cover for 30 minutes and drained
1 cup water
1 teaspoon salt
1 small cauliflower (about 1 pound after being trimmed of leaves and stems)
1 small onion, chopped
1 pound boneless leg or shoulder of lamb, trimmed of as much fat as possible and cut into ½-inch cubes
2 teaspoons *bahārāt* (page 524)
1 teaspoon fresh lemon juice
Freshly ground black pepper to taste
¼ cup tomato juice squeezed from a ripe tomato (optional)

1. In a medium-size heavy saucepan or casserole with a tight-fitting lid, melt 1 tablespoon of the *samna* and cook the rice over medium-high heat for 1 to 2 minutes, stirring. Pour in the water and salt. Bring to a boil, reduce the heat to very low, cover, and cook until half-cooked. Since rice varies in cooking time, taste the rice to see when it is half-cooked, that is, when it cracks a bit when biting down. Remove to a cooling platter and set aside.

2. Bring a large pot of water to a boil and cook the cauliflower whole until slightly resistant when pierced by a skewer, 5 to 7 minutes. Drain, cool, trim off remaining stems and leaves, and break into small florets. Set aside.

3. In a round, heavy-bottomed 6-quart enameled cast-iron casserole or Dutch oven 8 to 9 inches in diameter, heat the remaining tablespoon *samna* over medium-high heat, then cook the onion until translucent, 4 to 5 minutes, stirring a few times. Add the lamb, *bahārāt,* and lemon juice, season with salt and pepper, and brown, about 8 minutes, stirring. Pour in the tomato juice, if using, and stir for 2 minutes.

4. Put the cauliflower on top of the meat, packing it down tightly. Spoon the rice on top of the cauliflower, also packing it down. Cover, reduce the heat to very low, and cook until the lamb is tender, about 45 minutes. Remove from the heat and let it rest for 15 minutes. Place a large round serving platter over the top of the casserole and carefully invert in one very quick motion, holding both sides very tightly. Slowly and carefully lift the casserole. Serve.

Makes 4 servings

Tavuklu Pilavı (Turkey)

PILAF WITH CHICKEN

In Izmir, this dish is made on the wedding day by the bride's mother and sent to the son-in-law's home for the newlyweds to eat on their nuptial night. The Turkish food authority Nevin Halıcı reports that the chicken is meant to convey the thought that "our daughter has ceased to be ours; she now begins her new life in your home and she is henceforth yours." The pilaf expresses the hope that she will bear many children.

1 chicken leg and thigh (about 1¼ pounds)
3½ cups water
½ teaspoon cardamom seeds (not pods)
¼ cup (½ stick) unsalted butter
1½ cups long-grain rice, rinsed well or soaked in water to cover for 30 minutes and drained
1 teaspoon salt

1. Put the chicken in a medium-size saucepan and cover with the water. Bring to just below a boil over high heat and skim off the foam; do not let the water come to a boil. Before the chicken water starts to boil, reduce the heat to very low, add the cardamom seeds, and simmer for 2 hours. Drain the chicken (reserving 2 cups of the cooking water and saving the rest as chicken broth for other recipes) and remove the meat

from the bones once it is cool enough to handle, cutting into bite-size pieces.

2. Preheat the oven to 400°F. Place the chicken pieces in a baking dish and bake until heated through, about 10 minutes. Remove and set aside until needed, keeping it warm.

3. Meanwhile, in a large, heavy saucepan, melt the butter over medium-high heat, then cook the rice for 2 minutes, stirring constantly to coat all the grains. Bring the reserved chicken broth to a boil. Pour the boiling chicken broth into the saucepan with the rice, along with the salt. Cover and cook until the liquid is absorbed and the rice tender, about 12 minutes. Stir the reserved chicken pieces into the rice, tossing and fluffing well. Place a paper towel over the saucepan and cover with the lid. Leave for 10 minutes and serve.

Makes 4 to 6 servings

Safranlı Pilavı (Turkey)

SAFFRON PILAF

The Arab geographer Aḥmad Muḥammad al-Rāzī (888?–955?), sometimes confused with the famous Arab doctor known as Rhazes in the West, recognized the best saffron as coming from Toledo in Spain. There were other producers, and the use of saffron is usually associated with the cooking of the East. Traditionally, saffron has always been the most expensive spice, but at times it was abundant, as we know from the tenth-century description of the kitchen in Abbasid Iraq, where pots and pans were cleaned by using water, rubbing with brick dust, then with powdered dry potash and saffron and finally wiped dry with citron leaves.[85] *Medieval Muslim cooking used a great deal of saffron and even influenced the cooking of fourteenth- and fifteenth-century Italy, where one also finds a ubiquitous use of saffron.*

This pilaf is typically made to be eaten with fish. In Syria and Lebanon, a finely chopped onion would be fried in olive oil first, before adding the rice, and the final dish would be garnished with fried pine nuts. Armenians would throw in some toasted sesame seeds and almonds, and the pilaf would be called kirkoumov printz piliv.

2 pinches of saffron threads, toasted lightly (page 521) and powdered in a mortar
4 cups water
3 tablespoons *samna* (clarified butter; page 189)
2 cups long-grain rice, rinsed well or soaked in water to cover for 30 minutes and drained
2 teaspoons salt
1 small ripe plum tomato, peeled, seeded, and finely chopped

1. Stir the saffron into the water, using some of the water to extract all of the saffron from the mortar.

2. In a large, heavy casserole or saucepan with a tight-fitting lid, melt the *samna*, then cook the rice for 2 minutes, stirring to coat all the grains. Add the salt, tomato, and saffron water and bring to a boil. Reduce the heat to very low, cover, and cook until the water is absorbed and the rice tender with the grains separate, 12 to 25 minutes, depending on your rice. Serve.

Makes 4 to 6 servings

Nohutlu Pilavı (Turkey)

RICE PILAF WITH CHICKPEAS

The Sufi order of Muslim mystics in Turkey practiced an ascetic way of life, yet food occupied an important place. The order had huge kitchens to feed both the dervishes and the novices. Once the novice served one thousand days in the Sufi order, it was said that he was now "cooked" and could become a full member of the brotherhood. Being "cooked" meant one had reached the proper spiritual plane of enlightenment. This concept is reflected in Turkish cooking as well, where foods are cooked until they are soft. There is no al dente cooking in Turkish cuisine.

This concept of "cooked" is superbly told in the story of the chickpea by the famous thirteenth-century Turkish poet Mevlana Jalaluddin-i Rumi in his Mathnawi. *When the rock-hard chickpea is cooked in boiling water, it complains to the woman cooking it. She explains to it that this is necessary so that it can be eaten by human beings, thus becoming part of humanity and elevated to a higher form of life. The allegory of the chickpea is like the human soul, suffering before its embrace by the love of God. In Mevlana's poem, the whole universe is pictured as a huge pan with the stars as cooks.*[86]

In this recipe there is something elemental that embraces the soul. My friend Ihsan Gurdal is a culinary professional and a native of Turkey who, when reviewing my Turkish recipes for this book, was quite happy to see that I included this chickpea pilaf. Because it's so traditional and simple, he said, it is often overlooked by food writers. This pilaf is an excellent accompaniment to any of the köfte *recipes (pages 335–338).*

3 to 6 tablespoons unsalted butter, to your taste
2 cups long-grain rice, rinsed well or soaked in water to cover for 30 minutes and drained
1 cup drained cooked chickpeas
3 cups water
2 teaspoons salt
1 teaspoon freshly ground black pepper

1. In a large, heavy casserole or saucepan with a tight-fitting lid, melt the butter over medium-high heat, then cook the rice and chickpeas in the hot butter, stirring and turning the mixture frequently for 3 to 4 minutes.

2. Pour in the water, salt, and pepper. Stir, bring to a boil, cover, reduce the heat to very low, and simmer until the water is absorbed and the rice is tender, 12 to 25 minutes.

Makes 6 servings

Pilafi Simio (Simi, Dodocanese)

RICE PILAF WITH CHICKPEAS AND TOMATO RAGOUT WITH YOGURT FROM SIMI

Simi (or Symi) is a small island in the Dodecanese chain very near the Turkish coast and the much larger island of Rhodes. When the Ottoman Turks conquered the Dodecanese in 1522–1523, Simi avoided invasion by offering the sultan its beautiful sponges. This placated the Turks, and they accepted a yearly tribute of sponges in return for the limited independence of the islanders. The sultan declared Simi a free port and this enriched the island, which flourished in the seventeenth century.

Much of the cooking on Simi is Turkish influenced, as in this pilaf dish that I learned from a Simiot cook, Theo Tsatis, who owns a restaurant in the old town of Rhodes. It is a favorite of his, and although he doesn't serve it in his restaurant, he still asks his mother to make it for him. The yogurt used for the topping should be of a high quality; when the cool yogurt is placed on top of the hot food, the hot-cool contrast provides an extraordinarily appetizing affect.

½ cup extra virgin olive oil
1 medium-size onion, chopped
3 garlic cloves, crushed
2 celery stalks, chopped
½ cup dry white wine
2 pounds ripe tomatoes, peeled, seeded, and chopped, with their juices
4 to 8 quarts water, as needed
1½ cups dried chickpeas, picked over, soaked in water to cover overnight, and drained
1 cinnamon stick
Salt and freshly ground black pepper to taste
¾ pound baby carrots
2 tablespoons unsalted butter
2 cups long-grain rice, rinsed well or soaked in water to cover for 30 minutes and drained
3 cups boiling water
2 cups high-quality full-fat plain yogurt

1. In a large casserole or pot, heat the olive oil over medium-high heat, then cook the onion, garlic, and celery together until the onion is soft, about 6 minutes, stirring frequently. Pour in the wine and reduce for 2 minutes. Add the tomatoes and their juices, 4 quarts of the water, the chickpeas, and cinnamon stick and bring to a boil. Reduce the heat to medium and cook for 3 to 4 hours, adding more of the water if the ragout begins to dry out. After 3 hours, check the chickpeas; if they are still a little hard, add more water, season with salt and pepper, and continue cooking. Once the chickpeas are cooked, add the carrots and continue cooking until they are soft, about another hour. Adjust the heat if the carrots are cooking too quickly.

2. About 30 minutes after putting the carrots in, make the pilaf. In a large, heavy saucepan with a tight-fitting lid, melt the butter over medium-high heat, then cook the rice for 2 minutes, stirring to coat the grains. Pour in the boiling water and 1½ teaspoons salt. Bring to a boil, reduce the heat to very low, cover the top with paper towels, and place the lid on. Simmer until the water is absorbed and the rice is between al dente and tender, 12 to 25 minutes. Continue cooking if necessary or add more boiling water.

3. Serve by ladling some rice into a bowl, top with a ladle and a half of chickpea ragout, and then some spoonfuls of rich yogurt. Serve.

Makes 8 servings

Olleta de Arroz con Lentejas (Valencia)

VALENCIAN RICE AND LENTIL STEW

This traditional housewife preparation from the mountains behind Alicante in Valencia is much loved. An olleta *is a kind of Valencian stew that shows the industriousness and ingenuity of a poor people in concocting a nourishing winter dinner. You will find much in common in the* kushary *eaten by a Cairene on the other side of the Mediterranean (page 599), not in taste, but in spirit. Rice is also the favorite of laborers as is seen in* arròs empedrat, *the rice dish of the* turróneros, *the* turrón *or nougat factory workers in Jijona, a town north of Alicante in Valencia, which is made with white beans, garlic, tomato, and parsley.*

1 cup dried brown lentils, picked over and rinsed well
1½ pounds Swiss chard, trimmed of the stalks and leaves chopped
1 potato (about 10 ounces), peeled and cut into 10 pieces
1 turnip (about 1 pound), peeled and cut into 10 pieces
2¼ cups hot water
Salt and freshly ground black pepper to taste
½ cup extra virgin olive oil
1 dried red bell pepper (*ñora*; page 719)
1 head garlic, with some peel pulled off
1 large ripe tomato (about 10 ounces), peeled, seeded, and chopped
1 cup medium-grain rice

1. In a medium casserole or stockpot, cover the lentils, Swiss chard, potato, and turnip with the hot water, season with salt and pepper, and bring to a simmer over medium heat. Cook for 20 minutes, then reduce the heat to low.

2. Meanwhile, heat the olive oil in a small skillet over medium heat, then cook the dried red pepper for 6 minutes, stirring. Remove, chop, and set aside. Add the head of garlic and tomato to the skillet and cook for 10 minutes, shaking the skillet occasionally. Transfer the tomatoes and dried red pepper to the casserole.

3. Cook the *olleta* for another 40 minutes over low heat, then add the rice and cook until the rice has absorbed the liquid and is tender, about 20 minutes. Discard the head of garlic and serve immediately.

Makes 6 to 8 servings

Moros y Cristianos (Valencia)

MOORS AND CHRISTIANS

This is a typical plate of the Levante, another name for the Valencian coast. It means Moors and Christians, probably referring, as Penelope Casas, the author of several books on Spanish food, says, to the religious and cultural tension between Muslims and Christians before the expulsion of the Muslims and Jews between 1492 and the great expulsion of 1609–1614, the "white" rice being the Christians and the "black" beans representing the swarthy Moors—that is, Muslims. The use of bacon fat and olive oil in the same dish seems to point to the problem faced by Moriscos and Marranos (respectively, Muslim and Jewish converts to Christianity), especially when we remember their problems with the Grand Inquisitor (see page 540). There is another connection, too, as we see when we compare this preparation to mujaddara *(page 602) and* kushary *(page 599).*

For the beans

- **1 pound dried black beans (about 2 cups), picked over and soaked in water to cover overnight**
- **1 quart cold water**
- **1 medium-size onion, cut in half**
- **3 garlic cloves, crushed**
- **1 bay leaf**

To flavor the beans

- **¼ cup extra virgin olive oil**
- **2 large garlic cloves, finely chopped**
- **½ cup diced slab bacon**
- **1 medium-size onion, finely chopped**
- **2 teaspoons all-purpose flour**
- **1 teaspoon paprika**
- **2 teaspoons salt**

For the rice

- **6 tablespoons (¾ stick) unsalted butter**
- **1½ cups medium-grain rice, rinsed well or soaked in water for 30 minutes and drained**
- **2 cups vegetable broth (page 54)**
- **1 teaspoon salt**
- **¼ teaspoon finely chopped fresh tarragon leaves**
- **¼ teaspoon finely chopped fresh thyme leaves**
- **3 fresh chervil leaves**
- **Finely chopped fresh parsley leaves for garnish**

1. Drain the soaking beans and place them in a large pot with the water, onion halves, crushed garlic cloves, and bay leaf. Bring to a boil, reduce the heat to very low, cover, and simmer for 1 hour.

2. Meanwhile, heat the olive oil in a medium-size skillet over medium-high heat, then cook together the chopped garlic, bacon, and all of the chopped onion except for 2 tablespoons, for 5 minutes, stirring frequently. Add the flour and paprika, mix well, and transfer to a plate. Set aside.

3. After the beans have cooked 1 hour, stir in the bacon mixture and salt. Simmer for another hour, but check to see that the beans are not overcooking. When the beans are cooked, set aside or drain if there is any remaining liquid. Remove and discard the halved onion and bay leaf.

4. In a large enameled cast-iron casserole or saucepan, melt 3 tablespoons of the butter over medium-high heat. When the butter has melted, cook the reserved 2 tablespoons chopped onion until soft, about 2 minutes, stirring. Add the rice and cook, stirring to coat all the grains, about 1 minute. Pour in the vegetable broth, salt, tarragon, thyme, and chervil. Reduce the heat to low, cover, and cook until the broth is absorbed, about 18 minutes, but check for doneness after 12 minutes. Turn the heat off and let sit for 10 minutes.

5. Preheat the oven to 400°F. Butter a ring mold and fill with the rice, packing it down. Dot the top of the rice with the remaining 3 tablespoons butter. Place in the oven until hot (how long this takes depends on how much earlier the rice was cooked). Turn the rice out into a round platter and fill the center with the hot black beans. Sprinkle with parsley if desired and serve.

Makes 4 to 6 servings

✣ ✣ ✣

WHEAT, millet, and barley were important Mediterranean grains. City granaries often contained as much millet as they did wheat, and millet was used for military stores. Venice was saved from the Genoese naval attack during the War of Chiogga in 1372 by its stores of millet. No wheat was harvested in Vicenza during the winter of 1564–1565, and almost the entire population lived off millet. It was the same during Venice's extreme food shortage of 1569, when ration tickets allowed two millet loaves per person per day. Millet was grain for dogs, poor man's food, along with pulses, broad beans, peas, lentils, and rye. Even today millet, along with sorghum, is subsistence food, used mostly as fodder for animals or among the destitute tribes of the Sahara. The reason millet is poor food is that wheat and rice taste better and are more easily digested.

Barley was considered a bread cereal. Homer had called barley "the marrow of men's bones."[87] The Persian traveler Nāṣir-i Khusraw (1003–1061?) describes barley as the only cereal being grown around Hebron in Palestine.[88] In the Languedoc by 1200, it was used for making polenta, but also associated with bread making, as a baking ordinance from 1196 at Montpellier proves. The rich ate wheat bread, but the rest of the population ate a coarse barley and wheat mixture or the heavy and hard-to-digest barley bread. They were barley eaters on the Mediterranean coast, but in the mountains—in the Alps, the Rouergue, the Haut-Cerdagne, and the Aquitaine basin—rye and oats replaced barley.[89] On the Greek island of Zante (Zákinthos), a bad harvest meant the villagers ate black barley bread. In Troy, they ate oatmeal bread. In Corsica, the substitute for wheat or barley bread was chestnut bread, known as "tree bread." Occasionally rice replaced bread, and in North Africa they would eat sorghum, in the form of bread, couscous, or porridge.

❈ *Dashīsha Bulbūla* (Berber)

BERBER-STYLE BARLEY COUSCOUS

The Berbers are a Hamitic people, the native inhabitants of North Africa whom the Arab invaders encoun-

*tered in the seventh and eighth centuries during the early expansion of their empire. At that time most Berbers were Christians and lived in the narrow fertile strip along the North African coast. They were nomadic and seminomadic people for whom Roman and Byzantine civilizations held no attraction. Islam, on the other hand, seemed to have a special allure for the Berbers, who felt akin to the Semitic Arabs. Islam was successful in making Arabic the language of these semibarbarous Berber hordes, and by the ninth century the Berbers were thoroughly Islamicized. The food of the Berbers was primitive, and barley—*shᶜīr *in Arabic or* timzin *in Berber—was the staple grain. Along the coast, barley bread and sardines were eaten while Berbers of the mountains ate barley with vegetables and occasionally some meat, often game such as gazelle, jerboa, and hare, as well as locusts and lizards. The arrival of the Arabs into Berber lands undoubtedly brought with it new aesthetic considerations in terms of taste and the role of gastronomy in society. This Berber recipe shows that influence; this is not subsistence food.*

In classical Arabic, the word dashīsha *refers to a porridge made of wheat grains that are skillet griddled over an open fire and crushed before being boiled with butter. Today, in North Africa the word* dashīsha *refers to grains in general, although more specifically to barley cooked in the style of a couscous, as well as some soups and porridges made from grains such as wheat and barley. The barley is processed in the same manner as the wheat, being sorted, cleaned, and grilled in a platterlike skillet called a* ghanāᶜā *over a fire. The grains are then pounded, sieved, and dried in the open air. A further sieving through a finer sieve allows for the larger grains to be retained, the so-called* dashīsha. *An immature barley is favored, called* marmaz *(also known as* farık *in Tunisia), and after it is grilled in the* ghanāᶜā *this young barley is called* malthūth, *and is usually made into a barley couscous by the poor. The Berbers also call this grilled barley* tundjifin.

The bulbūla *in the name of the recipe seems to refer to a kind of earthenware cooking vessel with a long beak or tube, probably a reference to some local tradition, for it is commonly made in a* couscousière. *This particular recipe is typical among Moroccan Berbers in the Rif or Anti-Atlas Mountains. Barley couscous is common among the Berbers, who also make it with wheat, in which case it would simply be called* siksu badawī*—that is, Berber couscous.*

The preparation of barley couscous follows the same rules for making hard wheat couscous. Read the box "Preparing Couscous" on page 666. Peeled barley grains can be found in Middle Eastern markets and whole food stores.

3 cups (1½ pounds) peeled barley grains
3 teaspoons salt
12 cups water
12 tablespoons extra virgin olive oil
1 small chicken (about 2½ pounds), cut into 4 pieces
¾ pound lamb shoulder, cut up
1 medium-size onion, chopped
2 carrots (about 3 ounces each)
1 large turnip (about ¾ pound), quartered
1 cup drained cooked chickpeas
2 teaspoons freshly ground black pepper
½ teaspoon saffron threads, toasted (page 521) and crumbled
2 teaspoons turmeric
2 teaspoons paprika
1 cinnamon stick
2 tablespoons unsalted butter or *samna* (clarified butter; page 189)
Leaves from a half bunch fresh coriander (cilantro), finely chopped
2 tablespoons finely chopped fresh parsley leaves
One 10-ounce piece pumpkin, quartered
1 large fresh artichoke heart, quartered
1 cup dried fava beans, soaked 24 hours in water to cover and peeled
1 ripe tomato, peeled, seeded, and chopped
1 small head cabbage (about ¾ pound), quartered
⅓ cup golden raisins

1. Place half the barley in a platter or earthenware dish with shallow sides. Dissolve 1 teaspoon of the

salt in 1 cup of the water. Spread the grains around and begin moistening it with ½ cup of the salted water, a little at a time, until all of the water is used—do not pour the water in all at once. Every time you add water, rub it into the grains, breaking up any lumps. Use up to a ¼ cup of water at first, working the grains with your fingers to separate them and moisten them evenly. Work in a circular, rotating motion, raking with your fingers. If the mixture becomes too wet, add a little dry barley grains and start again. The barley should be evenly wet, not soggy, with the grains separate.

2. Arrange the barley on a large white dish towel or a section of a sheet and dry for 1 to 2 hours (depending on the humidity in the air). Repeat the moistening process of step 1 again with the remaining water and leave to dry another hour. Using your fingers, brush the barley grains with up to ¼ cup of the olive oil so they are all coated. Transfer the grains to the top portion of the *couscousière*. Set aside until needed.

3. Put 7 cups of the water in the bottom portion of the *couscousière* with the chicken, lamb, onion, carrots, turnip, chickpeas, the remaining 2 teaspoons salt, the pepper, saffron, turmeric, paprika, cinnamon stick, 6 tablespoons olive oil, and the butter. Turn the heat to high, place the top portion of the *couscousière* over the broth, and cover it, and cook 1 hour. Remove the top portion of the *couscousière* and transfer the barley to a platter and leave until it's cool, 30 to 40 minutes. Meanwhile, turn the heat off under the broth.

4. Place the barley in the top portion of the *couscousière* again. Mix the remaining 2 tablespoons olive oil with your fingers into the barley. Add the coriander, parsley, pumpkin, artichoke heart, fava beans, tomato, and cabbage to the broth, adding a little water if necessary. Replace the top portion of the *couscousière* on the bottom portion, bring the broth to a boil, and cook over medium-high heat until the meat is tender, about 1 hour.

5. Remove the top portion of the *couscousière* and transfer the barley to a platter and leave until it's cool. Stir the raisins into the barley. Meanwhile, turn the heat off under the now much reduced broth again. Once the barley is ready to be cooked a third time, check the meat and vegetables in the broth to see if they are tender. If they are cooked, which they should be, remove them from the broth with a slotted ladle and set aside in a baking dish covered with aluminum foil in a warm oven. Check the seasoning of the broth and correct. Place the barley in the top portion of the *couscousière* again. Add the remaining 4 cups water to the broth and replace the top portion of the *couscousière* on the bottom portion, bring the broth to a boil and cook until the barley is tender, about 1 hour.

6. Remove the barley and transfer to a serving platter. Arrange the vegetables and meat on top of the barley and serve.

Makes 8 servings

PETRUS de Crescentiis (1230?–1321) was a Bolognese landowner who advised hard-working people to eat bread made of less refined cereals—for example sorghum, which he said was better for peasants.[90] At the same time another Bolognese landowner and agronomist, Paganino Bonafede, considered only the cultivation of wheat without so much as mentioning other grains like millet and sorghum.[91] A sixteenth-century novella by Francesco Straparola, a Lombard, has a peasant woman from Padua named Tia who laments her city because "You eat wheat-bread and I eat millet and sorghum bread and polenta." The various inferior corns are suitable for polenta and flatbreads, important for rural diet. The use of *pasta*

Petrus de Crescentiis (1230?–1321), a Bolognese landowner and author of *Liber ruralium commodorum*, discusses tree planting and grafting in this miniature on vellum illuminated at Bruges, Belgium, about 1470. M.232, f.27. The Pierpont Morgan Library, New York. THE PIERPONT MORGAN LIBRARY/ART RESOURCE.

secca, made with durum wheat, which we know existed in twelfth-century Sicily, was most likely found predominantly in cities, and was food for the rich.[92] The introduction of maize to northern Italy helped reduce problems of hunger, and its use as polenta was a natural result.

Polenta (Veneto)

The word polenta *derives from the* puls, *a kind of porridge, of the Romans who originally made it with various grains such as barley or millet. Once maize was introduced from the New World to northern Italy, shortly after 1500, it replaced panic (foxtail millet), millet, and sorghum in the Veneto and polenta evolved into what we know it as today. One story attributes the arrival of maize in Italy to the diplomat Pietro Martire d'Angera who, in 1494, had brought a few seeds, given to him as a gift in Madrid, straight from Columbus, by the Milanese Cardinal Ascanio Sforza.[93] Whatever the story, we do know that maize, popularly called corn, was first known as* maizium *(from the Arawak-Carib word* mahiz*), and* sorgo-turco *(Turkish sorghum) or* grano-turco *(Turkish grain) and that it was being cultivated in Polesina di Rovigo and Basso Veronese in 1554, probably as a result of the suggestion of the Cremonese scientist Giovanni Lamo, who proposed its cultivation.[94] Once the doctor and botanist Pierandrea Mattioli published his important study* Discorsi di pedacio Discoride Anazarbeo della materia medicinale *in Venice in 1559 and talked about* seminano gli Indiani questo suo grano, il quale chiamano Mahiz in questo modo *(the Indians sow this grain, and call it maize) and about how it was grown, maize was planted throughout the Veneto and polenta naturally developed.[95]*

The first cornmeal in the Padua plain must have been an exciting phenomenon. Here was this food that could be a startling yellow, looking fresher than any bread the peasants would see. Some people believe that polenta is a northern Italian specialty, but polenta is as popular in southern Italy, especially around Benevento and Avellino, where polenta and sausages is a favorite dish. In the Veneto they prefer their polenta compact and dense while the Piedmontese like it soft. The southerners make it the same way the Piedmontese do, slowly stirring for a long time, and then eating it soft and hot. Polenta-like dishes are also made in Corsica with chestnut flour and in North Africa with hard wheat flour.

Polenta is traditionally made in an all-copper concave cauldron called a paioli, *stirring the cornmeal in one direction for almost an hour. Today there are other methods of cooking polenta including baking, and the method I use here, just as good and much easier than*

A cook serves polenta to two men in the Veneto of the eighteenth century. Pietro Longhi (1702–1785). *The Polenta.* Ca'Rezzonico Museum, Venice. ALINARI/ART RESOURCE.

the traditional one, was developed by San Francisco chef and author Carlo Middione.

2 quarts water
1 tablespoon salt
2 cups fine- or medium-ground cornmeal

1. In the bottom half of a double boiler, pour enough water to reach and cover the bottom of the top part. Bring this water to a boil, then reduce the heat so the water is just under a bubble.

2. Directly over a burner, bring the 2 quarts water to a boil in the top portion of a double boiler. Add the salt.

3. Using a wooden spoon, stir the water in the top of the double boiler until you have created a whirlpool. Now quickly pour the cornmeal into the center of the whirlpool in a continuous, steady stream, not too fast, not too slow. Do not stop stirring. Continue to stir at a slower pace once all the cornmeal is in the pot. Reduce the heat to low and stir for 3 to 5 minutes while the polenta bubbles slightly. It will thicken.

4. Place the lid on the top portion and fit it into the bottom half of the double boiler. Cook for 1½ hours, stirring in one direction every 30 minutes. When the polenta is done, it will be a thick Cream of Wheat consistency. It can be eaten like this or, if you intend on grilling it or eating it later, pour it into a baking dish to solidify, then cut into rectangles or squares.

Makes 8 servings

CONCLUSION

MEDITERRANEAN peoples were bedeviled for centuries with the constant, unending, and unrelieved preoccupation of finding food. The most basic food was bread, and bread was made from grain. Bread became the foundation of the diet and other foods, foods eaten with bread, were in the vernacular *companaticum*, accompaniments of bread. If there was no bread, there was famine.

The lessons of grain were simple: When scarcity appeared in one place, the price of grain rose. Traders in grain became rich, and their riches would later finance the Renaissance as well as the rice paddies of Lombardy and the kitchens of the dukes of Ferrara. Agriculture was the leading industry of the Mediterranean in the sixteenth century. Rice, barley, rye, oats, sorghum, millet, and maize all played an important role in the Mediterranean, even if they never became the overall staple that wheat did. The most desirable bread was wheat bread, the bread of princes, a bread made from soft wheat. But another kind of wheat, hard wheat, led to new food inventions, such as macaroni, couscous, and hardtack, that played a role in the alleviation of famine. These foods were, at first, foods for the rich, but they soon became common, and today one can hardly think of Italy without macaroni or North Africa without couscous. The story of macaroni, couscous, and hardtack, all made from hard wheat and today foods nearly synonymous with Mediterranean feasts, will be told in the next chapter.

❖ 10 ❖

HARD WHEAT AND ITS FAMOUS INVENTIONS

IN 1274, the most famous of medieval travelers, the Venetian Marco Polo, embarked on a voyage of discovery to the unknown lands of the East. Twenty-four years later he returned to Venice with fabulous stories about exotic places that became the major source of information about the East during the Renaissance. Legend has it that among the marvelous things he encountered in China was macaroni and that he introduced it to Europe—but legend it is. The real story of macaroni is a complex one and, appropriately, as slippery as a wet noodle. In this chapter the complicated story of macaroni—the generic term for all dried alimentary pastes made from hard wheat and water or eggs cooked in broth or water, also called pasta or noodles—will be set out as an inquiry into the meaning, origin, and importance of this food, as well as of two other important products also made from hard wheat—couscous and hardtack.[1]

MACARONI

THE invention of macaroni (what the Italians call *pasta secca*, and which specifies dried—versus fresh, *pasta fresca*—pasta) has been attributed to the Etruscans, the Chinese, the Greeks, and the Romans, as well as the Arabs. In this chapter I will try to lay out the history of macaroni as best we know it. But first we must ask what macaroni is and why it is important.

The way the term macaroni is used by scholars is determined by the kind of wheat used to make it. The mystery over the origin of macaroni is clouded by the fact that food writers traditionally have failed to discuss and distinguish the many varieties of wheat.[2] Establishing the locale or era for the origin of macaroni hinges on identifying not its particular shapes, nor that it is made of flour and water, but the kind of wheat used to make it. If mixing wheat flour and water together and stretching the dough into threads is what is meant by pasta, macaroni, or noodles, that definition tells us nothing; *it is not historically heuristic.* The reason scholars are interested in the origin of macaroni is that the answer can con-

A WARNING ABOUT WHEAT TALK

The discussion in this chapter is based on the distinction between hard wheat (Triticum turgidum *var.* durum) *and soft wheat or bread wheat* (T. aestivum) *in medieval times. In Roman times, and through the medieval era, flour was of much poorer quality than today. It was not thoroughly cleaned, and with the primitive milling technology that existed right up to the beginning of the modern era (c. 1700) the grain was coarsely ground. Sieves also had not improved over time, and even first grade flour was much coarser than what we think of as good breadmaking flour. Medieval milling technology was unable to grind hard wheat flour fine enough for bread baking, therefore wheat bread was made from soft wheat, also called bread wheat. This medieval hard wheat flour was used for other purposes than breadmaking, such as in porridges, and for the invention of new foods such as macaroni, couscous, and hardtack.*

But as any modern baker knows, today there are many varieties of wheat, including wheat blends, that can be used for breadmaking. All-purpose flour is a blend of soft and hard wheat to which nutrients have been added. Today's bread flour can be made from both soft and hard wheat.

tribute to a better understanding of the role a new food played in subsequent political and economic developments. Ascribing the word *macaroni* to an alimentary paste made from soft wheat, as many food writers do when discussing the history of macaroni, is incorrect, although quite commonly and understandably done because there is no unique word to indicate macaroni made with soft wheat. That filiform, round, cylindrical, or sheet dough products made from a mixture of water and the flour from cereal grains existed for a very long time is not in question.[3] That fact is not of interest to historians. After all, some Middle Eastern flatbreads are made of wheat flour and water and are rolled out as thin as lasagne. What is *historically* important about the invention of macaroni, the sine qua non of its definition, is that it is made with a particular *type* of wheat flour, *Triticum turgidum* var. *durum*. This wheat, which apparently evolved through cultivation from emmer wheat in an as yet undetermined location (Abyssinia has been suggested), is mixed with liquid to form an alimentary paste that is dried, then stored for long periods of time and cooked by boiling or (less commonly) steaming in or over water or broth. This particular kind of wheat, commonly known as hard wheat, semolina, or durum wheat, is unique because of its high gluten and low moisture content, which distinguishes it in a significant way from soft wheat or bread wheat *(Triticum aestivum),* the major wheat known by the ancient Greeks and Romans. These characteristics of hard wheat are important because, first, it prevents the stretching and breakage of pasta during the curing and drying process and, second, because it maintains its texture and taste better during the cooking process than does soft wheat.[4]

Did the Etruscans, Chinese, Greeks, Romans, or Arabs know about hard wheat? And if they did, did they invent any macaroni-like foods to take advantage of it? Before we can even begin to look at who invented macaroni, we must examine the current research concerning hard wheat. Knowledge of the literature of cytogenetics, molecular archeology, paleobotany, and agricultural history is essential in being able to talk intelligently about the origins of hard wheat and hard wheat food products such as macaroni. Robert Sallares explored this question in what is probably the fullest and most informed account of the grains of the ancient world, *The Ecology of the Ancient Greek World*, published in 1991. Sallares discusses the first appearance of hard wheat *(Triticum turgidum* var. *durum),* which he places in very ancient times, and argues that modern methods of molecular archeology can distinguish between soft wheat *(T. aestivum)* and hard wheat. But Professor Andrew M. Watson examined the sources that Sallares cites and points out that none of them actually supports this claim. In fact, it is impossible to determine whether carbonized grains and rachis internodes of free threshing wheat are hard wheat or soft wheat.[5]

Professors Daniel Zohary, Maria Hopf, and W. van Zeist, cytogeneticists and paleobotanists cited by Sallares, do offer a theory about the first appearance of hard wheat, but one based not on the identification of archeological remains but on deduction. Although taxonomists classify emmer as a hard wheat, the wheat designated as *Triticum turgidum* var. *durum* developed as a mutation from emmer. It is known that soft wheat is the result of hybridization of cultivated emmer *(T. dicoccum)* and a wild grass, *Aegilops squarrosa*. Zohary argues, convincingly, that this hybridization could not have occurred until sedentary agriculture using emmer had spread into the zones where *A. squarrosa* grew wild. He dates this occurrence somewhere around 6000–5000 B.C. He concludes that all of the earlier finds of naked wheat—and there are a number of these—must be of hard wheat, which is thus the more ancient grain. (Naked wheats are wheats where threshing releases the naked kernels of grain, in contrast to hulled wheats, where the product of threshing are spikelets not grains.) Zohary's deduction is based on the information currently available about the spread of agriculture in the Near East and on the present-day distribution of *A. squarrosa*. Andrew Watson argues that, in fact, we must assume that current hypotheses about the timing of the spread of agriculture in the Near East are at best tentative and likely to be overturned by future excavations; and it can in no way be supposed that the ancient distribution of *A. squarrosa* was the same as that of today.[6]

Professor Andrew M. Watson's book *Agricultural Innovation in the Early Islamic World: The Diffusion of Crops and Farming Techniques, 700–1100*, published in 1983, discusses the rise and spread of hard wheat. Watson was struck by the apparent absence in ancient writings on agriculture and natural history of any clear description of hard wheat. As these sources discuss grains in great detail, this omission is truly remarkable. Sallares addresses this by pointing out that second-century Greek physician Galen speaks of a type of wheat whose grain was particularly heavy, hard, and "vitreous." He thinks this must be hard wheat. Watson believes it could also be soft wheat, which, when grown in hot, dry places, produces grains with the characteristics described by Galen. Watson also points out that in a recent discussion of the grains described in Roman literature, Professor Renzo Landi, an agronomist at the University of Florence, has found nothing that seems to refer to hard wheat.[7]

Another factor influencing Watson's judgment on this matter is the absence in ancient literature of any description of the more obvious uses of hard wheat. With the kind of milling equipment available to the ancients, it would have been impossible to obtain a fine flour from the grains of hard wheat and thus virtually impossible to make bread from it. The obvious alternative uses for hard wheat are porridges, couscous, and *pasta secca*. According to the ancient writers, porridges were made from other grains, and there is no mention whatever of dishes resembling couscous or of *pasta secca*.[8] As best we can tell from the latest results of molecular archeology, the Romans and Greeks did not know hard wheat and therefore did not invent macaroni.[9]

Is it so important to know who invented macaroni and when? I believe it is because the invention of macaroni was not only of culinary interest but also historically important for three reasons. First, the perennial famines of the times could be reduced and controlled because dried pasta was a food with a very long shelf life. Second, governments and speculators could warehouse food supplies for long periods of time to counteract years of low production and to offset inflation caused by high prices and demand. Third, a plentiful supply of hard wheat (especially in the form of hardtack, but also *pasta secca*) allowed longer sea voyages, opening up an age of exploration.

So who invented macaroni? The invention of macaroni has been attributed to the Etruscans, the pre-Roman civilization of the Italian peninsula. The Italian culinary authority Massimo Alberini's claim that the Etruscans knew *pasta secca*, repeated by many authors, is now known to be false. He claimed that the painted stucco reliefs in the Tomba dei Rilievi at Cerveteri (Caere) show a table used to make the pasta dough, known as the *spianatora* (rolling out table) in Roman dialect, a rolling pin, knives, and even a little indented pasta wheel that cut crinkly-edged lasagne. Archeologists say that nothing of the sort is shown.[10] Furthermore, as I've mentioned, there is no evidence to suggest that the Etruscans grew hard wheat.

Let's turn to China. Did Marco Polo bring macaroni back from China? Did he bring back a hard wheat dried pasta? No, he didn't. Although he encountered wheat in China, what he actually brought back was another food from another country. In the kingdom of Fansur, on the western coast of Sumatra, Marco Polo encountered a food made from the starchy flour of the fruit of either the breadfruit tree *(Artocarpus altilis* syn. *A. communis)* or the sago tree *(Metroxylon laevis* syn. *M. rumphii*). He tells us in his diaries that the flour obtained from the tree is made into *lagana* (or *lasagne*) in strips and that its taste resembles that of barley.[11]

We know Marco Polo didn't discover macaroni in the Far East, for two reasons. First, it is clear that he is already familiar with lasagne and vermicelli and other pastas from his descriptions of the various alimentary pastes he encounters in the East. Furthermore, whenever he encounters wheat in the form of vermicelli or lasagne (undoubtedy soft wheat) he makes no mention of the most unique properties of hard wheat—namely its shelf life when made into various food products and its gluten content. In Peking (Beijing), he encountered a pasta made from wheat and tells us that the Chinese make it into lasagne and other pastas.[12] In comparison, the twelfth-century Chinese traveler Chau Ju-kua, while traveling in Spain before the birth of Marco Polo, notes that the wheat of Muslim Spain is kept in silos and does not spoil for ten years. This would hardly be notable if the Chinese knew of hard wheat.[13] Second, when Marco Polo describes the dough that people have long taken to be macaroni, he uses the words *vermicelli, lasagne,* and *lagana*. *Lagana* was not a word the Chinese or Sumatrans used, but was a word with which he was already familiar. In fact, Marco Polo was already familiar with *pasta secca* in Italy before he set out on his journey. *Lagana* was a Medieval Latin word that meant either a kind of thin crêpe or a sheet of dough. This word *lagana* is, in fact, proposed as the etymological root of *lasagne*, which it very well could be. Even today *lagana* is a word used in Calabria in southern Italy to mean a wide *tagliatelle*. *Lagana* may have been lasagne but was it macaroni—that is, *pasta secca*, the dried pasta made from hard wheat *(Triticum turgidum* var. *durum)* that is the defining element of what constitutes macaroni?[14]

Many food writers do not answer that question, ignoring the distinctions between wheat types, and simply see in the existence of the word *lagana* the proof that the Romans invented macaroni. They claim that the Medieval Latin word *lagana* used by Marco Polo referred to a *pasta secca* invented by the Romans. The medieval *lagana* is related, they say, to the classical word *laganum*, which they also take to mean the *pasta secca* known as lasagne. But an examination of the works of Horace, Celsus, Apicius, and Petronius, where the classical Latin words *laganum* or *lasanum* appear in various forms, shows that it does not mean *pasta secca*. The Latin word *laganum* is derived from the Greek *lasanon*, a word that can refer to a chamber pot, a cooking pot, a kind of trivet, or a large minced cake made with flour and oil.[15] The Greek use of the word *lasanon* appears in Hesychius to mean a kind of focaccia made of wheat and oil. In the Latin descriptions of *laganum* it seems to refer to a kind of cake or crêpe made of flour and oil that is deep-fried, not boiled, or a kind of *marmite* in which it perhaps was fried.[16] In Calabria, it also has come to mean, through the Latin, pasta sheets in which you roll *torta* or *pasticcio*.[17] More important, we know that as early as mid-fourteenth-century Sicily, *laganum* was a dough fried in oil and called *crispella* in the vernacular, while *lagana* was bread boiled in water and also called *lasagni* or *maccharruni*.[18] The fact that *lagana* can be a flat dough product and is derived from a Greek word has led some people to claim the ancient Greeks as the inventors of macaroni.

Did the ancient Greeks or Romans invent macaroni and did they know of hard wheat? It does not appear so. The classical *tracta*, a dough product taken by some writers to be macaroni, mentioned in the Roman writer Apicius's cookbook was not *pasta secca*. Classical Greek descriptions of *tracta* make it seem to be a dried dough product, perhaps a biscuit.[19]

Today, macaroni popularly refers to a tubular pasta three to five inches in length, but before the sixteenth century, macaroni meant not only *pasta secca* but also boiled bread. In fact, in the fourteenth century, the Sicilian lexicographer Angelo Senisio defined *maccheroni* as *panis lixis in aqua* (bread boiled in water), which is a description identical to the medieval Arab *tharīd* (page 560) that might be the root of one of the medieval Arabic words for macaroni, *iṭrīya*. Macaroni also once meant what we today call gnocchi. This sense was used in 1570, when the Renaissance chef Bartolomeo Scappi described making macaroni. He said that after you knead the dough you "*faccianosi i gnocchi cioè maccaroni*" (make gnocchi, that is, macaroni).[20]

The origin of macaroni lies not with the Etruscans, Greeks, Romans, or Chinese, but apparently with the Arabs. The earliest evidence of a true macaroni occurs at the juncture of medieval Sicilian, Italian, and Arab cultures.[21] The history of macaroni in Italy and Sicily is early indeed. An item on the dinner menu of the kitchen of the bishop of Luni in a document from August 17, 1188, mentions a food that might be macaroni. It doesn't specify what type of pasta nor how it is cooked.[22] Another unclear reference to what might be *pasta secca* is mentioned in a Genoese notary document of a woolmaker in 1244, who writes about "pasta made into strings."[23] A clearer reference to macaroni, used to mean *pasta secca* and not gnocchi or boiled bread, is in another Genoese notary document of a soldier named Ponzio Bastono dated 1279, whose inventory includes a *barixella una plena de maccaronis* (a chest full of macaroni), while one of the earliest mentions of vermicelli, meaning *pasta secca*, is found in a Pisan document from February 13, 1284, where a baker hires a helper *in faciendis et vendendis vermicellis* (in making and selling vermicelli).[24] Early recipes for vermicelli, such as the one in the anonymous fourteenth-century Tuscan cookery manuscript *Libro della cocina*, appear to be Arab influenced, as the recipe calls for a sauce of almond milk, sugar, and saffron with the boiled vermicelli.[25]

Sicily is another locus for the early appearance of macaroni. Italian cookery works of the fourteenth century also mention *pasta secca* by the generic name of *tria*, derived from the Arabic word *iṭrīya*. This was the word used to mean vermicelli by al-Idrīsī, the Arab court geographer of the Norman king of Sicily, Roger II, in his book completed in 1154, nearly one hundred and fifty years before Marco Polo (died 1323) returned from China.[26] This twelfth-century Sicilian pasta, the earliest clear reference we have to *pasta secca*, was exported to Calabria, and commercial contracts from Genoa between 1157 and 1160 recorded by the notary Giovanni Scriba show large imports of Sicilian pasta.[27] There are two other interesting descriptions of macaroni in fourteenth- and fifteenth-century Sicily from other sources. In the first, two Jesuit fathers tell us of the life of Guglielmo Cuffitella, some centuries after his death in 1404. He was born in Sicily and was known as William the Hermit and was beatified by Pope Paul III in 1537. In their description of his life they mention macaroni and lasagne: *Invitaverat Guillelmum aliquando compater suus Guiccionius ad prandium, eique aposuerat maccarones seu lagana cum pastillis* (William is asked whether he would like macaroni or lasagne pie). Although they are contemporaries, the *lagana* in this text refers to sheets of *pasta secca* that are boiled in water, unlike in Senisio, where they are fried in oil. In the second, Nicolo' Valle compiled a Sicilian-Latin dictionary in the late fifteenth century that was eventually published in 1510. He described macaroni *(maccarone)* as being boiled and its shape as round, identical to the Tunisian *muḥammaṣ*.[28] Boccaccio (1313–1375) mentions macaroni and ravioli in the *Decameron* in the mid-fourteenth century, as do numerous other sources.[29]

The word *iṭrīya* has a long history in Near Eastern languages. It derives originally from the Greek word *itrion* via the Aramaic, a word meaning a thin cake or a thin, unleavened dough product before the Christian era. In the fourteenth-century dictionary of the lexicographer al-Fīrūzābādī (1329–c. 1414), the *Mukhtār al-qāmūs, iṭrīya* is said to refer to a pasta-like thread made from flour and almost certainly made from hard wheat;[30] and the word is also used to designate a kind of *pasta secca* in the thirteenth-century cookery book of al-Baghdādī (written in 1226), the *Kitāb waṣf al-aṭʿima al-muʿtāda,* and in the medical treatise of Ibn Buṭlān (died c. 1068), the famed *Taqwīm al-ṣiḥḥa*, translated into Latin as the *Tacuinum sanitatis*.[31] Although Ibn Buṭlān wrote in the eleventh century, his manuscript was constantly revised until the fourteenth century. The first clear pictorial depictions of macaroni are in the Vienna, Paris, and Rome manuscripts of the *Tacuinum*. In the Vienna and Rome manuscripts it is called *trij*, and in the Paris manuscript it is called *formentini*. In all these illustrations the pasta depicted looks like fettuccine or *tagliatelle*.[32]

Iṭrīya also appears in the dictionaries of ninth-century lexicographer Ishu Bar ʿAlī (flourished ninth century) and al-Jawharī (died c. 1002–1003), and although it is clear that the word referred to pasta, it is not clear if this pasta was made from hard wheat.[33] It is quite hard to distinguish hard wheat in descriptions from medieval Arabic since there is no exact word that means hard wheat, although there are many words for wheat.[34] Bar ʿAlī describes a pasta that resembles a cloth, which might have been similar to lasagne, while al-Jawharī states that it is a sort of food similar to *ḥibrīya*, or hairs (flakes, perhaps).[35] Both of these might have been made from soft wheat, but it seems to the economic historian Professor Andrew Watson that these sources tell of early experimentation to make *pasta secca* from hard wheat.[36]

By the fifteenth century, macaroni was a commonly known, if not commonly eaten, food in Italy. In a Tuscan recipe from 1417, the merchant Saminiato de' Ricci casually mentions the making of lasagne and macaroni *(a fare lasangnie e maccheroni)*.[37] In fact, by the early sixteenth century, macaroni is common enough in Italy that Teofilo Folengo (1491–1544) can launch a literary style known as the *ars macaronica*, the macaronic way—a mixing of Mantuan patois,

Latin, and Italian—denoting something gross, crude, and rustic, like macaroni made with "flour and water and mixed with cheese and butter."[38]

Lasagne is thought to be one of the earliest forms of *pasta secca*. An intriguing line on the history of lasagne has been proposed by several scholars. They suggest that *lasagne* may be derived from the Arabic word *lawzīnaj*, a medieval Arabic word that denotes a thin cake of pastry, usually made with almonds. This cake was cut into ribbons, quadrangles, and rhomboids. It has been described as a food like *qaṭā'if* (page 722), a kind of pastry made from both soft and hard wheat and almond oil.[39] There are many medieval recipes for *lawzīnaj*, such as the one in the dietetic manual of Ibn Jazla (known as Gege in Latin), a Baghdad physician (d. 1100), called *Kitāb al-minhāj al-bayān fīmā yastaᶜmiluhu al-insān,* which was translated into Latin as the *Liber de ferculis et condimentis* (Book of dishes and seasonings). He writes that *lawzīnaj* is finer than *qaṭā'if* and more quickly digested, but less nutritious. It is made with ground almonds and sugar and melted with rose water until a kind of dough is formed from which the *lawzīnaj* is made. That both proposed etymologies for *lasagne*, one from the vulgar Latin and the other from medieval Arabic, seem to describe some kind of fried crêpe or cake leads me to believe that the circle of culinary borrowing is a lot more familiar than the proponents of either argument admit.[40]

The first written Italian lasagne recipe is found in an anonymous fourteenth-century cookery manuscript from the Angevin court in Naples, called *Liber de coquina* (Book of cooking). The sheets of lasagne are boiled and layered with ground spices and grated cheese in a bowl or on a trencher. In these medieval recipes "spices" can mean salt and pepper or sugar or some combination such as salt, pepper, cinnamon, cloves, nutmeg, and often saffron.[41] We also know that by the late 1370s, lasagne was being layered with cheese, as it is today, through a rather macabre description by Marchione di Coppo Stefani, who wrote that the corpses of the victims of the Black Death some thirty years before in Florence were layered in open pits like "lasagne."[42]

An Italian scholar, Luigi Sada, who has also authored several cookbooks, speculates that this early experimentation with hard wheat was found among nomadic Arabs who needed a transportable food that would not spoil.[43] I don't agree entirely with this line of thinking, but it does raise an interesting question: Was macaroni invented to solve the problem of food supply for people on the move? Rather than nomads, perhaps the inventor of macaroni was some unknown Arab general of military logistics who had the responsibility of feeding the large and rapidly moving armies of early Islam across the arid reaches of North Africa and the Middle East. In any case, it seems that macaroni may have been a wheat product invented to replace or improve on the then common barley products, such as the typical poor man's food, *sawīq. Sawīq* was a dried barley product used on long journeys that was reconstituted with water or milk when required. In affluent households, *sawīq* was made with fine wheat sweetened with sugar and other ingredients such as pomegranate seeds. A hard wheat macaroni may have been invented to provide a better-tasting food for people on the move, as well as for rich urban dwellers.

The very first macaroni products were likely to have been little balls of pasta, which were easily stored and could cook quickly in a region that lacked firewood and therefore the ability to keep fires going for a long time. This new food was also likely to have been made to resemble other grain foods Arabs were already familiar with, such as millet, barley, and rice. As far as extruded pastas go, like our contemporary tubular macaroni, their history before the twentieth century is unknown.

Spain is also a locus for the early history of macaroni. Aḥmad ibn Muḥammad al-Rāzī (888?–955?), the Arab geographer, describes the existence of hard wheat in Toledo, saying that "The air [of Toledo] is excellent and grain stays a long time without changing.[44] Although it's true that the Roman writer Varro (116–27? B.C.) also described wheat in the same manner, as being storable for fifty years, al-Rāzī's description can only be a description of hard wheat because his comment is not an isolated observation; it is repeated by other observers during the same period.[45]

In the anonymous thirteenth-century Hispano-Muslim cookbook *Kitāb al-ṭabīkh fī al-Maghrib wa'l-Āndalus*, we find some of the earliest references to macaroni. We are told that there are three ways of making it. It can be "made round like a coriander seed," "thin with the thinness of *kāghiṭ* [sheet of paper] and which is woman's food," and "lengthened in the mode of wheat" [*fidawsh*, vermicelli].[46] The coriander seed–type appears to be a form of *pasta secca*, called *maccarone* in fifteenth century Sicily, that later became known as *maghribiyya* in Syria, also known as the name of a dish (page 661), and the *muḥammaṣ* of Tunisia and the *burkūkis* of Algeria. The one with the thinness of *kāghiṭ* sounds much like lasagne. "It is cooked with zucchini, aromatics and fat; and then there is the kind like *qataif* [sic]." This *qataif* is the *qaṭā'if* mentioned above, a kind of pastry made from both soft and hard wheat and almond oil. The *Kitāb al-ṭabīkh* instructs the cook to cook *fidawsh* in the same manner as you would macaroni *(iṭrīya)*. From the word *al-fidawsh* came the Spanish word for spaghetti, *fideos*, as well as similar words in other Iberian and northern Italian dialects.[47] The *Kitāb al-ṭabīkh* gives a recipe for macaroni:

> Take shoulder, leg, breast and loin and some fat. Cut it up and put in a stewpot with salt, onion, black pepper, dry coriander and olive oil. Cook on a moderate heat until ripe. Immediately remove from the stewpot and clarify the sauce. Return to the pot and add butter, softened fat and sweet oil, bring to a boil and add the *fidawsh*, boiling furiously. Sprinkle with cinnamon and ginger and serve.[48]

This recipe certainly sounds like a remote ancestor of the contemporary Valencian recipe *fideuà al estilo de Gandía,* which uses fish instead of meat.

Fideuà al Estilo de Gandía (Valencia)

FIDEOS IN THE STYLE OF GANDÍA

This dish is essentially the pasta version of arròs a banda *(page 425). It is cooked in a paella pan with* fideos *no. 168, which are like thick two-inch-long spaghetti formed into nests. It is cooked with small additions of broth and water until done. Llorenç Millo, the Catalan culinary historian, tells us that* fideuà *began as a dish prepared by fishermen. The home of this dish is Gandía, a little town on the coast up the road from Denia, although my most memorable* fideuà *was at the Voramar restaurant on the* playa *(the strand) of Peñíscola.*

12 littleneck clams, scrubbed, soaked for 1 hour in cold water to cover with 1 tablespoon baking soda, and drained
3/4 cup extra virgin olive oil
1 large onion, chopped
6 large garlic cloves, 4 finely chopped and 2 peeled
4 ripe tomatoes (about 1 1/2 pounds), peeled, seeded, and finely chopped
5 cups water
1 cup dry white wine
Salt and freshly ground black pepper to taste
Bouquet garni, tied in cheesecloth, consisting of 1 bay leaf, 6 sprigs each fresh thyme and parsley, and 1 teaspoon fennel seeds or 1 fennel stalk with leaves
1 1/2 pounds fish for broth: 2 porgy (scup), butterfish, or Pacific kingfish, 5 fresh sardines, and 1 mackerel, cut up, and 1 bluefish or mahimahi head (or 1/2 pound bluefish fillet)

1 pound fresh shrimp with heads (½ pound headless shrimp), saving the heads and/or shells for the fish broth
Pinch of saffron threads, crumbled
1 teaspoon paprika
¼ teaspoon cayenne pepper
1 small onion, very finely chopped
2 tablespoons very finely chopped fresh parsley leaves
2¼ pounds mixed fish steaks or fillets (¾ pound monkfish, hake, cod, scrod, or pollack; ¾ pound striped bass, Atlantic kingfish, bluefish, Spanish mackerel, dogfish, or shark; ¾ pound red snapper, grouper, redfish, or wolffish)
2 dried chili peppers
¾ pound *fideos* no. 168, *gemelli* no. 63, *perciatelli*, or spaghetti broken into 2-inch lengths

1. Put the clams in a small pot and turn the heat to medium-high. Once the clams have all opened, about 6 minutes, remove. Remove the clams from the shells and set aside in the refrigerator. Strain the broth through a fine-mesh strainer and set aside. Discard the shells and any clams that remain tightly shut.

2. In a stockpot or large casserole, heat ¼ cup of the olive oil over medium heat, then cook the large onion, half of the chopped garlic cloves, and 3 of the chopped tomatoes until saucy, 10 to 12 minutes, stirring often so the garlic doesn't burn. Pour in the water, wine, and reserved clam broth and season with salt and pepper. Add the bouquet garni, cut-up fish for broth, and shrimp shells (keep the shrimp and all other fish refrigerated until needed). Bring to a boil, reduce the heat to low, and simmer for 2 hours. Strain the broth through a fine-mesh strainer (you should have about 6 cups).

3. In a mortar, pound together the whole garlic cloves, saffron, paprika, cayenne, and ½ teaspoon salt until completely mashed. Transfer to a 2-cup measuring glass and blend with 1 cup of the fish broth.

4. In a casserole, heat ¼ cup of the olive oil over medium-high heat, then cook the small onion, the remaining chopped garlic cloves and tomato, and the parsley until the onion is soft, about 6 minutes, stirring. Add the fish fillets and cook until all sides are well coated, 2 to 3 minutes. Add the reserved fish broth, bring to a boil, and cook for 2 to 3 minutes, shaking the casserole occasionally. Add the shrimp and cook another 2 minutes at a boil, shaking the casserole. Add the reserved clams just long enough to heat them, about 30 seconds. Remove the fish, shrimp, and clams with a slotted ladle, set aside, and keep warm, covered with a sheet of aluminum foil. Strain the fish broth, reserving 3 cups and storing the rest for another use.

5. In a paella pan or large skillet, heat the remaining ¼ cup olive oil over medium-high heat, then fry the crushed garlic cloves and chili peppers until the garlic begins to turn light brown. Remove and discard the garlic and chilies. Add the pasta, stirring well so the pasta is coated with oil, and cook for 2 minutes. Add the reserved fish broth and the garlic/saffron broth, bring to a boil, and cook for 10 minutes, uncovered. Do not stir the pasta, although you can shake the pan while there is plenty of liquid. Remove from the heat, cover, and let the pasta rest until tender, about 5 minutes. Serve the pasta as a first course and the fish as a second course.

Makes 4 to 6 servings

* * *

By the fourteenth century, two Catalan works, the anonymous cookbook *Libre de sent soví* and a medical treatise by Arnold of Vilanova, both speak of *aletria*, a word derived from the same Arabic word *iṭrīya*.[49] In the Catalan works, as with the early Italian cookery books, *aletria*, or macaroni, is boiled with almond milk.[50] Arnold of Vilanova has a recipe for "*alatria*," about which he says, *"et idem iudicium est de tri, quod vulgariter dicitur alatria"* (it is the same as *tri [fideus]*, which the common people call *alatria*).[51]

The word *macaroni* has an unknown etymology. At some point around the twelfth or thirteenth century it came to mean *pasta secca*, although the more familiar word *tria* or *trij* continued to be used it Italy.[52] In the Middle East, the word for macaroni during this period of time was either *rishta* (or *erişte* in Turkish), from the Persian word for "threads," or *iṭrīya*, as well as a few other words mentioned above. The fourteenth-century Arab traveler Ibn Baṭṭūṭa described the *rishta* he encountered in Anatolia as a kind of *shᶜiriyya,* a word that even today means vermicelli. Italian dictionaries admit the word *macaroni*'s *(maccherone)* obscure origin, suggesting as one possible derivation the Greek word *makaria*, meaning "food of the blessed." The suggestion that the word *macaroni* comes from the Greek may have its origins with the travel diaries of Ortensio Landi (1512–1553), a doctor from Modena who wrote about macaroni in Sicily and described it as having the name of the beatified *(il nome dal beatificare)*.[53] Another suggestion is that the word derives from *maccare*, a now archaic verb meaning "to knead."

Modern Arabic dictionaries usually tell us that the word *macaroni* is a loan word from Italian. On the other hand, Khmaïs Ouled-Abdessayed, a doctoral candidate in Arabic linguistics at the University of Tunis, suggests some circumstantial evidence that the word may derive from the Arabic. A very old form of *pasta secca*, still known today in Tunisia as *duwayda*, meaning "inchworm," is a kind of vermicelli broken into one-inch lengths. By taking the two ends of a strand of fresh *duwayda* and attaching them they are called *qaran*, coming from the Arabic verb *qarana*, "to attach," whose past participle is *ma-qrūn*. Once the ends of the *duwayda* are attached, they are referred to by the participial adjective *maq(a)rūna*, possibly giving us the word "macaroni."[54] Intriguing as this suggestion is, unfortunately I have never come across written evidence of such a pasta existing in medieval Tunisia, so we must withhold our judgment about this etymology. But we do know that *duwayda* did exist in fifteenth-century Tunisia and in the Ahaggar of the Sahara. In medieval Tunisia, *duwayda* was typically eaten with chicken on ᶜĀshūra, the tenth day of the Muslim month of Muharram, sacred to the Shias because Husayn, the son of ᶜAlī, the Prophet Muhammad's faithful follower and the fourth caliph, was martyred on this day at Karbala in Iraq, marking the origin of the Sunni-Shia schism.[55]

The evidence is clear that by the fourteenth century, macaroni was well known. In Sicily, there are documents from 1371 saying that the prices of *maccherone* and *lasagne* in Palermo are triple that of bread, and bourgeois households usually have a *sbriga*, a wooden instrument for beating, kneading, and compacting the pasta dough.[56] Much of the early history of macaroni focuses on Sicily. We don't know if that is where it was invented, but we do know that it was a food eaten by the privileged aristocracy and by the Jewish population. One historian, Professor Maurice Aymard, suggests that Sicilian Jews inherited the culinary practices of Arab-Norman Sicily, and this accounts for the prominent role that the manufacture of macaroni had in Sicily. Macaroni was common in Sicily by the fifteenth century, but not particularly so among the common people. Our evidence comes from the tax collector who taxed *vermicelli, maccaruni, cuscuso, lasagne, tagliarini,* and *tutti le cosi fini di semola* (all fine things made of semolina) in block. By 1597, *vivande di pasta* (pasta food) was divided into dry pasta *(pasta secca or axutta)* and fresh pasta *(bagnata)*.[57] By the late eighteenth century, macaroni was the food of the common people in Italy.[58]

Pasta Casareccio (Italy)

HOMEMADE PASTA

In southern Italy and Sicily, pasta secca *is traditionally made only with durum semolina (hard wheat) and water. Today, as in northern Italy, it is also made with white flour (soft, hard, or a blend of wheat), which is easier to work with, but heavier if eggs instead of water are used. Hard wheat flour, sold for pasta making as durum wheat or durum semolina, is sometimes labeled in supermarkets as "pasta flour." Bulk durum wheat flour can also be found through wholesalers, in whole food markets, and in Italian grocery stores. This recipe can be used for all the pasta recipes in the book.*

Making your own pasta is an easy task that requires only the purchase of a pasta rolling machine. You knead by hand, but use the machine for rolling. The electric pasta-extrusion machines have you put the flour and liquid into a receptacle; the machine kneads the dough and then extrudes it through a variety of dies so you can make flat and tubular pasta. These typically are unable to make wide lasagne pasta and do not knead the dough satisfactorily, to my mind, except for a few passable machines. I prefer to use an Italian-made pasta-rolling machine with an electric motor, although the hand-cranked ones are common.

3 cups durum semolina (pasta flour) or unbleached all-purpose flour
1 cup warm water (if using durum semolina) or 3 large eggs (if using all-purpose flour)
1 teaspoon salt
1 tablespoon extra virgin olive oil (2 tablespoons if using durum semolina)
All-purpose flour for dusting

1. Pour the flour onto a work surface. Make a well in the middle, piling up the flour around it so that it resembles the walls of a volcanic crater. Pour the water into the well (or break the eggs into it if using white flour) and sprinkle in the salt. Incorporate the water into the flour (or break the yolks with your fingers and begin to incorporate the eggs into the flour) a little at a time with your fingers, drawing more flour from the inside wall of the well. Make sure you don't break through the wall or the water (or eggs) might run out. Scrape any dough off your fingers and knead it into the dough.

2. Once the flour and water (or eggs) are combined and you can form the dough into a ball, knead for 8 to 10 minutes (see Note). As you press down while kneading, use the ball to pick up any loose clumps of dough. Don't add any more liquid until you've kneaded for at least 3 minutes. If the dough is too dry at this point and you must add water (add only water even if you are making egg pasta), do so only by wetting your hands, as many times as you need. If the dough is too wet—meaning, if there is any sign of stickiness—dust it with flour. Continue kneading, pressing down with the full force of both palms, until a smooth ball is formed. Wrap the dough in waxed paper or plastic wrap and leave for 30 minutes to 1 hour at room temperature if making egg pasta and 1 hour refrigerated if making durum wheat pasta.

3. Unwrap the ball of dough and dust with flour. Place on a floured work surface, pressing down with your palms to flatten it. With a rolling pin, roll the pasta out until it is about 12 inches in diameter, then cut it into thirds. Roll each third with the rolling pin until it is thin enough to fit into the widest setting of a pasta-rolling machine. Roll once at the widest setting. Close the setting one notch and roll again. Gather the sheet of pasta, fold it into thirds like a letter, and pass through the roller so you have a nice rectangle.

Continue ratcheting down the setting until the dough reaches the thickness you prefer or that is called for in the recipe. Dust the dough on both sides with flour at the slightest sign of stickiness. If necessary, continue to dust with flour as you roll through narrower and narrower settings; otherwise the dough will become hopelessly stuck together. By this time you will have a very long, thin ribbon of pliable dough that looks and even feels like a velvety chamois cloth.

4. Cut the ribbon into 10-inch lengths 3 to 5 inches wide for lasagne or run through whatever pasta-cutting attachment you have—for example, for spaghetti or fettuccine. (For making tubular pasta you will need an extruding machine.) Dust the pasta with flour and leave to rest in an airy place on white kitchen towels or a white sheet reserved for this purpose for 2 hours (for *pasta fresca*) before cooking, refrigerating, or freezing. Use refrigerated fresh pasta within 1 or 2 days; fresh pasta can be frozen for 6 months. Leave for 48 hours or longer for *pasta secca*.

NOTE: Eight to 10 minutes of kneading is sufficient if you plan to use a hand-cranked or electric pasta-rolling machine. If you are rolling by hand, knead for another 8 minutes.

Makes about 1½ pounds

Shakhshūkha al-Bisakra (Algeria)

FIERY HOT LASAGNE IN THE STYLE OF BISKRA

The meal eaten by the seigneurs and big merchants in the Dra region of Morocco described by Ḥasan al-Wazan, known as Leo Africanus (c. 1465–1550), of "roast mutton and gruel in a very fine puff pastry, layered like a lasagne, but more firm and thick than that pasta used for lasagne," followed by couscous, was a rare occurrence, but the lasagne that he mentions is interesting.[59] *He's comparing this preparation of rich merchants with lasagne, a food he must be familiar with from travels in North Africa. It is one of the earliest mentions of its being in North Africa with which I am familiar. Lasagne is known today in North Africa, as we can see by this traditional recipe from the Algerian oasis town of Biskra in the Sahara.*

Biskra sits on the northern edge of the great desert, but it is considered a southern town. This shakhshūkha *is a* pasta fresca *in the form of lasagne or pasta flakes, and not the vegetable-and-egg preparation that is becoming more familiar throughout the European Mediterranean as a kind of Tunisian ratatouille (called* shakshūka*), nor is it the Moroccan* salade composée *of tomatoes and peppers.*[60]

In Biskra, shakhshūkha *is the name of a very thin fresh lasagne preparation cooked in a* kiskis (couscousière) *with a blazing hot sauce of lamb brains, tomatoes, and spices. This recipe is typical in oasis towns where they also make a family of lasagne preparations, sometimes using mutton or chicken or ultra-thin lasagne sheets in various shapes known as* al-afṭīr wa'l-qiṣīl *(a kind of* faṭīr, *page 307, made of young barley or wheat).*[61] Al-afṭīr wa'l-qiṣīl *is the name used by the people of the Kabylia of Algeria to refer to a very thin pasta cut into strips like angel hair pasta, while in Algiers they call it* qaṭṭa wa ramī, *"cut and throw," meaning the pasta is cut into strips and thrown into boiling bouillon.*[62]

If you decide to make the lasagne in the top portion of a couscousière *and the sauce in the bottom portion, it is best to use lightly oiled fresh pasta sheets. This recipe assumes you will boil the lasagne. The reason you are boiling "no-boil" lasagne (if not using homemade lasagne sheets) is that the manufacturer assumes you will be baking the lasagne rather than cooking it in this manner. Because there are no guidelines for boiling times on packages of no-boil lasagne, you must check often to ensure that the pasta is cooked just past the al dente stage, which will be about 6 minutes.*

1 pound calf's or lamb's brains, any sinewy tissue removed if necessary
¼ cup fresh lemon juice
½ cup extra virgin olive oil
1 medium-size onion, finely chopped
Salt and freshly ground black pepper to taste
1 tablespoon *harīsa* (page 523)
2 teaspoons cayenne pepper
¼ teaspoon freshly ground cumin seeds
¼ teaspoon freshly ground caraway seeds
3 cups canned or fresh tomato puree
1 tablespoon tomato paste
1 cup drained cooked chickpeas
4 cups water
¾ pound boiling potatoes, peeled and diced
1 pound thin fresh homemade lasagne (page 628) or commercial "no-boil" (instant) lasagne
½ cup freshly grated Parmigiano-Reggiano or Gruyère cheese

1. Soak the brains in cold water to cover acidulated with 1 tablespoon of the lemon juice for 1 hour, changing the water every 15 minutes and adding another tablespoon lemon juice each time.

2. Place the brains in a medium-size pot of cold water to cover and bring to a very gentle boil. Reduce the heat to under a boil and poach the brains until firm to the touch, about 20 minutes. Drain, then dice once cool enough to handle. Set aside.

3. In the bottom part of a *couscousière* or in a large pot fitted with a colander if using freshly made lasagne, or in a large casserole if using no-boil lasagne, heat the olive oil over medium heat, then cook the onion until translucent, about 8 minutes, stirring occasionally. Add the salt and pepper, *harīsa*, cayenne, cumin, and caraway, stir well, add the tomato puree and tomato paste, chickpeas, and 1 cup of the water, and cook for 10 minutes. Add the remaining 3 cups water, cover, and cook for 15 minutes. Add the brains and potatoes and cook until the potatoes are tender, about 15 minutes.

4. Meanwhile, bring a large pot of water to a rolling boil if using no-boil lasagne, salt abundantly, and add the lasagne. Drain when cooked a bit more than al dente, about 6 minutes, and cut crosswise into squares. If using fresh lasagne, cut into small squares, toss with a little olive oil, place in the top portion of the *couscousière* or in the colander, and steam until the squares are soft, 10 to 15 minutes, tossing occasionally so they don't stick together.

5. Transfer the cooked lasagne to the bottom portion of the *couscousière* or pot or to the casserole, mix well with the brains and potatoes, and serve immediately with the grated cheese on top.

Makes 6 servings

Lasagne Cacate di Módica (Sicily)

SHITTY LASAGNE FROM MÓDICA

In order not to lead your mind astray, I won't offer a theory as to the name of this dish. But Sicilians do have a curious penchant for naming culinary preparations with vulgarities. This lasagne from the town of Módica, in the interior of Sicily, is called "shitty lasagne," rather a mild name given some of the filthier expressions I've encountered. According to the late nineteenth-century folklorist Salvatore Salomone-Marino, as reported by Pino Correnti, a renowned Sicilian culinary authority, Sicilian peasants traditionally prepared this dish for New Year's Eve. Mary Taylor Simeti, the author of several books on Sicilian food, relates an old Sicilian expression about this dish: Lasagni cacati e vinu a cannata bon sangu fannu pri tutta l'annata *(Shitty lasagne and wine by the pitcher make good blood for the whole of the year).*[63]

Traditionally, a peasant family would serve this as a piatto unico, *a one-pot meal, on New Year's Eve, not as a first course. This particular recipe is one where the effort to make* pasta casareccio, *homemade pasta, is justly rewarded. In Sicily, where they often make their own pasta, they might do the opposite and buy some from the store for this special occasion.*

1½ pounds homemade pasta (page 628)
½ pound ground beef
½ pound homemade *salsiccia fresca* (page 70) or commercial Italian sweet sausage, casings removed and meat crumbled
¼ cup extra virgin olive oil
¼ cup very finely chopped onion
1 garlic clove, very finely chopped
1 cup canned or fresh tomato puree
2 tablespoons tomato paste
½ cup hot water
Salt and freshly ground black pepper to taste
½ pound homemade ricotta cheese (page 467)
¼ to ½ cup freshly grated pecorino cheese or hard *ricotta salata*, to your taste

1. Prepare the lasagne dough. Roll the dough out into very thin sheets and, with a knife, cut them into 1-inch-wide strips. Lay the strips on a floured board or jelly-roll pan sprinkled with flour or semolina to dry for several hours.

2. In a medium-size skillet, cook the ground beef and sausage meat together over medium-high heat until there is no pink remaining, about 6 minutes, breaking up clumps of meat. Drain the meat with a slotted ladle, discarding the fat. Set the meat aside.

3. In a large skillet, heat the olive oil over medium heat, then cook the onion and garlic until the onion is translucent, about 3 minutes, stirring frequently so the garlic doesn't burn. Add the cooked beef and sausage, reduce the heat to low, and stir. Add the tomato puree, tomato paste, and hot water, season with salt and pepper, and cook until the consistency is thicker, about 30 minutes.

4. Meanwhile, bring a large pot of abundantly salted water to a boil and add the pasta when the water is rolling. Drain when al dente and transfer to a large serving platter. Cover with the meat sauce and sprinkle on the fresh ricotta. Toss well, sprinkle with the pecorino or *ricotta salata*, and serve.

Makes 4 to 6 servings

Fusilli con Aglio, Olio e Peperoncino (Campania and Basilicata)

FUSILLI WITH GARLIC, OLIVE OIL, AND RED CHILI PEPPERS

Some of the oldest and earliest forms of macaroni dishes are found in southern Italy, and they are often very simple concoctions. This simplicity was remarked upon by the German poet Johann Wolfgang von Goethe when he traveled to Naples in 1786–1788. He said that macaroni is simply cooked in water and seasoned with grated cheese and sold inexpensively everywhere in the city.[64] Strascinata, fusilli, *or* cavatelli *were once made with hard wheat flour, water, and a little yeast. This recipe is tasty because of the presence of a New World plant, the chili pepper, which is used here in some abundance. An otherwise bland food can become quite enticing to the palate without much expense or effort.*

6 garlic cloves, peeled
3 dried chili peppers, seeded
Salt to taste
3 tablespoons extra virgin olive oil
1 pound *fusilli*
¼ cup finely chopped fresh parsley leaves

1. In a mortar, pound the garlic and chili peppers together with some salt. Add the olive oil a little at a time while you continue pounding until homogeneous. Let it rest while you cook the *fusilli.*

2. Bring a large pot of abundantly salted water to a boil and cook the fusilli until al dente. Drain and mix carefully with the sauce. Add the parsley, toss gently again, and serve without cheese.

Makes 4 to 6 servings

Rigatoni alla Carrettiera (Sicily)

CART DRIVER'S RIGATONI

In Sicily, they make this "cart driver's"–style pasta very simply. The name implies that it is a kind of dish sold by street vendors, although there are many family versions of this dish throughout Sicily and central and southern Italy. The earliest print with which I am familiar depicting the selling of pasta from a street cart or stall is from the nineteenth century, when, indeed, pasta was sold to the public from street carts. This recipe is a family-style version from Sicily using rigatoni rather than spaghetti, and it yields many servings meant to feed many people before a grilled second course.

3 pounds very ripe tomatoes, peeled, seeded, and chopped
4 garlic cloves, finely chopped
4 to 6 dried chili peppers, to your taste, seeded and crumbled
15 large fresh basil leaves, finely chopped
1 cup extra virgin olive oil, plus a few more tablespoons for tossing
2 pounds rigatoni
Freshly grated pecorino cheese for sprinkling

1. Combine the tomatoes, garlic, chili peppers, and basil in a large bowl with the 1 cup of the olive oil and leave for 4 hours at room temperature.

2. Bring a large pot of abundantly salted water to a boil and add the pasta when the water is rolling. Drain well when al dente and toss with enough olive oil so the pasta doesn't stick together. Because water catches inside the rigatoni, continue draining for 1 minute by tossing it in the colander. Add the sauce, toss well, and serve with pecorino cheese if desired.

Makes 8 to 10 primi piatti *servings*

Maccheroni con Ricotta (Apulia)

MACARONI WITH RICOTTA

Macaroni recipes from the Italian peninsula in the Middle Ages and through the Renaissance were often cooked in broth as well as water. The macaroni was then usually flavored with cheese—ricotta, pecorino, caciocavallo, provola, *and Parmigiano-Reggiano being the most popular—as well as spices, cinnamon and saffron being the most common.*[65] *This recipe is perhaps a fleeting reminiscence of medieval cookery, and today usually served to children, although satisfying for everyone.*

¾ pound homemade ricotta cheese, preferably made from ewe's milk (page 467)
1 tablespoon sugar
Salt to taste
⅛ to ¼ teaspoon ground cinnamon, to your taste
1 pound short macaroni, such as *mezze* ziti, *tubetti, ditali,* or elbow macaroni
¼ cup milk (optional)

1. In a small bowl, stir the ricotta, sugar, salt, and cinnamon together.

2. Bring a large pot of abundantly salted water to a boil and cook the pasta until al dente. Drain, saving ¼ cup of the cooking water if not using the milk. Blend the ricotta with the milk or cooking water, beating with a fork. Toss the pasta with the ricotta and serve immediately.

Makes 4 to 6 servings

Ditaloni con Ricotta e Noci (Sicily)

DITALONI WITH RICOTTA AND NUTS

The popularity of macaroni and cheese is reflected in an old Italian expression, cacio sui maccheroni *(literally, cheese on the macaroni), meaning a person who arrives at an opportune moment. This popularity goes back to medieval days, especially with ricotta cheese, because of its supposed health benefits. According to the then prevailing dietetic thinking based on the Galenic theory of humors (see "An Essay on the Sources"), ricotta was an important nourishment for the body and suitable for people with vigorous temperaments.*[66] *Almonds and pistachios were grown in Sicily during the Arab era and they continue to be popular in macaroni preparations and in many sweets.*

1 pound homemade ricotta cheese (page 467)
Salt
1 pound *ditaloni* or *tubetti*
Freshly ground black pepper to taste
¼ cup roasted (page 709) and ground blanched almonds
¼ cup ground blanched pistachios

1. Pass the ricotta through a fine-mesh sieve and salt lightly. Check the taste.

2. Bring a large pot of water to a rolling boil, salt abundantly, and add the pasta. Drain when al dente, saving ¼ cup of the cooking water. Stir the water into the ricotta until well blended.

3. Toss the pasta and ricotta together with a grinding of pepper and serve the almonds and pistachios on the side, allowing each diner to sprinkle his own on top. Alternatively, toss the nuts with the pasta, then serve.

Makes 4 to 6 servings

Perciatelli con Pomodoro e Ricotta (Calabria)

PERCIATELLI WITH TOMATOES AND RICOTTA

The fifteenth-century chef known as Platina published a recipe for perciatelli *in his* De honesta voluptate et valetudine *(On honest indulgence and good health) of 1475, which he called* escicium siculum, *a food from Sicily, made with an iron rod that leaves a hole in the middle. This iron rod method of making* pasta secca *is found today in some parts of Italy, especially Calabria as well as Sicily, where, in the region of Syracuse and Noto, we find a kind of lasagne called* taccúna, *formed in a spiral around a thick stick such as a billiard cue or around an iron rod called a* ferreti.[67] *It is also found in Tunisia, where* maqrūnat al-ibra *is a pasta formed around a knitting needle, and typical of the cooking in the town of Testour.*[68]

The tomatoes in this preparation came long after the time of Platina. This dish looks very pretty if you serve it in a big platter or bowl with the tomato sauce poured over the pasta and then the pinkish ricotta over the tomatoes. Although I call for homemade or commercial fresh ricotta, which I believe improves the taste, your typical commercial ricotta will do fine.

3 tablespoons pork lard or *'nzugna* (page 281)
2 tablespoons extra virgin olive oil
1 small onion, chopped
3 cups fresh or canned crushed tomatoes
Salt to taste
2 tablespoons finely chopped fresh basil leaves
½ pound homemade ricotta cheese (page 467)
1¼ pounds *perciatelli*
Freshly ground Parmigianio-Reggiano cheese for sprinkling

1. In a medium-size skillet or casserole, melt the lard with the olive oil over medium-high heat, then cook the onion until translucent, about 5 minutes, stirring frequently. Add the tomatoes and season with salt. Reduce the heat to medium and cook until thicker, 20 minutes. Stir in the basil.

PRIESTS' HATS AND WOMEN'S CURLS

Pasta in the southern Italian province of Calabria is most often homemade, produced in a wide variety of shapes, and a popular serving on festival days. Its history is old, for we know that Calabrians were importing Sicilian pasta as early as the mid-twelfth century.[69] *The most common pastas today are* fusilli, paternostri *(our father), pasta shapes made with a special iron machine that forms small perforated dice; and* sagne e ricci e fimmina, *a curly edged kind of lasagne square.* Filatieddi, filatelli, *and* scilatielli *are all names of a pasta shaped into a long string about ⅛ inch thick. Cannelloni (which translates to "big cinnamon stick") are called in Calabrian dialect* cannaruòzzoli *or* canneroni. *There is a pasta called* cappieddi 'i prievidi *(priests' hats), which are formed into the shape of the three-cornered hats of the priests of Calabria.* Ferrazzuoli, fischietti, *or* maccarruni a firriettu *is a pasta formed by laying the sheets of dough on a thin iron device called a* firriettu *or* ferreti, *which is also known in Sicily and Sardinia (see page 77). The dough is pulled through, forming it into small perforated cylinders.* Nocchetedde *are pasta rectangles pinched in the middle to form a shape like little butterflies, called* farfalline. Laganedde *is the same thing as* tagliatelle. Rascatelli *(scraped pasta),* ricchielle *(curled pasta), and* ricchie 'i previti *(priests' curls) are all names for* cavatelli *(pulled pasta), a coin-sized flat piece of pasta that is rolled up.* Ricci di donna *(women's curls) is pasta formed by wrapping a thin thread of pasta dough around a knitting needle into a spiral. These pastas can be served with* sugo di agnello *(lamb sauce, page 641),* sugo di carne alla calabrese *(meat sauce),* sugo di maiale *(pork sauce, page 280),* sugo di pollo *(chicken sauce),* sugo di pomodoro *(tomato sauce, page 32),* sugo di funghi *(mushroom sauce), or* salsetta de alici e tonno *(tuna and anchovy sauce).*[70]

2. In a medium-size bowl, mix the ricotta with a third of the tomato sauce and blend the two well.

3. Meanwhile, bring a large pot of water to a rolling boil, salt abundantly, and add the pasta. Drain when al dente. Transfer to a serving platter and pour the tomato sauce over the pasta. Then pour the ricotta sauce on top with a sprinkling of Parmigiano-Reggiano and serve with more cheese at the table, if desired.

Makes 4 to 6 servings

Spaghetti ai "Chiuvetelli" (Campania)

SPAGHETTI WITH WILD MUSHROOMS

Some wild fungi are deadly poisonous, so it must have been with trepidation that people began to eat them regularly. But once peasants got hold of a morel or a truffle, which are not true mushrooms (that is, they are mushrooms that produce their fruiting bodies underground), a jewel of a taste was discovered. In southern Italy, there are also a variety of wild funghi, called chiuvetelli, *that grow on trees or in the ground and are eaten by the locals. Their scientific names are either* Armillariella mellea *or* Clitocybe tabescens. *The closest substitute one can find in an everyday market is, of course, the very expensive morel or truffle, but shiitake or oyster mushrooms will work fine in this recipe.*

3/4 pound fresh shiitake or oyster mushrooms, cleaned
6 tablespoons extra virgin olive oil
2 garlic cloves, finely chopped
Salt and freshly ground black pepper to taste
3/4 pound spaghetti
1/2 cup loosely packed fresh parsley leaves, ripped into pieces

1. Slice the stems of the mushrooms into pieces and the caps into quarters. Drop the mushrooms into boiling water for 2 minutes. Drain.

2. In a large skillet, heat the olive oil and garlic over medium heat. Once the garlic is sizzling, about 3 to 4 minutes, add the mushrooms, season with salt and pepper, and cook until the mushrooms are soft and dark, about 12 minutes.

3. Meanwhile, bring a large pot of water to a rolling boil, salt abundantly, and add the pasta. Drain when al dente, toss with the mushrooms and parsley in the skillet, and serve.

Makes 4 servings

Farfalle al Tonno (Campania)

FARFALLE WITH TUNA

Farfalle *is a flat, square sheet of macaroni pinched in the middle to make it look like a butterfly, hence the Italian name.*

Throughout the hilly landscapes of Campania the people have traditionally been very poor. Cooks would rely on conserved foods such as macaroni, cheeses, or tonno sott'olio, *tuna preserved in olive oil.*

This recipe comes from Consiglia De Ieso, the wife of my cousin Rinaldo De Ieso. Consiglia also happens to be a De Ieso, many times removed, from the little village of my grandfather, Pago Veiano near Benevento. This is a very easy preparation, perfect for a quick fam-

ily meal. One occasionally sees the mixing of fish with cheese in southern Italian cooking, a combination considered boorish by northern Italians.

Salt to taste
1 pound *farfalle*
One 6- to 7-ounce can tuna packed in olive oil (do not drain; you use the oil)
Handful of fresh basil or parsley leaves, ripped
½ cup extra virgin olive oil
⅓ cup freshly grated Parmigiano-Reggiano cheese
Freshly ground black pepper to taste

1. Bring a large pot of abundantly salted water to a boil and add the pasta when the water is rolling. Drain when al dente.

2. Meanwhile, empty the can of tuna with its oil into the pasta serving bowl. With a fork, break up the tuna and stir in the basil or parsley. Pour in the extra virgin olive oil. Add the hot drained pasta to the serving bowl along with the cheese and toss well with some freshly ground black pepper. Serve immediately.

Makes 4 to 6 servings

Vermicelli con le Vongole in Rosso (Campania)

VERMICELLI WITH RED CLAM SAUCE

The eating of clams with macaroni is relatively recent in southern Italy. In the Middle Ages, shellfish was mostly eaten boiled with a hot salsamento quod elixis piscis, *sauce for boiled fish, which was made of cinnamon, ginger, pepper, cloves, grains of paradise, galingale, saffron, and vinegar.*[71] *Gastropoda (single-shelled mollusks) such as limpets, abalone, and murex (a kind of whelk), and Lamellibranchiata (bivalves) such as oysters, mussels, scallops, and a variety of clams were popular then and are still today. According to Bartolomeo Scappi, probably the most famous chef of sixteenth-century Italy, many of the clams and oysters then eaten in Rome, and presumably in southern Italy, came from Genoa.*[72]

For this recipe, choose the smallest clams you can find. Some cooks remove the clams from their shells and chop them into the sauce, but I prefer the whole clams in their shells. Leaving out the tomato gives you vongole in bianco, *clams in white sauce.*

3 pounds littleneck clams (about 2 dozen), soaked in cold water to cover with 1 tablespoon baking soda for 1 hour, drained and scrubbed
Salt to taste
1½ pounds vermicelli
¼ cup extra virgin olive oil
4 garlic cloves, 2 crushed and 2 finely chopped
1 pound fresh or canned crushed tomatoes with their juices
3 tablespoons finely chopped fresh parsley leaves
Freshly ground black pepper to taste

1. Put the clams in a large casserole or pot and turn the heat to high. As the clams begin to open, 4 to 5 minutes for the first few, remove them to a bowl and continue cooking, shaking the casserole occasionally until the remaining clams open, another 1 to 4 minutes. Discard any clams that remain tightly shut. Strain the clam broth through a cheesecloth-lined strainer and set aside.

2. Meanwhile, bring a large pot of water to a rolling boil, salt abundantly, and add the pasta. Drain when al dente.

3. In a large casserole or skillet, heat the olive oil over medium-high heat, then cook the crushed garlic cloves until they begin to turn light brown. Remove and discard the garlic. Add the tomatoes, ¼ cup of the reserved clam juice, and the chopped garlic.

Reduce the heat to medium and simmer until the sauce is dense, about 20 minutes. Add the clams (in their shells) and parsley, season with pepper, cook for 1 minute, and add the vermicelli. Toss well, transfer to a serving bowl, and serve.

Makes 6 servings

Vermicelli con le Cozze in Bianco (Campania)

VERMICELLI WITH WHITE MUSSEL SAUCE

Cozze *is a word used in Campania for mussels. The word comes from the Medieval Latin word for mussel that was spoken in fourteenth-century Ragusa. It may have originally been an Apulian dialect word corresponding to the Italian* coccio, *an earthenware casserole, meant to convey the idea of the shell that carries the animal.*[73]

The mussels should be plump and the sauce coat the pasta just enough to give the illusion that it was made with cream. Mussels generally do not need to be purged because they cling to rocks and are not buried in the sand like other bivalves; but there is no harm in purging them as you did for the clams in the previous recipe.

¾ cup extra virgin olive oil
3 garlic cloves, finely chopped
¼ teaspoon red pepper flakes
4 pounds mussels (about 4 dozen), debearded and scrubbed
Salt to taste
¼ cup finely chopped fresh parsley leaves
1¼ pounds vermicelli

1. In a casserole large enough to hold all the mussels, heat the olive oil over medium heat, then cook the garlic and red pepper flakes, stirring, for 30 seconds. Add the mussels and salt and increase the heat to medium-high. Cover and cook until the mussels have opened, turning them now and then so they all open more or less about the same time (because they will not be in one layer), 6 to 7 minutes. Remove the mussels from the casserole, discarding any that remain tightly shut. Remove the mussels from their shells and set aside. Strain the mussel juice through a cheesecloth-lined strainer and return to the casserole. Reduce the mussel juice over medium-high heat for 4 minutes. Return the mussels to the casserole, stir in the parsley, and cook for 2 minutes. Turn off the heat until needed. The hot pasta will reheat the mussels sufficiently.

2. Meanwhile, bring a large pot of abundantly salted water to a boil and add the pasta when the water is rolling. Drain when al dente and transfer to the casserole. Toss well and serve from the casserole or transfer to a serving platter.

Makes 4 to 6 servings

Perciatelli con Sugo di Scòrfano (Campania)

PERCIATELLI WITH SCORPION-FISH SAUCE

The earliest written Italian macaroni recipes date from the fourteenth and fifteenth centuries. Their spicing and flavors were thoroughly Arab in inspiration, as we can see in a recipe from the Libro de arte coquinaria *(Book of the culinary art) of Maestro Martino da Como from the late fifteenth century, called* maccaroni siciliani. *The macaroni is made with fine white flour, egg whites, and rose water. Once it is made into a com-*

pacted dough, it is then flattened and rolled around an iron rod to form a maccherone pertusato*—that is, "macaroni with a narrow passage," or what is today called* perciatelli *or* bucatini*, a thick spaghetti with a hole in the middle. The pasta is sun-dried and can be kept for two or three years, and then cooked in boiling water or broth for some time before being served with fresh butter, grated cheese, and* spetie dolci*, sweet spices, probably sugar and cinnamon.*[74]

This Neapolitan recipe is also made with perciatelli *and seasoned with a more modern sauce made* from scòrfano*, scorpionfish, which in Marseilles is well known as* rascasse*, the essential fish for bouillabaisse. But scorpionfish is popular throughout the Tyrrhenian Sea and in Sicily it is made into a* zuppa di scòrfano*, with white wine, tomato, and red chili pepper.*

Scorpionfish are occasionally available in the United States, especially in fish stores in East Coast cities with Italian neighborhoods. After much experimenting, and consulting with my friend and fishmonger extraordinaire Salvatore Fantasia, I believe the taste of scorpionfish can be approximated by using a redfish (ocean perch), the North Atlantic fish closest in taste to scòrfano*, rockfish, wolffish (ocean catfish), or red snapper and dogfish (Cape shark) in combination.*

1 medium-size onion, sliced
2/3 cup extra virgin olive oil
3 garlic cloves, crushed
20 fresh basil leaves
1 pound redfish, rockfish, or wolffish fillets (or 1/2 pound red snapper fillet and 1/2 pound dogfish steak)
2/3 cup dry white wine
2 1/2 cups fresh or canned tomato puree
Salt and freshly ground black pepper to taste
1 1/4 pounds *perciatelli*

1. Put the onion, olive oil, garlic, and basil in a large casserole and turn the heat to medium. Cook, stirring occasionally, until the onion is translucent, about 10 minutes.

2. Add all the fish to the casserole and cook for 4 minutes, using all the wine by adding it at 1-minute intervals. Add the tomato puree, cover, reduce the heat to very low, and simmer until the fish is breaking apart, about 30 minutes. Continue to break up the fish with a wooden spoon and crumble further if necessary with a fork. Season with salt and pepper, cover, and leave over very low heat until needed, using a heat diffuser if necessary.

3. Meanwhile, bring a large pot of water to a rolling boil, salt abundantly, and add the pasta. Drain when al dente and toss with the sauce. Remove and discard the garlic, and serve.

Makes 6 servings

Penne e Carciofi (Campania)

PENNE AND ARTICHOKES

The early history of the introduction of the artichoke into the Mediterranean is confused because the Arabic word kharsūf*, from which the Italian word for the artichoke* (carciofi) *derives, can also be used to refer to the cardoon. It seems likely that the artichoke was developed in North Africa and then made its way to Spain and Sicily. There is evidence that the artichoke was grown in Sicilian gardens in the early fifteenth century and perhaps as early as the twelfth century. The earliest appearance of the artichoke in Campania was in the mid-fifteenth century, according to the Italian botanist Pierandrea Mattioli, who said it was brought to Naples from Sicily, where it seems to have been grown for the first time in Europe.*[75]

This simple dish is typical fare of the De Iesos, my grandfather's family, who are from Pago Veiano, a little village near Benevento. The artichokes are ideal when they are young.

Salt to taste
8 medium-size artichokes (about 6 ounces each)
Juice from 1 lemon
Salt to taste
1 pound penne
4 to 6 tablespoons extra virgin olive oil, to your taste
2 garlic cloves, finely chopped
Freshly ground black pepper to taste
1/4 cup water
1/4 cup finely chopped fresh parsley leaves

1. Trim the artichokes and remove the hearts (page 122). Slice the hearts thin and put into a bowl of water acidulated with the lemon juice until needed so the artichokes don't discolor.

2. Bring a large pot of water to a rolling boil, salt abundantly, and add the pasta. Drain when al dente.

3. Meanwhile, heat the olive oil in a large skillet over medium heat, then cook the garlic for 30 seconds, stirring constantly so it doesn't burn. Add the drained artichoke hearts, season with salt and pepper, and cook for 2 minutes. Add the water and cook until the artichokes are tender, 18 to 20 minutes, shaking the skillet occasionally. Sprinkle on the parsley and mix well. Toss the artichokes with the pasta and serve.

VARIATION

In step 3, rinse 4 salted anchovy fillets, add them when you add the artichokes, and sprinkle chopped fresh mint on top after the penne has been tossed with the parsley.

Makes 6 servings

Penne e Asparagi (Apulia)

PENNE AND ASPARAGUS

As late as the seventeenth century, asparagus preparations in Italy were still influenced by Arab culinary sensibilities. In Bartolomeo Stefani's L'arte di ben cucinare *(The art of good cooking), published in 1662, he gives a recipe for asparagus pie made with citron, cinnamon, sugar, egg yolks, cream, rose water, and crumbled* mostaccioli, *a sweet made from flour kneaded with honey, cooked wine, raisins, figs, and ground almonds.*[76] *Granted that this recipe is not meant to feed the same people that Stefani, head chef for the court of the Gonzagas, a princely Italian family from Mantua, was cooking for, it still demonstrates a different culinary sensibility, with its use of aromatic flavors and New World tomatoes instead of spices, one that has divorced itself from its Islamic past.*

This recipe is typical of homemade dishes in the Dáunia, the string of mountains where Molise, Apulia, and Campania meet. I have an attachment to this region because this is where the De Iesos, my grandfather's family, come from.

Salt to taste
1 pound thin asparagus, bottoms trimmed and cut into 1-inch lengths
1 pound penne
1/4 cup extra virgin olive oil
3 garlic cloves, lightly crushed
2/3 cup fresh or canned crushed tomatoes
Freshly ground black pepper to taste
1/4 cup freshly grated pecorino cheese
2 large eggs, lightly beaten

1. Bring a large pot of water to a rolling boil, salt abundantly, and boil or steam the asparagus until soft, about 10 minutes. Remove from the water and set aside, saving the cooking water.

2. In the same water you cooked the asparagus, cook the pasta once the water has returned to a furious boil and drain when al dente. Return the asparagus to the water for 1 minute to reheat it before you drain the pasta.

3. Meanwhile, heat the olive oil in a small skillet with the garlic cloves over medium-high heat. As the

garlic cloves begin to turn color, add the tomatoes and cook for 5 to 6 minutes, stirring frequently. Season with salt and pepper and remove the garlic cloves.

4. In a large bowl, stir a good amount of freshly and coarsely ground black pepper and half the cheese in with the beaten eggs. Add the pasta to the bowl along with the asparagus and toss gently. Add the tomato sauce and toss again, gently. Transfer the pasta to individual serving bowls or a large serving bowl, sprinkle the remaining cheese on top, and serve.

Makes 4 servings

Orecchiette con Broccoli Rape (Apulia)

"LITTLE EARS" WITH BROCCOLI RABE

The number of different kinds of pasta in Apulia is enormous, but orecchiette, *"little ears," is a favorite. Although traditionally made only with durum wheat, today a blend of durum wheat and white flour is usually used. The dough is kneaded vigorously and rolled into long strips that are then cut off and shaped with the thumb. If the dough is pushed with the thumb or a knife called a* rasaul *and rolled away in a quick movement, they are called* cavatelli, *popular in Apulia and Sicily. In Sicily,* cavatelli *are usually eaten with a sauce of eggplant, tomatoes, basil, and grated* ricotta salata *cheese, while in Apulia one finds beans or broccoli rabe. For more on pasta making, see page 628.*

This dish from Apulia uses bread crumbs to replace the more expensive Parmigiano-Reggiano cheese. One finds this use of bread crumbs with pasta, for sprinkling and stuffing, throughout the Mezzogiorno and Sicily, and it is traditionally cucina povera's *answer to the prohibitive expense of salted cheese.*

Broccoli rape or rabe is a sprouting broccoli also called friarelli, broccoli di foglia, broccoletti di rape, broccoli-rave, *or* cime di rapa *or just* rape *or* rabe *in Italian. (Be aware, though, that sometimes, both in English and Italian,* broccoli di rape *refers to turnip tops.)*

This dish is also made with arugula, beet greens, cauliflower, or spinach. The simplest of versions use only garlic and red pepper for seasoning.

¼ cup extra virgin olive oil
1 cup fresh bread crumbs
¼ cup golden or dark raisins
4 garlic cloves, finely chopped
¼ teaspoon red pepper flakes
8 salted anchovy fillets, rinsed
¾ pound store-bought or homemade *orecchiette* (page 628)
Salt to taste
1 pound broccoli rabe
¼ cup pine nuts
Salt to taste

1. In a small skillet, heat 2 tablespoons of the olive oil over medium heat, then brown the bread crumbs, stirring. Meanwhile, plump the raisins for 15 minutes in some tepid water to cover, then drain. In another skillet, place the garlic, red pepper flakes, and anchovy fillets in the remaining 2 tablespoons olive oil and heat for 1 minute over medium-high heat.

2. Meanwhile, bring a large pot of abundantly salted water to a boil, then add the pasta and broccoli rabe when the water is rolling. Drain when the pasta is al dente and add to the skillet with the anchovies. Add the drained raisins and pine nuts and stir. Sprinkle on the toasted bread crumbs, toss gently, and serve.

VARIATION

Cook the garlic and red pepper flakes in the olive oil. Add some chopped broccoli rabe that has been steamed for 5 to 10 minutes, and cook for 5 minutes, then toss with the cooked *orecchiette*.

Makes 4 servings

Orecchiette con "Recott-Asckuande" e "Recott Mazzadeche" (Apulia)

"LITTLE EARS" WITH SOUR RICOTTA AND HARD RICOTTA

This primitive preparation from Apulia is made with recott-asckuande, *a sour, slightly fermented ricotta reminiscent of the Syrian* shinklīsh *(page 188). Grated* recott mazzadeche, ricotta salata, *is sprinkled on top. Southern Italy, especially Sicily and Apulia, is well known for its mature ricotta cheeses that are hardened and available for grating. When buying* ricotta salata *in an Italian grocery, be sure to ask for the hard or grating version, not the soft* ricotta salata. *Use freshly made ricotta, sold in most Italian neighborhood markets, or make your own (page 467). This recipe is adapted from that of the Italian cookbook author Luigi Sada.*

Salt
3/4 pound store-bought or homemade *orecchiette* (page 628)
1 cup tomato sauce (page 32)
1/2 cup homemade ricotta cheese (page 467) or finely crumbled imported Greek or Balkan feta cheese
1/2 teaspoon freshly ground black pepper
3/4 cup freshly grated hard *ricotta salata*

1. Bring a large pot of abundantly salted water to a boil, cook the *orecchiette* until al dente, and drain.

2. Meanwhile, in a small bowl, stir together the tomato sauce, ricotta, and pepper. Transfer the pasta to a serving bowl or platter and sprinkle with the *ricotta salata*. Cover with the sauce while the pasta is still piping hot. Serve immediately.

Makes 4 servings

Orecchiette al Sugo d'Agnello (Apulia)

"LITTLE EARS" WITH LAMB SAUCE

This is an earthy farmhouse recipe with strong aromatic flavors that are very satisfying. The combination of pasta and lamb is not merely one of taste in Apulia. There was a natural cycle of production whereby the large number of sheep in the Apulia of the Middle Ages created enough manure to increase the yields of wheat fields far beyond other areas of Italy, and the surplus wheat was made into pasta for the benefit of rich feudal lords and the new class of rich farmers, both of whom were city and town dwellers.

1/2 cup (1 stick) unsalted butter
2 tablespoons extra virgin olive oil
1 sprig fresh rosemary
2 pounds boneless leg of lamb, trimmed of fat and cut into 1/2-inch cubes
Salt and freshly ground black pepper to taste
1 1/4 pounds store-bought or homemade *orecchiette* (page 628)
1/2 cup freshly grated Parmigiano-Reggiano cheese

1. In a large, heavy saucepan, heat the butter, olive oil, and rosemary sprig together over medium heat until the butter stops bubbling. Add the lamb cubes, cover, reduce the heat to low, and brown on all sides, about 10 minutes, stirring occasionally. Season with salt and pepper, increase the heat to medium, and cook for another 20 minutes, covered. Stir the lamb

occasionally and add a few tablespoons of water to keep the sauce at the same consistency. When the lamb is done, remove and discard the rosemary. Reduce the sauce for a few minutes until it is rich and darker. Scrape the sides and bottom of the saucepan well and stir into the sauce.

2. Meanwhile, bring a large pot of abundantly salted water to a boil and add the pasta when the water is rolling. Drain when al dente. Transfer to a warm serving platter. Cover the pasta with the lamb sauce. Toss with half the Parmigiano-Reggiano, sprinkle the remainder on top, and serve.

Makes 6 servings

"*Cavatieddi*" *con la Ruca* (Apulia)

CAVATELLI WITH ARUGULA

Cavatelli *is a kind of pasta popular in southern Italy and Sicily. It derives its name from the verb* cavare, *"to pull away." The pasta dough, once only made with hard wheat flour and water, but today with other flour, is rolled out into long ropes that are cut off in small segments to form small morsels that are then flattened into disks with the thumb to form a pasta called* orecchiette. *These disks are rolled away, doubling up on themselves, to become* cavatelli. Cavatieddi *is the Apulian dialect name for this rustic dish typical of home cooking. If you can't quite picture how* cavatelli *are made, try renting the Francis Ford Coppola film* Godfather III, *where, in one erotic scene, the Corleone cousins make* cavatelli. La ruca *is the dialect term for arugula.*

Salt
1 pound store-bought or homemade *cavatelli* (page 628)
1 pound arugula, washed and chopped
1 cup warm or hot tomato sauce (page 32)
Freshly grated pecorino cheese

Bring a large pot of water to a rolling boil, salt abundantly, and add the pasta. Cook for 2 minutes and add the arugula. Drain when the pasta is al dente and toss with the tomato sauce and pecorino cheese. Serve.

VARIATION

Instead of using tomato sauce and pecorino cheese, heat 1/4 cup extra virgin olive oil in a skillet over medium heat, then add 2 finely chopped garlic cloves and 4 rinsed salted anchovy fillets, stirring until they melt, about 1 minute. Drain the pasta and arugula and toss with the olive oil-and-anchovy sauce.

Makes 4 servings

Cavolfiore con Conchiglie (Sicily)

SEASHELL PASTA WITH CAULIFLOWER

Most varieties of pasta, and there are said to be about seven hundred or more, are relatively recent inventions. The combination of pasta with vegetables also appears to be recent. In Bartolomeo Scappi's Opera [dell'arte del cucinare], *published in 1570, pasta is usually cooked in broth with rose water, saffron, and cinnamon, among the typical flavorings used, and the cauliflower was simply boiled alone and not necessarily eaten with pasta. This preparation was suggested to me by Elenora Consoli, a food journalist at* La Sicilia *newspaper in Catania.[77] It is a very simple home-cooked preparation that serves time-pressed families well.*

1 small head cauliflower (about 1 pound after being trimmed of leaves and stalks), broken apart into florets
Salt
¼ cup extra virgin olive oil
½ pound *salsiccia fresca* (page 70) or commercial mild Italian sausage, casings removed
1 medium-size onion, chopped
Freshly ground black pepper to taste
Ground cinnamon to taste
¾ pound seashell pasta

1. Boil the cauliflower florets in lightly salted water until a skewer can glide easily to their centers, 8 to 10 minutes. Drain, saving the cooking water.

2. In a medium-size skillet, heat the olive oil over medium-high heat, then brown the sausage meat with the onion, about 10 minutes, stirring frequently to break the meat up. Add the cauliflower florets and season with pepper and cinnamon. Stir and cook for 5 or 6 minutes.

3. Meanwhile, bring the reserved cauliflower water to a boil and cook the pasta in it until al dente. Drain and add the pasta to the sauce. Stir well and serve.

Makes 6 servings

Spaghetti alla Puttanesca (Campania)

SPAGHETTI, WHORE'S STYLE

This famous Neapolitan pasta dish, it seems, was invented after World War II. Puttanesca *derives from a vulgar word for "prostitute." It is said that Neapolitan harlots would entice customers with plates of their favorite pasta. Given some of the other names this preparation is known by, that story might be fanciful. In Naples,* spaghetti alla puttanesca *is also known as* alla provenzale, alla martinique, alla marinara, *and* alla bonne femme.[78] *In fact, the Neapolitan culinary authority Jeanne Caròla Francesconi claims that the name is a post–World War II invention of the artist Eduardo Colucci.[79] If you want a hotter sauce, crumble the red pepper.*

5 tablespoons extra virgin olive oil
3 garlic cloves, 2 crushed and 1 finely chopped
1 pound ripe tomatoes, peeled, seeded, chopped, and drained
2 tablespoons capers, rinsed and chopped if large
20 imported black olives, pitted and cut in half
1 large dried chili pepper
1 teaspoon dried oregano
Freshly ground black pepper to taste
Salt to taste
1 pound spaghetti
12 salted anchovy fillets, rinsed and chopped
3 tablespoons finely chopped fresh parsley leaves

1. In a large casserole, heat the olive oil with the 2 crushed garlic cloves over medium-high heat until they begin to turn light brown, about 4 minutes. Remove and discard the garlic.

2. Add the tomatoes, capers, olives, chili pepper, oregano, black pepper, and chopped garlic. Cook over medium-high heat until the tomatoes are a bit thicker, 7 to 8 minutes, stirring almost constantly.

3. Meanwhile, bring a large pot of water to a rolling boil, salt abundantly, and add the pasta. Drain when al dente.

4. Reduce the heat under the sauce to low, add the anchovies and parsley, and simmer for 2 minutes. Discard the chili pepper. Transfer the spaghetti to the casserole with the sauce and toss well. Transfer to a serving platter or bowl and serve.

Makes 4 servings

Perciatelli con Animelle Fritte (Campania)

PERCIATELLI WITH FRIED SWEETBREADS

Sweetbreads are a delicate and rich-tasting meat—perfect with perciatelli. *Throughout the Mediterranean, offal is very popular and some, such as sweetbreads or brains, are highly prized for their mellow tastes. The cultural aversion to offal we see in postindustrial societies is not found (yet) in the Mediterranean. Food aversions in the Mediterranean are not so much about particular foods as about particular textures, cooking methods, and tastes—that is, different cuisines. So, for instance, an Arab would be averse to eating risotto, while an Italian might not be that keen on yogurt. As the Mediterranean becomes more "Euro," all this changes. Taste this preparation for sweetbreads and your ideas will change, too.*

1 pound veal sweetbreads, membranes removed
1 tablespoon white wine vinegar
Salt and freshly ground black pepper to taste
All-purpose flour for dredging
1 large egg, beaten
Dried bread crumbs for dredging
1 cup pure or virgin olive oil
2 garlic cloves, 1 crushed and 1 finely chopped
3/4 pound *perciatelli*
2 tablespoons finely chopped fresh parsley leaves

1. Place the sweetbreads in a medium-size pot and cover them with water. Add the vinegar. Turn the heat to medium-high and leave the water just below a boil for 20 minutes. Drain and cool the sweetbreads. Cut into bite-size pieces. Season the sweetbread pieces with salt and pepper. Dredge in the flour, tapping off any excess flour. Dip in the beaten egg and dredge in the bread crumbs, tapping off any excess. Set aside in the refrigerator for 30 minutes.

2. In a large skillet, heat the olive oil with the crushed garlic over medium-high heat until the garlic begins to turn light brown. Remove and discard the garlic. Once the olive oil is on the verge of smoking, fry the breaded sweetbread pieces until golden brown, about 3 minutes, turning once. Do not crowd the skillet; cook them in batches if you have to. Remove to drain on paper towels, salting lightly if desired, and keep warm, uncovered.

3. Meanwhile, bring a large pot of water to a rolling boil, salt abundantly, and add the pasta. Drain when al dente. Toss with the parsley, chopped garlic, and pepper to taste. Add the sweetbreads and toss again. Serve immediately.

Makes 4 servings

Ziti con Salsa d'Aragosta (Lazio)

ZITI WITH LOBSTER SAUCE

Lobster was an available shellfish for Italian fishermen of the Middle Ages. The Renaissance chef Bartolomeo Scappi, writing before 1570, suggests a simple boiled lobster. Another of his recipes is more involved. The boiled lobster meat is removed and pounded in a mortar into a forcemeat made of cheese, eggs, and herbs that is restuffed into the shell and fried in oil or butter.[80]

This recipe from Gaeta was given to me by Sal and Frances Fantasia, who are both from this coastal town south of Rome famous for its olives. They serve this ziti with lobster sauce as a primo piatto *followed by* rombo fritti *(fried turbot; page 358), as their* secondo.

1/2 cup extra virgin olive oil
1 small onion, finely chopped
3 garlic cloves, finely chopped
1/4 cup finely chopped fresh parsley leaves
7 to 8 ripe plum tomatoes (about 1 1/4 pounds), peeled, seeded, and chopped
One 1 1/2-pound live lobster
1 cup water
Salt to taste
1 pound ziti

1. In a deep stove-top casserole, heat the olive oil over medium heat, then cook the onion, garlic, and parsley together until the onion is translucent, about 7 minutes, stirring frequently so the garlic doesn't burn. Reduce the heat to low, add the tomatoes, and simmer until some liquid has evaporated, about 20 minutes.

2. Meanwhile, prepare the lobster. Holding the live lobster by the tail, dig the blade of a heavy, strong knife or cleaver into the crack between the two shell plates of the lobster 1 inch or so behind the head. This will kill the lobster immediately. Dig in deep with the knife. With your fingers, lift up and pull out the inedible portion under the head. The lobster may continue to move, but it's dead. Break the tail off and chop it into pieces with the shell with a cleaver. Crack the claws. Pull all the legs out.

3. Add all the lobster pieces, including the body, to the tomato sauce and simmer for 30 minutes. Add up to 1 cup water if the sauce gets too thick.

4. Meanwhile, bring a large pot of water to a rolling boil, salt abundantly, and add the pasta. Drain the pasta when al dente and transfer to a serving platter or bowl. Pour the lobster sauce over. You eat the lobster pieces with your hands.

Makes 4 servings

Maccheroni Arrosto (Liguria)

ROASTED MACARONI

I would argue that the very early appearance of pasta secca *(macaroni) in Genoa—as early as the thirteenth century, as we know from documents, and perhaps earlier—is attributable to the commercial links with Sicily in the twelfth and thirteenth centuries and not, at first, to the local industry. We know that macaroni was being manufactured near Trabia in Sicily by the mid-twelfth century and that the Sicilians were exporting it to Italy and even the Arab countries. Remember that in 1214, 41 percent of Genoese trade was with Sicily. Soon, though, the Genoese were also producing* pasta secca, *as they were in Pisa by 1284, in quantities and varieties large enough for Tommaso Garzoni, author of* Piazza universale di tutte le professioni del mondo *(published in Venice in 1585) to call them* paste di Genoa.[81]

In the fourteenth century, Genoese homes did not have ovens; breads and other foods were brought to public ovens for cooking. In bourgeois homes, the chore of taking the food to be baked to the public ovens fell upon Arab women slaves.[82] Baked macaroni at this time usually meant some kind of pie, like a lasagne pie—that is, the pasta was encased in pastry dough. The more common method of cooking pasta, as today, was by boiling in water or broth.

1/4 cup (1/2 stick) unsalted butter
1/2 pound ground veal
2 garlic cloves, finely chopped
Leaves from 1 sprig fresh rosemary, chopped
1/3 cup dry white wine
2 cups canned or fresh tomato puree
Salt and freshly ground black pepper to taste
3/4 cup beef broth (page 54)
1 1/2 pounds macaroni (any tubular pasta about 1 1/2 inches long)
1 cup freshly grated Parmigiano-Reggiano cheese

1. In a large casserole, melt 3 tablespoons of the butter over medium heat; when it stops bubbling, brown the veal with the garlic and rosemary, stirring constantly so the garlic doesn't burn and breaking up the veal, about 3 minutes.

2. Increase the heat to high and pour in the wine. Once the wine has evaporated, about 3 minutes, add the tomato puree, season with salt and pepper, and stir to blend well. Pour in the broth, reduce the heat to low, cover, and simmer until thick, about 30 minutes.

3. Preheat the oven to 350°F.

4. Meanwhile, bring a large pot of water to a rolling boil, salt abundantly, and add the pasta. Drain when just shy of al dente and toss with the sauce. Transfer several ladlefuls of macaroni and sauce at a time to a lightly oiled baking pan, interspersing them with the Parmigiano-Reggiano. Dot the top with the remaining tablespoon butter and bake until golden brown, 20 to 25 minutes.

Makes 6 to 8 servings

Spaghettini al Basilico Tritato (Liguria)

SPAGHETTINI WITH CHOPPED FRESH BASIL LEAVES

Two Arabic-derived words for macaroni were used to refer to the pasta of Genoa in the fourteenth century, in particular—the tria januensis *(Genoese vermicelli) and* fideli *(a kind of vermicelli). The expression* tria januenis *may not have been used by the Genoese themselves, but it was by others, such as the Neapolitans.*

We don't know when macaroni was first made with the most famous herb of Liguria, basil, but one story that has come down to us gives a glimpse of the importance of basil in Genoa. Francesco Marchese, a humanist ambassador from Genoa, said to the duke of Milan upon presenting him a tub of basil, "If treated well, basil gives off a nice scent; if dealt with harshly, it produces serpents and scorpions." This broad hint on how Milan should rule Genoa reveals the influence of humanist education and of basil in cooking.[83]

This easy recipe is typical of the Ligurian coast where basil grows profusely. For a perfect preparation, use the recommended pasta or a vermicelli or capellini *close to it. Make sure the basil leaves are quite dry before chopping.*

1 pound ripe tomatoes, peeled, seeded, and quartered
1/4 cup (1/2 stick) unsalted butter, at room temperature
2 tablespoons finely chopped onion
Salt and freshly ground black pepper to taste
3/4 pound *spaghettini* no. 9
Leaves from 1 bunch fresh basil, finely chopped (1/2 to 3/4 cup)
1/4 cup freshly grated Parmigiano-Reggiano cheese

1. Place the tomatoes in a medium-size skillet and turn the heat to medium. Simmer for 30 minutes, reducing the heat to low if it is bubbling too vigorously. Pass through a food mill or fine-mesh strainer and set aside.

2. Wash and dry out the skillet. In the skillet, melt 2 tablespoons of the butter over medium heat; when it starts to bubble, add the onion and cook until translucent, about 6 minutes, stirring a few times. Add the tomatoes, season with salt and pepper, and simmer over medium heat for 10 minutes.

3. Meanwhile, bring a large pot of water to a rolling boil, salt abundantly, and add the pasta. Drain when al dente. Transfer to a serving platter or bowl and toss with the remaining 2 tablespoons butter. Sprinkle the basil and half the cheese and toss again. Cover with the tomato sauce and toss again. Add the remaining cheese, toss once more, and serve.

Makes 4 servings

❖ *Tagliatelle con Ragù alla Bolognese* (Emilia-Romagna)

TAGLIATELLE WITH BOLOGNESE SAUCE

Tagliatelle, tagliolini, pappardelle, *tortellini, and lasagne are some of the pastas made from* sfoglia, *the "leaves" of egg-and-flour dough. Legend has it that the* tagliatelle *shape—strips of pasta about a half inch wide—was invented in 1487 by Maestro Zafirano, a cook from the village of Bentivoglio, on the occasion of the marriage of Lucrezia Borgia to the duke of Ferrara. The cook was said to be inspired by the beautiful blond hair of the bride.*[84] *Despite the appeal of this romantic notion, it seems likely that the invention of* tagliatelle *in Italy is earlier. In the* Compendium de naturis et proprietatibus alimentorum, *a list of local Emilian nomenclature for foods compiled in 1338 by Barnaba de Ritinis da Reggio di Modena, the entry for a pasta called* fermentini *indicates that it is cut into strips like* tagliatelle *and boiled.*[85]

The famous ragù *that accompanies* tagliatelle *is often bastardized by what I call international hotel cooking.*[86] *I have eaten horrible to adequate Bolognese sauces in as disparate places as a train station in Lübeck, Germany, and a hotel in Luxor, Egypt. Nowhere but Bologna, its home, can you find its flavor so inviting and its taste so rich. This recipe is one of the richest enhancements of the classic* ragù *from Bologna, which was once much simpler. The meat needs to be lean, otherwise there will be too much fat in the sauce. It can be ground in a food processor using very short bursts or pulses, resulting in a very finely chopped effect. Remember that "very finely chopped" means pieces no bigger than this "O," so you may consider using the food processor for all the ingredients, again using short bursts.*

3 tablespoons unsalted butter
3 tablespoons extra virgin olive oil
2 ounces pancetta, very finely chopped
1 ounce prosciutto, very finely chopped
1 ounce mortadella, very finely chopped
3 tablespoons dried porcini mushrooms, soaked in tepid water to cover for 15 minutes, drained, rinsed, and finely chopped
1 medium-size onion, very finely chopped
1 small garlic clove, very finely chopped
1 carrot, very finely chopped
1 celery stalk, very finely chopped
2 tablespoons very finely chopped fresh parsley leaves
1/4 pound lean beef sirloin, very finely chopped (not ground)
1/4 pound lean pork tenderloin, very finely chopped (not ground)
1/4 pound lean veal sirloin, very finely chopped (not ground)
2 chicken livers, membranes removed and very finely chopped
1/2 cup dry red wine
1/4 cup tomato sauce (page 32)
1 tablespoon water
1/4 cup beef broth (page 54)
Salt and freshly ground black pepper to taste
Pinch of freshly grated nutmeg
1/2 cup heavy cream
1 1/4 pounds *tagliatelle*

1. In a large, heavy skillet, melt the butter with the olive oil over medium-heat and cook the pancetta, prosciutto, and mortadella until the pancetta is soft and a bit rendered, about 10 minutes, stirring occasionally. Add the mushrooms, onion, garlic, carrot, celery, and parsley and cook until the vegetables have softened and turned color, about 10 minutes, stirring as needed. Add the beef, pork, veal, and chicken livers and brown, about 10 minutes.

2. Increase the heat to medium-high and add the wine. Once the wine has evaporated, reduce the heat to low and add the tomato sauce diluted with a little water and the beef broth. Season with salt, pepper, and nutmeg. Cover and simmer for 2 hours. Add the cream and cook another 10 minutes.

3. Meanwhile, bring a large pot of water to a rolling boil, salt abundantly, and add the pasta. Drain when al dente and transfer to a serving platter. Ladle the *ragù* on top and serve immediately. The *ragù* can be frozen for up to 4 months.

NOTE: A simpler preparation calls for cooking the onion with the celery and carrot in the oil and butter, adding the ground beef, but not the other meats, the wine, salt and pepper, nutmeg, and 1½ cups of tomato sauce. Follow the recipe above, eliminating all the ingredients except those called for in this note.

Makes 6 servings

Macaronia me Kima (Greece)
SPAGHETTI WITH GROUND MEAT AND TOMATO SAUCE

Although some people have claimed that the ancient Greeks knew of macaroni, there are two reasons why I don't believe this is so. First, the makaria *(a word sometimes taken to be the etymological root of* macaroni*) mentioned by the eighth-century* B.C. *Greek lexicographer Hesychius was wheat or barley bread soup.*[87] *Second, as I argued earlier (page 622), there is no conclusive evidence of the Greeks having known hard wheat, the sine qua non of macaroni. It is more likely that the medieval Greeks learned of hard wheat macaroni from the Arabs directly or by way of the Turks, or it was imported by the Italians at a later date.*

This traditional dish, which seems to evidence Venetian influence in its ragù di carne *and cinnamon, is a fairly common preparation in the home. It can also be expertly prepared in the more rural bus and truck-stop tavernas. This is important for the modern traveler to know because restaurant food in Greece is not generally to be recommended. When I first went to Greece in 1971, finding authentic Greek food was as natural as finding a Greek. Today, with Greece more thoroughly integrated into the European community and its tourism industry an important part of the economy, finding real Greek food outside of the home is exceedingly difficult. Greek restaurants cater to the palates of their most common visitor, the northern Europeans, and have diluted their original cuisine to a bland Greekish Euro-cuisine. The cooking that happens in the home is vastly different, infinitely better, and a treasure that a tourist with taste can only dream of unless lucky enough to be invited into that home. When I asked one sympathetic Greek restaurateur about this phenomenon, he said that it was the victory of poor taste, because tourists actually want Greek food, but once confronted with the real thing, they balk (usually because the northerner considers it too garlicky and too oily), hence tourist food* à la Grecque*. This negative phenomenon of tourism also appears on the Costa del Sol of Spain, but not, thankfully, in Italy or Turkey—yet.*

I first ate a dish like this many years ago on the island of Ios. Ios, a small volcanic island, was deathly quiet when I was there in April, and more or less devoid of tourists, excepting a handful of hippies. In the sixteenth century, Ios was the private preserve of the Pisani family of Venice, a family that provided a number of admirals to the fleet over the centuries, but there is today no trace of Venice's presence except a small ruined castle and perhaps some culinary surprises.

The small whitewashed village was a short walk up a steep hill from the tiny harbor, really not much more than a breakwater with a dock. In those days there were only two tavernas on the island, and the one I settled in served a beautiful roast baby lamb and spaghetti. This kind of spaghetti sauce is used with other pastas as well as rice. The Greeks do not like their spaghetti cooked al dente as do the Italians, preferring to cook it until soft as do the Arabs and Turks.

½ cup extra virgin olive oil
1 small onion, finely chopped
2 garlic cloves, 1 crushed and 1 sliced
1 pound ground beef
Salt and freshly ground black pepper to taste
½ cup dry red wine
1½ pounds canned or fresh chopped or crushed tomatoes
1 tablespoon tomato paste
1 bay leaf
1 cinnamon stick
1 whole clove
2 teaspoons sugar
1 tablespoon finely chopped fresh parsley leaves
1 pound spaghetti
¾ cup freshly grated *kefalotyri* cheese (page 716)

1. In a large casserole, heat the olive oil over medium-high heat, then cook the onion and crushed garlic until soft, about 4 minutes, stirring frequently so the garlic doesn't burn. Remove and discard the garlic.

2. Add the ground beef, season with salt and pepper, and cook until the meat loses its color, about 3 minutes, breaking up any lumps. Add the wine, tomatoes, tomato paste, sliced garlic, bay leaf, cinnamon stick, clove, sugar, and parsley. Reduce the heat to low and simmer until dense, about 1 hour.

3. Meanwhile, bring a large pot of water to a rolling boil, salt abundantly, and add the pasta. Drain the pasta when soft and toss with the sauce. Sprinkle the grated cheese on top and serve.

Makes 4 servings

Mʿakarūna bi'l-Laban (Arab Levant)

MACARONI WITH YOGURT

Contrary to the suggestion I made earlier about the as yet unproven etymology of macaroni, *Arabs will tell you that the word derives from the Italian. Then again, the Arab man on the street is mostly unaware of the early—Arab—history of* pasta secca. *In the medieval Arab world, the simplest way macaroni, in the form of spaghetti (vermicelli), was cooked was with lentils. The closest thing to a macaroni dish with yogurt like this one, in the medieval Middle East, might have been the Seljuk dish from Anatolia called* tutmaç, *described in the eleventh-century dictionary* Divanü Lugati't-Türk *of Mahmud el-Kaşgari as a kind of thick soup made with dumplings that may have been hard wheat* pasta secca *and yogurt. Another dish,* erişte *(from* rishta), *is described by the fourteenth-century Arab traveler Ibn Baṭṭūṭa, traveling in Anatolia, as vermicelli with horse and lamb meat cooked in milk.*[88]

In the Levant, pasta is served as a main course and never a first course, as the Italians would serve it. This is a rich and filling dish that could be accompanied by a simple vegetable.

¼ cup unsalted butter or *samna* (clarified butter; page 189)
½ pound lean ground lamb
1 pound onions, chopped
Salt to taste
1 teaspoon red Aleppo pepper (page 722) or ½ teaspoon cayenne pepper
½ pound spaghetti or *perciatelli*
6 garlic cloves, mashed in a mortar
1 cup high-quality full-fat plain yogurt
2 tablespoons *labna* (page 186)
1 tablespoon finely chopped fresh parsley leaves

1. In a large casserole, melt 1 tablespoon of the butter or *samna* over medium heat, then brown the lamb with the onions and salt, about 30 minutes, stirring. In a small skillet, heat 1 tablespoon of the butter or *samna* and dissolve the red pepper in it. Take off the heat.

2. Meanwhile, bring a large pot of water to a rolling boil, salt abundantly, and add the pasta. Drain the pasta when soft and toss with the remaining 2 tablespoons butter or *samna*.

3. Pour the spaghetti into the casserole with the meat sauce and toss with the mashed garlic and sauce. Whip the yogurt and *labna* together until smooth and pour over the spaghetti with the red pepper and butter. Toss well, sprinkle the parsley over, and serve.

Makes 2 to 4 servings

❈ *Duwayda Zarrāᶜ* (Tunisia)

PEASANT-STYLE VERMICELLI AND TURMERIC SOUP

Duwayda, *which means "inchworm" in Arabic, is a vermicelli broken into one-inch lengths. This form of macaroni appears to go back to the time of the Ḥafṣids (1228–1574), the most important dynasty in late medieval Ifriqiyya (the medieval Arabic name for Tunisia).*[89]

This is a simple farmer's (zarrāᶜ) *soup that might be eaten at midday. The spicing is typically Tunisian and quite nice on a cold winter day.*

½ cup extra virgin olive oil
1 medium-size onion, finely chopped
2 tablespoons tomato paste
6 cups water
3 bay leaves
½ teaspoon turmeric
1 tablespoon paprika
½ teaspoon freshly ground black pepper
2 tablespoons finely chopped celery leaves and some stalk
Salt to taste
6 to 8 ounces vermicelli, broken into 1-inch lengths

1. In a medium-size casserole, heat the olive oil over medium-high heat, then cook the onion until soft, about 4 minutes, stirring frequently. Dissolve the tomato paste in 1 cup of the water and add it to the casserole, along with the bay leaves, turmeric, paprika, pepper, celery leaves, and salt. Reduce the heat to medium and cook for 4 to 5 minutes, stirring.

2. Add the remaining 5 cups water and the vermicelli to the casserole and cook over medium heat until the pasta is soft, about 25 minutes, stirring occasionally.

Makes 4 servings

❈ *Duwayda Maṣbūba bi'l-Dajāj* (Tunisia)

BROKEN VERMICELLI AND CHICKEN WITH SPICY SAUCE

A Tunisian writer of the seventeenth century, Ibn Abī Dīnār al-Qayrawanī, describes how duwayda *was eaten with chicken in Tunis for ᶜĀshūra, the holiday during the Muslim month of Muharram, sacred to the Shias because Husayn, the son of ᶜAlī, married to the Prophet Muhammad's daughter, was martyred on this day at Karbala in Iraq in A.D. 680.*[90]

Among North Africans, Tunisians are noted for their appetizing variety of pasta dishes, many cooked in a couscousière. *This recipe is served on the ninth day of*

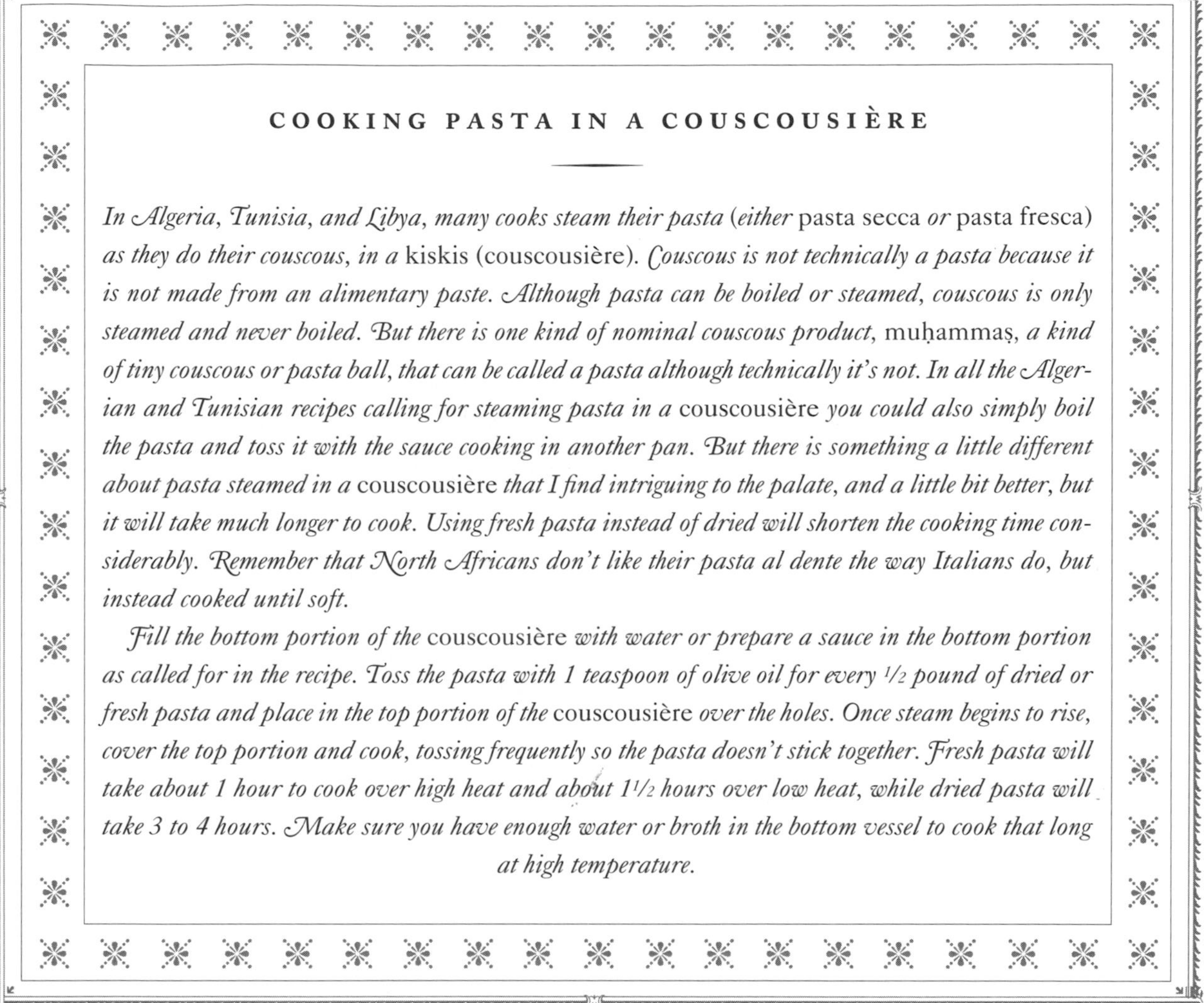

COOKING PASTA IN A COUSCOUSIÈRE

In Algeria, Tunisia, and Libya, many cooks steam their pasta (either pasta secca *or* pasta fresca) *as they do their couscous, in a* kiskis (couscousière). *Couscous is not technically a pasta because it is not made from an alimentary paste. Although pasta can be boiled or steamed, couscous is only steamed and never boiled. But there is one kind of nominal couscous product,* muḥammaṣ, *a kind of tiny couscous or pasta ball, that can be called a pasta although technically it's not. In all the Algerian and Tunisian recipes calling for steaming pasta in a* couscousière *you could also simply boil the pasta and toss it with the sauce cooking in another pan. But there is something a little different about pasta steamed in a* couscousière *that I find intriguing to the palate, and a little bit better, but it will take much longer to cook. Using fresh pasta instead of dried will shorten the cooking time considerably. Remember that North Africans don't like their pasta al dente the way Italians do, but instead cooked until soft.*

Fill the bottom portion of the couscousière *with water or prepare a sauce in the bottom portion as called for in the recipe. Toss the pasta with 1 teaspoon of olive oil for every ½ pound of dried or fresh pasta and place in the top portion of the* couscousière *over the holes. Once steam begins to rise, cover the top portion and cook, tossing frequently so the pasta doesn't stick together. Fresh pasta will take about 1 hour to cook over high heat and about 1½ hours over low heat, while dried pasta will take 3 to 4 hours. Make sure you have enough water or broth in the bottom vessel to cook that long at high temperature.*

ʿĀshūra, while mutton would be served on the tenth day.[91]

Make sure you use chicken thighs and not breast meat, which will dry out in this dish.

½ cup extra virgin olive oil
1 pound boneless chicken thighs, trimmed of fat and cut into small cubes
1 small onion, chopped
1 cup drained cooked chickpeas
2 tablespoons tomato paste dissolved in ½ cup water
2 teaspoons *harīsa* (page 523)
2 teaspoons ground red pepper
Salt to taste
5½ cups water (more as necessary)
¾ pound vermicelli, broken into 1-inch lengths (see Note on page 652 if using a *couscousière* to cook the pasta)
1 tablespoon *samna* (clarified butter; page 189)
Freshly ground black pepper to taste

1. In a large casserole or the bottom portion of a *couscousière*, heat the olive oil over high heat, then cook the chicken cubes and onion until golden, about 3 minutes, stirring a few times. Add the chickpeas, dissolved tomato paste, *harīsa*, red pepper, and salt. Stir, reduce the heat to medium-high, and cook for 5 minutes. Add 1½ cups of the water to barely cover

the pieces of meat. Bring to just below a boil, then reduce the heat to low, cover, and simmer for 1 hour.

2. When the chicken is almost cooked, add the remaining 4 cups water, bring to a boil, and add the vermicelli. Cook until the pasta is soft, about 15 minutes. Add the *samna*, season with black pepper, stir, and serve.

NOTE: If steaming the vermicelli in a *couscousière*, you will need to use fresh vermicelli or spaghetti. Break the vermicelli into 1-inch lengths and toss with 2 teaspoons olive oil, place in the top portion of a *couscousière*, and steam over the sauce cooking in the bottom portion for 1 hour, tossing occasionally. After 1 hour, transfer the pasta to the sauce and let cook together for 15 minutes.

Makes 4 servings

Maqarūna Jāriyya bi'l-Dibābish (Tunisia)

TEENY-TINY SEASHELL PASTA WITH SPICY LEGUMES

In the Maghrib, a typical winter meal is a small pasta cooked with legumes, the dish usually taking the name of the particular pasta being used. One of these dishes is ḥlālim, *named after the pasta used, a pasta shaped like a grain of rice and made of a dough of hard wheat flour, leavened bread dough, water, and salt, which is allowed to rise for two hours before being formed into the final pasta shape. The fermentation process gives a special taste and texture to the pasta. Another small pasta used for these winter soups is* maqarūna ʿaqīq, *a pasta shaped like an haricot bean.*

In this recipe, maqarūna jāriyya *are tiny seashell pasta and the finished dish is almost like a thick minestrone; the longer the pasta rests, the more sauce it absorbs until finally there is no liquid left.* Al-dibābish *refers to the soup being made of dried legumes instead of fresh.*[92] *The ideal pasta for this recipe is the* conchigliette piccole *no. 46 made by the Delverde company, available through Italian markets or it can be ordered by your local supermarket.*

1 cup dried fava beans, picked over, soaked overnight in cold water to cover, and drained
1/4 cup drained cooked chickpeas
1/4 cup extra virgin olive oil
1 small onion, chopped
1 cup canned or fresh tomato puree
1/2 cup water
1 tablespoon *harīsa* (page 523)
2 teaspoons freshly ground black pepper
3 tablespoons finely chopped fresh parsley leaves
2 celery stalks, finely chopped
2 quarts water
1 green bell pepper, seeded and chopped
Salt to taste
1/2 pound tiny seashell pasta
Freshly grated Parmigiano-Reggiano or Gruyère cheese to taste

1. In a medium-size pot, boil the drained fava beans in fresh water to cover generously until you can peel the skins off easily, about 15 minutes. Drain and peel, setting the beans aside. In a small saucepan, boil the chickpeas in water to cover for 5 minutes, drain, place in cold water, and rub them to remove their skins. Set aside with the fava beans.

2. In a large casserole, heat the olive oil over high heat, then cook the onion until browned slightly on the edges, 3 to 4 minutes, stirring almost constantly. Add the tomato puree, water, *harīsa*, black pepper, parsley, celery, and fava beans and chickpeas, stir, and cook for 2 minutes. Add 1 quart of the water and bring to a boil, then reduce the heat to low and simmer until the beans are tender, about 2 hours.

3. Add the remaining quart water, bring to a boil, and add the green pepper, salt, and pasta shells. Cook until the pasta is soft, 5 to 8 minutes. Check the salt and serve with the cheese on the side.

Makes 4 to 6 servings

Nawāṣar Mafawwra (Tunisia)

STEAMED PASTA SQUARES WITH LAMB AND CHICKPEAS IN A SPICY SAUCE

Nawāṣar *is a Tunisian pasta shape identical to the Italian* quadratini *or the Greek* hilopittes, *flat quarter-inch squares of macaroni. The name of this antique form of pasta has an interesting heritage.* Nawāṣar *is the plural of* nāṣra, *square silver coins that were a unit of coinage during the Almohad period (1130–1269) in Tunisia.*[93] *In Algeria, the same pasta is called* makarfta. *This pasta is cooked* mafawwra, *but although the word* mafawwra *comes from the root word* fawra, *meaning "to boil," the Tunisians actually steam the pasta squares in a* couscousière, *unlike the Italians, who boil* quadratini *for soups and minestrone.*

½ cup plus 2 teaspoons extra virgin olive oil
1 small onion, finely chopped
1 pound boneless leg of lamb, trimmed of fat and cut into 1-inch cubes
Salt and freshly ground black pepper to taste
2 teaspoons cayenne or red Aleppo pepper
1 tablespoon *harīsa* (page 523)
2 tablespoons tomato paste
1 cup drained cooked chickpeas
¾ pound small white potatoes, peeled
2 quarts water, or as needed
1 pound *nawāṣar (quadratini)*
2 tablespoons unsalted butter
3 hard-boiled eggs (optional), shelled and quartered

1. In the bottom part of a *couscousière* or pot that can fit a colander on top, heat ½ cup of the olive oil over high heat, then cook the onion until soft, about 2 minutes, stirring. Salt and pepper the lamb, then brown it with the onion on all sides, about 4 minutes, stirring frequently. Add the red pepper, *harīsa*, tomato paste, chickpeas, potatoes, and 1 quart of the water.

2. Toss the dry or fresh pasta squares with the remaining 2 teaspoons olive oil. Place the pasta loosely in the top part of the *couscousière* or in the colander. Place the top part or colander over the bottom part or pot. Steam the pasta over medium-high heat, covered, until you begin to see steam rising through the pasta, about 30 minutes, tossing the pasta occasionally. From that point, cook dried pasta for 3 hours, replenishing the broth with another quart of water, if necessary. If using fresh pasta, steam for 1 hour. Toss the pasta occasionally while it steams.

3. Transfer the pasta to a serving bowl and toss with the butter and sauce. Arrange the meat and potatoes around the pasta and garnish with the hard-boiled eggs if desired.

VARIATION

Cook the lamb and sauce in a casserole. After the lamb has cooked for 3 hours, add 1 quart water, bring to a boil, add the pasta, and cook until soft.

Makes 6 servings

Qrīṭfa (Tunisia)

This recipe from Gafsa, the oasis town in southwestern Tunisia, is ideally suited to the nomadic life. Nearly every ingredient is dried. At least one historian of pasta secca *believes that macaroni was invented by nomadic Bedouin utilizing the newly found properties of hard wheat: it could be dried, made small, and transported for long periods of time, up to many years.*[94] *On the other hand, I suspect that future historians may discover that it was some Arab general in charge of logistics who had to feed the armies of Islam as they exploded out of the Arabian Peninsula in the seventh century, sweeping across North Africa, southwestern Europe, and the Middle East over the next two centuries. Their food needs were enormous, the aridity of these regions meant they couldn't rely on local agriculture, and they needed food that was transportable, and could be stored for years. What better food than dried macaroni and dried legumes?*

This recipe is difficult—one of the few in this book—simply because so many of the ingredients are not available. The nawāṣar *can be replaced by the Italian soup pasta known as* quadratini, *which is identical. The* wazaf *are small dried fish, very common in coastal markets in Tunisia, and used for flavoring dishes.*[95] *It can be replaced with the* sardelle salate *(salted sardines) on page 434, salted anchovy fillets, or the small dried fish sold in Chinese or Japanese markets.* Qarnīṭ, *or dried octopus, is very hard to find. I've been told that the Japanese use dried octopus and one might find it in a Japanese market. The Greeks also use dried octopus, and you might have luck in their markets. The octopus is cleaned and dried in the sun. It shrivels until it is very small and can be stored. When it is used in cooking, it will rehydrate and swell up again. Its flavor is quite unique and pleasant. If you have bought a dried octopus in Tunisia as a souvenir, use it in cooking; if it doesn't swell up, it is old, and can simply be discarded after being used for its flavoring. If it isn't old, you can eat it. The remaining ingredients are easily found. If you decide to use a fresh octopus for this recipe, please see the Note below.*

I have not given an English name to this recipe because I can't think what it should be.

1 tablespoon tomato paste
2 quarts plus 1 cup water
½ cup dried fava beans, picked over, soaked in water to cover overnight, and drained
½ cup plus 1 tablespoon extra virgin olive oil
2 medium-size onions, chopped
1 bunch Swiss chard (about 1¼ pounds), stems removed and leaves ripped into pieces
1 *qarnīṭ* (small dried octopus)
1 cup *wazaf* (small dried fish) or substitute
½ cup drained cooked chickpeas
2 tablespoons dried brown lentils, picked over and rinsed
¼ pound dried apricots, quartered
1 teaspoon garlic powder
2 cups canned or fresh tomato puree
Salt to taste
1 pound *nawāṣar* (or substitute *quadratini* pasta)
2 tablespoons *samna* (clarified butter; page 189)

1. Dissolve the tomato paste in 1 cup of the water. Place the drained fava beans in a medium-size saucepan with fresh water to cover generously, bring to a boil, and boil until their skins can be peeled off, 5 to 15 minutes; check occasionally. Drain, peel the fava beans once you can handle them, and set aside.

2. In the bottom portion of a *couscousière* or a pot that can fit a colander on top, heat ½ cup of the olive oil over medium-high heat, then cook the onions until soft and golden, about 7 minutes, stirring. Pour the diluted tomato paste in with the onions, add the Swiss chard leaves, and cook until wilted, about 1 minute. Add the *qarnīṭ, wazaf*, chickpeas, fava beans, lentils, apricots, and garlic powder, stir, and pour in the 2 quarts water and the tomato puree. Reduce the heat to medium and season with salt.

3. Meanwhile, mix the *nawāṣar* with the remaining tablespoon olive oil, tossing well so every square is oiled; this way they won't stick together as they steam. Put the *nawāṣar* in the top portion of the *couscousière* or the colander, and the top portion or colander over the broth in the bottom portion or pot. Cover and

steam until tender, about 2½ hours. Mix the *nawāṣar* as well as the broth occasionally with a wooden spoon to distribute the flavors.

4. Remove the *nawāṣar* from the heat and stir to separate any pasta pieces from each other. Mix in 1 tablespoon of the *samna* and return to steam for another 30 minutes. Remove the pasta and transfer to a platter. Mix in the remaining tablespoon *samna* and toss. Cover with the sauce and serve.

NOTE: Wash and clean a 1½-pound fresh octopus, if that has not already been done. Put the octopus in a pot and cover with water and 1 cup vinegar. Bring to a boil, reduce the heat to medium, and simmer, covered, for half an hour. Drain and wash well in cold water, peeling off the skin. Add as directed in step 2 above.

Makes 6 servings

Rishta (Tunisia)

TUNISIAN PASTA WITH FAVA BEANS AND BELL PEPPERS

Rishta *is a name with a long history, derived from the Persian word for "threads," referring to any filiform* pasta secca. *In Algeria and Tunisia today,* rishta *is a fettuccine made, usually, with eggs.* Rishta jida *is a thinner pasta, 1 to 2 millimeters wide (what the Italians call* lingue*). A variety of dishes are made in Tunisia with* rishta, *such as* rishta jāriyya, *a soup of chickpeas, fava beans, turnips, carrots, onions, red pepper,* harīsa, *and* qadīd, *a preserved meat (pages 69 and 249).*

One geographer has claimed that in the Mediterranean, soil is unimportant, that everything is sun and rain. The green hillsides of the Atlas, the Alps, the Pyrenees, and the Kabylia are thick with grass and trees and comforting dishes such as those made of flour, beans, and oil. This rishta *recipe is from Sidi Boulbaba near Gabes. There are many varieties of* rishta *preparations, as there are many varieties of spaghetti preparations in Italy. One could concoct almost any combination of ingredients, perhaps using turnips, Swiss chard, carrots, or raisins. This preparation does not use any meat.*

2 pounds fresh fava beans
¾ cup extra virgin olive oil
1 medium-size onion, finely chopped
6 green bell peppers, seeded and thinly sliced
½ cup drained cooked chickpeas
1 pound canned or fresh tomatoes, peeled, seeded, and chopped
¼ cup finely chopped fresh parsley leaves
1 tablespoon *harīsa* (page 523)
2 teaspoons cayenne pepper
Salt and freshly ground black pepper to taste
¾ pound fettuccine

1. Peel the fava beans from their pods. Bring a medium-size pot of water to a boil and boil the fava beans for 3 to 4 minutes in order to easily remove their skins. You should have about 1½ cups of fava beans after their skins are removed. Discard the skins.

2. In a large casserole, heat the olive oil over medium-high heat, then cook the onion and bell peppers until soft, about 12 minutes, stirring occasionally. Add the fava beans, chickpeas, tomatoes, parsley, *harīsa*, and cayenne and season with salt and black pepper. Reduce the heat to low and simmer for 30 minutes, or until the vegetables are cooked the way you like.

3. Meanwhile, bring a large pot of water to a rolling boil, salt abundantly, and add the pasta. Drain when al dente and add to the vegetables in the casserole. Toss well, cook another 5 to 10 minutes, and serve.

Makes 6 servings

MACARONI IN THE MAGHRIB

Many people do not associate pasta with Arab cookery, but, in fact, the invention of macaroni may very well lie with the Arabs or Berbers in North Africa. Although the Italians eventually outstripped all other Mediterranean peoples in the variety and uses of pasta, Tunisians have claims to some of the earliest. Many pasta preparations in the Maghrib, especially in western Libya and southern Tunisia, are steamed over water or broth in a couscousière, *as one would cook couscous.*

Here are some of the varieties of macaroni found in North Africa:

- Rishta*:* *See page 655.*
- Nawāṣar*:* *See page 653.*
- Duwayda*: A Tunisian Arabic word meaning "vermicelli," coming from the identical root that the Italian comes from—*duwayda *and* verme *both mean "worms."* Duwayda bi'l-ᶜalūsh *is a lamb stew with vermicelli, onion, tomato puree, and red chili pepper while* duwayda zarrāᶜ *is a macaroni and turmeric soup (page 650).*
- Ḥlālim*: A soup pasta made of durum wheat, white flour, or bread dough, and water. The dough is soft like bread dough, and made with yeast. Pieces of the dough are rolled between the palms into strings about 1½ inches long, then small pieces are broken off and rolled with the fingers into 3-millimeter-wide cylinders, the size of pine nuts. It is used in soups with chickpeas, lentils, and haricot beans.*
- Tlītlū (*sometimes* tlītli): *A kind of pasta made the same way as* ḥlālim, *but the size of a rice grain, steamed in a* couscousière. *The preparation called* tlītlū *can also be made of millet.*
- Qaṭᶜa*: The same as* ḥlālim *but a little longer, which comes from the Bizerte region along the northern coast of Tunisia.*
- Maqarūna*: The term in Arabic is used in the same way as it is used in Italian: as a generic term for all forms of pasta. It is cooked in a variety of ways, such as* maqarūna bi'l-ṣalṣa, *with a sauce of grated Gruyère or other similar cheese, Parmesan cheese, dried garlic, tomato puree, and olive oil. Other recipes have chickpeas, onion, bay leaf, veal,* harīsa, *or beans, potatoes, turnips, etc.* Maqarūna *is often made with seafood.* Maqarūna ᶜaqīq *is a pasta shaped like a haricot bean, while* maqarūna jāriyya *are shaped like tiny seashells, what the Italians call* conchigliette piccole *(page 652).*[96]
- Muḥammaṣ*: This is usually described as a form of couscous, but it looks like round pasta. Its name derives from the word for chickpea* (ḥummuṣ), *although it is more the size of a peppercorn. It is one of the most important couscous/pasta products in Tunisia, and one of the oldest. It is made like couscous (page 659) or like pasta. It is sold in the U.S. under the name "moghrebiyya," toasted couscous, and by an Israeli firm as "Israeli couscous."*

- Shūrba*: This word means "soup" in Arabic and is the name of a soup of boiled pasta in Algeria and Tunisia, although its exact contents vary region to region. The pasta used in the soup is also called* shūrba, *which can mean either* capelli d'angeli, *or angel hair pasta, as well as referring to a couscous-like pasta that resembles the Sardinian* fregula *(page 484).*
- Ḥalazūn*: This is a small murex-shell pasta usually used with seafood-based preparations in Tunis.*

Macaroni is also found in Algeria and Morocco where it appears with several names. Made in Algeria with fine semolina, water or eggs or both, salt, and sometimes saffron and olive oil, it is called rishta. Rishta *is a medieval Arab macaroni that is still made, with lentils, in Syria and Lebanon, too.*[97] Drahmat *is a square pasta that may have originally been made with millet or another grain and is steamed in a manner like couscous.* Makarfta *is a square pasta, but the name is also used to refer to a kind of pasta like the Tunisian* tlītlū, *a rice-size pasta used in soups. It is also called* lisān al-ʿaṣfūr, *"little birds' tongues."*[98] Kaḥwa *starts as a filiform pasta rolled out between the palms of the hand and is then pinched off into small pieces like large couscous grains.*[99] Duwayda *is a kind of vermicelli. Algerian Jews used* duwayda *for festive occasions such as bar mitzvahs and other rites of passage. It is often steamed like couscous and served with chickpeas.*[100] Tashaʿrit *is the Moroccan Berber word for vermicelli. A dish called* qrātliyya *(the spelling is unsure) from Annaba, Algeria, is made of a pasta of flour, eggs, saffron, oil, and water and then a sauce of meat, onions, chickpeas, and cinnamon is used with meatballs.* Quṭā'if, *known in the Mashraq (the eastern Arab world) as a kind of shredded wheat used for pastries, is, in Algeria, a homemade fresh angel hair pasta* (capellini) *used often for fried pasta sweets.*[101] *In Morocco,* fidawsh *and* mukatfa *are words for vermicelli and* ṭarshta *is* tagliatelle.

Burkūkis *is a couscous better described as a pasta ball about 3 millimeters in diameter, identical to the Tunisian* muḥammaṣ, *but traditionally made in the Kabylia region of Algeria. It is usually steamed like couscous.*[102] Thimkataft *is a 1-centimeter-square pasta and also a generic term for a square pasta dish made in northern Algeria with tomatoes, peppers, and onions. Under the same name is a broken linguine-like pasta about 3 millimeters wide and 6 centimeters long.*

In Algeria are a variety of semolina doughs somewhere between pasta and crêpes. Trīd *and* ruqāq *are made of semolina, formed into sheets, and fried in a pan with a little oil, while* baghrīr, *made with yeast, and* ghrāyf *are more properly called crêpes.*

Eddeoueida *and* talia *are names for a kind of vermicelli used by the Tuareg of the Algerian Sahara, the latter name derived from* Italia.[103] *The making of vermicelli by hand is also an old tradition in the Libyan towns of Tripoli, Ghat, and Ghadames.*

❈ *Kunāfa Nābulsiyya* (Palestine)

SWEET CHEESE SEMOLINA PASTRY

Nablus is a town on the west bank of the Jordan River where they make a famous Arab dessert called kunāfa, *in which unsalted fresh white cheese is cooked between two layers of a kind of shredded wheat pastry made into the form of very thin vermicelli.* Kunāfa *is an old Arab preparation that is first mentioned in the* Riyāḍ al-nufūs, *a fabulously valuable manuscript for culinary matters, by the pious writer of tenth century Fāṭimid Tunisia (909–1171) Abū Bakr al-Mālikī, who describes this pastry in the ninth century.* Kunāfa *is described again in the medieval cookbooks of the anonymous Hispano-Muslim,* Kitāb al-ṭabīkh fī al-Maghrib wa'l-Āndalus, *the* Kitāb al-wuṣla ila l-ḥabīb fī waṣfi aṭ-ṭayyibāt wāṭ-ṭīb, *and Ibn Razīn al-Tujībī's* Kitāb faḍā-lat al-khiwān fī ṭayyibāt al-ṭᶜam wa'l-alwān.[104]

Although Nablus is the home of this pastry, I was told by a Syrian friend of "the world's best kunāfa*" being made in Jeble, a small town south of Latakia in northern Syria. There is no doubt that* kunāfa *is made in many places, including Turkey, but I was impressed with my friend's story about how Damascenes would make the four-hour drive to Jeble in order to arrive around four in the afternoon, about the time that a particular sweet maker set out his fresh* kunāfa.

Here in Jeble, this sweet maker did not use the cottage-type cheese used in most kunāfa, *but a fresh cheese made without salt that does not use any coloring, called* jubna ḥulwa, *sweet white cheese. He made his* kunāfa *in the normal way, in a large baking tray, cut the* kunāfa *into pieces, and then flipped the whole thing. There is quite a show when he flips the* kunāfa *and people come to watch it.*

Arriving like a culinary Indiana Jones in Jeble, I was met by my friend's sister, Mimi Halaby, who led me to the fabled shop in a hard-to-find alley of this hard-to-get-to coastal village in Syria. Once there (we arrived about 4 P.M.), I was invited to learn how to make kunāfa *from the master* kunāfa *maker himself, Ahmad Mathboot, who, with his sons Abdel-Rahman and Ibrahim, and nephew Housam Masloum, operate one of Syria's renowned sweet shops. Ahmad Mathboot Sweets is on Malik Faisal Street in the old town of Jeble, a town completely devoid of tourist facilities—no restaurants or hotels, and irregular bus service to Aleppo. The sweet shop also makes* shaᶜbiyyāt, *a sweet soft fresh white cheese (sort of a cross between farmer's cheese and ricotta) wrapped in phyllo pastry on a big tray and cut up and coated with sugar syrup.*

At Mr. Mathboot's shop they crumbled the fresh pastry on the top and bottom of the fresh white cheese and pan-fried it until brown on both sides. When it was done, both sides of the shredded wheat were golden brown and the cheese soft and hot. The shredded wheat pastry is made right at the shop. A batter of fine white semolina flour is mixed with some water and put in a device called a juzza, *a container with twelve very small funnels that rests above a large rotating hot plate over burners called a* furn. *As the batter streams out onto the turning hot plate, it forms rivulets of pastry-like contrails. Uniquely, and to perfect effect, Mr. Mathboot grinds his* qaṭā'ifi (kataifi), *unlike the Nablus sweet makers who keep it whole.*

If you are not inclined to order jubna ḥulwa *from the sources mentioned in the "Mediterranean Food Products Resources," you can mix a good-quality full-fat commercial mozzarella cheese that has been soaked in water to cover overnight with fresh mozzarella, and run both through a meat grinder. The fresh cheese should be dry, a little stringy, pliable, and slightly sour.*

¾ cup *samna* (clarified butter; page 189), melted
1 pound *kataifi* (shredded wheat pastry; page 716)
2 pounds *jubna ḥulwa* (sweet white cheese; page 716), crumbled
1½ cups sugar
¾ cup water

1. Using a pastry brush, grease a 12-inch round baking pan with 2 tablespoons of the *samna*. Toss the *kataifi* with 4 tablespoons of the *samna*, fluffing it with your fingers. Push through the coarse blade of a meat grinder three times, or process in a food processor with several short bursts. Toss the crumbled *kataifi* with 4 tablespoons of the *samna*. Push the cheese through the grinder or process with several short bursts in the food processor.

2. Sprinkle half of the *kataifi* evenly around the pan, pressing down slightly with the palms of your hands until it is about 3/8 inch thick. Lightly brown the bottom of the *kataifi* by moving the pan over high heat, about 3 minutes. Because the baking pan is larger than the burner, you must hold the pan with tongs and move it in a circular and even motion to make sure all parts are browned evenly.

3. Remove the pan from the burner. Sprinkle the cheese on top of the *kataifi* evenly and press down a little. Moisten your hands with a little hot water to keep them from sticking. Spread the remaining *kataifi* evenly on top, pressing the edges down so they cover the cheese that might escape from the sides, joining it to the *kataifi* on the bottom. Push the *kataifi* slightly away from the sides of the pan to make it look neat.

4. Continue browning the *kataifi* by moving the baking pan around so all parts of the bottom of the pan brown evenly over high heat, 5 to 8 minutes. Check by lifting the edges up carefully with a flexible spatula to see if it is browning evenly.

5. Place a large, flat pizza pan on top of the baking pan and quickly but carefully, with a firm grip, flip it over. Remove the baking pan and scrape out any cheese that may have oozed out and stuck to the sides of the pan. Grease the pan with the remaining 2 tablespoons *samna*, slide the *kunāfa* back in, and brown the other side, 5 to 8 minutes, over high heat, moving the pan continuously and evenly over all parts of the bottom. Remove the *kunāfa* and let it cool.

6. Prepare the sugar water by heating the sugar and water together in a medium-size saucepan until syrupy over medium-high heat, but not letting it come to a boil, about 10 minutes. Pour the sugar water over the *kunāfa* only after it has cooled a bit, but serve while it is still warm. Cut into portions and serve.

Makes 10 servings

COUSCOUS

COUSCOUS is a staple food in the Maghrib that requires very little in the way of utensils for its preparation. It is an ideal food for both nomadic and agricultural peoples. The preparation of couscous is one that symbolizes "happiness and abundance," in the words of one culinary anthropologist.[105]

One of the first written references to couscous is in the anonymous thirteenth-century Hispano-Muslim cookery book *Kitāb al-ṭabīkh fī al-Maghrib wa'l-Āndalus*.[106] There one finds a recipe from Marrakech, *alcuzcuz fitīyānī*, a couscous made for the young and described as "known all over the world."[107] The fact that the name is given with the Arabic article *al* is a flag to the linguist that the original couscous preparation probably was not an Arab dish, but a Berber dish, because the Arabic words *siksū, kuskus*, and *kusksi*, which all mean "couscous," do not take the article. In any case, we know that the Naṣrid royalty in Granada ate couscous, as mentioned in a culinary poem by the qadi (magistrate) of Granada, Abū ʿAbd Allah bin al-Azrak.[108] "Talk to me about *kuskusū*, it is a noble and distinguished dish."[109] There is a recipe for couscous in another Hispano-Muslim cookbook, the *Kitāb faḍālat al-khiwān* of Ibn Razīn al-Tujībī, a book from either the late eleventh or thirteenth century.[110]

The Arab traveler Leo Africanus (c. 1465–1550)

also mentioned couscous with some delight: "Of all things to be eaten once a day it's *alcuzcuçu* because it costs little and nourishes a lot."[111] The thirteenth-century *Kitāb al-wuṣla ila l-ḥabīb fī waṣfi aṭ-ṭayyibāt wāṭ-ṭib*, written or compiled by a Syrian historian from Aleppo, Ibn al-ᶜAdīm, identified as the grand-nephew of Saladin, the great Muslim warrior and opponent of the Crusaders, has four recipes for couscous; three are called *shᶜiriyya* and the fourth is called Maghribian couscous. *Shᶜiriyya* is a word used today in Lebanon to mean "broken vermicelli" or to refer to the rice-shaped pasta called orzo.

These very early references to couscous show that either it is not unique to the Maghrib or it spread with great rapidity to the Mashraq (the eastern Arab world). I believe it is unique to the Maghrib and that its appearance in the Levant is a curiosity. Personally, I agree with Professor Lisa Anderson of Columbia University, who suggests that the "couscous line" in North Africa is the Gulf of Sirte. In Tripolitania to the west, they eat couscous; and in Cyrenaica to the east, they eat Egyptian food.[112] Couscous was only a curiosity east of the Gulf of Sirte. In the Mashraq, one form of couscous is also known by the word *maghribiyya*, indicating that it is recognized as a food of the Maghrib (the western Arab world).[113] Even today couscous is not eaten that much by Libyans of Cyrenaica and western Egyptians, although it is known by them.[114] But in Morocco, Algeria, Tunisia, and Tripolitania couscous is a staple.

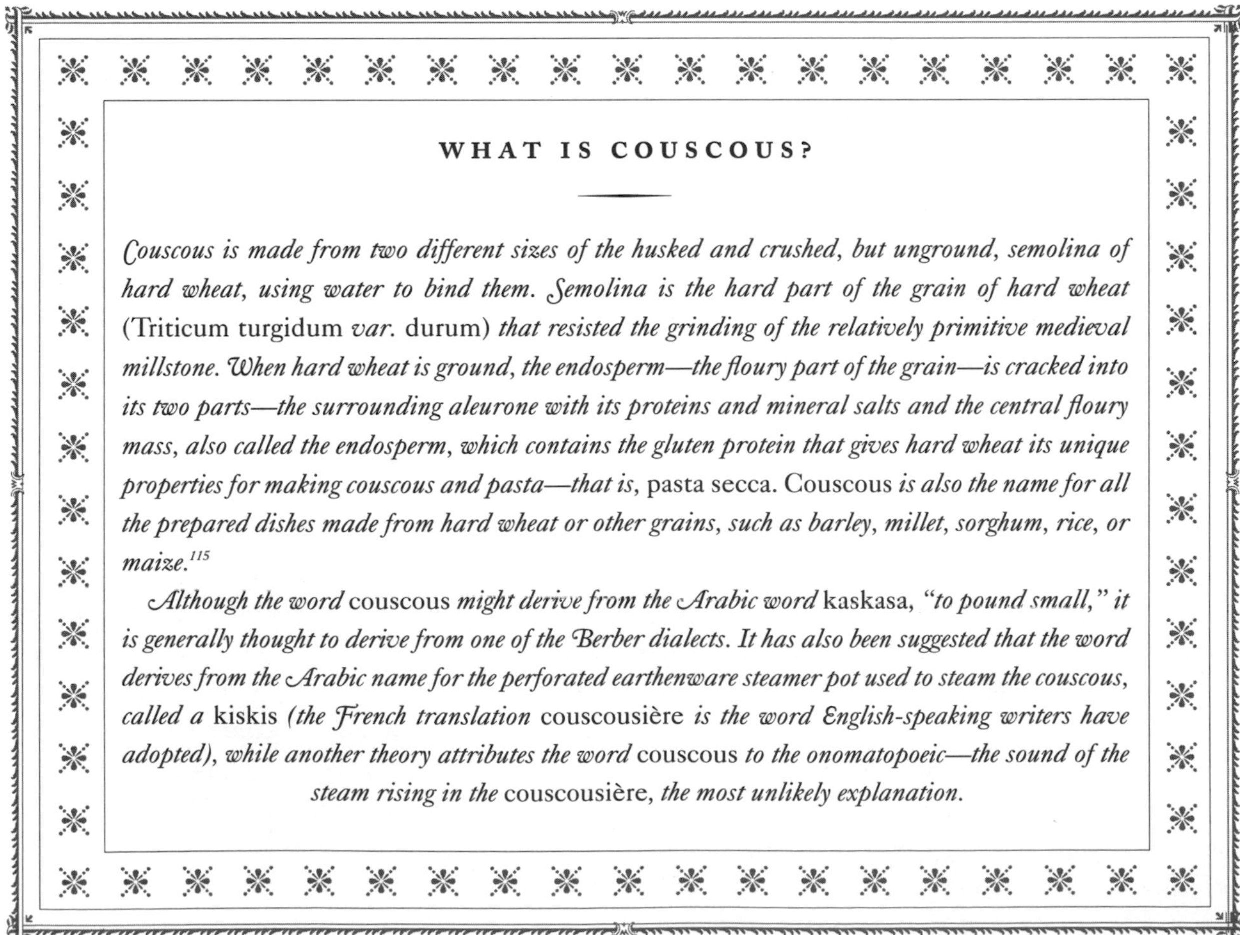

WHAT IS COUSCOUS?

Couscous is made from two different sizes of the husked and crushed, but unground, semolina of hard wheat, using water to bind them. Semolina is the hard part of the grain of hard wheat (Triticum turgidum *var.* durum) *that resisted the grinding of the relatively primitive medieval millstone. When hard wheat is ground, the endosperm—the floury part of the grain—is cracked into its two parts—the surrounding aleurone with its proteins and mineral salts and the central floury mass, also called the endosperm, which contains the gluten protein that gives hard wheat its unique properties for making couscous and pasta—that is,* pasta secca. Couscous *is also the name for all the prepared dishes made from hard wheat or other grains, such as barley, millet, sorghum, rice, or maize.*[115]

Although the word couscous *might derive from the Arabic word* kaskasa, *"to pound small," it is generally thought to derive from one of the Berber dialects. It has also been suggested that the word derives from the Arabic name for the perforated earthenware steamer pot used to steam the couscous, called a* kiskis *(the French translation* couscousière *is the word English-speaking writers have adopted), while another theory attributes the word* couscous *to the onomatopoeic—the sound of the steam rising in the* couscousière, *the most unlikely explanation.*

❈ *Maghribiyya* (Syria)

CHICKEN, LAMB, AND SEMOLINA BALL STEW

The Arabic name of this famous Syrian preparation means "from the Maghrib." This does not mean that the dish itself is from North Africa but that it recognizes the particular form of pasta secca *or couscous ball used in this chicken and meat stew as being originally from the Maghrib.* Maghribiyya *are little semolina balls about three millimeters in diameter. Although they are also known as* muḥammaṣ *in Tunisia and called "couscous," it is easier to think of them as pasta balls.*

Syrian butchers have a special cut of meat, either lamb or veal, used in this preparation called mawzāt, *derived from the Arabic word for a banana: it is the banana-shaped piece attached to the shin, a very succulent and tender cut of meat when stewed. The kind of onions used in Syria for this are red pearl onions, about the size of marbles. One can cook the* maghribiyya *in the top of a* couscousière, *but this takes so long that I opt in this recipe to boil the pasta, losing nothing to authenticity.*

This recipe takes time to prepare, but the result is one of the highlights of Syrian home cooking. My former wife, Najwa al-Qattan, made this for me on my birthday once and told me that the key to getting everything right is being careful with the amount of water you use. The maghribiyya *should be neither burnt nor soggy.*

¾ cup *samna* (clarified butter; page 189)
1 chicken (3½ pounds), cut into 8 pieces
1 pound boneless lamb shin meat, trimmed of tendons and cut into ¾-inch cubes
1 teaspoon freshly ground black pepper
1 teaspoon salt
1 teaspoon ground cinnamon
1 tablespoon freshly ground caraway seeds
20 ounces red pearl onions, peeled (page 720)
1¼ pounds *maghribiyya* (page 717)
One 15-ounce can chickpeas, drained
3 tablespoons unbleached all-purpose flour

1. In a large casserole, melt 6 tablespoons of the *samna* over medium-high heat, then lightly brown the chicken parts on all sides, about 8 minutes. Transfer the chicken to a stew pot or another casserole and just barely cover with water, about 4 cups. Set aside until needed.

2. Meanwhile, brown the lamb cubes in the same *samna* you cooked the chicken in over medium-high heat, about 4 minutes, seasoning with the black pepper, salt, cinnamon, and caraway, turning often so the meat is browned on all sides. Add to the chicken pot.

3. In the same *samna* you have fried the meat, cook the onions over medium-high heat until slightly soft, about 5 minutes, stirring. Transfer the onions to a small saucepan, barely cover with water, about 1 cup, and bring to a gentle boil over medium-high heat. Once it begins to boil, reduce the heat to medium-low and cook until tender, about 15 minutes. Set aside.

4. In a separate large casserole, melt 3 tablespoons of the *samna* over medium heat, then cook the *maghribiyya* until lightly golden, about 6 minutes, stirring or shaking the casserole frequently. Be careful you don't burn the pasta balls. Save this casserole and any remaining *samna* for later.

5. Meanwhile, bring a large pot of abundantly salted water to a boil and add the *maghribiyya* when the water is rolling. Drain when the *maghribiyya* is soft, not al dente as the Italians like it. Salt and pepper the *maghribiyya* and stir in the cooked chickpeas. Set aside until needed, keeping warm, or rewarming later.

6. Bring the broth with the chicken and lamb to a boil over medium-high heat. Reduce the heat to very low (use a heat diffuser if necessary) and cook the

chicken until it is nearly falling off the bone, about 3 hours, but check before then.

7. Once the chicken is cooked, melt the remaining 3 tablespoons *samna* in the large casserole you browned the *maghribiyya* in over medium-high heat and add the flour, stirring to form a roux. Slowly add up to 2 cups of mixed broth, ½ cup at a time, some taken from the chicken and lamb pot and some broth from the onion pan. Stir until the broth has thickened. Transfer the chicken, lamb, and onions to the large casserole and boil for 10 minutes.

8. Reheat the *maghribiyya* and chickpeas for 10 minutes. Transfer the *maghribiyya* and chickpeas to a serving platter and top with the chicken, lamb, and onions. Serve with slightly warmed *khubz ʿarabī* (Arab flatbread or pita bread).

Makes 8 servings

THERE is little in the way of archeological evidence of early use of couscous, mainly because the *kiskis* was probably a basket made from organic material set over a *marmite*-like terra-cotta bottom vessel and never survived.[116] Some shards of a *marmite*-like vessel have been found in the medieval Muslim stratum at Chellala in Algeria, but the dating is difficult.[117] Interestingly, the couscous recipes from the sixteenth and seventeenth centuries are no different from the ones today.

I believe couscous entered Tunisia sometime in the twelfth century, based on the monumental studies of Zīrīd (972–1148) and Ḥafṣid Tunisia (1228–1574) by historians Hady Roger Idris and Robert Brunschvig, who found no references to couscous in twelfth-century Zīrīd Tunisia and many references by thirteenth-century Ḥafṣid times.[118] The great Arab writer al-Muqaddasī (writing circa 985–990) never mentions couscous, although he is noted for writing about the foods he encountered.[119] But couscous is mentioned in connection with many saints of Ḥafṣid times, including Ibn Naji's description of *burkūkis* as a large-grained couscous with meat that is virtually identical to the *maghribiyya* mentioned in the recipe on page 661.[120] There is also an admiring description in the writings of Ibn Faḍallah of Tunisian pilgrims in Mecca in the fifteenth century who magically produced a plate of couscous, accompanied by melted butter, beef, and cabbage.[121]

By the fourteenth century, there are many references to *pasta secca* and couscous. In Pedro de Alcala's *Vocabulista*, published in Granada in 1505, he mentions *kouskoussou* as a *hormigos de massa* (coarse-ground wheat dough). Al-Maqqarī, a historian writing in Damascus in the seventeenth century and our principal authority for the literary history of Muslim Spain, relates a story told in the fifteenth century of a man in Damascus who helps someone from the Maghrib who fell sick. In a dream the Prophet tells him that he should feed the sick man *kouskoussoun*, a word used as a noun. A century earlier the famed Arab traveler Ibn Baṭṭūṭa (1308–1378?) also mentions couscous.[122]

One of the earliest appearances of couscous in northern Europe is in Brittany, when Charles de Clairambault, the naval commissioner, in a letter dated January 12, 1699, writes that the Moroccan ambassador, ʿAbd Allah bin ʿAisha, and his party of eighteen had brought their own flour and made *couscoussou* with dates and that it was a delicious dish they made for Ramadan.[123] But couscous made its appearance much earlier than that in Provence, where the traveler Jean-Jacques Bouchard writes in 1630 of eating in Toulon a "certain kind of pasta which is made of little grains like rice, and which puffs up considerably when cooked; it comes from the Levant and is called *courcoussou*."[124] Unexplained, and most intriguing, is his identification of the couscous as coming from the Levant and not North Africa.

Couscous is served with meat, fish, vegetables, and spices.[125] Cooked simply with sour milk and melted butter, it left the hungry traveler feeling full and was the traditional food of the poorest, namely the nomadic Berbers.[126] For centuries, black African women were employed as couscous cooks, a phenomenon that might be indicative of the sub-Saharan African origins of couscous. Even today in Morocco, the *dada*—young black Saharan and sub-Saharan women who serve as domestics, especially as cooks—are often employed to prepare couscous. The Tuareg, a Muslim Berber tribe of the Sahara, also employ young black servant women to make couscous.[127] Black slaves were also prominent as cooks in medieval Egyptian households and up until the nineteenth century.[128] In Muslim Spain, too, black slaves would prepare meals in aristocratic homes while the wives would prepare the food in poorer homes.[129]

The Berbers, to whom the invention of couscous is often attributed, call couscous *sekrou* or *seksu* and so do Moroccans of Arab origin, while it is known as *maftūl* or *maghribiyya* in the countries of the eastern Mediterranean and *suksukaniyya* in the Sudan. Various Berber tribes of Morocco have different names for couscous. The Abu Isaffen called it *shekshu*, while the Rif call it *sishtu* and the Beni Halima call it *sisu*.[130] In Algeria, couscous is called *kisksū* or *ṭʿām*, meaning "food" or "nourishment," indicating the importance of couscous as a daily staple. Even in western Sicily I have come across couscous called by this purely Algerian Arabic expression. In Tunisia, couscous is called *kiskisi, kisskiss, kuskusī*, and *kusksi*. Very large couscous grains are called *muḥammaṣ* or *burkūkis*, while very fine grains, usually used for sweet couscous dishes, are called *masfūf*.

There are also local names for certain kinds of couscous preparations, such as *burzqān* in Béja, Tunisia, where a fine-grain couscous is mixed with fresh butter, mutton, saffron, and chickpeas, sprinkled with hot milk, and garnished with raisins, almonds, pistachios, hazelnuts, and walnuts.[131] *Malthūth* is a barley couscous (page 613) used by the poor.[132] It is sorted carefully, cleaned, and grilled in a kind of platter called a *ghanāʿā*.[133] It is then pounded, sieved, and dried in the open air. A second sifting collects the barley. A further sieving through a finer sieve allows for the larger grains to be retained, *dashīsha*, as it is called in southern Algeria, also the name of a porridge made of pounded wheat and butter. The smaller grains that have fallen through can be used for barley couscous or *ʿaṣīda* (page 101) or *bazīn*, a kind of polenta with a sauce of bell peppers, chili peppers, tomatoes, *harīsa*, onions, and a little meat.[134] In southern Tunisia, ground fenugreek is sprinkled on the couscous.[135]

The best and most famous couscous is made from hard wheat. Hard wheat couscous was probably invented by Muslim Berbers in the eleventh- or twelfth-century Maghrib. But evidence is mounting that the process of couscous cookery, especially steaming grain over a broth in a special pot, might have originated before the tenth century in the area of West Africa where the medieval Sudanic kingdom thrived, today encompassing parts of the contemporary nations of Niger, Mali, Mauritania, Ghana, and Burkina Faso. Even today in the region of Youkounkoun of Guinea and Senegal, a millet couscous with meat or peanut sauce is made, as well as a rice couscous.[136]

Millet was also used for couscous by the Kel Ahaggar, a nomadic people of the desert of southern Algeria, who probably learned about it in the West African Sudanic kingdom, where it has been known for centuries.[137] Ibn Baṭṭūṭa journeyed to Mali in 1352, and in today's Mauritania he had a millet couscous: "When the traveler arrives in a village the negresses take out millet, sour milk, chickens, lotus-flour, rice, *founi* [*Digitaria exilis* Stapf], which resembles mustard grains, and they make a couscous."[138] Ibn Baṭṭūṭa also mentions rice couscous in the area of Mali in 1350.[139] Millet couscous was never as popular as hard wheat couscous because it took longer to cook and didn't taste as good.[140]

The suggestion of African origins of couscous was

originally made by Professor É. Lévi-Provençal in his monumental *Histoire de l'Espagne Musulmane*, and is also suggested in the early Arabic sources on West Africa.[141] Other studies, such as Professor Robert Hall's, using the tenth-century work of Ibn al-Faqīh's *Mukhtasar kitāb al-buldān*, also seem to support this idea.[142] In West Africa, one finds sorghum, *founi*, and finger millet *(Eleusine coracana)*, a cereal of Nigeria (also cultivated in India) made into couscous.[143] Sorghum was a popular grain for making couscous, and the Moroccan Berber word for sorghum, *illan* or *ilni*, is the same as the word in the West African language of Songhai, *illé*, lending further circumstantial evidence for an African genesis for couscous.[144] The argument that couscous was invented by the Muslims of Spain, an argument based on the fact that the first written couscous recipe is from Islamic Spain, I do not find compelling.

Kisskiss bi'l-Bisbās (Tunisia)
FENNEL COUSCOUS

The Tunisians are big eaters of couscous, and there are many varieties of hard wheat from which they can make it.[145] A family eats the couscous on a low table as part of its midday meal. Couscous and various soups are typical family fare during the winter. This recipe is one I had at the Couscous Diari factory, the world's largest couscous factory in Sfax, Tunisia. The company's North American representative, Samy Slimi, explained how to make it. Before proceeding, read about preparing couscous on page 666.

3 cups raw whole wheat couscous (about 1½ pounds)
4 teaspoons salt
6½ cups tepid water
1¼ cup extra virgin olive oil
1 medium-size onion, chopped
2 tablespoons tomato paste dissolved in ½ cup water
6 garlic cloves, finely chopped
2 tablespoons paprika
½ tablespoon freshly ground coriander seeds
½ tablespoon freshly ground caraway seeds
4 whole cloves
2 tablespoons hot *harīsa* (see Variation on page 524)
2 pounds fennel stalks, leaves, and some bulb, finely chopped
Leaves from ½ pound fresh coriander (cilantro; 2 bunches), finely chopped
½ pound scallions, white and green parts only, finely chopped
4 red potatoes (1½ pounds), peeled and diced
4 long green peppers (*peperoncino*)

1. Place half the couscous on a platter or earthenware dish with shallow sides (you could also use a large aluminum roasting pan, the kind you would use to roast a turkey). Dissolve 1 teaspoon of the salt in 1 cup of the water. Spread the couscous around and begin moistening it with the salted water a little at a time until all of the water is used—do not pour the water in all at once. Every time you add water, rub it into the grains, breaking up any lumps. Use up to ¼ cup of the water at first, working the grains with your fingers to separate and moisten them evenly. Work in a circular, rotating motion, constantly raking and forming the couscous into small marble shapes of soft dough. Rake them with one hand and with the other rub them into smaller pellets about 3 millimeters in diameter. If the mixture becomes too wet, add a little dry couscous and start again. Continue in this manner, adding more couscous and water, until all the grains are moistened. The couscous should be evenly wet, not soggy, and even-sized. If necessary, although I don't do it, shake the couscous through a large-holed, flat, and high-sided sieve, breaking up large pellets with one hand. You may want to sieve two or three times to make sure that each pellet is individual, although the same effect can be achieved by properly raking and rubbing with your fingers.

2. Arrange the couscous on a large white kitchen towel or a section of a sheet and dry for 1 to 2 hours (depending on the humidity in the air). Using your fingers, brush the little pellets of semolina with up to ¼ cup of the olive oil so they are all coated. Cut a piece of cheesecloth and with it cover the holes on the bottom of the *couscousière* and up the sides. The cheesecloth is not used to keep the couscous from falling through—it won't—but to facilitate transferring it during the several drying processes. Transfer the couscous to the top portion of the *couscousière*. Set aside until needed.

3. In the bottom portion of a *couscousière* (the *makfūl*), heat the remaining cup olive oil, then cook the onion until yellow and soft over medium heat, about 6 minutes, stirring a few times. Add the dissolved tomato paste, garlic, paprika, coriander seeds, caraway, cloves, the remaining 3 teaspoons salt, and the *harīsa* to the *couscousière*. Reduce the heat to low and simmer, adding up to 1½ cups water from time to time during the next 10 minutes.

4. Increase the heat to medium, add 2 cups water to the bottom portion, place the top portion on top, and steam the chopped fennel, coriander leaves, and scallions for 20 minutes, covered, fluffing once in a while with a fork. You may want to seal the two portions together with a rope made of flour and water (called the *qufila* in Arabic). Mix ½ cup flour with enough water to roll it out as you would play dough. (Some *couscousières* fit tight enough so that you need not make a seal. If you have improvised a *couscousière* with a pot and a colander, then you should make the seal.)

5. Remove the top of the *couscousière* and transfer the couscous to a cooling platter by picking up the ends of the cheesecloth and lifting it out. Break the grains up with your fingers, rubbing and aerating. Add the steamed vegetables and toss well. Add 2 cups water to the broth and return the couscous and vegetables to the top portion of the *couscousière*, then place on top of the *makfūl*, or bottom portion. Steam over medium heat for 20 minutes, covered, fluffing occasionally with a fork.

6. Transfer the couscous and vegetables to the platter again and leave to cool and dry for 1 hour.

7. Return the couscous to the top portion again and again place the top portion on top of the *makfūl*. Add the potatoes and green long peppers to the couscous. If a lot of steam is escaping from where the top and bottom parts of the *couscousière* meet, seal it with a rope made out of flour and water. Steam until the potatoes and peppers are tender, about 45 minutes, over medium heat.

8. Transfer the couscous to a serving bowl or platter and pour one to two ladlefuls of sauce over the couscous. Stir and let the grains absorb the broth. Serve.

Makes 6 to 8 servings

Kaskasū bi'l-Laḥm (Algeria)

COUSCOUS WITH LAMB

In Algeria, there are a wealth of terms for a variety of hard wheat products or prepared dishes, in the form of couscous or not. Fine semolina is also used for making baghrīr *and* ghrāyf, *a crêpe made with yeast, butter, and sugar and one made with melted butter and eggs, respectively. Algerians also have different names for different couscous dishes such as* būfawar *or* burkūkis, *a little semolina ball, the same as* muḥammaṣ *and* maghribiyya *(page 661). Among black Africans of southern Algeria, these large couscous grains are called* barbūsha.[146] Bazīn *is a dough made from fine hard wheat semolina or barley, similar to the Tunisian dish*

PREPARING COUSCOUS

The key to preparing an authentic couscous is patience and care. Experience will prove the best guide, but these instructions are meant to cut the time down for the novice.

There are two basic steps in preparing couscous before the cooking process: forming the couscous, and humidifying and drying the couscous. The first of these steps, forming the couscous—that is, preparing couscous from "scratch"—is rarely done anymore, even by Moroccans, Algerians, and Tunisians. Only poorer folk, some rural populations, and Berber tribes still make couscous from scratch. The original "from scratch" process involves rubbing and rolling together large grains of hard wheat semolina with finer grains of semolina sprayed with salted water to raise the humidity of the semolina so the two sizes affix to each other to form couscous, the large grain serving as a kind of nucleus for the smaller grains. But today when one buys couscous, whether you are buying it in North Africa or at a whole food store in this country, in a box or in bulk, this first step has been done, and it is this made-from-scratch couscous you are buying. I recommend buying the bulk couscous rather than the boxed couscous. Boxed couscous is usually precooked too much and the directions often (but not always) require you to boil the product. This so-called instant couscous is flavorless and should not be used for any of the recipes in this book. Couscous is always *steamed and* never *boiled. So when a recipe calls for couscous, you will find it sold in bulk bins at whole food or grain stores. At the time of this writing, bulk couscous is not sold in American supermarkets, only in whole food stores. In North Africa, there are a variety of couscous products, but in this country you are likely only to find fine wheat (white) couscous and whole wheat couscous.*

In Morocco, this rolling and rubbing process to form the couscous is done in a platter called a gas^{c}a, *a large earthenware faience platter traditional in Fez, but sometimes made of wood.*[147] *In Algeria, this platter is known by the same name, as well as* lyān. *In Morocco, the couscous is then dried in a* midūna, *a latticework basket of palm or esparto grass. Afterward it is transferred to a* tabaq, *a finer kind of basket. After drying a bit, the couscous is returned to the* midūna *for more rolling. The couscous is then sieved in three stages through sieves with progressively smaller holes called the* ghurbal qamiḥ, ghurbal kusksi, *and* ghurbal tala^{c} *in Morocco and Tunisia, and the* kharaj, rafaḍ, *and* tanay *in Algeria. It is sieved numerous times to form a uniform grain. The couscous is then left for four or five days to dry in the sun on a white sheet with occasional light sprays of water. It must be completely dry before storing. Today, modern North African couscous factories do all of this by machine, including the drying process.*

The second basic step, which is the only step you need to be concerned with for the couscous you buy, is the moistening process before cooking. Your ultimate goal is to have tender, light couscous swollen with the steam vapors of the particular broth the recipe calls for.

Put half the couscous on a large earthenware platter with shallow, angular sides and sprinkle or spray with some salted water (1 cup water salted with 1½ teaspoons salt for every 3 cups couscous) and olive oil (¼ cup olive oil for every 3 cups couscous). Work the grains with your fingers to separate and moisten them evenly. Work in a circular rotating motion, constantly raking and forming small "pearls" of soft dough. Rake with one hand and rub with the other, picking the couscous up with your hand and letting it fall back onto the platter, breaking up the lumps as you go. Rake the couscous to form pellets the size of peppercorns. If the mixture becomes too wet, add a little dry couscous and start again.

Add the remaining couscous and continue raking with your fingers, adding water and oil as needed. Continue in this manner until all the grains are moistened. The couscous should be evenly wet, not soggy, and uniform in size, about 3 millimeters in diameter. It may be necessary to shake the couscous through a flat sieve, breaking apart any pellets with your hand. You may wish to sieve two to three times to make sure each pellet is separate. On the other hand, you can get each pellet to its correct size by lengthening the raking and rubbing time. The final size of each pellet should, ideally, be about 1 millimeter in diameter and the pellets should be separate from one another. If you have not achieved this, rub and rake some more.

Arrange the couscous on white kitchen towels and leave to dry for 1 to 2 hours, depending on the humidity that day. With your fingers, rub the couscous with olive oil.

Couscous is steamed one, two, or three times over broth. The number of times one steams is based on cultural preferences. I always steam couscous at least twice, but only because that is how I was taught by Tunisian and Algerian friends. The couscous is never *submerged in the liquid; it is always steamed.*

Couscous is cooked in a special kind of cooking ensemble called a kiskis, *known by the French word* couscousière *in the West, except in Italy, where it is called a* couscousiera. *A* kiskis *consists of two parts: the bottom portion is a pot-bellied vessel for the broth while the top part fits snugly over the bottom part and has holes in its bottom for the steam to rise through, which cooks the couscous. In North Africa, it is often made of earthenware or aluminum. Fine kitchenware stores, such as Williams-Sonoma or Sur la Table sell aluminum* couscousières. *A makeshift* couscousière *can be made by placing a colander over a like-size pot. The Berbers of Morocco call this bottom portion the* ikineksu, *while the top portion is the* tikint; *the bottom portion of the* kiskis *or* couscousière *is called a* makfūl *in Tunisia, a* pignata *in western Sicily, and a* qidra *in Morocco and Algeria. The top portion is also called a* kiskis *in Morocco, Algeria, and Tunisia.*[148]

Cover the holes of the top portion of the couscousière *with cheesecloth and transfer the couscous on top of the cheesecloth. The reason I recommend using the cheesecloth is not that the grains fall through the holes (they don't) but because it is easier to move the couscous around for its several dry-*

ings. Add whatever spices, herbs, vegetables, meat, or fish the recipe calls for, if any, and bring the water or broth in the bottom portion of the couscousière *to a gentle boil. Mix the couscous gently. Mix 1/2 cup flour with enough water to form a dough that can be rolled out into a rope as you would roll out play dough. This flour-and-water rope is used to seal the top and bottom portions of the* couscousière *so steam doesn't escape. (This step is not always necessary and is up to the cook, depending on how much steam appears to be escaping.) Cook over low heat for 1 hour. Remove the couscous to a large platter and rub with salted water or butter or whatever the recipe calls for and leave to cool 15 to 30 minutes. This step is necessary; the initial steaming should not be too long because you do not want the couscous to become sticky and form a pasty dough.*

Traditionally, the cook knows the couscous is done when the sound of a spoon hit against the kiskis, *the top portion of the* couscousière, *makes a "heavy, coarse" (so they say) sound. The way I tell whether the couscous is done is by tasting it. The couscous should taste tender, not al dente and not mushy; the grains should be separate and taste moist, not wet and not dry. Put the couscous back into the top portion of the* couscousière *and steam another 30 minutes. This second steaming can continue until the couscous is fully cooked. The couscous can rest for 30 minutes, covered, if desired, before serving. Some Algerian cooks steam the couscous a third time.*

Now that you've read this process, I imagine you've decided that it is too much work. But let me say, lastly, that although this is really a lot of fun, you should not feel rushed when you make it, so preparing couscous for the first time is best done on a cold or rainy day when you know you'll be indoors. Once you've made the authentic North African couscous, you'll wonder what all the fuss is in my instructions. Why, it's so easy!

except it is not leavened. Diyūl, trīd, *and* rishta *are various terms for a variety of semolina pastry doughs or* pasta secca. Shakhshūkha al-Bisakra *(page 629) is the name of a lasagne dough made from fine semolina, water, and salt.* Dashīsha farīk *is a soup made of semolina of hard wheat and* farīk *(page 585). There are several preparations known as* dashīsha, *usually a kind of soup.*[149] *The famous* ḥarīra, *a semolina soup, is also found in Algeria. Dishes that carry the descriptive* shaṭīṭḥa *are preparations highly spiced with red pepper.*

The Algerian style of couscous, in its simplest form, is made of fine and medium semolina steamed over water and mixed with melted butter or samna. *Algerians make couscous a little bit differently from Tunisians. Tunisians like medium-size grains of couscous and Algerians prefer them fine. The Algerians mix butter and cinnamon into the couscous while Tunisians, especially Jewish cooks, might use olive oil. The couscous is steamed two or three times and butter and cinnamon are rolled into it each time.*

There are also big differences between the prepared couscous of northern Algeria and among the peoples of the Ahaggar in southern Algeria, where they often make couscous with a mixture of soft wheat, rye, and barley; in the north it is strictly semolina of hard wheat. The couscous of northern Algeria is often called ṭʿām *(literally meaning "food," showing the importance of couscous in daily life), a term rarely used in southern Algeria.*[150]

This recipe for couscous came about in a somewhat strange way. In the early 1990s, I was forced to cancel my research trip to Algeria previously organized by my friend Nacim Zeghlache, owing to political turmoil there. In its place Nacim had the idea of concocting an Algerian gastronomic feast with authentic dishes to be cooked at my house. In my kitchen, Nacim, who is from Sétif, got together with another Algerian, Abdou Ouahab, who is from Tlemcen. Both men are very good cooks, which at first glance might seem strange for Muslim men. But it is easily and amusingly explained. Many Muslim men came to America originally for university studies, and they so missed their mothers' cooking that they learned to cook by telephone—one hand on the frying pan and the other long-distance to Mom. Little did I realize how different and contested the making of couscous is even within Algeria.

When he was growing up, Nacim's family kept three rooms for the making of couscous grains. The family's favorite kind of wheat for couscous was white wheat formed into minuscule grains of couscous, although Nacim's father, and the older generation in general, prefer the whole wheat couscous. Nacim and Abdou made the couscous with my writing notes and refereeing as the two cooks constantly fought over the right way to make it. So, is this couscous from Sétif or Tlemcen? It's a compromise that will make you very happy, if the same cannot be said for my Algerian friends.

Before proceeding, read about preparing couscous on page 666.

9 cups raw couscous (about 4½ pounds)
2¼ to 2½ cups lightly salted warm water, as needed
1 cup extra virgin olive oil
2 medium-large onions (about 1 pound), grated
4 pounds lamb with bone in from the shoulder, ribs, and shank, trimmed of fat and cut into large chunks
3 large garlic cloves, grated or very finely chopped
1½ pounds ripe tomatoes, peeled, seeded, and crushed
1 teaspoon cayenne pepper
Salt and freshly ground black pepper to taste
2 quarts cold water
2 cups dried chickpeas (about 1 pound), picked over, soaked in water to cover overnight, and drained
1 pound turnip, peeled and cut into 1-inch cubes
4 large carrots, quartered lengthwise and sliced 1 inch thick
¾ pound green beans, ends trimmed and sliced ½ inch thick
3 medium-size zucchini, quartered lengthwise and sliced 1 inch thick
½ cup (1 stick) unsalted butter, at room temperature
1 teaspoon *harīsa* (page 523; optional) per diner

1. Place half the couscous on a platter or earthenware dish with shallow sides. (You could also use a large aluminum roasting pan, the kind you would use to roast a turkey.) Spread the couscous around and begin moistening with the warm salted water a little at a time until all of the water is used. Do not pour the water in all at once. Every time you add water, rub it into the grains, breaking up any lumps. You may or may not need all of the salted water. Use up to 1 cup at first, working the grains with your fingers to separate and moisten them evenly. Work in a circular, rotating motion, constantly raking and forming them into small marble shapes of soft dough. Rake with one hand and, with the other, rub them into smaller pellets about 3 millimeters in diameter. If the mixture becomes too wet, add a little dry couscous and start again. Continue in this manner, adding more couscous and water, until all the grains are moistened. The couscous should be evenly wet, not soggy, and even-sized. If necessary, shake the couscous through a large-holed, flat, and high-sided sieve, breaking up large pellets with one hand. You may want to sieve two or three times to make sure that each pellet is individual, although the same can be achieved by properly raking and rubbing with your fingers.

2. Arrange the couscous on a large white dish towel or a section of a sheet and dry for 1 to 2 hours

(depending on the humidity in the air). Using your fingers, brush the little pellets of semolina with some olive oil so they are all coated. Cut a piece of cheesecloth and with it cover the holes on the bottom of the *couscousière* and up the sides. The cheesecloth is not used to keep the couscous from falling through—it won't—but to facilitate transferring it during the several drying processes. Transfer the couscous to the top portion of the *couscousière*. Set aside until needed.

3. In the bottom of the *couscousière*, heat the olive oil over medium heat, then cook the onions until soft and golden, 10 to 12 minutes, stirring frequently. Add the lamb and brown on all sides for 15 minutes. Add the garlic, tomatoes, cayenne, salt, and pepper and mix well. Pour in the cold water and drained chickpeas, bring to a boil over high heat, and add the turnip. Reduce the heat a little to medium-high, so that the top of the bubbling broth is about 1 inch below the rim of the pot. After 20 minutes, add the carrots and keep at a boil. Add the green beans and zucchini 20 minutes after you put the carrots in.

4. Place the top part of the *couscousière* on top of the bottom vessel. You do not need to cover it. Seal the two together with a rope made of flour and water (called the *qufila* in Arabic). Mix ½ cup flour with enough water to roll it out as you would play dough. (Some *couscousières* fit tight enough so that you need not make a seal. If you have improvised a *couscousière* with a pot and a colander, then you should make the seal.) You may have to steam the couscous in two batches. Steam for 50 minutes, then remove to an aluminum roasting pan and rub together with your hands, breaking up lumps, so all the grains are separate.

5. Return the couscous to the *couscousière* to cook until the couscous is tender, another 50 minutes, adding water to the broth if you feel it is too thick and evaporated. Repeat the rubbing process again and for every batch you need to cook. At this point the lamb should be tender, almost falling off the bone. Turn the heat off, check the seasoning, and leave the broth in the pot.

6. Transfer the couscous to the aluminum pan and fold the butter into the couscous. Once the butter is melted, rub all the couscous together between the palms of your hands until everything is glistening. Mound the couscous attractively in a large serving bowl or platter. When diners serve themselves, have each person place three ladlefuls of couscous into a bowl. Top with meat and vegetables and two or three ladlefuls of broth. Add a teaspoon of *harīsa* if desired and let the bowl sit to absorb some broth before eating. In Tlemcen they like their couscous to be swimming in broth.

Makes 12 servings

Kusksi bi'l-ʿAṣbān (Tunisia)

COUSCOUS WITH "*ANDOUILLETTE*"

The origin of the homemade sausage, a kind of andouillette, *used in this Tunisian couscous may very well be a preparation that was born among Andalusian Muslims who settled in Tunisia after the Reconquest, especially in towns like Testour.*[151] *Although I have no proof, I am led to believe this because it is known that another famous Tunisian sausage,* mirqāz *(or merguez; page 249), apparently had its roots in Muslim Spain.*[152] *On the other hand, I've heard it described as a Tunisian Jewish specialty, which nevertheless may still have Iberian roots.*

The reason I call for such a range in the weight of the ʿaṣbān *is that normally a Tunisian family would use meat sparingly, for flavoring, yet whenever I have made my own* ʿaṣbān, *most guests develop a great love for these admittedly unusual sausages and eat far more than I expect. The yield for this recipe is for a large gathering of family or friends. I believe it is at its most satisfying in the late fall. Before proceeding read about preparing couscous on page 666.*

9 cups raw couscous (about 4½ pounds)
2 cups lightly salted warm water
3 to 5 pounds *ʿaṣbān* (page 72), to your taste
1 cup extra virgin olive oil
1 large onion, chopped
½ pound *liyya* (lamb fat; optional, page 717), chopped
¼ cup tomato paste
9 cups water
2 tablespoons *harīsa* (page 523)
1 tablespoon ground red Aleppo pepper (page 722) or 2 teaspoons cayenne pepper
1 pound baby carrots
1 pound small turnips, peeled and quartered
Salt to taste
1 pound boiling potatoes, peeled and quartered
2 cardoon stalks or 2 zucchini, peeled and quartered
1½ cups drained cooked chickpeas
¼ cup *samna* (clarified butter; page 189)
1 teaspoon *bahārāt* (page 525)
1 teaspoon freshly ground black pepper

1. Place half the couscous on a platter or earthenware dish with shallow sides. (You could also use a large aluminum roasting pan, the kind you would use to roast a turkey.) Spread the couscous around and begin moistening with the warm salted water a little at a time until all of the water is used. Do not pour the water in all at once. Every time you add water, rub it into the grains, breaking up any lumps. You may or may not need all of the salted water. Use up to 1 cup at first, working the grains with your fingers to separate and moisten them evenly. Work in a circular, rotating motion, constantly raking and forming them into small marble shapes of soft dough. Rake with one hand and with the other rub them into smaller pellets about 3 millimeters in diameter. If the mixture becomes too wet, add a little dry couscous and start again. Continue in this manner, adding more couscous and water, until all the grains are moistened. The couscous should be evenly wet, not soggy, and even-sized. If necessary, although I don't do it, shake the couscous through a large-holed, flat, and high-sided sieve, breaking up large pellets with one hand. You may want to sieve two or three times to make sure that each pellet is individual, although the same can be achieved by properly raking and rubbing with your fingers.

2. Arrange the couscous on a large white kitchen towel or a section of a sheet and dry for 1 to 2 hours (depending on the humidity in the air). Using your fingers, brush the little pellets of semolina with some olive oil so they are all coated. Cut a piece of cheesecloth and with it cover the holes on the bottom of the *couscousière* and up the sides. The cheesecloth is not used to keep the couscous from falling through—it won't—but to facilitate transferring it during the several drying processes. Transfer the couscous to the top portion of the *couscousière.* Set aside until needed.

3. Place the *ʿaṣbān* in a large pot of water and bring to a gentle boil. Keep the water just below a boil and simmer over low heat for 2 hours, without the water ever coming to a boil. Drain and set aside until needed.

4. In the bottom of the *couscousière* (called the *makfūl*) or a pot if you're using one, heat the olive oil over high heat, then cook the onion and lamb fat (if using) until translucent, about 5 minutes, stirring. Dissolve the tomato paste in 1 cup of the water and add to the *makfūl* or pot with the *harīsa* and red pepper. Reduce the heat to medium, stir, and cook for 10 minutes. Add the carrots, turnips, and the remaining 8 cups water and bring to a boil.

5. Place the top portion of the *couscousière* (the *kiskis*) with the couscous on top of the bottom portion. Seal the two together with a rope made of flour and water (called the *qufila* in Arabic). Mix ½ cup flour with enough water to roll it out as you would play

dough. (Some *couscousières* fit tight enough so that you need not make a seal. If you have improvised a *couscousière* with a pot and a colander, then you should make the seal.) As soon as steam begins to rise through the couscous grains, about 4 minutes, reduce the heat to medium, and cook 18 to 20 minutes, stirring and breaking up any lumps of couscous with a fork.

6. Remove the top of the *couscousière* and transfer the couscous to a cooling platter, break the grains up with your fingers, rubbing and aerating. Turn the heat off under the broth. Dry for 30 minutes to 1 hour.

7. Taste the broth and add salt, if necessary. Add water, too, if necessary. Add the potatoes, cardoons or zucchini and chickpeas to the broth. Return the couscous to the top portion of the *couscousière* and place over the broth. Reform the flour-and-water seal if using. Bring to a boil. As soon as the steam rises from the couscous, reduce the heat to medium and steam for 18 to 20 minutes. Remove the couscous to the cooling platter again and break up the grains with your fingers, rubbing and aerating. Turn off the heat under the broth, or keep over very low heat. Dry the couscous for 30 minutes.

8. Replace the couscous on top of the *couscousière* a third time. Bring the broth to a boil; when steam starts to rise, reduce the heat to medium. Steam the couscous for 20 minutes. Remove the top portion and add the cooked *ʿaṣbān* to the broth. Replace the top portion and continue cooking for 10 minutes.

9. Pour the couscous into a large serving platter or bowl, fluffing with a fork. (Tunisian cooks do this, impossibly, with their hands). Stir in a ladle of broth, the *samna, bahārāt*, and black pepper. Stir and fluff so that it is well blended. Mold the couscous attractively in the platter and scatter the *ʿaṣbān,* chickpeas, potatoes, carrots, zucchini, and turnips on top. Cover with aluminum foil and let rest for 10 minutes. Serve.

Makes 12 servings

Siksū bi'l-Dajāj wa'l-Ḥummuṣ (Morocco)

COUSCOUS WITH CHICKEN, CHICKPEAS, AND CARAMELIZED ONIONS

Although it is thought that the process of couscous cookery might have an African origin, and that the origin of the word may be Berber, the first reference to couscous being cooked with chicken comes from the anonymous thirteenth-century Hispano-Muslim cookbook Kitāb al-ṭabīkh fī al-Maghrib wa'l-Āndalus.[153]

This couscous, with its rich taste of carmelized onions, melting chicken, and fragrant spices with golden raisins and almonds, is made in homes ranging from Fez to Meknès to Casablanca. It is a sumptuous meal. I learned how to make this particular couscous in Sefrou, at the home of Mr. Gragui Houcine, where one of my dinner companions, Allal Chibane, an agronomist specializing in market gardening with the Moroccan Ministry of Agriculture, told me some of the secret intricacies of making couscous.

I have no idea if the practice still continues, but traditionally Berber women in Morocco, whose physical beauty was measured by plumpness, as was that of their menfolk, would add tesserint, *the root of a plant* (Telephium imperati *L.*) *to their couscous, and that root would contribute to their Rubenesque figures, or so it was thought.*[154] *Before proceeding, read about preparing couscous on page 666.*

4 cups raw couscous (about 2 pounds)
1½ to 2 cups lightly salted warm water as needed
4 large onions (about 4 pounds), sliced
1 cup extra virgin olive oil
5 teaspoons salt
1 recipe Moroccan spice mix (page 522)
⅓ cup sugar
1 cup drained cooked chickpeas

1 cup golden raisins, soaked in tepid water to cover for 15 minutes and drained
1½ teaspoons freshly ground black pepper
5 tablespoons *samna* (clarified butter; page 189)
1 cup blanched whole almonds
1 chicken (about 5 pounds), cut into 8 pieces
6 cups water
Pinch of saffron threads, crumbled
1 cinnamon stick

1. Place half the couscous on a platter or earthenware dish with shallow sides. (You could also use a large aluminum roasting pan, the kind you would use to roast a turkey.) Spread the couscous around and begin moistening with the warm salted water a little at a time until all of the water is used. Do not pour the water in all at once. Every time you add water, rub it into the grains, breaking up any lumps. You may or may not need all of the salted water. Use up to 1 cup at first, working the grains with your fingers to separate and moisten them evenly. Work in a circular, rotating motion, constantly raking and forming them into small marble shapes of soft dough. Rake with one hand and with the other rub them into smaller pellets about 3 millimeters in diameter. If the mixture becomes too wet, add a little dry couscous and start again. Continue in this manner, adding more couscous and water, until all the grains are moistened. The couscous should be evenly wet, not soggy, and even-sized. If necessary, shake the couscous through a large-holed, flat, and high-sided sieve, breaking up large pellets with one hand. You may want to sieve two or three times to make sure that each pellet is individual, although the same can be achieved by properly raking and rubbing with your fingers.

2. Arrange the couscous on a large white dish towel or a section of a sheet and dry for 1 to 2 hours (depending on the humidity in the air). Using your fingers, brush the little pellets of semolina with some olive oil so they are all coated. Cut a piece of cheesecloth and with it cover the holes on the bottom of the *couscousière* and up the sides. The cheesecloth is not used to keep the couscous from falling through—it won't—but to facilitate transferring it during the several drying processes. Transfer the couscous to the top portion of the *couscousière*. Set aside until needed.

3. Put the onions in a large casserole with ½ cup of the olive oil and 2 teaspoons of the salt. Cook the onions over medium heat for 15 minutes, stirring occasionally. Stir the spice mix and sugar into the onions. Cook for 30 minutes over medium-low to medium heat, adjusting the heat as necessary so the onions at no time are burning. Add the chickpeas and drained raisins and cook for 45 minutes, stirring occasionally. Correct the salt and stir in ¼ teaspoon of the black pepper.

4. In a small skillet, melt 1 tablespoon of the *samna* and cook the almonds over medium heat, stirring, until light brown. Remove and set the almonds aside.

5. Meanwhile, put the chicken, 5½ cups of the water, the remaining ½ cup olive oil, the saffron, cinnamon stick, the remaining 3 teaspoons salt, and the remaining 1¼ teaspoons black pepper in the bottom part of the *couscousière*. Bring to a boil. Reduce the heat to medium and place the top part (with the couscous) on the *couscousière*. Seal the two together with a rope made of flour and water (called the *qufila* in Arabic). Mix ½ cup flour with enough water to roll it out as you would play dough. (Some *couscousières* fit tight enough so that you need not make a seal. If you have improvised a *couscousière* with a pot and a colander, then you should make the seal.) Cover the top part and simmer for 1 hour, fluffing the couscous occasionally.

6. Remove the top part and spread the couscous, on a large baking tray or aluminum roasting pan. Sprinkle with the remaining ½ cup salted water, with a little extra salt added to it, and the remaining 4 tablespoons *samna* and leave to dry for 15 minutes. Turn the heat off under the chicken. Taste the chicken broth and correct the salt and pepper.

7. Replace the cheesecloth over the holes of the bottom of the *kiskis* (the top portion). Return the couscous to the *kiskis*, turn the heat to medium, reform the flour-and-water seal if desired, cover the top, and cook until the couscous is tender, about another 1¼ hours, fluffing the couscous with a fork occasionally.

8. When the couscous is done, remove to a platter and sprinkle 1 cup of the chicken broth into the couscous, stirring so it is distributed. Cover with a sheet of aluminum foil and leave for 10 minutes. Arrange the couscous on the platter with a slight well in the middle. Place the chicken in the center, cover with the caramelized onions and chickpeas, ladle some sauce on top, and sprinkle the almonds on top.

Makes 6 to 8 servings

❈ *Kuskusī bi'l-Ḥūt* (Tunisia)

DJERBAN-STYLE FISH COUSCOUS

The fishing off Tunisian coasts has been good since the days of the Carthaginians. In medieval times, the great Arab geographer al-Idrīsī (b. 1099?) commented on the abundance of fish off the coast of Sfax and Bizerte.[155] *Sfax was an important place for fish such as mullet, bream, bonito, monkfish, ray, saddled bream (maybe sheepshead bream), meagre, salema, sardine, and other fish hard to identify. In May and June, tuna was an important catch off the eastern coast of Tunisia. There was pearling, oystering, and sponge collecting off Sfax, as well as fish cookery that was considered the best in Tunisia.*[156] *Today, in a coastal town like Sfax, a poorer family has its couscous at midday, without the variety of fish in this recipe. Usually one inexpensive fish is used, such as gilt-head bream. The cook might cook the fish with chickpeas, quince, and tomato sauce spiced with red and black pepper, cinnamon, and rose petal powder. Along the coast of western Libya, the ancient Tripolitania, cooks making a fish couscous fry the fish first.*

This is the recipe I watched Chef Abderrazak al-Haouari, then of the Hotel Ulysse Palace in Djerba, prepare, and I was quite impressed with the technique and results. He used a special kiskis *(top portion of the* couscousière*) that had a receptacle for the fish inside the* kiskis *next to the couscous.*

Before proceeding, read about preparing couscous on page 666.

4 cups raw couscous (about 2 pounds)
1½ to 2 cups lightly salted warm water as needed
¾ cup extra virgin olive oil
1 large onion, coarsely chopped
½ pound (1 or 2) green bell peppers, seeded and chopped
One 6-ounce can tomato paste dissolved in 1 cup water
10 ounces Swiss chard, trimmed of heavy stems and leaves julienned
Leaves from 1 bunch fresh parsley (about 6 ounces), washed and chopped
1 head garlic (about 20 cloves), cloves peeled and lightly crushed
1 tablespoon *harīsa* (page 523)
½ teaspoon cayenne pepper
1 teaspoon freshly ground cumin seeds
Salt and freshly ground black pepper to taste
2 quarts fish broth (page 369)
1 large boiling potato, peeled and quartered
¼ pound baby carrots
½ pound turnips, peeled and quartered
2 zucchini, peeled and cut into thirds
2¾ pounds mixed fish fillets (at least 3 of the following: grouper, gray mullet, porgy, monkfish, shark, ocean catfish, hake, cod, halibut), cut into large pieces

1. Place half the couscous on a platter or earthenware dish with shallow sides. (You could also use a large aluminum roasting pan, the kind you would use

to roast a turkey.) Spread the couscous around and begin moistening with the warm salted water a little at a time until all of the water is used. Do not pour the water in all at once. Every time you add water, rub it into the grains, breaking up any lumps. You may or may not need all of the salted water. Use up to 1 cup at first, working the grains with your fingers to separate and moisten them evenly. Work in a circular, rotating motion, constantly raking and forming them into small marble shapes of soft dough. Rake with one hand and with the other rub them into smaller pellets about 3 millimeters in diameter. If the mixture becomes too wet, add a little dry couscous and start again. Continue in this manner, adding more couscous and water, until all the grains are moistened. The couscous should be evenly wet, not soggy, and even-sized. If necessary, shake the couscous through a large-holed, flat, and high-sided sieve, breaking up large pellets with one hand. You may want to sieve two or three times to make sure that each pellet is individual, although the same can be achieved by properly raking and rubbing with your fingers.

2. Arrange the couscous on a large white kitchen towel or a section of a sheet and dry for 1 to 2 hours (depending on the humidity in the air). Using your fingers, brush the little pellets of semolina with 2 tablespoons of the olive oil so they are all coated. Cut a piece of cheesecloth and with it cover the holes on the bottom of the *couscousière* and up the sides. The cheesecloth is not used to keep the couscous from falling through—it won't—but to facilitate transferring it during the several drying processes. Transfer the couscous to the top portion of the *couscousière*. Set aside until needed.

3. In the bottom of the *couscousière* (called the *makfūl*), heat the remaining 10 tablespoons olive oil over high heat, then cook the onion and green peppers until the onion is soft, about 6 minutes, stirring frequently. Add the dissolved tomato paste to the *makfūl* along with the Swiss chard, parsley, garlic cloves, *harīsa*, cayenne, cumin, salt, and black pepper. Reduce the heat to medium, stir, and cook for 10 minutes. Add the fish broth. Bring to a boil.

4. Place the top portion of the *couscousière* with the couscous on top of the bottom portion. Seal the two together with a rope made of flour and water (called the *qufila* in Arabic). (Some *couscousières* have a tight enough fit and you need not make a seal. If you have improvised a *couscousière* with a pot and a colander, then you should make the seal.) As soon as steam begins to rise through the couscous grains, about 4 minutes, reduce the heat to medium, cover, and cook 18 to 20 minutes, stirring and breaking up any lumps of couscous with a fork. Remove the top of the *couscousière* and transfer the couscous to a cooling platter by picking up the ends of the cheesecloth and lifting it out. Break the grains up with your fingers, rubbing and aerating. Turn the heat off under the broth. Dry the couscous for 30 minutes to 1 hour.

5. Taste the broth and add some salt, if necessary. Add more fish broth or water, if necessary. Return the couscous to the top portion of the *couscousière* and place over the broth. Reform the flour-and-water seal if you had to break it to add water or broth and if desired, and bring the broth to a boil. As soon as the steam rises from the couscous, reduce the heat to medium, and steam 18 to 20 minutes. Remove the couscous to the cooling platter again and break up the grains with your fingers, rubbing and aerating. Turn the heat off under the broth. Dry the couscous for 30 minutes to 1 hour.

6. Replace the couscous in the top of the *couscousière* a third time. Add the potato, carrots, turnips, and zucchini to the broth. Arrange the fish around on top of the couscous. (Do not place the fish on the bottom with the couscous on top because the fish would then cover the holes of the *kiskis*.) Cover, bring the

broth to a boil, and cook for 25 minutes over medium-high heat.

7. Check the fish and, if it is perfectly steamed, flaking easily but still maintaining its shape, remove to a platter. Pour the couscous into a large serving platter or bowl, fluffing with a fork (Tunisian cooks do this, impossibly, with their hands). Stir in a ladle or two or three of broth and black pepper to taste. Stir and fluff so that it is well blended. Mold the couscous attractively in the platter and scatter the fish and vegetables around on top. Cover with sheets of aluminum foil and let rest for 10 minutes. Remove the foil and serve with the remaining broth on the side.

Makes 8 to 10 servings

HARDTACK

THE third of the great inventions derived from hard wheat, after macaroni and couscous, was hardtack, also called ships' biscuit, and called *bizcocho* in thirteenth-century Spain, where it made its first identifiable appearance. It was a semolina biscuit that was cooked twice, the second time to make it hard and preservable, and it was stored in sacks. There are earlier references to *biscoctus* (from the word *bis* meaning "two" and the Latin *coctus*—cooked—signifying twice-cooked.)[157] One of the earliest of these references—and we cannot be sure this was a biscuit made of hard wheat—is in a charter from Tours in ninth-century France, where the *biscoctus* mentioned is said to have the characteristics of a Muslim country. After the siege of Ascalon in Palestine, the Crusaders entered Jerusalem with their camels and donkeys carrying *biscoctus* and flour, says the chronicler Petrus Tudebodus. But at some point it began to be made with hard wheat. Later the bread is called *panis africanus*, and by the end of the Middle Ages it is known as *panis Alexandrinus*.[158] *Bizcocho*, an unleavened biscuit that was rebaked and used on ships, was very easily conserved and favored by mariners, as we know from thirteenth-century notary records of naval affairs of Marseilles and Genoa.[159]

At some point, and we don't know when nor do we know how the change occurred, *bizcocho* came to mean in Spain not only hardtack but also the misnomer sponge cake—a light cake made with many eggs and a starch, such as, later, corn or potato starch. Even today, *bizcocho* can mean either sponge cake or biscuit (also called *galleta*) in Spanish, although in the late sixteenth century, *bizcocho* still meant only biscuit in Spanish.[160] But by the time it traveled to Sicily, where it came to be known as *pan di Spagna* (bread of Spain), it was also a sponge cake, and this was the meaning of *pan di Spagna*, sponge cake, that is, egg cake. It then spread to the rest of Italy with this name.[161] But the Italian *biscotto* and the French and English biscuit, derived from the same word, today only mean biscuits or cookies. The sponge cake from Spain may also have been introduced at about the same time to Liguria by Genoese merchants. In any case, the meaning of *bizcocho* was by that time that of a sponge cake (as well as hardtack). If the name is any indication, it appears the French learned how to make *pan di Spagna*, or sponge cake, from the Genoese and gave it the French name *génoise*, Genoese. Sponge cake is still known in Spain and in Catalonia, where it is called *bizcocho* and *pa di pessic*, respectively.

Pa de Pessic (Catalonia)

CATALAN SPONGE (EGG) CAKE

Although we don't know when the Spanish word bizcocho *came to mean sponge cake in addition to hardtack, it was probably the result of adding lots of eggs to the dough. This may have come about from the need to conserve eggs or very simply the desire to create a more savory bread or cake. This recipe from Catalonia is delicate, light, and although it has a lot of cornstarch, it is not starchy.*

1 cup granulated sugar
8 large egg yolks
¼ teaspoon pure vanilla extract
Zest from 1 lemon
½ cup unbleached all-purpose flour
½ cup cornstarch
¼ cup (½ stick) unsalted butter, melted
Confectioners' sugar for garnish
Ground cinnamon for garnish

1. Preheat the oven to 350°F. Beat the granulated sugar, egg yolks, vanilla, and lemon zest together in a large bowl. Work in the flour and cornstarch a spoonful at a time. Stir in the melted butter. The batter will be thick and very stiff.

2. Butter a 9-inch round cake pan on the bottom and sides. Spread the batter evenly in the pan. Bake for 35 minutes. Remove the cake from the pan to cool on a wire rack.

3. Once the cake is completely cooled, dust the top with confectioners' sugar. Decorate the top by making a diamond or heart, for instance. To make a heart stencil, fold a piece of stiff paper in half twice. Cut half a heart out along the edges. Open the paper, smoothing crinkled edges and gently place over the cake. Dust the heart cutout with ground cinnamon. Carefully remove the paper. Serve.

Makes 8 servings

CONCLUSION

THE invention of products such as macaroni, couscous, and hardtack, utilizing the unique properties of hard wheat, was important not only on the gastronomic level. First, these new foodstuffs, invented before the introduction of New World foods, helped control and reduce the strain of perennial famines because they had very long shelf lives. Second, governments and speculators could warehouse food supplies for long periods of time, counteracting the effects of low-production years and offsetting the inflation caused by higher prices and greater demand. Third, a plentiful supply of hard wheat (especially in the form of hardtack, but also *pasta secca*) allowed for longer sea voyages, opening up an age of exploration.

This chapter concludes Part III, A Measure of Mediterranean Gastronomy. I chose to consider the role of the two most important categories of foodstuffs as one measure of the Mediterranean. The story of food in the Mediterranean is a story of trade. The trade in these two foodstuffs—spices and grain—made the Mediterranean rich, and these riches allowed a new class to emerge and create a cuisine.

CONCLUSION
THE UNITY OF THE MEDITERRANEAN

THERE were two Mediterraneans—East and West, Turkish and Spanish, Islamic and Christian. The eastern Mediterranean, essentially the greater Ionian, was an Ottoman sea. After the occupation of Syria and Egypt in 1516–1517, the Turks became masters of the eastern Mediterranean. Their fleet grew stronger. Notably, the great sea battles of the sixteenth century took place where East met West, in the Sicilian Channel.[1] The Mediterranean was long dominated by two Muslim civilizations, first the Arabs and then the Ottoman Turks. But between 1450 and 1650, the dominant and subordinate positions of the Muslim civilizations in the East and the Latin civilization in the West, respectively, was in a process of slow reversal, and their economic and cultural differences became more pronounced. The East eventually lost its supremacy in various fields, and its influence in scientific achievements, as well as cultural transfers, diminished. Material civilization became less refined, Islam was beset with internal religious squabbles, technological advances slowed, large industry did not develop, banking suffered, and the supply of gold and silver dropped. The economic upheaval that resulted came at the time of the Age of Exploration and the opening up of the Atlantic, destroying in its wake the economic advantage that the Eastern Mediterranean had as a gateway to the riches of the Indies. Now the East looked to the West for technological advances. And the West looked to the East to find the markets for its surplus production.

Although the East and West were different, they had always been linked. The two basins of the Mediterranean acted as funnels for trade and commerce. It is said that trade created Mediterranean unity. This may be true, but East and West always maintained distinct identities and their own spheres of influence. For all the unity created by those human links of war, trade, and immigration, each population maintained its autonomy and its traditions, culinary and otherwise: Syrian food would never be mistaken for Provençal food.

As I hope it is somewhat evident by now, we can say that there are many Mediterraneans. There is the Mediterranean as defined by climate, another defined by the sea, and yet another defined by history. There is a human Mediterranean marked by the movements of its peoples, and it is this Mediterranean that can provide a unifying concept. The human Mediterranean reveals itself through literature, art and architecture, and gastronomy. The movement of peoples has also meant the continual repopulation of the Mediterranean. The population of Spain today is entirely different from what it was a thousand years ago—so, too, the island of Sicily, the peninsulas of Greece, and the towns of Israel. The movement of peoples is the driving force in the Mediterranean. Routes tying towns to mountain villages and ports to one another structure the human order of things. The Mediterranean is often painted as pastoral, but, in fact, agriculture is modest and serves the towns.

The Mediterranean can also be defined by the

familiar or the ubiquitous. This is a Mediterranean with which we are somewhat familiar, a Mediterranean of the Acropolis in Athens, or the Coliseum in Rome, or the writings of Cervantes, or the varied foods as we've encountered in this book. There are famous kings, battles, buildings, paintings, and culinary preparations. Of course, I'm speaking of a tourist Mediterranean. Maybe the companions to those "intermittent flares," as Fernand Braudel calls the great men, battles, and kings that make up history, are the simple, and not so simple, foods that reappear across the Mediterranean. Certainly the most ubiquitous figure throughout the Mediterranean, the most familiar figure, was the Jew.

THE WANDERING JEW

FOODS moved about the Mediterranean like immigrants, yet culinary preparations can be identified only locally for there is no pan-Mediterranean cuisine outside of a general impression given by the presence of olive oil, wine, wheat, garlic, vegetables, and herbs. Mountain dwellers, proletarians, and adventurers of all kinds were immigrants. The dockworkers and other laborers in Ragusa emigrated from the nearby mountains. In Marseilles, most immigrants were Corsicans. In Tunis, they were Moriscos coming from Andalusia. Venice, too, was an important city for immigrants, like the Albanians and Greek merchants.

The flow of immigrants was from the mountains to the plains and cities. There was a flow of people from Christian lands to the *dār al-Islām*. Artisans, artists, merchants, and soldiers left Italy for northern Europe, Arab countries, and even as far away as the Indies. By the end of the sixteenth century, five thousand Venetian families were living in the Middle East. Late-sixteenth-century Algiers was populated almost entirely by foreigners.

The quintessential immigrant was, of course, the Jew. The history of the Jewish people in the Mediterranean is one of persecution and expulsion, as is well known. But their lives were not ones of unmitigated victimization, and their role was of primary significance in the development of the region. Whenever the Jews were expelled, they were received somewhere else in the Mediterranean.[2] They might be persecuted in one land—Spain, for instance—only to be accepted in another, Turkey. Their role in the transmission of technology, such as gun carriages or printing, because of such enforced migration cannot be underestimated. After their expulsion from Spain, some Jews went to Salonika and Istanbul, where they built up vast retail businesses to compete with Ragusans, Armenians, and Venetians. A handful of Jews, after being expelled from Ancona on the Italian Adriatic by Pope Paul IV (1555), made a fortune on the other side of the sea in the Turkish port of Valona (Vlorë), in Albania. The Jews were driven from Castile and Portugal in 1492 and 1497, from Sicily in 1493, from Naples in 1540 and 1541, from Tuscany in 1571, and from Milan in 1597. In 1568, Jews were driven from Provence, to be accepted in Savoy. But the Jewish people had to adapt themselves to their new environments while maintaining their beliefs. Although some Jews would be ruined by one economy and they would make their fortunes in another, most Jews were as poor as other Mediterranean peoples. This is a distinct civilization that exerted influence, transferred cultural values, and resisted others. Fernand Braudel called the destiny of the Jews "one civilization against the rest."[3]

Immigrant Iberian Jews came to occupy leading positions in trade by the end of the fifteenth century in Cairo, Aleppo, Alexandria, Tripoli in the Lebanon (Syria), Salonika (Thessaloniki), and Istanbul. By the sixteenth century the Jews were handling large seaborne trade with Messina, Ragusa, Ancona, and Venice. One of the most profitable ventures of Christian pirates in the Levant became the search of Venetian, Ragusan, and Marseillaise vessels for Jewish merchandise. And the Jews soon found themselves in competition with the Armenians who were becoming the Levantine successors to the rich Italian merchants who once controlled the whole Mediterranean.

The Wandering Jew is not a figurative character spanning the centuries but often a real person, such as Jacob Sasportas, born in then Spanish-controlled Oran in Algeria. He became a rabbi in Tlemcen, then went to Marrakech and Fez. He was imprisoned, then escaped to Amsterdam, where he became a professor. He returned to North Africa, and in 1655 went to London as part of the embassy, then to Hamburg as a rabbi until 1673. He returned to Amsterdam, went to Leghorn, then back to Amsterdam, where he died. Anyone who has read Claudia Roden's excellent *The Book of Jewish Food* knows that the Wandering Jew still wanders; the author and her family are a living testament to the penetration of Jewish life into all Mediterranean cultures.

Jewish people did not always live apart or wear distinctive dress. They did not always inhabit a separate quarter of the city, the ghetto (from the name of the quarter that was assigned to them in Venice and whose name is supposed to be derived from its formerly being the foundry where iron was cast). Nor did they want to live only among themselves, witness their protest in Naples in 1540 against an order to "live together."

Sometimes the Jews were expelled, only to return. Genoa expelled Jews in 1516; they returned a year later. Movements to expel Jews were often reversed, as happened when Venice was preparing to expel its Jews in 1573. The Venetian *bailio* (consul) from Istanbul argued against this measure, which he considered madness, by pleading to the Council of Ten: "What pernicious act is this, to expel the Jews? Do you know what it may cost you in years to come? Who gave the Turk his strength and where else would he have found the skilled craftsmen to make the cannon, bows, shot, swords, shields and bucklers which enable him to measure himself against other powers, if not among the Jews who were expelled by the Kings of Spain?"[4]

Jews often spoke five or six languages and were essential participants in business transactions. Unintentionally, Jews were, until the thirteenth century and even later, the intermediaries through whom the West received Arab thought and science. Arabs rarely knew Latin and Europeans did not know Arabic, so Jews, who knew both, acted as translators. In fact, Jews had acted as translators for centuries.

In the fifteenth century, Jews developed an enthusiasm for printing. The first book printed in Portugal (in 1487) was the Pentateuch, also called the Torah, the first five books of the Old Testament. In 1565, Joseph Caro, a Sephardic rabbi who lived from 1488 to 1575, published in Venice a compilation of Jewish precepts covering all of material existence including dietary laws (kashruth) under the title *Shulḥan Arukh* in Hebrew, or *The Prepared Table*.[5]

The Spanish Jews brought with them to Istanbul and Salonika (Thessaloniki) their own language, Ladino, a Renaissance Spanish, and preserved many of their native Spanish customs. The same was true of the fourteenth- and fifteenth-century German Jews who brought Yiddish to Poland. As Braudel said, here's "proof that the soil of a man's native land may cling to his shoes."[6] Such memories survive in curious details: a student of Spanish literature of our own day has discovered among the Jews of Morocco knowledge of the words and melodies of medieval Spanish romances.

After their expulsion from Spain and Sicily, Jewish merchants made huge fortunes in Salonika (Thessaloniki), Bursa, Istanbul, and Adrianople (Edirne). Without the Jews, Leghorn (Livorno) would never have become the thriving port it did.[7] Jews were found in roles others either couldn't or wouldn't accept, such as money lending. They were travelers, and were found beyond the trading cities on the edges of the desert, Aleppo, Damascus, and Cairo. This was a world of caravans, a domain of Muslim and Jewish traders, where Europeans were a rarity.[8]

Spain expelled its Muslims and Jews because it was moving toward political unity, which in the fifteenth-century Mediterranean essentially meant religious unity, the only way people understood themselves as a civilization.[9] Even before the beginning of their expulsion from Spain in 1492, Jews found their way to the vibrant and accepting city of Ragusa. The first mention of a Jew in the archival documents of Ragusa is from 1281. In 1367, the first Jewish merchants begin to appear in the city. In the early fifteenth century, large numbers of Jews from Provence began to settle in Apulia and have regular contact with Ragusa. Jewish-Ragusan relations were generally good, and the Ragusans resisted Papal pressure to conform to the anti-Jewish nature of the Counter-Reformation.[10]

The Jews remained a cogent people throughout their Diaspora because of their traditions. During Passover, when the Jewish child asks at the Seder dinner, "Why is this night different from all other nights?" the answer about celebrating the flight of the Jews from Egypt, from slavery, is an evocation of a key moment in Jewish memory. Passover *(Pesach)* is the great Jewish holiday that celebrates the Jews' liberation from Egyptian bondage. It lasts eight days and no *ḥamez*, leavened foods, can be eaten. Because of this dietary prohibition, a great many specialized dishes were created. Tradition requires three kinds of *mazzot*, unleavened foods, a roast lamb bone, *huevos haminados* (hard-boiled eggs), and *ḥaroset* with romaine lettuce, "bitter herbs," and celery leaves.[11] The *ḥaroset*, a mixture or relish of fruits and nuts, was meant to represent the mortar that bound their people when enslaved by the Pharaohs. The Talmud enumerates a number of vegetables that there is a duty to eat on the night of the Seder. The Mishna, the canonical collection of Jewish law that constitutes part of the Talmud, names five: lettuce, chicory, wild chicory (according to Maimonides), *ḥarḥavina (Eryngium creticum)*, and *maror*, which seems to be *Sonchus oleraceus*, called in Arabic *murār*. It is a common weed, widespread in gardens, fallow fields, and roadsides in Israel. The soft leaves are eaten as a salad by the poor, some also eating the juicy root.[12]

In Jewish dietary laws (kashruth), we get a glimmer of the boundaries of the cuisines of the Jews in relation to their countries. In fact, if we can properly speak of a "Jewish cuisine," we can do so only by virtue of the fact that it developed as a result of kashruth.[13] Hebraic law concerning food is preoccupied with the rigorous codification of meats. The animal shares with the human the same vitality, designated by the Hebrew expression *ḥaya*, living. The regulation of meat as food among the Jews is a priori, of a certain fundamental value of life throughout the culture.[14] The koshering of food has to do mainly with the removal of blood from the animal in concurrence with the prohibition against its consumption in Leviticus 7:26–27 and 17:10–14. Leviticus 11:2–3 sets out what foods Jews can eat—namely animals whose hoofs are parted and cloven-footed, and who chew the cud. "Unclean" animals, forbidden for eating, are the camel, badger, hare, and pig. From the seas and rivers, Jews were allowed to eat fish only with fins and scales. Most birds were allowed, except birds of prey, such as eagles, falcons, hawks, and the osprey. Ravens, owls, vultures, gulls, and some other birds were also forbidden. Locusts, grasshoppers, and crickets could be eaten but not other insects.

The role of sacrifice, especially in relation to food preparation, is of paramount importance to Jews. The slaughter of an animal for food was designated by a special verb, *hullin*. That life was being surrendered was central to the sacrificial ritual and it was signified by the letting of the animal's blood. "For the life of the flesh is in the blood; and I have given it for you upon the altar to make atonement, by reason of the life" (Lev. 17:11). Jews, therefore, were forbidden to eat blood, since life belonged only to God (Lev. 17:10; Gen. 9:4; Lev. 3:17, 7:26; Deut. 12:16, 23; 15:23). A sacrifice was an offering.[15] The biblical teachings were important in the cooking of the Jews.

Wherever Jews appeared in the Mediterranean, they adopted the cuisines of their new home while adapting them to conform to their dietary laws. But Jews did have certain predilections that may have derived from Talmudic tradition or were cultural and culinary. The Jewish affinity for vegetables is attested to in the Bible, and the quintessential Egyptian vegetable *mulūkhiyya* is still also known as the "Jewish vegetable" (Jew's mallow, *Corchorus olitorius*). Vegetables were an important part of the diet in medieval times, and greengrocers and vegetable sellers are repeatedly mentioned in the Jewish letters that constitute the Geniza documents of the eleventh century in Cairo.[16] Economic factors, such as trade, also played a part in the cuisine of the Jews, for, like everyone else, they ate what was available because (except for grain and spices) little else came from afar.

The principal cuisine of the Mediterranean Jews can be called Sephardi, as opposed to the Ashkenazi Jewish cooking that resembles the various cuisines of central, northern, and eastern European cooking. *Sephardi* has come to imply Mediterranean Jewry, but strictly speaking the Sephardi are only the Iberian Jews who immigrated to Greece and Turkey. In any case, I use the term in its broader sense to mean Mediterranean Jews. I don't talk about so-called Israeli cuisine because at this time it is mostly inventive restaurant cooking. Sephardi cooking is characterized by the use of spices, olive oil, rice, pulses, and lamb. A sabbath meal is prepared on a Friday afternoon to bake in a slow oven overnight and is eaten for Saturday lunch. The Ashkenazi call the sabbath meal *cholent*, while eastern Mediterranean Jews call it *ḥamin* and usually make it with beans, fat meat, and potatoes. In North Africa, it is called *adafina, dafina*, or *tafīna*. Most Sephardi Jews use mutton instead of beef and rice instead of barley. Syrian Jews place the mixture inside a hollowed-out piece of pumpkin or squash. Sephardi and North African spices include whole hot red peppers, saffron or turmeric, and ground coriander seeds. Chickpeas are often added to the mixture, and North African Jews frequently throw in a handful of cracked wheat (*qamḥ*).[17]

Tafīna (Tunisian Jewish)

VEAL, CHICKPEA, AND POTATO STEW WITH TURMERIC

The sabbath adafina *of Spanish Jews was a kind of stew or hotpot, which belongs to the same family of dishes as* escudella *(page 170),* cocido *(page 541),* olla *(page 544),* l'ollada *(page 15),* cassoulet *(page 195),* pot-au-feu, *and* bollito misto. *In one of the most important historical cookbooks written in the past decade, David M. Gitlitz and Linda Kay Davidson, using archival material, tell the story of Spain's Marranos, the crypto-Jews who continued to follow their religion, in* A Drizzle of Honey: The Lives and Recipes of Spain's Secret Jews. *Spanish Jews for centuries made* adafina *on Friday nights to cook slowly and be eaten on the sabbath. During the Spanish Inquisition, the Marranos and Moriscos, converted Jews and Muslims, respectively, suffered all forms of doubt about the sincerity of their conversions to Christianity. One test of their purported newly found Christian belief was the public eating of pork, forbidden to true Muslims and Jews. Traditionally, the* adafina *was based on chicken or, more often, on veal or beef breast with hard-boiled eggs. During the Inquisition, it could be insisted that pork or pork fat was added to the* adafina *as a test to ferret out crypto-Jews. This was a serious matter, because a Christian neighbor could happen by on a Saturday (the Jewish sabbath) and one would be expected to generously offer the guest some* adafina. *Another level of suspicion con-*

cerned the mere fact that a stew was cooking unattended. A similar predicament existed for Muslim converts. If there was no pork in it, the Marrano or Morisco was suspected of being a crypto-Jew or Muslim and could suffer dire consequences.

Adafina *has died out among the Sephardic Jews who left for Turkey and Greece, but it is still popular among Algerian and Tunisian Jews (nearly all who have emigrated to Israel) as* tafīna, *a sumptuous meal reserved for festival days and most often made by Jewish housewives on Friday and kept warm over the ashes of a* kanūna, *a brazier, to be served for Saturday lunch. It is sometimes accompanied by couscous.*

1 pound veal bones
1 beef or veal foot or 4 lamb's feet
4 pounds veal breast, trimmed of fat
1 large onion, finely chopped
1 cup dried chickpeas (about 1/2 pound), picked over, soaked in water to cover overnight, and drained
1 pound small boiling potatoes, about the size of a lime, peeled and left whole
1 head garlic
2 large eggs
1 tablespoon salt
1 teaspoon freshly ground black pepper
1 cinnamon stick
1 tablespoon turmeric
1 bay leaf
1 cup extra virgin olive oil
2 1/2 quarts water

1. In a large casserole or the bottom portion of a *couscousière*, place the veal bones and feet. Cover with the veal breast and the remaining ingredients in the order in which they are listed.

2. Place the casserole over very low heat (or use a heat diffuser) just before sunset, about 6 P.M., leaving it partially covered. Cook slowly until noon the next day. Check two or three times to see that the water level is fine, which it should be. Serve with rice or couscous.

NOTE: If you feel uncomfortable with an unattended flame, preheat the oven to 170°F and place the casserole in until noon the next day.

Makes 4 servings

Ajlūk al-Qara[c] (Tunisian Jewish)

ZUCCHINI COMPOTE

An ajlūk *is a kind of vegetable side dish, a compote, served as part of an* ādū *(the Tunisian-Arabic expression for* mazza, *an assortment of olives, relishes, pickles, and prepared food served on small plates as an entire meal or to nibble). The word* ajlūk *is found only in northern Tunisia among Jews, according to Paula Wolfert. When I asked a Tunisian chef from Djerba in southern Tunisia about it, he had never heard the word.*[18] Ajlūk *dishes are like vegetable compotes, characterized by boiled vegetables.* Qara[c] *(squash) refers to all members of the Cucurbita family, in this case zucchini, but the dish is also delicious with pumpkin, both served with pieces of Arab flatbread for scooping up the vegetables. This recipe is adapted from the Tunisian cookbook of Edward Zeitoun.*

4 medium-size to large zucchini, sliced
2 teaspoons caraway seeds
4 garlic cloves, peeled
2 teaspoons *harīsa* (page 523)
2 teaspoons freshly ground coriander seeds
Salt to taste
Juice from 1 lemon
Extra virgin olive oil for drizzling
20 black olives for garnish

1. Boil the zucchini in lightly salted water to cover for 20 minutes. Drain in a colander and carefully

press out all the excess water, making sure you don't push the zucchini through the holes of the colander. Transfer to a platter and mash with a fork.

2. In a mortar, grind the caraway seeds to a powder. Add the garlic and pound until it's crushed. Add the *harīsa*, coriander, and salt and continue pounding to a paste. Slowly stir in the lemon juice, beating with a fork. This should amount to 1/4 cup of dressing.

3. Pour the dressing over the mashed zucchini, mixing with a fork. Taste and add salt if necessary. Drizzle some olive oil over the zucchini and garnish with the olives around the side of the serving platter.

Makes 4 servings

✣ ✣ ✣

JEWISH communities have existed throughout the Mediterranean since before the Roman era. For example, Jews were settled in Algeria since the first century, although their food had much in common with the Muslim community that eventually formed after the eighth century. The Algerian Jews ate jujube (*Ziziphus jujuba* Mill.) on New Year's Eve. The jujube is a small fruit a bit larger than a big olive, which I think tastes vaguely of dates flavored with apple and chocolate, called *sheyzaf* in the Mishna, and was introduced to the Maghrib in the third century. The mixture of garlic and onions is not only an age-old Mediterranean combination but also a favorite among the Algerian Jews. Garlic and onion, with the olive, form the foundation for the great majority of traditional North African Jewish recipes such as *ṭabikha*, a beef-and-onion stew, and *mḥaṭār*, a lamb or chicken-and-garlic stew made by the Jews of Constantine in Algeria. Garlic was important to the Jews because of its magical and medicinal properties, and the Talmud affirms the aphrodisiacal effects of garlic and recommends eating it for the sabbath dinner, perhaps because of its digestive properties.[19]

Ṭabikha (Algerian Jewish)

SPICY MEAT AND ONION STEW

In the Maghrib, for both Muslims and Jews, a ṭabikha *can refer to any cooked dish. In Tunisia, it usually refers to a green vegetable stew, a* ṭabikha al-khuḍra. *In Tataouine, in southern Tunisia, it is a specialty, a breakfast soup made with lentils and other vegetables. This is how I ate it in Djerba.*

Algerian Jewish cooking is very similar to that of the Muslim population, even though the Algerian Jews' presence in the region predates that of the Arabs by several hundred years. What distinguishes Jewish food are the preparations made for special occasions. ʿAsha, *or its full name* ʿasha bi'l-ʿayid, *or festival dinner, was traditionally eaten by the Jews of Oran on the coast of western Algeria, either on the first night of Passover or for the Jewish New Year. It is a kind of stew with head or breast of beef or lamb, cabbage, fresh fava beans, zucchini, tomato, onions, bay leaf, ground red chili pepper, and ground coriander seeds.*

Mḥaṭār *is a kind of blanquette of lamb made by the Jews of Constantine in eastern Algeria, with lots of garlic, mint, bay leaf, saffron, and eggs.* Kafta bi'l-qanawiyya *are meatballs with okra. A dish made by Jews and Muslims in Algeria and Tunisia is* tafīna, *which means "to bury" in Arabic, made with chicken or beef breast, turnips, onions, and red chili pepper. The name perhaps indicates that it is either buried in the* marmite *in which it cooks undisturbed or perhaps was once literally buried to cook. The Jews made it for the sabbath. Because it can't be cooked on the Jewish sabbath, it is prepared Friday night and left to cook for a*

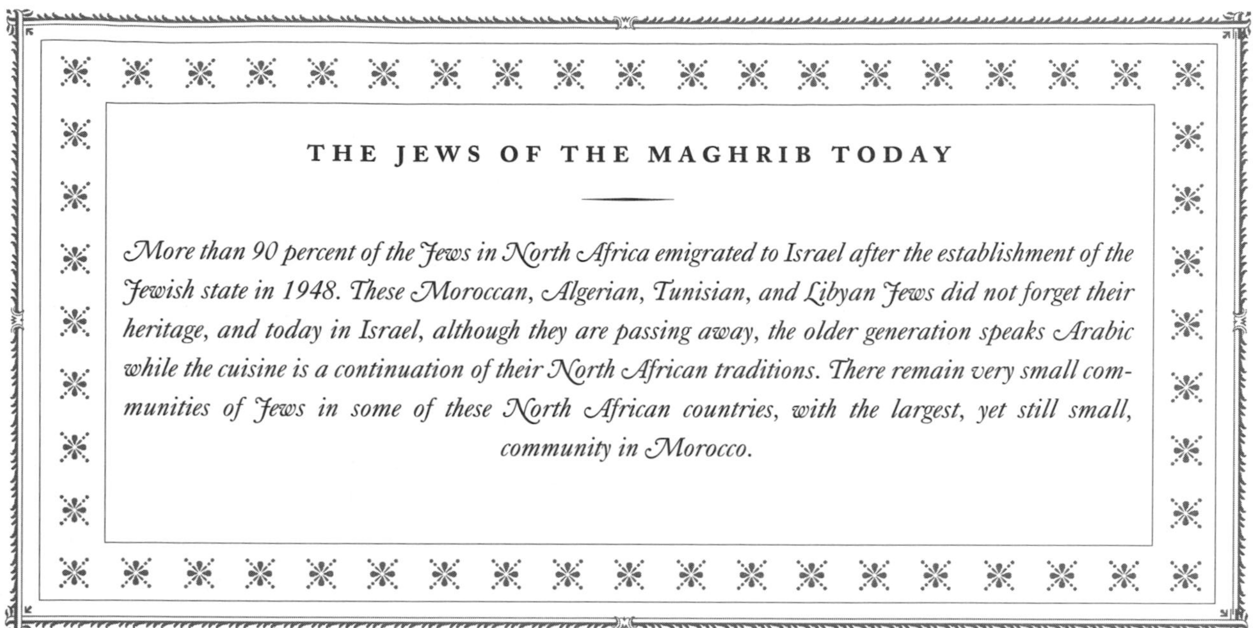

THE JEWS OF THE MAGHRIB TODAY

More than 90 percent of the Jews in North Africa emigrated to Israel after the establishment of the Jewish state in 1948. These Moroccan, Algerian, Tunisian, and Libyan Jews did not forget their heritage, and today in Israel, although they are passing away, the older generation speaks Arabic while the cuisine is a continuation of their North African traditions. There remain very small communities of Jews in some of these North African countries, with the largest, yet still small, community in Morocco.

long time. It figures in many Hebrew festival menus throughout the year and is derived from the Sephardic adafina, *a stew once made by the Jews of Spain.*

Ḥumra, *meaning "the red," the color of the finished dish, is a chicken-and-quince dish with onions, cinnamon, and nutmeg that is eaten on Yom Kippur by the Jews of Algiers. The French scholar Maxime Rodinson indicates that it is a preparation harking back to medieval times.*

This ṭabikha *is an Algerian Jewish dish of beef, onions, tomatoes, and red chili pepper, the name deriving from the Arabic for "cooked dish," in this case being cooked a long time over an enclosed fire. This dish is often prepared for wedding ceremonies, usually for the bride following her wedding eve bath, a Jewish custom in Constantine. It also is made for the bar mitzvah. For these reasons the dish is a prestigious one. The only vegetable in the dish is the onion, to symbolize the sweetness and unctuosity of the marriage and that it may not turn sour, to vinegar. The stew can be served with bread.*

¼ cup extra virgin olive oil
2 large onions, grated
3 garlic cloves, chopped
1 tablespoon *harīsa* (page 523)
Salt and freshly ground black pepper to taste
1 pound stew beef, trimmed of excessive fat and cubed
1 pound ripe tomatoes, peeled, seeded, and chopped
2 cups water
¼ cup finely chopped fresh coriander (cilantro) leaves

1. In a casserole or the bottom portion of a *couscousière*, heat the olive oil over medium-high heat, then cook the onions until translucent, about 10 minutes, stirring occasionally.

2. Add the garlic and *harīsa*, season with salt and pepper, and stir to mix well. Add the beef and brown on all sides for 2 to 4 minutes. Add the tomatoes and water, stir, reduce the heat to medium, cover, and cook for 45 minutes. Add the coriander and cook until the meat is tender, another 45 minutes.

Makes 4 to 6 servings

* * *

THE importance of food in the North African Judeo-Arabic culinary culture is reflected in certain festive meals. For example, festive meals are usually ragouts intended to be complete meals, such as the ragout of meat and haricot beans that is called *ʿasha*, meaning "the repast," the entire meal. Among Jews and Muslims in Algeria, but also throughout the Mediterranean, is what the anthropologist Joëlle Bahloul calls the culture of the *terrasse ensoleillée*, the terrace where food is salted or sun dried. Food selection is a cultural and social act, and the terrace where one conserves food is often shared with neighbors, perhaps a block of flats. It is an exclusively feminine activity. In the winter, beans are preserved in vinegar or lemon juice or salt and fruits are conserved in honey or sugar. In summer, beans and vegetables are dried and crushed or ground for making condiments such as the *harīsa*.[20]

The Jews of Algiers have a *kukla*, a kind of ball made of semolina bound together with beef fat and egg, seasoned with garlic and saffron, and traditional for the sabbath dinner. A very similar dish is made for festivals by the Palestinian Jews of Safad (Zefat) now in Israel, whose *kuklaya* is a meat platter. The Yiddish word *kugel*, or ball, is possibly derived from this dish, but it also could derive from the Judeo-Italian word *cugolo* from Leghorn (Livorno), meaning the same.[21] In winter, the Jews of Ain Beyda of the eastern Algerian steppe made a thick semolina soup, spicy with *harīsa* and cayenne pepper, using the large couscous balls called *muḥammaṣ*. The soup is called *ḥasū* and is eaten in the morning in place of coffee when it is very cold or snowing. *Tikurkabin* (the spelling is unsure) is another soup of *muḥammaṣ* bound with eggs and olive oil and plumped up partially in boiling bouillon. The soup also includes chickpeas, tomatoes, and onions. The same technique is found in the *kukla*, which is used in a *marmite* in cooking the *tafīna* (page 682).[22]

Essentially, Jewish cuisine is part and parcel of the host cuisine, although there are some good historical examples of the uniqueness of Jewish food, such as in Provence or Spain. Kalonimos ben Kalonimos, an Arlesian Jew of the first half of the fourteenth century, wrote a kind of satire of the customs of his co-religionists, titled *Eben Bohan*. Here we find descriptions of unique Jewish culinary habits such as a round fritter eaten with jam, made for the festival of the Maccabees. The Jews of Arles also made a cake of honey, milk, and flour fashioned in the form of a grid, like a ladder, and spread with honey and cherries.[23] In Spain, the town of Morella, in the province of Castellón in Valencia, was a thriving Jewish community famous for its bull "ham," *jamón de toro*.

An order from the council of Arles on October 21, 1427, proclaimed it dangerous for Christians to eat Jewish bread, namely unleavened bread. Since there was no difference between Christian and Jewish bread, it probably shows a general air of distrust of Jews throughout Provence. There also were separate Christian and Jewish butchers in Provence. Christian butchers sold all kinds of meat, Jewish ones did not sell pork and sold only meat butchered according to *de lege iudeorum* (Jewish law). In reality the relationship was more complex. Christian butchers would often supply the Jewish butchers, who in turn often sold to Christians.[24]

Jewish recipes, as we see in the following preparations from communities in Turkey, Spain, and Greece, could as easily be part of the local non-Jewish cuisines. What so often makes them Jewish, besides their being served at religious occasions, is the fact that Jewish cooks make them for a population who recognizes them as part of their culinary culture.

Espinaka Kotcha (Turkish Jewish)

SPINACH AND TOMATOES

Turkish Jews, according to Esther Benbassa's Cuisine Judeo-Espagole, *made* ravikos, *a spinach stem soup, for* shabat, *the sabbath day. The stems are cooked with broth, chopped tomatoes, rice, lemon, olive oil, and paprika.*[25] *The leaves are used in this preparation.*

2 pounds spinach, washed well
1 quart water
3 ripe tomatoes (about 1¼ pounds), peeled, seeded, and chopped
¼ cup extra virgin olive oil
1 cup beef or chicken broth (page 54)
Juice from 1 lemon
3 tablespoons long-grain rice, rinsed well or soaked in water to cover for 30 minutes and drained
2 teaspoons salt
2 teaspoons paprika
1 teaspoon sugar

1 Remove the stems from the spinach and save for making *ravikos* (see above). Bring the water to a boil in a large saucepan and cook the spinach for 5 minutes. Drain the spinach and place in a casserole with the tomatoes, olive oil, broth, lemon juice, rice, salt, paprika, and sugar.

2. Cover and cook over low heat for 30 minutes. Uncover and cook for another 15 minutes. Let it cook longer if there is liquid left. Serve hot.

Makes 4 servings

Keftes de Prassa y Carne (Turkish Jewish)

LEEK AND BEEF BURGERS

This is a Sephardic dish from Bursa, in Turkey. Claudia Roden, author of The Book of Jewish Food, *reports that this uniquely Jewish dish, which is unlikely to be found in a restaurant, is, in fact, made at a small establishment in the Grand Bazaar of Izmir, called the Kaşer Levi Lokantasi. These* keftes *are also very nice grilled with a brushing of olive oil.*

3 leeks, white and light green parts only, halved lengthwise, washed well, and finely chopped
1 pound ground beef, veal, or lamb
1 cup mashed potatoes (page 62)
1 large egg, beaten
1 teaspoon salt
Freshly ground black pepper to taste
½ cup sunflower or extra virgin olive oil

1. Boil the leeks for 10 minutes in water to cover. Drain and squeeze out as much water as possible. This is important, otherwise the patties will fall apart.

2. In a medium-size bowl, toss the leeks with all the other ingredients except the oil. Form into ten to twelve even-size patties, keeping your hands wet so the meat doesn't stick to them, and refrigerate for 1 hour.

3. In a large skillet, heat the oil over medium heat, then cook the patties until golden on both sides, 20 to 25 minutes. Serve.

NOTE: To grill the *keftes*, prepare a charcoal fire or preheat a gas grill on high heat for 20 minutes. Grill the *keftes* over the cool spot of the charcoal grill or reduce the heat of the gas grill to medium and cook until brown and springy to the touch, turning them several times, 20 to 25 minutes.

Makes 4 servings

Fritakas di Karne Blanca (Turkish Jewish)

CHICKEN BURGERS

This Sephardic dish would be typical for Passover among Turkish Jews. The heavy use of olive oil, as in this recipe, was considered typical of Mediterranean Jewish cooking in the Middle Ages.

1 pound ground chicken breast
1 matzo (about 6 inches square), soaked in water and squeezed dry
6 tablespoons finely chopped onion
1½ tablespoons finely chopped fresh dill
Salt and freshly ground black pepper to taste
¼ teaspoon freshly grated nutmeg
1 large egg, beaten
½ cup plus 1 tablespoon extra virgin olive oil

1. Mix all the ingredients except ½ cup of the olive oil in a medium-size bowl and form into eight to ten even-size patties. Refrigerate for 1 hour.

2. In a large skillet, heat the reserved olive oil over medium heat, then cook the patties until golden on both sides, 20 to 25 minutes. Serve.

Makes 4 servings

La Ensalada Sefardi (Spanish Jewish)

SEPHARDIC SALAD

This recipe was a presentation served at the famous Caballo Rojo restaurant in Córdoba, run by two brothers, Pepe and José Manuel, who claim to have researched these historical dishes. I cannot confirm that this is, in fact, a Sephardic dish, but it is really quite impressive anyway. It is a mélange of six different salads on one platter: a shredded salt cod with olive oil and sesame seeds; a salad of slightly boiled carrots dressed with olive oil, lemon, vinegar, and cumin seeds; roasted red peppers with cayenne, olive oil, and garlic; mashed tuna with vinegar and olive oil; very thin baby asparagus spears dressed with olive oil; and large mushrooms marinated with garlic.

For the salt cod
1 pound salt cod, prepared for cooking (page 436)
3 tablespoons extra virgin olive oil
½ teaspoon sesame seeds

For the carrots
¾ pound baby carrots
3 tablespoons extra virgin olive oil
½ teaspoon white wine vinegar
1 teaspoon fresh lemon juice
½ teaspoon cumin seeds

For the red bell peppers
3 red bell peppers
3 tablespoons extra virgin olive oil
1 garlic clove, very finely chopped
Pinch of cayenne pepper

For the remaining salads
One 6-ounce can imported tuna in olive oil
White wine vinegar for drizzling
Extra virgin olive oil for drizzling
½ pound very thin asparagus spears, bottoms trimmed
½ pound mushrooms
1 garlic clove, finely chopped

1. Prepare the salt cod. Place the salt cod in a pot and cover with cold water. Bring to a gentle boil, then turn off the heat and leave for 20 minutes. Drain and remove the bones and skin, if any. With a fork and knife, shred the salt cod. Transfer to a section of the

serving platter, pour the olive oil over the salt cod, and sprinkle with the sesame seeds.

2. Prepare the carrots. Bring a pot of lightly salted water to a boil and parboil the carrots until the tip of a knife can enter with slight resistance, about 5 minutes. Drain the carrots and toss with the olive oil, vinegar, lemon juice, and cumin seeds. Set aside until room temperature. Transfer to a section of the serving platter.

3. Prepare the bell peppers. Preheat the oven to 450°F. Place the peppers in a baking pan and roast until their skins char black, about 30 minutes. Remove from the oven; when they are cool enough to handle, seed, peel, and slice them into strips. Alternatively, use any high-quality roasted red peppers from a jar.

4. Toss the red peppers with the olive oil, garlic, and cayenne. Set aside until they reach room temperature. Transfer to the serving platter.

5. Prepare the remaining salads. Dress the tuna, without draining, with a little vinegar and olive oil on the serving platter.

6. Boil the asparagus in water to cover until completely soft, without any bite to it. Drain well, pat dry with paper towels, dress with a drizzle of olive oil, and arrange with all the spears pointing in one direction on the serving platter.

7. Boil the mushrooms whole in water to cover until soft. Drain, slice in half or into quarters, and dress with olive oil and garlic. Arrange each attractively on the serving platter with the other preparations and serve at room temperature.

Makes 4 servings

Kashkaval Pane (Greek Jewish)

BREADED FRIED CHEESE

This popular meze *is notable in Salonika (Thessaloniki), where there has been a significant Jewish population of Sephardim since 1492.*

3 tablespoons all-purpose flour
1 large egg
¼ cup milk
1 tablespoon unsalted butter
2 tablespoons extra virgin olive oil
Six ½-inch-thick slices *kashkaval* cheese (page 716)
Lemon wedges for garnish

1. Put the flour in a small bowl and beat in the egg until well blended. Slowly whisk in the milk until the batter is smooth. Refrigerate for 1 hour.

2. In a medium-size skillet, melt the butter with the olive oil over medium-high heat; once the bubbles have subsided but before any smoking occurs, dip the cheese slices in the batter and cook until the bottom is light brown, 3 to 4 minutes. Turn with a spatula, quickly and carefully, otherwise the batter crust may come off. Cook until the other side is light brown, another 3 to 4 minutes, and serve with a wedge of lemon.

Makes 2 to 4 servings

Patsas (Greek Jewish)

LAMB TROTTER SOUP

In the early 1970s I was living in Switzerland, and on spring break friends and I drove to Istanbul and then to

Athens. I learned then how cold April can be in the Mediterranean as we drove through Thessaloniki early one morning. Many years later I discovered that the lamb soup we ate then and loved so much was this one. My now vague memory of the soup was jump-started by a recipe given to me by Nikos Stavroulakis, whose book Cookbook of the Jews of Greece *is a classic of culinary anthropology. This recipe from the Jews of Salonika (Thessaloniki) was made in the winter for stevedores. It is a purely proletarian dish served as an early morning meal by special shops in the harbor where steaming* kazans *(cauldrons) of* patsas *would fortify the workers before their long day.*

5 pounds lamb bones, with some meat on them
3 quarts cold water
4 garlic cloves, thinly sliced
3 tablespoons extra virgin olive oil
Juice from 2 lemons
Salt and freshly ground black pepper to taste
Finely chopped fresh parsley leaves or dill for garnish
Sliced or chopped garlic (optional)

1. Put the lamb bones in a large pot and cover with the water. Bring to a boil; once it is boiling furiously, remove the foam from the surface with a skimmer. Keep the water at a boil and add the garlic, olive oil, lemon juice, salt, and pepper.

2. Reduce the heat to very low. Cover and place a heavy cleaver, pot, pan, lid, or rock on the lid to keep it tightly covered. Simmer overnight, about 12 hours.

3. The *patsas* can be served for breakfast in individual bowls with parsley or dill, more lemon juice, and sliced or chopped garlic if desired.

NOTE: If leaving the pot on an unattended flame makes you uncomfortable, preheat the oven to 180°F and place in the oven.

Makes 4 to 6 servings

MEDITERRANEAN FEAST

THE Mediterranean remained the center of the world through the sixteenth century. The influence of the Mediterranean spread to Africa through the reach of Islam. The Hispanic Mediterranean crossed to the New World, and the Turkish Mediterranean reached into the Balkans and as far away as India. In 1587, the last of the great corsairs, ʿUlujʿAlī, died. In 1589, King Henry III of France was dead, throwing the Mediterranean balance of power into confusion. In the 1590s, civil war erupted in Languedoc and Provence and the Ottoman Empire began its long, slow decline. In 1598, Philip II was dead; one of the longest reigns in Europe was over and an era ended. But it was not these men who made Mediterranean history. That history evolved as a long simmering ragout of peoples interacting on every geographical, economic, and cultural level.

The city-state, so important for the development of the Mediterranean region, was possible because urban merchants held a monopoly on the financial and technological elements of supplying them with their most important commodity brought from near and far—their daily food. The Italian city-states could not be challenged. But once the monarchs of large territories learned how to do the same in supporting large field armies for months at a time, the time of these great powers came to an end. Agents of the kings learned financial and transportation management, and with their large resources of manpower and material they could dominate the city-states, which lacked territory and manpower. The historian William McNeill considers this conflict between city-state and territorial state as the beginning of what we now call modernity.[26]

On the high seas, the city-states, especially Venice, had by 1580 failed to switch from galleys to the new form of gunnery available on roundships, and eventually the Atlantic navies outgunned the Mediterranean navies.[27]

The center of the world shifted to northern Europe, first to Amsterdam, later to London, and then, in the twentieth century, across the Atlantic to the United States. Although today's Mediterranean has receded in the world economy, it remains the center of our history and home of the foods we love so much. In a way, Mediterranean food has come full circle, now providing a paradigm for a heathy diet that maintains a respect for good taste.

We might think of the constant in Mediterranean food as the trinity of olive oil, wheat, and wine. But isn't there a culinary trinity of garlic, onion, and parsley that is just as important? And there is another trinity that should now be obvious: the historic one of war, plague, and famine that underlies all modern Mediterranean cuisines.

There is a rhythm to material life that coincides with the flux of human life. This rhythm has created the Mediterranean cuisines. In terms of food, the extant cookbooks from the thirteenth to sixteenth centuries are nothing but portrayals of the influence of Arab tastes on the evolution of European food. Platina reads like an extension of the thirteenth-century manuscript of Muḥammad ibn al-Ḥasan al-Baghdādī's the *Kitāb waṣf al-aṭʿima al-muʿtāda.* This brings us to the last Mediterranean trinity: the trinity of civilizations—Latin, Greek, and Arab—that gives us our Mediterranean feast.

I wrote this book in an attempt to extend one man's—Fernand Braudel's—vision, love, and scholarship, and I augmented it with my own research and love of Mediterranean food, in the hope of providing a guide to the Mediterranean that has not been attempted before. The weaving of history and gastronomy in *A Mediterranean Feast* was meant to reveal the culinary structure of the Mediterranean—its rugged contours, oppressive reality, and blue delight—through the eyes of geographers, travelers, historians, and cooks, what Braudel means by "total history." Braudel's writings were an attempt to seek out the "constant" of Mediterranean history, the structures and recurrent patterns of everyday life that provide the reference grid. For myself, and this book, the constant is the food of the Mediterranean, its cuisine and recipes. What, then, is the "plant of civilization" posed in the beginning of the book? I don't have an answer, but I'm inclined to say garlic because it is the plant whose aroma permeates all Mediterranean gastronomy.

Mediterranean civilization is capable of expanding globally. We certainly have seen this truth in the culinary sphere: We began with Latin, Greek, and Arab gastronomy then moved to Spain and Italy and France. Just as the economic importance of the Mediterranean was eventually eclipsed by northern Europe and later America, I believe that the gastronomic epicenter, which shifted centuries ago from Abbasid courts of Baghdad to the royal courts of Palermo, to the ecclesiastical and ducal kitchens of Renaissance Italy, and finally to the great chefs of France, will shift from France to America, if it hasn't already. It will take time, but eventually the most exciting cooking in the world will be in America.[28] Why? Because its possibilities are unlimited. Even today many American home cooks, when pressed, will tell you that they cook "international eclectic" food. But these same cooks ought to remember that "international eclectic" without an understanding of the cultures from which it derives is an empty cuisine, usually tasteless and compromised. For American cuisine to become a reality and excel, Americans need to learn about food and to be as passionate about it as about love, for cooking is love. We're not there yet, as we know from a glimpse of our huge supermarkets, 80 percent of whose shelves are filled with processed food products. As we learn more about how food is grown, produced, harvested, prepared, and cooked, we will learn more about how it should taste good.

For a Mediterranean feast, one must have at least a rudimentary grasp of the traditional and authentic Mediterranean recipes, which I have tried to provide in this book. These recipes arose as a human response to calamity and famine, and for the peoples of the Mediterranean, so many of whom are now in America, certainly perhaps by an amazing grace. If one is lucky enough to have a family that cherishes its culinary roots, all the better. For the rest of us, a little food history, a little caring about the food we eat, and a little attention paid to how we buy food and cook it—and caring for those with whom we share it—may open up possibilities to create and enjoy food as part of our new heritage.

AN ESSAY ON THE SOURCES

A HISTORY of Mediterranean cuisines has a rich literature to draw upon. But what can be learned from this culinary literature of the Middle Ages? Can the early cookbooks tell us something about regional culinary specialties or are they rather cosmopolitan, informing us more about aristocratic and bourgeois practices than those of the common folk? Certainly we learn what the rich ate, and almost nothing about the poor.

It is a given among culinary historians that there is the court cuisine and the food of the poor. I have no problem with the basic truth of this distinction, yet it is an oversimplification. Regionally, the rich sometimes ate what the poor ate—they shared a culinary culture. Henry of Navarre ate as much garlic as his servants.[1] Also, there were others besides the "rich" and the "poor," namely a class of small landowners, ecclesiastics, well-fed sailors, arquebusiers and light infantry, and the growing bourgeois for whom there was a regional cuisine.

The sources available to the culinary historian are enormous; unfortunately, there are almost no culinary historians. Many who claim to be culinary historians are, in fact, not trained in historical research and are generally unfamiliar with the current problems of historiography. On the other hand, the interest of professional historians in food seems to end in the field—that is, agricultural history seems to be the limit of the professional historian's interest in food. Historians, other than those working in the *Annales* tradition and a handful of others, are neither interested in nor have they written about the end product of agriculture, namely cuisine. As a result, most of the important sources and archives are unexamined by people studying cuisines. Furthermore, culinary historians have relied far too heavily on the extant cookbooks, which I review in this essay, providing a false picture of what people in the Middle Ages actually ate. But one must start somewhere and the books are the sources most readily available. The sources available to the historian tell us a story of Mediterranean cuisines in a somewhat confused way, but the outlines should be clear enough. This story draws upon works in Arabic, Latin, and a variety of other languages, not to mention the vast range of knowledge from art, botany, and a host of other subjects.

LATIN AND ARABIC SOURCES: COOKBOOKS, AGRICULTURAL TREATISES, AND HEALTH MANUALS

✣

A MEDITERRANEAN FEAST is a story of the Mediterranean from about 1450 to 1650. It looks at the antecedents of this period by considering a time span going back to about the ninth century. It is not a study of the classical Mediterranean. For that period one would, of course, need to be familiar with the writings of Athenaeus, Pliny, Columella, Theophrastus, Varro, Celsus, and many other writers. For the transition from late antiquity to the medieval era, the Arabic sources are the single most important for understanding the early development of contemporary Mediterranean cuisine. These sources are important for developing the thesis that the Mediterranean food of today, and especially the genesis of classical French and Italian cooking, has its roots not in the long-forgotten classical era of Rome and Greece but in Muslim culture. To my mind, medieval Arab cookery played a role in the development of European gastronomy identical to the role played by Arab agronomy, mathematics, astronomy, and other sciences in the subsequent development of the European sciences. The Mediterranean food we eat today, I have argued, has been shaped by three great historical revolutions: the Arab agricultural revolution (c. 700–1100), the Age of Exploration (c. 1255–1525), and the Italian Renaissance (c. 1350–1600).

Even a casual glance through the early Italian cookbooks provides an unmistakable mirror image of the medieval Arabic cookery works and other sources for culinary matters. The primary literature on Arab cookery comes from geographical works, the *adab* literature (writings during the Abbasid period on high culture, poetry, etc.), historical works and travel diaries, literature (such as the *Arabian Nights*), *ḥisba* works (writings of household accounts), and the cookbooks.[2]

The five major extant medieval Arab cookery works are the *Kitāb al-ṭabīkh fī iṣlāḥ al-aghdhiya al-maʿkūlāt wa-ṭayyib al-aṭʿima al-maṣnūʿāt* complied by Abū Muḥammad al-Muẓaffar ibn Nasr ibn Sayyār al-Warrāq in late tenth-century Abbasid Iraq; the *Kitāb waṣf al-aṭʿima al-muʿtāda*, complied by Muḥammad ibn al-Ḥasan al-Baghdādī about 1226 and translated into English by Professor A. J. Arberry and often called the Baghdad cookery book; the *Kitāb al-wuṣla ilā al-ḥabīb fī waṣf aṭ-ṭayyibāt wāṭ-ṭīb*, complied during the Ayyūbid period and attributed to the historian from Aleppo Ibn al-ʿAdīm (or ʿAmīd), who died in 1262 (this was the work studied in the famous article by the French scholar Maxime Rodinson and was translated into Turkish as early as the fifteenth century); the anonymous Egyptian work from the same period with nearly eight hundred recipes, *Kanz al-fawāhid fī tanwīha al-mawāhid*; and the sixteenth-century *Kitāb al-ṭibākha*, edited by H. Zayyat, by the Damascene Yūsūf b. Ḥasan ad-Dimashqī, known as Ibn al-Mabrad (d. 1503), translated into English in 1981 by Charles Perry.[3] Although I say these works are extant, there are others that I have not mentioned, and any interested student of this topic must begin by reading the famous article, mentioned above, by the French historian Maxime Rodinson, "Recherches sur les documents Arabes relatifs à la cuisine," in *Revue des Études Islamiques* (volumes 17–18, pp. 95–165), published in 1949.[4]

There are also several works from Muslim Spain: the anonymous Hispano-Muslim cookbook *Kitāb al-ṭabīkh fī al-Maghrib wa'l-Āndalus*, also called the Almohad cookbook; Ibn Razīn al-Tujībī's *Kitāb faḍāla at al-khiwān fī ṭayyibāt al-ṭʿam wa'l-alwān*; the earliest of the cookery works, which, according to its editor Fernando de la Granja Santamaria, is from the late eleventh century, although it has also been placed in the thirteenth century; and al-Arbūlī's book (see below). Another Hispano-Muslim work is Aḥmad b. Mubarākshah Shihāb al-Dīn's *Zahr al-ḥadīqa fī al-atʿima al-aniqa*, a manuscript that resides in the Landesbibliotek Gotha, Germany.[5]

Important features of the Arab influence on European cuisine, besides obvious linguistic connections, are sweetening with sugar, coloring with saffron, an emphasis on spices, and the use of rose water, oranges, lemons, pomegranates, and almonds, especially almond milk, as flavoring agents and liaisons for sauces. The abundance of sugar, both during cooking and sprinkling on afterward, is notable in both the Arab and European manuscripts. In contrast to the medieval recipes, sugar does not appear in the Roman cookery work of Apicius. Saffron, used so abundantly and frequently in medieval Arab and European texts, appears only three times in Apicius and its coloring potential is not mentioned. In coloring food, the Arabs were expanding, in a fashion, medieval alchemy by attempting to make the food look like gold, not to mention the fact that the Arabs considered yellow to be the color of gaiety. This alchemical search for an elixir swept over Europe at the same time cookery manuscripts began to appear in the thirteenth and fourteenth centuries.

The corollaries of the early culinary works are the agricultural treatises, pharmacological works, herbals, and dietetic manuals, the most important of which were translations of the medieval Arabic texts, widely available in the medieval world and critical to understanding Arab agriculture and dietetics. The most important were the anonymous *Calendar of Córdoba* from 961; Ibn Waḥshīya's (A.D. 903–904) *Al-filāḥa al-nabaṭīya* (Nabatean agriculture); and one of the most famous of medieval Arabic agricultural treatises, which had a wide influence, Ibn al-ᶜAwwām's (fl. twelfth century) *Kitāb al-filāḥa* (Book of farming). A short time earlier, Qusṭūs al-Rūmī (tenth century ?) wrote *Al-filāḥa al-rūmīya* (Greek or Byzantine agriculture). In thirteenth-century Ayyūbid Egypt, agricultural questions were addressed by Ibn Mammātī's (d. 1209) *Kitāb qawānīn al-dawāwīn*. A century later, Gamal al-Din al-Waṭwāṭ (1235–1318) wrote *Mabāhij al-fikar wa manāhij al-ᶜibar*, the fourth volume of which was devoted to plants and agriculture. In the fifteenth century, we have the *Nuzhat al-anām fī maḥāsin al-Shahm* by al-Badrī, who gives us the name in Syria of twenty-two varieties of apricots, fifty varieties of grapes, and six varieties of roses.[6]

Among the important pharmacological works are Ibn al-Baiṭār's (d. 1248) *Kitāb al-jāmiᶜ mufradāt al-adwiya wa'l-aghdhiya* (Book of the collection of simple drugs and nutrients) and Ibn al-Wāfid's (d. 1074) *Kitāb al-adwiya al-mufrada*, his main work on simple drugs following Galen and Dioscorides. Ibn al-Wāfid lived and conducted agricultural experiments in Spain. Arab physicians wrote important works dealing with health—for example, Māsawaih al-Mārdīnī (d. 1015), known as Mesuë the Younger in the West, whose book was a standard pharmacological textbook in Europe for centuries.

The medieval Arabic health manuals are equally important, and the most famous is the *Taqwīm al-ṣiḥḥa*, translated into Latin as *Tacuinum sanitatis*, of Ibn Buṭlān and the tenth century *Kitāb al-Manṣūrī*, translated into Latin as the *Liber de medicina ad Almansorum*, written by al-Rāzī (known as Rhazes in the West), the greatest clinician of the Middle Ages.[7] Ibn Buṭlān's health manual, along with the Salerno regimen, a handbook of domestic medicine, whose authorship is debated, became the foundations for modern Western medicine and played a great role in the formation of European dietetics, the medical practice of the time underlying all cuisine in the Middle Ages. Another important manual was written by the Egyptian doctor ᶜAlī ibn Riḍwān (died c. 1061). Many of these health and dietetic manuals contained culinary as well as medical recipes.

The medieval theories of dietetics in turn played a crucial role in the East to West culinary transference I describe. The cooking of food was very much linked to pharmacology and dietetics. In fact, a theory of taste was derived from the culinary documents understood in the light of the agricultural, medical, and pharmacological works. The Arabs had an aesthetic approach to food defined by four gustative flavors: sweet *(ḥulwa)*, sour *(ḥamiḍ)*, salt *(maliḥ)*, and bitter *(murr)*. It is arguable whether this aesthetic was passed on directly to Sicilians and Andalusians, in particular during their respective Arab Muslim eras, but it seems likely given the transference of other elements of material culture and the general revolution in scientific thought.[8]

All the cookery works, books, and manuals on dietetics and health in the Middle Ages presupposed the prevalent concept of medicine that was based on the so-called theory of humors. The theory of humors guided medieval cooks to such an extent that it may be legitimate to say that they were closer to pharmacologists than they are to today's cooks. This now disproved theory was a system of partly magical and partly medical notions based on ancient Egyptian hypotheses that postulated four fundamental elements of the world related to the four constituent elements of the human being. The four elements were earth, air, fire, and water. These elements had certain qualities—for example, water, which is moist and cool, or fire, which is warm and dry. These elements were opposites and their opposition kept nature in equilibrium. So, too, the human being could be kept in equilibrium with the proper diet. The four constitutive elements of the human being were related to the corporeal fluids, and each was identified with a color: bile was black, given to melancholy; blood was red, with the character of bloodiness; water was related to phlegm; and air was related to yellow bile. The basic organs of the body were also related to the humors as were qualities, natures, and seasons.[9] Through the four humors, nutrition interacted with the body. Medieval physicians spoke of human beings as having a certain complexion or temperament, used as a description of their state of being. Virtually all of the cookery manuscripts before the sixteenth century can be properly understood only in the context of this prevalent theory of dietetics. They were manuals of practical dietetics rather than gastronomic works per se.

The beginnings of medieval dietetics can be traced to the written contributions of the medical botany of Pedacius Dioscorides, who was born in the northwest of Roman Syria and wrote his *Materia medica* in the first century. About 850 it was translated into Arabic in Baghdad.[10] But the inhabitants of Arabia Deserta and Arabia Felix had accumulated a wealth of information and experience in the fields of economic botany, medical botany, and range management independent of Roman and Greek traditions. This heritage was collected by Abū Ḥanīfa al-Dīnawarī in the second half of the ninth century, and it showed no traces of the learning of Dioscorides' *Materia medica*.[11]

The *Al-Aqrābādhīn* (Medical formulary) of al-Kindī (800–870), a textbook by the famous Arab physician and pharmacologist, also showed no direct influence of Dioscorides' work.[12] Al-Kindī, whose influence was long felt in medicine, was considered by the sixteenth-century Italian physician Girolamo Cardano to be one of the twelve greatest minds ever to have lived. The medieval Arab philosopher Averroës (Ibn Rushd, 1126–1198) also wrote on food in his *Kitāb al-kulliyyāt* (Book of general principles of medicine).[13] Some other works deriving from Arab medical science were the Latin pseudo-Aristotelian *Secretum secretorum*, translated from the *Kitāb sirr al-asrār* (Book of the secrets of secrets). This Arabic work from 941 is described as a work of the ninth-century translator Yaḥyā ibn al-Biṭriq, who worked for the caliph al-Ma'mūn, the Latin translation coming from the mid-thirteenth century. The book recommends exercise for the appetite and advises the reader that one gets fat by resting, eating well—especially meats—drinking milk or sweet wine, and sleeping after eating.[14]

Perhaps even more important than Dioscorides' work was the anonymous *Herbarium apulei*, an herbal composed between the second and fourth centuries. The earliest known manuscript was written around 700 and is now in the Leiden University Library in the Netherlands. It was finally printed in Rome in 1481 by the Sicilian nobleman Giovan Filippo La Legname.

Herbals served as the foundation of European medical knowledge during the Dark Ages—that is, before the profound and lasting influence of Arabic medical learning that generally came to be accepted after 1200. The herbals were based on recipes that were remedies for various ailments. Over the centuries they were hand-copied and largely misunderstood, generally useless and disgusting. Not all the remedies in the *Herbarium apulei* are useless, though. For example, *herba scilla*, the medicinal squill of the Mediterranean region known as *Scilla maritima* L., contains glycosides that affect the heartbeat.[15] Another herbal that was useful, with its list of plants, in the Middle Ages was the *Herbolario vol-*

gare, wrongly attributed to Arnold of Vilanova (1240–1311), a celebrated Catalan doctor who served Pedro III and Alfonso III of Aragon and became an influential professor of medicine at the University of Montpellier. He was a remarkable man who knew Greek and Arabic, translating into Latin a work of the Muslim philosopher and medical encyclopaedist Ibn Sīnā (930–1037), known as Avicenna in the West, one of the most famous scientists of all time.[16] Avicenna's remarkable work, called the *Qānūn fī'l-ṭibb* (Canon of medicine), is an immense medical encyclopaedia with a great deal of dietetic information.

Dietetics was a wholly Arab science founded on the Arabic translations of the earlier Greek works, then unknown in Europe. One of the most important entrepôt for the introduction of Arabic science into Europe was the famous court of Frederick II in Palermo, who was also a patron of the University of Salerno where dietetics was studied from Arabic manuals. It should not be surprising, therefore, to see Arabic culinary texts being introduced and translated under the auspices of the Angevin king in Naples or Frederick's son Manfred when he became king of Sicily. The Arabic texts also appeared in the court in Valois.[17]

EUROPEAN AND TURKISH SOURCES: AGRICULTURAL TREATISES, PHARMACOLOGIES, HEALTH MANUALS, DIETETICS, AND COOKBOOKS

THE Arab agricultural treatises influenced European agronomy, which also drew upon the Roman tradition. The most important of these works was the *Liber ruralium commodorum* of Petrus de Crescentiis, a Bolognese landowner who advocated green manuring and was very aware of Italy's historic problem of winter forage for husbandry. Other important Italian writers on agriculture were Pagnino Bonafede (fl. 1360) and, later, the Florentine Michelangelo Tanaglia (d. 1512). One of the most important Spanish agricultural works was Gabriel Alonso de Herrera's *Obra de agricultura*, first published in 1513. De Herrera was familiar with Petrus de Crescentiis, as well as the classical writers Theophrastus, Pliny, and Columella, and wrote that barley was said to be nutritious and wheat flour with honey was a curative for scabs and mixed with honey and pork lard was placed on the nipples.[18]

There are important French works on dietetics and agriculture that can contribute to a history of Mediterranean food, such as Magninus Mediolanensis's *Regimen sanitatis*, written 1330–1340. He was physician to the bishop of Arras and his regimen was extensive, containing thirty-five recipes. He details the countries where certain foods are eaten and distinguishes between summer and winter preparations. Jean Bruyerin Champier's *De re cibaria*, written in 1560; the anonymous *Thresor de santé* from 1607; and *Diaeticon ployhistoricum* by Joseph Du Chesne in 1606 are all important works emanating from France during this period. Among the agricultural works are Quiqueran de Beaujeu's *De laudibus provinciae* of 1551, Charles Estienne's *Proedium rusticum* of 1554, and Olivier de Serres' *Le théâtre d'agriculture*, published in 1600.[19]

From Sicily a number of important agricultural works circulated. Antonio Venuto, a Sicilian from Noto, published a small book in Naples in 1516 called *De agricultura*, under the auspices of Federico Abbatelli, count of Cammarata and Harbor Master of Palermo for the kingdom of Sicily.[20] Abbatelli is an important name in the history of food because it was in his Palermo garden in 1487 that *arangii dulcibus* was grown, which may be a reference to sweet oranges before the generally accepted Portuguese introduction of the sweet orange.[21] Even though we have the book on agriculture written in the thirteenth century by Roberto of Palermo, Venuto's tract is the first on Sicilian agriculture independent of the Latin authors and deals with fruit-bearing trees. It was a best-seller in its time, with six editions published in Palermo up until 1589.[22]

In Italy, Taddeo Alderott (1223–1303) wrote *De regimine sanitatis*, saying that chewing fennel seeds, anise, or cloves stimulates the appetite. He talked about the relative properties of kid, milk-fed veal, piglets, mountain birds, eggs, and green cabbage, which should not be cooked too much. Pietro de Tossignano, writing at the end of the fourteenth century, suggested fresh anise bread, white wine, and cheese after dinner as foods that would ward off the plague. Giovanni da Ketham, in *Fasciculus medicinae*, published in 1491, recommended eating the small figs of Syria available in March. Ambrogio Oderico's *De sanitatte regenda consilium* gave dietetic advice in the second half of the fifteenth century that was relevant until the sixteenth century. Giacomo Castelvetro of Modena in 1614 wrote *Brief Account of all the Roots, Greens and Fruits that are Eaten in Italy either Raw or Cooked*, a list of Italian gastronomy, where he explains why the Italians eat more greens and fruits than meat. In 1569, Costanzo Felici wrote *On Salads and Plants that are in any way Used as Food for Man* and Salvatore Massonio wrote *Archidipno, or on Salad and its Use* in 1627.

In all the various medical, hygenic, and dietietic treatises, bread is *cum fere sit totius cibationis fundamentum* (almost always the most important food).[23] Although leavened white bread was the best bread, Fernand Braudel showed that it was rare until the early modern era, and gruel *(bouillie)*, flans, and *galettes* (flat cakes) coexisted with leavened bread during all of the Middle Ages.[24]

In Italy, the very earliest works related to food and cookery are often translations of Arab manuals and dietetics. There are about one hundred manuscripts from the fourteenth and fifteenth centuries dealing with cuisine, and a comprehensive and systematic study of these texts has never been undertaken.[25] Ibn Buṭlān's *Tacuinum sanitatis in medicina* is certainly the first, written in the eleventh century, and it resides in various archives. Ibn al-Wāfid had his work translated as *De medicinus et cibis simpicibus* by Gherardo of Cremona in the first half of the twelfth century. Constantine the African (d. 1087), a Tunisian merchant and doctor, translated at the convent in Monte Cassino several Arab and Greek medical books such as the *Kitāb al-adwiya al-mufrada wa'l-aghdhiya* (Book of simple drugs and nourishment) by the Jewish doctor Isḥāq ibn al-Isrāᶜīlī (died c. 932).[26] Constantine the African was the first great translator of Arabic to Latin, and thanks to him the vast corpus of Arabic medical literature came to be translated.

In Spain, the Arabs contributed a number of works that have come to be known as Hispano-Muslim cookbooks, although their predecessors are works on dietetics such as the *Kitāb al-aghdhiya* (Book of diet) by the Andalusian physician Abū Marwān ibn Zuhr (fl. twelfth century) who wrote the first scientific work on diet. Another manuscript from the Middle Ages is the *Al-kalām ᶜala al-aghdhiya* of al-Arbūlī, a scholar working during the Naṣrid reign in Granada. The work is from 1428 and today is in the Biblioteca Nacional de Madrid. Al-Arbūlī mentions the word *kaᶜk*, a kind of cake that is originally Egyptian, and not Persian, that may be the ancestor of the Sicilian *cassata* (page 302).[27] In Andalusia, it referred to a kind of round or twisted bread loaf or cake with a hole in the middle.[28]

Hispano-Muslim cookery refers to the cookery of the Muslim population in Spain. Spanish food was revolutionized in the ninth century with the arrival from Baghdad of the famous Ziryāb. He brought a new style of cooking, entertaining, and good living.[29] There is a dish of salted and grilled fava beans that people refer to as *ziryabi* in reference to this well-known Arab chef and fashion arbiter.[30] This was part and parcel of the general luxury of what were the richest cities in Europe, all Arab-ruled, Seville and Córdoba in Spain and Palermo in Sicily. Here one finds all the pleasures of the earth, especially in the luxurious gardens of paradise that bespeak calm and voluptuousness. A perfect example can be seen today in the garden of the Alcázar, the central palace of the Alhambra in Granada, built in the fourteenth century. The Arab poets of Spain and Sicily allude to the merriment accompanied by good wine with an anacreontic fervor, soirées in the country, and veritable orgies.[31]

The Turkish contribution to the early written culinary material is not very well known. One of the earliest written sources on pre-Islamic Turks are the inscriptions of the Orhun Relics that refer to a funeral ceremony of a ruler of the Göktürks, who established a large empire in Central Asia between the sixth and eighth centuries. From the Seljuk period (1077–1307), the *Divanü Lugati't-Türk* (Compilation of Turkish languages) of Mahmud el-Kaşgari, a dictionary compiled in the late eleventh century, gives the names of dishes such as *tutmaç*, a dumpling (possibly macaroni) soup and *yufka*, an unleavened pastry, as well as yogurt, and references to cooking in pits in the ground, to grills, skewers, and earthenware cooking pots. The other important work of the eleventh century is Yūsuf Khāṣṣ Ḥājib's *Kutadgu bilig* (Wisdom of royal glory), which mentions eating customs, feasts, and table service. The *Dede korkut hikayeleri* (The tales of Dede Korkut), complied toward the end of the fourteenth century, are twelve tales about the customs of the Oghuz Turks of southwestern Asia. It mentions various stews, kebabs, *togya çorbasi* (a soup made of wheat flour), and wine consumption. In the works of the famous thirteenth-century poet Mevlana Jalaluddin-i Rumi, the many references to food are categorized, such as meat stewed with vegetables.[32] The *Tabiat-name*, a fourteenth-century health manual written by Tutmacı for Umur Bey, the ruler of the Aydınoğlu principality, mentions many foods, such as *fatir*, which was a griddle-cooked bread. There are a number of other Turkish works related to health that contain information on food, as well as cooking manuscripts and diaries about food.[33] It was during the latter part of the Ottoman period (c. 1600–1923) that Turkish cuisine became very sophisticated.

In the Bibliothèque Nationale in Paris is a miscellaneous collected manuscript dedicated to Charles II of Anjou (1248–1309) containing the most important European gastronomic works of the Middle Ages: the *Liber ruralium commodorum* of Petrus de Crescentiis; a tractate called *Quomodo praeparanda et condienda omnia cibaria quae comuniter comeduntur*, believed to be French in origin, from the early fourteenth century; the anonymous *Liber de coquina* and a tract called *De valetudine conservanda*; the *Regimen sanitatis Salernitanum*; and a transcription of the *Liber de ferculis et condimentis*.[34] The last mentioned, the *Liber de ferculis et condimentis*, was a twelfth-century dietetic manual translated from the Arabic in Venice by Jambobino of Cremona from a work called *De cibis et medicinus simplicibus et compositis* written by Gege (also called Byngezla), son of al-Ghazzālī (known as Algazel in Latin), the greatest theologian of Islam. Gege, as he was known in Latin, was the Baghdad doctor Abū ᶜAli Yaḥyā ibn ᶜĪsā Ibn Jazla, who died in 1100, whose original work was titled *Kitāb al-minhāj al-bayān fīmā yastaᶜmiluhu al-insān* (The book of products used by man set forth).[35]

In this collection is the oldest Italian cookbook, the anonymous *Liber de coquina*, apparently written by someone familiar with the Neapolitan court then under the sphere of Charles II of Anjou, to whom the collection of food-related works bound together is dedicated.[36] The *Liber de coquina* itself, though, appears to be dedicated to Robert of Anjou, king of Sicily (Naples), son of Charles, therefore leading some people to call it a Sicilian cookbook.[37] But to call it a Sicilian or Italian cookbook is misleading. None of the early cookery manuscripts were cookbooks of regional recipes but were international in scope. The *Liber de coquina* is written in Latin but has some recipes with Arabic names, and recipes being used in France, England, southern Italy, Germany, Spain, and from Arab lands. This characterization is true of the other early cookery works mentioned in this essay. Two other cookbooks from fourteenth-century Italy, the *Libro della cocina*, written by an anonymous Tuscan, and the *Libro per cuoco*, by an anonymous Venetian, bring a wealth of information to the early history of Italian cuisine.[38] The *Libro per cuoco* improves on the early *Libro della cocina* by including measurements.[39] The earlier of the two is also notable for being clearly influenced by the Arab cuisine of the time—for instance, in the spicing of the recipe called *pastello di gambari*, a shrimp pie made with pine nuts, almonds, spices, and saffron.[40]

It is clear that these early European cookery works, especially in their use of spices such as saffron, and other ingredients not found at all or very sparsely in Apicius such as almond milk and rose water, are intimately related to Arab cookery—as related to Arab cookery as medieval European pharmacology and dietetics are related to the Arab sciences.

Some experts have suggested that these Italian cookery works might be attributed to the cook of the *brigata spendereccia* of Siena. The "Spendthrift's Club" was a band of young nobles in Siena during the second half of the thirteenth century who, in the fatalistic shadow of the Black Death, agreed to live a life of sumptuous delight, vanity, and profligacy by squandering their estates to live this life of luxury.[41] The Niccolò mentioned in Canto XXIX: 127–28 of Dante's *Inferno* is thought to be Niccolò de Salembeni, who invented dishes using expensive spices.[42]

In the fifteenth century, more cookery works make their appearance, including that of Bartolomeo Sacchi (1421–1481), who took a Latin name, Platina, as did many of his time who were enamored of the recently rediscovered classical era of Italy. He was a humanist who worked in ducal courts and became the Vatican librarian, and had his *De honesta voluptate et valetudine*, written in Latin, published in Rome in 1474.[43] The book was not just a cookbook but also a guide to good living, much like today's health and fitness books. It was not discovered until the twentieth century that five chapters of this work were actually written by Martino, the cook to Ludovico Trevisan, patriarch of Aquileia, in the Tuscan language and not Latin.[44]

After Platina, Cristoforo di Messisbugo's *Libro novo nel qual s'insegna a far d'ogni sorte di viviande* was published in Ferrara in 1549, a year after the death of the author, while Bartolomeo Scappi's *Opera* was published in Venice in 1570 by Michele Tramezzino. Scappi was chef to Pope Pius V, and probably Venetian, because of the dedication to a celebrated cook and carver of Venice and because he uses unmistakably Venetian language with terms of endearment and diminutives. There are a lot of Venetian recipes.

In 1560, Domenico Romoli's *La singola dottrina* was published in Venice and suggests matching food and wine. Venice was a major publishing center and many cookery works were published there—for example, the study of eating by Tommaso Garzoni, published in Venice 1585, called *Piazza universale di tutte le professioni del mondo*.[45] In 1516, the *Epulario, il quale tratta del modo del cucinare* of Giovanni Rosselli was published in Venice, and it delimited the revolution and simplification of the renaissance of Venetian and Italian cuisines. It was a practical book and had editions to 1750.[46]

As culinary history is not a popular field of study for professional historians, those who write about cuisine, who are consumers of scholarship, must rely on the serendipitous discoveries made by the occasional researcher who happens upon documents related to cuisine that might shed some light on particular areas, such as the *Ricettario* manuscript in the Biblioteca Nazionale Centrale di Firenze, where one comes across recipes for preparations such as *salsa saporita*, made of toasted bread pounded with vinegar, parsley, pepper, capers, anchovy, garlic, and a little sugar.[47] One of the major sources on Ligurian cuisine is found in such a manuscript called *Medicinalia quam plurima*, in the Biblioteca Universitaria di Genova, written in the second half of the fifteenth century by an anonymous Genoese or Ligurian.[48] There is also the unedited and unstudied MS. 226 of the Bibliothèque de Cessole of the Musée Massena de Nice that appears to be a cookery work from central Italy of the fourteenth century.[49]

Some of the earliest cookery works in medieval Europe were Catalan. The earliest was the *Libre de sent soví* from about 1324, and some of its recipes reappear in the fifteenth-century Italian cookery works, Maestro Martino's *Libro di arte coquinaria* (who called Catalan chefs the best in the world) and Platina's *De honesta voluptate et valetudine*. The author is anonymous, although he is Catalan and may have been a chef in England.[50] Colman Andrews, a noted authority on Catalan food, points out the clear Arab influences in the Catalan recipes.[51] Rudolf Grewe, who edited the *Libre de sent soví*, told me before he died that he believed the Arab connection with the development of European cuisine had long been overlooked and when that history was written, it would consider first of all the earliest Catalan and Italian cookery works and their relation to the still earlier Arab cookery works.[52]

Some other early Iberian works are the fourteenth-century *Llibre de cuina* in the Biblioteca de la Universidad Literaria de Valencia; the Catalan cookery work, dated 1331; the anonymous *Llibre del coc de la canonja de Tarragona* (Cookbook of the canon of Tarragona) that set down dietary rules and recommendations for ecclesiastics in the See of Tarragona and described common food products and dishes of the time; and the *Manual de mugeres en el qual se contienen muchas y diversas reçeutas muy buenas* from about 1475 to 1525 that has recipes and household advice for upper-class women.[53] In 1384, the Geronan priest Francesc Eiximenis discussed table manners, food service, and wine in one volume of his projected thirteen-part opus, *Lo Crestià* (The Christian). The fourth important Catalan work is the *Llibre de les dones, mes verament dit des consells*, from the fifteenth century written by the Valencian doctor to the Aragonese kings Alfonso V and Juan IV, Jaume Roig.[54]

The other great Catalan culinary text of the Middle Ages was the *Libre de coch*, ascribed to Ruperto de Nola and published in Barcelona in 1520. It may have been written earlier since some of its recipes refer to Lenten dietary restrictions that were abandoned in 1491. The *Libre de coch* is another cosmopolitan cookery book, not purely regional, and has Provençal and Italian recipes and even a few that apparently come from Istria or Dalmatia.[55]

The *Libro del arte de cozina*, by Diego Granado Maldonado, was published in Madrid in 1599, although much of the text is from Ruperto de Nola's *Libre de coch* and Bartolomeo Scappi's *Opera*. In fact, according to the study done by Jeanne Allard, of the 762 recipes in *Libro del arte de cozina*, 587 come from Scappi, 50 from Nola, and 125 are either original or from another source.[56] It is unclear who or what Diego Granado knew. He may have been familiar with the curious treatise on dietetics published in Basel in 1538 by the Greek doctor Simeon Sethos, who wrote in about 1075.[57] He admits that many of his recipes are German, French, and Castilian, but there are many Italian recipes, especially for fish, tortes, and sweets. His German-influenced recipes such as *lomo de vaca a la tudesca* (German-style beef loin) or *truchas a la tudesca* (German-style trout) might be attributable to the anonymous recipe book *Ain nützlichs Buchlin von der Speis des Menschen wölche Speis gesund su od nit zeniessen* from about 1500, as well as a Bohemian recipe book from 1591 and one from Flanders.[58] What is clear from Diego Granado's recipes is the influence of *la cocina arabigo-andaluza* on Spanish cuisine. The influence is not so much from Arabic literary or culinary works but emanates from centuries of Arab influence, custom, and tradition in the daily practical lives of the Andalusian populace and its material culture.[59] The recipes call for lots of vinegar, sugar, rose water, saffron, and cinnamon.[60] Some of his recipes, such as *sopas a la Lombarda con caldo de carne* (Lombardy soup with beef broth), have not even a remote similarity to any contemporary Lombard dish. The recipe for this soup is a mixture of white bread and pork fat roasted in the oven. A stuffing of beef and capon is pounded with grated cheese, sugar, pepper, and cinnamon. It is served with fresh *provatura* cheese, made from water buffalo milk, or other unsalted cheese.[61]

The master chef of King Philip III, Francisco Martínez Mo<n>tiño, wrote *Arte de cocina, pastelería, vizcochería y conservería*, published in Madrid in 1611. The cook is instructed to pay attention to cleanliness, taste, and speed. It was still being reprinted two hundred years later.[62] In 1614, Miguel Yelgo de Vázquez published his book that talked a lot about etiquette, *Estilo de servir a príncipes con ejemplos morales para servir a Dios*.[63]

The oldest culinary text in the French language is a manuscript in the Bibliothèque Nationale called *Enseingnemenz qui enseingnent a apareiller toutes manieres de viandes* (Instructions that teach the trimming of all kinds of meats). It was written about 1300.[64] Arab influence appears in the early French culinary texts as well, in, for example, the recipes for meatballs that are called *pommes* or *pommeaux*, a pommel, meant to capture the form of the Arab meatball, *kubayba* or *mudaqqaqa*.[65] Although it is true that *boulettes,* or quenelles, are familiar from ancient Rome (bearing the name *isicia* or *isiciata*), the medieval European *rissoles* stuffed with meat and other ingredients is a preparation similar to one from Arab cuisine.[66] Another early French text from 1306, the *Douet d'Arq*, has a recipe for eels in almond milk, a then popular Arab culinary method that appears in virtually every European cookbook of the period. In the recipe the almond milk is called "Provençal milk," made by dissolving the ground almonds in wine and water and cooking it with parsley, onions, and pieces of eel, seasoned with saffron and pepper.[67] Most famous of the early French texts are the *aide-mémoire* written in 1393 by a Parisian bourgeois for his very young wife, *Le Ménagier de Paris*, and the *Viandier*, written by Taillevent (Guillaume Tirel), the first of the great French chefs, in about the 1380s. Taillevent was the cook to King Philip VI by 1346.[68] Another great French cookbook was written about fifty years later, sometime around 1420, by Chiquart Amiczo, the chef to the duke of Savoy, called *Du fait de cuisine* (On the matter of cookery). Sometime around 1536 a small cookbook was published called *Petit traicté auquel verrez la maniere de faire cuisine comment on doibt abiller toutes sortes de viandes fort utile a ung chascun* (Small treatise showing the manner of how to cook) that was very different from the typical cookbooks of the Middle Ages because fish recipes dominated and butter was systematically used in place of the usual olive oil.[69]

Cookbooks played an important role in the transmission of culinary knowledge among the upper strata of society—maybe not as important as hands-on experience, but important enough if we believe the figures: it has been estimated that 90,000 copies of cookbooks were in circulation in France in the second half of the seventeenth century and 273,600 between 1700 and 1789.[70]

A systematic study of the corpus of the works cited in this essay and in the Bibliography has never been undertaken, and it would be a great contribution to our understanding of the food we eat if an ambitious scholar could make better sense of it all.

PRONUNCIATION GUIDE

This abbreviated guide is meant to help you pronounce words and names in this book. For full pronunciation guides, consult standard grammars or traveler's phrase books.

ARABIC

THE transliteration of Arabic words and names is fraught with difficulty. There is no standardized system outside the world of professional linguists and historians, so spellings can be quite inventive. I have followed the system used by Middle East historians as codified in the *International Journal of Middle East Studies* system, which has supplanted the *Encyclopaedia of Islam* system—namely, *qaf* = "q" not "k" nor "ḳ"; *jīm* = "j" not "dj"; the "l" of *al-* is not assimilated to the following consonant; *ta' marbūṭa* = "a" not "ah." Well-known names, though, are left in their familiar English transliterations—for example, "tabbouleh" rather than *"tabbūla,"* except for egregious transliterations (for example, *mulūkhiyya*, not "meloukia").

Another problem faced by the food writer is that native Arabic speakers who have written cookbooks have often mistransliterated words, sometimes inventing their own spellings to be picked up by Western writers; therefore all spellings were counterchecked against Wehr and Dozy (see Bibliography). When a word does not appear in standard dictionaries, I have tried to consult a native of that country. Words or names that are not *fuṣḥa* (from classic written Arabic) I have tried to spell the way they are pronounced.

Geographical names in North Africa and the Middle East are spelled according to Webster's New Geographical Dictionary and the comprehensive edition of *The Times Atlas of the World.*

In Arabic, when double consonants occur, both letters must be pronounced.

h = "h" almost like a sigh.

ḥ = like the first *h* in "high."

q = a guttural *k* sound from the back of the mouth, almost a glottal stop.

ṣ = a guttural sound as in "sod."

ḍ = a guttural sound as in "dod."

ṭ = a guttural sound as in "todd."

ẓ = a guttural sound as in "zod."

ᶜ= this symbol represents the Arabic "ayn," a glottal stop. The sound is similar to the *a* in "achoo," the expression of a sneeze, or the sound between the two words of the expression "oh oh!"

gh = this represents the Arabic "ghayn," also a glottal stop. The sound is similar to the noise made in the back of the throat before one spits phlegm, with a slight *r* sound.

kh = *ch* as in the Scottish "loch."

ā = long *a* as in "father."

ī = long *i* as in the *e* in "ear."

ū = long *u* as in the *oo* of "moon."

CATALAN

x = "ch" or "sh."

ll = "lli" as in "million."

ç = "sha."

FRENCH

ch = "sh" as in "shoot."
ç = *s* as in "sit."
g = like *s* in "pleasure" before *e*, *i*, and *y*; *g* as in "get" before *a*, *o*, and *u*.
gn = *ni* as in "onion."
h = silent.
j = like *s* in "pleasure."
qu = *k* as in "kick."
r = rolled *r* in the back of the mouth.
u = round your lips and say *ee* as in "feet"—that's the approximate sound.
ai, ay = *a* as in "gate."

GREEK

Greek names and words have been transliterated for pronunciation without the use of diacritical marks.

ITALIAN

In Italian, all vowels are pronounced. Two vowels next to each other are individually pronounced as separate syllables. Stress is on the vowel of the next to last syllable.

c = *ch* as in "choice," before *e* and *i*, elsewhere like *c* in "cat."
ch = *c* as in "cat."
g = *j* as in "jet" before *e* and *i*, elsewhere like *g* in "get."
gh = *g* as in "get."
gl = *lli* as in "million."
gn = *ni* as in "onion."
h = silent.
r = a trilled *r*.
s = sometimes like a *z*, mostly like *s* in "sit."
sc = *sh* before *i* and *e*; *sk* as in "skin" elsewhere.
a = short *a*.
e = like the *ai* in "hair" or the *e* in "get."
i = *ee* as in "feet."
o = *oa* as in "coat."
u = *oo* as in "foot."

LATIN

Dipthongs are always pronounced to form one sound. Consonants are the same as in English except for:

c is always pronounced as the *c* in "cat."
g is always pronounced as the *g* in "get."
j is always pronounced as the *y* in "yellow."
t is always pronounced as the *t* in "top."
v is always pronounced as a *w*.
th is pronounced as a *t*.
ch is pronounced as a *k*.
Never accent a word on the last syllable.

SERBO-CROATIAN

ć = *ch* as in "church."
č = *ch* as in "cheese."
š = *sh* as in "shoe."
ž = *s* as in "pleasure."

SPANISH

c = *th* as in "thick" before *e* and *i* (in Spain only, not in Latin America).
g = *ch* as in the Scottish "loch" before *e* and *i*.
h = silent.
j = *ch* as in the Scottish "loch."
ll = *lli* as in "million."
ñ = *ni* as in "onion."
qu = *k* as it "kick."
rr = a heavy trilled *r*.
z = *th* as in "thick."
u = *oo* as in "moon."
y = when alone or at end of word, *ee* as in "feet."

TURKISH

The three most important things to remember when seeing Turkish words is that a *c* is always pronounced as a *j* and the *j* is like a soft *z;* that ğ is never pronounced but indicates the vowel before it is lengthened; and the *i* without the dot, *ı,* is pronounced like "uh." The circumflex, used by Turks with vowels, has not been employed in this book.

i = *ee* as in "feet."
ı = the *er* sound in "sir" or "uh."
o = *o* as in "hot."
ö = *ur* as in "fur."
u = *oo* as in "shoe."
ü = like the French *u* as in "une."
c = *j* as in "jet."
ç = *ch* as in "choice."
g = *g* as in "get."
ğ = silent.
j = *z* as in "azure."
ş = *sh* as in "shoe."
v = the sound is in between a *v* and a *w* (wah).

VENETIAN

x = *z* as in "zoo."

ISLAMIC GLOSSARY

Abbasids A great dynasty from the classical Islamic era with its capital in Baghdad (750–1258).

Al-ḥamdu lillāh A common expression in Arabic that means "Praise be to God!"

ᶜĀshūra The tenth day of the Muslim month of Muharram, sacred to the Shias (Shi'ites) because Husayn (Hussein), the son of ᶜAlī, the son-in-law of the Prophet, was martyred on this day at Karbala in Iraq in 680.

ᶜAqiqa The traditional hair cutting of the newborn seven days after his birth.

Ayyūbids A dynasty founded by Saladin after defeating the Fāṭimids, from 1169 to the end of the fifteenth century.

Dār al-Islām Literally, the "house of Peace," territory under Muslim control. The rest of the world is known as *dār al-Ḥarb*, the "house of War," for it has not "surrendered" to the will of God. The expression also means "paradise."

Fāṭimids An Islamic dynasty from 909 to 1171 that founded the city of Cairo and once ruled Egypt, North Africa, Palestine, Syria, and Sicily.

Ḥajj The pilgrimage to Mecca undertaken by the faithful at least once in their lives.

Ḥaram or harem The harem is not a prostitutes' den, but is rather the name for the private living quarters in the homes of traditional Muslim families.

Hijra The emigration of the Propet Muhammad in 622 from Mecca to Medina; the beginning of the Muslim calender.

ᶜĪd al-adhā The great feast *(kabīr)*, or the feast of sacrifice. One of two festivals recognized by Islamic canonical law. This holiday celebrates the sacrifice of Abraham.

ᶜĪd al-fiṭr The little feast *(ṣaghīr)*, or the feast of the breaking of the Ramadan fast celebrated on the first of Shawwal. One of two festivals recognized by Islamic canonical law.

ᶜĪd al-kabīr See ᶜĪd al-adhā.

ᶜĪd al-ṣaghīr See ᶜĪd al-fiṭr.

Ifriqiyya Medieval Arabic name for modern Tunisia.

Koran or Quran The holy book of Islam, believed by Muslims to be the literal word of God. Muslims believe that the Koran is the fourth and last of the revealed scriptures of God, the others being the Torah of Moses, the Psalms of David, and the Gospel of Jesus.

Mamelukes Successors to the Ayyūbids in Egypt and Syria. A great dynasty from 1250 to 1517, ruled first by the Baḥrī line and then the Burjī line.

Marrano Christianized Jews of medieval Spain.

Mawlid al-Nabī Birthday festival of the Prophet Muhammad.

Morisco Christianized Muslims of medieval Spain.

Mustᶜarib "Would-be Arab," those Hispano-Romans who were allowed to practice their religion on condition of owing their allegiance to the Arab caliph.

Muwaḥḥadūn Hispano-Romans who converted to Islam.

Qāḍī or Qadi An Islamic judge.

Naṣrid The last Islamic dynasty in Spain with its capital in Granada from 1230 to 1492.

Ṭūlūnids A local dynasty in Egypt and Syria from 868 to 905.

Umayyad A great dynasty of classical Islamic civilization with its capital in Damascus (661–750).

Waqf (*awqāf*, pl.) Charitable trust for some pious purpose.

Zāwiyya In North Africa, a small cupolaed mosque over the tomb of a saint with a hospice and theological school.

THE MEDITERRANEAN PANTRY

Allspice Buy the berries rather than ground allspice so you can grind according to your needs and have fresher taste. Store in a cool, dry place.

Almonds Buy blanched whole almonds for convenience, although you will lose something in taste. Because nuts can go rancid, store in the freezer in zippered-top freezer bags. *To peel almonds*: Drop in boiling water for 3 to 5 minutes. Drain and squeeze the peel off. *To roast almonds*: Spread ¾ cup blanched whole almonds on a baking tray. Roast in a 450°F oven until they begin to turn brown in a few minutes. Remove immediately and cool. Store in the refrigerator until needed.

Almorí A Spanish condiment with roots in the medieval cooking of the Hispano-Muslims. There are a number of recipes, but a mock one is made by blending 1 tablespoon flour, 2 teaspoons honey, ½ teaspoon white wine vinegar, and salt to taste in a small bowl until it is a homogenous sticky paste. See page 530.

Anchovy The best are salted whole anchovies usually sold in bulk or large containers. They are infinitely better than the oil-packed anchovy fillets in the tiny cans. Salted anchovy fillets are an essential ingredient in Italian cooking and are never optional when you see them in the recipe. Salted anchovies are not available in supermarkets; you must seek out an Italian market or grocery.

Aniseed Used as a flavoring for alcoholic drinks such as Pernod, ouzo, *raki*, and *arak*, as well as breads, and in North African cooked dishes. Buy the seeds and store in a dark, cool place.

Arab bread See *KHUBZ ʿARABĪ* and *MARQŪQ*.

Artichokes Look for artichokes with relatively tight bracts. When working with artichokes, keep the hearts in water acidulated with vinegar or lemon juice to prevent them from discoloring. Canned and frozen artichoke hearts are adequate only if fresh artichokes are unavailable for recipes calling for hearts.

Arugula A bitter green, also called rocket, used in mixed salads. If you are unable to find it, it can be replaced with watercress.

Asparagus Look for firm, narrow stalks with firm tips. Trim or peel the bottom third.

Baccalà See SALT COD.

Bacon See CANADIAN OR IRISH BACON, and SMOKED BACON.

Bahārāt The name of any of a variety of spice mixes used in Middle Eastern and North African cooking. The *bahārāt* used in Levantine Arab cooking can be found in Middle Eastern markets or you can mix your own; see page 524. The *bahārāt* spice mix used in Tunisia is different; see page 525.

Basil An excellent herb for an herb garden or pot. In the winter you can bring basil indoors and have it fresh throughout the year. Do not substitute or bother to use dried basil; it has no flavor.

Basṭurma* or *pastırma A pressed and dried beef fillet seasoned with cumin, garlic, and other spices. It is used mostly in Turkey and Armenia, but found throughout the Levant. In this country it can be found in Middle Eastern markets.

Bay leaf Store in a cool, dark place. They keep for a long time. If a recipe calls for fresh bay leaves and you don't have any, soak dried leaves in tepid water for 30 minutes. Powder bay leaves by crumbling and then pounding in a mortar.

Beans A great variety of dried and fresh beans are called for in the recipes; however, you can use a common white or kidney bean in regional recipes calling for beans. Although I often call for soaking dried beans in water for some hours, it is not necessary; I tend to do it out of habit. If you know that the beans you usually use are not that old, there is no need to soak them. An excellent white bean, the *cannellini* bean, is packaged by the Castellani firm and imported to the United States where it is sold in most Italian markets. Other sources for dried beans are local Greek, Middle Eastern, and Indo-Pakistani markets. An excellent brand is Golchin, distributed by Overseas Food Dist., Inc., Sylmar, California 91342, (818) 896-6127.

Beets Look for smaller beets with their leaves still attached, which should be fresh looking and not limp. Beets can discolor other items readily so handle with care around clothing. Always cook the beets with their skins and part of their stems on before preparing them further, according to the recipe.

Bel paese A mild creamy Italian cheese that makes a good table or dessert cheese. Store in the refrigerator wrapped in plastic. Serve at room temperature.

Bell peppers Look for brightly colored, fleshy, firm peppers without blemishes that feel heavy when picked up. *To roast bell peppers*: Place in a preheated 425°F oven until the skins blister black, or do the same over a grill or burner. Let cool, then peel off blistered skin.

Beurre manié A mixture to help thicken sauces made by mashing together 1 tablespoon flour with 1 tablespoon butter until blended.

Black pepper The recipes call for freshly ground black pepper in all cases. Use whatever pepper you regularly use.

Bottarga Dried and salted fish roe, usually made of either tuna or gray mullet, and used in the cooking of Sicily and Sardinia, and some other cuisines. After years of telling people that I've never seen *bottarga* sold in the United States, I finally did see it in a delicatessen in California, but because it still is so rare, I provide a recipe on page 435.

Bouillon cubes I find concentrated bouillon cubes, such as the product made by Knorr, a convenient substitute when either I am not inclined to make my own homemade broth or I have run out. Canned low-sodium broth is also fine. Unfortunately, bouillon cubes tend to be very salty and you must remember this when using them. Homemade broth recipes are on pages 54–55, 369.

Brains A very delicate, bland, and soft meat that needs to soak in changes of cold water acidulated with lemon juice or vinegar before cooking. Cover the brains in water and poach for 20 minutes just under a boil.

Bread crumbs Make your own bread crumbs from stale bread or buy bags of bread crumbs from Italian markets. If using supermarket-variety bread crumbs, buy only the plain, not the ones described as Italian. Dry bread crumbs are bread crumbs made from stale or fresh bread that are dried further after grinding, while fresh bread crumbs are made from fresh or slightly stale bread and used immediately.

Bread A good bread is hard to find, but still better than twenty years ago when it was virtually impossible. One rule of thumb is that if the bread is wrapped in plastic and sliced, it is not suitable for any Mediterranean food, nor is sourdough bread. One problem with bread, and "rules of thumb," is that there are always exceptions. Rather than catalog all the breads of the Mediterranean, I can only suggest you might find top-quality bread in ethnic markets. Another place to look for bread is in the Yellow Pages under "Bakers—Retail," especially bakers who sell "Italian" bread wholesale and retail. Because there are upward of a thousand different breads in the Mediterranean, it might be worth your while to buy several of the better bread cookbooks and give them a try.

Broccoli The florets of fresh broccoli will be very green and tight. All parts of the broccoli will be firm and nothing will bend.

Broccoli rabe A bitter green much used in Italian cooking. Look for bright green leaves without blemishes.

Broth: See BOUILLON and pages 54–55, 369.

Bulgur A cracked wheat product found in Middle Eastern markets, natural food markets, and some supermarkets. Bulgur comes in coarse, medium, and fine grades. Coarse is usually used in dishes such as tabbouleh (page 578) or bulgur pilaf (page 577), while fine is used for kibbe (page 579).

***Butifarra (botifarra)* sausage** A Catalan veal sausage that will be all but impossible to find, but commercially made chicken sausage is close in taste to white *butifarra* sausage and readily available. Black *butifarra* is made with blood. One place, though, that sells authentic *butifarra* sausage by mail order is La Española, Inc., 25020 Doble Avenue, Harbor City, California 90710, (310) 539-0455, Fax (310) 539-5989.

Butter All the recipes that call for butter without exception use unsalted butter.

Cabbage Look for heavy cabbages with tight leaves. A popular cabbage in the Mediterranean is called Savoy cabbage in our supermarkets, but green cabbage is fine in all the recipes.

Caciocavallo A hard Italian cow's milk cheese usually in the shape of a gourd, tied off at the top to another gourd. It is a grating cheese that becomes sharper with aging. If unavailable, substitute an imported provolone. Wrap *caciocavallo* in plastic and store whole in the refrigerator. Do not grate until needed.

Canadian or Irish bacon These are the bacons most suited for use in Spanish cooking.

Capers Try to buy capers in bulk—they are significantly cheaper than the small jars of nonpareil capers. Store with their brine in a jar. Rinse before using.

Caraway Among Mediterranean cuisines, caraway seed is most used in Algerian, Tunisian, and Croatian cooking. Store in a cool, dark place.

Carrots Look for carrots that are bright orange and very stiff. If they bend without snapping, pass them by. Baby carrots are the best because they don't need to be peeled and they are sweeter than older carrots. Older carrots can be used in long-cooking stews.

Cayenne pepper Store in a cool, dark place.

Celery Look for tightly bunched, crisp stalks that snap rather than bend, and an unblemished root end.

Chestnuts *To peel fresh chestnuts*, make an "X" with a small paring knife on the flat sides. Place in a preheated 400°F oven until blackened, about 20 minutes. Cool and peel.

Chicken The best-tasting chickens are freshly killed free-range or semi-free-range chickens grown on a farm rather than in a chicken factory. However, these terms are misleading because if the chickens aren't eating properly, it hardly matters that they are free range. Free-range chickens are a bit harder to find than your everyday chicken but worth the effort, although very recently I've noticed some supermarkets beginning to carry these better-quality chickens. Also try specialty butchers and whole food stores.

Save parts of the chicken you don't use for making broth. I keep a large zippered-top freezer bag handy and toss in any of the necks and carcasses of the chicken, rather than throw them in the garbage. Chicken feet are terrific for adding to a homemade broth, so if you ever see a package in your supermarket, grab it and toss into the freezer until needed.

Whenever a recipe calls for boiling a chicken, as is the case in many of the Arab recipes, do not actually let the water come to boil, which will only toughen chicken. Rather, poach the chicken by allowing the water to just shimmer on the surface.

Chickpeas: Dried chickpeas must be soaked overnight and then boiled in water for about 3 hours. Some recipes call for "cooked chickpeas," for which the canned chickpeas are excellent.

Chili peppers Buy whole dried chili peppers instead of flakes. They will stay pungent longer. Store in a dark, cool place. Fresh chili peppers come in different sizes, varieties, and heat levels. Some people use rubber gloves to handle the hot peppers; although it makes sense, I always feel silly doing it, so I just remember to keep my fingers away from my mouth, eyes, and nose and wash well with soap and water when I'm done.

Chinese egg roll wrappers This pastry is perfect for various North African recipes. Egg roll wrappers can be found in Chinese, Korean, and Southeast Asian markets and many supermarkets.

Chives Look for dark green stalks that are not limp. Store in the refrigerator.

Chorizo sausage A Spanish chorizo sausage is not as hot as a Mexican chorizo sausage. Substitute a Portuguese *chouriço* sausage, Italian sweet sausage, or Polish kielbasa. See also La Española listed in "Mediterranean Food Products Resources."

Cinnamon Store in a dark, cool place. Keep ground cinnamon and cinnamon sticks in the pantry.

Clams Clams can be purged of grit and sand by soaking them in cold water with some baking soda for a couple of hours. If you are not adept at shucking clams, place them in the freezer until they crack open and then finish the job with a clam knife. The North American clams best suited for Mediterranean recipes are littlenecks.

Cloves Store in a dark, cool place.

Coconut flakes Wrap tightly and store in the freezer.

Confit de canard See DUCK.

Coriander Fresh coriander, also called cilantro or Chinese parsley, should smell strong and have bright green leaves. Discard the stems and use only the leaves in recipes. It is preferable not to refrigerate fresh coriander, to wash the leaves only as needed, and to use it quickly. In recipes calling for ground coriander, it is preferable to grind your own coriander seeds in a spice grinder (I use an inexpensive coffee grinder) or mortar rather than keeping ground coriander, which can become stale, unless, of course, you are regularly using lots of it.

Couscous See pages 659–674.

Crabs Fresh live crabs or frozen crab claws are fine to use. Picked crabmeat is sold by many fishmongers and, although expensive, might be worth it, given the labor involved in getting crabmeat.

Crème fraîche This is a full-fat fresh ripened cream, with the consistency of a very thick sour cream. It is used as a base for sauces in French cooking and with desserts. If your supermarket does not carry it, ask the store manager to stock it.

Cucumbers Look for firm, dark green vegetables. Many people don't seed cucumbers, but I prefer them without the bitter seeds. Cut in half lengthwise and scoop and scrape the seeds out with a teaspoon.

Cumin Store in a dark, cool place. Cumin seeds will keep longer than ground cumin. Grind the seeds in a spice grinder or mortar as needed.

Cuttlefish These cephalopods are related to squid,

except they are squatter and their flesh thicker. They are cleaned in the same way you clean squid, except that the plastic-like quill of the squid is a bone in the cuttlefish and the skin is harder to take off. They are often found in this country during the Christmas season, especially in Italian communities. They are usually sold frozen, which actually helps in the tenderizing process. See page 448 on cleaning cuttlefish.

Dandelion A popular wild green among Mediterranean peoples, more readily found in Italian and other ethnic markets, although increasingly in supermarkets. Should you wish to gather your own dandelion leaves, remember that they must be picked, root and all, while the leaves are young, before any flower has even begun to form. Trim the roots, wash, and follow the recipe. Do not pick dandelions from lawns using pesticides, from the median strips of highways, or near any congested road.

Dijon mustard Readily available in supermarkets. You can use any brand.

Dill Herb with an anise smell and flavor used abundantly in Greek and Turkish cooking. Store in the refrigerator if you are not using it regularly, although that will diminish its taste and smell.

Duck Defrost frozen ducks in the refrigerator over three days. Because of the need for duck fat in several recipes, such as the *confit de canard* (page 200), save all the duck fat collected from other recipes. Store in a jar in the refrigerator. At least one producer packages *confit de canard* for mail order: D'Artagnan, (800) 327-8246.

Eggplant Small Japanese, Italian, or baby eggplant are best for stuffing, while the more common, larger eggplant, with their deep purple skins, are best for other preparations. Eggplant have bitter juices that must be leached before using. Lay the eggplant pieces on some paper towels and sprinkle with salt. Leave them to drain for 30 minutes, then pat dry with paper towels.

Farīk or ***Fırik*** **(in Turkish)** An immature wheat, or green wheat, processed through smoldering on an open fire, pronounced FREE-ka, FREEK-y, or FREEK. *Farīk* can be found in Middle Eastern groceries and, although it is often cleaned, one still must make some effort cleaning it further by picking out stones and chaff and other grit. This might involve some time depending on the cleanliness of the original batch handled by the exporter or importer.

Fatback Pork fatback is used as a cooking fat and flavoring condiment. It can keep for a long time in the refrigerator.

Fava beans Fresh fava beans, which are in season in late spring, need to be removed from their thick, spongy green pods and then boiled ever so slightly to remove their skins before using. Look for thick, big pods without any large black blemishes. Dried fava beans need to be soaked, boiled, and peeled. They are either large or small. The small round fava beans are called *fūl ḥammām* in Arabic and are the ones used for making *fūl mudammas* (page 304). The fava bean is also known as the broad, horse, or Windsor bean. An excellent source for dried fava beans is Middle Eastern markets. The Golchin brand of dried fava beans, distributed by Overseas Food Dist., Inc. Sylmar, California 91342, (818) 896-6127, is excellent.

Feet Chicken feet, pig's feet, lamb's feet, veal feet—these are often the reason one stew or another tastes so good. If that bothers you, you must settle for second-rate Mediterranean food. But remember that feet are used for flavoring and are not, except in certain cases, eaten. I buy various feet and throw them into the freezer until I need them.

Fennel The fennel with the bulbous stem is a sweet, flavorful vegetable popular mostly with Italians. Look for white, fleshy bulbous stems without many blemishes, and firm stalks. Wild fennel is used in parts of the Mediterranean, especially Sicily, but the only place I have seen it growing here is in California.

Feta Sheep and goat's milk curd cheese; pure white and flaky, salted and stored in brine. Feta is found nearly everywhere today, produced domestically or imported from Greece, Bulgaria, Israel, and Romania. Most domestic feta, though, is made from cow's milk.

Fior de latte This fresh cheese refers to cow's milk mozzarella as opposed to *mozzarella di bufala*, water buffalo mozzarella, although today most mozzarella, in America and Italy, is made from cow's milk and both names are often used interchangeably for any fresh mozzarella.

Fish A Mediterranean reader would probably find the amount of information I provide about fish in the recipes somewhat strange. I do so because many Americans are at a complete loss when it comes to fish varieties and cookery, even those of us who live on the coasts. In all the recipes, the freshness of the fish is usually more important than the particular species of fish called for. I make extensive suggestions on possible substitutes. Rather than provide long and detailed instructions on determining when a fish is fresh, I suggest that you choose a fish store over the fish. A fishmonger who regularly sells fresh fish is the store you should give your business to. He or she will also guide you in cooking fish if you feel that a recipe doesn't give you the confidence. Because it is so difficult these days to find whole fish, seek out ethnic fishmongers because whole fish keep better than fillets. If a fish store smells "fishy," that is a bad sign—their fish is not fresh. A fish store should smell briny, like the ocean, or not at all. Also see HAKE, SMALL FISH, SARDINES.

Flour Unless specified, unbleached all-purpose flour is used in the recipes. A good source for various flours is Great Valley Mills, 687 Mill Road, Telford, Pennsylvania 18969.

Foie gras Many inferior canned foie gras are sold, but two excellent sources are D'Artagnan, (800) 327-8246, or, for even better products, from Valette, 46300 Gourdon-en-Quercy, France. Fax 011-33-65-41-30-57. If ordering from the French source, ask for *foie gras de canard* (duck) or *oie* (goose) *entier*.

Fontina This cheese from Val d'Aosta and the Piedmont region of Italy is made with whole cow's milk in the summer and, often, sheep's milk during other seasons. When you buy imported Italian fontina, ask for Val d'Aosta. It has a thin brown rind enclosing a soft pale cheese with tiny holes. Fontina Val d'Aosta is creamier, more flavorful, and more expensive than fontina Valbella, which has a brownish purple outside. Fontina is used in cooking, as it melts very well, and as a table cheese. I do not recommend Danish or Swedish fontina. Store in the refrigerator wrapped in plastic. Serve at room temperature.

Garlic Do not peel garlic until needed. Garlic does not need to be stored in the refrigerator. If it takes you longer than 5 seconds to peel garlic, you are doing it the wrong way. The easiest way to peel garlic is to line it up under the flat side of a chef's knife and press down to lightly crush the clove. The peel will crack and you pull it off. There are some new gadgets, such as the garlic roller, that work well for peeling a lot of garlic.

Ghee See *SAMNA*.

Goat A delicious meat that resembles mild lamb. Although I now occasionally find goat in my local supermarket, it is best to seek out Central and South American markets, Portuguese stores, and Muslim *ḥalāl* butchers, all of whom serve ethnic populations that eat goatmeat.

Goat cheese Both dried and fresh goat cheese are used in the recipes. Use whatever is available, and replace with sheep's milk cheese if necessary.

Goat's milk Available in whole food stores and supermarkets. Goat's milk makes excellent ricotta (page 467) and yogurt (page 184).

Gorgonzola An Italian blue cheese with a high fat content made from whole cow's milk. Taste before buying; it should not be bitter, but rich and creamy with a sharp flavor. Store in the refrigerator wrapped in plastic, but serve at room temperature.

Grains of paradise A spice from West Africa, also known as *melegueta (Aframomum melegueta)*, was the traditional medieval substitute for black pepper. You can use it as a substitute for or in addition to the black pepper called for in the recipes. It can be ordered from Dirigo Spice Corp., (617) 436-9540, or Frontier Cooperative Herb Co., Norway, Iowa, (800) 669-3275, and some whole food stores such as the Bread & Circus chain in New England. It is used in the Moroccan spice mix recipe (page 522).

Grape leaves Used for wrapping foods. They are easy to find, even in general supermarkets. Unravel carefully and lay out in front of you. Place a tablespoon of stuffing on the end closest to you and roll up one turn. Fold the side portions of the leaf in and over the roll, and continue rolling. Fresh grape leaves need to be boiled 5 minutes before using.

Graviera A Gruyère-type Greek cheese of sheep or cow's milk; salted, mild, used for grating and served with meals. It comes from Crete and Skyros in the northern Sporades.

Green beans Look for beans that are not too large, are unblemished, and that snap (that's why they call them snap beans). Trim both ends.

Gruyère A Swiss cow's milk cheese that finds its way into several recipes from Provence and even Algeria.

Hake The most popular fish in Spain. It can be replaced with cod, pollack, or halibut.

***Halloumi* cheese** *Halloum, halloumi*, or *hallūm* is a cheese very popular in Syria and Lebanon, although most production is from Cyprus. It is made from raw sheep's milk, sometimes mixed with goat's milk. The cheese is formed into blocks 6 × 4 × 1 inch thick. The *halloumi* cheese blocks are then cooked in the hot whey, after which they are salted, folded, and submerged in brine. It is an excellent frying or grilling cheese.

Harīsa A Tunisian spice paste; see page 523.

Hazelnuts (also called filberts) Store in a zippered-top freezer bag in the freezer. *To peel hazelnuts*: Boil for several minutes, drain, cool, and pinch off the skins.

Herbes de Provence I cannot recommend you buy the usually expensive and stale mixture of herbs sold with this name. In fact, *herbes de Provence* is a reference to the usual, but variable, mixed herbs available to the cook and used in the cooking of Provence, namely thyme, rosemary, bay leaf, basil, savory, aniseed, and lavender. Concoct whatever mixture you like from these herbs, using a minimum of three and preferably all of them, in the proportion called for in the recipe.

Hog casing See SAUSAGE CASING.

Hrūs A spice mix from Gabes, Tunisia, made with preserved onions, dried red peppers, rose petals, and cinnamon. It cannot be found in this country.

Ibores A Spanish goat cheese.

Idiazábal A Spanish sheep's milk cheese.

Ink See SQUID.

Jamīd Hard balls of sun-dried defatted, dehydrated yogurt. They are reconstituted by dissolving and diluting in water until a thick consistency. I have never found *jamīd* in this country, but it is worth asking at Middle Eastern groceries. If it is impossible to find, remember to get some as a souvenir when traveling in Jordan, or ask someone to bring some back. An alternative is to try asking for *KISHK* at a Middle Eastern market (a different product entirely). In place of *jamīd*, stir 3 tablespoons tahini (page 725) into 2 quarts stabilized yogurt (page 186).

Jamón de Trévelez A Spanish cured ham from the village of Trévelez in the province of Granada in Andalusia. Try La Española Meats, Inc. 25020 Doble Avenue, Harbor City, California 90710, (310) 539-0455; Fax (310) 539-5989.

Jamón serrano A Spanish cured ham (literally "mountain ham") that can be replaced with prosciutto. Try La Española (see above).

Jerusalem artichokes See SUNCHOKES.

Jibni See *JUBNA ḤULWA* and *JUBNA BAYḌĀ'*.

Jubna Arabic word for "cheese." *Jubna ʿakkawī* and *jubna nābulsī* are made by Indo-European Foods, Glendale, California 91201, (800) 682-1622.

Jubna bayḍā' See SYRIAN CHEESE.

Jubna ḥulwa An Arab sweet (unsalted) white cheese usually sold fresh and used for dessert making. See Karoun Dairies, page 730.

Juniper berries These berries are usually found dried and sold in jars from the spice rack of supermarkets. Store in a dark, cool place.

Kashkaval A cheese similar to *kasseri* (see below) and found in Greek and Middle Eastern markets.

Kasseri Mild, creamy, and cheddar or provolone-type in texture but saltier; made of whole sheep or goat's milk.

Kataifi A shredded wheat dough use for dessert making in the Middle East. An excellent frozen product is made (and sold under the Greek name *Kataifi*) by Athens Pastries and Frozen Foods, 13600 Snow Road, Cleveland, Ohio 44142-2596, (216) 676-8500.

Kefalotyri A very hard, salty, light yellow grating cheese made of sheep or goat's milk.

Khubz ʿarabī Arabic name for the flatbread sold in this country as pocket bread, pita bread, Arab bread, or Syrian bread. Store in the freezer.

Kid See GOAT.

Kielbasa Polish sausages that are a fine substitute for the sausages called for in Croatian and some Andalusian recipes.

Kishk This fermented and dried yogurt-and-bulgur mixture is sold in a powdered form usually, but also as hard dried balls as with *JAMĪD* (see above). Some Palestinians use *kishk* in place of *jamīd* when making *mansaf* (page 244). *Kishk* is more readily found in Middle Eastern markets than *jamīd*, but it is a different product.

Kunaifa or ***Kunāfa*** See *KATAIFI*.

Labna A strained yogurt product popular as a breakfast dip in the Arab Middle East. The water content of the yogurt is allowed to drip out over a period of time, and the yogurt becomes a thick spread. If your supermarket does not sell *labna* (also transliterated *lebany*, *lubny*, *labni*, and *labany*, or called "yogurt cheese"), ask the store manager to carry some. Or make your own; see page 186.

Lamb To my mind, American lamb is a very good-tasting product, and the best seems to come from Vermont, Colorado, and Wyoming. Further quality can be sought by buying the lamb from kosher or *ḥalāl* butchers. Items such as lamb's feet are generally not available in supermarket meat departments, so you are best off looking for lamb parts and quality lamb by scanning your Yellow Pages entry for "Meat-Retail" or "Meat-Wholesale" for *ḥalāl* or kosher butchers (the word *ḥalāl* will often appear in the name of the store) or "specialty" butchers. Try to avoid Australian and New Zealand lamb; they are of poorer quality and taste at the time of this writing.

Lard Pork lard is used in some recipes. It is an essential cooking fat in the recipes and never used in too great a quantity. It can be found in most supermarkets near the bacon, butter, or pork products. Also see *'Nzugna* on page 281.

Lasagnette See *PASTA SECCA*.

Lavash See *MARQŪQ*.

Laver Laver is a kind of seaweed or sea vegetable. It is harvested by the Maine Coast Sea Vegetables Company on Shore Road in Franklin,

Maine 04634, (207) 565-2907. The laver must be roasted in a preheated 350°F oven for 8 minutes before using in order to get its full nutty flavor. It can be used in place of marsh vegetables such as *salicornia* (glasswort).

Lebanese mountain bread See *MARQŪQ*.

Leek Look for firm stalks without blemishes. Leeks must be cleaned well in water. Remove the top dark green part of the stalk, which can be saved for making broth. Only the light green and white parts are used. Halve lengthwise and peel apart each leaf, washing well in water.

Lemon Use only freshly squeezed lemon juice when called for in the recipes. When using lemon zest, do not include any of the bitter white pith. If making the Egyptian lemonade (page 314) or preserved lemons (page 104), it is best to use the thin-skinned *daq* lemon. An equivalent lemon would be the Meyer lemon.

Lentil Several kinds of lentils are used in Mediterranean cooking: dark green lentils, red lentils, brown lentils, and unhulled red lentils that are black in color. Lentils do not require soaking, but some cooks like to rinse them first. Cooking times for lentils can range from 20 minutes to 1 hour, so you should continually monitor their cooking.

Lettuce Look for full leaves without blemishes that are not limp. If you prepare lettuce ahead of time, keep it in a pot of icy cold water. Drain and spin-dry in a salad spinner. Lettuce should have very little moisture, actually be dry, before the addition of dressing.

Lima beans Microwavable, frozen lima beans in a pouch are an excellent, perfectly workable replacement for fresh lima beans. For dried lima beans, try the Golchin brand distributed by Overseas Food Dist., Inc., Sylmar, California 91342, (818) 896-6127.

Liyya This is simply an Arabic word for rendered mutton or lamb fat that comes from the tail. In times past it was the most popular cooking fat, while today *SAMNA*, olive oil, or vegetable oil or shortening is often used. It is also spelled *alya* or *ilya*. When it is called for in a recipe, you can use the fat from any piece of lamb you happen to have or be using at the moment, or use beef suet or fat.

Lobster The most common lobster of the Mediterranean is the spiny lobster, without the distinctive claws of its North Atlantic counterpart. All the recipes in this book calling for lobster use the so-called Maine lobster *(Homarus americanus)*. Lobsters should be alive and kicking when purchased. If they are limp and lethargic, pass them by. Store the lobster in a brown paper bag in the refrigerator until needed. They can stay this way for quite some time. Never submerge the lobster in water: you will drown it because the water is not being oxygenated.

Macaroni See *PASTA SECCA*.

Maghribiyya See *MUḤAMMAṢ*.

Mahlepi A spice used in some Middle Eastern cookery, such as some recipes from Greece and Syria. It is made from the powdered pits of the St. Lucie's cherry, a kind of black cherry (*Prunus mahaleb* L.). It is found in Middle Eastern markets.

Manchego A Spanish sheep's milk cheese from La Mancha.

Manouri A soft, unsalted Greek white cream cheese similar to *MEZITHRA*; made of the whey of sheep and goat's milk; especially used for savory and sweet cheese pies and desserts.

Marjoram An excellent herb for an herb garden. The aromatic flavors are favored by Greek and Italian cooks. Replace fresh marjoram with fresh oregano but not dried.

Markouk See *MARQŪQ*.

Marqūq A kind of very thin Arab flatbread that can be found in Middle Eastern and Armenian markets in the U.S. with this name, or under the names *shrak, lavash*, Lebanese mountain bread, or *tannour* bread. All Middle Eastern markets sell this bread and an increasing number of supermarkets. If you are unable to find any, use Arab flatbread or pita bread *(khubz ʿarabī)* split into its two halves.

Marrow bones Marrow is the fatty meat inside bones. Most marrow bones are used in making broth and come from beef or veal.

Marsala A fortified wine from Sicily; use the dry variety for cooking purposes.

Mascarpone This Italian cheese looks like clotted cream. It has a very high fat content and is curdled with citric acid. It is sold in plastic tubs and fresh. Mascarpone is sometimes layered with other cheeses, such as Gorgonzola, or with herbs and nuts. Store in the refrigerator and use within three days.

Mastic The resin from an evergreen tree that grows on the Greek island of Chios. It is used in cooking as an odor purgative. It can be found in Middle Eastern markets.

Melokheya See *MULŪKHIYYA*.

Meloukia See *MULŪKHIYYA*.

Merguez See *MIRQĀZ*.

Mezithra (also Mitzithra, Mizithra, and Myzithra) There are two types of this Greek cheese: a soft, unsalted one, made of the whey from goat or sheep's milk used to make feta; it is used in sweet and savory pies and is like a soft ricotta or cottage cheese. The second kind is a lightly salted, semi-hard grating cheese.

Milk Unless specified, skim, low-fat, or whole milk can be used in the recipes.

Miloukia See *MULŪKHIYYA*.

Mint An excellent herb for an herb garden, although it is invasive. Mint is a powerful aromatic herb much loved in Arab cookery. Do not use dried mint when fresh mint is called for and vice versa; they serve two very different purposes.

Mirqāz Often transliterated as *merguez* in France and Tunisia, *mirqāz* are Tunisian sausages that are either dried or fresh. The fresh *mirqāz* sausage is made in this country by D'Artagnan, (800) 327-8246.

Mizuna A leafy green in the Brassica family (including mustard leaves, kale, broccoli, etc.). It can be used in a Greek *horta* (page 492).

Mortadella A large finely minced pork sausage known as bologna in this country. The mortadella made by Citterio in this country is excellent; ask for it.

Mozzarella A famous water buffalo's milk spun-curd cheese that is today more often made with cow's milk. Fresh mozzarella will be milky white and sold dripping in its whey. Packaged commercial mozzarella is rubbery, and neither moist nor flavorful, but people like to cook with it because it melts well. Store fresh mozzarella in a bowl of refrigerated water, changing the water once a day. It will stay fresh for three or more days.

Muḥammaṣ A couscous pasta ball used in Tunisian cooking. The identical product is used in several preparations in Lebanon, Syria, Jordan, and among Palestinians, although they call it *maghribiyya*. The balls are about the size of peppercorns or nonpareil capers. You can make the pasta-style ones yourself following the instruction in the recipe on page 661 or they can usually be found in a Middle Eastern market labeled in any of the following ways: couscous, Israeli couscous, toasted couscous or *moughrabiye*. Two excellent sources for this product are from the Indo-European Foods, Inc., Glendale, California 91201, (818) 247-1000, or a Jordanian product from the Canary Trading Co., Anaheim, California 92805, (714) 533-2744.

Mulūkhiyya The leaves of the mucilaginous vegetable called Jew's mallow *(Corchorus olitorius)*. It is popular in Egypt as a soup or with rabbit. *Mulūkhiyya* can be found, usually dried or frozen, in Middle Eastern markets and fresh at some farmer's markets.

Mushrooms Whenever a mushroom I call for is not available, replace with the common button or field mushroom. Dried mushrooms are used in cooking because they have high-intensity flavor; they must be soaked in water before using. Do not forage for mushrooms unless you have studied with a mycologist. In the Mediterranean, the favored mushrooms are wild, usually found in forests or woodlands, not the field mushrooms popular with Americans. Mushrooms are cleaned by brushing, not washing, because they will absorb too much water.

Mussels Many of the mussels sold today are cultivated. Mussels collected from rocks should be washed and the "beards" pulled off.

Noodles See *PASTA SECCA*.

Ñoras Dried red bell peppers used in Andalusian, Valencian, and Murcian cooking. They can be found in many supermarkets, especially in the southwestern United States.

Nutmeg Keep whole nutmeg and grate with a hand grater when needed. It will stay fresher and keep longer than ground nutmeg.

'Nzugna See page 281.

Octopus Fresh octopus can be found in ethnic food markets, especially Greek or Southeast Asian. Octopus sold in this country are already prepared and cleaned. This means that they have been "beaten"—that is, tenderized, usually by slamming them against rocks—and the beaklike mouth has been removed as well as any viscera in the head. Frozen octopus are sold in supermarkets. If your supermarket does not carry octopus, ask them to order you some. I have not found dried octopus in this country.

Okra Okra is a popular mucilaginous vegetable in the Middle East, Africa, and the American South. Unfortunately, most of the okra available in American markets is harvested much too big. The ideal size for Mediterranean cooking is about 1½ inches long, so choose the smallest ones available. They must be trimmed before eating.

Olive oil Olive oil is the key to Mediterranean cooking, therefore I recommend keeping three or four kinds of olive oil in the pantry to be used for different purposes. You may want a high-quality estate-bottled extra virgin olive oil for drizzling on foods or dipping. An inexpensive extra virgin is useful for sautéing. An olive oil (formerly called pure or virgin) or pomace oil, made from olive by-products, is good for deep-frying at high temperatures. There are many olive oils on the market, all imparting different tastes. I will not make brand recommendations, but the following is a sampling of inexpensive extra virgin olive oils that I have used on occasion: Bertolli, Berio, and Colavita are Italian olive oils that are excellent all-purpose oils, as is Italica, an equally good Spanish olive oil. Sapio (Bari) is a slightly yellowish green and very mild Italian oil that is excellent for cooking, especially sautéing. Marconi is a very yellowish green, very mild but slightly fruity Italian oil that is excellent for cooking and lightly drizzling on foods. San Giuliano Alghero is an Italian oil that is yellow greenish, very mild, and fruity; it can be used the same way as Marconi. Antica Italia is an oil from Partanna, Sicily, and it is green and fruity with a smooth taste. It is perfect for dipping, sautéing, drizzling on foods. Solon is a Greek oil that has an excellent price-value ratio. It is yellow and nutty. In the higher range, in terms of quality and price, are Nuñez de Prado, a Spanish oil from Baena, that is an unrefined, cloudy, fruity oil with a very distinctive taste, and Raineri, an excellent Italian oil. Although the Tuscan oils are commonly thought to be the best olive oils, Umbria makes fine oils, such as Dal Raccolto. The Tuscans oils tend to be very expensive. In North America, an excellent oil is made by Al-Mazara, a Mexican oil bottled by N. Sciabica and Sons of Modesto, California, for Corti Brothers, Sacramento, from Pendolino olives in Caborca.

Excellent oils are also made in Turkey, Syria, Lebanon, Tunisia, and most other Mediterranean countries, although availability is limited. When it comes to olive oils, taste and price are the final arbiters, so use an affordable olive oil that you like, not what someone tells you is the best.

Olives The best olives are the imported green and black olives that can be found in Greek, Italian, and Middle Eastern markets and are sold by weight or volume. I call for a number of different kinds of olives, but if you can't find them, use whatever imported green or black olives are available. Canned olives are not satisfactory for cooking Mediterranean food.

Onions Recipes calling for onions mean a standard yellow or Spanish onion. When I call for different size onions, use this guide: a small onion (3 to 5 ounces) is the size of a lime, a medium-size onion (6 to 9 ounces) is the size of a McIntosh apple, and a large onion (10 to 14 ounces) is the size of a softball. Vidalia and other sweet onions are excellent for Mediterranean dishes when you can find them. Red onions are called Calabrese in Italy and are called for in a number of recipes. *To peel white or red pearl onions*: Drop them in boiling water for 5 minutes, drain, cool, cut off the root end, and pop the onion out of its peel by squeezing.

Orange flower water A distilled water made from orange flowers. It can be found in Middle Eastern markets.

Oregano Fresh oregano is an easily grown herb for an herb garden. A strong aromatic herb greatly used in Italian cooking. Dried oregano is an acceptable substitute.

Oxtail If you are unable to find oxtail, ask the supermarket to order some for you; otherwise, replace with beef shank cut from the lower end of the leg.

Pancetta A cured Italian pork belly. Pancetta is found in Italian markets and sold as a cold cut. Supermarket delicatessens are beginning to carry pancetta, and you can request the manager of your market to do the same. In the event you are unable to find pancetta, use bacon parboiled in boiling water for 5 minutes.

Paprika Paprika in the recipes means a good-quality sweet paprika such as sweet Hungarian paprika. A special and excellent sweet paprika, *pimentón dulce*, used in Iberian cooking, is called La Chinata and made in the Extremadura region. It is worth your while to see if a spice company carries it. Store in a cool, dry place.

Parmigiano-Reggiano (Parmesan) This is probably the most famous Italian cheese and is ubiquitous with pasta and tomato sauce in Italian-American households. When cut fresh from a large wheel of cheese, Parmigiano-Reggiano is also a good eating cheese. Buy the imported variety called Parmigiano-Reggiano. The rind will be stamped with this name to assure you of its authenticity. Never grate Parmigiano-Reggiano until you need it, otherwise it will dry out and lose its flavor. For this reason, avoid the tasteless, canned domestic grated Parmesan varieties sold in supermarkets. The crusts of wheels of Parmigiano-Reggiano are used for flavoring minestrone; ask the supermarket to save you some. At the table, pass a chunk of Parmigiano-Reggiano with a hand-held grater for diners to grate the cheese themselves. Store wrapped in a zippered-top bag in the refrigerator.

Parsley Flat-leaf, also called Italian, parsley is used in this cookbook. The curly-leaf parsley is fine, but I do find it more bitter. Do not wash parsley until it is needed or, if you do, let it dry completely before storing. Store in the refrigerator to preserve its life if you must, although you will lose pungency. Never use dried parsley; it is completely devoid of taste and useless.

Pasta See *PASTA SECCA*

***Pasta secca* (also see *MUḤAMMAṢ*)** Follow the instructions on page 628 for cooking dry pasta. The widest variety of pasta products can usually be found in Italian markets. Before you buy a very expensive pasta product (I've seen some at nearly $6 a pound), ask yourself whether something made of wheat and water needs to cost so much. The best pasta products tend to be imported from Italy. There are some seven hundred varieties of *pasta secca* in the Mediterranean, and every culinary culture in the Mediterranean has pasta cookery, although the Italian is the most famous. You will encounter about twenty of these in this book, all of which can be found in a well-stocked Italian market, while the more common shapes will be found in a supermarket.

Pastırma See BASṬURMA.

Pâte feuilletée See PUFF PASTRY.

Peas Frozen and fresh peas can be used in the recipes interchangeably, but not canned peas.

Pecorino A hard Italian sheep's milk cheese used for grating. The most common pecorino is *Romano.* Never grate pecorino until you need it, otherwise it will dry out and lose its flavor. Store wrapped in plastic in the refrigerator. Buy only the imported Italian pecorino.

Pecorino *pepato* A Sicilian variety of pecorino with black peppercorns mixed into the curd. Store wrapped in plastic in the refrigerator.

Pecorino *Sardo* Today, a sheep and cow's milk pecorino made in Sardinia. Much of this pecorino is exported and it can be found in Italian markets in the United States. The young version, at three months old, is eaten as a table cheese, while at six months old it is usually grated. Replace with pecorino *Romano.*

Peppers A variety of peppers is used in Mediterranean cooking. *Peperoncini* are long green peppers. Red, yellow, and green bell peppers are popular vegetables in the Mediterranean (also see BELL PEPPERS). Look for firm brightly colored peppers without blemishes.

Phyllo pastry Phyllo (sometimes *filo*) is a pastry dough as thin as onion-skin paper. Because it is difficult to make well at home, I can recommend the excellent commercial phyllo dough sold in the freezer sections of supermarkets. For more on phyllo dough, see page 224.

***Pide* bread** This bread is used in Greek and Turkish cooking. Although the words *pide* (Turkish) and *pitta* (Greek) are found on what is called pita bread or Arab bread in this country, it is, in fact, a little different. It is not a pocket bread, but a flat bread used for *gyro* and *döner kebabı* (page 115). The letter and sound "p" does not exist in Arabic and therefore the pocket flatbread called pita bread is known in Arab lands as *khubz ᶜarabī.* Excellent *pide* breads are made by Krinos Foods, Inc., Long Island City, New York 11101, (800) 877-5757, and Royal Pita, Brooklyn, New York 11211, (718) 332-8569. *Pide*, readily found in the frozen foods section of Greek markets, must be defrosted and then heated before using, usually on a griddle.

Pigeon Pigeons or squab, as delicious as they are, are nearly impossible to find outside of specialty butchers, and when you do find them, they are expensive. Guinea hen or Cornish hen can be used in the place of pigeon.

Pine nuts The small white pine nuts used in Mediterranean cookery come from the umbrella pine (*Pinus pinea* L.), known also by the Italian name *pignoli.* Buying them in bulk from Middle Eastern markets is vastly cheaper than buying those in gourmet stores and supermarkets. Store in a plastic zippered-top freezer bag in the freezer.

Pistachio The best pistachios are a brilliant green color when crushed. Do not use pistachios that are dyed red. Pistachios can be found in Middle

Eastern markets in bulk or supermarkets, in the nut section. Store in the freezer.

Pita bread See *PIDE* BREAD and *KHUBZ ʿARABĪ*.

Pocket bread See *KHUBZ ʿARABĪ*.

Pomegranate The juice is made into a syrup, a molasses, that is important in southeastern Turkish and northern Syrian cooking. Pomegranate syrup can be found in Middle Eastern markets. The fruit is usually in season in the late fall, when you will want to make the recipes calling for it.

Pork skin Fresh pork skin can be bought from supermarket butchers if you ask them. If they're unavailable, use the skin from a piece of fatback or salt pork.

Potatoes Any baking potato is assumed when the recipe does not specify a particular kind of potato. But when a recipe does specify a potato, such as the Russian Banana or Yukon Gold, it is because that potato works particularly well in the recipe.

Preserved lemons See page 104.

Provolone A hard cow's milk cheese usually formed in a giant sausage shape. It is very similar in taste to *CACIOCAVALLO*. When you buy provolone, make sure you buy the mild imported version when using it for cooking purposes.

Puff pastry *(pâte feuilletée)* Good quality, frozen commercial puff pastry, such as that made by Pepperidge Farm, is found in the frozen foods section of most supermarkets. If you would like to make your own, follow the instructions in Julia Child's *The Way to Cook* (Alfred A. Knopf, 1989, pp. 389–391).

Qaṭā'if See *KATAIFI*.

Quince These fruits cannot be eaten raw; they must be cooked. If you cannot find them in your market, they can be replaced with Granny Smith apples, but the cooking time must be reduced.

Rabbit Rabbit is the lean, white meat par excellence, and it is increasing in popularity, albeit slowly, in America, where it can now be found in frozen food sections of supermarkets and sometimes fresh in bigger cities. Rabbit is a delicious tasting and favorite meat used in Mediterranean cooking.

Raisins Golden raisins (sultanas) and dark raisins can be stored in a jar in a cool, dark place.

Rās al-ḥanūt A Moroccan spice mix; see page 522.

Red Aleppo pepper This pepper is not as hot as some chili peppers. It is a coarse, rust-colored red, with a slight sweet smell. Red Aleppo pepper can be found in Middle Eastern markets. If you are unable to find any, try the excellent substitute mixture suggested by Paula Wolfert in *The Cooking of the Eastern Mediterranean*: 3 parts sweet Hungarian paprika and 1 part red chili pepper.

Rice Recipes call for raw short-, medium-, and long-grain rice. Short-grain rice is used for cooking Italian risottos, some Spanish rice cookery, and by some Arab cooks for stuffing vegetables. The most common Italian short-grain risotto rice available in this country is Arborio, found in Italian markets and some supermarkets. Ask the store manager to carry it. If you are unable to find Arborio rice, use medium-grain rice or any Chinese or Japanese short-grain rice.

Medium-grain rice is used mostly for Spanish rice cookery. This rice is prevalent in supermarkets and should not be difficult to find. The best of the Spanish rices is known as Calasparra.

Long-grain rice is used in Arab, Turkish, and Greek pilaf cookery. Various kinds, such as Basmati or Patna rice, are required for making pilafs where all the grains are separate. These rices can be found in Middle Eastern or Greek markets. Any unprocessed long-grain rice is satisfactory if you are unable to find specific rices. Do not use converted rice for any recipes. For more on rice cookery, see page 588.

Ricotta Italian markets often sell freshly made ricotta. Supermarkets sell ricotta in containers, including a low-fat kind, that is fine for cooking. Fresh ricotta will keep in the refrigerator for about three days. Store both in the refrigerator. The best fresh ricotta that I know of in this country is made by Liuzzi Cheese, 322 State Street, North Haven, Connecticut 06473, (203) 248-4356. On the other hand, you can make your own; see page 467.

Ricotta salata Although this term can refer to a pecorino, the type you will find in the market is a dried ricotta. It is placed in a perforated container and pressed for a long time and then left to dry in a special curing room. There are two varieties of *ricotta salata*, one for eating and another, harder one for grating. Store wrapped in plastic in the refrigerator.

Rose petals Used in North African cooking. See "Mediterranean Food Products Resources."

Rosemary An easily grown herb for your herb garden. The pungency of rosemary seems a natural accompaniment to lamb. The plant is not hardy and will not survive a particularly harsh winter. Dried rosemary is an acceptable substitute.

Saffron An expensive spice used in minute quantities for flavor and color. Store in a dark, cool place. Avoid powdered saffron, which is not as versatile as the threads (pistils), unless called for. If you ever find saffron being sold cheaply, it is not saffron but safflower, whose pistils look similar. Recipe writers usually call for saffron by the pinch, and I follow this convention, too. I actually counted how many pistils make up a pinch once, and it was about thirty, but you can be more, or less, generous than that if you like. See page 521 for more on saffron and how to use it.

***Sāj* bread** See *Marqūq*.

Salicornia If you are unable to find *salicornia* (see page 16), replace with Laver.

Salt Kosher and sea salts are best bought in large boxes so you don't run out. The recipes in this book universally call for salt to taste. That means that you must judge for yourself how salty you want your food. Salt a little, taste, and then salt again if necessary. Salt can often be the solution to dishes that seem bland.

Salt cod Salted and dried cod is called *baccalà* in Italian while stockfish is an air-dried cod. Salt cod needs to be soaked in at least two or three changes of cold water over two to three days. The amount of soaking depends on how salted the producer has made its product. For more on using salt cod, see page 436.

Salted lemon See Preserved lemons.

Saltwort Replace with Laver.

Samna Perhaps better known as ghee, the Hindi word *samna* is simply clarified butter used extensively as the cooking fat in North African and Middle Eastern cuisines. See page 189 for instructions on how to make and preserve it. Do not use commercially canned ghee, as it is of poor quality and often made from vegetables, not milk. In Syria they call clarified butter *samnī*.

Sardines There is no reason why you shouldn't be able to buy this quintessential Mediterranean fish, but unfortunately sardines are difficult to find because of lack of demand except in some ethnic communities near big cities. An excellent frozen sardine product is imported from Portugal that you might want to mention to your supermarket manager. Using ultra-frozen high technology, the Fripex-Sociedade de Conservação e Comércio de Peixe, Lda., Rua Marquês de Pombal, 120, 7520 Sines, Portugal, packages sardines and exports to the United States. Fresh sardines can be found in ethnic fish markets, especially Greek or Italian stores. Smelt can be used as a replacement for sardines, although the taste is entirely different; you might be better off with the larger mackerel.

Sausage casings Any supermarket that makes its own sausages will have sausage casings. Generally they do not sell it to the public because so few people make their own sausages, but if you ask the butcher, he or she will get you some. The casings are usually pork, preserved in salt, and already cleaned. All you need to do is attach one opening to a faucet and gently run the water through the casings to rinse the salt away. Store in the freezer or in their salt. A local *ḥalāl* butcher should be able to get you lamb casings. Sausage casings can also be ordered from The Sausage Maker, 1500 Clinton Street, Buffalo, New York 14206, (888) 490-8525; (716) 824-6510.

Savory Fresh savory and dried can be used interchangeably. It is a mild flavored herb often used in poultry cooking. Store in a cool, dark place.

Scallions Look for brightly colored scallions with firm, unblemished shoots. Trim the top one-third dark green portion of the scallion and the tip of the root end.

Semolina This is another name for hard wheat flour. It is usually sold in supermarkets as pasta flour and/or durum wheat and can also be bought in natural food stores.

Sesame seeds Used in Middle Eastern cooking, especially for making TAHINI (see page 725). Sesame seeds can be found in natural food stores and Middle Eastern markets.

Sherry Use a good-quality dry sherry for cooking.

***Shrak* bread** See *MARQŪQ*.

Shrimp Most shrimp sold in the United States are thawed, having been previously frozen and, as a result, rather tasteless. Occasionally, fresh shrimp from California, Florida, Maine, or Louisiana will appear in the market, and by all means you should be eating shrimp that day. Save the heads and shells for making broth.

Small fish Very small fish are popular in many Mediterranean countries. One can occasionally find these fish sold at ethnic fish markets, while the smallest frozen fish I've seen in my supermarket are three-inch-long smelt from Peru.

Smoked bacon Smoked bacon is used in Croatian and Serbian cooking. It can be ordered from the Hungarian Packing House, 213 East 82nd Street, New York, New York 10028, (212) 249-9360. Sometimes supermarkets sell smoked bacon. Use no-nitrate slab bacon in its place.

Snails Live snails are sometimes found in Italian markets and also Chinese markets. *To clean snails*: They must be purged over a period of time in several changes of cold water. Change the water once it becomes fouled and continue this repeated soaking until the water remains perfectly clear after one hour of soaking. This could take up to two days. For flavoring, some culinary cultures flavor the water they soak in with a variety of aromatics, such as orange peel.

Spaghetti See *PASTA SECCA*.

Spinach Remove the heavy stems from spinach and wash well in a pot of water to remove all sand and grit. The flatter leaved spinach with the red stems, sometimes called Italian spinach, is easier to clean and stem, and is not bagged, meaning you can buy more than the 10-ounce bags that seem standard.

Spleen A mild tasting variety meat that must be specially ordered from butchers.

Squid Some stores sell cleaned squid, a great time-saver, but be mindful that you get the tentacles. *To clean squid:* Grasp the head and tentacles and pull them out of the body. Cut the head and tentacles off just below the eyes. Discard the viscera and save the tentacles. Reach into the body cavity and remove the quill-like backbone and any other remaining viscera. Pinch a portion of the purplish skin and peel off. Wash the squid and follow the recipe instructions. For squid ink, see RJS Wholesale on page 731.

Stockfish See *SALT COD*.

Sumac A spice found in Middle Eastern markets. Store in a cool, dry place.

Sunchokes Also called Jerusalem artichokes, these tubers can turn black if cooked in aluminum pans.

Sunflower seed oil This oil is increasing in popularity in Turkey, over olive oil. It is also used in Venetian cuisine. If you can't find it, light olive oil mixed with a few tablespoons of peanut oil is a fine substitute.

Sweetbreads The thymus gland of a calf. Sweetbreads should be white when you buy them and soaked for an hour in cold water before cooking. Sweetbreads are a great delicacy, but hard to find outside of specialty butchers.

Swiss chard This leafy, spinachlike vegetable has either white or red stems. It should be washed well before using.

Syrian bread See *KHUBZ ʿARABĪ*.

Syrian cheese In Arabic this ubiquitous cheese is called *jubna bayḍā'* (also transliterated as *jibni beida*, "white cheese"). An excellent *jubna bayḍā'* can be obtained from Anoosh brand, A. B. A. Import Export Co., P. O. Box 1353, Arlington, Massachusetts 02174, (781) 646-9765. If you are unable to find it, use store-bought commercial mozzarella. A wide range of Syrian and Palestinian cheese products is sold by A to Z Food Distributors, see page 727.

Tābil A Tunisian spice mix based on coriander seeds; see page 522.

Tahini Sesame seed paste used for several recipes. Tahini can always be found in Middle Eastern markets and in many supermarkets.

Taleggio A semisoft whole cow's milk cheese from Lombardy, pale yellow and mild with a thin rind. As with all table cheeses, serve at room temperature. It melts well. Store wrapped in plastic in the refrigerator.

Thyme An excellent herb for an herb garden. You can use dried and fresh thyme interchangably.

Tomatoes Tomatoes used in the recipes are always assumed to be fresh, vine-ripened garden tomatoes. During the winter I assume you will use canned tomatoes, purees, and paste. Canned tomatoes in whatever form are an essential substitute for fresh during nonseasonal months and perfectly fine even in season. Tomato paste sold in tubes is more convenient than cans because you rarely use more than a tablespoon at a time. *To peel tomatoes*: Quickly drop them in boiling water for one minute, drain, and pinch off the peel.

Tripe In most Mediterranean cooking, a variety of tripe products is available, some used for stuffing like a sausage. Most tripe available in American markets is the honeycomb tripe that usually is sold cleaned, although it will need a good rinsing and long cooking time. Honeycomb tripe is not the stomach used for stuffing in Arab cooking.

Tuna The best canned tuna is the imported variety packed in olive oil. Canned tuna should never be cooked, merely heated.

Turmeric A spice of North African cooking that is used for coloring food and adding a pungent aroma. Store in a tightly closed jar in a dark, cool, dry place.

Turnip The smaller turnips with a little purple in their skins are sweeter than the older and bigger ones.

Ṭurshī Pickled vegetables served as accompaniments to other foods in North African and Middle Eastern cuisines. *Ṭurshī* can be found in Middle Eastern markets and some larger supermarkets.

Vermicelli See *PASTA SECCA*.

Vinegar Red and white wine vinegars range in quality. The best place to find high-quality vinegars are in ethnic markets and gourmet groceries.

Walnuts Store in a zippered-top freezer bag in the freezer.

White cheese See *SYRIAN CHEESE*.

Wine Use the same wine you would drink (unless it's expensive) in recipes calling for wine and not the so-called cooking wine sold in supermarkets.

Yogurt The yogurt sold in supermarkets is made from cow's milk that will curdle if heated too much; therefore, the yogurt must be stabilized for cooking purposes (page 186). For the fullest, most authentic flavor, use only full-fat plain yogurt. The highest quality yogurts will have a thin layer of buttery fat on top. Never use fruit yogurts for cooking. A high-quality yogurt is made by Stoneyfield Farm, Londonderry, New Hampshire 03053, (603) 437-4000.

Yufka A phyllo-type pastry dough used in Turkish and Armenian cooking. *Yufka* usually is a little thicker than phyllo and comes packaged as three 16-inch round sheets. Armenian and Turkish markets are most likely to carry *yufka* in their frozen foods sections. A source for *yufka* is Near East Importing Corp., Glendale, New York 11385, (718) 894-3600.

Zampone Stuffed pig's trotter. The foot and shin are boned and stuffed with ground pork snout and other ingredients. *Zampone* are made around Christmastime in this country and sold in Italian markets.

Zucchini and zucchini flowers Look for the smallest zucchini possible; large zucchini will taste woody. The flowers of a zucchini plant are regularly sold in many Mediterranean markets. In this country, they are found only at some farmer's markets; therefore, you may want to grow your own zucchini. A zucchini plant is a sprawling broad-leaved plant with bright yellow flowers. They are worth growing for the flowers, which can be stuffed, and are called for in a few recipes, as well as the vegetable. Because you grow your own, you can harvest the baby zucchini yourself and experience the delicious sweetness of the vegetable, at the same time understanding that the zucchini sold in markets are much too big.

MEDITERRANEAN FOOD PRODUCTS RESOURCES

NEARLY all of the recipes in this book can be made with ingredients you are likely to find in a supermarket. But for better quality and a wider range of products, you might want to go to your local farmer's market or seek out an Italian, Greek, or Middle Eastern market.

Finding a source for the Mediterranean products sometimes calls for ingenuity. If you live in or near a large metropolitan area with thriving ethnic neighborhoods, cities such as Los Angeles, Chicago, New York, and Boston, you will have no problem finding these products, and high-quality products, too. For others, the place to start is the Yellow Pages, and not only the food entries but also the church entries. Find a local Greek Orthodox church, a Roman Catholic church with an Italian congregation, or an Islamic mosque, and you can ask their office if they could connect you with people in the community who might know local food sources. This can be more rewarding than you imagine. In a small town in Syria, I encountered a delicious *jubna ḥulwa*, a sweet Syrian cheese used in dessert making. I assumed it would be all but impossible to find this back home, never having seen it sold even in Middle Eastern markets, but within a mile of where I lived at the time in Arlington, Massachusetts, a small cheese factory run by Arab-Americans made it. I still can't get over it. All in all, nearly all the products needed for making recipes in this book are easily found in a well-stocked supermarket. Unfortunately, this list will rapidly become outdated, but perhaps shopping on the Internet will become rewarding.

For the following sources, write or call asking for their catalogs. Not all these sources have catalogs, though.

A. B. A. Import Export Co.
P.O. Box 1353
Arlington, MA 02174
(781) 646-9765
Jubna bayḍā' (Syrian cheese) and other Middle Eastern cheeses.

Aphrodisia Products, Inc.
262 Bleeker Street
New York, NY 10014
(212) 989-6440
Rose petals.

Arax Market
603 Mt. Auburn Street
Watertown, MA 02172
(617) 924-3399
Middle Eastern products; zucchini corers, spices, red Aleppo pepper, bulgur, *farīk, muḥammaṣ (maghribiyya)*, flower waters, *mulūkhiyya*, nuts, *bahārāt, jubna bayḍā'* (Syrian cheese). No catalog, no mail order; local only.

Athens Pastries and Frozen Foods
13600 Snow Road
Cleveland, OH 44142-2596
(800) 837-5683; (216) 676-8500
Kunaifa (kataifi); phyllo; pitta/*pide* bread. Catalog available.

A to Z Food Distributers
16 Huntington Street
Brooklyn, NY 11231
(718) 855-8287; (Fax) (718) 855-8367
Jubna nābulsī, other Syrian and Palestinian cheeses. Catalog available.

The Baker's Catalogue, King Arthur Flour
P.O. Box 876
Norwich, VT 05055
(800) 827-6836
www.kingarthurflour.com
Yogurt-making equipment, glazed crockery bakeware, flour, semolina. Catalog available.

Bay Cities Importing Co.
1517 Lincoln Boulevard
Santa Monica, CA 90401
(310) 395-8279
Italian and Greek products; bottarga; olive oils.

The Bean Bag
818 Jefferson Street
Oakland, CA 94607
(800) 845-2326
Beans, including *borlotti.*

Boschetto Bakery
158 Salem Street
Boston, MA 02113
(617) 523-9350
Large round Tuscan bread. No catalog, no mail order; local only.

Bremen House
218 East 86th Street
New York, NY 10022
(212) 426-7341
Porcini mushrooms.

Bristol Farms
606 Fair Oaks Avenue
South Pasadena, CA 91030
(818) 441-5588
Various locations, various products.

Broadway Deli
1457 3rd Street Promenade
Santa Monica, CA 90401
(310) 451-0616
Bottarga.

Canary Trading Co.
1554 South Anaheim Boulevard
Anaheim, CA 92805
(714) 533-2744; Fax (714) 533-2746
Magribiyya and *muḥammaṣ* (pasta balls sold under the name "couscous"); importers of Middle Eastern products.

Cook's Garden
P. O. Box 535
Londonderry, VT 05148
(800) 457-9703; (802) 824-3400
www.cooksgarden.com
Herb and vegetable seeds. Catalog available.

Corti Brothers
5810 Folsom Boulevard
Sacramento, CA 95822
(916) 736-3800; Fax (916) 363-3663
Mediterranean products; olive oils, olives, vinegar. Newsletter available.

D'Artagnan
280 Wilson Avenue
Newark, NJ 07105
(800) 327-8246; Fax (973) 465-1870
www.dartagnan.com
Duck and goose fats, foie gras, *mirqāz (merguez)* sausages, *confit de canard*, pigeons, guinea hens, quail, partridge, rabbit. Catalog available.

Dean & DeLuca
560 Broadway
New York, NY 10012
(800) 221-7714; (212) 226-6800
www.dean-deluca.com
Italian products; cheeses, olives oils, polenta cornmeal, short- and medium-grain rices; huge catalog available.

Frontier Cooperative Herb Co.
P.O. Box 299
Norway, IA 52318
(800) 669-3275; Fax (800) 717-4372
www.frontiercoop.com
Grains of paradise, peppers. Catalog available.

G. B. Ratto & Co.
821 Washington Street
Oakland, CA 94607
(510) 832-6503; Fax (510) 836-2250
Mediterranean products. No catalog.

Gallo Brokerage
93 Willow Street
Wilkes Barre, PA 18702
(570) 822-9743; Fax (570) 822-6622
Sardinian pastas *(fregula* and *malloreddus)* and *carasau* bread. Catalog available.

Great Valley Mills
1774 County Line Road
Barto, PA 19504
(610) 754-7800; (800) 688-6455; Fax (610) 754-6490
Flours. Catalog available.

Hungarian Packing House
213 East 82nd Street
New York, NY 10028
(212) 249-9360
Smoked bacon.

Ideal Cheese Shop
1205 Second Avenue
New York, NY 10021
(800) 382-0109; (212) 688-7579
www.idealcheese.com
Huge catalog of cheeses.

Indo-European Foods
1000 Airway
Glendale, CA 91201
(818) 247-9722; (800) 682-1622
Arab cheeses, *maghribiyya* (pasta balls), Golchin brand of beans, and other Middle Eastern products. Catalog available.

Ital Foods
205 Shaw Road
P.O. Box 2563
South San Francisco, CA 94083
(650) 877-0724; Fax (650) 871-9437
Sardinian pastas *(fregula)* and Italian products. No catalog.

Italia Salami Co. Ltd.
65 Lewis Road
Guelph, Ontario, Canada N1H 6N1
(519) 821-7430; Fax (519) 837-0060
High-quality Italian salamis, especially *soppressa Veneta*. No catalog.

Karoun Dairies
5117 Santa Monica Boulevard
Los Angeles, CA 90029
(323) 666-6222
Jubna ḥulwa, Sicilian *tuma* and other Middle Eastern cheeses. Catalog available.

Krinos Foods, Inc.
4700 Northern Boulevard
Long Island City, NY 11101
(800) 877-5757; (Fax) (718) 361-9725; (718) 729-9000
Manouri cheese; Greek products, Turkish/Greek-style *pide/pitta* bread. Catalog available.

La Española
25020 Doble Avenue
Harbor City, CA 90710
(310) 539-0455; Fax: (310) 539-5989
Excellent source for all Spanish and Catalan sausages and food products including cheeses; *butifarra* and chorizo sausages. Catalog available.

Liuzzi Cheese
322 State Street
North Haven, CT 06473
(203) 248-4356
Fresh ricotta. No catalog, no mail order. Ask for where they distribute.

Maine Coast Sea Vegetables Co.
R. R. 1 Box 78
Franklin, ME 04634
www.seaveg.com
(207) 565-2907
Laver. Catalog available.

Mozzarella Company
2944 Elm Street
Dallas, TX 75226
(800) 798-2954; (214) 741-4072
Fresh mozzarella, *fior di latte*. Catalog available.

Nature's Own Charcoal
(800) 289-2427
Hardwood charcoal.

Near East Importing Corp.
8000 Cooper Avenue, Building 3
Glendale, NY 11385
(718) 894-3600; Fax (718) 326-2832
Turkish *yufka* dough and other Turkish products.

Oasis Date Gardens
59-111 Highway 111
P.O. Box 757
Thermal, CA 92274
(800) 827-8017
Medjool, deglet noor, khadrawy, barhi, halawi, zahidi, thoory, and honey dates. Mail order by UPS. Catalog available.

Old Fashion Lavash Bakery
2835 Newell Street
Los Angeles, CA 90039
(323) 663-5249; Fax (323) 663-8062
Marqūq (lavash) bread; Arab and Turkish/Armenian breads. Catalog available.

Overseas Food Distributors, Inc.
12381 Foot Hill
Sylmar, CA 91342
(818) 896-6127
Dried beans; Middle Eastern products. Catalog available.

Pacific Gourmet
2200 Jerrold Avenue
San Francisco, CA 94124
(415) 641-8400; Fax (415) 641-8309
Tunisian *malsūka* pastry for the making of *brīk* or a Moroccan *basṭīla*. Catalog available.

Penzeys Spices
P.O. Box 933
WI 9362 Apollo Drive
Muskego, WI 53150
(414) 679-7207; Fax (414) 679-7878
www.penzeys.com
Spices. Catalog available.

RJS Wholesale
804 Center Street
Jamaica Plain, MA 02130
(800) 757-2414; Tel. and Fax: (617) 524-5186.
Cuttlefish/squid ink; Spanish saffron. No catalog.

Rokko Trading Co., Inc.
5636 Bandini Boulevard
Bell, CA 90201
(310) 324-5888; Fax (323) 260-4977
Dried boiled anchovies for recipes calling for dried fish.

Royal Pita
705 Brighton Beach Avenue
Brooklyn, NY 11235
(718) 332-8569
Greek- and Turkish-style *pitta/pide* bread.

The Sausage Maker
1500 Clinton Street, Building 123
Buffalo, NY 14206
(716) 824-6510; Fax (716) 824-6465; (888) 490-8525
Sausage casings. Catalog available.

Sessa's
412-414 Highland Avenue
Somerville, MA 02144
(617) 776-6687
Italian products; fresh ricotta, fresh mozzarella, *fior di latte, caciocavallo, zampone, cotechino*, salami, Sardinian cheeses, Sicilian olives, pasta, salted anchovies. Mail order, but no catalog.

Sevran Bakery Corp.
598 Mt. Auburn Street
Watertown, MA 02172
(617) 924-9843
Homemade *mantı*, homemade *kaymak*, Syrian and Palestinian cheeses. No catalog, no mail order; local only.

Shatila Food Products
8505 West Warren
Dearborn, MI 48126
(800) 742-8452; (313) 934-1520
www.shatila.com
Arab pastry sweets. Catalog available.

Sierra Cheese Manufacturing Co.
84 Pine Street
Compton, CA 90221
(800) 243-0852; (323) 636-4270
Sicilian *tuma* cheese. Catalog available.

Simply Shrimp
7794 NW 44th Street
Sunrise, FL 33351
(800) 833-0888; Fax 954-741-6127
www.simplyshrimp.com
Fresh shrimp, grouper, swordfish, red snapper, tuna, salmon, sole, scallops delivered to your doorstep in Styrofoam boxes containing cold gel packs. Catalog available.

Stoneyfield Farm
10 Burton Drive
Londonderry, NH 03053
(800) 776-2697; (603) 437-4000
www.stoneyfield.com
High-quality full-fat yogurt. Catalog available.

Sur la Table
1765 Sixth Avenue South
Seattle, WA 98134-1608
(800) 240-0853
Baking stones, *ṭājin*s, paella pans, *couscousières*. Eight locations on the West Coast. Catalog available.

Timber Crest Farms
4701 Dry Creek Road
Healdsburg, CA 95448
(707) 433-8251; Fax (707) 433-8255
Nuts, dried fruit. Catalog available.

Titan Foods Retail
25-50 31st Street
Astoria, NY 11105
(718) 626-7771; Fax (718) 626-2327
Greek products. Catalog available.

Todaro Brothers
555 Second Avenue
New York, NY 10016
(212) 679-7766; Fax (212) 689-1679
Italian products; salami, cheeses, olive oils, polenta cornmeal, short- and medium-grain rices. Catalog available.

Vivande Porta Via
2125 Fillmore Street
San Francisco, CA 94115
(415) 346-4430; Fax (415) 346-2877
Italian products; olive oils, vinegars, polenta cornmeal, short- and medium-grain rices.

Williams-Sonoma
100 North Point
San Francisco, CA 94133
(800) 541-2233
www.williams-sonoma.com
Spanish *olla* (Catalan *cazuela*), *couscousières*, kitchen equipment. National chain, many locations. Catalog available.

Zingerman's Delicatessen
422 Detroit Street
Ann Arbor, MI 48104-3400
(734) 663-3354; Fax (734) 769 1260; (888) 636-8162
Italian, Spanish, French cheeses and olive oils; vinegars; French country bread, roasted peppers, capers, Calasparra rice, Fontina Val d'Aosta cheese. Catalog available.

NOTES

INTRODUCTION

1. Braudel 1981: 64.
2. Although her book is universally admired, it really is not about Mediterranean food but rather about French food. Only 4 percent of her recipes come from North Africa or the Levant, and she has this to say: "Paella is . . . . the Spanish equivalent of risotto, its great characteristic being the diversity of ingredients used and the mixture of all kinds of shell fish with chicken. . . . As with risotto there is no hard and fast rule for making Paella." See page 287; I believe one can conclude that it is an unusual statement; David 1950: 89.
3. See Herzfeld 1984: 440.
4. Braudel 1972–73: (2) 762.
5. Patton 1947: 59.
6. *Al-nafas* is an expression that means "the touch," used by Lebanese and Palestinians to refer to a cook who is a master of attaining the right taste. It is not a word in the written language but exists as part of colloquial speech.
7. Braudel 1972–73: (1) 166–67.
8. Revel 1982: 22. I accept this distinction with reservations; see page 693.

CHAPTER 1

1. Sura 47: 16ff.
2. Lopez 1976: 39–40.
3. Pliny, *Natural History*, XX, xxxiii: 78; Cato, *On Agriculture*, CLVI–CLVII, CLVII: 10–11. Cabbage is cooked with plenty of coriander and rue, then sprinkled with honey vinegar and a little silphium; Mnesitheus (4th century B.C.), quoted in Oribasius (4th century A.D.), *Medical Collections*, 4, 4, 1, in Dalby and Grainger 1996: 50–51. Romans were enthusiatic growers of cabbage and Pliny describes three kinds (*Natural History*, XIX, xli: 136): the curly one may be Savoy cabbage; the second had broad leaves like kale; the third had tight leaves like white cabbage, although he says it was the Greeks who so divided them.
4. Watson 1974: 14, 11.
5. Ibid., 16.
6. These were the plants studied in Watson 1983.
7. But some can also be blamed on Muslims too, such as the famous Arab philosopher and historian Ibn Khaldūn (1332–1406), who suggested false information about Muslim contributions either knowingly or unknowingly. Also see, for example, A. Reifenberg, *The Struggle Between the Desert and the Sown: The Rise and Fall of Agriculture in the Levant* (Jerusalem, 1955), p. 99 passim, quoted in Watson 1983.
8. Solignac 1953: 5ff, 223ff, points out one striking irrigation innovation developed by the Aghlabids in Qairouan. A recent example of a modern mistake is Dickie 1976: 92 n.9.
9. Solignac 1953; Glick 1970; Pipitone Cannone 1939: 273–82, 204–17. Also see a work that should be used with caution, Salmieri 1950: 23, 34, 38, 46, 59, 63, 73, 74; but also the excellent study by Pellegrini 1972: (1) 55–56 and the works of Agius listed in the bibliography.
10. Although the manpower for the Arab armies that conquered were more often than not nomadic Bedouin.
11. Mack Smith 1968: 9.
12. Amari 1986: (3) 5, pt. 3, 806ff.; Jamison 1957: 176, 220, 232–33.
13. Bresc 1972: 75.
14. Trasselli 1981: 21.
15. Watson 1983: 116.
16. P. A. Saccardo, *Cronologia della flora Italiana* (Padua, 1909), p. 78, cited in Watson 1983: 62, 176–7; Some commentators wrongly identify the Roman *blitum* as "spinach," such as Gowers 1993: 57, 97. The *blitum* mentioned by Plautus is *Amaranthus blitum* L., not spinach (*Spinacia oleracea* L.); see Watson 1983: 62, 176–77, and André 1981: 31.
17. Crescentiis [1230?–1321] 1495: bk. III, 7; Watson 1995: 63.
18. Ashtor 1978: 1026.
19. Excerpts from the *Liber ruralium commodorum*, bk. IV, cap. 25, in Stecchetti 1884.
20. Zohary and Hopf 1988: 160.
21. The artichoke is a development from the cultivated cardoon and, contrary to most writers' claim, was not known by the Greeks and Romans (see pages 235 and 261).
22. Glick 1970: 186; Braudel 1972–73: (1) 237.
23. See Grunebaum 1970: 55; Cahen 1953: 25–52; Al-Duri 1969: 6; and Varisco 1994. Robert B. Serjeant speculated on the influence Yemeni agriculturalists may have had in Spain. Yemen was the medieval Muslim province with the most highly developed irrigation systems, terraced mountainsides, great masonry cisterns, and skill in control of flood waters. Many Yemeni families, such as the Tujībī, Ḥimyarī, Kindī, and Maʿāfirī, settled in Spain where they may have influenced the development of the mountain districts; see Serjeant 1971: 537. The possible culinary connection is even more speculative, but certainly an area worthy of further research.
24. Simmonds 1979: 50; Watson 1994: 105–111. Also see Watson's "Botanical Gardens in the Early-Islamic World: Their Role in the Diffusion of Useful Plants,"

in *Corolla Torontonensis: Essays in Honour of Ronald Morton Smith* (Toronto: Tsar Publications, 1994).

25. See Ibn Ḥawqal's description in Amari 1880–81. Professor Henri Bresc also describes the gardens; see Bresc 1986: (2) 203 n. 26, and 1972: 69, suggesting that the market gardens of Norman Sicily, which were probably still in the hands of Muslim agriculturalists, were ploughed four times before planting.
26. Schimmel 1976: 15.
27. Sura 47: 15ff.
28. Sura 78; also see Gelfer-Jorgensen 1986: 92.
29. Sura 55: 48–76; Schimmel 1976: 29.
30. Sura 55: 68–69.
31. Sura 76: 12–22. In this sura is one of the most enticing images of paradise.
32. Hitti 1970: 454.
33. Pinder-Wilson 1976: 74 n.9.
34. Waines 1989: 8.
35. Arberry 1939: 193; Mantran 1962: 193; Perry 1985: 17.
36. Hitti 1970: 529; Glick 1970; Caracausi 1983; Agius and Hitchcock 1984; Agius 1984: 271–73; Pellegrini 1972; Dozy 1881/1991: (2); Corominas 1980.
37. Cook 1979: 213.
38. Part of this medieval *qanāt* still exists, and Oliver Asin, in *Historia del nombre Madrid*, links the actual name of Madrid to it; Serjeant 1971: 537. I have not seen Asin's book, but I imagine he argues that *Madrid* is the participial adjective of *dardara*, "the rush of water" made by water flowing through the *qanāt*s.
39. Watson 1974: 13; Watson 1983: 110.
40. McNeill 1974 argues that Sicily was less influential than Spain for the development of Latin learning from translations of Arabic versions of Greeks works because Sicily was insulated from other centers of Latin learning owing to the bitter and unremitting enmity between the popes and Frederick II, which stamped Frederick as a foul heretic in the eyes of Catholic Europe.
41. Bianchi-Giovini 1846: 53.
42. Esteban Hernández-Bermejo and García Sánchez 1998: 18–21.
43. Stouff 1970: 106.
44. Brutails 1981: 21; Stouff 1970: 106, 236, 261; *Goodman of Paris* 1928: 255; Piniés 1989: 117; Redon, Sabban, and Servanti 1991: 24, 34.
45. Éliane Thibaut-Comelade, correspondence with the author, November 18, 1992.
46. Simmonds 1979: 169–70.
47. Torres 1992: 74.
48. Wilson 1981: pt. 1, 13; see Riley-Smith 1973: 46–47; Tannahill 1973: 189; Runciman 1994: (1), 195, 197, 214, (2) 6, 18, (3) 13, 24, and 28, where we are told that in 1191 the Frankish Crusaders could barely survive: a silver penny bought thirteen beans or a single egg. A sack of grain cost the impossible hundred pieces of gold. They slaughtered their horses for food while the common soldiers ate grass and bare bones. The Crusaders were always hampered in their efforts to find food by the avarice of the Pisan merchants who controlled supply; Hitti 1970: 665–68 is wrong to claim that the Crusaders are responsible for some culinary introductions. That they encountered spices and sugar in the East is not in doubt, but whether they played a role in its diffusion is highly questionable.
49. Riley-Smith 1973: 80; Runciman 1997: (3) 295–96, and 1994: (2) 259.
50. Bloch 1961: (1) 142.
51. These are terms fraught with difficulty that I will not explore; see the excellent book by Susan Reynolds, *Fiefs and Vassals: The Medieval Evidence Reinterpreted* (Oxford: Oxford University Press, 1994), who points out that in the early thirteenth century, when King Frederick II of Sicily gave property to the church *in perpetuum feudum*, the word *fief* did not yet imply a category of property with rights and obligations but meant nothing more than one's property (p. 243). Reynolds argues that these terms are not helpful in understanding what feudalism was.
52. Wilhem Abel made an interesting calculation, in his classic work *Agricultural Fluctuation in Europe*, for understanding the food requirements for subsistence of a medieval smallholding family. Assuming that half the yield of the land has to go to the landlord, the church, and the tax collector, Abel estimates that a family needs a half-virgate of arable land (about fifteen acres). Under the best circumstances, in a three-field system there would be ten acres under cultivation in any one year. If half is already accounted for, it leaves the family with thirty bushels or 1,800 pounds of mixed grain. This provides a family of five with one pound of cereals per person per day, which is less than today's subsistence level as determined by the United Nation's Food and Agriculture Organization; Abel 1980: 32. The agricultural historian Slicher van Bath called it "direct agricultural consumption;" Slicher van Bath 1963: 24.
53. Goitein 1967: (1) 117–18; In the regions ruled by the Arabs there was nothing remotely akin to vassalage, though; Bloch 1961: (1) 188.
54. Bloch 1961: (1) 300, 247.
55. Schwanitz 1966: 53, 76.
56. Gies 1979: 111–14; 1981: 38–44, 47–50; Tannahill 1973: 107–18. The Mensa della Signoria of Florence made a blancmange in 1344 consisting of the meat from six capons, six pounds of lard, two pounds of sugar, three ounces of cloves, seven pounds of almonds, and one and a half pounds of pine nuts, Grieco 1992: 35.
57. Forbes 1956: 123–28. The millet was either common millet (*Panicum miliaceum*) or foxtail millet (also called panic by some; *P. italicum* syn. *Setaria italica*).
58. Montanari 1984: 308; 314.
59. Mazzi 1980: (1): 58.
60. Montanari 1984: 309. The question of the role of the growth of population in the agrarian social transformation is the subject of heated debate which I cannot get into here, see T. H. Aston and C. H. E. Philpin, eds., *The Brenner Debate: Agrarian Class Structure and Economic Development in Pre-Industrial Europe*, (Cambridge: Cambridge University Press, 1985).
61. In the Ottoman Empire, there was no private property in land, for all arable land was the personal patrimony of the sultan, with the exception of *waqf* (religious)

land, and therefore there was no hereditary nobility. The long and slow disintegration of the Ottoman Empire did not generate any refeudalization for there had not been a feudal system (as that term is generally understood when used for northern Europe) in the first place. See Anderson 1980: 361–94, although Anderson's point is well taken that there was no *de jure* private property, there was *de facto* private property because the people who worked the land could sell it.

62. White 1964: 43.
63. McNeill 1974: 16.
64. White 1964: 44. Another historian, Robert Sallares, challenged White's study by arguing against the notion of technological innovations as the most important factor in the rise in agricultural productivity. What really happened to European and Mediterranean agriculture, he said, was due to the new crops of oats and rye, providing more food for people and better food for horses. It was the evolution of the horse that was key to understanding feudalism in medieval Europe; Sallares 1991: 399–402. Another critic, Massimo Montanari, said White underestimated the quantity of vegetables, especially legumes such as fava beans, in the medieval diet that were grown in pastures and gardens; Montanari 1979: 161.
65. "Agriculture and Nutrition," in *Dictionary of the Middle Ages*. See Postan 1966 and its bibliography in particular for a thorough account of agrarian life in the Middle Ages.
66. Sallares 1991: 399–402.
67. White 1964: 28.
68. Bloch 1961: (1) 153.
69. White 1964: 1.
70. Ibid., 2. On warfare in the Middle Ages, see Beeler 1971; Contamine 1986; Oakeshott 1960; Parry and Yapp 1975.
71. Wallerstein 1974: 23. Also see Ladurie 1988: 244–87, who calls it the "little ice age."
72. Abel 1980: 4.
73. Lane 1973: 19; Abu-Lughod 1989: 237.
74. Abu-Lughod 1989: 237.
75. Abel 1980: 93.
76. Cipolla 1980: 109.
77. Wallerstein 1974: 15.
78. Ibid., 38.
79. McNeill 1974: 20. On this complex issue of modes of production and their relation to the development of capitalism, it is worth the interested reader's while to look at Rodinson 1978: 1–75.
80. Wallerstein 1974: 28–29; Dupuy and Dupuy 1970: 331.
81. Faccioli 1987: 47; Santich 1995: 117 translates *ova perdute* as "poached egg," which may be incorrect (it can also mean "scrambled eggs"), but see Maestro Martino in Faccioli 1987: 193.
82. Homer 1963: 106.
83. This is not the modern nation of the Sudan in northeast Africa, but the Sudanic kingdom of West Africa, the modern Mali, Niger, southern Algeria, and Mauritania.
84. Ladurie 1976: 60; Stouff 1996: 174.
85. Schwanitz 1966: 150 says that the tomato was an ancient cultivated plant in South America, presumably derived from *Lycopersicon pimpinellifolium*. But Harlan 1992: 225–26 disagrees, stating flatly that "there is not one shred of evidence that the tomato was known to South American Indians in pre-Columbian times." But the Mexican Indians knew the cultivated tomato, although no wild tomatoes grew in Mexico. Latini 1692: 390, 444; Faccioli 1987: 480; Willan 1977: 111–12, 105 misidentifies Leonardi as the source for the first tomato sauce recipe.
86. Braudel 1972–73: (1) 519.
87. The literature on the price revolution is vast. A good introduction is found in David Hackett Fischer's *The Great Wave: Price Revolutions and the Rhythm of History* (New York: Oxford University Press, 1996).
88. Braudel 1982: 101, 115. The role of take-out food in the late medieval and early modern Mediterranean would be a fertile area for a graduate student looking for a thesis topic.
89. Ibid., 115.
90. Runciman 1997: (3) 127; Ashtor 1976: 564, 565; Santich 1992: 138–39. Each *fattoro* might employ other *fattori* in other towns so they wouldn't need to constantly travel; see Congdon 1994: 12.
91. The Muslim merchant had sophisticated instruments of exchange such as the *suftaya* (or *suftaja*, bill of exchange) and the *ṣakh* or *ṣakk* (check), first mentioned in the ninth century, but describing events in the seventh century, to refer to food vouchers issued to the population of Medina for grain that was shipped from Egypt. Lieber 1968: 232. Lieber claims that there is no Persian or Arabic origin of the word (p. 240).
92. There were at least three men with the name Apicius, and although the presumed author Marcus Gabinus (or Gavinus) Apicius lived in the first century A.D., the work titled *De re coquinaria* was not compiled until the fourth or fifth century.

    I disagree entirely with the argument by Laurioux 1985: 43–76. Laurioux argues for a continuous culinary development from the time of Apicius to the earliest version of the *Viandier*. In denying the thesis originally proposed by Rodinson and supported by Peterson for an appraisal of the Arab role in the development of European cuisine, Laurioux cites "other documents" that link the third century to the fourteenth century in culinary terms and contradict the theory of a culinary revolution in the thirteenth and fourteenth centuries. These "other documents," though, are not compelling. They are sparse and are notable more for their poverty of imagination and taste than for linkage with the classical culinary tradition of Apicius. He admits that it is difficult to say how the spices listed in these documents were used. Furthermore, Laurioux seems unfamiliar with the vast body of medieval Arabic and Hispano-Muslim literature that supports the notion, which I argue for, of a culinary parallel to the Arab agricultural revolution studied by Watson. But, to his credit, Laurioux suggests a more complex story than the either/or of the continuity/revolution dichotomy in the development of European cuisine.

93. Redon, Sabban, and Servanti 1991: 13.
94. One of the foremost researchers in this area, Robert Sallares, admitted that "it is still a matter of debate whether ancient Greeks and Romans cultivated mainly durum wheat, from which pasta is now made, or the bread wheat generally used to make bread today"; Sallares 1995: 95. The whole area of molecular archeology and ancient history is both new and vast, although interested readers might like to look at recent articles in the magazines *Antiquity*, 62 (1992): 10–23 and *Scientific American*, 266, no. 5 (1992): 72–81.
95. Anthimus 1996; Redon, Sabban, and Servanti 1991: 15; Theuderich 1864–70: (2) 74.
96. See Laurioux 1985: 43–76.
97. Barber 1973: 37–45.
98. Stouff 1970: 256.
99. Mennell 1985: 52; Willan 1977: 31; Peterson 1980: 339 n.20.
100. Dalby 1996: 200.
101. Willan 1977: 19.
102. In this light, the claim that "the tastes of ancient Rome are still the tastes of Sicily today" is entirely wrong; see the introduction by Mary Taylor Simeti to Gozzini 1992: ix. Although Willan claims that Renaissance banquets were part of a deliberate evocation of the splendors of ancient Rome (which they sometimes were) and that Platina was familiar with Apicius, she offers no evidence or systematic argument; see Willan 1977: 31. Furthermore, given the dates of the first appearance and publication of Apicius in Italy, this claim is questionable; see Willan 1977: 31; Peterson 1980: 339 n.20. Even when Renaissance banquets evoked the classical era, they were also inadvertently utilizing an Islamic aesthetic.

    I have given a quick gloss on the knowledge of Latin learning. It was more thoroughgoing than I am implying in this short section; see Haskins 1927.
103. Rodinson 1971: 487, citing *Apolgia ad Guillelmum*, cap. 9, in Migne, *Patrologia latina*, t. 182, col. 910. Is this an early example of what Professor Edward W. Said called "orientalism"? "Orientalism" is a term used to describe the Western approach to the Orient, but also is used by Said to reflect that "collection of dreams, images, and vocabulary available to anyone who has tried to talk about what lies east of the [East-West] dividing line." It is an attitude that "shares with magic and mythology the self-containing, self-reinforcing character of a closed system, in which objects are what they are 'because' they are what they are"; Said 1979: 73, 70. So the Muslim, the epitome of the East, is truly "other," exotic but reprehensible. One sees this in gastronomic writing where the cuisine of the Arab Muslim is merely "Saracen" or "Moorish," or worse "Israeli" (such as the description of falafel as Israeli, truly culinary imperialism at work), as if the writers can't bare to let the word *Arab* form on their keyboard.
104. Rodinson 1971: 479–500; 1949: 95–165; 1990: 31–44; 1989: 15–25; 1986: 15–23; Vollenweider 1963: 59–88, 397–443; Heine 1988; Ashtor 1970: 1–24; 1968: 1017–53; Goitein 1983, vol. 4; 1971: 9–33; Peterson 1980: 317–41; Watson 1983.
105. Watson 1995: 70–71; Duby 1974: 17.
106. The erotic and humorous story of Alibech in Boccaccio's *Decameron* was typical of the image of the Muslim; Boccaccio 1972: (3) 10.
107. Rodinson 1990: 35. The Arabic book was titled *Kitāb al-minhāj al-bayān fimā yasta*ᶜ *miluhu al-insān* (The book of products used by man set forth or The pathway of explanation as to that which man uses). Scholars generally do not provide translations of the titles of medieval Arabic works because the translations usually give no indication of what the subject is of the book or manuscript.
108. These two earliest English recipe manuscripts are both in the British Library, catalogued as Additional 32085 and Royal 12.C.xii. Both manuscripts are from 1300–1340. They are reproduced with translation and critical comment in Hieatt and Jones 1986: 859–82.
109. From the anonymous *Kitāb waṣf al-aṭᶜima al-muᶜtāda*, compiled by Muḥammad ibn al-Ḥasan al-Baghdādī about 1226; see Arberry 1939: 198.
110. *Libro per cuoco* is a small cookery book in the Biblioteca Casanatense in Rome, written by an anonymous Venetian in the fourteenth century; see Frati 1899/1970: 29.
111. Even in the culinary sphere today, I am not aware of any major American publisher having published an Arab (or Middle Eastern) cookbook written by a Muslim Arab, although there are some books by minor publishers.
112. Watt 1972.
113. Jeanneret 1991: 111.
114. There is a vast body of literature concerning the Arab influence on Europe. Standard works include Watt 1972; Daniel 1979; various authors in Schacht 1979; Gibb 1988: 155–67; Levey 1971: 431–44; various authors in Agius and Hitchcock 1984; Crespi 1986; Peterson 1980: 317–41; Rodinson 1971: 479–500.
115. Curtis 1912: 308–309; Abulafia 1988: 54; Mack Smith 1968: (1) 25; Ibn Jubayr 1952: 340–41.
116. Watt 1972: 61.
117. Frazer 1935: (1) 140.
118. *Encyclopaedia of Islam*, 2nd ed., S. v., "*Ghidā*ᶜ," 1066.
119. Goitein 1983: (4) 227.
120. *Encyclopaedia of Islam*, 2nd ed., S. v., "*Ghidā*ᶜ," 1066.
121. Wilson 1981: 18.
122. *Encyclopaedia of Islam*, 2nd ed., S. v., "*Ghidā*ᶜ," 1066. Norman 1972; Wilson 1981: (7) 16, 18. All this permeates our language: both *alchemy* and *elixir* derive from the Arabic.
123. He was also concerned with the preparation of the different dishes and brought many recipes from the East, including many for asparagus; Lévi-Provençal 1967: (1) 271; Watt 1972: 24–25. Ziryāb seems to have been a kind of medieval Thomas Edison, Danny Kaye, August Escoffier, Robert Frost, Tony

Bennett, Vidal Sasson, and Carl Sagan rolled into one. Ziryāb is known as the musician who added the fifth string to the lute (although already described by the first century B.C. Chinese historian Se-me-Tsien; Harlan 1992: 33), and who knew thousands of songs. He may have been a black slave; see Hitti 1970: 514–15, 514 n.6.

124. The best overview of this literature can be found in Sarton 1927: (1).
125. Balletto 1986: 10–11.

CHAPTER 2

1. Camporesi 1996: 9.
2. Braudel 1981: 49; The French historian Emmanuel Le Roy Ladurie showed that the progressively later dates of the grape harvest can be attributed to people's preference for higher alcohol content or riper fruit; Ladurie 1988: 285–86.
3. Lane 1908: 327; Amari 1986: (3) 3, pt. 5, 920 n.5.
4. ᶜAlî al-Ballanûbî, Ibn Hamdis, and ᶜAbd ar-Rahmân di Trapani 1987:55.
5. Candolle 1959; Simmonds 1979: 67; Moldenke and Moldenke 1952: 88. Some botanists take var. *hardwickii* as the wild ancestor.
6. Brunner 1995: 28.
7. At Valladolid, 11,000 sheep were slaughtered between June and December 1586, with an average yield of 26 pounds. Similarly, 2,300 cattle were butchered in the same period with an average weight of 325 pounds; see Cipolla 1980: 126.
8. Brunner 1995: 29.
9. Cipolla 1980: 29.
10. A *comfit* is a candy with a piece of fruit, a root (usually licorice), and a nut preserved in sugar; Defourneaux 1979: 168.
11. So much of what scholars know today about sixteenth-century travel can be found in unique archives such as that of Simon y Cosme Ruiz, a rich Spanish merchant who wrote about 100,000 still-extant letters and had much business in Venice, or the postal records of Philip II's bureaucracy. In Venice there are the enormous records of the Archivio di Stato and the Marciana. The private archives of the Ruiz family are preserved in the Provincial Historical Archives of Valladolid; see Lapeyre 1958.
12. Presotto 1965: 313–435.
13. See Mary Kilbourne Matossian, *Poisons of the Past: Molds, Epidemics, and History* (New Haven: Yale University Press, 1989).
14. Cervantes 1950: 596.
15. *Libre de sent soví* 1979: 230.
16. Camporesi 1989.
17. *Māsh* may be *Phaseolus max* L., a leguminous plant with edible black grains; a kind of pea called Indian pea, or another leguminous plant called the mung bean (*Phaseolus aureus*), with green or yellow seeds. The word also refers to food in general (in the same manner that couscous is called *ṭᶜam,* "food" or "nourishment" in Tlemcen, Algeria), indicating that it is a staple, especially in rural areas.
18. Although the word *kissira* apparently derives from a word meaning "excellent wheat"; Dozy 1881/1991: (2) 475.
19. Busbecq 1927: 52.
20. Ibid., 110–11.
21. Parker 1972: 163–64.
22. Braudel 1981: 52.
23. Menjot 1984: 199–210, 201.
24. Montanari 1984: 320.
25. Croce 1978: 74.
26. From the *Trattato della natura de' cibi e del bere*, published in 1583 and quoted by Camporesi 1989: 169.
27. Ibid., 40. Reay Tannahill is entirely wrong to suggest otherwise in her *Food in History*; see Tannahill 1973: 106.
28. Cipolla 1980: 233, 234.
29. The claim that the introduction is later, in 1588, is mentioned in Cipolla 1980: 234, without a citation. Other reputable scholars suggest different locales for the discovery of the potato by Europeans, including the Altiplano of Peru and Quito in Ecuador; see Salaman 1949; McNeill 1991: 43–59. Also see Root 1980: 380, an unreliable author who must be used with care. Salaman 1949 has shown that our knowledge really is not as assured as we have been led to believe.
30. This paragraph is based on Salaman 1949.
31. Gual Camarena 1968: 259.
32. Faccioli 1987: 116, 698; Paganini 1857: 54.
33. Braudel 1981: 194, 197, 198.
34. Giuffrida 1975: 584.
35. Petroni 1976b: 12.
36. Cortelazzo and Zolli 1979–88.
37. Del Conte 1987: 190; but see Stouff 1970: 231.
38. *Encyclopaedia of Islam*, 2nd ed. S.v. "*Ghidāᶜ*," 1063. This important article was written by Professor Maxime Rodinson. As the word *maqāniq* is not *fuṣḥa* (that is, classical Arabic) but colloquial Arabic, one will occasionally see spellings with the "l" or "n" as an initial consonant.
39. Braudel 1972–73: (2) 741.
40. Defourneaux 1979: 113.
41. *Lazarillo de Tormes* 1969: 38, 41–43.
42. Angarano 1973: 29–32. The boiling then roasting of meat is a method common in Arab cookery. It would be interesting to explore the connection here, if any.
43. Root 1971: 583.
44. The Italian word *ragù* is generally thought to derive from the sixteenth-century French word *ragoût*, which in turn derives from a verb meaning "to revive the taste" (*ra-* "to revive"; *goût-* "taste"); see Cortelazzo and Zolli 1979–88.
45. Lane 1973: 349.
46. Bynum 1987: 3.
47. Ibid., 67, 4, 68.
48. Ibid., 245.
49. Ibid., 93.
50. Ibid., 114, 151.
51. Ladurie 1976: 111.
52. della Casa 1990: xi–xvi.
53. Homer 1996: 517. The suggestion that the fork was known in Roman times by virtue of passages in Petro-

nius' *Satyricon* is not tenable. These were forked instruments used in the kitchen and not table forks; see Henisch 1985: 185.
54. Runciman 1952a: 53. The fork may have appeared earlier on the Byzantine table, although I have not seen the so-called fourth-century Dumbarton Oaks silver fork.
55. Norwich 1989: 60.
56. Forbes 1956: 126; a reproduction is in Henisch 1985: 189.
57. *Opera nova che insegna apparechiar una mensa a uno convito*, Venice; Francesco di Alessandro Bindoni and Mapheo Pasini, 1526 (Biblioteca Vaticana, codex Rossiana 7659), cited in Benporat 1988: 41–42.
58. Braudel 1981: 209. An earlier painting, also of a Last Supper, depicting a fork, appears in the Pala d'Oro of St. Mark's Cathedral in Venice.
59. Cipolla 1980: 213 n.10.
60. Maffioli 1982: 100; also see Zorzi 1967: 2.
61. This obscure word comes from the *Qiṣṣat al-Harithi* of the *Bukhala*ᶜ, cited and analyzed in Agius 1984: 205.
62. Mantran 1965: 264.
63. Cipolla 1980: 213, 213 n.10. The classic work on manners is Norbert Elias's *The Civilizing Process*, Edmund Jephcott, trans. (Oxford, UK and Cambridge, USA: Blackwell, 1994).
64. Huizinga 1996: 44–45.
65. Casas 1988: 199.
66. The book was printed and reprinted in Venice from 1550 to 1559; Braudel 1981: 188.
67. del Conte 1987: 370. Waverly Root suggests that *zampone* existed at least from the 1500s, by virtue of an anonymous sixteenth-century painting of the Piazza Grande in the Palazzo Communale in Modena, where two *zampone* are depicted. I have not had an opportunity to examine this painting; Root 1971: 206.

CHAPTER 3

1. Huizinga 1996: 15.
2. The banquets of the rich are so extraordinary and rare, so removed from the daily life of the population, that they must be overlooked in generalizing about the European diet of the Middle Ages.
3. Finlay 1856: 135. The association of cactus fruit (prickly pears) with poverty is still evident, as witnessed by a comment made to me by a well-known food writer from a Mediterranean country upon seeing prickly pears in a market in Morocco: "Oh, but they must be poor to want to eat prickly pears."
4. Berengo 1956: 81.
5. According to Jean Bruyerin Champier in *De re cibaria* (1560), quoted in Flandrin and Hyman 1986: 226, 243 n.4.
6. Ibid., 244 n.11.
7. *Imaret* (mosque complexes) kitchens in central Anatolia in the sixteenth century are known to have had meals that seldom included meat, and ordinary peasants could probably not afford meat at all. But there is a paucity of data about daily consumption; see Islamoğlu-Inan 1987: 122. Also see Chapter 5, "Provisioning the Urban Monster."
8. Braudel 1981: 201, 202.
9. Cipolla 1980: 159.
10. Sanuto 1879–1903: vol. XLVI, col. 380.
11. Braudel 1972–73: (1) 602.
12. Wright 1992: 25; Camporesi 1989: 38. As far as I know, every food writer and independent food historian with whose writing I am familiar focuses on the extant cookery manuscripts that were produced for the uppermost echelons of society and devotes almost no attention to the actual diet of the masses.
13. Cipolla 1980: 212.
14. *Rerum Italicarum Scriptores*, IX, p. 128, quoted in Montanari 1994a: 56.
15. Bonvesin della Riva, *On the Marvels of the City of Milan*, collected in Lopez and Raymond 1990: 67.
16. Cipolla 1980: 213.
17. Faccioli 1987: 179–80.
18. Boccaccio 1972: (9) 8.
19. Pellegrini 1972: (1) 123; (2) 468; Cortelazzo and Zolli 1979–88: (5) 1467.
20. Pickersgill 1969: 447–48; Simmonds 1979: 267.
21. Ibn Riḍwān 1984: 16 n.74.
22. Sabadino degli Arienti, bk. 38: 227–30.
23. There must have been much conflicting advice because we know that Avicenna thought peaches were a wholesome food, while the Ancients believed pears were not because they produced colic and flatus; *School of Salernum* 1970: 181, and Ibn Riḍwān recommended eating apple, quince, prune, pomegranate, peach, and the fruits of Christ's-thorn (*Zizyphus spina-Christi* Willd.); Ibn Riḍwān 1984: 133.
24. Patrone 1981: 187, 184, 188.
25. Braudel 1981: 130; Lévi-Provençal 1967: (3) 420.
26. Agius 1984: 271.
27. Goitein 1967: (1) 72; Roden 1996: 440.
28. Bolens 1990: 59. Toussaint-Samat misses this point in her book; see Toussaint-Samat 1992: 143.
29. Agius 1984: 273.
30. Brunschvig 1947: (2) 272.
31. Rosenberger 1980: 484–85.
32. Brunschvig 1940/1947: (2) 272, 272 n.2.
33. Rosenberger 1980: 484.
34. al-Bakrī 1913/1965: 88.
35. Ibid., 18/trad 42–3.
36. Brunschvig 1940/1947: (1) 29, 27, 35.
37. Amari 1880–81; Talbi 1954: 299; Idris 1959: (2) 589.
38. Talbi 1954: 299; Idris 1959: (2) 589, 589 n.1 citing al-Burzulī's *Gamih masahil al-aḥkam*, the *Tuḥfa* of al-ʿUqbāni, and al-Mālikī, *Riyāḍ al-nufūs*.
39. Idris 1959: (2) 592, citing al-Mālikī.
40. Amari 1880–81: (1) 315–16; Idris 1959: (2) 592, 593. Idris claims *samāṣākhiyya* is "without doubt a bouillon of peppers and garlic," but this cannot be since peppers have not yet appeared in the Mediterranean at the time of al-Mālikī.
41. Brunschvig 1940/1947: (1) 25.
42. Ladurie 1976: 66; Brunschvig 1940/1947: (2) 258; manna is a sweetish sap from the European ash, used as a laxative and demulcent; storax is a balsam from the bark of an Asian tree used as an expectorant; scammony is the gum resin from the root of *Con-*

volvulus scammonia, a plant native to Syria and used pharmacologically as a purgative.

43. According to the great fourteenth-century philosopher Ibn Khaldūn (1332–1406), in his *Prolegomena*, the "first foods" of Ifriqiya (Tunisia) were barley and olive oil (Brunschvig 1940/1947: (2) 269, 270). An interesting *ḥisba* work (household accounts notebook) from North Africa (titled *Tuḥfat al-nāẓir wa-ghunyat al-dhakir fī ḥifẓ al-shaᶜair wa-taghyīr al-manākir*, cited in Talbi 1954: 294) sheds light on the Maghrib of the fifteenth century, along with a number of unedited manuscripts in the Zaytuna mosque of Tunis, such as the *ḥisba* of Muḥammad b. Aḥmad al-ᶜUqbanī al-Tilimsānī. He tells us that, under the ninth-century Tunisian dynasty of the Aghlabids, the sale of figs and raisins was from two sorts of baskets, the *qaratil* and the *silal*. Melons were sold from *qifāf* and dried fish were sold in jars. The butchers had the reputation of being particularly cunning. It was forbidden to mix lamb meat with other meat. Each piece had to be weighed separately. If a vendor cheated, he could be kicked out of the market. If the butcher mixed lamb and horse meat, his stall would be shut down. The same was true for the bread baker if he sold loaves of the wrong weight (Talbi 1954: 297; also see 299).
44. Idris 1959: (2) 458.
45. Brunschvig 1940/1947: (2) 156, 272 n.7, 218–19, 219, 271 n.4, 273, 220, 273, 221. The jujube was also popular in Languedoc and the Midi, where in 1561 Étienne Ferrières mentions shipping dried jujube; Caster 1962: 342.
46. Brunschvig 1940/1947: (2) 222.
47. *Ḥabb ᶜazīz* is the chufa or earth almond (*Cyperus esculentus* L.), whose small bean-sized tubers are edible. Both the Sicilian name *cabbasisa* and the Venetian name *bagigi* derive from the Arabic. See Brunschvig 1940/1947: (2) 222; Pellegrini 1972: (1) 186; Boerio 1856.
48. Edrisi 1866/1968: 106/trad 125.
49. Brunschvig 1940/1947: (2) 223.
50. Idris 1959: (2) 592. The *harīsa* mentioned here is a kind of porridge with pounded wheat, butter, meat, and spices, associated with the Sufis, and not the hot chili paste *harīsa* (page 523). There is a preparation from Tozeur that is also called *tozeur*, a Berber pan-cooked bread or pancake made from semolina, water, spices, and *hrūs* (page 500). It is formed into a small round loaf and cooked in a steel pan called a *ghanāᶜā*.
51. His travel diaries are in the Bibliothèque Muncipale de Lille in France.
52. Brunschvig 1936: 203; Brunschvig 1940/1947: (2) 271 n.4, 273.
53. Brunschvig 1936: 205.
54. Ibid., 6.
55. Brunschvig 1936: 75. Here is circumstantial evidence of the Muslim origin of the southern Italian *zeppole*, via Spain via Tunisia.
56. Lévi-Provençal 1967: (3) 417 n.4.
57. Ibid., (3) 418.
58. Perry 1984: 57–62. Kamman 1997: 1080 disagrees with this attribution, but she also seems unfamiliar with Perry's research.
59. Grewe 1992.
60. Dozy 1881/1991: (2) 507; also see the entries for *chochia* and *cochia* in Dozy's source Du Cange, *Glossarium medaie et infimae latinitatis* . . . , Niort: L. Favre, 1883–1887, 10 vols.
61. Dozy 1881/1991: (1) 641.
62. Manniche 1989: 158.
63. Alcala 1505.
64. Carrier 1987: 148.
65. Reboul n.d.: 70.
66. Mallos 1984: 60; Skoura 1967: 106; Alexiadrou 1989: 114.
67. The Turkish word may itself derive from the Persian *barg*, meaning "leaf"; see Dozy 1881/1991: (1) 75. Ayla Algar suggests another etymology, see note 38, page 753.
68. Algar 1985: 2.
69. Brunschvig 1940/1947: (2) 272. The *maqrūḍ* could be considered the original Fig Newton.
70. Caracausi 1983: 341, 340.
71. *Encyclopedia of Islam*, New ed., (x), S.v. "*Ṭabīkh*."
72. *Encyclopaedia of Islam*, 2nd ed., S.v. *"Ghidhāᶜ,"* 1063–64.
73. Ashtor 1968: 1037.
74. Ibid., 1023. This al-Baghdādī is not the same person who wrote the so-called thirteenth-century Baghdad cookery book.
75. de Biberstein Kazimirski 1860: (1) 484, Watson 1983: 62.
76. Man 1995: 9.
77. Watson 1983: 70. Watson notes that the word *ḥadaq*, used by the medieval Arab botanist Abū Ḥanīfa al-Dīnawarī (d. 895) for the eggplant, seems to derive from the Sanskrit words *vartaku* and *bantaku*, (p. 180).
78. Ibid., 70; literally "captain of leafy greens" (*ra'īs al-buqūl*), Ibn al-ᶜAwwām 1977: (2) 154.
79. Watson 1983: 64–65, 176–177; Lokotsch 1927: 833.
80. *Encyclopedia of Islam*, New ed., (10), S.v. "*Ṭabīkh*."
81. See the fascinating account in Hitti 1970: 505–11; Watson 1983: 89.
82. Montanari 1984: 317.
83. Sura 3: 100.
84. Cohen 1989: 13, 16; Najwa al-Qattan, conversation with the author, March 1989.
85. Stouff 1970: 131. The word *taula* appears to be adopted from the Arabic word for "table," although that word itself is thought to derive itself from the Italian word *tavola*.
86. Bökönyi 1974: 136.
87. Herodotus 1922–81: (III) 113.
88. Cohen 1989: 37.
89. Simmonds 1979: 55–56.
90. *Laban* means "milk" in North Africa, but in Syria and Lebanon it means "yogurt," *ḥalb* (coll.) being used to mean "milk," such as cow's milk.
91. As readers of Fernea and Goitein know, an outspoken public recognition of the cook is not typical in Arab cultures. Generally, there is a silent agreement

that so-in-so is an excellent cook. I have spent a good deal of time among Arab families and I don't recall any time when diners commented upon the food in the presence of the cook. But, in general, in conversations about food, men would often refer to a particular woman, perhaps a wife or mother, who was acknowledged among them as being "a very good cook"; see Elizabeth Warnock Fernea, *Guest of the Sheik* (New York: Anchor, 1969), p. 101, and Goitein 1983: 228.

92. Elliot 1965: 306.
93. Ibid., 306.
94. Professor William Cole, conversation with the author, October 1991.
95. Cervantes 1950: 498.
96. Elliot 1965: 306, 307.
97. Rios and March 1992: 70.
98. Molénat 1984: 313, 317.
99. This does not strike me as a likely explanation. Alcoholic beverages were always interpreted as forbidden by Muslim theologians. There are no halfway measures. But it is true that Muslims drank alcoholic beverages throughout the ages, and do even today, but it is still a forbidden practice to the faithful. Furthermore, even though Corominas suggests a Gothic etymology for the word, it does seem related to the Arabic word for "lid" or "small plate," *tabaq*, with the usual transformation of the phoneme "p" to "b" peculiar to the Arabic language; see Wehr 1976: 553; Corominas 1967: 556–57.
100. Rios 1987: 38.
101. Rios and March 1992: 26–27.
102. Defourneaux 1979: 64; 15; 16; 162–63.
103. Defourneaux 1979: 152, 153; Elliot 1965: 304. Also see page 000.
104. Isidore of Seville, *Etymology*, XX, 3, 19; see Isidore of Seville 1911: 2 vols.
105. See Lévi-Provençal 1928 and 1967, (3). Also see Grewe 1992, although his comments are based solely on an analysis of one anonymous thirteenth-century Hispano-Muslim cookbook written for the well-to-do.
106. A qadi is a Muslim magistrate.
107. Parvin 1985: 41–42.
108. Rodinson 1971: 492.
109. *Traduccion española de un manuscrito anónimo del siglo XIII* 1966: 130, 148, 151.
110. The *almogavar* are associated with professional Catalan-Aragonese mercenaries who operated in Sicily in the early fourteenth century. The word *almogavar* derives from the Arabic *al-mughāwir*, meaning "to carry out military actions"; see Pellegrini 1972: (1) 51, 95, 232, and Contamine 1986: 247–48 and 336–37, for an extensive bibliography on these commandos.
111. Luján 1988: 38.
112. Alberini 1990: 179.
113. Maffioli 1982: 236.
114. Jouveau 1976: 21.
115. Stouff 1996: 12, 16.
116. Guillaumond 1986: 37.
117. Flandrin and Hyman 1986: 234.
118. See *nāranjiyya* in Muḥammad ibn al-Ḥasan al-Baghdādī's *Kitāb waṣf al-aṭᶜima al-muᶜtāda*, compiled about 1226 and translated into English, Arberry 1939: 190.
119. Stouff 1970: 231. This appears to predate what Vollenweider claimed to be the earliest mention of ravioli, a description of *raviolo* in the *Cronica* of Salimbene of Parma from 1281, where it is written that "*in festo Sancte clare comedi primo 'raviolos' sine crusta de pasta*" (in the Holy festival the first course was ravioli pie); see Vollenweider 1963: 418, 419.
120. *"Liber de coquina"* 1968: 408, 409; Frati 1899/1970: 35; Anonimo Meridionale 1985: *Libro B*: no. 55 (p. 45); Faccioli 1987: 157.
121. Aliquot 1984: 136.
122. Grava 1984: 155.
123. Aliquot 1984: 136.
124. Stouff 1970: 259 is not sure about this meaning; for fish, the texts are in the Archives Départementales des Bouches-du-Rhône, p. 260. *Au gratin* cooking also apparently had a popularity in Muslim Spain of the thirteenth century, see Grewe 1992: 145.
125. Flandrin and Hyman 1986: 233.
126. Grava 1984: 155.
127. Ladurie 1976: 68.
128. Coulet 1992: 164, 166, 168.
129. Stouff 1970: 261; also see Stouff's excellent glossary of foods on pp. 467–77. Stouff's study was criticized by Flandrin and Hyman 1986 for its lack of attention to non-"objective" accounts, leaving Stouff with the false impression that there was a lack of specificity to the cooking of Provence (p. 231). Also see pp. 238–39.
130. Stouff 1970: 226, 230.
131. Vollenweider 1963: 442.
132. Flandrin and Hyman 1986: 245 n.12.
133. Ladurie 1976: 103.
134. Ladurie 1976: 42, 43. *Piquette* is a poor-quality wine made with water and the residue of pressed grapes.
135. Defourneaux 1979: 21; Andrews 1984.
136. Ladurie 1976: 64.
137. Locke 1953: 88, 111, 246–47.
138. Isidore of Seville 1911.
139. Stouff 1970: 51; 1996: 25. It is not clear what *menudeta* and *placentula* are. *Menudeta* might be a kind of cake, although Jean-Louis Flandrin suggests (using comparisons with other works) that it is a kind of dried dough cooked in liquid, such as soups. Yet another interpretation is that it is a kind of honey bonbon or a kind of semolina. *Placentula* appears to be a kind of cake, and probably close to the *fougasse*. But whether the fifteenth-century *fougasse* is similar to the *fougasse* of today is not known.
140. Bautier 1984: 40. She cites *Cartulaire de l'abbaye de Saint-Sernin de Toulouse*, C. Douais. Toulouse, 1887, app. 68, p. 538; also app. 33, p. 26 on minute descriptions of the bread baker. *Panis focacius, focacia, fogacia, fugatia, fogassa*, and *fouce* are names of a bread that appear frequently as a benefit title or in French charters since the ninth century, where we can see it in

the polytriptiques of Saint-Remi de Reims; Piniès 1989: 117.
141. Brutails 1891: 18–19.
142. Ashtor 1968: 1047.
143. Ibid., 1027.

PART II AN ECOLOGY OF MEDITERRANEAN GASTRONOMY

1. See Diamond 1997: 83–191.

CHAPTER 4

1. Braudel 1972–73: (1) 61.
2. Braudel incorrectly identifies Chrea in Algeria as the source of this offering, see Runciman 1994: (3) 61. Perry 1981c correctly argues that the words *sherbet* and *sorbet* (as well as the Italian *sorbetto*) do not derive from the Arabic word *shurba* (soup), which derives from the Persian compound of *shor* (salty, brackish) and *ba* (stew, dish cooked in water). Perry could have mentioned that *sherbet* is derived, though, from the Arabic *sharāb*, meaning the same or "beverage"; see Pellegrini 1972: (1) 123 n.173, and Caracausi 1983: 355–56. The Sicilian name for Mt. Etna is Mongibello, a contraction of the Latin and Arabic words for mountain, *mons* and *jabal*. For the development of sherbets in Muslim Andalusia, see Bolens 1992.
3. Braudel 1972–73: (1) 29.
4. Pla 1981: 8.
5. A quick review of the medieval appropriation of Roman and canon law can be found in Taylor 1966: (2) 260–309.
6. Ginzburg 1992: 3, 4, 15, 24, 57, 60, 153.
7. Hitti 1970: 515, citing al-Maqqarī.
8. Braudel 1981: 209, 210.
9. Matton 1957: 116.
10. Pellegrini 1972: (1) 198.
11. Dalby 1996: 190.
12. Braudel 1981: 210; Stouff 1970: 196.
13. Denti di Pirajno 1970: 195.
14. Goitein 1983: (4) 251–52.
15. Ashtor 1968: 1028.
16. Athenaeus 1969–93: (III) 96b.
17. Naso 1990.
18. Kaspar 1992: 488–92.
19. Braudel 1981: 210.
20. Braudel 1981: 211. It is thought that the cheese was originally made in Kavalla, the port opposite the island of Thásos in Greek Macedonia, which once had numerous residents originally from Wallachia; see Sada 1991: 98–99. On the other hand, some food writers believe the cheese had its origin in central Italy, especially the area around Naples.
21. *Larousse* 1987: 208, and Masui and Yamada 1996: 178, suggest that it is mentioned in Pliny. But a reading of Pliny, *Natural History*, XI, xcvii, 240–241, does not support this contention, except for the proximity of locales.
22. The product itself is older than the Turkish presence in Anatolia. In the writings of Galen, there appears to be a kind of yogurt and perhaps the classical Greek *pyriate* is a kind of yogurt as suggested by Dalby 1996: 66, 200.
23. Galen, *On the Properties of Foods* 3.15 quoted in Dalby 1996: 66.
24. Halıcı 1989: 10.
25. de Temmerman and Chedorge 1988: 140.
26. Busbecq 1927: 52.
27. Braudel 1972–73: (1) 66.
28. "Lombard" in the Middle Ages meant anyone from northern Italy.
29. Ladurie 1976: 11, 12.
30. *Encyclopaedia Britannica,* 11th ed. S.v. "Cathars."
31. Ladurie 1976: 13.
32. Ibid., 16.
33. Piniés 1989: 117. Rosenberger 1980: 486. The first appearance of maize in southwest France is said to have been in the sixteenth century, by virtue of Basque sailors returning from the New World; Wolfert 1983: 140. The *milhoca* that appears in twelfth-century France is sorghum; Watson 1983: 14.
34. Cited in Rosenberger 1980: 490.
35. See Corominas 1936: 1–81; 1954–57; and 1980.
36. Bonnaure 1988: 22.
37. Claustres 1990: 12.
38. Grigson 1970: 164; Root 1992: 303; Guy 1962: 208.
39. Guy 1962: 208; Root 1992: 304. It is thought that the haricot entered France for the first time in the early part of the sixteenth century, among the wedding presents brought by Catherine de'Medici; see Gidon 1936: 125–26. Barbara Wheaton makes the claim that the first reference to *Phaseolus* is in 1594, when it was mentioned by Olivier de Serres; see Wheaton 1983: 85–86. Wheaton also debunks the "myth of Catherine de' Medici's cooks" to whom many popular food writers attribute various culinary introductions to France; see pp. 43–51.
40. The *cigale de mer* is the flat lobster (*Scyllarrides latus*), sometimes called sea cricket by food writers but not the same as the mantis shrimp, also called sea cricket (see page 000).
41. Piniés 1989: 117.
42. Collier 1939: 270, 269, 271.
43. Abel 1980: 72.
44. Lapeyre 1958: 541; Braudel 1981: 212; Stouff 1970: 192.
45. Salaman 1940.
46. Salaman 1949: 134, 223.
47. Dozy 1881/1991: (2) 495.
48. Arnau de Vilanova 1947: 27, 198.
49. Grewe 1988: 107.
50. Stouff 1970: 14.
51. This box is based on Escudier 1953; Jouveau 1976; Chanot-Bullier 1988; Morard 1984; Reboul n.d.; Mascarelli: 1947; Barberousse n.d.
52. Stouff 1970: 14.
53. Professor Nikos Stavroulakis, conversation with the author, Khaniá, Crete, October 14, 1994. I have heard this claim verified by other Cretans, but find it curious because the ancient Greeks certainly knew spit-roasting as we know from Homer's *Odyssey* (Homer

1996: (3) (461–72) But meat was not a very common food in classical Greece; see Dalby 1996: 60. For more on Greek food in late antiquity see Kislinger 1996.

54. Mallos 1979: 23.
55. Yianilos 1970: 39.
56. Paradissis 1976: 7.
57. Chantiles 1975: xiii.
58. Dalby 1996: 34.
59. Professor Nikos Stavroulakis, conversation with the author, Khaniá, Crete, October 14, 1994.
60. Vyronis 1986: 481, 482–83. Although there are no studies of the vestigial culinary culture, Vyronis's study indicates the fertile ground to be explored for the notion of a Byzantine residue in Turkish Anatolia and who speaks of an "invisible" physical Byzantine residue (p. 463). Certainly the evidence is strong in the agricultural field, where he concludes that the "Byzantine agrarian practices and techniques determined Turkish agricultural life in Anatolia" (p. 477). As we have seen in other situations, agricultural evidence is the usual foundation for, at least, rural culinary culture. Another important work for researchers to examine in detail is the food and bread entries in A. Tietze's "Griechishe Lehnwörter im anatolishcen Türkishchen," *Oriens*, 8 (1955): 204–257.

    Turkmen cuisine was very simple, usually produced from their flocks, with products such as milk, yogurt, butter, and cheese, grains such as millet, fruit, honey, eggs, and a type of pancake cooked on a hot iron griddle. Vyronis states that the elaborate Turkish cuisine that came later was foreign to the Turkmen nomads and belonged to the native cuisine of the eastern Mediterranean. There is a similarity between the sweets of the Turks and those of the Byzantines, he argues, where one finds dough, sesame, nuts, honey, and fruits, as the Byzantine *pastilla* shows. The Turkish baklava, he argues, was known as *kopton* and Athenaeus gives a recipe (Athenaeus, XIV, 647–48). Cheese, *börek*, and *pastırma* were all known to the Byzantines, as was the roasting of meat on a spit. The above argument by Vyronis has been convincingly challenged by Charles Perry, who says that Vyronis misread the Greek text of Athenaeus and that the simple food of Turkic nomads may actually have been the mother of invention for more complex preparations, like layered doughs for bread; see Perry 1994: 87–91.
61. Skiotis 1975: 310–11.
62. Setton 1975.
63. Miller 1908: 211.
64. Today Rumelia refers to Greek Macedonia, but for the Greeks living under the Ottomans it meant all of the mainland north of the Peloponnesus.
65. Yianilos 1970: 153.
66. Tannahill 1973: 176, using Arberry 1939: 39–40.
67. Alberini 1990: 168.
68. Professor Nikos Stavroulakis, conversation with the author, Khaniá, Crete, October 14, 1994.
69. Yianilos is wrong in claiming Slavic etymology; Yianilos 1970: 131.
70. Athenaeus 1969–93: (III) 95–96.
71. Watson 1983: 177 n.3.
72. Vyronis 1986: 481, 482–83.
73. Braudel 1972–73: (1) 89.
74. Marino 1988: 42–43.
75. Patrone 1981: 158.
76. Ibid., 272–73, 274.
77. Waverly Root relates a *panarda* feast with thirty-five courses; Root 1971: 520.
78. See page 40.
79. Braudel 1972–73: (1) 86.
80. The famous merino sheep; see Lopez 1953: 161–68.
81. Cervantes 1950: 84.
82. *Traduccion española de un manuscrito anónimo del siglo XIII* 1966: 249. This translation has mistakes so it should be compared to the Arabic. Crone 1987 convincingly demonstrates that the "cinnamon" and "cassia" of antiquity were not the cinnamon and cassia of today. So the identity of this "Chinese cinnamon" should be taken as provisional until further research is done.
83. Braudel 1972–73: (1) 175.
84. Dozy 1881/1991: (1) 20. I have been unable to identify *berdi*, but it might be *Echinochloa stagnina* that contains sugar and is used for making sweet drinks, too. There is some confusion as to whether *cram-cram* is *Cenchrus biflorus* or *Pennisetum distichum*. Another staple is *Aristida pungens* Desf., in the northern Sahara; Lewicki 1974: 11, 154; Harlan 1992: 13, 187.
85. There are some studies, of course, especially Georg Jacob's *Altarabishes Beduinenleben. Nach den Quellen geschildert* (Berlin: Mayer, 1897), but none takes on the topic of culinary culture directly. Also see Charles Pellat's French translation of al-Djaḥiẓ's *Kitāb al-Bukhala*[c], titled *Le livre des avares* (Paris: G. P. Maisonneuve; Beirut: Commission Internationale pour la traduction des chefs d'oeuvres, 1951) and W. Robertson Smith, *Kinship and Marriage in Early Arabia,* new ed. (London: Darf, 1990).
86. Sura 16: 5–8.
87. Abu-Lughod 1988: 8.
88. Ibid., 6.
89. Ibid., 40.
90. Professor Lila Abu-Lughod, New York University, conversation with the author, July 1991; Dozy 1881/1991: (2) 261.
91. Professor Lisa Anderson, Columbia University, correspondence with the author, July 1995.
92. Professor Rahmani Mohamed, professor of agronomy, University of Hasan II, Morocco, comments delivered at "The Science and Gastronomy of Morocco's Healthy Traditional Mediterranean Cuisines," Oldways International Symposium, Casablanca, Morocco, October 2–8, 1994.
93. Brunschvig 1940/1947: (2) 270. Today *Ifriqiya* refers to all of Africa, but in Ibn Khaldūn's time it meant the eastern portion of Barbary while the western portion was known as the Maghrib.
94. Transliterated as *mirkas* by the Spanish translator. See *Kitāb al-ṭabīkh fī al-Maghrib wa'l-Āndalus* 1961–62:

15, although the Spanish translation leaves a lot to be desired.

95. Chef Moncef Meddeb, conversation with the author, January 25, 1997.
96. Professor Lila Abu-Lughod, New York University, e-mail to the author, November 25, 1997; Abu-Lughod 1988: 111, 40, 276 n.3.
97. al-Bakrī 1913/1965: 300. *Qaṭā'if* is a kind of batter that is cooked like a pancake and used to wrap sweet cheese or other kinds of sweets and dipped in honey or sugar water. Sometimes the batter is drizzled onto a spinning hot plate to form vermicelli-like strips that are also used for the preparation of sweets—for example *kunaifa* (*kunāfa,* see recipe on page 658).
98. Ibid., 339.

CHAPTER 5

1. McNeill 1974: 15, 21.
2. Chrysostomides 1970: 268, 298.
3. Nicol 1992: 40–41; Brown 1920: 68, 75.
4. Ashtor 1976: 536.
5. Norwich 1989: 12.
6. Braudel 1972–73: (1) 389.
7. Braudel 1982: 284.
8. Lane 1973: 307.
9. Braudel 1982: 286, 287. See also "Wheat" in Chapter 9.
10. Lane 1973: 306.
11. Cipolla 1980: 65.
12. Andrieux 1972: 133–34.
13. McNeill 1974: 175.
14. Lane 1973: 311, 317.
15. Newett 1902; Montanari 1994a: 72; also see Redon 1992.
16. Newett 1902: 248, 255, 256, 273.
17. Norwich 1989: 212.
18. Program Guided Tour, *Itinerari Secreti nel Palazzo Ducale a Venezia*, Palazzo Ducale, Venice, May 1991.
19. Lane 1973: 306.
20. All weight conversions are based on Appendix 1 of Lane 1934: 245–53.
21. Aymard 1966: 17.
22. Wright 1997; Targioni-Tozzetti 1853: 43.
23. The day-to-day affairs of the Venetian Republic were left to the Pregadi (Senate). At the base of the political structure was the Maggior Consiglio (Great Council), consisting of nearly 2,000 members. On the same level as the Senate was the Council of Ten, established in 1310 "to preserve the liberty and peace of the subjects of the Republic and to protect them from the abuses of personal power." The Council of Ten was elected by the Great Council. The executive arm of government was represented in the Collegio, a cabinet where state business was conducted. Although the Doge presided over all these institutions he was effectively blockaded by the Minor Consiglio or Signoria (Minor Council), whose approval he needed; Norwich 1989: 282–83; Lane 1973: 89–95.
24. Alberini 1990: 17.
25. Lane 1973: 14; McNeill 1974: 66. In the Arab world, the equivalent type of foreign merchant's inn was called a *khan, wikāla*, or *funduq*. The Rialto Bridge, built between 1588 and 1591, is today, as it was four centuries ago, a market area. One of the architects bidding on the Rialto Bridge project was Andrea Palladio (1508–1580), as well as other famous architects. But a much less distinguished architect won the bidding, Antonion de Ponte. Although I don't believe the Rialto Bridge is an architectural wonder, it is interesting. Each end sits on 6,000 piles driven into the mud.
26. Alberini 1990: 16.
27. Boccaccio 1972: (6) 4.
28. Benporat 1988: 41–44, 45; Alberini 1990: 25, 26.
29. See Wright 1992: 193. *'Ntammaru* in Sicilian means "to mature in vinegar; to marinate; to season," derived from the Arabic *āntamar* or *ṭ'am* or *th'am*—that is, "appetite, food." *'Ntammaru* can also be a condiment; see De Gregorio and Seybold 1903: 243.
30. Apicius 1958: (1) 9, 2.
31. "*Liber de coquina*" 1968: 413.
32. *Libro per cuoco*, in Frati 1899/1970: (lxxx) 44. Carol Field misidentified this work as being from the sixteenth century; Field 1990: 126.
33. Anonimo Meridionale 1985: *Libro B:* no. 8 (p. 36).
34. Especially the works of Professor Maxime Rodinson; see Rodinson 1956; 1990: 31–44; 1971: 479–500; 1949: 95–165; and also Peterson 1980: 317–41.
35. A picture of an antique *bigolo* is reproduced in Bugialli 1988: 209.
36. *Bigoli* is also known as *menuèi*; Boerio 1856; Alberini 1990; Coltro 1983; Da Mosto 1985; Maffioli 1982.
37. Interestingly, one finds the same new peas used in traditional Provençal housewife cookery, called *mange-tout*; see Reboul n.d.: 279. The names *mange-tout, magnatuto*, and *mangiatutto* can also refer to snow pea pods (*Pisum sativum* L. ssp. *sativum* f. *macrocarpon*).
38. Braudel 1982: 202.
39. Faccioli 1987: 77.
40. Cortelazzo and Zolli 1979–88; Stouff 1970: 231; "*Liber de coquina*" 1968: 397; Frati 1899/1970: 25.
41. Waverly Root, who thought this etymology nonsense, was characteristically wrong. The derivation can be drawn as far back as the Greeks, who also fattened pigs and oxen with figs. Horace also spoke of *ficis pastum iecur anseris albi*; Horace 1966: I (8) 88.
42. Braudel 1981: 192.
43. The pluck are the heart, liver, lungs, and windpipe of an animal; Maffioli 1982: 78–80.
44. Montanari 1984: 315; Matazone da Calignano 1960: 794, v. 99–102; Pullan 1971: 278.
45. Giovanni Villani, *The Chronicle of Giovanni Villani*, collected in Lopez and Raymond 1990: 73; Cipolla 1980: 210.
46. Braudel 1981: 212, citing Parenti, 120.
47. Rodinson 1990: 37.
48. Quaglia 1980: 450, 452.
49. *Specie*, which means "spices," refers to many things that we today don't consider spices, such as silk, pharmaceuticals, and other items of trade; Braudel 1982: (2) 98, 140.
50. Braudel 1972–73: (1) 58.

51. Ladurie 1976: 145.
52. See De Gislain 1984: 89–101.
53. Lane 1973: 19.
54. Braudel 1972–73: (1) 220, (2) 762.
55. Baratier 1973: 154.
56. Collier and Billioud 1954: (3) 398. This is nearly forty pounds less than Braudel's estimate for twenty years earlier.
57. Gleijeses, *A Napoli*, 1977: 89.
58. See *timballo di lasagne alla Napoletana* and *lasagne di Giovedì Grasso* in Wright 1995: 44–45, 69.
59. Salmieri 1950; Cortelazzo and Zolli 1979–88.
60. Gleijeses, *A Napoli*, 1977: 21, translation by Carlo De Ieso.
61. Ibid., 24.
62. Pliny, *Natural History*, XVIII, 117; Montanari 1979: 156–57.
63. Cortelazzo and Zolli 1979–88; Root 1971: 182–83; Athenaeus 1969–93: (1) iii, 100–101.
64. Andrews 1984: 3, 23.
65. Braudel 1981: 143.
66. Lazarillo de Tormes 1969: 39.
67. See note 47, page 000.
68. Hamilton 1929: 431.
69. Pike 1962: 370–71.
70. Pike 1966: 20.
71. Argan (*Argania sideroxylon* Roem. et Schult.) is a kind of evergreen from which the oil is extracted. It is edible and used in several Moroccan preparations.
72. Dozy 1881/1991: (1) 126–27; Arberry 1939: 191, 23.
73. Marín 1981: 200–04.
74. Rios and March 1992: 134.
75. Ibid.
76. The Old World contribution to the foods of the *Cucurbitaceae* consists of gourds, cucumber, cantaloupe, cassaba, and watermelon. The squash mentioned by Ruperto de Nola may have been another member of the *Cucurbitaceae*, the bottle gourd (*Lagenaria siceraria* Mol. Standl. syn. *Lagenaria vulgaris* Sér.), which is thought to be native to Africa, although archeological remains have been found in both Peru and Mexico dating from 7000 B.C. (Vavilov believes it has an Indo-Chinese center of origin; 1992: 331). It appears that the seeds of this gourd, which are able to survive salt water for very long periods, floated to the New World; Heiser 1990: 180. Other possibilities are that the squash mentioned here is the bitter gourd (*Momordica charantia* L.), luffa or dishcloth gourd (*Luffa acutangula* Roxb.), or snake gourd (*Trichosanthes anguina* L.). The word *gourd* is also used in English translations of the Bible to refer to a few other plants; Vavilov 1992: 331; Phillips & Rix 1993: 192–93; Moldenke and Moldenke 1952: passim.
77. Wright 1992: 204. The kingdom of Aragon, once it united with Catalonia in 1137, grew into a leading Mediterranean power and gained possession of the Balearic Islands, Sicily, Sardinia, and Naples during the next two centuries.
78. Goitein 1983: (4) 234, the original source being G. Salmon, *Noms de plantes en arabe* . . . (1906), p. 70; Gitlitz and Davidson 1999: 5–6.
79. Wolfert 1973: 97–107; Carrier 1987: 84–86.
80. Dozy 1881/1991: (1) 86; Brunot 1952: (2) 52.
81. Simonet 1975: 426.
82. This notion is reinforced by the *pestelas* of the Yemeni Jews, a sesame seed–topped pastry filled with pine nuts and onion, and delicately flavored, also called *burekas*; see *Encyclopedia Judaica*, S.v. "Food," 1424.
83. Grewe 1992: 146.
84. Paula Wolfert, conversation with the author, January 24, 1997.
85. Paula Wolfert, e-mail correspondence with the author, January 6, 1998. Wolfert had originally misread Laoust, whose "*bestila*" referred not to *basṭīla*, the pigeon pie, but to one of a number of *ṭājins*, stews, that he was describing.
86. Braudel 1991: 114.
87. Roden 1974: 91.
88. Smouha 1955: 47.
89. Palmer 1982: 9.
90. *Encyclopaedia of Islam*, 2nd ed., S.v. "*Ghidā*ᶜ," 1065.
91. Bautier 1984: 44.
92. It is also spelled *b'stila, bisteeya, bistayla, pastilla*, among a few others. The correct transliteration is *basṭīla*.
93. Guiral 1984: 121.
94. Faccioli 1987: 32, 33.
95. Simmonds 1979: 261–62; Tolkowsky 1938: 113ff; Ibn al-ᶜAwwām 1977: (1) 320–22.
96. Simmonds 1979: 222; Watson 1983: 55–57.
97. Simmonds 1979: 245.
98. Watson 1983: 83.
99. Guiral 1984: 119, 120, 121, 123.
100. *Libre de sent soví* 1979: 96 (no. 52); on the etymology of *marzipan* and its relation to Arabic, see Pellegrini 1972: (2) 590–99; Calera 1992: 200.
101. Ashtor 1981: 95.
102. Algozina 1977: 128–32.
103. Ahmad 1975: 88. The contemporary historian of Sicily, Carmelo Trasselli, went so far as to argue that the very spirit of the Renaissance penetrated feudal Sicily through its urban patrician class; Trasselli 1981: 12.
104. Bresc 1986: (2) 586 n.44; also see García Sánchez 1981–82: 151, 151 n.58.
105. da Aleppo and Calvaruso 1910; this etymology was also dismissed by another great Italian etymologist G. Alessio, see Cortelazzo and Zolli 1979.
106. da Aleppo and Calvaruso 1910: 130; de Gregorio and Seybold 1903: 232; Amari 1986: (3), pt. 5, 892 n.2.
107. Archivio di Stato di Palermo, Not. Inc. Sp. 1; 30.1.1409, *in festo Pascatis de Cassatis judeorum*, cited in Bresc 1986: (2) 163.
108. Amari 1986: (3) pt. 5, 919 n.2, 808 n.4; (2), pt. 2, bk. 4, 509, 509 n.6.
109. Abū Marwān ᶜAbd al-Malik b. Zuhr 1992: 49; García Sánchez 1981–82: 151, 151 n.58; Arié: 1974–75: 305.
110. Bresc 1986: (2) 586 n.42.
111. Pellegrini 1972: (1) 203, 206–207.
112. Michele De Vio, *Felicis et fidelissimae urbis Panormitanae selecta aliquot ad civitatis decus et commodum*

spectantia Privilegia (Palermo, 1706), p. 107, quoted in Bresc 1986: (2) 586.

113. Busbecq 1927: 89. See page 327 for more on the Janissaries.
114. Brothwell 1998: 105.
115. Wissa Wassef 1971: 346. Charles Perry is dubious of the Coptic roots of the word; Perry 1993: 48.
116. Professor Janet Abu-Lughod, Graduate Faculty, New School for Social Research, conversation with the author, New York, June 1991. See Professor Abu-Lughod's book on Cairo, published by Princeton University Press. The eccentric mini-debate in *Petits Propos Culinaires*, 43 (1993), a journal for food aficionados published in England, fails to distinguish between *ḥamām* meaning "pigeon" and *ḥammām* meaning "bath," and leads the discussants to all kinds of confusions.
117. *Insight Guides: Egypt* 1989: 58.
118. The other claimant for the oldest university in the world is in the Kairaouine Mosque in Fez, Morocco, completed by 862. The controversy stems from the criteria for a university as distinguished from a theological school.
119. Watson 1983: 95.
120. Tannahill 1973 cites the medieval Arabic recipe for *maghmūma* (also called *muqaṭṭaᶜa*) translated in Arberry 1939: 39–40 as the root of all the Middle Eastern moussakas. The claim does not seem farfetched, although it is pure speculation.
121. Chau Ju-kua 1911: 144.
122. The Mamelukes (Arabic for "slave") were originally slaves in tenth-century Fāṭimid Egypt, trained as soldiers. When they finally replaced the Ayyūbids in 1250, many were already freed.
123. Ashtor 1968: 1051; 1970: 3.
124. Professor Elisabeth Wickett and Hamida Abdel-Magid, conversation with the author, October 6, 1991.
125. Watson 1983: 55–57.
126. Gozzini 1994: 12; Pliny, *Natural History*, Book XII, vii. 15, who is clear in stating that the fruit is not eaten, so it surely is not the lemon. Also see Watson 1983: 42–50.
127. Dalby 1996: 144 repeats the view of Tolkowsky 1938: 100–103, which is strange because he tells the reader that that source is unsound (252 n.34), and although he seems to be aware of the compelling argument against this notion in Zohary and Hopf (1988), he does not go further and seems unaware of the argument in Watson 1983.
128. Watson 1983: 42–50; 167 n.1–171 n.49. On the controversy about the relationship of this work with the Byzantine *Geoponika* of the tenth century, see Watson 1983: 221 n.1.
129. Watson 1983: 46, citing Sarton 1927: (2) 432–33.
130. Ashtor 1968: 1041 claims that the Egyptians, although they knew of the lemon, did not yet know it as a popular and drinkable fruit. But the evidence (in the following note) indicates otherwise.
131. Watson 1983: 46, 169 n.28; Sarton 1927 (1) 468; Goitein 1967: (1) 121, 428 n.42.
132. *Burtuqal* derives from *Portugal*, where it was thought that the first sweet orange entered the Mediterranean. But there is evidence that the sweet orange appears earlier than the usual attribution to Portuguese traders; see note 21 for "An Essay on the Sources."
133. The Sublime Porte, or Bab-i Ali, was so-called by Westerners because the phrase was used in Ottoman documents, referring to the Islamic customary laws of the petitioner waiting by the house, palace, tent, or door (*porte*, from the French) before being received by the sultan or caliph, who would then adjudicate on the issue at hand. On the provisioning of Istanbul, see Güçer 1949–50: 153–62. The provisioning of Istanbul is an old and much researched topic among historians of the Ottoman Empire, and there is a significant literature, much of which is explored in the Güçer article cited above and in Mantran 1965; 1962; and Murphey 1988: 217–63, which review the literature. *Etmek* is an archaic form of *ekmek*, bread.
134. Braudel 1972–73: (1) 350.
135. İnalcık 1960: 145.
136. Murphey 1988: 219; *Encyclopaedia of Islam*, 2nd ed., S.v. "*Maṭbakh.*"
137. Murphey 1988: 229.
138. Mantran 1962: 196.
139. Ḥājib 1983.
140. Ibid., 197 n.1.
141. Mantran 1965: 265.
142. Ibid., 266.
143. See Halil İnalcık's article in *Encyclopaedia of Islam*, 2nd ed. S.v. "*Maṭbakh,*" 809a–813b. The Topkapı Palace kitchens can be visited today. They are on the eastern wall of the Inner Palace. The kitchens were built in three stages from the fifteenth to the sixteenth centuries. Today they house a collection of Chinese porcelain, but the great cauldrons, the *kazan*s, can still be seen.
144. *Encyclopaedia of Islam*, 2nd ed. S.v. "*Maṭbakh.*"
145. Mantran 1962: 189, 190, 192.
146. Ibid., 193.
147. Perry 1994: 89–90.
148. Arsel 1996: 210.
149. *Encyclopaedia of Islam*, 2nd ed. S.v., "*Maṭbakh,*" 809a–813b. The *futuwwa* or *fütüvvet* was a semireligious movement.
150. Algar 1985: 5.
151. Professor Najwa al-Qattan, UCLA, conversation with the author, May 1997.
152. Mantran 1962: 197.
153. Braudel 1986: 42.
154. Mantran 1965: 264; see also page 82 on the introduction of the fork.
155. Mantran 1962: 203.
156. Alberti 1889: 148–49, 160.
157. Mantran 1965: 267.
158. Mantran 1962: 205, 209. Various dates are given for the introduction of coffee. The earliest date for its introduction to Istanbul is 1505; Arsel 1996: 59. McNeill 1974: 302 n.69 suggests 1555 as a date of the introduction of coffee to Istanbul. Hattox 1991:

22–23 points out that coffee was being used in the Yemen in the mid-fifteenth century. Maffioli 1982: 252, without a source, says that coffee came from the Yemen in the fourteenth century, that it appeared in Mecca a century later, in Cairo a century after that where the first coffee house was opened, and in Venice by 1640. This can't be true because coffee is not mentioned in any of the agricultural texts from the Rasūlid period in Yemen (1229–1454); Varisco 1994: 157. Maffioli quotes, again without citation, Gianfranco Morosini, the Venetian diplomat in Constantinople, who informed the Senate in 1585 that the Turks drink a "black water, boiling, that they made from seeds, that they call *cavee* which has the virtue they say of awakening a man." Also see Braudel 1981: 256.

159. Halıcı 1989: 9.
160. Algar 1985: 1. Also see Sabban-Serventi 1989: 29–50.
161. *Shakhshūka* does not appear in either Dozy 1881 1991 or Wehr 1976; see *Contemporary Turkish/ English Dictionary* 1983: 359.
162. Halıcı 1989: 56
163. Bibliothèque Nationale 1908: (I) plate 82. As for Muslim soldiers using their weapons for cooking, I am not familiar with any iconographical or literary evidence. In both Anthony North's *An Introduction of Islamic Arms* (London: HMSO, 1985) and Robert Elgood's *Islamic Arms and Armour* (London: Scolar Press, 1979), there is no mention of weapons being used as cooking utensils, but that in itself is not conclusive evidence that they were not so used.
164. Homer 1996: (3) 37, 73, 519, 528, (14) 484ff.
165. Polo 1993: (1) 17 n.2.
166. Judith E. Tucker, "Revisiting Reform: Women and the Ottoman Law of Family Rights," Internet document, http://sfswww.georgetown.edu/sfs/programs/ccas/asj/tucker.htm, December 4, 1997.
167. Athenaeus 1969–93: (VII) 314e.
168. al-Bakrī 1913: 203.
169. Krekić 1972: 58.
170. Ibid., 106.
171. Ibid., 108.
172. Krekić 1980: I: 40.
173. Krekić 1972: 108.
174. Schwanitz 1967: 54; Phillips & Rix 1993: 33; Watson 1996: 153–55; *Taylor's Guide to Vegetables & Herbs* 1961: 307–08; Harlan 1992: 70; Heiser 1990: 178; Vavilov 1992: 340.
175. Serafino Razzi 1595/1903: 183.
176. Krekić 1972: 109.
177. McNeill 1974: 255 n.8, 56.
178. Krekić 1980: XIX: 376–77.
179. Krekić 1972: 100.
180. Ibid., 103.
181. Ibid., 145.
182. Ibid., 157.
183. Krekić 1961: 96, 103, 317.
184. Ibid., 117.
185. Giacchero 1984: 89.
186. Epstein 1996: 25–26, 113.
187. Ibid., 219.
188. Ibid., 28, 97, 150, 231.
189. Cipolla 1980: 194, 196. A controversy exists among legal scholars and historians about the untranslated term *commenda*.
190. Ibid., 197.
191. The carrack, from the Arabic plural for merchant ship *ququr*, was a sailing ship with many beams, the main mast being quite prominent with a large sail.
192. Epstein 1996: 295.
193. Pike 1962: 370.
194. de Quevedo 1969: 140.
195. Epstein 1996: 102, 267, 268.
196. Accame, Torre, and Pronzati 1994 and Lingua 1989 make no mention of the sociopolitical history of Genoa and cuisine. Andrews 1996 also makes no mention of it. In fact, the Arab influence in Genoa is not well known among food writers, even though the seminal article by G.-B. Pellegrini was written in 1961, "*Contributo allo studio dell'influsso linguistico arabo in Liguria*"; see Pellegrini 1972: (1) 333–400.
197. Epstein 1996: xvi, 16, 98, 319–20.
198. Pike 1962: 349.
199. "Almohad" derives from *al-muwaḥḥadūn*, "those who affirm God's unity."
200. Pike 1962: 355.
201. Ibid., 359.
202. Epstein 1996: 272, 296, 309–11, 308.
203. The two best scholarly works are Patrone 1990 and Balletto 1986.
204. Darrell Corti, conversation with the author, June 18, 1997.

CHAPTER 6

1. Quoted in Purcell 1995: 135.
2. Scappi 1570/1981: 3, cap. LXXXI.
3. Root 1974: 63.
4. Buonassisi 1991: 222.
5. Epstein 1996: 98.
6. George, Athanassiou, and Boulos 1967: 17.
7. Braudel 1972–73: (1) 139.
8. Luján 1988: 56.
9. Faccioli 1987: 773.
10. Defourneaux 1979: 77.
11. Epstein 1996: 98. A tartan is a small one-masted ship with a large lateen sail and a foresail. A shallop was a large, heavy kind of sloop fitted with one or two masts with fore and aft sails. A felucca is a typical small boat of the Nile propelled by oars or a lateen sail and used for coastline voyages. A *caramusali* is the name of a kind of Turkish merchantman. A *scafi* is a light boat, a kind of skiff. A *bargue* is a kind of bark, a three-masted ship with a square-rigged foremast and mainmast and a fore-and-aft rigged mizzenmast. A xebec is derived from the Arabic word *shabbāk,* a kind of fishing boat.
12. Lane 1934: 1.
13. Lane 1934: 37–38.
14. Braudel 1981: 403; for more on the technical development of the lateen rig, also see Lane 1934: 37–38.
15. Ibid., 119. This section is based on Lane's writings.

16. Lane 1973: 120. Occasionally rare portolan charts come on the market for the collector, such as the Francesco Oliva Portolan Chart of the Mediterranean, Messina 1614, that was offered in 1995 for $125,000.
17. Ibid., 120.
18. Lane 1934: 2–3.
19. Ibid., 4–5.
20. Ibid., 6–7.
21. Ibid., 9.
22. Ibid., 10.
23. Ibid., 13.
24. Ibid., 15–16.
25. Ibid., 17–19, 21.
26. Ibid., 19 n.32, 20.
27. Ibid., 21.
28. Ibid., 22, 24–26.
29. Ibid., 27.
30. Ibid., 29–30.
31. Ibid., 37–38.
32. Ibid., 41–44. It has been suggested that the word *carrack* derives from the Arabic words *qarāqīr,* or *ḥarāqa*, meaning "merchant ships"; see *Merriam-Webster's New Collegiate Dictionary, Ninth Edition* (Springfield, MA: Merriam-Webster, 1983) and Pellegrini 1972: (1) 362.
33. Also see Tenenti 1985.
34. Lane 1934: 47–48.
35. Ibid., 72, 74.
36. Ibid., 218, 88–89.
37. Ibid., 143.
38. Ibid., 108.
39. Ibid., 193.
40. Faccioli 1987: 54.
41. Goitein 1971: 10.
42. Archestratus' work is known only in fragments through the writings of Athenaeus. Plato, *Letter*, 7.326b.
43. Edrisi 1866/1968: 126 (107); Brunschvig 1940/1947: (2) 228.
44. Aliquot 1984; Grava 1984.
45. Chantiles 1979: xiii; Kochilas 1990: 134.
46. Athenaeus, 1969–93: (VII), 293.
47. Anonimo Meridionale 1985: *Libro A:* no. 74, (p. 19).
48. *Bouille*, boil, and *peis*, fish. Also see Littré 1881.
49. Davidson 1988: 27; Dauzat, Dubois, and Mitterand 1971.
50. Oliver 1967: 163–87. As far as I know there is no scholarly basis for these extravagant claims.
51. Ibid., 178.
52. David 1962: 298.
53. See Bini 1967–70 for the definitive treatment on most of the fish mentioned in this book.
54. Jacobs 1991: 237.
55. Bosworth 1967: 15; Hitti 1970: 528.
56. Vincent 1975: 451.
57. Dufourcq 1965: 546, 547.
58. Hamilton 1929: 430.
59. Defourneaux 1979: 78.
60. Pike 1962: 359.
61. Hamilton 1929: 431.
62. Ibid., 433.
63. Hémardinquer 1970: 85–86.
64. Hamilton 1929: 435–36.
65. Ibid., 437.
66. Ruperto de Nola 1520/1929.
67. Mittwoch 1933: 89.
68. Hamilton 1929: 437.
69. Ibid., 439.
70. Palmer 1982: 9. See page 294.
71. Hamilton 1929: 439 n.33.
72. Lane 1966: 264.
73. Ibid., 51. The word *mattress* derives from the Arabic word *al-maṭraḥ*, a place where something is thrown, namely a cushion or mat.
74. Ibid., 264–65.
75. Ibid., 265–66.
76. Ibid., 382.
77. Aymard and Bresc 1975: 566.
78. Beck-Bossard 1981: 311–19; Bresc 1986: (1) 261.
79. Giuffrida 1975: 584.
80. Bresc 1986: (1) 261. I am indebted to Dr. W. L. Klawe, chief scientist of the InterAmerican Tropical Tuna Commission, La Jolla, California, for providing a great deal of material on the tuna.
81. Bresc 1986: (1) 261, 263 n.4; and Mary Taylor Simeti, conversation with the author, Palermo, Sicily, August 1989.
82. Bresc 1986: (1) 262 n.54.
83. Aymard and Bresc 1975: 562.
84. Bresc 1986: (1) 261.
85. Ibid., 261–62.
86. Ibid., 262.
87. Archestratus fragment 34 in Athenaeus 1969–93: (VII), 314.
88. Pliny, *Natural History*, bk. XXXII, vi. 16–17.
89. Corominas 1980.
90. Bresc 1986: (1) 261.
91. Agius 1986: 37–51.
92. Bresc 1986: (1) 262, 262 n.54.
93. Ibid., 263.
94. Redon, Sabban, and Servanti 1991: 22.
95. Lentini 1987: 32, 33.
96. Bresc 1986: (1) 262.
97. Ibid., 269, 270.
98. Ibid., 265, 268, 262 n.50.
99. Ibid., 268.
100. Ibid., 269–73.
101. The literature on the history of tuna fishing in Sicily is larger than one would expect. The standard introduction is Lentini 1987. Researchers can look at the notes in Consolo 1987 for more information.
102. Athenaeus 1969–93: (VII) 302.
103. Amari 1880–81: 41, 42.
104. al-Bakrī 1965: 89. Al-Idrīsī in the twelfth century also describes good fishing in Sfax and Bizerte; Edrisi 1866/1968: 126 (107) and 134 (115).
105. Edrisi 1866/1968: 126 (107). Fishing had been an important industry in Roman Tunisia as well, as we know from Pliny the Younger, *Letters*, IX, 33, and the magnificent Roman mosaics in the Bardo Museum in Tunis and the Sousse Museum.
106. Brunschvig 1940/1947: (2) 228.

107. Edrisi 1866/1968: 134 (115).
108. Talbi 1954: 297.
109. Goitein 1983: (4) 250–51; 1967: (1) 430 n.86.
110. Ashtor 1968: 1033; Canard 1959: 121.
111. George, Athanassiou, and Boulos 1967: 1.
112. Goitein 1967: (1) 126–27.
113. Reported by Ibn Ḥawqal, in Canard 1959: 121.
114. Braudel 1986: 37.
115. Goitein 1967: (1) 126.
116. Dr. Haniya Baha ad-Din, conversation with the author, Alexandria, Egypt, October 1991.
117. Najwa al-Qattan, conversation with the author, Kuwait, December 1980.
118. Goitein 1967: (1) 126.
119. Sal Fantasia, conversation with the author, Cambridge, MA, November 1989.
120. "Lent," Britannica Online. <http://www.eb.com:180/cgi-bin/g?DocF=micro/344/43.html>.
121. Collier and Billioud 1954: (3) 401–402, 403.
122. Baratier 1973: 154.
123. Guiral 1984: 121.
124. Stouff 1996: 155, 149.
125. Anonimo Meridionale 1985: *Libro A*: no. 74 (p. 19); Frati 1899/1970: 8.
126. Stouff 1996: 205.
127. Grava 1984: 155.
128. Stouff 1996: 146–48, 156–57.
129. Redon, Sabban, and Servanti 1991: 34; Menjot 1984: 203.
130. Ladurie 1976: 56, 58, 60.
131. Scully 1988: 201.
132. Ibid., 104, 119, 121, 124, 135, 143; Baratier 1973: 154.
133. Faber 1883: 99, 151.
134. Lane 1973: 60.
135. Faber 1883: 151. See page 176 for the *bottarga* recipe.
136. Ibid., 151, 153.
137. Cecchetti 1885: pt. 1 (2), 86, 97.
138. Faccioli 1987: 87.
139. Scappi 1570/1981: (III), cap. LXII, 117. I've translated *melangole* as "pomegranate," although it may mean "oranges."
140. The herbs are probably parsley, basil, marjoram, and one other, while the spices could mean salt, pepper, saffron, and nutmeg. *Liber de coquina* excerpts in Faccioli 1987: 39.
141. Martinez Sopena and Carbajo Serrano 1984: 339.
142. Lladonosa i Giró 1984: 58.
143. See page 421.
144. Menjot 1984: 203.
145. Malpica Cuello 1984: 103–117.
146. Caster 1962: 341.
147. Hamilton 1929: 436.
148. Abū Marwān ʿAbd al-Malik b. Zuhr 1992: 63, 66.
149. Vincent 1975: 452.
150. *Kitāb al-ṭabīkh fī al-Maghrib wa'l-Āndalus* 1961–62: 40.
151. Clara Ma. G. de Amezúa, conversation with the author, Seville, Spain, October 1992.
152. Caracausi 1983: 106 *Arangium: Videas ibi est lumias acetositate sua saporandis.*
153. Faccioli 1987: 198.
154. Arberry 1939: 40–41.
155. Hamilton 1929: 431.
156. Rios and March 1992: 150; Corominas 1967: 43.
157. Stouff 1996: 144, 145; Caster 1962: 313.
158. Stouff 1970: 202, 212.
159. Faber 1883: 148.
160. Pryor 1988.
161. Abel 1980: 39.
162. A continental shelf is the shallow part of the seafloor adjacent to and surrounding the land. The biological resources of an ocean are ultimately related to the production of organic matter by plants. The shallow waters of continental shelves have high production rates of organic matter because of a high nutrient content and sunlight for photosynthesis, and therefore are a place where fish congregate. Many shelf areas are abundant in nutrients because of upwelling, which brings deep, nutrient-rich waters to the surface so that phytoplankton that the fish feed on have high levels of nutrients to use for photosynthesis. The area off Newfoundland is unique, though, because it is not an upwelling region. Newfoundland has high phytoplankton production of organic material >500mgC/m2/d (milligrams of carbon per square meter per day) off its northeast continental shelf. It's not known for sure why, but an educated guess is that the high biological production is the result of enhanced vertical mixing at the shelf's edges, resulting in an enhanced flux of nutrients over the sides of the shelf. The freshwater discharge from the St. Lawrence watershed into the Gulf of St. Lawrence and Scotian Shelf, which can be considered an extended estuarine shelf system along with the inshore and offshore branches of the Labrador Current, play an important role in controlling the circulation of nutrient-rich waters in this region; Sheila Griffin, Department of Earth Systems Science, University of California, Irvine, e-mail correspondance with the author, January 4, 1999.
163. *Baccalà*, from Old Dutch and *stoccafisso* from the Middle Dutch through the Norwegian. See Cortelazzo and Zolli 1979–88 and *Oxford English Dictionary* 1971.
164. Braudel 1981: 218.
165. Faccioli 1987: 190.
166. Colman Andrews, e-mail communication with the author, April 1, 1997.
167. Martí i Oliver 1989: G, 125, 243.
168. "Octopus," Britannica Online, <http://www.eb.com:180/cgi-bin/g?DocF=micro/434/69.html>.
169. Caster 1962: 277, 313, 27 n.80 (Antonio Petino studied saffron in the Abruzzi at the end of the Middle Ages; earlier in time it had been grown elsewhere, such as Arab Sicily), 319, 325, 320 n.73.
170. Ibid., 320, 320 n.73; *Libre de sent soví* 1979: ap. I, 57.
171. Morize 1914: 313–448.
172. Braudel 1982: 534.
173. Ladurie 1976: 81.
174. Andrews 1988: 142.
175. Dante 1986: 128–29.

176. Anonimo Meridionale 1985: *Libro A*: no. 67 (pp. 17–18).
177. Field 1990: 482.
178. Pliny, *Natural History*, bk. IX, 189–193; Apicius, 1969: bk. IX, v; Faccioli 1987: 37.
179. Sparkes 1995: 153 misinterprets this device, calling it a fish trap.
180. Braudel 1981: 215.
181. Cecchetti 1885: 97, 189.
182. *Libre de sent soví* 1979: recipe 196, 202–03; "*Liber de coquina*" 1968: 415–16; Faccioli 1987: 62.
183. "*Liber de coquina*" 1968: 416.
184. Guerrini 1887: recipe 34.
185. Pellegrini 1972: (1) 353. Andrews 1996: 11 implies that the Genoese are responsible for this etymological interpretation, but to my knowledge the scholars who work in this area of neolatin etymology are professional academic linguists, not all of whom are Italian, let alone Genoese, and who presumably adhere to the canons of objective scholarship.
186. Platina 1998: 427.
187. Aristophanes 1971: 49.
188. Athenaeus 1969–93: (III) 108.
189. Monchicourt 1913a: 76.
190. "Barbary pirate," Britannica Online, <http://www.eb.com:180/cgi-bin/g?DocF=micro/51/51.html>.
191. Dufourcq 1965: 85 (text in archives from Jaime II, October 15, 1325).
192. Monchicourt 1913a: 76.
193. Braudel 1972–73: (2) 867.
194. Dufourcq 1978: 174.
195. Abulafia 1984: 14.
196. Braudel 1972–73: (2) 880.
197. Gozzini 1994: 12.

CHAPTER 7

1. Author's translation, Goethe 1982: 240.
2. Theodore Tsatis, conversation with the author, Rhodes, Greece, October 1994.
3. Patrone 1981: 158, 358.
4. See Argenti 1958.
5. Ibid., (3) 477.
6. Finlay 1856: 86, 85. Also see Argenti 1958: 482, 503.
7. Finlay 1856: 91. Aglaia Kremezi, conversation with the author, October 1994. During a research trip, Ms. Kremezi discovered preparations such as tragacanth (*Astragalus creticus*) or *Parnassi dragante*, sweets that might have some Venetian connection. Her research was subsequently published as part of the Oxford Symposium on Food in 1995.
8. Kochilas 1990: 270; Dalby 1996: 181.
9. Ahmad 1975: 88. The contemporary historian of Sicily, Carmelo Trasselli, went so far as to argue that the very spirit of the Renaissance penetrated feudal Sicily through its urban patrician class; Trasselli 1981: 12.
10. Koenigsberger 1951: 73.
11. Ibid., 79.
12. Aymard and Bresc 1975: 565 referring to documents from 1371. Dining out or taking out food was not typical among the Jews. The Talmud denounced those who dined out (Pesachim, 49b); see Abrahams 1981: 143.
13. Ahmad 1975: 38.
14. Pinder-Wilson 1976: 74 n.9.
15. The earliest descriptions are in Ibn Ḥawqal (writing c. 988). A rich, untapped, source for the history of the kitchen garden in Sicily is the *Adamo Citella* (1299–1300) in the Archivio Communale di Palermo, cited in Bresc 1986: (1) 26. Also see Amari 1986: (3) iii, 872; Sturtevant 1919: 339–40.
16. Bresc 1986: (2) 162. Epstein 1992 argues against Bresc and the historical orthodoxy that Sicily's decline is rooted in the wars between the Angevins and Aragonese in the fourteenth century. Epstein argues that the plagues were the decisive factor, leading to a rise in wages, lower rents (impoverishing the lesser aristocrats), and an increase in productivity as lands reverted to pasturage. Epstein argues that neither wars nor exploitation by foreign merchants was the principal cause of Sicily's pauperization, but shows how there was interregional fluctuation in the fortunes of Sicilians affected by government regulation, taxes, climate, and so forth.
17. In Sicily, the principal olives are the *ogliaro*, grown mainly in Palermo and Messina, the *neba* or *zaituni* (from the Arabic word for olive) in the Syracuse region, the *di Termini* or *Calamignara*, grown around Termini Imerese, Catania, and Syracuse, the *caltabellottese*, grown around that town, and the *cerasuolo*, found near Alcamo, Trapani, and Calatifimi. See Francolini 1923: 55.
18. Aymard and Bresc 1975: 565.
19. Bresc 1986: (2) 163.
20. Pellegrini 1972: (1) 73, 138, 281; Caracausi 1983: 400–402.
21. Athenaeus 1969–93 (IV) 147; (I) 27d. Cheese making is also mentioned by a number of Roman writers, but the Roman man of letters, Varro (116–27? B.C.), seems clear in his *De re rustica* that one uses rennet to make cheese, which of course is not necessarily the case in the making of ricotta; Varro 1993: (II) xi.
22. Professor Santi Correnti, University of Catania, interview with the author, Torre Archirafi, Sicily, July 1989.
23. The Latin translation was done at the court of the Sicilian king Manfred, son of Frederick II, in Palermo in the mid- to late thirteenth century and is now held in the Bibliothèque Nationale in Paris.
24. Giuffrida 1975: 583–84.
25. Ibid.
26. Trasselli 1981: 21.
27. Waern 1910: 77–83; De Candolle 1885: 219–20; Goitein 1971: 15.
28. Dante 1986: 118–120.
29. Correnti 1976–85.
30. Pomar 1988: 76.
31. He also states that the fruit is edible; Watson 1983: 70, 179 n.2.
32. Watson 1983: 70–71; Bresc 1972: 73 n.2. The suggestion by Del Conte 1987: 173 that the eggplant was known in eleventh-century Sicily is not supported by any evidence, although it may be true.

33. Heiser 1990: 182; Caracausi 1983: 287; Pellegrini 1972: (1) 193; Cortelazzo and Zolli 1979–88: (3) 737.
34. George Duby linked the increase of stock raising in France at the end of the thirteenth century to "the growing demand for meat, leather and wool originating in the cities"; Wallerstein 1974: 109 n.153.
35. Giuffrida 1975: 590.
36. Stouff 1970: 192.
37. Cohen 1989: 56. The figure for Rome comes from Braudel.
38. Because there were fewer people alive to work they were able to bargain for better pay. The plague was transmitted by fleas inhabiting rats, and when people shopped for food they sought deratted food. Traditionally, there was a proportional relationship between what they were paid and the price of deratted food, such as uncontaminated grain and meat. But rats ate from and contaminated grain stores and not meat. Logically, meat consumption among a decimated population now receiving higher salaries and fearful of contaminated grain increased with the greater availability and relative safety of meat; Giuffrida 1975: 593.
39. Aymard and Bresc 1975: 563.
40. Montanari 1994a: 76–77.
41. Cancila 1983: 59 n.39.
42. Braudel 1972–73: (1) 382.
43. Fois 1984; 184; Perisi 1989: 103–105.
44. Fois 1984: 185.
45. Ibid., 185–87.
46. Andrews 1988: 8. Corominas claims it derives from the Mozarab without mention of the Arabic; Corominas 1980: 615.
47. Star-gazer is known as *pesce prete* in Italian, while *salici* might be Sardinian dialect for ray or maybe blenny; see Davidson 1981: 134; weever is *aragno* and *salema* is a kind of bream.
48. Fois 1984: 189.
49. Also known in Corsica as *lonza*.
50. Morris 1980: 113–14.
51. Hopkins 1977: 103, 114.
52. Chatto and Martin 1987: 32.
53. al-Bakrī 1913/1965: 117.
54. Vincent 1975: 449.
55. Runciman 1958.
56. This is far from a settled matter. Although Redhouse seems pretty clear on the Turkish, both the sources used by Dozy, Shaw's *Reizen door Barbarijen* (Utrecht, 1773) and Beaussier, *Dictionnaire pratique arabe-français* (Algier, 1871) do not mention any Turkish etymology. Paula Wolfert, conversation with the author, December 10, 1993, and January 25, 1997, who reports that one of the folkloric explanations for the word is onomatopoeic, that the spiciness of the *lablābī* is such that it leads one to make the same noise as the ram in coitus.
57. George Lucas used Matmata as a site for some opening scenes in the movie *Star Wars*. Some of the *kasr*s have been turned into tourist inns.
58. Brunschvig 1940/1947: (1), 269, 220.
59. Martí i Oliver 1989: 188; Ripoll 1984: 16.
60. Brunschvig 1940/1947: (2) 156, 272 n.7, 218–19, 219, 271 n.4, 273, 220, 273, 221.
61. Quoted in Braudel 1982: 30.
62. Wright 1992: 73.

CHAPTER 8

1. Norman 1990: 10–11.
2. Crone 1987: 8, 10.
3. Ibid., 37, 261.
4. Ibid., 38, 42.
5. Ibid., 51, 71.
6. Braudel 1981: 130. The statement by Scully 1995: 9 that the medieval diet was not monotonous is false unless qualified to mean only the food available to the richest.

   I cannot agree with the claim made by Barbara Santich, in *The Original Mediterranean Cuisine: Medieval Recipes for Today*, that spices were not used to counteract the monotony of the diet. Her claim that the medieval diet was dominated by salted meats and fish is entirely incorrect. The diet was dominated by inferior grains and vegetables of the *Cruciferae* family, not by protein-laden foods, except during the period immediately after the Black Death. It's true, though, that because of the expense, the spices used in such abundance were consumed by the rich (until the introduction of New World chili peppers). The poor continued to have monotonous food; Santich 1995: 30.
7. McNeill 1974: 255 n.8. The section on medieval spices in Heyd 1959 is a good introduction to spices. But this edition, which is the only one I had access to, is a very inaccurate translation of *Geschichte des Levantehandels im Mitelalter*. The Leipzig edition of 1923 is better. Also see Lopez and Raymond 1990: 109, which reproduces Francesco di Balduccio Pegolotti's list of spices from *The Practice of Commerce* from 1310–1340. Also see Braudel 1981: 220; Montanari 1984: 315; Patrone 1981: 142, 144.
8. Frati 1899/1970: 2–3. Spices were measured by the light pound, equal to 0.66 English pounds. My reasoning is based on the weight estimates made in Lane 1934, app. I, 245, 245n.1, 249–51. Scully 1995: 84 incorrectly argues that spice use in noble medieval cookery was not huge as he offers only one source as an example.
9. Ashtor 1976: 567, 569; Lane 1966: 29. Madelein Pelner Cosman, in *Fabulous Feasts: Medieval Cookery and Ceremony*, is completely wrong to suggest that spices were used in "sparing amounts" in medieval cookery; Cosman 1976: 47. Santich explains this spice use as being in conformity with time-honored traditions going back to the ancient world, but there is simply no evidence for that position; Santich 1992: 31.
10. Peterson 1980: 317–41.
11. Braudel 1981: 221.
12. Cited in Peterson 1980: 318.
13. Montanari 1994a: 60–61.
14. *Goodman of Paris* 1393/1928: 248. The Power translation is an abridgement. Jacobs 1975: 63 is wrong in implying that fresh meat was not available.

15. Montanari 1994a: 61–62.
16. Ibid., 62.
17. Braudel 1981: 221.
18. Stouff 1970: 106ff.
19. Stouff 1970: 261, 259.
20. Pliny, *Natural History*, XIX, 112–113; Millo 1984: 20; Andrews 1988: 30.
21. Although Sicily was once known for its saffron export, by the fifteenth century there was no mention of saffron in the documents; Caster 1962: 277, 313, 278 n.80 (Antonio Petino studied saffron in the Abruzzi at the end of the Middle Ages; earlier in time it had been grown elsewhere, such as Arab Sicily), 319, 325, 320 n.73.
22. Braudel 1982: 168.
23. Caster 1962: 281, 363.
24. Laurioux 1985: 46.
25. Martha Rose Shulman, conversation with the author, December 22, 1997.
26. Stecchetti 1884: 45. The spices called for in this recipe might have been a concoction of cinnamon, nutmeg, salt, and pepper.
27. Contini 1988: 133.
28. Lane 1973: 71.
29. Crone 1987: 70–71.
30. Lieber 1968: 230, using G. C. Torrey, *The Commercial Technical Terms in the Koran* (Leyden, 1892).
31. Madan, Kapur, and Gupta 1966.
32. The first tomato to reach Italy was a yellow tomato called *pomi d'oro*, apple of gold, transformed into *poma amoris*, apple of love. There is speculation that the word might derive from *pomi di moro*, Moorish apple, following the belief that its introduction was associated with the Arabs. The early tomato fruits seen by Europeans were also orange, pink, green, and red. Also see Wilson 1981: (7)16.
33. Guerrini 1887: 33.
34. Aliquot 1984: 132.
35. Caster 1962: 363.
36. Ibid., 366–67.
37. Ibid., 367–68.
38. The records for the spice trade are enormous—for example, the notary archives of the Haute-Garonne has a full four-year record (1531–1535) of the sales made by the grocer Nicolas Guerrier; Caster 1962: 368, 372, 375; Lane 1966: 27 n.8.
39. Wehr 1976; Dozy 1881/1991: (1) 141.
40. Unpublished recipe, Paula Wolfert for International Olive Oil Council, Foodcom, Inc. New York, NY, 1993.
41. Skhiri 1968: 23.
42. Daniel 1979: 317–18; Hitti 1970: 555–56.
43. Wolfert 1973: 25.
44. There are many varieties of "mixed spices," such as *āfāḥ,* a spice mix from Djerid in the governate of Gabes, Tunisia, comprising coriander seed, caraway, cumin, aniseed, cinnamon, rose petals, turmeric, red pepper, dried garlic, cloves, black pepper, and gall. Gall is also known as oak apple, an excrescence caused mostly on oak trees by the insects of the genus *Cynips*. Gall is used in medicine and for tannin, an astringent complex phenolic substance of plant origin used for dyeing; see Kouki 1971: 568.
45. Lane 1973: 287.
46. The yards are long spars tapered toward the ends to support the head of a sail; Lane 1973: 71.
47. Lane 1973: 71. The notion that European merchants in the Levant lived as closed communities, separate from the native population, has been challenged by Congdon 1994: 19–20, who argues that there was a good deal of intercommunal cooperation, in contradistinction to the argument made in various works by E. Ashtor (see Bibliography).
48. *Traduccion española de un manuscrito anónimo del siglo XIII* 1966: 21.
49. Cook 1979: 227.
50. *Contemporary Turkish-English Dictionary* 1983: 359.
51. Nacim Zeghlache, conversation with the author, Cambridge, MA, July 1992.
52. Dozy 1881/1991: (1) 741.
53. Charles Perry suggests a similarity with the Greek *halmyros*, "briny," or perhaps Persian influences given the use of Persian words in some medieval recipes. Perry goes on to point out that the *Kitāb waṣf al-aṭᶜima al-muᶜtāda*, compiled by Muḥammad ibn al-Ḥasan al-Baghdādī about 1226, has recipes for both Byzantine-style *murri* and North African *murri*; Perry 1981b: 103 n.5. Although Perry doesn't mention it, I believe the Latin derivation is clear from its use in Cato, who says *oleas orcites, posias; eae optime conduntur vel virides in muria* . . . (of, olives, the orcite and posea, which are excellent when preserved green in brine . . .); Cato, *On Agriculture*, vii and lxxxviii. *Al-murri* also is mentioned in the twelfth-century manual by Abū Marwān ᶜAbd al-Malik b. Zuhr 1992: 55, and the anonymous seventeenth-century medical glossary *Tuḥfat al-aḥbāb. Glossaire de la matière médicale marocaine*, H. P. J. Renaud and G. Colin, eds. and trans. (Paris 1934), no. 386, p. 167.
54. Lane 1966: 33.
55. Braudel 1981: 222. The statement in Scully 1995: 205 that pepper lost favor in aristocractic cooking and was replaced by grains of paradise is incorrect. Grains of paradise became a pepper substitute not because of taste but because of a classic supply and demand economy.
56. *Beledi* (ginger native to the west coast of India, from the Arabic "country-style" or "common"), *micchino* (ginger having passed through the Mecca spice market), and *colombino* (from the name of the port of Kulam in the princely state of Travancore on India's southwestern coast along the Arabian Sea, in today's Kerala state); see Ashtor 1980: 758; Scully 1988: 241.
57. Guinaudeau 1962: 115, Guinaudeau-Franc 1981: 122. *Qidra* refers to the earthenware *marmite* itself, similar to the Spanish *olla*; see Dozy 1881/1991: (2) 321. Der Haroutunian 1985: 26.
58. Laoust 1920: 79 n.3.
59. Paula Wolfert, conversation with the author, October 1994.
60. Dozy 1881–1991: (1) 410. Although al-Maqqarī was writing in the seventeenth century, he is generally rec-

ognized as being reliable for details of the earlier period of Islamic Spain.

61. Braudel 1991: 114.
62. Contini 1988: 6.
63. Patrone 1981: 158, 167, 439, 171–76.
64. The evidence comes from many sources, including the October 1564 report of a Portuguese spy that this traffic is 25,000 quintals (1,400 tons) of pepper.
65. Braudel 1972–73: (1) 551; Ashtor 1976: 567, 569; Lane 1966: 29.
66. Lane 1966: 26–27.
67. The *tercio* is a tactical combat formation developed to solve the problem that medieval combat formations faced with the increasing use of firearms and artillery. It was formed of three *colunelas* or columns of about 1,000 men each. A *cabo de colunela* or colonel commanded each column, which evolved into the modern battalion or regiment, while the *tercio* became the modern division.
68. Sereni 1997: 181.
69. Cipolla 1980: 222.
70. Lieber 1968: 232, 239, 239 n.1.
71. Zambrini 1863: 45–46.
72. Rodinson 1990: 31. For the last three mentioned dishes, see Zambrini 1863: 35, 72; and Frati 1899/1970: 48.
73. Rodinson 1989: 19.
74. "*Liber de coquina*" 1968: 407.
75. *Early English Recipes Selected from the Harleian Ms. 279 of about 1430 A.D.* (Cambridge: Cambridge University Press, 1937).
76. Alazdi 1902: 40.
77. Maxime Rodinson's article on *ma'mūniyya* has been translated into English, and he covers the problems of etymology quite thoroughly there. There is another recipe for *"mahmuniyya"* from an unpublished book of the fifteenth century, the *Zahr al-ḥadīqa* . . . by Aḥmad ibn Mubarākshah Shihāb al-Dīn, which is known from a manuscript in the library of Gotha, Germany; see Rodinson 1989: 17, 18.
78. "Un libro de cocina del siglo XIV" 1935: 177.
79. Poliakov 1961: (2) 180.
80. Braudel 1972–73: (1) 52.
81. al-Rāzī 1953: 82.
82. Grewe 1992: 145; *Traduccion española de un manuscrito anónimo del siglo XIII* 1966: 183–84.
83. Rios 1984: 19–28.
84. Ibn al-ʿAwwām 1977: (2) 242–44.
85. Corominas 1967: 524.
86. Wallerstein 1974: 42.

CHAPTER 9

1. Berger 1985: 124–5.
2. Montanari 1994a: 104–105.
3. Montanari 1984: 307. In note 3, there is an example of a labor contract from 1201 concerning the *decimam de pane* in the Archivio di Stato di Modena, Monastero di San Pietro, VI, 2.
4. Martinez Sopena and Carbajo Serrano 1984: 337.
5. Bautier 1984: 33, 34. In Sicily alone there are hundreds of breads, many of which are detailed in a wonderful book by Antonio Uccello, called *Pani e dolci di sicilia* (Palermo: Sellerio, 1976).
6. Uccello 1976.
7. Pellegrini 1972: (1) 204, 206; Braccini 1979: 42–87 argues for a German etymology for the word *pizza*.
8. Morelli 1956: 234. Giovanni di Pagolo Morelli's chronicle is from 1393–1421.
9. Montanari 1984: 308–309.
10. Ibid., 309.
11. Panic, or foxtail millet (*panicum*), was an important cereal grass of the Middle Ages. Also see Montanari 1984: 310. The origins of buckwheat (*Fagopyrum sagittatum* or F. *Esculentum*) were long thought to be in central Asia, somewhere between Lake Baikal and Manchuria. Recent research now leans toward southwest China and the Himalayan region as the center of origin (see Ohmi Ohnishi, "Search for the Wild Ancestor of Buckwheat. III. The Wild Ancestor of Cultivated Common Buckwheat, and of Tartary Buckwheat," *Economic Botany*, 52, no. 2 (1998), pp. 123–33). It is considered a cereal although it does not belong to the same *Gramineae* family. Buckwheat is known as *grano saraceno* in Italian and *sarrasin* in French, leading the late food writer Waverly Root to assume its Arab or Muslim origins. But the term "Saracen" was used by Europeans of the Middle Ages to describe many things that simply came from the East, whether they were known to be Arab or not. According to the contemporary Italian botanist Valerio Giacomini, who has made a thorough study of buckwheat, there are three possible ways buckwheat arrived in Europe: the first route goes through southern Russia, Poland, and Germany, reaching Belgium and France where buckwheat appears; the second runs through Turkey to Greece, Hungary, and southern Russia; and the third through the maritime contacts of Venice, which might explain in part the ascription of "Saracen." In any case, the origin of buckwheat is unknown even if its name in Latin languages suggests an Arab provenance. There is a legend that Joost van Gistele brought it back with him from his journey to the Holy Land in 1485. The Arab, and even central Asian, origin has been contradicted by recent archeological research. It has come to light through pollen analysis that buckwheat grew in the Netherlands and northwest Germany long before the beginning of our era. The first documentary evidence is of four *malder boicweyts* supplied in 1394 in Middelaar, near Mook (Netherlands) to the Duke of Gelre (Silcher). This date is the earliest documentary evidence we have for buckwheat in Europe; see Slicher van Bath 1963: 264; Root 1980: 39–40; Bianchini and Corbetta 1976: 28–29.
12. Ashtor 1968: 1020.
13. Cohen 1989: 99.
14. Ashtor 1968: 1020. The medieval Middle Eastern diet was characterized by the predominance of wheat, that is, "white" bread. In the European Mediterranean bread was usually made with bran or inferior flours. The famous Arab doctor al-Rāzī (d. 925) mentions

that bread made with flour that is not cleaned of bran *(nukhālah)* provokes melancholy and, therefore, he warns against bread with the bran. Ibn Jazla said unleavened bread was less nourishing than bread made of the best flour. Hibatallāh ibn Jumai[c] (d. 1198), the private doctor to Saladin, recommended eating only white bread; Ibn Riḍwān 1984: 90 n.8.

15. Rodinson 1949: 133, 136.
16. Ibid., 136.
17. Cancila 1983: 207, 61, 207. The reasons for the rise of Sicilian pauperism is debated by historians. The French historian Henri Bresc (see Bresc 1986, vols. 1 and 2) argues that Sicily's decline is rooted in the wars between the Angevins and Aragonese in the fourteenth century. Stephan Epstein (see Epstein 1992) argues that the plagues were the decisive factor, leading to a rise in wages, lower rents (impoverishing the lesser aristocrats), and an increase in productivity as lands reverted to pasturage. Epstein argues that neither wars nor exploitation by foreign merchants were the principal cause of Sicily's pauperization, but shows how there was interregional fluctuation in the fortunes of Sicilians affected by government regulation, taxes, climate, and so forth.
18. Cipolla 1980: 27, 28, 28 n.43; Braudel 1981: 133.
19. "*Liber de coquina*" 1968: 409; *Libre de sent soví* 1979: 224.
20. *Goodman of Paris* 1928: 245, 276.
    A cook they hadde with him for the nones,
    to boille the chiknes with the mary-bones,
    And poudre-marchant tart, and galingale.
    Wel coude he knowe a draughte of London ale.
    He coude roste, and sethe, and broille, and frye,
    Maken mortreux, and wel bake a pye.
    —Chaucer, *Prologue, Canterbury Tales*, 384.
21. Rodinson 1949: 134.
22. The reference can be found in A. J. Wensinck, *Concordance et indices de la tradition musulmane: Les six livres, le musnad al-darimi, le muwatta de Malik, le musnad de Ahmad ibn Hanbal*, 2nd ed. (Leiden: E. J. Brill, 1992), vol. 1, p. 290.
23. *Encyclopaedia of Islam*, 2nd ed., S.v. *"Ghidā[c]."* Crone 1987: 109, 112.
24. Agius 1984: 271–73.
25. Wolfert 1973: 119; Guinaudeau 1962: 57, 157.
26. Professor Dionysius Agius, correspondence with the author, June 13, 1994.
27. Bérard 1896: 103.
28. Field 1990: 493; Sada 1994: 37; Middione 1987: 64; Arberry 1939: 25, 25 n.1. The twelfth-century Italian dietetic manual *Liber de ferculis et condimentis*, which was translated from the Arabic, has a recipe *sanbasuc* that would certainly lend plausibility to this theory; see Rodinson 1971: 492 n.63 (the *Liber de ferculis et condimentis* manuscript is in the Bibliothèque Nationale, Paris, Ms. Latin 9328, f. 159v.).
29. Alberini 1990: 69.
30. See de Biberstein Kazimirski 1960: (1) 533; Traina 1890; Pellegrini 1972: (1) 204; ʿAbd el Wahab Pacha 1951: 76.
31. A recipe can be found in Wright 1992: 70.
32. Vidossi 1960: 317, 317 n.57. This practice is rooted in Greek Sicily, see Athenaeus 1969–93: (XIV) 647.
33. Marinoni 1955; Pellegrini 1972: (1); Pasqualino 1785; Amari 1986: (3), pt. 5.
34. Arberry 1939: 25–26.
35. Ibid., 25, 25 n.1.
36. Rodinson 1971: 492 n.63.
37. *Traduccion española de un manuscrito anónimo del siglo XIII* 1966: 242.
38. Bolens 1990: 160. Ayla Algar points out that the etymology of the word *börek* is uncertain. She refers to an account that attributes the invention of the *börek* to Bugra Khan (d. 994), a ruler of eastern Turkistan; see Algar 1985: 2. Also see note 67, page 739.
39. Braudel 1972–73: (1) 422.
40. Romano 1956. Also see Romano 1953: (2) 149–56.
41. Braudel 1972–73: (1) 423.
42. Boissonade 1905: 332.
43. Ladurie 1976: 45.
44. Teissier 1869: 54.
45. Cecchetti 1885: pt. 1 (2), 5.
46. Braudel 1972–73: (1) 598.
47. Sereni 1997: 381–82.
48. It has been argued that Braudel overestimated the consumption of grain—still it was huge. See Murphey 1988: 229, 254 n.47.
49. One must be careful in using Arabic dictionaries for root meanings because words often have multiple root meanings and therefore one must know the context.
50. Rodinson 1949: 107, 134 n.1, 136 n.1, 153, 153 n.3; Arberry 1939: 190, 195.
51. Wolfert 1994: 261–64 lists fifty varieties.
52. This *kubbaybī* is related to earlier types of meatball preparations that might have medieval roots. A number of Arabic cookbooks published in the nineteenth and early twentieth centuries are said by Maxime Rodinson to share certain character traits with the cookery of the Middle Ages. The sixth edition of one in particular, published in Beirut in 1885, called *Tadhkirat al-khawātin wa'l-ustādh al-ṭabbākhīn* has a chapter called *kubayba*, which consists of recipes for ground meat mixed with bulgur; Rodinson 1949: 106–107.
53. Today the Egyptian government encourages the use of *farīk* as more nutritious than rice and adaptable to Egyptian soil and farming techniques. Rice, which has to be imported, is a drain on Egypt's foreign currency reserves. In Tunisia today, "*farīk*" is also used to refer to young barley.
54. Arberry 1939: 46.
55. The rice spoken of in this book is Asiatic rice (*Oryza sativa* L.) and not African rice (*O. glaberrima* Steud.), which has been cultivated in West Africa for several millennia.
56. Alberini 1990: 77. Rice may very well have been grown earlier in northern Italy since we do have references to its cultivation in thirteenth-century Roussillon, to the west; see Watson 1983: 156 n.19.
57. Cipolla 1980: 72.
58. Watson 1983: 15–19.
59. Ashtor 1968: 1018; Canard 1959: 118.

60. Ashtor 1968: 1018; Ibn al-ʿAwwām 1977: (2) 60–61.
61. Canard 1959: 125.
62. Ibid., 129.
63. Corominas notes that rice was grown in the southeast of the Iberian Peninsula in the seventh century, when the area was under Byzantine rule. He does not provide any sources for the claim though, see Corominas 1980: (1) 431.
64. Messedaglia 1974: (1) 136.
65. Quiqueran de Beaujeu, *La Provence louée*, pp. 329, 333, cited in Collier and Billioud 1954: (3) 390.
66. Braudel 1981: 110.
67. *Encyclopaedia of Islam*, 2nd ed., S. v. "*Filāḥa*."
68. Lewis 1961: 89.
69. Norwich 1989: 453.
70. Contini 1988: 154.
71. Boerio 1856: 609. I'm not sure what Boerio is trying to get at: "*birron*" is not an Arabic word, but it may be Persian.
72. Faccioli 1987: 535.
73. My claim is not new; see Denti di Pirajno 1970: 134, and Maffioli 1982: 222. Also see, for the growing of saffron and rice in Arab Sicily, the extracts of Yāqūt's (b. 1178) *Muʿgham al-buldān*, in Amari 1880–81: (1) 201, and al-Qazwīnī's (c. 1203–83) *Āṭār al-bilād* (Notable things in countries and news about men) in Amari 1880–81: (2) 238, par. 140, as well as al-Muqqadasī's description of Sicilian saffron cited in Lewis 1951: 211; Wright 1992: 111.
74. Watson 1983: 17; 156 n.17
75. Goitein 1967: (1) 119; 424 ns. 22, 23, 24, 25, 26.
76. Professor Elisabeth Wickett, conversation with the author, Cairo, October 6, 1991; Hamida Abdel-Magid, conversation with the author, Cairo, October 6, 1991.
77. Thorne 1995: 5–6.
78. Ibn Baṭṭūṭa 1853–58/1969: (3) 131. He likens the Indian daily eating of *kishri* to the daily eating of *ḥarīra* (a wheat flour porridge cooked in milk or *samna* usually eaten for breakfast in Morocco, see Carrier 1987:124–133) in the Maghrib. *Kushary* is clearly related to the Iraqi *kishry*, and the origin is certainly the Hindi kedergee or rice and pulses.
79. Burton 1857: (1) 178, (2) 63.
80. Heiser 1990: 117.
81. Rodinson 1949: 124 n.1.
82. Ashtor 1968: 1023.
83. Ibid., 1037.
84. Rodinson 1989.
85. Al-Rāzī 1953: 82; *Encyclopaedia of Islam*, 2nd ed., S.v. "*Maṭbakh*."
86. "FOCUS on Turkey: Food and Spirituality," internet hypertext document, December 2, 1997, http://www.focusmm.com.au/~focus/tr_ye_13.htm.
87. Homer, 1996: (2) 324.
88. Ashtor 1968: 1018. Job's tears are the hard white seeds of an Asian grass (*Coix lacryma-jobi*) that is sometimes described as pearl barley, which it is not, nor is it a kind of millet or sorghum, so this barley is probably the real thing.
89. Ladurie 1976: 45, 46.
90. Montanari 1984: 311.
91. L. Frati, ed., *Rimatori bolognesi del trecento* (Bologna, 1915), vss. 169–70, p. 108, quoted in Montanari 1994a: 53.
92. Montanari 1984: 311.
93. Alberini 1990: 119.
94. Fussell 1992: 17; Beltrami 1955: 21. One of the first depictions of maize is from the 1554 edition of a book by the cosmographer Giambattista Ramusio; Sereni 1997: 181. Agricultural historians, following British usage, generally use the term "corn" to refer generically to a variety of grains such as einkorn and millet, as well as wheat; Alberini 1990: 119.
95. Sandri 1985: 16.

CHAPTER 10

1. Couscous is also the name of a preparation of steamed grains other than that made of hard wheat.
2. Virtually all food writers have made this mistake and omission, including serious researchers such as Perry 1981a.
3. Montanari 1989: 62–64.
4. Dick and Matsuo 1988: 523.
5. Sallares 1991; Professor Andrew Watson, e-mail correspondence with the author, June 9, 1997; Sallares 1991: 318 says that "the most recent research, employing more sophisticated techniques, focusing on more distinctive spikelet fragments rather than on the grains themselves, and employing electron microscopes, has concluded that it is possible to differentiate bread wheat and durum wheat and that the progenitors of both had evolved by c. 5000 B.C." In support of this statement he gives four references. In fact, Watson points out, none of the references cited gives any support whatever to this statement. Sallares uses W. van Zeist, "Macroscopic traces of food plants in south-western Asia," *Philosophical Transactions of the Royal Society*, B 275 (1976), pp. 27–41, who states, on the contrary, that "in summary one must conclude that it seems impossible to determine whether carbonized grains and rachis internodes of free threshing wheat are of *T. durum* [hard wheat] or *T. aestivum* [bread wheat]." Sallares also cites J. R. Harlan, who stresses the virtual impossibility of distinguishing the carbonized remains of the two but hopes that "the real story will some day be unravelled." (see J. R. Harlan, "The Early History of Wheat; Earliest Traces to the Sack of Rome," in L. T. Evan and W. J. Peacock, eds., *Wheat Science: Today and Tomorrow* (Cambridge, 1981), p.6). Sallares's third reference, D. Zohary, "The Origin of Cultivated Cereals and Pulses in the Middle East," *Chromosomes Today*, 4 (1973), pp. 307–21, is completely agnostic about the identification of archeological finds of naked wheats, and D. Zohary and M. Hopf, *Domestication of Plants in the Old World* (Oxford, 1988), who Sallares cites, using pages 44–45, do not discuss naked wheats on the pages mentioned. Although he tells us that the suitability of durum wheat for making pasta rests on its gliadin : glutin ratio (glieden : glutanin in Sallares)

among its proteins, and that naked tetraploid wheats existed in classical Greece, there is a conspicuous absence in classical sources of pasta-type foods and Sallares believes that, given the state of the classical Greek culinary arts, it seems unlikely that they had durum wheat but just didn't think of inventing pasta (p. 319). Given this statement, he then goes on to claim (p. 320) that Pliny's *alica* is a semolina-based food, a kind of groats, saying that semolina particles called *aphairema* in the Campanian dialect of Greek were preferred for its manufacture, and it was similar to bulgur. But Sallares also says that Pliny said it could be made with any kind of wheat but mainly emmer. Watson 1983: 157 n.3 is unequivocal in stating that it is wrong to claim that *alica* mentioned in classical texts is hard wheat. Sallares still has not shown that durum wheat is widespread or actually used in pasta products, outside of simply stating that tetraploid wheats existed.

6. Professor Andrew Watson, e-mail correspondence with the author, June 9, 1997.
7. Renzo Lanzi, "Le coltivazioni agrarie in Italia dalla prehistoria agli splendori dell'Imperio Romano," in *L'alimentazione nell'antichitá* (Parma, 1985), pp. 51–77.
8. Watson was also influenced by Jane M. Renfrew's book, *Paleoethnobotany*, published in 1973, which seemed to represent the most up-to-date scholarship of the time. Renfrew saw no botanical evidence of hard wheat before late Roman times. Another influence on Watson was the writings of Professor Hans Helbaek, who, using the most sophisticated techniques available, did not identify any hard wheat in the remains he analyzed from many dozens of prehistoric and ancient sites.
9. In the end, none of this is a settled matter at the time of this writing. Even Robert Sallares, in a recent work, takes a point of view contrary to the one he argued for in his book on the ecology of ancient Greece by admitting that "it is still a matter of debate whether ancient Greeks and Romans cultivated mainly durum wheat, from which pasta is now made, or the bread wheat generally used to make bread today"; Robert Sallares, "Molecular Archeology and Ancient History," in John Wilkins, David Harvey, and Mike Dobson, eds., *Food in Antiquity* (Exeter: Exeter University Press, 1996), p. 95.
10. Alberini 1977: 16; Professor Phyllis Pray Bober, Leslie Clark Professor Emeritus in Humanities and Classical and Near Eastern Archeology and Art History, Bryn Mawr College, Philadelphia, conversation with the author, December 1993. Also see Mingazzini 1954.
11. Polo 1982; Ramusio 1978–88: (3) 264; Polo 1993: (2) 305. I do not accept the recent revisionist history of Marco Polo by Frances Wood, "Did Marco Polo Go to China?" who argued that Marco Polo never made it to China. The anomalies she points out have long been a focus of learned debate, and I believe are adequately addressed by scholars, especially Sir Henry Yule in his annotated edition of Marco Polo's travels.
12. Ramusio 1978–88: (3) 186; Polo 1993: (1) 438 n.4, called "vermicelli" there rather than the correct *in lasagne*.
13. Polo 1982; 1993: (2) 305; Chau Ju-kua 1911: 142. This in itself is not entirely conclusive because at least one classical author, Varro, mentions that wheat in Spain can be kept for fifty years, but also says millet can be kept for 100 years; cf. Varro, *On Agriculture*, I. lvii.
14. Hard wheat used to be designated *Triticum durum* Desf., but is currently designated *T. turgidum* var. *durum,* Dick and Matsuo 1988: 508.
15. Petronius, *Satriycon*, 41: 9, *Ab hoc ferculo Trimalco ad lasanum surrexit* (he was going to the bathroom).
16. The word as used in Horace, *Satires*, 1, 6, 115; Celsus, 2, 22, 1; and Apicius' recipe *patina Apiciana*, cited by André 1981: 211 as being a general word designating minced or stretched dough, a kind of crêpe that is often deep-fried in oil. Also see, for the Greek, Chantraine 1968–80: 64, where *lasanon* is a large minced cake cooked with flour and oil ("LXX et grec posterieur cit. d'Aristophnaes," *Assemblée* 843 in Ath. 110a); Sereni 1958: (5) 359–61.
17. Dorsa 1876: 44.
18. This was confirmed by Uguccione da Pisa, a grammarian whose manuscript *Derivazioni* was used to comment on Senisio, the fourteenth-century Sicilian lexicographer's *Declarus*; see Marinoni 1955: 79, 150v, 84, 163v, 175–76. On the similarities and uses of a bread–pasta concurrence, see the comments on *tharīd* on page 560.
19. Perry 1982: 37–39; Hill and Bryer 1995: 44–54.
20. Marinoni 1955: 84; Scappi 1570/1981: bk. 3, cap. CCLV.
21. Montanari 1994b: 140; Watson 1974: 8–35; 1983; 1981: 29–58; Alessio 1958–59; 261–80; Sereni 1958: (4) 272–95, (5) 353–77, (6) 398–422.
22. The document is an *ordo cocarie domini episcopi Lunensis*; Balletto 1986: 50.
23. Lopez 1975: 381–83; Alberini 1994: 35–36.
24. Herlihy 1973: 39 n.15.
25. Guerrini 1887: no. 33.
26. This universal geography is called *Nuzʿhat al-mushtāq* and was written by al-Idrīsī under the patronage of Roger II, and for this reason is also known as the *Kitāb al-Rujārī* or *Book of Roger*; see Amari 1880–81: (1) 35–42.
27. Mantovano 1985.
28. *Acta Sanctorum Aprilis [Acta de B. Guillelmo Eremitae]* 1675: (9), t.1, 383. The two priests, Godefrido Henschenio and Daniele Papebrochio, wrote their account of William the Hermit several centuries later. Also see Du Cange, Dominus, *Glossarium mediae et infimae latinitatis . . .* (Niort, 1883–87) (5) p.159; Marinoni 1955: 84, 79. Valle 1990: *maccarone hic pastillus li uel globulus. li aglobo farine dilactato deide lixo ca seus super infunditur.*

29. Alessio 1958–59: 263–64; Boccaccio 1972: (VIII) 3.
30. Watson 1983: 22, citing al-Fīrūzābādī [1329–c. 1414], *Mukhtār al-qāmūs,* (Cairo, 1963), p. 383.
31. Arberry 1939: 45. Ibn Buṭlān's *Taqwīm al-ṣiḥḥa* was composed in Arabic in the eleventh century, translated into Latin under the auspices of King Manfred of Sicily in the thirteenth century, but, unfortunately, frequently revised until the fourteenth century.
32. The illustrations are reproduced in the Medieval Health Handbook: *Tacuinum Sanitatis* 1976: plates XLII, 232, 233.
33. Watson 1983: 158 n.23, citing al-Jawharī [d. c. 1010], *Tāj al-lugha wa ṣiḥāḥ al-ᶜarabīya*, 2 vols. (Bulaq, 1865).
34. Watson 1983: 20–23. Today there are words for "hard wheat" in Arabic and Berber such as the name *tourki* in the Fezzan and *amekkaoui* in the Ahaggar of the Sahara; see Erroux n.d.: 25.
35. Cited in Sereni 1958: (5) 364 without a source. Bar ᶜAlī's dictionary appears to give a Syriac equivalent of the Arabic *iṭrīya* (root: *t-r-y*). His work is not easily accessible, but see Bar ᶜAlī, *Syrisch arabische Glossen*, Georg Hoffman, ed. (Kiel, 1874), a copy of which is in the University of California, Los Angeles research library and the New York Public Library, which is unfortunately missing volume 2. I have not examined this work but rely on correspondence between Professor David Lane and Professor Andrew Watson (provided by Professor Watson) on this matter.
36. Watson 1983: 158 n.23. Several scholars have incorrectly placed the first codification of *pasta secca* in the ninth century. Professors Massimo Montanari and Giuseppe Mantovano cite the so-called ninth-century cookbook of Ibn al-Mibrad as describing a "dish common between the old Bedouin tribes and the Berbers," namely *pasta secca*. Both scholars have made a mistake: Ibn al-Mibrad is the pseudonym of Yūsūf b. Ḥasan ad-Dimashqī who wrote in the sixteenth century A.D. which is the ninth century A.H. (year of the hegira in the Islamic calendar); see Montanari 1989: 61; Mantovano 1985: 285.
37. Balletto 1986: 56.
38. Messedaglia 1974: (2) 175ff.
39. Dozy 1881/1991: (2) 557, where *lawzīnaj* (L-w-z-y-n-j) is a food like "ktaief" (i.e., *qaṭā'if*) made with almond oil. Dozy's sources are al-Aghani, *Alii Ispahanensis Liber Cantilenarum magnus*, Ioanne Godofredo Ludovico Kosegarten, ed. (Greifswalde, 1840), vol. 1: 61, 10, and Bar ᶜAlī, *Syrisch arabische Glossen*, Georg Hoffman, ed. (Kiel, 1874).
40. Rodinson 1986: 16; Vollenweider 1963: 440–43.
41. See Wright 1995: 6.
42. "And then more bodies were put on top of them, with a little more dirt over those; they put layer on layer just like one puts layers of cheese in a lasagna." Marchione di Coppo Stefani was born in Florence in 1336 and he wrote his Florentine Chronicle in the late 1370s and early 1380s. "Rubric 643: Concerning A Mortality In The City of Florence In Which Many People Died," *Cronaca fiorentina. Rerum Italicarum Scriptores*, vol. 30, Niccolo Rodolico, ed. Citta di Castello: 1903–13 in Plague and Public Health in Renaissance Europe, http://jefferson.village.virginia.edu/osheim/intro.html.
43. Mantovano 1985: 285.
44. al-Rāzī 1953: 82, quoted in Watson 1983: 21. This al-Rāzī is not the famous doctor known as Rhazes in the West.
45. Varro, *On Agriculture*, I.57.
46. *Kitāb al-tabīkh fī al-Maghrib wa'l-Āndalus* 1961–62: 12–256. Also see *Traduccion española de un manuscrito anónimo del siglo XIII* 1966, although the translation is not accurate.
47. Such as *fidelli, sfidelli*, and *fidellini*; see Corominas 1936: 1–81 and 1954–57. Also see Garulo 1983: 224, where the entry for *fideo* is related to *zarcillo*, either a vine tendril, a dropped earring, or a hoop of a barrel, the point twisted and tender vine shoot. The word comes from the verb "to bud" derived from the Arabic *fāḍ*, "to grow," "to expand." The word appears in Ibn al-Jatib; see Simonet 1888/1975.
48. *Traduccion española de un manuscrito anónimo del siglo XIII* 1966: 207.
49. Arnau de Vilanova 1947: (2) 135, 137; *Libre de sent soví* 1979: 182, 184.
50. Lladonosa i Giró 1984: 95.
51. Arnau de Vilanova 1947: (2) 135 n.3, 135–36. *Tria* is the same as *alatria*. Arnold of Vilanova's recipe for pasta, which is cooked in oil or water: *De forment, e de farines, e de tot menjar quis fa de pasta frita ho cuyt en aygua. Ffoment cuyt no deu hom soven mengar, per ço cor moltipica e engenera en lo ventre los vermens qui son apetatz lombrics, e, encara, engenera apilacions, e fa disposicio e hordonament a aver peres ho arenes en la vexigua e en los royons. Açò matex fa[n] farines fetes de farina de forment e tota res qui sia fet de pasta frita ho cuyta en aygua.*
That this is probably a hard wheat pasta is indicated by his use of the word *semola* earlier.
52. Alessio 1958–59; Sereni 1958. Exactly when this occurs is unknown. The attribution of the origin of *pasta secca* to the Arabs has been questioned with a cautionary note by Montanari 1994b: 141. Citing Rosenberger, he notes that the very notion of pasta seems absent from Arabic gastronomy. It seems that Montanari has misread Rosenberger, who appears to make exactly the opposite claim; Rosenberger 1989: 87. Rosenberger focuses on medieval Arab words for varieties of pasta appearing in the sources, overlooking instances of *pasta secca* in contemporary Arab cookery; see Wright 1993.
53. Faccioli 1987: 277, who called the etymology "fanciful."
54. This section is derived from Wright 1996–97.
55. Brunschvig 1947: (2) 272; in Tuareg, a language of the Ahaggar, *duwayda* was known as *eddouida* and *talia* (from "Italia" or *tagliatelle*) both mean vermicelli; de Foucauld 1951: (1) 223.
56. Also spelled *isbriga* or *ysbriga*. Aymard and Bresc 1975: 541; The vermicelli of Trapani in the sixteenth century was 50 percent more expensive than in Palermo; Bautier 1984: 41.

57. Aymard and Bresc 1975: 541, 542; Bautier 1984: 41.
58. Goethe 1982: 320.
59. Rosenberger 1980: 493.
60. Nancy Harmon Jenkins reports that she was told in Morocco that *shakhshūka* was a term used by Moroccan Jews; see Jenkins 1994: 61. But the term *shakhshūka* is not Arabic, it does not appear in either Dozy 1881/1991 nor Wehr 1976, but in fact derives from the Turkish dish made with peppers, onions, and eggs called *şakşuka*; see *Contemporary Turkish-English Dictionary* 1983: 359.
61. Another kind of semolina preparation in Algeria is called *zimbū* (or *zembo*). In the Ahaggar (Tamanrasset) region of Algeria, wives prepare *zimbū*, a roasted green wheat mixed with water and eaten cold, after the evening prayers. It is eaten by all portions of the population, infants and adults, town dwellers and nomads, as a light dish, a fortifier. *Zimbū* can be made with barley, millet, and sorghum, too. Some Imouhar call it *jembou*, a term used in everyday language among black Saharans and which can mean "flour"; see Gast 1968: 59. Could *zimbū* have anything to do with the preparation known in Liguria as *lasagne cö zembe*, a meat, mascarpone, or ricotta-stuffed ravioli? The Ligurian *zembe* literally means "lasagne with humps"—that is, ravioli made with a special device called a *cannella da ravieu* (cinnamon stick for ravioli) in Ligurian dialect, a kind of rolling pin with square crimping edges that quickly forms the stuffed ravioli. The Arab influence on Ligurian dialect is noted in Pellegrini 1972: (1) 333–400.
62. Tamzali 1986: 91.
63. Correnti 1976–85: 150; Salomone-Marino 1924; Simeti 1989: 155.
64. Goethe 1982: 320.
65. See Cristoforo Messisbugo's recipes (published in 1549) for macaroni and Antoni Latini's from his *Lo scalco alla moderna* from 1692, in Faccioli 1987: 306–307; 697–98.
66. Medieval Health Handbook: *Tacuinum Sanitatis* 1976: XXXI, Paris, f.59 and 221. Vienna, f. 62.
67. Wright 1995: 91.
68. Skhiri 1968: 26.
69. Amari and Schiaparelli 1883: 28.
70. Angarano 1973: 29–32.
71. Patrone 1981: 339.
72. Scappi 1570/1981: bk. 3, cap. CXC.
73. Cortelazzo and Zolli 1979–88.
74. Faccioli 1987: 158.
75. Bresc 1972: 73; Wright 1997; Targioni-Tozzetti 1853: 43.
76. Faccioli 1987: 663.
77. Scappi 1570/1981: bk. 2, cap. CLXXIII, CLXXIIII; bk. 3, cap. CCXXXIX; Elenora Consoli, conversation with the author, Catania, Sicily, August 1989.
78. Gleijeses, *A Napoli*, 1977: 55. The Italian culinary authority Vincenzo Buonassisi suggests that the dish arose from the post-World War II chaos on Ischia, while Paula Wolfert relates a story that the dish was served by respectable women to the men with whom they were having affairs.
79. Francesconi 1992: 164.
80. Scappi 1570/1981: bk. 3, cap. CLXXV.
81. Al-Idrīsī [c. 1099 ?–1154 ?], *Kitāb al-Rujārī*, in Amari 1880–81: 35–42; Epstein 1996: 97. This is Alessio's position as well; see Alessio 1958–59: 266. Genoese-Sicilian trade dwindled to nothing between 1232 and 1240 as a result of retaliation by Frederick II for political reasons; Epstein 1996: 121; Herlihy 1973: 39 n.15; Alessio 1958–59: 267.
82. Epstein 1996: 267.
83. Ibid., 295.
84. Boni 1969: 101; Kaspar 1992: 78; Veronelli 1973: 32; Root 1971: 197; Alberini 1994: 180–82.
85. Sereni 1958: (5) 361–62.
86. An excellent and thorough introduction to *ragù* can be found in Kaspar 1992: 33–57.
87. Alessio 1958–59: 267.
88. Arsel 1996: 38, 234.
89. Brunschvig 1940/1947: (2) 272; Gobert 1940b: 579.
90. Brunschvig 1940/1947. (2) 272; Gobert 1940b: 579.
91. Hubert 1984: 110.
92. Dozy 1881/1991: (2) 153.
93. I believe these might have been the distinctive square silver coins that became known as *milares* by western Europeans that were minted in Tunis; see Spufford 1988: 171, and Harry W. Hazard, "*The Numismatic History of Late Medieval North Africa*," Numismatic Studies, 7, New York: American Numismatic Society (1952).
94. This is proposed in Luigi Sada, *Spaghetti e compagni*, (Bari, 1982).
95. *Wazaf* (sometimes transliterated as "ouzaf") are the fry of either *Engraulis meletta* Cuv., a kind of anchovy, or they are sardine (*Sardinella aurita* Val.). They are commonly sold dried in Tunisian fish markets and used as a condiment in cooking.
96. Dozy 1881/1991: (2) 153.
97. Rodinson 1949: 138 n.9.
98. Possibly derived from the word *darmak*, meaning "flour of the best quality;" see Dozy 1881/1991: (1) 437.
99. Although the name appears to refer to coffee beans, in fact the derivation is probably *kahūrāt*, a kind of legume; see Dozy 1881/1991: (2) 504.
100. Bahloul 1983: 160.
101. Fried pasta sweets are found commonly in Sicily too, an Arab heritage; see Wright 1992: 229–30.
102. The word *burkūkis* is originally Berber. It is a type of pasta/couscous that can be boiled as well as steamed; see Laoust 1920: 78 n.4.
103. Foucauld 1951: (1) 223. Both words are originally Arabic: *eddeouetda*, again, comes from *duwayda*, meaning "worms," while *talia* signifies either "Italian" or "*tagliatelle*."
104. Dozy 1881/1991: (2) 502; Amari 1880; *Traduccion española de un manuscrito anónimo del siglo XIII* 1966: 223; Rodinson 1949: 105, 126, 140; Bolens 1990: 231, 305 n.19.
105. See Wright 1996b; Valensi 1975: 606.
106. Wright, "Couscous," 1996.

107. *Traduccion española de un manuscrito anónimo del siglo XIII* 1966: 203.
108. Lévi-Provençal 1967: (3) 421, quoting Makkari (i.e., al-Maqqarī), *Analectes*, vol. 2, pp. 202–205.
109. Rosenberger 1980: 483.
110. Bolens 1990: 157.
111. Rosenberger 1980: 483.
112. Professor Lisa Anderson, Columbia University, correspondence with the author, July 19, 1995. Culinary boundaries are never exact: one certainly finds couscous made by some Bedouin tribes of Egypt's Western Desert.
113. Rodinson 1949: 95–165.
114. Gobert 1940b: 480.
115. See Wright, "Couscous," 1996.
116. See *Encyclopaedia of Islam*, 2nd ed., S.v. "*Kuskusū*;" Gobert 1940b: 480 n.7.
117. Rosenberger 1980: 483.
118. Brunschvig 1940/1947; Idris 1959. French historian Charles-Emmanuel Dufourcq's claim that couscous was known in eighth-century Andalusia appears to be wrong for the reasons given above; Dufourcq 1978: 105.
119. Idris 1959: (2) 589.
120. Brunschvig 1940/1947: (2) 271 n.4, citing Ibn Naji (or Nagi), *Maʿālim al-iman fī maʿrifat ahl al-Qayrawan* (Tunis, A.H. 1320), vol. IV, pp. 173, 177 mentioning couscous.
121. Brunschvig 1940/1947: (2) 271, citing Ibn Faḍlallah [1300–1348], *Masālik al-abṣār fi mamālik al-amṣār*, Gaudefroy-Demombynes, trans. (Paris, 1927).
122. Wright 1993; also see Gobert 1955: 514–15; Pérès 1943: 140–41; Dozy 1881/1991: (2) 476.
123. *Les sources inédites de l'histoire du Maroc* 1953: (5) 46–47.
124. Flandrin and Hyman 1986: 234.
125. The most painstaking and detailed description of the making of hard wheat couscous can be found in Gast 1968: 78–101.
126. Moreau and Andry 1942: 305, 308.
127. Gast 1968: 95. The Tuareg, whose skin coloring ranges from nearly white to dark skinned, are pastoralists who range from Touat, Algeria, to Timbuktu, Mali, to Fezzan, Libya, and northern Nigeria.
128. Lane 1908: 136.
129. Lévi-Provençal 1967: (3) 418.
130. Laoust 1920: 78 n.3.
131. Gobert 1940b: 509; Kouki 1971: 563.
132. Burnet and Viscontini 1939: 229.
133. The word means "singing," perhaps to capture the crackling sounds of the grains in the pan. In some parts of Tunisia this grill pan is called *ḥamas*.
134. Burnet and Viscontini 1939: 229; Kouki 1971: 589.
135. Burnet and Viscontini 1939: 228.
136. Schnell 1957: 96.
137. Gast 1968: 94.
138. Ibn Baṭṭūṭa 1853–58/1969: (4) 394. The lotus flower is *Rhamnus nabeca. Founi* or *fonio* is *Digitaria exilis* Stapf.
139. Schnell 1957: 137.
140. Gast 1968: 77. Another reason it wasn't popular is that it doesn't taste as good.
141. Lévi-Provençal 1967: (3) 421.
142. Hall 1991: 165.
143. *Founi* or *fonio* is *Digitaria exilis* Stapf, Schnell 1957: 153–54; Harlan 1992: 71; Facciola 1998: 175.
144. Rosenberger 1980: 482, Laoust 1920: 268 n.1. Songhai is a language in the Nilo-Saharan family of West Africa.
145. For example, according to Burnet and Viscontini 1939: (28) 227, *biskri* and *mahoudi* (*Triticum durum* var. *leucomelan*), *sbei* (*T. durum* var. *melanopus*), *hamia* (*T. durum* var. *apiculatum*), *agili* (*T. durum* var. *affine*).
146. Dozy 1881/1991: (1) 64.
147. Today most couscous consumed in North Africa is factory made and the home making of couscous is diminishing.
148. Laoust 1920: 95.
149. In the thirteenth century, the word appears to have meant any kind of coarse flour; Aubaile-Sallenave 1994: 117.
150. Gast 1968: 95.
151. Skhiri 1968: 21–28.
152. *Kitāb al-ṭabīkh fī al-Maghrib wa'l-Āndalus* 1961–62: 15.
153. *Traduccion española de un manuscrito anónimo del siglo XIII* 1966: 204.
154. Dozy 1881/1991: (1) 138.
155. Edrisi 1968: 126 (107), 134 (115).
156. Brunschvig 1940/1947: (2) 228.
157. Corominas 1980; Dozy 1881/1991: (1) 90.
158. Bautier 1984: 41.
159. Luján 1988: 51; Bautier 1984: 41.
160. Corominas 1967: 97.
161. Cortelazzo and Zolli 1979–88: (4) 870.

CONCLUSION

1. Tripoli (1511, 1551), Djerba (1510, 1520, 1560), Tunis (1535, 1573, 1574), Bizerte (Bizerta) (1573, 1574), Malta (1565), Lepanto (Návpaktos) (1571), Modon (Methóni) (1572), Coron (Koróni) (1534), and Prévesa (1538).
2. The reasons behind Jewish expulsion from Spain are hotly debated by scholars, who argue for either race or religion as the motivating cause.
3. Braudel 1972–73: (2) 802.
4. Ibid., 808.
5. Bahloul 1983: 13; *Encyclopaedia Judaica*, S.v., "*Shulkan Arukh*."
6. Braudel 1972–73: (2) 809.
7. Braudel 1982: 159.
8. Ibid., 163.
9. I think the argument made by Professor Benzion Netanyahu, in his *The Origins of the Inquisition in Fifteenth Century Spain* (New York: Random House, 1995), that race, not religion, was the motivation behind the expulsion of the Jews is overstated. After all, the Muslims were expelled, too.
10. Krekić 1980: XXI, 260–62.

11. *Cooking the Sephardic Way* 1971: 128BB.
12. *Encyclopaedia Judaica*, S.v., "*Maror.*"
13. Claudia Roden grapples with the question of whether there is a Jewish cuisine by treating her subject as a personal odyssey; see Roden 1996. Also see Feeley-Harnik 1994.
14. Bahloul 1983: 45.
15. *Encyclopaedia Judaica*, S.v., "Sacrifice."
16. Goitein 1983: (4) 234; 1967: (1) 119.
17. *Encyclopaedia Judaica*, S.v., "Food."
18. The standard Arabic dictionaries do not have an entry for *ajlūk* either. Could the word be derived from *jāl*, an emigrant from Spain?
19. Bahloul 1983: 15, 90, 91, 92.
20. Ibid., 128.
21. Ibid., 139, 142; Cohen 1912: 492.
22. Bahloul 1983: 151.
23. Stouff 1970: 52.
24. Ibid., 53, 145–46.
25. Benbassa 1984: 116.
26. McNeill 1974: 57.
27. Ibid., 129.
28. I use the word *Mediterranean* in this paragraph in the extended way used by Braudel, who would consider the reach of Mediterranean culture to extend to the Hispanic cultures of South and Central Americas and to the Muslim cultures of the Far East.

AN ESSAY ON THE SOURCES

1. Stouff 1970: 261 n.3.
2. See Heine 1988: 14–16; Marín 1981: 193, 201; and Perry 1981b, where there is an excellent description of three of these medieval Arab cookbooks.
3. Also see Heine 1988; Rodinson 1949: 95–165; Perry 1985: 17–22; Perry 1981b: 96–105.
4. Two new editions have recently been published: *Kitāb al-wuṣla ilā al-ḥabīb fī waṣf al-ṭayyibāt wā'-ṭīb* was edited by S. Maḥjūb and D. al-Khatīb and published in Aleppo in 1988, while the *Kanz al-fawāhid fī tanwīha al-mawāhid* was edited by M. Marín and David Waines in 1993 and published by Dar al-Nasr and Franz Steiner in Beirut and Stuttgart.
5. An anonymous work from Morocco with which I am not familiar is the *Al–ṭabkh al-Maghribī fī ᶜaṣr al-muwaḥḥadīn*, Microfilm no. 810, Rabat: Archive de la Bibliothèque Générale. The *Kitāb al-ṭabīkh fī al-Maghrib wa'l-Āndalus* was published in a poor Spanish translation some years ago (see Bibliography). A new critical edition and translation was being prepared as part of the "Medieval Iberian Peninsula Text and Studies" series to be published by E. J. Brill publishers, Leiden.
6. *Encyclopaedia of Islam*, 2nd ed., S.v., "*Filaḥa.*"
7. Many important medical works were translated under the auspices of King Manfred of Sicily, known as the lover of science, in the thirteenth century. The court of Manfred, son of Frederick II, continued the tradition of the Arabophilia of the Norman and Swabian kings of Sicily. The Norman and Swabian court at Palermo was a major center for the translation of Arab scientific works into Latin.
8. *Encyclopaedia of Islam*, 2nd ed., S.v., "*Ghidāᶜ*," 1070.
9. Balletto 1986: 18 n.11.
10. Ibn al-Baiṭār 1991: 7–9.
11. Ibid., 10.
12. Ibid., 10, although the translation was going on at the same time in Baghdad. The same conclusion was reached by Levey 1967.
13. Bolens 1990: 115.
14. Manzalaoui 1977: 570, 574.
15. Pseudo-Apuleius 1481/1979: (1) lxi.
16. *Herbolario Volgare* 1522/1979.
17. Rodinson 1990: 37.
18. Postan 1966: 136, 367, 368, 378; de Herrera 1539/1970: 33.
19. Weiss-Amer 1992: 75; Flandrin and Hyman 1986: 225.
20. Trasselli 1981: 3.
21. Bresc 1972: 73. One credible source even puts the introduction of the sweet orange in the fourteenth century, see Forbes 1955: (2) 46. We know that Arab Sicilian poets of the twelfth century described oranges as "appearing like fires among the emerald branches," but we can't tell if these were bitter or sweet oranges, see Amari 1986: 3 (3), 779.
22. Trasselli 1981: 23.
23. Balletto 1986: 20.
24. Bolens 1980: 462.
25. Redon, Sabban, and Servanti 1991: 15.
26. This is a tenth-century work by this Jewish physician and philosopher, who wrote mostly in Arabic. It was translated into Latin in 1087 as the *Liber dietetarium universalium*, which was influential; Rodinson 1971: 489; Bolens 1990: 158.
27. Dozy 1881/1991: (2) Some linguists see an Arabic derivation while others believe *cassata* derives from the Latin word for cheese. The matter is unsettled, but see the box on page 302.
28. Diaz Garcia 1978–79: 17.
29. Dufourcq 1978: 107. Also see Chapter 1.
30. Hierro 1989: 27.
31. Dufourcq 1978: 119.
32. This paragraph is based on Halıcı 1989: 9–11; 16. Halıcı also mentions the first Turkish cookery book, a work titled *Tabh-i et'ime* (Instruction in cookery) and believed to have been translated from the Arabic *Kitāb al-ṭabīkh* (Book of cookery) in the fifteenth century by Şirvani. In the eighteenth century, there are two other books, *Ağidiye risalesi* (The manual of nourishment) by Abdullah Efendi, and the anonymous *Yemek risalesi* (A manual of dishes).
33. Arsel 1996: 62–68. On these pages are listed the most important Turkish works.
34. Faccioli 1973: (5), no. 1, 995.
35. Rodinson 1990: 33. Ibn Jazla's work could also be translated as "The pathway of explanation as to that which man uses." Scholars generally do not provide translations of the titles of medieval Arabic works because the translations give no indication to what the subject of the book or manuscript is about.
36. Faccioli 1987: 20. In calling it the oldest Italian cookbook I am, of course, not considering the cookery work of Apicius or the works referred to by Athenaeus.

37. Peterson 1980: 338 n.9; also see "*Liber de coquina*" 1968: 369–435.
38. The French scholar Marianne Mulon has shown that the *Liber de coquina* and the *Libro della cucina* are related texts. "*Liber de coquina*" 1968: 369–435.
39. Faccioli 1987: 71.
40. Guerrini 1887: no. 58. Although the influence is Arab, it might very well be from Hispano-Muslim cuisine.
41. This occurred in the shadow of the Black Death, which was claiming nearly half of the population of Italy.
42. Rodinson 1990: 38.
43. Platina appears to be the first Italian in 1,000 years to be familiar with the cookery manuscript of Apicius.
44. Mention should be made of an early Italian work not appearing in Faccioli 1987, the anonymous *Cuoco napolitanno* (New York, Morgan Library, Buhler 36) that shows Catalan influences and that may be related to Maestro Martino; see Milham 1995: 61–66.
45. Maffioli 1982: 43, although his dates are wrong; therefore use Faccioli 1987.
46. Maffioli 1982: 93.
47. Stufa 1965: 75.
48. Biblioteca Universitaria di Genova, ms. F VI 4.
49. Redon, Sabban, and Servanti 1991: 17 n.3.
50. *Libre de sent soví* 1979.
51. Andrews 1988: 19.
52. Dr. Rudolf Grewe, conversation with the author, New York, June 1990.
53. "Un libro de cocina del siglo XIV" 1935; *Llibre del coc de la seu de Tarragona* 1331/1935; Andrews 1988: 18; *Manual de mugeres en el qual se contienen muchas y diversas reçeutas muy buenas.* Alicia Martínez Crespo, ed. Salamanca: Universidad, 1995. This manuscript is Mss. Parmense 834 in the Biblioteca Palatina in Parma, Italy.
54. Lladonosa i Giró 1984: 12.
55. Ruperto de Nola 1520/1929. Andrews 1988: 19 argues that the date of 1491 might be wrong, that it could be as early as 1477, and it is argued by Nèstor Luján that this little Ruperto might be Roberto of the village of Nola near Naples. This possibility might explain some of the recipes; see Luján 1979: 28–31.
56. Allard 1987: 37.
57. Granado 1599/1971: xxvi.
58. Ibid., xxx.
59. Ibid., xxxvi.
60. Ibid., 12–13.
61. Ibid., 104.
62. Luján 1988: 37; Rios and March 1992.
63. Luján 1988: 40.
64. Lozinski 1933: 55.
65. Rodinson 1971: 492.
66. Ibid.
67. *Douet d'Arq*, a little culinary treatise written in French in 1306, published in *Bibliothéque de l'Ecole des Chartes*, 1860, pp. 209–227, quoted in Stouff 1970.
68. There were many editions of the *Viandier*. Scully cites 1370 as the date when he becomes the king's chef; see Scully 1988 and 1995.
69. Hyman and Hyman 1992: 60, 61.
70. Peterson 1994: 206.

BIBLIOGRAPHY

COOKBOOKS AND DIETETICS

70 Médecins de France. n.d. *Le trésor de la cuisine du bassin Méditerranéen*. Prosper Montagne, ed. n.p.: Editions de la Tournelle.

Abdennour, Samia. 1985. *Egyptian Cooking: A Practical Guide*. Cairo: American University in Cairo.

Accame, Franco. 1995. *Mandilli de saea: Cento piatti liguri e la loro storia illustrata*. 7th ed. Genoa: de Ferrari.

Accame, Franco, Silvio Torre, and Virgilio Pronzati. 1994. *Il grande libro della cucina ligure*. Genoa: de Ferrari.

Adami, Italia. 1977. *Le ricette della mia cucina genovese e ligure*. Florence: del Riccio.

Adami, Pietro. 1985. *La cucina carnica*. Padua: Franco Muzzio.

Agnelli, Susanna, ed. 1979. *Il grande libro della cucina regionale*. Milan: Fabbri.

Agnetti, V. 1909. *La nuova cucina delle specialita regionali*. Milan: Societa Editoriale Milanese.

Aguilar, Jeanette. 1966. *The Classic Cooking of Spain*. New York: Holt, Rinehart, & Winston.

Albani, Tito, and Gianni Bonacina. 1977. *Vini e cibi della calabria*. Chiaravalle Centrale: Effe Emme.

Albanian Cookbook. 1977. Worcester: Women's Guild, St. Mary's Albanian Orthodox Church.

Alberini, Massimo. 1965. *Liguri a tavola: Itinerario gastronomico da nizza a lerici*. Milan: Longanesi.

———. 1966. *Storia del pranzo all'italiana: Dal triclinio allo snack*. Milan: Rizzoli.

———. 1972. *4000 anni a tavola: Dalla bistecca preistorica al pic-nic sulla luna*. Milan: Fratelli.

———. 1974. *Cento ricette storiche*. Florence: Sansoni.

———. 1977. *Pasta & Pizza*. With recipes compiled by Anna Martini. Elisabeth Evans, trans. New York: St. Martin's.

———. 1990. *Antica cucina veneziana*. Casale Monferrato: Piemme.

Alexiadrou, Vefa. 1989. *Greek Cuisine*. Thessaloniki: Vefa Alexiadrou.

Algar, Ayla Esen. 1985. *The Complete Book of Turkish Cooking*. London and New York: Kegan Paul International.

Allegranzi, Antonio. 1980. *La cucina del pesce dal po a trieste*. Padova: Franco Muzzio.

Almanaccu Siciliannu. 1988. *Cucina siciliana*. 3 vols. Marina di Patti: Pungitoppo.

Anadol, Cemal. 1995. *Türk Yemekleri Ansiklopedisi: Türkiye 'de ilk defa Anadolu Yemekleri ve Saray Yemekleri*. Istanbul: Türkmen. [in Turkish]

Andrews, Colman. 1988. *Catalan Cuisine: Europe's Last Great Culinary Secret*. New York: Atheneum.

———. 1996. *Flavors of the Riviera: Discovering Real Mediterranean Cooking*. New York: Bantam.

Anonimo Meridionale. 1985. *Due libri di cucina*. Ingemar Boström, ed. Acta Universitatis Stockholmiensis 11. Stockholm: Almqvist & Wiksell International.

Anthimus. 1996. *De obseruatione ciborum* (On the observance of foods). Mark Grant, ed. and trans. Totnes: Prospect.

Anthony, Dawn, Elaine and Selwa. 1978. *Lebanese Cookbook*. Secaucus, NJ: Chartwell.

Apicius. 1958. *The Roman Cookery Book*. B. Flower and E. Rosenbaum, trans. London: Harrap.

———. 1969. *De re coquinaria [On the art of cooking]*. M. E. Milham, ed. Leipzig: Teubner.

———. 1977. *Cookery and Dining in Imperial Rome*. Joseph Dommers Vehling, ed. and trans. New York: Dover.

Apostolo, Franca Colonna Romano. 1988. *Sicilia in bocca . . . e nel cuore: Alimentazione sana=tradizione siciliana*. Palermo: FAP Grafica.

Arberry, A. J., trans. 1939. "A Baghdad Cookery Book." *Islamic Culture*, 13, no. 1 (January): 21–47 and no. 2 (April): 189–214.

Ardakoç, Berrin. 1993. *Türk sofrası: Alaturka-Alafranga Yemek ve Tatlı Kitabı*. Istanbul: Geçit. [in Turkish]

Arnau de Vilanova [Arnold of Vilanova] 1947. *Obres catalanes*. Vol. 2: *Escrits Mèdics*. Barcelona: Barcino.

Arsel, Semahat, dir. 1996. *Timeless Tastes: Turkish Culinary Culture*. Istanbul: Divan.

Artusi, Pellegrino. 1975. *Italianissimo: Italian Cooking at its Best*. New York: Liveright.

Barber, R. W. 1973. *Cooking and Recipes from Rome to the Renaissance*. London: Allen Lane.

Barberousse, Michel. n.d. *Cuisine provençale*. Seguret: Michel Barberousse.

Barron, Rosemary. 1991. *Flavors of Greece*. New York: William Morrow.

Bartelletti, N. Sapio. 1985. *La cucina siciliana nobile e popolare: Ricette-storia-aneddoti-curiosita*. Milano: Franco Angeli.

Başan Ghillie. 1997. *Classic Turkish Cooking*. New York: St. Martin's.

Batmanglij, Najmieh. 1986. *Food of Life: A Book of Ancient Persian and Modern Iranian Cooking and Ceremonies*. Washington, DC: Mage Publishers.

Bazán, Condesa de Pardo. n.d. [c. 1910]. *La cocina Española Antigua*. Madrid: Renacimiento.

Behague, Dominique. 1986. *Recueil de la gastronomie languedocienne*. Ingersheim: Editions S.A.E.P.

Benbassa, Esther. 1984. *Cuisine Judéo-Espagnole: Recettes et traditions*. Paris: Éditions du Scribe.

Benghiat, Suzy. 1984. *Middle Eastern Cookery*. London: Weidenfeld and Nicolson.

Benkirane, Fettouma. 1979. *La nouvelle cuisine Marocaine*. Paris: J. P. Taillandier.

———. 1985. *Secrets of Moroccan Cookery*. Shirley Kay, trans. Paris: J. P. Taillandier-Sochepress.

Bennani-Smires, Latifa. 1991. *La cuisine Marocaine . . . plus*. Casablanca: Al Madariss.

Bettoja, Jo, with Jane Garmey. 1991. *Southern Italian Cooking: Family Recipes from the Kingdom of the Two Sicilies*. New York: Bantam.

Black, Maggie. 1992. *The Medieval Cookbook*. New York: Thames and Hudson.

Blanc, Jacques et Paul-Louis Meissonnier. 1988. *Les meilleures recettes de la cuisine du Languedoc Roussillon par ses chefs*. Cahors: Éditions Gamma.

Boni, Ada. 1950. *The Talisman Italian Cook Book*. Matilde La Rosa, trans. New York: Crown.

———. 1969. *Italian Regional Cooking*. Maria Langdale and Ursula Whyte, trans. New York: Bonanza Books.

———. 1989. *Il Talismano della Felicita*. Roma: Colombo.

Bonino, Marialusa. n.d. *Odor di basilico: Le autentiche ricette della cucina ligure*. 9th ed. Genoa: e.r.g.a.

Bonnaure, André. 1988. *La cuisine en Languedoc*. N.p.: Collot.

Bouayed, Fatima-Zohra. 1983. *La cuisine algérienne*. Paris: Messidor/Temps Actuels.

Bourin, Jeanne, with Jeannine Thomassin. 1983. *Les recettes de Mathilde Brunel: Cuisine médiévale pour table d'aujourd'hui*. Malesherbes: Flammarion.

Bouterin, Antoine, and Joan Schwartz. 1994. *Cooking Provence: Four Generations of Recipes and Traditions*. New York: Macmillan.

Boxer, Arabella. 1981. *Mediterranean Cookbook*. London: Penguin.

Bozzi, Ottorina Perna. 1979. *Vecchia brianza in cucina*. Florence: Martello-Giunti.

Bruning, H. F., Jr., and Cav. Umberto Bullo. 1973. *Venetian Cooking: 200 Authentic Recipes from a Great Regional Cuisine Adapted for American Cooks*. New York: Macmillan; London: Collier Macmillan.

Bugialli, Giuliano. 1982. *Classic Techniques of Italian Cooking*. New York: Simon & Schuster.

———. 1988. *Bugialli on Pasta*. New York: Simon and Schuster.

Buonassisi, Vincenzo. 1991. *Il nuovo codice della pasta*. Milan: Biblioteca Universale Rizzoli.

Calera, Ana Maria. 1991. *Cocina valenciana (Alicante, Castellón, Valencia)*. León: Editorial Everest.

———. 1992. *Cocina andaluza*. León: Editorial Everest.

Calingaert, Efrem Funghi, and Jacquelyn Days Serwer. 1983. *Pasta and Rice Italian Style*. New York: Charles Scribner's Sons.

Camporesi, Carla Geri. 1993. *Ricette tradizionali fiorentine*. Lucca: Maria Pacini Fazzi.

Capnist, Giovanni. 1985. *La cucina polesana*. Milan: Franco Muzzio.

Carbonaro, Carmen. 1970. *Recipes of Maltese Dishes*. 4th ed. Malta: National Press-Pietà.

Cardella, Antonio. 1981. *Sicilia e le isole in bocca*. Palermo: Edikronos.

———. 1987. *Trapani in bocca*. Palermo: La Nuova Edrisi.

Caredda, Gian Paolo. 1995. *Gastronomia in sardegna*. 3rd ed. Cagliari: Edizioni della Torre.

Carluccio, Antonio. 1986. *A Taste of Italy*. Boston: Little, Brown.

Carnacina, Luigi, and Luigi Veronelli. 1966. *La buona vera cucina italiana*. Milan: Rizzoli.

———. 1978–80. *La cucina rustica regionale*. 4 vols. 5th ed. Milan: Rizzoli.

Carrier, Robert. 1987. *A Taste of Morocco: A Culinary Journey with Recipes*. New York: Clarkson Potter.

Carter, Elizabeth. 1989. *Majorcan Food and Cookery*. London: Prospect Books.

Casas, Penelope. 1985. *Tapas: The Little Dishes of Spain*. New York: Alfred A. Knopf.

———. 1988. *The Foods and Wines of Spain*. New York: Alfred A. Knopf.

Cascino, Francesco Paolo. 1980. *Cucina di sicilia*. Palermo: Misuraca.

Cass, Elizabeth. 1968. *Spanish Cooking*. London: Andre Deutsch for the Cookery Book Club.

Cavalcanti, Ottavio. 1979. *Il libro d'oro della cucina e dei vini di calabria e basilicata*. Milan: Mursia.

Cerrahoğlu Abdurraham. 1994. *Sofra Nimetleri: Uygulamali Yemek Kitabı*. Istanbul: Timaş Yayınları. [in Turkish]

Cervio, Vincenzo. 1593. *Il trinciante*. Rome: Giulio Burchioni.

Chamberlain, Samuel, with Narcissa Chamberlain. 1958. *Italian Bouquet: An Epicurean Tour of Italy*. New York: Gourmet.

Chanot-Bullier, C. 1988. *Vielles recettes de cuisine provençale—vieii receto de cousino prouvençalo*. 4th ed. Marseilles: Tacussel.

Chantiles, Vilma Liacouras. 1979. *The Food of Greece*. New York: Avenel.

Chatto James, and W. L. Martin. 1987. *A Kitchen in Corfu*. London: Weidenfeld and Nicolson.

Chines, A., and A. Pisa. 1970. *Cucina di putiri fari: Piccolo breviario della cucina siciliana facile e fattibile*. Palermo: S. F. Flaccovio.

Claustres, Francine. 1990. *Connâitre la cuisine du Languedoc*. Lucon: Sud Ouest.

Clavel, Jean, ed. 1988. *Vins and cuisine de terroir en Languedoc*. Toulouse: Privat.

Cocina andaluza. 1990. Madrid: Susaeta Ediciones.

Codacci, Leo. 1981. *Civiltà della tavola contadina: 190 "ricette" e tanti buoni consigli*. Florence: Sansoni.

Colonna Romano, Franca. 1975. *Sicilia al tappo*. Palermo: Il Vespro.

Coltro, Dino. 1983. *La cucina tradizionale veneta*. Rome: Newton Compton.

Consoli, Eleonora. 1986. *Sicilia: La cucina del sole*. 2 vols. Catania: Tringale.

Consoli Sardo, Maria. 1978. *Cucina nostra*. Palermo: Flaccovio.

Contini, Mila. 1988. *Veneto in bocca*. N.p. [probably Palermo]: La Nuova Ed.ri.si.

Contoli, Corrado. 1963. *Romagna gastronomca*. Bologna: Calderini.

Cooking the Sephardic Way. 1971. Los Angeles: Sephardic Sisterhood, Temple Tifereth Israel.

Coppini, Remo. 1983. *Umbria a tavola: Aneddoti, folclore, tradizioni, usanze e . . . ricette*. Perugia: Guerra.

Corey, Helen. 1962. *The Art of Syrian Cookery: A Culinary Trip to the Land of Bible History—Syria and Lebanon*. Garden City: Doubleday.

Coria, Giuseppe. 1981. *Profumi di sicilia: Il libro della cucina siciliana*. Palermo: Vito Cavallotto.

Correnti, Pino. 1971. *La gastronomica nella storia e nella vita del popolo siciliano*. Milan: Ecotour.

———. 1976–85. *Il libro d'oro della cucina e dei vini di Sicilia*. Milan: Mursia.

Couffignal, Huguette. 1976. *La cuisine des pays d'Oc*. Paris: Solar.

Coulbaux, Paul. 1963. *200 maneras de preparar los Huevos usted mismo*. Fernando Moreno Sánchez, trans. Madrid: Espasa-Calpe.

d'Alba, Tommaso. 1980. *La cucina siciliana di derivazione araba*. Palermo: Vittorietti.

Dalby, Andrew, and Sally Grainger, 1996. *The Classical Cookbook*. Los Angeles: J. Paul Getty Museum.

Da Mosto, Ranieri. 1985. *II veneto in cucina*. Florence: Giunti-Martello.

David, Elizabeth. 1950. *A Book of Mediterranean Food*. London: John Lehmann.

———. 1962. *French Provincial Cooking*. New York: Harper & Row.

———. 1982. *Italian Food*. Harmondsworth: Penguin.

David, Suzy. 1984. *The Sephardic Kosher Kitchen*. Middle Village, NY: Jonathan David.

de Amezúa, Clara Ma. G., Ángeles Arenillas, and José Carlos Capel. 1988. *From Spain with Olive Oil*. Madrid: Técnicos Editoriales y Consultores for ASOLIVA and ICEX.

de Croze, Austin. 1928. *Les plats régionaux de France*. Paris: Montaigne.

de Padua, Jacobus Philippus. 1962. *El libro agregà de serapiom*. Gustav Ineichen, ed. Parte 1: testo. Venice; Rome: Istituto per la Collaborazione Culturale.

Del Conte, Anna. 1987. *Gastronomy of Italy*. New York: Prentice-Hall.

delle Cinqueterre, Berengario. 1975. *The Renaissance Cookbook: Historical Perspectives Through Cookery*. Crown Point, IN: Dunes Press.

Denti di Pirajno, Alberto. 1970. *Siciliani a tavola: Itinerario gastronomico da messina a porto empedocle*. Milan: Longanesi.

———. 1985. *Il gastronomo educato*. 3rd ed. Vicenza: Neri Pozza.

Deplano, Francesco. 1988. *Sardegna in bocca*. Palermo: La Nuova Ed.ri.si.

der Haroutunian, Arto. 1983. *North African Cookery*. London: Century.

de' Medici, Lorenza. 1989. *The Renaissance of Italian Cooking*. New York: Fawcett Columbine.

———. 1992. *Tuscany: The Beautiful Cookbook*. San Francisco: Collins.

de' Medici, Lorenza, and Patrizia Passigli. 1988. *Italy, the Beautiful Cookbook: Authentic Recipes from the Regions of Italy*. Los Angeles: Knapp.

de' Medici Stucchi, Lorenza. 1988. *Cuisines de la mediterranée*. Marina Gagliano, trans. Paris: Flammarion.

di Napoli Oliver, Fiammetta. 1976. *La grande cucina siciliana*. Milan: Moizzi.

di Stefano, Bianca. 1987. *Cucina che vai natura che trovi: Ricette, tradizione e folklore della cucina rustica siciliana*. Palermo: Edikronos.

Doménech, Ignacio. n.d. [c. 1915]. *La nueva cocina elegante Española*. 2nd ed. Madrid: Helénica.

Doméneck, Alejndro, with Irena Kirshman, ed. 1974. *Spanish and Portuguese Cooking: Favorite Recipes from the Iberian Peninsula*. 'Round the world cooking library. New York: Drake.

Donati, Stella, ed. 1979. *Il grande manuale della cucina regionale*. Bergamo: Sogarco.

"Du fait de cuisine par Maistre Chiquart (1420)." 1985. Terence Scully, ed. *Vallesia: Bulletin Annuel de la Bibliothèque et des Archives Cantonales du Valais, des Musées de Valère et de la Majorie*. 40, 101–231.

Emi, Timur. 1990. *Günümüzün Yemek Kitabı*. Istanbul: Serhat. [in Turkish]

Eren, Neşet. 1969. *The Art of Turkish Cooking: Or, Delectable Delights of Topkapi*. New York: Doubleday.

Escudier, Jean-Noël. 1953. *La veritable cuisine provencale et niçoise*. Toulon: Éditions Gallia.

Fàbrega, Jaume. 1985. *La cuina gironina*. Barcelona: Graffiti Edicions i Editorial Laia.

Faccioli, Emilio, ed. 1987. *L'arte della cucina in Italia: Libri di ricette e trattati sulla civilità della tavola dal XIV al XIX secolo*. Turin: Giulio Einaudi.

Farah, Madelain. 1985. *Lebanese Cuisine*. Portland, OR: Lebanese Cuisine.

Famous Turkish Cookery n.d. Tepebaşı-İstanbul: Minyatür.

Feast of Italy. 1973. New York: Galahad.

Ferhi, Youcef. 1957. *Grand recettes de la cuisine algérienne*. Paris: Bordas.

Field, Carol. 1985. *The Italian Baker*. New York: Harper & Row.

———. 1990. *Celebrating Italy*. New York: William Morrow.

Fiori, Maria Falchi. 1985. *Le ricette della mia cucina sarda*. Florence: Riccio.

Fiorio Saba, Franca. 1977. *La cucina sarda*. Florence: Sansoni.

Francesconi, Jeanne Caròla. 1992. *La cucina napoletana*. Rome: Newton Compton.

Frati, Ludovico. 1899/1970. *Libro di cucina del secolo XIV*. Livorno: Raffaello. Reprinted Bologna, Testi Antichi di Gastronomia 7.

Fytrakis, Eva. 1981. *Greek Cooking*. Diana Reid, trans. Athens: Aegean.

Galizia, Anne, and Helen Caruana. 1972. *Recipes from Malta: A guide to Traditional Maltese Cooking*. Valletta: Progress Press.

Galluzzi, Maria, Alessandra Iori, Narsete Iori, and Marco Iannotta. 1987. *La cucina ferrarese*. Milan: Franco Muzzio.

Gitlitz, David M., and Linda Kay Davidson. 1999. *A Drizzle of Honey: The Lives and Recipes of Spain's Secret Jews*. New York: St. Martin's.

Gleijeses, Vittorio. 1977. *A Napoli si mangia cosi'*. Naples: Società Editrice Napoletana.

Göknar, Şükran. 1992. *Türk Islâm Sofrası*. Istanbul: Kitsan. [in Turkish]

González Pomata, Antonio. 1990. *Cocina alicantina*. León: Editorial Everest.

Goodman of Paris, the: A Treatise on Moral and Domestic Economy by a Citizen of Paris (c. 1393). 1928. Eileen Power, trans. London: George Routledge and Sons.

Gosetti, Fernanda. 1989. *La grande cucina regionale italiana: I primi piatti*. Milan: Fabbri Editori.

———. 1990. *La grande cucina regionale italiana: I pesci*. Milan: Fabbri Editori.

Gosetti della Salda, Anna. 1988. *Le ricette regionali italiane*. Milan: Casa Editrice "Solares."

Gozzini, Ilaria Giacosa. 1992. *A Taste of Ancient Rome*. Anna Herklotz, trans. Chicago: University of Chicago Press.

Granado, Diego. 1599/1971. *Libro del arte de cocina*. Madrid: Luiz Sanchez. Reprinted Madrid: La Sociedad de Bibliofilos Españoles.

Grasso, J. C. 1984. *The Best of Southern Italian Cooking*. Woodbury, NY: Barron's.

Gray, Patience. 1987. *Honey from a Weed: Fasting and Feasting in Tuscany, Catalonia, the Cyclades and Apulia*. New York: Harper & Row; Prospect Books.

Grigson, Jane. 1970. *Charcuterie & French Pork Cookery*. London: Penguin.

Grimaldi, Gianni. 1987. *Liguria in bocca*. Palermo: La Nuova Edrisi.

Guerrini, O. 1887. *Frammento di un libro di cucina del sec. XIV edito nel dì delle nozze carducci-gnaccarini*. Bologna: Nicola Zanichelli.

Guida Gastronomica d'Italia. 1931. Milan: Touring Club Italiano.

Guida Gastronomica e dei vini d'Italia. 1973. N.p.: "La Navicella."

Guinaudeau, Z. 1962. *Fès vu par sa cuisine*. Rabat: E. Laurent.

Guinaudeau-Franc, Zette. 1981. *Les secrets des cuisines en terre marocaine*. Paris: Jean-Pierre Taillandier.

Haase, Richard. 1985. *Jewish Regional Cooking*. London: Macdonald.

Hadjiat, Salima. 1990. *La cuisine d'Algerie*. Paris: Publisud.

Hal, Fatéma. 1995. *Les saveurs & les gestes: Cuisines et traditions du Maroc*. Paris: Stock.

Halıcı, Nevin. 1989. *Nevin Halıcı's Turkish Cookbook*. E. M. Samy, trans. London: Dorling Kindersley.

Hammond, Richard, and George Martin. 1957. *Eating in Italy: A Pocket Guide to Italian Food and Restaurants*. New York: Charles Scribner's Sons.

Harris, Valentina. 1988. *Traveller's Guide to the Food of Italy*. New York: Henry Holt.

———. 1989. *Recipes from an Italian Farmhouse*. New York: Simon & Schuster.

Hieatt, Constance B., and Robin F. Jones. 1986. "Two Anglo-Norman Culinary Collections Edited from British Library Manuscripts Additional 32085 and Royal 12.C.xii." *Speculum*, 61, no. 4 (October): 859–82.

Hierro, Miguel Salcedo. 1989. *La cocina andaluza: Premio nacional de gastronomia 1979*. Seville: Centro Andaluz del Libro.

Howe, Robin. 1953. *Italian Cooking*. London: Andre Deutsch.

Iddison, Philip. 1990. "Leaves from a Turkish Notebook." *Petits Propos Culinaire*, 34 (March): 21–30.

Ifergan, Jeanne. 1990. *Savoir préparer la cuisine juive d'Afrique du nord*. Paris: Idées Recettes.

Il cucchiaio d'argento: Il libro fondamentale della cucina italiana. 1952. 3rd ed. Milan: Domus.

Il cuoco piedmontese. 1832. 6th ed. Milan: Giovani Silvestri.

Isnard, Léon. n.d. *L'Afrique gourmande: Encyclopédie culinaire de l'Algérie de la Tunisie et du Maroc*. 2nd ed. Oran: L. Fouque.

Italian Academy of Cookery. 1987. *The Great Italian Cookbook*. New York: International Culinary Society.

al-Jābirī, Lamia. n.d. *Shaḥiyya ṭayibba*. Damascus [?]: Dar Ṭlas. [in Arabic]

Jaffin, Leone. 1987. *150 recettes et mille et un souvenirs d'une Juive d'Algérie: Récit culinaire*. Paris: Encre.

Jarret, Enrica, and Vernon Jarret. 1975. *The Complete Book of Pasta*. New York: Dover.

Jenkins, Nancy Harmon. 1994. *The Mediterranean Diet Cookbook: A Delicious Alternative for Lifelong Health*. New York, Bantam.

Johnston, Mireille. 1976. *Cuisine of the Sun: Classic Recipes from Nice and Provence*. New York: Random House.

Jouveau, René. 1976. *La cuisine provençale de tradition populaire*. Nîmes: Bene.

Kaak, Zeinab. 1976. *La sofra ou l'art de préparer la véritable cuisine tunisienne*. Tunis: STD.

Kamman, Madeleine. 1997. *The New Making of a Cook: The Art, Techniques, and Science of Good Cooking*. New York: William Morrow.

Kapetanović, Ružica, and Alojzije Kapetanović. 1993. *Croatian Cuisine*. Rev. ed. Scottsdale: Associated Book Publishers.

Karapandža, Stevo. 1986. *Croatian Cookery*. Ellen Elias-Bursać, trans. Zagreb: Grafčki Zavod Hrvatske; Pittsburgh: Croatian Fraternal Union of America.

Karsenty, Irène, and Lucienne Karsenty. 1969. *Le livre de la cuisine pied-noir*. Paris: Planète.

Kaspar, Lynn Rossetto. 1992. *The Splendid Table: Recipes from Emilia-Romagna, the Heartland of Northern Italian Food*. New York: William Morrow.

Kershner, Ruth. 1977. *Greek Cooking*. New York: Weathervane.

Khayat, Marie Karam, and Margaret Clark Keatinge. 1961. *Food from the Arab World*. Beirut: Khayats.

Kochilas, Diane. 1990. *The Food and Wine of Greece*. New York: St. Martin's Press.

Koşay, Hămit Z., and Akile Ülkücan. 1961. *Anadolu Yemekleri ve Türk Mutfaği*. Ankara: Milli Eğitim Basimevi. [in Turkish]

Kouki. Mohamed. 1971. *La cuisine tunisienne d' "ommok sannafa."* Tunis: Maison Tunisienne de l'Edition.

———. 1993. *Cuisine et patisserie tunisiennes*. Tunis: Dar Ettourath Ettounsi.

Kramarz, Inge. 1972. *The Balkan Cookbook*. New York: Crown.

La vera cuciniera genovese. 1948. Emanuele Rossi, comp. Milan: Bietti.

La cuisine tunisienne. 1974. Tunis: Societe Tunisienne de Diffusion and Paris: Jean-Pierre Taillandier.

Ladies of the Philoptochos Society, Holy Trinity Greek Orthodox Church, Charleston, South Carolina, comp. 1957. *Popular Greek Recipes*. Charleston: Greek Orthodox Ladies Philoptochos Society.

L'antica cuciniera genovese. 1983. Genoa: Nuova Editrice Genovese.

Lanza, Anna Tasca. 1993. *The Heart of Sicily: Recipes and Reminiscences of Regaleali—A Country Estate*. New York: Clarkson Potter.

Larousse: Les fromages. 1987. Paris: Larousse.

Latini, Antonio. 1692. *Lo scalco alla moderna*. Naples: Ant. Parrino e Michele Luigi Mutii.

Levi, Zion, and Hani Agabria. 1988. *The Yemenite Cookbook*. New York: Seaver Books.

"*Liber de coquina*." 1969. In Marianne Mulon. "Deux traités inédits d'art culinaire médiéval," *Bulletin Philologique et Historique (jusqu'à 1610)*, 1: 369–435.

Libre de sent soví. 1979. Rudolf Grewe, ed. Barcelona: Editorial Barcino.

Lingua, Paola. 1989. *La cucina dei genovesi*. Milan: Franco Muzzi.

Llibre del coc de la seu de Tarragona. 1331/1935. Joan Serra i Vilaró, ed. Barcelona: La Acadèmíca, Hs. de Serra i Russell.

Lodato, Nuccia. 1978. *Le ricette della mia cucina siciliana*. Milan: Edizioni del Riccio.

Lo Monte, Mimmetta. 1983. *La bella cucina: Traditional Recipes from a Sicilian Kitchen*. New York: Beaufort Books.

———. 1990. *Mimmetta Lo Monte's Classic Sicilian Cookbook*. New York: Simon & Schuster.

Lo Pinto, Maria. 1948. *The Art of Italian Cooking*. New York: Doubleday.

Lorini, Tebaldo. 1985. *Mugello in cucina: Storie, prodotti, tradizioni, ricette*. Borgo S. Lorenzo: Toccafondi.

Loubat, Bernard, and Jeannette Bertrandy. 1994. *La bonne cuisine provençale*. Paris: Solar.

Lozinski, Grégoire. 1933. *La bataille de caresme et de charnage*. Paris: Ancienne Honoré Champion.

M. F. 1828. *La cucina caserecchia con cinque utili trattati delle frutta, de'vini, de'gelati, de'rosolj e della manifattura de'dolci*. 7th ed. Naples: Sav. Giordano.

Machlin, Edda Serva. 1981. *The Classic Cuisine of Italian Jews*. New York: Everett House.

Macmiadhacháin, Anna, et al. 1979. *The Mediterranean Cookbook*. Secaucus: Chartwell.

Maffioli, Giuseppe. 1970. *La cucina per l'amore*. Turin Dellavalle.

———. 1981a. *La cucina padovana*. Milan: Franco Muzzio.

———. 1981b. *La cucina padovana*. Milan: Franco Muzzio.

———. 1982. *La cucina veneziana*. Padua: Franco Muzzio.

———. 1983. *La cucina trevigiana*. Padua: Franco Muzzio.

Malgieri, Nick. 1990. *Great Italian Desserts*. Boston: Little, Brown.

Mallo, Beppe. 1979. *Calabria e lucania in bocca*. Palermo: II Vespro.

Mallos, Tess. 1979. *The Complete Middle East Cookbook*. New York: McGraw-Hill.

———. 1984. *Greek Cookbook*. Sydney: Lansdowne Press.

Man, Rosamond. 1995. *Mezze*. Reading, UK: Garnet.

Mangione, Felice. 1982. *Sicilia a tavola*. Marina di Patti: Pungitopo.

March, Lourdes. 1985. *El Libro de la paella y de los arroces*. Madrid: Alianza Editorial.

Marjanović-Radica, Dika. 1973. *Dalmatinska Kuhinja*. Sarajevo: Veselin, Masleša. [in Serbo-Croatian]

Mark, Theonie. 1972. *Greek Islands Cooking*. Boston: Little, Brown.

Martí i Oliver, Jaume. 1989. *Receptari de cuina de segle XVIII*. Joan Miralles and Francesca Cantallops, eds. Biblioteca Marian Aguiló 12. Barcelona: Departament de Filologia Catalan i Lingüística General, Universitat de les Illes Balears.

Mascarelli, Benoit. 1947. *La table en Provence & sur la cote d'Azur*. Paris: Jacques Haumont.

Masui, Kazuko, and Tomoko Yamada. 1966. *French Cheeses*. Eyewitness Handbooks. New York: DK Publishing.

McDouall, Robin. 1971. *Mediterranean Cooking for Pleasure*. London: Paul Hamlyn.

Médecin, Jacques. 1983. *Cuisine niçoise: Recipes from a Mediterranean Kitchen*. Peter Graham, ed. and trans. London: Penguin Books.

Middione, Carlo. 1987. *The Food of Southern Italy*. New York: William Morrow.

Mirodan, Vladimir. 1989. *The Balkan Cookbook*. Gretna: Pelican.

Montiño, Francisco Martínez. 1611/1809. *Arte de cocina, pastelería, vizcochería y conservería*. Madrid: Don Joseph Doblado.

Morard, Marius. 1984. *Manuel complet de la cuisineaire provençale*. Marseilles: Lafitte Reprints.

Muffoletto, Anna. 1982. *The Art of Sicilian Cooking*. New York: Gramercy.

Muzannar, Ibrahim. 1981. *Fan al-ṭabkh al-ʿarabī*. Beirut [?]: Muktabat Lubnān. [in Arabic]

Nahoum, Aldo. 1971. *The Art of Israeli Cooking*. New York: Holt, Rinehart and Winston.

Naso, Irma. 1990. *Formaggi del medioevo*. La "Summa lacticiniorum" *di pantaleone da confienza*. Turin: Il Segnalibro.

Navarro Rubio, P. 1975. *Atlas del arte culinario*. Barcelona: Ediciones Jover.

Nebbia, Antonio. 1792. *Il cuoco maceratese*. 5th ed. Macerata: Lucca Giannini.

Nicolaou, Nearchos. 1980. *Cooking from Cyprus: The Island of Aphrodite*. 4th ed. Nicosia: Nearchos Nicolaou.

Nicolau, M. del Carme. 1972. *Catalan Cooking*. Anna Lankester, trans. Barcelona: Miguel Arimany.

Norman, Barbara. 1966. *The Spanish Cookbook*. New York: Athenaeum.

Obejda, Khadidja. 1983. *253 recettes de cuisine algérienne*. Paris: Jacques Grancher.

Orga, Irfan. 1963. *Turkish Cooking*. London: Andre Deutsch.

Ortega, Simone. 1989. *Mil ochenta recetas de cocina*. Madrid: Alianza Editorial.

Paradissis, Chrissa. 1976. *The Best Book of Greek Cookery*. Athens: Efstathiadis Group.

Paramichael-Kontronmpa, Allas. 1985. *Roditikes Syntages: Paradosiakes Trophes tes Rodoy*. Athens: Lykeion Essenidon Rodoy. [in Greek]

Perisi, Giuseppina. 1989. *Cucine di sardegna*. Padua: Franco Muzzio.

Perl, Lila. 1967. *Rice, Spice and Bitter Oranges: Mediterranean Foods and Festivals*. Cleveland and New York: World.

Petroni, Paolo. 1976a. *Il libro della vera cucina marinara*. Florence: Bonechi.

———. 1976b. *Il libro della vera cucina bolognese*. Florence: Bonechi.

———. 1978. *Il libro della vera cucina emiliana*. Florence: Bonechi.

Pierotti, G. 1927. *Cucina toscana*. Florence: Edizioni dell'ente per le attività toscane.

Pisa, A., and A. Chines. 1970. *Cucina d'un putiri fari: Piccolo breviario di ricette siciliane strane, insolite e divertenti*. Palermo: S. F. Flaccovio.

Platina [Bartolomeo de Sacchi di Piadena]. 1967. *De honesta voluptate*, vol. V. N.p.: Mallinckrodt Chemical Works.

———. 1998. *On Right Pleasure and Good Health*. A Critical Edition and Translation of *De Honesta Voluptate et Valetudine*. May Ella Milham, ed. and trans. Tempe, AZ: Medieval & Renaissance Texts & Studies, The Renaissance Society of America.

Pohren, D. E. 1972. *Adventures in Taste: The Wines and Folk Food of Spain*. Morón de la Frontera Sevilla: Society of Spanish Studies, Finca Espartero.

Pomar, Anna. 1988. *La cucina tradizionale siciliana*. N.p.: Giuseppe Brancato.

Pomata, Antonio González. 1990. *Cocina alicantina*. León: Everest.

Prezzolini, Giuseppe. 1955. *Spaghetti Dinner*. New York: Abelard-Schuman.

Rabiha. 1925. *La bonne cuisine turque facile et economique des mets les plus usités et renommés du pays*. 2nd ed. N.p.: Société Anonyme de Papeterie et d'Imprimerie.

Ramazani, Nesta. 1974. *Persian Cooking: A Table of Exotic Delights*. New York: Quadrangle.

Ramazanoğlu, Gülseren. 1993. *Turkish Cookery*. 4th ed. Istanbul: Ramazanoğlu.

Ratto, G. B., and Giovanni Ratto. 1947. *La cuciniera genovese: Ossia la vera maniera di cucinare alla genovese*. 13th ed. Genoa: Pagano.

ar-Razi, Abu Bakr Muhammad ibn Zakariya. n.d. [c. 1465?]. *Liber tertius almansori aut libaldoni*. In versi italiani. N.p.[in Biblioteca Nazionale Marciana, Venice].

Reboul, J.-B. n.d. *La cuisinière provençale*. 24th ed. Marseilles: Tacussel.

Recipe Club of Saint Paul's Greek Orthodox Cathedral. 1990. *The Complete Book of Greek Cooking*. New York: Harper & Row.

Redon, Odile, Françoise Sabban, and Silvano Servanti. 1991. *La gastronomie au moyen âge: 150 recettes de France et d'Italie*. Rennes: Stock.

Rios, Alicia, and Lourdes March. 1992. *The Heritage of Spanish Cooking*. New York: Random House.

Ripoll, Luis. 1984. *Cocina de la Baleares: 620 recetas de Mallorca, Menorca e Ibiza-Formentera*. 3rd ed. Palma de Mallorca: Libro de intéres turístico.

Rivieccio Zaniboni, Maria. 1975. *Cucina e vini di napoli e della campania*. Milan: Mursia.

Roden, Claudia. 1974. *A Book of Middle Eastern Food*. New York: Vintage.

———. 1987. *Mediterranean Cookery*. New York: Alfred A. Knopf.

———. 1996. *The Book of Jewish Food: An Odyssey from Samarkand to New York*. New York: Alfred A. Knopf.

Root, Waverly. 1971. *The Food of Italy*. New York: Vintage.

———. 1974. *The Best of Italian Cooking*. New York: Grosset & Dunlap.

———. 1992. *The Food of France*. New York: Vintage.

Rousseau, Francesca. 1978. *L'Italia in 455 ricette: La cucina regionale italiana*. Florence: Le Lettere.

Ruperto de Nola. 1520/1929. *Libro de guisados*. Dionisio Pérez ("Post-Thebussem"), ed. Madrid: Los Clàsicos Olvidados.

Russo, Baldo. 1988. *Sapore di sicilia*. Palermo: La Nuova ED.RI.SI.

Sada, Luigi. 1979. *Puglie in bocca*. Palermo: Il Vespro.

———. 1991. *La cucina della terra di Bari*. Padua: Franco Muzzio.

———. 1994. *La cucina pugliese*. Rome: Newton Compton.

Salaman, Rena. 1987. *The Cooking of Greece and Turkey*. London: Martin Books for J. Sainsbury.

Salaparuta, Enrico Alliata, Duca di. 1971. *Cucina vegetariana e naturismo crudo: Manuale di gastrosofia naturista con raccolta di 1030 formule scelte d'ogni paese*. Palermo: Esse.

Samia, Ilias, Ghalib Yaḥshushī, and Joseph Maḥfuẓ. n.d. *Kitāb al-maṭbakh al-Lubnāniyya wa'l-ᶜArabiyya*. Beirut [?]: al-mu ᶜassassa al-Lubnāniyya al-ᶜArabiyya li'ttawzīᶜ wa'l-ṭibāᶜa wa'l-nashr. [in Arabic]

Sandri, Amedeo. 1985. *La polenta nella cucina veneta*. 2nd ed. Padua: Franco Muzzio.

Sandri, Amedeo, and Maurizio Fallopi. 1982. *Veneti e "bacalà."* Milan: Nuova Edritrice Periodici Italiani.

Santich, Barbara. 1995. *The Original Mediterranean Cuisine: Medieval Recipes for Today*. Chicago: Chicago Review Press.

Santini, Aldo. 1988. *La cucina livornese*. Padua: Franco Muzzio.

Scappi, Bartolomeo. 1570/1981. *Opera [dell'arte del cucinare]*. Testi Antichi di Gastronomia 12. Sala Bolognese: Arnaldo Forni Editore.

Scott, David. 1983. *Recipes for an Arabian Night: Traditional Cooking from North Africa and the Middle East*. New York: Pantheon.

Scully, D. Eleanor, and Terence Scully. 1995. *Early French Cookery: Sources, History, Original Recipes and Modern Adaptations*. Ann Arbor: University of Michigan Press.

Scully, Terence. 1995. "Mixing it Up in the Medieval Kitchen." In Mary-Jo Arn, ed., *Medieval Food and Drink*. Acta vol. 21. Binghamton: Center for Medieval and Early Renaissance Studies, State University of New York at Binghamton. pp. 1–26.

Scully, Terence, ed. 1988. *The "Viandier" of Taillevent: An Edition of all Extant Manuscripts*. Ottawa: University of Ottawa.

Seijo Alonso, Francisco G. 1977. *Gastronomia de la provincia de Alicante*. Alicante: Villa.

Sigal, Jane. 1994. *Backroad Bistros, Farmhouse Fare: A French Country Cookbook*. New York: Doubleday.

Simeti, Mary Taylor. 1989. *Pomp and Sustenance: Twenty-Five Centuries of Sicilian Food*. New York: Alfred A. Knopf.

Skoura, Sophia. 1967. *The Greek Cook Book*. Helen Georges, trans. New York: Crown.

Smouha, Patricia. 1955. *Middle Eastern Cooking*. London: Andre Deutsch.

Spontini, G. C. Zonghi. 1982. *Della cucina erotica: Dall'antica roma al rinascimento a oggi la gastronomia che dà più forza e poesia all'amore*. Turin: MEB.

Stavroulakis, Nicholas. 1986. *Cookbook of the Jews of Greece*. Port Jefferson: Cadmus.

Stecchetti, Lorenzo (Dott. O. Guerrini). 1884. *La tavola e la cucina nei secoli XIV e XV*. Florence: G. Barbèra.

Stubbs, Joyce M. 1963. *The Home Book of Greek Cookery: A Selection of Traditional Greek Recipes*. London: Faber and Faber.

Stufa, Maria Luisa Incontri Lotteringhi della. 1965. *Pranzi e conviti: La cucina toscana dal XVI secolo ai giorni d'oggi*. Florence: Olimpia.

Taglienti, Maria Luisa. 1955. *The Italian Cookbook*. New York: Random House.

Tamzali, Haydee. 1986. *La cuisine en Afrique du nord*. Paris: Vilo.

Testa, Itala, ed. 1994. *Cucina di sardegna*. Cagliari: Edi-Sar.

Theuderich [King of the Franks]. 1864–70. "Epistula Anthimi viri inlustris comitis et legatarii ad gloriosissimum Theudericum regem Francorum (de observatione ciborum)" and "Die Diätetik des Anthimus." In Valentin Rose, *Anecdota græca et græcolatina*, 2, pp. 43–98. Berlin: Ferd. Duemmler.

Thibaut i Comelade, Eliana. 1986. *La cuina medieval a l'abast*. Barcelona: Edicions de la Magrana.

———. 1989. *La cuisine catalane*. 2 vols. 3rd ed. Malakoff: L. T. Editions J. Lanore.

Torres, Marimar. 1992. *The Catalan Country Kitchen: Food and Wine from the Pyrenees to the Mediterranean Seacoast of Barcelona*. Reading, MA: Addison-Wesley.

Tselementes, Nicholas. 1954. *Greek Cookery*. New York: D.C. Divry.

Turabi Effendi. 1862/1987. *Turkish Cookery Book: A Collection of Receipts*. facs. Rottingdean: Rottingdean Cooks Books.

Turkish Cookery. 1990. Istanbul: Net Turistik Yayinlar.

Tzabar, Naomi, and Shimon Tzabar. 1966. *Yemenite & Sabra Cookery*. Gerald Sevel, trans. 2nd ed. Tel-Aviv: Sadan.

Uccello, Antonio. 1976. *Pani e dolci di sicilia*. Palermo: Sellerio.

"Un libro de cocina del siglo XIV." 1935. José Osset Merle, ed. *Boletin de la Sociedad Castellonese de Cultura*, 16, no. 3: 156–77.

Vada, Simonetta Lupi. 1985. *Step by Step Cookbook Italian Seafood and Salad and More*. Secaucus: Chartwell.

———. 1986. *The Flavors of Italy*. Tucson AZ: HP Books.

Vehel, J. n.d *La cuisine tunisienne*. Tunis: J. Saliba.

Venos, Fannie, and Lillian Prichard. 1950. *Can the Greeks Cook!* Richmond: Dietz Press.

Veronelli, Luigi. 1973. *The World of Food: Italy*. New York: World.

Waines, David. 1989. *In a Caliph's Kitchen*. London: Riad el-Rayyes.

Waldron, Maggie. 1983. *Barbecue & Smoke Cookery*. San Francisco: 101 Productions.

al-Warrāq, Ibn Sayyār. 1987. *Kitāb al-ṭabīkh*. Kaj Öhrnberg and Sahban Mroueh, eds. Studia Orientalia 60. Helsinki: Societas Orientalis Fennica. [in Arabic]

Wason, Betty. 1963. *The Art of Spanish Cooking*. New York: Doubleday.

Willan, Anne. 1977. *Great Cooks and Their Recipes: From Taillevent to Escoffier*. New York: McGraw-Hill.

Wolfert, Paula. 1973. *Couscous and Other Good Food From Morocco*. New York: Harper & Row.

———. 1983. *The Cooking of South-West France*. New York: Harper & Row.

———. 1985. *Mediterranean Cooking*. New York: Ecco Press.

———. 1988. *Paula Wolfert's World of Food: A Collection of Recipes from Her Kitchen, Travels, and Friends*. New York: Harper & Row.

———. 1994. *The Cooking of the Eastern Mediterranean: 215 Healthy, Vibrant, and Inspired Recipes*. New York: HarperCollins.

———. 1998. *Mediterranean Grains and Greens: A Book of Savory Sun-Drenched Recipes*. New York: HarperCollins.

Women of St. Paul's Greek Orthodox Church, Hempstead, Long Island, New York. 1961. *The Art of Greek Cookery*. New York: Doubleday.

Wright, Clifford A. 1992. *Cucina Paradiso: The Heavenly Food of Sicily*. New York: Simon & Schuster.

———. 1995. *Lasagne*. Boston: Little, Brown.

———. 1996. *Grill Italian*. New York: Macmillan.

Wright, Jeni. 1981. *The Encyclopedia of Italian Cooking*. New York: Crescent Books.

Yassine, Sima Osman, and Sadouf Kamal. 1984. *Middle Eastern Cuisine*. Beirut: Dar el-ilm lil-Malayin.

Yazgan, Mehmet, ed. 1992. *Turkish Cuisine*. Anita Gillet, trans. Istanbul: Yazgan Turizm.

Yianilos, Theresa Karas. 1970. *The Complete Greek Cookbook: The Best from Three Thousand Years of Greek Cooking*. New York: Avenel Books.

Yıldız, Gülsev. 1994. *Türk Mutfağinin Izahlı Yemek ve Tatlı Kitabı*. Istanbul: Şenyıldız Yayınevi. [in Turkish]

Zambrini, Francesco, ed. 1863. *Il libro della cucina de secolo XIV*. Testo di lingua non mai fin qui stampato. Bologna: Romagnoli.

Zeitoun, Edmond. 1977. *250 recettes classiques de cuisine tunisienne*. Paris: Jacques Grancher.

OTHER WORKS

ʿAbd el Wahab Pacha. 1951. "Pantelleria, île arab." *Proceedings of the Royal Society of Historical Studies*, 1.

Abdul-Wahab, Hassen Husny. 1905. *La domination Musulmane en Sicile*. Tunis: J. Picard.

Abel, Wilhelm. 1980. *Agricultural fluctuations in Europe: From the Thirteenth to the Twentieth Centuries*. Olive Ordish, trans. New York: St. Martin's.

Abrahams, Israel. 1981. *Jewish Life in the Middle Ages*. New York: Atheneum.

Abrate, Mario. 1957. "Creta—colonia veneziana nei secoli XIII-XV." *Economia e Storia*, 4 no. 3 (July-September): 251–77.

Abulafia, David. 1984. "The Role of Trade in Muslim-Christian Contact during the Middle Ages." In Dionisius A. Agius and Richard Hitchcock, eds., *The Arab Influence in Medieval Europe:* Folia Scholastica Mediterranea. Reading: Ithaca Press.

———. 1987. *Italy, Sicily, and the Mediterranean 1100–1400*. London: Variorum.

———. 1988. *Frederick II A Medieval Emperor*. London: Allen Lane, Penguin Press.

———. 1990. "End of Muslim Sicily." In James M. Powell, ed., *Muslims under Latin Rule 1100–1300* (pp. 103–33). Princeton: Princeton University Press.

Abu-Lughod, Janet. 1971. *Cairo: 1001 Years of the City Victorious*. Princeton: Princeton University Press.

———. 1989. *Before European Hegemony: The World System A.D. 1250–1350*. Oxford: Oxford University Press.

Abu-Lughod, Lila. 1988. *Veiled Sentiments: Honor and Poetry in a Bedouin Society*. Berkeley: University of California Press.

Abū Marwān ʿAbd al-Malik b. Zuhr. 1992. *Kitāb al-agḏiya (Tratados de los alimentos)*. Expiración García Sánchez, ed. and trans. Madrid: Consejo Superior de Investigaciones Científicas, Instituto de Cooperacíon con el Mundo Arabe.

Acta Sanctorum Aprilis [Acta de B. Guillelmo Eremitae]. 1675. Godefrido Henschenio and Daniele Papebrochio. Vol. 9 (tome 1). 66 vols. Antwerp: Michaelem Cnobarum.

Agius, Dionisius A. 1984. *Arabic Literary Works as a Source of Documentation for Technical Terms of the Material Culture*. Islamkundliche Untersuchungen Band 98. Berlin: Klaus Schwarz.

———. 1984. *The Arab Influence in Medieval Europe*: Folia Scholastica Mediterranea. Reading: Ithaca Press.

———. 1986. "Italo-Sicula Elements of Nautical Terms Found in Medieval and Post-Medieval Arabic." *Scripta Mediterranea*, 7: 37–51.

———. 1990. "Arab Expertise in Cultivation as Reflected in the Siculo-Arabic Agricultural Terminology." *Le Muséon,* 103, fasc. 1–2: 167–76.

Agusti, Miquel. 1617/1988. *Llibre dels secrets de agricultura casa rústica i pastoril*. Barcelona: Alta Fulla.

Ahmad, Aziz. 1975. *A History of Islamic Sicily*. Islamic Surveys 10. Edinburgh: Edinburgh University Press.

Alazdi, Muhammad ibn Ahmad Abulmutahhar. 1902. *Abulkasim, ein Bagdader Sittenbild*. Adam Mez, ed. Heidelberg: Carl Winter.

Alberini, Massimo. 1994. *Maccheroni e spaghetti: Storia letteratura aneddoti 1244–1994*. Casale Monferrato: Piemme.

Alberti, Tommaso. 1889. *Viaggio a Costantinopoli*. A. Bacchi della Lega, ed. Bologna: Romagnoli dall'Acqua.

Alcala, Pedro de. 1505. *Vocabulista aravigo en letra castellana*. Granada: J. Varela.

da Aleppo, P. Gabriele Maria, and G. M. Calvaruso. 1910. *Le fonti arabiche nel dialetto siciliano*. Rome: Ermanno Loescher, 1910.

Alessio, Giovanni. 1958–59. "Storia linguistica di un antico cibo rituale: 'i maccheroni,' " *Atti della Accademia Pontaniana*, nuova serie, 8: 261–80.

Algozina, Rosaria Papa. 1977. *Sicilia Araba*. Catania: Edizioni Greco.

Alî al-Ballanûbî, Ibn Hamdis, and ʿAbd ar-Rahmân di Trapani. 1987. *Poeti arabi di sicilia*. Francesca Maria Corrao, ed. Milan: Arnoldo Mondadori.

Aliquot, H. 1984. "Les épices à la table des papes d'Avignon au XIV e siecle." *Manger et Boire au Moyen Âge*, Actes du Colloque de Nice, 1, no. 27: 131–50: *Aliments et Société*. Centre d'Études Médiévales de Nice: Centre National de la Recherche Scientifique, Les Belles Lettres.

Allard, Jeanne. 1987. "Diego Granado Maldonado." *Petits Propos Culinaire*, 25 (March): 35–41.

Allen, W. E. D. 1963. *Problems of Turkish Power in the Sixteenth Century*. London: Central Asian Research Centre.

Amari, Michele, ed. 1880–81. *Biblioteca arabo-sicula*, versione italiana. 2 vols. Turin: Ermanno Loescher.

Amari, Michele. 1986. *Storia dei musulmani di sicilia*, 3 vols. in 5 parts. Catania: Dafni.

Amari, M., and C. Schiaparelli, eds. 1883. *L'Italia descritta nel* "Libro del re Ruggiero" *compilato da Edrisi*. Rome: Salviucci.

Anderson, Perry. 1980. *Lineages of the Absolutist State*. London: Verso.

André, Jacques. 1956. *Lexique des termes de botanique en Latin*. Paris: C. Klincksieck.

———. 1981. *L'Alimentation et la cuisine a Rome*. Paris: Les Belles Lettres.

Andrews, E. A. 1851. *Latin-English Lexicon*. Harper & Brothers: New York.

Andrews, Jean. 1984. *Peppers: The Domesticated Capsicums*. Austin: University of Texas.

Andrieux, Maurice. 1972. *Daily Life in Venice at the Time of Casanova*. Mary Fitton, trans. New York: Praeger.

Angarano, Francesco Antonio. 1973. *Vita tradizionale dei contadini e pastori calabresi*. Biblioteca de "Lares," vol. 41. Florence: Leo S. Olschki.

Antonlini, Piero. 1983. *I manducanti: Storia e civilta' dell'uomo a tavola*. Venice: Rebellato.

Archivio di Stato, Campo dei Frari, Venezia. 1419–21. Senato I-R no. 53, Deliber. Miste, MCCCCXXI, XXIII, and Senato Misti, reg. 53 doppio f. 488, Dec. 23, 1421.

Argenti, Philip P. 1958. *The Occupation of Chios by the Genoese and Their Administration of the Island, 1346–1566*. 3 vols. Cambridge: Cambridge University Press.

Arié, Rachel. 1974–75. "Remarques sur l'alimentation des Musulmans d'Espagne au cours du bas moyen âge." *Cuadernos de Estudios Medievales*, 2–3: 299–312.

Aristophanes. 1971. *The Complete Plays*. Moses Hadas, ed. New York: Bantam.

Arndt, Alice. 1995. "The Historical Development of the Cuisine of Turkey from the Steppes of Central Asia to the Shores of the Mediterranean with Attention to the Culinary Contributions of the Sephardic Jews." *Culinary Historians of Boston Newsletter*, 15, no. 4 (March): 3–12.

Arte della cucina e alimentazione nelle opere a stampa della Biblioteca Nazionale Marciana dal XV al XIX Secolo. 1987. Anna Alberati, Mirella Canzian, Tiziana Plebani, Marcello Brusegan, eds. Ministero per i Beni Culturali e Abientali, Biblioteca Nazionale Marciana-Venezia Rome: Istituto Poligrafico e Zecca dello Stato.

Ashtor, E. 1968. "Essai sur l'alimentation des diverses classes sociales dans l'Orient médiéval," *Annales: Économies. Sociétés. Civilisations*, 23, no. 5 (September–October): 1017–53.

———. 1970. "The Diet of Salaried Classes in the Medieval Near East." *Journal of Asian History*, 4, no. 1: 1–24.

———. 1976. "Observations on Venetian Trade in the Levant in the XIVth Century." *Journal of European Economic History*, 5, no. 3 (Winter): 533–86.

———. 1980. "The Volume of Mediaeval Spice Trade." *Journal of European Economic History*, 9, no. 3 (Winter): 753–63.

———. 1981. "Levantine Sugar Industry in the Late Middle Ages: A Case of Technological Decline." In A. L. Udovitch, ed., *The Islamic Middle East, 700–1900: Studies in Economic and Social History* (pp. 91–132). Princeton Studies on the Near East. Princeton, NJ: Darwin Press.

———. 1983. *Levant Trade in the Later Middle Ages*. Princeton: Princeton University Press.

———. 1986. *East-West Trade in the Medieval Mediterranean*. London: Variorum Reprints.

Asín Palacios, Miguel, ed. 1943. *Glosario de voces romances registradas por un botánico anónimo hispano-musulmán (siglos XI–XII)*. Madrid and Granada: Escuelas de Estudios Árabes de Madrid y Granada.

Asso, Ignacio de. 1798. *Historia de la economia politica de Aragon*. Zaragossa: Francisco Magallon.

Athenaeus. 1969–93. *The Deipnosophists*. Charles Burton Gulick, trans. Loeb Classical Library. 7 vols. Cambridge: Harvard University Press.

Aubaile-Sallenave, Françoise. 1984. "L'Agriculture musulmane aux premiers temps de la conquête: apports et emprunts, à propos de *Agricultural innovation in the early Islamic world* de Andrew M. Watson." *Journal d'Agriculture Traditionelle et de Botanique Appliquée*. 31, no. 3–4: 245–56.

———. 1994. "'*Al-Kishk*': The Past and Present of a Complex Culinary Practice." In Sami Zubaida and Richard Tapper, eds., *Culinary Cultures of the Middle East*. pp. 105–139. London: I. B. Tauris with Centre of Near and Middle Eastern Studies, School of Oriental and African Studies, University of London.

Aymard, Maurice. 1966. *Venise, Raguse et le commerce du blé pendant la seconde moitié du XIVe siècle*. Paris: S.E.V.P.E.N.

———. 1972. "Une famille de l'aristocratie sicilienne aux XVIe et XVIIe siècles: Les ducs de Terranova." *Revue Historique*, 501 (January–March): 29–66.

———. 1975. "Histoire de l'alimentation: l'Italie." *Mélanges de l'École Française de Rome: Moyen Âge-Temps Modernes*, 87, no. 2: 455–460.

———. 1976. "Il commercio dei grani nella Sicilia del '500." *Archivio Storico per la Sicila Orientale*, 22, fasc. 1–3: 19.

———. 1979. "Toward the History of Nutrition: Some Methodological Remarks." *Food and Drink in History: Selections from the Annales. Économies. Sociétés, Civilisations* (pp. 1–16). Robert Forster and Orest Ranum, eds., Elborg Forster and Patricia M. Ranum, trans. Vol. 5. Baltimore: Johns Hopkins University.

Aymard, Maurice and Henri Bresc. 1975. "Nourritures et consommation en Sicile entre XIVe et XVIIIe siècle." *Mèlanges de l'École Française de Rome: Moyen Âge-Temps Modernes*, 87, n.2: 535–81.

Badi, Méri. 1985. *La cocina judeo-español*. Barcelona: Muchnik.

Baehrel, René. 1961. *Une croissance: La Basse-Provence rurale (fin XVIe siècle-1789)*. Paris: S.E.V.P.E.N.

Bahloul, Joëlle. 1983. *Le culte de la table dressé: Rites et traditions de la table juive algérienne*. Paris: A.-M. Métailié.

al-Bakrī, Abū ʿUbayd. 1913/1965. *Description de l'Afrique septentrionale*. Mac Guckin de Slane, trans. Algiers: Adolphe Jourdan. Reprinted Paris: Adrien-Maisonneuve.

———. 1968. *Jughrāfīyat al-Andalus wa Ūrūbā (The geography of Andalusia and Europe from the book* Al-Masālik wal-Mamalik [*The routes and the countries*]) ʿAbd al-Raḥmān ʿAlī al-Ḥajjī, ed. Beirut: Dar al-Irshad. [in Arabic]

Balfet, Helene. 1975. "Bread in Some Regions of the Mediterranean Area: A Contribution to the Studies of Eating Habits." In Margaret L. Arnott, ed., *Gastronomy: The Anthropology of Food and Food Habits*. The Hague: Mouton.

Balletto, Laura. 1986. "Dieta e gastronomia nel medioevo Genovese." *Saggi e Documenti VII*. vol. 2 (pp. 7–76). Civico Istituto Colombiano 9. Genoa: Civico Istituto Columbiano.

Bandello, Matteo. 1890. *The Novels of Bandello*. John Payne, trans. 6 vols. London: Villon Society.

Baratier, Edouard. 1973. *Histoire de Marseille*. Toulouse: Edouard Privat.

Barbari, Hermolai. 1530. *In Dioscoridem corollariorum libri quinque*. Cologne: Ioan. Soterem.

Barkan, Ömer Lutfi. 1954. "La *Méditerranée* de Fernand Braudel vue d'Istamboul." *Annales: Économies. Sociétés. Civilisations*, 9, no. 2 (April–June): 189–200.

Basini, Gian Luigi. 1970. *L'uomo e il pane: Risorse, consumi e carenze alimentari della popolazione modenese nel cinque e seicento*. Milan: A. Giuffré.

Battisti, Carlo, and Giovanni Alessio. 1950–57. *Dizionario etimologico italiano*. 5 vols. Florence: G. Barbèra.

Bautier, Anne-Marie. 1960. "Les plus anciennes mentions de moulins hydrauliques industriels et de moulins a vent." *Bulletin Philologique et Historique*, 2: 567–625.

———. 1984. "Pain et pâtisserie dans les textes médiévaux latins antérieurs au XIIIè siècle." *Manger et Boire au Moyen Âge*. Actes du Colloque de Nice; 1, no. 27: 33–65. *Aliments et Société*. Centre d'Études Médiévales de Nice: Centre National de la Recherche Scientifique, Les Belles Lettres.

Bautier, Robert-Henri. 1945. "Marchands siennois et 'draps d'outremonts' aux foires de Champagne (1294)," *Annuaire-Bulletin de la Société de l'Histoire de France*, pp. 87–107.

Beaussier, Marcelin. 1959. *Dictionnaire pratique arabe-français*. 2 ed. 2 vols. Algiers: J. Carbonel.

Beck-Bossard, Corinne. 1981. "L'Alimentazione in un villagio siciliano del XIV secolo, sulla scorta delle fonte archeologiche." *Archeologia Medievale*, 8: 311–19.

Beeching, Jack. 1982. *The Galleys at Lepanto*. London: Hutchinson.

Beeler, John. 1971. *Warfare in Feudal Europe 730–1200*. Ithaca: Cornell University Press.

Beltrami, Daniele. 1955. *Saggio di storia dell'agricoltura nella repubblica di Venezia durante l'età moderna*. Rome, Venice: Istituto per la Collaborazione Culturale.

Benjamin of Tudela. n.d. *The Itinerary of Rabbi Benjamin of Tudela*. A. Asher, ed. and trans. Vol. 1. New York: Hakesheth.

Bennassar, B. 1961. "L'alimentation d'une ville espagnole au XVIe siècle. Quelques données sur les approvisionnements et la consommation de Valladolid." *Annales: Économies. Sociétés. Civilisations*, 16, no. 4 (July–August): 728–40.

Bennett, M. K. 1954. *The World's Food: A Study of the Interrelations of World Populations, National Diets, and Food Potentials*. New York: Harper.

Benoist, J. O. 1984. "Le gibier dans l'alimentation seigneuriale (XIème–XVème siècles)." *Manger et Boire au Moyen Âge*. Actes du Colloque de Nice, 1, no. 27: 75–87. *Aliments et Société*. Centre d'Études Médiévales de Nice: Centre National de la Recherche Scientifique, Les Belles Lettres.

Benporat, Claudio. 1988. "A Discovery at the Vatican—the First Italian Treatise on the Art of the 'Scalco' (Head Steward)." *Petits Propos Culinaire*, 30 (November): 41–45.

Bérard, Victor. 1896. *La Turquie et l'hellénisme contemporain*. Paris: Germer Baillière.

Berengo, Marino. 1956. *La società veneta alla fine del settecento*. Florence: G. C. Sansoni.

Bergasse, Louis, and Gaston Rambert. 1954. *Histoire du commerce de Marseille* Vol. 4. Gaston Rambert, gen. ed. Paris: Plon.

Berger, Pamela. 1985. *The Goddess Obscured: Transformation of the Grain Protectress from Goddess to Saint*. Boston: Beacon Press.

Bianchi-Giovini, A. 1846. *Sulla dominazione degli arabi in Italia*. Milan: Civelli.

Bianchini, F., and F. Corbetta. 1976. *The Complete Book of Fruits and Vegetables*. Italia and Alberto Mancinelli, trans. New York: Crown.

Bibliothèque Nationale (France). Departement des manuscrit. 1908. *Evangiles avec peintures byzantines du XIe siècle: Reproduction des 361 miniatures du Manuscrit grec 74 de la Bibliotheque nationale*. H. Omont, ed. Vol. I. Paris: Berthaud freres.

Bini, Giorgio. 1967–70. *Atlante dei pesci delle coste italiane*. 8 vols. Rome: Mondo Sommerso.

Bloch, Marc. 1961. *Feudal Society*. L. A. Manyon, trans. 2 vols. Chicago: University of Chicago Press.

Boccaccio, Giovanni. 1972. *The Decameron*. G. H. McWilliam, trans. London: Penguin.

Boerio, Giuseppe. 1856. *Dizionario del dialetto veneziano*. Venice: Giovanni Cecchini.

Bois, D. 1927–37. *Les plantes alimentaires chez tous les peuples et à travers les âges*. 4 vols. Paris: Paul Lechevalier.

Boissonade, P. 1905. "La production et commerce des céréales, des vins et des eaux-de-vie en Languedoc, dans la seconde moitié du XVIIe siècle." *Annales du Midi*, 17: 329–60.

———. 1982. *Life and Work in Medieval Europe: The Evolution of Medieval Economy from the Fifth to the Fifteenth Century*. Eileen Power, trans. Westport: Greenwood.

Bolens, Lucie. 1980. "Pain quotidien et pains de disette dans l'Espagne Musulmane." *Annales: Économies. Sociétés. Civilisations*, nos. 3–4 (May–August): 462–76.

———. 1990. *La cuisine andalouse, un art de vivre: XIe–XIIIe siècle*. Paris: Albin Michel.

———. 1992. "Les sorbets Andalous (XIe–XIIIe siècles) ou conjurer la nostalgie par la douceur." In Carole Lambert, ed. *Du Manuscrit à la Table: Essais sur la cuisine au moyen âge et répertoire des manuscrits médiévaux contenant des recettes culinaires* (pp. 257–72). Montréal: Les Presses de l'Université de Montréal; Paris: Champion-Slatkine.

Bono, Salvatore. 1964. *I corsari barbareschi*. Turin: ERI.

———. 1992. *Siciliani nel Maghreb*. Mazara del Vallo: Liceo Ginnasio 'Gian Giacomo Adria'.

Bökönyi, Sàndor. 1974. *History of Domestic Mammals in Central and Eastern Europe*. Lili Halápy, trans. Budapest: Akadémiai Kiadó.

Borlandi, Franco. 1942. *Per la storia della popolazione della Corsica*. Milan: Istituto per gli Studi di Politica Internazionale.

Boscolo, Alberto. 1978. *Sardegna, Pisa e Genova*. Collana Storica di fonti e Studi 24. Genoa: Istituto di Paleografia e Storia medievale, Università di Genoa.

Bosworth, Clifford Edmund. 1967. *The Islamic Dynasties: A Chronological and Genealogical Handbook*. Edinburgh: Edinburgh University Press.

Boüard, Michel de. 1938. "Problèmes de subsistences dans un état médiéval: Le marché et le prix des céréales au royaume angevin de sicile (1266–1282)." *Annales d'Histoire Economique et Sociale*, 10: 483–501.

Bourdeau, Louis. 1894. *Histoire de l'alimentation*. Paris: Felix Alcan.

Bovill, E. W. 1968. *The Golden Trade of the Moors*. London: Oxford University Press.

Braccini, Giovanna Princi. 1979. "Etimo germanico e itinerario italiano di *pizza*." *Archivio Glottologico Italiano*, 64: 42–89.

Bradford, Ernle. 1961. *The Great Siege*. London: Hodder and Stoughton.

Braudel, Fernand. 1970. "Alimentations et catégories de l'histoire." In *Pour une histoire de l'alimentation* (pp. 15–19). Jean-Jacques Hémardinquer, ed. Paris: Armand Colin.

———. 1972–73. *The Mediterranean and the Mediterranean World in the Age of Philip II*. 2 vols. Siân Reynolds, trans. New York: Harper & Row.

———. 1981. *Civilization and Capitalism 15th–18th Century:* Vol. 1: *The Structures of Everyday Life: The Limits of the Possible*. Siân Reynolds, trans. London: Collins.

———. 1982. *Civilization and Capitalism 15th–18th Century:* Vol. 2: *The Wheels of Commerce*. Siân Reynolds, trans. London: Collins.

———, ed. 1986. *La Méditerranée*. Paris: Arts et Métiers Graphiques.

———. 1991. *Out of Italy: 1450–1650*. Siân Reynolds, trans. Paris: Flammarion.

Bresc, Henri. 1972. "Les jardins de Palerme (1290–1460)." *Mélanges de l'École Française de Rome: Moyen Âge-Temps Modernes*, 84, no. 1: 55–127.

———. 1986. *Un monde Méditerranéen. Économie et société en Sicilie 1300–1450*. 2 vols. Rome: École Française de Rome: Palermo: Accademia di Scienze, Lettre e Arti di Palermo.

Bresc-Bautier, Genevieve, Henri Bresc, and Pascal Herbeth. 1984. "L'Equipement de la cuisine et de la table en Provence et en Sicile (XIVe–XVe Siècles), Étude comparée." *Manger et Boire au Moyen Âge*. Actes du Colloque de Nice (15–17 Octobre). Centre d'Études Médiévales de Nice, no. 28 lère serie. Nice: Les Belles Lettres, t. 2: *Cuisine, Manieres de Table, Regimes Alimentaires*.

Brookes, John. 1987. *Gardens of Paradise: The History and Design of the Great Islamic Gardens*. London: Weidenfeld and Nicolson.

Brothwell, Don, and Patricia Brothwell. 1998. *Food in Antiquity: A Survey of the Diet of Early Peoples*. Expanded ed. Baltimore: Johns Hopkins University Press.

Brown, Horatio F. 1920. "The Venetians and the Venetian Quarter in Constantinople to the Close of the Twelfth Century." *Journal of Hellenic Studies*, 40: 68–88.

Brunner, Karl. 1995. "Continuity and Discontinuity of Roman Agricultural Knowledge in the Early Middle Ages." In Del Sweeney, ed., *Agriculture in the Middle Ages: Technology, Practice, and Representation*. (pp. 21–40). Philadelphia: University of Pennsylvania Press.

Brunot, L. 1952. *Textes arabes de Rabat*. Vol. 2. Paris: Glossaire.

Brunschvig, Robert. 1936. *Deux récits de voyage inédits en Afrique du Nord au XVe siècle, ᶜAbdalbasit b. Halil et Adorne*. Paris: Larose.

———. 1940/1947. *La Berbérie Orientale sous les Ḥafṣides: Des origines à la fin du XVe siècle*. 2 vols. Publications de l'Institut d'Études Orientales d'Alger VIII. Paris: Adrien-Maisonneuve.

Brutails, Jean-Auguste. 1891. *Étude sur la condition des populations rurales du Roussillon au moyen âge*. Paris: Imprimerie Nationale.

Burnet, Et., and M. Viscontini. 1939. "Le pain et les céréales dans l'alimentation tunisienne." *Archives de l'Institut Pasteur de Tunis*, 27: 85–95 and 28, no. 2 (June): 221–68.

Burton, Richard F. 1857. *Personal Narrative of a Pilgrimage to El Medinah and Meccah*. 2nd ed. 2 vols. London: Longman, Brown, Green, Longmans, and Robert.

Busbecq, Ogier Ghiselin de. 1927. *The Turkish Letters*. Edward Seymour Forster, trans. Oxford: Clarendon Press.

Busquet, Raoul. 1945. *Histoire de Marseille*. Paris: Robert Laffont.

Bynum, Caroline Walker. 1987. *Holy Feast and Holy Fast: The Religious Significance of Food to Medieval Women*. Berkeley: University of California Press.

Byrne, Eugene H. 1920. "Genoese Trade with Syria in the Twelfth Century." *American Historical Review*, 25, no. 2 (January): 191–219.

Cahen, Claude. 1953. "L'Évolution de l'*iqta*ᶜ du IXe au XIIIe siècle: contribution à une histoire comparée des sociétés médiévales." *Annales: Économies. Sociétés. Civilisations*, 8, no. 1 (January–March): 25–52.

———. 1971. "Notes pour une histoire de l'agriculture dans les pays Musulmans médiévaux." *Journal of the Economic and Social History of the Orient*, 14: 63–68.

Camporesi, Piero. 1980. *Alimentazione, Folklore, Società*. Parma: Pratiche.

———. 1989. *Bread of Dreams*. David Gentilcore, trans. Cambridge: Polity.

———. 1996. *The Land of Hunger*. Tania Croft-Murray, trans. Cambridge: Polity.

Canard, M. 1956. "Quelques notes relatives à la Sicile sous les premiers Califes Fatimites." *Studi Medievali in Onore di Antonino de Stefano*. Palermo: Societa Siciliana per la Storia Patria; pp. 569–76.

———. 1959. "Le riz dans le Proche Orient aux premiers siècles d'Islam," *Arabica*, 6, facs. 2: 113–31.

Cancila, Orazio. 1983. *Baroni e popolo nella sicilia del grano*. Palermo: G. B. Palumbo.

Capuozzo, Toni, and Michele Neri. 1985. *Feste e sagre dei paesi italiani*. Milan: Arnoldo Mondadori Editore.

Caracausi, Girolamo. 1983. *Arabismi medievali di sicilia*. Supplementi 5. Palermo: Centro di studi filologi e linguistici siciliani.

Caracciolo, Domenica. 1805. "Riflessioni sull'economia e l'estrazione de frumenti della Sicilia." *Scrittori classici italiani di economia politica*, parte moderna, 40. Milan: G. G. Destefanis.

Caredda, Gian Paolo. 1990. *Sagre e feste in sardegna*. Genoa: Sagep.

Castelvetro, Giacomo. 1989. *The Fruits, Herbs & Vegetables of Italy*. Gillian Riley, trans. London: Viking Penguin

Caster, Gilles. 1962. *Le commerce du pastel et de l'épicerie a Toulouse de 1450 environ a 1561*. Toulouse: Edouard Privat.

Catalan Dictionary: English-Catalan/Catalan-English. 1993. London: Routledge.

Cato. 1993. *On Agriculture*. William Davis Hooper, trans. Loeb Classical Library. Cambridge: Harvard University Press.

Cavailles, Henri. 1931. *La vie pastorale et agricole dans le Pyrenees des Gaves, de l'Adour et des Nestes*. Paris: Armand Colin.

Cave, Roy C., and Herbert H. Coulson. 1965. *A Source Book for Medieval Economic History*. New York: Biblo and Tannen.

Ca' da Mosto, Alvise da. 1937. *The Voyages of Cadamosto*. G. R. Crone, trans. 2nd series, vol. 80. London: Hakluyt Society Works.

Ceccaldi, Mathieu. 1982. *Dictionnaire Corse-Français*. Paris: Klincksieck.

Cecchetti, Bartolomeo. 1885. *La vita dei veneziani nel 1300*. Part 1: *La città, la laguna*; Part 2: *Il vitto*. Venice: Fratelli Visentini.

Celsus. 1935–38. *De medicina*. W. G. Spencer, trans. 3 vols. Loeb Classical Library. Cambridge: Harvard University Press.

Cervantes Saavedra, Miguel de. 1950. *The Adventures of Don Quixote*. J. M. Cohen, trans. London: Penguin Books.

Chalandon, Ferdinand. 1907. *Histoire de la domination Normande en Italie et en Sicile*. 2 vols. Paris: Alphonse Picard.

Chantraine, Pierre. 1968–80. *Dictionnaire étymologique de la langue grecque*. 4 vols. Paris: Klincksieck.

Charrière, E. ed. 1848–60. *Négociations de la France dans le Levant*. 4 vols. Paris: Imprimerie Nationale.

Chau Ju-kua. 1911. *His Work on the Chinese and Arab Trade in the Twelfth and Thirteenth Centuries, entitled Chu-fan-chï*. Friedrich Hirth and W. W. Rockhill, eds and trans. St. Petersburg: Imperial Academy of Sciences.

Chaunu, Pierre. 1959. *Seville et l'Alantique (1504–1650)*, vol. 8, pt. 2 (1): *La Conjoncture (1504–1592)*. Paris: S. E. V. P. E. N.

Cherubini, Giovanni. 1972. *Agricoltura e sociatà rurale nel medioevo*. Florence: Sansoni.

Chevalier, Aug. 1932. "Les production végétales du Sahara." *Revue de Botanique Appliquée et d'Agriculture Tropicale*, 12, no. 133–134 (September–October): 742–43.

———. 1939. "Les origines et l'evolution de l'agriculture Méditerranéenne." *Revue de Botanique Appliquée et d'Agriculture Tropicale*, 19, no. 217–218 (September–October): 613–62.

Chronicon Salernitanum. 1956. A Critical Edition with Studies on Literary and Historical Sources and on Language. Ulla Westerbergh, ed. Studia Latina Stockholmiensia III. Stockholm: Almqvist and Wiksell.

Chrysostomides, Julian. 1970. "Venetian Commercial Privileges under the Paleologi." *Studi Veneziani*, 12: 267–356.

Ciccaglione, F. 1913. "La vita economia siciliana nel periodo normanno-svevo." *Archivo Storico per la Sicilia Orientale*, 10, no. 3: 321–45.

Cipolla, Carlo M. 1967. *Money, Prices, and Civilization in the Mediterranean World*. New York: Gordian Press.

———. 1980. *Before the Industrial Revolution: European Society and Economy, 1000–1700*. 2nd ed. New York: W. W. Norton.

Clément-Mullet, J. J. 1865. "Sur les noms des céréales chez les anciens et en particular chez les Arabes." *Journal Asiatique*, 6th ser. vol. 5: 185–226.

Cleray, Edmond. 1921. "Le voyage de Pierre Lescalopier "Parisien" de Venise a Constantinople, l'an 1574." *Revue d'Histoire Diplomatic*, 35: 21–55.

Cohen, Amnon. 1989. *Economic Life in Ottoman Jerusalem*. Cambridge: Cambridge University Press.

Cohen, Marcel. 1912. *Le parler arabe des Juifs d'Alger*. Paris: Champion.

Collier, Basil. 1939. *Catalan France*. London: J. M. Dent & Sons.

Collier, Raymond, and Joseph Billioud 1954. *Histoire du commerce de Marseille*. Gaston Rambert, gen. ed. Vol. 3. Paris: Plon.

Comet, Georges. 1989. "Dur ou tendre? Propos sur le blé médiéval." *Médiévales. Langue, Textes, Histoire*, 16–17: 103–12.

Condesa de Pardo Bazan, ed. n.d. *La cocina espanola antigua*. Madrid: Renacimento.

Congdon, Eleanor A. 1994. "Venetian Merchant Activity within Mamluk Syria (886–893/1481–1487)." *Al-Masaq: Studia Arabo-Islamica Mediterranea*, 7: 1–33.

Consiglio, Alberto. 1959. *La storia dei maccheroni con cento ricette e con Pulcinella Mangiamaccheroni*. Roma: Moderne.

Consolo, Vincenzo. 1987. *La pesca del tonno in sicilia*. Palermo: Sellerio.

Contamine, Philip. 1986. *War in the Middle Ages*. Michael Jones, trans. Oxford: Basil Blackwell.

Contemporary Turkish-English Dictionary. 1983. Istanbul: Redhouse.

Cook, M. A. 1979. "Economic Developments." In Joseph Schacht, ed., with C. E. Bosworth, *The Legacy of Islam*. 2nd ed. pp. 210–43 Oxford: Oxford University Press.

Coppola, Gauro. 1973. "L'agricoltura di alcune pievi della pianura irrigua milanese nei dati catastali della metà del secolo XVI." *Contributi dell'Istituto di storia economica e sociale*. Milan: Università Cattolica del Sacro Cuore.

Corominas, Joan. 1936. "Mots catalans d'origen arabic." *Bulleti de Dialectolgia Catalana*, 24: 1–81.

———. 1954–57. *Diccionario critico-etimológico de la lengua castellana*. 4 vols. Berne: Francke.

———. 1967. *Breve diccionario etimologico de la lengua Castellana*. 2nd ed. Madrid: Editorial Gredos.

———. 1980. *Diccionari etimològic i complementari de la llengua Catalana*. 9 vols. Barcelona: Curial Editions Catalanes.

Correnti, Santi. 1976. *La Sicilia del seicento: Società e cultura*. Milan: Mursia.

Corridore, Francesco. 1899. *Storia documentata della populazione del regno di sardegna*. Turin: Carlo Clausen.

Cortelazzo, Manlio, and Paolo Zolli. 1979–88. *Dizionario etimologico della lingua italiana*. 5 vols. Bologna: N. Zanichelli.

Cosman, Madeleine Pelner. 1976. *Fabulous Feasts: Medieval Cookery and Ceremony*. New York: George Braziller.

Coulet, Noël. 1966. "Commerce et marchands dans un village provençal du XVe siècle. La leyde de Puyloubier."

Études Rurales, nos. 22–23–24 (July–December): 99–118.

———. 1992. "La cuisine dans la maison Aixoise du XVe Siècle (1402–1453)." In Carole Lambert, ed., *Du manuscrit à la table: Essais sur la cuisine au moyen âge et répertoire des manuscrits médiévaux contenant des recettes culinaires* (pp. 163–172). Montréal: Les Presses de l'Université de Montréal; Paris: Champion-Slatkine.

Crescentiis, Petrus de. 1495. *Liber ruralium commodorum*. Venice: Matteo Cordeca'.

Crespi, Gabriele. 1986. *The Arabs in Europe*. New York: Rizzoli.

Crino, Sebastiano. 1923. "Come si coltivava la canna da zucchero in Sicilia." *L'Agricoltura Coloniale*, 17, no. 3 (March): 81–89.

Croce, G. C. 1978. *Le sottilissime astuzie di Bertoldo*. P. Camporesi, ed. Turin: G. Einaudi.

Crowther, Geoff, and Hugh Finlay. 1992. *Morocco, Algeria & Tunisia: A Travel Survival Kit*. 2nd ed. Hawthorn: Lonely Planet.

Cunsolo, Felice. 1965. *Gli italiani a tavola*. Milano: Mursia.

———. 1975. *Guida Gastronomica d'Italia*. Novara: Istituto Geografico De Agostini.

Curtis, Edmund. 1912. *Roger of Sicily and the Normans in Lower Italy 1016–1154*. New York: G. P. Putnam's.

Cvijić, Jovan. 1918. *La Péninsule Balkanique*. Paris: Armand Colin.

Dagher, Shawky M. 1991. *Traditional Foods in the Near East*. FAO Food and Nutrition Paper 50. Rome: Food and Agriculture Organization of the United Nations.

Dalby, Andrew. 1996. *Siren Feasts: A History of Food and Gastronomy in Greece*. London and New York: Routledge.

Dalmazia, Veneta e Romana. 1941. Rome: Società Nazionale 'Dante Alighieri.'

Daniel, Norman. 1975. *The Arab Impact on Sicily and Southern Italy in the Middle Ages*, no. 4. Cairo: Istituto Italiano di Cultura per la R.A.E.

———. 1979. *The Arabs and Mediaeval Europe*. 2nd ed. London and New York: Longman; Beirut: Librairie du Liban.

Dante Alighieri. 1986. *The Divine Comedy*. Allen Mandelbaum, trans. New York: Bantam.

Dauzat, Alber, Jean Dubois, and Henri Mitterand. 1971. *Nouveau dictionnaire étymologique et historique*. Paris: Larousse.

David, Elizabeth. 1981. "Mad, Mad, Despised and Dangerous." *Petits Propos Culinaires*, 9 (October): 7–13.

Davidson, Alan. 1979. *North Atlantic Seafood*. New York: Viking.

———. 1981. *Mediterranean Seafood*. 2nd ed. Baton Rouge: Louisana State University Press.

———. 1988. "The Harlot of Marseilles." *Petits Propos Culinaire*, 29 (July): 26–33.

Davies, Timothy. 1983. "Changes in the Structure of the Wheat Trade in Seventeenth-Century Sicily and the Building of New Villages." *Journal of European Economic History*, 12, no. 2 (Fall): 371–404.

de Biberstein Kazimirski, A. 1860. *Dictionnaire Arabe-Français*. 2 vols. Paris: G.-P. Maisonneuve.

De Candolle, Alphonse. 1959. *Origin of Cultivated Plants*. New York: Hafner.

Deerr, Noel. 1949. *The History of Sugar*. London: Chapman and Hall.

de Foucauld, Le Père Charles. 1951. *Dictionnaire Touareg-Français: dialecte de l'Ahaggar*. 2 vols. Paris: Imprimerie Nationale De France.

Defourneaux, Marcelin. 1979. *Daily Life in Spain in the Golden Age*. Newton Branch, trans. Stanford: Stanford University Press.

De Gislain, G. 1984. "Le role des étangs dans l'alimentation médiévale." *Manager et Boire au Moyen Âge*. Actes du Colloque de Nice, *Aliments et Société*; 1 no. 27: 89–101 Centre d'Études Médiévales de Nice: Centre National de la Recherche Scientifique, Les Belles Lettres.

de Gregorio, G. and Chr. F. Seybold. 1903. "Glossario delle voci siciliane di origine araba." *Studi Glottologici Italiani*, 3: 225–51.

de Herrera, Gabriel Alonso. 1539/1970. *Obra de agricultura*. Madrid: Atlas.

de la Ferriere, Hector, ed. 1885–95. *Lettres de Catherine de Medicis*. 10 vols. Paris: Imprimerie Nationale.

della Casa, Giovanni. 1990. *Galateo*. Konrad Eisenbichler and Kenneth R. Bartlett, trans. Canada: Dovehouse.

De Maddalena, Aldo. 1964. "Il mondo rurale italiano nel cinque e nel seicento," *Rivista storica italiana*. 76 fasc. 2: 349–426.

de Quevedo, Francisco. 1969. *The Swindler (El Buscón)*, in *Two Spanish Picaresque Novels*. Michael Alpert, trans. London: Penguin.

de Temmerman, Geneviève and Didier Chedorge. 1988. *The A-Z of French Food: L'ABC de la gastronomie française*. Paris: Editions Scribo.

de Vega, Luis Antonio. 1970. *Guia gastronomica de España*. 3rd ed. Madrid: Editora Nacional.

Diamond, Jared. 1997. *Guns, Germs, and Steel: The Fates of Human Societies*. New York: W. W. Norton.

"Diari della città di Palermo, dal secolo XVI al XIX: Pubblicati sui manoscritti della Biblioteca Comunale." 1849. In Gioacchino di Marzo, G. ed. *Biblioteca storica e letteraria di sicilia*. vol. 2, (pp. 59–61). Palermo: Luigi Pedone Lauriel.

Diaz Garcia, Amador. 1978–79. "Un tratado Nazari sobre alimentos: *Al-kalām ʿalā l-agḏiya* de al-Arbūlī. Edicìon, Traduccion y estudio, con glosario." In *Cuadernos de Estudios Medievales* VI–VII.: 5–37.

Dick, J. W., and R. R. Matsuo. 1988. "Durum Wheat and Pasta Products." In Y. Pomeranz, ed., *Wheat: Chemistry and Technology*. 3rd ed. (1) vol. 2, pp. 507–47. St. Paul: American Association of Cereal Chemists.

Dickie, James. 1976. "The Islamic Garden in Spain." In Elisabeth B. Macdougall and Richard Ettinghausen, eds., *The Islamic Garden*. Dumbarton Oaks Colloquium on the History of Landscape Architecture IV (pp. 89–105). Washington, DC: Dumbarton Oaks.

Dictionary of the Middle Ages. S. v., "Agriculture and Nutrition."

Di Gregorio, Pasquale. 1904. *Vicende storiche dell'agricoltura siciliana*. Palermo: Priulla.

Dion, Roger. 1969. *Histoire de la vigne et du vin en France: Des origines au XIXe siècle*. Paris: Ch. Poisson.

Dolader, Miguel Angel Motis. 1996. "L'alimentation juive médiévale," In Jean-Louis Flandrin and Massimo Montanari, *Histoire de l'alimentation* (pp. 367–87). Bari: Gius. Laterza; Paris: Fayard.

Doménech, I., and F. Martì. 1982. *Ayunos y abstinencias*. Barcelona: Alta Fulla.

Dorsa, Vincenzo. 1876. *La tradizione greco-latina nei dialetti della calabria citeriore*. Cosenza: Migliaccio.

Dozy, R. 1881/1991. *Supplément aux dictionnaires arabes*. 2 vols. Leiden: Brill. Reprinted Beirut: Librarie du Liban.

Dozy, R., and Dr. W. H. Engelmann. 1869. *Glossaire des mot Espagnols et Portugais derivés de l'arabe*. Leiden: E. J. Brill and Paris: Maisonneuve.

Duby, Georges, 1974. *The Early Growth of the European Economy: Warriors and Peasants from the Seventh to the Twelfth Century*. Howard B. Clarke, trans. Ithaca: Cornell University Press.

———. 1976. *Rural Economy and Country Life in the Medieval West*. Cynthia Postan, trans. Columbia: University of South Carolina Press.

———, ed. 1988. *A History of Private Life*. II: *Revelations of the Medieval World*. Arthur Goldhammer, trans. Cambridge: Belknap Press of Harvard University Press.

Dufourcq, Charles-Emmanuel. 1965. *L'Espagne catalane et le Maghrib aux XIIIe et XIVe siècles: De la bataille de las Navas de Tolosa (1212) à l'avènement du sultan mérinide Abou-l-Hasan (1331)*. Paris: Presse Universitaires de France.

———. 1978. *La vie quotidienne dans l'Europe médiévale sous domination Arabe*. Paris: Hachette.

Duncan, R. M. 1946. "Meaning of *Pimienta* in Medieval Spanish." *Hispanic Review*, 14: 66–68.

Dupont, André. 1942. *Les relations commerciales entre les cités maritimes de Languedoc et les cités Méditerranéennes d'Espagne et d'Italie du Xeme au XIIIeme siècle*. Nîmes: Chastanier Frère & Almeras.

Dupuy, R. Ernest, and Trevor N. Dupuy. 1970. *The Encyclopedia of Military History*. New York: Harper & Row.

Duran, Khalid. 1992. "Andalusia's Nostalgia for Progress and Harmonious Heresy." *Middle East Report*, 22, no. 5 (September/October): 20–23.

al-Duri, A. A. 1969. "The Origins of iqta in Islam." *Al-Abhath* 22.

Durliat, Marcel. 1977. *Languedoc Méditerranéen et Roussillon*. Paris: Arthaud.

Edrisi. 1866/1968. *Description de l'Afrique et de l'Espagne*. R. Dozy and M. J. de Goeje, eds. and trans. Leyden: E. J. Brill.

Eléxpuru, Inés. 1991. *Al-Andalus: Magia y seduccion culinarus*. Madrid: Instituto Occidental de Cultura Islamica.

Elliot, J. H. 1965. *Imperial Spain 1469–1716*. London: Edward Arnold.

Encyclopedia Britannica, 11th ed.

Encyclopédie Berbère.

Encyclopedia of Islam, 2nd ed.

Encyclopedia of Islam, new ed.

Encyclopedia Judaica.

Epstein, Stephan R. 1992. *An Island for Itself: Economic Development and Social Change in Late Medieval Sicily*. New York: Cambridge University Press.

Epstein, Steven A. 1996. *Genoa & the Genoese, 958–1528*. Chapel Hill: University of North Carolina Press.

Erroux, J. n.d. *Les blés des oasis Sahariennes*. Algiers: Université d'Alger, Institut de Recherches Sahariennes.

Esteban Hernández Bermejo, J., and Expiración García Sánchez. 1998. "Economic Botany and Ethnobotany in al-Andalus (Iberian Peninsula: Tenth-Fifteenth Centuries). An Unknown Heritage of Mankind." *Economic Botany*, 52: 16–26.

Estienne, Charles. 1536. *De re hortensi libellus, vulgaria herbarum, florum, ac fruticum, qui in hortis conseri solent nomina Latinis vocibus efferre docens ex probatis autoribus*. Paris: Roberti Stephani.

Ettinghausen, Richard. 1976. "The Man-Made Setting." In Bernard Lewis, ed., *Islam and the Arab World: Faith-People-Culture*, (pp. 57–72). New York: Alfred A. Knopf in association with American Heritage Publishing.

Faber, G. L. 1883. *The Fisheries of the Adriatic and the Fish Thereof: A Report of the Austro-Hungarian Sea-Fisheries*. London: Bernard Quaritch.

Facciola, Stephen. 1998. *Cornucopia II: A Source Book of Edible Plants*. Vista, CA: Kampong.

Faccioli, Emilio. 1973. "La cucina." In *Storia d'Italia: I Documenti*. Ruggiero Romano and Corrado Vivanti, coord. vol. 5 (1) (pp. 938–1030). Turin: Einaudi.

———. 1981. "Le fonti letterarie della storia dell'alimentazione nel basso medioevo." *Archeologia Medievale*, 8: pp. 59–70.

Faridi, Hamed. 1988. "Flat Breads." In Y. Pomeranz, ed., *Wheat: Chemistry and Technology*. 3rd ed. vol. 2, (457–505). St. Paul: American Association of Cereal Chemists.

Feeley-Harnik, Gillian. 1994. *The Lord's Table: The Meaning of Food in Early Judaism and Christianity*. Washington: Smithsonian Institution Press.

Finlay, George. 1856. *History of Greece under Othoman and Venetian Domination*. London: William Blackwood.

First International Food Congress, Turkey, 25–30 September 1986. Kültür ve Turizm Bakanlığı Yayını. Ankara: Nurol Mataacılık.

al-Fīrūzābādī. 1964. *Mukhtār al-qāmūs*. Cairo: Isa al-Babi al-Halabi. [in Arabic]

Flandrin, Jean-Louis. 1989. "Les pâtes dans la cuisine provençale." *Médiévales. Langue, Textes, Histoire*, 16–17: 65–75.

Flandrin, Jean-Louis, and Philip Hyman. 1986. "Regional Tastes and Cuisines: Problems, Documents, and Discourses on Food in Southern France in the 16th and 17th Centuries." *Food and Foodways*, 1: 221–51.

Flandrin, Jean-Louis, and Massimo Montanari. 1996. *Histoire de l'alimentation*. Bari: Gius. Laterza; Paris: Fayard.

Fois, B. 1984. "Annotazioni sull'alimentazione nella Sardegna del trecento: i prodotti, le vivande, prezzi, e salari." *Manger et Boire au Moyen Âge*. Actes du Colloque de Nice, 1, no. 27: 183–97. *Aliments et Société*. Centre D'Études Médiévales de Nice: Centre National de la Recherche Scientifique, Les Belles Lettres.

Forbes, R. J. 1955. *Studies in Ancient Technology*. Vol. 2. Leiden: E. J. Brill.

———. 1956. "Food and Drink." In Charles Singer et al., eds., *A History of Technology* (Vol. 2, pp. 103–46). Oxford: Oxford University Press.

Francolini, Francesco. 1923. *Olivicoltura*. Turin: Unione Tipografico Editrice Editrice Torinese.

Frazer, James George. 1935. *The Golden Bough: A Study in Magic and Religion*. 3rd ed. Vol. 1: *The Magic Art and the Evolution of Kings*. New York: Macmillan.

Fussell, Betty. 1992. *The Story of Corn*. New York: Alfred A. Knopf.

Gabrieli, Francesco. 1964. "Greeks and Arabs in the Central Mediterranean Area." *Dumbarton Oaks Papers*, no. 18 (pp. 57–65). Washington, DC: Dumbarton Oaks Center for Byzantine Studies.

———. 1979. "Islam in the Mediterranean World." In Joseph Schacht, ed., with C. E. Bosworth, *The Legacy of Islam*. 2nd ed. pp. 63–104. Oxford: Oxford University Press.

Galusso, Giuseppe. 1992. *Economia e società nella Calabria del cinquecento*. 3rd ed. Naples: Guida.

García Sánchez, Expiración. 1980. "Ibn al-Azraq: Uryuza sobre ciertas perferencias gastronómicas de los granadinos." *Andalucía Islamica*, 1: 141–62.

———. 1981–82. "La alimentación en la Andalucía Islámica. Estudio histórico y bromatológico. I: Cereales y leguminosas." *Andalucía Islamica*, 2–3: 139–77.

Garulo, Teresa. 1983. *Los Arabismos en il lexico Andaluz*. Instituto Hispano-Arabe de Cultura.

Gast, Marceau. 1968. *Alimentation des populations de L'Ahaggar: Étude ethnographique*. Mémoires du Centre de Recherches Anthropologiques Préhistoriques et Ethnographiques, Conseil de la Recherche Scientifique en Algérie. VIII. Paris: Art et Métiers.

Gelfer-Jorgensen, Mirjam. 1986. *Medieval Islamic Symbolism and the Paintings in the Cefalu Cathedral*. Leiden: E. J. Brill.

George, C. J., V. A. Athanassiou, and I. Boulos. 1967. *The Fishes of the Coastal Waters of Lebanon*. Miscellaneous Papers in the Natural Sciences, no. 4. Beirut: American University of Beirut.

Giacchero, Giulio. 1984. *Storia delle assicurazioni marittime; L'esperienza genovese dal medioeveo all' etá contemporanea*. Genova: Sagep.

Gibault, Georges. 1907. *Le cardon et l'artichaut*. Paris: Gibault.

———. 1912. *Histoire des légumes*. Paris: Librarie Horticole.

Gibb, Sir Hamilton. 1988. "The Influence of Islamic Culture on Medieval Europe." In Sylvia L. Thrupp, ed., *Change in Medieval Society: Europe North of the Alps 1050–1500* (pp. 155–67). Toronto: University of Toronto and Medieval Academy of America.

Gidon, F. 1936. "Le haricot est-il arrivé en France dans la corbeille de mariage de Catherine de Médices?" *La Presse Médicale*, January 18, 1936, pp. 125–26.

Gies, Joseph, and Frances Gies. 1979. *Life in a Medieval Castle*. New York: Harper & Row.

———. 1981. *Life in a Medieval City*. New York: Harper & Row.

Ginzburg, Carlo. 1992. *The Night Battles: Witchcraft & Agrarian Cults in the Sixteenth and Seventeenth Centuries*. John & Anne Tedeschi, trans. Baltimore: Johns Hopkins University Press.

Gioeni, Giuseppe. 1885. *Saggio di etimologie siciline*. Archivio storico siciliano Xa. Palermo: Tipographia dello "Statuto."

Giofrè, Domenico. 1951. "La relazioni fra Genova e Madera nel I decennio del secolo XVI." *Studi Colombiani*, 3: 435–59.

Girard, Alain. 1977. "Le triomphe de la cuisinère bourgeoise: Livres culinaires, cuisine et société en France aux XVII et XVIII siècles." *Revue d'Histoire Moderne et Contemporaine*, 24 (October–December): 497–523.

Giuffrida, Antonino. 1975. "Considerazioni sul consumo della carne a Palermo nei secoli XIV e XV." *Mélanges de l'École Française de Rome: Moyen Âge-Temps Modernes,* 87, no. 2: 583–95.

Gleijeses, Vittorio. 1977. *Feste, farina, e forca.* 3rd ed. Naples: Società Editrice Napoletana, 1977.

Glick, Thomas F. 1970. *Irrigation and Society in Medieval Valencia*. Cambridge: Belkap Press of Harvard University Press.

Gobert, E. G. 1940a. *Usages et rites alimentaires des Tunisiens*. Tunis: Bascone & Muscat.

———. 1940b. "Usages et rites alimentaires Tunisiens leur aspect domestique, physiologique et social." *Archives de l'Institute Pasteur de Tunis*, 29, no. 4 (December): 475–589.

———. 1955. "Les references historiques des nourritures Tunisiennes." *Les Cahiers de Tunisie*, 12: 500–42.

Goethe, J. W. 1982. *Italian Journey: 1776–1778*. W. H. Auden and Elizabeth Mayer, trans. San Francisco: North Point.

Goitein, S. D. 1967. *A Mediterranean Society: The Jewish Communities of the Arab World as Portrayed in the Documents of the Cairo Geniza*, Vol. 1: *Economic Foundations*. Berkeley: University of California Press.

———. 1971. "Sicily and Southern Italy in the Cairo Geniza Documents." *Archivio Storico per la Sicilia Orientale*, 67, no. 1: 9–33.

———. 1983. *A Mediterranean Society: The Jewish Communities of the Arab World as Portrayed in the Documents of the Cairo Geniza*, Vol. IV: *Daily Life*. Berkeley: University of California Press.

Goodwin, Godfrey. 1990. *Islamic Spain*. Architectural Guides for Travelers. San Francisco: Chronicle.

Goody, Jack. 1989. *Cooking, Cuisine and Class: A Study in Comparative Sociology*. Cambridge: Cambridge University Press.

Gottschalk, Alfred. 1948. *Histoire de l'alimentation et de la gastronomie depuis la préhistoire jusqu'à nos jours*. 2 vols. Paris: Hippocrate.

Gowers, Emily. 1993. *The Loaded Table: Representations of Food in Roman Literature*. Oxford: Clarendon.

Grava, Y. 1984. "Notes martégales sur le ravitaillement et la consommation du poisson à la cour pontificale d'Avignon au cours du XIVè siècle." *Manger et Boire au Moyen Âge.* Actes du Colloque de Nice, 1, no. 27: 153–70. *Aliments et Société.* Centre d'Études Médiévales de Nice: Centre National de la Recherche Scientifique, Les Belles Lettres.

Grewe, Rudolf. 1988. "The Arrival of the Tomato in Spain and Italy: Early Recipes." In *First International Food Congress, Turkey,* 25–30 September 1986 (pp. 106–13). Ankara: Kültür ve Turizm Bakanliği Yayını.

———. 1992. "Hispano-Arabic Cuisine in the Twelfth Century." In Carole Lambert, ed., *Du manuscript à la table: Essais sur la cuisine au moyen âge et répertoire des manuscrits médiévaux contenant des recettes culinaires* (pp. 141–48). Montréal: Les Presses de l'Université de Montréal; Paris: Champion-Slatkine.

Grieco, Allen J. 1992. "From the Cookbook to the Table: A Florentine Table and Italian Recipes of the Fourteenth and Fifteenth Centuries." In Carole Lambert, ed., *Du manuscrit à la table: Essais sur la cuisine au moyen âge et répertoire des manuscrits médiévaux contenant des recettes culinaires* (pp. 29–38). Montréal: Les Presses de l'Université de Montréal; Paris: Champion-Slatkine.

Grunebaum, G. von. 1970. *Classical Islam: A History, 600–1258.* London: G. Allen and Unwin.

Gual Camarena, Miguel. 1968. *Vocabulario del comercio medieval.* Tarragona: Excelentísima Diputación Provincial.

Güçer, Lütfi. 1949–50. "Le problème de l'approvisionnement d'Istanbul en céréales vèrs le milieu du XVIII ème siècle," and "Le commerce interieur des céréales dans l'Empire Ottoman pendant la seconde moitié du XVI ème siècle." *Revue de la Faculté des Sciences Économiques de l'Université d'Istabul,* 11 nos. 1-4 (October): 153–62, 163–88.

Guillaumond, Catherine. 1986. "L'eau dans l'alimentation et la cuisine arabe du IXème au XIIIème siècles." In P. Louis, ed., *L'homme et l'eau en méditerranée et au proche orient.* Vol. III: *L'eau dans les techniques* (pp. 29–37) Lyon: Maison de l'Orient.

Guiral, J. 1984. "Le sucre a Valence aux XVè et XVIè siècles." *Manger et Boire au Moyen Âge.* Actes du Colloque de Nice, 1, no. 27: 119–29. *Aliments et Société.* Centre d'Études Médiévales de Nice: Centre National de la Recherche Scientifique, Les Belles Lettres.

Gunnis, Rupert. 1936. *Historic Cyprus: A Guide to its Towns and Villages, Monasteries and Castles.* London: Methuen.

Guy, Christian. 1962. *An Illustrated History of French Cuisine: From Charlemagne to Charles de Gaulle.* Elisabeth Abbott, trans. New York: Bramhall House.

Ḥājib, Yūsuf Khāṣṣ. 1983. *Wisdom of Royal Glory (Kutuadgu Bilig): A Turkish-Islamic Mirror for Princes.* Robert Dankoff, trans. Chicago: Chicago University Press.

Hall, Robert. 1991. "Savoring Africa in the New World." In Herman Viola and Carolyn Margolis, *Seeds of Change: A Quincentennial Commemoration.* Washington, DC and London: Smithsonian Institution Press.

Hamilton, Earl J. 1929. "Wages and Subsistence on Spanish Treasure Ships, 1503–1660." *Journal of Political Economy,* 37, no. 4 (August): 429–50.

———. 1934. *American Treasure and the Price Revolution in Spain, 1501–1650.* Cambridge: Harvard University Press.

Harlan, Jack R. 1986. "Plant Domestication: Diffuse Origins and Diffusions." In C. Barigozzi, ed., *The Origin and Domestication of Cultivated Plants. Developments in Agricultural and Managed-Forest Ecology* (pp. 21–34). Amsterdam: Elsevier.

———. 1992. *Crops & Man.* 2nd ed. Madison: American Society of Agronomy and Crop Science Society of America.

Harrap's Shorter French and English Dictionary. 1991. Rev. ed. Edinburgh: Harrap's and New York: Prentice-Hall.

Harrison, S. G., G. B. Masefield, and Michael Wallis. 1969. *The Oxford Book of Food Plants.* Oxford: Oxford University Press.

Hartmann, Fernande. 1923. *L'agriculture dans l'ancienne Égypte.* Paris: Libraires-Imprimeries Réunies.

Haskins, Charles Homer. 1924. *Studies in the History of Mediaeval Science.* Cambridge: Harvard University Press.

———. 1927. *The Renaissance of the Twelfth Century.* Cambridge: Harvard University Press.

Hattox, Ralph S. 1991. *Coffee and Coffeehouses: The Origins of a Social Beverage in the Medieval Near East.* Seattle: University of Washington Press.

Hawkes, J. G. 1983. *The Diversity of Crop Plants.* Cambridge: Harvard University Press.

Heers, Jacques. 1955. "Il commercio nel Mediterraneo alla fine del secolo XIV a nei primi anni del XV." *Archivio Storico Italiano,* 113, no. 406: 157–209.

———. 1981. *Esclaves et domestiques au moyen âge dans le monde méditerranéen.* Paris: Arthéme Fayard.

Hehn, Victor. 1976. *Cultivated Plants and Domesticated Animals in their Migration from Asia to Europe.* Amsterdam: John Benjamins.

Heine, Peter. 1988. *Kulinarische Studien: Untersuchungen zur Kochkunst im arabisch-islamischen Mittelalter Mit Rezepten.* Wiesbaden: Otto Harrassowitz.

Heiser Jr., Charles B. 1990. *Seed to Civilization: The Story of Food.* Cambridge, MA: Harvard University Press.

Helbaek, Hans. 1969a. "Plant Collecting, Dry Farming, and Irrigation Agriculture in Prehistoric Deh Luran." In Frank Hole, Kent V. Flannery, and James A. Neeley, eds., *Prehistory and the Ecology of the Deh Luran Plain: An Early Village Sequence from Khuzistan, Iran* (pp. 386–426). Ann Arbor: Museum of Anthropology, University of Michigan.

———. 1969b. "Palaeo-ethnobotony." In Don Brothwell and Eric Higgs, eds., *Science in Archeology: A Survey of Progress and Research* (pp. 206–14). Rev. ed. New York: Praeger.

Hémardinquer, Jean-Jacques. 1970. "Sur les galères de Toscane au XVe siècle." In Jean-Jacques Hémardinquer, ed., *Pour une histoire de l'alimentation* (pp. 85–92). Paris: Armand Colin.

Henisch, Bridget Ann. 1985. *Fast and Feast: Food in Medieval Society.* University Park: Pennsylvania State University.

Herbolario Volgare. 1522/1979. Erminio Caprotti and William T. Stearn, intro. Verona: Il Polifilo.

Herlihy, David. 1958. "The Agrarian Revolution in Southern France and Italy. 801–1150." *Speculum*, 33, no. 1 (January): 23–41.

———. 1973. *Pisa in the Early Renaissance: A Study of Urban Growth*. Port Washington: Kennikat.

———. 1985. *Medieval Households*. Cambridge: Harvard University Press.

Herzfeld, Michael. 1984. "The Horns of the Mediterraneanist Dilemma." *American Ethnologist*, 11, no. 3 (August): 439–54.

Herodotus. 1922–81. *Herodotus*. A. D. Godley. trans. Rev. ed. Loeb Classical Library. 4 vols. Cambridge: Harvard University Press.

Heyd, W. 1959. *Histoire du commerce du Levant au Moyen-âge*. Furcy Raynaud, trans. and ed. 2 vols. Amsterdam: Adolf M. Hakkert.

Hill, George. 1940–52. *A History of Cyprus*. 2 vols. Cambridge and New York: Cambridge University Press.

Hill, Stephen, and Anthony Bryer. 1995. "Byzantine Porridge: *Tracta, Trachanás*, and *Tarhana*." In John Wilkins, David Harvey, and Mike Dobson, eds., *Food in Antiquity* (pp. 44–54). Exeter: University of Exeter Press.

Hitti, Philip K. 1970. *History of the Arabs from the Earliest Times to the Present*. 10th ed. New York: St. Martin's.

Hodgson, Marshall G. S. 1924. *The Venture of Islam: Conscience and History in a World Civilization*. Vol. 2: *The Expansion of Islam in the Middle Periods*. Chicago: University of Chicago.

Hoepli, Manuali. 1896. *Dizionario milanese-italiano*. Milan: Ulrico Hoepli.

Homer. 1996. *The Odyssey*. Robert Fagles, trans. New York: Penguin.

Homer, Sidney. 1963. *A History of Interest Rates*. New Brunswick: Rutgers University Press.

Hopkins, Adam. 1977. *Crete: Its Past, Present and People*. London: Faber and Faber.

Horace. 1966. *Satires, Epistles and Ars Poetica*. H. Rushton Fairdough, trans. Loeb Classical Library. Cambridge: Harvard University Press.

Howe, Sonia E. n.d. *In Quest of Spices*. 2nd ed. London: Herbert Jenkins.

Hubert, Annie. 1984. *Le pain et l'olive: aspects de l'alimentation en Tunisie*. Paris: Centre National de la Recherche Scientifique.

Hughes, Spike, and Charmian Hughes. 1986. *The Pocket Guide to Italian Food and Wine*. New York: Simon & Schuster.

Huizinga, Johan. 1996. *The Autumn of the Middle Ages*. Rodney J. Payton and Ulrich Mammitzsch, trans. Chicago: University of Chicago Press.

Hyman, Philip, and Mary Hyman. 1992. "Les livres de cuisine et le commerce des recette en France aux Xve et XVIe siécles." In Carole Lambert, ed., *Du manuscrit à la table: Essais sur la cuisine au moyen âge et répertoire des manuscrits médiévaux contenaut des recettes culinaires* (pp. 59–68). Montréal: Les Presses de l'Université de Montréal; Paris: Champion-Slatkine.

Ibn al-ʿAwwām. 1977. *Kitāb al-filāḥa (Le livre de l'agriculture)*. J.-J. Clément-Mullet, trans. 2nd ed. 2 vols. Tunis: Editions Bouslama.

Ibn al-Baiṭār. 1991. *The Cilician Dioscorides' Plant* Materia Media *as Appeard in Ibn al-Baitar, the Arab Herbalist of the 13th Century*. Mohamed Nazir Sankary, ed. Aleppo: Institute for the History of Arab Science, University of Aleppo Publications.

———. 1877–83. *Traité des simples*. L. Leclerc, trans. 3 vols. Notices et extrits des manuscrit de la Bibliothèque Nationale. Paris: Bibliothèque Nationale.

Ibn Baṭṭūṭa. 1853–58/1969. *Voyages d'Ibn Battûta*. C. Defremery and B. R. Sanguinetti, eds. and trans. 4 vols. Paris: Anthropos.

Ibn Jubayr. 1952. *The Travels of Ibn Jubayr*. R. J. C. Broadhurst, trans. London: Jonathan Cape.

———. 1956. *Voyages*. Maurice Gaudefroy-Demombynes, trans. Vol. 3. Paris: Paul Geuthner.

Ibn Manẓūr. 1955. *Lisān al-ʿArab*. 15 vols. Beirut: Dar Sader and Dar Beyrouth. [in Arabic]

Ibn Riḍwān. 1984. *On the Prevention of Bodily Ills in Egypt. Medieval Islamic Medicine.* Michael W. Dols, trans. Berkeley: University of California Press.

Idris, Hady Roger. 1959. *La Berbérie Orientale sous les Zīrīdes*. Xe-XIIe siècles. 2 vols. Paris: Adrien-Maisonneuve.

Il nuovo dizionario inglese garzanti. 1984. Milan: Garzanti.

İnalcık, Halıl. 1960. "Bursa and the Commerce of the Levant." *Journal of Economic and Social History of the Orient,* 3, no. 2.

Insight Guides: Egypt. 1989. Hisham Youssef and John Rodenbeck, eds. Singapore: APA Publications.

Isidore of Seville. 1911. *Etymologiarum sive originum Libri XX*. M. W. Lindsay, ed. 2 vols. Oxford: Oxford University Press.

Islamoğlu-Inan, Huri. 1987. "State and Peasants in the Ottoman Empire: A Study of Peasant Economy in North-Central Anatolia during the Sixteenth Century." In Huri Islamoğlu-Inan, ed., *The Ottoman Empire and the World Economy*. Cambridge: Cambridge University Press and Paris: Éditions de la Maison des Science de l'Homme.

Istituto nazionale di sociologia rurale. 1984. *Gastronomia e societa*. Milan: Franco Angeli.

Jacob, Georg. 1897. *Altarabishes Beduinenleben. Nach den Quellen geschildert*. Berlin: Mayer & Müller.

Jacobs, Jay. 1975. *Gastronomy*. New York: Newsweek.

Jacobs, Michael. 1991. *A Guide to Andalusia*. London: Penguin.

Jamison, Evelyn. 1957. *Admiral Eugenius of Sicily: His Life and Work and the Authorship of the* Epistola ad Petrum *and the* Historia Hugonis Falcandi Siculi. London: Oxford University Press for the British Academy.

Jasny, Naum. 1944. *The Wheats of Classical Antiquity*. Johns Hopkins University Studies in Historical and Political Science Series 62, no. 3. Baltimore: Johns Hopkins.

Jeanneret, Michel. 1991. *A Feast of Words: Banquets and Table Talk in the Renaissance*. Jeremy Whiteley and Emma Hughes, trans. Chicago: University of Chicago Press.

Kalligas, Haris. 1990. *Byzantine Monemvasia. The Sources*. Monemvasia: Akroneon.

Kasaba, Reşat. 1992. " 'By Compass and Sword!' The Meanings of 1492." *Middle East Report*, 22, no. 5 (September/October): 6–10.

Kedar, Benjamin. 1984. *Crusade and Mission: European Approaches towards the Muslims*. Princeton: Princeton University Press.

"King Mutton, a Curious Egyptian Tale of the Mamluk Period." 1990. Joshua Finkel, trans. *Petits Propos Culinaire*, 33 (March): 26–46.

Kislinger, Ewald. 1996. "Les chrétiens d'Orient: Règles et réalités alimentaires dans le monde byzantin." In Jean-Louis Flandrin and Massimo Montanari, *Histoire de l'alimentation* (pp. 325–44). Bari: Gius. Laterza; Paris: Fayard.

Kitāb al-ṭabīkh fī al-Maghrib wa'l-Āndalus. 1961–62. A. Huici Miranda, ed. *Revista del Instituto de Eśtudios Islamicos en Madrid*, 9–10, Arabic section (pp. 12–256). [in Arabic]

Koenigsberger, Helmut. 1951. *The Government of Sicily Under Philip II of Spain*. London: Staples.

Koran. 1980. N. J. Dawood, trans. London: Penguin.

Krekić, Bariša. 1961. *Dubrovnik (Raguse) et le Levant au Moyen Âge*. Paris: Mouton.

———. 1972. *Dubrovnik in the 14th and 15th Centuries*. Norman: University of Oklahoma Press.

———. 1980. *Dubrovnik, Italy and the Balkans in the Late Middle Ages*. London: Variorum Reprint.

Labib, Subhi Y. 1965. *Handelsgeschichte Ägyptens im Spätmittelalter (1171–1517)*. Wiesbaden: Franz Steiner.

"La cucina del vescovo di Luni." *Giornale lingustico di archeologia, storia e letteratura*, 9 (January): 161–65.

Ladurie, Emmanuel Le Roy. 1976. *The Peasants of Languedoc*. John Day, trans. Urbana: University of Illinois.

———. 1988. *Times of Feast, Times of Famine: A History of Climate Since the Year 1000*. Barbara Bray, trans. New York: Farrar, Straus and Giroux.

Lambert, Carole. 1992. "Astuces et flexibilité des recetter culinaires médiévales Françaises." In Carole Lambert, ed., *Du manuscrit à la table: Essais sur la cuisine au moyen âge et répertoire des manuscrits médiévaux contenant des recettes culinaires* (pp. 215–25). Montréal: Les Presses de l'Université de Montréal; Paris: Champion-Slatkine.

Lane, Edward William. 1863–93. *An Arabic-English Lexicon*. 8 vols. London: Williams and Norgate.

———. 1908. *The Manners and Customs of the Modern Egyptians*. London and Toronto: J. M. Dent; New York: E. P. Dutton.

Lane, Frederick Chapin. 1934. *Venetian Ships and Shipbuilders of the Renaissance*. Baltimore: Johns Hopkins.

———. 1940. "The Mediterranean Spice Trade: Its Revival in the Sixteenth Century." *American Historical Review*, 45: 581–90.

———. 1966. *Venice and History*. Baltimore: Johns Hopkins.

———. 1973. *Venice: A Maritime Republic*. Baltimore: Johns Hopkins University Press.

Laoust, E. 1920. *Mots et choses Berbères dialectes du Maroc*. Paris: Augustin Challamel.

Lapeyre, Henri. 1958. *Une famille de marchands les Ruiz*. Paris: Armand Colin.

La Primaudaie, M. F. Elie de. 1868. *Les Arabes en Sicilie et en Italie. Les Norman en Sicilie et en Italie: Études historiques et geographiques d'apres des documents nouveaux et inedits*. Paris: Challamel Aine.

Larenaudie, Marie-Josèphe. 1952. "Les famines en Languedoc aux XIVe et XVe siècles." *Annales du Midi*, 64, no. 17 (January).

Lauer, J.-P., V. Laurent Täckholm, and E. Åberg. 1949–50. "Les plantes découvertes dans les souterrains de l'enceinte du roi Zoser à Saqqarah (IIIe dynastie)." *Bulletin de l'Institut d'Egypte*, 32: 121–57.

Laurioux, Bruno. 1985. "Spices in the Medieval Diet: A New Approach." *Food and Foodways*, 1: 43–76.

———. 1988. "Entre savoir et pratiques: Le livre de cuisine à la fin du moyen âge." *Médiévales*, 14 (Spring): 59–71.

———. 1989. *Le moyen âge à table*. Paris: Adam Biro.

Lazarillo de Tormes. 1969. In *Two Spanish Picaresque Novels*. Michael Alpert, trans. London: Penguin.

Lentini, Rosario. 1987. "Economia e storia delle tonnare di Sicilia." In Vincenzo Consolo, ed., *La pesca del tonno in Sicilia* (pp. 32–56) Palermo: Sellerio.

Les sources inédites de l'histoire du Maroc. 1953. 2nd series, vol. 5. Paris: Paul Geuthner.

Levey, Martin. 1971. "Influence of Arabic Pharmacology on Medieval Europe." *Oriente e occidente nel medioevo: filosofia e scienza* (pp. 431–44). Accademia Nazionale dei Lincei, Fondazione Alessandro Volta, Atti dei Convegni 13. Convegno Internazionale, 9–15 April 1969. Rome: Accademia dei Lincei.

Levey, Martin, and Noury al-Khaledy, trans. and eds. 1967. *The Medical Formulary of Al-Samarqandī and the Relation of Early Arabic Simples to Those Found in the Indigenous Medicine of the Near East and India*. Philadelphia: University of Pennsylvania Press.

Lévi-Provençal, É. 1928. *Documents inédits d'histoire Almohade*. Paris: Paul Geuthner.

———. 1967. *Histoire de l'Espagne Musulmane*. 3 vols. Paris: G. P. Maisonneuve & Larose.

Lewicki, Tadeusz. 1974. *West African Food in the Middle Ages*. Cambridge: Cambridge University Press.

Lewis, Archibald R. 1951. *Naval Power and Trade in the Mediterranean, A.D. 500–1100*. Princeton: Princeton University Press.

Lewis, Bernard. 1961. *The Emergence of Modern Turkey*. London: Oxford University Press.

———. 1982. *The Muslim Discovery of Europe*. New York: W. W. Norton.

———. 1987. ed. and trans. *Islam from the Prophet Muhammad to the Capture of Constantinople*. II: *Religion and Society*. Oxford: Oxford University Press.

Lieber, Alfred E. 1968. "Eastern Business Practices and Medieval European Commerce." *Economic History Review*, 21, no. 2 (August): 230–43.

Lingua, Paola. 1984. *Andrea Doria*. Milan: Nuova.

Littré, É. 1881. *Dictionnaire de la langue Français*. Paris: Hachette.

Lladonosa i Giró, Josep. 1984. *La cocina medieval*. Barcelona: Editorial Laia.

Locke, John. 1953. *Locke's Travels in France, 1675–1679.* John Lough, ed. Cambridge: Cambridge University Press.

Lokotsch, Karl. 1927. *Etymolisches Wörterbuch der Europäischen (Germanischen, Romanischen und Slavischen) Wörter Orientalischen Ursprungs.* Indogermanische Bibliothek. Heidelberg: Carl Winter's Universitätsbuchhandlung.

Lombardini, Gabriele. 1963. *Pane e denaro a Bassano: Prezzi del grano e politica dell'approvvigionamento tra il 1501 e il 1799.* Vicenza: Neri Pozza.

Lopez, Roberto Sabatino. 1936. *Studi sull'economia genovese nel medio evo.* Turin: S. Lattes & C.

———. 1938. *Storia delle colonie genovesi nel Mediterraneo.* Bologna: Nicola Zanichelli.

———. 1953. "The Origin of Merino Sheep." In *Joshua Starr Memorial Volume: Studies in History and Philology* (pp. 161–68). New York: Conference on Jewish Relations.

———. 1975. "Chi ha inventato gli spaghetti?" In R. Lopez, ed., *Su e giù per la storia di Genova*, no. 20 (pp. 381–83). Genoa: Collana storica di fonti e studi.

———. 1976. *The Commercial Revolution of the Middle Ages 950–1350.* Cambridge: Cambridge University Press.

Lopez, Robert S., and Irving W. Raymond. 1990. *Medieval Trade in the Mediterranean World.* New York: Columbia University Press.

Lorenzetti, Giulio. 1956. *Venice and its Lagoon.* Rome: Istituto Poligrafico dello Stato.

Lozach, Jean. 1935. *Le delta du Nil: Étude de géographie humaine.* Cairo: E. & R. Schindler.

Luján, Nèstor. 1979. *El menjar.* Barcelona: Dopesa 2.

———. 1981–82. "Assaig sobre l'arròs a catalunya." *Congrès Català de la Cuina.* Barcelona: Generalitet de Catalunya, Departmento de Comerc, I Turisme.

———. 1988. *La vida cotidiana en el siglo de oro español.* 4th ed. Barcelona: Planeta.

Luzzatto, Gino. 1954. *Studi de storia economica veneziana.* Padua: Cedam.

———. 1961a. *Storia economica di Venezia dall'XI al XVI secolo.* Venice: Centro internazionale delle arti e del costume.

———. 1961b. *An Economic History of Italy from the Fall of the Roman Empire to the Beginning of the Sixteenth Century.* Philip Jones, trans. London: Routledge and Kegan Paul.

Macadam, Alta. 1981. *Blue Guide: Sicily.* London and Tonbridge: Ernest Benn and Chicago: Rand McNally.

Mack Smith, Denis. 1968. *A History of Sicily: Medieval Sicily 800–1713.* 2 vols. New York: Dorset.

Madan, C. L., B. M. Kapur, and U.S. Gupta. 1966. "Saffron." *Economic Botany*, 20, no. 4 (October-December).

Maffioli, G. n.d. *Venetian Gastronomy.* N.p.: Regione del Veneto.

Maimonides, Moses. 1940. *Šarḥ asmā' al-ᶜuqqār (L'explication des nomes des drogues).* Max Meyerhof, ed. and trans. Mémoires présenté a l'Institut d'Égypte. XLI. Cairo: L'institut Français d'archéologie orientale.

Malpica Cuello, A. 1984. "El pescado en el reino de Granada a fines de la edad media: Especies y nivel de consumo." *Manger et Boire au Moyen Âge.* Actes du Colloque de Nice, 1, no. 27: 103–107. *Aliments et Société.* Centre d'Études Médiévales de Nice: Centre National de la Recherche Scientifique, Les Belles Lettres.

Manfroni, Camillo. 1897. *Storia della marina italiana.* Vol. 2: *Dalla caduta di Constantinopoli alla battaglia di Lepanto.* Rome: Forzani.

Mangelsdorf, Paul C. 1974. *Corn: Its Origin, Evolution, and Improvement.* Cambridge: Harvard University Press.

Manniche, Lise. 1989. *An Ancient Egyptian Herbal.* Austin: University of Texas Press with British Museum Publications.

Mantovano, Giuseppe. 1985. *La cucina italiana: Origine, storia e segreti.* Rome: Newton Compton.

Mantran, Robert. 1962. *Istanbul dans la seconde moitié du XVIIe siècle.* Bibliothéque archélogique et historique de l'Institut Français d'Archéologie d'Istanbul 12. Paris: Adrien Maisonneuve.

———. 1965. *La vie quotidienne a Constantinople au temps du Soliman le Magnifique et de ses successeurs (XVIe et XVIIe siècles).* Paris: Hachette.

Manzalaoui, M. A., ed. 1977. *Secretum secretorum: Nine English Versions.* Oxford: Oxford University Press for the Early English Text Society.

March, Lourdes. 1989. "The Valencian Paella-its Origin, Tradition and Universality." *Oxford Symposium on Food and Cookery 1988: The Cooking Pot.* Proceedings. London: Prospect.

Marengo, Emilio. 1901. *Genova e Tunisi (1388–1515).* Rome: Artigianelli di San Giuseppe.

Margen, Sheldon, and the Editors of the University of California at Berkeley Wellness Letter. 1992. *The Wellness Encyclopedia of Food and Nutrition: How to Buy, Store, and Prepare Every Variety of Fresh Food.* New York: Rebus.

Marín, Manuela. 1981. "Sobre buran y buraniyya." *Al-Qantara*, 2, fasc. 1 and 2: 193–207.

———. 1986. "Materiaux pour l'histoire de l'alimentation hispano-maghrebine: *Ali b. Ibrahim al-Andalusi et son "Urguzat al-Fawakih," Islão e Arabismo na Península ibérica* (pp. 297–304). Actas do XI Congresso da Uniao europeia de arabistas & islamologos. Évora: Universidade de Évora.

Marín, Manuela, and David Waines, eds. 1994. *La alimentación en las culturas islamicas.* Madrid: Agencis Española de Cooperación International.

Marino, John A. 1988. *Pastoral Economics in the Kingdom of Naples.* Baltimore: Johns Hopkins University Press.

Marinoni, A., ed. 1955. *Dal* Declarus *di A. Senisio: I vocaboli siciliani.* Collezione di testi siciliani dei secoli XIV e XV 6. Palermo: Centro di Studi Filologici e Linguistici Siciliani.

Marling, William E., and Clare F. Marling. 1971. *The "Marling" Menu-Master for France: A Comprehensive Manual for Translating the French Menu into American English.* Orinda, CA: Altarinda Books.

———. 1971. *The "Marling" Menu-Master for Italy: A Comprehensive Manual for Translating the Italian Menu into American English*. Orinda, CA: Altarinda Books.

———. 1973. *The "Marling" Menu-Master for Spain: A Comprehensive Manual for Translating the Spanish Menu into American English*. No place: William E. and Clare F. Marling.

Marotta, Giuseppe. 1965. *L'oro di napoli*. Milan: Bompiani.

Martínez Llopis, Manuel. 1981. *Historia de la gastronomia Española*. Madrid: Editora Nacional.

Martinez Sopena, P., and Ma. J. Carbajo Serrano. 1984. "L'alimentation des paysans Castillans du XIe au XIIIe siecle d'apres les *fueros*." *Manger et Boire au Moyen Âge*. Actes du Colloque de Nice, 1, no-27: 335–47. *Aliments et Société*. Centre d'Études Médiévales de Nice: Centre National de la Recherche Scientifique, Les Belles Lettres.

Masson, Michel. 1988. "A propos de quelques mots grecs relatifs a l'alimentation." *Revue de Philologie*, 62: 25–39.

Masson, Paul. 1967. *Histoire du commerce Français dans le Levant au XVIIe siècle*. New York: Burt Franklin.

Matazone da Calignano. 1960. "Detto dei villani." G. Contini, ed. In *Poeti del Duecento*. Vol. 1. Milan and Naples: R. Ricciardi.

Matton, Raymond. 1957. *La Créte au cours de siècles*. Athens: Istitut Français d'Athenes.

Mazzi, Maria Serena. 1980. "Note per una storia dell'alimentazione nell'Italia medievale." In *Studi di storia medievale e moderna per Ernesto Sestan*. Vol. 1: *Medioevo* (pp. 57–102). Florence: Leo S. Olschki.

McNeill, William H. 1974. *Venice: The Hinge of Europe 1081–1797*. Chicago: University of Chicago Press.

———. 1991. "American Food Crops in the Old World." In Herman J. Viola and Carolyn Margolis, eds., *Seeds of Change: A Quincentennial Celebration* (pp. 43–59). Washington, DC: Smithsonian Institution Press.

McPhee, John. 1966. *Oranges*. New York: Farrar, Straus and Giroux.

Medieval Health Handbook. 1976. *Tacuinum Sanitatis*. Luisa Cogliati Arano, ed. Oscar Ratti and Adele Westbrook, trans. New York: George Braziller.

Menjot, D. 1984. "Notes sur le marché de l'alimentation et la consommation alimentaire a Murcie à la fin du moyen âge." *Manger et Boire au Moyen Âge*. Actes du Colloque de Nice, 1, no. 27: 199–210. *Aliments et Société*. Centre d'Études Médiévales de Nice: Centre National de la Recherche Scientifique, Les Belles Lettres.

Mennell, Stephen. 1985. *All Manners of Food: Eating and Taste in England and France from the Middle Ages to the Present*, Oxford: Basil Blackwell.

Messedaglia, Luigi. 1974. *Vita e costume della rinascenza in Merlin Cocai*. 2 vols. Medioevo e Umanesimo 14. Padua: Antenore.

M'Hamsadji. 1956. "Usages et rites alimentaires d'une contrée rurale d'Algerie." *Annales de l'Institut d'Études Orientales*, 14: 257–329.

Migliari, Maria Luisa, and Alida Azzola. 1978. *Storia della gastronomia*. Novara: Edipem.

Milham, Mary Ella. 1995. "Martino and his *De re coquinaria*." In Mary-Jo Arn, ed, *Medieval Food and Drink* (pp. 61–66). Acta vol. xxi. Binghamton, NY: Center for Medieval and Early Renaissance Studies, Binghamton, State University of New York.

Miller, William. 1908. *The Latins in the Levant: A History of Frankish Greece (1204–1566)*. New York: E. P. Dutton.

Millo, Llorenç. 1984. *La taula i la cuina*. Valencia: Diputació Provencial de València.

Mingazzini, Paolino. 1954. "Gli antichi conoscevano i maccheroni?" *Archeologia Classica*, 6: 292–94.

Mintz, Sidney W. 1985. *Sweetness and Power: The Place of Sugar in Modern History*. New York: Penguin.

Mistral, Frédéric. 1879. *Lou tresor dóu felibrige ou dictionnaire provençal-français*. Aix-en-Provence: Veuve Remondet-Aubin; Avignon: Roumanille; Paris: H. Champion.

Mitchell, Tim. 1991. "America's Egypt: Discourse of the Development Industry." *Middle East Report*, (March–April): 18–36.

Mittwoch, Eugen. 1933. "P. de Konings Bearbeitung der Heilmittellehre von Ibn Gazla." In Institut für Geschichte der Medizin und der Naturwissenschaften in Berlin, ed., *Quellen und Studien zur Geschichte der Naturwissenschaften und der Medizin* (pp. 85–91[293–99]). Berlin: Julius Springer.

Moldenke, Harold N., and Alma L. Moldenke. 1952. *Plants of the Bible*. New York: Dover.

Molénat, J. P. 1984. "Menus des pauvres, menus des confreres a Tolede dans la deuxieme moitié du XVè siecle." *Manger et Boire au Moyen Âge*. Actes du Colloque de Nice, 1, no. 27: 313–18. *Aliments et Société*. Centre d'Études Médiévales de Nice: Centre National de la Recherche Scientifique, Les Belles Lettres.

Monchicourt, Ch. 1913a. *L'expédition Espagnole de 1560 contre l'ile de Djerba*. Paris: Ernest Leroux.

———. 1913b. *La region du Haut Tell en Tunisie*. Paris: Armand Colin.

Montanari, Massimo. 1979. *L'alimentazione contadina nell'alto medioevo*. Naples: Liguori.

———. 1984. "Rural Food in Late Medieval Italy." In *Bäuerliche Sachkultur des Spätmittelalters: Internationaler Kongress Krems an der Donau 21. bis 24. September 1982* (pp. 307–20). Vienna: Österreichischen Akademie der Wissenschaften.

———. 1989. "Note sur l'histoire des pâtes en Italie." *Médiévales. Langue, textes, histoire*, vols. 16–17: 61–64.

———. 1994a. *The Culture of Food*. Oxford and Cambridge, MA: Blackwell.

———. 1994b. *Alimentazione e cultura nel medioevo*. Bari: Laterza.

Moore, R. W. 1952. "The Renaissance." In Michael Huxley, ed., *The Root of Europe: Studies in the Diffusion of Greek Culture* (pp. 61–72). London: The Geographical Magazine.

Moreau, Jean, and Robert Andry. 1942. "Un aliment Nord-Africain: Le couscous, composition, fabrication, préparation." *Archives de l'Institute Pasteur de Tunis*, 31, no. 3–4 (December): 302–10.

Morelli, Giovanni di Pagolo. 1956. *Ricordi*. Florence: Le Monnier.

Moreno, Diego. 1989. "Châtaigneraie 'historique' et châtaigneraie traditionnelle: Notes pour l'identification d'une pratique culturale." *Médiévales. Langue, textes, histoire* 16–17: 147–69.

Moreno, Eduardo Manzano. 1984. "Christian-Muslim Frontier in Al-Andalus: Idea and Reality." In Dionisius A. Agius and Richard Hitchcock, eds., *The Arab Influence in Medieval Europe*: Folia Scholastica Mediterranea (pp. 83–99). Reading: Ithaca Press.

Morize, Jean. 1914. "Aigue-Mortes au XIIIe siècle." *Annales du Midi*, 26: 313–448.

Morris, Jan. 1980. *The Venetian Empire: A Sea Voyage*. New York: Harcourt Brace Jovanovich.

Mortillaro, Vincenzo. 1983. *Dizionario siciliano-italiano*. Palermo: Vittorietti.

Moss, H. St L. B. 1952. "Greece and the Early Mediaeval West." In Michael Huxley, ed., *The Root of Europe: Studies in the Diffusion of Greek Culture* (pp. 35–43). London: The Geographical Magazine.

Mugoni, Pietro. 1985. *Economia e società nella sardegna medievale*. Oristano: S'Alvure Oristano.

Murphey, Rhoads. 1988. "Provisioning Istanbul: The State and Subsistence in the Early Modern Middle East." *Food and Foodways* 2: 217–63.

Newett, Margaret M. 1902. "The Sumptuary Laws of Venice in the Fourteenth and Fifteenth Centuries." In T. F. Tout Manchester, and James Tait, eds., *Historical Essays by Members of Owens College* (pp. 245–77). London: Longmans, Green and Co.

Nicol, Donald M. 1992. *Byzantium and Venice: A Study in Diplomatic and Cultural Relations*. Cambridge: Cambridge University Press.

Norman, Barbara. 1972. *Tales of the Table: A History of Western Cuisine*. Englewood Cliffs, NJ: Prentice-Hall.

Norman, Jill. 1990. *The Complete Book of Spices*. London: Dorling Kindersley.

Norwich, John Julius. 1967. *The Normans in the South 1016–1130*. London: Longman.

———. 1970. *The Kingdom in the Sun 1130–1194*. London: Longman.

———. 1989. *A History of Venice*. New York: Vintage.

Oakeshott, R. Ewart. 1960. *The Archaeology of Weapons: Arms and Armor from Prehistory to the Age of Chivalry*. New York: Frederick A. Praeger.

Oliva, Salvador, and Angela Buxton. 1983–85. *Diccionari Angles-Català; Català-Angles*. Barcelona: Enciclopèdia Catalana.

Oliver, Raymond. 1967. *Gastronomy of France*. Claude Durrell, trans. Cleveland: The Wine and Food Society with World Publishing.

Ostrogorsky, George. 1969. *History of the Byzantine State*. Rev. ed. New Brunswick: Rutgers University Press.

Oxford English Dictionary. 1971. Oxford: Oxford University Press.

Paganini, P. Angelo. 1857. *Vocabolario domestico genovese-italiano*. Genoa: Gaetano Schenone.

Palmer, Maria del Carmen Simon. 1982. *La alimentation y sus circunstancias real Alcazar de Madrid*. Madrid: Instituto de Estudios Madrileños.

Pansier, P. 1927. *Histoire de la langue Provençale a Avignon du XIIme au XIXme siècle*. Avignon: Aubanel Frères.

Parain, Charles. 1936. *La Méditerranée: Les hommes et leurs travaux*. Paris: Gallimard.

Parker, Geoffrey. 1972. *The Army of Flanders and the Spanish Road, 1567–1659*. Cambridge: Cambridge University Press.

Parry, V. J., and M. E. Yapp, eds. 1975. *War, Technology and Society in the Middle East*. London: Oxford University Press.

Parvin, Jo Ann. 1985. "Andalusian Poyos." *Petits Propos Culinaire*, 21 (November): 41–44.

Pasquali, Gianfranco. 1984. *Agricoltura e società rurale in romagna nel medioevo*. Bologna: Pàtron.

Pasqualino, Michele. 1785. *Vocabulario siciliano, etimologico, italiano, e latino*. Palermo: Dalle Reale Stamperia.

Patrone, Anna Maria Nada. 1981. *Il cibo del ricco ed il cibo del povero: Contributo alla storia qualitativa dell'alimentazione. L'area pedemontana negli ultimi secoli del medio evo*. Turin: Centro Studi Piemontesi.

———. 1990. "I consumi possibili." In *Storia dell'economia italiana*. Vol. 1: *Il medioevo dal Crollo al Trionfo* (pp. 193–212). Turin: Giulio Einaudi.

Patton Jr., George S. 1947. *War As I Knew It*. Boston: Houghton Mifflin.

Peers, Edgar Allison, et al. 1966. *Cassell's Spanish Dictionary*. New York: Funk & Wagnalls.

Pellegrini, Giovan Battista. 1972. *Gli arabismi nelle lingue neolatine con speciale riguardo all'Italia*. 2 vols. Brescia: Paideia.

Pérès, H. 1943. *Bulletin des Études Arabes* (Algiers), 15 (November–December): 140–41.

Perry, Charles. 1981a. "The Oldest Mediterranean Noodle: A Cautionary Tale." *Petits Propos Culinaire*, 9 (October): 42–45.

———. 1981b. "Three Medieval Arabic Cook Books." In *Oxford Symposium 1981: National & Regional Styles of Cookery, Proceedings* (pp. 96–105). London: Prospect.

———. 1981c. "Shorba: A Linguistic-Chemico-Culinary Inquiry." *Petits Propos Culinaire*, 7 (March): 23–24.

———. 1982. "What Was Tracta?" *Petits Propos Culinaires*, 12: 37–39.

———. 1984. "Puff Paste Is Spanish." *Petits Propos Culinaires*, 17 (June): 57–62.

———. 1985. "*Kitab al-Tibakhah*: A Fifteenth-Century Cookbook." *Petits Propos Culinaire*, 21 (November): 17–22.

———. 1987. "The Ṣalṣ of the Infidels." *Petits Propos Culinaire*, 26 (July): 55–59.

———. 1989. "Isfidhabaj, Blancmanger and No Almonds," *Petits Propos Culinaire*, 31 (March): 25–28.

———. et al. 1993. "Ful Medames," *Petits Propos Culinaire*, 43 (May): 47–48.

———. 1994. "The Taste for Layered Bread among the Nomadic Turks and the Central Asian Origins of Baklava." In Sami Zubaida and Richard Tapper, eds., *Culinary Cultures of the Middle East* (pp. 87–91). London: I. B. Tauris with Centre of Near and Middle Eastern Studies, School of Oriental and African Studies, University of London.

Pertusi, Agostino, ed. 1973–74. *Venezia e il levante fino al secolo XV*. Florence: Leo S. Olschki.

Peterson, Toby. 1980. "The Arab Influence on Western European Cooking." *Journal of Medieval History*, 6 (September): 317–41.

———. 1994. *Acquired Taste: The French Origins of Modern Cooking*. Ithaca and London: Cornell University Press.

Petronius. 1977. *Satyricon*. J. P. Sullivan, trans. Harmondsworth: Penquin.

Phillips, Roger, and Martyn Rix. 1993. *Vegetables*. New York: Random House.

Pianigiani, Ottorino. 1907. *Vocabolario etimologico della lingua italiana*. Rome and Milan: Albrighi, Segati.

Piccinni, Gabriella. 1982. "Note sull'alimentazione medievale." *Studi Storici* (Rome), 23 (July-September): 603–15.

Pickersgill, Barbara. 1969. "The Domestication of Chili Peppers." In Peter J. Ucko and G. W. Dimbleby, eds., *The Domestication and Exploitation of Plants and Animals* (pp. 443–50). Chicago: Aldine.

Pike, Ruth. 1962. "The Genoese in Seville and the Opening of the New World," *Journal of Economic History*. 22 no. 3 (September): 348–78.

———. 1966. *Enterprise and Adventure: The Genoese in Seville and the Opening of the New World*. Ithaca: Cornell University Press.

Pinder-Wilson, Ralph. 1976. "The Persian Garden: *Bagh* and *Chahar Bagh*." In *The Islamic Garden* (pp. 71–85). Washington, DC: Dumbarton Oaks Trustees for Harvard University.

Piniés, Jean-Pierre. 1989. "Ethnographie." In *Languedoc Méditerranéen: Aude, Gard, Hérault* (pp. 117–120). Paris: Christine Bonneton.

Pino-Branca, Alfredo. 1938. *La vita economica degli stati italiani nei secoli XVI, XVII, XVIII (secondo le relazioni degli ambasciatori veneti)*. Catania: Studio Editoriale Moderno.

Pinto, Giuliano. 1981. "Le fonti documentarie bassomedievali." *Archeologia Medievale*, 8: 39–58.

Pipitone Cannone, A. 1939. "Governo delle acque e case rurale nella Sicilia musulmana." *Problemi Mediterranei*, 16: 273–82, 204–17.

Pla, Josep. 1981. *El que hem menjat*. Barcelona: Edicions Destino.

———. 1983. *Obra completa*. Vol. 31: *Articles amb Cua*. 2nd ed. Barcelona: Edicions Destino.

Pliny. 1938–1962. *Natural History*. H. Rackham, W. H. S. Jones, D. E. Eichman, Loeb Classical Library, 10 vols. Cambridge: Harvard University Press.

Plouvier, Liliane. 1992. "Le 'letuaire,' une confiture du bas moyen âge." In Carole Lambert, ed., *Du manuscrit à la table: Essais sur la cuisine au moyen âge et répertoire des manuscrits médiévaux contenant des recettes culinaires* (pp. 243–56). Montréal: Les Presses de l'Université de Montréal; Paris: Champion-Slatkine.

Poliakov, Léon. 1961. *Histoire de l'antisemitisme: De mahomet aux marranes*. Paris: Calmann-Lévy.

Polo, Marco. 1982. *Milione. Le divisament dou monde*. Gabriella Ronchi, ed. Milan: Arnoldo Mondadori.

———. 1993. *The Travels of Marco Polo: The Complete Yule-Cordier Edition,* 2 vols. New York: Dover.

Porcaro, Giuseppe. 1985. *Sapore di napoli: Storia della pizza napoletana*. Naples: Adriano Gallina.

Porceddu, E., and D. Lafiandra. 1986. "Origin and Evolution of Wheats." In C. Barigozzi, ed., *The Origin and Domestication of Cultivated Plants* (pp. 143–78). Developments in Agricultural and Managed-Forest Ecology 16. Amsterdam: Elsevier.

Postan, M. M. 1966. *The Cambridge Economic History of Europe*. Vol. 2: *The Agrarian Life of the Middle Ages*. 2nd ed. Cambridge: Cambridge University Press.

———. 1967. "Investment in Medieval Agriculture." *Journal of Economic History*, 27, no. 4 (December): 576–87.

Presotto, Danilo. 1965. "Genova 1656–1657: Cronache di una pestilenza." *Atti della Societá Ligure di Storia Patria*, 79, fasc. 2: 313–435.

Pryor, John H. 1988. "*In Subsidium Terrae Sanctae*: Exports of Foodstuffs and War Materials from the Kingdom of Sicily to the Kingdom of Jerusalem, 1265–1284." In B. Z. Kedar and A. L. Udovitch, eds., "The Medieval Levant: Studies in Memory of Eliyahu Ashtor (1914–1984)." *Asian and African Studies*, 22, nos. 1–3 (November): 127–46.

Pseudo-Apuleius. 1481/1979. *Herbarium Apulei 1481*. Erminio Caprotti and William T. Stearn, intro. Verona: Il Polifilo.

Pullan, Brian. 1971. *Rich and Poor in Renaissance Venice: The Social Institutions of a Catholic State to 1620*. Cambridge: Harvard University Press.

Purcell, Nicolas. 1995. "Eating Fish: The Paradoxes of Seafood." In John Wilkins, David Harvey, and Mike Dobson, eds., *Food in Antiquity* (pp. 132–49). Exeter: University of Exeter Press.

Quaglia, A. M. Pult. 1980. "Controls over Food Supplies in Florence in the late XVIth and Early XVIIth Centuries." *Journal of European Economic History*, 9, no. 2 (Fall): 449–57.

Ramusio, Giovanni Battista. 1978–88. *Navigazioni e viaggi. I Milleni*. 3 vols. Turin: G. Einaudi.

al-Rāzī, Aḥmad ibn Muḥammad. 1953. *"La Description de l'Espagne d'Aḥmad al-Rāzī."* É. Lévi-Provençal, trans. *Al Andalus,* 18: 51–108.

Rebora, Giovanni. 1987. "La cucina medievale italiana tra Oriente e Occidente." *Miscellanea Storica Ligure*, 19, nos. 1–2: 1431–579.

Redhouse, James W., Sir. 1978. *A Turkish and English Lexicon Shewing in English the Significations of the Turkish Terms*. Istanbul: Cagri Yayinlari.

Redon, Odile. 1992. "La réglementation des banquets par les lois somptuaires dans les villes d'Italie (XIIIe-XVe siècles)." In Carole Lambert, ed., *Du manuscrit à la table: Essais sur la cuisine au moyen âge et répertoire des manuscrits médiévaux contenant des recettes culinaires* (pp. 109–19). Montréal; Les Presses de l'Université de Montréal: Paris: Champion-Slatkine.

Redon, Odile, and Bruno Laurioux. 1989. "La constitution d'une nouvelle catégorie culinaire? Les pâtes dans les livres de cuisine italiens de la fin au moyen âge."

Médiévales. Langue, textes, histoire. Vols. 16–17: 51–60.

Renfrew, Jane M. 1973. *Paleoethnobotany: The Prehistoric Food Plants of the Near East and Europe*. New York: Columbia University Press.

Revel, Jean-Francois. 1982. *Culture and Cuisine: A Journey Through the History of Food*. Helen R. Lane, trans. New York: Da Capo.

Reynolds, Susan. 1994. *Fiefs and Vassals: The Medieval Evidence Reinterpreted*. Oxford: Oxford University Press.

Reynolds, Robert L. 1945. "In Search of a Business Class in Thirteenth-Century Genoa." *Journal of Economic History*, Supplement 5 (December): 1–19.

Richard, J.-M. 1892. "Thierry d'Hireçon, agriculteur artésian (13..-1328)." *Bibliothèque de l'École des Chartes*, 53 (July–October): 383–416 and (November–December) 571–604.

Riley-Smith, Jonathan. 1973. *The Feudal Nobility and the Kingdom of Jerusalem 1174–1277*. Hamden, CT: Archon.

Rios, Alicia. 1984. "The cocido madrileno; A case of culinary adhocism." *Petits Propos Culinaire*, 18 (November): 19–28.

———. 1987. *"El Arte del Tapeo." Petits Propos Culinaire*, 27 (October): 37–45.

Roden, Claudia. 1980. "Early Arab Cooking and Cookery Manuscripts." *Petits Propos Culinaires*, 6 (October): 16–27.

Rodinson, Maxime. 1949. "Recherches sur les documents Arabes relatifs à la cuisine." *Revue des Études Islamiques*, 17–18. pp. 95–165.

———. 1956. "Sur l'etymologie de 'losange.' " In *Studi orientalistici in onore di Giorgio Levi Della Vida* Vol. 2. Istituto per l'Oriente 52. Rome: Istituto per l'Oriente.

———. 1971. "Les influences de la civilisation Musulmane sur la civilisation Européenne médiévale dans les domaines de la consommation et de la distraction: L'alimentation." *Oriente e occidente nel medioevo: Filosofia e scienza* (pp. 479–500). Accademia Nazionale dei Lincei, Fondazione Alessandro Volta, Atti dei Convegni 13. Convegno Internazionale, 9–15 April 1969. Rome: Accademia dei Lincei.

———. 1978. *Islam and Capitalism*. Brian Pearce, trans. Austin: University of Texas.

———. 1979. "The Western Image and Western Studies of Islam." In Joseph Schacht, ed., with C. E. Bosworth. 1986. *The Legacy of Islam*. 2nd ed. Oxford: Oxford University Press. pp. 9–62.

———. 1986. "On the Etymology of 'Losange.' " Charles Perry, trans. *Petits Propos Culinaire*, 23 (July): 15–23.

———. 1989. *"Ma'mūniyya* East and West." Barbara Inskip, trans. *Petits Propos Culinaire*, 33 (November): 15–25.

———. 1990. "*Romania* and Other Arab Words in Italian." *Petits Propos Culinaire*, 34 (March): 31–44.

Rohlfs, Gerhard. 1956–59. *Vocabolario dei dialetti salentini (Terra d'Otranto)*. Vols. 41, 48. Munich: Verlag der Bayerischen Akademie der Wissenschaften.

Romano, Ruggiero. 1953. A propos du commerce du blé dans la Méditerranée des XIVe et XV siècles." *In Éventail de l'histoire vivante: Hommage à Lucien Febvre* (vol. 2, pp. 149–56). Paris: Armand Colin.

———. 1956. *Commerce et prix du blé à Marseille au XVIIIe siècle*. Paris: A. Colin.

Romier, Lucien. 1922. *Le royaume de Catherine de Médicis*. Vol. 1: *La France à la veille des guerres de religion*. Paris: Perrin.

Root, Waverly. 1980. *Food: An Authoritative, Visual History and Dictionary of the Foods of the World*. New York: Fireside.

Rosenberger, Bernard. 1980. "Cultures complémentaires et nourritures de substitution au Maroc (XVe-XVIIIe siècle)." *Annales: Économies. Sociétés. Civilisations*, nos. 3–4 (May–August): 477–503.

———. 1989. "Les pâtes dans le monde Musulman." *Médiévales. Langue, textes, histoire*, vols. 16–17: 77–98.

———. 1996. "La cuisine arabe et son apporte à la cuisine européenne." In Jean-Louis Flandrin and Massimo Montanari, *Histoire de l'alimentation* (pp. 345–65). Bari: Gius. Laterza; Paris: Fayard.

Rucquoi, A. 1984. "Alimentation des riches, alimentation des pauvres dans une ville Castillane au XVe siècle." *Manger et Boire au Moyen Âge*. Actes du Colloque de Nice, 1, no. 27: 297–312. *Aliments et Société*. Centre d'Études Médiévales de Nice: Centre National de la Recherche Scientifique, Les Belles Lettres.

Runciman, Steven. 1952a. "Byzantium and the High Middle Ages." In Michael Huxley, ed., *The Root of Europe: Studies in the Diffusion of Greek Culture* (pp. 53–60). London: The Geographical Magazine.

———. 1952b. "Byzantium and the East." In Michael Huxley, ed. *The Root of Europe: Studies in the Diffusion of Greek Culture* (pp. 73–84). London: The Geographical Magazine.

———. 1958. *The Sicilian Vespers: A History of the Mediterranean World in the Later Thirteenth Century*. Cambridge: Cambridge University Press.

———. 1994–1997. *A History of the Crusades*. 3 vols. London: The Folio Society.

Sabadino degli Arienti. n.d. *Le Porrettane*. Book 38. Rome: Salerno.

Sabbadini, Remigio. 1916. " 'Maccheroni' 'Tradurre' (per la 'Crusca')." *Rendiconti del Reale Istituto Lombardo di Scienze e Lettere*. series 2. 49: 219–221.

Sabban-Serventi, Françoise. 1989. "Ravioli cristallins et tagliatelle rouges: Les pâtes chinoises entre XIIe et XVe siècle." *Médiévales*, vols. 16–17: 29–50.

Said, Edward W. 1979. *Orientalism*. New York: Vintage.

Saige, Gustave. 1881. *Les Juifs de Languedoc*. Paris: Alphonse Picard.

Saint Basil. 1963. *Exegetic Homilies*. Sister Agnes Clare Way, trans. Washington, DC: Catholic University of America Press.

Salaman, Redcliffe N. 1940. "Why Jerusalem Artichoke?" *Journal of the Royal Horticultural Society*, 65: 338–48, 376–83.

———. 1949. *The History and Social Influence of the Potato*. Cambridge: Cambridge University Press, 1949.

Sallares, Robert. 1991. *The Ecology of the Ancient Greek World*. London: Gerald Duckworth.

———. 1995. "Molecular Archeology and Ancient History." In John Wilkins, David Harvey, and Mike Dobson, eds., *Food in Antiquity* (pp. 87–100). Exeter: University of Exeter Press.

Salmieri, Giuseppe. 1950. "Voci lessicali arabo-sicule." In F. G. Arezzo, *Sicilia miscellanea di studi storici, giuridici ed economici sulla Sicilia. Glossario di voci siciliane derivate dal greco, latino, arabo, spagnulo, francese, tedesco, etc*. Palermo: Greco.

Salomone-Marino, Salvatore. 1924. *Costumi ed usanze dei contadini di Sicilia*. Florence: R. Sandron.

Sanderson, John. 1931. *The Travels of John Sanderson in the Levant (1584–1602)*. William Foster, ed. London: The Hakylut Society.

Santich, Barbara. 1992. "Les elements distinctifs de la cuisine médiévale méditerranéenne." In Carole Lambert, ed., *Du manuscrit à la table: Essais sur la cuisine au moyen âge et répertoire des manuscrits médiévaux contenant des recettes culinaires* (pp. 133–39). Montréal: Les Presses de l'Université de Montréal; Paris: Champion-Slatkine.

Sanuto, Marino. 1879–1903. *I Diari*. Vol. 46 Venice: Fratelli Visentini.

Sapori, Armando. 1946. *Studi di storia economica medievale* (secoli XIII-XIV-XV). 2 vols. Florence: G. C. Sansoni.

———. 1970. *The Italian Merchant in the Middle Ages*. Patricia Ann Kennen, trans. New York: W. W. Norton.

Sarton, George. 1927. *Introduction to the History of Science*. Vol. 1: *From Homer to Omar Khayyam*. Baltimore: William & Wilkins for the Carnegie Institution of Washington.

Sauer, Jonathan D. 1993. *Historical Geography of Crop Plants: A Select Roster.* Boca Raton: CRC Press.

Scarlata, Marina. 1981. "L'approvvigionamento alimentare di una nave negli scali mediterranei del XIV secolo." *Archeologia medievale*, 8: 305–10.

Schacht, Joseph, ed. with C. E. Bosworth. 1979. *The Legacy of Islam*. 2nd ed. Oxford: Oxford University Press.

Schevill, Ferdinand. 1909. *Siena: The Story of a Medieval Commune*. New York: Charles Scribners Sons.

Schimmel, Annemarie. 1976. "The Celestial Garden in Islam." In Elisabeth B. Macdougall and Richard Ettinghausen, eds. *The Islamic Garden* (pp. 13–39). Dumbarton Oaks Colloquium on the History of Landscape Architecture IV. Washington, DC: Dumbarton Oaks.

Schnell, R. 1957. *Plantes alimentaires et vie agricole de l'Afrique noire: Essai de phytogéographie alimentaire*. Paris: Larose.

School of Salernum: Regimen Sanitatis Salernitanum. 1970. John Harrington, trans., with Francis R. Packard and Fielding H. Garrison. New York: Augustus M. Kelley.

Schwanitz, Franz. 1967. *The Origin of Cultivated Plants*. Cambridge: Harvard University Press.

Sciannameo, Nicola, ed. 1987. *The Province of Cagliari*. 2 vols. Milan: Cinisello B. for the Provincia di Cagliari.

Scully, Terence. 1995 *The Art of Cookery in the Middle Ages*. Woodbridge: The Boydell Press.

Seijo Alonso, Francisco G. 1977. *Gastronomia de la provincia de valenciana*. Alicante: Villa.

Sella, Domenico. 1961. *Commerci e industrie a Venezia nel secolo XVII*. Venice and Rome: Istituto per la Collaborazione Culturale.

Serafino Razzi, Fra. 1595/1903. *La storia di Raugia*. Lucca: Vincentio Busdraghi; Dubrovnik: A. Pasarić.

Sereni, Emilio. 1958. "Note di storia dell'alimentazione nel Mezzogiorno. I Napoletani da 'mangiafoglia' a 'mangiamaccheroni'." *Cronache Meriodionali*, 4, anno V (April): 272–95; 5, anno V. (May): 353–77; 6, anno V. (June): 398–422.

———. 1961. *Storia del paesaggio agrario italiana*. Bari: P. Laterza.

———. 1997. *History of the Italian Agricultural Landscape*. R. Burr Litchfield, trans. Princeton: Princeton University Press.

Serjeant, Robert B. 1971. "Agriculture and Horticulture: Some Cultural Interchanges of the Medieval Arabs and Europe." *Oriente e occidente nel medioevo: filosofia e scienza* (pp. 535–48). Accademia Nazionale dei Lincei, Fondazione Alessandro Volta, Atti dei Convegni 13. Convegno Internazionale, 9–15 April 1969. Rome: Accademia dei Lincei.

Serres, Olivier de. 1605/1804–5. *Le théâtre d'agriculture et mesnage des champs*. Paris: Huzard.

Seton-Williams, Veronica, and Peter Stocks. 1988 *Blue Guide: Egypt*. London: A & C Black; New York: W. W. Norton.

Setton, Kenneth M. 1948. *Catalan Domination of Athens, 1311–1388*. Cambridge, MA: Medieval Academy of America.

———. 1975. *Athens in the Middle Ages*. London: Variorum Reprints.

Sharman, Fay, and Brian Chadwick. 1985. *The Taste of Italy: A Dictionary of Italian Food and Wine*. London: Macmillan.

Shatzmiller, J. 1984. "Droit féodal et législation rabbinique: La cuisson du pain chez les Juifs du moyen âge." *Manger et Boire au Moyen Âge*. Actes du Colloque de Nice, no. 27: 67–74. *Aliments et Société*. Centre d'Études Médiévales de Nice: Centre National de la Recherche Scientifique, Les Belles Lettres.

Shneidman, J. Lee. 1970. *The Rise of the Aragonese-Catalan Empire, 1200–1350*. 2 vols. New York: New York University Press.

Simmonds, N. W. ed. 1979. *Evolution of Crop Plants*. London: Longman.

Simonet, D. Francisco Javier. 1888/1975. *Glosario de voces ibéricas y latinas usadas entre los mozárabes*. Beirut: Librarie du Liban.

Skhiri, Fathia. 1968. "Les traditions culinaries andalouses à Testour." In *Cahiers des Arts et Traditions Populaires* (Tunis), 2: 21–28.

Skinner, Patricia. 1997. *Health and Medicine in Early Medieval Southern Italy.* The Medieval Mediterranean: Peoples, Economies and Cultures 400–1453, vol. 11 Leiden: Brill.

Skiotis, Dennis N. 1975. "Mountain Warriors and the Greek Revolution." In V. J. Parry and M. E. Yapp, eds., *War, Technology and Society in the Middle East* (pp. 308–29). London: Oxford University Press.

Slessarev, Vsevolod. 1967. "*Ecclesiae Mercatorum* and the Rise of Merchant Colonies." *Business History Review*, 41, no. 2 (Summer): 177–97.

Slicher van Bath, B. H. 1963. *The Agrarian History of Western Europe A.D. 500–1850*. Olive Ordish, trans. London: Edward Arnold.

Soler, J. 1979. "The Dietary Prohibitions of the Hebrews." In Robert Forster and Orest Ranum, eds., *Food and Drink in History: Selections from the Annales: Économies. Sociétés. Civilisations* (vol. 5, pp. 943–55). Elborg Forster and Patricia M. Ranum, trans. Baltimore: Johns Hopkins University.

Solignac, Marcel. 1953. *Recherches sur les installations hydrauliques de Kairouan et des steppes tunisiennes du VIIe au XIe siècle (J. C.)*. L'institut d'études orientales de la faculte des lettres d'Alger, vol. 13. Algiers: La Typo-Litho et Jules Carbonel.

Sparkes, Brian. 1995. "A Pretty Kettle of Fish." In John Wilkins, David Harvey and Mike Dobson, eds., *Food in Antiquity* (pp. 150–61) Exeter: University of Exeter Press.

Spufford, Peter. 1988. *Money and Its Use in Medieval Europe*. Cambridge: Cambridge University Press.

Stouff, Louis. 1970. *Ravitaillement et alimentation en Provence aux XIVe et XVe siècles*. Paris; the Hague: Mouton.

———. 1986. *Arles à la fin du moyen-âge*. 2 vols. Aix-en-Provence: Université de Provence; Lille: Université Lille III.

———. 1996. *La table provençale: Boire et manger en Provence à la fin du moyen âge*. Avignon: A. Barthélemy.

Sturtevant, E. Lewis. 1919. *Sturtevant's Notes on Edible Plants*. U. P. Hedrick, ed. Albany: State of New York, Department of Agriculture.

Sussarello, Maria Laura Fois. 1991. *Memorie di un'alimentazione antica Sassari e la sua provincia*. Sassari: Stampacolor.

Tagliaferri, Amelio. 1966. *L'economia veronese secondo gli estimi dal 1409 al 1635*. Milan: A. Giuffrè.

Talbi, M. 1954. "Quelques données sur la vie sociale en occident Musulman d'après un traité de *Ḥisba* du XVe siècle." *Arabica*, 294–306.

Tannahill, Reay. 1973. *Food in History*. New York: Stein and Day.

Targioni-Tozzetti, Antonio. 1853. *Cenni storici sulla introduzione de varie piante nell'agricoltura ed orticoltura toscana*. Florence: Tipografia Galileiana.

Taylor, F. Sherwood. 1966. "The Moslem Carriers." In Michael Huxley, ed., *The Root of Europe: Studies in the Diffusion of Greek Culture* (pp. 44–53). London: The Geographical Magazine.

Taylor, Henry Osborn. 1966. *The Medieval Mind: A History of the Development of Thought and Emotion in the Middle Ages*. 4th ed. 2 vols. Cambridge: Harvard University Press.

Taylor's Guide to Vegetables & Herbs. 1961. Boston: Houghton Mifflin.

Teissier, Octave. 1869. *Histoire de Toulon au moyen âge*. Paris: Dumoulin.

Tenenti, Alberto. 1967. *Piracy and the Decline of Venice, 1580–1615*. Janet and Brian Pullan, trans. Berkeley: University of California Press.

———, and Branislava Tenenti. 1985. *Il prezzo del rischio: L'assicurazione mediterranea vista da Ragusa: 1563–1591*. Rome: Jouvence.

Thiriet, Freddy. 1968. "Quelques réflexions sur les enterprises vénitiennes dans les pays du sudest européen." *Revue des Études Sud-Est Européennes*, 6, no. 3: 395–405.

Thorne, John. 1995. "Khichri/Kusharu/Kedgeree." *Simple Cooking*, 42 (Spring): 5–6.

Tilly, Charles. 1992. "The Europe of Columbus and Bayazid." *Middle East Report*, 22, no. 5 (September/October): 2–5.

Tolkowsky, S. 1938. *Hesperides: A History of the Culture and Use of Citrus Fruits*. London: John Bale Sons and Curnow.

Tongas, Gérard. 1942. *Les relations de la France avec l'empire Ottoman durant la première moitié du XVIIe siècle et l'ambassade à Constantinople de Philippe de Harlay, Comte de Césy (1619–1640)*. Toulouse: F. Boisseau.

Tore, Gianfranco. 1975. "Ricerche sull'alimentazione e sul consume alimentare nella sardegna del XVIII e XIX secolo." *Mélanges de l'École Française de Rome: Moyen Âge–Temps Modernes*, 87, n.2: 597–615.

Toubert, Pierre. 1960. "Les statuts communaux et l'histoire des campagnes lombardes au XIVe siècle." *Mélanges d'archéologie d'histoire*, 72: 487.

Toussaint-Samat, Maguelonne. 1992. *History of Food*. Anthea Bell, trans. Cambridge, MA: Basil Blackwell.

Trabut, L. 1900a. *État de l'horticulture en Algérie*. Algiers: de Giralt.

———. 1900b. *L'olivier*. Alger-Mustapha: Giralt.

———. 1935. *Répertoire de noms indigènes des plantes spontanées, cultivées en Afrique du Nord*. Algiers: J. Carbonel.

Traduccion española de un manuscrito anónimo del siglo XIII sobre la cocina hispano-magribi. 1966. Ambrosio Huici Miranda, trans. Madrid: Maestre.

Traina, Antonino. 1890. *Nuovo vocabolario siciliano-italiano*. Palermo: Lorenzo Finocchiaro e Fiorenza Orazio.

Trasselli, Carmelo. 1981. *Siciliani fra quattrocento e cinquecento*. Messina: Michele Intilla.

———. 1982. *Storia dello zucchero siciliano*. Caltanissetta: Salvatore Sciascia.

Tutin, T. G. et al., eds. 1976. *Flora europaea*. Vol. 4: *Plantaginaceae to Compositae (and Rubiaceae)*. Cambridge: Cambridge University Press.

Ucko, Peter J., and G. W. Dimbleby, eds. 1969. *The Domestication and Exploitation of Plants and Animals*. Chicago: Aldine.

Ukers, William H. 1922. *All about Coffee*. New York: The Tea and Coffee Trade Journal Company.

Usher, Abbott Payson. 1913. *The History of the Grain Trade in France 1400–1710*. Cambridge: Harvard University Press.

———. 1943. *The Early History of Deposit Banking in Mediterranean Europe*. Vol. 1. Cambridge: Harvard University Press.

Valensi, Lucette. 1975. "Consommation et usages alimentaires en Tunisie aux XVIIIe et XIXe siècles." *Annales: Économies. Sociétés. Civilisations*, nos. 2–3 (March–June): 600–609.

Valle, Niccolo'. 1510/1990. *Vallilium: Primo dizionaro siculo–latino del XVI secolo.* Palermo: Librarie Siciliane.

Varisco, Daniel Martin. 1994. *Medieval Agriculture and Islamic Science: The Almanac of a Yemeni Sultan.* Seattle: University of Washington Press.

Varro. 1993. *On Agriculture.* William Davis Hooper, trans. Loeb Classical Library. Cambridge: Harvard University Press.

Vasiliev, A. A. 1935. *Byzance et les Arabes.* Tome 1: *La Dynastie d'Amorium.* Corpus Bruxellense Historiae Byzantinae 1. Bruxelles: Editions de l'Institut de Philologie et d'Histoire Orientales.

———. 1952. *History of the Byzantine Empire 324–1453.* Vol. 1. Madison: University of Wisconsin Press.

Vavilov, N. I. 1951. *The Origin, Variation, Immunity, and Breeding of Cultivated Plants.* no. XII. Waltham: Chronica Botanica.

———. 1960. *Agroecological Survey of the Main Field Crops.* Marc Paenson and Z. S. Cole, trans. N. p. Israel Program for Scientific Translations for the National Science Foundation, Washington, DC and the U.S. Department of Agriculture.

———. 1992. *Origin and Geography of Cultivated Plants.* Doris Löve, trans. Cambridge: Cambridge University Press.

Vedel, Jacques. 1975. "La consommation alimentaire dans le haut Languedoc aux XVIe et XVIIIe siècles." *Annales: Économies. Sociétés. Civilisations*, no. 2–3 (March–June): 478–490.

Ventura, Angelo. 1964. *Nobiltà e popolo nella società veneta del '400 e '500.* Bari: Laterza.

Vidossi, Giuseppe. 1960. *Saggi e scritti minori di folklore.* Turin: Bottega d'Ernsmo.

Vincent, Bernard. 1975. "Consommation alimentaire en Andalousie Orientale (les achats de l'Hôpital Royal de Guadix, 1581–1582." *Annales: Économies. Sociétés. Civilisations*, nos. 2–3 (March–June): 445–53.

Visser, Margaret. 1986. *Much Depends on Dinner: The Extraordinary History and Mythology, Allure and Obsessions, Perils and Taboos of an Ordinary Meal.* New York: Collier Books.

"Vita di Don Pietro di Toledo scritta da scipione miccio." 1846. *Archivio storico italiano*, 9: 1–89.

Vollenweider, Alice. 1963. "Der Einfluss der italienischen auf die französische Kochkunst im Spiegel der Sprache." *Vox Romanica: Annales Helvetici explorandis linguis romanicis destinati*, 22, no. 1 (January–June): 59–88 and no. 2 (July–December): 397–443.

Vyronis, Speros, Jr. 1986. *The Decline of Medieval Hellenism in Asia Minor and the Process of Islamization from the Eleventh through the Fifteenth Century.* Berkeley: University of California Press.

Waern, Cecilia. 1910. *Medieval Sicily: Aspects of Life and Art in the Middle Ages.* London: Duckworth.

Wallerstein, Immanuel. 1974. *The Modern World-System* I: *Capitalist Agriculture and the Origins of the European World-Economy in the Sixteenth Century.* Studies in Social Discontinuity. San Diego: Academic Press.

Watson, Andrew M. 1974. "The Arab Agricultural Revolution and Its Diffusion, 700–1100." *Journal of Economic History*, 34, no. 1 (March): 8–35.

———. 1981. "A Medieval Green Revolution: New Crops and Farming Techniques in the Early Islamic World." In A. L. Udovitch, ed., *The Islamic Middle East, 700–1900: Studies in Economic and Social History* (pp. 29–58). Princeton Studies on the Near East. Princeton, NJ: Darwin Press.

———. 1983. *Agricultural Innovation in the Early Islamic World: The Diffusion of Crops and Farming Techniques, 700–1100.* Cambridge: Cambridge University Press.

———. 1994. "Botanical Gardens in the Early Islamic World." In E. Robbins and S. Sandahl, eds., *The Ronald Smith Festschrift* (pp. 105–11). Toronto: Tsar.

———. 1995. "Arab and European Agriculture in the Middle Ages: A Case of Restricted Diffusion." In Del Sweeney, ed., *Agriculture in the Middle Ages: Technology, Practice, and Representation* (pp. 62–75). Philadelphia: University of Pennsylvania Press.

Watson, Benjamin. 1996. *Taylor's Guide to Heirloom Vegetables.* Boston: Houghton Mifflin.

Watt, W. Montgomery. 1965. *A History of Islamic Spain.* Edinburgh: Edinburgh University Press.

———. 1972. *The Influence of Islam on Medieval Europe.* Islamic Surveys 9. Edinburgh: Edinburgh University Press.

Weaver, William Woys. 1997. *Heirloom Vegetable Gardening: A Master Gardener's Guide to Planting, Growing, Seed Saving, and Cultural History.* New York: Henry Holt.

Wehr, Hans. 1976. *A Dictionary of Modern Written Arabic.* 3rd ed. Ithaca: Spoken Language Services.

Weiss-Amer, Melitta. 1992. "The Role of Medieval Physicians in the Diffusion of Culinary Recipes and Cooking Practices." In Carole Lambert, ed., *Du manuscrit à la table: Essais sur la cuisine au moyen âge et répertoire des manuscrits médiévaux contenant des recettes culinaires* (pp. 69–80). Montréal: Les Presses de l'Université de Montréal; Paris: Champion-Slatkine.

Wells, Patricia. 1987. *The Food Lover's Guide to France.* New York: Workman.

Westbury, Lord. 1963. *Handlist of Italian Cookery Books.* Biblioteca di bibliografia Italiana. XLII. Florence: Leo S. Olschki.

Wheaton, Barbara Ketchum. 1983. *Savoring the Past: The French Kitchen and Table from 1300 to 1789.* Philadelphia: University of Pennsylvania Press.

White, K. D. 1970. *Roman Farming.* London: Thames and Hudson.

White, Lynn Townsend. 1938. *Latin Monasticism in Norman Sicily.* Cambridge, MA: Medieval Academy of America.

———. 1964. *Medieval Technology and Social Change.* Oxford: Oxford University Press.

Wilson, C. Anne. 1981. "The Saracen Connection: Arab Cuisine and the Medieval West: Parts 1 and 2." *Petits Propos Culinaires*, 7 (March): 13–22 and 8 (June): 19–28.

Wissa Wassef, Cérès. 1971. *Pratiques rituelles et alimentaires des Coptes*. Cairo: Institute français d'archéologie orientale du Caire.

Wolff, Philippe. 1954. *Commerce et marchands de Toulouse (vers 1350–vers 1450)*. Paris: Plon.

Wright, Clifford A. 1990. "Cuscusù: A Paradigm of Arab-Sicilian Cuisine." *Journal of Gastronomy*, 5, no. 4 (Spring): 19–37.

———. 1993. "The Discovery and Dispersal of Hard Wheat (*Triticum durum*) and its Inventions: Pasta and Couscous and their Varieties in Tunisia." Paper delivered at the Sixth Oldways International Symposium, "Tunisia: The Splendors and Traditions of its Cuisines and Culture." Djerba, Sousse, and Tunis. December 4 to December 10, 1993.

———. 1996. "Couscous." *Encyclopaedia of the Modern Middle East*. New York: Macmillan for Columbia University.

———. 1996–97. *"Cucina Arabo-Sicula* and *Maccharruni." Al-Mashāq: Studia Arabo-Islamica Mediterranea*, 9: 151–77.

———. 1997. "Did the Ancients Know the Artichoke? A Review of the Evidence." Submitted to *Journal d'agriculture traditionnelle et de botanique appliquée*.

Zamorano, Rodrigo. 1989. *Reasons for the Seasons: Weather Prediction in the Year 1513*. Harry Andrew Marriner, trans. Bogota: Harry Andrew Marriner.

Zanetti, Dante. 1964. *Problemi alimentari di una economia preindustriale: Cereali a pavia dal 1398 al 1700*. Turin: Paolo Boringhieri.

Zohary, Daniel. 1973. "The Origin of Cultivated Cereals and Pulses in the Middle East." In J. Wahrman and K. R. Lewis, eds., *Chromosomes Today. Vol. 4: Proceedings of the Jerusalem Chromosome Conference* (pp. 307–20), September 11–15, 1972. New York: John Wiley; Jerusalem: Israel Universities Press.

———, and Marcia Hopf. 1988. *Domestication of Plants in the Old World: The Origin and Spread of Cultivated Plants in West Asia, Europe, and the Nile Valley*. Oxford: Clarendon Press.

Zorzi, Elio. 1967. *Osterie veneziane*. Venice: Filippi.

Zubaida, Sami, and Richard Tapper, eds. 1994. *Culinary Cultures of the Middle East*. London: I. B. Tauris with Centre of Near and Middle Eastern Studies, School of Oriental and African Studies, University of London.

GENERAL INDEX

Page numbers in *italics* refer to maps and illustrations.

INDEX OF RECIPES